Statutory Instruments
1987

PART I

SECTION 1

Published by Authority

LONDON

HER MAJESTY'S STATIONERY OFFICE

1988

ISBN 0 11 840283 8

HMSO publications are available from:

HMSO Publications Centre
(Mail and telephone orders only)
PO Box 276, London, SW8 5DT
Telephone orders 01-873 9090
General enquiries 01-873 0011
(queuing system in operation for both numbers)

HMSO Bookshops
49 High Holborn, London, WC1V 6HB   01-873 0011 (Counter service only)
258 Broad Street, Birmingham, B1 2HE   021-643 3740
Southey House, 33 Wine Street, Bristol, BS1 2BQ   (0272) 264306
9-21 Princess Street, Manchester, M60 8AS   061-834 7201
80 Chichester Street, Belfast, BT1 4JY   (0232) 238451
71 Lothian Road, Edinburgh, EH3 9AZ   031-228 4181

HMSO's Accredited Agents
(see Yellow Pages)

and through good booksellers

Price for two sections £167 net

Printed in the United Kingdom for Her Majesty's Stationery Office
Dd 500250 3/89 C7 G409 10170

Contents of the Edition

PART I

SECTION 1

SECTION 2

PART II

PART III

Preface to the Edition

CONTENTS

1. The annual edition of *Statutory Instruments* contains the full text of the statutory instruments that were registered in the year 1987 and were classified as general**(a)**. It also gives certain particulars of those that were classified as local**(b)**. Certain instruments that are not statutory instruments are reproduced in Appendices.

2. The statutory instruments are arranged according to their SI numbers, that is to say, in order of their registration as statutory instruments**(c)**.

3. Publication is in three Parts as follows:

Part I

Contains the text of the statutory instruments registered between 1st January and 30th April, preceded by a list of the instruments showing their SI numbers and titles. Next is an Appendix containing the text of certain instruments not registered as statutory instruments, including Orders in Council made under the royal prerogative or otherwise falling outside the definition of statutory instrument, Letters Patent and Royal Instructions relating to overseas territories and Royal Proclamations that are of a legislative nature. At the end of the Part are a table of modifications to legislation and an index.

Part II

Contains similar material in respect of the period 1st May to 31st August. Its table and index are cumulative.

Part III

Contains similar material in respect of the period 1st September to 31st December, except that the table of modifications and index are replaced by the features required by regulation 10 of the Statutory Instruments Regulations 1947 to be included in the annual edition of *Statutory Instruments*. These features relate to the statutory instruments in all three Parts, and are as follows:

> **Classified List of Local Instruments.** This gives particulars, including the SI numbers, of all the statutory instruments that were classified as local and registered in the year, the instruments being grouped in classes according to their subject-matter.

> **Tables of Effect.** Table A gives particulars of the Acts of Parliament, and Table B particulars of the general instruments and certain prerogative instruments, whose operation was affected by the instruments contained in the edition. The tables incorporate the information already given in the tables of modifications to legislation in Parts I and II. Table B also gives particulars of general instruments whose operation was expressly affected by the Public General Acts of the year, or that became spent or expired during the year.

> **Numerical and Issue List.** This gives particulars of all statutory instruments that were printed and put on sale by the Queen's Printer of Acts of Parliament in pursuance of the Statutory Instruments Act 1946**(d)** during the year with, in each

---

(a) But *see* para 4 below as to Northern Ireland

(b) Reg 4 of the Statutory Instruments Regulations 1947 (SI 1948/1) provides that, in general, an instrument that is in the nature of a local and personal or private Act shall be classified as local and an instrument that is in the nature of a public general Act shall be classified as general

(c) Reg 3 of the Statutory Instruments Regulations 1947 provides for instruments to be numbered in a separate series of each calendar year. In addition, certain instruments are given a subsidiary number:

   C   Commencement orders (bringing an Act or part of an Act into operation)

   L   Instruments relating to fees or procedure in courts in England and Wales

   S   Instruments made by a Scottish authority and applying to Scotland only

   NI Orders in Council made under para 1 of Sch 1 to the Northern Ireland Act 1974

(d) 1946 c.36

case, the date of the first issue by HMSO. The Table in this edition also includes, for the first time, the number and title of those local statutory instruments which were not issued (i.e. not printed and put on sale) by HMSO.

Index. This is cumulative, covering all three Parts.

4. **Northern Ireland.** Orders in Council made under paragraph 1 of Schedule 1 to the Northern Ireland Act 1974(a) are excluded pursuant to paragraph 1(8) of that Schedule, but they are listed in the Numerical and Issue List in Part III of the annual edition. All such Orders in Council are included in the annual volumes of Northern Ireland statutes.

DEFINITION OF STATUTORY INSTRUMENT

5. To determine whether an instrument is a statutory instrument, it is necessary to refer to section 1 of the Statutory Instruments Act 1946, regulation 2 of the Statutory Instruments Regulations 1947 and article 1 of the Statutory Instruments (Confirmatory Powers) Order 1947(b). Under those provisions:

as regards an instrument made under an Act passed before 1st January 1948, the matter is governed by definitions contained in the repealed Rules Publication Act 1893(c);

as regards an instrument made under an Act passed on or after 1st January 1948, an instrument is a statutory instrument if it is an Order in Council, or if it is made by a Minister of the Crown and the Act provides that the power is exercisable by statutory instrument.

Power to make instruments has, by various Acts, been conferred on persons other than Ministers.

CITATION OF INSTRUMENTS

6. For the purpose of citation, statutory instruments are given a title. In addition, a statutory instrument may be identified by its year and number: by this method, the first instrument in Part I would be cited as "SI 1987/1".

7. Where a statutory instrument refers to another statutory instrument it contains a lettered footnote identifying the instrument referred to by means of its year and number.

PROOF OF INSTRUMENTS

8. Under section 2 of the Documentary Evidence Act 1868(d), as read with section 2 of the Documentary Evidence Act 1882(e), evidence of proclamations, orders or regulations made by certain authorities may be given in court by the production of a copy purporting to be printed by the Government Printer or under the superintendence or authority of Her Majesty's Stationery Office. The Act of 1868 has been extended by numerous Acts to instruments made by other authorities(f). The texts printed in this edition may therefore be produced as prima facie evidence so far as they come within the scope of the 1868 Act as extended.

INFORMATION ABOUT INSTRUMENTS

9. The *Index to Government Orders* contains, under subject headings, summaries of all powers to make subordinate legislation conferred by statute on Her Majesty in Council, the Privy Council, government departments and certain other public bodies. Below each summary are listed the general instruments that have been made in exercise

---

(a) 1974 c.28   (b) SI 1948/2   (c) 1893 c.66   (d) 1868 c.37   (e) 1882 c.9
(f) Extensions of the Act of 1868 are listed in the *Chronological Table of the Statutes*

of the power and are in force. Details are also given of certain instruments made under prerogative powers. The work includes a Table of Statutes listing, under each statute, the sections that confer powers to make subordinate legislation, and showing in relation to each section the subject-heading of the *Index* under which the power is set forth. The *Index* is published every two years by HMSO, and a *Supplement* is issued in the years when no *Index* is published.

10. The *Table of Government Orders* lists all general statutory rules and orders and statutory instruments in numerical order, together with certain instruments made under prerogative powers, and gives the history of those that have been affected by subsequent legislation, whether Acts or subordinate legislation. Where an instrument has been amended the *Table* indicates which provisions have been affected. The *Table of Government Orders* is published annually by HMSO and is cumulative. A *Noter-Up* is issued towards the end of each year.

11. The annual *List of Statutory Instruments*, published in paperback by HMSO, is a companion to this edition and contains:
- a list of all general and local statutory instruments issued by HMSO arranged under subject headings;
- a numerical list of the same instruments, with subject headings and month of publication;
- a list of instruments with subsidiary numbers;
- an alphabetical index of the titles of all issued instruments; and
- a list of Northern Ireland Statutory Rules, and associated indexes.

12. Copies of local instruments issued recently by HMSO may be obtained from that Office (see addresses on reverse of title page). Copies of other local instruments from 1922 onwards **(a)** may be obtained at prevailing prices either from the Statutory Publications Office, Queen Anne's Chambers, 28 Broadway, London SW1H 9JS, or (up to 1957) from the Head of Search Department, Public Record Office, Chancery Lane, London WC2A 1LR, or the British Library, Official Publications and Social Sciences Service, Great Russell Street, London WC1B 3DG.

AUTHORITY FOR PUBLICATION

13. The annual edition is published in pursuance of regulation 10 of the Statutory Instruments Regulations 1947, and is prepared under the direction of the Statute Law Committee. Any comments or suggestions should be addressed to the Editor, Statutory Publications Office, Queen Anne's Chambers, 28 Broadway, London SW1H 9JS.

(a) There are, unfortunately, gaps in these collections, notably for the years 1942, 1950, 1951 and up to no. 940 of 1952

Abbreviations

Act of Adj	..	Act of Adjournal
AS	..	Act of Sederunt
addnl	..	additional
admin	..	administration
am, amdg, amdt		amended, amending, amendment
appx	..	appendix
art(s)	..	article(s)
assocn(s)	..	association(s)
authy, authies	..	authority, authorities
bd(s)	..	boards
c. ..	..	chapter(s)
C ..	..	Commencement
CAP	..	Common Agricultural Policy
Cm, Cmd, Cmnd		Command Paper
Co	..	Company
Commn(s)	..	Commission(s)
Commr(s)	..	Commissioner(s)
contd	..	continued
ct(s)	..	court(s)
ctee(s)	..	committee(s)
dept	..	department
devpt	..	development
E ..	..	England
EEC	..	European Economic Community
ext	..	extended, extension
GB	..	Great Britain
gen	..	general, generally
GLC	..	Greater London Council
govt	..	government
HC	..	House of Commons
HL	..	House of Lords
HM	..	Her Majesty, Her Majesty's
incl	..	included, including
instrt	..	instrument
Is ..	..	Island(s), Isle(s)
LP	..	Letters Patent
Ltd	..	Limited
met	..	metropolitan
Min(s)	..	Minister(s)
misc	..	miscellaneous
mod, mod(s)	..	modified, modification(s)
Nat	..	National
NHS	..	National Health Service
NI..	..	Northern Ireland
no.	..	number
O ..	..	Order(s)
O in C, O of C..		Order(s) in Council, Order(s) of Council
p., pp.	..	page(s)
para(s)	..	paragraph(s)
plc	..	public limited company
prerog	..	prerogative
prosp	..	prospectively
prov	..	provisional, proviso
provn(s)	..	provision(s)
Pt ..	..	Part
r ..	..	repealed, revoked
R ..	..	Royal
RAF	..	Royal Air Force
reg(s)	..	regulation(s)
retrosp	..	retrospectively
Rev	..	Statutory Rules and Orders and Statutory Instruments Revised (Third Edition, 1948)
Rev 1903	..	Statutory Rules and Orders (Second Revised Edition, 1903)
revn	..	revocation
RN	..	Royal Navy
S ..	..	Scotland
s., ss.	..	section(s)
SI	..	Statutory Instrument(s)
SR & O ..	..	Statutory Rule(s) and Order(s)
Sch(s)	..	Schedule(s)
Secy	..	Secretary
supn	..	superannuation
temp	..	temporarily, temporary
transfd	..	transferred
UK	..	United Kingdom of Great Britain and Northern Ireland
UN	..	United Nations
USA	..	United States of America
VAT	..	value added tax
vol	..	volume
W ..	..	Wales

List of Instruments in Part I

STATUTORY INSTRUMENTS

OTHER INSTRUMENTS

*Numbered as SI 1987/511 by virtue of the House of Commons Members' Fund Act 1948 s. 3(3)

STATUTORY INSTRUMENTS

1987 No. 1

REPRESENTATION OF THE PEOPLE

The Parish and Community Meetings (Polls) Rules 1987

Made - - - -	*5th January 1987*
Laid before Parliament	*16th January 1987*
Coming into force	*16th February 1987*

In exercise of the powers conferred upon me by paragraph 18(5) of Part III of, and paragraph 34(5) of Part V of, Schedule 12 to the Local Government Act 1972(**a**) and section 36 of the Representation of the People Act 1983(**b**), I hereby make the following Rules:—

Citation and extent

1.—(1) These Rules may be cited as the Parish and Community Meetings (Polls) Rules 1987.

(2) These Rules do not extend to Scotland and Northern Ireland.

Commencement

2. These Rules shall come into force on 16th February 1987 except that they shall not have effect in relation to a poll consequent on a parish or community meeting which has been demanded before that date.

Revocations

3. The Parish and Community Meetings (Polls) Rules 1973(**c**), the Parish and Community Meetings (Polls) (Amendment) Rules 1976(**d**) and the Parish and Community Meetings (Polls) (Amendment) Rules 1983(**e**) are hereby revoked except that those Rules shall apply to any poll which has been demanded before these Rules come into force.

Returning officer

4.—(1) If a poll consequent on a parish or community meeting is required to be taken, the chairman of the meeting shall notify the district council in which the parish or community is situate of the fact and that council shall appoint an officer of the council to be returning officer.

(2) The chairman of the meeting shall give the returning officer such particulars as will enable him to give notice of the poll.

(3) The returning officer shall appoint an office for the purpose of the poll.

(**a**) 1972 c.70; those paragraphs were amended by paragraph 14 of Schedule 8 to the Representation of the People Act 1983 (c.2).
(**b**) 1983 c.2; the power in section 36 is referred to in section 187(1) of that Act.
(**c**) S.I. 1973/1911.
(**d**) S.I. 1976/2067.
(**e**) S.I. 1983/1151.

Poll rules

5. In the application of the Local Elections (Parishes and Communities) Rules 1986**(a)** to a poll consequent on a parish or community meeting, adaptations, alterations and exceptions shall be made to those rules so that the poll shall be conducted in accordance with the rules in the Schedule to these Rules.

Application of provisions in the Act of 1983

6. In the application of those provisions of the Representation of the People Act 1983 referred to in section 187(1) of that Act**(b)** to the election of the chairman of a parish meeting or to a poll consequent on a parish or community meeting the following adaptations, alterations and exceptions shall have effect:—

(a) where the poll is to be taken on any question other than that of the election of the chairman of a parish meeting or of an appointment to any other office, the only provisions of those referred to in section 187(1) which are to apply are sections 60, 66**(c)**, 113, 114, 115, 119**(d)**, 160(4) and (5), 168**(e)**, 169**(f)**, 173**(g)**, 174(5) and (6), 176**(h)**, 177, 179, 180, 181**(i)**, 186 and 189;

(b) references to the proper officer of the authority for which the election was held shall be taken as references to the returning officer;

(c) references to the authority for which the election was held shall be taken as references to the parish and references to the area thereof shall be construed accordingly except that in section 130(6) for the words "area of the authority for which the election was held" there shall be substituted "district in which the parish is situate";

(d) in sections 60(2) and 99(1), for the words "local government election" there shall be substituted "election under the local government Act";

(e) in section 66, subsection (4) and any reference to an election agent or the proxy for an elector shall be omitted and in subsections (2)(b), (3)(b), (c) and (d) and (5) after the words "the candidate for whom" there shall be inserted "or the manner in which";

(f) in section 136(2)(b)**(j)**, for the words "£2,500" there shall be substituted "£1,500";

(g) references to an election under the local government Act shall be deemed to include a reference to a poll consequent on a parish or community meeting.

Douglas Hurd

Home Office
5th January 1987

One of Her Majesty's Principal Secretaries of State

(a) S.I. 1986/2215.
(b) Section 187(1) was repealed in part by Schedule 5 to the Representation of the People Act 1985 (c.50) ("the Act of 1985").
(c) Section 66(6) was amended by paragraph 3 of Schedule 3 to the Act of 1985.
(d) Subsections (2) and (3) of section 119 were substituted by section 19(4) of the Act of 1985.
(e) Section 168 was amended by paragraph 8 of Schedule 3 to, and paragraph 57 of Schedule 4 to, the Act of 1985.
(f) Section 169 was amended by paragraph 9 of Schedule 3 to the Act of 1985 and repealed in part by Schedule 5 to that Act.
(g) Section 173(a) was repealed in part by Schedule 5 to the Act of 1985.
(h) Section 176 was amended by paragraph 61 of Schedule 4 to the Act of 1985 and repealed in part by Schedule 5 to that Act.
(i) Section 181 was amended by paragraph 63 of Schedule 4 to the Act of 1985 and repealed in part by Schedule 5 to that Act and Schedule 2 to the Prosecution of Offences Act 1985 (c.23).
(j) Section 136(2)(b) was amended by paragraph 48(b) of Schedule 4 to the Act of 1985.

Rule 5

SCHEDULE

POLL RULES

Arrangement of rules

APPENDIX OF FORMS

Form of ballot paper on a question of appointment to an office and directions as to printing the ballot paper.

Form of ballot paper on a question other than that of appointment to an office and directions as to printing the ballot paper.

Form of directions for the guidance of the voters in voting where the poll is on a question of appointment to an office.

Form of directions for the guidance of the voters in voting where the poll is on a question other than that of appointment to an office.

Form of declaration to be made by the companion of a blind voter.

Timetable

1. The proceedings at the poll shall be conducted in accordance with the following Table.

TIMETABLE

Proceeding	*Time*
Delivery of notices of withdrawals of candidature	Not later than noon on the fourth day after the day on which the poll was demanded.
Notice of poll	Not later than the fifth day before the day of the poll.
Polling	Between the hours of 4 in the afternoon and 9 at night on the day fixed by the returning officer which shall not be earlier than the fourteenth day nor later than the twenty-fifth day after the day on which the poll was demanded.

Computation of time

2.—(1) In computing any period of time for the purposes of the Timetable—

(a) a Saturday or Sunday,

(b) Christmas Eve, Christmas Day, Maundy Thursday, Good Friday or a bank holiday, or

(c) a day appointed for public thanksgiving or mourning,

shall be disregarded, and any such day shall not be treated as a day for the purpose of any proceedings up to completion of the poll nor shall the returning officer be obliged to proceed with the counting of the votes on such a day.

(2) In this rule "bank holiday" means a day which is a bank holiday under the Banking and Financial Dealings Act 1971(**a**) in England and Wales.

Withdrawal of candidates

3.—(1) A candidate may withdraw his candidature by notice of withdrawal signed by him and attested by one witness and delivered at the office appointed by the returning officer.

(2) If the number of remaining candidates after any withdrawals under this rule does not exceed the number of persons to be elected, such candidates shall be deemed to be elected and the returning officer shall as soon as possible give public notice of the abandonment of the poll which shall—

(a) refer to the meeting at which the poll was demanded and the offices in respect of which the poll was demanded;

(b) set out the full names, home addresses and (if required) descriptions of the candidates;

(c) indicate which of those candidates has withdrawn;

(d) state that no poll will be taken; and

(e) list the candidates deemed to be elected,

and the returning officer shall send a copy of that notice to each of the candidates and the chairman of the meeting at which the poll was demanded.

(**a**)   1971 c.80.

The ballot papers

4.—(1) The ballot of every voter shall consist of a ballot paper.

(2) Every ballot paper shall be in the appropriate form in the Appendix, and shall be printed in accordance with the appropriate directions in that Appendix and—

(a) if the poll is taken on the question of appointment to any office, shall contain the full names, home addresses and (if required) descriptions of the candidates arranged alphabetically in the order of their surnames and, if there are two or more of them with the same surname, of their other names;

(b) if the poll is taken on any other question, shall state the question or questions on which the poll is to be taken;

(c) shall be capable of being folded up;

(d) shall have a number printed on the back; and

(e) shall have attached a counterfoil with the same number printed on it.

(3) Where a poll on the question of appointment to any office and a poll on any other question are taken together, ballot papers of a different colour shall be used for each poll.

The official mark

5.—(1) Every ballot paper shall be marked with an official mark, which shall perforate the ballot paper.

(2) The official mark shall be kept secret, and the same official mark shall not be used at consecutive polls in the same parish or community.

Prohibition of disclosure of vote

6. No person who has voted at the poll shall, in any legal proceeding to question the poll, be required to state how or for whom he has voted.

Use of schools and public rooms

7.—(1) The returning officer may use, free of charge, for the purpose of taking the poll or counting the votes—

(a) a room in a school maintained or assisted by a local education authority or a school in respect of which grants are made out of moneys provided by Parliament to the person or body of persons responsible for the management of the school;

(b) a room the expense of maintaining which is payable out of any rate.

(2) The returning officer shall make good any damage done to, and defray any expense incurred by the persons having control over, any such room as mentioned above by reason of its being used for the purpose of taking the poll or counting the votes.

(3) The use of a room in an unoccupied house for that purpose or those purposes does not render a person liable to be rated or to pay any rate for the house.

Notice of poll

8. The returning officer shall give public notice of the poll which refers to the parish or community meeting at which a poll was demanded and states—

(a) the day and hours fixed for the poll;

(b) if the poll is taken on the question of appointment to any office, the name of the office, the number of vacancies, the particulars of each candidate who has not withdrawn (the order of the names of the candidates and particulars being the same as in the ballot papers) and the name of the proposer of each candidate;

(c) if the poll is taken on any other question, the particulars of the question and the name and address of the proposer of the resolution in respect of which the poll is being taken; and

(d) the situation of each polling station and the description of the persons entitled to vote there.

Provision of polling stations

9.—(1) The returning officer shall provide a sufficient number of polling stations and, if more than one polling station is provided, shall allot the electors to the polling station in such manner as he thinks most convenient, subject to the following provisions of this rule.

(2) One or more polling stations may be provided in the same room.

(3) The polling station allotted to electors from any parliamentary polling district wholly or partly within the parish or community shall, in the absence of special circumstances, be in the parliamentary polling place for that district, unless that place is outside the parish or community.

(4) The returning officer shall provide each polling station with such number of compartments as may be necessary in which the voters can mark their votes screened from observation.

Appointment of presiding officers and clerks

10.—(1) The returning officer shall appoint and may pay a presiding officer to attend at each polling station and such clerks as may be necessary for the purposes of the poll, but he shall not appoint any person who has been employed by or on behalf of a candidate in or about the poll.

(2) The returning officer may, if he thinks fit, preside at a polling station and the provisions of these rules relating to a presiding officer shall apply to a returning officer so presiding with the necessary modifications as to things to be done by the returning officer to the presiding officer or by the presiding officer to the returning officer.

(3) A presiding officer may do, by the clerks appointed to assist him, any act (including the asking of questions) which he is required or authorised by these rules to do at a polling station except order the arrest, exclusion or removal of any person from the polling station.

Equipment of polling stations

11.—(1) The returning officer shall provide each presiding officer with such number of ballot boxes and ballot papers as in the returning officer's opinion may be necessary.

(2) Every ballot box shall be so constructed that the ballot papers can be put in it, but cannot be withdrawn from it, without the box being unlocked.

(3) The returning officer shall provide each polling station with—

(a) materials to enable voters to mark the ballot papers;

(b) instruments for stamping on them the official mark;

(c) copies of the register of electors for the parish or community or such part of it as contains the names of the electors allotted to the station.

(4) A notice in the appropriate form in the Appendix, giving directions for the guidance of voters in voting, shall be printed in conspicuous characters and exhibited inside and outside every polling station.

(5) Where the poll is taken on the question of appointment to any office, there shall be exhibited in every compartment of every polling station the notice "Vote for . . . . candidates only as [*insert name of office*]. Put no other mark on the ballot paper, or your vote may not be counted.".

Appointment of polling and counting agents

12.—(1) Each candidate may, before the commencement of the poll, appoint—

(a) one polling agent to attend at each polling station for the purpose of detecting personation, and

(b) one counting agent to attend at the counting of the votes.

(2) Notice in writing of the appointment, stating the names and addresses of the persons appointed, shall be given by the candidate to the returning officer and shall be so given not later than the third day (computed like any period of time in the Timetable) before the day of the poll.

(3) If an agent dies, or becomes incapable of acting, the candidate may appoint another agent in his place, and shall forthwith give to the returning officer notice in writing of the name and address of the agent appointed.

(4) In the following provisions of these rules references to polling agents and counting agents shall be taken as references to agents whose appointments have been duly made and notified and who are within the permitted numbers.

(5) Any notice required to be given to a counting agent by the returning officer may be delivered at or sent by post to the address stated in the notice of appointment.

(6) A candidate may himself do any act or thing which any polling or counting agent of his, if appointed, would have been authorised to do, or may assist his agent in doing any such act or thing.

(7) Where by these rules any act or thing is required or authorised to be done in the presence of the polling or counting agents, the non-attendance of any agent or agents at the time and place appointed for the purpose shall not, if the act or thing is otherwise duly done, invalidate the act or thing done.

Notification of requirement of secrecy

13. The returning officer shall make such arrangements as he thinks fit to ensure that—

(a) every person attending at a polling station (otherwise than for the purpose of voting or assisting a blind voter to vote or as a constable on duty there) has been given a copy in writing of the provisions of subsections (1), (3) and (6) of section 66**(a)** of the Representation of the People Act 1983, subject to the adaptations, alterations and exceptions set out in rule 6*(e)* of the Parish and Community Meetings (Polls) Rules 1987; and

(b) every person attending at the counting of the votes (other than any constable on duty at the counting) has been given a copy in writing of the provisions of subsections (2) and (6) of that section (as so subject).

Admission to polling station

14. The presiding officer shall regulate the number of voters to be admitted to the polling station at the same time, and shall exclude all other persons except—

(a) where the poll is taken on the question of appointment to any office, the candidates and their wives and husbands;

(b) where the poll is taken on any other question, the proposer of the resolution in respect of which the poll is taken;

(c) the polling agents appointed to attend at the polling station;

(d) the clerks appointed to attend at the polling station;

(e) the constables on duty; and

(f) the companions of blind voters.

Keeping of order in station

15.—(1) It is the presiding officer's duty to keep order at his polling station.

(2) If a person misconducts himself in a polling station, or fails to obey the presiding officer's lawful orders, he may immediately, by the presiding officer's order, be removed from the polling station—

(a) by a constable in or near that station, or

(b) by any other person authorised in writing by the returning officer to remove him,

and the person so removed shall not, without the presiding officer's permission, again enter the polling station during the day.

(a)   Section 66(6) was amended by paragraph 3 of Schedule 3 to the Representation of the People Act 1985 (c.50).

(3) Any person so removed may, if charged with the commission in the polling station of an offence, be dealt with as a person taken into custody by a constable for an offence without warrant.

(4) The powers conferred by this rule shall not be exercised so as to prevent a voter who is otherwise entitled to vote at a polling station from having an opportunity of voting at that station.

Sealing of ballot boxes

16. Immediately before the commencement of the poll, the presiding officer shall show the ballot box empty to such persons, if any, as are present in the polling station, so that they may see that it is empty, and shall then lock it up and place his seal on it in such a manner as to prevent its being opened without breaking the seal and shall place it in his view for the receipt of ballot papers, and keep it so locked and sealed.

Questions to be put to voters

17.—(1) The presiding officer may, and if required by a candidate or his polling agent shall, put to any person applying for a ballot paper at the time of his application, but not afterwards, the following questions or either of them—

(i) "Are you the person registered in the register of local government electors for this [parish] [community] as follows?" *(read the whole entry from the register.)*

(ii) "Have you already voted at the present poll?"

(2) A ballot paper shall not be delivered to any person required to answer the above questions or either of them unless he has answered the questions or question satisfactorily.

(3) Save as by this rule authorised, no inquiry shall be permitted as to the right of any person to vote.

Challenge of voter

18.—(1) If at the time a person applies for a ballot paper for the purpose of voting in person, or after he has applied for a ballot paper for that purpose and before he has left the polling station, a candidate or his polling agent—

(a) declares to the presiding officer that he has reasonable cause to believe that the applicant has committed an offence of personation, and

(b) undertakes to substantiate the charge in a court of law,

the presiding officer may order a constable to arrest the applicant, and the order of the presiding officer shall be sufficient authority for the constable to do so.

(2) A person against whom a declaration is made under this rule shall not by reason of it be prevented from voting.

(3) A person arrested under the provisions of this rule shall be dealt with as a person taken into custody by a constable for an offence without a warrant.

Voting procedure

19.—(1) A ballot paper shall be delivered to a voter who applies for one, and immediately before delivery—

(a) the ballot paper shall be stamped with the official mark;

(b) the number and name of the elector as stated in the copy of the register of electors shall be called out;

(c) the number of the elector shall be marked on the counterfoil; and

(d) a mark shall be placed in the register of electors against the number of the elector to denote that a ballot paper has been received but without showing the particular ballot paper which has been received.

(2) The voter, on receiving the ballot paper, shall forthwith proceed into one of the compartments in the polling station and there secretly mark his paper and fold it up so as to conceal his vote, and shall then show to the presiding officer the back of the paper, so as to disclose the official mark, and put the ballot paper so folded up into the ballot box in the presiding officer's presence.

(3) The voter shall vote without undue delay, and shall leave the polling station as soon as he has put his ballot paper into the ballot box.

Votes marked by presiding officer

20.—(1) The presiding officer, on the application of a voter—

(a) who is incapacitated by blindness or other physical cause from voting in manner directed by these rules, or

(b) who declares orally that he is unable to read,

shall, in the presence of the polling agents, cause the voter's vote to be marked on a ballot paper in manner directed by the voter, and the ballot paper to be placed in the ballot box.

(2) The name and number on the register of electors of every voter whose vote is marked in pursuance of this rule, and the reason why it is so marked, shall be entered on a list (in these rules called "the list of votes marked by the presiding officer").

Voting by blind persons

21.—(1) If a voter makes an application to the presiding officer to be allowed on the ground of blindness to vote with the assistance of another person by whom he is accompanied (in these rules referred to as "the companion"), the presiding officer shall require the voter to declare orally whether he is so incapacitated by his blindness as to be unable to vote without assistance.

(2) If the presiding officer—

(a) is satisfied that the voter is so incapacitated, and

(b) is also satisfied by a written declaration made by the companion (in these rules referred to as "the declaration made by the companion of a blind voter") that the companion—

  (i) is a qualified person within the meaning of this rule, and

  (ii) has not previously assisted more than one blind person to vote at the poll,

the presiding officer shall grant the application, and then anything which is by these rules required to be done to or by that voter in connection with the giving of his vote may be done to, or with the assistance of, the companion.

(3) For the purposes of this rule, a person shall be qualified to assist a blind voter to vote, if that person is either—

(a) a person who is entitled to vote at the poll; or

(b) the father, mother, brother, sister, husband, wife, son or daughter of the blind voter and has attained the age of 18 years.

(4) The name and number in the register of electors of every voter whose vote is given in accordance with this rule and the name and address of the companion shall be entered on a list (in these rules referred to as "the list of blind voters assisted by companions").

(5) The declaration made by the companion—

(a) shall be in the form in the Appendix;

(b) shall be made before the presiding officer at the time when the voter applies to vote with the assistance of a companion and shall forthwith be given to the presiding officer who shall attest and retain it.

(6) No fee or other payment shall be charged in respect of the declaration.

Tendered ballot papers

22.—(1) If a person, representing himself to be a particular elector named on the register applies for a ballot paper after another person has voted as the elector, the applicant shall, on satisfactorily answering the questions permitted by law to be asked at the poll, be entitled, subject to the following provisions of this rule, to mark a ballot paper (in these rules referred to as "a tendered ballot paper") in the same manner as any other voter.

(2) A tendered ballot paper shall—

(a) be of a colour differing from the other ballot papers;

(b) instead of being put into the ballot box, be given to the presiding officer and endorsed by him with the name of the voter and his number in the register of electors, and set aside in a separate packet.

(3) The name of the voter and his number on the register of electors shall be entered on a list (in these rules referred to as the "tendered votes list").

Spoilt ballot papers

23. A voter who has inadvertently dealt with his ballot paper in such manner that it cannot be conveniently used as a ballot paper may, on delivering it to the presiding officer and proving to his satisfaction the fact of the inadvertence, obtain another ballot paper in the place of the ballot paper so delivered (in these rules referred to as "a spoilt ballot paper"), and the spoilt ballot paper shall be immediately cancelled.

Adjournment of poll in case of riot

24.—(1) Where the proceedings at any polling station are interrupted or obstructed by riot or open violence, the presiding officer shall adjourn the proceedings till the following day and shall forthwith give notice to the returning officer.

(2) Where the poll is adjourned at any polling station—

(a) the hours of polling on the day to which it is adjourned shall be the same as for the original day; and

(b) references in these rules to the close of the poll shall be construed accordingly.

Procedure on close of poll

25.—(1) As soon as practicable after the close of the poll, the presiding officer shall, in the presence of the polling agents, make up into separate packets, sealed with his own seal and the seals of such polling agents as desire to affix their seals—

(a) each ballot box in use at the station, sealed so as to prevent the introduction of additional ballot papers and unopened, but with the key attached,

(b) the unused and spoilt ballot papers placed together,

(c) the tendered ballot papers,

(d) the marked copies of the register of electors,

(e) the counterfoils of the used ballot papers,

(f) the tendered votes list, the list of blind voters assisted by companions, the list of votes marked by the presiding officer, a statement of the number of voters whose votes are so marked by the presiding officer under the heads "physical incapacity" and "unable to read", and the declarations made by the companions of blind voters,

and shall deliver the packets or cause them to be delivered to the returning officer to be taken charge of by him; but if the packets are not delivered by the presiding officer personally to the returning officer, the arrangements for their delivery shall require the returning officer's approval.

(2) The marked copies of the register of electors shall not be in the same packet as the counterfoils of the used ballot papers.

(3) The packets shall be accompanied by a statement (in these rules referred to as "the ballot paper account") made by the presiding officer showing the number of ballot papers entrusted to him, and accounting for them under the heads of ballot papers issued and not otherwise accounted for, unused, spoilt and tendered ballot papers.

Attendance at counting of votes

26.—(1) The returning officer shall make arrangements for counting the votes in the presence of the counting agents as soon as practicable after the close of the poll, and shall give to the counting agents notice in writing of the time and place at which he will begin to count the votes.

(2) No person other than—

(a) the returning officer and his clerks,

(b) where the poll is taken on the question of appointment to any office, the candidates and their wives or husbands,

(c) where the poll is taken on any other question, the proposer of the resolution in respect of which the poll is taken,

(d) the counting agents,

may be present at the counting of the votes, unless permitted by the returning officer to attend.

(3) A person not entitled to attend at the counting of the votes shall not be permitted to do so by the returning officer unless he is satisfied that the efficient counting of the votes will not be impeded.

(4) The returning officer shall give the counting agents all such reasonable facilities for overseeing the proceedings, and all such information with respect to them, as he can give them consistently with the orderly conduct of the proceedings and the discharge of his duties in connection with them.

(5) In particular, where the votes are counted by—

(a) sorting the ballot papers according to the candidate for whom the vote is given and then counting the number of ballot papers for each candidate, or

(b) sorting the ballot papers according to votes for or against the question and then counting the number of ballot papers in each category,

the counting agents or the person referred to in paragraph (2)(c) above shall be entitled to satisfy themselves that the ballot papers are correctly sorted.

The count

27.—(1) The returning officer shall—

(a) in the presence of the counting agents open each ballot box, count and record the number of ballot papers in it and verify each ballot paper account;

(b) where two polls have been taken together, separate the ballot papers relating to each poll and count and record the number of ballot papers relating to each poll; and

(c) then mix together the whole of the ballot papers relating to the poll or each poll, as the case may be, which were contained in the ballot boxes.

(2) The returning officer shall not count any tendered ballot paper.

(3) The returning officer, while separating, counting and recording the number of ballot papers and counting the votes, shall keep the ballot papers with their faces upwards and take all proper precautions for preventing any person from seeing the numbers printed on the back of the papers.

(4) The returning officer shall verify each ballot paper account by comparing it with the number of ballot papers recorded by him, and the unused and spoilt ballot papers in his possession and the tendered votes list (opening and resealing the packets containing the unused and spoilt ballot papers and the tendered votes list) and shall draw up a statement as to the result of the verification, which any counting agent may copy.

(5) The returning officer shall so far as practicable proceed continuously with counting the votes, allowing only time for refreshment, except that he may, in so far as he thinks necessary, exclude the hours between 7 in the evening and 9 on the following morning.

(6) During the time so excluded the returning officer shall—

(a) place the ballot papers and other documents relating to the poll under his own seal and the seals of such of the counting agents as desire to affix their seals; and

(b) otherwise take proper precautions for the security of the papers and documents.

Re-count

28.—(1) A candidate may, if present when the counting or any re-count of the votes is completed, require the returning officer to have the votes re-counted or again re-counted but the returning officer may refuse to do so if in his opinion the request is unreasonable.

(2) No step shall be taken on the completion of the counting or any re-count of votes until the candidates present at its completion have been given a reasonable opportunity to exercise the right conferred by this rule.

Rejected ballot papers

29.—(1) Any ballot paper—

(a) which does not bear the official mark, or

(b) on which votes are given for more candidates than the voter is entitled to vote for or on which votes are given for and against the same question, or

(c) on which anything is written or marked by which the voter can be identified except the printed number on the back, or

(d) which is unmarked or void for uncertainty,

shall, subject to paragraphs (2) and (3) below, be void and not counted.

(2) Where the voter is entitled to vote for more than one candidate or on more than one question, a ballot paper shall not be deemed to be void for uncertainty as respects any vote as to which no uncertainty arises and that vote shall be counted.

(3) A ballot paper on which the vote is marked—

(a) elsewhere than in the proper place, or

(b) otherwise than by means of a cross, or

(c) by more than one mark,

shall not for such reason be deemed to be void (either wholly or as respects that vote) if an intention that the vote shall be for one or other of the candidates or for or against any question clearly appears, and the way the paper is marked does not itself identify the voter and it is not shown that he can be identified by it.

(4) The returning officer shall—

(a) endorse the word "rejected" on any ballot paper which under this rule is not to be counted; and

(b) in the case of a ballot paper on which any vote is counted under paragraph (2) above, endorse the words "rejected in part" on the ballot paper and indicate which vote or votes have been counted;

and shall add to the endorsement the words "rejection objected to" if any objection is made by a counting agent to his decision.

(5) The returning officer shall draw up a statement showing the number of ballot papers rejected, including those rejected in part, under the several heads of—

(a) want of official mark;

(b) voting for more candidates than voter is entitled to or for and against the same question;

(c) writing or mark by which voter could be identified;

(d) unmarked or void for uncertainty;

and the statement shall record the number of ballot papers rejected in part.

Decisions on ballot papers

30. The decision of the returning officer on any question arising in respect of a ballot paper shall be final, but shall be subject to review on an election petition.

Equality of votes

31. Where, after the counting of the votes (including any re-count) is completed, an equality of votes is found to exist between any candidates or for and against any question and the addition of a vote would entitle any of those candidates to be declared elected or would decide the question, the returning officer shall forthwith decide either between those candidates or that question by lot, and proceed as if the candidate or answer in favour of or against the question on whom or on which the lot falls had received an additional vote.

Declaration of result

32. When the result of the poll has been ascertained the returning officer shall forthwith—

(a) in the case of a poll on the question of appointment to any office—

   (i) declare to be elected the candidate or candidates to whom more votes have been given than to the other candidates, up to the number of appointments to be made;

   (ii) give notice of the name of each person elected to the chairman of the meeting at which the poll was demanded; and

   (iii) give public notice of the name of each candidate elected and of the total number of votes given for each candidate (whether elected or not) together with the number of rejected ballot papers under each head shown in the statement of rejected ballot papers;

(b) in the case of a poll on any other question—

   (i) declare the number of votes given for and against the question and whether the proposal to which the question relates has been carried or not;

   (ii) give notice of the result of the poll to the chairman of the meeting at which the poll was demanded; and

   (iii) give public notice of the declaration under sub-paragraph (i) above, together with the number of rejected ballot papers under each head shown in the statement of rejected ballot papers.

Sealing up of ballot papers

33.—(1) On the completion of the counting, the returning officer shall seal up in separate packets the counted and rejected ballot papers, including ballot papers rejected in part.

(2) The returning officer shall not open the sealed packets of tendered ballot papers or of counterfoils or of marked copies of the register of electors.

Delivery of documents to district council

34. The returning officer shall then forward to the proper officer of the council of the district in which the parish or community is situate the following documents—

(a) the packets of ballot papers in his possession,

(b) the ballot paper accounts and the statements of rejected ballot papers and of the result of the verification of the ballot paper accounts,

(c) the tendered votes lists, the lists of blind voters assisted by companions, the lists of votes marked by the presiding officer and the related statements, and the declarations made by the companions of blind voters,

(d) the packets of counterfoils,

(e) the packets containing marked copies of the register of electors,

endorsing on each packet a description of its contents, the date of the poll to which they relate and the name of the parish or community for which the poll was held.

Orders for production of documents

35.—(1) An order—

(a) for the inspection or production of any rejected ballot papers, including ballot papers rejected in part, in the custody of the proper officer of the council of the district in which the parish or community is situate; or

(b) for the opening of a sealed packet of counterfoils or the inspection of any counted ballot papers in his custody,

may be made by a county court, if the court is satisfied by evidence on oath that the order is required for the purpose of instituting or maintaining a prosecution for an offence in relation to ballot papers, or for the purpose of an election petition.

(2) An order for the opening of a sealed packet of counterfoils or for the inspection of any counted ballot papers in the custody of the proper officer referred to in paragraph (1) above may be made by an election court.

(3) An order under this rule may be made subject to such conditions as to—

(a) persons,

(b) time,

(c) place and mode of inspection,

(d) production or opening,

as the court making the order may think expedient; but in making and carrying into effect an order for the opening of a packet of counterfoils or for the inspection of counted ballot papers, care shall be taken that the way in which the vote of any particular elector has been given shall not be disclosed until it has been proved—

(i) that his vote was given; and

(ii) that the vote has been declared by a competent court to be invalid.

(4) An appeal lies to the High Court from any order of a county court under this rule.

(5) Any power given under this rule to a county court may be exercised by any judge of the court otherwise than in open court.

(6) Where an order is made for the production by the proper officer referred to in paragraph (1) above of any document in his possession relating to any specified poll—

(a) the production by him or his agent of the document ordered in such manner as may be directed by that order shall be conclusive evidence that the document relates to the specified poll; and

(b) any endorsement on any packet of ballot papers so produced shall be prima facie evidence that the ballot papers are what they are stated to be by the endorsement.

(7) The production from proper custody of a ballot paper purporting to have been used at any poll and of a counterfoil marked with the same printed number and having a number marked on it in writing, shall be prima facie evidence that the elector whose vote was given by that ballot paper was the person who at the time of the poll had affixed to his name in the register of electors the same number as the number written on the counterfoil.

(8) Save as by this rule provided, no person shall be allowed to inspect any rejected or counted ballot papers in the possession of the proper officer referred to in paragraph (1) above or open any sealed packets of counterfoils.

Retention and public inspection of documents

36.—(1) The proper officer of the council of the district in which the parish or community is situate shall retain for six months amongst the records of the council all documents relating to a poll forwarded to him in pursuance of these rules by a returning officer, and then, unless otherwise directed by an order of a county court or an election court, shall cause them to be destroyed.

(2) The documents, except ballot papers and counterfoils, shall be open to public inspection at such time and in such manner as the district council may determine.

(3) The proper officer referred to in paragraph (1) above shall, on request, supply copies of or extracts from the documents open to public inspection on payment of such fees and subject to such conditions as may be determined by the district council.

Countermand or abandonment of poll on death of candidate

37.—(1) If before the result of the poll is declared proof is given to the returning officer's satisfaction that a candidate who has not withdrawn has died, then the returning officer shall countermand notice of the poll or, if polling has begun, direct that the poll be abandoned.

(2) Where the poll is abandoned by reason of a candidate's death, the proceedings at or consequent on that poll shall be interrupted, and the presiding officer at any polling station shall take the like steps (so far as not already taken) for the delivery to the returning officer of ballot boxes and of ballot papers and other documents as he is required to take on the close of the poll in due course, and the returning officer shall dispose of ballot papers and other documents in his possession as he is required to do on the completion in due course of the counting of the votes, but—

(a) it shall not be necessary for any ballot paper account to be prepared or verified; and

(b) the returning officer, without taking any step or further step for the counting of the ballot papers or of the votes shall seal up all the ballot papers, whether the votes on them have been counted or not, and it shall not be necessary to seal up counted and rejected ballot papers in separate packets.

(3) The provisions of these rules as to the inspection, production, retention and destruction of ballot papers and other documents relating to a poll apply to any such documents relating to a poll abandoned by reason of a candidate's death, with the following modifications—

(a) ballot papers on which the votes were neither counted nor rejected shall be treated as counted ballot papers; and

(b) no order shall be made for the production or inspection of any ballot papers or for the opening of a sealed packet of counterfoils unless the order is made by a court with reference to a prosecution.

(4) Where a poll is countermanded or abandoned by reason of a candidate's death, the district council in which the parish or community is situate may by order make any appointment, or make provision for the holding of a parish meeting or do such other thing as appears to them to be expedient in the circumstances.

Interpretation

38.—(1) Where a poll is held in part only of a parish or community, any reference in these rules to a parish or community shall be construed as reference to a part of a parish or part of a community, as the case may be.

(2) A public notice required by these rules to be given by the returning officer shall be given by posting the notice in some conspicuous place or places in the parish or community, and may also be given in such other manner as he thinks desirable for publicising it.

(3) Any reference in these rules to a proper officer of a council means any officer appointed for that purpose by that council.

APPENDIX

Note. — The forms contained in this Appendix may be adapted as far as circumstances require.

Rule 4

FORM OF BALLOT PAPER ON A QUESTION OF APPOINTMENT TO AN OFFICE

Form of front of ballot paper

VOTE FOR .... CANDIDATE(S) ONLY

Counterfoil
No.

*The counterfoil is
to have a number
to correspond with
that on the back of
the ballot paper.*

1	**BROWN** JOHN EDWARD Brown, 2 The Cottages, Barlington, Grayshire Labour	
2	**BROWN** THOMAS WILLIAM Brown, 15 Barchester Road, Barlington, Grayshire Liberal	
3	**JONES** William David Jones, The Grange, Barlington, Grayshire Conservative	
4	**MERTON** Hon. George Travis, commonly called Viscount Merton, Barlington, Grayshire	
5	**SMITH** Mary Smith, School House, Barlington, Grayshire Schoolteacher, Progressive	
6	**WILLIAMS** Elizabeth Williams, 3 Ivy Lane, Barlington, Grayshire Housewife	

Form of back of ballot paper

No.

Poll on appointment of [*insert name of office*] for the Parish of .... on
.... 19...

Note. — The number on the ballot paper is to correspond with that on the counterfoil.

Directions as to printing the ballot paper

1. Nothing is to be printed on the ballot paper except in accordance with these directions.

2. So far as practicable, the following arrangements shall be observed in the printing of the ballot paper:—

(a) no word shall be printed on the face except the direction "VOTE FOR .... CANDIDATE(S) ONLY" and the particulars of the candidates;

(b) no rule shall be printed on the face except the horizontal rule separating the direction mentioned in paragraph *(a)* above from the particulars of the candidates and the horizontal rules separating the particulars of the candidates from one another and the vertical rules separating those particulars from the numbers on the left-hand side and the spaces on the right where the vote is to be marked;

(c) the whole space between the top and the bottom of the paper shall be equally divided between the direction mentioned in paragraph *(a)* above and each of the candidates by the horizontal rules mentioned in paragraph *(b)* above.

3. The direction mentioned in paragraph 2*(a)* above shall be printed in large capitals.

4. The surname of each candidate shall in all cases be printed by itself in large capitals, and his full particulars shall be set out below it and shall be printed in ordinary type except that small capitals shall be used—

(a) if his surname is the same as another candidate's, for his other names; and

(b) if his other names are also the same as the other candidate's, either for his home address or for his description unless each of them is the same as that of another candidate with the same surname and other names.

5. The number on the back of the ballot paper shall be printed in small characters.

Rule 4

FORM OF BALLOT PAPER ON A QUESTION OTHER THAN THAT OF APPOINTMENT TO AN OFFICE

Form of front of ballot paper

Counterfoil No.	Question[s]	Answer[s]	
		Yes	No
The counterfoil is to have a number to correspond with that on the back of the ballot paper	[*Insert question or questions to be asked*]		

Form of back of ballot paper

No.

Poll consequent on Parish/Community Meeting for the Parish/Community of .... on .... 19...

Note. — *The number on the ballot paper is to correspond with that on the counterfoil.*

Directions as to printing the ballot paper

1. Nothing is to be printed on the ballot paper except in accordance with these directions.

2. So far as practicable, the following arrangements shall be observed in the printing of the ballot paper:—

(a) no word shall be printed on the face except the words "Question[s]" and "Answer[s]", the question or questions to be asked and the words "Yes" and "No" underneath "Answer[s]";

(b) no rule shall be printed on the face except the vertical rules separating the questions from the answers and the answers from each other and, where more than one question is asked, a horizontal rule separating the answers to each question; and

(c) an equal amount of space shall be allocated for the answer "Yes" and the answer "No" to each question.

3. The number on the back of the ballot paper shall be printed in small characters.

Rule 11

FORM OF DIRECTIONS FOR THE GUIDANCE OF THE VOTERS IN VOTING WHERE THE POLL IS ON A QUESTION OF APPOINTMENT TO AN OFFICE

GUIDANCE FOR VOTERS

1. When you are given a ballot paper, make sure it is stamped with the official mark.

2. Go to one of the compartments. Mark a cross (X) in the box on the right hand side of the ballot paper opposite the name(s) of the candidate(s) you are voting for.

3. Fold the ballot paper in two. Show the official mark to the presiding officer, but do not let anyone see your vote. Put the ballot paper in the ballot box and leave the polling station.

4. Vote for …. candidate(s) only. Put no other mark on the ballot paper or your vote may not be counted.

5. If by mistake you spoil a ballot paper, show it to the presiding officer and ask for another one.

Rule 11

FORM OF DIRECTIONS FOR GUIDANCE OF THE VOTERS IN VOTING WHERE THE POLL IS ON A QUESTION OTHER THAN THAT OF APPOINTMENT TO AN OFFICE

GUIDANCE FOR VOTERS

1. When you are given a ballot paper, make sure it is stamped with the official mark.

2. Go to one of the compartments. Mark a cross (X) in the column of the ballot paper which is headed "Yes" or in that headed "No" according to whether you wish to vote for or against the question(s) opposite to which you mark your cross. Put no other mark on the ballot paper or your vote may not be counted.

3. Fold the ballot paper in two. Show the official mark to the presiding officer, but do not let anyone see your vote. Put the ballot paper in the ballot box and leave the polling station.

4. If by mistake you spoil a ballot paper, show it to the presiding officer and ask for another one.

Rule 21(5)

FORM OF DECLARATION TO BE MADE BY THE COMPANION OF A BLIND VOTER

I, A. B., of ...., having been requested to assist C.D. whose number on the register is .... to record his vote at the poll now being held in this [parish] [community] hereby declare that [I am entitled to vote as an elector at the said poll] [I am the ....*........ of the said voter and have attained the age of 18 years], and that I have not previously assisted any blind person [except E.F., of ....] to vote at the said poll.

(Signed) A.B.,

day of   19

I, the undersigned, being the presiding officer for the .... polling station for [................... ward of the] Parish/Community of .... hereby certify that the above declaration, having been first read to the above-named declarant, was signed by the declarant in my presence.

(Signed) G.H.,

day of   19   .
minutes past   o'clock [p.m.]

NOTE: — If the person making the above declaration knowingly and wilfully makes therein a statement false in a material particular, he will be guilty of an offence.

*State the relationship of the companion to the voter.

EXPLANATORY NOTE

(This note is not part of these Rules)

These Rules replace the Parish and Community Meetings (Polls) Rules 1973, as amended, ("the 1973 Rules") which are revoked by Rule 3 of these Rules. These Rules provide for the conduct of a poll consequent on a parish or community meeting (Rule 5 and the Schedule).

The rules in the Schedule to these Rules, like the rules in the Schedule to the 1973 Rules, apply with adaptations, alterations and exceptions the elections rules which apply for the election of parish or community councillors. The relevant rules for those elections are now the Local Elections (Parishes and Communities) Rules 1986 and the elections rules in Schedule 2 to those Rules are applied in the Schedule to these Rules. The provisions about computation of time (rule 2), notices in polling stations (rule 11 and the Appendix) and the notification of the requirement of secrecy (rule 13) differ from the 1973 Rules. In addition, the Appendix to the rules no longer prescribes forms the content of which is sufficiently described in the text of the rules.

Rule 6 modifies certain provisions of the Representation of the People Act 1983 in their application to the election of a chairman of a parish meeting and to a poll consequent on a parish or community meeting.

STATUTORY INSTRUMENTS

1987 No. 2 (S. 1)

NATIONAL HEALTH SERVICE, SCOTLAND

The National Health Service (Food Premises) (Scotland) Regulations 1987

Made - - - -	*6th January 1987*
Laid before Parliament	*16th January 1987*
Coming into force	*7th February 1987*

The Secretary of State, in exercise of powers conferred on him by section 1(2)(a) of the National Health Service (Amendment) Act 1986(**a**), and of all other powers enabling him in that behalf, hereby makes the following regulations:

Citation, commencement and interpretation

1.—(1) These regulations may be cited as the National Health Service (Food Premises) (Scotland) Regulations 1987 and shall come into force on 7th February 1987.

(2) In these regulations -

"the food legislation" means the Milk and Dairies (Scotland) Acts 1914 to 1949(**b**), the Food and Drugs (Scotland) Act 1956(**c**), and the Control of Food Premises (Scotland) Act 1977(**d**) and any regulations or order made under those Acts;

"health authority" means a Health Board constituted under section 2 of the National Health Service (Scotland) Act 1978(**e**), the Common Services Agency constituted under section 10 of that Act(**f**) or a State Hospital Management Committee constituted under section 91 of the Mental Health (Scotland) Act 1984(**g**).

Occupiers or owners of health service premises

2. For the purposes of the food legislation a health authority shall be treated as both the owner and occupier of premises used by that authority.

New St. Andrew's House
Edinburgh
6th January 1987

Glenarthur
Minister of State,
Scottish Office

(**a**) 1986 c.66. (**b**) 1914 c.46, 1922 c.54 and 1949 c.34; *see* section 16(4) of the Milk (Special Designations) Act 1949 (c.34). (**c**) 1956 c.30. (**d**) 1977 c.28. (**e**) 1978 c.29; section 2 was amended by the Health and Social Services and Social Security Adjudications Act 1983 (c.41), Schedule 7, paragraph 1. (**f**) Section 10 was amended by the Health Services Act 1980 (c.53), Schedule 6, paragraph 2. (**g**) 1984 c.36.

EXPLANATORY NOTE

(This note is not part of the Regulations)

These regulations provide that health authorities in Scotland shall, for the purposes of the food legislation (as defined in these regulations) and of any regulations or order made under that legislation, be treated as both owners and occupiers of premises used by them.

1987 No. 3

TELECOMMUNICATIONS

The Public Telecommunication System Designation (Swindon Cable Limited) Order 1987

Made - - - -	5th January 1987
Laid before Parliament	8th January 1987
Coming into force	6th February 1987

Whereas the Secretary of State has granted to Swindon Cable Limited a licence ("the Licence") under section 7 of the Telecommunications Act 1984(**a**) ("the Act"), to which section 8 of the Act applies, for the running of the telecommunication systems specified in Annex A to the Licence ("the Applicable Cabled Systems");

Now, therefore, the Secretary of State, in exercise of the powers conferred on him by sections 9 and 104 of the Act, hereby makes the following Order:

1.—(1) This Order may be cited as the Public Telecommunication System Designation (Swindon Cable Limited) Order 1987 and shall come into force on 6th February 1987.

(2) The Public Telecommunication System Designation (Swindon Cable Limited) Order 1985(**b**) is hereby revoked.

2. Each of the Applicable Cabled Systems is hereby designated as a public telecommunication system.

Geoffrey Pattie
Minister of State,
Department of Trade and Industry

5th January 1987

(**a**) 1984 c.12.
(**b**) S.I. 1985/1596, made under sections 9 and 104 of the Act.

EXPLANATORY NOTE

(This note is not part of the Order)

The Secretary of State granted to Swindon Cable Limited on 31st December 1986 a licence under section 7 of the Telecommunications Act 1984 ("the Act") to run the telecommunication systems specified in Annex A to that licence, in Swindon, Wiltshire. A copy of the licence was laid before Parliament on 8th January 1987. The licence replaces a licence previously granted to Swindon Cable Limited on 29th July 1985 ("the 1985 Licence") which will be revoked. This Order replaces the Public Telecommunication System Designation (Swindon Cable Limited) Order 1985 which applies to the 1985 licence and designates the telecommunication systems specified in the new licence as public telecommunication systems. Consequently, by virtue of section 9(3) of the Act, Swindon Cable Limited will continue to be a public telecommunications operator when the Order comes into force.

A copy of the new licence may be obtained from the Office of Telecommunications, Atlantic House, Holborn Viaduct, London EC1N 2HQ.

STATUTORY INSTRUMENTS

1987 No. 4

OFFSHORE INSTALLATIONS

The Offshore Installations (Safety Zones) (Amendment) Order 1987

Made - - - -	*7th January 1987*
Coming into force	*9th January 1987*

The Secretary of State, in exercise of the power conferred on him by section 21(1) of the Oil and Gas (Enterprise) Act 1982(**a**), and of all other powers enabling him in that behalf, hereby makes the following Order:

1. This Order may be cited as the Offshore Installations (Safety Zones) (Amendment) Order 1987 and shall come into force on 9th January 1987.

2. In column 1 of the Schedule to the Offshore Installations (Safety Zones) (No. 69) Order 1986(**b**) for the designation "21/10–FE" there shall be substituted the designation "22/6–FE".

Alastair Goodlad
Parliamentary Under Secretary of State,
Department of Energy

7th January 1987

EXPLANATORY NOTE

(This note is not part of the Order)

This order amends the Offshore Installations (Safety Zones) (No. 69) Order 1986 by changing the designation of the offshore installation to which the Order applies. This is necessary because the designation of the installation has been changed.

(**a**) 1982 c.23.
(**b**) S.I. 1986/1199.

STATUTORY INSTRUMENTS

1987 No. 5

NATIONAL HEALTH SERVICE, ENGLAND AND WALES

The National Health Service (General Medical and Pharmaceutical Services) Amendment Regulations 1987

Made - - - -	*6th January 1987*
Laid before Parliament	*9th January 1987*
Coming into force	
For the purposes of regulation 2(4)	*1st August 1987*
For all other purposes	*1st February 1987*

The Secretary of State for Social Services, in exercise of powers conferred upon him by sections 29, 41 and 42 of the National Health Service Act 1977**(a)** and of all other powers enabling him in that behalf, hereby makes the following regulations:—

Citation and commencement

1. These regulations may be cited as the National Health Service (General Medical and Pharmaceutical Services) Amendment Regulations 1987 and shall come into force for the purposes of regulation 2(4) on 1st August 1987 and for all other purposes on 1st February 1987.

Amendment of regulations

2.—(1) Schedule 3A to the National Health Service (General Medical and Pharmaceutical Services) Regulations 1974**(b)** (drugs and other substances not to be prescribed for supply under pharmaceutical services) shall be amended in accordance with the following paragraphs of this regulation.

(2) The following entries shall be omitted:—

Fenoprofen Tablets 200 mg
Maalox Tablets
Maalox TC Tablets
Progesic Tablets 200 mg.

(3) The following entries shall be inserted at the appropriate point in the alphabetical order:—

Actonorm Gel
Angiers Junior Paracetamol Tablets
Catarrh—Ex Tablets
Dextromethorphan Hydrobromide Solution 3.75 mg/5 ml

(a) 1977 c.49; section 29 was amended by the Health Services Act 1980 (c.53) ("the 1980 Act"), section 7 and Schedule 1, paragraph 42 and by the Health and Social Services and Social Security Adjudications Act 1983 (c.41), Schedule 6, paragraph 2; section 41 was amended by the 1980 Act, section 20(1) and Schedule 1, paragraph 53 and Schedule 7; section 42 was amended by the 1980 Act, section 21(1) and Schedule 1, paragraph 54; sections 29, 41 and 42 were each modified by S.I. 1985/39.

(b) S.I. 1974/160; relevant amending instruments are S.I. 1985/290 and 1712.

Dextromethorphan Hydrobromide Solution 7.5 mg/5 ml
Haliborange Tablets
Hot Blackcurrant Cold Remedy (Beechams)
Hot Lemon Cold Remedy (Beechams)
Librofem Tablets
Mentholatum Nasal Inhaler
Night Nurse Capsules
Panacron Nasal Spray
Paxidal Tablets
Resolve Granules
Robitussin Cough Soother
Robitussin Cough Soother Junior Formula
Robitussin Plus Liquid
Seclodin Capsules
Seven Seas Malt and Cod Liver Oil
Simeco Suspension
Simeco Tablets.

(4) The following entry shall be inserted at the appropriate point in the alphabetical order:—

Normax Capsules.

Signed by authority of the Secretary of State for Social Services.

Tony Newton
6th January 1987   Minister of State, Department of Health and Social Security

---

EXPLANATORY NOTE

(This note is not part of the Regulations)

These Regulations amend the National Health Service (General Medical and Pharmaceutical Services) Regulations 1974 ("the 1974 Regulations"), which regulate the terms on which doctors and chemists provide general medical services and pharmaceutical services under the National Health Service Act 1977.

Schedule 3A to the 1974 Regulations contains a list of drugs and other substances for which a doctor may not issue a prescription for supply under pharmaceutical services and which may not be dispensed under those services. These Regulations add some drugs to, and delete others from, that list.

STATUTORY INSTRUMENTS

1987 No. 6

NATIONAL HEALTH SERVICE, ENGLAND AND WALES

The Health Education Authority (Establishment and Constitution) Order 1987

Made - - -	*7th January 1987*
Laid before Parliament	*13th January 1987*
Coming into force	*3rd February 1987*

The Secretary of State for Social Services, in exercise of powers conferred upon him by section 11 of the National Health Service Act 1977(a) and of all other powers enabling him in that behalf, hereby makes the following Order:—

Citation and commencement

1. This Order may be cited as the Health Education Authority (Establishment and Constitution) Order 1987 and shall come into force on 3rd February 1987.

Establishment of the Health Education Authority

2. There is hereby established a special health authority which shall be known as the Health Education Authority (in this Order referred to as "the Authority").

Functions of the Authority

3.— (1) Subject to and in accordance with such directions as the Secretary of State may give to the Authority, the Authority shall perform the functions specified in paragraph (2) of this Article and such other functions as the Secretary of State may direct the Authority to perform on his behalf.

(2) The functions referred to in paragraph (1) of this Article are—
  (a) advising the Secretary of State for Social Services on matters relating to health education;
  (b) undertaking health education activity;
  (c) for that purpose planning and carrying out national and regional or local programmes or other activities in co-operation with health authorities, Family Practitioner Committees, local authorities and local education authorities, voluntary organisations and other persons or bodies concerned with health education;
  (d) sponsoring research and evaluation in relation to health education;
  (e) assisting the provision of appropriate training in health education;
  (f) preparing, publishing or distributing material relevant to health education;
  (g) providing a national centre of information and advice on health education;

(a) 1977 c.49; section 11 was amended by the Health Services Act 1980 (c.53), Schedule 1, paragraph 31.

(h) exercising the Secretary of State's functions—

    (i) under section 23(1) of the National Health Service Act 1977 with respect to arranging with any person or body (including a voluntary organisation) for that body to assist in providing any service under that Act;

    (ii) under section 23(2) of that Act with respect to making available to certain persons or bodies (including voluntary organisations) facilities and services of persons employed in connection with such facilities;

    (iii) under section 23(3) of that Act with respect to the agreement of terms and the making of payments in respect of facilities or services provided under section 23 of that Act;

insofar as such services are provided under that Act in pursuance of the functions specified above.

Constitution of the Authority

4. The Authority shall consist of such number of members not exceeding 20 as the Secretary of State may from time to time determine, all of whom shall be appointed by the Secretary of State and of whom—

(a) one shall be Chairman;

(b) one shall be appointed on nomination by the Secretary of State for Education and Science.

Norman Fowler

7th January 1987   Secretary of State for Social Services

EXPLANATORY NOTE

(This note is not part of the Order)

This Order provides for the establishment and constitution of a special health authority to be known as the Health Education Authority for the purpose of carrying out certain specified functions relating to health education (Article 3(2)) and such other functions as the Secretary of State may direct.

STATUTORY INSTRUMENTS

1987 No. 7

NATIONAL HEALTH SERVICE, ENGLAND AND WALES

The Health Education Authority Regulations 1987

Made - - - -		*7th January 1987*
Laid before Parliament		*13th January 1987*
Coming into force - -		*3rd February 1987*

The Secretary of State for Social Services, in exercise of powers conferred by paragraphs 12 and 16 of Schedule 5 to the National Health Service Act 1977(a) and of all other powers enabling him in that behalf, hereby makes the following regulations:

Citation, commencement and interpretation

1.—(1) These regulations may be cited as the Health Education Authority Regulations 1987 and shall come into force on 3rd February 1987.

(2) In these regulations unless the context otherwise requires—

"the Authority" means the Health Education Authority established by the Health Education Authority (Establishment and Constitution) Order 1987 (**b**);

"member" means the Chairman or other member of the Authority.

Tenure of office of member

2. Subject to any provisions applied by these regulations as to termination of and disqualification for membership, the tenure of office of a member shall be for such period not exceeding four years as the Secretary of State shall specify on making the appointment.

Termination of tenure of office

3.—(1) A member may resign his office at any time during the period for which he was appointed by giving notice in writing to the Secretary of State.

(2) Where the Secretary of State is satisfied that it is not in the interests of the Authority or the health service that a person whom he has appointed as a member should continue to hold that office, he may forthwith terminate that member's tenure of office.

Application of regulations relating to membership and procedure

4. The provisions of regulations 5(4), (6) and (7) (termination of tenure of office), regulation 6 (eligibility for reappointment), regulation 7 (disqualification for appointment), regulation 8 (cessation of disqualification), regulation 9 (election of vice-chairman), regulation 10 (powers of vice-chairman), regulation 11 (appointment of

---

(**a**) 1977 c.49.   (**b**) S.I. 1987/6.

committees and sub-committees), regulation 12 (arrangements for the exercise of functions), regulation 13 (meetings and proceedings), regulation 14 (disability of chairman and members in proceedings on account of pecuniary interests) of and Schedule 1 (rules as to meetings and proceedings of Authorities) to the National Health Service (Regional and District Health Authorities: Membership and Procedure) Regulations 1983(a) shall apply in relation to the Authority as if any reference in those provisions to an Authority included a reference to the Authority.

Reports and papers by the Authority

5.   The Authority shall make reports to the Secretary of State in such manner and at such time, being at least once a year, as the Secretary of State may direct and shall furnish to the Secretary of State such information as he may from time to time require.

Norman Fowler
7th January 1987   Secretary of State for Social Services

EXPLANATORY NOTE

(This note is not part of the Regulations)

These Regulations provide for the tenure of office of the Chairman and other members of the special health authority known as the Health Education Authority. They also provide for the procedure of and report to the Secretary of State by that Authority.

(a) S.I. 1983/315.

STATUTORY INSTRUMENTS

1987 No. 8

PRICES

The Price Marking (Petrol) (Amendment) Order 1987

Made - - -	*7th January 1987*
Laid before Parliament	*16th January 1987*
Coming into force	*1st March 1987*

The Secretary of State, after consulting in accordance with section 4(3) of the Prices Act 1974(**a**) with the organisations therein referred to, in exercise of his powers under that section and of all other powers enabling him in that behalf, hereby makes the following Order:—

1. This Order may be cited as the Price Marking (Petrol) (Amendment) Order 1987 and shall come into operation on 1st March 1987.

2. The Price Marking (Petrol) Order 1980(**b**) is hereby amended—

(*a*) in Article 2 by deleting paragraph (1) and substituting therefor the following paragraph:

"(1) In this Order, a grade of petrol means one of the following grades, that is to say, 2 star, 3 star or 4 star as mentioned in the British Standard specification for leaded petrol (gasoline) for motor vehicles B.S. 4040: 1985 published by the British Standards Institution on 31st May 1985 or as the case may be Premium or Regular as mentioned in the British Standard specification for unleaded petrol (gasoline) for motor vehicles B.S. 7070: 1985 published by the British Standards Institution on 31st October 1985."; and

(*b*) in paragraph 8(2) in Part III of the Schedule by inserting the word "leaded" before the word "petrol" in the second place in which it occurs.

Lucas of Chilworth
Parliamentary Under-Secretary of State,
Department of Trade and Industry

7th January 1987

(**a**) 1974 c.24; section 4 was amended by the Price Commission Act 1977 (c.33), section 16(1).
(**b**) S.I. 1980/1121.

EXPLANATORY NOTE

(This note is not part of the Order)

This Order amends the Price Marking (Petrol) Order 1980 by—

    (a) bringing grades of unleaded petrol mentioned in the British Standard (B.S. 7070) within the scope of the Order;

       and

    (b) updating the reference to the British Standard (B.S. 4040) which sets out the specifications for grades of leaded petrol.

Copies of British Standards can be obtained from any of the sales outlets operated by the British Standards Institution (BSI), or by post from the BSI at Linford Wood, Milton Keynes, MK14 6LE.

STATUTORY INSTRUMENTS

1987 No. 11 (S. 2)

HOUSING, SCOTLAND

The Housing Revenue Account Rate Fund Contribution Limits (Scotland) Order 1987

Made - - - -	*7th January 1987*
Laid before Parliament	*20th January 1987*
Coming into force	*11th February 1987*

The Secretary of State, in exercise of the powers conferred on him by section 23A of the Housing (Financial Provisions) (Scotland) Act 1972(**a**) and of all other powers enabling him in that behalf, hereby makes the following order:

Citation and commencement

1. This order may be cited as the Housing Revenue Account Rate Fund Contribution Limits (Scotland) Order 1987 and shall come into force on 11th February 1987.

Rate fund contribution limit

2. The amount of contribution out of its general fund which each of the local authorities listed in Column 1 of the Schedule hereto may estimate that it will carry to the credit of its housing revenue account for the year 1987-88 shall not exceed the amount set out in relation to that authority in Column 2 thereof.

New St. Andrew's House
Edinburgh
7th January 1987

Ian Lang
Parliamentary Under Secretary of State,
Scottish Office

(**a**) 1972 c.46; section 23A was inserted by section 8 of the Rating and Valuation (Amendment) (Scotland) Act 1984 (c.31).

Article 2   SCHEDULE

Column 1 District Councils	Column 2 £m
Berwickshire	Nil
Ettrick & Lauderdale	Nil
Roxburgh	0.084
Tweeddale	Nil
Clackmannan	0.322
Falkirk	1.097
Stirling	0.438
Annandale & Eskdale	0.177
Nithsdale	0.277
Stewartry	0.084
Wigtown	Nil
Dunfermline	0.712
Kirkcaldy	0.836
North East Fife	Nil
City of Aberdeen	2.319
Banff & Buchan	0.111
Gordon	0.194
Kincardine & Deeside	0.127
Moray	Nil
Badenoch & Strathspey	0.039
Caithness	0.138
Inverness	0.330
Lochaber	0.687
Nairn	0.038
Ross & Cromarty	0.220
Skye & Lochalsh	0.028
Sutherland	0.061
East Lothian	0.525
City of Edinburgh	1.821
Midlothian	0.407
West Lothian	0.746
Argyll & Bute	0.088
Bearsden & Milngavie	0.125
Clydebank	0.409
Clydesdale	0.339
Cumbernauld & Kilsyth	0.152
Cumnock & Doon Valley	0.353
Cunninghame	0.799
Dumbarton	0.463
East Kilbride	0.050
Eastwood	0.066
City of Glasgow	19.977
Hamilton	0.913
Inverclyde	0.663
Kilmarnock & Loudoun	0.599
Kyle & Carrick	0.606
Monklands	1.005

Column 1 District Councils	Column 2 £m
Motherwell	1.374
Renfrew	1.343
Strathkelvin	0.363
Angus	Nil
City of Dundee	1.397
Perth & Kinross	Nil
Islands Councils	
Orkney Islands	0.052
Shetland Islands	0.527
Western Isles	0.241

EXPLANATORY NOTE

(This note is not part of the Order)

This order limits the amount of contribution from the rates to the housing revenue account which local authorities may include in their estimates for the year 1987-88.

STATUTORY INSTRUMENTS

1987 No. 12 (S. 3)

COURT OF SESSION, SCOTLAND

Act of Sederunt (Rules of Court Amendment No. 1) (Drug Trafficking) 1987

Made - - - -	*8th January 1987*
Coming into force	*12th January 1987*

The Lords of Council and Session, under and by virtue of the powers conferred on them by section 16 of the Administration of Justice (Scotland) Act 1933(**a**), section 21(2) of the Drug Trafficking Offences Act 1986(**b**) and of all other powers enabling them in that behalf, do hereby enact and declare:

Citation and commencement

1.—(1) This Act of Sederunt may be cited as the Act of Sederunt (Rules of Court Amendment No. 1) (Drug Trafficking) 1987 and shall come into force on 12th January 1987.

(2) This Act of Sederunt shall be inserted in the Books of Sederunt.

Amendment of the Rules of the Court of Session

2.—(1) The Rules of the Court of Session(**c**) shall be amended in accordance with the following sub-paragraphs.

(2) After Section 8C of Chapter IV of the Rules of the Court of Session, insert the following Section:–

"SECTION 8D
REGISTRATION AND ENFORCEMENT OF ORDERS OF THE HIGH COURT IN ENGLAND AND WALES UNDER THE DRUG TRAFFICKING OFFENCES ACT 1986

249S. Interpretation

(1) In this Section–

"the Act of 1986" means the Drug Trafficking Offences Act 1986;

"Keeper of the Registers" means the Keeper of the Registers of Scotland.

(2) Words and expressions which are used in this section and are used in the Act of 1986 have the same meaning as in that Act, unless the context otherwise requires.

249T. Applications for registration

(1) An application under section 21(1) of the Act of 1986 for registration of an order to which section 20 of that Act applies, shall be made by petition presented to the Outer House.

(2) There shall be produced with a petition under paragraph (1) a certified copy of the order which is sought to be registered.

(**a**) 1933 c.41.   (**b**) 1986 c.32.   (**c**) S.I. 1965/321, as amended by S.I. 1986/1941.

(3) Rules 192 and 195 to 197 shall not apply to a petition under this section.

(4) The motion to grant the prayer of a petition under paragraph (1) shall not require an appearance for the petitioner unless the court so requires.

(5) Where the court requires an appearance under paragraph (4), the hearing shall be in chambers.

249U. Registration

(1) The court, on being satisfied that the application meets the requirements of the Act of 1986, shall–

    (a) grant decree and warrant for the registration of the order sought to be registered;

    (b) where necessary, grant decree of the order sought to be registered in accordance with Scots Law and grant decree and warrant for registration of that decree; and

    (c) where warrant for execution is sought, grant decree and warrant for registration in the Books of Council and Session.

(2) Where the court grants decree under paragraph (1), the Deputy Principal Clerk shall enter the order in a register for the registration of orders under the Act of 1986.

(3) Where decree and warrant for execution has been granted under paragraph (1)(c), upon presentation by the petitioner to the Keeper of the Registers of–

    (a) a certified copy of the interlocutor granting such decree and warrant for registration; and

    (b) a certified copy of the order to be registered,

the same shall be registered in the Register of Judgments of the Books of Council and Session whereupon the Keeper of the Registers shall issue an extract of the registered order and decree with warrant for execution.

249V. Intimation of registration

(1) Intimation of a decree and warrant for registration and of registration of an order under rule 249U shall be made by the petitioner in Form 62 to the person against whom the decree and warrant for registration was granted.

(2) Service of the intimation under paragraph (1) shall be made in accordance with rule 74A(**a**), 74B or 75, as the case may be, and an execution of service shall be lodged in process.

249W. Suspension of enforcement

Where an order has been registered under rule 249U, the court may on the application of the person against whom the order may be enforced by note in the process of the petition, if satisfied that it is sought to have the order set aside or quashed in the High Court in England and Wales–

    (a) suspend enforcement of the registered order; and

    (b) sist any proceedings for enforcement of the registered order.

249X. Modification and cancellation of registration

(1) An application to modify or cancel the registration of an order registered under rule 249U shall be made–

    (a) by the petitioner, by motion in the process of the petition; and

    (b) by any other interested party, by note in the process of the petition.

(2) There shall be produced with the application a certified copy of the order which modifies or revokes the registered order or which causes that order to cease to have effect.

(3) The court shall, on being satisfied that the registered order has been modified, revoked or has ceased to have effect, pronounce an interlocutor so modifying or cancelling the registration, as the case may be.

(**a**) Rule 74A was added by S.I. 1984/472 and amended by S.I. 1985/1600 and 1986/1941.

(4) Where the court pronounces an interlocutor under paragraph (3), the Deputy Principal Clerk shall modify or cancel the registration in the register kept under rule 249U(2) in accordance with that interlocutor.

249Y. Applications for inhibition and arrestment

(1) An application under section 22(1) of the Act of 1986 for warrant for inhibition or arrestment shall be made by the prosecutor–

(a) by motion in the process of the petition for registration under rule 249U where the prayer of the petition has previously been granted; or

(b) in the prayer of that petition.

(2) A motion under paragraph (1)(a) shall not require an appearance for the prosecutor unless the court so requires, in which case the hearing shall be in chambers.".

(3) In the Appendix, after Form 61, insert the following form:—

"FORM 62   Rule 249V(1)

**Intimation of decree and warrant for registration of an order of
the High Court in England and Wales under the Drug Trafficking Offences Act 1986**

IN THE COURT OF SESSION

in

PETITION

of

[AB]   (*address*)

under section 21 of the Drug
Trafficking Offences Act 1986

for

registration of an order of the High
Court of Justice in England and Wales

Dated the .... day of .... 19 ....

TO (*name of person against whom the order was made and decree and warrant for registration granted*).

TAKE NOTICE that an interlocutor dated the .... day of 19 ...., a certified copy of which is attached, was pronounced in the Court of Session granting decree and warrant for registration in the Court of Session [and for registration in the Register of Judgments of the Books of Council and Session] of the order of the High Court of Justice in England and Wales dated the .... day of .... 19 .... that (*briefly describe order*).

The order was registered in the Court of Session on (*date*).

[The order was registered in the Register of Judgments of the Books of Council and Session on (*date*) and an extract of the registered order and decree with warrant for execution has been issued by the Keeper of the Registers. Diligence in execution of the order may now be taken against you to enforce the order.]

Dated this .... day of .... 19 ....

(*Signed*)
Petitioner [or Solicitor for petitioner].

(*Address*)".

Edinburgh
8th January 1987

Emslie
Lord President,
I.P.D.

EXPLANATORY NOTE

(This note is not part of the Act of Sederunt)

This Act of Sederunt amends the rules of the Court of Session to make provision for registration and enforcement in Scotland of orders of the High Court in England and Wales under the Drug Trafficking Offences Act 1986.

STATUTORY INSTRUMENTS

1987 No. 16

ROAD TRAFFIC

The "Pelican" Pedestrian Crossings Regulations and General Directions 1987

Made - - - -	*12th January 1987*
Laid before Parliament	*28th January 1987*
Coming into force	*18th February 1987*

ARRANGEMENT

PART I: GENERAL

PART II: REGULATIONS

SCHEDULES TO PART II

PART III: GENERAL DIRECTIONS

Direction

The Secretary of State for Transport, the Secretary of State for Scotland and the Secretary of State for Wales, acting jointly in exercise of the powers conferred by sections 64 and 65(1) of the Road Traffic Regulation Act 1984(a), and acting separately in exercise of the powers conferred by section 25 of that Act, and of all other enabling powers, and after consultation with representative organisations in accordance with section 134(2) of that Act, hereby make the following Regulations and give the following Directions:

PART I

GENERAL

Citation and commencement

1. This Instrument may be cited as the "Pelican" Pedestrian Crossings Regulations and General Directions 1987 and shall come into force on 18th February 1987.

(a) 1984 c.27.

Revocation

2. The "Pelican" Pedestrian Crossings Regulations and General Directions 1969(**a**) and the "Pelican" Pedestrian Crossings (Amendment) Regulations and General Directions 1979(**b**) are hereby revoked.

Interpretation

3.—(1) In this Instrument–

(a) any reference to a numbered regulation is a reference to the regulation bearing that number in the Regulations contained in Part II of this Instrument; and

(b) except where otherwise stated, any reference to a numbered Schedule is a reference to the Schedule to the Regulations contained in Part II of this Instrument bearing that number.

(2) In this Instrument the following expressions have the meanings hereby respectively assigned to them–

"the 1984 Act" means the Road Traffic Regulation Act 1984;

"the 1969 Regulations" means the "Pelican" Pedestrian Crossing Regulations 1969;

"appropriate authority" means, in relation to a trunk road, the appropriate Secretary of State and, in relation to any other road, the local authority who established the crossing;

"appropriate Secretary of State" means, in relation to a crossing established or to be established on a road in–

(a) England, the Secretary of State for Transport;

(b) Scotland, the Secretary of State for Scotland; or

(c) Wales, the Secretary of State for Wales;

"carriageway" means–

(a) where it is in a highway, a way constituting or comprised in the highway being a way over which the public have a right of way for the passage of vehicles; and

(b) where it is in any other road to which the public has access, that part of the road to which vehicles have access,

but does not, in either case, include any central reservation (whether within the limits of a crossing or not);

"central reservation" means any provision which separates one part of a carriageway from another part of that carriageway, and includes a refuge for pedestrians;

"crossing" means a crossing for pedestrians established either:

(a) in the case of any road other than a trunk road, by a local authority under the provisions of section 23 of the 1984 Act; or

(b) in the case of a trunk road, by the appropriate Secretary of State in discharge of the duty imposed on him by section 24 of the 1984 Act;

"indicator for pedestrians" means the traffic sign of that description prescribed by regulation 2(1) and Schedule 1;

"one-way street" means any road on which the driving of vehicles otherwise than in one direction is prohibited at all times;

"pedestrian" means a foot passenger;

"pedestrian light signals" means the traffic signs of that description prescribed by regulation 2(1) and Schedule 1;

" "Pelican" crossing" means a crossing–

(a) at which there are traffic signs of the size, colour and type prescribed, or treated as if prescribed, by regulation 2(1) and Schedule 1; and

(b) the presence and limits of which are indicated, or are treated as indicated, in accordance with regulation 2(2) and Schedule 2;

" "Pelican" controlled area" means, in relation to a "Pelican" crossing, the area of the carriageway in the vicinity of the crossing and lying on both sides of the crossing or only one side of the crossing, the presence and limits of which are indicated, or are treated as indicated, in accordance with regulation 3 and Schedule 2;

"primary signal" means the traffic sign prescribed as a vehicular light signal by regulation 2(1) and Schedule 1 erected on or near the carriageway facing traffic approaching the "Pelican" crossing and sited between the stop line and the line of

(**a**) S.I. 1969/888.   (**b**) S.I. 1979/401.

studs indicating the limits of the crossing in accordance with Schedule 2 nearest to the stop line;

"refuge for pedestrians" means an area of a carriageway to which vehicles do not have access and on which pedestrians may wait after crossing one part of that carriageway and before crossing the other part;

"secondary signal" means the traffic sign prescribed as a vehicular light signal by regulation 2(1) and Schedule 1 erected on or near the carriageway facing traffic approaching the "Pelican" crossing but sited beyond the furthest edge of the "Pelican" crossing as viewed from the direction of travel of such traffic;

"stop line" means, in relation to the driver of a vehicle approaching a "Pelican" crossing, the transverse white line which is parallel to the limits of the crossing as indicated in accordance with Schedule 2 and on the same side of the crossing as the driver;

"stud" means any mark or device on the carriageway, whether or not projecting above the surface thereof;

"a system of staggered crossings" means two "Pelican" crossings provided on a road where there is a central reservation in the road, each separately constituted as a "Pelican" crossing, one such crossing being on one side of the central reservation and the other such crossing being on the other side and which together do not form a straight line across the road.

(3) Any reference in this Instrument to a vehicular light signal is–

(a) where a primary signal has been erected without a secondary signal, a reference to the light signal displayed by the primary signal; and

(b) where a secondary signal has been erected as well as a primary signal, a reference to the light signal displayed by both the primary signal and the secondary signal or by either the primary signal operating without the secondary signal or by the secondary signal operating without the primary signal.

PART II

REGULATIONS

Citation

1. The Regulations contained in this Part of this Instrument may be cited as the "Pelican" Pedestrian Crossings Regulations 1987.

"Pelican" crossings

2.—(1) The provisions of Schedule 1 shall have effect as respects the size, colour and type of the traffic signs which are to be placed at or near a crossing for the purpose of constituting it a "Pelican" crossing.

(2) The provisions of Schedule 2 shall have effect for regulating the manner in which the presence and limits of a crossing are to be indicated for the purpose of constituting it a "Pelican" crossing.

(3) Any crossing which, immediately before the coming into operation of these Regulations, was constituted as a "Pelican" crossing in accordance with the 1969 Regulations shall, notwithstanding the revocation of those Regulations, be treated as constituted in accordance with these Regulations for so long as the traffic signs situated at or near it and the manner in which its presence and limits are indicated comply with the 1969 Regulations.

"Pelican" controlled areas

3.—(1) The provisions of Schedule 2 shall have effect as respects the size, colour and type of the traffic signs which shall be placed in the vicinity of a "Pelican" crossing for the purpose of constituting a "Pelican" controlled area in relation to that crossing and of indicating the presence and limits of that area.

(2) A stop line shall indicate to vehicular traffic proceeding towards a "Pelican" crossing the position at which a driver of a vehicle shall stop it for the purpose of complying with regulations 16 and 17.

(3) Where the appropriate authority is satisfied in relation to a particular area of carriageway in the vicinity of the "Pelican" crossing that, by reason of the layout or character of the roads in the vicinity of the crossing, the application of such a prohibition as is mentioned in any of regulations 12, 13, 14, 19 and 20 to that particular area or the constitution of that particular area as a "Pelican" controlled area by the placing of traffic signs in accordance with Schedule 2 would be impracticable, it shall not be necessary for that area to be constituted a "Pelican" controlled area but if, by virtue of this paragraph, it is proposed that no area, on either side of the limits of a "Pelican" crossing (not on a trunk road), is to be constituted a "Pelican" controlled area by 18th February 1989, a notice in writing shall be sent by the appropriate authority to the appropriate Secretary of State stating the reasons why it is proposed that no such area should be constituted.

(4) Where immediately before the coming into operation of these Regulations, the approach for vehicular traffic to a "Pelican" crossing has been indicated by a pattern of studs placed and white lines marked on the carriageway in accordance with the provisions of paragraph 3 of Schedule 2 to the 1969 Regulations, then, notwithstanding the revocation effected by article 2 of Part I of this Instrument, that approach may until 18th February 1989 continue to be so indicated for so long as the said pattern of studs and white lines does not lie within a "Pelican" controlled area or in the vicinity of such an area on the same side of the crossing as that pattern.

Variations in dimensions

4.—(1) Any variation in–

(i) a dimension (other than as to the height of a letter) specified in any of the diagrams in Parts II and III of Schedule 1; or

(ii) a dimension as to the height of a letter specified in the diagram in Part III of that Schedule,

shall be treated as permitted by these Regulations if the variation–

(a) in the case of a dimension of less than 10 millimetres, does not exceed 1 millimetre;

(b) in the case of a dimension of 10 millimetres or more but less than 50 millimetres, does not exceed 10% of that dimension;

(c) in the case of a dimension of 50 millimetres or more but less than 300 millimetres, does not exceed 7½% of that dimension; or

(d) in the case of a dimension of 300 millimetres or more, does not exceed 5% of that dimension.

(2) Any variation in a dimension specified in any of the diagrams in Schedule 2 shall be treated as permitted by these Regulations if the variation–

(a) in the case of a dimension of 300 millimetres or more, does not exceed 20% of that dimension; or

(b) in the case of a dimension of less than 300 millimetres, where the actual dimension exceeds the dimension so specified, does not exceed 30% of the dimension so specified, and where the actual dimension is less than the dimension so specified, does not exceed 10% of the dimension so specified.

Box for housing equipment

5. Apparatus designed to control or to monitor, or to control and monitor, the operation of the vehicular light signals and pedestrian light signals may be housed in one or more boxes attached to the post or other structure on which such signals are mounted.

Additional traffic signs

6. In addition to the traffic signs prescribed in regulation 2(1) and Schedule 1, the traffic signs specified in diagrams 610, 611, 612, 613 and 616 in Schedule 1 to the Traffic Signs Regulations 1981 (a) may be placed at or near a "Pelican" crossing.

(a) S.I. 1981/859, to which there are no relevant amending instruments.

Significance of traffic signs

7.   Regulations 8 to 10 are made under section 64 of the 1984 Act and shall have effect for the purpose of prescribing the warnings, information, requirements and prohibitions which are to be conveyed to traffic by the traffic signs of the size, colour and type prescribed by regulations 2(1) and 6 and Schedule 1.

Significance of vehicular light signals

8.—(1) The vehicular light signal at a "Pelican" crossing shall convey the following information, requirements and prohibitions–

(a) the steady green light shall convey the information that vehicular traffic may proceed across the crossing;

(b) except as provided in sub-paragraph (d) below, the steady amber light shall convey the prohibition that vehicular traffic shall not proceed beyond the stop line, or, if the stop line is not for the time being visible, beyond the post or other structure on which is mounted the primary signal facing such traffic on the side of the carriageway on which vehicles approach the crossing except in the case of any vehicle which when the steady amber light is first shown is so close to the stop line, post or structure that it cannot safely be stopped before passing the line, post or structure;

(c) except as provided in sub-paragraph (d) below, the red light shall convey the prohibition that vehicular traffic shall not proceed beyond the stop line, or, if the stop line is not for the time being visible, beyond the post or other structure on which is mounted the primary signal facing such traffic on the side of the carriageway on which vehicles approach the crossing;

(d) on any occasion when a vehicle is being used for fire brigade, ambulance or police purposes and the observance of the prohibitions conveyed by the steady amber and red lights (as specified in sub-paragraphs (b) and (c) above respectively) would be likely to hinder the use of the vehicle for the purpose in question, then sub-paragraphs (b) and (c) above shall not apply to that vehicle. In the circumstances described in the preceding part of this sub-paragraph, the steady amber light and the red light shall each convey the information that the vehicle may only proceed beyond the stop line or (as the case may be) the post or other structure if the driver–

(i) accords precedence to any pedestrian who is on that part of the carriageway which lies within the limits of the crossing or on a central reservation which lies between two crossings which do not form a system of staggered crossings; and

(ii) subject to sub-paragraph (i) above, does not proceed in such a manner or at such a time as is likely to cause danger to any other vehicle approaching or waiting at the crossing, or in such a manner as to compel the driver of any such vehicle to change its speed or course in order to avoid an accident; and

(e) the flashing amber light shall convey the information that vehicular traffic may proceed across the crossing but that every pedestrian if he is on the carriageway or a central reservation within the limits of that crossing (but not if he is on a central reservation which lies between two crossings which form a system of staggered crossings) before any part of a vehicle has entered those limits, has the right of precedence within those limits over that vehicle, and the requirement that the driver of a vehicle shall accord such precedence to any such pedestrian.

(2) Vehicular traffic passing the vehicular light signal in accordance with the foregoing provisions of this regulation shall proceed with due regard to the safety of other users of the road and subject to the direction of any police constable in uniform or traffic warden who may be engaged in the regulation of traffic.

Significance of pedestrian traffic signals

9.—(1) The pedestrian traffic signal at a "Pelican" crossing shall convey to pedestrians the warnings and information specified in the following paragraphs of this regulation.

(2) The pedestrian light signal shall convey to pedestrians the following warnings and information–

   (a) the red light shall convey to a pedestrian the warning that he should not in the interests of safety use the crossing;

   (b) the steady green light shall convey to a pedestrian the information that he may use the crossing and drivers of vehicles may not cause their vehicles to enter the limits of the crossing; and

   (c) the flashing green light shall convey–

      (i) to a pedestrian who is already on the crossing when the flashing green light is first shown the information that he may continue to use the crossing, and that if he is on the carriageway or on a central reservation within the limits of that crossing (but not if he is on a central reservation which lies between two crossings which form part of a system of staggered crossings) before any part of a vehicle has entered those limits he has the right of precedence within those limits over that vehicle; and

      (ii) to a pedestrian who is not already on the crossing when the flashing green light is first shown the warning that he should not in the interests of safety start to cross the carriageway.

   (3) When the word "WAIT" shown by the indicator for pedestrians is illuminated it shall convey to a pedestrian the same warning as that conveyed by the red light shown by the pedestrian light signal, that is to say, that he should not in the interests of safety use the crossing.

   (4) Any audible signal emitted by any device for emitting audible signals provided in conjunction with the steady green light for pedestrians, and any tactile signal made by any device for making tactile signals similarly provided, shall convey to a pedestrian the same information as that conveyed by the steady green light, that is to say, that he may use the crossing and drivers of vehicles may not cause their vehicle to enter the limits of the crossing.

Significance of additional traffic signs

   10. The traffic signs referred to in regulation 6 shall convey the information, prohibitions or requirements mentioned in relation thereto in the captions to the diagrams in Schedule 1 to the Traffic Signs Regulations 1981 mentioned in that regulation.

Movement of traffic and precedence of pedestrians

   11. Regulations 12 to 20 are made under section 25 of the 1984 Act and shall have effect with respect to the movement of traffic (including pedestrians) and the precedence of pedestrians over vehicles at and in the vicinity of a "Pelican" crossing.

Prohibition on stopping in areas adjacent to "Pelican" crossings

   12.—(1) For the purposes of this regulation and the next two following regulations, the expression "vehicle" shall not include a pedal bicycle not having a sidecar attached thereto, whether additional means of propulsion by mechanical power are attached to the bicycle or not.

   (2) Save as provided in regulations 13 and 14, and subject to regulation 15, the driver of a vehicle shall not cause the vehicle or any part thereof to stop in a "Pelican" controlled area.

   13. A vehicle shall not by regulation 12 be prevented from stopping in any length of road on any side thereof–

   (a) if the driver has stopped for the purpose of complying with regulation 16, 17 or 19(b);

   (b) if the driver is prevented from proceeding by circumstances beyond his control or it is necessary for him to stop in order to avoid an accident; or

   (c) for so long as may be necessary to enable the vehicle, if it cannot be used for such purpose without stopping in that length of road, to be used for fire brigade, ambulance or police purposes or in connection with any building operation, demolition or excavation, the removal of any obstruction to traffic, the maintenance, improvement or reconstruction of that length of road, or the laying, erection, alteration, repair or cleaning in or near to that length of road of any sewer or of any main, pipe or apparatus for the supply of gas, water or electricity, or of any telecommunication apparatus kept installed for the purposes of a telecommunications code system or of any other telecommunication apparatus lawfully kept installed in any position.

14.—(1) A vehicle shall not by regulation 12 be prevented from stopping in a "Pelican" controlled area–

(a) if the vehicle is stopped for the purpose of making a left or right turn; or

(b) if the vehicle is a public service vehicle being used–

    (i) in the provision of a service which is a local service within the meaning of the Transport Act 1985(**a**) ; or

    (ii) to carry passengers for hire or reward at separate fare otherwise than in the provision of a local service,

but excluding in each case any such vehicle being used on an excursion or tour, and the vehicle is waiting, after having proceeded past the "Pelican" crossing in relation to which the "Pelican" controlled area is indicated, in order to take up or set down passengers.

(2) In sub-paragraph (b) of paragraph (1) of this regulation "local service" and "excursion or tour" have respectively the same meanings as in the Transport Act 1985.

Saving for crossings constituted in accordance with 1969 Regulations

15. In relation to any crossing which, immediately before the coming into operation of these Regulations, was constituted as a "Pelican" crossing in accordance with the 1969 Regulations, for a period of two years commencing on the date these Regulations come into operation regulations 12, 13 and 14 shall not apply and regulation 9 of the 1969 Regulations shall, notwithstanding the repeal of those Regulations, continue to have effect but only for so long during that period as the crossing remains so constituted.

Prohibition against the proceeding of vehicles across a "Pelican" crossing

16. When the vehicular traffic light signal is showing a red light, the driver of a vehicle shall not cause the vehicle or any part thereof to proceed beyond the stop line, or, if that line is not for the time being visible, beyond the post or other structure on which is mounted the primary signal facing the driver on the side of the carriageway on which vehicles approach the crossing.

Precedence of pedestrians over vehicles on a "Pelican" crossing

17. When the vehicular traffic light signal at a "Pelican" crossing is showing a flashing amber light, every pedestrian, if he is on the carriageway, or a central reservation within the limits of that crossing (but not if he is on a central reservation which lies between two crossings which form part of a system of staggered crossings) before any part of the vehicle has entered those limits, shall have precedence within those limits over that vehicle and the driver of a vehicle shall accord such precedence to any such pedestrian.

Prohibition against the waiting of vehicles and pedestrians on a "Pelican" crossing

18.—(1) The driver of a vehicle shall not cause the vehicle or any part thereof to stop within the limits of a "Pelican" crossing unless either he is prevented from proceeding by circumstances beyond his control or it is necessary for him to stop in order to avoid an accident.

(2) No pedestrian shall remain on the carriageway within the limits of a "Pelican" crossing longer than is necessary for the purpose of passing over the crossing with reasonable despatch.

Prohibition against overtaking at a "Pelican" crossing

19. The driver of a vehicle while it or any part of it is in a "Pelican" controlled area and it is proceeding towards the limits of a "Pelican" crossing in relation to which the area is indicated (hereinafter referred to as "the approaching vehicle") shall not cause that vehicle, or any part of it–

(**a**) 1985 c.67.

(a) to pass ahead of the foremost part of another moving motor vehicle being a vehicle proceeding in the same direction wholly or partly within that area; or

(b) subject to the next succeeding regulation, to pass ahead of the foremost part of a stationary vehicle on the same side of the crossing as the approaching vehicle, which stationary vehicle is stopped for the purpose of complying with regulation 16 or 17.

For the purposes of this regulation–

(i) the reference to another moving motor vehicle is, in a case where only one other motor vehicle is proceeding in the same direction in a "Pelican" controlled area, a reference to that vehicle, and, in a case where more than one other motor vehicle is so proceeding, a reference to such one of those vehicles as is nearest to the limits of the crossing; and

(ii) the reference to a stationary vehicle is, in a case where only one other vehicle is stopped for the purpose of complying with regulation 16 or 17, a reference to that vehicle, and, in a case where more than one other vehicle is stopped for that purpose, a reference to such one of those vehicles as is nearest to the limits of the crossing.

20. Nothing in paragraph (b) of regulation 19 shall apply so as to prevent the approaching vehicle from passing ahead of the foremost part of a stationary vehicle within the meaning of that paragraph, if the stationary vehicle is stopped for the purpose of complying with regulation 16 or 17 in relation to a "Pelican" crossing which is a separate crossing from the "Pelican" crossing towards the limits of which the approaching vehicle is proceeding.

Regulation 2(1)

SCHEDULE 1

THE SIZE, COLOUR AND TYPE OF TRAFFIC SIGNS AT A "PELICAN" CROSSING

PART I

Traffic signs

1. The traffic signs which are to be placed at or near a crossing for the purpose of constituting it a "Pelican" crossing shall consist of a combination of–

(a) vehicular light signals;

(b) pedestrian light signals; and

(c) indicators for pedestrians,

of the size, colour and type prescribed by the following provisions of this Schedule, together with any additional traffic signs placed at or near the crossing pursuant to regulation 6.

Vehicular light signals

2. The vehicular light signals shall be as follows–

(a) three lights shall be used, one red, one amber, and one green;

(b) the lamps showing the aforesaid lights shall be arranged vertically, the lamp showing the red light being the uppermost and that showing the green light the lowermost;

(c) each lamp shall be separately illuminated and the effective diameter of the lens thereof shall be not less than 195 millimetres nor more than 220 millimetres;

(d) the height of the centre of the amber lens from the surface of the carriageway in the immediate vicinity shall, in the case of signals placed at the side of the carriageway or on a central reservation, be not less than 2.4 metres nor more than 4 metres and, in the case of signals placed elsewhere and over the carriageway, not less than 6.1 metres nor more than 9 metres;

(e) the centres of the lenses of adjacent lamps shall be not less than 305 millimetres nor more than 360 millimetres apart;

(f) the lamp showing the amber light shall be capable of showing a steady light or a flashing light such that it flashes at a rate of not less than 70 nor more than 90 flashes per minute; and

(g) no lettering or symbols shall be used upon the lens.

Pedestrian light signals

3.—(1) The pedestrian light signals shall be of the size, colour and type shown in the diagrams in Part II of this Schedule.

(2) The height of the lower edge of the container enclosing the light signals from the surface of the carriageway in the immediate vicinity shall be not less than 2.1 metres nor more than 2.6 metres.

(3) The said signals shall be so designed that–

(a) the red figure shown in the said diagrams can be internally illuminated by a steady light;

(b) the green figure shown in the said diagrams can be internally illuminated by a steady light or by a flashing light at a rate of not less than 70 nor more than 90 flashes per minute; and

(c) when one signal is illuminated the other signal is not illuminated.

(4) A device for emitting audible signals may be provided for use when the green figure is illuminated by a steady light.

Indicator for pedestrians

4.—(1) The indicator for pedestrians shall be of the size, colour and type shown in the diagram in Part III of this Schedule.

(2) The indicator for pedestrians shall be so designed and constructed that "WAIT" as shown on the diagram can be illuminated and that there is incorporated in the indicator a device, which may be a push button or pressure pad and which is hereinafter in this Schedule referred to as "a push button", which can be used by pedestrians with the effect hereinafter described.

(3) The instruction for pedestrians shown in the diagram may be internally illuminated.

(4) A device for making tactile signals may be provided for use when the green figure shown in the diagram is illuminated by a steady light.

Sequence of signals

5.—(1) The vehicular light signals and pedestrian light signals and the indicators for pedestrians when they are placed at or near any crossing shall be so designed and constructed that–

(a) before the signals and indicators are operated by the pressing of a push button or as described in paragraph 6 of this Schedule the vehicular light signal shows a steady green light, the pedestrian light signal shows a red light, the word "WAIT" in the indicator for pedestrians is not illuminated, any device for making tactile signals is inactive, and any device for emitting audible signals is silent;

(b) when a push button is pressed–

(i) after the expiration of the vehicle period but before the vehicular light signals are showing a steady amber light, the signals and indicators, unless they are working as described in paragraph 6 of this Schedule, are caused to show lights in the sequences specified in descending order in column 1 in the case of vehicular light signals, in column 2 in the case of pedestrian light signals and in column 3 in the case of the indicators for pedestrians, of either Part IV or Part V of this Schedule;

(ii) when the vehicular light signals are showing a steady amber light or a red light when the signal to pedestrians shows a red or steady green light, there is no effect;

(iii) when the pedestrian light signals are showing a flashing green light, the word "WAIT" in each of the indicators for pedestrians is illuminated immediately and the signals and indicators are caused to show lights in the sequence specified in sub-paragraph (i) of this paragraph at the end of the next vehicle period; and

(iv) after the pedestrian light signals have ceased to show a flashing green light and before the end of the next vehicle period, the word "WAIT" in each of the indicators for pedestrians is illuminated immediately and the signals and indicators are caused to show lights in the sequence specified in sub-paragraph (i) of this paragraph at the end of the vehicle period;

(c) the periods during which lights are shown by the signals and the indicators, commence and terminate in relation to each other as shown in either Part IV or Part V of this Schedule as if each horizontal line therein represented one moment in time, subsequent moments occurring in descending order, but the distances between the horizontal lines do not represent the lengths of the periods during which the lights shown by the signals and the indicator are, or are not, lit.

(2) Where a device for emitting audible signals has been provided pursuant to paragraph 3(4) of this Schedule, it shall be so designed and constructed that a pulsed sound is emitted throughout every period when the pedestrian light signals are showing a steady green light, and at the same time the vehicular light signals are showing a red light, but only during such periods and at no other times, save that such a device need not operate during the hours of darkness.

(3) Where a device for making tactile signals has been provided pursuant to paragraph 4(4) of this Schedule, it shall be so designed and constructed that a regular movement perceptible to touch by pedestrians is made throughout every period when the pedestrian light signals are showing a steady green light, and at the same time the vehicular light signals are showing a red light, but only during such periods and at no other times.

(4) In this paragraph "vehicle period" means such period as may be fixed from time to time in relation to a "Pelican" crossing, which commences when the vehicular light signals cease to show a flashing amber light and during which the vehicular traffic light signals show a green light.

Operation by remote control

6.   The vehicular light signals, pedestrian light signals, indicators for pedestrians, any device for making tactile signals, and any device for emitting audible signals, when they are placed at or near any crossing may also be so designed and constructed that they can by remote control be made to operate–

(a) as if a push button has been pressed; and

(b) so that the pressing of a push button has no effect, other than causing the word "WAIT" in each of the indicators for the pedestrians to be illuminated, until normal operation is resumed.

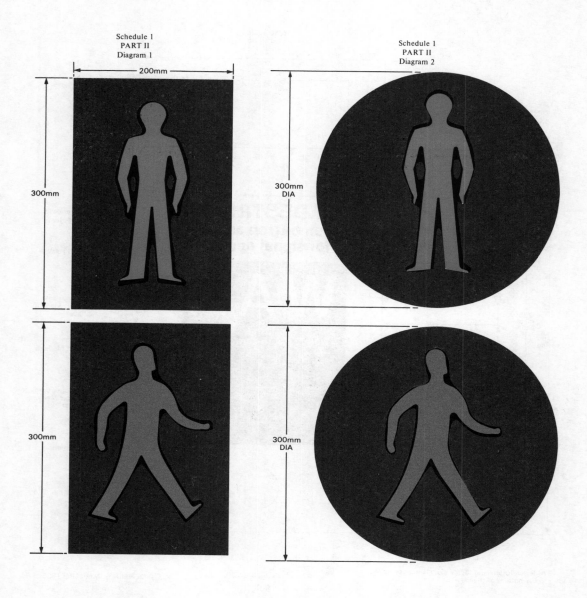

Schedule 1
PART II
Diagram 1

200mm

300mm

300mm

Schedule 1
PART II
Diagram 2

300mm
DIA

300mm
DIA

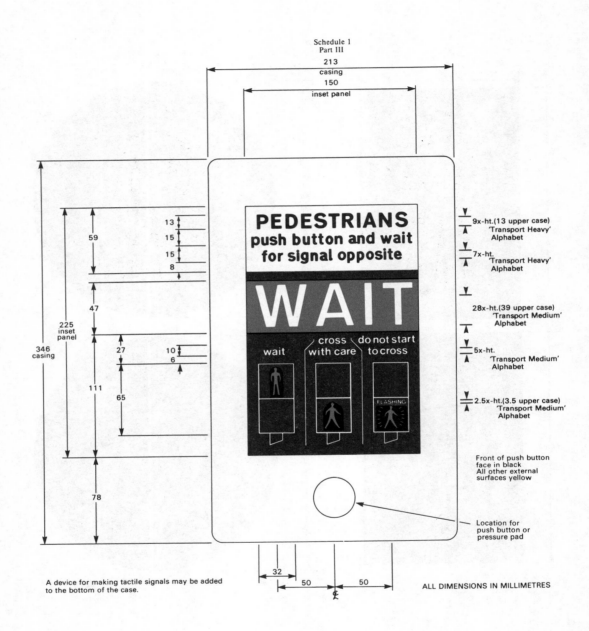

Schedule 1
Part III

213
casing

150
inset panel

PEDESTRIANS
push button and wait
for signal opposite

WAIT

cross | do not start
wait | with care | to cross

FLASHING

9x-ht.(13 upper case)
'Transport Heavy'
Alphabet

7x-ht.
'Transport Heavy'
Alphabet

28x-ht.(39 upper case)
'Transport Medium'
Alphabet

5x-ht.
'Transport Medium'
Alphabet

2.5x-ht.(3.5 upper case)
'Transport Medium'
Alphabet

Front of push button
face in black
All other external
surfaces yellow

Location for
push button or
pressure pad

346
casing

225
inset panel

59

13
15
15
8

47

27
10
6

111

65

78

32
50
50

A device for making tactile signals may be added
to the bottom of the case.

ALL DIMENSIONS IN MILLIMETRES

SCHEDULE 1

PART IV
SEQUENCE OF OPERATION OF VEHICULAR AND PEDESTRIAN LIGHT SIGNALS AND INDICATOR FOR PEDESTRIANS (BUT NOT THE AUDIBLE SIGNALS)

Sequence of vehicular traffic light signals	Sequence of pedestrian signals	
	Pedestrian light signals	Indicator for pedestrians
(1)	(2)	(3)
Green light	Red light	The word "WAIT" is illuminated
Amber light		
Red light		
	Green light	The word "WAIT" is not illuminated
Flashing amber light	Flashing green light	The word "WAIT" is illuminated
	Red light	
Green light		

SCHEDULE 1

PART V
ALTERNATIVE SEQUENCE OF OPERATION OF VEHICULAR AND PEDESTRIAN LIGHT SIGNALS AND INDICATOR FOR PEDESTRIANS (BUT NOT THE AUDIBLE SIGNALS)

Sequence of vehicular traffic light signals	Sequence of pedestrian signals	
	Pedestrian light signals	Indicator for pedestrians
(1)	(2)	(3)
Green light	Red light	The word "WAIT" is illuminated
Amber light		
Red light		
	Green light	The word "WAIT" is not illuminated
Flashing amber light	Flashing green light	The word "WAIT" is illuminated
	Red light	
Green light		

Regulation 2(2)   **SCHEDULE 2**

THE MANNER OF INDICATING THE PRESENCE AND LIMITS OF A "PELICAN" CROSSING AND "PELICAN" CONTROLLED AREA

General

1.   In this Schedule, and except where otherwise stated, any reference to a numbered diagram is a reference to the diagram bearing that number in this Schedule.

2.—(1) Every crossing which is a "Pelican" crossing on a road which is not a one-way street shall have its limits indicated, subject to the following provisions of this Schedule, by the pattern of studs on or in and lines on the carriageway in the manner shown–

  (a) in diagram 1 where there is no central reservation;

  (b) in diagram 2 where there is a central reservation, but the crossing does not form part of a system of staggered crossings; and

  (c) in diagram 3 where the crossing forms part of a system of staggered crossings.

(2) Every crossing which is a "Pelican" crossing on a road which is a one-way street shall have its limits indicated, subject to the following provisions of this Schedule, by the pattern of studs on or in and lines on the carriageway in the manner shown–

  (a) in diagram 4 where there is no central reservation;

  (b) in diagram 5 where there is a central reservation but the crossing does not form part of a system of staggered crossings; and

  (c) in diagram 6 where the crossing forms part of a system of staggered crossings.

Manner of indicating the limits of the crossing

3.   The limits of a "Pelican" crossing shall be indicated by two lines of studs in the positions shown, and in accordance with the measurements in, the diagram corresponding to the type of crossing.

4.   The two lines of studs indicating the limits of the crossing need not be at right angles to the edge of the carriageway, but shall form straight lines and shall as near as is reasonably practicable be parallel to each other.

Manner of indicating a "Pelican" controlled area and provision as to placing the stop line

5.   Subject to paragraph 8 of this Schedule, the presence and limits of a "Pelican" controlled area shall be indicated by the pattern of lines placed in the positions shown, and in accordance with the measurements, in the diagram corresponding to the type of crossing, and in accordance with the provisions of paragraphs 6 and 7 of this Schedule.

6.   Where the crossing is on a road which is not a one-way street the pattern of lines shall consist of–

(1) a stop line placed on the carriageway parallel to the nearer row of studs indicating the limits of the crossing and extending, in the manner indicated in the appropriate diagram, across the part of the carriageway used by vehicles approaching the crossing from the side on which the stop line is placed;

(2) two or more longitudinal white broken lines (hereinafter referred to as "zig-zag lines") placed on the carriageway or, where the road is a dual-carriageway road, on each part of the carriageway, each zig-zag line containing not less than 8 nor more than 18 marks and extending away from the crossing in the manner indicated in the appropriate diagram;

(3) subject to sub-paragraph (4) of this paragraph, where a central reservation is provided the road marking shown in diagram 1040.1 in Schedule 2 to the Traffic Signs Regulations 1981 (**a**) may be placed on the carriageway between the zig-zag lines on the approaches to the central reservation;

(4) where a central reservation is provided connecting crossings which form part of a system of staggered crossings, the road markings mentioned in sub-paragraph (3) of this paragraph shall be placed on the carriageway in the manner indicated in diagram 3.

7.   Where the crossing is on a road which is a one-way street the pattern of lines shall consist of:

(1) a stop line placed parallel to the nearer row of studs indicating the limits of the crossing and extending–

  (a) in the case of a crossing of the type shown in diagram 4 or 5, from one edge of the carriageway to the other; and

---

(**a**) S.I. 1981/859, to which there are no relevant amending instruments.

(b) in the case of a crossing of the type shown in diagram 6, from the edge of the carriageway to the central reservation;

(2) two or more zig-zag lines placed on the carriageway, each containing not less than 8 and not more than 18 marks, and extending away from the crossing;

(3) subject to sub-paragraph (4) of this paragraph, where a central reservation is provided the road marking shown in diagram 1041 in Schedule 2 to the Traffic Signs Regulations 1981 may be placed on the carriageway between the zig-zag lines on the approaches to the central reservation; and

(4) where a central reservation is provided connecting crossings which form part of a system of staggered crossings, the road markings mentioned in sub-paragraph (3) of this paragraph shall be placed on the carriageway in the manner indicated in diagram 6.

8.—(1) Where the appropriate authority is satisfied in relation to a particular area of carriageway in the vicinity of a "Pelican" crossing that by reason of the layout of, or character of, the roads in the vicinity of the crossing it would be impracticable to lay the pattern of lines as shown in the diagrams in, and in accordance with paragraphs 5 to 7 of, this Schedule any of the following variations as respects the pattern shall be permitted–

(a) the number of marks contained in each zig-zag line may be reduced from 8 to not less than 2; and

(b) a mark contained in a zig-zag line may be varied in length so as to extend for a distance not less than 1 metre and less than 2 metres, but where such a variation is made as respects a mark each other mark in each zig-zag line shall be of the same or substantially the same length as that mark, so however that the number of marks in each zig-zag line shall not be more than 8 nor less than 2.

(2) The angle of the stop line in relation to the nearer line of studs indicating the limits of a crossing may be varied, if the appropriate authority is satisfied that such variation is necessary having regard to the angle of the crossing in relation to the edge of the carriageway at the place where the crossing is situated.

(3) The maximum distance of 3 metres between the stop line and the nearer line of studs indicating the limits of the crossing shown in the diagrams in this Schedule may be increased to such greater distance, not in any case exceeding 10 metres, as the appropriate authority may decide.

(4) Where by reason of regulation 3(3) an area of carriageway in the vicinity of a "Pelican" crossing is not constituted a "Pelican" controlled area by the placing of a pattern of lines as provided in the foregoing provisions of this Schedule, a stop line shall nevertheless be placed on the carriageway as previously provided in this Schedule.

Colour and dimensions of road markings and studs

9. The road markings shown in the diagrams in this Schedule shall be white in colour, and may be illuminated by reflecting material.

10.—(1) The studs shown in the diagrams shall be either white, silver or light grey in colour and shall not be fitted with reflective lenses.

(2) The said studs shall be either circular in shape with a diameter of not more than 110 millimetres or less than 95 millimetres or square in shape with each side being not more than 110 millimetres or less than 95 millimetres.

(3) Any stud which is fixed or embedded in the carriageway shall not project more than 18 millimetres above the carriageway at its highest point nor more than 6 millimetres at its edges.

11. Where in any diagram in this Schedule a dimension or measurement is indicated in brackets against a dimension or measurement not indicated in brackets any dimension or measurement indicated in brackets may be treated as an alternative to the dimension or measurement not so indicated.

Supplementary

12. The foregoing provisions of this Schedule shall be regarded as having been complied with in the case of any pattern of studs or white lines if most of the studs or lengths of white lines comply notwithstanding that one or more studs or some of the lengths of white lines may not comply with those provisions by reason of discoloration, temporary removal, displacement or for some other reason so long as the general appearance of the pattern of studs or white lines is not thereby materially impaired.

Schedule 2　Diagram 1

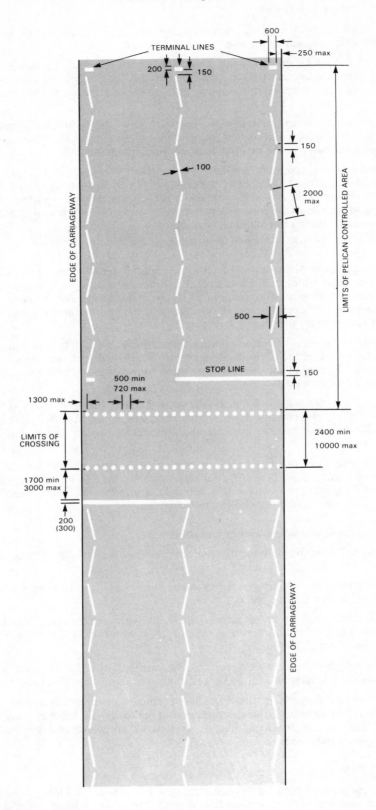

NOTE:- Each zigzag line need not contain the same number of marks.

ALL DIMENSIONS IN MILLIMETRES

Schedule 2 Diagram 2

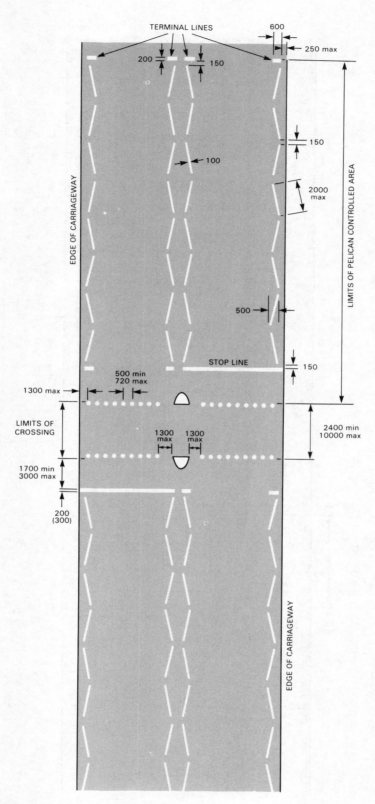

NOTE:- Each zigzag line need not contain the same number of marks.

ALL DIMENSIONS IN MILLIMETRES

Schedule 2   Diagram 3

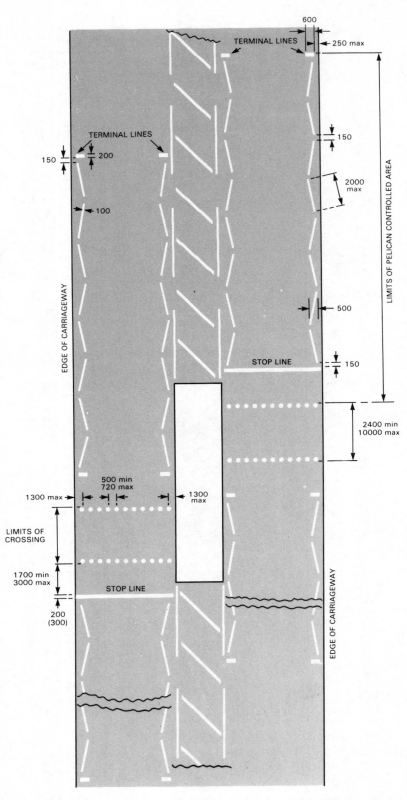

NOTE:- Each zigzag line need not contain the same number of marks.
The stagger may be reversed as required

ALL DIMENSIONS IN MILLIMETRES

Schedule 2   Diagram 4

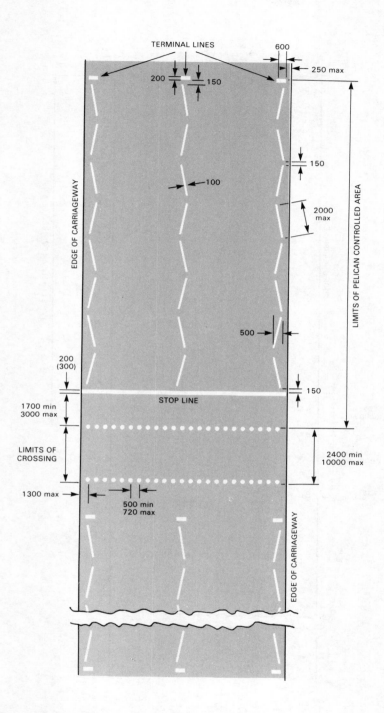

NOTE:- Each zigzag line need not contain the same number of marks.

ALL DIMENSIONS IN MILLIMETRES

Schedule 2   Diagram 5

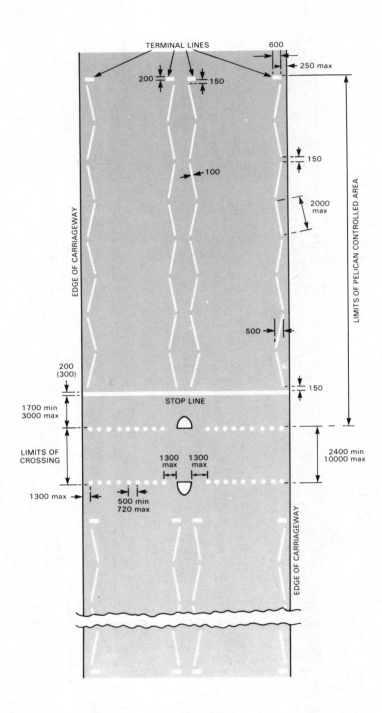

NOTE:- Each zigzag line need not contain the same number of marks.

ALL DIMENSIONS IN MILLIMETRES

Schedule 2   Diagram 6

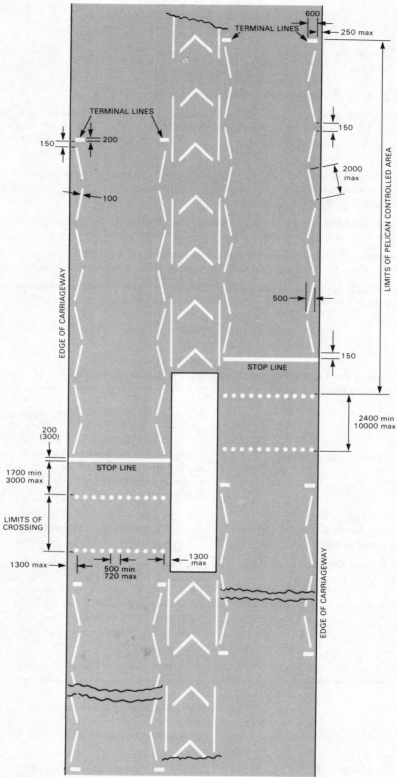

NOTE:- Each zigzag line need not contain the same number of marks. The stagger may be reversed as required
ALL DIMENSIONS IN MILLIMETRES

PART III
GENERAL DIRECTIONS

Citation

1. The Directions contained in this Part of this Instrument may be cited as the "Pelican" Pedestrian Crossings General Directions 1987.

Number and manner of placing of vehicular light signals

2.—(1) There shall be placed at a "Pelican" crossing which is on a road which is not a one-way street and which is of the type specified in column 1 of Part I of the Table below, the vehicular light signals facing each direction of traffic specified in relation thereto in column 2 of Part I of the said Table.

(2) There shall be placed at a "Pelican" crossing which is on a one-way street and which is of a type specified in column 1 of Part II of the said Table the vehicular light signals specified in relation thereto in column 2 of Part II of the said Table.

(3) The vehicular light signals referred to in paragraphs (1) and (2) shall be placed as primary signals or secondary signals as specified in column 2 of the said Table.

(4) One or more additional vehicular light signals may be placed either as a primary signal or as a secondary signal on the side of, or over, the carriageway or on any central reservation.

(5) Every vehicular light signal placed at a "Pelican" crossing pursuant to the provisions of this direction shall face the stream of traffic which it is intended to control.

TABLE

PART I

PELICAN CROSSINGS ON ROADS WHICH ARE NOT ONE-WAY STREETS

(1) *Type of crossing*	(2) *Vehicular light signals required facing each direction of traffic*
Crossing on a road without a central reservation.	One primary signal on the side of the carriageway nearest to the direction of vehicular traffic and one secondary signal on the side of the carriageway furthest away from the direction of vehicular traffic.
Crossing on a road with a central reservation which does not form part of a system of staggered crossings.	One primary signal on the side of the carriageway nearest to the direction of vehicular traffic and one secondary signal on the central reservation.
Crossing which forms part of a system of staggered crossings.	One primary signal on the side of the carriageway nearest to the direction of vehicular traffic and one primary signal on the central reservation.

PART II

PELICAN CROSSINGS ON ROADS WHICH ARE ONE-WAY STREETS

(1) *Type of crossing*	(2) *Vehicular light signals required*
Crossing on a road without a central reservation.	One primary signal on each side of the carriageway.
Crossing on a road with a central reservation which does not form part of a system of staggered crossings.	One primary signal on each side of the carriageway and one secondary signal on the central reservation.
Crossing which forms part of a system of staggered crossings.	One primary signal on the side of the carriageway and one primary signal on the central reservation.

Number and manner of placing of pedestrian light signals and indicators for pedestrians

3.—(1) At least one pedestrian light signal and at least one indicator for pedestrians shall be placed at each end of a "Pelican" crossing.

(2) Where there is a central reservation in a crossing, one or more additional indicators for pedestrians shall be placed on the central reservation.

(3) Each pedestrian light signal at either end of the crossing shall be so placed as to be clearly visible to any person who is about to use the crossing at the other end of the crossing.

(4) Each indicator for pedestrians shall be so placed that the push button in the indicator is readily accessible to pedestrians who wish to press it.

Additional traffic signs

4. The traffic signs specified in diagrams 610 and 611 in Schedule 1 to the Traffic Signs Regulations 1981 shall be placed only on a central reservation in a crossing, or on a central reservation which lies between two crossings which form part of a system of staggered crossings.

Colouring of containers and posts

5.—(1) The containers of the vehicular light signals and of the pedestrian light signals shall be coloured black and may be mounted with a backing board and if so mounted the backing board shall be coloured black and may have a white border not less than 45 millimetres nor more than 55 millimetres in width which may be of a reflective material.

(2) Where a vehicular light signal, a pedestrian light signal or an indicator for pedestrians is mounted on a post specially provided for the purpose, that part of the post which extends above ground level shall be coloured grey and may have one white band not less than 140 millimetres nor more than 160 millimetres in depth, the lower edge of the band being not less than 1.5 metres nor more than 1.7 metres above the level of the surface of the ground in the immediate vicinity.

(3) Any box attached to a post or other structure on which pedestrian light signals or vehicular light signals are mounted and housing apparatus designed to control, or to monitor, or to control and monitor, the operation of such signals shall be coloured grey, yellow or black, or a combination of any of those colours.

Approval for mechanisms and sequence adjustments

6.—(1) Vehicular light signals, pedestrian light signals and indicators for pedestrians may be placed at or near any "Pelican" crossing only if the apparatus (including the content of all instructions stored in, or executable by, it) used to secure that the signals and indicators comply with the relevant provisions of the Regulations is of a type approved in writing by or on behalf of the Secretary of State.

(2) Such signals may be retained in place notwithstanding the subsequent withdrawal of any approval relating to any such apparatus.

Special Cases

7. Nothing in these Directions shall be taken to limit the power of the Secretary of State by any special direction to dispense with, add to or modify any of the requirements of the Directions in relation to any particular case.

Signed by authority of the Secretary of State.

Peter Bottomley
Parliamentary Under Secretary of State,
Department of Transport

7th January 1987

Malcolm Rifkind
Secretary of State for Scotland

12th January 1987

Nicholas Edwards
Secretary of State for Wales

12th January 1987

EXPLANATORY NOTE

(This note is not part of the Instrument)

This Instrument revokes and re-enacts with amendments the provisions of the "Pelican" Pedestrian Crossing Regulations and General Directions 1969 and the "Pelican" Pedestrian Crossings (Amendment) Regulations and General Directions 1979.

The changes of substance to the "Pelican" Pedestrian Crossing Regulations 1969 (as amended) are as follows:

1.   The permitted variations in certain dimensions are increased (regulation 4 and Schedule 2).

2.   Provision is made for zig-zag markings to be placed on the carriageway in the vicinity of a "Pelican" crossing for the purpose of making that carriageway a "Pelican" controlled area in relation to a "Pelican" crossing (Schedule 2, paragraphs 5 to 8).

3.   Regulation 5 provides that certain apparatus may be housed in a box attached to the post or structure on which the vehicular light signals are mounted.

4.   Regulation 6 provides that certain traffic signs may be placed as additional traffic signs at or near a "Pelican" crossing. Regulation 10 prescribes their significance.

5.   Provision is made that the prohibition on proceeding when the vehicular light signals show a red light and the requirement for precedence for pedestrians when the signals show a flashing amber light apply if the primary signal is operating without the secondary signal and the secondary signal is operating without the primary signal (regulations 8, 16 and 17 together with the definition of vehicular light signal in article 3(2) in Part I of this Instrument). "Primary signal" and "secondary signal" are defined in article 3(2) in Part I. Provision is made that the prohibitions on proceeding beyond the stop line when the vehicular light signals are showing red or steady amber apply, if the stop line is not visible, as prohibitions on proceeding beyond the post or other structure on which the primary signal is mounted (regulations 8(1)(b) and (c) and 16). There is an exemption (regulation 8(1)(d)) for emergency services vehicles.

6.   When the vehicular light signal is showing a flashing amber light and likewise when the pedestrian light signal is showing a flashing green light a pedestrian has precedence over vehicles if he is on the carriageway or a central reservation within the limits of the crossing, but not if he is on a central reservation which lies between two crossings which form part of a system of staggered crossings (regulations 8(1)(a), 9(2)(c) and 17). "Central reservation" and "system of staggered crossings" are defined in article 3(2) in Part I.

7. Regulation 12 prohibits vehicles (other than certain pedal cycles) from stopping in "Pelican" controlled areas, subject to the exceptions in regulations 13 and 14, and, in relation to "Pelican" crossings in existence before these Regulations come into operation, subject also to regulation 15.

8. Regulation 19 introduces a prohibition against the overtaking in a "Pelican" controlled area of another moving or stationary vehicle by drivers of vehicles proceeding towards a "Pelican" crossing.

9. Regulation 20 modifies the prohibition as to overtaking a stationary vehicle in the case of a system of staggered crossings.

10. As from 18th February 1989 the manner of indicating the vehicular approaches to a "Pelican" crossing and the requirements with respect to the stopping of vehicles on the approach to a "Pelican" crossing will cease to have effect (regulation 3 and Schedule 2, paragraph 3). Instead of studs, zig-zag lines will have to be used.

11. The device which is used by pedestrians to activate the sequence of signals may be a pressure pad as well as a push button (Schedule 1, para 4(2)). There is also provision for the indicator for pedestrians to include a device for making tactile signals (Schedule 1, para 4(4)).

12. Provision is made that on two-way roads hatched markings may be placed on the carriageway where there is a central reservation, but such a marking must be provided where the central reservation connects two crossings which form part of a system of staggered crossings (Schedule 2, paragraph 6(3) and diagram 3). Chevron markings in place of hatched markings are to be used in similar situations in one-way streets (Schedule 2, paragraph 7(3) and diagram 6).

13. The provision to omit the stop line (formerly contained in paragraphs 5 and 9 of Schedule 2 to the 1969 Regulations) is discontinued, and the stop line becomes mandatory in all cases.

Apart from the changes of substance mentioned above, Schedule 2, which prescribes the manner of indicating the presence and limits of a "Pelican" crossing, is redrafted so that reference is made to diagrams and so as to include the manner of indicating the presence and limits of a "Pelican" controlled area.

Regulation 2(3) provides a saving provision whereby "Pelican" crossings established before the coming into operation of these Regulations shall continue to be constituted as "Pelican" crossings if they complied with the 1969 Regulations. And regulation 3(4) provides a saving provision for approaches to "Pelican" crossings until 18th February 1989.

The changes of substance to the "Pelican" Pedestrian Crossings General Directions 1969 as amended are as follows:

1. The General Directions provide that vehicular light signals shall be placed either as primary or as secondary signals (direction 2).

2. Direction 4 makes provision for the placing of the additional traffic signs referred to in regulation 6.

3. The requirement formerly contained in the amended paragraph 6(1) of the 1969 Directions for approval of the Secretary of State to the use of signals which operate with the alternative phasing specified in Table 2 in Part IV of Schedule 1 to the Regulations is discontinued.

STATUTORY INSTRUMENTS

1987 No. 17

SOCIAL SECURITY

The Supplementary Benefit (Housing Requirements and Resources) Amendment Regulations 1987

Made - - -	*13th January 1987*
Coming into force	*26th January 1987*

The Secretary of State for Social Services, in exercise of the powers conferred on him by sections 2(2) and 34(1)(a) of, and paragraphs 1(2) and 2(1) of Schedule 1 to the Supplementary Benefits Act 1976(b) and of all other powers enabling him in that behalf, with the consent of the Treasury (c), and after reference to the Social Security Advisory Committee of the proposals other than that which the Committee has agreed should not be referred to it (d), hereby makes the following regulations of which a draft has, in accordance with section 33(3) of that Act, been laid before Parliament and approved by a resolution of each House of Parliament:—

Citation and Commencement

1. These regulations may be cited as the Supplementary Benefit (Housing Requirements and Resources) Amendment Regulations 1987 and shall come into force on 26th January 1987.

Amendment of the Supplementary Benefit (Requirements) Regulations 1983

2.—(1) The Supplementary Benefit (Requirements) Regulations 1983(e) shall be amended in accordance with the following provisions of this regulation.

(a) *See* the definitions of "prescribed" and "regulations".
(b) 1976 c.71, as amended by section 6(1) of and Part I of Schedule 2 to the Social Security Act 1980 (c.30).
(c) *See* Section 33(3) of the Supplementary Benefit Act 1976.
(d) *See* Section 10(1) of the Social Security Act 1980, as amended by the Social Security Act 1986 (c.50), Schedule 10, paragraph 98, and section 61(1)(b) of the latter Act.
(e) S.I. 1983/1399; the only relevant amending instrument is S.I. 1984/1102.

(2)   In regulation 14 (housing requirements), the following paragraph shall be inserted after paragraph (5):—

"(5A) Where—

(a)   for the purposes of section 48(5) of the General Rate Act 1967(**a**), it appears to a rating authority or it is determined in pursuance of subsection (6) of that section 48 that the hereditament including the home is a mixed hereditament and that only a proportion of the rateable value of the hereditament is attributable to use for the purpose of a private dwelling, or

(b)   in Scotland, an assessor acting pursuant to section 45(1) of the Water (Scotland) Act 1980(**b**) has apportioned the net annual value of the premises including the home between the part occupied as a dwelling and the remainder,

the amounts applicable under regulation 15 or 17 shall be such proportion of the amounts applicable in respect of the hereditament or premises as a whole as is equal to the proportion of the rateable value of the hereditament attributable to the part of the hereditament used for the purposes of a private dwelling or, in Scotland, the proportion of the net annual value of the premises apportioned to the part occupied as a dwelling house.".

(3)   The following regulation shall be substituted for regulation 15 (mortgage payments):—

"Interest on loans to acquire an interest in the home

15.—(1) Subject to paragraphs (2) to (10) the following amounts shall be applicable under this regulation:—

(a)   if the claimant or, if he is a member of a married or unmarried couple, he or his partner is aged 60 or over, 100 per cent. of the eligible interest in his case;

(b)   if the claimant or, if he is a member of a married or unmarried couple, he and his partner are aged under 60

(i)   where the claimant has been in receipt of an allowance in respect of a continuous period of not less than 16 weeks, 100 per cent. of the eligible interest in his case;

(ii)   in any other case, 50 per cent. of the eligible interest in that case.

(2)   Where in a case to which paragraph (1)(b)(ii) applies —

(a)   either:—

(i)   the claim for an allowance is refused, or

(ii)   an award of an allowance is terminated on appeal or review

solely because the claimant's resources exceed his requirements by virtue of the fact that only 50 per cent. of the eligible interest in his case is applicable to him under paragraph (1)(b)(ii), and

---

(**a**) 1967 c.9.   (**b**) 1980 c.45.

(b) the claimant or his partner makes a further claim no later than 20 weeks after—

    (i) where the original claim for an allowance was refused, the date of that claim, or

    (ii) where an award of an allowance was terminated on appeal or review, the date of the claim in respect of which that award was made,

the amount applicable under this regulation commencing on a date not before the expiry of 16 weeks from the date specified in head (i) or (ii), as the case may be, shall be 100 per cent. of the eligible interest in that case and until that date shall be the amount specified in paragraph (1)(b)(ii).

(3) Subject to paragraphs (4) and (5), in this regulation, "eligible interest" means the amount of interest on a loan, whether or not secured by way of a mortgage or, in Scotland, under a heritable security, taken out to defray money applied for the purpose of —

(a) acquiring an interest in the home; or

(b) paying off another loan but only to the extent that interest on that other loan would have been eligible interest had the loan not been paid off.

(4) Subject to paragraph (5) and regulation 14(5A) and to any restriction imposed under regulation 21, the amount of eligible interest in any case shall be the amount, calculated on a weekly basis, of —

(a) where, or in so far as, section 26 of the Finance Act 1982(a) applies to the payments of interest on the loan, the interest which is payable after deduction of a sum equal to income tax thereon at the basic rate for the year of assessment in which the payment of interest becomes due;

(b) in any other case the interest which is payable on the loan without deduction of such a sum.

(5) Where a loan is applied only in part for a purpose specified in paragraph (3), only such proportion of the interest payable thereon as is equal to the proportion of the loan applied for that purpose shall qualify as eligible interest.

(a) 1982 c.39.

(6)   Where, under the terms of a loan taken out for a purpose specified in paragraph (3), interest is payable on accumulated arrears of interest (whether or not those arrears have been consolidated with the outstanding capital), the amount of such interest shall be applicable under this regulation as if it were eligible interest but only in so far as it represents interest on arrears incurred during any period —

(a)   when paragraph (1)(b)(ii) applied in that case, or

(b)   when the claimant was not entitled to benefit which fell within the period of 20 weeks specified in paragraph (2)(b);

and in either case only to the extent that arrears do not exceed 50 per cent. of the eligible interest that otherwise would have been payable during the period in question.

(7)   Where a person who was formerly one of a married or unmarried couple —

(a)   has taken out, either solely or jointly with his former partner, a loan secured on their home for a purpose other than one specified in paragraph (3), and

(b)   has left the home and either cannot or will not pay the interest on the loan,

and, if that person's former partner has to pay the interest on the loan in order to continue to live in the home, there shall be applicable to the former partner under this regulation the amount of interest on the loan calculated as if it were a loan taken out for a purpose specified in paragraph (3).

(8)   Where an amount is applicable under this regulation, if, notwithstanding that the amount of interest payable is reduced by virtue of —

(a)   a reduction in interest rates, or

(b)   a reduction in the amount of loan capital outstanding,

the amount of instalments which the borrower is liable to pay remains constant, the amount applicable shall not be adjusted to take account of the new amount of interest payable except where regulation 87(3) of the Social Security (Adjudication) Regulations 1984(a) so provides.

(9)   Notwithstanding paragraph (1)(b)(ii), where a claimant is or, if he is a member of a married or unmarried couple he and his partner are, aged under 60 and he or, either of them, was in receipt of an allowance immediately before the 26th January 1987, there shall be applicable under this regulation 100 per cent. of the eligible interest in that case for so long as he or either of them remain in receipt of an allowance.

(a) S.I. 1984/451; there are no relevant amending instruments.

(10)   For the purpose of paragraphs (1) and (9) —

(a) a person shall be treated as being in receipt of an allowance during the following periods:—

(i)   any period in respect of which it was subsequently held on appeal or review, that he was so entitled; and

(ii) any period of 8 weeks or less in respect of which he was not in receipt of an allowance and which fell immediately between periods in respect of which he was in receipt thereof or to which head (i) above applies;

(b) a person shall be treated as not being in receipt of an allowance during any period other than a period to which sub-paragraph (a)(ii) above applies in respect of which it is subsequently held on appeal or review that he was not so entitled;

(c) where the requirements and resources of a person, A, were, in respect of a past period, aggregated and treated as those of another person, B —

(i)   under paragraph 3(1) of Schedule 1 to the Act (aggregation in the case of married or unmarried couples), or

(ii) under paragraph 3(2) of that Schedule 1 (aggregation of dependants) and there are now aggregated with A's requirements and resources under that paragraph 3(2) those of another person which were previously so aggregated with B's,

and if A makes a claim for an allowance within 8 weeks of the cessation of aggregation, A shall be treated as having been in receipt of an allowance for the same period as B had been or had been treated, for the purpose of paragraph (1), as having been.".

(4)   In regulation 17(1) (interest on loans for repairs and improvements), for the words from "the amount" to the end there shall be substituted the words "an amount in respect of interest payable on a loan which is taken out, with or without security, for the purpose of —

(a) carrying out repairs or improvements to the home, or

(b) paying off another loan but only to the extent that interest on that other loan would have been applicable under this regulation had the loan not been paid off,

and which is used for that purpose or is to be so used within 6 months of the date of receipt or such further period as an Adjudication officer considers reasonable, and the amount applicable under this regulation shall be calculated as if the loan were a loan to which regulation 15 applied.".

(5)   In regulation 21 (restrictions where amounts excessive) for paragraphs (1) and (2) there shall be substituted the following paragraph —

"   (1)   Subject to paragraphs (3) and (4), the amounts applicable under regulations 15 to 18 shall be regarded as excessive and shall be restricted and the excess not allowed if and to the extent that —

(a) the home, excluding any part which is let or is normally occupied by boarders, is unnecessarily large for the assessment unit, any persons to whom regulation 4(2)(e) of the Supplementary Benefit (Aggregation) Regulations 1981(a) applies and any other non-dependants; or

(b) the immediate area in which the home is located is unnecessarily expensive; or

(c) the outgoings of the home in respect of which the amounts are applicable under those regulations as aforesaid are unreasonably high by comparison with the outgoings of suitable alternative accommodation in the area.".

Amendment of the Supplementary Benefit (Resources) Regulations 1981

3.—(1)   The Supplementary Benefit (Resources) Regulations 1981(b) shall be amended in accordance with the following provisions of this regulation.

(2)   In regulation 2(1) (interpretation), after the definition of "Tax Act" there shall be inserted the following definition:—

"the 1983 Requirements Regulations" means the Supplementary Benefit (Requirements) Regulations 1983(c);

(3)   In regulation 11 (treatment of income other than earnings) —

(a) in paragraph (2) there shall be added the following sub-paragraph —

"   (w)   any payment received under an insurance policy taken out to insure against the risk of being unable during any period to maintain payments on a loan to which regulation 15 or 17 of the 1983 Requirements Regulations applies, less any amount which falls to be disregarded by virtue of paragraph (4)(o).";

(b) in paragraph (4) there shall be added the following sub-paragraph —

"   (o)   in the case of a loan specified in regulations 15(3) or 17(1) of the 1983 Requirements Regulations, any payment received under a policy specified in paragraph (2)(w) and used to meet repayments in respect of that loan, to the extent that it does not exceed —

(i) subject to paragraph (4B), the amount, calculated on a weekly basis, of the claimant's eligible interest under regulations 15 or 17 of the 1983 Requirements Regulations,

---

(a) S.I. 1981/1524; the relevant amending instrument is S.I. 1983/1000.
(b) S.I. 1981/1527; the relevant amending instruments are S.I. 1982/1125, 1126, 1127, 1983/503, 505, 1240, 1985/613, 1986/1292, 1293.
(c) S.I. 1983/1399; the relevant amending instruments are S.I. 1984/282, 1102, 1103, 2034, 1985/1247, 1835, 1986/1292.

(ii) the amount of the payment, calculated on a weekly basis, due on the loan attributable to the repayment of capital, and

(iii) an amount equal to the amount, calculated on a weekly basis, of the premiums due on that policy.'';

(c) the following paragraph shall be inserted after paragraph (4A) —

" (4B)   Payments to which paragraph (4)(o) applies shall be disregarded by virtue of head (i) of that provision only for any period during which there is applicable to the claimant as a housing requirement 50 per cent. of his eligible interest by virtue of regulation 15(1)(b)(ii) of the 1983 Requirements Regulations.''.

Signed by authority of the Secretary of State for Social Services.

John Major
Minister of State,
Department of Health and Social Security

8th January 1987

We consent,

Mark Lennox Boyd
Tim Sainsbury
Two of the Lords Commissioners of
Her Majesty's Treasury

13th January 1987

EXPLANATORY NOTE

(This note is not part of the Regulations)

These Regulations amend Part IV of the Supplementary Benefit (Requirements) Regulations 1983 (which sets out the housing requirements of supplementary benefit claimants) in the following respects:—

— they amend regulation 14 so that, where the home is included in a hereditament or premises of which a part only is rated or assessed as a dwelling the amounts applicable under regulations 15 and 17 are limited to the proportion of the amounts applicable in respect of the hereditaments or premises as a whole equal to the proportion so rated or assessed;

— a new regulation 15 is substituted by which restrictions are placed on the amount of mortgage interest which will be met as a housing requirement during the first 16 weeks of benefit where the claimant or his partner is aged less than 60 and he was not in receipt of benefit prior to coming into force of this regulation;

— regulation 17 is amended so that interest on loans for repairs or improvements on the home is treated in the same way as interest on a loan which qualifies under regulation 15;

— regulation 21 is amended so that the amounts applicable as housing requirements under regulations 15 to 18 are restricted where the outgoings of the claimant's home are unreasonably high by comparison with the outgoings of suitable alternative accommodation in the locality.

In addition, regulation 3 of these regulations amends the Supplementary Benefit (Resources) Regulations 1981 to provide that any income received under the terms of an insurance policy taken out to insure against the risk of the claimant being unable to meet the interest on a loan to which regulation 15 or 17 of the Requirements Regulations applies, is subject to certain exceptions, to be taken into account in full as a resource.

The Report of the Social Security Advisory Committee dated 13th August 1986 on the proposals relevant to those regulations and a statement showing the extent to which these regulations give effect to the Committee's recommendations, and, in so far as they do not give effect to them, the reasons why not are contained in Command Papers 35 and 36 published by Her Majesty's Stationery Office. The Committee agreed not to have referred to them the proposal as to having regard to any foster children when determining whether the home is unnecessarily large and so the housing requirements for that home ought to be restricted.

1987 No. 18

NATIONAL HEALTH SERVICE, ENGLAND AND WALES

The National Health Service (Food Premises) Regulations 1987

Made - - - -	*14th January 1987*
Laid before Parliament	*16th January 1987*
Coming into force	*7th February 1987*

The Minister of Agriculture, Fisheries and Food, the Secretary of State for Social Services, and the Secretary of State for Wales, acting jointly, in exercise of powers conferred by section 1(2)(a), (3), (4) and (7)(a) of the National Health Service (Amendment) Act 1986 (**a**), and of all other powers enabling them in that behalf, hereby make the following Regulations:

Citation, commencement and interpretation

1.—(1) These Regulations may be cited as the National Health Service (Food Premises) Regulations 1987 and shall come into force on 7th February 1987.

(2) In these Regulations:

"the food legislation" means the Food Act 1984 (**b**) and any regulations or orders made under it;

"health authority" has the meaning assigned to it by section 128 of the National Health Service Act 1977 (**c**).

Occupiers or owners of health service premises for the purposes of the food legislation

2. A health authority shall be treated as both the owner and occupier of premises used by the health authority for the purposes of the food legislation.

(**a**) 1986 c.66.
(**b**) 1984 c.30.
(**c**) 1977 c.49.

In Witness whereof the Official Seal of the Minister of Agriculture, Fisheries and Food is hereunto affixed on 14th January 1987.

Michael Jopling
Minister of Agriculture, Fisheries and Food

12th January 1987

Norman Fowler
Secretary of State for Social Services

9th January 1987

Nicholas Edwards
Secretary of State for Wales

EXPLANATORY NOTE

(This note is not part of the Regulations)

These Regulations provide that health authorities in England and Wales shall be treated as both owners and occupiers of premises used by them for the purposes of the Food Act 1984 and any Regulations or Order made under that Act.

STATUTORY INSTRUMENTS

1987 No. 19

PLANT HEALTH

The Potatoes (Prohibition on Landing) (Great Britain) Order 1987

Made - - - -	*14th January 1987*
Laid before Parliament	*16th January 1987*
Coming into force	*6th February 1987*

The Minister of Agriculture, Fisheries and Food in relation to England, the Secretary of State for Scotland in relation to Scotland and the Secretary of State for Wales in relation to Wales, in exercise of the powers conferred by sections 2 and 3(1) and (2) of the Plant Health Act 1967(a), as read with section 20 of the Agriculture (Miscellaneous Provisions) Act 1972(b), and now vested in them (c), and of all other powers enabling them in that behalf, hereby make the following Order:—

Title, extent, commencement and interpretation

1.—(1) This Order may be cited as the Potatoes (Prohibition on Landing) (Great Britain) Order 1987, shall apply to Great Britain and shall come into force on 6th February 1987.

(2) In this Order "potato" means any plant or any part of a plant, including tubers and true seed, of *Solanum tuberosum* L. or other tuber-forming species or hybrids of the genus *Solanum* L.

Prohibition on landing

2. The landing in Great Britain of:—
  (a) any potatoes grown in the Federal Republic of Germany whether consigned from the Federal Republic of Germany or from any other country, and
  (b) any potatoes consigned from the Federal Republic of Germany
is hereby prohibited.

Application of the Import and Export (Plant Health) (Great Britain) Order 1980

3. The provisions of Articles 12 (examination, sampling and marking), 13 and 15 (action when plants are, or are likely to be, landed), 16 (powers of an officer of Customs and Excise), 17 (licences) and 19 (service of notices) of the Import and Export (Plant Health) (Great Britain) Order 1980(d) shall apply to the prohibition contained in Article 2 of this Order.

(a) 1967 c.8; sections 2(1), 3(1) and (2) were amended by the European Communities Act 1972 (c.68), section 4(1) and Schedule 4, paragraph 8.   (b) 1972 c.62.   (c) In the case of Secretary of State for Wales by virtue of S.I. 1978/272.   (d) S.I. 1980/420, to which there are amendments not relevant to this Order.

In Witness whereof the Official Seal of the Minister of Agriculture, Fisheries and Food is hereunto affixed on 13th January 1987.

(L.S.)

Michael Jopling
Minister of Agriculture, Fisheries and Food

John J. Mackay
Parliamentary Under-Secretary of State,
Scottish Office

13th January 1987

Nicholas Edwards
Secretary of State for Wales

14th January 1987

EXPLANATORY NOTE

(This note is not part of the Order)

This Order prohibits the landing in Great Britain of potatoes grown in or consigned from the Federal Republic of Germany from 6th February 1987.

The following provisions of the Import and Export (Plant Health) (Great Britain) Order 1980 apply to the prohibition on landing contained in Article 2:—

(a) an officer of the appropriate Minister authorised for the purposes of that Order has the powers of entry; examination and sampling and powers to enable remedial action to be taken when plants or flowers are landed or are likely to be landed in contravention of this order (Articles 12 and 13 of that Order);

(b) officers of Customs and Excise may detain plants and flowers for examination (Article 16 of that Order);

(c) the landing of a plant or flower which is prohibited by this Order may be authorised by licence (Article 17 of that Order).

Any person who lands potatoes in contravention of this order with intent to evade the prohibition contained in it is guilty of an offence under section 50(2) of the Customs and Excise Management Act 1979 (c.2) and may be detained. A person guilty of such offence is liable, on summary conviction, to a penalty of £2,000 or of three times the value of the goods, whichever is the greater, or to imprisonment for a term not exceeding 6 months, or to both, and, on conviction on indictment, to a penalty of any amount, or to imprisonment for a term not exceeding 2 years, or to both.

STATUTORY INSTRUMENTS

1987 No. 26 (S. 4)

FOOD

COMPOSITION AND LABELLING

The Condensed Milk and Dried Milk (Scotland) Amendment Regulations 1987

Made - - - -	*12th January 1987*
Laid before Parliament	*26th January 1987*
Coming into force	
Regulations 1 and 4	*16th February 1987*
Regulations 2 and 3	*1st January 1988*

The Secretary of State, in exercise of the powers conferred upon him by sections 4, 7, 56 and 56A of the Food and Drugs (Scotland) Act 1956(**a**) and of all other powers enabling him in that behalf, and after consultation in accordance with section 56(6) of the said Act with such organisations as appear to him to be representative of interests substantially affected by these Regulations, hereby makes the following Regulations:

Title and commencement

1. These Regulations may be cited as the Condensed Milk and Dried Milk (Scotland) Amendment Regulations 1987, and shall come into force–

(a) as respects regulations 1 and 4 on 16th February 1987, and

(b) as respects regulations 2 and 3 on 1st January 1988.

Amendment of the Condensed Milk and Dried Milk (Scotland) Regulations 1977

2. The Condensed Milk and Dried Milk (Scotland) Regulations 1977(**b**) are hereby further amended–

(a) by substituting for regulations 5 and 6 thereof the following regulations:–

"**Labelling and description of condensed milk and dried milk products for retail sale**

5.—(1) Without prejudice to the provisions of the Food Labelling (Scotland) Regulations 1984(**c**) and subject to paragraph (2) below and regulation 6, no person shall sell by retail, or consign or deliver pursuant to a sale by retail, any condensed milk product or dried milk product in a container unless that container is correctly marked or labelled with the following particulars:–

(a) a reserved description of the product, which shall be the name prescribed by law for that product for the purposes of regulation 7(1) of the Food Labelling (Scotland) Regulations 1984;

(**a**) 1956 c.30; section 4(1) was amended by the European Communities Act 1972 (c.68), Schedule 4, paragraph 3(1); section 56 was amended by the Criminal Justice Act 1982 (c.48), Schedule 15, paragraph 8; section 56A was added by the European Communities Act 1972, Schedule 4, paragraph 3(2).   (**b**) S.I. 1977/1027, amended by S.I. 1982/1209, 1983/270 and 1985/1068.   (**c**) S.I. 1984/1519, to which there are amendments not relevant to these Regulations.

(b) in the case of a dried milk product which is an instant preparation containing added lecithins in accordance with paragraph (c) of the proviso to regulation 9, the word "instant" added to the reserved description;

(c) in the case of any condensed milk product containing not less than 1.0 per centum milk fat and any dried milk product containing not less than 1.5 per centum milk fat, the milk fat content or minimum milk fat content expressed as a percentage;

(d) in the case of any condensed milk product, the milk solids not fat content or minimum milk solids not fat content expressed as a percentage;

(e) in the case of any condensed milk product, directions for dilution or reconstitution, or relevant information as to usage where the product is intended for use in its unaltered state;

(f) in the case of any dried milk product containing not less than 1.5 per centum milk fat, directions for dilution or reconstitution and an indication of the fat content of the product after dilution or reconstitution as directed;

(g) in the case of any unsweetened condensed milk product which has been subjected to ultra heat treatment and aseptically packed, the expression "UHT" or "ultra heat treated";

(h) in the case of any condensed milk product containing not more than 1.0 per centum milk fat and any dried milk product containing not more than 1.5 per centum milk fat, the warning "not to be used for babies except under medical advice".

(2) Where the condensed milk product or dried milk product is packed in units each weighing less than 20 grammes within an outer packaging, the particulars required by paragraphs (1)(b) to (h) above may appear on the outer packaging only.

Labelling and description of condensed milk and dried milk products for non-retail sale

5A. Subject to regulation 6A, no person shall sell otherwise than by retail, or consign or deliver pursuant to a sale otherwise than by retail, any condensed milk product or dried milk product in a container unless that container is correctly marked or labelled with the following particulars:-

(a) a reserved description of the product;

(b) the name or business name and the address of the manufacturer or packer or of a seller established within the Community;

(c) in the case of a product imported from a country outside the Community, the name of the country of origin;

(d) the date of manufacture or some marking by which the batch can be identified;

(e) in the case of any dried milk product containing any added permitted anti-caking agent in accordance with paragraph (d) of the proviso to regulation 9, the declaration "for use in vending machines only".

Manner of marking or labelling for retail sale

6.—(1) Regulations 32(1) and 34(1) and (2) of the Food Labelling (Scotland) Regulations 1984 (which relate to the manner of marking or labelling of food) shall apply to the particulars with which a condensed milk product or dried milk product is required to be marked or labelled by regulation 5 as if they were particulars with which food is required to be marked or labelled by the Food Labelling (Scotland) Regulations 1984.

(2) Any indication of minimum durability required by regulation 21 of the Food Labelling (Scotland) Regulations 1984 shall appear in the labelling of the condensed milk product or dried milk product sold by retail or consigned or delivered pursuant to a sale by retail in the same field of vision as the particulars required by regulation 5(1)(a), (b), (c) and (d).

Manner of marking or labelling for non-retail sale

6A. The particulars with which any condensed milk product or dried milk product is required to be marked or labelled by–

(a) regulation 5A, shall be clearly visible, easily legible and in indelible characters;

(b) paragraphs (a), (c) and (d) of regulation 5A shall be in English, either exclusively or in addition to any other language, or otherwise in a form easily understood by the purchaser;

(c) paragraph (c) of regulation 5A, may appear in an accompanying document.";

(b) by substituting for paragraph (c) of the proviso to regulation 9 thereof, the following paragraph:–

"(c) any dried milk product which contains not less than 1.5 per centum milk fat and which is an instant preparation may contain not more than 0.5 per centum of the added permitted emulsifier lecithins E322;".

Amendment of the Food Labelling (Scotland) Regulations 1984

3. The Food Labelling (Scotland) Regulations 1984 are hereby further amended by substituting for sub-paragraph (d) of paragraph (2) of regulation 5 thereof the following sub-paragraph:—

"(d) any condensed milk product or dried milk product as defined in the Condensed Milk and Dried Milk (Scotland) Regulations 1977 which is ready for delivery to a catering establishment, other than any such product which is specially prepared for infant feeding and in the labelling of which there appears a clear statement that such food is intended for consumption by infants and no statement to the effect that such food is intended for consumption by any other class of person;".

Transitional provisions

4. In any proceedings brought before 1st January 1988 under the Condensed Milk and Dried Milk (Scotland) Regulations 1977, the accused shall not be convicted of an offence–

(a) against regulation 5 unless the prosecution prove that the act alleged to constitute the offence would have constituted an offence against regulation 5 or 5A as substituted for that regulation by regulation 2 of these Regulations if it had been in force when the act was done;

(b) against regulation 6 unless the prosecution prove that the act alleged to have constituted an offence would have constituted an offence against regulation 6 or 6A as substituted for that regulation by regulation 2 of these Regulations if it had been in force when the act was done.

Glenarthur
Minister of State,
Scottish Office

New St. Andrew's House
Edinburgh
12th January 1987

EXPLANATORY NOTE

(This note is not part of the Regulations)

These Regulations, which apply to Scotland only, implement Council Directive No. 83/635/EEC (O.J. No. L357, 21.12.83, p.37) which amended for the second time Directive 76/118/EEC on the approximation of the laws of the Member States relating to certain partly or wholly dehydrated preserved milk for human consumption. For this purpose, they further amend the Condensed Milk and Dried Milk (Scotland) Regulations 1977 ("the principal Regulations") by substituting for original regulations 5 and 6, new regulations 5, 5A, 6 and 6A to make separate provision for retail and non-retail sales of condensed milk and dried milk products (regulation 2(a)). They also amend the Food Labelling (Scotland) Regulations 1984 so as to apply Part III of those Regulations, not only to products prepared for infant feeding and labelled accordingly, but also to products ready for delivery to the ultimate consumer (regulation 3).

In relation to retail sales, the requirements in new principal regulation 5 for labelling products with specified particulars, make the following changes of substance:–

(a) for dried milk products, the drying process need no longer be declared;

(b) the requirement to give a warning in respect of baby feeding, which expired on 31st December 1980, is reinstated for wholly skimmed products.

In relation to non-retail sales, new principal regulation 5A requires products to be labelled with a specified description and particulars of the Community manufacturer, packer or seller, the country of origin for imports to the Community, the date of manufacture or batch identification and, in the case of dried milk products containing permitted anti-caking agent, a declaration that they are for use in vending machines, where this is the intention.

The manner of marking or labelling is prescribed by new principal regulations 6 and 6A for retail sales and non-retail sales respectively.

These Regulations also amend principal regulation 9 to provide that only specified dried milk products which are instant preparations may contain lecithins E322 to the prescribed maximum percentage (regulation 2(b)).

The substantive changes made by regulations 2 and 3 come into force on 1st January 1988. Until then regulation 4 (which with regulation 1 comes into force on 16th February 1987) provides that an accused shall not be convicted of an offence against regulations 5 or 6 of the principal Regulations unless it is proved that his act would have constituted an offence against the respective substituted provisions had they then been in force.

STATUTORY INSTRUMENTS

1987 No. 27

ROAD TRAFFIC

The Community Drivers' Hours (Passenger and Goods Vehicles) (Temporary Exception) Regulations 1987

Made - - - -	*16th January 1987*
Laid before Parliament	*16th January 1987*
Coming into force	*17th January 1987*

The Secretary of State for Transport, being a Minister designated (**a**) for the purpose of section 2(2) of the European Communities Act 1972 (**b**) in relation to the regulation and supervision of the working conditions of persons engaged in road transport, in exercise of the powers conferred by that section, hereby makes the following Regulations:

1. These Regulations may be cited as the Community Drivers' Hours (Passenger and Goods Vehicles) (Temporary Exception) Regulations 1987 and shall come into force on 17th January 1987.

2. Pursuant to Article 13(2) of Council Regulation (EEC) No. 3820/85 of 20th December 1985 on the harmonisation of certain social legislation relating to road transport (**c**) until 16th February 1987 that Regulation shall apply to transport operations to which it applies with the exception of Articles 6, 8 and 9.

Signed by authority of the Secretary of State.

Peter Bottomley
Parliamentary Under Secretary of State,
Department of Transport

16th January 1987

(**a**) S.I. 1975/1707.
(**b**) 1972 c.68.
(**c**) OJ No. L370, 31.12.85, p.1.

EXPLANATORY NOTE

(This note is not part of the Regulations)

Article 13(2) of Council Regulation (EEC) No. 3820/85 of the 20th December 1985 on the harmonisation of certain social legislation relating to road transport provides that Member States may in urgent cases grant a temporary exception for a period not exceeding 30 days to transport operations carried out in exceptional circumstances. These Regulations provide that until the 16th February 1987 the Regulation shall apply to transport operations to which it applies with the exception of Articles 6, 8 and 9. The exceptional circumstances for the making of the Regulations are the severe weather conditions and the effects and consequences of the severe weather conditions.

STATUTORY INSTRUMENTS

1987 No. 28

ROAD TRAFFIC

The Drivers' Hours (Passenger and Goods Vehicles) (Exemption) Regulations 1987

Made - - - -	*16th January 1987*
Laid before Parliament	*16th January 1987*
Coming into force	*17th January 1987*

The Secretary of State for Transport, in exercise of the powers conferred by section 96(10) of the Transport Act 1968(**a**) and now vested in him (**b**) and of all the enabling powers, after consultation with representative organisations in accordance with section 101(6) of that Act, hereby makes the following Regulations:—

1. The Regulations may be cited as the Drivers' Hours (Passenger and Goods Vehicles) (Exemption) Regulations 1987 and shall come into force on 17th January 1987.

2. A driver who during any working day or any working week spends time in driving passenger or goods vehicles and who spends time driving or on duty during that day or week to meet the special need occasioned by severe weather conditions or the effects or consequences of severe weather conditions is exempted from the requirements of the domestic drivers' hours code in respect of that day or that week.

Peter Bottomley
Parliamentary Under Secretary of State,
Department of Transport

Signed by authority of the Secretary of State
16th January 1987

EXPLANATORY NOTE

(This note is not part of the Regulations)

These Regulations exempt from the remaining requirements of section 96(1) to (6) of the Transport Act 1968 a driver who during any working day or any working week spends time in driving passenger or goods vehicles and who spends time driving or on duty during that day or week to meet the special need occasioned by severe weather conditions or the effects or consequences of severe weather conditions in respect of that day or that week.

(**a**) 1968 c. 73; Part VI of the Transport Act 1968 is modified by S.I. 1970/257, 1971/818 and 1986/1459.
(**b**) S.I. 1970/1681, 1979/571 and 1981/238.

STATUTORY INSTRUMENTS

1987 No. 29

INDUSTRIAL TRAINING

The Industrial Training Levy (Construction Board) Order 1987

Made -   -   -   -   *16th January 1987*
Coming into force on the day after the day on which it is made

Whereas proposals made by the Construction Industry Training Board for the raising and collection of a levy have been submitted to, and approved by, the Manpower Services Commission under section 11(1) of the Industrial Training Act 1982 (**a**) ("the 1982 Act") and thereafter submitted by the said Commission to the Secretary of State under that subsection;

And whereas in pursuance of section 11(3) of the 1982 Act the said proposals include provision for the exemption from the levy of employers who, in view of the small number of their employees, ought in the opinion of the Secretary of State to be exempted from it;

And whereas the proposals are made in pursuance of section 11(4)*(b)* of the 1982 Act and the Secretary of State is satisified that those proposals falling within section 11(5)*(b)* of the said Act ("the relevant proposals") are necessary as mentioned in the said section 11(5), and that the condition mentioned in section 11(6)*(a)* of the 1982 Act is satisfied in the case of the relevant proposals;

And whereas the following Order falls within section 11(7)*(b)* of the 1982 Act;

And whereas a draft of the following Order was laid before Parliament in accordance with section 12(6) of the 1982 Act and approved by resolution of each House of Parliament;

Now, therefore, the Secretary of State, in exercise of the powers conferred by sections 11(2), 12(3) and 12(4) of the 1982 Act and of all other powers enabling him in that behalf, hereby makes the following Order:—

Citation and commencement

1. This Order may be cited as the Industrial Training Levy (Construction Board) Order 1987 and shall come into force on the day after the day on which it is made.

(**a**) 1982 c.10.

Interpretation

2.—(1) In this Order unless the context otherwise requires:—

(a) "assessment" means an assessment of an employer to the levy;

(b) "the Board" means the Construction Industry Training Board;

(c) "business" means any activities of industry or commerce;

(d) "construction establishment" means an establishment in Great Britain engaged wholly or mainly in the construction industry for a total of twenty-seven or more weeks in the period of twelve months that commenced on 6th April 1985 or, being an establishment that commenced to carry on business in the said period, for a total number of weeks exceeding one half of the number of weeks in the part of the said period commencing with the day on which business was commenced and ending on the last day thereof;

(e) "the construction industry" does not include any activities of an establishment which have been transferred from the industry of the Board to the industry of another industrial training board by one of the transfer orders, but save as aforesaid means any one or more of the activities which, subject to the provisions of paragraph 2 of the Schedule to the industrial training order, are specified in paragraph 1 of that Schedule as the activities of the construction industry or, in relation to an establishment whose activities have been transferred to the industry of the Board by one of the transfer orders, any activities so transferred;

(f) "the twenty-second levy period" means the period commencing with the day upon which this Order comes into operation and ending on 31st March 1987;

(g) "employer" means a person who is an employer in the construction industry at any time in the twenty-second levy period;

(h) "the industrial training order" means the Industrial Training (Construction Board) Order 1964 (**a**);

(i) "the levy" means the levy imposed by the Board in respect of the twenty-second levy period;

(j) "notice" means a notice in writing;

(k) "the transfer orders" means—

   (i) the Industrial Training (Transfer of the Activities of Establishments) Order 1975 (**b**);

   (ii) the Industrial Training (Transfer of the Activities of Establishments) (No. 2) Order 1975 (**c**);

   (iii) the Industrial Training (Transfer of the Activities of Establishments) Order 1976 (**d**);

   (iv) the Industrial Training (Transfer of the Activities of Establishments) (No. 2) Order 1976 (**e**);

   (v) the Industrial Training (Transfer of the Activities of Establishments) (No. 3) Order 1976 (**f**);

   (vi) the Industrial Training (Transfer of the Activities of Establishments) Order 1977 (**g**);

(**a**) S.I. 1964/1079, amended by S.I. 1980/1274, 1982/922.   (**b**) S.I. 1975/434.
(**c**) S.I. 1975/1157.   (**d**) S.I. 1976/396.   (**e**) S.I. 1976/1635.
(**f**) S.I. 1976/2110.   (**g**) S.I. 1977/1951.

   (vii) the Industrial Training (Transfer of the Activities of Establishments) Order 1978(**a**);

  (viii) the Industrial Training (Transfer of the Activities of Establishments) (No. 2) Order 1978(**b**);

    (ix) the Industrial Training (Transfer of the Activities of Establishments) (No. 3) Order 1978(**c**);

     (x) the Industrial Training (Transfer of the Activities of Establishments) Order 1979(**d**);

    (xi) the Industrial Training (Transfer of the Activities of Establishments) (No. 2) Order 1980(**e**);

   (xii) the Industrial Training (Transfer of the Activities of Establishments) Order 1981(**f**); and

  (xiii) the Industrial Training (Transfer of the Activities of Establishments) Order 1985(**g**);

(2) Any reference in this Order to an establishment that commences to carry on business or that ceases to carry on business shall not be taken to apply where the location of the establishment is changed but its business is continued wholly or mainly at or from the new location, or where the suspension of activities is of a temporary or seasonal nature.

Imposition of the levy

3.—(1) The levy to be imposed by the Board on employers in respect of the twenty-second levy period shall be assessed in accordance with the provisions of this Article and of the Schedule to this Order.

(2) The levy shall be assessed by the Board separately in respect of each construction establishment of an employer, but in agreement with the employer one assessment may be made in respect of any number of such establishments, in which case those establishments shall be deemed for the purposes of that assessment to constitute one establishment.

Assessment notices

4.—(1) The Board shall serve an assessment notice on every employer assessed to the levy, but one notice may comprise two or more assessments.

(2) An assessment notice shall state the amount of the levy payable by the person assessed to the levy, and that amount shall be equal to the total amount of the levy assessed by the Board under the provisions of this Order in respect of each establishment included in the notice.

(3) An assessment notice shall state the Board's address for the service of a notice of appeal or of an application for an extension of time for appealing.

(4) An assessment notice may be served on the person assessed to the levy either by delivering it to him personally or by leaving it, or sending it to him by post, at his last known address or place of business in the United Kingdom or, if that person is a corporation, by leaving it, or sending it by post to the corporation, at such address or place of business or at its registered or principal office.

(**a**) S.I. 1978/448.	(**b**) S.I. 1978/1225.	(**c**) S.I. 1978/1643.
(**d**) S.I. 1979/793.	(**e**) S.I. 1980/1753.	(**f**) S.I. 1981/1041.
(**g**) S.I. 1985/1662.		

Payment of the levy

5.—(1) Subject to the provisions of this Article and of Articles 6 and 7 of this Order, the amount of the levy payable under an assessment notice served by the Board shall be due and payable to the Board one month after the date of the assessment notice.

(2) The amount of an assessment shall not be recoverable by the Board until there has expired the time allowed for appealing against the assessment by Article 7(1) of this Order and any further period or periods of time that the Board or an industrial tribunal may have allowed for appealing under paragraph (2) or (3) of that Article or, where an appeal is brought, until the appeal is decided or withdrawn.

Withdrawal of assessment

6.—(1) The Board may, by a notice served on the person assessed to the levy in the same manner as an assessment notice, withdraw an assessment if that person has appealed against that assessment under the provisions of Article 7 of this Order and the appeal has not been entered in the Register of Appeals kept under the appropriate Regulations specified in paragraph (5) of that Article.

(2) The withdrawal of an assessment shall be without prejudice—

(a) to the power of the Board to serve a further assessment notice in respect of any establishment to which that assessment related; or

(b) to any other assessment included in the original assessment notice, and such notice shall thereupon have effect as if any assessment withdrawn by the Board had not been included therein.

Appeals

7.—(1) A person assessed to the levy may appeal to an industrial tribunal against the assessment within one month from the date of the service of the assessment notice or within any further period or periods of time that may be allowed by the Board or an industrial tribunal under the following provisions of this Article.

(2) The Board by notice may for good cause allow a person assessed to the levy to appeal to an industrial tribunal against an assessment at any time within the period of four months from the date of the service of the assessment notice or within such further period or periods as the Board may allow before such time as may then be limited for appealing has expired.

(3) If the Board shall not allow an application for extension of time for appealing, an industrial tribunal shall upon application made to the tribunal by the person assessed to the levy have the like powers as the Board under the last foregoing paragraph.

(4) In the case of an establishment that ceases to carry on business in the twenty-second levy period on any day after the date of the service of the relevant assessment notice, the foregoing provisions of this Article shall have effect as if for the period of four months from the date of the service of the assessment notice mentioned in paragraph (2) of this Article there were substituted the period of six months from the date of the cessation of business.

(5) An appeal or an application to an industrial tribunal under this Article shall be made in accordance with the Industrial Tribunals (England and

Wales) Regulations 1965 (**a**) except where the establishment to which the relevant assessement relates is wholly in Scotland, when the appeal or application shall be made in accordance with the Industrial Tribunals (Scotland) Regulations 1965 (**b**).

(6) The powers of an industrial tribunal under paragraph (3) of this Article may be exercised by the President of the Industrial Tribunals (England and Wales) or by the President of the Industrial Tribunals (Scotland) as the case may be.

Evidence

8.—(1) Upon the discharge by a person assessed to the levy of his liability under an assessment, the Board shall if so requested issue to him a certificate to that effect.

(2) The production in any proceedings of a document purporting to be certified by the Secretary of the Board or any other person, being a member, officer or servant of the Board authorised to act in that behalf, to be a true copy of an assessment or other notice issued by the Board, or purporting to be a certificate such as is mentioned in the foregoing paragraph of this Article, shall, unless the contrary is proved, be sufficient evidence of the document and of the facts stated therein.

Signed by order of the Secretary of State

David Trippier
Parliamentary Under Secretary of State,
Department of Employment

16th January 1987

(**a**)   S.I. 1965/1101, amended by S.I. 1967/301.
(**b**)   S.I. 1965/1157, amended by S.I. 1967/302.

Article 3   SCHEDULE

Interpretation

1.   In this Schedule, unless the context otherwise requires—

   (a) "agriculture" has the same meaning as in section 109(3) of the Agriculture Act 1947 (**a**) or, in relation to Scotland, as in section 86(3) of the Agriculture (Scotland) Act 1948 (**b**) ;

   (b) "average number", in relation to any category and description of persons employed at or from a construction establishment of an employer, means the number that is equal to the average of the numbers of the persons of that category and description specified in the first and second columns of the Appendix to this Schedule employed, or treated as employed under the provisions of paragraph 2*(c)* of this Schedule, at or from the establishment by the employer on the relevant dates or, in the case of an establishment that commenced to carry on business after the first of the relevant dates but before the second, the number of persons of that category and description specified as aforesaid and employed by the employer at or from the establishment on the second of the relevant dates;

   (c) "charity" has the same meaning as in section 360 of the Income and Corporation Taxes Act 1970 (**c**) ;

   (d) "clerical or miscellaneous worker" includes—

      (i) a clerk and other office staff, including those working in sales, computers and stores, and supervisors of these staff;

      (ii) a storeman;

      (iii) a transport worker (but not a motor mechanic);

      (iv) an operative or conversion fitter (excluding a gas fitter, a plumber or a heating and ventilating fitter), engaged in the conversion of appliances to natural gas or in the preliminary work;

      (v) a terrazzo worker, including a terrazzo layer;

      (vi) any other person (including a foreman, a ganger and a chargehand) mainly employed as a manual worker not comprised in any other category and description of worker specified in this Schedule or the appendix thereto;

   (e) "craftsman (building)" means—

      (i) a bricklayer, including a specialist bricklayer;

      (ii) a carpenter joiner, including a carpenter, a joiner, a formwork carpenter, a joiner bench hand, a woodworking machinist or woodworking operative and a setter out;

      (iii) a mason, including a monumental mason, a stone carver and a stone polisher;

      (iv) a mason pavior, including a person involved in cutting and carving stone and who is following or has completed a course of further education being the City and Guilds of London Institute Course No. 588 on Masonry at Craft Level;

      (v) a painter, including a painter and decorator, an industrial painter, a french polisher and a signwriter;

      (vi) a plasterer, including a solid or fibrous plasterer, a moulder and a dry-lining or partition operative;

      (vii) a roof slater and tiler;

      (viii) any other person (including a foreman, a ganger and a chargehand) mainly employed as a manual worker, otherwise than as a labourer or general operative, in any of the trades specified in this sub-paragraph;

(**a**)   1947 c.48.   (**b**)   1948 c.45.   (**c**)   1970 c.10.

(f) "craftsman (mechanical engineering services)" means—
    (i) a gas fitter;
    (ii) a heating and ventilating fitter, including a heating fitter;
    (iii) an oil burner mechanic;
    (iv) a pipe fitter;
    (v) a plumber, including a chemical plumber, a plumber welder and a hot water fitter;
    (vi) a refrigeration mechanic;
    (vii) a welder, including an oxy-acetylene, metallic-arc or shielded-arc welder;
    (viii) any other person (including a foreman, a ganger and a chargehand) mainly employed as a manual worker, otherwise than as a labourer or general operative, in any of the trades specified in this sub-paragraph;

(g) "craftsman (electrical engineering services)" means—
    (i) an electrician, including a cable jointer;
    (ii) any other person (including a foreman, a ganger and a chargehand) mainly employed as a manual worker, otherwise than as a labourer or general operative, in any of the trades specified in this sub-paragraph;

(h) "craftsman (miscellaneous)" means—
    (i) a thermal insulation operative or ductwork erector;
    (ii) any other person (including a foreman, a ganger and a chargehand) mainly employed as a manual worker, otherwise than as a labourer or general operative, in either of the trades specified in this sub-paragraph or in any other trade not specified in this Schedule or the appendix thereto;

(i) "specialist building operative" means—
    (i) a floor or wall tiler, including a mosaic worker and a tile fixer;
    (ii) a ceiling fixer, including a suspended ceiling erector and a metal fixer (ceiling systems);
    (iii) a mastic asphalter, including a mastic asphalt spreader;
    (iv) a floor coverer, including a parquet floorer and a vinyl, linoleum or carpet layer;
    (v) a floorer, including a granolithic or other in situ floor finisher;
    (vi) a glazier, including a double glazier, a window fixer, a patent glazier, a leaded light worker and a glass production or processing worker;
    (vii) a demountable partition erector;
    (viii) a steeplejack, including a lightning conductor erector;
    (ix) a demolisher, including a general labourer using a compressed air drill or pneumatic punching machine or spade, a sorter, an improver, a mattockman, a topman, a burner topman, a burner groundsman, a shorer (timber) and a shorer's mate;
    (x) any other person (including a foreman, a ganger and a chargehand) mainly employed as a manual worker, otherwise than as a labourer or general operative, in any of the trades specified in this sub-paragraph;

(j) "a labour-only agreement" means any agreement, not being a contract of service or of apprenticeship, made between an employer and any other person or persons whereby the services (including any incidental use of tools) of such person or persons, or of any other person or persons were rendered to the employer in his trade or business;

(k) "the relevant dates" means 3rd October 1985 and 3rd April 1986;

(l) "a skilled building and civil engineering worker" means—
    (i) a concretor, including a bar bender and fixer, a pre-cast concrete

erector and fixer, a pre-stressing or pre-tensioning operative, a concrete placer, a vibrator or finisher;

(ii) a diver, including a surface, demand or helmet diver and a life linesman;

(iii) an excavation operative, including a heading driver, a manhole builder, a pipe layer, a pipe jointer and a timberman;

(iv) a mechanical plant operator, including a mechanical equipment, compressor, air tool or paving machine operator, a mixerman, a potman, a banksman, a slinger, a plant driver, a dumper driver, a crane driver, an excavation plant operator, an earthmoving plant operator, a pumpman, an oiler and a greaser;

(v) a piling or well drilling operative, including a borer driver, a vibrator or specialist piling operative, a well or rock driller and a shaft sinker;

(vi) a tunnel miner, including a soft-heading miner;

(vii) a blacksmith, including a marker-out;

(viii) a steel erector;

(ix) a repetitive process factory worker;

(x) a gas distribution mains layer, including a service layer;

(xi) a plant mechanic, including a plant maintenance mechanic, a contractors' plant mechanic and a motor mechanic;

(xii) a tar pavior;

(xiii) a labourer or general operative mainly employed in any of the trades specified in this sub-paragraph or in sub-paragraph *(e), (f), (g), (h), (i),* or *(n)* of this paragraph who was entitled to extra payment for skill or responsibility under a Working Rule Agreement;

(xiv) any other person (including a foreman, a ganger and a chargehand) mainly employed as a manual worker, otherwise than as a labourer or general operative, in any of the trades mentioned in this sub-paragraph;

(m) "a person employed in a managerial, administrative, professional or technical capacity" includes—

(i) a manager, including a contracts, site, area, sales or office manager;

(ii) an accountant or company secretary;

(iii) an estimator, surveyor or buyer;

(iv) an engineer or architect;

(v) a technical, planning or laboratory assistant, a draughtsman, a tracer or a design detailer;

(vi) a work study officer;

(vii) a personnel officer, a training officer or an instructor;

(viii) a person occupying the position of foreman or of works supervisor being a person who is not mainly employed as a manual worker whether in handling materials or otherwise;

(n) "a roof sheeter or felter" includes—

(i) a roof sheeter and cladder, an asbestos roofer, a galvanised or protected steel sheeter or an aluminium sheeter;

(ii) a roofing felt fixer and a roofing felt layer;

(iii) any other person (including a foreman, a ganger and a chargehand) mainly employed as a manual worker, otherwise than as a labourer or general operative, in any of the trades specified in this sub-paragraph;

(o) "trainee" means a person (including an apprentice) who is learning a managerial, administrative, professional, technical or manual skill and whose employer has undertaken to provide training for him in that skill for a specified period of not less than twelve months;

(p) "Working Rule Agreement" means any agreement as to pay, being an agreement between—

  (i) parties who are or represent employers or organisations of employers or associations of such organisations; and

  (ii) parties who are or represent organisations of employees or associations of such organisations;

but includes also any award modifying or supplementing such an agreement.

2. For the purposes of this Schedule the following provisions shall have effect—

  (a) no regard shall be had to any person employed wholly in the supply of food or drink for immediate consumption or in agriculture or who was normally working for an aggregate of less than 8 hours weekly;

  (b) no regard shall be had to a company director remunerated solely by fees but, save as aforesaid, the provisions of this Schedule shall apply to a company director (including a person occupying the position of director by whatever name he is called) as they apply to other persons and accordingly such a person shall be taken to be comprised in the category appropriate to the work in which he was mainly engaged;

  (c) in the case of a construction establishment that is taken over (whether directly or indirectly) by a employer in succession to, or jointly with another person, the person or persons carrying on the establishment on the day upon which this Order comes into operation shall be treated as the employer of any person who was employed on either or both of the relevant dates, or at any time in the period of twelve months that commenced on 6th April 1985 at or from the establishment under a contract of service or of apprenticeship or under a labour-only agreement, by the person then carrying on the establishment.

Basic assessment rules

3.—(1) Subject to the exemptions in paragraphs 4 and 5(1) below, the amount to be assessed by way of levy in respect of a construction establishment, other than a brick-manufacturing establishment, (being an establishment carrying on business in the twenty-second levy period) shall be the aggregate of the amount (if any) by which 2% of the labour-only payments exceeds 2% of labour-only receipts and the amount of the occupational levy.

(2) For the purposes of sub-paragraph (1) above:—

  (a) "2% of labour-only payments" means the sum which (rounded down where necessary to the nearest £1) represents 2% of all payments made to any persons by the employer during the period of 12 months that commenced on 6th April 1985 under labour-only agreements in respect of work carried out at or from the establishment;

  (b) "2% of labour-only receipts" means the sum which (rounded down where necessary to the nearest £1) represents 2% of all payments received by the employer during the period of 12 months that commenced on 6th April 1985 from any other employers in the construction industry under labour-only agreements in respect of work carried out at or from the establishment;

  (c) "the amount of the occupational levy" means the sum of the amounts (rounded down in each case where necessary to the nearest £1) produced by multiplying the appropriate amount in the third column of the appendix to this Schedule by the average number of persons employed by the employer at or from the establishment under contracts of service or apprenticeship in each relevant category and description of employment, less the amount (if any) by which 2% of labour-only receipts exceeds 2% of labour-only payments, provided that the amount of the occupational levy shall not exceed an amount equal to 1% of the aggregate of the emoluments and payments intended to be disbursed as emoluments which have been paid or are payable by the employer to or in respect of persons employed in the industry in respect of the period of twelve months which commenced on 6th April 1985.

(3) Subject to the exemptions in paragraphs 4 and 5(2) below, the amount to be assessed by way of levy in respect of a brick-manufacturing establishment (being an establishment carrying on business in the twenty-second levy period) shall be equal to 0.05% of the aggregate of the emoluments and payments intended to be disbursed as emoluments which have been paid or are payable by the employer to or in respect of persons employed at or from the establishment under contracts of service or apprenticeship in respect of the period of 12 months which commenced on 6th April 1985.

(4) For the purposes of this paragraph and paragraph 5 below "a brick-manufacturing establishment" means a construction establishment engaged wholly or mainly in the manufacture of bricks from clay or calcium silicate for building purposes but excluding bricks made for refractory purposes.

Exemption of charities

4.   A charity shall be exempt from the levy.

Exemption of small employers

5.—(1) There shall be exempt from the levy an employer in whose case the aggregate amount of—

(a) the sum of the emoluments of all the persons employed at or from the construction establishment or establishments of the employer (not being a brick-manufacturing establishment or brick-manufacturing establishments) in the period of 12 months that commenced on 6th April 1985, and

(b) all such sums (if any) as were paid in the said period by the employer to any person under a labour-only agreement at or from the said establishment or establishments,

was less than £15,000.

(2) There shall be exempt from the levy, in respect of brick-manufacturing establishments, an employer in whose case the sum of the emoluments of all the persons employed at or from the brick-manufacturing establishments of the employer in the period of 12 months that commenced on 6th April 1985 was less than £100,000.

(3) For the purposes of sub-paragraphs (1)(a) and (2) above "emoluments" means all emoluments assessable to income tax under Schedule E of the Income and Corporation Taxes Act 1970 (other than pensions), being emoluments from which tax under that Schedule is deductible, whether or not tax in fact falls to be deducted from any particular payment thereof.

(4) For the purposes of sub-paragraphs (1) and (2) above, Article 3(2) of this Order shall be disregarded.

Cessation of business

6.   The amount of the levy imposed in respect of a construction establishment that ceases to carry on business in the twenty-second levy period shall be in the same proportion to the amount that would otherwise be due in accordance with the foregoing provisions of this Schedule as the number of days between the commencement of the said levy period and the date of cessation of business (both dates inclusive) bears to the number of days in the said levy period.

APPENDIX

Category	Description	Amount Per Capita
1.	A person employed in a managerial, administrative, professional or technical capacity	£44
2.	A clerical or miscellaneous worker	NIL
3.	A craftsman (building)	£75
4.	A craftsman (mechanical engineering services)	£95
5.	A craftsman (electrical engineering services)	£85
6.	A skilled building and civil engineering worker	£25
7.	A labourer or general operative not entitled to extra payment for skill or responsibility under a Working Rule Agreement	£18
8.	A craftsman (miscellaneous)	£20
9.	A specialist building operative	£50
10.	A roof sheeter or felter	£55
11.	A scaffolder	£58
12.	A cavity wall insulation operative, a fencer or fence erector	£33
13.	A trainee in any of the categories 1–6 and 8–12 above	NIL

EXPLANATORY NOTE

(This note is not part of the Order)

This Order gives effect to proposals of the Construction Industry Training Board which were submitted to and approved by the Manpower Services Commission, and thereafter submitted by the Manpower Services Commission to the Secretary of State. The proposals are for the imposition of a levy on employers in the construction industry for the purpose of raising money towards meeting the expenses of the Board.

A levy is to be imposed on employers limited to 1 per cent of payroll in respect of employees employed by them under contracts of service or apprenticeship and to 2 per cent of payments made by the employers to persons under labour-only agreements.

A levy of 0.05 per cent of payroll is to be imposed on employers with brick-manufacturing establishments in respect of persons employed by them at or from the establishments under contracts of service or of apprenticeship.

This levy is in respect of the twenty-second levy period commencing with the date on which this Order comes into operation and ending on 31st March 1987.

The levy will be assessed by the Board, and there will be a right of appeal against an assessment to an industrial tribunal.

STATUTORY INSTRUMENTS

1987 No. 30

NORTHERN IRELAND

The Northern Ireland (Emergency Provisions) Act 1978 (Continuance) Order 1987

Laid before Parliament in draft

Made - - - - -	*14th January 1987*
Coming into force	*25th January 1987*

Whereas a draft of this Order has been approved by resolution of each House of Parliament:

Now, therefore, in exercise of the powers conferred upon me by section 33(3)(*a*) of the Northern Ireland (Emergency Provisions) Act 1978 **(a)**, I hereby make the following Order:—

1. This Order may be cited as the Northern Ireland (Emergency Provisions) Act 1978 (Continuance) Order 1987 and shall come into force on 25th January 1987.

2. In this Order "the temporary provisions of the Act of 1978" means all the provisions of the Northern Ireland (Emergency Provisions) Act 1978, except sections 5 and 28 to 36, Part III of Schedule 4, Schedules 5 and 6 and, so far as they relate to offences which are scheduled offences by virtue of the said Part III, sections 2, 6 and 7.

3. The temporary provisions of the Act of 1978, except section 12 and Schedule 1, shall continue in force for a period of six months beginning with 25th January 1987.

Tom King
One of Her Majesty's Principal
Secretaries of State

Northern Ireland Office
14th January 1987

(a) 1978 c. 5.

EXPLANATORY NOTE

(This note is not part of the Order)

This Order continues in force the temporary provisions of the Northern Ireland (Emergency Provisions) Act 1978, except section 12 and Schedule 1 (which relate to the detention of terrorists), for a period of six months beginning with 25th January 1987. These provisions are currently in force by virtue of the Northern Ireland (Emergency Provisions) Act 1978 (Continuance) (No. 2) Order 1986 (S.I. 1986/1146).

STATUTORY INSTRUMENTS

1987 No. 31

SOCIAL SECURITY

The Social Security (Hospital In-Patients) Amendment Regulations 1987

Made - - - -	*15th January 1987*
Laid before Parliament	*23rd January 1987*
Coming into force - -	*13th February 1987*

The Secretary of State for Social Services, in exercise of the powers conferred upon him by section 85(1) of and Schedule 20**(a)** to the Social Security Act 1975**(b)** and of all other powers enabling him in that behalf, after agreement by the Social Security Advisory Committee that proposals to make these regulations shall not be referred to it**(c)**, hereby makes the following regulations:—

Citation and commencement

1. These regulations may be cited as the Social Security (Hospital In-Patients) Amendment Regulations 1987 and shall come into force on 13th February 1987.

Amendment of the Social Security (Hospital In-Patients) Regulations 1975

2.—(1) The Social Security (Hospital In-Patients) Regulations 1975**(d)** shall be amended in accordance with the following provisions of this regulation.

(2) In regulation 6 (adjustment of personal benefit after 52 weeks in hospital) paragraph (4) shall be omitted.

(3) In regulation 7 (adjustment of personal benefit after 104 weeks in hospital) paragraphs (3) and (4) shall be omitted.

(4) In regulation 11 (adjustment of dependency benefit where dependant is the husband or wife of the beneficiary and is in hospital) paragraph (2) shall be omitted.

(5) In regulation 18 (priority of adjustments)

(a) in paragraph (1) the words " Except in any case to which paragraph (2) applies ", shall be omitted;

(b) paragraph (2) shall be omitted.

(6) In regulation 19 (treatment of age addition) for the words " has not a child or children or a wife who resides with him " there shall be substituted " is neither residing with a child or children nor with a spouse ".

(a) *See* the definition of " Regulations ".   (b) 1975 c.14.
(c) *See* section 10(2)(*b*) of the Social Security Act 1980 (c.30).
(d) S.I. 1975/555; the relevant amending instruments are S.I. 1977/342, 1693, 1979/223, 1984/1699 and 1986/903.

(7) In Schedule 1 (beneficiary to be regarded as having a dependant if any of these benefits is or would be payable)—

(a) in paragraph (b) the words from " otherwise than " to the end, shall be omitted;

(b) for paragraph (c) there shall be substituted:—

" (c) a retirement pension of any category where a beneficiary and spouse are residing together.";

(c) paragraphs (d) to (f) shall be omitted.

Signed by authority of the Secretary of State for Social Services

John Major

15th January 1987   Minister of State, Department of Health and Social Security

EXPLANATORY NOTE

(This note is not part of the Regulations)

The Social Security (Hospital In-Patients) Regulations 1975, which these regulations amend, provide for benefits payable under the Social Security Act 1975 to be adjusted while the beneficiary, or dependant, is undergoing treatment as an in-patient. The amending regulations secure that men and women are treated equally in these respects.

STATUTORY INSTRUMENTS

1987 No. 32

SOCIAL SECURITY

The Family Income Supplements (Computation) Regulations 1987

Made	- - -	*19th January 1987*
Coming into force	-	*7th April 1987*

The Secretary of State for Social Services, in exercise of the powers conferred on him by sections 2(1), 3(1) and (1A) and 10(1) and (3A) of the Family Income Supplements Act 1970(**a**), and of all other powers enabling him in that behalf, hereby makes the following Regulations of which a draft has, in accordance with section 10(5) of that Act, been laid before Parliament and approved by resolution of each House of Parliament:—

Citation and commencement

1. These Regulations may be cited as the Family Income Supplements (Computation) Regulations 1987 and shall come into force on 7th April 1987.

Prescribed amount

2.—(1) The prescribed amount for any family for the purposes of section 1(2) of the the Family Income Supplements Act 1970 shall be the amount specified in paragraph (2) or (3) below as the case may be.

(2) Where the family includes only one child the prescribed amount shall be —

    (a) £100.70, if the child is aged under 11;

    (b) £101.75, if the child is aged under 16 but not less than 11;

    (c) £102.80, if the child is aged 16 or over.

(**a**) 1970 c.55; section 2(1) was amended by paragraph 3 of Schedule 4 to the Child Benefit Act 1975 (c.61) and section 3 was amended by paragraph 4 of that Schedule; section 10(3A) was inserted by section 7(5)(b) of the Social Security Act 1980 (c.30) and applies section 166(2) and (3) of the Social Security Act 1975 (c.14).

(3)   Where the family includes more than one child the prescribed amount shall be the aggregate of whatever would be applicable under paragraph (2) above if the first child were the only child plus, for each additional child —

(a) aged under 11, £11.90;

(b) aged under 16 but not less than 11, £12.95;

(c) aged 16 or over, £14.00.

Maximum amount of family income supplement

3.—(1) The weekly rate of family income supplement shall not exceed the amount specified in paragraph (2) or (3) below as the case may be.

(2)   Where the family includes only one child the weekly rate of family income supplement shall not exceed —

(a) £25.85, if the child is aged under 11;

(b) £26.40, if the child is aged under 16 but not less than 11;

(c) £26.90, if the child is aged 16 or over.

(3)   Where the family includes more than one child, the weekly rate of family income supplement shall not exceed the aggregate of whatever would be applicable under paragraph (2) above, if the first child were the only child plus, for each additional child —

(a) aged under 11, £2.60;

(b) aged under 16 but not less than 11, £3.15;

(c) aged 16 or over, £3.65.

Revocation

4.   The Family Income Supplements (Computation) Regulations 1986(**a**) are hereby revoked.

Signed by authority of the Secretary of State for Social Services

John Major
Minister of State,
Department of Health and Social Security

19th January 1987

(**a**) S.I. 1986/1120.

EXPLANATORY NOTE

(This note is not part of the Regulations)

Sections 2 and 3 of the Family Income Supplements Act 1970 provide for a family income supplement of one half of the difference between a family's weekly resources and an amount prescribed by regulations, but subject to a prescribed maximum. These Regulations increase the amounts prescribed and also raise the maximum with effect from 7th April 1987.

The amounts currently prescribed for a family with one child are £98.60 where the child is under 11; £99.60 where the child is between 11 and 16; and £100.60 where the child is 16 or over. Where the family includes more than one child those amounts are increased by £11.65, £12.65 or £13.65 for each additional child according to age. Instead of the above amounts regulation 2 now specifies —

(a) £100.70 as the prescribed amount for a family whose first or only child is under 11, plus £11.90 for every other child under that age.

(b) £101.75 for a family whose first or only child is between 11 and 16, plus £12.95 for every other child between those ages and £11.90 for every child under 11.

(c) £102.80 for a family whose first or only child is 16 or over, plus £14.00 for every other such child, £12.95 for every child between 11 and 16 and £11.90 for every child under 11.

The current maximum weekly rate for a family with one child is £25.30 where the child is under 11; £25.80 where the child is between 11 and 16; and £26.30 where the child is 16 or over. Where there is more than one child the maximum is increased by £2.55, £3.05 or £3.55 for each child depending on age. In place of the above amounts regulation 3 now specifies as the maximum weekly rates for a family in group (*a*), (*b*) and (*c*) above, £25.85, £26.40 and £26.90 respectively, plus for every child after the first, if under 11 £2.60, if between 11 and 16 £3.15 and if 16 or over £3.65.

The Family Income Supplements (Computation) Regulations 1986 in which the current amounts are specified, are revoked by regulation 4.

STATUTORY INSTRUMENTS

1987 No. 33

TERMS AND CONDITIONS OF EMPLOYMENT

The Statutory Sick Pay (Rate of Payment) Regulations 1987

Made	- - -	*9th January 1987*
Coming into force	-	*6th April 1987*

The Secretary of State for Social Services in exercise of the powers conferred upon him by section 7(1A) of the Social Security and Housing Benefits Act 1982(**a**) and section 89(1) of the Social Security Act 1986(**b**), and of all other powers enabling him in that behalf, by this instrument, which contains only regulations made under section 89(1) of the Social Security Act 1986 and provisions consequential upon section 67(1) of that Act and before the end of a period of 12 months from the commencement of those sections, makes the following Regulations:—

Citation, commencement and interpretation

1.—(1) These Regulations may be cited as the Statutory Sick Pay (Rate of Payment) Regulations 1987 and shall come into force on 6th April 1987.

(2) In these Regulations, "the 1982 Act" means the Social Security and Housing Benefits Act 1982.

(3) Unless the context otherwise requires any reference in a regulation to a numbered paragraph is a reference to the paragraph of that regulation bearing that number.

Substitution of provisions in section 7(1) of the 1982 Act

2. For subsection (1)(*a*) to (*c*) of section 7 of the 1982 Act there shall be substituted the following subsection:—

"(1) Statutory sick pay shall be payable by an employer at the weekly rate of —

(a) £47.20, in a case where the employee's normal weekly earnings under his contract of service with that employer are not less than £76.50; or

(b) £32.85, in any other case.".

(**a**) 1982 c.24; section 7(1A) was inserted by section 67(1) of the Social Security Act 1986 (c.50).
(**b**) 1986 c.50.

Transitional provisions

3.—(1) Subject to paragraph (2), where for any employee 5th April 1987 was a day of incapacity for work forming part of a period of incapacity for work and statutory sick pay was payable to him during that period of incapacity for work at the weekly rate of £39.20, for any day of incapacity for work —

(a) which falls on or after 6th April 1987, and

(b) which falls within the same period of incapacity for work, and

(c) in respect of which his employer is liable to make to him a payment of statutory sick pay,

that payment shall, notwithstanding section 7(1) of the 1982 Act, be made to him at the weekly rate of £39.20.

(2) For the purpose of determining in accordance with paragraph (1) whether a day of incapacity for work forms part of a period of incapacity for work, and for that purpose only, section 2(3) of the 1982 Act shall be omitted.

(3) Where a period of entitlement as between an employer and an employee is running at 6th April 1987 and the employee's normal weekly earnings under his contract of service with that employer are not less than or treated in accordance with Article 3(a) of the Statutory Sick Pay Up-rating Order 1986(a) as not less than £74.50 they shall be treated as not less than £76.50 for the remainder of that period.

Signed by authority of the Secretary of State for Social Services

9th January 1987

John Major
Minister of State,
Department of Health and Social Security

EXPLANATORY NOTE

(This note is not part of the Regulations)

These Regulations are either made under section 89(1) of the Social Security Act 1986 ("the 1986 Act") or are consequential upon section 67(1) of that Act. Neither of those provisions have been in force for 12 months. Accordingly, the Regulations are exempt, by section 61(5) of the 1986 Act from reference to the Social Security Advisory Committee and are made without reference to that Committee.

Regulation 2 replaces the three rates of statutory sick pay with two rates.

Regulation 3 contains transitional provisions for those in receipt of the middle rate of statutory sick pay immediately before it was abolished and for those in receipt of the higher rate on 6th April 1987 whose normal weekly earnings were between £74.50 and £76.50 (inclusive).

(a) S.I. 1986/67.

STATUTORY INSTRUMENTS

1987 No. 36

SOCIAL SECURITY

The Supplementary Benefit (Single Payments) Amendment Regulations 1987

Made - - - -	*20th January 1987*
Laid before Parliament	*20th January 1987*
Coming into force	
Regulations 1 and 3	*21st January 1987*
Regulation 2	*26th January 1987*

The Secretary of State for Social Services, in exercise of the powers conferred upon him by sections 3, 14(2)(a) and 34(1)(a) of the Supplementary Benefits Act 1976(b), section 166(2) and (3) of the Social Security Act 1975(c) and of all other powers enabling him in that behalf, without having referred any proposals on the matter to the Social Security Advisory Committee since it appears to him that by reason of urgency it is inexpedient to do so(d), hereby makes the following Regulations:-

Citation, commencement and interpretation

1.—(1) These Regulations which may be cited as the Supplementary Benefit (Single Payments) Amendment Regulations 1987 shall come into force as follows:-

(a)   regulations 1 and 3 on 21st January 1987;

(b)   regulation 2 on 26th January 1987.

(2)   In these Regulations—

"the Single Payments Regulations" means the Supplementary Benefit (Single Payments) Regulations 1981(e).

Amendment of regulation 26A of the Single Payments Regulations

2.   In regulation 26A(5)(a) (definition of a period of exceptionally cold weather) for the words "minus 1.5 degrees Celsius" there shall be substituted "0 degrees Celsius".

Supplementary provision for cases before amendment of regulation 26A comes into force

3.   In any case where a claim under regulation 26A of the Single Payments Regulations (exceptionally cold weather) is made or treated as made in respect of the period of 7 days ending immediately before regulation 2 of these Regulations comes

---

(a) *See* the definitions of "prescribed" and "regulations".   (b) 1976 c.71, as amended by section 6(1) of, and Part I of Schedule 2 to, the Social Security Act 1980 (c. 30).   (c) 1975 c.14; this section was applied by section 33(2) of the Supplementary Benefits Act 1976.   (d) *See* section 61(1)(a) of the Social Security Act 1986 (c.50).   (e) S.I. 1981/1528; the relevant amending Regulations are S.I. 1982/914, 1983/1000 and 1986/1961.

into force, the average mean daily temperature recorded for that period at the designated station shall be treated as equal to minus 1.5 degrees Celsius.

Signed by the authority of the Secretary of State for Social Services.

John Major
20th January 1987   Minister of State, Department of Health and Social Security

---

EXPLANATORY NOTE

(This note is not part of the Regulations)

These Regulations further amend the Supplementary Benefit (Single Payments) Regulations 1981 relating to single payments for exceptionally cold weather. They substitute for the average temperature of minus 1.5 degrees Celsius a temperature of 0 degrees Celsius; and for the purposes of a claim made under regulation 26A in respect of a period of 7 days ending on 25th January 1987, they provide for the average temperature to be treated as equal to minus 1.5 degrees Celsius.

These Regulations will be referred to the Social Security Advisory Committee under section 61(2) of the Social Security Act 1986.

STATUTORY INSTRUMENTS

1987 No. 37

HEALTH AND SAFETY

The Dangerous Substances in Harbour Areas Regulations 1987

Made - - - -	*15th January 1987*
Laid before Parliament	*26th February 1987*
Coming into force	*1st June 1987*

ARRANGEMENT OF REGULATIONS

38. Vessels and vehicles loaded with explosives to be taken out of harbours and harbour areas.

39. Harbour craft carrying explosives not to carry passengers.

40. Electro-explosive devices.

41. Deteriorated explosives.

42. Records relating to explosives to be kept.

PART X: MISCELLANEOUS AND GENERAL

43. Power of a statutory harbour authority to make byelaws.

44. Enforcement of these Regulations.

45. Defence in proceedings for contravening these Regulations or byelaws.

46. Power to grant exemptions from these Regulations.

47. Repeals, revocations, modifications and savings.

SCHEDULES

1. The classification of and hazard warning signs for dangerous substances.

2. Examples of substances and articles not to be treated as being in Class 4.2 (spontaneously combustible substances).

3. List of specified dangerous substances.

4. Flag indicating that a vessel is carrying a dangerous substance.

5. Hazard warning panels.

6. Provisions relating to byelaws.

7. Procedure for explosives licence applications.

8. Repeals, revocations and savings.

The Secretary of State for Transport in the exercise of the powers conferred by sections 15(1), (2), (3)(a) and (c), (4), (5)(b), (6)(a) and (b) and (9), 43(2), (4), (5), (6) and (9), 80(1) and (4) and 82(3)(a) of, and paragraphs 1(1) to (4), 2(1), 3, 4, 6, 7, 9, 11, 12, 13(2), 14, 15(1), 16, 18(a), 20, 21(a) to (c) and 22 of Schedule 3 to, the Health and Safety at Work etc. Act 1974(a) ("the 1974 Act") and section 97(5) of the Explosives Act 1875(b) and now vested in him(c) and of all other enabling powers;

(a) for the purpose of giving effect without modifications to proposals submitted to him by the Health and Safety Commission under section 11(2)(d) of the 1974 Act after the carrying out by the said Commission of consultations in accordance with section 50(3) of that Act; and

(b) it appearing to him that the repeal of the instruments referred to in paragraphs (1)(d), (5) and (6) of regulation 47 and Parts II and III of Schedule 8 below provided for by section 80(1) of the 1974 Act is expedient, after the carrying out by him of consultations in accordance with subsection (4) of that section,

hereby makes the following Regulations:

(a) 1974 c.37; sections 15, 43 and 80 were amended by the Employment Protection Act 1975 (c.71), Schedule 15, paragraphs 6, 12 and 19 respectively.

(b) 1875 c.17; section 97(5) was extended by the Emergency Laws (Miscellaneous Provisions) Act 1947 (c.10 (11 and 12 Geo. 6)) and the Visiting Forces and International Headquarters (Application of Law) Order 1965 (S.I. 1965/1536).

(c) S.I. 1979/571 and 1981/238.

PART I

INTERPRETATION AND APPLICATION

Citation and commencement

1.   These Regulations may be cited as the Dangerous Substances in Harbour Areas Regulations 1987 and shall come into force on 1st June 1987.

Interpretation

2.—(1) In these Regulations, unless the context otherwise requires–

"approved list" means the list described in regulation 4 of the Classification, Packaging and Labelling of Dangerous Substances Regulations 1984(**a**);

"barge" includes any lighter or similar vessel whether self-propelled or not;

"berth" means any dock, pier, jetty, quay, wharf or similar structure (whether floating or not) or buoy berth in each case within a harbour or harbour area, at which a vessel may tie up, and–

(a) includes any plant or premises, other than a vessel, used for purposes ancillary or incidental to the loading or unloading of a dangerous substance within the curtilage of that berth, but

(b) does not include a monobuoy or in regulations 18, 21(6) and 27(1) any other buoy berth;

"classification" where the reference is to the classification of a dangerous substance means either–

(a) the classification for the purposes of–

(i) the Merchant Shipping (Dangerous Goods) Regulations 1981(**b**), or

(ii) the Classification, Packaging and Labelling of Dangerous Substances Regulations 1984 in relation to substances which are dangerous for conveyance within the meaning of those Regulations; or

(b) the classification specified in column 2 of Part I of Schedule 1 to these Regulations corresponding to the most hazardous of the characteristic properties of that substance specified in column 1 of that Part;

"Compatibility Group" and "Compatibility Group letter" have the same meaning as in regulation 2(1) of the Classification and Labelling of Explosives Regulations 1983(**c**);

"consignor" means the original consignor;

"dangerous substance" means a substance or article described in regulation 3;

"Division" and "Division number" have the same meaning as in regulation 2(1) of the Classification and Labelling of Explosives Regulations 1983;

"dumb craft" means a vessel not possessing mechanical means of propulsion and includes a dumb barge and a dracone;

"explosive" means in relation to an article or substance which falls within regulation 3, either goods of Class 1 in the IMDG Code or explosives of Class 1 in Part I of Schedule 1;

"explosives licence" means a licence issued by the Health and Safety Executive for the purposes of Part IX of these Regulations;

"freight container" means a container as defined in regulation 2(1) of the Freight Containers (Safety Convention) Regulations 1984(**d**) other than a container within the definition of "portable tank" in these Regulations;

"handling" in relation to a dangerous substance includes the operations of loading, unloading and transferring that substance and cleaning, purging, gas-freeing and ballasting any tank on a vessel which contains a dangerous substance or its vapour;

"harbour" means any harbour, whether natural or artificial, and any port, haven, estuary, tidal or other river, canal or inland navigation waterway navigated by sea-going vessels, in each case outside a harbour area, and includes–

(**a**)   S.I. 1984/1244, amended by S.I. 1986/1922.   (**b**) S.I. 1981/1747, amended by S.I. 1986/1069.
(**c**)   S.I. 1983/1140.   (**d**) S.I. 1984/1890.

(a) a dock, wharf or other works in or at which vessels can obtain shelter, or ship and unship goods or passengers;

(b) harbour land, being land adjacent to a harbour as defined above and occupied wholly or mainly for the purposes of activities carried on within the harbour;

(c) a monobuoy connected to one or more storage facilities in a harbour as defined above and its monobuoy area;

"harbour area" means–

(a) (i) all areas of water within the statutory jurisdiction of a statutory harbour authority, other than the areas of water referred to in sub-paragraph (b),

(ii) any berth, abutting any of the areas of water falling within head (i) above, where the loading or unloading of any dangerous substance takes place (whether or not that berth is for other purposes under the statutory jurisdiction of the harbour authority),

(iii) any land, within the statutory jurisdiction of a statutory harbour authority or occupied by a statutory harbour authority, used in connection with the loading or unloading of vessels,

(iv) a monobuoy connected to one or more storage facilities in a harbour area as defined above and its monobuoy area,

but excluding–

(b) areas of water which are within the statutory jurisdiction of another statutory harbour authority where those areas of water are used primarily by vessels using berths or land within the harbour area of that other statutory harbour authority (for the purpose of these Regulations the harbour area of that other statutory harbour authority is known as "an overlapping harbour area");

"harbour authority" means–

(a) in relation to a harbour area, the statutory harbour authority by reference to which that harbour area is defined,

(b) in relation to a harbour, any person being, or claiming to be–

(i) the proprietor of that harbour, or

(ii) entrusted with the duty, or invested with the duty, or invested with the power of improving, managing, maintaining or regulating that harbour;

"harbour craft" means a self-propelled craft which is used wholly or mainly within a harbour or harbour area or within such places and on adjoining inland waterways;

"harbour master" means the harbour master, dock master or other officer duly appointed by the harbour authority to act in such capacity or any person having authority so to act;

"hazard warning panel" means the panel required by regulation 11 and specified in Schedule 5;

"hazard warning sign" means in relation to a dangerous substance, the hazard warning sign specified and coloured as in column 3 of Part I of Schedule 1 for the classification of the substance specified in the corresponding entry in column 2 of that Part and which is further described in Part II of that Schedule;

"the IMDG Code" has the same meaning as in regulation 1(2) of the Merchant Shipping (Dangerous Goods) Regulations 1981;

"liquid" includes liquefied gas except in Schedule 1;

"loading" and "unloading" in relation to a dangerous substance means the actual operations of loading and unloading a vessel and includes any acts of ullaging, sounding or sampling carried out in connection with such operations and the handling of substances ancillary to such operations;

"master" includes any person, other than a pilot, having charge of a vessel;

"military explosive" has the same meaning as in regulation 2(1) of the Classification and Labelling of Explosives Regulations 1983;

"monobuoy" means a mooring buoy at which a dangerous substance may be loaded onto or unloaded from a vessel and which is connected to one or more storage facilities in a harbour or harbour area and includes the pipeline or pipelines by which it is so connected;

"monobuoy area" means the area of water surrounding a monobuoy where loading or unloading of dangerous substances takes place but does not extend to the area of water surrounding the pipeline or pipelines connected to it;

"operator" shall be construed in accordance with regulation 4;

"petroleum-spirit" means petroleum-spirit within the meaning of section 23 of the Petroleum (Consolidation) Act 1928(**a**);

"portable tank" means–

(a) a portable tank with a capacity of 450 litres or more, and

(b) a tank container and the carrying tank of a road tanker both as defined in the Dangerous Substances (Conveyance by Road in Road Tankers and Tank Containers) Regulations 1981(**b**);

"receptacle" includes any form of packaging used for the transport of a dangerous substance, but does not include a freight container, a portable tank or a vehicle;

"statutory harbour authority" means a "harbour authority" within the meaning of section 57 of the Harbours Act 1964(**c**), except that a person shall not be a statutory harbour authority for the purposes of these Regulations in respect of a harbour area which is inside the harbour area of another statutory harbour authority and which is used wholly or mainly for vessels bringing or receiving goods of either or both of the following descriptions, that is to say goods which have been manufactured or produced by that person or which are to be used by that person for the manufacture or production of goods or electricity, and for this purpose there shall be treated as carried on by a company the activities of manufacture or production carried on by–

(a) a holding company or subsidiary of that company,

(b) the members of a consortium who between them own, directly or indirectly, more than half the issued share capital of that company;

"storage tank" means a fixed tank designed for the storage of substances in bulk;

"tank barge" means a barge constructed or adapted to carry liquids in bulk;

"towing" includes the propulsion of a dumb craft by pushing;

"UN list" means Chapter 2 of the Recommendations prepared by the United Nations Committee of Experts on the Transport of Dangerous Goods;

"vessel" means every description of vessel, however propelled or moved, and includes a hovercraft, a hydrofoil vessel, anything constructed or adapted to carry persons or goods by water and a flying boat or seaplane on or in the water.

(2) Where in these Regulations a duty is imposed upon the master of a vessel, then, in relation to a dumb craft, that duty shall be imposed—

(a) while the dumb craft is being towed, upon the master of the towing vessel;

(b) at any other time, upon the operator of the dumb craft.

(3) For the purpose of these Regulations a substance is–

(a) carried by, loaded into or unloaded from a vessel in bulk if it is, without any intermediate form of containment, carried in, loaded into or unloaded from the vessel's hold, tank or cargo space, which is a structural part of or permanently attached to the vessel;

(b) stored in bulk if it is stored without any intermediate form of containment in a storage tank.

(4) Any reference in these Regulations to the quantity of any explosive shall be construed as a reference to the net mass of explosive substance therein contained.

(5) Unless the context otherwise requires, any reference in these Regulations to—

(a) a numbered regulation or Schedule is a reference to the regulation or Schedule in these Regulations so numbered;

(b) a numbered paragraph is a reference to the paragraph so numbered in the regulation or Schedule in which the reference appears; and

(c) any specified document shall operate as a reference to that document as revised or re-issued from time to time.

(**a**) 1928 c.32.   (**b**) S.I. 1981/1059.   (**c**) 1964 c.40.

Meaning of "dangerous substance"

3.—(1) Subject to paragraphs (2) and (3), "dangerous substance" means any substance (including any preparation or other mixture) which by reason of its characteristic properties, being properties specified in column 1 of Part I of Schedule 1, creates a risk to the health or safety of any person when the substance is in a harbour or harbour area and includes, whether or not it would otherwise be a dangerous substance, any substance or article which is within the definition of "dangerous goods" in regulation 1(2) of the Merchant Shipping (Dangerous Goods) Regulations 1981.

(2) Nothing in paragraph (1) shall require a substance or article which is brought into a harbour or harbour area from inland and which is not or is not to be loaded onto a vessel as cargo, to be defined as a dangerous substance to which these Regulations apply, unless either–

(a) it has characteristic properties, being properties specified in column 1 of Part I of Schedule 1, which create a risk to the health or safety of any person when the substance is in the harbour or harbour area; or

(b) it is "dangerous for conveyance" within the meaning of sub-paragraph (b) in the definition of "dangerous substance" in regulation 2(1) of the Classification, Packaging and Labelling of Dangerous Substances Regulations 1984 as extended by regulation 3(5) of those Regulations.

(3) The following are not dangerous substances within the meaning of these Regulations–

(a) a substance which is intended for use as food within the meaning of section 131(1) of the Food Act 1984(**a**) or section 58(1) of the Food and Drugs (Scotland) Act 1956(**b**) and which, if it is intended for use as an additive within the meaning of the Food Labelling Regulations 1980(**c**) or the Food Labelling (Scotland) Regulations 1981(**d**), is intended to be supplied to the public;

(b) a substance which is intended for use as an animal feeding stuff within the meaning of section 66(1) of the Agriculture Act 1970(**e**);

(c) a substance which is intended for use as a cosmetic product within the meaning of regulation 4(1) of the Cosmetic Products (Safety) Regulations 1984(**f**) (including any aerosol containing a cosmetic product);

(d) a substance which is intended for use as–

(i) a medicinal product as defined in section 130 of the Medicines Act 1968(**g**), or

(ii) a substance specified in an order made under section 104 or 105 of the Medicines Act 1968 which is for the time being in force and which directs that specified provisions of that Act shall have effect in relation to that substance as such provisions have effect in relation to medicinal products within the meaning of that Act;

(e) a substance which is a controlled drug within the meaning of the Misuse of Drugs Act 1971(**h**) and which is not excepted from section 4(1)(b) of that Act (which makes it unlawful to supply a controlled drug) by regulations made under section 7(1)(a) of the Act;

(f) a substance which is a sample taken by an authority responsible for the enforcement of any requirement imposed by or under any enactment.

(4) Substances and articles, including those mentioned in Schedule 2 and similar substances and articles which, when assembled in large mass, are liable to spontaneous oxidative heating over a long period of time shall not be treated as dangerous substances of Class 4.2 (spontaneously combustible substances) for the purposes of these Regulations.

(5) For the purposes of these Regulations vessels which have carried a liquid dangerous substance in bulk and portable tanks which have contained a liquid dangerous substance shall be deemed to be still carrying or containing that dangerous substance, as the case may be, until in the case of a vessel it has been gas-freed, inerted or cleaned and in the case of a portable tank it has been purged or cleaned, so that any of the substance or its vapour that remains is not sufficient to create a risk to the health or safety of any person.

(**a**) 1984 c.30.   (**b**) 1956 c.30.   (**c**) S.I. 1980/1849.   (**d**) S.I. 1981/137.   (**e**) 1970 c.40.
(**f**) S.I. 1984/1260.   (**g**) 1968 c.67.   (**h**) 1971 c.38.

Meaning of "operator"

4.—(1) "Operator" means in relation to a road vehicle–

    (a) a person who holds, or is required by section 60 of the Transport Act 1968(**a**) to hold, a licence for the use of that vehicle for the carriage of goods on a road; or

    (b) where no such licence is required, the keeper of the vehicle.

(2) "Operator" means in relation to any other mode of transport and in relation to a berth or a storage tank, the person who has for the time being day-to-day control of its running.

(3) "Operator" means in relation to a portable tank (other than the carrying tank of a road tanker) which is being conveyed by road, either–

    (a) the owner of the tank or his agent, if that person–

        (i) has a place of business in Great Britain; and

        (ii) is identified as the owner of or, as the case may be, as the agent of the owner of the tank on the portable tank itself or on a document carried on the vehicle; or

    (b) if no person satisfies the requirements set out in sub-paragraph (a) above, the operator of the vehicle on which the portable tank is carried.

(4) For the purpose of paragraph (3), a person to whom a portable tank is leased or hired shall be treated as the owner of that portable tank.

Application of these Regulations

5.—(1) These Regulations shall apply in every harbour and harbour area in Great Britain and to any premises or activities in any part of a harbour area in the territorial waters adjacent to Great Britain to which or in relation to which sections 1 to 59 and 80 to 82 of the Health and Safety at Work etc. Act 1974(**b**) apply by virtue of Article 5 (but only in so far as it relates to monobuoys) and 7 of the Health and Safety at Work etc. Act 1974 (Application outside Great Britain) Order 1977(**c**), but not (except as provided in regulation 33) elsewhere.

(2) These Regulations shall apply to or in relation to any dangerous substance except to–

    (a) petroleum-spirit, intended for use as a fuel for any internal combustion engine and not wholly or partly for the purpose of sale, in a receptacle which conforms to the requirements of either–

        (i) the Petroleum-spirit (Motor Vehicles, &c.) Regulations 1929(**d**), or

        (ii) the Petroleum-Spirit (Plastic Containers) Regulations 1982(**e**),

    and which does not exceed the quantity specified in those Regulations;

    (b) a dangerous substance used solely in connection with the operation of a vessel of less than 50 tons gross tonnage or a vehicle and carried in–

        (i) a tank forming part of or attached to that vehicle or vessel,

        (ii) the fuel tank of an outboard motor or in a battery, or

        (iii) fuel pipes associated with any of the above;

    (c) a dangerous substance when carried–

        (i) by a vessel as part of the stores of that vessel,

        (ii) by a vehicle or vessel or in a freight container as part of the equipment of that vehicle, vessel or freight container or for safety purposes,

        (iii) by a vessel as a result of the use of a fumigant;

    (d) a small quantity of a dangerous substance for the personal use of any person within the harbour or harbour area;

    (e) a dangerous substance which–

        (i) passes through a harbour or harbour area by land to or from a storage facility or a factory within the meaning of section 175, excluding sub-section (2)(n), of the Factories Act 1961(**f**) whether within or adjacent to the harbour or harbour area,

        (ii) is stored on land, or

(iii) is within a factory as defined above,

other than a dangerous substance which is to be, or which has been, loaded on board or unloaded from a vessel within the harbour or harbour area or which is used ancillary to such loading or unloading;

(f) a dangerous substance, other than an explosive, when carried by a harbour craft in the course of harbour engineering operations;

(g) a nuclear explosive device or any component thereof.

(3) Only regulation 16 shall apply to or in relation to a liquid petroleum fuel, other than petroleum-spirit, which is carried in a tank (and associated fuel pipes) which forms part of or is attached to, and which is used solely in connection with the operation of, a vessel.

(4) The duties imposed by regulations 16, 17(1) and 18 shall not extend to–

(a) the master or crew of a sea-going ship; or

(b) the employer of such persons,

in relation to the normal ship board activities of a ship's crew under the direction of the master.

(5) These Regulations shall not prejudice–

(a) any action of Her Majesty's Commissioners of Customs and Excise or any requirement for approval of, authority from, clearance by or notification to, Her Majesty's Commissioners of Customs and Excise or the necessity to comply with any order or conditions imposed by Her Majesty's Commissioners of Customs and Excise;

(b) any action duly taken by a person in pursuance of a direction given to him under section 12 of the Prevention of Oil Pollution Act 1971(a), or any action taken under subsection (4) or (5) of that section.

PART II

ENTRY OF DANGEROUS SUBSTANCES INTO HARBOUR AREAS

Notice of entry of dangerous substances

6.—(1) Subject to paragraphs (4) and (5) and to regulation 9, a dangerous substance shall not be brought into a harbour or harbour area unless–

(a) in the case of a vessel, the master or agent; or

(b) in the case of any other mode of transport, the operator,

has given to the harbour master and, if the substance is to be brought to a berth, to the berth operator, notice containing the particulars referred to in paragraph (3) not less than 24 hours, or such longer time in respect of both notices as the harbour master may for operational reasons require but which shall not exceed 14 days, before the substance is brought in or, if it is not reasonably practicable to give 24 hours notice, such shorter time in respect of both notices as the harbour master and berth operator may together agree.

(2) Where a vessel carrying a dangerous substance is to enter a harbour area not to load or unload there but on the way to loading or unloading in an overlapping harbour area or in an abutting harbour area then the notice required under paragraph (1) shall be given to the harbour master of that harbour area and to the harbour master and, if the substance is to be brought to a berth, to the berth operator of that overlapping or abutting harbour area.

(3) Any notice required under paragraph (1) may be given up to six months in advance and shall be in writing or in such other form as the harbour master may agree and shall contain such information as is adequate to evaluate the risk created by the substance to the health and safety of any person and, in the case of a notice given by the master or agent of a vessel, shall in addition contain the following information, namely–

(a) 1971 c.60.

(a) where the International Maritime Organisation recommends that the vessel should have a certificate of fitness, whether it has a current certificate of fitness;

(b) in the case of a vessel which is an oil tanker required to have valid cargo–ship safety construction and safety equipment certificates under a Safety of Life at Sea Convention whether it has such valid safety certificates.

(4) Notice need not be given under paragraph (1) in respect of–

(a) a radioactive substance in a package which is exempt from the requirements of Part II of the Radioactive Substances (Carriage by Road) (Great Britain) Regulations 1974(a) by virtue of regulation 20 of those Regulations;

(b) a dangerous substance carried by a vessel which is to pass through the harbour area and will not load or unload either in that harbour area or in an overlapping harbour area or in an abutting harbour area;

(c) a dangerous substance in a pipeline;

(d) a dangerous substance carried by a British or foreign warship; or

(e) without prejudice to sub-paragraph (d) above, explosives carried by any other vessel in the service of the Crown, where either–

(i) the master of the vessel has informed the harbour master that the quantity of explosives carried is within the limit of any condition to which the entry into or the carrying or handling within the harbour or harbour area of explosives will be subject, or

(ii) those explosives are for use at sea and no handling of the explosives takes place while the vessel is in the harbour or harbour area.

(5) Where it appears to a harbour master necessary for securing the health or safety of any person, he may exempt any person from the prohibition in paragraph (1) in so far as it relates to the giving of notice to him or to a berth operator in his harbour or harbour area and any such exemption may be granted subject to conditions and to a limit of time and may be revoked at any time.

(6) A harbour master granting or revoking an exemption shall make a record thereof as soon as is reasonably practicable thereafter including any conditions and limit of time attached thereto.

Harbour master's powers of prohibition, removal and regulation relating to dangerous substances

7.—(1) Subject to paragraph (7) and without prejudice to any powers that may be given to him by byelaws made under regulation 43, a harbour master may if in his opinion the condition of any dangerous substance is such as to create a risk to the health or safety of any person and having regard to the matters set out in paragraph (3) give directions as set out in paragraph (5) to the person having control of that substance or of any freight container, portable tank or receptacle containing that substance or of any vehicle or vessel carrying that substance.

(2) Subject to paragraph (7) and without prejudice to any powers that may be given to him by byelaws made under regulation 43, a harbour master may if in his opinion the condition of–

(a) any freight container, portable tank or receptacle containing a dangerous substance;

(b) any vehicle or vessel carrying a dangerous substance,

is such as to create a risk to the health or safety of any person from that substance and having regard to the matters set out in paragraph (3) give directions as set out in paragraph (5) to the person having control of that freight container, portable tank, receptacle, vehicle or vessel or of any dangerous substance contained or carried therein.

(3) In determining whether to give any directions under paragraph (1) or (2) in any particular case, a harbour master shall have regard to all the circumstances of that case and, in particular, he shall have regard to the safety of any person, whether that person is within or outside the harbour or harbour area.

(4)(a) Where a harbour master has given directions under paragraph (1) or (2) or both, the Secretary of State may, for the purposes of securing the safety of any

_____
(a) S.I. 1974/1735.

person, give directions to that harbour master requiring him to give such other directions under this paragraph as may be specified by the Secretary of State.

(b) The directions given by the harbour master under this paragraph shall be given to such person having control of a dangerous substance or of a freight container, portable tank or receptacle containing a dangerous substance or of a vehicle or vessel carrying a dangerous substance as may be specified by the Secretary of State and shall concern such of the matters set out in paragraph (5) as may be specified by the Secretary of State and when given shall cause the directions originally given by the harbour master under paragraph (1) or (2) or both to cease to have effect.

(5) The directions referred to in paragraphs (1), (2) and (4) may–

(a) regulate or prohibit the entry into;

(b) require the removal from;

(c) regulate the handling, movement or position within;

the harbour or harbour area of that substance, freight container, portable tank, receptacle, vehicle or vessel.

(6) Where the harbour master intends to give a direction requiring a dangerous substance to be removed by land from the harbour or harbour area, he shall, before giving the direction, consult the chief officer of police for the police district in which the harbour or harbour area is situated.

(7) A person to whom directions are given under this regulation shall comply with those directions.

(8) Paragraphs (1) and (2) shall not apply to any vessel in the service of the Crown or to any dangerous substance, freight container, portable tank or receptacle being carried by such a vessel.

(9) A harbour master shall not by virtue of this regulation be under any duty to examine the condition of any substance, freight container, portable tank, receptacle, vehicle or vessel.

(10) Directions may be given by the harbour master under paragraphs (1) and (2) in any such reasonable manner as he may think fit.

PART III

MARKING AND NAVIGATION OF VESSELS

Flags and lights to be displayed by vessels

8.—(1) Subject to regulation 9, where a vessel is carrying a dangerous substance specified in Schedule 3 in at least the quantity, if any, specified in that Schedule, the master of that vessel shall ensure that it displays–

(a) in the case of a vessel with a mast–

(i) during the day between sunrise and sunset, a flag complying with the requirements of Parts I and II of Schedule 4, and

(ii) when moored or anchored at night between sunset and sunrise and also during the day in restricted visibility an all-round red light giving a clear, uniform and unbroken light visible in conditions of good night-time visibility all round the horizon for a distance of at least 2 nautical miles;

(b) in the case of a vessel without a mast–

(i) during the day between sunrise and sunset, a flag complying with the requirements of Parts I and III of Schedule 4, and

(ii) when moored or anchored at night between sunset and sunrise and also during the day in restricted visibility, an all-round red light.

(2) Any flag or light required by paragraph (1) to be displayed shall be positioned so as to be as conspicuous as is reasonably practicable and, in the case of a light, so that it is above any other light being displayed by the vessel.

(3) It shall be a sufficient compliance with this regulation if–

(a) when a dumb craft is being towed, the towing vessel displays the flag required under the foregoing paragraphs; or

(b) when a dumb craft is moored or anchored that flag or light is displayed by an attendant vessel.

Regulations 6 and 8 not to apply to certain ferry-boats

9. Regulations 6 and 8 shall not apply to any ferry-boat which for the time being operates entirely within smooth or partially smooth waters within the meaning of the Merchant Shipping (Smooth and Partially Smooth Waters) Rules 1977(**a**).

Vessels to keep a safe distance from moored or anchored vessels displaying the flag or light required by regulation 8

10.—(1) A master shall not bring his vessel alongside a moored or anchored vessel which is displaying any flag or light required by regulation 8 without–

(a) the permission of the berth operator and the master of that vessel if it is at a berth;

(b) the permission of the harbour master and the master of that vessel if it is elsewhere, and

shall otherwise keep his vessel at a safe distance from that vessel.

(2) The permission, referred to in paragraph (1), of the berth operator and of the harbour master may relate to a named vessel, to a class of vessels or to vessels generally.

Marking of barges

11.—(1) The operator of a barge which is carrying 3,000 kilograms or more of one or more dangerous substances, or in the case of a tank barge any quantity of a dangerous substance, shall ensure that it displays hazard warning panels which shall be arranged so as to be visible on each side of the barge and each such panel shall–

(a) be weather resistant and durably marked so as to comply with the provisions of Schedule 5 (which relates to the required form, colour, information and specification);

(b) be either rigid or fixed so as to be rigid;

(c) be marked on or securely attached to the barge in a substantially vertical plane and if that means of attachment is by a frame that frame shall carry no other hazard warning panel; and

(d) have its lower edge at least one metre above the deck or if that is not reasonably practicable as high above the deck as is reasonably practicable.

(2) In addition to complying with paragraph (1), where a tank barge is carrying different dangerous substances in separate tanks, the operator of that tank barge shall ensure that each tank which contains a dangerous substance displays two labels which shall–

(a) be weather resistant and durably marked on one side only so as to comply with the provisions of Schedule 5;

(b) be marked on or securely attached to the outside of the tank, or on a frame immediately above the tank, in a substantially vertical plane so that there is a label visible on each side of the barge; and

(c) have their centres as close as is reasonably practicable to a position midway between the front and rear of the tank in which the dangerous substance to which the labels relate is being carried.

(3) Where one or more dangerous substances have been carried and all tanks and compartments have been emptied and cleaned or purged so that any dangerous substance or its vapour which remains is not sufficient to create a risk to the health or safety of any person, then the operator shall ensure that the hazard warning panels and labels are either–

(a) completely covered or completely removed; or

(**a**) S.I. 1977/252, amended by S.I. 1977/632, 1978/801, 1984/955.

(b) in the case of hazard warning panels only, partly covered or partly removed so as to leave visible only the telephone number and the text referred to in paragraph 3(c) and (d) of Schedule 5 respectively.

(4) Where two or more dangerous substances have been carried and the tanks or compartments which were carrying one of them have been emptied and cleaned or purged so that any of the dangerous substance or its vapour which remains is not sufficient to create a risk to the health or safety of any person, then the operator shall ensure that–

(a) the labels referring to the substance which has been removed are completely covered or completely removed; and

(b) the hazard warning panels are changed, if necessary, so as to comply with paragraph 3 of Schedule 5.

Control of harbour craft

12.—(1) The operator of a harbour craft which is carrying a dangerous substance or which is towing a vessel which is carrying a dangerous substance shall ensure that–

(a) the master of that harbour craft is competent to perform the duties required of him; and

(b) the master and any other person on duty on the harbour craft are not under the influence of drink or a drug to such an extent that their capacity to carry out their duties is impaired.

(2) The master of any harbour craft referred to in paragraph (1) shall control that craft and any vessel being towed by it with due care and diligence.

Provision and use of radios

13.—(1) This regulation applies to–

(a) a vessel, other than a dumb craft, of 50 tons gross tonnage or more carrying a dangerous substance;

(b) a vessel towing one or more dumb craft where the combined gross tonnage of all the dumb craft being towed is 50 tons or more and at least one is carrying a dangerous substance.

(2) The master of a vessel to which this regulation applies shall ensure that all times it is in a harbour or harbour area it is provided with a radio capable of receiving and transmitting in the very high frequency band.

(3) The master of a vessel to which this regulation applies shall ensure that a listening watch is kept on the operational frequency of the harbour authority at all times except–

(a) when the vessel is at a berth; or

(b) for short periods when the radio is tuned to another frequency for operational purposes.

Anchoring and mooring of vessels

14.—(1) The master of a vessel which is carrying a dangerous substance or on board which any dangerous substance is to be loaded shall anchor or moor his vessel only at such places and at such times as the harbour master may from time to time direct and shall ensure that any conditions the harbour master may impose with regard to anchoring or mooring are complied with.

(2) The harbour master shall, before giving any directions as to the berthing of a vessel at a berth not operated by the harbour authority, consult the operator of that berth.

(3) When he has anchored or moored his vessel, the master shall ensure that it is not moved except–

(a) if the harbour master, after consultation with the berth operator if the vessel is at a berth, so permits or directs;

(b) in an emergency or for the safety of persons on the vessel or on the berth; or

(c) to comply with the terms of an explosives licence.

(4) The master shall ensure that any directions given by the harbour master as to the movement of his vessel are complied with.

(5) While the vessel is at a berth, the berth operator shall ensure that adequate fenders are kept between the vessel and the berth.

(6) This regulation shall not apply in respect of any vessel on which the only dangerous substance or substances are one or more explosives in Division 1.4.

(7) Nothing in paragraph (2) or (3)(a) shall prejudice the power of the harbour master to give directions under any other enactment which applies to the case.

Mobility of vessels

15.—(1) The master of a vessel, other than a dumb barge, carrying a dangerous substance specified in Schedule 3 in the quantity, if any, specified in that Schedule shall ensure that the vessel is in a state of readiness to be moved at any time tidal conditions permitting.

(2) The harbour master may, if he is satisfied that the health or safety of any person will not be prejudiced, exempt by a certificate in writing, a master, other than the master of a vessel carrying any explosive specified in sub-paragraph (a) of Schedule 3, from the requirements of paragraph (1), and any such exemption may be granted subject to conditions and to a limit of time and may be revoked at any time by a certificate in writing.

PART IV

HANDLING DANGEROUS SUBSTANCES

General duties of persons handling dangerous substances

16.   Every person who has to any extent control of, or who is engaged in, the handling of a dangerous substance shall ensure that, so far as is reasonably practicable, nothing in the manner in which that substance is handled is such as might create a risk to the health or safety of any person.

Additional duties of employers, self-employed persons and berth operators

17.—(1) The employer of a person engaged in the handling of a dangerous substance shall–
  (a) ensure that that employee is provided with such information, instruction, training and supervision as are necessary to ensure his health and safety and to enable him to perform any operation in which he is involved with due regard to the health and safety of others;
  (b) provide that employee, where necessary, with adequate safety equipment and protective clothing; and
  (c) keep a record of the training received by that employee in accordance with this paragraph while that employee is in his employment and on request by that employee give a copy of that record to him.

(2) A self-employed person engaged in the handling of a dangerous substance shall ensure that–
  (a) he has such information, instruction, training and supervision as are necessary to ensure his health and safety and to enable him to perform any operation in which he is involved with due regard to the health and safety of others; and
  (b) he has, where necessary, adequate safety equipment and protective clothing.

(3) The operator of a berth where any dangerous substance is loaded or unloaded shall ensure that–
  (a) the handling of dangerous substances on the berth is adequately supervised, and
  (b) persons present on the berth are provided with such information and instruction as are necessary to ensure their health and safety and to enable them to perform any operation in which they are involved with due regard to the health and safety of others.

Precautions to be taken against fire or explosion

18.—(1) Where a dangerous substance may give rise to a risk of fire or explosion, every person engaged in the handling of that substance and both the owner and the operator of any berth on which that substance is kept or handled, shall observe all the precautions necessary for preventing, and for minimising the effect of, any such fire or explosion.

(2) Without prejudice to the generality of paragraph (1)–

(a) the owner of the berth shall ensure that adequate means for fighting fires are available;

(b) the berth operator shall ensure that adequately trained personnel are available sufficient to operate the fire-fighting equipment that would be required to provide first-aid fire-fighting appropriate to the type and quantity of the dangerous substance being loaded or unloaded;

(c) the operator and the owner of the berth shall ensure that ready access by the emergency services is available at all times to any vessel at a berth which is carrying, loading or unloading any such dangerous substance.

(3) No person shall smoke, use naked lights or any other source of ignition or carry any source of ignition within any area in which such activities have been prohibited by the harbour authority or the berth operator.

(4) In this regulation, "owner of the berth" means any person having overall control and management of the berth, and includes a lessee.

PART V

LIQUID DANGEROUS SUBSTANCES IN BULK

Fitness of vessels

19.—(1) The master of a vessel to which any of the Codes mentioned in paragraph (2) applies shall not carry, load or unload any liquid dangerous substance in bulk in a harbour or harbour area unless either–

(a) the vessel has a valid certificate of fitness for the carriage of the substance in bulk issued under the terms of whichever is appropriate of those Codes issued under the authority of the government of the country of registration of the vessel and he complies with any conditions of carriage laid down in that certificate; or

(b) the harbour master has given his permission in writing.

(2) The Codes referred to in paragraph (1)(a) are the following–

(a) "Bulk Chemical Code" namely, the IMO Code for the Construction and Equipment of Ships Carrying Dangerous Chemicals in Bulk;

(b) "Gas Carrier Code" namely, the IMO Code for the Construction and Equipment of Ships Carrying Liquefied Gases in Bulk;

(c) "Gas Carrier Code for Existing Ships" namely, the IMO Code for Existing Ships Carrying Liquefied Gases in Bulk;

(d) "International Bulk Chemical Code" namely, the IMO International Code for the Construction and Equipment of Ships Carrying Dangerous Chemicals in Bulk; and

(e) "International Gas Carrier Code" namely, the IMO International Code for the Construction and Equipment of Ships Carrying Liquefied Gases in Bulk,

all published by the International Maritime Organisation (formerly the Inter-Governmental Maritime Consultative Organisation).

(3) The operator of a vessel which is a barge shall ensure that the barge does not carry, load or unload any liquid dangerous substance in bulk in a harbour or harbour area unless either–

(a) the barge–

(i) has been approved for the carriage of the substance in question by a recognised classification society, a naval architect or some other person who, by reason of his qualifications, training and experience is competent to do so; and

(ii) complies with any conditions imposed by the harbour authority;

   or

(b) the harbour master has given his permission in writing.

Permission for transfer between vessels

20. The master of a vessel carrying a liquid dangerous substance in bulk shall not cause or permit that substance to be transferred by pipeline to another vessel unless the harbour master and, where the vessel is at a berth, the berth operator have given permission in writing for that transfer to take place.

Safety precautions for loading, unloading or transfer

21.—(1) The operator ot any berth where any liquid dangerous substance is loaded or unloaded in bulk shall, after consultation with the harbour authority, prepare a list showing the main safety precautions to be taken before and during such loading or unloading but this duty shall not extend to any transfer to which paragraph (4) applies.

(2) The master of the vessel and the operator of the berth where any liquid dangerous substance is loaded or unloaded in bulk shall ensure that the safety precautions in the list referred to in paragraph (1) are carried out.

(3) The loading or unloading of any liquid dangerous substance in bulk shall not begin unless the master of the vessel or a person designated by him and the berth operator or a person designated by him (who shall not be the same person as the person designated by the master) have both signed two copies of the list referred to in paragraph (1) to confirm that the relevant precautions set out on the list have been or, in the case of those which are to continue during loading or unloading, are being taken and each shall keep one of those copies available for inspection throughout the loading or unloading.

(4) A liquid dangerous substance shall not be transferred by pipeline between two vessels unless the masters of those vessels have–

(a) consulted each other on the appropriate safety precautions to be taken;

(b) prepared a list showing the main safety precautions to be taken before and during the transfer; and

(c) both signed two copies of that list to confirm that the relevant precautions set out therein have been or, in the case of those which are to continue during the transfer, are being taken.

(5) The master of each vessel involved in the transfer referred to in paragraph (4) shall–

(a) carry out the appropriate safety precautions in the list referred to in paragraph (4)(b); and

(b) keep one signed copy of that list available for inspection throughout the transfer.

(6) The berth operator shall ensure, so far as is reasonably practicable, that at all times when a vessel loading, carrying or unloading a liquid dangerous substance in bulk is at the berth, means of giving an effective warning of an emergency to people in the vicinity are installed at the berth.

Certain operations on vessels forbidden without prior permission

22.—(1) The master of any vessel carrying or which has recently carried a liquid dangerous substance in bulk shall ensure that none of the following operations are commenced–

(a) the discharge from the vessel's tanks of ballast or slops contaminated with any dangerous substance;

(b) the cleaning or ventilation of any tank which was last used to carry a dangerous substance; or

(c) the pumping overside of bilges contaminated with any dangerous substance,

unless the conditions specified in paragraph (3) have been complied with.

(2) The master of any vessel carrying or which has recently carried any flammable liquid in bulk shall ensure that none of the following operations is commenced–

(a) the gas freeing of any tank which was last used to carry the substance;

(b) the cleaning of any such tank with water, steam, detergents or other chemicals;

(c) the purging of any such tank with an inert gas; or

(d) the washing of a tank with crude oil during unloading,

unless the conditions specified in paragraph (3) have been complied with.

(3) The conditions referred to in paragraphs (1) and (2) are as follows–

(a) where the vessel is at a berth–

(i) the berth operator has given his permission, and

(ii) the harbour master has given his permission (which may relate to any or all of the following, namely, named vessels, named berths or specified operations), or has been notified and has not objected on grounds of safety; or

(b) where the vessel is not at a berth, the harbour master has given his permission.

PART VI

PACKAGING AND LABELLING

Freight containers

23.—(1) Any person bringing a freight container containing any dangerous substance into a harbour or harbour area from inland shall ensure that that container is accompanied by a certificate, given by the person responsible for loading the dangerous substance into the freight container, certifying that the substance has been safely packed inside that container.

(2) A person opening a freight container containing any dangerous substance shall take sufficient precautions to protect himself and others in the vicinity from the effect of any spillage or escape of any dangerous substance and shall adequately ventilate the interior before entering the freight container or unloading anything from that container and, if he is an employee, his employer shall also ensure that he takes such precautions.

Portable tanks and receptacles

24. Where a dangerous substance is brought into a harbour or harbour area from inland in–

(a) a portable tank, the operator of the tank shall ensure that it is correctly filled and either–

(i) in the case of a portable tank to which the Dangerous Substances (Conveyance by Road in Road Tankers and Tank Containers) Regulations 1981 applies, complies with the requirements of regulation 6 of those Regulations; or

(ii) in any other case, the portable tank is suitable for the purpose and complies with the requirements of sub-paragraphs (a) to (c) of regulation 7 of the Classification, Packaging and Labelling of Dangerous Substances Regulations 1984.

(b) a receptacle, the consignor of that substance shall ensure that–

(i) the receptacle is designed, constructed, maintained and closed so as to prevent any of the contents escaping when subjected to the stresses and strains of normal handling or transport except that this shall not prevent the fitting of a suitable safety device,

(ii) the receptacle and any fastenings are, in so far as they are likely to come into contact with the substance, made of materials which are neither liable to be adversely affected by the substance nor liable in conjunction with the substance to form any other substance which is itself a risk to health or safety,

(iii) the receptacle is correctly filled, and

(iv) in the case of a receptacle containing a compressed gas, the receptacle has been appropriately tested.

Labelling

25.—(1) Where a dangerous substance is brought into a harbour or harbour area from inland in a freight container, portable tank or receptacle the consignor of that freight container, portable tank or receptacle, as the case may be, shall ensure that–

(a) any such freight container is clearly and durably labelled to show on each vertical side the hazard warning sign of each Class of dangerous substance contained therein;

(b) any such receptacle which is liable to be individually handled while in the harbour or harbour area and any such portable tank is clearly and durably labelled to show the hazard warning signs of each Class of dangerous substance contained therein, and, in respect of each dangerous substance contained therein, either–

(i) the name given in the IMDG Code or the approved list or if there is no name given, the chemical name or the common name, or

(ii) in the case of a dangerous substance which is a mixture prepared by its manufacturer of two or more other substances, the designation for such preparations given in accordance with either the IMDG Code or the Classification, Packaging and Labelling of Dangerous Substances Regulations 1984.

(2) It shall be a sufficient compliance with paragraph (1), if a freight container, portable tank or receptacle which, while in the harbour or harbour area, is or will be required to be labelled in accordance with any of the following provisions, is labelled in accordance with those provisions, namely–

(a) the Dangerous Substances (Conveyance by Road in Road Tankers and Tank Containers) Regulations 1981;

(b) the Classification and Labelling of Explosives Regulations 1983;

(c) the Classification, Packaging and Labelling of Dangerous Substances Regulations 1984 relating to the labelling for conveyance by road;

(d) the Radioactive Substances (Carriage by Road) (Great Britain) Regulations 1974;

(e) the Merchant Shipping (Dangerous Goods) Regulations 1981;

(f) Regulations for the Safe Transport of Radioactive Materials published by the International Atomic Energy Agency;

(g) the Technical Instructions for the Safe Transport of Dangerous Goods by Air published by the Council of the International Civil Aviation Organisation;

(h) the European Agreement concerning the International Carriage of Dangerous Goods by Road (ADR) signed at Geneva on 30th September 1957;

(i) Regulations concerning the International Carriage of Dangerous Goods by Rail (RID).

(3) As soon as is practicable after all the dangerous substances and any residue have been removed from any freight container or portable tank the person in charge of that removal shall ensure that all labels which indicate that dangerous substances are contained therein are obliterated or removed from any such freight container or portable tank.

PART VII

EMERGENCY ARRANGEMENTS AND UNTOWARD INCIDENTS

Preparation of emergency plans by harbour authorities

26.—(1) A harbour authority shall, before dangerous substances are handled in the harbour or harbour area, prepare and keep up to date, after consulting the emergency services and any other body which appears to it to be appropriate, an effective emergency plan for dealing with emergencies which involve, affect or could affect dangerous substances that are brought into or are handled in the harbour or harbour area as the case may be.

(2) Port users and berth operators shall if requested by the harbour authority co-operate with the harbour authority in preparing its plan.

(3) A harbour authority shall notify the contents of its plan to those responsible for putting it into effect.

(4) Until 1st December 1987 it shall be a sufficient compliance with paragraph (1) if the harbour authority prepares its emergency plan in accordance with that paragraph by that date.

Emergency arrangements at berths

27.—(1) The berth operator shall ensure that at all times when a vessel loading, carrying or unloading a dangerous substance is at the berth and at any other time when there are risks from dangerous substances—

(a) means of rapid communication with the emergency services are available; and

(b) adequate means of escape from that berth are provided for use in an emergency.

(2) Subject to paragraph (5), as soon as practicable after the berthing of a vessel which is carrying or is to be loaded with any dangerous substance, and before the loading or unloading of that substance begins, the berth operator shall notify the master of that vessel of emergency arrangements at the berth and the means by which the alarm can be raised, and shall provide him with a written notice of the signals to be used in an emergency and of the arrangements for summoning the emergency services.

(3) The operator of any berth where any dangerous substance is being loaded on board or unloaded from a vessel in bulk or where any such substance is stored in bulk before loading or after unloading, shall ensure that such information is immediately available to the emergency services as will enable them to know—

(a) the identity, quantity and location of each such substance which is for the time being on the berth; and

(b) the nature of the dangers to which each such substance may give rise and the emergency action that should be taken.

(4) Subject to paragraph (5), the operator of any berth where any dangerous substance other than in bulk is being loaded on board or unloaded from a vessel or where any such substance is stored before loading or after unloading, shall ensure that such information is immediately available to the emergency services as will enable them to know the identity, quantity and location of each such substance which is for the time being on the berth.

(5) Paragraphs (2) and (4) shall apply to any quantity of explosives and to 25 kilograms or more of one or more dangerous substances.

Untoward incidents

28.—(1) In this regulation, "untoward incident" means an incident involving or threatening the containment of a dangerous substance which might, irrespective of where such incident occurs, create in the harbour or harbour area a risk of serious personal injury or a risk to the safety of a vessel.

(2) The master of a vessel carrying a dangerous substance shall immediately inform the harbour master and, if the vessel is at a berth, the berth operator of any untoward incident which occurs or has occurred on the vessel.

(3) The berth operator shall immediately inform the harbour master and the master of any vessel at the berth of any untoward incident which occurs on the berth.

(4) Where an untoward incident occurs during the operation of handling a dangerous substance, the person having control of that operation shall stop the operation as soon as it is safe to do so and shall immediately report the incident to the harbour master, to the operator of any berth and the master of any vessel which might be affected by the incident and, where appropriate, the emergency services.

(5) Where an operation has been stopped in accordance with paragraph (4), it shall not be resumed until such corrective measures have been taken as make it safe to resume the operation and the harbour master has authorised resumption of the operation.

PART VIII

STORAGE OF DANGEROUS SUBSTANCES

Application of this Part

29. The provisions of this Part shall apply to the storage of any dangerous substance within a harbour or harbour area ancillary to loading or unloading within that harbour or harbour area, except that regulations 30 and 31 shall not apply–

(a) where the Highly Flammable Liquids and Liquefied Petroleum Gases Regulations 1972(**a**) apply to that storage;

(b) in the case of petroleum-spirit, or any other substance to which the provisions of section 1 of the Petroleum (Consolidation) Act 1928 were applied by the Petroleum (Carbide of Calcium) Order 1929(**b**), the Petroleum (Mixtures) Order 1929(**c**) and the Petroleum (Liquid Methane) Order 1957(**d**), to the extent that the storage is regulated by or under the Petroleum (Consolidation) Act 1928.

Storage tanks

30.—(1) The operator of any storage tank and, where the tank is on a berth, the berth operator shall, before it is used for the storage of a dangerous substance in bulk, consult the appropriate fire authority with respect to the fire precautions that should be taken.

(2) Where before 1st June 1987 a storage tank was used for the storage of a dangerous substance in bulk, it shall be a sufficient compliance with paragraph (1) if the berth operator consults the fire authority in accordance with that paragraph before 1st December 1987.

(3) The operator of any storage tank shall both before it is used for the storage of any dangerous substance in bulk and during such use ensure that the tank (including any associated equipment) is–

(a) properly designed, of adequate strength and of good construction from sound and suitable materials;

(b) suitable for the storage in bulk of that substance;

(c) properly maintained; and

(d) sited in a safe place.

(4) The operator of a storage tank who transfers a dangerous substance into that tank shall ensure that–

(a) the substance is compatible with any other substance (whether dangerous or not) already in the tank;

(b) the substance does not cause a risk to the health or safety of any person by chemical or physical attack on the tank (including any associated equipment); and

(c) the tank is filled safely and is not over-filled.

(**a**) S.I. 1972/917.   (**b**) S.R. & O. 1929/992.   (**c**) S.R. & O. 1929/993.
(**d**) S.I. 1957/859.

Storage of freight containers, portable tanks and receptacles containing dangerous substances

31.   A person who stores a freight container, portable tank or receptacle containing a dangerous substance shall ensure that–

(a) so far as is reasonably practicable the conditions under which that freight container, portable tank or receptacle is stored are not such as might create a risk from that dangerous substance to the health or safety of any person; and

(b) the area in which it is stored is kept free from rubbish, vegetation and other matter where that might create any such risk.

Parking of road vehicles carrying dangerous substances

32.—(1) Every berth operator shall so far as is reasonably practicable designate a suitable parking area for road vehicles carrying dangerous substances that use the berth and in so far as the berth operator is unable to designate a suitable parking area for such vehicles he shall notify the harbour authority thereof who shall take all reasonably practicable steps to designate such a parking area.

(2) The driver of any vehicle which is carrying a dangerous substance shall not–

(a) where a parking area has been designated by the berth operator or the harbour authority, leave his vehicle unattended except in that area;

(b) park the vehicle (whether attended or not) at a place or in a manner as may be liable to create a risk to the health or safety of any person.

PART IX
EXPLOSIVES

Application of this Part

33.—(1) Subject to paragraph (2), regulations 34 to 36 shall, in addition to their application in every harbour and harbour area under regulation 5, apply to–

(a) the loading on board or unloading from a vessel (other than a vessel which is an offshore installation within the meaning of section 1(4) of the Mineral Workings (Offshore Installations) Act 1971(**a**)) of any explosive on any part of the coast of Great Britain or in any tidal water; and

(b) the loading on board or unloading from a vessel of any explosive within territorial waters to which sections 1 to 59 and 80 to 82 of the Health and Safety at Work etc. Act 1974 are applied by article 7 of the Health and Safety at Work etc. Act 1974 (Application outside Great Britain) Order 1977.

(2) Regulations 34 to 36 shall not apply in relation to–

(a) explosives–

(i) in Division 1.4; or

(ii) in any other division (except explosives in Compatibility Group L), where the total quantity of explosive involved does not exceed 10 kilograms;

(b) explosives that are to be used immediately by a vessel at sea;

(c) explosives to be dumped at sea in accordance with the terms of a licence granted under Part II of the Food and Environment Protection Act 1985(**b**) or, in the case of a military explosive, with the consent of the Secretary of State;

(d) explosives of less than 1 tonne in quantity intended for immediate use in connection with harbour works or for wreck dispersal in the harbour or harbour area, if–

(i) the consent in writing of the harbour master has been obtained, and

(ii) the explosives are carried and used in accordance with any conditions attached to that consent;

(**a**) 1971 c.61; section 1 was substituted by section 24 of the Oil and Gas Enterprise Act 1982 (c.23).
(**b**) 1985 c.48.

(e) a berth which forms part of a factory or magazine either licensed under the Explosives Act 1875 or lawfully existing whether under that Act or by virtue of a certificate of exemption granted pursuant to the Explosives Act 1875 (Exemptions) Regulations 1979(a);

(f) explosives carried by a British or foreign warship;

(g) without prejudice to sub-paragraph (f) above, explosives carried by any other vessel in the service of the Crown, where those explosives are for use at sea and no handling of the explosives takes place while the vessel is in the harbour or harbour area;

(h) explosives within the limits of any dockyard port defined by an Order in Council made under the Dockyard Ports Regulation Act 1865(b) or within the limits of the Marchwood berth and anchorage at Southampton.

Need for an explosives licence

34.—(1) Subject to paragraph (2), a person shall not–

(a) bring any explosive into a harbour or harbour area;

(b) carry or handle any explosive within a harbour or harbour area; or

(c) load or unload any explosive in circumstances to which this regulation applies by virtue of regulation 33(1),

unless there is in existence an explosives licence permitting that activity and the conditions attached to the licence are complied with.

(2) If an application for an explosives licence is made before 6th April 1988, then explosives may be carried or handled in circumstances where, but for the provisions of this paragraph, an explosives licence would be required, until such time as the licence is issued or refused or until 31st December 1991 whichever is the earlier, if the explosives are carried or handled in accordance with the byelaws relating to such explosives which were in force immediately before the coming into operation of these Regulations or, in the case of military explosives, in accordance with the Conveyance in Harbours of Military Explosives Regulations 1977(c) as in force immediately before the coming into operation of these Regulations.

Applications for explosives licences

35.—(1) An application for an explosives licence or for any alteration in the terms of an existing explosives licence shall be made to the Health and Safety Executive and the applicant shall be–

(a) in a case to which regulation 34(1)(a) and (b) relates, the harbour authority or, if he informs the harbour authority of his intention, a berth operator; or

(b) in a case to which regulation 34(1)(c) relates, a person having an interest in the activities for which the licence is required,

and in either case the application shall be made in accordance with the procedure specified in Schedule 7 unless the Executive otherwise agrees.

(2) The Executive may make a charge for work carried out in connection with an application for an explosives licence or for any alteration in the terms of an existing licence of £150 plus £25 for each man-hour expended (excluding time spent in travelling and any typing, messenger or ancillary work) and that charge shall be payable by the applicant prior to the issue of the decision.

Consideration of licence applications

36.—(1) In considering an application for an explosives licence or for any alteration in the terms of an existing licence, the Health and Safety Executive shall take account of any comments or objections received by it pursuant to paragraphs 3 and 5 of Schedule 7 and may reject the application altogether or may grant the licence or amending licence which may be subject to such conditions as it thinks fit and any such licence or amending licence may be with or without limit of time and may be varied or revoked in writing at any time.

(a) S.I. 1979/1378.   (b) 1865 c.125.   (c) S.I. 1977/890.

(2) Nothing in paragraph (1) shall prevent the Executive from granting a provisional explosives licence or a provisional amending licence in cases of urgency and any such licence or amending licence may have effect for a period of up to 6 months from the date on which it was granted unless revoked in writing by the Executive before its date of expiry.

Security of explosives

37.—(1) The operator of a berth at which explosives are carried or handled shall appoint a berth explosives security officer who shall ensure in respect of the berth that adequate precautions are taken to secure explosives against loss, theft or wrongful use and a harbour authority in whose harbour or harbour area explosives are carried or handled shall appoint a harbour explosives security officer who shall do likewise in respect of those parts of the harbour or harbour area for which there is no berth explosives security officer.

(2) Any person handling or having custody of explosives in a harbour or harbour area shall take adequate precautions to secure those explosives against loss, theft or wrongful use, and shall comply with any instructions given to him for that purpose by an explosives security officer and shall co-operate with the explosives security officer in the execution of his duties.

(3) Any person having custody of explosives in a harbour or harbour area who transfers the custody of those explosives to some other person shall obtain a written receipt from that other person recording that transfer.

(4) Where explosives are dropped overboard (otherwise than intentionally as part of the activities of persons at work) or lost, the person who had previously had custody of those explosives shall forthwith report the occurrence to the harbour master and either to the berth explosives security officer, if the incident took place at a berth, or to the harbour explosives security officer and shall take such steps as are reasonably practicable to recover those explosives.

Vessels and vehicles loaded with explosives to be taken out of harbours and harbour areas

38. When loading of a vessel or a vehicle with explosives has been completed, the master of the vessel or the operator of that vehicle, as the case may be, shall ensure that the vessel or vehicle is taken out of the harbour or harbour area as soon as is reasonably practicable unless the harbour master and, where the vessel or vehicle is at a berth, the berth operator otherwise agree.

Harbour craft carrying explosives not to carry passengers

39.—(1) Subject to paragraph (2), the master of a harbour craft shall ensure that while the harbour craft is carrying explosives it does not carry any passengers.

(2) Paragraph (1) shall not apply–
(a) where the only explosives carried are–
   (i) explosives in Division 1.4, Compatibility Group S, or
   (ii) ships' pyrotechnic signals which are being carried to another vessel and which contain a total of less than 1 kilogram of explosives; or
(b) where the only passengers carried are carried in connection with the harbour works for which the explosives are carried or who are to handle the explosives being carried.

Electro-explosive devices

40. A person shall not bring an electro-explosive device into a harbour or harbour area unless it is so constructed and packed as to be safe for carriage.

Deteriorated explosives

41. Where in any harbour or harbour area explosives have deteriorated or have undergone any change which might significantly increase the risks attendant upon their carriage and handling within the harbour or harbour area, the person having custody of those explosives shall–

(a) notify the Health and Safety Executive and the harbour master and, where the explosives are at a berth, the berth operator of the deterioration or change;

(b) agree with the harbour master any additional precautions to be taken before moving or handling them; and

(c) take those precautions.

Records relating to explosives to be kept

42.—(1) The harbour authority shall keep a record of all explosives handled within the harbour or harbour area, other than shop goods fireworks, in any calendar year and that record shall distinguish between exports, imports and explosives in transit and be preserved for 5 years after making.

(2) The berth operator shall co-operate with the harbour authority in the preparation of such record.

(3) In a case to which regulation 34(1)(c) relates, the licensee shall keep a record of all explosives, other than shop goods fireworks, loaded or unloaded there in any calendar year and that record shall distinguish between exports, imports and explosives in transit and be preserved for 5 years after making.

PART X

MISCELLANEOUS AND GENERAL

Power of a statutory harbour authority to make byelaws

43.—(1) Subject to the provisions of Schedule 6, a statutory harbour authority may make in respect of the harbour area, byelaws prohibiting the entry or regulating the entry, carriage, handling and storage of dangerous substances.

(2) Byelaws shall not conflict with these Regulations or with any other relevant statutory provision.

(3) Byelaws shall be restricted to matters relating to the harbour area.

(4) Byelaws may contain their own provisions for enforcement.

Enforcement of these Regulations

44.—(1) Subject to paragraph (2), the Health and Safety Executive shall be responsible for enforcing these Regulations.

(2) A statutory harbour authority shall be responsible for enforcing Parts II and III of these Regulations and regulations 19, 20, 32(2) and 38 in the harbour area against persons other than itself.

Defence in proceedings for contravening these Regulations or byelaws

45. In any proceedings for an offence of contravening these Regulations (other than for an offence under regulation 16, 31(a) or 32(1)) or of contravening any byelaw made under these Regulations, it shall be a defence for any person to prove that he took all reasonable precautions and exercised all due diligence to avoid the commission of that offence.

Power to grant exemptions from these Regulations

46.—(1) Subject to paragraph (2), the Health and Safety Executive may, by a certificate in writing, exempt any person or class of persons, from any requirement or prohibition imposed by or under these Regulations, and any such exemption may be granted subject to conditions and to a limit of time and may be revoked at any time by a certificate in writing.

(2) The Executive shall not grant any such exemption unless, having regard to the circumstances of the case and in particular to—

(a) the conditions, if any, which it proposes to attach to the exemption; and

(b) any other requirements imposed by or under any enactment which apply to the case;

it is satisfied that neither the health or safety of persons, nor the security of any explosive, likely to be affected by the exemption, will be prejudiced in consequence of it.

(3) The Secretary of State for Defence may, in the interests of national security by a certificate in writing, exempt from all or any requirements or prohibitions imposed by these Regulations–

(a) Her Majesty's forces;

(b) visiting forces within the meaning of any of the provisions of Part 1 of the Visiting Forces Act 1952(a);

(c) any headquarters or organisation designated for the purposes of the International Headquarters and Defence Organisations Act 1964(b);

(d) any person engaged in the carriage, keeping or supply of any military explosives, if that person is under the direct supervision of a representative of the Ministry of Defence,

and any such exemption may be granted subject to conditions and to a limit of time and may be revoked by a certificate in writing at any time.

Repeals, revocations, modifications and savings

47.—(1) Subject to paragraph (3), the following provisions and the byelaws made thereunder are hereby repealed except in so far as they apply to Northern Ireland–

(a) sections 34, 36 (only in so far as that section applies within harbours and harbour areas) and 115 of the Explosives Act 1875;

(b) section 4 of the Explosives Act 1923(c);

(c) sections 7 and 8 of the Petroleum (Consolidation) Act 1928(d); and

(d) section 71(5) of the Harbours Docks and Piers Clauses Act 1847(e).

(2) The Conveyance in Harbours of Military Explosives Regulations 1977 are hereby revoked except in so far as they apply to Northern Ireland.

(3) The provisions mentioned in column 2 of Part I of Schedule 8 of the byelaws mentioned in the corresponding entry in Column 1 of that Part (being byelaws made under section 7 of the Petroleum (Consolidation) Act 1928) shall continue in force after the commencement of these Regulations as if that section had not been repealed, but shall cease to have effect on 31st December 1989 unless they have been repealed before that date.

(4) In the Fire Certificates (Special Premises) Regulations 1976(f) after regulation 3 there shall be inserted the following regulation–

"Premises for which a fire certificate is not required

3A. Notwithstanding regulation 3(1), a fire certificate shall not be required for any berth to which the Dangerous Substances in Harbour Areas Regulations 1987 (S.I. 1987/37) apply".

(5) The provisions mentioned in column 2 of Part II of Schedule 8 of the local Acts and byelaws (being Acts passed and byelaws made before 31st July 1974) mentioned in column 1 of that Part are hereby repealed in so far as they apply within harbours and harbour areas and, within those harbours and harbour areas to the extent that they apply in relation to dangerous substances to which these Regulations apply.

(6) The provisions mentioned in column 2 of Part III of Schedule 8 of the byelaws (being byelaws made before 31st July 1974) mentioned in column 1 of that Part are hereby repealed with effect from 31st December 1989, in so far as they apply within harbours and harbour areas and, within those harbours and harbour areas to the extent that they apply in relation to dangerous substances to which these Regulations apply.

(7) The provisions of any local Act passed before 31st July 1974 or of any byelaws made before 31st July 1974 which conflict with the provisions of these Regulations or of

---

(a) 1952 c.67.   (b) 1964 c.5.   (c) 1923 c.17.
(d) 1928 c.32.   (e) 1847 c.27.   (f) S.I. 1976/2003.

any explosives licence granted under these Regulations shall cease to have effect and that Act or those byelaws shall be modified accordingly.

Signed by authority of the Secretary of State

Michael Spicer
Parliamentary Under Secretary of State,
Department of Transport

15th January 1987

Regulations 2(1), 3(1) and (2)   ## SCHEDULE 1

THE CLASSIFICATION OF AND HAZARD WARNING SIGNS FOR DANGEROUS SUBSTANCES

PART I
TABLE OF CHARACTERISTIC PROPERTIES, CLASSIFICATIONS AND HAZARD WARNING SIGNS

(1) *Characteristic properties of the substance*	(2) *Classification*	(3) *Hazard warning sign*
An explosive substance, that is to say– (a) a solid or liquid substance, or (b) a mixture of solid or liquid substances or both, which is capable by chemical reaction in itself of producing gas at such a temperature and pressure and at such a speed as could cause damage to surroundings or which is designed to produce an effect by heat, light, sound, gas or smoke or a combination of these as a result of non-detonative self-sustaining exothermic chemical reactions; including one or more such substances contained in an article. (See Note 1).	Class 1: Division 1.1, 1.2 or 1.3	(The Division number "1.2" and Compatibility Group letter "E" shown are only examples).
	Division 1.4	 (The Compatibility Group letter "G" shown is only an example). For explosives of hazard classification code 1.4S, "1.4S" may appear in the upper half of the label or may be shown on its own without the orange label. The orange label may be dispensed with for fireworks of Divison 1.4 provided the word "FIREWORK" followed by the hazard classification code is shown.

(1) *Characteristic properties of the substance*	(2) *Classification*	(3) *Hazard warning sign*
	Division 1.5	 (The Compatibility Group letter "D" shown is only an example).
Explosive substances defined as above which have a predominant hazard appropriate to another Class but which nevertheless present a significant hazard from explosion.	According to the predominant hazard	 (The hazard warning sign shown above should appear on packages in addition to the hazard warning sign of the main classification).
A substance which– (a) has a critical temperature below 50°C or which at 50°C has a vapour pressure of more than 3 bar absolute; and (b) is conveyed at a pressure of more than 500 millibar above atmospheric pressure or in liquefied form; other than a toxic gas or a flammable gas.	Class 2 (Non-flammable compressed gas)	COMPRESSED GAS
A substance which has a critical temperature below 50°C or which at 50°C has a vapour pressure of more than 3 bar absolute and which is toxic.	Class 2 (Toxic gas)	TOXIC GAS

(1) *Characteristic properties of the substance*	(2) *Classification*	(3) *Hazard warning sign*
A substance which has a critical temperature below 50°C or which at 50°C has a vapour pressure of more than 3 bar absolute and is flammable. (See Note 2).	Class 2 (Flammable gas)	FLAMMABLE GAS
A liquid with a flash point of 55°C or below except a liquid which– (a) has a flash point equal to or more than 21°C and less than or equal to 55°C and (b) when tested at 55°C in the manner described in Schedule 2 to the Highly Flammable Liquids and Liquefied Petroleum Gases Regulations 1972 (a) does not support combustion. (See Notes 3 to 5).	Class 3 (Flammable liquid)	FLAMMABLE LIQUID
A solid which is readily combustible under conditions encountered in a harbour or harbour area or which may cause or contribute to fire through friction.	Class 4.1 (Flammable solid)	FLAMMABLE SOLID
A substance which is liable to spontaneous heating under conditions encountered in a harbour or harbour area or to heating in contact with air being then liable to catch fire.	Class 4.2 (Spontaneously combustible substance)	 SPONTANEOUSLY COMBUSTIBLE

(a) S.I. 1972/917.

(1) *Characteristic properties of the substance*	(2) *Classification*	(3) *Hazard warning sign*
A substance which in contact with water is liable to become spontaneously combustible or to give off a flammable gas.	Class 4.3 (Substance which in contact with water emits flammable gas)	
A substance other than an organic peroxide, which, although not itself necessarily combustible, may by yielding oxygen or by a similar process cause or contribute to the combustion of other material.	Class 5.1 (Oxidizing substance)	
A substance which is– (a) an organic peroxide; and (b) an unstable substance which may undergo exothermic self-accelerating decomposition.	Class 5.2 (Organic Peroxide)	
A substance known to be so toxic to man as to afford a hazard to health under conditions encountered in a harbour or harbour area or which, in the absence of adequate data on human toxicity, is presumed to be toxic to man.	Class 6.1 (Toxic substance)	
A substance known to be toxic to man or, in the absence of adequate data on human toxicity, is presumed to be toxic to man but which is unlikely to afford a serious acute hazard to health under conditions encountered in a harbour or harbour area.	Class 6.1 (Harmful substance)	

(1) *Characteristic properties of the substance*	(2) *Classification*	(3) *Hazard warning sign*
A substance which contains disease-producing micro-organisms.	Class 6.2 (Infectious substance)	
A substance of specific activity of more than 70 Becquerels per gram (0.002 microcuries per gram) (See Note 6).	Class 7 (Radioactive substance)	
A substance which by chemical action will— (a) cause severe damage when in contact with living tissue, or (b) materially damage other freight or equipment if leakage occurs.	Class 8 (Corrosive substance)	

(1) *Characteristic properties of the substance*	(2) *Classification*	(3) *Hazard warning sign*
Two or more dangerous substances having different classifications.	Multi-load	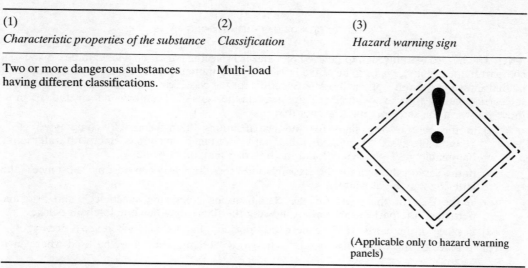 (Applicable only to hazard warning panels)

Note 1

Where explosives of more than one division are carried in a freight container or barge, the division with the lowest number should be shown on the hazard warning sign. When explosives of Division 1.5 and Division 1.2 are carried together in a freight container or barge, the hazard warning sign displayed on the freight container or barge should be that for Division 1.1.

Note 2

An aerosol which is flammable in accordance with paragraph 2 of Part III of Schedule 1 to the Classification, Packaging and Labelling of Dangerous Substances Regulations 1984 shall have the classification of a flammable gas. Other aerosols need not be classified as flammable gas or flammable liquid.

Note 3

Viscous preparations which comply with the conditions in Part III of Schedule 2 to the Classification, Packaging and Labelling of Dangerous Substances Regulations 1984 shall not be required to be classified as a flammable liquid.

Note 4

The flash point shall be determined in accordance with one of the methods described in Part IV of Schedule 1 to the Classification, Packaging and Labelling of Dangerous Substances Regulations 1984.

Note 5

For the purposes of Schedule 3, liquids having a flash point not exceeding 60°C shall be treated as being in Class 3.

Note 6

The hazard warning sign to be employed should be the appropriate one required by the regulations for the Safe Transport of Radioactive Materials published by the International Atomic Energy Agency.

PART II
SPECIFICATION OF HAZARD WARNING SIGNS

1. The hazard warning sign to be used on a hazard warning panel, on a label to be affixed to a compartmented tank barge or to be affixed to a freight container, portable tank or receptacle shall be that shown in column 3 of Part I of this Schedule for the classification of the substance shown in the corresponding entry in column 2 of that Part, and the signs shall conform in form and colour to those shown in the said column 3, except that–

    (a) in the case of the signs for the classifications "non-flammable compressed gas", "flammable gas", "flammable liquid" and "substance which in contact with water emits flammable gas", the symbol and the lettering may be in white;

    (b) in the case of the sign for the classification "spontaneously combustible substance", the lettering may be in white;

    (c) in the case of the signs for the classifications "oxidizing substance" and "organic peroxide" the part of the symbol showing the flame may be completely in black;

    (d) in place of the word "toxic", the word "poison" may be used wherever it occurs;

    (e) in place of the word "flammable", the word "inflammable" may be used wherever it occurs;

    (f) the sign may show the class number in accordance with the IMDG Code and in the case of Classes 1 and 7 must show the Class number.

2. Each hazard warning sign shall be in the form of a square set with its sides at an angle of 45° to the vertical and the length of the sides shall be–

    (a) in the case of signs on hazard warning panels, not less than 200 millimetres;

    (b) in the case of signs on the labels for compartmented tank barges, not less than 95 millimetres;

    (c) in the case of signs, other than those for substances in Class 7, to be affixed to a freight container, portable tank or receptacle, not less than 100 millimetres, except that, in the case of receptacles that are of such dimensions that they can only bear smaller signs, the sign should be as large as is reasonably practicable;

    (d) in the case of signs for substances in Class 7 to be affixed to a freight container, portable tank or receptacle, 100 millimetres.

3. Hazard warning signs to be affixed to a freight container, portable tank or receptacle shall have a line of the same colour as the symbol, 5 millimetres inside the edge and running parallel to it. (The broken line which surrounds each sign delineates the edge of that sign and need not be shown.)

4. Hazard warning signs to be affixed to hazard warning panels and labels for compartmented tank barges shall, for any part of the sign that is not black have a black border–

    (a) in the case of signs for hazard warning panels, at least 2 millimetres wide;

    (b) in the case of signs for labels, at least 1 millimetre wide.

SCHEDULE 2   Regulation 3(4)

EXAMPLES OF SUBSTANCES AND ARTICLES NOT TO BE TREATED AS IN CLASS 4.2

(Spontaneously combustible substances)

1. Rubber scrap and rubber shoddy, in powdered or granulated form.
2. Copra.
3. Cotton waste, oily.
4. Cotton, wet.
5. Fibres, animal or vegetable, burnt, wet or damp.
6. Fibres or fabrics, animal or vegetable, with animal or vegetable oil.
7. Fish meal (unstabilised).
8. Iron oxide, spent, or iron sponge, spent (obtained from coal gas purification).
9. Paper, treated with unsaturated oils, incompletely dried (includes carbon paper).
10. Seed cakes (seed expellers) containing more than 1.5% oil and not more than 11% moisture.
11. Wool waste, wet.
12. Rags, oily.
13. Textile waste, wet.
14. Seed cakes, containing not more than 1.5% oil and not more than 11% moisture.

SCHEDULE 3   Regulations 8(1) and 15(1)

LIST OF SPECIFIED DANGEROUS SUBSTANCES

The dangerous substances referred to in regulations 8(1) and 15(1) are as follows–

(a) more than 10 kilograms of explosives in Division 1.1 or 250 kilograms in the aggregate of explosives in Division 1.2, 1.3 and 1.5; when explosives in Division 1.1 are carried simultaneously in the ship with explosives in Division 1.2, 1.3 or 1.5, the overall limit is 10 kilograms;

(b) more than 25 tonnes of sodium chlorate or potassium chlorate, or more than 500 tonnes of ammonium nitrate of Class 5.1;

(c) bulk liquefied gases of Class 2, including the remnants of such gases which remain after their discharge from a tank which has not subsequently been gas-freed or inerted;

(d) bulk liquids of Class 3 with a flashpoint, when determined in accordance with one of the methods described in Part IV of Schedule 1 to the Classification, Packaging and Labelling of Dangerous Substances Regulations 1984, not exceeding 60°C, including the remnants of such liquids which remain after their discharge from a tank which has not subsequently been gas-freed or inerted;

(e) bulk liquids of Classes 4, 5, 6.1 and 8 of UN Packing Groups I and II in the UN list;

(f) bulk liquids of Class 6.1, UN Packing Group III in the UN list, if such liquids have a harmful inhalation risk.

Regulation 8(1)   **SCHEDULE 4**

FLAG INDICATING THAT A VESSEL IS CARRYING A DANGEROUS SUBSTANCE

PART I
SHAPE AND COLOUR OF FLAG

1. The shape of the flag shall be as shown in the diagram below.

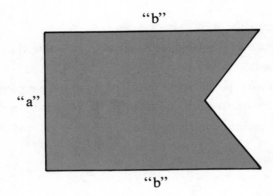

2. The flag shall be red in colour.

PART II
MATERIAL AND SIZE OF FLAG ON VESSELS WITH A MAST

1. The flag shall be made of fabric.

2. The side of the flag marked "a" on the diagram shown in Part I of this Schedule shall be not less than 75 centimetres in length and the sides of the flag marked "b" on the said diagram shall have equal lengths of not less than 90 centimetres.

PART III
MATERIAL AND SIZE OF FLAG ON VESSELS WITHOUT A MAST

1. The flag shall be made of metal.

2. The side of the flag marked "a" on the diagram shown in Part I of this Schedule shall be not less than 45 centimetres in length and the sides of the flag marked "b" on the said diagram shall have equal lengths of not less than 54 centimetres.

SCHEDULE 5

Regulations 2(1) and 11

HAZARD WARNING PANELS

Form and colour of hazard warning panels

1. Each hazard warning panel shall be in the form and colour of the following diagram–

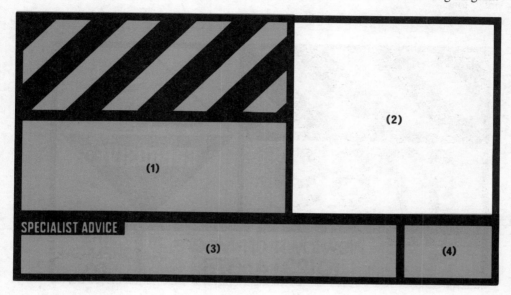

2. Any reference in paragraph 3 of this Schedule to a space number is a reference to the space so numbered in the diagram in paragraph 1.

Information about substances on a barge or tank barge

3. The following information shall be shown on each hazard warning panel when a barge or tank barge is carrying a dangerous substance–

(a) in space (1)–

    (i) where only one substance is being carried and that substance is specified in the approved list or the UN list, the substance identification number for that substance, except that the chemical name, an accepted common name or the trade name of the substance may also be included;

    (ii) where only one substance is being carried and that substance is not specified in the approved list or the UN list, the chemical name, an accepted common name or the trade name of the substance;

    (iii) where more than one dangerous substance is being carried, the word "Multi-load"; and

(b) in space (2)–

    (i) where only one dangerous substance is being carried and that substance is specified in the approved list or the UN list, the hazard warning sign for the classification of that substance;

    (ii) where only one dangerous substance is being carried and that substance is not specified in the approved list or the UN list, the hazard warning sign specified in column 3 of Part I of Schedule 1 for the most hazardous of the characteristic properties of the substance;

    (iii) where more than one dangerous substance is being carried and all of those substances are of the same classification, the hazard warning sign for that classification specified in column 3 of Part I of Schedule 1;

    (iv) where more than one dangerous substance is being carried and all those substances are not of the same classification, the hazard warning sign for multi-load specified in column 3 of Part I of Schedule 1;

(c) in space (3), the telephone number at which or by means of which specialist advice can be obtained at all times when the substance is being carried; and

(d) in space (4), the name of the manufacturer or owner of the substance, his house symbol, or both, may be shown but otherwise the space shall be left blank.

Specification for hazard warning panels

4. The specifications for hazard warning panels shall be those set out in the diagrams below with dimensions in millimetres; larger measurements may be used, but in that case they shall be kept in the same proportions to each other except that the lettering and figures may remain as shown in the diagram, or be of intermediate size. The diagonal lines in the top left may be thinner and may slope in the opposite direction.

For single loads–

For multi-loads–

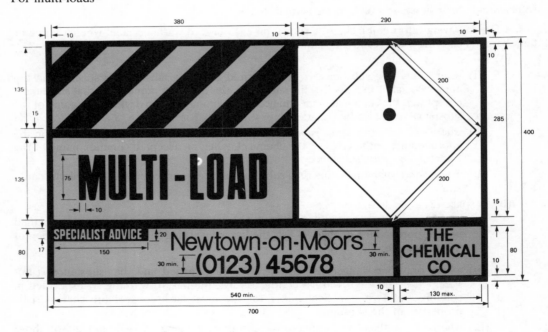

Labels for compartmented tank barges

Form of labels

5. In the case of a tank barge which has separate tanks which are being used to carry different dangerous substances at the same time the label to be attached to each tank in accordance with regulation 11(2) shall be in the form and colour of the following diagram except that where all the dangerous substances being carried are of the same classification, space (2) may be omitted.

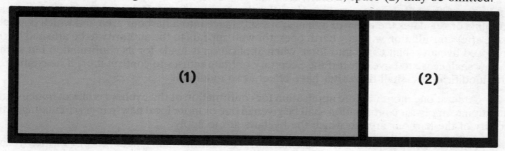

6. Any reference to a space number in paragraphs 5 and 7 of this Part is a reference to the space so numbered in the diagram in paragraph 5.

Information to be shown on labels

7. The following information shall be shown on each label–

(a) in space (1)–

    (i) where the substance is specified in the approved list or the UN list, the substance identification number of that substance, except that the chemical name, an accepted common name or the trade name of the substance may also be included, or

    (ii) where the substance is not specified in the approved list or the UN list, the chemical name, an accepted common name or the trade name of the substance;

(b) in space (2)–

    (i) where the substance is specified in the approved list or the UN list, the hazard warning sign for the classification of that substance,

    (ii) where the substance is not specified in the approved list or the UN list, the hazard warning sign specified in column 3 of Part I of Schedule 1 of the most hazardous of the characteristic properties of the substance;

(c) where all the substances being carried have the same classification, space (2), if included in the label, may be left blank.

Specification for labels

8. The specification for labels is set out below with dimensions in millimetres; larger measurements may be used but in that case they shall be kept in the same proportions to each other except that the lettering and figures may remain as shown in the diagram or be of intermediate size.

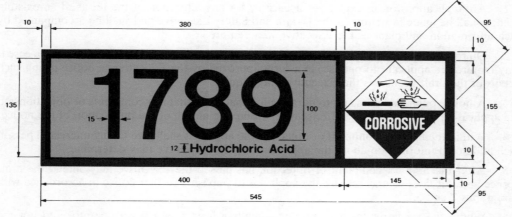

Colour of hazard warning panels and labels

9. Where in this Schedule parts of hazard warning panels are shown as coloured orange that colour shall match the colour in the British Standard Specification BSS No. 381C (1980) No. 557 Light Orange.

Regulation 43(1)

SCHEDULE 6

PROVISIONS RELATING TO BYELAWS

1.   In this Schedule, "byelaws" means byelaws made by a statutory harbour authority for all or any of the purposes set out in regulation 43(1).

2.   Byelaws shall be made under the common seal of the statutory harbour authority and shall not have effect until they are confirmed by the Secretary of State: Provided that a byelaw which prohibits or regulates the entry of a dangerous substance into a harbour area and which has been made after consultation with any berth operator who appears to the authority to be affected by the proposed byelaw, shall come into force when application is made for its confirmation but such a byelaw shall cease to have effect if the Secretary of State refuses to confirm it or, if he confirms it with modifications, shall thereafter have effect as so modified.

3.   At least one month before application for confirmation of the byelaws is made, notice of the intention to apply for confirmation shall be given in one or more local newspapers circulating in the vicinity of the harbour area to which the byelaws are to apply.

4.   For at least one month before application for confirmation is made, a copy of the byelaws shall be deposited at the offices of the statutory harbour authority by whom the byelaws are made and shall at all reasonable hours be open to public inspection without payment.

5.   The Secretary of State may confirm, with or without modifications, or refuse to confirm, any byelaw submitted for confirmation, and subject to the proviso in paragraph 2 above may fix the date on which the byelaw is to come into operation and subject as aforesaid if no date is fixed the byelaw shall come into operation at the expiration of one month from the date of its confirmation:

Provided that where the Secretary of State proposes to confirm a byelaw with a modification which appears to him to be substantial he shall inform the statutory harbour authority and require it to take any steps he considers necessary for informing persons likely to be concerned with the modification and shall not confirm the byelaw until such period has elapsed as he thinks reasonable for consideration of, and comment upon, the proposed modification by the statutory harbour authority and by other persons who have been informed of it.

6.   The Secretary of State shall not under the foregoing provisions of this Schedule confirm, whether or not with modifications, or refuse to confirm, a byelaw except after consultation with the Health and Safety Commission.

7.   A copy of the byelaws, when confirmed, shall be printed and shall be deposited at the offices of the statutory harbour authority by whom the byelaws are made, and shall at all reasonable hours be open to public inspection without payment.

Regulations 35(1) and 36(1)

SCHEDULE 7

PROCEDURE FOR EXPLOSIVES LICENCE APPLICATIONS

1.   An application for an explosives licence or for any alteration of the terms of an existing licence shall be made in writing to the Health and Safety Executive and shall be accompanied by such information and plans as the Executive may require.

2.   On receipt of an application, the Executive may prepare a draft licence and in such a case it may require the applicant to publish, in a form approved by the Executive, a notice giving such details of the draft licence as the Executive may require.

3.   A notice published pursuant to paragraph 2 shall state that any comments or objections on the application must be sent to the Executive within one month of the publication of the notice.

4.   Within the time for comment or objection the applicant shall give to any interested person such additional information about the application as the Executive may determine.

5.   After the time for comment or objection has passed the Executive may amend the draft licence and if it does so may require the applicant to publish a further notice in accordance with paragraphs 2 and 3.

6.   Where the applicant for a licence or amending licence is a berth operator and not the harbour authority, he shall send a copy of the application to the harbour authority.

SCHEDULE 8   Regulation 47(3), (5) and (6)

REPEALS, REVOCATIONS AND SAVINGS

PART I
PETROLEUM BYELAWS HAVING EFFECT UNTIL 31ST DECEMBER 1989

(1) *Title of Byelaws*	(2) *Byelaws having effect until 31st December 1989*
Bristol Petroleum Spirit and Carbide of Calcium Byelaws 1951, as amended	5 and 17
Gloucester and Sharpness Canal, Lee Navigation, the Regent's Canal Dock, the River Severn Navigation, the Weaver Navigation and Keadby Jetty Petroleum Spirit and Carbide of Calcium Byelaws 1962	6 and 7
Port of Liverpool Petroleum Spirit Byelaws 1961	7, 9, 10 and 11
Port of London Petroleum Spirit Byelaws 1929, as amended	7, 8, 9, 10 and 17
Port of London Liquid Methane Byelaws 1965	8 and 9
Harbour and Port of Manchester Petroleum Spirit and Carbide of Calcium Byelaws 1950, as amended	3, 6, 7, 15 and 16
Port of Southampton Petroleum Spirit Byelaws 1975	5.1
Weymouth and Melcombe Regis Harbour Petroleum Spirit and Carbide of Calcium Byelaws 1949	3

PART II
LOCAL ACTS AND OTHER HARBOUR BYELAWS REPEALED

Title of Instrument	*Extent of Repeal*
Aberdeen Harbour Byelaws for the Discharge and Loading of Petroleum in Bulk 1929	The whole byelaws except 1, 2 and 4
Arbroath Harbour General Byelaws 1921	Byelaw 48
Port of Bristol General Byelaws 1956	Byelaws 28 and 29
Port of Bristol, Loading, Discharging, Transport etc. of Petroleum (other than Petroleum Spirit) Byelaws 1951, as amended.	The whole byelaws except 1, 2, 5 and 18
Caernarvon Harbour Byelaws for Petroleum in Bulk (other than Petroleum Spirit) 1950	The whole byelaws
Cattewater Harbour Petroleum or Mineral Oil (other than Dangerous Petroleum) Byelaws 1924	The whole byelaws
Chichester Harbour Conservancy Act 1971 (a)	Section 85
Clyde Port Authority Order Confirmation Act 1965 (b)	Sections 90 and 95
Forths Ports Authority Order Confirmation Act 1969 (c)	Sections 68 and 77
Goole Docks Byelaws 1912	Byelaws 19, 20, 30 and 31
Grimsby Docks Byelaws 1939	Byelaw 41
Harwich Harbour Act 1974 (d)	Sections 40 and 42
Immingham Dock Byelaws 1929	Byelaw 41
Ipswich Dock Act 1971 (e)	Section 79
King's Lynn Docks and Railway Company Byelaws 1935	Byelaws 20, 27 and 28

(a) 1971 c.1xx.   (b) 1965 c.xlv.   (c) 1969 c.xxxiv.
(d) 1974 c.i.   (e) 1971 c.xiv.

Title of Instrument	Extent of Repeal
River Lee (Dangerous Goods) Byelaws 1937	The whole byelaws except byelaws 2, 3, 6, 7 and 19
Port of Liverpool Common Petroleum and Fuel Oil Byelaws 1937	Byelaws 2 to 6, 8 to 10, 13, 15 and 16
Port of London Act 1968 (**a**)	Sections 150 to 152 and 166
Harbour and Port of Manchester Petroleum Byelaws 1929	The whole byelaws except byelaws 1, 2, 5, 6, 7 and 18
Mersey Dock Acts (Consolidation) Act 1858 (**b**)	Sections CCXIX and CCXX
Newlyn Pier and Harbour (Petroleum and Carbide of Calcium) Byelaws 1908	The whole byelaws
Plymouth Great Western Docks General Byelaws 1894	Byelaws 3 and 16
Poole Harbour Byelaws 1901	Byelaw 28
Port and Harbour of Preston General Byelaws 1960	Byelaws 52 and 53
Rothesay Harbour Act 1831 (**c**)	Section XXX
Shoreham Harbour Byelaws 1965	Byelaw 42
Sunderland Corporation Act 1972 (**d**)	Sections 59 and 65
Teesport Oil Berths Byelaws 1952	Byelaws 3 to 5, 16 and 17
Tees and Hartlepools Port Authority Act 1966 (**e**)	Sections 86 and 92
Torbay Harbour Act 1970 (**f**)	Sections 38 and 46
Troon Harbour Byelaws and Regulations 1920	Byelaws XL11
Port of Tyne Reorganisation Scheme 1967 Confirmation Order 1968 (**g**)	Articles 35 and 77
Port of Tyne Byelaws 1884	Byelaws 82 and 85
Whitstable Harbour Byelaws 1928	Byelaw 36
Zetland County Council Act 1974 (**h**)	Sections 36 and 45

PART III
BYELAWS REPEALED WITH EFFECT FROM 31ST DECEMBER 1989

Title of Byelaws	Extent of Repeal
Harbour and Port of Manchester Byelaws 1966	Byelaw 61 and regulations, made under that byelaw.
Shoreham Harbour Butane Byelaws 1969	The whole byelaws.

(**a**) 1968 c.xxxii.   (**b**) 1858 c.xcii.   (**c**) 1831 c.xxxiv.   (**d**) 1972 c.xxiii.
(**e**) 1966 c.xxv.   (**f**) 1970 c.liii.   (**g**) S.I. 1968/942.   (**h**) 1974 c.viii.

EXPLANATORY NOTE

(This note is not part of the Regulations)

These Regulations provide for the control of carriage, loading, unloading and storage of dangerous substances in harbours and harbour areas. The Regulations are divided into 10 parts.

Part I (Interpretation and application – Regulations 1 to 5)

In addition to defining the terms used, the Regulations are applied to harbours and harbour areas in Great Britain and to those parts of harbour areas which are within the territorial waters adjacent to Great Britain.

Part II (Entry of dangerous substances into harbour areas – Regulations 6 and 7)

A person who intends to bring a dangerous substance into a harbour or harbour area, either from inland or from the sea, is required to give the harbour master advance notice of his intention. The harbour master is empowered to prohibit, require the removal of or regulate the entry of a dangerous substance into the harbour area if in his opinion the condition of the dangerous substance, its container or of the vehicle or vessel carrying it, is such as to create a risk to health or safety.

Part III (Marking and navigation of vessels – Regulations 8 to 15)

Vessels carrying certain dangerous substances are required to show a red flag during the daytime and, when moored or anchored, a red light at night. The regulations also make provision for the marking of barges and for the navigation of vessels carrying dangerous substances within the harbour or harbour area.

Part IV (Handling of dangerous substances – Regulations 16 to 18)

The regulations in this Part impose duties on every person who handles a dangerous substance in a harbour or harbour area to do so safely and to take all necessary precautions to avoid fire or explosion.

These regulations also impose duties upon employers, self-employed persons and berth operators to ensure that persons handling dangerous substances are properly trained.

Part V (Liquid dangerous substances in bulk – Regulations 19 to 22)

The regulations in this Part impose duties relating to the carriage, loading and unloading of dangerous substances in bulk. They require that vessels so used are suitable and that suitable safety precautions are taken. They also require that permission is obtained from the harbour master and, where the vessel is at a berth, the berth operator before certain specified activities are carried out.

Part VI (Packaging and Labelling – Regulations 23 to 25)

The regulations in this Part require freight containers from inland containing dangerous substances to be accompanied by a certificate certifying that they have been properly packed and require precautions to be taken so that all freight containers can be unloaded safely. Portable tanks and receptacles from inland containing dangerous substances are required to be suitable for the purpose and to be labelled in accordance with relevant international transport rules or domestic legislation.

Part VII (Emergency arrangements and untoward incidents – Regulations 26 to 28)

These regulations require each harbour authority which handles dangerous substances in its harbour area to prepare an emergency plan for dealing with emergencies involving those dangerous substances. Berth operators are also required to take safety precautions when a vessel carrying, loading or unloading dangerous substances is at the berth. Duties are imposed on masters of vessels and berth operators to notify any untoward incident involving a dangerous substance which might create a risk of serious personal injury to persons within the harbour or harbour area.

Part VIII (Storage of dangerous substances – Regulations 29 to 32)

The regulations in this Part apply to the storage of dangerous substances in harbour areas ancillary to their being loaded onto or unloaded from a vessel. The operator of any storage tank to which this Part applies, which is used for such purposes is required to consult the fire authority and to take appropriate safety precautions. The regulations also impose requirements to ensure the safe storage of such substances in freight containers, portable tanks and receptacles and to ensure the safe parking of vehicles containing dangerous substances.

Part IX (Explosives – Regulations 33 to 42)

The regulations in this Part prohibit, with certain exceptions, explosives from being brought into or handled in a harbour area unless such activities are covered by an explosives licence granted by the Health and Safety Executive. An explosives licence is also required for loading on board or unloading from a vessel of explosives when this occurs on any part of the coast or in the tidal waters of Great Britain or within the territorial waters adjacent to Great Britain.

The procedure to be followed for the application and grant of explosives licences is set out and the fee payable by the applicant is specified.

The regulations also impose requirements relating to the security of explosives, safety precautions and for the keeping of records.

Part X (Miscellaneous and general – Regulations 43 to 47)

These regulations empower harbour authorities to make byelaws relating to dangerous substances. The procedure for making byelaws which requires the consent of the Secretary of State for Transport is set out in Schedule 6.

The Regulations provide that the harbour authority shall be the enforcing authority for certain of the Regulations which relate to operations within the harbour area (namely Parts II and III of the Regulations and regulations 19, 29, 32(2) and 38) and that the Health and Safety Executive shall be the enforcing authority for the remaining regulations.

The Regulations also provide for a defence in the case of contraventions of certain of the regulations and of byelaws made under them and for exemptions to be granted by the Health and Safety Executive or by the Secretary of State.

The Regulations repeal as respects Great Britain the provisions mentioned in paragraphs (1) and (2) of regulation 47 and the byelaws made under them and with effect from 31st December 1989 the byelaws relating to petroleum mentioned in Part I of Schedule 8.

The local Acts and byelaws mentioned in Part II of Schedule 8 are repealed and those in Part III of that Schedule are repealed with effect from 31st December 1989.

Relevant documents

Copies of relevant documents may be obtained as follows–

Regulation	Document Quoted	Published by	Available from
2(1)	International Maritime Dangerous Goods Code – ISBN 92-801-1125-6	International Maritime Organisation (IMO)	IMO, 4 Albert Embankment, London SE1 7SR
2(1) Schedule 3 Schedule 5	Transport of Dangerous Goods – Recommendations of the Committee of Experts on the Transport of Dangerous Goods ISBN 92-1-139022-2	United Nations	HMSO

Regulation	Document Quoted	Published by	Available from
19(1)	Code for the construction and equipment of ships carrying dangerous chemicals in bulk – ISBN 92-801-1182-5	IMO	IMO
19(1)	Code for the construction and equipment of ships carrying liquefied gases in bulk – ISBN 92-801-1165-5	IMO	IMO
19(1)	Code for existing ships carrying liquefied gases in bulk – ISBN 92-801-1051-9 plus supplement – ISBN 92-801-1101-9	IMO	IMO
19(1)	International code for the construction and equipment of ships carrying dangerous chemicals in bulk (IBC) – ISBN 92-801-1162-0	IMO	IMO
19(1)	International code for the construction and equipment of ships carrying liquefied gases in bulk (IGC) – ISBN 92-801-1163-9	IMO	IMO
25(1) Schedule 1	Regulations for the Safe Transport of Radioactive Materials – ISBN 92-012-3185-7	International Atomic Energy Agency	HMSO
25(1)	Technical Instructions for the Safe Transport of Dangerous Goods by Air and Supplement – ISBN 0-940394-18-9	Council of the International Civil Aviation Organisation (ICAO)	International Aeradio Ltd, Aeradio House, Hayes Road, Southall, Middlesex UB2 5NG
25(1)	European Agreement concerning the International Carriage of Dangerous Goods by Road (ADR) – ISBN 0-11-550735-3	Department of Transport	HMSO
25(1)	1. Regulations concerning the International Carriage of Dangerous Goods by Rail (RID) – ISBN 0-11-550681-0 2. Amendment No 1 – ISBN 0-11-550745-0	Department of Transport	HMSO
Schedule 5	British Standard – BS Specification 381C 1980	British Standards Institution (BSI)	BSI, Linford Wood, Milton Keynes MK14 6LE

STATUTORY INSTRUMENTS

1987 No. 38 (S. 5)

COURT OF SESSION, SCOTLAND
TEINDS

The Court of Session etc. Fees Amendment Order 1987

Made - - - -	*13th January 1987*
Laid before Parliament	*30th January 1987*
Coming into force	*23rd February 1987*

The Secretary of State, in exercise of the powers conferred on him by section 2 of the Courts of Law Fees (Scotland) Act 1895(**a**), and of all other powers enabling him in that behalf, and with the concurrence of the Treasury, hereby makes the following Order:

1. This Order may be cited as the Court of Session etc. Fees Amendment Order 1987 and shall come into force on 23rd February 1987.

2. In Part I of the Table of Fees in the Schedule to the Court of Session etc. Fees Order 1984(**b**) the following amendments shall be made:–

(a) for the entry in column 1 of item C1 there shall be substituted the following:–

"**1.** Petition of whatever nature presented to Inner or Outer House other than a petition under item C2 of this table, whether in respect of the first or any subsequent step of process, and any application for registration or recognition of a judgment from a Contracting State under the Civil Jurisdiction and Judgments Act 1982(**c**) – inclusive fee";

(b) for the entry in column 1 of item G4 there shall be substituted the following:–

"**4.** Certificate under the Judgments Extension Act 1868(**d**) or under the Civil Jurisdiction and Judgments Act 1982".

Ian Lang
Parliamentary Under Secretary of State,
Scottish Office

New St. Andrew's House
Edinburgh
18th December 1986

We concur,

Mark Lennox-Boyd
Tim Sainsbury

13th January 1987   Two of the Lords Commissioners of Her Majesty's Treasury

---

(**a**) 1895 c.14; section 2 was substituted by section 4 of the Divorce Jurisdiction, Court Fees and Legal Aid (Scotland) Act 1983 (c.12).   (**b**) 1984/256; the Table of Fees in the Schedule to that Order was substituted by S.I. 1986/450.   (**c**) 1982 c.27.   (**d**) 1868 c.54.

EXPLANATORY NOTE

(This note is not part of the Order)

This Order provides for the charging of fees in the Court of Session relating to registration and enforcement of judgments from certain European countries in terms of the Civil Jurisdiction and Judgments Act 1982.

1987 No. 39 (S. 6)

SHERIFF COURT, SCOTLAND

The Sheriff Court Fees Amendment Order 1987

Made - - - -	*13th January 1987*
Laid before Parliament	*30th January 1987*
Coming into force	*23rd February 1987*

The Secretary of State, in exercise of the powers conferred on him by section 2 of the Courts of Law Fees (Scotland) Act 1895(**a**), and of all other powers enabling him in that behalf, and with the concurrence of the Treasury, hereby makes the following Order:

1. This Order may be cited as the Sheriff Court Fees Amendment Order 1987 and shall come into force on 23rd February 1987.

2. In Part II of the Table of Fees in the Schedule to the Sheriff Court Fees Order 1985(**b**) for the entry in column 1 of paragraph 14 there shall be substituted the following:–

"Enforcement of United Kingdom Judgments

14. Any proceedings under the Inferior Courts Judgments Extension Act 1882(**c**) or under sections 12 or 18 of the Civil Jurisdiction and Judgments Act 1982(**d**)".

Ian Lang
New St. Andrew's House
Edinburgh
18th December 1986
Parliamentary Under Secretary of State,
Scottish Office

We concur,

Mark Lennox-Boyd
Tim Sainsbury
13th January 1987
Two of the Lords Commissioners of Her Majesty's Treasury

EXPLANATORY NOTE

(This note is not part of the Order)

This Order provides for the charging of fees in the Sheriff Court relating to enforcement of judgments from certain European countries in terms of the Civil Jurisdiction and Judgments Act 1982.

(**a**) 1895 c.14; section 2 was substituted by section 4 of the Divorce Jurisdiction, Court Fees and Legal Aid (Scotland) Act 1983 (c.12).　(**b**) S.I. 1985/827; the Table of Fees in the Schedule to that Order was substituted by S.I. 1986/451.　(**c**) 1882 c.31.　(**d**) 1982 c.27.

STATUTORY INSTRUMENTS

1987 No. 40 (S. 7)

COURT OF SESSION, SCOTLAND

Act of Sederunt (Sessions of Court and Sederunt Days) 1987

Made - - - -	*20th January 1987*
Coming into force	*1st January 1988*

The Lords of Council and Session, under and by virtue of the powers conferred on them by section 2 of the Administration of Justice (Scotland) Act 1948(**a**) and by section 4(2) of the Administration of Justice (Scotland) Act 1933(**b**), and of all other powers enabling them in that behalf, do hereby enact and declare:

Citation and commencement

1. This Act of Sederunt may be cited as the Act of Sederunt (Sessions of Court and Sederunt Days) 1987 and shall come into force on 1st January 1988.

Sessions of court 1988

2. The ordinary sessions of the Court of Session during 1988 shall extend—
(a) from Tuesday 5th January to Saturday 26th March;
(b) from Tuesday 26th April to Saturday 16th July;
(c) from Tuesday 27th September to Wednesday 21st December.

Sederunt days

3. The ordinary sessions of the Court of Session shall extend to and include each Thursday of each vacation (Easter and Summer).

And the Lords appoint this Act of Sederunt to be inserted in the Books of Sederunt.

Emslie
Lord President,
I.P.D.

Edinburgh
20th January 1987

EXPLANATORY NOTE

(This note is not part of the Act of Sederunt)

This Act of Sederunt makes provision for the ordinary business of the Court of Session to be done between the dates specified in paragraph 2 and on each Thursday of each vacation (Easter and Summer).

(**a**) 1948 c. 10 (12, 13 & 14 Geo. 6).   (**b**) 1933 c. 41.

STATUTORY INSTRUMENTS

1987 No. 45

SOCIAL SECURITY

The Social Security Benefits Up-rating Order 1987

Made	- - -	*20th January 1987*

Coming into force
Articles 1(1), 8 and 10(2)	*1st April 1987*
remainder	*6th April 1987*

Whereas, the Secretary of State for Social Services having made a review under section 63(1) of the Social Security Act 1986(**a**), a draft of the following order was laid before Parliament in accordance with the provisions of section 63(2) and section 83(3)(*d*) of that Act and approved by resolution of each House of Parliament.

Now, therefore, the Secretary of State for Social Services, with the consent of the Treasury (**b**), in exercise of the powers conferred upon him by section 63 of the Social Security Act 1986, and of all other powers enabling him in that behalf, hereby makes the following order:—

Citation, commencement and interpretation

1.—(1)   This order may be cited as the Social Security Benefits Up-rating Order 1987 and shall come into force in the case of Articles 1(1), 8 and 10(2) on 1st April 1987 and in the case of all other Articles on 6th April 1987.

(2)   In this order, unless the context otherwise requires—

"the 1975 Act" means the Social Security Act 1975(**c**);

"the 1986 Act" means the Social Security Act 1986; and

"the Pensions Act" means the Social Security Pensions Act 1975(**d**).

Alterations in rates or amounts of certain benefits under the 1975 Act

2.—(1)   In this Article, "Schedule 4" means Schedule 4 to the 1975 Act (**e**).

(**a**) 1986 c.50.
(**b**) *See* section 83(5) of the Social Security Act 1986.
(**c**) 1975 c.14.
(**d**) 1975 c.60.
(**e**) Schedule 4 was amended by section 21(1) and (2) of, and Schedules 4 and 5 to, the Child Benefit Act 1975 (c.61), section 22(2) of, and paragraphs 62 and 63 of Schedule 4 to, the Social Security Pensions Act 1975, paragraph 13 of Schedule 1 to the Social Security Act 1979 (c.18) and the Social Security Benefits Up-rating Order 1986 (S.I. 1986/1117).

(2)   The sums specified in paragraph (3) below shall be altered from and including the respective dates specified in Article 4 below; and Schedule 4 shall accordingly have effect as set out in the Schedule to this order.

(3)   The sums mentioned in paragraph (2) above are the sums specified in Parts I, III, IV and V of Schedule 4 (contributory periodical benefits, non-contributory periodical benefits, increase of benefits for dependants and rate or amounts of industrial injuries benefits, respectively), except—

(a) in Part I the sum specified for child's special allowance;

(b) in Part III the sums specified for guardian's allowance and age addition;

(c) in column (2) of Part IV the sums specified by way of increase for a dependent child; and

(d) in Part V sums specified in respect of a dependent child.

Increase of rates or amounts of certain benefits under the Pensions Act
3.—(1)   The sums mentioned in paragraphs (2) to (5) below shall be increased from and including the respective dates specified in Article 4 below.

(2)   In section 6(1)(a) of the Pensions Act (basic component of Category A retirement pension)—

(a) so far as the sum is relevant for the purpose of calculating under section 14(6) of the 1975 Act the rate of sickness benefit, for the sum of £37.05 there shall be substituted the sum of £37.85;

(b) except so far as mentioned in sub-paragraph (a) above, for the sum of £38.70 there shall be substituted the sum of £39.50.

(3)   It is hereby directed that the sums which are the additional components in the rates of long-term benefits calculated by reference to any final relevant year earlier than the tax year 1986/1987 shall be increased by 2.1 per cent. of their amount apart from this order.

(4)   It is hereby directed that the sums payable by way of increases of retirement pensions under Schedule 1 to the Pensions Act (increase of pension where pensioner defers retirement) shall be increased by 2.1 per cent.

(5)   It is hereby declared that an amount equal to 2.1 per cent. of the aggregate amount of the sums —

(a) payable by virtue of section 35(6) of the Pensions Act (which provides for increases in a person's guaranteed minimum pension if payment of his occupational pension is postponed after he attains pensionable age) to a person who is also entitled to a Category A or Category B retirement pension (including sums payable by virtue of section 36(3)); and

(b) payable to such a person as part of his Category A or Category B retirement pension by virtue of an order made under section 126A of the 1975 Act (**a**) or section 63 of the 1986 Act,

shall be payable by way of an increase of such a person's Category A or Category B retirement pension.

Dates on which sums specified for rates or amounts of benefit under the 1975 Act or the Pensions Act are altered by this order

4.—(1)   The alterations made by this order in the sums specified for rates or amounts of benefit under the 1975 Act or the Pensions Act shall take effect for each case on the date specified in relation to such case in the following provisions of this Article.

(2)   In relation to the case of a person over pensionable age who has not retired from regular employment and for whom the rate of unemployment benefit, sickness benefit or invalidity pension falls to be calculated in accordance with section 14(6) or 15(4) of the 1975 Act (**b**), the increases in the sums mentioned in Articles 2, 3 and 6 for Category A and B retirement pension and graduated retirement benefit (together with, where appropriate, increases for dependants) shall take effect on 9th April 1987 and in relation to all other cases the increases in such sums shall take effect on 6th April 1987.

(3)   The increase mentioned in Article 3(5) shall take effect on 6th April 1987.

(4)   The alterations in the amounts of maternity allowance, widow's allowance, widowed mother's allowance, widow's pension, Category C and D retirement pension, attendance allowance, invalid care allowance (except in a case where the Secretary of State has made arrangements for it to be paid on a Wednesday), and industrial death benefit by way of widow's and widower's pension and allowance in respect of children (together with, where appropriate, increases for dependants) shall in all cases take effect on 6th April 1987.

(5)   The sums specified for the rate of mobility allowance, invalid care allowance (in a case where the Secretary of State has made arrangements for it to be paid on a Wednesday), disablement benefit (together with increases of disablement pension), maximum disablement gratuity under section 57(5) of the 1975 Act, increase of unemployability supplement under section 59 of the 1975 Act and maximum, under section 91(1) of the 1975 Act, of the aggregate of weekly benefit payable for successive accidents, shall be increased in all cases with effect from 8th April 1987.

(**a**) Section 126A was inserted by section 12 of the Social Security Act 1979 and repealed by the Social Security Act 1986, section 86, Schedule 11.

(**b**) Section 14(6) is amended by the Social Security Pensions Act 1975 (c.60), section 65(1), Schedule 4, paragraph 39(*b*), and the Social Security Act 1979, section 21(4), Schedule 3, paragraph 6; and section 15(4) is amended by the Social Security Pensions Act 1975, section 65(1), Schedule 4, paragraph 40(*c*) and the Social Security Act 1979, section 21(4), Schedule 3, paragraph 7.

(6)   In relation to the case of a person whose weekly rate of Category A or B retirement pension falls to be increased under the provisions of section 28(7) or 29(8) of the 1975 Act (**a**) by reference to the weekly rate of invalidity allowance to which he was previously entitled, the increase in the sum specified for the appropriate rate of invalidity allowance shall take effect on 6th April 1987 and in relation to all other cases the increase in such sum shall take effect on 9th April 1987.

(7)   The alterations in the rates or amounts of unemployment and sickness benefit, invalidity pension and severe disablement allowance (together with, where appropriate, increase for dependants), shall take effect in all cases on 9th April 1987.

Increase in rates of certain benefits under the Industrial Injuries and Diseases (Old Cases) Act 1975

5.   In the Industrial Injuries and Diseases (Old Cases) Act 1975(**b**) the sum of £23.25 referred to in section 2(6)(*c*) (maximum weekly rate of lesser incapacity allowance supplementing workmen's compensation) and section 7(2)(*b*) (industrial diseases benefit schemes: weekly rate of allowance payable where disablement is not total) shall be further increased; and from and including 8th April 1987 the reference to that sum in section 2(6)(*c*), and from and including 9th April 1987 the reference to that sum in section 7(2)(*b*), shall accordingly have effect as references to £23.75.

Increase in rate of graduated retirement benefit and increments thereof

6.—(1)   In the National Insurance Act 1965(**c**) the sum of 5.06 pence referred to in section 36(1) (graduated retirement benefit) shall be increased by 2.1 per cent.; and from and including 6th April 1987 the reference in that provision to that sum shall accordingly have effect as a reference to 5.17 pence.

(2)   It is hereby directed that the aggregate amount of any increases of graduated retirement benefit payable under Schedule 2 to the Social Security (Graduated Retirement Benefit) (No.2) Regulations 1978(**d**) (increases for deferred retirement) shall be increased by 2.1 per cent.

Increase in the rate of child benefit

7.   In regulation 2 of the Child Benefit and Social Security (Fixing and Adjustment of Rates) Regulations 1976(**e**) (weekly rates of child benefit) —

(a)   in paragraph (1) for "£7.10" there shall be substituted "£7.25";

(b)   in paragraph (2) for "£4.60" there shall be substituted "£4.70".

(**a**) Section 28(7) is amended by the Social Security (No.2) Act 1980 (c.39), section 3(3).
(**b**) 1975 c.16. Sections 2(6)(c) and 7(2)(b) were amended by the Social Security Benefits Up-rating Order 1986 (S.I. 1986/1117).
(**c**) 1965 c.51. Section 36 was repealed by the Social Security Act 1973 (c.38) but subsection (1) is now continued in force by regulation 3 of the Social Security (Graduated Retirement Benefit) (No.2) Regulations 1978 (S.I. 1978/393) in the modified form set out in the Schedule to those regulations as amended by Article 6 of the Social Security Benefits Up-rating Order 1986 (S.I. 1986/1117).
(**d**) S.I. 1978/393.
(**e**) S.I. 1976/1267; the relevant amending instruments are S.I. 1977/1328, 1980/110, 1985/1243 and 1986/1172.

Statutory Sick Pay

8. The sums specified in section 7(1) of the Social Security and Housing Benefits Act 1982(**a**) are —

    (a) in paragraph (*a*), £46.75 and £74.50 respectively;

    (b) in paragraph (*b*), £39.20, £74.50 and £55.50 respectively;

    (c) in paragraph (*c*), £31.60.

Earnings Limits

9.—(1) The sum specified in subsection (1) of section 30 of the 1975 Act is £75 and the sums specified —

    (a) in paragraph (*a*) of that subsection, are £4, 5 pence and 10 pence respectively, and

    (b) in paragraph (*b*) of that subsection are £4, 5 pence, 10 pence, £4, 5 pence and 5 pence respectively.

(2) The sums specified in section 41(2B) of the 1975 Act(**b**) are £85, £10, and £85 respectively.

Revocations

10.—(1) The Social Security Benefits Up-rating Order 1986(**c**) is hereby revoked.

(2) Articles 2 and 3(*b*) of the Statutory Sick Pay Up-rating Order 1986(**d**) are hereby revoked.

Signed by authority of the Secretary of State for Social Services.

John Major
Minister of State,
Department of Health and Social Security

19th January 1987

We consent.

Michael Neubert
Mark Lennox Boyd
Two of the Lords Commissioners of
Her Majesty's Treasury

20th January 1987

(**a**) 1982 c.24; the sums specified in section 7(1) as enacted were increased by S.I. 1983/123, 1947, 1984/2037 and 1986/67.
(**b**) Section 41(2B) was inserted by the Health and Social Security Act 1984 (c.48), s.13, Schedule 5, paragraph 3(c).
(**c**) S.I. 1986/1117.
(**d**) S.I. 1986/67.

SCHEDULE

Article 2(2)

SCHEDULE 4 TO THE 1975 ACT AS AMENDED BY THIS ORDER

SCHEDULE 4

RATES OF BENEFITS, GRANTS AND INCREASES FOR DEPENDANTS

PART I

CONTRIBUTORY PERIODICAL BENEFITS (SECTIONS 14–31)

Description of benefit	Weekly rate
1. Unemployment or sickness benefit (section 14).	(*a*) unemployment benefit .... £31.45. (*b*) sickness benefit .... £30.05.
3. Invalidity allowance (section 16).	(*a*) higher rate .... £8.30. (*b*) middle rate .... £5.30. (*c*) lower rate .... £2.65. (the appropriate rate being determined in accordance with section 16(2)(**a**)).
4. Maternity allowance (section 22).	£30.05.
5. Widow's allowance (section 24).	£55.35.
9. Category B retirement pension where section 29(7)(*a*)(i) applies.	£23.75.
10. Child's special allowance (section 31).	£8.05.

(**a**) Section 16(2) was amended by paragraph 10 of Schedule 1 to the Social Security Act 1979.

Part III

Non-contributory Periodical Benefits (Sections 34–40)

Description of benefit	Weekly rate
1. Attendance allowance (section 35).	(*a*) higher rate .... £31.60. (*b*) lower rate .... £21.10. (the appropriate rate being determined in accordance with section 35(3)(**a**)).
2. Severe disablement allowance (section 36).	£23.75.
3. Invalid care allowance (section 37).	£23.75.
3A. Mobility allowance (section 37A).	£22.10.
4. Guardian's allowance (section 38).	£8.05.
5. Category C retirement pension (section 39).	(*a*) lower rate .... £14.20. (*b*) higher rate .... £23.75. (the appropriate rate being determined in accordance with section 39(2)).
5A. Category D retirement pension (section 39)(**b**).	The higher rate for Category C retirement pensions under paragraph 5 above.
6. Age addition (to a pension of any category, and otherwise under section 40).	£0.25.

(**a**) Section 35(3) was amended by section 2(4) of the Social Security Act 1979.
(**b**) Paragraph 5A was inserted by section 12(2) of the Social Security Act 1985 (c.53).

Part IV

Increases for dependants (Sections 41–49)

Benefit to which increase applies (1)	Increase for qualifying child (2)	Increase for adult dependant (3)
	£	£
1. Unemployment or sickness benefit — (a) unemployment benefit, where the beneficiary is under pensionable age.	—	19.40
(b) unemployment benefit, where the beneficiary is over pensionable age.	8.05	23.75
(c) sickness benefit, where the beneficiary is under pensionable age.	—	18.60
(d) sickness benefit, where the beneficiary is over pensionable age.	8.05	22.70
2. Invalidity pension	8.05	23.75
3. Maternity allowance	—	18.60
4. Widow's allowance	8.05	—
5. Widowed mother's allowance	8.05	—
6. Category A or B retirement pension	8.05	23.75
7. Category C retirement pension	8.05	14.20
8. Child's special allowance	8.05	—
9. Severe disablement allowance	8.05	14.20
10. Invalid care allowance	8.05	14.20

Description of benefit, etc.	Rate or amount
2. Maximum disablement gratuity under section 57(5).	£4,290.00
3. Disablement pension under section 57(6) (weekly rates).	For the several degrees of disablement set out in column (1) of the following Table, the respective amounts in that Table using — (*a*) column (2) for any period during which the beneficiary is over the age of 18 or is entitled to an increase of benefit in respect of a child or adult dependant; (*b*) column (3) for any period during which the beneficiary is not over the age of 18 and not so entitled;

TABLE

Degree of disablement	Amount	
(1) Per cent.	(2) £	(3) £
100	64.50	39.50
90	58.05	35.55
80	51.60	31.60
70	45.15	27.65
60	38.70	23.70
50	32.25	19.75
40	25.80	15.80
30	19.35	11.85
20	12.90	7.90

Description of benefit, etc.	Rate or amount
4. Unemployability supplement under section 58 (increase of weekly rate of disablement pension).	£39.50
5. Increase under section 59 of weekly rate of unemployability supplement (early onset of incapacity for work).	(*a*) if on the qualifying date the beneficiary was under the age of 35, or if that date fell before 5th July 1948 .... £8.30 (*aa*) if head (*a*) above does not apply and on the qualifying date the beneficiary was under the age of 40 and he had not attained pensionable age before 6th April 1979 .... £8.30 (*b*) if heads (*a*) and (*aa*) above do not apply and on the qualifying date the beneficiary was under the age of 45 .... £5.30

PART V — *continued*

RATE OR AMOUNT OF INDUSTRIAL INJURIES BENEFIT

Description of benefit, etc.	Rate or amount
	(*bb*) if heads (*a*), (*aa*) and (*b*) above do not apply and on the qualifying date the beneficiary was under the age of 50 and had not attained pensionable age before 6th April 1979 .... £5.30
	(*c*) in any other case £2.65
7. Maximum increase under section 61 of weekly rate of disablement pension where constant attendance needed.	(*a*) except in cases of exceptionally severe disablement £25.80
	(*b*) in any case £51.60
8. Increase under section 63 of weekly rate of disablement pension (exceptionally severe disablement).	£25.80
10. Increase under section 64 of weekly rate of disablement pension (dependent children).	£8.05
12. Increase under section 66(2) of weekly rate of disablement pension (adult dependant).	£23.75
13. Widow's pension under section 68 (weekly rates) —	
(*a*) initial rate	£55.35
(*b*) higher permanent rate	£40.05
(*c*) lower permanent rate	30 per cent. of the sum specified in section 6(1)(*a*) of the Pensions Act.
14. Widower's pension under section 69 (weekly rate).	£40.05
15. Weekly rate of allowance under section 70 in respect of children.	In respect of each qualifying child ...£8.05
16. Maximum under section 91(1) of aggregate of weekly benefit payable for successive accidents.	(*a*) for any period during which the beneficiary is over the age of 18 or is entitled to an increase in benefit in respect of a child or adult dependant £64.50
	(*b*) for any period during which the beneficiary is not over the age of 18 and not so entitled £39.50

EXPLANATORY NOTE

(This note is not part of the Order)

This Order, a draft of which has been laid before and approved by resolution of each House of Parliament, is made as a consequence of a review under section 63(1) of the Social Security Act 1986. It alters, with effect from dates in the week beginning 6th April 1987 which are specified in Articles 4 to 6, the rates and amounts of certain benefits and other sums.

Article 2 alters the benefits and increases of benefit (except age addition and certain benefits in respect of children which are also subject to the provisions of section 17(1) of the Child Benefit Act 1975) specified in Parts I, III, IV and V of Schedule 4 to that Act; Article 3 increases the rates and amounts of certain benefits under Part II of the Social Security Pensions Act 1975 (including increases of Category A or B retirement pension payable by reference to the increases of increments in guaranteed minimum pensions payable by virtue of section 35(6) of that Act); Article 4 specifies the date from which the rates or amounts of benefits are altered; Article 5 increases the rates laid down in the Industrial Injuries and Diseases (Old Cases) Act 1975 for the maximum weekly rate of lesser incapacity allowance supplementing workmen's compensation and the weekly rate of allowance under the Industrial Diseases Benefit Schemes where disablement is not total; Article 6 increases the rate of graduated retirement pension under the National Insurance Act 1965; Article 7 provides for the weekly rates of child benefit and one-parent benefit to be increased; Article 8 specifies the weekly rates of statutory sick pay payable as at 1st April 1987 under section 7(1) of the Social Security and Housing Benefits Act 1982; Article 9 specifies earnings limits for retirement pensions and child dependency increases.

In accordance with section 63(11) of the Social Security Act 1986, a copy of the report of the Government Actuary (Cmnd. 24) giving his opinion on the likely effect on the National Insurance Fund of the making of this Order was laid before Parliament with the draft Order.

STATUTORY INSTRUMENTS

1987 No. 46

SOCIAL SECURITY

The Social Security (Contributions, Re-rating) Order 1987

Made -	-	-	-	*20th January 1987*
Coming into force				*6th April 1987*

Whereas the Secretary of State for Social Services, as a result of carrying out in the tax year 1986–87 a review of the general level of earnings pursuant to subsections (2) and (3) of section 120 of the Social Security Act 1975(**a**), has determined that an Order should be made under that section amending Part I of the said Act by altering the rates of Class 2 and Class 3 contributions, the amount of earnings below which an earner may be excepted from liability for Class 2 contributions and the lower and upper limits of profits or gains to be taken into account for Class 4 contributions:

And whereas the Secretary of State, for the purposes of adjusting amounts payable by way of Class 1 contributions, has determined that an Order should be made under section 123A(1) and (2) of that Act(**b**) amending section 4(6B) and (6E) of that Act(**c**) by altering the weekly earnings figures therein specified:

And whereas a draft of the following Order was laid before Parliament in accordance with the provisions of sections 120(4), 121(2) and 123A(6) of that Act and approved by resolution of each House of Parliament:

Now, therefore, the Secretary of State for Social Services, in conjunction with the Treasury so far as relates to matters with regard to which the Treasury has so directed(**d**), in exercise of powers conferred upon him by sections 120(5) and (6), 121(2) and 123A(1) and (2) of the said Act and of all other powers enabling him in that behalf, hereby makes the following Order:

Citation, commencement and interpretation

1.—(1) This Order may be cited as the Social Security (Contributions, Re-rating) Order 1987 and shall come into force on 6th April 1987.

(2) In this Order "the Act" means the Social Security Act 1975.

Weekly earnings figures for primary and secondary earnings brackets

2.—(1) Section 4 of the Act (incidence of Class 1 contributions) shall be amended in accordance with the provisions of this article.

(2) In subsection (6B) (primary earnings brackets)–

    (a) for the figure £59.99 specified in respect of Bracket 1 there shall be substituted the figure £64.99;

(**a**) 1975 c.14.
(**b**) Section 123A was inserted by section 7(5) of the Social Security Act 1985 (c.53), and amended by section 74(1) and (2) of the Social Security Act 1986 (c.50).
(**c**) Section 4(6B) and (6E) was inserted by section 7(2) of the Social Security Act 1985; the relevant amending instrument is S.I. 1986/25.
(**d**) *See* the Social Security Act 1975, section 166(5).

(b) for the figures £60.00 and £94.99 specified in respect of Bracket 2 there shall be substituted respectively the figures £65.00 and £99.99;

(c) for the figure £95.00 specified in respect of Bracket 3 there shall be substituted the figure £100.00.

(3) In subsection (6E) (secondary earnings brackets)–

(a) for the figure £59.99 specified in respect of Bracket 1 there shall be substituted the figure £64.99;

(b) for the figures £60.00 and £94.99 specified in respect of Bracket 2 there shall be substituted respectively the figures £65.00 and £99.99;

(c) for the figures £95.00 and £139.99 specified in respect of Bracket 3 there shall be substituted respectively the figures £100.00 and £149.99;

(d) for the figure £140.00 specified in respect of Bracket 4 there shall be substituted the figure £150.00.

Rate of, and small earnings exception from, Class 2 contributions

3. In section 7 of the Act (Class 2 contributions)–

(a) in subsection (1) (weekly rate) for "£3.75"(**a**) there shall be substituted "£3.85";

(b) in subsection (5) (small earnings exception) for "£2,075"(**b**) there shall be substituted "£2,125".

Amount of Class 3 contributions

4. In section 8(1) of the Act (amount of Class 3 contributions) for "£3.65"(**c**) there shall be substituted "£3.75".

Lower and upper limits for Class 4 contributions

5. In sections 9(2) and 10(1) of the Act (Class 4 contributions recoverable under Tax Acts and regulations)–

(a) for "£4,450" (lower limit)(**d**) wherever that amount appears there shall be substituted in each of those sections "£4,590";

(b) for "£14,820" (upper limit)(**e**) there shall be substituted in each of those sections "£15,340".

Signed by authority of the Secretary of State for Social Services.

John Major
Minister of State,
Department of Health and Social Security

19th January 1987

Michael Neubert
Mark Lennox-Boyd
Two of the Lords Commissioners of
Her Majesty's Treasury

20th January 1987

(**a**) *See* S.I. 1986/25, article 3(a). (**b**) *See* S.I. 1986/25, article 3(b). (**c**) *See* S.I. 1986/25, article 4.
(**d**) *See* S.I. 1986/25, article 5(a). (**e**) *See* S.I. 1986/25, article 5(b).

EXPLANATORY NOTE

(This note is not part of the Order)

This Order increases the amounts of weekly earnings specified in the earnings brackets in section 4(6B) and (6E) of the Social Security Act 1975, determining the appropriate percentage rate at which Class 1 contributions are payable under that Act (article 2). It increases the rates of Class 2 and Class 3 contributions payable under that Act (articles 3(a) and 4). It increases the amount of earnings below which an earner may be excepted from liability for Class 2 contributions (article 3(b)), and the lower and upper limits of profits or gains between which Class 4 contributions are payable (article 5).

In accordance with sections 121(1) and 123A(6A) of the Social Security Act 1975, a copy of the report by the Government Actuary (Cmnd. 24), giving his opinion on the likely effect on the National Insurance Fund of the making of the Order was laid before Parliament with a draft of it.

STATUTORY INSTRUMENTS

1987 No. 48

SOCIAL SECURITY

The Social Security (Treasury Supplement to and Allocation of Contributions) (Re-rating) Order 1987

Made - - - - -	*20th January 1987*
Coming into force	*6th April 1987*

Whereas a draft of this Order was laid before Parliament in accordance with the provisions of section 167(1) of the Social Security Act 1975 **(a)** and approved by resolution of each House of Parliament:

Now, therefore, the Secretary of State for Social Services, with the consent of the Treasury, in exercise of the powers conferred upon him by sections 1(5A) and 134(4A) and (5A) of the Social Security Act 1975 **(b)** and of all other powers enabling him in that behalf, hereby makes the following Order:—

Citation and commencement

1. This Order may be cited as the Social Security (Treasury Supplement to and Allocation of Contributions) (Re-rating) Order 1987 and shall come into operation on 6th April 1987.

Alteration of Treasury supplement to contributions

2. In section 1(5) of the Social Security Act 1975 (Treasury supplement to contributions) **(c)** for the words "9 per cent." **(d)** there shall be substituted the words "7 per cent.".

(a) 1975 c. 14; section 167(1) was amended by the Social Security (Contributions) Act 1981 (c. 1), section 4(5), and by the Social Security Act 1986 (c. 50), section 74(4).

(b) Section 1(5A) was inserted by the Social Security (Contributions) Act 1981, section 2(2), and was amended by the Social Security (Contributions) Act 1982 (c. 2), section 2(2); section 134(4A) was inserted by the Social Security (Contributions) Act 1981, section 3(3); section 134(5A) was inserted by the Social Security Act 1986, section 74(3).

(c) Section 1(5) was amended by the Social Security (Miscellaneous Provisions) Act 1977 (c. 5), section 24(6) and Schedule 2, and by the Employment Protection Act 1975 (c. 71), section 40(1).

(d) *See* S.I. 1984/1904, article 2.

Percentage rates of appropriate national health service and employment protection allocations

3.—(1) Section 134(4) of the Act**(a)** (allocation of contributions) shall be amended in accordance with the provisions of this article.

(2) In the definition of "the appropriate national health service allocation"—

(*a*) in paragraph (*a*) (primary Class 1 contributions) for the words "0.75 per cent."**(b)** there shall be substituted the words "0.85 per cent.";

(*b*) in paragraph (*b*) (secondary Class 1 contributions) for the words "0.6 per cent." there shall be substituted the words "0.7 per cent.";

(*c*) in paragraph (*c*) (Class 2 contributions) for the words "11.5 per cent." **(c)** there shall be substituted the words "15.5 per cent.";

(*d*) in paragraph (*d*) (Class 3 contributions) for the words "11.5 per cent." **(d)** there shall be substituted the words "15.5 per cent.";

(*e*) in paragraph (*e*) (Class 4 contributions) for the words "0.95 per cent." **(e)** there shall be substituted the words "1.15 per cent.".

(3) In the definition of "the appropriate employment protection allocation"—

(*a*) in paragraph (i) (primary Class 1 contributions) for the words "0.25 per cent." **(f)** there shall be substituted the words "0.07 per cent.";

(*b*) in paragraph (ii) (secondary Class 1 contributions) for the words "0.2 per cent." there shall be substituted the words "0.06 per cent.".

Signed by authority of the Secretary of State for Social Services.

John Major
Minister of State,
Department of Health and
Social Security

19th January 1987

Michael Neubert
Mark Lennox Boyd
Two of the Lords Commissioners
of Her Majesty's Treasury

20th January 1987

(a) Section 134(4) was amended by the Employment Protection Act 1975, section 40(1), by the Social Security (Contributions) Act 1982, section 3(3) and by the Social Security Act 1985 (c. 53), section 29(1) and Schedule 5, paragraph 11.

(b) *See* the Social Security (Contributions) Act 1982, section 3(2)(*a*).

(c) *See* the Social Security (Contributions) Act 1981, section 3(2)(*b*).

(d) *See* the Social Security (Contributions) Act 1981, section 3(2)(*c*).

(e) *See* the Social Security (Contributions) Act 1982, section 3(2)(*b*).

(f) *See* S.I. 1982/1790, article 6.

EXPLANATORY NOTE

(This note is not part of the Order)

This Order decreases the Treasury supplement to contributions paid under the Social Security Act 1975 from 9 per cent. to 7 per cent. (article 2). It increases the percentage rates of the appropriate national health service allocation and reduces the percentage rates of the appropriate employment protection allocation (article 3).

STATUTORY INSTRUMENTS

1987 No. 49

SOCIAL SECURITY

The Supplementary Benefit Uprating Regulations 1987

Made - - -		*20th January 1987*
Coming into force -		*6th April 1987*

The Secretary of State for Social Services, in exercise of the powers conferred on him by sections 2(2) and 34(1)(**a**) of, and paragraph 2(1) and (4) of Schedule 1 to the Supplementary Benefits Act 1976(**b**) and of all other powers enabling him in that behalf, with the consent of the Treasury (**c**) and, so far as is required (**d**), after agreement by the Social Security Advisory Committee that the proposals to make these regulations should not be referred to it (**e**), hereby makes the following regulations of which a draft has, in accordance with section 33(3) of that Act, been laid before Parliament and approved by a resolution of each House of Parliament:—

Citation, commencement and interpretation

1.—(1) These regulations may be cited as the Supplementary Benefit Uprating Regulations 1987 and shall come into force on 6th April 1987.

(2) In these regulations "Requirements Regulations" means the Supplementary Benefit (Requirements) Regulations 1983(**f**).

Amendment of amounts specified in the Requirements Regulations

2.—(1) The Requirements Regulations shall be amended in accordance with the following provisions of this regulation.

(2) In regulation 5 (normal requirements of relevant persons) —

    (a) in paragraph (1)(*c*) for "£1.30" there shall be substituted "£1.40";

    (b) in paragraph (2)(*d*) for "£0.75" there shall be substituted "£0.70"; and

    (c) in paragraph (3)(*b*) for "£0.80" there shall be substituted "£0.85".

(**a**) *See* the definitions of "prescribed" and "regulations".
(**b**) 1976 c.71, as amended by section 6(1) of, and Part I of Schedule 2 to, the Social Security Act 1980 (c.30).
(**c**) *See* section 33(3) of the Supplementary Benefits Act 1976.
(**d**) These requirements apply only to regulation 2(2).
(**e**) *See* section 61(1)(b) of the Social Security Act 1986 (c.50).
(**f**) S.I. 1983/1399; the relevant amending instruments are S.I. 1984/1102, 1103, 1985/1247, 1835, 1986/1173, 1292.

(3)   In regulation 9(12) (personal expenses of boarders) for "£9.05" there shall be substituted "£9.25" and —

    (a)   in sub-paragraph (*a*), in head (i) for "£21.90" and in head (ii) for "£19.60" there shall be substituted "£22.30" and "£20.00" respectively;

    (b)   in sub-paragraph (*b*), in head (i) for "£10.95" and in head (ii) for "£9.80" there shall be substituted "£11.15" and "£10.00" respectively; and

    (c)   in sub-paragraph (*c*), in head (i) for "£9.80", in head (ii) for "£5.90", in head (iii) for "£5.05" and in head (iv) for "£3.30" there shall be substituted "£10.00", "£6.00", "£5.15" and "£3.35" respectively.

(4)   In regulation 16(1) (maintenance and insurance), for "£1.85" there shall be substituted "£1.95".

(5)   In regulation 22(3) (reduction in amounts where the home is occupied by a non-dependant) —

    (a)   in sub-paragraph (*a*), in head (i) for "£2.80", in head (ii) for "£7.80" and in head (iii) for "£2.80", there shall be substituted "£2.90", "£8.05" and "£2.90" respectively; and

    (b)   in sub-paragraphs (*b*), (*c*) and (*d*) for "£2.80" there shall be substituted "£2.90".

(6)   In regulation 23(1) (non-householder's contribution) for "£3.90" there shall be substituted "£4.05".

(7)   In Schedule 1 (normal requirements), for the amount specified in column (2) of that Schedule in relation to each provision specified in column (1) thereof, such amount being set out in column 2 of the First Schedule to these regulations, there shall be substituted the amount set out in relation to that provision in column 3 of that First Schedule.

(8)   In Schedule 4 in paragraphs 14 and 17 (diet and hospital fares) for the amount specified in column (2) of that Schedule in relation to each provision specified in column (1) thereof, such amount being out in column 2 of the Second Schedule to these regulations, there shall be substituted the amount set out in relation to that provision in column 3 of that Second Schedule.

Signed by authority of the Secretary of State for Social Services.

John Major
Minister of State,
Department of Health and Social Security

19th January 1987

We consent,

Michael Neubert
Mark Lennox Boyd
Two of the Lords Commissioners of
Her Majesty's Treasury

20th January 1987

THE FIRST SCHEDULE   Regulation 2(7)

AMOUNTS SUBSTITUTED IN SCHEDULE 1 TO THE REQUIREMENTS REGULATIONS

Column 1	Column 2	Column 3
Provision of Schedule 1 to the Requirements Regulations	Old Amount	New Amount
Paragraph A (couples) —		
sub-paragraph (*a*)	£60.65	£61.85
sub-paragraph (*b*)	£48.40	£49.35
Paragraph B (householders) —		
sub-paragraph (*a*)	£37.90	£38.65
sub-paragraph (*b*)	£29.80	£30.40
Paragraph 1 (non-householders not less than 18 or less than 18 with a dependant) —		
sub-paragraph (*a*)	£30.35	£30.95
sub-paragraph (*b*)	£23.85	£24.35
Paragraph 2 (non-householders less than 18 without a dependant) —		
sub-paragraph (*a*)	£23.25	£23.70
sub-paragraph (*b*)	£18.40	£18.75
Paragraph 3 (dependants) —		
sub-paragraph (*a*)	£23.85	£24.35
sub-paragraph (*b*)	£18.40	£18.75
sub-paragraph (*c*)	£15.30	£15.60
sub-paragraph (*d*)	£10.20	£10.40

Regulation 2(8) THE SECOND SCHEDULE

Amounts substituted in Schedule 4 to the Requirements Regulations

Column 1	Column 2	Column 3
Provision of Schedule 4 to the Requirements Regulations	Old Amount	New Amount
Part II – Items other than heating		
Paragraph 14 (diet) —		
sub-paragraph (*a*)	£3.70	£3.80
sub-paragraph (*b*)	£1.60	£1.65
sub-paragraph (*c*)	£1.60	£1.65
sub-paragraph (*d*)	£10.65	£10.85
Paragraph 17 (hospital fares) —		
sub-paragraph (*b*)(i)	£15.00	£15.30
sub-paragraph (*b*)(ii)	£10.85	£11.05
sub-paragraph (*c*)(i)	£7.25	£7.40
sub-paragraph (*c*)(ii)	£3.10	£3.15
sub-paragraph (*d*)(i)	£16.10	£16.45
sub-paragraph (*d*)(ii)	£10.65	£10.85
sub-paragraph (*d*)(iii)	£7.55	£7.70
sub-paragraph (*d*)(iv)	£2.45	£2.50
sub-paragraph (*e*)(i)	£30.15	£30.75
sub-paragraph (*e*)(ii)	£22.05	£22.50
sub-paragraph (*e*)(iii)	£22.60	£23.05
sub-paragraph (*e*)(iv)	£16.10	£16.45

EXPLANATORY NOTE

(This note is not part of the Regulations)

These Regulations alter certain amounts specified in the Supplementary Benefit (Requirements) Regulations 1983 for the purpose of determining entitlement to supplementary benefit under the Supplementary Benefit Act 1976. They vary amounts for a person's normal requirements (regulation 2(2) and (7)). They increase certain allowances for personal expenses for persons in board and lodging accommodation (regulation 2(3)); the weekly amount payable for maintenance and insurance of the home (regulation 2(4)); the reduction to be made in certain payments in respect of housing where the home is occupied by non-dependants (regulation 2(5)); the amount of the non-householder's contribution (regulation 2(6)); certain amounts of additional requirements relating to diet and the reduction made in certain circumstances to amounts paid in respect of fares for hospital visiting (regulation 2(8)).

STATUTORY INSTRUMENTS

1987 No. 50

REGISTRATION OF BIRTHS, DEATHS, MARRIAGES, ETC.

ENGLAND AND WALES

The Registration of Births, Deaths and Marriages (Fees) Order 1987

Made - - - -	*21st January 1987*
Laid before Parliament	*30th January 1987*
Coming into force	*1st April 1987*

The Secretary of State for Social Services in exercise of the powers conferred by section 5(1) and (2) of, and paragraphs 1 and 2 of Schedule 3 to, the Public Expenditure and Receipts Act 1968 (**a**) and now vested in him (**b**) and of all other powers enabling him in that behalf, hereby makes the following order:

Citation and commencement

1. This Order may be cited as the Registration of Births, Deaths and Marriages (Fees) Order 1987 and shall come into force on 1st April 1987.

Fees payable

2. The fees payable under each of the enactments specified in column 2 of the Schedule to this Order in respect of the matters specified in column 3 shall be the fees specified in relation thereto in column 4 and each of those enactments shall have effect accordingly.

Revocation of Order

3. The provisions of this Order shall have effect in place of the provisions of the Registration of Births, Deaths and Marriages (Fees) Order 1985 (**c**) (under which the fees payable were as respectively set out in column 5 of the Schedule to this Order) and that Order is accordingly revoked.

Signed by authority of the Secretary of State for Social Services.

Trumpington
Parliamentary Under Secretary of State,
Department of Health and Social Security

21st January 1987

(**a**)   1968 c.14; paragraph 1 of Schedule 3 was amended by paragraph 21 of Schedule 9 to the Friendly Societies Act 1974 (c.46) and by paragraph 33 of Schedule 2 to the Social Security (Consequential Provisions) Act 1975 (c.18). By virtue of section 2(2) of the Marriage Act 1983 (c.32) the reference to the Marriage Act 1949 (c.76) in the said Schedule 3 includes a reference to that Act as amended by the 1983 Act.
(**b**) *See* the Secretary of State for Social Services Order 1968 (S.I. 1968/1699), article 2 (transferring all functions of the Minister of Health to the Secretary of State).
(**c**) S.I. 1985/1960.

I/1g

Article 2

SCHEDULE

FEES PAYABLE

(1)	(2) Enactment specifying fees	(3) Matter for which fee is payable	(4) New fee	(5) Old fee
1855 c.81	Places of Worship Registration Act 1855			
	Section 5	Certification of place of meeting for religious worship	£12.00	£12.00
1887 c.40	Savings Banks Act 1887 Section 10 (**a**)	Certificate of birth, death or marriage, for purposes of certain Acts	£1.50	£1.50
1938 c.69	Young Persons (Employment) Act 1938			
	Section 5	Copy of entry in birth register for purposes of that Act	£1.50	£1.50
1944 c.31	Education Act 1944 Section 94(1)	Copy of entry in birth register for purposes of certain Acts	£1.50	£1.50
1949 c.76	Marriage Act 1949 Section 27(6)	Entry in marriage notice book	£10.00	£8.00
	Section 27(7) (**b**)	Attendance of superintendent registrar other than at his office for purpose of being given notice of marriage of house-bound or detained person	£24.00	£22.00
	Section 32(5) (**c**)	Licence for marriage	£28.00	£26.00
	Section 41(6)	Registration of building for solemnization of marriages	£70.00	£65.00
	Section 51(1) (**d**)	Fee of registrar for attending marriage–		
		(i) at a register office	£11.00	£10.00
		(ii) at a registered building or at the place where a house-bound or detained person usually resides	£20.00	£18.00
	Section 51(2) (**e**)	Fee of a superintendent registrar attending marriage at the place where a house-bound or detained person usually resides	£24.00	£22.00
	Section 57(4) (**f**)	Sum paid to incumbent, etc. for every entry contained in quarterly certified copies of entries of marriage	£1.20	£1.20
	Section 63(1)(b)	Certified copy of entry issued under that subsection–		
		(i) when application is made at the time of registering or to a registrar	£2.00	£2.00
		(ii) in any other case	£5.00	£5.00
	Section 64(2)(a)	General search of indexes of register books kept by superintendent registrars	£12.00	£12.00

(**a**) Section 10 was amended by Part III of Schedule 6 to the Post Office Act 1969 (c.48) and by Schedule 4 to the Trustee Savings Banks Act 1985 (c.58) and is applied by regulation 32 of the Savings Certificates Regulations 1972 (S.I. 1972/641) and by regulation 25 of the Premium Savings Banks Regulations 1972 (S.I. 1972/765).
(**b**) Section 27(7) was inserted by paragraph 5(c) of Schedule 1 to the Marriage Act 1983.
(**c**) Section 32(5) was amended by article 4(2) of the Registration of Births, Deaths and Marriages (Fees) Order 1968 (S.I. 1968/1242).
(**d**) Section 51(1) was so numbered by paragraph 15 of Schedule 1 to the Marriage Act 1983.
(**e**) Section 51(2) was inserted by paragraph 15 of Schedule 1 to the Marriage Act 1983.
(**f**) Section 57(4) was amended by paragraph 40 of Schedule 29 to the Local Government Act 1972 (c.70).

(1)	(2) Enactment specifying fees	(3) Matter for which fee is payable	(4) New fee	(5) Old fee
	Section 64(2)(c)	Certified copy of entry issued under that subsection	£5.00	£5.00
	Section 65(2)(c)	Certified copy of entry, following a search of indexes kept at General Register Office	£5.00	£5.00
1950 c.28	Shops Act 1950 Section 35(1)	Copy of entry in birth register for purposes of that Act	£1.50	£1.50
1953 c.20	Births and Deaths Registration Act 1953			
	Section 13(2)	Issue of certificate of baptism	£1.00	£1.00
	Section 30(2)(c)	Certified copy of entry following search of indexes kept at General Register Office	£5.00	£5.00
	Section 31(2)(a)	General search of indexes kept by superintendent registrars	£12.00	£12.00
	Section 31(2)(c)	Certified copy of entry isued under that subsection	£5.00	£5.00
	Section 32(c)	Certified copy of entry in registers kept by registrars	£2.00	£2.00
	Section 33(1)	(i) Short certificate of birth obtained at the time of registration, or if more than one such certificate is obtained, the first of these	NIL	NIL
		(ii) Any other short certificate of birth obtained from a registrar	£1.50	£1.50
		(iii) A short certificate of birth obtained in any other case	£2.50	£2.50
1961 c.34	Factories Act 1961 Section 178(1)	Extract of entry in birth register for purposes of that Act	£1.50	£1.50
1974 c.46	Friendly Societies Act 1974 Section 106(2) and Schedule 5, paragraph 8	Certificate of birth or death for purposes of certain Acts	£1.50	£1.50
1975 c.14	Social Security Act 1975 Section 160(2)(a)	Certificate of birth, death or marriage for purposes of certain Acts	£1.50	£1.50

EXPLANATORY NOTE

(This note is not part of the Order)

This Order increases certain of the fees payable under the Acts relating to the registration of births, deaths and marriages and associated matters and it consolidates the provisions for the new fees with the provisions of the Births, Deaths and Marriages (Fees) Order 1985 relating to those which are not changed. It also revokes that Order. The fees increased relate only to marriages.

The increases take effect on 1st April 1987 and the fees payable both before and from that date are set out in the Schedule.

(a) Section 160 is applied by section 11 of the Industrial Injuries and Diseases (Old Cases) Act 1975 (c.16) and section 9(1) of the Child Benefit Act 1975 (c.61).

STATUTORY INSTRUMENTS

1987 No. 51

WEIGHTS AND MEASURES

The Weights and Measures (Local and Working Standard Capacity Measures and Testing Equipment) Regulations 1987

Made - - - -	*21st January 1987*
Laid before Parliament	*26th January 1987*
Coming into force	*16th February 1987*

The Secretary of State, in exercise of his powers under sections 4(5) and (6), 5(9), 86(1) and 94(1) of the Weights and Measures Act 1985 (**a**) and of all other powers enabling him in that behalf, hereby makes the following Regulations:—

PART I

GENERAL

Citation, commencement and revocation

1.—(1) These Regulations may be cited as the Weights and Measures (Local and Working Standard Capacity Measures and Testing Equipment) Regulations 1987 and shall come into operation on 16th February 1987.

(2) The Weights and Measures (Local Standards: Limits of Error) Regulations 1970 (**b**), the Working Standards and Testing Equipment (Testing and Adjustment) Regulations 1970 (**c**), the Weights and Measures (Local Standards: Periods of Validity) Regulations 1979 (**d**), the Working Standards and Testing Equipment (Testing and Adjustment) (Amendment) Regulations 1979 (**e**) and the Weights and Measures (Local and Working Standard Capacity Measures) Regulations 1983 (**f**) are hereby revoked insofar as they relate to capacity measures and capacity testing equipment.

Interpretation

2.—(1) In these Regulations:—

"the Act" means the Weights and Measures Act 1985;

"discrimination threshold" means the smallest change which produces a perceptible change in the indication;

"linearity" means the horizontal band within which the graph of the meter error of a reference meter lies over the authorised range of flowrates;

"multifiller" means a device consisting of a number of calibrated measures, capable of dispensing simultaneously known quantities of water, used for the testing of capacity measures;

(**a**) 1985 c.72.
(**c**) S.I. 1970/1714.
(**b**) S.I. 1970/1710; relevant amending instrument is S.I. 1983/1654.
(**d**) S.I. 1979/1436.   (**e**) S.I. 1979/1719.   (**f**) S.I. 1983/1654.

"reference meter" means a meter for use in testing measuring equipment used for the measurement of liquid fuel delivered from road tankers; and

"repeatability" means the ability of reference meters to indicate, under defined conditions of use, closely similar quantities on repeated measurings.

(2) The abbreviations of, and symbols for, units of measurement used in these Regulations refer to the relevant units as follows:—

Imperial System		Metric System	
fluid ounce	fl oz	millilitre	ml
pint	pt	litre	l
gallon	gal		

PART II

WORKING STANDARD CAPACITY MEASURES

3.—(1) Working standard capacity measures provided pursuant to section 5(1) of the Act for use by inspectors of weights and measures shall be tested by one of the following methods:—

Method 1

(a) where the test relates to an indicated imperial measurement not exceeding 1 gal or an indicated metric measurement not exceeding 5 l, by transfer of water from an equivalent local standard capacity measure;

(b) in any other case by transfer of water from a local standard capacity measure of maximum possible capacity in relation to the working standard used the requisite number of times;

Method 2

by pouring water of a known temperature into the measure under test, when the measure is resting on a horizontal surface—

(a) where the nominal capacity of the measure is defined by a line, until the bottom of the meniscus coincides with the top of that line or with the top of any graduation line or tolerance mark being tested; or

(b) where the nominal capacity of the measure is defined by its brim, until the surface water coincides with the brim;

and in either case determining the weight of the water on a suitable weighing machine (the discrimination threshold of which in grams shall not be more than one-fifth of the equivalent amount in millilitres of the appropriate limit of error set out in Schedule 1 to these Regulations) and calculating therefrom the capacity of the measure in accordance with British Standard 1797: 1968 (**a**) or British Standard 6696: 1986 (**b**).

(2) A working standard capacity measure shall be tested as a measure of any amount in Schedule 3 to the Act which it is designed to measure and the

---

(**a**) Tables for use in the calibration of Volumetric Glassware, SBN 580 00129 6, published by the British Standards Institution in February 1952, and revised in April 1968.

(**b**) British Standard Methods for use and testing of capacity volumetric glassware, ISBN 0 580 15076 3, published by the British Standards Institution on 28th February 1986.

accuracy of any tolerance marks adjacent to any graduation tested shall also be tested.

4. Every working standard capacity measure—

    (a) which is made of glass shall have been tested within 12 months before use;

    (b) which is made of metal and

        (i) is of 50 l or less or 10 gal or less shall have been tested within 6 months before use;

        (ii) is of more than 50 l or 10 gal shall have been tested within 24 months before use.

PART III

TESTING EQUIPMENT

Reference meters

5.—(1) Reference meters shall be tested either—

    (a) by means of a local or working standard capacity measure which is of sufficient size to hold at least one minute's delivery of the meter under test; or

    (b) by means of a weighing machine which can weigh at least one minute's delivery of the meter under test.

(2) The capacity measure or the weighing machine used to test a reference meter shall have a discrimination threshold of not less than 0.01 per cent. of the quantity delivered by the meter under test.

In a test under paragraph (1)*(b)* above, the density of the test liquid shall be determined to an accuracy of 0.01 per cent.

6. A reference meter shall have been tested over the range of flowrates and liquids for which it is intended to be used within 24 months before use, and the results of the test shall be such that

    (a) the repeatability shall be such that the range of five consecutive tests with the same liquid at the same flowrate does not exceed 0.05 per cent. of the quantity delivered on each test;

    (b) the linearity shall be such that the range of the means of any five consecutive tests with the same liquid within the flowrate range shall not exceed 0.1 per cent. of the quantity delivered on each test; and

    (c) notwithstanding the application of corrections when a reference meter is used to test meter measuring systems in accordance with the Measuring Equipment (Liquid Fuel delivered from Road Tankers) Regulations 1983 **(a)**, the accuracy of the mean of any five consecutive tests shall not exceed 0.5 per cent. of the quantity delivered on any test.

7. A reference meter shall have been tested at a single flowrate within 6 months before use, and the mean of five consecutive measurements at the same flowrate shall not differ by more than 0.05 per cent. of the quantity delivered on each test from the mean quantity delivered at the same flowrate with liquid of the same viscosity when the meter was last tested in accordance with Regulation 6 above.

(a) S.I. 1983/1390, amended by S.I. 1986/1210.

Multifillers

8. Every measure in a multifiller shall be tested in the manner in which it is to be used by discharging water into a working standard capacity measure or into a container and determining the volume of water delivered on a suitable weighing machine.

9. Every multifiller shall have been tested within 6 months before use and shall have been adjusted so that the quantity delivered does not lie outside the limit of error permitted for a working standard of the same nominal capacity.

Burettes and pipettes

10. Burettes and pipettes shall have been tested within 12 months before use and shall have been adjusted so that the error in volume does not exceed the limit of error permitted for a working standard of the same nominal capacity.

11. A pipette shall be tested as a measure of its maximum purported capacity, and (if applicable) as a measure of at least one amount indicated by a subdivision, by filling it to the level of the graduation, discharging it, and weighing the water discharged.

12. A burette shall be tested as a measure of its maximum purported capacity, and (if applicable) as a measure of at least two amounts indicated by subdivisions, by filling it to the level of the graduation, discharging it, and weighing the water discharged.

Displacement plungers

13. A displacement plunger shall be tested by measuring either the volume or the weight of water displaced when the displacement plunger is immersed in water up to the line which indicates the nominal volume.

14. A displacement plunger shall have been tested within 12 months before use and shall have been adjusted so that the error in volume does not exceed the limit of error set out in Schedule 2 to these Regulations.

PART IV

Working Standard Capacity Measures and Testing Equipment

15.—(1) Where an inspector has reasonable cause to believe that any working standard capacity measure or testing equipment referred to in these Regulations is not accurate within the relevant limits of error, he shall test it before use.

(2) Where testing reveals an error which exceeds the relevant limit shown in Schedule 1 or 2 to these Regulations, the measure or testing equipment shall not be further used until it has been so adjusted that any error is within that limit.

PART V

Local Standard Capacity Measures

Prescribed limits of error

16. The error on local standard capacity measures shall not exceed the limits of error shown in Schedule 3 to these Regulations.

Periods of validity of certificates of fitness of local standard capacity measures

17. The periods prescribed in the case of local standard capacity measures for the purposes of section 4(6) of the Act (which relates to periods of validity of certificates of fitness of local standards) shall be:

(a) ten years, in the case of a capacity measure up to and including 500 ml or 1 pint;

(b) five years, in the case of a capacity measure over 500 ml or 1 pint.

Lucas of Chilworth
Parliamentary Under-Secretary of State,
Department of Trade and Industry

21st January 1987

Regulations 3 and 15   SCHEDULE 1

WORKING STANDARD CAPACITY MEASURES AND TESTING EQUIPMENT
(excluding proving tanks, graduated measuring cylinders, displacement plungers and reference meters)

(a) Imperial		(b) Metric	
Indicated capacity of or tolerance mark relating to—	Limit of error in millilitres	Indicated capacity of or tolerance mark relating to—	Limit of error in millilitres
¼ gill or less	0.2	1 ml or 2 ml	0.1
⅓ gill	0.3	5 ml or 10 ml	0.2
⅖ gill or		20 ml or 25 ml	0.2
½ gill	0.4	50 ml	0.3
4 fl oz	0.5	100 ml	0.4
1 gill (5 fl oz)	0.6	125 ml	0.5
6 fl oz	0.7	150 ml	0.6
⅓ pt, 8 fl oz		175 ml	0.7
or ½ pt	0.8	200 ml or 250 ml	0.8
1 pt	1.0	500 ml	1.0
1 quart or			
½ gal	2.0	1 l or 2 l	2.0
1 gal	5.0	2.5 l	2.5
2 gal	10.0	5 l	5.0
5 gal	20.0	10 l	10.0
more than 5 gal	0.1 per cent.	more than 10 l	0.1 per cent.

PROVING TANKS

The permitted limit of error on proving tanks shall be 0.02 per cent. of the nominal capacity.

GRADUATED MEASURING CYLINDERS

Nominal Capacity Metric	Limit of error
5 ml	0.2 ml
10 ml	0.2 ml
25 ml	0.25 ml
50 ml	0.5 ml
100 ml	0.8 ml
250 ml	1.5 ml
500 ml	2.0 ml
1000 ml	4.0 ml
2000 ml	8.0 ml
Imperial	
¼ gal	4.0 ml
½ gal	8.0 ml

SCHEDULE 2   Regulations 14 and 15

DISPLACEMENT PLUNGERS

Nominal volume	Limit of error
not exceeding 2 ml	0.1 ml
over 2 ml but not exceeding 25 ml	0.2 ml
over 25 ml but not exceeding 50 ml	0.3 ml
over 50 ml but not exceeding 100 ml	0.4 ml
over 100 ml but not exceeding 125 ml	0.5 ml
over 125 ml but not exceeding 150 ml	0.6 ml
over 150 ml but not exceeding 175 ml	0.7 ml
over 175 ml but not exceeding 250 ml	0.8 ml
over 250 ml but not exceeding 500 ml	1.0 ml

Regulation 16　　　　　　　SCHEDULE 3

LOCAL STANDARD CAPACITY MEASURES

(a) Imperial		(b) Metric	
Local Standard of—	Limit of Error	Local Standard of—	Limit of Error
⅙, ⅕ or ¼ gill	0.12 ml	1 or 2 ml	0.04 ml
⅓ gill	0.15 ml	5 ml	0.06 ml
⅖ or ½ gill	0.20 ml	10 ml	0.08 ml
4 fl oz	0.25 ml	20 or 25 ml	0.12 ml
1 gill	0.30 ml	50 ml	0.15 ml
6 fl oz	0.35 ml	100 ml	0.20 ml
⅓ pt, 8 fl oz or ½ pt	0.4 ml	125 ml	0.25 ml
1 pt	0.5 ml	150 ml	0.30 ml
1 quart or ½ gal	1.0 ml	175 ml	0.35 ml
1 gal	2.5 ml	200 or 250 ml	0.4 ml
more than 1 gal	0.02 per cent. of the nominal capacity	500 ml	0.5 ml
		1 l or 2 l	1.0 ml
		2.5 l	1.2 ml
		5 l	2.5 ml
		10 l	5 ml
		more than 10 l	0.02 per cent. of the nominal capacity

EXPLANATORY NOTE

(This note is not part of the Regulations)

These Regulations replace the Weights and Measures (Local Standards: Limits of Error) Regulations 1970, the Working Standards and Testing Equipment (Testing and Adjustment) Regulations 1970, the Weights and Measures (Local Standards: Periods of Validity) Regulations 1979, the Working Standards and Testing Equipment (Testing and Adjustment) (Amendment) Regulations 1979 and the Weights and Measures (Local and Working Standard Capacity Measures) Regulations 1983 insofar as they relate to local and working standard capacity measures and related testing equipment.

They prescribe the methods of testing and adjusting, and the limits of error for, working standard capacity measures and testing equipment used for measuring by inspectors of weights and measures. They also make provision for limits of error for local standard capacity measures and for the periods of validity of certificates of fitness of these local standards.

The Regulations make the following changes of substance:

(a) working standard capacity measures used for measuring need only be tested within one year before use in the case of glass measures, six months in the case of metal measures of 50 litres, 10 gallons or less, and two years in the case of metal measures exceeding 50 litres or 10 gallons (previously at intervals of not more than six months) (Regulation 4);

(b) the prescribed limits of error for working standards consisting of graduated measuring cylinders have been relaxed (Regulation 15(2)); and

(c) limits of error are now prescribed for a wider range of displacement plungers up to 500 ml (previously there were errors for ¼, ⅜, ½ or 1 fluid ounce only) (Schedule 2).

Copies of British Standards (see Regulation 3(1)) can be obtained from any of the sales outlets operated by the British Standards Institution (BSI) or by post from the BSI at Linford Wood, Milton Keynes, MK14 6LE.

1987 No. 52

HEALTH AND SAFETY

The Health and Safety (Explosives and Petroleum Fees) (Modification) Regulations 1987

Made - - - -	*22nd January 1987*
Laid before Parliament	*30th January 1987*
Coming into force	*20th February 1987*

The Secretary of State, in exercise of the powers conferred on him by sections 15(1) and (3)(a), 43(2), (4), (5), (6) and (9), and 82(3)(a) of the Health and Safety at Work etc. Act 1974 **(a)** ("the 1974 Act") and of all other powers enabling him in that behalf and for the purpose of giving effect without modifications to proposals submitted to him by the Health and Safety Commission under section 11(2)(d) of the 1974 Act after the carrying out by the said Commission of consultations in accordance with section 50(3) of that Act, hereby makes the following Regulations:-

Citation and commencement

1. These Regulations may be cited as the Health and Safety (Explosives and Petroleum Fees) (Modification) Regulations 1987 and shall come into force on 20th February 1987.

Modification and repeal of statutory provisions

2. The provisions specified in column 1 of Schedule 1 to these Regulations (which relate to fees payable in respect of the matters described in the corresponding entry in column 2 of the Schedule) are hereby modified or repealed, as the case may be, to the extent specified in the corresponding entry in column 3 of that Schedule.

Prescribed fees and maximum fees

3.—(1) Where any application in relation to a provision specified in column 1 of Part I of Schedule 2 to these Regulations is made for a purpose specified in column 2 of that Part, the fee specified in the corresponding entry in column 3 of that Part shall be payable by the applicant to the Health and Safety Executive.

(2) The fee or maximum fee payable under each provision in column 1 of Part II of Schedule 2 to these Regulations for a purpose described in the corresponding entry in column 2 of that Part shall be that specified in the corresponding entry in column 3 of that Part.

(a) 1974 c.37; sections 15(1) and 43(6) were substituted respectively by paragraphs 6 and 12 of Schedule 15 to the Employment Protection Act 1975 (c.71).

Date from which licence etc. takes effect to determine whether old or new fees apply

4. Notwithstanding the provisions of section 4 of the Petroleum (Consolidation) Act 1928 **(a)** or section 1(4) of the Petroleum (Transfer of Licences) Act 1936 **(b)** the fees for petroleum licences substituted by these Regulations shall be payable for any licence first having effect or any transfer or renewal of a licence taking effect on or after 20th February 1987, irrespective of the date of the application for that licence, transfer or renewal.

Revocations

5. The instruments specified in column 1 of Schedule 3 to these Regulations are hereby revoked to the extent specified in the corresponding entry in column 3 of that Schedule.

Northern Ireland

6. These Regulations shall not apply to Northern Ireland.

Signed by order of the Secretary of State
22nd January 1987

David Trippier
**Parliamentary Under Secretary of State,
Department of Employment**

SCHEDULE 1

Regulation 2

LEGISLATION MODIFIED OR REPEALED

(1) *Statutory provisions modified or repealed*	(2) *Matter to which provision in column 1 relates*	(3) *Extent of modification or repeal*
Explosives Act 1875 c.17.		
Section 15 (relevant amending instrument is S.I. 1985/1108)	Grant of an explosives store licence	For "£36", substitute "that from time to time fixed by or determined under regulations made in accordance with section 43(2) of the Health and Safety at Work etc. Act 1974".
Section 18 (relevant amending instrument is S.I. 1985/1108)	Renewal of an explosives store licence	For "£36", substitute "that from time to time fixed by or determined under regulations made in accordance with section 43(2) of the Health and Safety at Work etc. Act 1974".

(a) 1928 c.32.   **(b)** 1936 c.27.

SCHEDULE 1 - *continued*

(1) *Statutory provisions modified or repealed*	(2) *Matter to which provision in column 1 relates*	(3) *Extent of modification or repeal*
Section 21 (relevant amending instrument is S.I. 1985/1108)	Registration and renewal of registration of premises used for keeping of explosives	In the first place where it occurs, for "£6" substitute "that from time to time fixed by or determined under regulations made in accordance with section 43(2) of the Health and Safety at Work etc. Act 1974" and, in the second place where it occurs, for "£6" substitute "that from time to time fixed by or determined under those regulations.".
Section 26 (relevant amending instruments are S.I. 1974/1885 and S.I. 1983/1450)	Fees for licences	For "the maximum fee which such authority are authorised to fix" substitute "that from time to time fixed by or determined under regulations made in accordance with section 43(2) of the Health and Safety at Work etc. Act 1974".

Petroleum (Consolidation) Act 1928 c.32.

Section 4 (relevant amending instrument is S.I. 1974/1942)	Licence to keep petroleum-spirit	For "shown in the scale set out in the First Schedule to this Act or such lower scale as the Secretary of State may, with the consent of the Treasury, prescribe by regulations" substitute "fixed by or determined under regulations made in accordance with section 43(2) of the Health and Safety at Work etc. Act 1974".
Schedule 1 (relevant amending instrument is S.I. 1983/1640)	Rate of fees payable in respect of licences to keep petroleum-spirit.	Repeal the whole schedule.

Petroleum (Transfer of Licences) Act 1936 c.27.

Section 1(4) (relevant amending instruments are S.I. 1974/1942 and S.I. 1983/1640)	Transfer of petroleum-spirit licence	For "a fee of £4" substitute "the fee from time to time fixed by or determined under regulations made in accordance with section 43(2) of the Health and Safety at Work etc. Act 1974".

SCHEDULE 2

Regulation 3

FEE

PART 1

(1) *Provision under which a licence is granted*	(2) *Purpose of application*	(3) *Fee*
Explosives Act 1875 c.17.		
Section 6 (as applied to explosives other than gunpowder by sections 39 and 40)	Factory licence	£470; plus £26 additional fee for each building or other place in which explosives are to be made or kept.
	Factory amending licence	£85; plus £6 additional fee for each building or other place to be specified in the amending licence and in which explosives are to be made or kept.
	Replacement of one of the above licences if lost	£12.50.
Section 12 (as applied to explosives other than gunpowder by sections 39 and 40)	Magazine licence	£345; plus £26 additional fee for each building or other place in which explosives are to be kept.
	Magazine amending licence	£31; plus £6 additional fee for each building or other place to be specified in the amending licence and in which explosives are to be kept.
	Replacement of one of the above licences if lost	£12.50.
Section 40(9)	Licence for importation of explosives	£26.50.
	Licence for importation of a consignment of explosives which are not to be distributed in Great Britain but imported for transhipment only	£26.50.
	Replacement of one of the above licences if lost	£13.
	The issue of a new licence replacing the original and incorporating an amendment	£9.

Regulation 3   PART II

                                    FEE OR MAXIMUM FEE

(1) *Provision under which a fee or maximum fee is payable*	(2) *Purpose of application*	(3) *Fee or Maximum fee*
Explosives Act 1875 c.17.		
Section 15 (see note 1)	A store licence	£36.
Section 18 (see note 1)	Renewal of a store licence	£36.
Section 21 (see note 1)	Registration and renewal of registration of premises for the keeping of explosives with a local authority	£6.
Petroleum (Consolidation) Act 1928 c.32.		
Section 4 (see notes 2 and 3)	Licence to keep petroleum spirit of a quantity – not exceeding 2,500 litres	£20 for each year of licence.
	exceeding 2,500 litres, but not exceeding 50,000 litres	£30 for each year of licence.
	exceeding 50,000 litres	£59 for each year of licence.
Petroleum (Transfer of Licences) Act 1936 c.27.		
Section 1(4)	Transfer of petroleum spirit licence	£5.

Note:

(1)   Part 1 of the Explosives Act 1875 (which includes sections 15, 18 and 21) is applied to explosives other than gunpowder by sections 39 and 40 of that Act.

(2)   In the case of a solid substance for which by virtue of an Order in Council made under section 19 of the Petroleum (Consolidation) Act 1928 a licence is required, the fee payable under this Schedule shall be calculated as if one kilogram of the substance were equivalent to one litre.

(3)   The fee payable for a licence of more or less than one year's duration shall be the fee set out above increased or decreased, as the case may be, proportionately according to the duration of the period for which the licence is granted or renewed.

SCHEDULE 3   Regulation 5
REVOCATIONS

(1) *Instrument revoked*	(2) *Reference*	(3) *Extent of revocation*
The Explosives (Fees for Importation) Order 1958	S.I. 1958/136	The whole instrument in so far as it applies to Great Britain.
The Explosives and Related Matters (Fees) Regulations 1983	S.I. 1983/1450	The whole instrument.
The Petroleum (Regulation) Acts 1928 and 1936 (Fees) Regulations 1983	S.I. 1983/1640	The whole instrument.
The Explosives (Licensing of Stores and Registration of Premises) Fees Regulations 1985	S.I. 1985/1108	The whole instrument.

EXPLANATORY NOTE

(This note is not part of the Regulations)

1.   The Regulations supersede and revoke the Regulations listed in Schedule 3 to the extent specified in column 3 of that Schedule. They fix or determine the fees or maximum fees payable in respect of an application for –

    (a) a licence (and an amending licence) of a factory for explosives;

    (b) a licence (and an amending licence) of a magazine for explosives;

    (c) licences (and amending licences) for importation and transhipment of explosives;

    (d) replacement of one of the above-mentioned licences;

    (e) an explosives store licence or renewal of an explosives store licence;

    (f) registration or renewal of registration of premises for the keeping of explosives;

    (g) licence to keep a quantity of petroleum spirit;

    (h) **transfer of a petroleum spirit licence.**

(Regulation 3 and Schedule 2)

In the case of amendment or replacement of an import or transhipment licence the fee is fixed for the first time.

2.   The Regulations modify and repeal provisions in the Explosives Act 1875, the Petroleum (Consolidation) Act 1928 and the Petroleum (Transfer of Licences) Act 1936 (Regulation 2 and Schedule 1).

3. Regulation 3 and Schedule 2 to these Regulations change the fees previously fixed as follows:-

(a) *Explosives*

(1) Item	(2) Previous fee	(3) New fee
Factory licence (each building)	£25	£26
Magazine licence (each building)	£25	£26
Factory amending licence	£29	£85
Magazine amending licence	£29	£31
Replacement of licences above	£12	£12.50
Amendment of Import/Transhipment licence	£ 0	£ 9
Replacement of Import/Transhipment licence	£ 0	£13

(b) *Petroleum Spirit*

(1) Item	(2) Previous fee	(3) New fee
A licence to keep a quantity –		
not exceeding 2500 litres	£17 per annum	£20 per annum
exceeding 2500 litres, not exceeding 50,000 litres	£26 per annum	£30 per annum
exceeding 50,000 litres	£51 per annum	£59 per annum
Transfer of a licence	£4 each	£5 each

4. The Regulations do not apply to Northern Ireland (Regulation 6).

STATUTORY INSTRUMENTS

1987 No. 53

OFFSHORE INSTALLATIONS

The Offshore Installations (Safety Zones) (Revocation) Order 1987

Made - - -	*22nd January 1987*
Coming into force	*24th January 1987*

The Secretary of State, in exercise of the power conferred on him by section 21(1) of the Oil and Gas (Enterprise) Act 1982(**a**), and of all other powers enabling him in that behalf, hereby makes the following Order:—

1. This Order may be cited as the Offshore Installations (Safety Zones) (Revocation) Order 1987 and shall come into force on 24th January 1987.

2. The Offshore Installations (Safety Zones) Orders specified in the Schedule hereto are hereby revoked.

Alick Buchanan-Smith
Minister of State,
Department of Energy

22nd January 1987

(**a**) 1982 c.23.

Article 2   SCHEDULE

OFFSHORE INSTALLATIONS (SAFETY ZONES) ORDERS REVOKED

Order	Reference	Name of installation to which Order relates
The Offshore Installations (Safety Zones) (No. 103) Order 1986	S.I. 1986/1842	Penrod 92
The Offshore Installations (Safety Zones) (No. 102) Order 1986	S.I. 1986/1841	Pentagone 84
The Offshore Installations (Safety Zones) (No. 100) Order 1984	S.I. 1984/2011	Transworld 58

EXPLANATORY NOTE
(*This note is not part of the Order*)

This Order revokes the Offshore Installations (Safety Zones) Orders specified in the Schedule. The installations specified in the Schedule which were protected by the safety zones established by those Orders have been removed and accordingly those Orders are no longer required.

STATUTORY INSTRUMENTS

1987 No. 54

OFFSHORE INSTALLATIONS

The Offshore Installations (Safety Zones) Order 1987

Made - - -	*22nd January 1987*	
Coming into force -	*24th January 1987*	

The Secretary of State, in exercise of the powers conferred on him by section 21(1), (2) and (3) of the Oil and Gas (Enterprise) Act 1982(**a**) (hereinafter referred to as "the Act"), and of all other powers enabling him in that behalf, hereby makes the following Order:—

1. This Order may be cited as the Offshore Installations (Safety Zones) Order 1987 and shall come into force on 24th January 1987.

2.—(1) A safety zone is hereby established around the installation specified in Column 1 of the Schedule hereto (being an installation maintained in waters to which section 21 of the Act(**b**) applies) having a radius of five hundred metres from the point as respects that installation which has the co-ordinates of latitude and longitude according to European Datum (1950) specified in Columns 2 and 3 of the Schedule.

(2) The prohibition under section 21(3) of the Act on a vessel entering or remaining in a safety zone without the consent of the Secretary of State shall not apply to a vessel entering or remaining in the safety zone established under paragraph (1) above —

(*a*) in connection with the laying, inspection, testing, repair, alteration, renewal or removal of any submarine cable or pipe-line in or near that safety zone;

(*b*) to provide services for, to transport persons or goods to or from, or under the authority of a government department to inspect, any installation in that safety zone;

(*c*) if it is a vessel belonging to a general lighthouse authority performing duties relating to the safety of navigation;

(*d*) in connection with the saving or attempted saving of life or property;

(*e*) owing to stress of weather; or

(*f*) when in distress.

Alick Buchanan-Smith
Minister of State,
Department of Energy

22nd January 1987

(**a**) 1982 c.23.   (**b**) *See* section 21(9).

Article 2(1)   SCHEDULE

SAFETY ZONE

1	2	3
Name or other designation of the offshore installation	Latitude North	Longitude East
Well 16/21a–7z	58° 14′ 41·80″	01° 06′ 17·94″

EXPLANATORY NOTE

(*This note is not part of the Order*)

This Order establishes, under section 21 of the Oil and Gas (Enterprise) Act 1982, a safety zone, having a radius of 500 metres from a specified point, around the installation specified in the Schedule to this Order and maintained in waters to which the section applies (these include territorial waters and waters in areas designated under section 1(7) of the Continental Shelf Act 1964 (c.29)).

Vessels (which for this purpose include hovercraft, submersible apparatus and installations in transit) are prohibited from entering or remaining in the safety zone except with the consent of the Secretary of State or in the circumstances mentioned in Article 2(2) of the Order.

STATUTORY INSTRUMENTS

1987 No. 55

OFFSHORE INSTALLATIONS

The Offshore Installations (Safety Zones) (No. 2) Order 1987

Made - - -	*22nd January 1987*
Coming into force -	*24th January 1987*

The Secretary of State, in exercise of the powers conferred on him by section 21(1), (2) and (3) of the Oil and Gas (Enterprise) Act 1982(**a**) (hereinafter referred to as "the Act"), and of all other powers enabling him in that behalf, hereby makes the following Order:—

1. This Order may be cited as the Offshore Installations (Safety Zones) (No. 2) Order 1987 and shall come into force on 24th January 1987.

2.—(1) A safety zone is hereby established around the installation specified in Column 1 of the Schedule hereto (being an installation maintained in waters to which section 21 of the Act(**b**) applies) having a radius of five hundred metres from the point as respects that installation which has the co-ordinates of latitude and longitude according to European Datum (1950) specified in Columns 2 and 3 of the Schedule.

(2) The prohibition under section 21(3) of the Act on a vessel entering or remaining in a safety zone without the consent of the Secretary of State shall not apply to a vessel entering or remaining in the safety zone established under paragraph (1) above —

(*a*) in connection with the laying, inspection, testing, repair, alteration, renewal or removal of any submarine cable or pipe-line in or near that safety zone;

(*b*) to provide services for, to transport persons or goods to or from, or under the authority of a government department to inspect, any installation in that safety zone;

(*c*) if it is a vessel belonging to a general lighthouse authority performing duties relating to the safety of navigation;

(*d*) in connection with the saving or attempted saving of life or property;

(*e*) owing to stress of weather; or

(*f*) when in distress.

Alick Buchanan-Smith
Minister of State,
Department of Energy

22nd January 1987

(**a**) 1982 c.23.   (**b**) *See* section 21(9).

Article 2(1)

SCHEDULE

Safety Zone

1	2	3
Name or other designation of the offshore installation	Latitude North	Longitude East
Well 16/21a–16	58° 13′ 42·66″	01° 08′ 57·88″

EXPLANATORY NOTE

(This note is not part of the Order)

This Order establishes, under section 21 of the Oil and Gas (Enterprise) Act 1982, a safety zone, having a radius of 500 metres from a specified point, around the installation specified in the Schedule to this Order and maintained in waters to which the section applies (these include territorial waters and waters in areas designated under section 1(7) of the Continental Shelf Act 1964 (c.29)).

Vessels (which for this purpose include hovercraft, submersible apparatus and installations in transit) are prohibited from entering or remaining in the safety zone except with the consent of the Secretary of State or in the circumstances mentioned in Article 2(2) of the Order.

STATUTORY INSTRUMENTS

1987 No. 56

OFFSHORE INSTALLATIONS

The Offshore Installations (Safety Zones) (No. 3) Order 1987

Made - - -	*22nd January 1987*
Coming into force -	*24th January 1987*

The Secretary of State, in exercise of the powers conferred on him by section 21(1), (2) and (3) of the Oil and Gas (Enterprise) Act 1982(**a**) (hereinafter referred to as "the Act"), and of all other powers enabling him in that behalf, hereby makes the following Order:—

1. This Order may be cited as the Offshore Installations (Safety Zones) (No. 3) Order 1987 and shall come into force on 24th January 1987.

2.—(1) A safety zone is hereby established around the installation specified in Column 1 of the Schedule hereto (being an installation maintained in waters to which section 21 of the Act(**b**) applies) having a radius of five hundred metres from the point as respects that installation which has the co-ordinates of latitude and longitude according to European Datum (1950) specified in Columns 2 and 3 of the Schedule.

(2) The prohibition under section 21(3) of the Act on a vessel entering or remaining in a safety zone without the consent of the Secretary of State shall not apply to a vessel entering or remaining in the safety zone established under paragraph (1) above —

(*a*) in connection with the laying, inspection, testing, repair, alteration, renewal or removal of any submarine cable or pipe-line in or near that safety zone;

(*b*) to provide services for, to transport persons or goods to or from, or under the authority of a government department to inspect, any installation in that safety zone;

(*c*) if it is a vessel belonging to a general lighthouse authority performing duties relating to the safety of navigation;

(*d*) in connection with the saving or attempted saving of life or property;

(*e*) owing to stress of weather; or

(*f*) when in distress.

Alick Buchanan-Smith
Minister of State,
Department of Energy

22nd January 1987

(**a**) 1982 c.23.   (**b**) *See* section 21(9).

Article 2(1)   SCHEDULE

SAFETY ZONE

1	2	3
Name or other designation of the offshore installation	Latitude North	Longitude East
Well 16/21b–4A	58° 12′ 39·97″	01° 10′ 34·00″

EXPLANATORY NOTE

(This note is not part of the Order)

This Order establishes, under section 21 of the Oil and Gas (Enterprise) Act 1982, a safety zone, having a radius of 500 metres from a specified point, around the installation specified in the Schedule to this Order and maintained in waters to which the section applies (these include territorial waters and waters in areas designated under section 1(7) of the Continental Shelf Act 1964 (c.29)).

Vessels (which for this purpose include hovercraft, submersible apparatus and installations in transit) are prohibited from entering or remaining in the safety zone except with the consent of the Secretary of State or in the circumstances mentioned in Article 2(2) of the Order.

STATUTORY INSTRUMENTS

1987 No. 57

OFFSHORE INSTALLATIONS

The Offshore Installations (Safety Zones) (No. 4) Order 1987

Made	- - -	*22nd January 1987*	
Coming into force -		*24th January 1987*	

The Secretary of State, in exercise of the powers conferred on him by section 21(1), (2) and (3) of the Oil and Gas (Enterprise) Act 1982(**a**) (hereinafter referred to as "the Act"), and of all other powers enabling him in that behalf, hereby makes the following Order:—

1. This Order may be cited as the Offshore Installations (Safety Zones) (No. 4) Order 1987 and shall come into force on 24th January 1987.

2.—(1) A safety zone is hereby established around the installation specified in Column 1 of the Schedule hereto (being an installation maintained in waters to which section 21 of the Act(**b**) applies) having a radius of five hundred metres from the point as respects that installation which has the co-ordinates of latitude and longitude according to European Datum (1950) specified in Columns 2 and 3 of the Schedule.

(2) The prohibition under section 21(3) of the Act on a vessel entering or remaining in a safety zone without the consent of the Secretary of State shall not apply to a vessel entering or remaining in the safety zone established under paragraph (1) above —

(*a*) in connection with the laying, inspection, testing, repair, alteration, renewal or removal of any submarine cable or pipe-line in or near that safety zone;

(*b*) to provide services for, to transport persons or goods to or from, or under the authority of a government department to inspect, any installation in that safety zone;

(*c*) if it is a vessel belonging to a general lighthouse authority performing duties relating to the safety of navigation;

(*d*) in connection with the saving or attempted saving of life or property;

(*e*) owing to stress of weather; or

(*f*) when in distress.

Alick Buchanan-Smith
Minister of State,
Department of Energy

22nd January 1987

(**a**) 1982 c.23.   (**b**) *See* section 21(9).

Article 2(1)   SCHEDULE

SAFETY ZONE

1	2	3
Name or other designation of the offshore installation	Latitude North	Longitude East
Well 16/21b–12	58° 15′ 09·71″	01° 03′ 25·45″

EXPLANATORY NOTE

(This note is not part of the Order)

This Order establishes, under section 21 of the Oil and Gas (Enterprise) Act 1982, a safety zone, having a radius of 500 metres from a specified point, around the installation specified in the Schedule to this Order and maintained in waters to which the section applies (these include territorial waters and waters in areas designated under section 1(7) of the Continental Shelf Act 1964 (c.29)).

Vessels (which for this purpose include hovercraft, submersible apparatus and installations in transit) are prohibited from entering or remaining in the safety zone except with the consent of the Secretary of State or in the circumstances mentioned in Article 2(2) of the Order.

STATUTORY INSTRUMENTS

1987 No. 58

OFFSHORE INSTALLATIONS

The Offshore Installations (Safety Zones) (No. 5) Order 1987

Made   -   -   -   *22nd January 1987*

Coming into force -   *24th January 1987*

The Secretary of State, in exercise of the powers conferred on him by section 21(1), (2) and (3) of the Oil and Gas (Enterprise) Act 1982(**a**) (hereinafter referred to as "the Act"), and of all other powers enabling him in that behalf, hereby makes the following Order:—

1. This Order may be cited as the Offshore Installations (Safety Zones) (No. 5) Order 1987 and shall come into force on 24th January 1987.

2.—(1) A safety zone is hereby established around the installation specified in Column 1 of the Schedule hereto (being an installation maintained in waters to which section 21 of the Act(**b**) applies) having a radius of five hundred metres from the point as respects that installation which has the co-ordinates of latitude and longitude according to European Datum (1950) specified in Columns 2 and 3 of the Schedule.

(2) The prohibition under section 21(3) of the Act on a vessel entering or remaining in a safety zone without the consent of the Secretary of State shall not apply to a vessel entering or remaining in the safety zone established under paragraph (1) above —

(*a*) in connection with the laying, inspection, testing, repair, alteration, renewal or removal of any submarine cable or pipe-line in or near that safety zone;

(*b*) to provide services for, to transport persons or goods to or from, or under the authority of a government department to inspect, any installation in that safety zone;

(*c*) if it is a vessel belonging to a general lighthouse authority performing duties relating to the safety of navigation;

(*d*) in connection with the saving or attempted saving of life or property;

(*e*) owing to stress of weather; or

(*f*) when in distress.

Alick Buchanan-Smith
Minister of State,
Department of Energy

22nd January 1987

(**a**) 1982 c.23.   (**b**) *See* section 21(9).

Article 2(1)   SCHEDULE

SAFETY ZONE

1	2	3
Name or other designation of the offshore installation	Latitude North	Longitude East
Well 16/21b–14	58° 13′ 36·41″	01° 03′ 39·29″

EXPLANATORY NOTE

(*This note is not part of the Order*)

This Order establishes, under section 21 of the Oil and Gas (Enterprise) Act 1982, a safety zone, having a radius of 500 metres from a specified point, around the installation specified in the Schedule to this Order and maintained in waters to which the section applies (these include territorial waters and waters in areas designated under section 1(7) of the Continental Shelf Act 1964 (c.29)).

Vessels (which for this purpose include hovercraft, submersible apparatus and installations in transit) are prohibited from entering or remaining in the safety zone except with the consent of the Secretary of State or in the circumstances mentioned in Article 2(2) of the Order.

STATUTORY INSTRUMENTS

1987 No. 59

OFFSHORE INSTALLATIONS

The Offshore Installations (Safety Zones) (No. 6) Order 1987

Made	-	-	-	22nd January 1987
Coming into force	-			24th January 1987

The Secretary of State, in exercise of the powers conferred on him by section 21(1), (2) and (3) of the Oil and Gas (Enterprise) Act 1982(**a**) (hereinafter referred to as "the Act"), and of all other powers enabling him in that behalf, hereby makes the following Order:—

1. This Order may be cited as the Offshore Installations (Safety Zones) (No. 6) Order 1987 and shall come into force on 24th January 1987.

2.—(1) A safety zone is hereby established around the installation specified in Column 1 of the Schedule hereto (being an installation maintained in waters to which section 21 of the Act(**b**) applies) having a radius of five hundred metres from the point as respects that installation which has the co-ordinates of latitude and longitude according to European Datum (1950) specified in Columns 2 and 3 of the Schedule.

(2) The prohibition under section 21(3) of the Act on a vessel entering or remaining in a safety zone without the consent of the Secretary of State shall not apply to a vessel entering or remaining in the safety zone established under paragraph (1) above —

(*a*) in connection with the laying, inspection, testing, repair, alteration, renewal or removal of any submarine cable or pipe-line in or near that safety zone;

(*b*) to provide services for, to transport persons or goods to or from, or under the authority of a government department to inspect, any installation in that safety zone;

(*c*) if it is a vessel belonging to a general lighthouse authority performing duties relating to the safety of navigation;

(*d*) in connection with the saving or attempted saving of life or property;

(*e*) owing to stress of weather; or

(*f*) when in distress.

Alick Buchanan-Smith
Minister of State,
Department of Energy

22nd January 1987

(**a**) 1982 c.23.   (**b**) *See* section 21(9).

Article 2(1)   SCHEDULE

                                      SAFETY ZONE

1	2	3
Name or other designation of the offshore installation	Latitude North	Longitude East
Balmoral Template	58° 13′ 45·70″	01° 06′ 31·22″

EXPLANATORY NOTE

(This note is not part of the Order)

This Order establishes, under section 21 of the Oil and Gas (Enterprise) Act 1982, a safety zone, having a radius of 500 metres from a specified point, around the installation specified in the Schedule to this Order and maintained in waters to which the section applies (these include territorial waters and waters in areas designated under section 1(7) of the Continental Shelf Act 1964 (c.29)).

Vessels (which for this purpose include hovercraft, submersible apparatus and installations in transit) are prohibited from entering or remaining in the safety zone except with the consent of the Secretary of State or in the circumstances mentioned in Article 2(2) of the Order.

STATUTORY INSTRUMENTS

1987 No. 61

OFFSHORE INSTALLATIONS

The Offshore Installations (Safety Zones) (No. 7) Order 1987

Made - - -		*22nd January 1987*
Coming into force -		*24th January 1987*

The Secretary of State, in exercise of the powers conferred on him by section 21(1), (2) and (3) of the Oil and Gas (Enterprise) Act 1982(**a**) (hereinafter referred to as "the Act"), and of all other powers enabling him in that behalf, hereby makes the following Order:—

1. This Order may be cited as the Offshore Installations (Safety Zones) (No. 7) Order 1987 and shall come into force on 24th January 1987.

2.—(1) A safety zone is hereby established around the installation specified in Column 1 of the Schedule hereto (being an installation maintained in waters to which section 21 of the Act(**b**) applies) having a radius of five hundred metres from the point as respects that installation which has the co-ordinates of latitude and longitude according to European Datum (1950) specified in Columns 2 and 3 of the Schedule.

(2) The prohibition under section 21(3) of the Act on a vessel entering or remaining in a safety zone without the consent of the Secretary of State shall not apply to a vessel entering or remaining in the safety zone established under paragraph (1) above —

(*a*) in connection with the laying, inspection, testing, repair, alteration, renewal or removal of any submarine cable or pipe-line in or near that safety zone;

(*b*) to provide services for, to transport persons or goods to or from, or under the authority of a government department to inspect, any installation in that safety zone;

(*c*) if it is a vessel belonging to a general lighthouse authority performing duties relating to the safety of navigation;

(*d*) in connection with the saving or attempted saving of life or property;

(*e*) owing to stress of weather; or

(*f*) when in distress.

Alick Buchanan-Smith
Minister of State,
Department of Energy

22nd January 1987

(**a**) 1982 c.23.   (**b**) *See* section 21(9).

Article 2(1)

SCHEDULE

Safety Zone

1	2	3
Name or other designation of the offshore installation	Latitude North	Longitude East
Indefatigable 49/24 N	53° 17′ 20·28″	02° 43′ 22·34″

EXPLANATORY NOTE

(This note is not part of the Order)

This Order establishes, under section 21 of the Oil and Gas (Enterprise) Act 1982, a safety zone, having a radius of 500 metres from a specified point, around the installation specified in the Schedule to this Order and maintained in waters to which the section applies (these include territorial waters and waters in areas designated under section 1(7) of the Continental Shelf Act 1964 (c.29)).

Vessels (which for this purpose include hovercraft, submersible apparatus and installations in transit) are prohibited from entering or remaining in the safety zone except with the consent of the Secretary of State or in the circumstances mentioned in Article 2(2) of the Order.

STATUTORY INSTRUMENTS

1987 No. 62

OFFSHORE INSTALLATIONS

The Offshore Installations (Safety Zones) (No. 8) October 1987

Made	- - -	*22nd January 1987*
Coming into force	-	*24th January 1987*

The Secretary of State, in exercise of the powers conferred on him by section 21(1), (2) and (3) of the Oil and Gas (Enterprise) Act 1982(**a**) (hereinafter referred to as "the Act"), and of all other powers enabling him in that behalf, hereby makes the following Order:—

1. This Order may be cited as the Offshore Installations (Safety Zones) (No. 8) Order 1987 and shall come into force on 24th January 1987.

2.—(1) A safety zone is hereby established around the installation specified in Column 1 of the Schedule hereto (being an installation maintained in waters to which section 21 of the Act(**b**) applies) having a radius of five hundred metres from the point as respects that installation which has the co-ordinates of latitude and longitude according to European Datum (1950) specified in Columns 2 and 3 of the Schedule.

(2) The prohibition under section 21(3) of the Act on a vessel entering or remaining in a safety zone without the consent of the Secretary of State shall not apply to a vessel entering or remaining in the safety zone established under paragraph (1) above —

(*a*) in connection with the laying, inspection, testing, repair, alteration, renewal or removal of any submarine cable or pipe-line in or near that safety zone;

(*b*) to provide services for, to transport persons or goods to or from, or under the authority of a government department to inspect, any installation in that safety zone;

(*c*) if it is a vessel belonging to a general lighthouse authority performing duties relating to the safety of navigation;

(*d*) in connection with the saving or attempted saving of life or property;

(*e*) owing to stress of weather; or

(*f*) when in distress.

Alick Buchanan-Smith
Minister of State,
Department of Energy

22nd January 1987

(**a**) 1982 c.23.   (**b**) *See* section 21(9).

Article 2(1)   SCHEDULE

SAFETY ZONE

1	2	3
Name or other designation of the offshore installation	Latitude North	Longitude East
Well 30/24–24	56° 16′ 05·14″	02° 39′ 49·04″

EXPLANATORY NOTE

(This note is not part of the Order)

This Order establishes, under section 21 of the Oil and Gas (Enterprise) Act 1982, a safety zone, having a radius of 500 metres from a specified point, around the installation specified in the Schedule to this Order and maintained in waters to which the section applies (these include territorial waters and waters in areas designated under section 1(7) of the Continental Shelf Act 1964 (c.29)).

Vessels (which for this purpose include hovercraft, submersible apparatus and installations in transit) are prohibited from entering or remaining in the safety zone except with the consent of the Secretary of State or in the circumstances mentioned in Article 2(2) of the Order.

STATUTORY INSTRUMENTS

1987 No. 63

MERCHANT SHIPPING
MARINE POLLUTION

The Merchant Shipping (Fees) Regulations 1987

Made - - - -	*22nd January 1987*
Laid before Parliament	*30th January 1987*
Coming into force	*1st February 1987*

The Secretary of State, in exercise of the powers conferred by:—
  (i) section 5(3) of the Merchant Shipping Act 1948**(a)**,
  (ii) section 33 of the Merchant Shipping (Safety Convention) Act 1949**(b)**,
  (iii) section 26 of the Merchant Shipping (Load Lines) Act 1967**(c)**,
  (iv) section 6 of the Fishing Vessels (Safety Provisions) Act 1970**(d)**,
  (v) section 84 of the Merchant Shipping Act 1970**(e)**,
  (vi) section 17 of and Schedule 5 to the Merchant Shipping Act 1974**(f)**,
  (vii) section 21(1) and (3)(r) of the Merchant Shipping Act 1979**(g)**,
  (viii) section 5(1) and (8) of, and paragraph 2(j) of the Schedule to the Merchant Shipping Act 1983**(h)**,
  (ix) article 3(1)(a) of the Merchant Shipping (Prevention of Oil Pollution) Order 1983**(i)**
and now vested in him**(j)** and of all other powers enabling him in that behalf, and with the consent and approval of the Treasury (except in respect of the powers conferred by the Acts of 1948 and 1974) hereby makes the following Regulation:—

1. These Regulations may be cited as the Merchant Shipping (Fees) Regulations 1987 and shall come into force on 1st February 1987.

2.—(1) In these Regulations:
    "the Act of 1948" means the Merchant Shipping Act 1948;
    "the Act of 1949" means the Merchant Shipping (Safety Convention) Act 1949;
    "the Act of 1967" means the Merchant Shipping (Load Lines) Act 1967;
    "the Act of 1970" means the Merchant Shipping Act 1970;
    "the Act of 1979" means the Merchant Shipping Act 1979;

(a) 1948 c.44.
(b) 1949 c.43; section 33 was extended by section 2(4) of the Merchant Shipping Act 1964 (c.47), which was amended by S.I. 1980/539.
(c) 1967 c.27.
(d) 1970 c.27.
(e) 1970 c.36.
(f) 1974 c.43.
(g) 1979 c.39.
(h) 1983 c.13.
(i) S.I. 1983/1106, to which there is an amendment not relevant to these Regulations.
(j) See S.I. 1970/1537.

"the principal Act" means the Merchant Shipping Act 1894(**a**); and

"tons" means gross tons and the gross tonnage of a ship having alternative gross tonnages shall be taken to the larger of those tonnages.

(2) Subject to regulation 3 below the following Regulations are hereby revoked:—

the Merchant Shipping (Fees) Regulations 1985(**b**);

the Merchant Shipping (Fees) (Amendment No. 2) Regulations 1985(**c**);

the Merchant Shipping (Fishing Vessels) (Radios) (Fees) Regulations 1986(**d**);

the Merchant Shipping (Fees) (Amendment No. 1) Regulations 1986(**e**).

3. Nothing in these Regulations shall apply to—

(a) any work involved in carrying out a service before these Regulations come into force; and

(b) any service started prior to 15th November 1985:

Provided that if the fee that would be chargeable under these Regulations if they applied would be less than the fee payable under or by virtue of the Regulations referred to in regulation 2(2) above then such lesser fee shall be payable.

4. Where a fee is determined by the amount of work involved on or off the ship:

(a) travelling time in excess of 4 hours for each visit to a ship in the United Kingdom shall be disregarded;

(b) travelling time includes the time taken to travel from the United Kingdom to a ship overseas subject to a maximum of 10 hours in any 24 hour period;

(c) (i) travelling time in the United Kingdom in respect of the survey of a fishing vessel under the Fishing Vessels (Safety Provisions) Rules 1975(**f**), and an inspection under the Merchant Shipping (Crew Accommodation) (Fishing Vessels) Regulations 1975(**g**) shall be disregarded;

(ii) time spent by a surveyor in the office in respect of the survey for the renewal of a fishing vessel certificate under the Fishing Vessels (Safety Provisions) Rules 1975, or an inspection under the Merchant Shipping (Crew Accommodation) (Fishing Vessels) Regulations 1975 shall in either case be charged for at a flat rate of £74.

(d) the cost of travelling and subsistence incurred in visiting a ship outside the United Kingdom shall be charged additionally to the hourly rate;

(e) where the work is carried out in conjunction with a non-statutory survey for which fees are not payable under these Regulations, the work involved shall be the extra time taken to ensure compliance with the requirements for which fees are charged under these Regulations;

(f) any specific costs incurred in respect of computer or outside services shall be charged additionally to the hourly rate.

5.— (1) The fees payable for the services specified in the Schedule to these Regulations shall be the fees specified in relation thereto in that Schedule.

(2) The fee in the case of a survey or periodical inspection for the issue, renewal or endorsement of a certificate shall cover the issue or endorsement of that certificate.

Signed by authority of
the Secretary of State
21st January 1987

Michael Spicer
Parliamentary Under Secretary of State,
Department of Transport

(**a**) 1894 c.60.
(**b**) S.I. 1985/1607.
(**c**) S.I. 1985/1727.
(**d**) S.I. 1986/680.
(**e**) S.I. 1986/837.
(**f**) S.I. 1975/330, amended by S.I. 1976/432, 1977/313, 1978/1598.
(**g**) S.I. 1975/2220.

We consent to and approve the making of these Regulations,

Tim Sainsbury
Tony Durant

22nd January 1987   Two of the Lords Commissioners of Her Majesty's Treasury

SCHEDULE   Regulation 5

PART I

SURVEYS, INSPECTIONS AND APPLICATIONS FOR EXEMPTION

1. In this Part of the Schedule "the statutory requirements" means any provision of the following:

(1) *Primary Legislation*

The principal Act, Parts III and V, the Act of 1948, the Act of 1949, the Act of 1967, the Act of 1970, and the Act of 1979, sections 20 and 21.

(2) *Statutory Instruments*

TITLE	S.I. Number	Amended by S.I.
A. CREW		
Merchant Shipping (Provisions and Water) Regulations 1972	1871	1975/733 1978/36
Merchant Shipping (Code of Safe Working Practices) Regulations 1980	686	
Merchant Shipping (Means of Access) Regulations 1981	1729	1983/117
Merchant Shipping (Health and Safety: General Duties) Regulations 1984	408	
B. CREW ACCOMMODATION		
Merchant Shipping (Crew Accommodation) Regulations 1978	795	1979/491
C. DANGEROUS GOODS		
Merchant Shipping (Dangerous Goods) Regulations 1981	1747	1986/1069
D. DIVING AND SUBMERSIBLES		
Merchant Shipping (Submersible Craft Construction and Survey) Regulations 1981	1098	
E. FIRE AND LIFE SAVING		
Merchant Shipping (Life-Saving Appliances) Regulations 1980	538	1981/577 1986/1072
Merchant Shipping (Fire Appliances) Regulations 1980	544	1981/574 1985/1194 1986/1070
Merchant Shipping (Musters) Regulations 1980	542	1981/578 1986/1071
Merchant Shipping (Fire Protection) Regulations 1984	1218	1985/1193 1986/1070

(2) *Statutory Instruments (continued)*

TITLE	S.I. Number	Amended by S.I.
Merchant Shipping (Fire Protection) (Ships built before 25th May 1980) Regulations 1985	1218	1986/1070
Merchant Shipping (Fire Protection) (Non-United Kingdom) (Non-SOLAS) Rules 1986	1248	
F. FISHING VESSELS		
Merchant Shipping (Provisions and Water) (Fishing Vessels) Regulations 1972	1872	1975/733
Merchant Shipping (Crew Accommodation) (Fishing Vessels) Regulations 1975	2220	
Fishing Vessels (Certification of Deck Officers and Engineer Officers) Regulations 1984	1115	
Fishing Vessels (Safety Provisions) Rules 1975	330	1976/432 1977/313 1978/1598
G. LOAD LINES		
Merchant Shipping (Load Lines) Rules 1968	1053	1970/1003 1979/1267 1980/641
Merchant Shipping (Load Lines) (Length of Ship) Regulations 1968	1072	
Merchant Shipping (Load Lines) (Deck Cargo) Regulations 1968	1089	
Merchant Shipping (Load Lines) (Exemption) Order 1968	1116	
Merchant Shipping (Load Lines) (Particulars of Depth of Loading) Regulations 1972	1841	
Merchant Shipping (Grain) Regulations 1985	1217	
H. MEDICAL STORES		
Merchant Shipping (Medical Stores) Regulations 1986	144	
I. RADIO AND NAVIGATIONAL EQUIPMENT		
Merchant Shipping (Radio Installations) Regulations 1980	529	1981/582 1984/346 1984/1223 1985/1216 1986/1075
Merchant Shipping (Navigational Equipment) Regulations 1980	530	1981/579 1984/1203
Merchant Shipping (Navigational Equipment) Regulations 1984	1203	1985/659
Merchant Shipping (Radio Installations Surveys) Regulations 1981	583	
Merchant Shipping (Radio) (Fishing Vessels) Rules 1974	1919	
J. SHIPS—CONSTRUCTION AND EQUIPMENT		
Anchors and Chain Cables Rules 1970	1453	
Merchant Shipping (Passenger Ship Construction) Regulations 1980	535	1984/1220 1985/660 1986/1074
Merchant Shipping (Closing of Openings in Hulls and Watertight Bulkheads) Regulations 1980	540	
Merchant Shipping (Pilot Ladders and Hoists) Regulations 1980	543	1981/581
Merchant Shipping (Automatic Pilot and Testing of Steering Gear) Regulations 1981	571	

(2) *Statutory Instruments (continued)*

TITLE	S.I. Number	Amended by S.I.
Merchant Shipping (Cargo Ship Construction and Survey) Regulations 1981	572	1984/1219 1985/663
Merchant Shipping (Application of Construction and Survey Regulations to other Ships) Regulations 1985	661	
Merchant Shipping (Cargo Ship Construction and Survey) Regulations 1984	1217	1986/1067
Merchant Shipping (Cargo Ship Safety Equipment Survey) Regulations 1981	573	1985/211
Merchant Shipping (Passenger Ship Classification) Regulations 1981	1472	
Merchant Shipping (Passenger Ship Construction and Survey) Regulations 1984	1216	1986/1074
K. OIL POLLUTION Merchant Shipping (Prevention of Oil Pollution) Regulations 1983	1398	1985/2040
Merchant Shipping (Reception Facilities) Order 1984	862	

2. Subject to any additional charge payable under Part X of this Schedule, the fees for the services in this Part of the Schedule shall be determined by the amount of work involved, charged at an hourly rate of £45.50, except in the case of any service in connection with:

(a) the Merchant Shipping (Provisions and Water) (Fishing Vessels) Regulations 1972 and the Merchant Shipping (Provision and Water) Regulations 1972, when the hourly rate shall be £30;

(b) the Fishing Vessels (Safety Provisions) Rules 1975 when the hourly rate shall be £37;

(c) the Merchant Shipping (Crew Accommodation) (Fishing Vessels) Regulations 1975 when the hourly rate shall be £37; and

(d) the Merchant Shipping (Radio Installations) Regulations 1980, the Merchant Shipping (Navigational Equipment) Regulations 1980, the Merchant Shipping (Radio Installations Surveys) Regulations 1981 and the Merchant Shipping (Radios) (Fishing Vessels) Rules 1984 when the hourly rate shall be £49.

3. Subject to paragraph 4 below, the services in this Part of this Schedule are:

(a) any survey or inspection of a ship or its equipment for the issue, amendment, endorsement or renewal of a certificate in accordance with or showing compliance with any of the statutory requirements;

(b) any other inspection of a ship or its equipment under section 76(1) of the Act of 1970, on the application of the owner for the purpose of seeing that the ship complies with any of the statutory requirements;

(c) any other inspection otherwise than on the application of the owner to ensure compliance with the statutory requirements where a previous inspection (whether or not the owner's application) has revealed a failure to comply with any of those requirements;

(d) any inspection or survey where the ship or any of its equipment subject to the statutory requirements has been damaged, changed or modified for the purpose of seeing that the ship complies with the statutory requirements after such damage, change or modification;

(e) any application for an exemption in accordance with the provisions of any of the statutory requirements;

(f) arranging the appointment of a surveyor not employed by the Department of Transport to undertake a survey or inspection outside the UK in accordance with the statutory requirements.

4. Where a fee is specified in or covered by another part of this Schedule for any survey, inspection or certificate in connection with any of the statutory requirements, the fee shall be payable in accordance with that Part and not this.

PART II

TONNAGE MEASUREMENT

Fees for Measurement of Ship's Tonnage

1. The fees prescribed in this Part include the survey and certification under section 6 and the inspection of markings under section 7(1) of the principal Act.

2. In this Part:—

"the Regulations" means the Merchant Shipping (Tonnage) Regulations 1982(a) and references to specific Regulations shall be construed accordingly;

"sister ship" means a ship which corresponds in all major respects relevant to the measurement for tonnage with a ship the tonnage of which has been previously ascertained under the Regulations, and for which the calculation for tonnage is available to the Certifying Authority to which, prior to the commencement of its measurement for tonnage, application has been made in writing by or on behalf of the owner of the ship requesting it to be treated as a sister ship.

3. The fee to be charged for the tonnage measurement of ships (not being a ship to which paragraph 4 below refers to) shall be that set out in the following Table:

Table A

A ship which exceeds (tons):	*A ship which does not exceed (tons):*	*Fee* £
	90	335
90	180	503
180	270	669
270	450	838
450	900	1,114
900	1,450	1,389
1,450	1,800	1,533
1,800	2,700	1,677
2,700	3,600	1,951
3,600	4,500	2,228
4,500	6,000	2,504
6,000	7,000	2,791
7,000	8,000	3,066
8,000	9,000	3,343
9,000	10,000	3,616
10,000	11,000	3,834
11,000	12,000	4,035
12,000	13,000	4,252
13,000	14,000	4,454
14,000	15,000	4,672
15,000	16,000	4,875
16,000	17,000	5,019
17,000	18,000	5,150
18,000	19,000	5,226
19,000	20,000	5,425
20,000	21,000	5,569
21,000	22,000	5,712
22,000	23,000	5,845
23,000	24,000	5,989
24,000	25,000	6,132
25.000	27,500	6,408
27,500	30,000	6,683
30,000	32.500	6,972
32,500	35,000	7,243
35,000	40,000	7,797
40,000	45,000	8,361
45,000	50,000	9,056
50,000	55,000	9,750
55,000	60,000	10,445
60,000		11,141

(a) S.I. 1982/841.

4.—(1)(a) The fee to be charged for the tonnage measurement of a ship in accordance with Part II of the Regulations (that is to say, the International Tonnage Convention, 1969) shall be 70% of the fees set out in Table A.

(b) The fees for a sister ship, or a foreign ship with an International Tonnage Certificate (1969) transferring to the United Kingdom register, shall be determined by the amount of work involved, charged at an hourly rate of £45.50 subject to the maximum fee chargeable under sub-paragraph (1)(a) above.

(2)(a) The fees to be charged for the tonnage measurement of a ship in accordance with either Schedule 5, Part I, paragraph 2(2) (single tonnage) or Schedule 5, Part III, paragraph 12 (modified tonnage) of the Regulations shall be 100% of the fees set out in Table A.

(b) The fees for a sister ship shall be determined by the amount of work involved, charged at an hourly rate of £45.50 subject to the maximum fee chargeable under sub-paragraph (2)(a) above.

(3)(a) The fees to be charged for the tonnage measurement of a ship in accordance with Schedule 5, Part III, paragraph 13 (alternative tonnages) shall be 150% of the fees set out in Table A.

(b) The fees for a sister ship shall be determined by the amount of work involved charged at an hourly rate of £45.50 subject to the maximum fee chargeable under sub-paragraph (3)(a) above.

(4)(a) The fees to be charged for the tonnage measurement of a ship in accordance with Part VI of the Regulations (gross tonnage for Interim Scheme for tonnage measurement for certain ships) shall be 80% of the fees set out in Table A.

(b) The fees for a sister ship shall be determined by the amount of work involved charged at an hourly rate of £45.50 subject to the maximum fee chargeable under sub-paragraph (4)(a) above.

(5) The fees to be charged for the tonnage measurement or measurement of a pleasure yacht under 13.7 metres (45 feet) in overall length in accordance with Schedule 5, Part IV and Appendix 5 shall:

(i) when undertaken in the United Kingdom, not exceed £117 and

(ii) when undertaken outside the United Kingdom, not exceed £234.50.

(6) The fees to be charged for the tonnage measurement of a ship to which Schedule 5, Part I, paragraph 2(3) of the Regulations (girthing of a loaded ship) applies, shall be 50% of the fees set out in Table A.

(7) The fee to be charged for the remeasurement of a ship for tonnage purposes, verification of changes in any of the registered particulars, or any other services associated with the tonnage measurement shall be determined by the amount of work involved charged at an hourly rate of £45.50 subject to the maximum fee shown for a ship of that tonnage in Table A.

PART III

CERTIFICATES OF COMPETENCY AS AN OFFICER

The fee for the issue or endorsement of any certificate of competency as an officer shall (except as provided in section C of Part IV below, be £10.

PART IV

EXAMINATION CONDUCTED BY THE DEPARTMENT OF TRANSPORT FOR CERTIFICATES OF COMPETENCY AS AN OFFICER, AND OTHER SERVICES

SECTION A

Fees for examinations for certificates of competency as skipper or other officer of fishing vessel

Service	Fee
1. (i) For examination for a certificate of competency on each occasion on which a candidate presents himself for the whole examination as:	
(a) skipper	£249
(b) second hand	£105

Service	Fee
(ii) Where a candidate is examined in any part of the written but not in the practical oral part of the examination mentioned above or vice versa	50% of the appropriate fee in 1, subject to a minimum fee of £105

2. For examination for a certificate of competency on each occasion on which a candidate presents himself for the practical oral part of the examination as:

(a) deck officer (fishing vessel) Class 1	£85
(b) deck officer (fishing vessel) Class 2	£70
(c) deck officer (fishing vessel) Class 3	£85
(d) engineer officer (fishing vessel) Class 1	£85
(e) engineer officer (fishing vessel) Class 2	£70

3. For examination for a sight test certificate where it is a requirement for a candidate for an examination for a certificate of competency as skipper or second hand or as a deck officer (fishing vessel) in cases 1(i)(a) or (b) or 2(a), (b) or (c) above and for the grant of a certificate to a person passing the examination ... £15

SECTION B

Fees for examinations for certificates of competency as master, deck officer or marine engineer officer

Service	Fee

1. For examination for a certificate of competency on each occasion on which a candidate presents himself for the whole examination as:

(a) deck officer class 1 (master mariner)	£455
(b) deck officer class 2	£221
(c) deck officer class 4	£161

2. Where a candidate in case 1(a), (b) or (c) is examined in any part of the written but not in the practical oral part of the examination, or vice versa	50% of the appropriate fee in 1, subject to a minimum of £105

3. For examination for a certificate of competency on each occasion on which a candidate presents himself for the practical oral part of the examination as:

(a) deck officer class 5	£70
(b) marine engineer officer class 1	£85
(c) marine engineer officer class 2	£85
(d) marine engineer officer class 3	£85
(e) marine engineer officer class 4	£70

4. For examination on each occasion on which a candidate presents himself for the practical oral part for a command endorsement as:

(a) master (extended European)	£85
(b) master (limited European)	£85
(c) tugmaster	£85
(d) tugmaster (limited European)	£85
(e) master (restricted) and master (restricted) extended European	£85
(f) master (restricted) limited European	£85

5. For examination of a class 1, class 2 or class 4 marine engineer officer for the endorsement of his steam certificate to the effect that he is qualified to act in the capacity stated in his certificate on board a motor vessel, or vice versa, for the practical oral part of the examination:

marine engineer officer class 1	£85
marine engineer officer class 2	£85
marine engineer officer class 4	£70

Service   *Fee*

6. For examination for a service endorsement to a certificate of competency as marine engineer officer   £70

7. For examination for a sight test certificate where it is a requirement for a candidate for an examination for a certificate of competency as deck officer or for a command endorsement in cases 1(a), (b), or (c) or 3(a) or 4(a), (b), (c), (d), (e) or (f) and for the grant of a certificate to a person passing the examination   £15

SECTION C

Removal of Endorsements, and Dangerous Cargo Endorsement

1. Removal of a 'For Standby, Seismic, and Oceanographic Survey Vessels Only' endorsement from a certificate of competency   £31

2. Removal of a 'For Tug Service Only' endorsement from a certificate of competency   £31

3. For a dangerous cargo endorsement to a certificate of competency or service   £31

SECTION D

Miscellaneous

1. For examination for an electronic navigation systems certificate or an electronic navigation systems (fishing) certificate and for the grant of a certificate to a person passing the examination   £31

2. For examination for a certificate of qualification as efficient deck hand except where the examination is sat at a centre specially approved by the Secretary of State, and for the grant of a certificate to a person passing the examination   £15

3. For the grant of a certificate of qualification as efficient deck hand where the examination was set at a centre specially approved by the Secretary of State   £8

4. For examination for a certificate of proficiency in survival craft except where the examination is sat at a centre specially approved by the Secretary of State, and for the grant of a certificate to a person passing the examination   £15

5. For the grant of a certificate of proficiency in survival craft where the examination was sat at a centre specially approved by the Secretary of State   £8

6. For examination for a licence as Marine Engine Operator or Senior Marine Engine Operator and for the grant of a certificate to a person passing the examination   £60

SECTION E

Fees for Examinations for Certificates of Competency as A.B.

1. For Schedule 3 to the Merchant Shipping (Certificates of Competency as A.B.) Regulations 1970**(a)**, there shall be substituted the following:—

(a) S.I. 1970/294; the relevant amending instrument is S.I. 1983/1167.

"SCHEDULE 3

FEES

Service	Fee
1. For sitting the examination specified in regulation 4(1)(c), except in cases to which paragraph 3 of this Schedule applies or where the examination is sat at a centre specially approved by the Secretary of State	£15
2. For the grant of a certificate of competency, except in cases to which paragraph 3 of this Schedule applies	£8
3. For sitting the said examination and for the grant of a certificate of competency in the case of a person making application therefore under regulation 5(6) and passing the examination	£15
4. For a copy of a certificate of competency issued pursuant to regulation 10, except where the loss or destruction of the original certificate was occasioned by the wreck or loss of a ship or by a fire on board ship, in which case no fee shall be payable	£8"

PART V

REGISTRATION ETC OF SHIPS AND SUBMERSIBLE CRAFT

Fees for Registration, Transfer and Mortgage of Ships (excluding Vessels not exceeding 10 Tons Employed Solely in Fishing) and Inspection of the Register Book

1. In this Part:

"ship" does not include vessels not exceeding 10 tons employed solely in fishing;

"submersible craft" means a submersible craft as defined in the Merchant Shipping (Registration of Submersible Craft) Regulations 1976**(a)**.

Service	Fee
2.—(1) First registry, registry anew or re-registry of a ship, or the transfer of registry of a ship from one port to another, where the ship:	
does not exceed 1,500 tons	£145
exceeds 1,500 tons	£210
(2) Registry of the transfer of ownership of a ship by bill of sale or by transmission, or of the mortgage of a ship or the transfer or the discharge of such a mortgage, where the ship:	
does not exceed 1,500 tons	£45
exceeds 1,500 tons	£80
(3) Each inspection of the register book	£5
(4) For the issue of a certificate of registration on the Small Ships Register, including an amended certificate or a duplicate copy of a certificate	£10
(5) On application to register a submersible craft	£30

PART VI

COPIES OF DOCUMENTS

Fees for Copies of, or Extracts from, Documents Admissible in Evidence

1. Supplying a certified copy of the particulars entered by the registrar in the register book on the registry of a ship, together with a certified statement showing the ownership of the ship at the time being   £15

(a) S.I. 1976/940, to which there is an amendment not relevant to these Regulations.

Service   *Fee*

2. Supplying a certified copy of any declaration or document, a copy of which is made evidence by the Merchant Shipping Acts or for a certified copy of or extracts from a document declared by the Merchant Shipping Acts to be admissible as evidence:—

    (a) if the declaration or document relates to the registry of a ship, for each folio of 90 words or part thereof   £6

    (b) in any other case, for each page or portion thereof   £6

PART VII

WRECK

Fees of Receivers of Wreck

Service   *Fee*

1. Wreck taken by the Receiver into his custody $7\frac{1}{2}$% of the value thereof

2. Services rendered by a Receiver in respect of any vessel in distress, not being a wreck, or in respect of the cargo or other articles belonging thereto   £50 for each day during which the Receiver is employed on that service

PART VIII

SEAMEN'S DOCUMENTS

Fees for the Issue of British Seamen's Cards and Discharge Books

1. In this Part "the Regulations" means the Merchant Shipping (Seamen's Documents) Regulations 1972(a); and the person to whom a British Seaman's Card or a discharge book has been issued is referred to as the holder of it.

Service   *Fee*

2.—(1) For the issue of a British Seaman's Card:—

    (a) to a British Seaman under regulation 5 of the Regulations:

        (i) on postal application   £15

        (ii) Other   £35

    (b) to a person who would, but for the provisions of regulation 9 of the Regulations, be regarded as the holder of a British Seaman's Card:

        (i) on postal application   £15

        (ii) Other   £35

    (c) to a person who has ceased to be regarded as the holder of a British Seaman's Card because it has been lost, destroyed or defaced through shipwreck or fire at sea   No fee

(2) For the issue of a discharge book under paragraph 1 or paragraph 2 of regulation 19 of the Regulations to a seaman—

    (a) who, in accordance with regulation 18(1)(b) of the Regulations, produces a Seaman's Record Book (as defined in regulation 1(2)(h) of the Regulations), which has been issued to him, or a discharge book of which he would, but for the provisions of regulation 25(b) of the Regulations, be regarded as the holder:

        (i) on postal application   £15

        (ii) Other   £35

    (b) to whom a Seaman's Record Book (as so defined) has been issued or who was the holder of a discharge book, which in either case has been lost, destroyed or defaced through shipwreck or fire at sea   No fee

---

(a) S.I. 1972/1295, to which there are amendments not relevant to these Regulations.

PART IX

ENGAGEMENT AND DISCHARGE OF SEAMEN

Fees for the Engagement and Discharge of Seamen

1. In this Part "the Crew Agreements Regulations" means the Merchant Shipping (Crew Agreements, Lists of Crew and Discharge of Seamen) Regulations 1972(**a**) and the Merchant Shipping (Crew Arrangements, Lists of Crew and Discharge of Seamen) (Fishing Vessels) Regulations 1972(**b**).

2. For the engagement and discharge of seamen before a Superintendent pursuant to the Crew Agreements Regulations, or for any service rendered in connection with a crew agreement at the request of the owner, agent or master:—

Service	*Fee*
(a) Where the service is performed elsewhere than in a Marine Office:—	
(i) On Monday to Friday (excluding Public Holidays) between 9.00 am and 5.00 pm	The fee will be determined by the amount of work involved, including travelling time, charged at an hourly rate of £21 subject to a minimum fee of £21
(ii) At all other times	200% of the appropriate fee under (1) above
These fees are exclusive of travel and subsistence expenses which will be charged additionally	
(b) Where the service is performed in a Marine Office:—	
(i) On Monday to Friday (excluding Public Holidays) between 9.00 am and 5.00 pm	The fee will be determined by the amount of work involved charged at an hourly rate of £21, subject to a minimum fee of £5.25
(ii) At all other times	200% of the appropriate fee under (1) above.

PART X

ADDITIONAL CHARGES

Fees in Respect of Surveys, or Inspection of Ship's Provisions or Water, in or outside the United Kingdom for Waiting Time Attendance at Unusual Hours, Weekends and Public Holidays

When a surveyor or inspector is unable to start an inspection at the appointed hour, unless this is for reasons over which the applicant, his agent or supplier has no control or where (except for similar reasons) a survey or inspection is disrupted, an additional fee in accordance with the following Table shall be payable:

Provided that where the surveyor or inspector is able to avoid waiting time by carrying out other available survey or inspection work in the vicinity, for which the appropriate fees have been paid, such additional fees will not be payable.

(**a**) S.I. 1972/918, to which there are amendments not relevant to these Regulations.
(**b**) S.I. 1972/919, to which there are amendments not relevant to these Regulations.

Table

	Inspection of ship's provisions	Fishing vessels (any survey or inspection)	Other surveys inspections and tests etc
	£ per hour or part thereof	£ per hour or part thereof	£ per hour or part thereof
1. For waiting time prior to the commencement of and during the course of a survey or inspection:			
for periods not in excess of one hour	No fee	No fee	No fee
for periods in excess of one hour—			
for surveys in the United Kingdom	30.00	37.00	45.50
for surveys abroad	60.00	74.00	91.00
2. For abortive visits in the United Kingdom: for the time wasted in excess of one hour at the place of survey or inspection plus the time occupied in travelling to and from the place of survey	30.00	37.00	45.50
3. When a surveyor or inspector is called upon to perform services in the United Kingdom at unusual hours: for work undertaken during the following hours including time occupied in travelling:			
Mondays to Fridays inclusive between 6pm and 8am and all day Saturday	15.00	18.50	22.75
Sundays and Public Holidays	30.00	37.00	45.50

Table *(continued)*

	Inspection of ship's provisions	*Fishing vessels (any survey or inspection)*	*Other surveys inspections and tests etc*
	£ per hour or part thereof	*£ per hour or part thereof*	*£ per hour or part thereof*
4. When a surveyor or inspector is called upon to perform services outside the United Kingdom which involve working total hours in any one week in excess of normal weekly employment hours, for the excess hours of work	12.30	12.30	12.30

EXPLANATORY NOTE

(This note is not part of the Regulations)

These Regulations revoke and replace the Merchant Shipping (Fees) Regulations 1985 as amended. The Regulations prescribe an increase in fees of around 10% for surveys and inspections (Part I) and tonnage measurement (Part II) except fees for radio and navigational equipment surveys to which an increase of 18% is applied.

Fishing vessel radio survey fees and fishing vessel survey fees, for which there is no longer a separate part in these Regulations, have been restructured and are now made chargeable at an hourly rate instead of a fixed fee as before (Part I).

Fees for examinations have also been restructured (Parts III and IV of the Schedule). The Department of Transport now only conduct practical oral examinations and a limited number of written examinations. The Department of Transport continues to issue and endorse certificates. The fees in Parts III and IV have been increased by around 10%.

A two tier system of fees has been introduced in respect of seamen's documents taking into account the introduction of provision for postal applications (Part VIII).

Fees for other services (Parts VI, VII, IX and X) have been increased by amounts varying from 10% to 20%. Fees for registration (Part V) are unchanged.

STATUTORY INSTRUMENTS

1987 No. 64

BANKS AND BANKING

The Banking Act 1979 (Advertisements)(Amendment) Regulations 1987

Made - - - -	*22nd January 1987*
Laid before Parliament	*26th January 1987*
Coming into force	*16th February 1987*

The Treasury, in exercise of the powers conferred upon them by section 34(1) and (2) of the Banking Act 1979**(a)** and of all other powers enabling them in that behalf, and after consultation with the Bank of England, hereby make the following Regulations:–

1. These Regulations may be cited as the Banking Act 1979 (Advertisements) (Amendment) Regulations 1987 and shall come into force on 16th February 1987.

2. The Banking Act 1979 (Advertisements) Regulations 1985**(b)** shall be amended in regulation 2(4)(e) by inserting after the words "The Stock Exchange (Listing) Regulations 1984**(c)**" the words "or (as the case may be) for the purposes of any listing rules made pursuant to section 142(6) of the Financial Services Act 1986**(d)**.".

Tim Sainsbury
Michael Neubert

22nd January 1987   Two of the Lords Commissioners of Her Majesty's Treasury

---

EXPLANATORY NOTE

(This note is not part of the Regulations)

These Regulations amend the Banking Act 1979 (Advertisements) Regulations 1985 in regulation 2(4)(e), which disapplies the 1985 Regulations in relation to any issue of an application form for securities if there is provided with it a statement of the approved listing particulars for the purposes of the Stock Exchange (Listing) Regulations 1984 (S.I. 1984/716) or the form shows where such particulars can be obtained or inspected. Reference is now made to such particulars for the purposes of the 1984 Regulations or, as the case may be, of any listing rules made pursuant to section 142(6) of the Financial Services Act 1986 (c.60). With effect from 16th February 1987 such rules will for certain purposes supersede the 1984 Regulations, and reference in regulation 2(4)(e) to both the rules and those Regulations is made to cover transitional cases.

(a) 1979 c.37.   **(b)** S.I. 1985/220.   **(c)** S.I. 1984/716.   **(d)** 1986 c.60.

1987 No. 65

BANKS AND BANKING

The Banking Act 1979 (Exempt Transactions) (Amendment) Regulations 1987

Made - - - -	*22nd January 1987*
Laid before Parliament	*26th January 1987*
Coming into force	*16th February 1987*

The Treasury, in exercise of the powers conferred upon them by section 2(1) and (5) of the Banking Act 1979**(a)** and of all other powers enabling them in that behalf, hereby make the following Regulations:—

1. These Regulations may be cited as the Banking Act 1979 (Exempt Transactions) (Amendment) Regulations 1987 and shall come into force on 16th February 1987.

2.—(1) The Banking Act 1979 (Exempt Transactions) Regulations 1986**(b)** shall be amended as follows.

(2) In Regulation 1(2) (interpretation)—

  (a) for the definition of "company" there shall be substituted—

    " "company" means a body corporate, including a body corporate constituted under the law of a country or territory outside the United Kingdom;", and

  (b) after the definition of "the Listing Regulations" there shall be inserted—

    " "the listing rules" means any rules made pursuant to section 142(6) of the Financial Services Act 1986**(c)**;".

(3) In Regulation 14 (sterling debt securities)—

  (a) in sub-paragraph (a)(i) for the words "Listing Regulations" there shall be substituted the words "listing rules", and

  (b) in sub-paragraph (c)(i) after the words "Listing Regulations" in both places where they occur there shall be inserted the words "or (as the case may be) the listing rules".

(4) In Regulation 15(e)(iii) (sterling commercial paper)—

  (a) for the words "Listing Regulations" where they first occur there shall be substituted the words "listing rules", and

  (b) after the words "Listing Regulations" where they next occur there shall be inserted the words "or (as the case may be) the listing rules".

Tim Sainsbury
Michael Neubert
22nd January 1987   Two of the Lords Commissioners of Her Majesty's Treasury

---

(a) 1979 c.37.
(b) S.I. 1986/1712.
(c) 1986 c.60.

EXPLANATORY NOTE

(This note is not part of the Regulations)

These Regulations amend the Banking Act 1979 (Exempt Transactions) Regulations 1986 in consequence of the commencement on 16th February 1987 of Part IV of the Financial Services Act 1986 and the repeal on that date of related provisions.

In Regulation 1(2) of the 1986 Regulations, the definition of "company" (which depends on certain statutory provisions to be partially repealed by the 1986 Act) is replaced with a single definition. There is inserted in that Regulation a definition of "the listing rules", to mean rules made pursuant to section 142(6) of the Financial Services Act 1986. Such rules will for certain purposes supersede the Stock Exchange (Listing) Regulations 1984 (S.I. 1984/716).

In Regulations 14 and 15, references to the new listing rules are substituted for references to the 1984 Regulations and, where appropriate, reference both to the rules and to Regulations is made to cover transitional cases.

1987 No. 66

OFFSHORE INSTALLATIONS

The Offshore Installations (Safety Zones) (No. 9) Order 1987

Made - - -	*22nd January 1987*
Coming into force -	*24th January 1987*

The Secretary of State, in exercise of the powers conferred on him by section 21(1), (2) and (3) of the Oil and Gas (Enterprise) Act 1982(a) (hereinafter referred to as "the Act"), and of all other powers enabling him in that behalf, hereby makes the following Order:—

1. This Order may be cited as the Offshore Installations (Safety Zones) (No. 9) Order 1987 and shall come into force on 24th January 1987.

2.—(1) A safety zone is hereby established around the installation specified in Column 1 of the Schedule hereto (being an installation maintained in waters to which section 21 of the Act(b) applies) having a radius of five hundred metres from the point as respects that installation which has the co-ordinates of latitude and longitude according to European Datum (1950) specified in Columns 2 and 3 of the Schedule.

(2) The prohibition under section 21(3) of the Act on a vessel entering or remaining in a safety zone without the consent of the Secretary of State shall not apply to a vessel entering or remaining in the safety zone established under paragraph (1) above —

(*a*) in connection with the laying, inspection, testing, repair, alteration, renewal or removal of any submarine cable or pipe-line in or near that safety zone;

(*b*) to provide services for, to transport persons or goods to or from, or under the authority of a government department to inspect, any installation in that safety zone;

(*c*) if it is a vessel belonging to a general lighthouse authority performing duties relating to the safety of navigation;

(*d*) in connection with the saving or attempted saving of life or property;

(*e*) owing to stress of weather; or

(*f*) when in distress.

Alick Buchanan-Smith
Minister of State,
Department of Energy

22nd January 1987

(**a**) 1982 c.23.   (**b**) *See* section 21(9).

SCHEDULE

Article 2(1)

SAFETY ZONE

1	2	3
Name or other designation of the offshore installation	Latitude North	Longitude East
Well 30/24–32	56° 16′ 37·29″	02° 39′ 05·67″

EXPLANATORY NOTE

(This note is not part of the Order)

This Order establishes, under section 21 of the Oil and Gas (Enterprise) Act 1982, a safety zone, having a radius of 500 metres from a specified point, around the installation specified in the Schedule to this Order and maintained in waters to which the section applies (these include territorial waters and waters in areas designated under section 1(7) of the Continental Shelf Act 1964 (c.29)).

Vessels (which for this purpose include hovercraft, submersible apparatus and installations in transit) are prohibited from entering or remaining in the safety zone except with the consent of the Secretary of State or in the circumstances mentioned in Article 2(2) of the Order.

1987 No. 67
OFFSHORE INSTALLATIONS
The Offshore Installations (Safety Zones) (No. 10) Order 1987

Made - - -		*22nd January 1987*
Coming into force -		*24th January 1987*

The Secretary of State, in exercise of the powers conferred on him by section 21(1), (2) and (3) of the Oil and Gas (Enterprise) Act 1982(**a**) (hereinafter referred to as "the Act"), and of all other powers enabling him in that behalf, hereby makes the following Order:—

1. This Order may be cited as the Offshore Installations (Safety Zones) (No. 10) Order 1987 and shall come into force on 24th January 1987.

2.—(1) A safety zone is hereby established around the installation specified in Column 1 of the Schedule hereto (being an installation maintained in waters to which section 21 of the Act(**b**) applies) having a radius of five hundred metres from the point as respects that installation which has the co-ordinates of latitude and longitude according to European Datum (1950) specified in Columns 2 and 3 of the Schedule.

(2) The prohibition under section 21(3) of the Act on a vessel entering or remaining in a safety zone without the consent of the Secretary of State shall not apply to a vessel entering or remaining in the safety zone established under paragraph (1) above —

(*a*) in connection with the laying, inspection, testing, repair, alteration, renewal or removal of any submarine cable or pipe-line in or near that safety zone;

(*b*) to provide services for, to transport persons or goods to or from, or under the authority of a government department to inspect, any installation in that safety zone;

(*c*) if it is a vessel belonging to a general lighthouse authority performing duties relating to the safety of navigation;

(*d*) in connection with the saving or attempted saving of life or property;

(*e*) owing to stress of weather; or

(*f*) when in distress.

3. The Offshore Installations (Safety Zones) (No. 81) Order 1986(**c**) is hereby revoked.

Alick Buchanan-Smith
Minister of State,
Department of Energy

22nd January 1987

(**a**) 1982 c.23.   (**b**) *See* section 21(9).   (**c**) S.I. 1986/1465.

SCHEDULE   Article 2(1)

SAFETY ZONE

1	2	3
Name or other designation of the offshore installation	Latitude North	Longitude East
Rowan Gorilla II	53° 28′ 09·60″	01° 54′ 52·60″

EXPLANATORY NOTE

(*This note is not part of the Order*)

This Order establishes, under section 21 of the Oil and Gas (Enterprise) Act 1982, a safety zone, having a radius of 500 metres from a specified point, around the installation specified in the Schedule to this Order and maintained in waters to which the section applies (these include territorial waters and waters in areas designated under section 1(7) of the Continental Shelf Act 1964 (c.29)).

Vessels (which for this purpose include hovercraft, submersible apparatus and installations in transit) are prohibited from entering or remaining in the safety zone except with the consent of the Secretary of State or in the circumstances mentioned in Article 2(2) of the Order.

The Order also revokes the Offshore Installations (Safety Zones) Order which created a safety zone around the installation specified in the Schedule to this Order on its previous location.

STATUTORY INSTRUMENTS

1987 No. 68

OFFSHORE INSTALLATIONS

The Offshore Installations (Safety Zones) (No. 11) Order 1987

Made - - -		*22nd January 1987*
Coming into force -		*24th January 1987*

The Secretary of State, in exercise of the powers conferred on him by section 21(1), (2) and (3) of the Oil and Gas (Enterprise) Act 1982(**a**) (hereinafter referred to as "the Act"), and of all other powers enabling him in that behalf, hereby makes the following Order:—

1. This Order may be cited as the Offshore Installations (Safety Zones) (No. 11) Order 1987 and shall come into force on 24th January 1987.

2.—(1) A safety zone is hereby established around the installation specified in Column 1 of the Schedule hereto (being an installation maintained in waters to which section 21 of the Act(**b**) applies) having a radius of five hundred metres from the point as respects that installation which has the co-ordinates of latitude and longitude according to European Datum (1950) specified in Columns 2 and 3 of the Schedule.

(2) The prohibition under section 21(3) of the Act on a vessel entering or remaining in a safety zone without the consent of the Secretary of State shall not apply to a vessel entering or remaining in the safety zone established under paragraph (1) above —

  (*a*) in connection with the laying, inspection, testing, repair, alteration, renewal or removal of any submarine cable or pipe-line in or near that safety zone;

  (*b*) to provide services for, to transport persons or goods to or from, or under the authority of a government department to inspect, any installation in that safety zone;

  (*c*) if it is a vessel belonging to a general lighthouse authority performing duties relating to the safety of navigation;

  (*d*) in connection with the saving or attempted saving of life or property;

  (*e*) owing to stress of weather; or

  (*f*) when in distress.

Alick Buchanan-Smith
Minister of State,
Department of Energy

22nd January 1987

(**a**) 1982 c.23.   (**b**) *See* section 21(9).

SCHEDULE

Article 2(1)

SAFETY ZONE

1	2	3
Name or other designation of the offshore installation	Latitude North	Longitude East
Drillstar	57° 13′ 13·00″	01° 37′ 42·00″

EXPLANATORY NOTE

(This note is not part of the Order)

This Order establishes, under section 21 of the Oil and Gas (Enterprise) Act 1982, a safety zone, having a radius of 500 metres from a specified point, around the installation specified in the Schedule to this Order and maintained in waters to which the section applies (these include territorial waters and waters in areas designated under section 1(7) of the Continental Shelf Act 1964 (c.29)).

Vessels (which for this purpose include hovercraft, submersible apparatus and installations in transit) are prohibited from entering or remaining in the safety zone except with the consent of the Secretary of State or in the circumstances mentioned in Article 2(2) of the Order.

STATUTORY INSTRUMENTS

1987 No. 69

OFFSHORE INSTALLATIONS

The Offshore Installations (Safety Zones) (No. 12) Order 1987

Made - - -		*22nd January 1987*
Coming into force -		*24th January 1987*

The Secretary of State, in exercise of the powers conferred on him by section 21(1), (2) and (3) of the Oil and Gas (Enterprise) Act 1982(**a**) (hereinafter referred to as "the Act"), and of all other powers enabling him in that behalf, hereby makes the following Order:—

1. This Order may be cited as the Offshore Installations (Safety Zones) (No. 12) Order 1987 and shall come into force on 24th January 1987.

2.—(1) A safety zone is hereby established around the installation specified in Column 1 of the Schedule hereto (being an installation maintained in waters to which section 21 of the Act(**b**) applies) having a radius of five hundred metres from the point as respects that installation which has the co-ordinates of latitude and longitude according to European Datum (1950) specified in Columns 2 and 3 of the Schedule.

(2) The prohibition under section 21(3) of the Act on a vessel entering or remaining in a safety zone without the consent of the Secretary of State shall not apply to a vessel entering or remaining in the safety zone established under paragraph (1) above —

    (*a*) in connection with the laying, inspection, testing, repair, alteration, renewal or removal of any submarine cable or pipe-line in or near that safety zone;

    (*b*) to provide services for, to transport persons or goods to or from, or under the authority of a government department to inspect, any installation in that safety zone;

    (*c*) if it is a vessel belonging to a general lighthouse authority performing duties relating to the safety of navigation;

    (*d*) in connection with the saving or attempted saving of life or property;

    (*e*) owing to stress of weather; or

    (*f*) when in distress.

Alick Buchanan-Smith
Minister of State,
Department of Energy

22nd January 1987

(**a**) 1982 c.23.   (**b**) *See* section 21(9).

SCHEDULE

Article 2(1)

SAFETY ZONE

1	2	3
Name or other designation of the offshore installation	Latitude North	Longitude East
M G Hulme Jr	59° 35′ 16·56″	01° 28′ 43·43″

EXPLANATORY NOTE

(This note is not part of the Order)

This Order establishes, under section 21 of the Oil and Gas (Enterprise) Act 1982, a safety zone, having a radius of 500 metres from a specified point, around the installation specified in the Schedule to this Order and maintained in waters to which the section applies (these include territorial waters and waters in areas designated under section 1(7) of the Continental Shelf Act 1964 (c.29)).

Vessels (which for this purpose include hovercraft, submersible apparatus and installations in transit) are prohibited from entering or remaining in the safety zone except with the consent of the Secretary of State or in the circumstances mentioned in Article 2(2) of the Order.

1987 No. 70

OFFSHORE INSTALLATIONS

The Offshore Installations (Safety Zones) (No. 13) Order 1987

Made	- - -	*22nd January 1987*
Coming into force	-	*24th January 1987*

The Secretary of State, in exercise of the powers conferred on him by section 21(1), (2) and (3) of the Oil and Gas (Enterprise) Act 1982(**a**) (hereinafter referred to as "the Act"), and of all other powers enabling him in that behalf, hereby makes the following Order:—

1. This Order may be cited as the Offshore Installations (Safety Zones) (No. 13) Order 1987 and shall come into force on 24th January 1987.

2.—(1) A safety zone is hereby established around the installation specified in Column 1 of the Schedule hereto (being an installation maintained in waters to which section 21 of the Act(**b**) applies) having a radius of five hundred metres from the point as respects that installation which has the co-ordinates of latitude and longitude according to European Datum (1950) specified in Columns 2 and 3 of the Schedule.

(2) The prohibition under section 21(3) of the Act on a vessel entering or remaining in a safety zone without the consent of the Secretary of State shall not apply to a vessel entering or remaining in the safety zone established under paragraph (1) above —

(*a*) in connection with the laying, inspection, testing, repair, alteration, renewal or removal of any submarine cable or pipe-line in or near that safety zone;

(*b*) to provide services for, to transport persons or goods to or from, or under the authority of a government department to inspect, any installation in that safety zone;

(*c*) if it is a vessel belonging to a general lighthouse authority performing duties relating to the safety of navigation;

(*d*) in connection with the saving or attempted saving of life or property;

(*e*) owing to stress of weather; or

(*f*) when in distress.

Alick Buchanan-Smith
Minister of State,
Department of Energy

22nd January 1987

(**a**) 1982 c.23.　　　　(**b**) *See* section 21(9).

SCHEDULE

Article 2(1)

SAFETY ZONE

1	2	3
Name or other designation of the offshore installation	Latitude North	Longitude East
Ocean Bounty	57° 42′ 28·30″	01° 44′ 53·28″

EXPLANATORY NOTE

(This note is not part of the Order)

This Order establishes, under section 21 of the Oil and Gas (Enterprise) Act 1982, a safety zone, having a radius of 500 metres from a specified point, around the installation specified in the Schedule to this Order and maintained in waters to which the section applies (these include territorial waters and waters in areas designated under section 1(7) of the Continental Shelf Act 1964 (c.29)).

Vessels (which for this purpose include hovercraft, submersible apparatus and installations in transit) are prohibited from entering or remaining in the safety zone except with the consent of the Secretary of State or in the circumstances mentioned in Article 2(2) of the Order.

STATUTORY INSTRUMENTS

1987 No. 71

OFFSHORE INSTALLATIONS

The Offshore Installations (Safety Zones) (No. 14) Order 1987

Made	- - -		*22nd January 1987*
Coming into force	-		*24th January 1987*

The Secretary of State, in exercise of the powers conferred on him by section 21(1), (2) and (3) of the Oil and Gas (Enterprise) Act 1982(**a**) (hereinafter referred to as "the Act"), and of all other powers enabling him in that behalf, hereby makes the following Order:—

1. This Order may be cited as the Offshore Installations (Safety Zones) (No. 14) Order 1987 and shall come into force on 24th January 1987.

2.—(1) A safety zone is hereby established around the installation specified in Column 1 of the Schedule hereto (being an installation maintained in waters to which section 21 of the Act(**b**) applies) having a radius of five hundred metres from the point as respects that installation which has the co-ordinates of latitude and longitude according to European Datum (1950) specified in Columns 2 and 3 of the Schedule.

(2) The prohibition under section 21(3) of the Act on a vessel entering or remaining in a safety zone without the consent of the Secretary of State shall not apply to a vessel entering or remaining in the safety zone established under paragraph (1) above —

   (*a*) in connection with the laying, inspection, testing, repair, alteration, renewal or removal of any submarine cable or pipe-line in or near that safety zone;

   (*b*) to provide services for, to transport persons or goods to or from, or under the authority of a government department to inspect, any installation in that safety zone;

   (*c*) if it is a vessel belonging to a general lighthouse authority performing duties relating to the safety of navigation;

   (*d*) in connection with the saving or attempted saving of life or property;

   (*e*) owing to stress of weather; or

   (*f*) when in distress.

Alick Buchanan-Smith
Minister of State,
Department of Energy

22nd January 1987

(**a**) 1982 c.23.   (**b**) *See* section 21(9).

SCHEDULE   Article 2(1)

SAFETY ZONE

1	2	3
Name or other designation of the offshore installation	Latitude North	Longitude West
Sedco 7/4	57° 57′ 04·53″	00° 08′ 24·17″

EXPLANATORY NOTE

(This note is not part of the Order)

This Order establishes, under section 21 of the Oil and Gas (Enterprise) Act 1982, a safety zone, having a radius of 500 metres from a specified point, around the installation specified in the Schedule to this Order and maintained in waters to which the section applies (these include territorial waters and waters in areas designated under section 1(7) of the Continental Shelf Act 1964 (c.29)).

Vessels (which for this purpose include hovercraft, submersible apparatus and installations in transit) are prohibited from entering or remaining in the safety zone except with the consent of the Secretary of State or in the circumstances mentioned in Article 2(2) of the Order.

STATUTORY INSTRUMENTS

1987 No. 72

OFFSHORE INSTALLATIONS

The Offshore Installations (Safety Zones) (No. 15) Order 1987

Made	-	-	-	*22nd January 1987*
Coming into force	-		*24th January 1987*

The Secretary of State, in exercise of the powers conferred on him by section 21(1), (2) and (3) of the Oil and Gas (Enterprise) Act 1982(**a**) (hereinafter referred to as "the Act"), and of all other powers enabling him in that behalf, hereby makes the following Order:—

1. This Order may be cited as the Offshore Installations (Safety Zones) (No. 15) Order 1987 and shall come into force on 24th January 1987.

2.—(1) A safety zone is hereby established around the installation specified in Column 1 of the Schedule hereto (being an installation maintained in waters to which section 21 of the Act(**b**) applies) having a radius of five hundred metres from the point as respects that installation which has the co-ordinates of latitude and longitude according to European Datum (1950) specified in Columns 2 and 3 of the Schedule.

(2) The prohibition under section 21(3) of the Act on a vessel entering or remaining in a safety zone without the consent of the Secretary of State shall not apply to a vessel entering or remaining in the safety zone established under paragraph (1) above —

(*a*) in connection with the laying, inspection, testing, repair, alteration, renewal or removal of any submarine cable or pipe-line in or near that safety zone;

(*b*) to provide services for, to transport persons or goods to or from, or under the authority of a government department to inspect, any installation in that safety zone;

(*c*) if it is a vessel belonging to a general lighthouse authority performing duties relating to the safety of navigation;

(*d*) in connection with the saving or attempted saving of life or property;

(*e*) owing to stress of weather; or

(*f*) when in distress.

3. The Offshore Installations (Safety Zones) (No. 89) Order 1986(**c**) is hereby revoked.

Alick Buchanan-Smith
Minister of State,
Department of Energy

22nd January 1987

(**a**) 1982 c.23.   (**b**) *See* section 21(9).   (**c**) S.I. 1986/1584.

SCHEDULE   Article 2(1)

SAFETY ZONE

1	2	3
Name or other designation of the offshore installation	Latitude North	Longitude East
Stadrill	61° 09′ 43·00″	01° 06′ 42·60″

EXPLANATORY NOTE

(This note is not part of the Order)

This Order establishes, under section 21 of the Oil and Gas (Enterprise) Act 1982, a safety zone, having a radius of 500 metres from a specified point, around the installation specified in the Schedule to this Order and maintained in waters to which the section applies (these include territorial waters and waters in areas designated under section 1(7) of the Continental Shelf Act 1964 (c.29)).

Vessels (which for this purpose include hovercraft, submersible apparatus and installations in transit) are prohibited from entering or remaining in the safety zone except with the consent of the Secretary of State or in the circumstances mentioned in Article 2(2) of the Order.

The Order also revokes the Offshore Installations (Safety Zones) Order which created a safety zone around the installation specified in the Schedule to this Order on its previous location.

STATUTORY INSTRUMENTS

1987 No. 74

ANIMALS

ANIMAL HEALTH

The Diseases of Animals (Approved Disinfectants) (Amendment) Order 1987

Made - - - -	*16th January 1987*
Coming into force	*31st January 1987*

The Minister of Agriculture, Fisheries and Food, the Secretary of State for Scotland and the Secretary of State for Wales, acting jointly, in exercise of the powers conferred on them by sections 1, 7(1)(a), (b) and (c) and (2) and 23(f) and (g) of the Animal Health Act 1981(**a**) and of all other powers enabling them in that behalf, hereby order as follows:—

Title and commencement

1. This Order may be cited as the Diseases of Animals (Approved Disinfectants) (Amendment) Order 1987 and shall come into force on 31st January 1987.

Amendment

2. The Diseases of Animals (Approved Disinfectants) Order 1978(**b**) shall be amended as follows:—

   (a) for the provisions of Schedule 1 to that Order (which lists disinfectants approved by the Minister) there shall be substituted the provisions of Schedule 1 to this Order;

   (b) for the provisions of Schedule 2 to that Order (which lists disinfectants subject to transitional provisions) there shall be substituted the provisions of Schedule 2 to this Order; and

   (c) in Article 6(2) of that Order (which relates to disinfectants subject to transitional provisions) for the words "31st December 1986" there shall be substituted the words "30th June 1987".

Revocation

4. The Diseases of Animals (Approved Disinfectants) (Amendment) Order 1986(**c**) and the Diseases of Animals (Approved Disinfectants) (Amendment) (No. 2) Order 1986(**d**) are revoked.

(**a**) 1981 c.22.
(**b**) S.I. 1978/32; relevant amending instruments are S.I. 1986/5 and 1290.
(**c**) S.I. 1986/5.
(**d**) S.I. 1986/1290.

In witness whereof the Official Seal of the Minister of Agriculture, Fisheries and Food is hereunto affixed on 14th January 1987.

Michael Jopling
Minister of Agriculture, Fisheries and Food

16th January 1987

John J. Mackay
Parliamentary Under-Secretary of State, Scottish Office

14th January 1987

Nicholas Edwards
Secretary of State for Wales

Article 2(a)

Articles 4 and 5

SCHEDULE 1

PROVISIONS TO BE SUBSTITUTED FOR SCHEDULE 1

"SCHEDULE 1"

APPROVED DISINFECTANTS

Disinfectant	Foot-and-Mouth Disease Orders	Swine Vesicular Disease Order	Fowl Pest Orders	Tuberculosis Orders	General Orders
			Orders in respect of which use is approved; and dilution rates		
Action Approved Disinfectant	240	200	80	25	145
Agri Disinfex	250	300	125	30	180
Agridyne 2	250	300	125	30	180
*Agrimar Iodophor Disinfectant	250	300	125	30	180
Agrimar Longstay	—	—	100	100	120
Agrimar White Fluid	—	—	30	90	100
Agrisan Master Approved Disinfectant	120	250	59	—	59
Alodine	240	250	100	15	110
Ani-Odophor GT	240	160	91	25	145
Antec Black Fluid	—	—	41	—	80
Antec Farm Fluid	219	100	39	24	29
*Antec Farm Fluid S	700	200	200	50	115
Antec Iodine Active Steriliser	250	300	125	30	180
Antec Long Life	—	—	60	—	60
Antec Long Life 200	—	160	200	—	90
Antec Long Life 250S	500	200	250	48	90
Antec Long Life Extra	—	—	71	75	85
Antec New Formula Black Fluid	—	—	52	—	60
Antec New Formula Farm Fluid	300	110	70	30	65
Antec New Formula White Fluid	—	—	45	83	103
Antec Santec 1000	1000	80	160	30	90
Antec Virkon S	1300	200	280	30	120
Antec White Fluid	—	—	30	90	100
Applied 8–57 White Disinfectant	—	—	—	49	89
Arrow Agricultural Hydroclean Bactericidal Cleaner Disinfectant	30	—	—	—	—
Aviary Disinfectant	240	200	80	25	145
Basol 99	—	—	20	20	20
Battles Black Disinfectant Fluid	—	—	45	—	60

*Additions to Schedule.

SCHEDULE 1 – *continued*

Orders in respect of which use is approved; and dilution rates

Disinfectant	Foot-and-Mouth Disease Orders	Swine Vesicular Disease Order	Fowl Pest Orders	Tuberculosis Orders	General Orders
Battles Iofarm Iodophor Disinfectant and Dairy Detergent Steriliser	250	300	125	30	180
Battles Universal Disinfectant Fluid	300	—	60	37	—
Battles White Disinfectant Fluid	—	—	50	50	60
Betaphors 25	240	180	90	30	160
Biocid 30	250	300	125	30	180
Biokil Plus	40	—	50	—	40
*Black Disinfectant	—	—	41	—	80
Capriclense	240	200	80	25	145
Carbo White Disinfectant	50	—	—	49	89
Castrol Solvex ICD 109	—	—	—	—	—
Centaur New Approved Agricultural Disinfectant	250	300	125	30	180
Century Black Disinfectant	—	—	20	—	—
Citric Acid BP	500	—	—	—	—
Clearsol	—	—	—	45	—
Combat 2	250	300	125	30	180
Compass Agricultural Disinfectant	50	—	100	50	100
Compass Lysol BP 1968	9	—	39	39	49
*Convoy Liquid Disinfectant	250	150	80	60	85
Crown Special Detergent Disinfectant	240	200	80	25	145
CS Disinfectant	—	—	65	—	40
Davrisol 76	—	—	30	90	100
Defender	—	—	30	90	100
Delsanex Iodel FD	215	234	130	26	147
Dexadyne	240	—	91	—	—
Dexstar Halo-Giene	20	90	200	20	199
Disteola	240	300	80	25	100
Downland White Disinfectant	—	—	—	49	89
Durak 100 P	—	—	60	65	70
Eley's Economic Farm Fluid	250	20	100	25	70
Equivite All-Purpose Disinfectant	250	300	125	30	180
Evans White Disinfectant	—	—	—	49	89
FAM	240	250	100	15	110
FAM 30	250	300	125	30	180
FAM 30C	405	485	200	48	290

*Additions to Schedule.

SCHEDULE 1 – *continued*

Disinfectant	Foot-and-Mouth Disease Orders	Swine Vesicular Disease Order	Fowl Pest Orders	Tuberculosis Orders	General Orders
	Orders in respect of which use is approved; and dilution rates				
Famclor	200	500	59	12	70
Famosan	120	200	59	—	59
*Farm Aid 200	75	75	100	75	200
Farm Disinfex	—	—	30	90	100
Farmicide	40	—	50	65	40
Fensol	—	—	60	85	70
Ficare Blue Star	—	—	100	—	150
Ficare Gold Star	275	330	141	33	200
Formalin BP (Containing not less than 34% formaldehyde)	9	9	To be used undiluted	—	—
Formula H	—	—		—	—
Gliddons Iodophor Detergent Sanitizer and Disinfectant	250	300	125	30	180
Gloquat SD Extra	20	25	50	—	—
Glu-Cid	—	—	100	—	9
Gower Agri 30	250	300	125	30	180
Gower Agriclor	200	500	59	12	70
Gower Farm Disinfectant	—	—	30	90	100
GPC 8	80*	—	200	—	20
GR 218	400	200	—	—	—
Halamid	20	90	200	20	199
Hitec Farm Supreme	100	120	50	12	73
Hitec Five Star	405	485	200	48	290
Hitec Hygiene Supreme	—	—	50	—	5
Hullite Disinfectant Fluid	—	—	—	49	89
Hullite Farm Disinfectant Fluid	—	—	30	90	100
Hy-Co AFD	—	—	30	90	100
Hydrochlor	—	100	250	—	210
Hykil X	219	100	39	24	29
Iodet	240	250	100	15	110
Iofarm	240	250	100	15	110
Iosan Farm Disinfectant	240	180	80	15	80
Izal Germicide	—	—	41	75	90
Jeyes Fluid	—	—	30	—	50

*Additions to Schedule.

SCHEDULE 1 – *continued*

Disinfectant	Orders in respect of which use is approved; and dilution rates				
	Foot-and-Mouth Disease Orders	Swine Vesicular Disease Order	Fowl Pest Orders	Tuberculosis Orders	General Orders
Kaylass General Farm Disinfectant	250	300	125	30	180
Kilcrobe WO Disinfectant Fluid Special Grade	—	—	—	—	99
Killgerm Black Disinfectant RW Co-efficient 18/22	250	260	41	—	80
Killgerm Iodair	—	—	61	39	49
Killgerm Lysol BP	—	—	50	66	100
Killgerm White Farm Disinfectant	—	448	21	—	450
Kirby Chlor	60	—	271	—	20
Kryptol	—	50	—	—	—
Lifeline	175	—	75	—	—
LPH Disinfectant	—	—	50	39	50
Lysol BP Evansol	10	—	66	45	49
Lysovet	250	260	61	—	—
Marstan Dairy Hygiene Iodair	—	—	—	—	—
Master SVD Solution	—	9	250	—	—
Micro Chlor	—	100	100	—	210
Microdine	160	140	30	—	110
Microfec	—	—	60	90	100
Microl-Plus	—	—	70	65	70
Microsan	—	—	100	—	—
Microzol	—	—	150	100	120
*New Formula Pet Protect	75	—	100	75	200
Newmarket Fluid	240	75	80	22	145
Novagen FP	250	180	125	30	180
Nutosan	250	300	125	30	180
Nutriken Iodophor Disinfectant	250	300	125	30	180
Orbicide	330	300	200	—	—
Ortho-phosphoric acid (Technical Grade)	—	—	—	—	25
Ovitek Biocidal Solution Concentrate	—	—	50	—	—
Parakil	—	—	100	100	120
Parasept	—	—	61	—	—
Pennine Iodophor Detergent Steriliser	250	260	100	75	200
Peratol	75	75	80	11	90
Phiodin	220	180	—	—	—

*Additions to Schedule.

SCHEDULE 1 – *continued*

Disinfectant	Foot-and-Mouth Disease Orders	Orders in respect of which use is approved; and dilution rates			
		Swine Vesicular Disease Order	Fowl Pest Orders	Tuberculosis Orders	General Orders
Phorpass	240	280	90	30	85
Phorpass 75	380	300	180	100	180
Polykil + Disinfectant	—	300	—	—	180
Premiere White Disinfectant	—	—	—	49	89
Ropolik	240	250	100	15	110
Rygenitas Farm Disinfectant	—	—	30	90	100
Ryodac	250	300	125	30	180
Ry-odophor SP	240	160	91	25	145
Safeguard Abattoir Sanitiser	20	—	10	—	3
Safeguard Iodophor Concentrate	100	—	100	—	74
SEP 55	—	—	100	100	120
Sodium Carbonate (Decahydrate) Complying with BS 3674 of 1963	24	100	—	—	—
Sodium Hydroxide	—	100	—	—	—
Sorex White Farm Disinfectant	75	75	21	66	100
Sorgene 5	—	—	100	75	200
Sorgene Clear	—	—	100	100	120
Sorgene White	—	—	30	90	100
Special Ropolik	250	300	125	30	180
Sterilite Farm Disinfectant	—	—	30	90	100
Sterilite WD White Disinfectant	—	—	—	49	89
Sudol	500	—	60	65	70
Sulphamic Acid	—	—	—	—	—
Superblack	—	—	41	—	80
Superdine	250	300	125	30	180
Superkill	—	50	100	—	—
Superlin Black Disinfectant	—	—	—	70	70
Superlysol	—	—	50	39	49
*Superphenol	—	—	100	100	120
Superwhite	—	—	21	66	100
Surgiclene	250	300	125	30	180
SWC General White	—	—	30	90	100
SWC Iodine	250	300	125	30	180
SWC Poultry Terminal	—	—	100	100	120
*Tegodor	—	—	51	—	—

*Additions to Schedule.

SCHEDULE 1 – *continued*

Disinfectant	Orders in respect of which use is approved; and dilution rates				
	Foot-and-Mouth Disease Orders	Swine Vesicular Disease Order	Fowl Pest Orders	Tuberculosis Orders	General Orders
Tegodor 73	—	—	51	—	135
Tekresol	—	—	90	80	95
Texol	—	—	—	—	180
Total Farm Disinfectant	250	300	125	30	145
Tynedale Dairy Hygiene Disinfectant Plus	240	160	91	25	70
Unidol	—	—	60	65	100
Unilite	—	—	30	90	120
Unisep	—	—	100	100	100
Universal	240	100	100	25	89
Valley White Disinfectant	—	—	—	49	100
Vanodine Farm Disinfectant	—	—	30	90	80
Vapulin Black Disinfectant	—	—	41	—	55
Vesphene D39	10	—	50	70	—
*VH Parvocide Plus	—	—	150	—	—
*VH 150 Avicide	—	—	150	—	—
VH 1000 Virucide	1000	80	160	30	90
VH6 Virucide	219	100	39	24	29
VH7 Virucide	—	100	250	—	210
Vykil All Purpose Detergent Disinfectant	240	200	80	25	145
*Whelm Powder Disinfectant	450	300	130	30	180
White Cresanol	—	—	30	90	100
Young's Disinfectant and Dairy Detergent Steriliser	250	300	125	30	180
Young's Farm Septol	—	—	40	89	99
Young's Iodophor Farm Disinfectant	215	234	130	26	147
Zenasan Farm Disinfectant	—	—	30	90	100

*Additions to Schedule.

SCHEDULE 2

PROVISIONS TO BE SUBSTITUTED FOR SCHEDULE 2

Article 2(b)

"SCHEDULE 2

Articles 4 and 6

APPROVED DISINFECTANTS SUBJECT TO TRANSITIONAL PROVISIONS

Disinfectant	Orders in respect of which use is approved; and dilution rates				
	Foot-and-Mouth Disease Orders	Swine Vesicular Disease Order	Fowl Pest Orders	Tuberculosis Orders	General Orders
Antec New Formula Farm Fluid S	700	200	200	50	115
Ciba Geigy White Fluid	—	—	30	90	100
Dellaphen General Purpose Soluble Disinfectant	—	—	60	65	70
Delsol	—	—	100	100	120
Farm Disinfectant	—	—	30	90	100
Lenfectant White Fluid	—	—	—	49	89
Leonard Smith's Approved Special Detergent Disinfectant	240	200	80	25	145
Unifarm Universal Disinfectant	240	100	100	25	100
Warden Black Disinfectant	—	—	—	160	60

".

EXPLANATORY NOTE

(This note is not part of the Order)

This Order amends the Diseases of Animals (Approved Disinfectants) Order 1978 by substituting new schedules for Schedules 1 and 2 to that Order (Article 2(*a*) and (*b*)). Schedule 1, which lists approved disinfectants, includes newly approved disinfectants, and Schedule 2 lists disinfectants which are now omitted from Schedule 1 but which may nevertheless continue to be used as approved disinfectants until 30th June 1987 (Article 2(*c*)).

1987 No. 91

TERMS AND CONDITIONS OF EMPLOYMENT

The Statutory Maternity Pay (Compensation of Employers) Regulations 1987

Made - - -		*27th January 1987*
Laid before Parliament		*4th February 1987*
Coming into force -		*6th April 1987*

The Secretary of State for Social Services, with the concurrence of the Inland Revenue insofar as their concurrence is required, in exercise of powers conferred on him by sections 49(1) and 84(1) of, and paragraphs 1 and 5 of Schedule 4 to, the Social Security Act 1986**(a)** and section 166(1) of the Social Security Act 1975**(b)** and of all other powers enabling him in that behalf, hereby makes the following regulations:—

Citation, commencement and interpretation

1.—(1) These regulations may be cited as the Statutory Maternity Pay (Compensation of Employers) Regulations 1987 and shall come into force on 6th April 1987.

(2) In these regulations—
"contributions payments" means any payments which an employer is required, by or under any enactment, to make in discharge of any liability in respect of primary or secondary Class 1 contributions;

"regulation 2", "regulation 3", "regulation 4" and "regulation 5" mean, respectively, regulations 2, 3, 4 and 5 of these regulations;

"statutory sick pay" has the same meaning as in Part I of the Social Security and Housing Benefits Act 1982**(c)**;

and other expressions have the same meaning as in the Social Security Act 1986.

(3) For the purposes of regulations 4 and 5 "the Secretary of State" shall include a reference to the Commissioners of Inland Revenue acting on his behalf.

Right of employers to prescribed amount

2. An employer who has made a payment of statutory maternity pay shall be entitled to an amount, determined in accordance with the provisions of regulation 3, which he shall be entitled to deduct or, as the case may be, receive in accordance with the provisions of regulation 4 or 5.

Determination of the amount an employer shall be entitled to under regulation 2

3. In respect of a payment of statutory maternity pay made in the tax year commencing 6th April 1987, an employer shall be entitled under regulation 2 to an amount equal to 7 per cent. of the payment, that percentage being the total amount of

---

(a) 1986 c.50.
(b) 1975 c.14; *see* section 83(1) of the Social Security Act 1986.
(c) 1982 c.24.

secondary Class 1 contributions estimated by the Secretary of State as to be paid in respect of statutory maternity pay and statutory sick pay by all employers in that year, expressed as a percentage of the total amount of statutory maternity pay and statutory sick pay estimated by him to be paid by all employers in that year.

Deductions from contributions payments

4. An employer who has made a payment of statutory maternity pay may recover—
  (i) the amount so paid, and
  (ii) the amount determined in accordance with regulation 3,
by making one or more deductions from his contributions payments except where and insofar as—
  (a) the contributions payments relate to earnings paid before the beginning of the income tax month in which the payment of statutory maternity pay was made;
  (b) the contributions payments are made by him later than 6 years after the end of the tax year in which the payment of statutory maternity pay was made;
  (c) the amount of the payment of statutory maternity pay or the amount determined in accordance with regulation 3 have been paid to him under regulation 5 by the Secretary of State; or
  (d) the employer has made a request in writing under regulation 5 that the amount of the payment of statutory maternity pay or the amount determined in accordance with regulation 3 be paid to him and he has not received notification by the Secretary of State that the request is refused.

Payments to employers by the Secretary of State

5.—(1) If the total amount which an employer is or would otherwise be entitled to deduct under regulation 4 exceeds the total amount which the employer is liable to pay by way of primary and secondary Class 1 contributions in respect of the earnings paid in an income tax month, and the Secretary of State is satisfied that that is so, then provided that the employer has in writing requested him to do so, the Secretary of State shall pay the employer such amount as the employer was unable to deduct.

(2) If an employer is not liable to pay any primary or secondary Class 1 contributions but would otherwise be entitled to deduct an amount under regulation 4, and the Secretary of State is satisfied that that is so, then provided the employer has in writing requested him to so do, the Secretary of State shall pay the employer that amount.

Date when certain contributions are to be treated as paid

6. Where an employer has made a deduction from a contributions payment under regulation 4, the date on which it is to be treated as having been paid for the purposes of paragraph 5 of Schedule 4 to the Social Security Act 1986 (amount deducted to be treated as paid and received towards discharging liability in respect of Class 1 contributions) is—
  (a) in a case where the deduction did not extinguish the contributions payment, the date on which the remainder of the contributions payment or, as the case may be, the first date on which any part of the remainder of the contributions payment, was paid; and
  (b) in a case where the deduction extinguished the contributions payment, the fourteenth day after the end of the income tax month during which there were paid the earnings in respect of which the contributions payment was payable.

Signed by authority of the Secretary of State for Social Services.

John Major

23rd January 1987   Minister of State, Department of Health and Social Security

The Commissioners of Inland Revenue hereby concur.
By Order of the Commissioners of Inland Revenue.

B. Pollard
A.J.G. Isaac

27th January 1987   Two of the Commissioners of Inland Revenue

---

EXPLANATORY NOTE

(This note is not part of the Regulations)

These regulations provide for compensation of employers who have made payments of statutory maternity pay under the Social Security Act 1986.

They are made under section 49(1) of, and paragraphs 1 and 5 of Schedule 4 to, the Social Security Act 1986, all of which come into force on 6th April 1987 (see the Social Security Act 1986 (Commencement No. 4) Order 1986, S.I. 1986/1959 (C.73)). As the regulations are made before the end of a period of 12 months from the coming into force of the above provisions, they are exempted by section 61(5)(a) of the Social Security Act 1986 from the requirement under section 10(1) of the Social Security Act 1980 (c.30) to refer proposals to the Social Security Advisory Committee and are made without reference to that Committee.

Regulations 2 and 3 provide that an employer who has made a payment of statutory maternity pay shall be entitled to a sum equal to a percentage of the statutory maternity pay he has paid.

Regulation 4 provides that, subject to specified exceptions, an employer may recover the amount of the statutory maternity pay he has paid and the additional sum to which he is entitled under regulations 2 and 3 by making one or more deductions from the payments of Class 1 contributions which he is required to make under the Social Security Act 1975 (c.14).

Regulation 5 specifies circumstances in which the Secretary of State is to pay to an employer a sum which the employer has paid as statutory maternity pay or to which he is entitled under regulations 2 and 3.

When a deduction has been made under regulation 4, the amount deducted is treated under paragraph 5 of Schedule 4 to the Social Security Act 1986 as having been paid towards discharging the liability for contributions under the 1975 Act. Regulation 6 makes provision for determining the date on which it is to be treated as having been paid.

1987 No. 92

TERMS AND CONDITIONS OF EMPLOYMENT

The Statutory Sick Pay (Additional Compensation of Employers) Amendment Regulations 1987

Made - - - -	*27th January 1987*
Laid before Parliament	*4th Februry 1987*
Coming into force	*6th April 1987*

The Secretary of State for Social Services, with the concurrence of the Inland Revenue insofar as their concurrence is required, in exercise of the powers conferred upon him by sections 9(1A), 26(1), 45(2) and 47 of the Social Security and Housing Benefits Act 1982 (**a**) and of all other powers enabling him in that behalf, hereby makes the following regulations:

Citation, commencement and interpretation

1.—(1) These regulations may be cited as the Statutory Sick Pay (Additional Compensation of Employers) Amendment Regulations 1987 and shall come into force on 6th April 1987.

(2) In these regulations "the principal regulations" means the Statutory Sick Pay (Additional Compensation of Employers and Consequential Amendments) Regulations 1985 (**b**).

Amendment of regulation 1(2) of the principal regulations

2. In regulation 1(2) of the principal regulations (interpretation) after the definition of regulation 2, regulation 3, regulation 4 and regulation 5 there shall be inserted–

" "statutory maternity pay" has the same meaning as in Part V of the Social Security Act 1986 (**c**);"

Substitution for regulation 3 of the principal regulations

3. For regulation 3 of the principal regulations (determination of amount) there shall be substituted the following regulation–

"**3.** In respect of a payment of statutory sick pay made in the tax year commencing 6th April 1987, an employer shall be entitled under regulation 2 to an amount equal to 7 per cent. of the payment, that percentage being the total amount of secondary Class 1 contributions estimated by the Secretary of State as to be paid in respect of statutory maternity pay and statutory sick pay by all employers in that year, expressed as a percentage of the total amount of statutory maternity pay and statutory sick pay estimated by him to be paid by all employers in that year.".

(**a**) 1982 c.24; section 9(1A) was inserted by the Social Security Act 1985 (c.53), section 19(1)(a), and amended by the Social Security Act 1986 (c.50), section 67(2).
(**b**) S.I. 1985/1411.
(**c**) 1986 c.50.

Signed by authority of the Secretary of State for Social Services.

John Major
Minister of State,
23rd January 1987   Department of Health and Social Security

The Commissioners of Inland Revenue hereby concur.
By Order of the Commissioners of Inland Revenue.

B. Pollard
A. J. G. Isaac
27th January 1987   Two of the Commissioners of Inland Revenue

---

EXPLANATORY NOTE

(This note is not part of the Regulations)

These regulations amend the Statutory Sick Pay (Additional Compensation of Employers and Consequential Amendments) Regulations 1985 by inserting a new regulation 3 into those regulations (regulation 2).

The new regulation 3 provides that, for the tax year beginning on 6th April 1987, the rate of an employer's additional compensation in respect of any payment of statutory sick pay made by him is to be 7 per cent., that rate having been determined by reference to the aggregate of secondary Class 1 contributions paid in respect of statutory sick pay and statutory maternity pay.

As these regulations are made under section 9 of the Social Security and Housing Benefits Act 1982 they are exempted by paragraph 15A of Schedule 3 to the Social Security Act 1980 (c.30) (see also paragraph 107 of Schedule 10 to the Social Security Act 1986) from the requirement under section 10(1) of the Social Security Act 1980 to refer proposals to the Social Security Advisory Committee and are made without reference to that Committee.

STATUTORY INSTRUMENTS

1987 No. 93 (S. 8)

BETTING, GAMING AND LOTTERIES

The Betting, Gaming and Lotteries Act 1963 (Variation of Fees) (Scotland) Order 1987

Made - - - -	*19th January 1987*
Laid before Parliament	*5th February 1987*
Coming into force	*2nd March 1987*

The Secretary of State, in exercise of the powers conferred on him by paragraph 20(1A) of Schedule 1 to the Betting, Gaming and Lotteries Act 1963(**a**) and of all other powers enabling him in that behalf, hereby makes the following Order:

1. This Order may be cited as the Betting, Gaming and Lotteries Act 1963 (Variation of Fees) (Scotland) Order 1987, shall extend to Scotland only and shall come into force on 2nd March 1987.

2. Paragraph 20(1) (fees for grant or renewal of bookmakers' permits, betting agency permits and betting office licences) of Schedule 1 to the Betting, Gaming and Lotteries Act 1963 shall be amended as follows:–

(a) in paragraph (b) (grant of betting agency permit), for the words "five pounds" there shall be substituted "£100"; and

(b) for paragraph (c) (renewal of bookmaker's permit, betting agency permit or grant or renewal of betting office licence) there shall be substituted–

"(c) in the case of the grant of a betting office licence, £80;

(d) in the case of the renewal of a bookmaker's permit or betting agency permit, £12;

(e) in the case of the renewal of a betting office licence, £15;".

Ian Lang
Parliamentary Under Secretary of State,
Scottish Office

New St. Andrew's House
Edinburgh
19th January 1987

(**a**) 1963 c.2; paragraph 20(1A) was inserted by the Betting, Gaming and Lotteries (Amendment) Act 1984 (c.25), section 3.

EXPLANATORY NOTE

(This note is not part of the Order)

This Order amends the fees payable to the appropriate authority under paragraph 20(1) of Schedule 1 to the Betting, Gaming and Lotteries Act 1963 for the grant and renewal of betting agency permits and betting office licences and the renewal of bookmakers' permits. The fee for the grant of a betting agency permit is increased from £5 to £100 (article 2(a)), and for the grant of a betting office licence from £1 to £80 (article 2(b)). The fee for the renewal of a bookmaker's permit or betting agency permit is increased from £1 to £12, and of a betting office licence from £1 to £15 (article 2(b)).

STATUTORY INSTRUMENTS

1987 No. 95

BETTING, GAMING AND LOTTERIES

The Betting, Gaming and Lotteries Act 1963 (Variation of Fees) Order 1987

Made - - - -	*27th January 1987*
Laid before Parliament	*5th February 1987*
Coming into force - -	*2nd March 1987*

In pursuance of paragraph 20(1A) of Schedule 1 to the Betting, Gaming and Lotteries Act 1963**(a)**, I hereby make the following Order:

1.—(1) This Order may be cited as the Betting, Gaming and Lotteries Act 1963 (Variation of Fees) Order 1987 and shall come into force on 2nd March 1987.

(2) This Order shall not extend to Scotland.

2.   Paragraph 20(1) (grant or renewal of permit or licence) of Schedule 1 (bookmakers' permits, betting agency permits and betting office licences) to the Betting, Gaming and Lotteries Act 1963 shall be amended as follows –

(a) in paragraph (b) (grant of betting agency permit) for the words "five pounds" there shall be substituted "£100"; and

(b) for paragraph (c) (renewal of bookmaker's permit or betting agency permit or grant or renewal of betting office licence) there shall be substituted –

"(c) in the case of the grant of a betting office licence, £80;

(d) in the case of the renewal of a bookmaker's permit or betting agency permit, £12;

(e) in the case of the renewal of a betting office licence, £15;".

Douglas Hurd
One of Her Majesty's Principal Secretaries of State

Home Office
27th January 1987

(a) 1963 c.2; paragraph 20(1A) was inserted by section 3 of the Betting, Gaming and Lotteries (Amendment) Act 1984 (c.25).

EXPLANATORY NOTE

(This note is not part of the Order)

This Order amends the fees payable in England and Wales to the appropriate authority under paragraph 20(1) of Schedule 1 to the Betting, Gaming and Lotteries Act 1963 for the grant and renewal of betting agency permits and betting office licences and the renewal of bookmakers' permits. The fee for the grant of a betting agency permit is increased from £5 to £100 (Article 2(a)) and for the grant of a betting office licence from £1 to £80 (Article 2(b)). The fee for renewal of a bookmaker's permit or betting agency permit is increased from £1 to £12 and of a betting office licence from £1 to £15 (Article 2(b)).

1987 No. 96

EDUCATION, ENGLAND AND WALES

The Education (Training Grants) Regulations 1987

Made - - - -		*26th January 1987*
Laid before Parliament		*5th February 1987*
Coming into force		*1st March 1987*

In exercise of the powers conferred on the Secretary of State by sections 50 and 63 of the Education (No. 2) Act 1986(a), read with section 114 of the Education Act 1944(b), and (as respects the revocation made by regulation 13) by sections 3(a) and 4 of the Education Act 1962(c), I hereby make the following Regulations:-

Citation and operation

1. These Regulations may be cited as the Education (Training Grants) Regulations 1987 and shall come into force on 1st March 1987.

Interpretation

2.—(1) In these Regulations –

"authority" means a local education authority;

"determine" means determine by notice in writing;

"eligible training" means training of a kind mentioned in regulation 4;

"expenditure" means expenditure of a kind mentioned in regulation 5;

"expenditure incurred by an authority" includes expenditure incurred –

(a) by the governors of an aided school,

(b) by the persons responsible for the maintenance of a further education establishment, or

(c) by persons employing youth and community workers

and reimbursed by the authority;

"further education establishment" means a further education establishment provided by an authority or designated by or under regulations(d) made under section 27 of the Education Act 1980(e) as an establishment substantially dependent for its maintenance on assistance from local education authorities;

"grant" means a grant in pursuance of these Regulations;

"higher rate" means 70 per cent;

"lower rate" means 50 per cent;

(a) 1986 c.61.   (b) 1944 c.31 (section 114(1) defines "prescribed"); S.I.1964/490, 1970/1536 and 1978/274.   (c) 1962 c.12. Sections 3 and 4 are set out, as substituted, in Schedule 5 to the Education Act 1980 (c.20).   (d) Regulations in which such establishments are currently designated are the Education (Teachers) Regulations 1982 (S.I.1982/106) and the Education (Schools and Further Education) Regulations 1981 (S.I.1981/1086), to which there are relevant amendments in S.I.1983/262.   (e) 1980 c.20.

"qualified teacher" means a person who, in pursuance of the regulations(a) relating to the employment of teachers from time to time in force under section 27 of the Education Act 1980, is qualified to be employed as a teacher at a school to which that section applies;

"trainee" means a person undergoing eligible training in respect of whom grant is payable under these Regulations; and

"training in a national priority area" means eligible training of a kind approved by the Secretary of State for the purpose of these Regulations as training eligible for grant at the higher rate.

(2)   In these Regulations a reference to a regulation is a reference to a regulation contained therein and a reference in a regulation to a paragraph is a reference to a paragraph of that regulation.

Employment connected with leisure-time facilities

3.   All categories of employment connected with leisure-time facilities, excluding those of a solely administrative, secretarial, clerical or manual nature, are hereby prescribed for the purpose of the definition of "youth and community worker" in section 50(4) of the Education (No. 2) Act 1986.

Grants by the Secretary of State

4.   The Secretary of State is hereby authorised, subject to and in accordance with these Regulations, to make grants to authorities to facilitate and encourage –

(a)   the further training as teachers of qualified teachers, whether or not they are employed as such;

(b)   the training or further training as teachers of persons other than qualified teachers who are employed as teachers by an authority, by the governors of an aided school or by the persons responsible for the maintenance of a further education establishment;

(c)   the training of qualified teachers (whether or not they are employed as such) and other persons who are employed as teachers by an authority, by the governors of an aided school or by the persons responsible for the maintenance of a further education establishment as –

(i)   youth and community workers;

(ii)   educational psychologists;

(iii)   education authority inspectors;

(iv)   education advisers;

(d)   the training or further training of those employed –

(i)   as youth and community workers;

(ii)   as educational psychologists;

(iii)   as education authority inspectors;

(iv)   by an authority as education advisers.

Expenditure in respect of which grants are payable

5.   Grants shall be payable only in respect of expenditure incurred by an authority on or after 1st April 1987 on –

(a)   tuition fees, examination fees and residential and other charges payable in respect of eligible training;

(b)   travelling, subsistence and other incidental expenses of a trainee;

(c)   that part of the remuneration of persons whose employment is necessary to free the trainee for training which relates to the period during which their employment is so necessary;

(d)   the cost of providing (including the provision of premises), planning, co-ordinating, monitoring and evaluating eligible training:

(a) The Regulations currently in force are the Education (Teachers) Regulations 1982.

Provided that where such costs are incurred for such purposes and for other purposes grant shall be payable only on such proportion of those costs as is attributable to the provision, planning, co-ordinating, monitoring or evaluation of eligible training.

Conditions for payment of grant

6.   It shall be a condition for the payment of grant to any authority that the authority shall have submitted to the Secretary of State proposals for expenditure to be incurred by them on eligible training –

   (a)   in such form,

   (b)   at such time,

   (c)   containing such particulars of expenditure which the authority proposes to incur on training in each national priority area (including such training on which the authority does not propose to claim grant), and

   (d)   containing such particulars of expenditure which the authority proposes to incur in respect of such other eligible training (including such training on which the authority does not propose to claim grant)

as the Secretary of State may determine.

7.—(1)   The Secretary of State shall notify the authority in writing of –

   (a)   the maximum amount of expenditure to be incurred by the authority on training in each national priority area that will, subject to regulation 9, be eligible for grant at the higher rate, and

   (b)   the maximum amount of expenditure to be incurred by the authority on eligible training that will be eligible for grant at the lower rate

which maximum amount may, in any case, be nil.

(2)   Where it appears to the Secretary of State that an authority does not expect to incur expenditure up to, or wishes to incur expenditure in excess of, a maximum amount notified under paragraph (1) the Secretary of State may, after consulting the authority, by notice in writing to the authority reduce or increase the maximum amount of expenditure so notified. A notice given under this paragraph shall, for the purposes of these Regulations, be deemed to be a notice of the maximum amount of expenditure to be incurred by the authority on training in the national priority area concerned under paragraph (1)(a) or on eligible training under paragraph (1)(b), as the case may be.

8.—(1)   Grant at the higher rate shall, subject to regulation 9, be payable on any expenditure incurred by an authority on training in a national priority area up to the maximum amount for such expenditure notified for that area under regulation 7(1)(a).

(2)   Grant at the lower rate shall be payable on expenditure incurred by an authority on eligible training up to the maximum amount for such expenditure notified under regulation 7(1)(b).

9.—(1)   Where an authority incurs expenditure on training in a national priority area in excess of the maximum notified for that area under regulation 7(1)(a), then, if that authority has incurred, on training in such other national priority areas as may be determined by the Secretary of State for this purpose before or at the time of making such notification, expenditure less than the maximum so notified, grant on that excess expenditure shall be payable at the higher rate up to the aggregate amount of the shortfall of expenditure in those other areas, subject to a limit in respect of each other area of 10% of the maximum amount so notified for that area.

(2)   Any expenditure incurred by an authority on training in a national priority area not eligible for grant at the higher rate under regulation 8(1) or paragraph (1) shall be eligible for grant at the lower rate to the extent that the expenditure can be accommodated within the maximum notified under regulation 7(1)(b).

10.—(1)   No payment of grant shall be made except in response to a claim in writing from an authority to the Secretary of State, authenticated by the officer of the authority responsible for the administration of their financial affairs or his deputy.

(2)   Claims for the payment of grant shall relate to expenditure over one or more quarters.

(3)   Claims which relate to expenditure during the quarters commencing on 1st April, 1st July and 1st October in any year shall specify the expenditure in respect of which grant is claimed which it is estimated has been or will be incurred by the authority during that quarter and shall be accompanied by an estimate of expenditure which the authority expects to incur in the remainder of the financial year.

(4)   Each authority that has received or seeks to receive a payment of grant in respect of expenditure incurred during the year ending on 31st March shall, during the quarter commencing on 1st April or as soon as practicable thereafter –

(a)   submit to the Secretary of State a claim which shall specify the expenditure in respect of which grant has been or is being claimed which has been incurred by the authority during that year; and

(b)   secure the submission to the Secretary of State of a certificate, signed by the auditor appointed by the Audit Commission to audit the accounts of the authority or any auditor qualified for such appointment by virtue of section 13(5) and (6) of the Local Government Finance Act 1982(a), certifying that in his opinion the particulars stated in the claim submitted by the authority pursuant to this paragraph are fairly stated and that grant at the rate claimed is properly payable pursuant to these Regulations.

(5)   No payment of grant shall be made in respect of expenditure by an authority incurred in the quarter beginning on 1st October in any year or any subsequent quarter, if grant was paid to the authority in respect of expenditure in the year ending on the preceding 31st March but the Secretary of State has not received the auditor's certificate referred to in paragraph (4) for that year.

(6)   Any under-payment or over-payment of grant which remains outstanding following receipt of the auditor's certificate referred to in paragraph (4) shall, without prejudice to the recovery of any over-payment from any subsequent payment of grant to the authority, be adjusted by payment between the authority and the Secretary of State.

(7)   In this regulation, a "quarter" means a period of three calendar months commencing on 1st January, 1st April, 1st July or 1st October in any year.

11.   Any authority to whom a payment of grant has been made shall, if so requested by the Secretary of State, furnish him with such further information as may be determined by him to enable him to verify that any grant paid has been properly paid under these Regulations.

Further Conditions and Requests

12.—(1)   The Secretary of State may from time to time determine further conditions on the fulfilment of which the making of any payment in pursuance of these Regulations shall be dependent.

(2)   Where conditions have been determined in pursuance of this regulation no grant shall be payable unless such conditions have been fulfilled.

(3)   The Secretary of State may from time to time after consulting the authority concerned determine further requests with which any authority to whom a payment has been made in pursuance of these Regulations shall comply.

Revocation and Transitional Provisions

13.   The Education (Grants for Teacher Training) (No. 2) Regulations 1985(b) are hereby revoked but nothing in this revocation shall prevent the Secretary of State making payments of grant in respect of training to which those regulations applied carried out on or before 31st March 1987.

Angela Rumbold
Minister of State,
26th January 1987   Department of Education and Science

(a) 1982 c.32.   (b) S.I. 1985/1883.

EXPLANATORY NOTE

(This note is not part of the Regulations)

These Regulations make provision for the payment by the Secretary of State to local education authorities of grants to encourage and facilitate the training of teachers, youth and community workers, educational psychologists, education authority inspectors and education advisers employed by an authority. The kind of training eligible for grant is set out in Regulation 4.

The expenditure on which grant is payable includes fees and charges payable in respect of eligible training, the costs of providing the eligible training and the remuneration of necessary staff to replace the trainee (Regulation 5). It includes, in addition to expenditure incurred by the authority itself, expenditure incurred by governors of aided schools and by persons who maintain further education establishments assisted by the authority and by persons employing youth and community workers, where such expenditure is reimbursed by the authority.

Authorities wishing to claim grant are required to submit proposals for expenditure on eligible training in such form and containing such particulars (including particulars of training in a national priority area) as the Secretary of State may determine. "National priority area" is defined in Regulation 2(1) to mean eligible training of a kind approved by the Secretary of State for the purpose of the Regulations as training eligible for grant at the higher rate. The Secretary of State will then notify authorities of the maximum level of expenditure eligible for grant at the higher rate of 70% in each national priority area and the maximum level of expenditure that will be eligible for grant at the lower rate of 50%. Provision is made for varying the maximum levels and for payment of grant at the higher rate on expenditure in a national priority area in excess of the maximum notified for that area where less expenditure has been incurred on another area. (Regulations 6 to 9).

Claims for grant are to be made quarterly and the manner of making claims and the other requirements relating thereto are set out in Regulation 10. Authorities are required to furnish the Secretary of State with such further information as he may determine (Regulation 11).

The Secretary of State may determine further conditions on the fulfilment of which the payment of grant shall be dependent. He may also determine further requests with which authorities to whom grant has been paid must comply (Regulation 12).

"Youth and community worker" is defined by section 50(4) of the Education (No. 2) Act 1986 as meaning a person who is employed (whether or not by a local education authority) in such category of employment connected with leisure-time facilities as may be prescribed by regulations. Regulation 3 prescribes for this purpose all categories of employment connected with such facilities except those of a solely administrative, secretarial, clerical or manual nature. "Leisure-time facilities" is defined in the 1986 Act as meaning only those which local education authorities are, by virtue of a scheme of further education or the requirements of section 53(1) of the Education Act 1944, under a duty to provide.

The Education (Grants for Teacher Training) (No. 2) Regulations 1985 are revoked, but grant may still be paid where training to which those Regulations applied has been carried out before 31st March 1987.

STATUTORY INSTRUMENTS

1987 No. 97

ROAD TRAFFIC

The Community Drivers' Hours (Passenger and Goods Vehicles) (Temporary Exception) (Revocation) Regulations 1987

Made - - - -	*28th January 1987*
Laid before Parliament	*30th January 1987*
Coming into force	*2nd February 1987*

The Secretary of State for Transport, being a Minister designated**(a)** for the purposes of section 2(2) of the European Communities Act 1972**(b)** in relation to the regulation and supervision of the working conditions of persons engaged in road transport, in exercise of the powers conferred by that section, hereby makes the following Regulations:—

1. These Regulations may be cited as the Community Drivers' Hours (Passenger and Goods Vehicles) (Temporary Exception) (Revocation) Regulations 1987 and shall come into force on 2nd February 1987.

2.—(1) The Community Drivers' Hours (Passenger and Goods Vehicles) (Temporary Exception) Regulations 1987**(c)** are hereby revoked.

(2) On and after 2nd February 1987 no account shall be taken of any time spent driving or on duty before that date for the purpose of the application of Articles 6, 8 or 9 of Council Regulation (EEC) No. 3820/85 of 20th December 1985 on the harmonisation of certain social legislation relating to road transport**(d)**.

Peter Bottomley
Signed by authority of the Secretary of State
28th January 1987
Parliamentary Under Secretary of State,
Department of Transport

(**a**) S.I. 1975/1707.
(**b**) 1972 c.68.
(**c**) S.I. 1987/27.
(**d**) OJ No. L 370, 31.12.85, p.1.

EXPLANATORY NOTE

(This note is not part of the Regulations)

These Regulations revoke the Community Drivers' Hours (Passenger and Goods Vehicles) (Temporary Exception) Regulations 1987.

STATUTORY INSTRUMENTS

1987 No. 98

ROAD TRAFFIC

The Drivers' Hours (Passenger and Goods Vehicles) (Exemption) (Revocation) Regulations 1987

Made - - -	*28th January 1987*
Laid before Parliament	*30th January 1987*
Coming into force -	*2nd February 1987*

The Secretary of State for Transport, in exercise of the powers conferred by section 96(10) of the Transport Act 1968(a) and now vested in him(b) and of all other enabling powers, after consultation with representative organisations in accordance with section 101(6) of that Act, hereby makes the following Regulations:—

1. These Regulations may be cited as the Drivers' Hours (Passenger and Goods Vehicles) (Exemption) (Revocation) Regulations 1987 and shall come into force on 2nd February 1987.

2.— The Drivers' Hours (Passenger and Goods Vehicles) (Exemption) Regulations 1987(c) are hereby revoked.

Signed by authority of the Secretary of State

Peter Bottomley
Parliamentary Under Secretary of State,
Department of Transport

28th January 1987

EXPLANATORY NOTE

(This note is not part of the Regulations)

These Regulations revoke the Drivers' Hours (Passenger and Goods Vehicles) (Exemption) Regulations 1987.

(a) 1968 c.73; Part VI of the Transport Act 1968 is modified by S.I. 1970/257, 1971/818 and 1986/1459.
(b) S.I. 1970/1681, 1979/571 and 1981/238.
(c) S.I. 1987/28.

STATUTORY INSTRUMENTS

1987 No. 101

TOWN AND COUNTRY PLANNING, ENGLAND AND WALES

The Town and Country Planning (Fees for Applications and Deemed Applications) (Amendment) Regulations 1987

Made - - - -	*28th January 1987*
Coming into force	*25th February 1987*

The Secretary of State for the Environment, in exercise of the powers conferred upon him by section 87 of the Local Government, Planning and Land Act 1980(**a**) and of all other powers enabling him in that behalf, hereby makes the following regulations:

Citation and commencement

1.—(1) These regulations may be cited as the Town and Country Planning (Fees for Applications and Deemed Applications) (Amendment) Regulations 1987.

(2) These regulations shall come into force on the twenty-eighth day after the day on which they are made.

General increase in fees

2.—(1) The Town and Country Planning (Fees for Applications and Deemed Applications) Regulations 1983(**b**) ("the 1983 regulations") shall have effect with the amendments relating to the amounts of fees that are set out in this regulation.

(2) In Part I of Schedule 1 there shall be substituted for "£53"–

(a) in relation to fees due after the commencement of these regulations but before 1st July 1987, "£60"; and

(b) in relation to fees due on or after 1st July 1987, "£66".

(3) The scale of fees set out in Part II of Schedule 1 shall have effect with the substitution for a reference to a sum mentioned in the first column of the Table below–

(i) in relation to fees due after the commencement of these regulations but before 1st July 1987, of a reference to the relevant sum specified in the second column; and

(ii) in relation to fees due on or after 1st July 1987, of a reference to the relevant sum specified in the third column.

(**a**) 1980 c.65.
(**b**) S.I. 1983/1674, amended by S.I. 1985/1182.

Sum currently specified	Increased sum for the period until 1st July 1987	Increased sum from 1st July 1987
Fees and multipliers		
£27	£30	£33
£53	£60	£66
Maxima		
£270	£300	£330
£315	£355	£390
£1,325	£1,500	£1,650
£2,650	£3,000	£3,300
£4,050	£4,500	£4,950

(4) In Schedule 2,–

    (a) in relation to fees due after the commencement of these regulations but before 1st July 1987, "£16" shall be substituted for "£14" and "£60" for "£53"; and

    (b) in relation to fees due on or after 1st July 1987, "£18" shall be substituted for "£14" and "£66" for "£53".

Miscellaneous amendments

3. The 1983 regulations shall also have effect subject to the miscellaneous amendments set out in Schedule 1 hereto.

Substitution of a new fee Schedule

4. In relation to fees due on or after 1st July 1987 there shall be substituted for Part II of Schedule 1 to the 1983 regulations the new Part II set out in Schedule 2 hereto (which reflects the increased amounts mentioned in column 3 of the Table in regulation 2 and other amendments made to Part II by these regulations).

Revocations

5.—(1) In the Town and Country Planning (Fees for Applications and Deemed Applications) (Amendment) Regulations 1985 (**a**), regulations 2(c)(iii), (iv) and (vi) and (e) are revoked from the commencement of these regulations, and regulation 2(d) and the Schedule are revoked on 1st July 1987.

(2) Regulations 2(2)(a), (3) and (4)(a) of, and paragraph 7 of Schedule 1 to, these regulations cease to have effect on 1st July 1987.

Regulation 3

SCHEDULE 1

MINOR AMENDMENTS TO THE 1983 REGULATIONS

Invalid application: refund of fees

1. In regulation 3, there shall be added as paragraph (5),–

    "(5) Any fee paid pursuant to this regulation shall be refunded if the relevant application is rejected as invalidly made.".

Consolidation of permissions for mineral working: exemption from fee

2. There shall be inserted as regulation 7A–

    "**7A.** Regulation 3 shall not apply to impose a fee in relation to an application to a local planning authority for permission to carry out development consisting of the winning and working of minerals where the application–

(**a**) S.I. 1985/1182.

(a) is for a permission which consolidates two or more subsisting permissions; and

(b) does not seek permission for development which is not authorised by a subsisting permission.".

Refund of fees on deemed applications

3. In regulation 8,–

(a) at the beginning of paragraph (2) there shall be inserted, "Subject to paragraph (13)";

(b) at the end of paragraph (10) there shall be added "or if the Secretary of State decides that the enforcement notice is a nullity";

(c) at the end of paragraph (12) there shall be added "(whether because there is no subsisting use of the land in relation to which he may grant planning permission or for any other reason)"; and

(d) there shall be added as paragraph (13),–

"(13)(a) Where planning permission is deemed to have been applied for by virtue of section 88B (3) of the 1971 Act (**a**) and–

(i) an enforcement notice is varied under section 88A otherwise than to take account of a grant of planning permission under section 88B; and

(ii) the amount of the fee calculated in accordance with Schedule 1 would have been a lesser amount if the original notice had been in the terms of the varied notice,

the fee payable shall be that lesser amount; and any excess amount already paid shall be refunded.

(b) In determining a fee under sub-paragraph (a) no account shall be taken of any change in fees which takes effect after the making of the deemed application.".

Advertisement consent: exemption from, and refund of, fees

4. In regulation 9,–

(a) in paragraph (1) for "1969" there shall be substituted "1984 ("the 1984 regulations")";

(b) in paragraph (10) (conditions for exemption) there shall be substituted for sub-paragraph (a)(ii)–

"(ii) in any other case, the date of refusal, or where an appeal is made to the Secretary of State pursuant to regulation 22 of the 1984 regulations, the date on which the appeal is determined,"; and

(c) there shall be added as paragraphs (11) and (12),–

"(11) No fee is payable under this regulation in respect of an application for consent to display an advertisement if the application is occasioned by a direction under regulation 15 of the 1984 regulations disapplying regulation 14 in relation to the advertisement in question.

(12) Any fee paid pursuant to this regulation shall be refunded if the relevant application is rejected as invalidly made.".

Multiple applications for approval of reserved matters

5. Paragraph 5 of Part I of Schedule 1 shall be omitted and there shall be inserted the following two paragraphs–

"5.—(1) This paragraph applies where–

(a) an application is made for approval of one or more reserved matters ("the current application"); and

(b) the applicant has previously applied for such approval under the same outline planning permission and paid fees in relation to one or more such applications; and

(c) no application has been made under that permission other than by or on behalf of the applicant.

(2) Where this paragraph applies and the amount of the fees paid as mentioned in sub-paragraph (1)(b) is not less than the amount which would be payable if the applicant were by his current application seeking approval of all the matters reserved by the outline permission (and in relation to the whole of the development authorised by the permission), the amount of the fee payable in respect of the current application shall be–

(a) if the fee is due after the commencement of these regulations but before 1st July 1987, £60;

(b) if the fee is due on or after 1st July 1987, £66.

(**a**) This is a reference to the Town and Country Planning Act 1971 (c.78).

(3) Where–

    (i) this paragraph applies;

    (ii) a fee has been paid as mentioned in sub-paragraph (1)(b) at a rate lower than that prevailing at the date of the current application; and

    (iii) sub-paragraph (2) would apply if that fee had been paid at the rate applying at that date,

the amount of the fee in respect of the current application shall be the relevant amount specified in sub-paragraph (2).

Applications under section 31A of the 1971 Act

5A.   Where application is made pursuant to section 31A of the 1971 Act(**a**) the amount of the fee payable in respect of the application shall be £30 if the fee is due before 1st July 1987, and £33 if it is due on or after that date.".

Land in the area of two or more authorities

6.   Paragraph 6 of Part I of Schedule 1 shall be omitted and there shall be inserted the following two paragraphs–

"**6.**—(1) This paragraph applies where applications are made for planning permission or for the approval of reserved matters in respect of the development of land lying in the areas of–

    (a) two or more local planning authorities in a metropolitan county or in Greater London; or

    (b) two or more district planning authorities in a non-metropolitan county; or

    (c) one or more such local planning authorities and one or more such district planning authorities.

(2) Where this paragraph applies a fee shall be payable under these regulations only to the local planning authority or district planning authority in whose area the largest part of the relevant land is situated: and the amount of that fee shall be–

    (i) where the applications relate wholly or partly to a county matter within the meaning of paragraph 32 of Schedule 16 to the Local Government Act 1972(**b**), and all the land is situated in a single non-metropolitan county, the amount which would have been payable if application had fallen to be made to one authority in relation to the whole development;

    (ii) in any other case, one and a half times the amount which would have been payable if application had fallen to be made to a single authority.

6A.—(1) This paragraph applies where application for planning permission is deemed to have been made by virtue of section 88B(3) of the 1971 Act in respect of such land as is mentioned in paragraph 6(1).

(2) Where this paragraph applies, the fee payable to the Secretary of State shall be a fee of the amount which would be payable by virtue of paragraph 6(2) if application for the like permission had been made to the relevant local or district planning authority on the date on which notice of appeal was given in accordance with section 88(3) of the 1971 Act.".

Development in connection with oil or gas exploration

7.   In Part II of Schedule 1 there shall be inserted as item 7A–

"**7A.** The carrying out of any operations connected with exploratory drilling for oil or natural gas.	(a) Where application is made before 1st July 1987, £60 for each 0.1 hectare of the site area subject to a maximum of £4,500;
	(b) in any other case, £66 for each 0.1 hectare of the site area subject to a maximum of £4,950.".

(**a**) Section 31A is inserted by paragraph 4 of Schedule 11 to the Housing and Planning Act 1986 (c.63).
(**b**) 1972 c.70.

SCHEDULE 2   Regulation 4

NEW PART II OF SCHEDULE 1 TO THE 1983 REGULATIONS
SCALE OF FEES PAYABLE ON OR AFTER 1ST JULY 1987

Category of development	*Fee payable*

I. Operations

1. The erection of dwellinghouses (other than development within category 6 below).

(a) Where the application is for outline planning permission, £66 for each 0.1 hectare of the site area, subject to a maximum of £1,650;

(b) in other cases, £66 for each dwellinghouse to be created by the development, subject to a maximum of £3,300.

2. The erection of buildings (other than dwellinghouses, buildings coming within category 3, category 4 or category 7 or buildings in the nature of plant or machinery).

(a) Where the application is for outline planning permission, £66 for each 0.1 hectare of the site area, subject to a maximum of £1,650;

(b) in other cases–

  (i) where no floor space is to be created by the development, £33;

  (ii) where the area of gross floor space to be created by the development does not exceed 40 sq metres, £33;

  (iii) where the area of gross floor space to be created by the development exceeds 40 sq metres but does not exceed 75 sq metres, £66; and

  (iv) where the area of gross floor space to be created by the development exceeds 75 sq metres, £66 for each 75 sq metres, subject to a maximum of £3,300.

3. The erection, on land used for the purposes of agriculture, of buildings (other than glasshouses) to be used for agricultural purposes.

(a) Where the application is for outline planning permission, £66 for each 0.1 hectare of the site area, subject to a maximum of £1,650;

(b) in other cases–

  (i) where the area of gross floor space to be created by the development does not exceed 465 sq metres, nil;

  (ii) where the area of gross floor space to be created by the development exceeds 465 sq metres but does not exceed 540 sq metres, £66;

  (iii) where the area of gross floor space to be created by the development exceeds 540 sq metres, £66 for the first 540 sq metres and £66 for each 75 sq metres in excess of that figure, subject to a maximum of £3,300.

4. The erection of glasshouses on land used for the purposes of agriculture.

(a) Where the area of gross floor space to be created by the development does not exceed 465 sq metres, nil;

(b) where the area of gross floor space to be created by the development exceeds 465 sq metres, £390.

5. The erection, alteration or replacement of plant or machinery.

£66 for each 0.1 hectare of the site area, subject to a maximum of £3,300.

Category of development	*Fee payable*
6. The enlargement, improvement or other alteration of existing dwellinghouses.	(a) Where the application relates to one dwellinghouse, £33; (b) where the application relates to 2 or more dwellinghouses, £66.
7. (a) The carrying out of operations (including the erection of a building) within the curtilage of an existing dwellinghouse, for purposes ancillary to the enjoyment of the dwellinghouse as such, or the erection or construction of gates, fences, walls or other means of enclosure along a boundary of the curtilage of an existing dwellinghouse; or (b) the construction of car parks, service roads and other means of access on land used for the purposes of a single undertaking, where the development is required for a purpose incidental to the existing use of the land.	£33.
8. The carrying out of any operations connected with exploratory drilling for oil or natural gas.	£66 for each 0.1 hectare of the site area, subject to a maximum of £4,950.
9. The carrying out of any operations not coming within any of the above categories.	£33 for each 0.1 hectare of the site area, subject to a maximum of– (a) in the case of operations for the winning and working of minerals, £4,950; (b) in other cases, £330.

II. Uses of Land

Category of development	*Fee payable*
10. The change of use of a building to use as one or more separate dwellinghouses.	(a) Where the change is from a previous use as a single dwellinghouse to use as two or more single dwellinghouses, £66 for each additional dwellinghouse to be created by the development, subject to a maximum of £3,300; (b) in other cases, £66 for each dwellinghouse to be created by the development, subject to a maximum of £3,300.
11. (a) The use of land for the disposal of refuse or waste materials or for the deposit of material remaining after minerals have been extracted from land; or (b) the use of land for the storage of minerals in the open.	£33 for each 0.1 hectare of the site area, subject to a maximum of £4,950.
12. The making of a material change in the use of a building or land (other than a material change of use coming within any of the above categories).	£66.
13. The continuance of a use of land, or the retention of buildings or works on land, without compliance with a condition subject to which a previous planning permission has been granted (including a condition requiring the discontinuance of the use or the removal of the building or works at the end of a specified period).	£33.

Nicholas Ridley
28th January 1987   Secretary of State for the Environment

EXPLANATORY NOTE

(This note is not part of the Regulations)

These regulations further amend the Town and Country Planning (Fees for Applications and Deemed Applications) Regulations 1983.

The main change is that fees currently payable under the 1983 Regulations on planning applications are increased by two stages. The table in regulation 2 sets out the main figures and the increased figures. A replacement fee schedule set out in Schedule 2 shows most of the fees chargeable from 1st July 1987.

Two new fee categories are introduced. A new paragraph 5A is added to Part I of Schedule 1 to the 1983 regulations to provide for a standard fee of £30 (increasing to £33 on 1st July 1987) for applications under section 31A of the 1971 Act (change of conditions). A distinct fee category is introduced in paragraph 7A for planning permission connected with oil or natural gas exploration. The fee will be £60 for each 0.1 hectare of the site up to a maximum of £4,500, with an increase on 1st July 1987 in line with similar fees. Without specific provision, the fee would initially have been £30 for each 0.1 hectare subject to a maximum of £300.

Schedule 1 also sets out other miscellaneous amendments to the 1983 regulations. These provide for the refund of fees where an application is invalid (paragraphs 1 and 4) or where it is connected with an enforcement notice which is found to be invalid (paragraph 3). They also exempt from fee applications to consolidate existing permissions for mineral operations (paragraph 2) and applications to display advertisements occasioned by the withdrawal of deemed consent (paragraph 4). Account is also taken of the impact of the Local Government Act 1985 (c.51) on planning responsibilities in a case where a site is in the area of two authorities (paragraph 6) and the provision for reduced fees on successive applications for approval of reserved matters is revised to take account of fee increases (paragraph 5).

STATUTORY INSTRUMENTS

1987 No. 102

MEDICAL PROFESSION

The General Medical Council (Registration (Fees) (Amendment) Regulations) Order of Council 1987

Made - - - *29th January 1987*

Coming into force *1st February 1987*

At the Council Chamber, Whitehall, the 29th day of January 1987

By the Lords of Her Majesty's Most Honourable Privy Council

Whereas in pursuance of section 32 of the Medical Act 1983(a) the General Medical Council have made the Medical Practitioners Registration (Fees) (Amendment) Regulations 1986:

And whereas by subsection (8) of the said section such regulations shall not have effect until approved by Order of the Privy Council;

Now, therefore, Their Lordships, having taken the said regulations into consideration, are hereby pleased to approve the same as set out in the Schedule to this Order with effect from 1st February 1987.

This Order may be cited as the General Medical Council (Registration (Fees) (Amendment) Regulations) Order of Council 1987.

G. I. de Deney
Clerk of the Privy Council

(a) 1983 c.54.

SCHEDULE

THE MEDICAL PRACTITIONERS REGISTRATION (FEES) (AMENDMENT) REGULATIONS 1986

The General Medical Council in exercise of their powers under section 32 of the Medical Act 1983 hereby make the following regulations:—

Citation, commencement and interpretation

1.—(1) These regulations may be cited as the Medical Practitioners Registration (Fees) (Amendment) Regulations 1986 and shall come into operation on 1st February 1987.

(2) In these regulations "the principal regulations" means the Medical Practitioners Registration (Fees) Regulations 1985(a).

Amendment of principal regulations

2. For Regulations 3(2) and 4(2) of the principal regulations there shall be substituted the following:—

"3. (2) The scrutiny fee shall be:—
(a) For applications under section 19:
  (i) in the case of a person who has been provisionally registered £22
  (ii) In the case of any other person £42
(b) For applications under section 21 ....£20
(c) For applications by virtue of section 25 ....£140
    except in the case of a person who has obtained a primary United Kingdom qualification, when no fee shall be payable
(d) For applications under section 27 ....£42.";

"4. (2) The fees for the making of entries in the register shall be:—
(a) On provisional registration under section 15 of the Act £30
(b) On provisional registration under section 21 of the Act £56
(c) On full registration under section 3 of the Act:
  (i) in the case of a person who is or has at any time been provisionally registered £55
  (ii) in the case of any other person £85
    except in the case of a person who is already fully registered when no fee shall be payable
(d) On full registration under section 19 of the Act:
  (i) in the case of a person who is or has at any time been provisionally registered £84
  (ii) in the case of any other person £140
(e) On full registration by virtue of section 25 of the Act £140
(f) On registration under section 27 of the Act ....£140."

Given under the official seal of the General Medical Council this 3rd day of December, nineteen hundred and eighty-six.

J. N. Walton,
President

(a) Approved by S.I. 1986/149.

EXPLANATORY NOTE

(This note is not part of the Order)

The regulations approved by this Order increase, by approximately 40 per cent, the fees payable to the General Medical Council by overseas qualified medical practitioners in respect of the scrutiny of applications from such practitioners for registration and the making of entries in the register of medical practitioners, with effect from 1st February 1987.

STATUTORY INSTRUMENTS

1987 No. 106

SOCIAL SECURITY

The Social Security (Contributions) Amendment Regulations 1987

Made - - - -	*30th January 1987*
Laid before Parliament	*6th February 1987*
Coming into force	*6th April 1987*

The Secretary of State for Social Services, in exercise of the powers conferred upon him by section 1 of the Social Security Pensions Act 1975(**a**), and section 168(1) of, and Schedule 20 to, the Social Security Act 1975(**b**) and of all other powers enabling him in that behalf, hereby makes the following regulations:

Citation and commencement

1. These regulations, which may be cited as the Social Security (Contributions) Amendment Regulations 1987, amend the Social Security (Contributions) Regulations 1979(**c**) and shall come into force on 6th April 1987.

Amendment of regulation 7 of the Social Security (Contributions) Regulations 1979

2. In regulation 7 of the Social Security (Contributions) Regulations 1979 (lower and upper earnings limits for Class 1 contributions)–

(a) for the words "6th April 1986" there shall be substituted the words "6th April 1987"; and

(b) for "£38" and "£285" there shall be substituted respectively "£39" and "£295".

Signed by authority of the Secretary of State for Social Services.

John Major
30th January 1987   Minister of State, Department of Health and Social Security

---

EXPLANATORY NOTE

(This note is not part of the Regulations)

These Regulations further amend the Social Security (Contributions) Regulations 1979 by increasing the weekly lower and upper earnings limits for Class 1 contributions for the tax year beginning 6th April 1987.

(**a**) 1975 c.60; section 1 was amended by section 74(6) of the Social Security Act 1986 (c.50).
(**b**) 1975 c.14; see the Social Security Pensions Act 1975, section 66(2).
(**c**) S.I. 1979/591; the relevant amending instrument is S.I. 1985/1726.

STATUTORY INSTRUMENTS

1987 No. 114

ANIMALS

PREVENTION OF CRUELTY

The Welfare of Livestock (Prohibited Operations) (Amendment) Regulations 1987

Made - - - - -	*31st January 1987*
Coming into force	*1st February 1987*

The Minister of Agriculture, Fisheries and Food, the Secretary of State for Scotland and the Secretary of State for Wales, acting jointly, in exercise of the powers conferred by section 2 of the Agriculture (Miscellaneous Provisions) Act 1968**(a)** and now vested in them**(b)** and of all other powers enabling them in that behalf, after consultation in accordance with the said section 2 with such persons appearing to them to represent any interests concerned as they consider appropriate, hereby make the following regulations, of which a draft has been approved by a resolution of each House of Parliament:—

Title and commencement

1. These regulations may be cited as the Welfare of Livestock (Prohibited Operations) (Amendment) Regulations 1987 and shall come into operation on the day after the day on which they are made.

Amendment

2. The Welfare of Livestock (Prohibited Operations) Regulations 1982**(c)** shall be amended as follows:—

(a) after regulation 3 (prohibited operations) there shall be inserted the following regulation—

"3A. Subject to the provisions of regulation 4(a) no person shall perform, or cause or permit to be performed, the following operation in relation to sheep for the time being situated on agricultural land, namely tooth grinding of sheep."; and

---

(a) 1968 c. 34.
(b) In the case of the Secretary of State for Wales, by virtue of S.I. 1978/272.
(c) S.I. 1982/1884.

(b) for paragraph (a) of regulation 4 (exemptions) there shall be substituted the following paragraph—

    "(a) any act lawfully done under the Animals (Scientific Procedures) Act 1986**(a)**".

In Witness whereof the Official Seal of the Minister of Agriculture, Fisheries and Food is hereunto affixed on 31st January 1987.

Michael Jopling
Minister of Agriculture, Fisheries and Food

John J. Mackay
Parliamentary Under-Secretary of State, Scottish Office

26th January 1987

Nicholas Edwards
Secretary of State for Wales

28th January 1987

EXPLANATORY NOTE

(*This note is not part of the Regulations*)

The Welfare of Livestock (Prohibited Operations) Regulations 1982 prohibited a number of operations in relation to livestock for the time being situated on agricultural land.

These Regulations amend the 1982 Regulations by prohibiting the tooth grinding of sheep for the time being situated on agricultural land, subject to an exemption where this operation is lawfully done under the Animals (Scientific Procedures) Act 1986 (Regulation 2(*a*) and (*b*)).

(a) 1986 c. 14.

STATUTORY INSTRUMENTS

1987 No. 116

HEALTH AND SAFETY

The Gas Cylinders (Pattern Approval) Regulations 1987

Made - - - -	*30th January 1987*
Laid before Parliament	*10th February 1987*
Coming into force	*3rd March 1987*

The Secretary of State, being the Minister designated (**a**) for the purposes of section 2(2) of the European Communities Act 1972 (**b**) in relation to the regulation of design, construction, verification and inspection of pressure vessels, in exercise of the powers conferred on him by that section, and of all other powers enabling him in that behalf, hereby makes the following Regulations:

Citation, commencement and extent

1. These Regulations, which extend to Great Britain, may be cited as the Gas Cylinders (Pattern Approval) Regulations 1987, and shall come into force on 3rd March 1987.

Interpretation

2.—(1) In these Regulations, unless the context otherwise requires–

"the Executive" means the Health and Safety Executive;

"the Framework Directive" means the Council Directive No. 76/767/EEC (**c**) concerning the approximation of the laws of the Member States relating to common provisions for pressure vessels and methods of inspecting them;

"provisional fee" means the fee referred to in Regulation 5;

"Separate Directives" means Council Directives No. 84/525/EEC (**d**), No. 84/526/EEC (**e**) and No. 84/527/EEC (**f**) concerning the approximation of the laws of the Member States relating to seamless steel gas cylinders, seamless unalloyed aluminium and aluminium alloy gas cylinders, and welded unalloyed steel gas cylinders respectively; and any reference in these Regulations to the relevant Separate Directive is a reference to the Separate Directive which relates to the type of gas cylinder concerned.

(2) References in these Regulations to EEC pattern approval of a type of gas cylinder include references to EEC pattern approval of a family of gas cylinders, that is to say, gas cylinders from the same factory differing only in length within the following limits–

(a) the minimum overall length must not be less than 3 times the external diameter of the cylinder,

(b) the maximum overall length must not be more than 1.5 times the overall length of the cylinder tested.

(3) Unless the context otherwise requires, any reference in these Regulations to–

(a) a numbered Regulation, is a reference to the Regulation so numbered in these Regulations,

---

(**a**) S.I. 1977/1718.   (**c**) OJ No. L262, 27.9.1976, p.153.   (**e**) OJ No. L300, 19.11.84, p.20.

(**b**) 1972 c.68.   (**d**) OJ No. L300, 19.11.84, p.1.   (**f**) OJ No. L300, 19.11.84, p.48.

(b) a numbered paragraph, is a reference to the paragraph so numbered in the Regulation in which that reference appears.

Application for approval

3.—(1) An application by a manufacturer for EEC pattern approval of a type of gas cylinder may be made to the Executive.

(2) The application shall be made in writing and shall contain such information and be supported by such documents as the Framework Directive and the relevant Separate Directive require, and such further information and supporting documents as the Executive may reasonably require.

(3) The manufacturer shall make available to the Executive such samples of gas cylinders as the relevant Separate Directive requires.

Grant of EEC pattern approval

4.—(1) On receiving an application under Regulation 3, the Executive shall, on payment of the provisional fee, carry out or cause to be carried out on its behalf such checks, examinations and tests as are required for EEC pattern approval under the Framework Directive and the relevant Separate Directive.

(2) If the results of the checks, examinations and tests are satisfactory, the Executive shall grant EEC pattern approval and issue an EEC pattern approval certificate to the applicant.

(3) The certificate issued shall–

(a) be in accordance with the model set out in the relevant Separate Directive, and

(b) be accompanied by the technical annex specified in that Directive, and such descriptions and drawings as are necessary to identify the pattern and, where it is appropriate, to explain how it functions.

(4) The Executive shall not proceed with an application under this Regulation in any case where to its knowledge an application for EEC pattern approval in respect of the same pattern of gas cylinder has previously been made to another authority which, under the law of any Member State, is authorised to grant such approval for the purposes of the Framework Directive and the relevant Separate Directive.

Fees

5.—(1) The provisional fee payable under Regulation 4 shall be equal to the amount which the Executive estimates it will incur in, or in connection with, carrying out or causing to be carried out the functions referred to in that Regulation in respect of the application concerned.

(2) Where the costs incurred by the Executive are greater than the provisional fee, the difference between those costs and that fee shall be payable by the manufacturer to the Executive, and where those costs are less than the provisional fee, the difference between those costs and that fee shall be repayable by the Executive to the manufacturer.

(3) For the purposes of estimating the provisional fee and ascertaining the costs incurred by it the Executive may determine the cost of employing an officer for any period on work appropriate to his grade by reference to the average cost to it of employing officers of his grade for that period.

Withdrawal of approval

6. The Executive shall withdraw an EEC pattern approval granted under Regulation 4 if it has reason to believe that–

(a) the approval should not have been granted, or

(b) gas cylinders of the type for which the approval was granted fail to conform to the approval and either–

(i) the cylinders concerned constitute a safety hazard, or

(ii) the manufacturer has failed to comply with a written request from the Executive to make within the period specified in the request, the appropriate manufacturing changes necessary to conform to the approval;

except that the approval need not be withdrawn if the changes are minimal, or have no fundamental effect on the design of the cylinder or on manufacturing methods.

Notices of withdrawal or refusal

7.   On taking a decision refusing to grant EEC pattern approval or withdrawing an approval the Executive shall, as soon as practicable thereafter, send to the manufacturer a notice in writing of that decision stating the exact grounds on which it was based and informing the manufacturer of his right to apply for a review under Regulation 8 and of the time limit for making such an application referred to in paragraph (2) of that Regulation.

Review

8.—(1) A manufacturer who is aggrieved by a decision of the Executive refusing to grant EEC pattern approval or withdrawing an approval may apply to the Secretary of State for a review of the decision.

(2) An application for review shall be made by written notice to the Secretary of State and shall be lodged not later than 14 days from the date on which the manufacturer received the notice from the Executive referred to in Regulation 7.

(3) A notice of application for review shall state the grounds on which the application is made and shall be accompanied by–

(a) a copy of the manufacturer's application for EEC pattern approval and of every other document submitted to the Executive by the manufacturer in connection with the application, and

(b) a copy of the notice from the Executive referred to in Regulation 7.

(4) On an application for review the Secretary of State shall have the power to do anything which the Executive is authorised or required to do by paragraph (1) of Regulation 4 and shall, if he determines to grant EEC pattern approval, issue a certificate of approval in accordance with paragraph (3) of that Regulation.

(5) On an application for review the Secretary of State may–

(a) hold an inquiry in connection therewith, and

(b) appoint an assessor for the purpose of assisting with the review or any such inquiry.

(6) If, on conducting a review, the Secretary of State confirms the decision of the Executive, he may require payment of any fees, and costs which he has incurred in conducting the review from the manufacturer and for the purposes of this paragraph the Secretary of State may determine the cost of employing an officer for any period on work appropriate to his grade by reference to the average cost to the Secretary of State of employing officers of his grade for that period.

9.—(1) Subject to paragraph (2), no manufacturer shall affix to a gas cylinder–

(a) a pattern approval mark described in the Framework Directive or any mark liable to be confused with such a mark unless the cylinder is of a type for which EEC pattern approval is in force;

(b) a pattern approval mark described in one of the Separate Directives or any mark liable to be confused with such a mark unless the cylinder is of a type for which EEC pattern approval, granted for the purposes of that Directive, is in force.

(2) Paragraph (1) does not apply to a sample cylinder to be submitted to the Executive in connection with an application for pattern approval.

(3) Paragraph (1) shall have effect as if it were a health and safety regulation made under section 15 of the Health and Safety at Work etc. Act 1974 (**a**) and the provisions of that Act as regards enforcement and offences shall apply to that paragraph.

(4) It shall be a defence to a charge of committing an offence under sub-paragraphs (a) and (b) of paragraph (1) for the manufacturer to show that he neither knew nor had

---

(**a**)   1974 c.37; section 15 was amended by the Employment Protection Act 1975 (c.71), Schedule 15, p.6.

reasonable grounds to believe that the cylinder was not of a type, in relation to an offence charged under sub-paragraph (a), for which EEC pattern approval was in force or, in relation to an offence charged under sub-paragraph (b), for which EEC pattern approval, granted for the purposes of the Separate Directive in question, was in force.

Signed by order of the Secretary of State.

David Trippier
Parliamentary Under Secretary of State,
Department of Employment

30th January 1987

EXPLANATORY NOTE

(This note is not part of the Regulations)

These Regulations implement those provisions of Council Directives 76/767/EEC (OJ No. L262 p.153), 84/525/EEC (OJ No. L300 p.1), 84/526/EEC (OJ No. L300 p.20) and 84/527/EEC (OJ No. L300 p.48) which relate to the pattern approval of gas cylinders. The Regulations:

(a) enable manufacturers to make applications for pattern approval to the Health and Safety Executive (Regulation 3);

(b) provide for the Executive to grant pattern approval and issue a certificate of such approval if satisfied that a type of gas cylinder conforms with the appropriate requirements of the Directives (Regulation 4);

(c) empower the Executive to withdraw approval if it should not have been granted or if gas cylinders of the type for which an approval was granted fail to conform with it (Regulation 6);

(d) enable manufacturers to apply to the Secretary of State for a review of a decision by the Executive to refuse or withdraw pattern approval (Regulation 8);

(e) make it an offence for a manufacturer to affix a pattern approval mark described in the Directives to a gas cylinder if it is not of a type for which the appropriate pattern approval is in force (Regulation 9).

STATUTORY INSTRUMENTS

1987 No. 117

LONDON GOVERNMENT

The London Government Reorganisation (Housing Association Mortgages) Order 1987

Made - - - -	*2nd February 1987*
Laid before Parliament	*6th February 1987*
Coming into force	*28th February 1987*

Whereas the London Residuary Body, acting pursuant to section 67(1)(a) of the Local Government Act 1985(**a**), has submitted proposals to the Secretary of State for the transfer of certain rights and liabilities (being rights and liabilities of that Body which are likely to subsist for longer than the period of five years beginning with 1st April 1986) to the councils of districts and London boroughs:

And whereas the Secretary of State has decided to give effect to those proposals with modifications:

Now, therefore, the Secretary of State, in exercise of the powers conferred on him by sections 67(3) and 100(2) and (4) of that Act, and of all other powers enabling him in that behalf, hereby makes the following order:

Citation, commencement and interpretation

1.—(1) This order may be cited as the London Government Reorganisation (Housing Association Mortgages) Order 1987, and shall come into force on 28th February 1987.

(2) In this order–

"the relevant council", in relation to any mortgaged land, means the council of the district or London borough in which the land is situated, or, if it is situated in the City, the Common Council; and

"the transfer date"–

(a) is 28th February 1987 in relation to any mortgage in connection with a project in respect of which the London Residuary Body has made an advance before that date, and

(b) is 30th April 1987 in relation to any other mortgage to which article 2 applies.

Transfer of housing association mortgages

2.—(1) This article applies to any mortgage granted by a housing association to secure a loan by the Greater London Council in connection with a housing project approved by the Secretary of State for the purposes of section 29(1) of the Housing Act 1974(**b**) other than one in respect of which no housing association grant under section 49(2) or (3) of the Housing Associations Act 1985(**c**) remains payable.

(**a**) 1985 c.51.
(**b**) 1974 c.44. Section 29(1) was repealed by the Housing (Consequential Provisions) Act 1985 (c.71), Schedule 1, and re-enacted in section 41(1) of the Housing Associations Act 1985 with effect from 1st April 1986.
(**c**) 1985 c.69. Section 49(2) and (3) re-enacts in part section 30(1) of the Housing Act 1974 as amended by paragraph 4 of Schedule 18 to the Housing Act 1980 (c.51).

(2) Subject to article 4, all rights and liabilities of the London Residuary Body in respect of any mortgage to which this article applies, and all records relating exclusively to such rights and liabilities, shall on the transfer date vest in the relevant council on the terms mentioned in paragraph (3).

(3) In relation to any mortgage to which this article applies, the relevant council shall pay to the London Residuary Body a sum equal to the aggregate of all amounts outstanding by way of principal and interest in respect of advances made to the association by that Body or the Greater London Council.

Prescribed expenditure

3. For the purposes of Part VIII of the Local Government, Planning and Land Act 1980 (**a**) (prescribed expenditure) and notwithstanding section 80 of that Act, the only amount which any relevant council shall be taken to have paid in respect of the transfer by this order of any mortgage to which article 2 applies shall be equal to the amount of principal outstanding on the transfer date in respect of any advance made by the London Residuary Body.

Land situated in more than one area

4. Where in respect of any mortgage to which article 2 applies the mortgaged land is situated in the areas of more than one relevant council–

    (a) the rights, liabilities and records in respect of the mortgage shall vest in those councils jointly on such terms, and

    (b) any amount falling by virtue of article 3 to be treated as prescribed expenditure shall be so treated in respect of each council in such proportion,

as may be agreed between those councils or, failing such agreement, determined by a person so agreed on, or appointed in default of agreement by the Secretary of State; and the sum payable by virtue of article 2(3) shall be recoverable by the London Residuary Body from those councils jointly or severally.

Nicholas Ridley
Secretary of State for the Environment

2nd February 1987

EXPLANATORY NOTE

(This note is not part of the Order)

Article 2 of this order transfers to the councils of districts and London boroughs any rights and liabilities vested in the London Residuary Body in respect of mortgages by housing associations in connection with projects other than those on which no housing association grant under the Housing Associations Act 1985 remains payable, and makes provision for payments to that Body by such councils in respect of such transfers.

Article 3 makes consequential provision for the treatment of sums payable for the purposes of Part VIII (prescribed expenditure) of the Local Government, Planning and Land Act 1980, and article 4 for the terms of transfer where the land subject to a transferred mortgage is situated in the areas of different councils.

(**a**) 1980 c.65.

STATUTORY INSTRUMENTS

1987 No. 118

LOCAL GOVERNMENT, ENGLAND AND WALES

The Local Government Reorganisation (Capital Money) (Greater London) Order 1987

Made - - - -	*2nd February 1987*
Laid before Parliament	*6th February 1987*
Coming into force	*27th February 1987*

The Secretary of State for the Environment, in exercise of the powers conferred upon him by sections 49, 77 and 101 of the Local Government Act 1985**(a)** and of all other powers enabling him in that behalf, hereby makes the following Order:—

PART I

Citation and commencement

1. This Order may be cited as the Local Government Reorganisation (Capital Money) (Greater London) Order 1987 and shall come into force on 27th February 1987.

Interpretation

2.—(1) In this Order except where the context otherwise requires—

"the abolished council" means the Greater London Council;

"the 1985 Act" means the Local Government Act 1985;

"the 1980 Act" means the Local Government, Planning and Land Act 1980**(b)**;

"direct capital receipts" means monies described in paragraph (2)(a);

"disposal" means disposal by operation of law or otherwise;

"education balances" means those transferred capital receipts which are not attributable to sums received by the abolished council from the disposal of land or other property or by way of repayment of grants and advances of a capital nature which remained unapplied immediately before 1st April 1986;

"housing advances" means sums advanced by the abolished council by way of loan for the purchase, construction, repair or improvement of dwellings;

"housing assets" means relevant land held by the abolished council for the purposes of section 92 of the Housing Act 1957**(c)**;

"housing receipts" means those direct capital receipts which are attributable to the disposal of housing assets or the repayment of housing advances and grants for the purchase, construction, repair or improvement of dwellings;

"other property" means any vehicle, vessel, movable and immovable plant, machinery and apparatus;

(a) 1985 c.51.
(b) 1980 c.65.
(c) 1957 c.56; the abolished council was a housing authority for the purposes of section 92 by virtue of section 21(4) of the London Government Act 1963 (c.33).

"reimbursable capital money" means capital money as defined in paragraph (2) which is payable by the Residuary Body to the Exchequer or to the European Commission by virtue of the relevant land, other property, grant or advance having been financed either in whole or in part by grants from the Exchequer or the Commission;

"relevant land" means any land other than—

    (a) land held as an investment of a superannuation fund maintained under regulations made under section 7 of the Superannuation Act 1972**(a)**; and

    (b) land in respect of which a housing association is the mortgagor and the Residuary Body is the mortgagee;

"the rating authorities" means the rating authorities in Greater London other than The Temples;

"the Residuary Body" means the London Residuary Body;

"transferred capital receipts" means monies described in paragraph (2)(b).

(2) For the purposes of section 77 of the 1985 Act and this order, except article 9, "capital money" means—

    (a) money received by the Residuary Body—

        (i) which is attributable to the disposal of relevant land or other property by that Body;

        (ii) which is attributable to amounts left outstanding in accordance with section 9 of the Housing Act 1980**(b)** in connection with the disposal of housing assets by the abolished council; and

        (iii) by way of repayments of grants and advances of a capital nature; and

    (b) such amount of the monies vested in the Residuary Body on the abolition date by virtue of section 62 of the 1985 Act as equals the aggregate of—

        (i) the net aggregate of those parts of the amounts shown as cash (whether credit or debit) in the accounts of the abolished council referred to in paragraph (3) for the financial year ended 31st March 1986, made up and balanced in accordance with regulation 6 of the Accounts and Audit Regulations 1983**(c)**, which are attributable to the functions of the abolished council as a local education authority; and

        (ii) the amount shown as cash in the abolished council's Supplies Reserve Fund for that financial year.

(3) The accounts referred to in paragraph (2)(b) are—

    (a) the Direct Labour Operation of the Architect's Department Account;

    (b) the Inner London Education Authority Building and Equipment Renewal and Repair Fund;

    (c) the Insurance Fund;

    (d) the Insurance Reserve Fund;

    (e) the Mechanical and Electrical Engineering Maintenance Direct Labour Organisation Account; and

    (f) the Special No. 1 Precept Account.

(4) Where the amount vested as mentioned in paragraph (2)(b) is less than the aggregate of the amounts shown as cash in the accounts of the abolished council for the financial year ended 31st March 1986 the Residuary Body shall be deemed for the purposes of this order to have had vested in it under section 62 such additional sum as makes that amount equal to that aggregate.

(a) 1972 c.11.
(b) 1980 c.51.
(c) S.I. 1983/1761, to which there are amendments not relevant to this Order.

PART II

Interpretation

3.—(1) In this Part—

"net capital residue" means the direct capital receipts of the Residuary Body in the financial year in question other than those receipts which are attributable to—

(a) the disposal of relevant land or other property purchased by that Body; or

(b) repayments of grants and advances of a capital nature in respect of—

(i) grants or advances made by that Body; and

(ii) grants or advances made to authorities to whom Part VIII of the 1980 Act applies or to the London Transport Executive,

less the amount payable in that year by way of reimbursable capital money.

(2) For the purposes of this Part, the population of the area of a rating authority shall be taken to be the number estimated by the Registrar General and certified by him to the Secretary of State by reference to the 30th June which falls 21 months before the beginning of the financial year in question.

Additions to net capital receipts

4.—(1) For the purposes of section 72(3) of the 1980 Act, each rating authority's net capital receipts for each financial year commencing with the financial year beginning 1st April 1986 shall be treated as if they included an amount determined in accordance with the formula—

$$\frac{SA}{T} + \frac{YB}{Z} \quad \text{where—}$$

S equals the population of the area of the rating authority in question;

T equals the population of the area of all the rating authorities;

A equals that part of the net capital residue for the financial year in question which does not consist of housing receipts;

Y equals that part of the amount of prescribed expenditure first specified for that year in accordance with section 72(1) of the 1980 Act in relation to the rating authority in question which is referable to the Housing Investment Programme;

Z equals the aggregate of those parts of the amounts of prescribed expenditure so specified in relation to each of the rating authorities which are referable to the Housing Investment Programme; and

B equals that part of the net capital residue for that year which consists of housing receipts.

(2) For the purposes of section 72(3) of the 1980 Act, each rating authority's net capital receipts for the financial year ending 31st March 1987 shall be treated as if they included (in addition to any amount ascertained in accordance with paragraph (1)) an amount determined in accordance with the formula—

$$\frac{SC}{T} \quad \text{where—}$$

S and T have the same values as in paragraph (1) and C is an amount equal to that which, if the abolished council had been an authority to whom Part VIII of the 1980 Act applied,

(a) would have been regarded as capital receipts for the purposes of that Part of that Act; and

(b) immediately before 1st April 1986 remained unused for the purpose of authorising prescribed expenditure by that council,

less the amount which would have been attributable to the functions of the abolished council as a local education authority.

(3) For the purposes of section 72(3) of the 1980 Act, the net capital receipts of the Inner London Education Authority for the financial year ending 31st March 1987 shall be treated as if they included the amount last mentioned in paragraph (2).

(4) Regulations under sections 72(3)(d) and 75 of the 1980 Act apply in relation to amounts to be included in the net capital receipts of any authority by virtue of this article as they apply to other receipts of the authority.

PART III

Grant to The Trust for London

5. On or before 31st March 1987 the Residuary Body shall pay by way of grant to The Trust for London (an eligible charity for the purposes of section 49 of the 1985 Act) the sum of ten million pounds.

Distribution of other capital money

6.—(1) In respect of each financial year commencing with the financial year beginning 1st April 1986 the Residuary Body shall pay to each rating authority an amount which shall be determined in accordance with the Schedule to this order.

(2) The Residuary Body shall pay to the Inner London Education Authority—

    (a) the transferred capital receipts; and

    (b) an amount which shall be calculated by applying to the transferred capital receipts the rate agreed between the Residuary Body and the Authority on 28th April 1986 as if those receipts were an amount of principal and the rate were a weekly rate of interest in respect of the period beginning on 1st April 1986 and ending on the day on which the payment required by subparagraph (a) is made.

PART IV

Administrative arrangements—notifications

7.—(1) Subject to paragraph (2), on or before 30th June and on or before 31st December in each financial year beginning with the financial year commencing 1st April 1986 the Residuary Body shall notify each rating authority of its estimate and revised estimate, respectively, of—

    (a) the amounts of capital money to be received in the current and next succeeding financial years;

    (b) the amounts to be paid to that authority in those years in accordance with this order;

    (c) the amounts which, in accordance with article 4(1), are to be treated as included in the authority's net capital receipts for those years; and

    (d) the classes of disposals and repayments to which the amounts referred to in subparagraph (c) relate.

(2) Paragraph (1) shall apply to the financial year ending 31st March 1987 with the omission of any reference to 30th June and revised estimates and with the substitution of 28th February for 31st December.

(3) On or before 28th February 1987 the Residuary Body shall notify each rating authority and the Inner London Education Authority of its estimate of the amount which, in accordance with article 4(2) and (3), respectively, is to be treated as included in the authority's net capital receipts and of the classes of disposals and repayments to which that amount relates.

(4) On or before 30th June in each financial year commencing with the financial year beginning 1st April 1987, the Residuary Body shall notify each rating authority of the amount determined for the preceding financial year in accordance with article 4(1) for that authority and on or before 30th June 1987 that Body shall notify each rating authority and the Inner London Education Authority of the amount determined in its case for the preceding financial year in accordance with article 4(2) and (3), respectively, together with an indication of the classes of disposals and repayments to which that amount relates.

(5) At the same time as it notifies an authority of any of the matters referred to in paragraphs (1), (3) and (4) the Residuary Body shall send a copy of such notification to the Secretary of State.

(6) For the purposes of paragraphs (1), (3) and (4), disposals and repayments shall be classified in accordance with Schedule 1 to the Local Government (Prescribed Expenditure) Regulations 1983**(a)**,

Administrative arrangements—distribution of capital money

8.—(1) The payment required by article 6(2) shall be made no later than 28 days after the date upon which the accounts of the abolished council for the financial year ended 31st March 1986 are made up and balanced in accordance with regulation 6 of the Accounts and Audit Regulations 1983 or 14 days after this order comes into force, whichever is the later.

(2) The Residuary Body shall notify the Inner London Education Authority of the amount of the parts of that payment which are referable to the education balances and to the amount referred to in article 6(2)(b) and shall send a copy of such notification to the Secretary of State.

(3) Within seven days of making any payment in accordance with article 6(2), the Residuary Body shall notify the Secretary of State of the amount paid.

(4) The Residuary Body shall use its best endeavours to secure that payments required by article 6(1) are made on or before the last day of the financial year in question. Any part of a payment not so made ("the residual amount") shall be paid no later than 30th June in the next financial year.

(5) Residual amounts shall be deemed to vest in the rating authority entitled to them on the last day of the financial year in question and shall thereafter be regarded as interest-free loans to the Residuary Body by the relevant rating authorities.

(6) On or before 1st July in each financial year commencing with the financial year beginning 1st April 1987 the Residuary Body shall notify the Secretary of State of the amounts paid in respect of the preceding financial year by virtue of article 6(1).

Application of capital money

9.—(1) Subject to paragraph (2), money received by an authority by virtue of this order shall be applied for any purpose for which capital money received by a local authority on the disposal of land under Part VII of the Local Government Act 1972**(b)** may properly be applied.

(2) The education balances and the amount referred to in article 6(2)(b) shall be carried to the general fund kept by the Inner London Education Authority in accordance with section 72(1) of the 1985 Act.

2nd February 1987

Nicholas Ridley
Secretary of State for the Environment

(**a**) S.I. 1983/296; Schedule 1 was substituted by S.I. 1985/257.
(**b**) 1972 c.70.

SCHEDULE

Article 6(1)

Formula for determining payments to be made by the Residuary Body

The formula for each financial year commencing with the financial year beginning 1st April 1986 is—

$$\frac{PY}{Z}+\frac{RS}{T} \quad \text{where—}$$

P is ascertained by applying the formula—

$$E-\frac{GH}{J} \quad \text{where—}$$

E is an amount equal to the housing receipts for the financial year in question, less—

(a) the amount which is attributable to the repayment of housing advances, other than reimbursable capital money;

(b) an amount equal to that part of the reimbursable capital money received in that year which is attributable to housing receipts;

(c) an amount equal to the expenditure incurred by the Residuary Body in that year for facilitating the disposal of housing assets; and

(d) an amount equal to the loans outstanding immediately before the first day of that year which that Body had raised for the purpose of financing expenditure incurred by them for facilitating the disposal of housing assets;

G is the amount paid in that year by virtue of article 5;

H is an amount equal to the housing receipts for that year which are attributable to the disposal of housing assets; and

J is an amount equal to the direct capital receipts for that year which are attributable to the disposal of relevant land;

R is ascertained by applying the formula—

$$F-\frac{GK}{J} \quad \text{where—}$$

F is an amount equal to the direct capital receipts for that year which are not housing receipts, less—

(a) the amount which is attributable to the repayment of the advances referred to in article 2(2)(a)(ii) which are not housing advances, other than reimbursable capital money;

(b) an amount equal to that part of the reimbursable capital money received in that year which is not attributable to housing receipts;

(c) an amount equal to the expenditure incurred by the Residuary Body in that year for facilitating the disposal of other property and relevant land other than housing assets; and

(d) an amount equal to the loans outstanding immediately before the first day of that year which that Body had raised for the purpose of financing expenditure incurred by them for facilitating the disposal of other property and relevant land other than housing assets;

K is an amount equal to the direct capital receipts for that year which are attributable to the disposal of relevant land but which are not housing receipts; and

Y,Z,S and T have the same meanings as in article 4:

Provided that—

(a) if P is less than zero but R is greater than zero the formula shall be—

$$\frac{(P+R)\,S}{T};$$

(b) if R is less than zero but P is greater than zero the formula shall be—

$$\frac{(P+R)\,Y}{Z}; \text{ and}$$

(c) if both P and R are zero or less than zero or if the application of either of the formulae specified in subparagraphs (a) and (b) produces a negative result the Residuary Body shall not make any payment to the rating authorities under article 6(1).

EXPLANATORY NOTE

(This note is not part of the Order)

This Order is primarily concerned with the distribution of capital receipts by the London Residuary Body to rating authorities in Greater London following the abolition of the Greater London Council: and with the enhancement of capital spending power under Part VIII of the Local Government, Planning and Land Act 1980 on account of such receipts. It also provides for the making of a grant to The Trust for London and for the transfer to the Inner London Education Authority of certain sums held by the abolished council.

Part I of the order defines terms used in the order. In particular, "capital money" is defined for the purposes of section 77 of the Local Government Act 1985 and the order.

Part II provides for notional additions to the net capital receipts of rating authorities (other than The Temples) and the Inner London Education Authority for the purposes of section 72(3) of the 1980 Act, to authorise further capital expenditure. For the financial year beginning on 1st April 1986 and subsequent years, the additions are based on the amounts derived from the disposal by the London Residuary Body of certain land and other property which it inherited on abolition and from the repayment to it of certain grants and advances of a capital nature but do not include amounts payable to the Exchequer or the European Commission by way of reimbursement of grant. For the financial year 1986/87 the additions also include amounts based on the capital receipts of the Greater London Council which had not been used before 1st April 1986.

Part III of the order provides for the making of a grant of £10 millions to The Trust for London and for the payment to the Inner London Education Authority of an amount which represents the part of the Greater London Councils's revenue balances and unapplied capital receipts at the abolition date which is attributable to its functions as a local education authority. Receipts of the Residuary Body from the disposal of certain land and other property are to be passed to the rating authorites in accordance with a formula which is contained in the Schedule to the order. The formula permits the Residuary Body to retain amounts which reflect its expenditure on facilitating disposals and on financing loans raised for that purpose; and amounts payable to the Exchequer or the European Commission by way of reimbursement of grant.

Part IV of the order requires the Residuary Body to notify the rating authorities, the Inner London Education Authority and the Secretary of State of the amounts, both notional and actual, which are likely to be available for distribution and which are, in fact, distributed. The Residuary Body is required to use its best endeavours to secure that payments to the rating authorities are made on or before the last day of the financial year in question. To the extent that payments are not so made, they are treated as interest-free loans from the rating authorities to the Residuary Body.

The rating authorities are required to use money received under the order for purposes for which they may use capital money which they have received on the disposal of land under Part VII of the Local Government Act 1972. Some of the money received by the Inner London Education Authority under the order is to be used for those purposes; the rest is to be carried to its general fund.

STATUTORY INSTRUMENTS

1987 No. 119

PREVENTION AND SUPPRESSION OF TERRORISM

The Prevention of Terrorism (Supplemental Temporary Provisions) (Amendment) Order 1987

Made - - -	*2nd February 1987*
Laid before Parliament	*10th February 1987*
Coming into force -	*1st April 1987*

In exercise of the powers conferred upon me by sections 13 and 14(7) of and paragraph 1(6) of Schedule 3 to the Prevention of Terrorism (Temporary Provisions) Act 1984(**a**), I hereby make the following Order:

1. This Order may be cited as the Prevention of Terrorism (Supplemental Temporary Provisions) (Amendment) Order 1987 and shall come into force on 1st April 1987.

2. Schedule 2 to the Prevention of Terrorism (Supplemental Temporary Provisions) Order 1984(**b**) (which designates certain ports for the purposes of Article 11 of that Order) shall be amended by the insertion of "Poole Harbour" after "Plymouth" in the list of designated seaports and hoverports.

Douglas Hurd
One of Her Majesty's Principal Secretaries of State

Home Office
2nd February 1987

(**a**) 1984 c. 8.　　　　(**b**) S.I. 1984/418.

EXPLANATORY NOTE

(This note is not part of the Order)

This Order amends the Prevention of Terrorism (Supplemental Temporary Provisions) Order 1984 by adding Poole Harbour to the list of seaports and hoverports which are designated ports for the purposes of Article 11 of the 1984 Order. Article 11 inter alia requires the owners or agents of a ship or aircraft carrying passengers for reward coming from the Republic of Ireland, Northern Ireland or any of the Channel Islands or the Isle of Man or going to any of those places not to arrange for the ship or aircraft to call at or leave any port in Great Britain other than one listed in Schedule 2 to the 1984 Order, and thereby a designated port, for the purpose of embarking or disembarking passengers without the approval of an examining officer.

STATUTORY INSTRUMENTS

1987 No. 122

LANDLORD AND TENANT

The Assured Tenancies (Prescribed Amount) Order 1987

Made - - - -	*2nd February 1987*
Laid before Parliament	*4th February 1987*
Coming into force	*25th February 1987*

The Secretary of State for the Environment, as respects England, and the Secretary of State for Wales, as respects Wales, in exercise of the powers conferred upon them by section 56B(6)**(a)** of the Housing Act 1980**(b)**, and of all other powers enabling them in that behalf, hereby make the following Order:—

1. This Order may be cited as the Assured Tenancies (Prescribed Amount) Order 1987 and shall come into force on 25th February 1987.

2. The prescribed amount for the purposes of section 56B of the Housing Act 1980 is—

    (a) in the case of a dwelling-house in Greater London, £7,000; and

    (b) in the case of a dwelling-house elsewhere in England or Wales, £5,000.

3. The Assured Tenancies (Prescribed Amount) Order 1986**(c)** is hereby revoked.

Nicholas Ridley
Secretary of State for the Environment
2nd February 1987

Nicholas Edwards
Secretary of State for Wales
2nd February 1987

(a) *See* the definition of "the prescribed amount".
(b) 1980 c.51; section 56B was inserted by section 12(2) of the Housing and Planning Act 1986 (c.63).
(c) S.I. 1986/2180.

EXPLANATORY NOTE

(This note is not part of the Order)

Assured tenancies are tenancies which would otherwise have been protected tenancies or housing association tenancies under the Rent Act 1977 (c.42). They are subject to Part II of the Landlord and Tenant Act 1954 (c.56), as modified by Schedule 5 to the Housing Act 1980.

For a dwelling-house to be let on an assured tenancy, one of two sets of conditions must be fulfilled. Under the conditions dealt with in section 56B of the Housing Act 1980, works must have been carried out involving expenditure of a prescribed amount attributable to the dwelling-house. Attributable expenditure includes money spent on works to the dwelling-house itself and to land or buildings let with it. In the case of a flat, it also includes a proportion of money spent on works to the structure and common parts of the building.

This Order increases the amounts from those prescribed in the Assured Tenancies (Prescribed Amount) Order 1986, which is revoked, by £2,000 in the case of Greater London and £1,000 elsewhere.

STATUTORY INSTRUMENTS

1987 No. 123 (C.1)

VIDEO RECORDINGS

The Video Recordings Act 1984 (Commencement No. 4) Order 1987

Made	- - -	*3rd February 1987*

In exercise of the powers conferred upon me by section 23(2) of the Video Recordings Act 1984(a), I hereby make the following Order:

1.—(1) This Order may be cited as the Video Recordings Act 1984 (Commencement No. 4) Order 1987.

(2) This Order does not extend to Scotland.

(3) In this Order—

"the Act" means the Video Recordings Act 1984;

"the 1985 Order" means the Video Recordings Act 1984 (Commencement No. 2) Order 1985(b).

2.—(1) Subject to paragraph (2) below, sections 9 and 10 of the Act shall come into force on 1st March 1987 for the purpose of prohibiting the supply, the offer to supply or the possession for the purpose of supply of a video recording to which Article 3(a) of the 1985 Order does not apply and which contains a video work which satisfies the requirements in paragraph (3) below.

(2) Where a video recording to which paragraph (1) above applies contains another video work not being a work which satisfies the requirements in paragraph (3) below, sections 9 and 10 of the Act shall come into force for the purpose set out in paragraph (1) above only in respect of the video work which satisfies those requirements.

(3) The requirements which a video work must satisfy are that—

(a) its visual images, when shown as a moving picture, are substantially the same as the moving picture produced on showing a film registered, or deemed to have been registered, under Part II of the Films Act 1960(c) on or after 1st January 1980;

(b) its visual images are accompanied by sound which comprises or includes words predominantly in the English language; and

(c) no classification certificate has been issued in respect of it.

Home Office	*Douglas Hurd,*
3rd February 1987	One of Her Majesty's Principal Secretaries of State

---

(a) 1984 c.39.   **(b)** S.I. 1985/1264.

(c) 1960 c.57. The Films Act 1960 was repealed by section 7(1) of, and Schedule 2 to, the Films Act 1985 (c.21) but the register under Part II continues to be kept under section 7(3) of the 1985 Act for the purpose set out therein.

EXPLANATORY NOTE

(This note is not part of the Order)

This Order brings sections 9 and 10 of the Video Recordings Act 1984 into force in England, Wales and Northern Ireland for certain purposes on 1st March 1987. The sections are brought into force in Scotland on the same day and for the same purposes by the Video Recordings Act 1984 (Scotland) (Commencement No. 4) Order 1987.

Sections 9 and 10 create the offences of supplying, offering to supply and possession for the purpose of supply of a video recording containing an unclassified video work. This Order brings these sections into force in respect of an unclassified English language video work which has been sold, let on hire or offered for sale or hire in the United Kingdom to the public in video form before 1st September 1985 (and to which Article 3(a) of the Video Recordings Act 1984 (Commencement No. 2) Order 1985 (S.I. 1985/1264) does not therefore apply) and of which a film version was registered on or after 1st January 1980 under Part II of the Films Act 1960 (c.57).

NOTE AS TO EARLIER COMMENCEMENT ORDERS

(This note is not part of the Order)

Provision	Date of Commencement	S.I. No.
Sections 1, 4, 5, 7, 8, 22 and 23	10.6.85	As to England, Wales and Northern Ireland, 1985/883; As to Scotland, 1985/904.
Sections 2, 3, 6, 11 to 17 and 21	1.9.85	As to England, Wales and Northern Ireland, 1985/1264; As to Scotland, 1985/1265.
Sections 9 and 10 as to certain purposes	1.9.85	As to England, Wales and Northern Ireland, 1985/1264: As to Scotland, 1985/1265.
as to certain other purposes	1.9.86	As to England, Wales and Northern Ireland, 1986/1125; As to Scotland, 1986/1182.
Sections 18 and 19 as to England, Wales and Northern Ireland	1.9.85	1985/1264.
Section 20 as to Scotland	1.9.85	1985/1265.

1987 No. 125

TRANSPORT

The London Regional Transport (Levy) Order 1987

Made -   -   -   -   3rd February 1987

Coming into force in accordance with article 1

The Secretary of State for Transport, in exercise of the powers conferred by section 13(4) of the London Regional Transport Act 1984(**a**) and of all other enabling powers, hereby makes the following Order, a draft of which has been laid before and approved by a resolution of the Commons House of Parliament pursuant to section 13(9) of that Act.

Citation and commencement

1.   This Order may be cited as the London Regional Transport (Levy) Order 1987 and shall come into force on the day after it is made.

Interpretation

2.   In this Order–

"the 1984 Act" means the London Regional Transport Act 1984;

"the year 1987/8" means the period of twelve months beginning with 1st April 1987;

"the estimated grant" means the Secretary of State's estimated expenditure in the year 1987/8 on grants to London Regional Transport under section 12 of the 1984 Act;

"the ratepayer proportion" means the proportion of the estimated grants which it appears to the Secretary of State appropriate to recover from the ratepayers of Greater London;

"the estimated penny rate product of a rating area" means, in relation to the rating areas listed in the left hand column of the Schedule (which are the rating areas comprised in Greater London) an estimate of the amount, calculated as provided in section 12(4) of the General Rate Act 1967(**b**), which would be produced by a rate of a penny in the pound levied in the rating area in question and each such estimate (which has been transmitted to the Secretary of State pursuant to section 12(4) of that Act) is shown in the right hand column of the Schedule opposite the rating area to which it relates; and

"the estimated penny rate product of Greater London" means the total of the estimated penny rate products of the rating areas comprised in Greater London (shown at the bottom of the right hand column of the Schedule).

Amount in the pound

3.   The amount in the pound for the purpose of section 13(4) of the 1984 Act in respect of the year 1987/8 shall be 7·77 pence.

(**a**)   1984 c.32.
(**b**)   1967 c.9; section 12 applies to a demand issued under section 13(2) of the 1984 Act by virtue of section 14 thereof.

Factors taken into account

4. The factors taken into account in determining the amount in the pound specified in article 3 are as follows–

(1) the estimated grant which is £239 million;

(2) the ratepayer proportion which is 65·63%; and

(3) the estimated penny rate product of Greater London which is £20,186,201.

Method of calculation

5. The method of calculation employed in determining the amount in the pound specified in article 3 is as follows–

(1) the unrounded amount in the pound is obtained by the formula

$$\frac{\text{the estimated grant} \times \text{the ratepayer proportion}}{\text{the estimated penny rate product of Greater London}}$$

and accordingly the calculation is–

$$\frac{£239,000,000 \times 0·6563}{£20,186,201} = 7·7704417 \text{ pence;}$$

(2) the unrounded amount in the pound is rounded to two places of decimals to give 7·77 pence.

John Moore
Secretary of State for Transport

3rd February 1987

SCHEDULE

Article 2

Rating Area	Estimated penny rate product of the rating area (£)
Barking & Dagenham	262,000
Barnet	612,500
Bexley	319,000
Brent	494,000
Bromley	518,000
Camden	1,147,000
City of London	2,660,000
City of Westiminster	3,275,000
Croydon	697,000
Ealing	575,000
Enfield	487,500
Greenwich	320,000
Hackney	360,000
Hammersmith & Fulham	361,200
Haringey	354,000
Harrow	349,000
Havering	375,500
Hillingdon	601,800
Hounslow	495,000
Inner Temple	4,250
Islington	522,000
Kensington & Chelsea	705,000
Kingston upon Thames	291,000
Lambeth	588,000
Lewisham	343,000
Merton	306,000
Middle Temple	2,651
Newham	336,300
Redbridge	363,000
Richmond upon Thames	329,000
Southwark	584,000
Sutton	295,000
Tower Hamlets	510,000
Waltham Forest	308,500
Wandsworth	435,000
Total (estimated penny rate product of Greater London)	20,186,201

EXPLANATORY NOTE

(This note is not part of the Order)

Section 13 of the London Regional Transport Act 1984 provides that the Secretary of State may, in respect of any year, make a levy on the rating authorities for all the rating areas in Greater London to recover a contribution from Greater London ratepayers towards his estimated expenditure in that year on grants to London Regional Transport, and for the purpose of raising the levy the Secretary of State may issue a demand for payments to the rating authorities. Such a demand shall require the rating authorities to levy as part, or as an additional item of the rate, a rate of an amount in the pound specified by Order in respect of the year to which the demand relates.

This Order specifies an amount of 7·77 pence in the pound in respect of the year 1987/8 (article 3). As required by section 13(7) of the London Regional Transport Act 1984 this Order sets out the factors taken into account (article 4) and the method of calculation employed (article 5) in determining the amount in the pound.

STATUTORY INSTRUMENTS

1987 No. 129

OFFSHORE INSTALLATIONS

The Offshore Installations (Life-saving Appliances and Fire-fighting Equipment) (Amendment) Regulations 1987

Made - - - -	*3rd February 1987*
Laid before Parliament	*5th February 1987*
Coming into force	*1st March 1987*

The Secretary of State, in exercise of the powers conferred on him by section 6 of the Mineral Workings (Offshore Installations) Act 1971(**a**) and of all other powers enabling him in that behalf, and after consulting with organisations appearing to him to be representative of those persons who will be affected, hereby makes the following Regulations:—

1. These Regulations may be cited as the Offshore Installations (Life-saving Appliances and Fire-fighting Equipment) (Amendment) Regulations 1987 and shall come into force on 1st March 1987.

2. The following table shall be substituted for the table set out in sub-paragraph (*a*) of the Schedule to the Offshore Installations (Life-saving Appliances) Regulations 1977(**b**) and for the table set out in sub-paragraph (*a*) of the Schedule to the Offshore Installations (Fire-fighting Equipment) Regulations 1978(**c**):—

"TABLE

Time spent	Rate per hour or part thereof
On any day except a Saturday, Sunday or public holiday—	
between 8 a.m. and 6 p.m.	£45.50
before 8 a.m. or after 6 p.m.	£68.25
On a Saturday	£68.25
On a Sunday or public holiday	£91.00"

3rd February 1987

Alick Buchanan-Smith
Minister of State, Department of Energy

(**a**) 1971 c.61; section 1 was repealed and re-enacted by the Oil and Gas (Enterprise) Act 1982 (c.23), section 24; section 6 was amended by Schedule 3, paragraph 8 of that Act, and it should also be read with section 44(5) of the Petroleum and Submarine Pipe-lines Act 1975 (c.74). (**b**) S.I. 1977/486, amended by S.I. 1984/419 and 1985/1612. (**c**) S.I. 1978/611, amended by S.I. 1984/419 and 1985/1612.

EXPLANATORY NOTE

(This note is not part of the Regulations)

The Offshore Installations (Life-saving Appliances) Regulations 1977 prohibit the presence of any person on an installation to which the Regulations apply unless the life-saving appliances on that installation have been examined by a person acting at the direction of the Secretary of State. The Offshore Installations (Fire-fighting Equipment) Regulations 1978 contain a similar prohibition in respect of the fire-fighting equipment provided on an offshore installation. Both the 1977 and the 1978 Regulations require the owner of an installation on which an examination is carried out to pay a fee to the Secretary of State, comprising a sum based on the time spent by the examiner in carrying out the examination and in travelling to and from the installation, calculated in accordance with a table set out in the Schedule to the Regulations, and the cost of his travelling and subsistence expenses. These Regulations substitute in the 1977 Regulations and the 1978 Regulations a new table specifying the rates payable in respect of the time spent by an examiner. These new rates replace those having effect by virtue of the Offshore Installations (Life-saving Appliances and Fire-fighting Equipment) (Amendment) Regulations 1985 which were as follows:—

Time spent	Rate per hour or part thereof
On any day except a Saturday, Sunday or public holiday—	
between 8 a.m. and 6 p.m.	£41.50
before 8 a.m. or after 6 p.m.	£62.25
On a Saturday	£62.25
On a Sunday or public holiday	£83.00

STATUTORY INSTRUMENTS

1987 No. 130

PENSIONS

The Pensions Increase (Review) Order 1987

Made	- - -	*2nd February 1987*
Laid before Parliament		*9th February 1987*
Coming into force	-	*6th April 1987*

Whereas by virtue of section 23(2)(**a**) of the Social Security Pensions Act 1975(**b**) a direction has been given(**c**) under section 63(2) and section 83(3) of the Social Security Act 1986(**d**) by the Secretary of State for Social Services that the sums mentioned in section 63(1)*(b)* are to be increased:

Now therefore the Treasury, in exercise of the powers conferred by section 59(1), (2) and (5) of the Social Security Pensions Act 1975(**e**) and now vested in them(**f**), and all other powers enabling them in that behalf, hereby make the following Order:—

Citation and commencement

1. This Order may be cited as the Pensions Increase (Review) Order 1987 and shall come into force on 6th April 1987.

Interpretation

2.— (1) In this Order—

"the 1971 Act" means the Pensions (Increase) Act 1971(**g**);

"the 1974 Act" means the Pensions (Increase) Act 1974(**h**);

"the 1975 Act" means the Social Security Pensions Act 1975;

"basic rate" has the meaning given by section 17(1) of the 1971 Act as amended by section 1(3) of the 1974 Act;

"the existing Orders" means the Pensions Increase (Annual Review) Order 1972(**i**), the Pensions Increase (Annual Review) Order 1973(**j**), the Pensions Increase (Annual Review) Order 1974(**k**), the Pensions Increase (Annual Review) Order 1975(**l**), the Pensions Increase (Annual Review) Order 1976(**m**), the Pensions Increase (Annual

(**a**) Section 23(2) was amended by Schedule 10, paragraph 91 of the Social Security Act 1986 (c.50).

(**b**) 1975 c. 60.

(**c**) The direction is contained in S.I. 1987/45.

(**d**) 1986 c. 50; section 1 of the Social Security and Housing Benefits Act 1983 (c. 36) made provision for increases to reflect actual, rather than estimated, rises in the general level of prices.

(**e**) Section 59 was amended and section 59A was added by section 11 of the Social Security Act 1979 (c. 18). Section 59 was also amended by Schedule 5, paragraph 33 to the Social Security Act 1985. Section 59(1) was further amended by Schedule 10, paragraph 93 of the Social Security Act 1986 (c. 50).

(**f**) S.I. 1981/1670.

(**g**) 1971 c. 56.

(**h**) 1974 c. 9.

(**i**) S.I. 1972/1298.

(**j**) S.I. 1973/1370.

(**k**) S.I. 1974/1373.

(**l**) S.I. 1975/1384.

(**m**) S.I. 1976/1356.

Review) Order 1977(**a**), the Pensions Increase (Annual Review) Order 1978(**b**), the Pensions Increase (Review) Order 1979(**c**), the Pensions Increase (Review) Order 1980(**d**), the Pensions Increase (Review) Order 1981(**e**), the Pensions Increase (Review) Order 1982(**f**), the Pensions Increase (Review) Order 1983(**g**), the Pensions Increase (Review) Order 1984(**h**), the Pensions Increase (Review) Order 1985(**i**) and the Pensions Increase (Review) Order 1986(**j**);

"official pension" has the meaning given by section 5(1) of the 1971 Act;

"pension authority" has the meaning given by section 7(1) of the 1971 Act;

"qualifying condition" means one of the conditions laid down in section 3 of the 1971 Act as amended by section 3(2) and (3) of the 1974 Act;

"widow's pension" means a pension payable in respect of the services of the pensioner's deceased husband.

(2) For the purposes of this Order the time when a pension "begins" is that stated in section 8(2) of the 1971 Act, and the "beginning date" shall be construed accordingly.

(3) Where, for the purposes of this Order, it is necessary to calculate the number of complete months in any period an incomplete month shall be treated as a complete month if it consists of at least 16 days.

Pension increases

3. The annual rate of an official pension may, if a qualifying condition is satisfied or the pension is a widow's pension, be increased by the pension authority in respect of any period beginning on or after 6th April 1987 as follows:—

(1) a pension beginning before 28th July 1986 may be increased by 2.1 per cent of the basic rate as increased by the amount of any increase under section 1 of the 1971 Act or the existing Orders;

(2) a pension beginning on or after 28th July 1986 and before 6th April 1987 may be increased by 2.1 per cent multiplied by $\frac{A}{B}$ where

   (a) A is the number of complete months in the period between the beginning date of the pension and 6th April 1987, and

   (b) B is 8.

Increases in certain lump sums

4. In respect of any lump sum or instalment of a lump sum which became payable before 6th April 1987 but after 27th July 1986 there may be paid an increase of 2.1 per cent of the amount of the lump sum or instalment (as increased by the amount under section 1 of the 1971 Act or under the existing Orders) multiplied by $\frac{A}{B}$ where

   (a) A is the number of complete months in the period between the beginning date for the lump sum or, if later, 28th July 1986 and the date on which it became payable; and

   (b) B is 8.

Reductions in respect of guaranteed minimum pensions

5. The amount by reference to which any increase in the rate of an official pension provided for by this Order is to be calculated shall, in the case of a person—

   (a) who is entitled to a guaranteed minimum pension on 6th April 1987, and

   (b) whose entitlement to that guaranteed minimum pension arises from an employment from which (either directly or by virtue of the payment of a transfer credit) entitlement to the official pension also arises,

(**a**) S.I. 1977/1387.   (**b**) S.I. 1978/1211.   (**c**) S.I. 1979/1047.
(**d**) S.I. 1980/1302.   (**e**) S.I. 1981/1217.   (**f**) S.I. 1982/1178.
(**g**) S.I. 1983/1264.   (**h**) S.I. 1984/1307.   (**i**) S.I. 1985/1575.
(**j**) S.I. 1986/1116.

be reduced by an amount equal to the rate of the guaranteed minimum pension unless the Treasury(a) shall, in accordance with the provisions of section 59A of the 1975 Act, otherwise direct.

Tony Durant
Mark Lennox-Boyd
Two of the Lords Commissioners
of Her Majesty's Treasury

2nd February 1987

(a) *See* S.I. 1981/1670, articles 2(1)*(c)* and 3(5).

EXPLANATORY NOTE
(This note is not part of the Order)

Under section 59 of the Social Security Pensions Act 1975 as amended by section 11 of the Social Security Act 1979 and as modified by section 59A of the 1975 Act (introduced by section 11(4) of the 1979 Act) the Treasury (in whom the functions conferred by those provisions are now vested) are required to provide by order for the increase in the rates of public service pensions. The increase is the percentage (or in some circumstances a fraction of the percentage) by which the Secretary of State for Social Services has, by directions given under the provisions of section 23(2) of the Social Security Pensions Act 1975 (as amended by Schedule 10, paragraph 91 of the Social Security Act 1986), increased the sums referred to in section 63(1)(*b*) of the Social Security Act 1986. These are the sums which are the additional components in the rates of long term benefits, namely the additional pension entitlements accruing to employees in respect of earnings after 5th April 1978.

For pensions which began before 28th July 1986 the increase is 2.1 per cent. For pensions which began on or after 28th July 1986 the increases are as follows:

Pensions Beginning	*Percentage Increase*	*Pensions Beginning*	*Percentage Increase*
28th July 1986 to 21st August 1986	2.10%	22nd November 1986 to 21st December 1986	1.05%
22nd August 1986 to 21st September 1986	1.84%	22nd December 1986 to 21st January 1987	0.79%
22nd September 1986 to 21st October 1986	1.58%	22nd January 1987 to 21st February 1987	0.53%
22nd October 1986 to 21st November 1986	1.31%	22nd February 1987 to 21st March 1987	0.26%

Deferred lump sums beginning on or before 21st March 1987 and which become payable after 5th April 1987 receive the same percentage increase as pensions which began on the same date. Article 4 of the Order provides for increases on certain deferred lump sums which became payable after 27th July 1986 and before 6th April 1987.

The Order also makes provision for the amount by reference to which any increase in the rate of an official pension is to be calculated to be reduced by the amount equal to the rate of the guaranteed minimum pension entitlement deriving from the employment which gives rise to the official pension. This is required by section 59(5) of the Social Security Pensions Act 1975 but by virtue of section 59A of that Act and the Transfer of Functions (Minister for the Civil Service and Treasury) Order 1981 the Treasury is empowered to direct that in respect of specified cases or classes of case either no such reduction be made or the reduction shall be less than the rate of the guaranteed minimum pension.

STATUTORY INSTRUMENTS

1987 No. 133

FOOD

AUTHORITIES

The Authorised Officers (Meat Inspection) Regulations 1987

Made - - - -	*1st February 1987*
Coming into force	*22nd February 1987*

The Minister of Agriculture, Fisheries and Food, the Secretary of State for Social Services and the Secretary of State for Wales, acting jointly, in exercise of the powers conferred on them by section 73(2) of the Food Act 1984**(a)** and of all other powers enabling them in that behalf, hereby make the following Regulations:-

Title and comencement

1.   These Regulations may be cited as the Authorised Officers (Meat Inspection) Regulations 1987 and shall come into force on 22nd February 1987.

Authorised Officers

2.   Pursuant to section 73(2) of the Food Act 1984 any officer of a council, being a person having any of the qualifications specified in the Schedule to these Regulations, may be authorised under that Act to act in relation to the examination and seizure of meat.

Revocation of Authorised Officers (Meat Inspection) Regulations 1978

3.   The Authorised Officers (Meat Inspection) Regulations 1978**(b)** are hereby revoked.

In Witness whereof the Official Seal of the Minister of Agriculture, Fisheries and Food is hereunto affixed on 1st February 1987.

Michael Jopling
Minister of Agriculture, Fisheries and Food

30th January 1987

Trumpington
for the Secretary of State for Social Services

28th January 1987

Nicholas Edwards
Secretary of State for Wales

(a) 1984 c.30.   **(b)** S.I. 1978/884.

THE SCHEDULE   Regulation 2

QUALIFICATIONS OF AUTHORISED OFFICERS

1. Registered Medical Practitioner.

2. Member of the Royal College of Veterinary Surgeons.

3. The holder of a valid—

(a) Certificate or Diploma of the former Public Health Inspectors Education Board, or

(b) Certificate of the former Royal Sanitary Institute and Sanitary Inspectors Examination Joint Board, or

(c) Certificate of the former Sanitary Inspectors Examination Board, or

(d) Certificate in Meat Inspection of the Royal Society for the promotion of Health, or

(e) Diploma in Environmental Health of the former Environmental Health Officers Education Board, or

(f) Certificate of Registration of the Environmental Health Officers Registration Board, or

(g) Diploma in Environmental Health of the Institution of Environmental Health Officers, or

(h) Certificate of Competency in the Inspection of Meat and other Foods of the former Royal Sanitary Association of Scotland, or

(i) Certificate or Diploma of the former Royal Sanitary Association of Scotland, or

(j) Diploma in the Inspection of Meat and other Foods of the Royal Environmental Health Institute of Scotland, or

(k) Certificate for Meat Detention Officers in Northern Ireland of the Royal College of Veterinary Surgeons.

EXPLANATORY NOTE

(This note is not part of the Regulations)

These Regulations come into force on 22nd February 1987 and prescribe the qualifications to be held by an officer of a council authorised under the Food Act 1984 to act in relation to the examination and seizure of meat. They revoke and re-enact the Authorised Officers (Meat Inspection) Regulations 1978 and prescribe two additional alternative qualifications, that of a Diploma in Environmental Health of the Institution of Environmental Health Officers and a Diploma in the Inspection of Meat and other Foods of the Royal Environmental Health Institute of Scotland.

STATUTORY INSTRUMENTS

1987 No. 134

CUSTOMS AND EXCISE

GENERAL RELIEFS

The Agricultural Levy Reliefs (Frozen Beef and Veal) Order 1987

Made - - - -	*4th February 1987*
Laid before the House of Commons	*6th February 1987*
Coming into force	*27th February 1987*

The Minister of Agriculture, Fisheries and Food, the Secretary of State for Scotland, the Secretary of State for Northern Ireland (being the Secretaries of State respectively concerned with agriculture in Scotland and Northern Ireland) and the Secretary of State for Wales, acting jointly, in exercise of the powers conferred by section 4 of the Customs and Excise Duties (General Reliefs) Act 1979 (a), as applied in relation to agricultural levies of the Economic Community by section 6(5) of the European Communities Act 1972 (b), and now vested in them (c), and of all other powers enabling them in that behalf, hereby make the following Order:

1. This Order may be cited as the Agricultural Levy Reliefs (Frozen Beef and Veal) Order 1987 and shall come into force on 27th February 1987.

2. In this Order, unless the context otherwise requires–

"the Board" means the Intervention Board for Agricultural Produce established under section 6 of the European Communities Act 1972;

"entered for home use" means entered for home use within the meaning of the Customs and Excise Management Act 1979 (d) or regulation 13 of the Customs Warehousing Regulations 1979 (e);

"international organisations established in the Economic Community" means the following–

Delegation of the Commission of European Communities;

Intergovernmental Maritime Organisation;

International Coffee Organisation;

International Labour Office;

International Sugar Organisation;

International Tin Council;

International Wheat Council;

(a) 1979 c.3.

(b) 1972 c.68; section 6(5) was amended, so far as is relevant to this Order, by section 19(1) of, and paragraph 4 of Schedule 2 to, the Customs and Excise Duties (General Reliefs) Act 1979; by virtue of section 6(8) of the European Communities Act 1972 the reference to the Ministers in section 6(5) of that Act is to be construed as if contained in Part I of the Agriculture Act 1957 (c.57).

(c) In the case of the Secretary of State for Wales, by virtue of S.I. 1978/272.

(d) 1979 c.2.

(e) S.I. 1979/207.

United Nations Children's Fund;

United Nations Development Programme;

United Nations Information Centre;

United Nations High Commission for Refugees;

Western European Union;

Commonwealth Secretariat;

"licence" means an import licence issued by the Board under the provisions of Council Regulation (EEC) No. 805/68(**a**) on the common organisation of the market in beef and veal, as amended(**b**), Commission Regulation (EEC) No. 3183/ 80(**c**) laying down common detailed rules for the application of the system of import and export licences and advance fixing certificates for agricultural products, as amended(**d**), and Commission Regulation (EEC) No. 2377/80(**e**) on special detailed rules for the application of the system of import and export licences in the beef and veal sector, as amended (**f**) ;

"local authorities" means–

(a) in Greater London the Inner London Education Authority, the councils of London boroughs and the Common Council of the City of London,

(b) in England and Wales outside Greater London the county and metropolitan district councils,

(c) in Scotland the councils of islands areas and regions,

(d) in Northern Ireland Education and Library Boards;

"the Minister" means the Minister of Agriculture, Fisheries and Food;

"the quota" means the Community quota for the levy-free importation of frozen beef and veal provided for by Council Regulation (EEC) No. 3929/86(**g**) opening, allocating and providing for the administration of a Community tariff quota for frozen beef and veal falling within subheading 02.01 A II b) of the Common Customs Tariff (1987);

"the reference period" means the period from 1st October 1984 to 30th September 1986;

"the Second Lomé Convention" means the second ACP-EEC Convention signed at Lomé on 31st October 1979 between the African, Caribbean and Pacific States of the one part and the Economic Community and its Member States of the other part as set out in Council Regulation (EEC) No. 3225/80(**h**) and extended by Council Regulations (EEC) Nos. 485/85(**i**) and 690/86(**j**);

"the Third Lomé Convention" means the third ACP-EEC Convention signed at Lomé on 8th December 1984 between the African Caribbean and Pacific States of the one part and the Economic Community and its Member States of the other part as set out in Council and Commission Decision 86/125/EEC/ECSC(**k**).

3.—(1) The Minister shall determine the allocation to persons established within the United Kingdom of its share of the quota.

(2) The determination mentioned in paragraph (1) of this article shall be made by the Minister by allocating an amount not exceeding one third of the United Kingdom's share to Government Departments and local authorities, and allocating the remainder as follows–

(a) as to 70% thereof to importers of frozen beef and veal by reference to the amounts of frozen beef and veal which such importers have imported from outside the Economic Community and entered for home use during the reference period, other than amounts imported free of duty pursuant to the Second Lomé Convention or the Third Lomé Convention;

(**a**) O.J. No. L148, 28.6.68, p.24 (O.J./S.E. 1968 (I) p.187).

(**b**) The relevant amending instrument is Council Regulation (EEC) No. 425/77 (O.J. No. L61, 5.3.77, p.1).

(**c**) O.J. No. L338, 13.12.80, p.1.

(**d**) The relevant amending instrument is Commission Regulation (EEC) No. 3913/86 (O.J. No. L364, 23.12.86, p.31).

(**e**) O.J. No. L241, 13.9.80, p.5.

(**f**) The amendments are not relevant to this Order.

(**g**) O.J. No. L365, 24.12.86, p.3.

(**h**) O.J. No. L347, 22.12.80, p.1.

(**i**) O.J. No. L61, 1.3.85, p.1.

(**j**) O.J. No. L63, 5.3.86, p.1.

(**k**) O.J. No. L86, 31.3.86, p.1.

(b) as to 20% thereof to exporters of fresh chilled or frozen beef and veal by reference to the amounts of fresh chilled or frozen beef and veal which such exporters have exported during the reference period from the United Kingdom to countries outside the Economic Community or to one of the following destinations–

(i) seagoing vessels, or aircraft serving on international routes, including routes between Member States of the Economic Community;

(ii) international organisations established in the Economic Community;

(iii) armed forces stationed in the territory of a Member State but not serving under its flag;

(iv) drilling or extraction platforms, including workpoints providing support services for such operations, situated within the area of the European Continental shelf, or within the area of the continental shelf of the non-European part of the Community, but beyond a three mile zone starting from the base line used to determine the width of the territorial sea of a Member State of the Economic Community; and

(c) as to the remaining 10% thereof to purchasers of frozen beef and veal from the Board by reference to the amounts of frozen beef and veal which they have purchased from the Board during the reference period, other than frozen beef and veal sold by the Board on condition that it should be exported from the Economic Community.

Any such allocation shall be made subject to such conditions as appear to the Minister to be expedient to secure the object or prevent abuse of the relief.

4. Any entitlement to relief under the United Kingdom's share of the quota shall be subject to–

(a) the production of the licence in respect of the goods on which relief is sought appropriately endorsed by the Board with a statement that the amount of frozen beef or veal appearing in the licence may be imported free of levy under the quota; and

(b) the observance by the importer of any conditions subject to which the allocation was made.

5. A licence endorsed with the statement referred to in article 4(a) of this Order shall not be issued to an importer unless the Board is satisfied, after taking into account any levy-free imports of beef or veal authorised under previous licences issued to that importer, that the amount of levy-free beef or veal allocated to him in pursuance of this Order will not be exceeded by the import of beef or veal under that licence.

6. Goods shall be treated as forming part of the quota when they are entered for home use under the authority of a licence endorsed with the statement referred to in article 4(a) of this Order.

In Witness whereof the Official Seal of the Minister of Agriculture, Fisheries and Food is hereunto affixed on 4th February 1987.

Michael Jopling
Minister of Agriculture, Fisheries and Food

4th February 1987

John J. Mackay
Parliamentary Under-Secretary of State, Scottish Office

4th February 1987

Tom King
Secretary of State for Northern Ireland

3rd February 1987

Nicholas Edwards
Secretary of State of Wales

EXPLANATORY NOTE

(This note is not part of the Order)

This Order, which applies throughout the United Kingdom, requires the Minister of Agriculture, Fisheries and Food to allocate to persons established within the United Kingdom its share of a quota for the levy-free import of frozen beef and veal under the provisions of Council Regulation (EEC) No. 3929/86 (O.J. No. L365, 24.12.86, p.3).

This Order provides that not more than one third of the United Kingdom's share of the quota shall be allocated to Government Departments and local authorities (article 3(2)), and that the remainder shall be allocated—

(a) as to 70% thereof, to importers of frozen beef and veal by reference to the amounts of frozen beef and veal which they have imported from outside the European Economic Community into the United Kingdom during the reference period other than amounts imported free of duty pursuant to the Second Lomé Convention, as extended, or to the Third Lomé Convention (article 3(2)(a));

(b) as to 20% thereof, to exporters of fresh chilled or frozen beef or veal by reference to the amounts of fresh chilled or frozen beef or veal which they have exported during the reference period to destinations outside the European Economic Community and other similar destinations (article 3(2)(b)); and

(c) as to 10% thereof, to purchasers of frozen beef or veal from the Intervention Board for Agricultural Produce by reference to the amounts of frozen beef and veal which they have purchased from the Board during the reference period other than frozen beef and veal sold by the Board on condition that it should be exported from the European Economic Community (article 3(2)(c)).

For the purposes of (a), (b) and (c) above the reference period is the period from 1st October 1984 to 30th September 1986 (article 2).

The Order comes into force on 27th February 1987.

STATUTORY INSTRUMENTS

1987 No. 135 (S. 10)

ANIMALS

ANIMAL HEALTH

The Brucellosis (Scotland) Amendment Order 1987

Made - - - -	*28th January 1987*
Coming into force - -	*9th February 1987*

The Secretary of State, in exercise of the powers conferred on him by sections 1, 6, 8, 86(1) and 87(2) of the Animal Health Act 1981(**a**), and of all other powers enabling him in that behalf, hereby makes the following Order:

Title and commencement

1. This Order may be cited as the Brucellosis (Scotland) Amendment Order 1987 and shall come into force on 9th February 1987.

Amendment

2. The Brucellosis (Scotland) Order 1979(**b**) shall be amended as follows:–

  (a) in the definition of "cattle dealer" in article 2(1) the words ",and not for the purpose of rearing, fattening or breeding" shall be deleted;

  (b) for article 20 (control of premises used by cattle dealers) there shall be substituted the following article:–

"Control of premises used by cattle dealers and others for the keeping of cattle

  20. No premises shall be used–

      (a) by a cattle dealer for the keeping of cattle in connection with his business as a dealer; or

      (b) by any person who regularly purchases pregnant cattle for resale within 30 days of their expected date of calving or within 30 days of their having calved for the keeping of any such cattle so purchased,

other than premises which have been approved for the purpose by a veterinary inspector or officer of the Secretary of State.";

  (c) for article 21 (animals other than cattle) there shall be substituted the following article:–

"Control of infection from other animals

21.—(1) Where a veterinary inspector or officer of the Secretary of State reasonably believes that an animal kept on any premises is, or may be, infected with brucellosis, he may by notice in writing served on the owner or other person in charge of cattle kept on any premises or on the occupier or person in charge of such premises, require him to keep the animal under control in such manner as may be specified in the notice or to confine it to such part of the premises as may be so specified.

(**a**) 1981 c.22; for the extension of the Act to brucellosis *see* S.I. 1971/531.
(**b**) S.I. 1979/1596, to which there are amendments not relevant to this Order.

(2) A notice served under paragraph (1) above in respect of an animal kept on any premises shall remain in force until such time as the animal dies or it is withdrawn by a further notice in writing served by a veterinary inspector on such owner, occupier or person.

(3) For the purposes of paragraphs (1) and (2) above "animal" means any kind of mammal except man.".

John J. MacKay
New St. Andrew's House, Edinburgh
Parliamentary Under Secretary of State,
28th January 1987
Scottish Office

EXPLANATORY NOTE

(This note is not part of the Order)

This Order amends the Brucellosis (Scotland) Order 1979 ("the 1979 Order"). Article 20 of the 1979 Order prohibits a cattle dealer from using any premises for the keeping of cattle in connection with his business as a dealer unless they have first been approved by a veterinary inspector or officer of the Secretary of State. This Order extends that provision so as to prohibit any person who regularly purchases pregnant cattle for resale within 30 days of their expected date of calving or within 30 days of their having calved from using any premises for keeping any such cattle unless they have been similarly approved. It also amends the definition of "cattle dealer" so as to remove the exemption previously enjoyed by those dealers who intend to rear, fatten or breed cattle.

Article 21 of the 1979 Order allowed notice to be given to owners or persons in charge of cattle kept on any premises or to the occupiers of such premises, requiring them to ensure that cattle did not come into contact with other animals. This Order substitutes for this a provision enabling a veterinary inspector or officer of the Secretary of State to require the occupier or person in charge of any premises on which is kept any animal he reasonably believes is infected with brucellosis, or the owner or other person in charge of cattle kept on those premises, to keep that animal under control in a specified manner or to confine it to a specified part of the premises.

STATUTORY INSTRUMENTS

1987 No. 136

HOVERCRAFT

The Hovercraft (Fees) (Amendment) Regulations 1987

Made - - - - *4th February 1987*

Coming into force - - *25th February 1987*

The Secretary of State for Transport, with the approval of the Treasury and in exercise of his powers under Article 35 of the Hovercraft (General) Order 1972**(a)** and of all other powers enabling him in that behalf, hereby makes the following Regulations:—

1. The Regulations may be cited as the Hovercraft (Fees) (Amendment) Regulations 1987 and shall come into force on 25th February 1987.

2. The Schedule to the Hovercraft (Fees) Regulations 1985**(b)** shall be amended as follows:—

(1) In paragraph 10, in sub-paragraphs (1) and (2) for "£41·50" there shall be substituted "£45·50".

(2) In paragraph 11, for "£41·50" there shall be substituted "£45·50".

Signed by authority of the Secretary of State.

Michael Spicer
Parliamentary Under Secretary of State,
4th February 1987   Department of Transport

We approve the making of these Regulations,

Mark Lennox-Boyd
Tim Sainsbury
4th February 1987   Two of the Lords Commissioners of Her Majesty's Treasury

---

EXPLANATORY NOTE

(This note is not part of the Regulations)

These Regulations amend the Hovercraft (Fees) Regulations 1985 by prescribing increased fees payable to the Secretary of State for the issue of operating permits for hovercraft, and exemptions, under the Hovercraft (General) Order 1972. The increase is of 9·64 per cent.

(a) S.I. 1972/674.   **(b)** S.I. 1985/1605.

STATUTORY INSTRUMENTS

1987 No. 137

EDUCATION, ENGLAND AND WALES

The Remuneration of Teachers (Primary and Secondary Education) (Amendment) Order 1987

Made - - - -	*4th February 1987*
Coming into force	*17th February 1987*

WHEREAS:

(1) in pursuance of section 2(2) of the Remuneration of Teachers Act 1965 (**a**) ("the Act"), the Committee constituted under section 1 of the Act for the purpose of considering the remuneration payable to teachers in primary and secondary schools maintained by local education authorities and to other persons employed by such authorities as teachers in the provision of primary and secondary education (except teachers in an establishment maintained by a local authority in the exercise of a social services function) ("the Committee") have transmitted to the Secretary of State for Education and Science ("the Secretary of State") recommendations agreed on by them with respect to the remuneration of such teachers ("primary and secondary education teachers");

(2) there are in force Orders made under sections 2(4) and (6) of the Act with respect to the remuneration of the teachers in question, such Orders being those specified in Schedule 1 to this Order;

(3) it appears to the Secretary of State that effect can most conveniently be given to the recommendations of the Committee by amending the scales and other provisions set out in the document referred to in the said Orders, namely the document published by Her Majesty's Stationery Office on 7th October 1983 under the title "Scales of Salaries for Teachers: Primary and Secondary Education, England and Wales 1983" (**b**) ("the 1983 Document"), as amended by the said Orders;

(4) in pursuance of section 2(5) of the Act, the Secretary of State has prepared a draft Order setting out the amendments to the 1983 Document which, in his opinion, are requisite for giving effect to the recommendations of the Committee, and

(5) the Secretary of State, as required by section 2(6) of the Act, has consulted the Committee with respect to the draft Order and the Committee have made no representations with respect thereto:

Now, therefore, the Secretary of State, in pursuance of sections 2(6) and 7(2) and (3) of the Act, hereby makes the following Order, which is in the form of the draft:

1.—(1) This Order may be cited as the Remuneration of Teachers (Primary and Secondary Education) (Amendment) Order 1987.

(2) This Order shall come into force on 17th February 1987.

2. The scales and other provisions contained in the 1983 Document, as amended, are hereby further amended, with effect from 1st April 1985, in the manner specified in Schedule 2 to this Order and, with effect from 1st April 1986, in the manner specified in Schedule 3 to this Order.

(**a**) 1965 c.3.
(**b**) ISBN 0 11 270550 2.

3. The Remuneration of Teachers (Primary and Secondary Education) (Amendment) Order 1985 (**a**) and the Remuneration of Teachers (Primary and Secondary Education) (Amendment) (No. 2) Order 1985 (**b**) are hereby revoked.

SCHEDULE 1

ORDERS IN FORCE RELATING TO THE REMUNERATION OF PRIMARY AND SECONDARY EDUCATION TEACHERS

Order	Reference
The Remuneration of Teachers (Primary and Secondary Education) Order 1983.	S.I. 1983/1463.
The Remuneration of Teachers (Primary and Secondary Education) (Amendment) Order 1984.	S.I. 1984/1650.
The Remuneration of Teachers (Primary and Secondary Education) (Amendment) Order 1985.	S.I. 1985/38.
The Remuneration of Teachers (Primary and Secondary Education) (Amendment) (No. 2) Order 1985.	S.I. 1985/944.
The Remuneration of Teachers (Primary and Secondary Education) (Amendment) Order 1986.	S.I. 1986/559.

SCHEDULE 2

AMENDMENTS EFFECTIVE FROM 1ST APRIL 1985 (**c**)

1. In section 12 (London Area Allowances)–
   (a) in paragraph (1) for the sum of £1,038 there shall be substituted the sum of £1,110;
   (b) in paragraph (2) for the sum of £678 there shall be substituted the sum of £726 and the word "serving" shall be inserted after the word "teachers";
   (c) paragraph (3) shall be deleted;
   (d) in paragraph (4) for the sum of £264 there shall be substituted the sum of £282 and the words "and not in receipt of a London Area Allowance under section 12(3) above" shall be deleted.

SCHEDULE 3

AMENDMENTS EFFECTIVE FROM 1ST APRIL 1986(**d**)

1. In section 8*(c)* for the sum of £867 there shall be substituted the sum of £915.

2. In section 9*(c)*–
   (a) in paragraph (i) for the sum of £1,830 there shall be substituted the sum of £1,932;
   (b) in paragraph (ii) for the sum of £1,545 there shall be substituted the sum of £1,629;

3. In section 10–
   (a) in paragraph *(a)*(i) for the sum of £810 there shall be substituted the sum of £855;
   (b) in paragraph *(a)*(ii) for the sum of £549 there shall be substituted the sum of £579;

(**a**) S.I. 1985/38.
(**b**) S.I. 1985/944.
(**c**) The provisions amended by paragraph 1(a) and (b) of this Schedule were last amended by S.I. 1985/38 and that amended by paragraph 1(d) was last amended by S.I. 1985/944.
(**d**) The provisions amended by paragraphs 1 to 6, 9 and 10 of this Schedule were last amended by Schedule 3 to S.I. 1986/559, and the provisions amended by paragraphs 7 and 8 by Schedule 2 thereto.

(c) in paragraph *(c)* for the sum of £735 there shall be substituted the sum of £774;

(d) in paragraph *(e)*(i) for the sum of £696 there shall be substituted the sum of £741;

(e) in paragraph *(e)*(ii) for the sum of £462 there shall be substituted the sum of £492.

4. In section 14(2)*(a)* and *(b)* for the sum of £561 there shall in each case be substituted the sum of £591.

5. In section 20 for the sum of £633 there shall be substituted the sum of £669.

6. For Appendix 1 there shall be substituted the following Appendix–

APPENDIX I

Scales of Salaries

1. Qualified Teachers (excluding Head Teachers and Deputy Head Teachers) in schools, other than special schools and Unqualified Teachers to whom section 7(2) applies–

Incremental Point	Scales				
	1	2	3	4	Senior Teacher
	£	£	£	£	£
0	6,423	7,302	8,910	10,533	11,349
1	6,696	7,560	9,204	10,986	11,778
2	6,900	7,824	9,501	11,349	12,201
3	7,107	8,085	9,804	11,778	12,627
4	7,302	8,364	10,170	12,201	13,053
5	7,560	8,637	10,533	12,627	13,656
6	7,824	8,910	10,986	13,053	14,151
7	8,085	9,204	11,349	13,656	14,838
8	8,364	9,501	11,778	14,151	15,330
9	8,637	9,804	12,201		
10	8,910	10,170	12,627		
11	9,204	10,533			
12	9,501	10,986			
13	9,804				

Note 1

Where a teacher paid on Scale 1 is entitled to be classed as a good honours graduate for salary purposes under the conditions set out in annex F to Appendix III, the scale shall be extended by two increments as follows–

Incremental Point	Salary
	£
14	10,170
15	10,533

Note 2

Teachers entitled to be paid a personal salary of £3,609 per annum on 31 March 1975 as good honours graduates on Scale 2 under the provisions of Appendix I to the 1974 Primary and Secondary Salaries Document (**a**) shall be paid a personal salary of £11,349.

Note 3

In the case of a teacher to whom section 10*(b)* applies, this paragraph shall have effect subject thereto and the additional increment there referred to shall, if he is a Senior Teacher, equal the amount of the last increment on the relevant scale, and in any other case equal the amount of the next increment in the incremental sequence common to all the above scales.

(**a**) ISBN 0 11 270279 1.

2. Qualified Teachers (excluding Head Teachers and Deputy Head Teachers) in special schools

Incremental Point	Scales			
	1	2(S)	3(S)	Senior Teacher
	£	£	£	£
0	6,423	8,085	9,804	11,349
1	6,696	8,364	10,170	11,778
2	6,900	8,637	10,533	12,201
3	7,107	8,910	10,986	12,627
4	7,302	9,204	11,349	13,053
5	7,560	9,501	11,778	13,656
6	7,824	9,804	12,201	14,151
7	8,085	10,170	12,627	14,838
8	8,364	10,533	13,053	15,330
9	8,637	10,986	13,656	
10	8,910	11,349		
11	9,204	11,778		
12	9,501			
13	9,804			

Note 1

Where a teacher paid on Scale 1 is entitled to be classed as a good honours graduate for salary purposes under the conditions set out in annex F to Appendix III, the scale shall be extended by two increments as follows–

Incremental Point	Salary
	£
14	10,170
15	10,533

Note 2

Teachers entitled to be paid a personal salary of £3,927 per annum on 31st March 1975 as good honours graduates on Scale 2(S) under the provisions of Appendix I to the 1974 Primary and Secondary Salaries Document shall be paid a personal salary of £12,201 per annum.

Note 3

In the case of a teacher to whom section 10*(b)* applies, this paragraph shall have effect subject thereto and the additional increment there referred to shall, if he is a Senior Teacher, equal the amount of the last increment on the relevant scale, and in any other case equal the amount of the next increment in the incremental sequence common to all the above scales.

3. Qualified Deputy Head Teachers

(a) Schools, other than special schools–

Incremental Point	Group					
	Below 4	4	5	6	7	8
	£	£	£	£	£	£
0	7,905	9,252	10,308	11,757	12,426	13,053
1	8,199	9,546	10,668	12,123	12,789	13,419
2	8,490	9,840	11,040	12,480	13,158	13,779
3	8,775	10,143	11,397	12,846	13,524	14,148
4	9,066	10,458	11,757	13,179	13,878	14,517
5	9,354	10,761	12,123			
6	9,645	11,067	12,480			
7	9,933	11,382	12,846			
8	10,242	11,691				
9	10,548	12,000				
10	10,857					
11	11,163					

Incremental Point	Group					
	9	10	11	12	13	14
	£	£	£	£	£	£
0	13,779	14,694	15,447	16,326	16,821	17,592
1	14,148	15,072	15,822	16,692	17,202	17,967
2	14,517	15,447	16,185	17,076	17,574	18,345
3	14,883	15,822	16,557	17,448	17,952	18,723
4	15,288	16,185	16,929	17,820	18,324	19,104

(b) Special schools

Incremental Point	Group							
	3(S)	4(S)	5(S)	6(S)	7(S)	8(S)	9(S)	10(S)
	£	£	£	£	£	£	£	£
0	9,075	10,461	12,453	12,891	13,347	13,785	14,664	15,342
1	9,354	10,812	12,813	13,248	13,704	14,145	15,018	15,693
2	9,639	11,160	13,167	13,596	14,052	14,496	15,378	16,047
3	9,915	11,511	13,524	13,947	14,403	14,850	15,729	16,404
4	10,212	11,859	13,872	14,313	14,766	15,201	16,089	16,764
5	10,512	12,204						
6	10,812	12,558						
7	11,109	12,903						
8	11,403							
9	11,700							
10	12,000							
11	12,297							

Note 1

In the case of a teacher to whom section 10*(b)* applies, this paragraph shall have effect subject thereto and the additional increment there referred to shall equal the last increment on the scale in this paragraph applicable to him.

4. Qualified Head Teachers

(a) Schools, other than special schools

Incremental Point	Group						
	1	2	3	4	5	6	7
	£	£	£	£	£	£	£
0	10,956	11,436	11,967	12,720	13,785	14,751	15,666
1	11,271	11,739	12,273	13,083	14,151	15,129	16,044
2	11,580	12,048	12,588	13,449	14,520	15,489	16,407
3	11,892	12,363	12,894	13,806	14,883	15,867	16,776
4	12,195	12,675	13,203	14,175	15,243	16,236	17,148

Incremental Point	Group						
	8	9	10	11	12	13	14
	£	£	£	£	£	£	£
0	16,785	18,075	19,260	20,787	22,251	23,442	24,795
1	17,154	18,459	19,626	21,165	22,737	23,937	25,284
2	17,535	18,828	20,013	21,555	23,217	24,420	25,770
3	17,901	19,206	20,385	21,939	23,700	24,903	26,259
4	18,273	19,587	20,766	22,332			

(b) Special schools

Incremental Point	Group							
	3(S)	4(S)	5(S)	6(S)	7(S)	8(S)	9(S)	10(S)
	£	£	£	£	£	£	£	£
0	12,999	13,773	15,327	15,843	16,983	17,796	18,585	19,404
1	13,302	14,124	15,693	16,212	17,346	18,171	18,963	19,788
2	13,599	14,490	16,059	16,572	17,718	18,531	19,347	20,172
3	13,917	14,850	16,416	16,929	18,075	18,900	19,737	20,562
4	14,217	15,207	16,782	17,301	18,450	19,272	20,124	20,955

Note 1

In the case of a teacher to whom section 10*(b)* applies, this paragraph shall have effect subject thereto and the additional increment there referred to shall equal the last increment on the scale in this paragraph applicable to him.

5.   Unqualified Teachers other than those to whom sub-sections 7(2)*(a)*, 8*(a)* and 9*(a)* of Part III apply

Incremental Point	Scale		
	A	B	C
	£	£	£
0	5,604	5,604	6,012
1	5,712	5,712	6,117
2	5,814	5,814	6,231
3	5,928	5,928	6,339
4	6,039	6,039	6,465
5		6,153	6,690
6		6,261	6,921
7		6,396	7,158
8			7,386
9			7,641
10			7,905
11			8,169

Note 1

Scale C may be extended by one or two increments of £264 to a maximum of £8,433, or £8,697 as the case may be, in the case of a teacher who, in the opinion of the local education authority, possesses a qualification of particular value in the performance of his duties.

Note 2

Unqualified teachers shall be placed on Scales A, B or C in accordance with the following Table–

Employment authorised under	Scale applicable
Paragraphs 5 and 6 of Schedule 4 to the Education (Teachers) Regulations 1982 **(a)**	A
Paragraphs 1, 2 and 4 of Schedule 4 to the Education (Teachers) Regulations 1982	B
Paragraph 3 of Schedule 4 to the Education (Teachers) Regulations 1982	C

Note 3

In the case of an unqualified deputy head teacher or an unqualified head teacher who is paid on a scale set out in this paragraph and is entitled to an allowance under section 8 or, as the case may be, section 9, that allowance shall be increased–

  (a) in the case of the deputy head teacher of a special school, to £915;

  (b) in the case of a head teacher of a special school, to £1,932;

  (c) in the case of any other head teacher, to £1,629.

(a) S.I. 1982/106.

6. Unqualified Deputy Head Teachers of Special Schools, to whom sub-section 8*(a)* of Part III applies

Incremental Point	Group						
	3(S)	4(S)	5(S)	6(S)	7(S)	8(S)	9(S)
	£	£	£	£	£	£	£
0	8,256	9,654	11,532	11,943	12,627	13,101	13,947
1	8,538	9,972	11,874	12,279	12,972	13,449	14,304
2	8,820	10,308	12,219	12,624	13,320	12,797	14,655
3	9,096	10,653	12,558	12,960	13,677	14,142	15,009
4	9,384	10,986	12,897	13,305	14,019	14,484	15,366
5	9,666	11,331					
6	9,951	11,664					
7	10,242	12,006					
8	10,536						
9	10,833						
10	11,139						
11	11,436						

7. Unqualified Head Teachers of Special Schools, to whom sub-section 9*(a)* of Part III applies

Incremental Point	Group						
	3(S)	4(S)	5(S)	6(S)	7(S)	8(S)	9(S)
	£	£	£	£	£	£	£
0	11,976	12,840	14,475	14,952	16,092	17,037	17,826
1	12,288	13,191	14,847	15,318	16,470	17,409	18,201
2	12,600	13,569	15,216	15,693	16,842	17,787	18,582
3	12,909	13,932	15,588	16,062	17,214	18,177	18,957
4	13,230	14,295	15,951	16,440	17,601	18,546	19,332

7. In Appendix II, Part A, paragraph 6(3)–

(a) for sub-paragraph *(c)*, there shall be substituted the following sub-paragraph–

"*(c) the year beginning* 1 *April* 1982–
for the period 1 April 1986 to 31 March 1988 on *(a)* the average of unit totals for 1984, 1985 and 1986 or *(b)* the unit total for 1986 or *(c)* the estimated unit total for 1986, whichever is the greatest. Where a new head or deputy head teacher is appointed during the period 1 April 1986 to 31 March 1988, the head or deputy head teacher scale applicable shall be based on whichever of *(a)* or *(b)* is the greater;"

(b) after sub-paragraph *(f)*, there shall be inserted the following sub-paragraph–

"*(g) the year beginning* 1 *April* 1986–
from the date of opening or reorganisation until 31 March 1990, on the estimated unit total for 1990.".

8. In Part B of Appendix II, in paragraphs 3 and 4 there shall be substituted for the date 1985 wherever it appears the date 1986.

9. In Appendix III, paragraph 10(3)*(a)*(i), for the sum of £7,041 there shall be substituted the sum of £7,560.

10. In Appendix III, paragraph 12(1)*(a)*, for the sums of £141, £249 and £276 there shall be substituted the sums of £150, £264 and £291 respectively.

Kenneth Baker
4th February 1987   Secretary of State for Education and Science

EXPLANATORY NOTE

(This note is not part of the Order)

This Order amends, with effect from 1st April 1985 (Schedule 2) and 1st April 1986 (Schedule 3) the provisions contained in the document setting out the scales and other provisions for determining the remuneration of teachers in primary and secondary schools maintained by local education authorities and certain other teachers employed by such authorities. This document, entitled "Scales of Salaries for Teachers: Primary and Secondary Education, England and Wales 1983", which has been amended by the Orders listed in Schedule 1, is published by Her Majesty's Stationery Office and may be obtained from Government Bookshops and through booksellers. The Order gives effect to recommendations of the appropriate Burnham Committee under section 2 of the Remuneration of Teachers Act 1965 and revokes two earlier amending Orders that are now spent. The increase in the Fringe Area allowance (section 12(4)) renders unnecessary the special provision for certain teachers in certain parts of that area and section 12(3) is accordingly deleted with effect from 1st April 1985.

The retrospective effect of the Order is authorised by section 7(3) of the Act.

STATUTORY INSTRUMENTS

1987 No. 143

FOREIGN COMPENSATION

The Foreign Compensation Commission (Union of Soviet Socialist Republics) Rules Approval Instrument 1987

Made - - - -	*4th February 1987*
Laid before Parliament	*9th February 1987*
Coming into force	*2nd March 1987*

Whereas the Foreign Compensation Commission have, in exercise of their powers under section 4(2) and (3) of the Foreign Compensation Act 1950**(a)**, after consultation with the Council on Tribunals in accordance with the Tribunals and Inquiries Act 1971**(b)**, made rules of procedure and submitted them to the Lord Chancellor for his approval:

Now, therefore, the Lord Chancellor, in exercise of the powers conferred on him by section 4(2) and 8(3) of the said Act, after consultation with the Council on Tribunals, in accordance with section 10 of the Tribunals and Inquiries Act 1971**(b)**, hereby approves the said rules in the form set out in the Schedule hereto.

This Instrument may be cited as the Foreign Compensation Commission (Union of Soviet Socialist Republics) Rules Approval Instrument 1987 and shall come into force on 2nd March 1987.

Hailsham of St. Marylebone, C.

Dated 4th February 1987

(a) 1950 c.12.
(b) 1971 c.62.

SCHEDULE

Arrangement of Rules

The Foreign Compensation Commission, in exercise of their powers under section 4(2) and (3) of the Foreign Compensation Act 1950(a), after consultation with the Council on Tribunals in accordance with section 10 of the Tribunals and Inquiries Act 1971, hereby make the following Rules:–

Citation and application

1.—(1) These Rules may be cited as the Foreign Compensation Commission (Union of Soviet Socialist Republics) Rules 1987.

(2) These Rules shall apply to all applications under the Foreign Compensation (Union of Soviet Socialist Republics) (Registration and Determination of Claims) Order 1986(b) from the date they come into force and no rules heretofore made by the Commission shall thereafter apply to such applications.

Interpretation

2.—(1) In these Rules, unless the context otherwise requires:–

"bond claim" means a claim in respect of a bond under Part II of the Order;

"the Commission" means the Foreign Compensation Commission;

"Commissioner" means the Chairman or other member of the Commission;

"determination" means the determination of a claim under rule 9 or rule 29 of these rules;

"Legal Officer" means a Legal Officer appointed by the Commission to represent the interests of the Fund and any person authorised by the Commission to act in that behalf;

"the Order" means the Foreign Compensation (Union of Soviet Socialist Republics) (Registration and Determination of Claims) Order 1986(b);

"personal injury claim" means a claim in respect of personal injury or death under Part V of the Order;

"personal representative" means the person to whom a grant of probate or confirmation or letters of administration shall have been made in any part of the United Kingdom;

"pleading" means the application (or any other document accepted by the Commission in lieu thereof), an Answer, a reply and any particulars delivered in respect of such documents;

"property claim" means a claim in respect of property under Part IV of the Order;

"Registrar" means a Registrar appointed by the Commission and any person authorized to act in that behalf;

(2) Expressions defined in the Order shall have the meanings therein assigned to them.

Claims

3. Unless the Commission otherwise order, a claim shall be made by an application in the appropriate form issued or approved by the Commission, which shall be signed by the applicant or, in the case of a corporation, by the secretary or a director. Applications shall be addressed to the Commission and delivered by prepaid post or by hand.

Time and form of applications

4.—(1) No application shall be entertained unless–

(a) being an application in respect of a bond claim, it has reached the Commission on or before 31st March 1987;

(b) being an application in respect of a property claim or of a personal injury claim, it has reached the Commission on or before 30th June 1987.

(2) An applicant shall be deemed to have complied with paragraph (1) if he shall have delivered to the Commission on or before the relevant date the application form issued

(a) 1950 c.12.
(b) S.I. 1986/2222.

by the Commission duly completed and signed or such other document as the Commission may accept as giving sufficient notice of the claim:

Provided that if the application was not made on the form issued by the Commission the Commission may require the applicant to complete an application in the appropriate form within a period specified by the Commission.

(3) A claim which has been withdrawn shall not be further entertained except with the leave of the Commission.

Estates of deceased persons

5. Where a person has died who was qualified to make an application under the Order, an application may be made in respect of a claim on behalf of his estate notwithstanding that there is no personal representative, by any person who—

(a) has taken out a grant of probate or administration in respect of that estate in any part of the Commonwealth other than the United Kingdom; or

(b) is named as an executor in the last will of the deceased person; or

(c) appears to the Commission to be the widower, widow, child, grandchild, parent, brother or sister of the deceased person:

Provided that—

(i) the Commission shall not accept more than one application on behalf of the same estate;

(ii) the Commission may at any time as regards any applicant require a grant of probate or administration to be obtained in the United Kingdom and may set a time limit within which such grant of probate or administration shall be obtained and produced to the Commission;

(iii) upon the obtaining of such a grant the person to whom it is made, if not already an applicant, shall be substituted as applicant by order of the Commission on his signing all appropriate forms.

Minors

6.—(1) Applications may be made on behalf of a minor by his parent or guardian, or any person appointed for the purpose by his parent or guardian, or a person appointed by the Commission.

(2) Upon any such minor attaining full age, the application shall be carried on in his name unless he shall withdraw it in writing upon or within three months after his attaining full age.

Unincorporated associations

7.—(1) Where an application under the Order is made in respect of any property of an unincorporated association, charitable or otherwise, the Commission may appoint any two or more persons who appear to them to be suitable to represent the interests of the association to make or continue an application on its behalf.

(2) The Commission may at any time discharge any appointment so made or appoint any other person in addition to, or in substitution for, any person previously so appointed.

(3) No person shall be appointed under the preceding paragraphs of this rule without his consent in writing.

(4) Any person for the time being so appointed shall for all the purposes of these Rules be deemed to be an applicant.

Bond claims

8.—(1) The Commission shall register a claim in respect of a bond if—

(a) they are satisfied the claim has been made in proper form by an applicant entitled to claim;

(b) the application is supported by a statutory declaration in Form A in the Appendix; and

(c) the bond to which the application relates has been delivered to the Commission.

(2) Without prejudice to the requirements of sub-paragraphs (b) and (c) of paragraph (1), the Commission may at any time give such directions as they think fit regarding the production by the applicant of written evidence in support of his application.

(3) Rules 9 to 11, 13, 18, 20 to 23 and 28 to 37 of these Rules shall not apply to bond claims.

Unopposed property and personal injury claims

9.—(1) With or without prior consultation with the Commission, the Legal Officer may at any time file with the Registrar a statement recommending the Commission to admit a property claim or a personal injury claim in the sum claimed or at a sum agreed in writing by the applicant, and the Commission may determine the claim accordingly.

(2) Before making a determination under the provisions of paragraph (1), the Commission may require an applicant to make or obtain a statutory declaration of the statements by which he has supported his claim.

Answer

10. If the Legal Officer does not make a recommendation under the provisions of rule 9 or the Commission do not accept a recommendation so made, then unless the Commission otherwise direct, the Legal Officer shall file an Answer, a copy of which shall be served on the applicant, stating which facts in the application he admits and which facts he denies and any other facts or submissions on which he relies.

Reply, written argument and evidence

11.—(1) If the applicant wishes to reply to the Answer, he shall deliver his reply within 28 days of service of the Answer unless the Commission otherwise direct.

(2) Such reply shall contain any additional facts and submissions upon which he relies and shall be accompanied by any further evidence he wishes to put before the Commission.

(3) A copy of such reply shall be served by the Registrar on the Legal Officer who may make written submissions to the Commission thereon.

Further particulars

12. The Commission may direct the Legal Officer or an applicant to give further particulars of any pleading. If the applicant thereafter fails to comply with any such directions within the time specified the Commission may treat the claim in question as withdrawn.

Adjudication

13.—(1) The Commission may if they think fit direct that a claim shall be the subject of an oral hearing.

(2) If the Commission make such a direction, notice of not less than 21 days, unless the applicant otherwise agrees, shall be given to the applicant and the Legal Officer by the Registrar of the date of the hearing and of any adjournment thereof.

(3) If the Commission do not direct an oral hearing, the Commission shall proceed to a determination of the claim under rule 29.

(4) Subject to any directions given by the Commission, every oral hearing shall be in public.

Amendments

14.—(1) A pleading may be amended only with the leave of the Commission.

(2) A copy of the proposed amendment shall be delivered to the Registrar who shall serve a copy on the applicant or the Legal Officer, as the case may be.

Change of applicant

15.—(1) Subject to the provisions of rule 16, an applicant may only be removed from or added to a subsisting application by order of the Commission. An application for such removal or addition shall be in writing and shall state the reasons therefor and particulars of the proposed new applicant and shall be served on the Legal Officer and any applicant who may be affected.

(2) If the Legal Officer or any applicant desires to oppose such application he shall so inform the Commission and the proposed new applicant within 28 days of the service on him of such application.

Death of applicant or devolution or transfer of claims

16.—(1) Upon the death of an applicant or upon any devolution or transfer of any claim, the application may, subject to this rule, be continued as regards any claim not already determined by–

(a) the personal representative of the deceased applicant;

(b) a person claiming to be entitled to continue the application or any claim therein in lieu of any applicant by virtue of any devolution or transfer from the said applicant.

(2) After the expiration of three months from the date of the death of the deceased applicant or from the devolution or transfer of any claim, the application or claim in question may be continued as in paragraph (1) of this rule only with the leave of the Commission.

(3) No person shall be entitled to continue an application or claim under paragraphs (1) and (2) of this rule unless he shall first produce his full particulars and evidence of his title to the satisfaction of the Commission and signs or executes the application form already filed with the Commission.

(4) Failing the grant of leave under paragraph (2), or the taking of action under paragraph (3) of this rule, the Commission shall dismiss the claim.

(5) Nothing in the rule shall be deemed to affect any application or claim surviving to a joint applicant.

Language of proceedings and translations

17.—(1) All applications to, and all proceedings of, the Commission under the Order shall be in the English language.

(2) The Commission may order an English translation to be made of any document. Any translation submitted by the applicant may be certified by the Registrar to be a true translation.

(3) The Commission may appoint interpreters to interpret oral evidence or to translate documents.

Evidence

18. The Commission shall not be bound by rules of evidence and may admit in evidence any document or statement whether on oath or not which they deem to have probative value, but no such document or statement may without leave of the Commission be used unless it has been disclosed to the applicant or the Legal Officer, as the case may be, and he has been given a reasonable opportunity to make submissions to the Commission thereon.

Associated applications

19. Where there are pending at the same time two or more applications which could, in the opinion of the Commission, be conveniently taken together, the Commission may, on the application of an applicant or the Legal Officer or of their own motion, order that such several applications or parts thereof be determined at the same time. Upon making such an order the Commission shall give any consequential directions that may be required.

Oaths, affirmations and answers

20. The Commission shall have power at an oral hearing to administer an oath to or take the affirmation of any applicant or witness and to require any such person to take such oath or make such affirmation and to answer any question to which the Commission may lawfully require an answer.

Reports or information

21. The Commission may on an application by the applicant or the Legal Officer in that behalf or of their own motion order that a report or information be provided by any person nominated by the Commission on any matter affecting any claim and a copy thereof shall be supplied to the applicant and the Legal Officer who shall be entitled to comment thereon.

Summonses to witnesses and orders to forward documents

22.—(1) A summons for any person to attend to give evidence and to produce documents at an oral hearing shall be in Form B and an order to forward documents shall be in Form C, with such variations as circumstances may require.

(2) Where an applicant or the Legal Officer desires a summons or order to issue, the Registrar may issue the same and, in the case of a summons in Form B, shall specify therein a sum to be tendered to the person to be summoned to attend which shall be reasonably sufficient to cover his expenses in travelling to and from the place of hearing.

(3) An applicant or the Legal Officer, as the case may be, shall serve with the summons an undertaking in Form D to pay to the person summoned to attend compensation for loss of time and any additional expenses which may be certified by the Registrar to have been reasonably incurred.

(4) Each summons or order shall contain the name of one person only and shall be served personally a reasonable time before the date fixed for hearing.

(5) No summons or order issued pursuant to this rule shall be valid unless it is served upon the person named therein within 12 weeks from the date of signature by the Registrar and unless the conditions therein with regard to compensation for loss of time and expenses are complied with.

(6) A person served with a summons to attend to give evidence may apply to the Commission to set aside the same whereupon the Registrar shall send notice of the application to set aside the summons to the person at whose instance it was issued, and after taking into account the representations of both parties the Commission shall direct that the summons be confirmed or order that it be set aside.

Taking evidence abroad

23. The Commission may give such directions for the taking of evidence abroad and for the manner thereof as may be deemed expedient.

Extension of time

24. The time appointed by these Rules, other than any time appointed by paragraph (1) of rule 4, for doing any act or taking any step in proceedings–

(a) shall, if the act is to be done or the step taken by a person normally resident outside the United Kingdom, be extended by 28 days; and

(b) may be extended, if the Commission so order, for any period in their discretion notwithstanding that the time appointed has already expired.

Orders and directions and dismissal of applications

25. Without prejudice to any other provision for orders or directions in these Rules, the Commission may on an application by the applicant or the Legal Officer in that behalf or of their own motion make any order or give any direction in connection with any application or may dismiss any application.

Service by post

26. Save as otherwise provided in these Rules, any notice or other document required or authorised to be served on any person for the purpose of these Rules may be sent by pre-paid post to that person at his last ordinary or permanent address notified to the Commission or other address for service specified in any notice given under these Rules, and if so sent it shall be deemed to have been duly served on the date of such posting. The address of a solicitor instructed by an applicant to act generally in relation to his claim shall be deemed to be an address for service specified as aforesaid.

Copies of notices and applications

27. All notices and applications to the Commission or to the Registrar shall be in writing and shall be sent by pre-paid post or delivered by hand and a copy thereof shall be served by the Registrar on the applicant or the Legal Officer, as the case may be.

Rights of audience

28. The following persons only may address the Commission–
    (a) an applicant other than a corporation;
    (b) the Legal Officer;
    (c) counsel retained by or on behalf of an applicant or the Legal Officer;
    (d) a solicitor acting generally in the proceedings for an applicant (in this paragraph referred to as "a solicitor on the record"), any solicitor employed by a solicitor on the record, any solicitor engaged as an agent by a solicitor on the record, and any solicitor employed by a solicitor so engaged;
    (e) in the case of an applicant other than a corporation, any person who satisfies the Commission that he is a relative or friend of the applicant he proposes to represent and that he has the authority of the applicant to represent him in that behalf;
    (f) in the case of an applicant corporation, counsel or solicitor as aforesaid, or, if the Commission give leave, a director or the secretary.

Determinations

29.—(1) A determination of every property claim and personal injury claim not previously withdrawn shall be made by the Commission, and notice in writing thereof shall be given to every applicant and the Legal Officer. It shall not be necessary for the Commission to meet for the purpose of announcing their determination.

(2) Subject to the provisions of rules 30 and 31, all determinations of the Commission shall be final.

Review

30.—(1) The Commission may direct that a determination be reviewed if in their opinion the interests of justice so require.

(2) Before reviewing any determination, the Commission shall serve upon the applicant notice of intention to review.

(3) On review, the Commission may invite the applicant and the Legal Officer to submit additional written evidence or argument or to attend an oral hearing but subject as hereinafter provided neither the applicant nor the Legal Officer shall be entitled on review to have an oral hearing or to submit any additional evidence or argument.

(4) On review, an applicant shall be entitled to submit additional written evidence and argument if the Commission propose to disallow or reduce the amount of a claim and the Legal Officer shall be so entitled if the Commission propose to increase the amount of a claim or to allow a claim which has been disallowed.

(5) The Commission shall give the applicant and the Legal Officer notice of any such proposal as is referred to in paragraph (4) and any written evidence or argument shall be served upon the Commission before the expiration of 28 days from the service of the notice of such proposal.

(6) There shall not be more than one review of any determination.

(7) If it appears to the Commission that an applicant has died and no grant of representation to his estate has been produced to them, the Commission may review the determination of a claim made by the deceased applicant without serving any notice of intention to review or may, if they think fit, by order appoint such person as they think proper to represent the estate of the deceased applicant for the purpose of such review, and in that case the foregoing provisions of this rule shall apply to the person so appointed as they apply to an applicant and notice of intention to review shall be served upon that person.

(8) Where the Commission receive no acknowledgement within 28 days from the date of posting of the notice of intention to review, or within such further period as may be specified therein for replying thereto, the provisions of paragraph (7) of this rule shall apply as if the applicant had died.

Revocation of determinations

31. Notwithstanding the provisions of rules 29 and 30, if it shall appear to the Commission that the determination by the Commission of any claim (whether such determination shall have been reviewed by the Commission or not) has been affected by any alteration of the provisions of the Order or as a result of any proceedings questioning the said determination under section 3 of the Foreign Compensation Act 1969**(a)** or otherwise, the Commission may revoke the said determination either wholly or in part and in lieu thereof or of the part revoked make a fresh determination. Any such revocation shall be made after giving reasonable prior notice thereof to the applicant and the Legal Officer and after consideration of any submission in writing or, subject to the leave of the Commission, any oral evidence or argument on behalf of either party.

Composition of Commission

32.—(1) Subject to the provisions of Article 11 of the Order and of this rule, any determination, order, direction or other act of the Commission may be made, given or done by a single Commissioner.

(2) Any review of a determination in accordance with the provisions of rules 30 and 31 shall be conducted by not less than two Commissioners.

Selection of Commissioners

33.—(1) The Chairman, or in his absence the next senior Commissioner, may select any Commissioners required to hear and determine any particular application or group of applications or any matter arising therein, or to conduct any review of a determination, and may from time to time vary the Commissioners selected, and where more than one Commissioner is required shall appoint the Commissioner who is to preside.

(2) If in the course of any hearing one or more of the Commissioners so appointed becomes unable to attend another Commissioner may, with the consent of the applicant, in like manner be appointed.

Majority decision

34. In case of disagreement the opinion of the majority of the Commissioners hearing or determining an application or conducting the review of a determination shall prevail. If the opinions shall be equally divided the opinion of the presiding Commissioner shall prevail.

Admissions by Legal Officer

35. In determining any application the Commission shall not be bound by any admission or concession by the Legal Officer on any question of fact or of law.

(a) 1969 c.20.

Amendment of determinations, orders and directions

36. Clerical mistakes or errors in determinations, orders or directions, arising from any accidental slip or omission may at any time, without review, be corrected by the Commission of their own motion after giving notice to the applicant and the Legal Officer or on the application of the applicant or the Legal Officer after giving notice to the other of them.

Non-compliance with Rules

37. Non-compliance with any of these Rules shall not render void any proceedings unless the Commission shall so direct.

Transitional provisions

38. All applications made to the Commission and all directions given or orders made by the Commission in respect of such applications and all other steps taken by the applicant or the Commission in respect of such applications under the Foreign Compensation Commission Rules, 1956**(a)** shall be deemed to have been duly made, given or taken under these Rules.

APPENDIX

FORM A

I ....

of ....

*as Trustee for .... who died

on .... do solemnly and

sincerely declare as follows:–

I am and was/the said deceased was* on 14th July 1986 the beneficial owner of the bond(s) to which this application under the Foreign Compensation (Union of Soviet Socialist Republics) (Registration and Determination of Claims) Order 1986, relates, AND I make this solemn declaration conscientiously believing the same to be true and by virtue of the provisions of the Statutory Declarations Act 1835.

DECLARED at ....⎤
                                                                                          ⎪   ....
         ....⎬   Signature
                                                                                          ⎪
         ....⎦

this .... day of ....

Before me, ...
              a Solicitor/Commissioner for Oaths.

*delete as required

(a) S.I. 1956/962.

FORM B

FOREIGN COMPENSATION ACT 1950

SUMMONS TO ATTEND TO GIVE EVIDENCE
FOREIGN COMPENSATION COMMISSION

IN THE MATTER OF AN APPLICATION pending before the Foreign Compensation Commission

by

Applicant

To

of

You are hereby summoned to attend at .... on the .... day of .... 19...... at .... in the .... noon and so from day to day until the above matter has been heard to give evidence in the above application.

And also to bring with you and produce at the time and place aforesaid (specify documents to be produced)

.... dated this .... day of .... 19........

Registrar

This summons is issued at the request of * ....

You are not obliged to attend unless on the service of this summons the said * .... tenders to you the sum of £........ on account of your expenses, and gives you a written undertaking to pay to you such further sum in respect of expenses and loss of time as the Registrar to the Commission may certify to be reasonable.

If you fail to attend as aforesaid the Chairman of the Commission may certify your absence to the High Court which may if it thinks fit punish you as for a contempt of Court.

You may if you think fit apply in writing to the Commission, for just cause, particulars whereof must be stated, for an order to set aside this summons. Any such request must be delivered by hand or sent by post addressed to the Registrar of the Commission at .... within seven days after service of this summons. If the cause is ill-health a medical certificate must be enclosed with the request.

This summons is of no validity unless served upon you within twelve weeks from the date of its signature above.

Receipt of Expenses

I hereby acknowledge the receipt of the sum of £........ on account of my expenses and of the required written undertaking.

Signed**

---

* Fill in the name of the person requesting the summons.
** To be signed by the person to whom the summons is directed.

FORM C

FOREIGN COMPENSATION ACT 1950

ORDER TO FORWARD DOCUMENTS
FOREIGN COMPENSATION COMMISSION

IN THE MATTER OF AN APPLICATION pending before the Foreign Compensation Commission

by

Applicant

To

of

You are hereby required to deliver by hand or forward by post to the Registrar of the Commission at .... on or before the .... day of .... 19...... the following documents:–

If the said documents or any of them are not in your possession, custody or power or if you claim to have legal objection to the production of the documents or any of them you must on or before the last-mentioned date forward as above directed a declaration signed by yourself giving the reasons for your inability or objection to forward each of the documents to which such reasons apply.

If you know the name and/or address of the person in whose possession, custody or power the said documents or any of them now are or have been you must give it.

Dated this .... day of .... 19......

Registrar

This order is issued at the request of *..

If you fail without reasonable excuse to comply with this Order the Chairman of the Commission may certify your failure to the High Court which may if it thinks fit punish you as for a contempt of Court.

This Order is of no validity unless served upon you within twelve weeks from the date of its signature as above.

The Commission will refund to you the cost of forwarding the said documents.

---

* Fill in the name of the person requesting the summons.

FORM D

FOREIGN COMPENSATION ACT 1950

FORM OF UNDERTAKING TO PAY EXPENSES AND COMPENSATION FOR LOSS OF TIME
FOREIGN COMPENSATION COMMISSION

In addition to the sum of £ .... paid to the said * ....
in respect of expenses I hereby undertake to pay to the said * .... such further sum
in respect of expenses and/or loss of time as the Registrar of the Commission may certify to be
reasonable.

Signature of the person
applying for the summons in
Form B

*Insert name of witness

The seal of the Foreign Compensation Commission was hereunto affixed this 2nd day
of February 1987.

A. W. E. Wheeler
Chairman of the Commission

D. H. Wright
Secretary

EXPLANATORY NOTE

(This note is not part of the Instrument)

By this Instrument the Lord Chancellor approves rules made by the Foreign
Compensation Commission to govern the procedure to be followed by the Commission
in the disposal of applications under the Foreign Compensation (Union of Soviet
Socialist Republics) (Registration and Determination of Claims) Order 1986. They are
substantially based on those made under previous Orders providing for the registration
and determination of claims. Reflecting the terms of the Order, hearings will be conducted
on the papers, subject to the Commission's power to direct an oral hearing if they think
fit.

STATUTORY INSTRUMENTS

1987 No.149

CUSTOMS AND EXCISE

The Excise Duties (Small Non-Commercial Consignments) Relief (Amendment) Regulations 1987

Made - - - -	*9th February 1987*
Laid before Parliament	*16th February 1987*
Coming into force	*9th March 1987*

The Commissioners of Customs and Excise, being a department designated for the purposes of section 2(2) of the European Communities Act 1972(**a**) in relation to excise matters of the European Communities(**b**), in exercise of the powers conferred upon them by the said section 2(2) and of all other powers enabling them in that behalf, hereby make the following Regulations:

1. These Regulations may be cited as the Excise Duties (Small Non-Commercial Consignments) Relief (Amendment) Regulations 1987 and shall come into force on 9th March 1987.

2. In regulation 3(2) of the Excise Duties (Small Non-Commercial Consignments) Relief Regulations 1986(**c**)–

(a) in sub-paragraph (2)(a) for "£58" there shall be substituted "£71"; and

(b) in sub-paragraph (2)(b) for "£27" there shall be substituted "£32".

Peter Jefferson Smith
Commissioner of Customs and Excise

King's Beam House
Mark Lane, London EC3R 7HE
9th February 1987

(**a**) 1972 c.68.
(**b**) S.I. 1980/865.
(**c**) S.I. 1986/938.

EXPLANATORY NOTE

(This note is not part of the Order)

Under the Excise Duties (Small Non-Commercial Consignments) Relief Regulations 1986 certain small consignments of a non-commercial character may be admitted into the United Kingdom without payment of excise duty. The present Regulations increase the maximum sterling value of such a consignment to £71 when imported from another Member State and to £32 when imported from a third country. It implements, for intra-community consignments, the requirements of Article 1(a) of Council Directive 74/651/EEC (O.J. No. L354, 30.12.74, p.57) which was added by Council Directive 78/1034/EEC (O.J. No. L366, 28.12.78, p.33) and, for consignments from third countries, the requirements of Article 4 of Council Directive 78/1035/EEC (O.J. No. L366, 28.12.78, p.34). These Articles provide, for the purposes of the Directives, that the equivalent of the European Currency Unit in national currency is fixed at the rates obtaining on 1st October each year to have effect from 1st January the following year.

Parallel increased limits for value added tax purposes are found in the Value Added Tax (Small Non-Commercial Consignments) Relief (Amendment) Order 1987 (S.I. 1987/154).

STATUTORY INSTRUMENTS

1987 No. 150

VALUE ADDED TAX

The Value Added Tax (General) (Amendment) Regulations 1987

Made - - - -	*9th February 1987*
Laid before the House of Commons	*16th February 1987*
Coming into force	*9th March 1987*

The Commissioners of Customs and Excise, in exercise of the powers conferred on them by section 16(7) of the Value Added Tax Act 1983**(a)** and of all other powers enabling them in that behalf, hereby make the following Regulations:

1. These Regulations may be cited as the Value Added Tax (General) (Amendment) Regulations 1987 and shall come into force on 9th March 1987.

2. The Value Added Tax (General) Regulations 1985**(b)** shall be amended in accordance with the following provisions of these Regulations.

3. In Regulation 53—
    (a) in sub-paragraph (b) (i) for "£45" there shall be substituted "£55";
    (b) in sub-paragraph (b) (ii) for "£165" there shall be substituted "£200"; and
    (c) in sub-paragraph (b) (iii) for "£207" there shall be substituted "£250".

4. In Regulation 55(1)—
    (a) in sub-paragraph (b)(i) for "£45" there shall be substituted "£55";
    (b) in sub-paragraph (b)(ii) for "£165" there shall be substituted "£200"; and
    (c) in sub-paragraph (b)(iii) for "£207" there shall be substituted "£250".

King's Beam House, Mark Lane,
London, EC3 7HE
9th February 1987

Peter Jefferson Smith
Commissioner of Customs and Excise

(a) 1983 c.55.
(b) S.I. 1985/886, as amended by S.I. 1985/1650, and to which there are other amendments not relevant to these Regulations.

EXPLANATORY NOTE

(This note is not part of the Regulations)

These Regulations amend Regulations 53 and 55 of the Value Added Tax (General) Regulations 1985 (as amended) to provide revised values of goods that can be purchased under the retail export schemes by Community travellers.

They implement the requirements of Article 7 of Directive 69/169/EEC (O.J. No. L133, 4.6.69, p.6). (Article 7 was added by Directive 78/1032/EEC (O.J. No. L366, 28.12.78, p.28) and amended by Directive 85/348/EEC (O.J. No. L183, 16.7.85, p.24)). The equivalent of the European Currency Unit in national currency is fixed at the rates obtaining on 1 October each year to have effect from 1 January of the following year.

1987 No. 151

NATIONAL HEALTH SERVICE, ENGLAND AND WALES

The Welsh Health Promotion Authority (Establishment and Constitution) Order 1987

Made - - - -	*6th February 1987*
Laid before Parliament	*10th February 1987*
Coming into force	*3rd March 1987*

The Secretary of State for Wales, in exercise of powers conferred upon him by section 11 of the National Health Service Act 1977 (**a**) and of all other powers enabling him in that behalf, hereby makes the following Order:

Citation and commencement

1. This Order may be cited as the Welsh Health Promotion Authority (Establishment and Constitution) Order 1987 and shall come into force on 3rd March 1987.

Establishment of the Welsh Health Promotion Authority

2. There is hereby established a special health authority which shall be known as the Welsh Health Promotion Authority (in this Order referred to as "The Authority").

Functions of the Authority

3.—(1) Subject to and in accordance with such directions as the Secretary of State may give to the Authority, the Authority shall perform in Wales the functions specified in paragraph (2) of this Article and such other functions as the Secretary of State may direct the Authority to perform on his behalf.

(2) The functions referred to in paragraph (1) of this Article are–

(a) advising the Secretary of State on matters relating to health promotion;

(b) undertaking health promotion activity;

(c) for that purpose planning and carrying out national or local programmes or other activities in co-operation with health authorities, Family Practitioner Committees, local authorities and local education authorities, voluntary organisations and other persons or bodies concerned with or having an interest in health promotion;

(d) sponsoring research and evaluation in relation to health promotion;

(e) assisting the provision of appropriate training in health promotion;

(f) preparing, publishing or distributing material relevant to health promotion;

(g) providing a national centre of information and advice on health promotion;

(h) exercising the Secretary of State's functions–

(i) under section 23(1) of the National Health Service Act 1977 with respect to arranging with any person or body (including a voluntary organisation) for that body to assist in providing any service under that Act;

(**a**) 1977 c.49; section 11 was amended by the Health Services Act 1980 (c.53), Schedule 1, paragraph 31.

(ii) under section 23(2) of that Act with respect to making available to certain persons or bodies (including voluntary organisations) facilities and services of persons employed in connection with such facilities;

(iii) under section 23(3) of that Act with respect to the agreement of terms and the making of payments by or to the Secretary of State in respect of arrangements made or facilities or services provided under section 23 of that Act,

insofar as such arrangements or services are made or provided in pursuance of the functions specified above.

Constitution of the Authority

4. The Authority shall consist of a Chairman and fourteen other members, all of whom shall be appointed by the Secretary of State.

Nicholas Edwards
6th February 1987   Secretary of State for Wales

EXPLANATORY NOTE

(This note is not part of the Order)

This Order provides for the establishment and constitution of a special health authority, to be known as the Welsh Health Promotion Authority, for the purpose of carrying out certain specified functions relating to health promotion (Article 3(2)) and such other functions as the Secretary of State may direct.

STATUTORY INSTRUMENTS

1987 No. 152

NATIONAL HEALTH SERVICE, ENGLAND AND WALES

The Welsh Health Promotion Authority Regulations 1987

Made - - - -	*6th February 1987*
Laid before Parliament	*10th February 1987*
Coming into force	*3rd March 1987*

The Secretary of State for Wales, in exercise of powers conferred upon him by paragraphs 12 and 16 of Schedule 5 to the National Health Service Act 1977(a) and of all other powers enabling him in that behalf, hereby makes the following Regulations:–

Citation, commencement and interpretation

1.—(1) These Regulations may be cited as the Welsh Health Promotion Authority Regulations 1987 and shall come into force on 3rd March 1987.

(2) In these Regulations unless the context otherwise requires—

"the Authority" means the Welsh Health Promotion Authority established by the Welsh Health Promotion Authority (Establishment and Constitution) Order 1987(b);

"member" means the Chairman or other member of the Authority.

Tenure of office of member

2. Subject to any provisions applied by these Regulations as to termination of and disqualification for membership, the tenure of office of a member shall be for such period not exceeding four years as the Secretary of State shall specify on making the appointment.

Termination of tenure of office

3.—(1) A member may resign his office at any time during the period for which he was appointed by giving notice in writing to the Secretary of State.

(2) Where the Secretary of State is satisfied that it is not in the interests of the Authority or the health service that a person whom he has appointed as a member should continue to hold that office, he may forthwith terminate that member's tenure of office.

(a) 1977 c.49.   (b) S.I. 1987/151.

Application of Regulations relating to membership and procedure

4. The provisions of Regulations 5(4), (6) and (7) (termination of tenure of office), Regulation 6 (eligibility for reappointment), Regulation 7 (disqualification for appointment), Regulation 8 (cessation of disqualification), Regulation 9 (election of vice-chairman), Regulation 10 (powers of vice-chairman), Regulation 11 (appointment of committees and sub-committees), Regulation 12 (arrangements for the exercise of functions), Regulation 13 (meetings and proceedings), Regulation 14 (disability of chairman and members in proceedings on account of pecuniary interests) of and Schedule 1 (rules as to meetings and proceedings of Authorities) to the National Health Service (Regional and District Health Authorities: Membership and Procedure) Regulations 1983(**a**) shall apply in relation to the Authority as if any reference in those provisions to an Authority included a reference to the Authority.

Reports and papers by the Authority

5. The Authority shall make reports to the Secretary of State in such manner and at such time, being at least once a year, as the Secretary of State may direct and shall furnish to the Secretary of State such information as he may from time to time require.

Nicholas Edwards
6th February 1987   Secretary of State for Wales

EXPLANATORY NOTE

(This note is not part of the Regulations)

These Regulations provide for the tenure of office of the Chairman and other members of the special health authority known as the Welsh Health Promotion Authority. They also provide for the procedure of and report to the Secretary of State by that Authority.

(**a**) S.I. 1983/315.

STATUTORY INSTRUMENTS

1987 No. 153

PUBLIC HEALTH, ENGLAND AND WALES
PUBLIC HEALTH, SCOTLAND
PUBLIC HEALTH, NORTHERN IRELAND
CONTAMINATION OF FOOD

The Food Protection (Emergency Prohibitions) (England) (No. 2) Amendment Order 1987

Made - - - -	*8th February 1987*
Laid before Parliament	*10th February 1987*
Coming into force	*16th February 1987*

Whereas the Minister of Agriculture, Fisheries and Food is of the opinion, in accordance with section 1(1)(a) of the Food and Environment Protection Act 1985(a), that there has been or may have been an escape of substances of such descriptions and in such quantities and such circumstances as are likely to create a hazard to human health through human consumption of food;

And whereas the said Minister is of the opinion, in accordance with section 1(1)(b) of the said Act, that in consequence of the said escape of substances food which is or may be in the future in the area described in the Schedule to the Food Protection (Emergency Prohibitions) (England) (No. 2) Order 1986(b), or which is derived or may be in the future derived from anything in that area, is, or may be, or may become, unsuitable for human consumption;

Now, therefore, the said Minister, in exercise of the powers conferred on him by the said section 1(1) and section 24(3) of the said Act, and of all other powers enabling him in that behalf, hereby makes the following Order:–

Title and commencement

1. This Order may be cited as the Food Protection (Emergency Prohibitions) (England) (No. 2) Amendment Order 1987 and shall come into force on 16th February 1987.

Partial revocation and amendment

2. The Food Protection (Emergency Prohibitions) (England) (No. 2) Order 1986 is revoked to the extent that it imposes prohibitions on–

    (a) the slaughter of a sheep which–

        (i) was moved from a place in accordance with a consent given under section 2(1) of the Food and Environment Protection Act 1985 which consent was subject to the condition that the sheep to which it applies should be marked with a red mark; and

        (ii) has been examined and marked by an ear-tag by a person authorised in that behalf by one of the Ministers; and

---

(a) 1985 c.48.
(b) S.I. 1986/1689, amended by S.I. 1986/2208.

(b) the supply or having in possession for supply of meat, or food containing meat, derived from such a sheep,

and accordingly that Order is further amended in accordance with the following provisions of this Order.

3. Article 4 shall be re-numbered article 4(1) and after that paragraph there shall be inserted the following paragraph–

"(2) Paragraph (1) above shall not apply in the case of any sheep which–

(a) was moved from any place in accordance with a consent given under the said section 2(1) which consent was subject to the condition that the sheep to which it applies should be marked with a red mark; and

(b) has been examined and marked by an ear-tag by a person authorised in that behalf by one of the Ministers.".

4. In article 6(2)(b)(i), after the words "blue mark" there shall be inserted the words "or with a red mark".

In witness whereof the Official Seal of the Minister of Agriculture, Fisheries and Food is hereunto affixed on 8th February 1987.

Michael Jopling
Minister of Agriculture, Fisheries and Food

EXPLANATORY NOTE

(This note is not part of the Order)

The Food Protection (Emergency Prohibitions) (England) (No. 2) Order 1986 contains emergency prohibitions restricting various activities in order to prevent human consumption of food which has been or which may have been rendered unsuitable for that purpose in consequence of the escape of radioactive substances from a nuclear reactor situated at Chernobyl in the USSR.

This Order excepts from the prohibition on slaughter in the area designated by that Order and from the prohibition on slaughter and supply throughout the United Kingdom any sheep (and in the latter case any meat derived from such sheep) identified by a red paint mark which have been examined and subsequently marked by an ear-tag by an official of the Ministry of Agriculture, Fisheries and Food, Scottish Office or Welsh Office (articles 3 and 4).

STATUTORY INSTRUMENTS

1987 No. 154

VALUE ADDED TAX

The Value Added Tax (Small Non-Commercial Consignments) Relief (Amendment) Order 1987

Made - - - -	*9th February 1987*
Laid before the House of Commons	*16th February 1987*
Coming into force	*9th March 1987*

Whereas it appears to the Treasury expedient that the relief from value added tax provided by this Order should be allowed with a view to conforming with Article 1a of Council Directive No. 74/651/EEC(**a**) (as amended by Council Directive 78/1034/EEC(**b**) and as last amended by Council Directive No. 85/349/EEC(**c**)) on the tax reliefs to be allowed on the importation of certain goods when sent in small consignments from a State which is a member of the European Economic Community to another such State and with Article 4 of Council Directive No. 78/1035/EEC(**d**) (as last amended by Council Directive 85/576/EEC(**e**)) on the tax reliefs to be allowed on the importation of certain goods when sent in small consignments from a State which is not a member of the European Economic Community to a State which is a member thereof:

Now, therefore, the Lords Commissioners of Her Majesty's Treasury, by virtue of the powers conferred on them by section 19(1) of the Value Added Tax Act 1983(**f**) and of all other powers enabling them in that behalf, hereby make the following Order—

1. This Order may be cited as the Value Added Tax (Small Non-Commercial Consignments) Relief (Amendment) Order 1987 and shall come into force on 9th March 1987.

2. In Article 3(2) of the Value Added Tax (Small Non-Commercial Consignments) Relief Order 1986(**g**)—

    (a)   in sub-paragraph (a) for "£58" there shall be substituted "£71"; and

    (b)   in sub-paragraph (b) for "£27" there shall be substituted "£32".

Peter Lloyd
Tim Sainsbury
9th February 1987   Two of the Lords Commissioners of Her Majesty's Treasury

---

(**a**) O.J. No. L354, 30.12.74, p.57.   (**b**) O.J. No. L366, 28.12.78, p.33.   (**c**) O.J. No. L183, 16.7.85, p.27.   (**d**) O.J. No. L366, 28.12.78, p.34.   (**e**) O.J. No. L372, 31.12.85, p.30.   (**f**) 1983 c.55.   (**g**) S.I. 1986/939.

EXPLANATORY NOTE

(This note is not part of the Order)

Under the Value Added Tax (Small Non-Commercial Consignments) Relief Order 1986 certain small consignments of a non-commercial character may be admitted into the United Kingdom without payment of value added tax. The present Order increases the maximum sterling value of such a consignment to £71 when imported from another Member State and to £32 when imported from a third country. It implements, for intra-Community consignments, the requirements of Article 1a of Directive 74/651/EEC (as amended) and, for consignments from third countries, the requirements of Article 4 of Directive 78/1035/EEC (as amended). The equivalent of the European Currency Unit in national currency is fixed at the rates obtaining on 1 October each year to have effect from 1 January the following year.

Parallel increased limits for excise duty purposes are found in the Excise Duties (Small Non-Commercial Consignments) Relief (Amendment) Regulations 1987 (S.I. 1987/149).

STATUTORY INSTRUMENTS

1987 No. 155

VALUE ADDED TAX

The Value Added Tax (Imported Goods) Relief (Amendment) Order 1987

Made - - - -	*9th February 1987*
Laid before the House of Commons	*16th February 1987*
Coming into force	*9th March 1987*

Whereas it appears to the Treasury expedient that the relief from value added tax provided by this Order should be allowed with a view to conforming with Article 90 of Council Directive No. 83/181/EEC(**a**), determining the scope of Article 14(1)(d) of Council Directive No. 77/388/EEC(**b**) as regards exemption from value added tax on the final importation of certain goods:

Now, therefore, the Lords Commissioners of Her Majesty's Treasury, by virtue of the powers conferred on them by section 19(1) of the Value Added Tax Act 1983(**c**) and of all other powers enabling them in that behalf, hereby make the following Order–

1. This Order may be cited as the Value Added Tax (Imported Goods) Relief (Amendment) Order 1987 and shall come into force on 9th March 1987.

2. In Group 8, Item 8 of Schedule 2 to the Value Added Tax (Imported Goods) Relief Order 1984(**d**) for "£6" there shall be substituted "£7".

Peter Lloyd
Tim Sainsbury
9th February 1987   Two of the Lords Commissioners of Her Majesty's Treasury

---

EXPLANATORY NOTE

(This note is not part of the Order)

This Order amends the Value Added Tax (Imported Goods) Relief Order 1984 which provides for relief from value added tax on final importation of certain goods into the United Kingdom. It increases the maximum value for such relief on a postal consignment of goods from £6 to £7. This implements the requirements of Article 90 of Council Directive 83/181/EEC. The equivalent of the European Currency Unit in national currency is fixed at the rates obtaining on 1 October each year to have effect on 1 January the following year.

(**a**) O.J. No. L105, 23.4.83, p.38.
(**b**) O.J. No. L145, 13.6.77, p.1.
(**c**) 1983 c.55.
(**d**) S.I. 1984/746.

1987 No. 156

POLICE

The Police (Injury Benefit) Regulations 1987

Made - - - -	*4th February 1987*
Laid before Parliament	*17th February 1987*
Coming into force	*17th March 1987*

In exercise of the powers conferred on me by sections 1, 3, 4 and 6 of the Police Pensions Act 1976(**a**), and after consultation with the Police Negotiating Board for the United Kingdom, I hereby, with the consent of the Treasury(**b**), make the following Regulations:

PART I

PRELIMINARY

Citation

1. These Regulations may be cited as the Police (Injury Benefit) Regulations 1987.

Commencement

2. These Regulations shall come into force on 17th March 1987 and shall have effect as from 25th November 1982.

Interpretation

3.—(1) Subject to the following provisions of these Regulations, these Regulations shall be construed as one with the Police Pensions Regulations 1973(**c**) (hereinafter referred to as "the principal Regulations").

(2) Without prejudice to paragraph (1)–

  (a) in these Regulations–

    (i) "taxable allowances" includes all taxable allowances payable by virtue of regulations from time to time in force under section 33 of the Police Act 1964(**d**) or section 26 of the Police (Scotland) Act 1967(**e**);

    (ii) "total remuneration", in relation to a member of a police force, means the sum of his pensionable pay and taxable allowances payable to him;

    (iii) notwithstanding Regulation 13(3) of the principal Regulations, "totally disabled" means incapable by reason of the disablement in question of earning any money in any employment and "total disablement" shall be construed accordingly; and

---

(**a**) 1976 c.35, as amended by section 2(3) of the Police Negotiating Board Act 1980 (c.10).
(**b**) Formerly the Minister for the Civil Service: *see* S.I. 1981/1670.
(**c**) S.I. 1973/428; the relevant amending instruments are S.I. 1978/1348, 1983/996, 1985/156, 1986/1379.
(**d**) 1964 c.48.   (**e**) 1967 c.77.

(b) in the case of a person who is totally disabled, Regulation 13(1) of the principal Regulations shall have effect, for the purposes of these Regulations, as if the reference to "that disablement being .... likely to be permanent" were a reference to the total disablement of that person being likely to be permanent.

PART II

BENEFIT ON DISABLEMENT OR DEATH

Disablement gratuity

4.—(1) This Regulation shall apply to a person who–
   (a) receives or received an injury without his own default in the execution of his duty, whether before, on or after 25th November 1982; and
   (b) on or after that date ceases or has ceased to be a member of a police force; and
   (c) on or after that date and within 12 months of so receiving that injury, becomes or became totally and permanently disabled as a result thereof.

(2) Subject to the following provisions of these Regulations, the police authority for the force in which a person to whom this Regulation applies last served shall pay to him a gratuity of an amount equal to whichever is the lesser of the following amounts, namely–
   (a) five times the annual value of his pensionable pay on his last day of service as a member of a police force;
   (b) the sum of four times his total remuneration during the 12 months ending with his last day of service as a member of a police force and the amount of his aggregate pension contributions in respect of the relevant period of service.

Death gratuity

5.—(1) Subject to paragraph (2), this Regulation shall apply to a member of a police force who–
   (a) receives or received an injury without his own default in the execution of his duty, whether before, on or after 25th November 1982; and
   (b) was serving as such a member on or after that date; and
   (c) within 12 months of so receiving that injury dies or has died as a result thereof.

(2) In the case of a person who had ceased to serve as a member of a police force before his death, this Regulation shall only apply to him if his death also occurred before any decision by a duly qualified medical practitioner under Regulation 71 of the principal Regulations that he was totally and permanently disabled as a result of that injury.

(3) Subject to the following provisions of these Regulations, where a member to whom this Regulation applies–
   (a) leaves a widow (unless, by reason of Regulation 33(2) or 34 of the principal Regulations, she would not qualify for a special award under Regulation 28 thereof); or
   (b) does not leave any such widow, but leaves a child (unless, by reason of Regulation 42 of the principal Regulations, that child would not qualify for a special allowance under Regulation 38 thereof); or
   (c) does not leave any such widow or child, but leaves a dependent relative to whom a special pension may be paid under Regulation 36 of the principal Regulations,
the police authority shall pay to his widow or, as the case may be, to the child or dependent relative a gratuity of an amount equal to whichever is the lesser of the following amounts, namely–
      (i) five times the annual value of his pensionable pay on his death or, if earlier, on his last day of service as a member of a police force;
      (ii) the sum of four times his total remuneration during the 12 months ending with his death, or, if earlier, with his last day of service as a member of a

police force and the amount of his aggregate pension contributions in respect of the relevant period of service.

(4) Where a member of a police force to whom this Regulation applies leaves two or more children or two or more dependent relatives, then the amount of the gratuity so payable shall be divided by the police authority among the children or dependent relatives (as the case may be) in their discretion.

PART III
GENERAL

Gratuities paid in anticipation

6. Where, before 17th March 1987, a police authority pays to any person a gratuity in respect of the death or disablement of a member of a police force as the result of an injury received by him in the execution of his duty, and the gratuity is at any time thereafter certified by the police authority as having been so paid in anticipation of the coming into force of these Regulations–

(a) nothing in these Regulations shall entitle that person to any further payment in respect of the death or disablement of the member in question; and

(b) for the purposes of these Regulations, the gratuity shall be treated as if it were a gratuity paid to that person under these Regulations.

Abatement in respect of gratuities payable under the principal Regulations

7.—(1) The amount of any gratuity payable to a member of a police force under Regulation 4 shall be reduced by deducting therefrom the amount of any gratuity paid to him under Regulation 20(4), 21(4) or 22 of the principal Regulations.

(2) The amount of any gratuity payable to any person under Regulation 5 in respect of the death of a member of a police force shall be reduced by deducting therefrom–

(a) the amount of any gratuities paid to the member or his estate under Regulation 20(4), 21(4), 22 or 43 of the principal Regulations;

(b) in the case of a widow, where a gratuity under Regulation 28(2) of the principal Regulations is payable to her or her estate–

(i) unless sub-paragraph (ii) below applies, the amount of the gratuity;

(ii) where the said amount falls to be calculated in accordance with Regulation 29(3) of the principal Regulations, an amount equal to the amount of the gratuity which would be payable to her or her estate under the said Regulation 28(2) if–

(A) the said Regulation 29 had not applied;

(B) the husband had died while serving as a member of a police force (whether or not he was in fact so serving when he died); and

(C) the husband's average pensionable pay was greater than $2\frac{1}{4}$ times the annual amount of the ill-health pension which would have been payable under Regulation 20 of the principal Regulations to the husband if he had retired on the grounds of permanent disability on the day on which he had died (whether or not it was in fact greater); and

(c) in the case of any other person, the amount of any gratuity paid to that person or his estate in respect of the death of that member under Regulation 39 or Regulation 43 of the principal Regulations.

(3) In any case where, by reason of Regulation 5(4) a payment in respect of the death of a member of a police force falls to be divided among two or more persons, that payment shall, before it is so divided, be reduced by deducting therefrom the amount of any gratuities paid as mentioned in paragraph (2).

Abatement in respect of damages or compensation

8.—(1) The police authority shall take into account against any gratuity payable under these Regulations any damages or compensation which are recovered by any person in respect of the death or disability to which the gratuity relates and the gratuity may be withheld or reduced accordingly.

(2) For the purposes of this Regulation–

    (a) a person shall be deemed to have recovered damages–

        (i) whether they are paid in pursuance of a judgment or order of the court or by way of settlement or compromise of his claim and whether or not proceedings are instituted to enforce the claim; or

        (ii) if they are recovered for that person's benefit in respect of a claim under the Fatal Accidents Act 1976 (**a**);

    (b) "compensation" does not include an award of compensation made to a person by the Criminal Injuries Compensation Board if the amount of the award was reduced by the amount of any gratuity paid or payable to him under these Regulations.

(3) Without prejudice to paragraph (1), where any payment in respect of a gratuity under these Regulations is made to a person and that person subsequently recovers any damages or compensation in respect of the death or disability to which the gratuity relates, the police authority shall be entitled to recover from that person an amount not exceeding–

    (a) where the amount of the payment made by the police authority is less than the net amount of the damages or compensation, the amount of that payment;

    (b) where the amount of that payment is not less than the net amount of the damages or compensation, an amount equal to the net amount of the damages or compensation.

(4) So far as any amount recoverable under this Regulation represents a payment made by the police authority from which income tax has been deducted before the payment, the proper allowance shall be made in respect of the amount so deducted; and, in this Regulation, "the net amount", in relation to damages or compensation recovered by any person, means the amount of the damages or compensation after deducting tax payable in the United Kingdom or elsewhere to which the damages or compensation are subject.

(5) No proceedings shall be brought to recover any amount paid in respect of a gratuity under this Regulation–

    (a) after the death of the person to whom the payment was made, or

    (b) after the expiration of 2 years from the date on which the final determination of the amount of the damages or compensation first came to the knowledge of the police authority.

Admissibility of certificates in evidence

9.   A certificate issued by a police authority–

    (a) certifying that a gratuity has been paid as mentioned in Regulation 6; or

    (b) stating the date on which the final determination of a right to and the amount of any damages or compensation first came to its knowledge,

shall be received in evidence in any proceedings, and the said gratuity shall be deemed to have been so paid or, as the case may be, the said date shall be deemed to be the date so stated until the contrary is proved.

Application of principal Regulations

10.—(1) Without prejudice to Regulation 3(2), and subject to the preceding provisions of these Regulations, the principal Regulations shall apply, subject to the necessary modifications, in relation to awards under these Regulations as they would apply in the circumstances of the case to the corresponding award under those Regulations.

(**a**) 1976 c.30.

(2) For the purposes of this Regulation, "the corresponding award" means–
- (a) in relation to a gratuity payable under Regulation 4, a gratuity payable under Regulation 22 of the principal Regulations;
- (b) in relation to a gratuity payable under Regulation 5–
    - (i) in the case of a widow, a gratuity payable under Regulation 28 of those Regulations;
    - (ii) in the case of a child, a gratuity payable under Regulation 39 of those Regulations;
    - (iii) in the case of a dependent relative, a gratuity payable under Regulation 43 of those Regulations.

(3) Without prejudice to the foregoing, Part VIII of the principal Regulations (determination of questions) shall apply for the purposes of determining eligibility for awards under these Regulations as it applies to the determination of questions under those Regulations, and as if the questions to be referred by the police authority to a duly qualified medical practitioner under Regulation 71(2) of those Regulations were the following–
- (a) whether the person concerned is totally disabled;
- (b) whether that total disablement is likely to be permanent;
- (c) whether the disablement is the result of an injury received in the execution of duty; and
- (d) the date on which the person became totally disabled.

Home Office
2nd February 1987

Douglas Hurd
One of Her Majesty's Principal Secretaries of State

We consent

Mark Lennox-Boyd
Tim Sainsbury
4th February 1987
Two of the Lords Commissioners of Her Majesty's Treasury

EXPLANATORY NOTE

(This note is not part of the Regulations)

These Regulations make provision for enhanced benefits in case of death or total disablement resulting from an injury received by a member of a police force in the execution of his duty. The benefit is in the form of a gratuity payable, in the case of death, to the widow, child or dependent relative of the member and, in the case of disablement, to the member himself. The gratuity is to be abated by the amount of any gratuity under Regulation 20, 21, 22, 28, 39 or 43, as the case may be, of the Police Pensions Regulations 1973 (the principal Regulations) and by the amount of any damages or compensation recovered in respect of the death or disability in question.

The Regulations are to be construed with the principal Regulations, which are applied in relation to awards under these Regulations with necessary modifications.

The Regulations come into force on 17th March 1987 and have effect as from 25th November 1982 (retrospection is authorised by section 1(5) of the Police Pensions Act 1976).

STATUTORY INSTRUMENTS

1987 No. 157

POLICE

The Police Cadets (Pensions) (Amendment) Regulations 1987

Made - - - - *2nd February 1987*

Laid before Parliament *17th February 1987*

Coming into force - - *17th March 1987*

In exercise of the powers conferred on me by section 35 of the Police Act 1964**(a)**, as extended by section 13 of the Superannuation (Miscellaneous Provisions) Act 1967**(b)** and sections 12 and 15 of the Superannuation Act 1972**(c)**, and after consulting the Police Negotiating Board for the United Kingdom in accordance with section 2(3) of the Police Negotiating Board Act 1980**(d)**, I hereby make the following Regulations:

1. These Regulations may be cited as the Police Cadets (Pensions) (Amendment) Regulations 1987.

2. These Regulations shall come into force on 17th March 1987 and shall have effect as from 25th November 1982.

3. In the Police Cadets (Pensions) Regulations 1973**(e)**, after Regulation 7 there shall be inserted the following Regulation—

"Dependent relative's special pension

7A.—(1) This Regulation shall apply where a police cadet dies or has died as the result of an injury received without his own default in the execution of his duty as a police cadet and, in such case, shall apply—

(*a*) to a parent or (without prejudice to the following sub-paragraph) to a brother or sister of the police cadet who had attained the age of 19 years before the police cadet's death, or

(*b*) subject to his having attained the age of 19 years, to any child of the police cadet, whether or not he had attained that age before the police cadet's death,

being a person who was substantially dependent on the police cadet immediately before his death (hereinafter referred to as a dependent relative).

(2) A dependent relative to whom this Regulation applies may be granted a special pension if the police authority, having regard to all the circumstances of the case, in their discretion so determine, and Regulation 36 of the principal Regulations **(f)** and Part XIII thereof shall apply as if the police cadet had been a regular policeman at the time that he received the injury.".

Douglas Hurd

Home Office One of Her Majesty's Principal Secretaries of State
2nd February 1987

(a) 1964 c.48. **(b)** 1967 c.28. **(c)** 1972 c.11. **(d)** 1980 c.10.
(e) S.I. 1973/430, to which there are amendments not relevant to these Regulations.
(f) The Police Pensions Regulations 1973 (S.I. 1973/428).

EXPLANATORY NOTE

(This note is not part of the Regulations)

These Regulations amend the Police Cadets (Pensions) Regulations 1973 with effect from 25th November 1982 (retrospection is authorised by sections 12 and 15 of the Superannuation Act 1972). They provide for the payment, at the discretion of the police authority, of a dependent relative's special pension in case of death resulting from an injury received by a police cadet in the execution of duty, similar to that payable in the case of a regular policeman under the Police Pensions Regulations 1973.

STATUTORY INSTRUMENTS

1987 No. 158

POLICE

The Police Cadets (Injury Benefit) Regulations 1987

Made - - - -	*6th February 1987*
Laid before Parliament	*17th February 1987*
Coming into force - -	*17th March 1987*

In exercise of the powers conferred on me by section 35 of The Police Act 1964**(a)**, as extended by section 13 of the Superannuation (Miscellaneous Provisions) Act 1967**(b)** and sections 12 and 15 of the Superannuation Act 1972**(c)**, and after consulting the Police Negotiating Board for the United Kingdom in accordance with section 2(3) of the Police Negotiating Board Act 1980**(d)**, I hereby make the following Regulations—

Citation

1. These Regulations may be cited as the Police Cadets (Injury Benefit) Regulations 1987.

Commencement

2. These Regulations shall come into force on 17th March 1987 and shall have effect as from 25th November 1982.

Interpretation

3.—(1) Subject to the following provisions of these Regulations, these Regulations shall be construed as one with the Police Cadets (Pensions) Regulations 1973**(e)**(hereinafter referred to as " the principal Regulations ").

(2) Notwithstanding Regulation 3(4) of the principal Regulations, in these Regulations " totally disabled " means incapable by reason of the disablement in question of earning any money in any employment and " total disablement " shall be construed accordingly.

(3) In the case of a person who is totally disabled, Regulation 13(1) of the Police Pensions Regulations 1973**(f)**, as applied by Regulation 3(2) of the principal Regulations, shall have effect, for the purposes of these Regulations, as if the reference to " that disablement being . . . likely to be permanent " were a reference to the total disablement of that person being likely to be permanent.

Injury benefit

4.—(1) The Police (Injury Benefit) Regulations 1987**(g)** shall apply, subject to the necessary modifications, in relation to—

(*a*) a person who—
(i) receives or received an injury without his own default in the execution of his duty, whether before, on or after 25th November 1982; and
(ii) on or after that date ceases or has ceased to serve as a police cadet; and
(iii) on or after that date and within 12 months of so receiving that injury, becomes or became totally and permanently disabled as a result thereof; and

---

(a) 1964 c.48.   **(b)** 1967 c.28.   **(c)** 1972 c.11.   **(d)** 1980 c.10.
(e) S.I. 1973/430; the relevant amending instruments are S.I. 1983/990 and 1987/157.
(f) S.I. 1973/428, to which there are amendments not relevant to these Regulations.   **(g)** S.I. 1987/156.

(*b*) a police cadet who—
  (i) receives or received an injury without his own default in the execution of his duty, whether before, on or after 25th November 1982; and
  (ii) was serving as a police cadet on or after that date; and
  (iii) within 12 months of so receiving that injury, dies or has died as a result thereof,

as they apply in the case of a person such as is mentioned in Regulation 4(1) or, as the case may be, Regulation 5(1) of those Regulations, and as if references in those Regulations to any of the provisions of the Police Pensions Regulations 1973 included references to those provisions as applied in relation to police cadets by the principal Regulations.

(2) These Regulations shall have effect in relation to a police cadet notwithstanding Regulation 4(3) of the principal Regulations; and accordingly there shall be inserted therein after the words " any enactment " the words " other than the Police Cadets (Injury Benefit) Regulations 1987 ".

Douglas Hurd

Home Office
6th February 1987

One of Her Majesty's Principal Secretaries of State

EXPLANATORY NOTE

(This note is not part of the Regulations)

These Regulations make provision for enhanced benefits in case of death or total disablement resulting from an injury received by a police cadet in the execution of duty similar to that made in relation to members of police forces by the Police (Injury Benefit) Regulations 1987.

The Regulations come into force on 17th March 1987 and have effect as from 25th November 1982 (retrospection is authorised by sections 12 and 15 of the Superannuation Act 1972).

STATUTORY INSTRUMENTS

1987 No. 159

POLICE

The Special Constables (Injury Benefit) Regulations 1987

Made - - - -	*6th February 1987*
Laid before Parliament	*17th February 1987*
Coming into force	*17th March 1987*

In exercise of the powers conferred on me by section 34 of the Police Act 1964(**a**) (read with section 1(2) of the Police Pensions Act 1961(**b**)), as amended and extended by sections 12 and 15 of the Superannuation Act 1972(**c**), I hereby make the following Regulations:

Citation

1. These Regulations may be cited as the Special Constables (Injury Benefit) Regulations 1987.

Commencement

2. These Regulations shall come into force on 17th March 1987 and shall have effect as from 25th November 1982.

Interpretation

3.—(1) Subject to the following provisions of these Regulations, these Regulations shall be construed as one with the Special Constables (Pensions) Regulations 1973(**d**) (hereinafter referred to as "the principal Regulations").

(2) Notwithstanding Regulation 3(3) of the principal Regulations, in these Regulations "totally disabled" means incapable by reason of the disablement in question of earning any money in any employment and "total disablement" shall be construed accordingly.

(3) In the case of a person who is totally disabled, Regulation 13(1) of the Police Pensions Regulations 1973(**e**), as applied by Regulation 3(2) of the principal Regulations, shall have effect, for the purposes of these Regulations, as if the reference to "that disablement being .... likely to be permanent" were a reference to the total disablement of that person being likely to be permanent.

Injury Benefit

4. The Police (Injury Benefit) Regulations 1987(**f**) shall apply, subject to the necessary modifications, in relation to:

    (a) a person who–

(**a**) 1964 c.48.   (**b**) 1961 c.35.   (**c**) 1972 c.11.
(**d**) S.I. 1973/431, to which there are amendments not relevant to these Regulations.
(**e**) S.I. 1973/428, to which there are amendments not relevant to these Regulations.
(**f**) S.I. 1987/156.

(i) receives or received an injury without his own default in the execution of his duty, whether before, on or after 25th November 1982; and

(ii) on or after that date ceases or has ceased to hold office as a special constable; and

(iii) on or after that date and within 12 months of so receiving that injury, becomes or became totally and permanently disabled as a result thereof; and

(b) a special constable who–

(i) receives or received an injury without his own default in the execution of his duty, whether before, on or after 25th November 1982; and

(ii) was holding office as such on or after that date; and

(iii) within 12 months of so receiving that injury, dies or has died as a result thereof,

as they apply in the case of a person such as is mentioned in Regulation 4(1) or, as the case may be, Regulation 5(1) of those Regulations, and as if references in those Regulations to any of the provisions of the Police Pensions Regulations 1973 included references to those provisions as applied in relation to special constables by the principal Regulations.

Home Office
6th February 1987

Douglas Hurd
One of Her Majesty's Principal Secretaries of State

EXPLANATORY NOTE

(This note is not part of the Regulations)

These Regulations make provision for enhanced benefits in case of death or total disablement resulting from an injury received by a special constable in the execution of duty similar to that made in relation to members of police forces by the Police (Injury Benefit) Regulations 1987.

The Regulations come into force on 17th March 1987 and have effect as from 25th November 1982 (retrospection is authorised by sections 12 and 15 of the Superannuation Act 1972).

1987 No. 160 (C. 2) (S. 11)

VIDEO RECORDINGS

The Video Recordings Act 1984 (Scotland) (Commencement No. 4) Order 1987

Made - - - - *3rd February 1987*

The Secretary of State, in exercise of the powers conferred on him by section 23(2) of the Video Recordings Act 1984(**a**), hereby makes the following Order:

1.—(1) This Order may be cited as the Video Recordings Act 1984 (Scotland) (Commencement No. 4) Order 1987.

(2) This Order shall extend to Scotland only.

(3) In this Order—

"the Act" means the Video Recordings Act 1984; and

"the 1985 Order" means the Video Recordings Act 1984 (Scotland) (Commencement No. 2) Order 1985(**b**).

2.—(1) Subject to paragraph (2) below, sections 9 and 10 of the Act shall come into force on 1st March 1987 for the purpose of prohibiting the supply, the offer to supply or the possession for the purpose of supply of a video recording to which article 3(a) of the 1985 Order does not apply and which contains a video work which satisfies the requirements in paragraph (3) below.

(2) Where a video recording to which paragraph (1) above applies contains another video work not being a work which satisfies the requirements in paragraph (3) below, sections 9 and 10 of the Act shall come into force for the purpose set out in paragraph (1) above only in respect of the video work which satisfies those requirements.

(3) The requirements which a video work must satisfy are that—

(a) its visual images, when shown as a moving picture, are substantially the same as the moving picture produced on showing a film registered, or deemed to have been registered, under Part II of the Films Act 1960(**c**) on or after 1st January 1980;

(b) its visual images are accompanied by sound which comprises or includes words predominantly in the English language; and

(c) no classification certificate has been issued in respect of it.

Ian Lang

New St. Andrew's House, Edinburgh
3rd February 1987

Parliamentary Under Secretary of State,
Scottish Office

(**a**) 1984 c.39.
(**b**) S.I. 1985/1265.
(**c**) 1960 c.57; the Films Act 1960 was repealed by section 7(1) of, and Schedule 2 to, the Films Act 1985 (c.21) but the register under Part II continues to be kept under section 7(3) of the 1985 Act for the purpose set out therein.

EXPLANATORY NOTE

(This note is not part of the Order)

This Order brings sections 9 and 10 of the Video Recordings Act 1984 into force in Scotland for certain purposes on 1st March 1987. The sections are brought into force in England, Wales and Northern Ireland on the same day and for the same purposes by the Video Recordings Act 1984 (Commencement No. 4) Order 1987 (S.I. 1987/123).

Sections 9 and 10 create the offences of supplying, offering to supply and possession for the purpose of supply of a video recording containing an unclassified video work. This Order brings these sections into force in respect of an unclassified English language video work which has been sold, let on hire or offered for sale or hire in the United Kingdom to the public in video form before 1st September 1985 (and to which article 3(a) of the Video Recordings Act 1984 (Scotland) (Commencement No. 2) Order 1985 does not therefore apply) and of which a film version was registered on or after 1st January 1980 under Part II of the Films Act 1960.

NOTE AS TO EARLIER COMMENCEMENT ORDERS

(This note is not part of the Order)

Provision	Date of Commencement	S.I. No.
Sections 1, 4, 5, 7, 8, 22 and 23	10.6.85	As to England, Wales and Northern Ireland, 1985/883;
		As to Scotland, 1985/904.
Sections 2, 3, 6, 11 to 17 and 21	1.9.85	As to England, Wales and Northern Ireland, 1985/1264;
		As to Scotland, 1985/1265.
Sections 9 and 10–		
as to certain purposes	1.9.85	As to England, Wales and Northern Ireland, 1985/1264;
		As to Scotland, 1985/1265.
as to certain other purposes	1.9.86	As to England, Wales and Northern Ireland, 1986/1125;
		As to Scotland, 1986/1182.
Sections 18 and 19 as to England, Wales and Northern Ireland	1.9.85	1985/1264.
Section 20 as to Scotland	1.9.85	1985/1265.

STATUTORY INSTRUMENTS

1987 No. 163

CHILDREN AND YOUNG PERSONS

The Child Abduction and Custody (Parties to Conventions) (Amendment) Order 1987

Made -   -   -   -   10th February 1987

At the Court at Buckingham Palace, the 10th day of February 1987

Present

The Queen's Most Excellent Majesty in Council

Her Majesty, in exercise of the powers conferred on Her by section 2 of the Child Abduction and Custody Act 1985(**a**), is pleased, by and with the advice of Her Privy Council, to order, and it is hereby ordered, as follows:

1. This Order may be cited as the Child Abduction and Custody (Parties to Conventions) (Amendment) Order 1987.

2. The Child Abduction and Custody (Parties to Conventions) Order 1986(**b**) is amended by deleting Schedule 1 thereto and substituting therefor the following–

(**a**) 1985 c.60.
(**b**) S.I. 1986/1159.

"SCHEDULE 1   Article 2

CONVENTION ON THE CIVIL ASPECTS OF INTERNATIONAL CHILD ABDUCTION, THE HAGUE, 25th OCTOBER 1980

Contracting States to the Convention	Territories specified in Declarations under Article 39 or 40 of the Convention	Date of Coming into Force as between the United Kingdom and the State or Territory
Australia	Australian States and mainland Territories	1st January 1987
Canada	Ontario	1st August 1986
	New Brunswick	1st August 1986
	British Columbia	1st August 1986
	Manitoba	1st August 1986
	Nova Scotia	1st August 1986
	Newfoundland	1st August 1986
	Prince Edward Island	1st August 1986
	Quebec	1st August 1986
	Yukon Territory	1st August 1986
	Saskatchewan	1st November 1986
	Alberta	1st February 1987
The French Republic	—	1st August 1986
The Hungarian People's Republic	—	1st September 1986
The Grand Duchy of Luxembourg	—	1st January 1987
The Portuguese Republic	—	1st August 1986
The Swiss Confederation	—	1st August 1986 "

G. I. de Deney
Clerk of the Privy Council

EXPLANATORY NOTE

(This note is not part of the Order)

This Order amends the Child Abduction and Custody (Parties to Conventions) Order 1986 in order to specify that the Convention on the Civil Aspects of International Child Abduction, The Hague, 25th October 1980 (Cm. 33) has entered into force for Australia, Luxembourg and the Canadian Provinces of Saskatchewan and Alberta.

STATUTORY INSTRUMENTS

1987 No. 164

FOREIGN COMPENSATION

The Foreign Compensation (Financial Provisions) Order 1987

Made - - - -	*10th February 1987*
Laid before Parliament	*18th February 1987*
Coming into force	*18th March 1987*

At the Court at Buckingham Palace, the 10th day of February 1987

Present

The Queen's Most Excellent Majesty in Council

Her Majesty, by virtue and in exercise of the powers conferred upon Her in that behalf by section 7(2) of the Foreign Compensation Act 1950(**a**) and section 3(3) of the Foreign Compensation Act 1962(**b**) or otherwise in Her Majesty vested, is pleased, by and with the advice of Her Privy Council, to order, and it is hereby ordered, as follows:—

1. This Order may be cited as the Foreign Compensation (Financial Provisions) Order 1987 and shall come into force on 18th March 1987.

2. The Foreign Compensation Commission shall pay into the Consolidated Fund not later than 31st March 1987 out of the compensation fund named in Column 1 of the Schedule to this Order the amount specified in Column 2 of the Schedule which is hereby determined to be the amount of the expenses of the Commission during the period 1st October 1985 to 30th September 1986 attributable to the discharge by the Commission of their functions in relation to the distribution of sums from that compensation fund.

G. I. de Deney
Clerk of the Privy Council

(**a**) 1950 c.12.
(**b**) 1962 c.4 (11 & 12 Eliz. 2).

SCHEDULE

Column 1	Column 2
Name of Fund	*Amount*
	£
The Czechoslovakia Compensation Fund	383,995

EXPLANATORY NOTE

(This note is not part of the Order)

This Order, which is made under section 7(2) of the Foreign Compensation Act 1950 and section 3(3) of the Foreign Compensation Act 1962, directs the Foreign Compensation Commission to pay into the Consolidated Fund, out of the funds paid to the Commission for the purpose of being distributed under the said Acts, an amount in respect of the Commission's expenses during the period 1st October 1985 to 30th September 1986 in relation to the distribution of those funds.

STATUTORY INSTRUMENTS

1987 No. 165

PENSIONS

The Naval, Military and Air Forces etc. (Disablement and Death) Service Pensions Amendment Order 1987

Made - - -	*10th February 1987*
Laid before Parliament	*18th February 1987*
Coming into force -	*6th April 1987*

At the Court at Buckingham Palace, the 10th day of February 1987

Present

The Queen's Most Excellent Majesty in Council

WHEREAS Her Majesty deems it expedient to amend the Naval, Military and Air Forces etc. (Disablement and Death) Service Pensions Order 1983(a) and to do so by Order in Council in pursuance of section 12(1) of the Social Security (Miscellaneous Provisions) Act 1977(b):

NOW, THEREFORE, Her Majesty, in exercise of the powers conferred by the said section 12(1) and of all other powers enabling Her in that behalf, is pleased, by and with the advice of Her Privy Council, to order, and it is hereby ordered, as follows:—

Citation, commencement and interpretation

1.—(1) This Order, which may be cited as the Naval, Military and Air Forces etc. (Disablement and Death) Service Pensions Amendment Order 1987, shall come into force on 6th April 1987.

(2) In this Order, the expression "the principal Order" means the Naval, Military and Air Forces etc. (Disablement and Death) Service Pensions Order 1983.

Amendment of article 18 of the principal Order

2. In article 18 of the principal Order (unemployability allowances) in paragraph (2) for the amount "£1,326" there shall be substituted the amount "£1,352".

Amendment of Schedules to the principal Order

3.—(1) In Schedule 1 to the principal Order (rates of pension and other grants payable in respect of disablement)—

    (a) for Tables 1 and 3 of Part II there shall respectively be substituted the Tables set out in Schedules 1 and 2 hereto;

(a) S.I. 1983/883, as amended by S.I. 1983/1116, 1521, 1984/1154, 1687, 1985/1201, 1986/592.
(b) 1977 c. 5.

(b) for Tables 1 and 2 of Part III there shall respectively be substituted the Tables set out in Schedules 3 and 4 hereto;

(c) for Part IV there shall be substituted the Part set out in Schedule 5 hereto.

(2) In Schedule 2 to the principal Order (rates of pension and other grants payable in respect of death)—

(a) for Table 1A of Part II there shall be substituted the Table set out in Schedule 6 hereto;

(b) for the amount "£2,623" in the second column of Table 1B of Part II there shall be substituted the amount "£2,677";

(c) for the amounts "£50.30" and "£11.61" in the second and third columns of Table 3 of Part II there shall respectively be substituted the amounts "£51.35" and "£11.85";

(d) for Table 5 of Part II there shall be substituted the Table set out in Schedule 7 hereto;

(e) for Part III there shall be substituted the Part set out in Schedule 8 hereto.

G. I. de Deney
Clerk of the Privy Council

SCHEDULE 1

Article 3(1)(a)

Table to be substituted for Table 1 of Part II of Schedule 1 to the principal Order

Table 1: Yearly Rates of—

A. Retired Pay and Pensions for Disabled Officers and Nurses for all Ranks in Groups 1–9 of Part I of this Schedule

B. Disablement Addition on a Pension Basis (Article 43(3)(a)) for all Ranks in Groups 1–9 of Part I of this Schedule and Groups 2 and 3 of Part I or Schedule 2

Degree of Disability	Yearly Rate
Per cent.	£
100	3398
90	3058
80	2718
70	2379
60	2039
50	1699
40	1359
30	1019
20	680

Article 3(1)(a)   SCHEDULE 2

Table to be substituted for Table 3 of Part II of Schedule 1 to the principal Order

Table 3: Weekly Rates of Pension for Disabled Other Ranks Groups 10–15

Degree of Disability	Weekly Rate
Per cent.	£
100	64.50
90	58.05
80	51.60
70	45.15
60	38.70
50	32.25
40	25.80
30	19.35
20	12.90

Article 3(1)(b)   SCHEDULE 3

Table to be substituted for Table 1 of Part III of Schedule 1 to the principal Order

Table 1: Gratuities payable for specified minor injuries

Description of Injury	Assessments	Groups 1–9	Groups 10–15
For the loss of:—	Per cent.	£	£
A. FINGERS			
Index Finger—			
More than 2 phalanges, including loss of whole finger	14	3278	3248
More than 1 phalanx, but not more than 2 phalanges	11	2624	2599
1 phalanx or part thereof	9	2185	2165
Guillotine amputation of tip without loss of bone	5	1307	1297
Middle Finger—			
More than 2 phalanges, including loss of whole finger	12	2839	2814
More than 1 phalanx, but not more than 2 phalanges	9	2185	2165
1 phalanx or part thereof	7	1746	1731
Guillotine amputation of tip without loss of bone	4	1093	1083
Ring or little finger—			
More than 2 phalanges, including loss of whole finger	7	1746	1731
More than 1 phalanx, but not more than 2 phalanges	6	1532	1517
1 phalanx or part thereof	5	1307	1297
Guillotine amputation of tip without loss of bone	2	654	649
B. TOES:—			
Great toe—			
through metatarso-phalangeal joint	14	3278	3248
part with some loss of bone	3	868	863
1 other toe—			
through metatarso-phalangeal joint	3	868	863
part, with some loss of bone	1	439	434
2 toes, excluding great toe—			
through metatarso-phalangeal joint	5	1307	1297
part, with some loss of bone	2	654	649
3 toes, excluding great toe—			
through metatarso-phalangeal joint	6	1532	1517
part, with some loss of bone	3	868	863
4 toes, excluding great toe—			
through metatarso-phalangeal joint	9	2185	2165
part, with some loss of bone	3	868	863

SCHEDULE 4   Article 3(1)(b)

Table to be substituted for Table 2 of Part III of Schedule 1 to the principal Order

Table 2: Gratuities Payable to Members of the Armed Forces for Disablement Assessed at Less than 20 Per cent, not being a Minor Injury Specified in Table 1

	Estimated duration of the disablement within the degree referred to								
	Temporary less than a year			*Temporary more than a year*			*Indeterminate*		
Group	*Per cent.*			*Per cent.*			*Per cent.*		
	1–5	6–14	15–19	1–5	6–14	15–19	1–5	6–14	15–19
	£	£	£	£	£	£	£	£	£
1	191	425	742	381	847	1483	1144	2543	4449
3	189	420	735	377	838	1467	1132	2516	4402
4	187	416	727	373	829	1451	1120	2489	4355
5	185	413	721	371	823	1441	1112	2471	4323
6	184	410	716	368	817	1430	1104	2453	4292
7, 8	182	405	708	364	808	1414	1092	2426	4245
9	180	401	700	360	799	1399	1080	2399	4197
10	181	402	702	362	802	1403	1079	2397	4189
11	181	401	701	361	801	1400	1077	2392	4180
12	180	401	699	360	799	1397	1075	2387	4171
13	180	400	698	360	797	1394	1073	2382	4163
14	179	399	696	359	796	1391	1070	2377	4154
15	179	398	695	358	794	1388	1068	2372	4145

SCHEDULE 5   Article 3(1)(c)

Part to be substituted for Part IV of Schedule 1 to the principal Order

PART IV

RATES OF ALLOWANCES PAYABLE IN RESPECT OF DISABLEMENT

Description of Allowance	*Rate*	
	Groups 1–9	*Groups 10–15*
1. Education allowance under article 13	£120.00 per annum (maximum)	£120.00 per annum (maximum)
2. Constant attendance allowance—		
(a) under article 14(1)(*b*).........................	£2690 per annum (maximum)	£51.60 per week (maximum)
(b) under article 14(1)(*a*).........................	£1345 per annum (maximum)	£25.80 per week (maximum)
3. Exceptionally severe disablement allowance under article 15..................................	£1345 per annum	£25.80 per week
4. Severe disablement occupational allowance under article 16.................................	£673 per annum	£12.90 per week
5. Allowance for wear and tear of clothing—		
(a) under article 17(1)(*a*).........................	£56.00 per annum	£56.00 per annum
(b) under article 17(1)(*b*) and 17(2)........	£88.00 per annum	£88.00 per annum

SCHEDULE 5—*contd.*

Description of Allowance	Rate Groups 1–9	Groups 10–15
6. Unemployability allowances		
(a) personal allowance under article 18(1)(*a*)...	£2187 per annum	£41.95 per week
(b) additional allowances for dependants by way of—		
(i) increase of allowance in respect of a wife, husband or unmarried dependant living as a spouse, under article 18(5)(*b*)	£1238 per annum (maximum)	£23.75 per week (maximum)
(ii) allowance in respect of an adult dependant under article 18(5)(*c*).	£1238 per annum (maximum)	£23.75 per week (maximum)
(iii) increase of allowance in respect of each child under article 18(5)(*d*)......................................	£420 per annum	£8.05 per week
7. Invalidity allowance under article 19—		
(a) if—		
(i) the relevant date fell before 5th July 1948; or		
(ii) on the relevant date the member was under the age of 35; or		
(iii) on the relevant date the member was under the age of 40 and had not attained the age of 65, in the case of the member being a man, or 60, in the case of the member being a woman, before 6th April 1979 and the period in respect of which payment of the allowance is to relate begins on or after 6th April 1979....................	£433 per annum	£8.30 per week
(b) if—		
(i) on the relevant date the member was under the age of 45; or		
(ii) on the relevant date the member was under the age of 50 and had not attained the age of 65, in the case of the member being a man, or 60, in the case of the member being a woman, before 6th April 1979 and the period in respect of which payment of the allowance is to relate begins on or after 6th April 1979	£276 per annum	£5.30 per week
(c) if heads (a) and (b) do not apply, and on the relevant date the member was a man under the age of 60 or a woman under the age of 55................	£138 per annum	£2.65 per week
8. Comforts allowance—		
(a) under article 20(1)(*a*).........................	£579 per annum	£11.10 per week
(b) under article 20(1)(*b*).........................	£289 per annum	£5.55 per week
9. Allowance for lowered standard of occupation under article 21	£1345 per annum (maximum)	£25.80 per week (maximum)

SCHEDULE 5—*contd.*

Description of Allowance	Rate Groups 1–9	Groups 10–15
10. Age allowance under article 22 where the degree of pensioned disablement is—		
(a) 40 to 50 per cent.	£235 per annum	£4.50 per week
(b) over 50 per cent., but not exceeding 70 per cent.	£365 per annum	£7.00 per week
(c) over 70 per cent., but not exceeding 90 per cent.	£524 per annum	£10.05 per week
(d) over 90 per cent.	£730 per annum	£14.00 per week
11. Treatment allowances— increase of personal allowance under article 23(3)	£730 per annum (maximum)	£14.00 per week (maximum)
12. Part-time treatment allowance under article 25	£25.40 per day (maximum)	£25.40 per day (maximum)
13. Mobility supplement under article 26A	£24.55 per week	£24.55 per week

SCHEDULE 6   Article 3(2)(a)

Table to be substituted for Table 1A of Part II of Schedule 2 to the principal Order

Table 1: Yearly Rates of Pensions for Widows of Officers

A.—Pensions other than pensions awarded under article 11(1) or (2) of the 1921 (Officers) Order or article 11(1) of the 1921 (Warrant Officers) Order, of the 1920 Warrant or of the 1921 Order

Group (1)	Rate (2) £	Rate (3) £
1		
2		
3		
4		2677
5		
6	2677	
7		
8		949
9		846
10		744
11		659

Article 3(2)(d)

SCHEDULE 7

Table to be substituted for Table 5 of Part II of Schedule 2 to the principal Order

Table 5: Maximum Yearly Rates of Pension for Relatives of 1914 World War Officers

Group (1)	Rate (2)
	£
1	
2	
3	
4	2677
5	
6	
7	
8	949
9	846
10	744
11	659

Article 3(2)(e)

SCHEDULE 8

Part to be substituted for Part III of Schedule 2 to the principal Order

PART III

RATES OF PENSIONS, OTHER THAN WIDOWS' PENSIONS AND ALLOWANCES, PAYABLE IN RESPECT OF DEATH

Description of Pension of Allowance	Rate	
	Groups 1–11	Groups 12–17
1. Pension under article 30 to unmarried dependant who lived as a spouse	£2571 per annum (maximum)	£49.30 per week (maximum)
2. Rent allowance under article 31	£19.55 per week (maximum)	£19.55 per week (maximum)
3. Allowance under article 32 to elderly widow or widower or unmarried dependant who lived as a spouse—		
(a) if age 65 but under 70	£287 per annum	£5.50 per week
(b) if age 70 but under 80	£574 per annum	£11.00 per week
(c) if age 80 or over.................................	£722 per annum	£13.85 per week
4. Pension to widower under article 34.........	£3287 per annum (maximum)	£51.35 per week (maximum)
5. Allowances in respect of children—		
(a) under article 35(1) in respect of each child..	£605 per annum	£11.60 per week
(b) under article 35(3)	£662 per annum	£12.70 per week
6. Pension under article 36 to a motherless or fatherless child of a member......................	£662 per annum	£12.70 per week
7. Pension or allowance under article 37(3) to or in respect of a child over the age limit	£2060 per annum (maximum)	£39.50 per week (maximum)

SCHEDULE 8—*contd.*

Description of Allowance	Rate	
	Groups 1–11	*Groups* 12–17
8. Education allowance under article 38	£120 per annum (maximum)	£120 per annum (maximum)
9. Pensions to parents—		
(a) minimum rate under article 40(3).....	£15 per annum	£0.25 per week
(b) under paragraphs (a) and (b) of article 40(3)—		
(i) where there is only one eligible parent	(i) Groups 1–10 £75 per annum (maximum) (ii) Group 11 £60 per annum (maximum)	£1.00 per week (maximum)
(ii) where there is more than one eligible parent.............................	(i) Groups 1–10 £100 per annum (maximum) (ii) Group 11 £85 per annum (maximum)	£1.38 per week (maximum)
(c) increase under article 40(3)(*c*)..........	£20 per annum (maximum)	(i) where there is only one eligible parent— £0.38 per week (maximum) (ii) where there is more than one eligible parent —£0.62 per week (maximum)
(d) under paragraph (d) of article 40(4)..	—	£1.00 per week (maximum)
10. Pensions to other dependants—		
(a) under article 41(2)............................	£54 per annum (maximum)	£1.00 per week (maximum)
(b) for each juvenile dependant under article 41(3).......................................	(i) Groups 1–10 £26 per annum (maximum) (ii) Group 11 £20 per annum (maximum)	£0.30 per week (maximum)
(c) aggregate rate under article 41(3)......	(i) Groups 1–10 £75 per annum (maximum) (ii) Group 11 £65 per annum (maximum)	£1.00 per week (maximum)

EXPLANATORY NOTE

(*This note is not part of the Order*)

This Order, which takes effect from 6th April 1987, further amends the Naval, Military and Air Forces etc. (Disablement and Death) Service Pensions Order 1983 ("the principal Order") which makes provision for pensions and other awards in respect of disablement or death due to service in the naval, military and air forces during the 1914 World War and after 2nd September 1939.

Article 2 of this Order raises the maximum amount of annual earnings which may be received by a disabled person while he is deemed to be unemployable for the purposes of unemployability allowances under article 18 of the principal Order and article 3(1) and (2) substitutes Schedules in the principal Order thereby varying the rates of retired pay, pensions, gratuities and allowances in respect of disablement or death due to service in the armed forces.

STATUTORY INSTRUMENTS

1987 No. 168

NORTHERN IRELAND

The Local Elections (Northern Ireland) (Amendment) Order 1987

Made - - - *10th February 1987*

Coming into force in accordance with Article 2

At the Court at Buckingham Palace, the 10th day of February 1987

Present

The Queen's Most Excellent Majesty in Council

Whereas a draft of this Order has been approved by resolution of each House of Parliament:

Now, therefore, Her Majesty in exercise of the powers conferred by section 38(1)(a) and (4) of the Northern Ireland Constitution Act 1973(a), is pleased, by and with the advice of Her Privy Council, to order, and it is hereby ordered, as follows:—

Citation and extent

1.—(1) This Order may be cited as the Local Elections (Northern Ireland) (Amendment) Order 1987.

(2) This Order extends to Northern Ireland only.

Commencement

2.—(1) Subject to paragraphs (2) to (7), this Order shall come into force on the sixth day after the day on which it is made.

(2) The provisions of—

(a) Articles 5 and 6,

(b) paragraphs 5, 6, 32 to 34, 36 to 39, 42 and 46 to 50 of Schedule 1, and

(c) Schedules 2 and 3,

shall not have effect for the purposes of an election in respect of which the notice of election is published before the sixth day after the day on which this Order is made.

(3) The provisions of paragraphs 18, 22, 25 to 27, 30, 51, 56 and 57 of Schedule 1 shall not have effect for the purposes of an offence committed, or alleged to have been committed, before the sixth day after the day on which this Order is made.

(4) The provisions of paragraphs 7 to 11, 13, 15, 52 and 58 of Schedule 1 shall not have

---

(a) 1973 c.36; section 38 was amended by paragaph 6 of Schedule 2 to the Northern Ireland Act 1982 (c.38) and the powers in section 38(1) are referred to in section 5(1) of the Elections (Northern Ireland) Act 1985 (c.2).

effect for the purposes of an election the result of which is declared before the sixth day after the day on which this Order is made.

(5) The provisions of paragraphs 12 and 24 of Schedule 1 shall not have effect for the purposes of an application made under sections 49 and 107, respectively, of the Act of 1962 before the sixth day after the day on which this Order is made.

(6) Paragraph 14 of Schedule 1 shall not have effect for the purposes of an order made under section 50 of the Act of 1962 which was made before the sixth day after the day on which this Order is made.

(7) Paragraph 44 of Schedule 1 shall come into force on the expiry of three months after the day on which this Order is made.

Interpretation

3.—(1) The Interpretation Act (Northern Ireland) 1954**(a)** shall apply to Articles 1 and 2 and the following provisions of this Order as it applies to a Measure of the Northern Ireland Assembly.

(2) The "Act of 1962" means the Electoral Law Act (Northern Ireland) 1962**(b)**.

Miscellaneous amendments to Act of 1962

4. The Act of 1962 shall have effect subject to the amendments specified in Schedule 1.

Amendments to the Local Elections (Northern Ireland) Order 1985

5.—(1) Article 6(6) (manner of voting) of the Local Elections (Northern Ireland) Order 1985**(c)** shall be omitted.

(2) For Article 6(7) of that Order there shall be substituted the following paragraph:

"(7) If a local elector is not entitled as an elector to an absent vote at the election but cannot reasonably be expected to go in person to the polling station allotted to him under the local elections rules by reason of the particular circumstances of his employment either as a constable or by the returning officer, on the date of the poll for a purpose connected with the election, he may vote in person at any polling station in the district electoral area.".

(3) At the end of Article 6 of that Order there shall be added the following paragraphs:—

"(9) For the purposes of the provisions of this Order and the Act of 1962, a person entitled to vote as an elector at a local election is entitled as an elector to vote by post or entitled to vote by proxy at the election if he is shown in the absent voters list for the election as so entitled; and references in those provisions to entitlement as an elector to an absent vote at a local election are references to entitlement as an elector to vote by post or entitlement to vote by proxy at the election.

(10) Parts I and III of Schedule 2 shall have effect as if contained in Part VII of the Act of 1962.".

(4) Article 14 (voting offences) of that Order shall be omitted.

(5) For Part I (voting by post and by proxy) of Schedule 2 to that Order there shall be substituted the provisions set out in Schedule 2.

(6) Part II (forms) of Schedule 2 to that Order shall be omitted.

(7) Part III (issue and receipt of postal ballot papers) of Schedule 2 to that Order shall have effect subject to the amendments specified in Schedule 3.

Transitional provisions for absent voters

6.—(1) In relation to any person who, immediately before 16th February 1987, was entitled to vote by post or by proxy for an indefinite period at local elections by virtue of an application under paragraph 2(1) of Part I of Schedule 2 to the Local Elections

---

(a) 1954 c.33 (N.I.).
(b) 1962 c.14 (N.I.).
(c) S.I. 1985/454.

(Northern Ireland) Order 1985 (which Part is to be replaced by the Part set out in Schedule 2 to this Order and is hereafter referred to as the "replaced Part"), paragraphs 1 to 4 of Part I of Schedule 2 to that Order, as substituted by Schedule 2 to this Order ("the Part which is substituted"), shall have effect—

(a) as if an application by him under paragraph 1 of the Part which is substituted so to vote at local elections had been granted on the date of the coming into force of that Part,

(b) where immediately before 16th February 1987, an appointment of a person to vote for him as proxy at local elections was in force, as if the appointment had been made in respect of such elections under paragraph 3 of the Part which is substituted on the date of the coming into force of that Part, and

(c) where the application treated as granted by virtue of sub-paragraph (a) is an application to vote by post, as if he had specified in the application as the address to which his ballot paper is to be sent the address provided by him for the purpose under the replaced Part.

(2) Where an appointment of a person to vote as proxy for another at local elections is treated by virtue of paragraph (1) as made under paragraph 3 of the Part which is substituted, and immediately before 16th February 1987 the proxy was entitled, in pursuance of an application for an indefinite period, so to vote by post at local elections, paragraph 4 of that Part shall have effect—

(a) where the proxy's application was based on his entitlement as elector to vote by post, as if an application by him under paragraph 4(4)(a) of that Part to vote by post as proxy at local elections had been granted on the date of the coming into force of that part, and

(b) where the proxy's application was based on the situation of the address to which his ballot paper was to be sent, as if an application by him under paragraph 4(4)(b) of that Part to vote by post as proxy at local elections had been granted on the date of the coming into force of that Part.

G. I. de Deney
Clerk of the Privy Council

Article 4

SCHEDULE 1

Amendments to the Act of 1962

1. In section 32(1)(a) (corrupt and illegal practices list) **(a)** the words "or local" shall be omitted.

2. In section 34(4) (appointment of election agent), after the word "appointment" there shall be inserted the words "(or, at a local election, a deemed appointment)".

3. At the end of section 36(1) (offices of election agent and sub-agent) there shall be added the words:
"At a local election, this subsection shall have effect as if after the words 'appointment of the agent' there were inserted the words 'is declared to him'.".

4. After subsection (3) of section 37 (default in appointing election agent) there shall be inserted:
"(3A) At a local election the deemed appointment of a candidate as his own election agent may be revoked as if it were an actual appointment.".

5. At the end of section 39(2) (payment of expenses at an election through election agent)**(b)** there shall be added the words:
"At a local election, this subsection shall have effect as if for the words '£2' there were substituted the words '£20'.".

6. In section 41(2) (prohibition of unauthorised expenses)**(c)** after the sum "50p" there shall be inserted the words "or, at a local election, £5".

7. At the end of section 41(5)**(d)** there shall be added the words:
"At a local election, paragraph (b) of this subsection shall have effect as if for the words 'fourteen' and 'send' there were substituted 'twenty-one' and 'deliver', respectively.".

8. At the end of section 43(1) (time for sending in and paying claims) **(e)** there shall be added the words:
"At a local election, this subsection, subsection (3) and section 44(4) shall have effect as if for the word 'fourteen' there were substituted 'twenty-one'.".

9. At the end of section 46 (return as to expenses at an election)**(f)** there shall be added the following subsection:
"(7) At a local election, subsections (1) and (5) shall have effect as if for the word 'transmit' in each place where it occurs there were substituted 'deliver' and for the word 'transmitted' in subsection (5) there were substituted 'delivered'.".

10. At the end of section 47 (declarations as to expenses at an election) there shall be added the following subsection:
"(4) At a local election, subsections (1) and (2) shall have effect as if for the word 'transmitted' in each place where it occurs in subsection (1) and the proviso to

---

(a) Section 32(1) was repealed in part by Schedule 3 to the Electoral Law (Northern Ireland) Order 1972 (S.I. 1972/1264 (N.I. 13)).

(b) Section 39 was extended by Article 13(1) of the Electoral Law (Northern Ireland) Order 1972 (S.I. 1972/1264 (N.I. 13)) and the sum in section 39(2) substituted by virtue of section 10 of, and Schedule 1 to, the Decimal Currency Act 1969 (c.19).

(c) The sum in section 41(2) was substituted by virtue of section 10 of, and Schedule 1 to, the Decimal Currency Act 1969 (c.19).

(d) Section 41(5) was extended by Article 13(1) of the Electoral Law (Northern Ireland) Order 1972 (S.I. 1972/1264 (N.I. 13)).

(e) Section 43 was extended by Article 13(1) of the Electoral Law (Northern Ireland) Order 1972 (S.I. 1972/1264 (N.I. 13)) and subsection (4) of that section was repealed by Part II of Schedule 7 to the Judicature (Northern Ireland) Act 1978 (c.23).

(f) Section 46 was extended by Article 13(1) of the Electoral Law (Northern Ireland) Order 1972 (S.I. 1972/1264 (N.I. 13)).

subsection (2) there were substituted 'delivered' and for the words 'transmits' and 'transmit or cause to be transmitted' in subsection (2) there were substituted respectively 'delivers' and 'deliver'.".

11. At the end of section 48(1) (penalty for sitting or voting after failure to transmit return and declarations)**(a)** there shall be added the words:

"At a local election this subsection shall have effect as if for the word 'transmitted', in each place where it occurs, there were substituted 'delivered'.".

12. After section 49(1) (authorised excuses for failure as respects return and declarations) there shall be added the following subsection:

"(1A) Where a person makes an application under this section in respect of the return and declaration as to election expenses at a local election, he shall notify the Director of Public Prosecutions for Northern Ireland of the application and the Director or his assistant or any barrister or solicitor duly appointed as the Director's representative may attend the hearing of the application and make representations at the hearing in respect of it.".

13. At the end of section 49(2) there shall be added the words:

"At a local election this subsection shall have effect as if for the word 'transmit', in each place where it occurs, there were substituted 'deliver'.".

14. At the end of section 50(3) (power of court to require information from election agent or sub-agent) there shall be added the words:

"At a local election this subsection shall have effect as if for the words 'five hundred pounds' there were substituted 'the amount of the maximum fine to which he would be liable if at the time the order is made he were convicted of a summary offence on conviction of which he was liable to a fine of level 5 on the standard scale'.".

15. At the end of section 52(1) (inspection of returns and declarations)**(b)** there shall be added the words:

"and this subsection shall have effect as if for the word 'sent' there were substituted 'delivered'.".

16. At the end of section 55 (duty on and licences for carriages, etc., used at elections) there shall be added the words "other than a local election".

17. At the end of section 73 (attendance of Director of Public Prosecutions at trial of election petition)**(c)** there shall be added the words:

"At the trial of a petition relating to a local election, this section shall have effect as if for the word 'shall' there were substituted 'may and, if the election court so requests him, shall'.".

18. At the end of section 86 (punishment for corrupt withdrawal) there shall be added the words:

"In respect of a petition relating to a local election, this section shall have effect as if for the words from 'to a fine' to 'and such fine' there were substituted 'to a fine, or to both, or on summary conviction, to imprisonment for a term not exceeding 6 months, or to a fine not exceeding the statutory maximum or to both'.".

(a) Section 48 was extended by Article 13(1) of, and subsection (2A) was inserted by Article 13(2) of, the Electoral Law (Northern Ireland) Order 1972 (S.I. 1972/1264 (N.I. 13)).

(b) Section 52(1) was amended by Article 10 of the Local Elections (Northern Ireland) Order 1985 (S.I. 1985/454).

(c) Section 73 was amended by Article 9(1) of the Prosecution of Offences (Northern Ireland) Order 1972 (S.I. 1972/538 (N.I. 1)).

19. In section 92 (further provision as to costs of petition)—

(a) at the end of subsection (1) there shall be added the words:

"In respect of a petition relating to a local election, this subsection shall have effect as if the reference to subsection (2) were omitted."; and

(b) in subsection (2) the words from "and, in relation to a local" to the end shall be omitted.

20. At the end of section 96 (provisions applying to all persons reported personally guilty of a corrupt or illegal practice)(**a**) there shall be added the following subsection:

"(5) In respect of the report of an election court at the trial of a local election petition, this section shall have effect subject to the following amendments:

(a) in subsection (1) the words from 'and whether' to 'indemnity' and from 'It shall be the duty' to 'is given' shall be omitted; and

(b) for subsection (2) there shall be substituted:

'(2) The report shall be laid before the Director of Public Prosecutions for Northern Ireland.'.".

21. At the end of section 97 (disciplinary action on report of corrupt practice)(**b**) there shall be added the following subsection:

"(4) In respect of the report of an election court at the trial of a local election petition, subsections (1), (2) and (3) shall have effect as if for the words from 'whether' to 'for Northern Ireland to', in each place where those words occur, there were substituted 'the court shall'.".

22. At the end of section 105 (prosecution and trial of electoral misdemeanours)(**c**) there shall be added the following subsection:

"(8) In respect of the prosecution and trial of an electoral misdemeanour committed or alleged to have been committed at a local election, this section shall have effect subject to the following amendments:

(a) in subsection (1) the words, 'subject to subsection (2),' and from 'A person charged with personation' to the end of the subsection shall be omitted;

(b) subsections (2) and (6) shall be omitted; and

(c) in subsection (5) for the words 'the offences specified in paragraphs 24 to 26' there shall be substituted 'the offence specified in paragraph 26(2)' and for the words 'charged with any of the electoral offences specified in paragraphs 24 to 26' there shall be substituted 'to whom section 111(2A)(c)(i) applies charged with the offence specified in paragraph 26(2)'.".

23. At the end of section 106 (prosecution of offences disclosed on election petition) there shall be added the following subsection:

"(10) This section shall not apply to electoral misdemeanours committed or alleged to have been committed at a local election.".

24. After section 107(1) (power to except innocent act from being illegal practice, payment, employment or hiring) there shall be added the following subsection:

"(1A) Where a person makes an application under this section for relief in respect of an act or omission at a local election, he shall notify the Director of Public Prosecutions for Northern Ireland of the application and the Director or his assistant or any barrister or solicitor duly appointed as the Director's representative may attend the hearing of the application and make representations at the hearing in respect of it.".

25. At the end of section 108 (penalties for corrupt practices) there shall be added the following subsection:

"(4) Subsections (1) to (3) above shall not apply to a person convicted of a corrupt practice at a local election and such a person shall be liable—

(**a**) Section 96(1) was amended by Article 9(1) of the Prosecution of Offences (Northern Ireland) Order 1972 (S.I. 1972/538 (N.I. 1)).

(**b**) Section 97 was amended by Article 9(1) of the Prosecution of Offences (Northern Ireland) Order 1972 (S.I. 1972/538 (N.I. 1)).

(**c**) Section 105(1) was amended by paragraph 66 of Schedule 6 to the Magistrates' Courts (Northern Ireland) Order 1981 (S.I. 1981/1675 (N.I. 26)).

(a) on conviction on indictment—

    (i) in the case of a corrupt practice under paragraph 4 of Schedule 9 or paragraphs 8 or 9 of that Schedule in relation to the offence in paragraph 4, to imprisonment for a term not exceeding two years, or to a fine, or to both;

    (ii) in any other case, to imprisonment for a term not exceeding one year, or to a fine, or to both;

(b) on summary conviction, to imprisonment for a term not exceeding 6 months, or to a fine not exceeding the statutory maximum, or to both.".

26. At the end of section 109 (penalty for illegal practices) there shall be added:

"In respect of an illegal practice at a local election this section shall have effect as if for the words 'one hundred pounds' there were substituted 'level 5 on the standard scale'.".

27. After section 111(2) (penalties for electoral offences by officers and other persons), there shall be inserted the following subsection:

"(2A) Subsections (1) and (2) above shall not apply to a person convicted of an electoral offence at a local election or in connection with the registration of local electors and such a person shall be liable—

(a) in the case of an offence under paragraph 24, 24A, 25, 28, 29, 30, 31 or 32A of Schedule 9, on summary conviction to a fine not exceeding level 5 on the standard scale;

(b) in the case of an offence under paragraph 26(1) or 33 of Schedule 9, on summary conviction to a fine not exceeding level 3 on the standard scale;

(c) in the case of an offence under paragraph 26(2) of Schedule 9—

    (i) if the person guilty of the offence is the Chief Electoral Officer or any person to whom functions are delegated by him under this Act, a presiding officer or a clerk appointed to assist in taking the poll, counting the votes or assisting at the proceedings in connection with the issue or receipt of postal ballot papers, on conviction on indictment to a fine, or to imprisonment for a term not exceeding 2 years, or to both, or on summary conviction, to a fine not exceeding the statutory maximum, or to imprisonment for a term not exceeding 6 months, or to both;

    (ii) if the person guilty of the offence is any other person, on summary conviction to a fine not exceeding level 5 on the standard scale or to imprisonment for a term not exceeding 6 months, or to both;

(d) in the case of an offence under paragraph 27 of Schedule 9, on summary conviction to a fine not exceeding level 5 on the standard scale or to imprisonment for a term not exceeding 6 months;

(e) in the case of an offence under paragraph 32 of Schedule 9, on summary conviction to a fine not exceeding level 4 on the standard scale.".

28. At the end of section 111(3)(a) there shall be added:

"In respect of a breach of official duty at a local election, this subsection shall have effect as if for the words 'the Clerk of the Crown' there were substituted 'any presiding officer, any person either appointed to assist in the conduct of the election or who so assists in the course of his employment'.".

29. At the end of section 112(1) (incapacities resulting from convictions for corrupt and illegal practices) there shall be added:

"In respect of a person convicted of a corrupt practice at a local election this subsection shall have effect as if the words 'on indictment or by an election court' were omitted.".

(a) Section 111 was amended by Schedule 2 to the Electoral Law (Northern Ireland) Order 1972 (S.I. 1972/1264 (N.I. 13)).

30. At the end of section 118 (time limit for prosecutions)(**a**) there shall be added the following subsection:

"(3) In respect of the prosecution of an electoral misdemeanour committed or alleged to have been committed at a local election, this section shall have effect subject to the following amendments:

    (a) in subsection (1) the words, 'whether before an election court or otherwise,' shall be omitted, and

    (b) for subsection (2) there shall be substituted:

        '(2) For the purposes of this section, the making of a complaint shall be deemed to be the commencement of a proceeding.'.".

31. At the end of section 120(4) (provisions as to Director of Public Prosecutions)(**b**) there shall be added:

"In respect of the costs of an election petition relating to a local election, this subsection shall have effect as if the words 'so far as they are not in the case of any prosecution paid by the defendant' were omitted.".

32. At the end of section 129 (computation of time) there shall be added:

"In respect of a local election and an election petition relating to a local election the foregoing provisions shall not have effect and any period of time shall be computed as follows:

    (a) where the day or the last day on which anything is required or permitted to be done by or in pursuance of Parts VI and IX is any of the days mentioned in paragraph (b), the requirement or permission shall be deemed to relate to the first day thereafter which is not one of those days; and in computing any period of not more than 7 days for the purposes of those Parts any of the days so mentioned shall be disregarded;

    (b) the days referred to in paragraph (a) are Saturday, Sunday, Christmas Eve, Maundy Thursday or a public holiday.".

33. In section 130(1) (interpretation)(**c**) before the definition of "Chief Electoral Officer" there shall be inserted the following definition—

" 'absent voters list' means, in relation to any local election, the list kept under paragraph 2(4) of Part I of Schedule 2 to the Local Elections (Northern Ireland) Order 1985 (as substituted by Schedule 2 to the Local Elections (Northern Ireland) (Amendment) Order 1987) for that election;".

34. In rule 2 of the local elections rules in Schedule 5 to the Act of 1962 (computation of time)(**d**), after the word "Sunday" there shall be inserted ", Christmas Eve, Maundy Thursday".

35. In rule 16(2)(d) of the local elections rules in Schedule 5 (the ballot papers)(**d**), for the words "on the face" there shall be substituted "on it".

36. In rule 21(1) of the local elections rules in Schedule 5 (postal ballot papers)(**d**) for the words "provided by them for the purpose" there shall be substituted "shown in the absent voters list".

37. Rule 24 of the local elections rules in Schedule 5 to the Act of 1962 (list of proxies and postal voters)(**d**) shall be omitted.

(**a**) Section 118(1) was repealed in part by Part V of the Schedule to the Statute Law Revision (Northern Ireland) Act 1976 (c.12).

(**b**) Section 120 was amended by Article 9(1) of the Prosecution of Offences (Northern Ireland) Order 1972 (S.I. 1972/538 (N.I. 1)) and the functions of the Ministry of Finance were transferred by Article 5(2) of, and Schedule 1 to, the Northern Ireland (Modification of Enactments—No. 1) Order 1973 (S.I. 1973/2163).

(**c**) Section 130(1) was amended by Schedule 2 to the Electoral Law (Northern Ireland) Order 1972 (S.I. 1972/1264 (N.I. 13)) and other provisions not relevant to this Order.

(**d**) The rules in Schedule 5 were substituted by Schedule 1 to the Local Elections (Northern Ireland) Order 1985 (S.I. 1985/454).

38. In rule 25(1)(b) of the local elections rules in Schedule 5 (issue of official poll cards)(**a**) for the words from "his application" to the end there shall be substituted "he is entitled to vote by post as proxy at the election".

39. For rule 28 of the local elections rules in Schedule 5 (declaration of secrecy)(**a**) there shall be substituted:

"Notification of requirement of secrecy
   28. The returning officer shall make such arrangements as he thinks fit to ensure that—

    (a) every person attending at a polling station (otherwise than for the purpose of voting or assisting a blind voter to vote or as a constable on duty there) has been given a copy in writing of the provisions of paragraph 27(1) and (3) of Schedule 9 and a statement of the penalty prescribed by section 111(2A)(d) (as inserted by paragraph 27 of Schedule 1 to the Local Elections (Norther Ireland) (Amendment) Order 1987); and

    (b) every person attending at the counting of the votes (other than any constable on duty at the counting) has been given a copy in writing of the provisions of paragraph 27(2) of Schedule 9 and a statement of the penalty prescribed by section 111(2A)(d) (as inserted by paragraph 27 of Schedule 1 to the Local Elections (Northern Ireland) (Amendment) Order 1987).".

40. In rule 29 of the local elections rules in Schedule 5 (admission to polling station)(**a**):

    (a) paragraph (1)(e) shall be omitted, and

    (b) in paragraph (3) the words ", a member of Her Majesty's forces (including Her Majesty's reserve or auxilliary forces)" and sub-paragraph (b) shall be omitted.

41. In rule 34(6) of the local elections rules in Schedule 5 (voting procedure)(**a**):

    (a) in sub-paragraph (a) for the words "Article 12" there shall be substituted "Articles 8 and 12"; and

    (b) after sub-paragraph (e), the following sub-paragraph shall be added:
       "(f) a British seaman's card issued in accordance with regulations made under section 70 of the Merchant Shipping Act 1970(**b**)".

42. In rule 37(1)(b) of the local elections rules in Schedule 5 (tendered ballot papers)(**a**) the words "named in the list of persons" shall be omitted.

43. In the Appendix of forms to the local elections rules in Schedule 5(**a**), in form 9 (form of certificate of employment), paragraph (b) (members of Her Majesty's forces) shall be omitted.

44. In paragraph 7 (provisions as to security for costs) of Schedule 8 (election courts):

    (a) in sub-paragraph (2)(b) for the words "five hundred pounds" there shall be substituted "£2,500";

    (b) at the end of sub-paragraph (3) there shall be added:
       "In respect of a petition relating to a local election the following provisions shall have effect in substitution for the foregoing provisions of this sub-paragraph:
          'Within the prescribed time after giving the security the petitioner shall serve on the respondent in the prescribed manner—
            (a) a notice of the presentation of the petition and of the amount and nature of the security, and
            (b) a copy of the petition.'.";

    (c) at the end of sub-paragraph (4) there shall be added:

(**a**) The rules in Schedule 5 were substituted by Schedule 1 to the Local Elections (Northern Ireland) Order 1985 (S.I. 1985/454).
  (**b**) 1970 c.36.

"In respect of a petition relating to a local election this sub-paragraph shall have effect as if the words ', not exceeding five days after service of the notice,' were omitted.";

(d) sub-paragraph (5) shall be omitted; and

(e) at the end of sub-paragraph (7) there shall be added:

"In respect of a petition relating to a local election this sub-paragraph shall have effect as if the words 'not exceeding five days' were omitted.".

45. In paragraph 12 (witnesses) of Schedule 8:

(a) at the beginning of sub-paragraph (5) there shall be inserted the words "Except in respect of the trial of a local election petition,"; and

(b) in sub-paragraph (7)(a) after the words "to answer" there shall be inserted the words ", other than a witness at a trial of a local election petition,".

46. At the beginning of paragraph 5 (misdemeanours as to proxy voting)(**a**) of Schedule 9 (electoral misdemeanours) there shall be inserted the words "Except at a local election" and the words "or local" in sub-paragraph (a) shall be omitted.

47. In paragraph 10 (offences in connection with legal incapacity to vote)(**b**) of Schedule 9:

(a) at the beginning of sub-paragraph (1) there shall be inserted the words "Except at a local election" and the words "or votes by post at a local election" and "or local" shall be omitted; and

(b) in sub-paragraph (2) the words "or local government electoral area" shall be omitted.

48. In paragraph 11 (offences in connection with voting in person)(**c**) of Schedule 9:

(a) in sub-paragraph (b) the words "or local" shall be omitted; and

(b) sub-paragraphs (c) and (d) shall be omitted.

49. In paragraph 12 (proxy offences)(**d**) of Schedule 9:

(a) at the beginning of sub-paragraph (1) there shall be inserted the words "Except at a local election" and the words "(at a local election, whether in person or by post)" shall be omitted; and

(b) sub-paragraph (2)(d) shall be omitted.

50. For paragraph 12A (supplementary provisions about voting offences)(**e**) of Schedule 9 there shall be substituted the following paragraph—

"12A.—(1) A person shall be guilty of an illegal practice if—

(a) he votes in person or by post, whether as an elector or as proxy, or applies to vote by proxy or by post as elector, at a local election or at local elections, knowing that he is subject to a legal incapacity to vote at the election or, as the case may be, at such elections; or

(b) he applies for the appointment of a proxy to vote for him at any local election or at local elections knowing that he or the person to be appointed is subject to a legal incapacity to vote at the election or, as the case may be, such elections; or

(c) he votes, whether in person or by post, as proxy for some other person at a local election, knowing that that person is subject to a legal incapacity to vote.

For the purposes of this sub-paragraph references to a person being subject to a legal incapacity to vote do not, in relation to things done before polling day at the election

---

(**a**) Paragraph 5 was amended by Article 14 of the Local Elections (Northern Ireland) Order 1985 (S.I. 1985/454).

(**b**) Paragraph 10 was amended by Article 14 of the Local Elections (Northern Ireland) Order 1985.

(**c**) Paragraph 11 was amended by Article 14 of the Local Elections (Northern Ireland) Order 1985.

(**d**) Paragraph 12 was amended by Article 14 of the Local Elections (Northern Ireland) Order 1985.

(**e**) Paragraph 12A was inserted by Article 14 of the Local Elections (Northern Ireland) Order 1985.

or first election at which or for which they are done, include his being below voting age if he will be of voting age on that day.

(2) A person shall be guilty of an illegal practice if—

(a) he votes as elector otherwise than by proxy either—

   (i) more than once in the same district electoral area at any local election; or

   (ii) in more than one district electoral area at an ordinary election of councillors for a local government district; or

   (iii) in any district electoral area at such an ordinary election as mentioned above, when there is in force an appointment of a person to vote as his proxy at the election in some other district electoral area; or

(b) he votes as elector in person at a local election at which he is entitled to vote by post; or

(c) he votes as elector in person at a local election, knowing that a person appointed to vote as his proxy at the election either has already voted in person at the election or is entitled to vote by post.

(3) A person shall be guilty of an illegal practice if—

(a) he votes as proxy for the same elector either—

   (i) more than once in the same district electoral area at any local election; or

   (ii) in more than one district electoral area at an ordinary election of councillors for a local government district; or

(b) he votes in person as proxy for an elector at a local election at which he is entitled to vote by post as proxy for that elector; or

(c) he votes in person as proxy for an elector at a local election knowing that the elector has already voted in person at the election.

(4) A person shall also be guilty of an illegal practice if he votes at a local election in any district electoral area as proxy for more than two persons of whom he is not the husband, wife, parent, grandparent, brother, sister, child or grandchild.

(5) A person shall also be guilty of an illegal practice if he knowingly induces or procures some other person to do an act which is, or but for that other person's want of knowledge would be, an offence by that other person under the foregoing provisions of this paragraph.

(6) For the purposes of this paragraph a person who has applied for a ballot paper for the purpose of voting in person, or who has marked, whether validly or not, and returned a ballot paper issued for the purpose of voting by post, shall be deemed to have voted, but for the purpose of determining whether an application for a ballot paper constitutes an offence under sub-paragraph (4), a previous application made in circumstances which entitle the applicant only to mark a tendered ballot paper shall, if he does not exercise that right, be disregarded.

(7) Where a person is alleged to have committed an offence under sub-paragraph (2)(a)(i) or (3)(a)(i) by voting on a second or subsequent occasion, he shall not be deemed by sub-paragraph (6) to have voted by applying on a previous occasion for a ballot paper for the purpose of voting in person unless he then marked a tendered ballot paper under rule 37(4) of the local elections rules.

(8) In respect of an illegal practice under this paragraph—

(a) the court before whom a person is convicted may, if they think it just in the special circumstances of the case, mitigate or entirely remit any incapacity imposed by virtue of section 112; and

(b) a candidate shall not be liable, nor shall his election be avoided, for an illegal practice under this paragraph of any agent of his other than an offence under sub-paragraph (5).".

51. In paragraph 13(1)(b) (offence at meetings held with reference to local elections) of Schedule 9 for the words "on or within three weeks before" there shall be substituted "in the period beginning with the last day on which notice of election may be published under rule 1 of the local elections rules and ending with".

52. At the end of paragraph 16 (failure to send certain statements, declarations, returns or copies) of Schedule 9 there shall be added:

"In respect of the application of the provisions of sections 41(5)(b), 46 and 47 at a local election, this paragraph shall have effect as if for "send" there were substituted "deliver".

53. After paragraph 24 (offences in connection with service declarations) of Schedule 9 there shall be inserted the following paragraph:

"24A. A person who makes a statement which he knows to be false in any declaration or form used for any of the purposes of Part I of Schedule 2 to the Local Elections (Northern Ireland) Order 1985 (as substituted by Schedule 2 to the Local Elections (Northern Ireland) (Amendment) Order 1987) or attests an application under that Part when he knows that he is not authorised to do so or that it contains a statement which is false shall be guilty of an electoral offence.".

54. In paragraph 29(4) (prohibition of certain payments) of Schedule 9 after the words "any election" there shall be inserted ", other than a local election,".

55. In paragraph 31(2) (prohibition of use of certain premises as committee rooms) of Schedule 9 before the words "This sub-paragraph applies to" there shall be inserted "Except in respect of a committee room in connection with a local election" and at the end of the sub-paragraph there shall be added "At a local election this sub-paragraph applies only to the premises referred to at (iv) above".

56. After paragraph 32 (officials not to act for candidates) of Schedule 9 there shall be inserted—

"32A.—(1) A person to whom this paragraph applies shall be guilty of an electoral offence if, without reasonable cause, he is guilty of any act or omission in breach of his official duty.

(2) The persons to whom this paragraph applies are—

    (a) the Chief Electoral Officer and any person to whom functions are delegated by him under this Act,

    (b) any presiding officer or any person either appointed to assist in the conduct of the election or who so assists in the course of his employment, and

    (c) any postmaster or his deputy;

and 'official duty' shall for the purposes of this paragraph be construed accordingly, but shall not include duties imposed otherwise than by the law relating to local elections or the registration of local electors.".

57. At the beginning of paragraph 34 (attempts etc.) of Schedule 9 there shall be inserted the words "Except at a local election" and at the end of the paragraph there shall be added:

"Without prejudice to any other enactment a person who does any of the acts described in sub-paragraphs (a) or (b) shall be guilty of the electoral offence in question and shall be liable to be punished accordingly.".

58. In form 5 (form of declaration as to election expenses required by section 47) of Schedule 10 (forms), in paragraph 2 after the word "transmitted" there shall be inserted "(or at a local election, delivered)".

Article 5(5)

SCHEDULE 2

Provisions substituted for Part I of Schedule 2 to the Local Elections (Northern Ireland) Order 1985

"PART I

VOTING BY POST, BY PROXY AND BY POST AS PROXY

Absent vote at local elections for indefinite period

1.—(1) Where a person applies to the Chief Electoral Officer to vote by post, or to vote by proxy, at local elections for an indefinite period, the Chief Electoral Officer shall grant the application (subject to sub-paragraph (6)) if—

  (a) he is satisfied that the applicant is eligible for an absent vote at such elections for an indefinite period,

  (b) he is satisfied that the applicant is or will be registered in the register of local electors, and

  (c) the application meets the requirements set out in paragraphs 5 to 11.

(2) For the purposes of this paragraph, a person is eligible for an absent vote at local elections for an indefinite period—

  (a) if he is or will be registered as a service elector,

  (b) if he cannot reasonably be expected—

   (i) to go in person to the polling station allotted or likely to be allotted to him under the local elections rules, or

   (ii) to vote unaided there,

   by reason of blindness or other physical incapacity,

  (c) if he cannot reasonably be expected to go in person to that polling station by reason of the general nature of his occupation, service or employment or that of his spouse, or

  (d) if he cannot go in person from his qualifying address to that polling station without making a journey by air or sea.

(3) The Chief Electoral Officer shall keep a record of those whose applications under this paragraph have been granted showing—

  (a) in the case of those who may vote by post, the addresses provided by them in their applications as the addresses to which their ballot papers are to be sent, and

  (b) in the case of those who may vote by proxy, the names and addresses of those appointed as their proxies.

(4) The Chief Electoral Officer shall remove a person from the record kept under sub-paragraph (3)—

  (a) if he applies to the Chief Electoral Officer to be removed,

  (b) in the case of any registered person, if he ceases to be registered at the same qualifying address or ceases to be, or becomes, registered as a service elector, or

  (c) if the Chief Electoral Officer gives notice that he has reason to believe there has been a material change of circumstances.

(5) A person shown in the record kept under sub-paragraph (3) as voting by post or, as the case may be, voting by proxy may subsequently alter his choice (subject to sub-paragraph (6)) on an application to the Chief Electoral Officer that meets the requirements set out in paragraphs 5 to 11 and the Chief Electoral Officer shall amend the record accordingly.

(6) A person applying to vote by post must provide an address in the United Kingdom as the address to which his ballot paper is to be sent.

Absent vote at a particular local election and absent voters list

2.—(1) Where a person applies to the Chief Electoral Officer to vote by post, or to vote by proxy, at a particular local election, the Chief Electoral Officer shall grant the application (subject to sub-paragraph (5)) if—

    (a) he is satisfied that the applicant's circumstances on the date of the poll will be or are likely to be such that he cannot reasonably be expected to vote in person at the polling station allotted or likely to be allotted to him under the local elections rules,

    (b) he is satisfied that the applicant is or will be registered in the register of local electors, and

    (c) the application meets the requirements set out in paragraphs 5 to 11.

(2) Sub-paragraph (1) does not apply to a person who is included in the record kept under paragraph 1, but such a person may, in respect of a particular local election apply to the Chief Electoral Officer—

    (a) for his ballot paper to be sent to a different address in the United Kingdom, or

    (b) to vote by proxy

if he is shown in the record so kept as voting by post.

(3) The Chief Electoral Officer shall grant an application under sub-paragraph (2) if it meets the requirements set out in paragraphs 5 to 11.

(4) The Chief Electoral Officer shall, in respect of each local election, keep a special list ("the absent voters list") consisting of—

    (a) a list of—

        (i) those whose applications under sub-paragraph (1) to vote by post at the election have been granted, together with the addresses provided by them in their applications as the addresses to which their ballot papers are to be sent, and

        (ii) those who are for the time being shown in the record kept under paragraph 1 as voting by post (excluding those so shown whose applications under sub-paragraph (2) to vote by proxy at the election have been granted), together with the addresses provided by them in their applications under that paragraph or, as the case may be, sub-paragraph (2) as the addresses to which their ballot papers are to be sent, and

    (b) a list ("the list of proxies") of those whose applications under this paragraph to vote by proxy at the election have been granted or who are for the time being shown in the record kept under paragraph 1 as voting by proxy, together with the names and addresses of those appointed as their proxies.

(5) A person applying to vote by post must provide an address in the United Kingdom as the address to which his ballot paper is to be sent.

Proxies at local elections

3.—(1) Subject to the provisions of this paragraph, any person is capable of being appointed proxy to vote for another (in this paragraph and paragraph 4 referred to as "the elector") at any local election and may vote in pursuance of the appointment.

(2) A person is not capable of being appointed to vote, or voting, as proxy at a local election—

    (a) if he is subject to any legal incapacity (age apart) to vote at the election as an elector, or

    (b) if he is neither a Commonwealth citizen nor a citizen of the Republic of Ireland.

(3) A person is not capable of voting as proxy at any such election unless on the date of the poll he has attained the age of eighteen.

(4) A person is not entitled to vote as proxy at the same local election in any district electoral area on behalf of more than two electors of whom that person is not the husband, wife, parent, grandparent, brother, sister, child or grandchild.

(5) Where the elector applies to the Chief Electoral Officer for the appointment of a proxy to vote for him at local elections for an indefinite period, the Chief Electoral

Officer shall make the appointment if the application meets the requirements set out in paragraphs 5 to 11 and he is satisfied that the elector is or will be—

    (a) registered in the register of local electors, and

    (b) shown in the record kept under paragraph 1 as voting by proxy at local elections,

and that the proxy is capable of being and willing to be appointed to vote as proxy at such elections.

(6) Where the elector applies to the Chief Electoral Officer for the appointment of a proxy to vote for him at a particular local election, the Chief Electoral Officer shall make the appointment if the application meets the requirements set out in paragraphs 5 to 11 and he is satisfied that the elector is or will be—

    (a) registered in the register of local electors, and

    (b) entitled to vote by proxy at that election by virtue of an application under paragraph 2,

and that the proxy is capable of being and willing to be appointed.

(7) The appointment of the proxy under this paragraph is to be made by means of a proxy paper in the form in the Appendix to this Part, or a form to the like effect, issued by the Chief Electoral Officer.

(8) The appointment may be cancelled by the elector by giving notice to the Chief Electoral Officer and shall also cease to be in force on the issue of a proxy paper appointing a different person to vote for him at a local election or local elections in the same district electoral area.

(9) Subject to sub-paragraph (8) the appointment shall remain in force—

    (a) in the case of an appointment for a particular election, for that election, and

    (b) in any other case, while the elector is shown as voting by proxy in the record kept under paragraph 1 in pursuance of the same application under that paragraph.

Voting as proxy

4.—(1) A person entitled to vote as proxy at a local election may do so in person at the polling station allotted to the elector under the local elections rules unless he is entitled to vote by post as proxy for the elector at the election, in which case he may vote by post.

(2) Where a person in entitled to vote by post as proxy for the elector at any election, the elector may not apply for a ballot paper for the purpose of voting in person at the election.

(3) For the purposes of this Order and the Act of 1962, a person entitled to vote as proxy for another at a local election is entitled so to vote by post if he is included in the list kept under sub-paragraph (8) in respect of the election.

(4) Where a person applies to the Chief Electoral Officer to vote by post as proxy at local elections for an indefinite period, the Chief Electoral Officer shall (subject to sub-paragraphs (9) and (11)) grant the application if—

    (a) the applicant is included in the record kept under paragraph 1 in respect of the district electoral area, or

    (b) the address provided by the applicant in his application as the address to which his ballot paper is to be sent is not in the same ward as the elector's qualifying address,

and the application meets the requirements set out in paragraphs 5 to 11.

(5) The Chief Electoral Officer shall keep a record of those whose applications under sub-paragraph (4) have been granted showing the addresses provided by them in their applications as the addresses to which their ballot papers are to be sent.

(6) Where a person applies to the Chief Electoral Officer to vote by post as proxy at a particular election and the application meets the requirements set out in paragraphs 5 to

11, the Chief Electoral Officer shall (subject to sub-paragraphs (9) and (11)) grant the application if—

    (a) he is satisfied that the applicant's circumstances on the date of the poll will be or are likely to be such that he cannot reasonably be expected to vote in person at the polling station allotted or likely to be allotted to the elector under the local elections rules, or

    (b) the applicant is, or the Chief Electoral Officer is satisfied that he will be, included in respect of the district electoral area in the absent voters lists for that election.

(7) Where, in the case of a particular election, a person included in the record kept under sub-paragraph (5) applies to the Chief Electoral Officer for his ballot paper to be sent to a different address in the United Kingdom, the Chief Electoral Officer shall grant the application if it meets the requirements set out in paragraphs 5 to 11.

(8) The Chief Electoral Officer shall, in respect of each local election keep a special list of—

    (a) those who are for the time being included in the record kept under sub-paragraph (5), together with the addresses provided by them in their applications under that sub-paragraph or, as the case may be, sub-paragraph (7) as the addresses to which their ballot papers are to be sent, and

    (b) those whose applications under sub-paragraph (6) have been granted in respect of the election concerned, together with the addresses provided by them in their applications as the addresses to which their ballot papers are to be sent.

(9) The Chief Electoral Officer shall not grant any application under this paragraph unless—

    (a) he is satisfied that the elector is or will be registered in the register of local electors, and

    (b) there is in force an appointment of the applicant as the elector's proxy to vote for him at local elections or, as the case may be, the election concerned.

(10) The Chief Electoral Officer shall remove a person from the record kept under sub-paragraph (5)—

    (a) if he applies to the Chief Electoral Officer to be removed,

    (b) where he was included in the record on the ground mentioned in sub-paragraph (4)(a), if he ceases to be included in any record kept under paragraph 1 in respect of the district electoral area or becomes so included in pursuance of a further application under that paragraph,

    (c) if the elector ceases to be registered as mentioned in sub-paragraph (9)(a), or

    (d) if the appointment of the person concerned as the elector's proxy ceases to be in force (whether or not he is re-appointed).

(11) A person applying to vote by post as proxy must provide an address in the United Kingdom as the address to which his ballot paper is to be sent.

General requirements for applications

5.—(1) Applications under paragraph 1, 2, 3 or 4 shall, in addition to the address which is required by paragraph 1(6), 2(5) or 4(11) (as the case may be) in the case of a person applying to vote by post, state:—

    (a) the applicant's full name,

    (b) except in the case of an application under paragraph 4, the address in respect of which the applicant is or will be registered in the register,

    (c) in the case of an application under paragraph 4, the address of the applicant, together with the name of the elector for whom he acts as proxy and the address of that elector for the purposes of paragraph (b), and

    (d) in the case of an application under paragraph 1(1), 2(1), 4(4) or (6), the grounds on which the applicant claims to be entitled to an absent vote;

and the application shall be signed by the applicant.

For the purposes of paragraph (b), the address in respect of which the applicant is or will be registered includes, in the case of a service elector, the address at which he would be resident but for his service as a member of the forces or employment as a Crown servant.

(2) An application to vote by proxy under paragraph 1(1) or (5) or 2(1) or (2) shall include an application for the appointment of a proxy which meets the requirements of paragraph 9.

(3) An application under this Part to the Chief Electoral Officer shall be made in writing and sent by post or delivered to his office or to the address specified by him for the purpose.

(4) An application under paragraph 1, 2, 3 or 4 shall comply with such further requirements of this Part as applies to such an application and with the requirements as to time set out in paragraph 11.

Additional requirements for applications on grounds of physical incapacity

6.—(1) An application under paragraph 1(2)(b) shall specify the physcial incapacity by reason of which the application is made.

(2) Subject to sub-paragraph (4), such an application shall be attested and signed by—
  (a) a registered medical practitioner;
  (b) a first level nurse trained in general nursing registered in Part I of the register maintained under section 10(1) of the Nurses, Midwives and Health Visitors Act 1979(**a**) in accordance with Article 2 of, and Schedule 1 to, the Nurses, Midwives and Health Visitors (Parts of the Register) Order 1983(**b**);
  (c) a Christian Science practitioner;
  (d) in the case of an application in which the applicant states that he is registered in a home for persons in need within the meaning of the definition in Article 2(2) of the Health and Personal Social Services (Northern Ireland) Order 1972(**c**) or a nursing home within the meaning of the definition in section 10(1) of the Nursing Homes and Nursing Agencies Act (Northern Ireland) 1971(**d**) which is required to be registered under Schedule 5 to that Order or Part I of that Act, as the case may be, by the person registered under that Order or that Act respectively as carrying on that home;
  (e) in the case of an application in which the applicant states that he is resident in residential accommodation provided under Article 15 of the Health and Personal Social Services (Northern Ireland) Order 1972, by the officer in charge of that accommodation; or
  (f) in the case of an application in which the applicant states that he resides in premises forming part of a group of premises—
    (i) which are provided for persons of pensionable age or physically disabled persons, and
    (ii) for which there is a resident warden,
    by that warden.

(3) The person attesting the application under sub-paragraph (2) shall state—
  (a) his name and address and the qualification by virtue of which he is authorised to attest the application;
  (b) that, to the best of his knowledge and belief, the applicant is suffering from the physical incapacity specified in the application and that he cannot reasonably be expected to go in person to his allotted polling station or to vote unaided there, by reason of that incapacity; and
  (c) that to the best of his knowledge and belief, the physical incapacity specified in the application is likely to continue either indefinitely or for a period specified by the person attesting the application.

(**a**) 1979 c.36.
(**b**) S.I. 1983/667.
(**c**) S.I. 1972/1265 (N.I. 14); that definition was repealed in part by the Health and Personal Social Services (Northern Ireland) Order 1978 (S.I. 1978/1907 (N.I. 26)), Schedule 2.
(**d**) 1971 c.32 (N.I.); that definition was repealed in part by the Health and Personal Social Services (Northern Ireland) Order 1972, Schedule 18.

(4) Sub-paragraphs (2) and (3) shall not apply where—
  (a) the application is based on the applicant's blindness and the applicant is registered as a blind person by a Health and Social Services Board, which is specified in the application, or
  (b) the applicant is in receipt of a mobility allowance under section 37A of the Social Security (Northern Ireland) Act 1975(a) and the reference number of such an allowance is set out in the application.

(5) The fact that an applicant is either—
  (a) registered with a Health and Social Services Board as a blind person, or
  (b) in receipt of a mobility allowance,

shall be deemed sufficient evidence that he is eligible for an absent vote on the grounds set out in paragraph 1(2)(b).

(6) In this paragraph and paragraphs 7 and 8 "his allotted polling station", in relation to an elector, means the polling station allotted or likely to be allotted to him under the local elections rules.

Additional requirements for applications based on occupation, service or employment
7.—(1) An application under paragraph 1(2)(c) shall state—
  (a) whether the occupation, service or employment, in respect of which it is made, is that of the applicant or his spouse;
  (b) the nature of the occupation, service or employment in respect of which it is made;
  (c) where the person in respect of whose occupation, service or employment it is made (in this paragraph referred to as "the employed person") is self-employed, that fact; and in any other case the name of that person's employer;
  (d) why the applicant cannot reasonably be expected to go in person to his allotted polling station (within the meaning of paragraph 6(6)) by reason of the general nature of the occupation, service or employment referred to in paragraph (b).

(2) Such an application shall be attested and signed—
  (a) where the employed person is self-employed, by a person who—
    (i) is aged 18 years or over;
    (ii) resides in the United Kingdom;
    (iii) knows the employed person; and
    (iv) is not related to him, and
  (b) in any other case, by the employer of the employed person or by another employee to whom this function is designated by the employer.

For the purposes of paragraph (a) above and paragraph (i) of sub-paragraph (3), one person is related to another if he is the husband, wife, parent, grandparent, brother, sister, child or grandchild of the other.

(3) The person attesting an application under sub-paragraph (2) shall—
  (a) where the applicant is the employed person, certify that the statements included in the application in accordance with the requirements of paragraphs (a) to (d) of sub-paragraph (1) are true; or
  (b) where the applicant is the spouse of the employed person, certify that the statements included in the application in accordance with the requirements of paragraphs (a) to (c) of sub-paragraph (1) are true;

and in addition, he shall state:—
    (i) in the case of a person who attests an application under paragraph (a) of sub-paragraph (2), his name and address, and that he is aged 18 years or over, resides in the United Kingdom, knows the employed person, but is not related to him, or

---

(a) 1975 c.15; section 37A was inserted by Article 24(1) of the Social Security Pensions (Northern Ireland) Order 1975 (S.I. 1975/1503 (N.I. 15)).

(ii) in the case of a person who attests an application under paragraph (b) of that sub-paragraph, either that he is the employer of the employed person or the position he holds in the employment of that employer.

Additional requirements for applications in respect of a particular election

8.—(1) An application under paragraph 2(1) shall set out why the applicant's circumstances on the date of the poll for the election in respect of which it is made will be or are likely to be such that he cannot reasonably be expected to vote in person at his allotted polling station (within the meaning of paragraph 6(6)).

(2) Except in respect of an application to which sub-paragraph (4) applies, such an application shall be signed and attested by a person who—

    (a) is aged 18 years or over,

    (b) resides in the United Kingdom,

    (c) knows the applicant but is not related to him, and

    (d) has not attested under this sub-paragraph any other application in respect of the election for which the application he attests is made.

For the purposes of paragraph (c) above and paragraph (d) of sub-paragraph (3), one person is related to another if he is the husband, wife, parent, grandparent, brother, sister, child or grandchild of the other.

(3) The person attesting an application under sub-paragraph (2) shall state—

    (a) his full name and address,

    (b) that he is aged 18 years or over,

    (c) that he resides in the United Kingdom,

    (d) that he knows the applicant, but is not related to him, and

    (e) that he has not attested under sub-paragraph (2) any other application in respect of the election for which the application he attests is made;

and shall certify that, to the best of his knowledge and belief, the statement included in the application in accordance with the requirements of sub-paragraph (1) is true.

(4) This sub-paragraph applies in respect of an application under paragraph 2(1) which—

    (a) states that it is made on the grounds that the applicant cannot reasonably be expected to vote in person at his allotted polling station (within the meaning of paragraph 6(6)) because he will be or is likely to be physically ill on the date of the poll,

    (b) specifies that illness, and

    (c) is attested and signed by one of the persons specified in paragraphs (a), (b) and (c) of paragraph 6(2).

(5) The person attesting the application under sub-paragraph (4) shall state—

    (a) his name and address and the qualification by virtue of which he is authorised to attest it; and

    (b) that, to the best of his knowledge and belief, the applicant is suffering from the physical illness specified in the application, that he will be or is likely to be so suffering on the date of the poll, and that he cannot reasonably be expected to vote in person at his allotted polling station by reason of that illness.

Additional requirements for applications for appointment of a proxy

9. An application for the appointment of a proxy under paragraph 3(5) or (6) shall state the full name and address of the person whom the applicant wishes to appoint as his proxy, together with his family relationship, if any, with the applicant, and—

    (a) if it is signed only by the applicant, shall contain a statement by him that he has consulted the person so named and that that person is capable of being and willing to be appointed as his proxy, or

    (b) if it is also signed by the person to be appointed, shall contain a statement by that person that he is capable of being and willing to be appointed to vote as the applicant's proxy.

Additional requirements for applications by proxies to vote by post at a particular election

10.   An application under paragraph 4(6) shall set out why the applicant's circumstances on the date of the poll for the election in respect of which it is made will be or are likely to be such that he cannot reasonably be expected to vote in person at the polling station allotted or likely to be allotted to the elector under the local elections rules.

Closing dates for applications

11.—(1) An application—

    (a) to vote by post or proxy under paragraph 1(1);

    (b) by an absent voter to alter his choice as to the manner of absent voting under paragraph 1(5);

    (c) for the appointment of a proxy under paragraph 3(5); or

    (d) from a proxy to vote by post under paragraph 4(4),

shall be disregarded for the purposes of any particular election if it is received by the Chief Electoral Officer after noon on the thirteenth day before the date of the poll at that election.

(2)   Subject to sub-paragraphs (3) and (4), an application—

    (a) to vote by post or proxy under paragraph 2(1);

    (b) by a postal voter for his ballot paper to be sent to a different address or to vote instead by proxy at a particular election under paragraph 2(2);

    (c) for the appointment of a proxy under paragraph 3(6);

    (d) from a proxy to vote by post under paragraph 4(6); or

    (e) from a postal proxy for his ballot paper to be sent to a different address at a particular election under paragraph 4(7),

shall be disallowed if it is received by the Chief Electoral Officer after noon on the thirteenth day before the date of the poll at the election for which it was made.

(3) Sub-paragraph (2) shall not apply to an application—

    (a) to which sub-paragraph (4) of paragraph 8 applies and which is attested in accordance with sub-paragraph (5) of that paragraph, and

    (b) in which, in addition to those requirements, the applicant states that on the thirteenth day before the date of the poll at the election for which the application is made (calculated in accordance with sub-paragraph (6)) he could not reasonably have foreseen that he would be or was likely to be physcially ill on the date of the poll and the attester states that, so far as he is aware, that statement is true;

and such an application shall be disallowed if it is received by the Chief Electoral Officer after noon on the sixth day before the date of the poll at the election for which it was made.

(4) Sub-paragraph (2) shall not apply to an application to vote by post or proxy under paragraph 2(1) in which the applicant's circumstances on the date of the poll for the election in respect of which it is made are stated to be his employment, either as a constable or by the Chief Electoral Officer, on that date for a purpose connected with that election; and such an application may be disallowed if it is received by the Chief Electoral Officer after noon on the thirteenth day before that date.

(5) An application—

    (a) under paragraph 1(4)(a), by an elector to be removed from the record kept under paragraph 1(3), and

    (b) under paragraph 4(10)(a), by a proxy to be removed from the record kept under paragraph 4(5), and

a notice under paragraph 3(8) of the cancellation of a proxy's appointment may be disregarded for the purposes of any particular election if it is received by the Chief Electoral Officer after noon on the thirteenth day before the date of the poll at that election.

(6) In computing a period of days for the purposes of this paragraph, Saturday, Sunday, Christmas Eve, Maundy Thursday or a public holiday shall be disregarded.

Grant or refusal of applications

12.—(1) Where the Chief Electoral Officer grants an application under paragraph 1, 2, 3 or 4 he shall, where practicable, notify the applicant of his decision.

(2) Where the Chief Electoral Officer disallows an application under paragraph 1, 2, 3 or 4 he shall notify the applicant of his decision and shall date such notification.

(3) Where under paragraph 11(1) or (5) the Chief Electoral Officer disregards an application for the purposes of any particular election, he shall, where practicable, notify the applicant of this.

Cancellation of proxy appointment

13. Where the appointment of a proxy is cancelled by notice given to the Chief Electoral Officer under paragraph 3(8) or ceases to be in force under that provision or is no longer in force under paragraph 3(9)(b), the Chief Electoral Officer shall—

(a) notify the person whose appointment as proxy has been cancelled or ceases to be or is no longer in force, unless the Chief Electoral Officer has previously been notified by that person that he no longer wishes to act as proxy, and

(b) remove his name from the record kept under paragraph 1(3)(c).

Inquiries by Chief Electoral Officer

14.—(1) The Chief Electoral Officer may, at such times as he thinks fit, make inquiries of a person—

(a) who is shown in the record kept under sub-paragraph (3) of paragraph 1 by virtue of an application under that paragraph on the grounds set out in sub-paragraph (2)(b) or (c) of that paragraph, or

(b) who immediately before 16th February 1987 was entitled to vote by post or by proxy for an indefinite period at local elections by virtue of his entitlement so to vote at parliamentary elections where that entitlement was based on the grounds set out in paragraphs (b)(i), (c) or (h) of section 19(1) of the Representation of the People Act 1983(a) and in respect of whom paragraph 1 has effect, by virtue of Article 6(1) of the Local Elections (Northern Ireland) (Amendment) Order 1987, as if an application under that paragraph so to vote had been granted on the date of the coming into force of that paragraph 1,

for the purpose of determining whether there has been a material change of circumstances.

(2) In the case of a person—

(a) who is shown in the record kept under sub-paragraph (3) of paragraph 1 by virtue of an application under that paragraph on the grounds set out in sub-paragraph (2)(c) of that paragraph, or

(b) to whom sub-paragraph (1)(b) applies and whose application to be treated as an absent voter was based on the ground set out in paragraph (b)(i) or (h) (general nature of applicant's occupation, service or employment or that of his spouse) of section 19(1) of the Representation of the People Act 1983,

the Chief Electoral Officer shall make the inquiries referred to in sub-paragraph (1) not later than three years after the date of the granting of the application or the last such inquiries, as the case may be.

In respect of a person to whom sub-paragraph (1)(b) applies, 16th February 1987 shall be treated as the date of the granting of the application.

(3) The Chief Electoral Officer may treat the failure by a person of whom inquiries have been made under sub-paragraph (1) or (2) to respond to such inquiries within one month of the date on which they were made as sufficient evidence of a material change in circumstances.

(a) 1983 c.2.

Records and lists kept under paragraphs 1, 2 and 4

15.—(1) Subject to the provisions of this paragraph, the records kept under paragraphs 1(3) and 4(5) and the lists kept under paragraphs 2(4) and 4(8) shall be in such form as the Chief Electoral Officer thinks fit.

(2) In that part of the absent voters list referred to in paragraph 2(4)(a), the address to which the ballot paper is to be sent to a person who is entitled to vote by post as an elector shall be placed on the right hand side of his name and electoral number.

(3) In that part of the absent voters list referred to in paragraph 2(4)(b) (the list of proxies), the name and address of the proxy shall be placed on the right hand side of the elector's name and electoral number.

(4) In the list kept under paragraph 4(8) (those proxies who are entitled to vote by post), the name of the proxy, together with the address to which his ballot paper is to be sent, shall be placed on the right hand side of the elector's name and electoral number.

(5) The Chief Electoral Officer shall make available for inspection at his office during ordinary office hours a copy of the records kept under paragraphs 1(3) and 4(5).

(6) As soon as practicable after the day referred to in paragraph 11(1), the Chief Electoral Officer shall publish the lists kept under paragraphs 2(4) and 4(8) by making a copy of them available for inspection at his office during ordinary office hours; and he shall continue to make a copy of those lists so available until the date of the poll.

(7) As soon as practicable after the publication of the lists referred to in sub-paragraph (6) above, the Chief Electoral Officer shall, on request, supply free of charge a copy of them to each candidate or his election agent:

Provided that, if such a request is made before any issue of postal ballot papers, he shall before that issue supply a copy of those lists or so much of them as relates to that issue.

(8) In this paragraph, "electoral number" means a person's number in the register to be used at the election or, pending publication of the register, his number (if any) in the electors lists for that register.

Marked register for polling stations

16. To indicate that an elector or his proxy is entitled to vote by post and is for that reason not entitled to vote in person, the letter "A" shall be placed against the name of that elector in any copy of the register, or part of it, provided for a polling station.

Forms

17. The Chief Electoral Officer shall supply free of charge as many copies of forms for use in connection with applications made under paragraph 1, 2, 3 or 4 as appear to that Officer reasonable in the circumstances to any person who satisfies that Officer of his intention to use the forms in connection with an election.

Notifications

18. Where the Chief Electoral Officer is required by a provision in this Part to notify any person, such notification shall be in writing and may be sent by post—

(a) in the case of a person other than a service elector, to the address provided by that person for the purpose of such notification or of any record, or if there is no such address, to the last known place of abode of that person;

(b) in the case of a service elector, to any address provided by him for the purpose of such notification or of any record or to the address provided for the purpose by the appropriate Government department (within the meaning of section 59(3) of the Representation of the People Act 1983).

Publication of documents

19.—(1) Any failure to publish a document in accordance with this Part shall not invalidate the document, but this provision shall not relieve the Chief Electoral Officer from any penalty for such a failure.

(2) Where a document is made available for inspection, any person may make a copy of, or take extracts from, such document.

APPENDIX

Form of proxy paper

District electoral area ....

Polling district...

Name of Proxy..

Address..

....

is hereby appointed as proxy for

(Name of elector)...

who is qualified to be registered for

(Qualifying address)..

to vote for him/her at

*[the local election for the above district electoral area on (date)...................................]

*[any local election for the above district electoral area]

*[This proxy appointment is not valid until ....]

Signature...

*Delete whichever is   Chief Electoral Officer
inappropriate

Address...

....

....

Date..

Your Right to Vote as Proxy

1.   This proxy paper gives you the right to vote as proxy on behalf of the elector whose name is given above.

2.   Your appointment as proxy may be for a particular election only, or it may be for an indefinite period. If it is for a particular election, you have the right to vote as proxy only at the election specified in the proxy paper. If it is for an indefinite period, you have the right to vote as proxy at any local election until the Chief Electoral Officer informs you to the contrary.

3.   When the elector applied for you to be appointed as proxy EITHER he or she was asked to state that he or she had consulted you and that you were capable of being and willing to be appointed as proxy OR you signed a statement stating that you were capable of being and willing to be appointed. You are capable of being appointed as proxy if you are at least 18 years old on polling day, a British or other Commonwealth citizen or a citizen of the Republic of Ireland and not for any reason disqualified from voting. If for some reason you are not capable of being, or willing to be, appointed as proxy, please write to the elector asking him to cancel the appointment.

4.   You may vote as proxy at the polling station allotted to the elector on whose behalf you are appointed. However, you may not vote as proxy at the same election for more than two electors of whom you are not the husband, wife, parent, grandparent, brother, sister, child or grandchild. Shortly before polling day you will be sent a proxy poll card telling you where the polling station is. You do not need to take either the poll card or this proxy paper to the polling station but you may find it helpful to do so. Remember that the elector may still vote in person. If he or she applies for a ballot paper at the polling station before you do you will not be able to vote as proxy on his or her behalf.

5.   If you cannot vote in person at the polling station the Chief Electoral Officer may be able to allow you to vote as proxy by post. If your appointment is for an indefinite period, you may apply to vote by post throughout the period your appointment is in force if you live in a different ward from the elector's qualifying address. If you are registered for the same ward as the elector, you may apply if you are entitled to vote by post or proxy on your own behalf. In addition, you may vote by post at a particular election if the Chief Electoral Officer is satisfied that you cannot reasonably be expected to vote in person at the elector's polling station. But the Chief Electoral Officer cannot allow an application to vote by post at a particular election if he receives it after midday on the thirteenth working day before the poll.".

Article 5(7)

SCHEDULE 3

Amendments to Part III of Schedule 2 to the Local Elections
(Northern Ireland) Order 1985

1. In paragraph 1 (interpretation) after the definition of "issue" there shall be inserted the following definition:—

" 'list of postal proxies' means the list kept under paragraph 4(8) of Part I of this Schedule (as substituted by Schedule 2 to the Local Elections (Northern Ireland) (Amendment) Order 1987);".

2. For paragraph 4 (declaration of secrecy) there shall be substituted the following paragraph:

"Notification of requirement of secrecy

4. The returning officer shall make such arrangements as he thinks fit to ensure that every person attending the proceedings in connection with the issue and receipt of postal ballot papers has been given a copy in writing of the provisions of paragraph 27(4) of Schedule 9 to the Act of 1962 and a statement of the penalty prescribed by section 111(2A)(d) of that Act (as inserted by paragraph 27 of Schedule 1 to the Local Elections (Northern Ireland) (Amendment) Order 1987).".

3. In paragraph 6(1) (marking of postal ballot paper) for the words "list of postal voters" there shall be substituted "absent voters list".

4. In paragraph 7 (refusal to issue postal ballot paper) for the words from "the list of postal voters" to "list of proxies" there shall be substituted "either the absent voters list or the list of postal proxies or in each of those lists relate to the same elector".

5. In paragraph 11 (sealing up of special lists and counterfoils) for the words "list of postal voters", in each place where those words occur, there shall be substituted "absent voters list and of the list of postal proxies".

EXPLANATORY NOTE

(This note is not part of the Order)

This Order amends the Electoral Law Act (Northern Ireland) 1962 ("the 1962 Act") and the Local Elections (Northern Ireland) Order 1985 ("the 1985 Order") to make changes to the law in respect of local elections in Northern Ireland equivalent to those changes in respect of parliamentary elections which were made by the Representation of the People Act 1985 (c.50) ("the 1985 Act").

Schedule 1 to this Order includes amendments to the 1962 Act equivalent to those made to the Representation of the People Act 1983 (c.2) ("the 1983 Act") by sections 14 and 19 of, and Schedules 2, 3, 4 and 5 to, the 1985 Act. In addition, paragraph 41 of that Schedule amends the list of documents, one of which must be produced at a polling station before a ballot paper can be delivered to a voter; the amendment corresponds to that made for parliamentary elections by Regulation 13 of the Representation of the People (Northern Ireland) Regulations 1986 (S.I. 1986/1091) ("the 1986 Regulations"). Paragraph 50 of that Schedule (together with paragraphs 46 to 49) makes provision for voting offences at local elections in Northern Ireland equivalent to that made for such offences at parliamentary elections there by section 61 of the 1983 Act (as amended by the Elections (Northern Ireland) Act 1985 (c.2) and the 1985 Act). Paragraph 54 of that Schedule disapplies an offence which is already repealed as respects parliamentary elections.

Schedule 2 to this Order replaces the provisions about entitlement to vote by post or by proxy in Part I of Schedule 2 to the 1985 Order. The new provisions correspond to the provisions in respect of parliamentary elections made by sections 6 to 9 of the 1985 Act and Part IV of the 1986 Regulations. The absent voting forms prescribed by Part II of Schedule 2 to the 1985 Order are revoked by Article 5(6) of this Order because the new provisions set out the contents of applications to vote by post or by proxy or by post as proxy but do not prescribe forms as such.

Schedule 3 to this Order makes consequential amendments to Part III of Schedule 2 to the 1985 Order, which concerns the procedure on the issue and receipt of postal ballot papers. It also replaces the requirement to make a declaration of secrecy before attending such proceedings with a duty on the returning officer to notify persons so attending of the requirement of secrecy.

STATUTORY INSTRUMENTS

1987 No. 169

INCOME TAX

The Double Taxation Relief (Taxes on Income) (Ivory Coast) Order 1987

Made - - - *10th February 1987*

At the Court at Buckingham Palace, the 10th day of February 1987

Present

The Queen's Most Excellent Majesty in Council

Whereas a draft of this Order was laid before the House of Commons in accordance with the provisions of section 497(8) of the Income and Corporation Taxes Act 1970(**a**), and an Address has been presented to Her Majesty by that House praying that an Order may be made in the terms of that draft:

Now, therefore, Her Majesty, in exercise of the powers conferred upon Her by section 497 of the said Income and Corporation Taxes Act 1970, and of all other powers enabling Her in that behalf, is pleased, by and with the advice of Her Privy Council, to order, and it is hereby ordered, as follows:—

1. This Order may be cited as the Double Taxation Relief (Taxes on Income) (Ivory Coast) Order 1987.

2. It is hereby declared—

(a) that the arrangements specified in the Convention set out in the Schedule to this Order have been made with the Government of the Republic of the Ivory Coast with a view to affording relief from double taxation in relation to income tax, corporation tax or capital gains tax and taxes of a similar character imposed by the laws of the Ivory Coast; and

(b) that it is expedient that those arrangements should have effect.

G. I. de Deney
Clerk of the Privy Council

(**a**) 1970 c.10; section 497 was amended and extended by sections 98(2) and 100(1) of the Finance Act 1972 (c.41) and section 10 of the Capital Gains Tax Act 1979 (c.14).

SCHEDULE

CONVENTION BETWEEN THE GOVERNMENT OF THE UNITED KINGDOM OF
GREAT BRITAIN AND NORTHERN IRELAND AND THE GOVERNMENT OF THE
REPUBLIC OF THE IVORY COAST FOR THE AVOIDANCE OF DOUBLE TAXATION
AND THE PREVENTION OF FISCAL EVASION WITH RESPECT TO TAXES ON INCOME
AND CAPITAL GAINS

The Government of the United Kingdom of Great Britain and Northern
Ireland and the Government of the Republic of the Ivory Coast;

Desiring to conclude a Convention for the avoidance of double taxation and
the prevention of fiscal evasion with respect to taxes on income and capital
gains;

Have agreed as follows:

ARTICLE 1

Personal scope

This Convention shall apply to persons who are residents of one or both of
the Contracting States.

ARTICLE 2

Taxes covered

(1) This Convention shall apply to taxes on income and on capital gains
imposed by a Contracting State irrespective of the manner in which they are
levied.

(2) There shall be regarded as taxes on income and on capital gains all taxes
imposed on total income, on total capital gains, or on elements of income or of
capital gains, including taxes on gains from the alienation of movable or
immovable property, as well as taxes on capital appreciation.

(3) The existing taxes which are the subject of this Convention are:
   (a) in the United Kingdom of Great Britain and Northern Ireland:
      (i) the income tax;
      (ii) the corporation tax; and
      (iii) the capital gains tax;
      (hereinafter referred to as "United Kingdom tax");
   (b) in the Republic of the Ivory Coast:
      (i) the tax on industrial and commercial profits and on agricultural
      profits (l'impôt sur les bénéfices industriels et commerciaux et sur
      les bénéfices agricoles);
      (ii) the tax on non-commercial profits (l'impôt sur les bénéfices non
      commerciaux);

(iii) the tax on salaries and wages (l'impôt sur les traitements et salaires);

(iv) the tax on income from movable capital (l'impôt sur le revenu des capitaux mobiliers); and

(v) the general income tax (l'impôt général sur le revenu);

(hereinafter referred to as "Ivory Coast tax").

(4) This Convention shall also apply to any identical or substantially similar taxes which are imposed by either Contracting State after the date of signature of this Convention in addition to, or in place of, the existing taxes. The competent authorities of the Contracting States shall notify each other of any substantial changes which have been made in their respective taxation laws.

ARTICLE 3

General definitions

(1) For the purposes of this Convention, unless the context otherwise requires:

(a) the term "United Kingdom" means Great Britain and Northern Ireland, including any area outside the territorial sea of the United Kingdom which in accordance with international law has been or may hereafter be designated, under the laws of the United Kingdom concerning the Continental Shelf, as an area within which the rights of the United Kingdom with respect to the sea bed and subsoil and their natural resources may be exercised;

(b) the term "the Ivory Coast" means the national territory of the Republic of the Ivory Coast including any area outside the territorial sea of the Ivory Coast which in accordance with international law has been or may hereafter be designated, under the laws of the Ivory Coast concerning the Continental Shelf, as an area within which the rights of the Ivory Coast with respect to the sea bed and subsoil and their natural resources may be exercised;

(c) the term "national" means:

(i) in relation to the United Kingdom, any individual who has under the law in the United Kingdom the status of United Kingdom national, provided he has the right of abode in the United Kingdom; and any legal person, partnership, association or other entity deriving its status as such from the law in force in the United Kingdom;

(ii) in relation to the Ivory Coast, any individual who possesses Ivory Coast nationality and any legal person, partnership, association or other entity deriving its status as such from the law in force in the Ivory Coast;

(d) the terms "a Contracting State" and "the other Contracting State" mean the United Kingdom or the Ivory Coast, as the context requires;

(e) the term "person" comprises an individual, a company and any other body of persons;

I/1n*

(f) the term "company" means any body corporate or any entity which is treated as a body corporate for tax purposes;

(g) the terms "enterprise of a Contracting State" and "enterprise of the other Contracting State" mean respectively an enterprise carried on by a resident of a Contracting State and an enterprise carried on by a resident of the other Contracting State;

(h) the term "international traffic" means any transport by a ship or aircraft operated by an enterprise which has its place of effective management in a Contracting State, except when the ship or aircraft is operated solely between places in the other Contracting State;

(i) the term "competent authority" means, in the case of the United Kingdom the Commissioners of Inland Revenue or their authorised representative, and in the case of the Ivory Coast the Minister of Finance (Ministre des Finances) or his authorised representative.

(2) As regards the application of this Convention by a Contracting State any term not otherwise defined shall, unless the context otherwise requires, have the meaning which it has under the laws of that Contracting State relating to the taxes which are the subject of this Convention.

ARTICLE 4

Fiscal domicile

(1) For the purposes of this Convention, the term "resident of a Contracting State" means any person who, under the law of that State, is liable to tax therein by reason of his domicile, residence, place of management or any other criterion of a similar nature.

(2) Where by reason of the provisions of paragraph (1) of this Article an individual is a resident of both Contracting States, then his status shall be determined in accordance with the following rules:

(a) he shall be deemed to be a resident of the Contracting State in which he has a permanent home available to him; if he has a permanent home available to him in both States, he shall be deemed to be a resident of the State with which his personal and economic relations are closer (centre of vital interests);

(b) if the State in which he has his centre of vital interests cannot be determined, or if he has not a permanent home available to him in either State, he shall be deemed to be a resident of the State in which he has an habitual abode;

(c) if he has an habitual abode in both States or in neither of them, he shall be deemed to be a resident of the State of which he is a national;

(d) if he is a national of both States or of neither of them, the competent authorities of the Contracting States shall settle the question by mutual agreement.

(3) Where by reason of the provisions of paragraph (1) of this Article a person other than an individual is a resident of both Contracting States, then it shall be deemed to be a resident of the State in which its place of effective management is situated.

ARTICLE 5

Permanent establishment

(1) For the purposes of this Convention, the term "permanent establishment" means a fixed place of business through which the business of an enterprise is wholly or partly carried on.

(2) The term "permanent establishment" includes especially:

(a) a place of management;

(b) a branch;

(c) an office;

(d) a factory;

(e) a shop;

(f) a workshop;

(g) a mine, an oil or gas well, a quarry or any other place of extraction of natural resources; and

(h) a building site or temporary construction or assembly project or supervisory activities in connection therewith, where such site, temporary project or activities continue for a period of more than six months, or where such temporary project or activities, being incidental to the sale of machinery or equipment, continue for a period not exceeding six months and the charges payable for the temporary project or activities exceed 10 per cent of the sale price of the machinery or equipment.

(3) Notwithstanding the preceding provisions of this Article, the term "permanent establishment" shall be deemed not to include:

(a) the use of facilities solely for the purpose of storage or display of goods or merchandise belonging to the enterprise;

(b) the maintenance of a stock of goods or merchandise belonging to the enterprise solely for the purpose of storage or display;

(c) the maintenance of a stock of goods or merchandise belonging to the enterprise solely for the purpose of processing by another enterprise;

(d) the maintenance of a fixed place of business solely for the purpose of carrying on, for the enterprise, any other activity of a preparatory character.

(4) Notwithstanding the provisions of paragraphs (1) and (2) of this Article, where a person, other than an agent of an independent status to whom paragraph (6) of this Article applies, is acting in a Contracting State on behalf of an enterprise of the other Contracting State, that enterprise shall be deemed to have a permanent establishment in the first-mentioned State if the person:

(a) has and habitually exercises in that State an authority to conclude contracts on behalf of the enterprise; or

(b) has no such authority, but habitually maintains in the first-mentioned State a stock of goods or merchandise from which he regularly delivers goods or merchandise on behalf of the enterprise.

(5) An insurance enterprise of a Contracting State shall, except with regard to reinsurance, be deemed to have a permanent establishment in the other Contracting State if it collects premiums in the territory of that other State or insures risks situated in that territory through an employee or representative who does not enter into the category of persons referred to in paragraph (6) of this Article.

(6) An enterprise shall not be deemed to have a permanent establishment in a Contracting State merely because it carries on business in that State through a broker, general commission agent or any other agent of an independent status, provided that such a person is acting in the ordinary course of his business. However if such an agent is required to devote the whole or substantially the whole of his time to the business of the enterprise he shall not be considered as an independent agent within the meaning of this paragraph.

(7) The fact that a company which is a resident of a Contracting State controls or is controlled by a company which is a resident of the other Contracting State, or which carries on business in that other State (whether through a permanent establishment or otherwise), shall not of itself constitute either company a permanent establishment of the other.

ARTICLE 6

Income from immovable property

(1) Income derived by a resident of a Contracting State from immovable property (including income from agriculture or forestry) situated in the other Contracting State may be taxed in that other State.

(2) The term "immovable property" shall have the meaning which it has under the law of the Contracting State in which the property in question is situated. The term shall in any case include property accessory to immovable property, livestock and equipment used in agriculture and forestry, rights to which the provisions of general law respecting landed property apply, usufruct of immovable property and rights to variable or fixed payments as consideration for the working of, or the right to work, mineral deposits, sources and other natural resources; ships, boats and aircraft shall not be regarded as immovable property.

(3) The provisions of paragraph (1) of this Article shall apply to income derived from the direct use, letting, or use in any other form of immovable property.

(4) The provisions of paragraphs (1) and (3) of this Article shall also apply to the income from immovable property of an enterprise and to income from immovable property used for the performance of independent personal services.

ARTICLE 7

Business profits

(1) The profits of an enterprise of a Contracting State shall be taxable only in that State unless the enterprise carries on business in the other Contracting

State through a permanent establishment situated therein. If the enterprise carries on business as aforesaid, the profits of the enterprise may be taxed in the other State but only so much of them as is attributable to that permanent establishment.

(2) Where an enterprise of a Contracting State carries on business in the other Contracting State through a permanent establishment situated therein, there shall in each Contracting State be attributed to that permanent establishment the profits which it might be expected to make if it were a distinct and separate enterprise engaged in the same or similar activities under the same or similar conditions and dealing wholly independently with the enterprise of which it is a permanent establishment.

(3) In determining the profits of a permanent establishment, there shall be allowed as deductions expenses which are incurred for the purposes of the permanent establishment, including an allocation of executive and general administrative expenses incurred for the purposes of the enterprise as a whole, whether in the State in which the permanent establishment is situated or elsewhere, calculated in proportion to the turnover realised in each of the establishments of the enterprise or according to any other acceptable criterion.

(4) In so far as it has been customary in a Contracting State, according to its law, to determine the profits to be attributed to a permanent establishment on the basis of an apportionment of the total profits of the enterprise to its various parts, nothing in paragraph (2) of this Article shall preclude that Contracting State from determining the profits to be taxed by such an apportionment as may be customary; the method of apportionment adopted shall, however, be such that the result shall be in accordance with the principles of this Article.

(5) Where profits include items which are dealt with separately in other Articles of this Convention, then the provisions of those Articles shall not be affected by the provisions of this Article.

ARTICLE 8

Shipping and air transport

(1) Profits from the operation of ships or aircraft in international traffic shall be taxable only in the Contracting State in which the place of effective management of the enterprise is situated.

(2) If the place of effective management of a shipping enterprise is aboard a ship or boat, then it shall be deemed to be situated in the Contracting State in which the home harbour of the ship or boat is situated, or, if there is no such home harbour, in the Contracting State of which the operator of the ship or boat is a resident.

(3) The provisions of paragraph (1) of this Article shall also apply to profits from the participation in a pool, a joint business or an international operating agency.

With respect to profits derived by the air transport company Air-Afrique the provisions of this paragraph and of paragraph (1) of this Article shall only apply to the share of profits attributed to the Ivory Coast.

ARTICLE 9

Associated enterprises

(1) Where

(a) an enterprise of a Contracting State participates directly or indirectly in the management, control or capital of an enterprise of the other Contracting State; or

(b) the same persons participate directly or indirectly in the management, control or capital of an enterprise of a Contracting State and an enterprise of the other Contracting State;

and in either case conditions are made or imposed between the two enterprises in their commercial or financial relations which differ from those which would be made between independent enterprises, then any profits which would, but for those conditions, have accrued to one of the enterprises, but, by reason of those conditions, have not so accrued, may be included in the profits of that enterprise and taxed accordingly.

(2) Where a Contracting State includes in the profits of an enterprise of that State—and taxes accordingly—profits on which an enterprise of the other Contracting State has been charged to tax in that other State and the profits so included are profits which would have accrued to the enterprise of the first-mentioned State if the conditions made between the two enterprises had been those which would have been made between independent enterprises, then that other State shall make an appropriate adjustment to the amount of the tax charged therein on those profits. In determining such adjustment, due regard shall be had to the other provisions of this Convention and the competent authorities of the Contracting States shall if necessary consult each other.

ARTICLE 10

Dividends

(1) Dividends paid by a company which is a resident of a Contracting State to a resident of the other Contracting State may be taxed in that other State.

(2) However, such dividends may also be taxed in the Contracting State of which the company paying the dividends is a resident and according to the laws of that State, but if the recipient is the beneficial owner of the dividends, the tax so charged shall not exceed:

(a) 18 per cent of the gross amount of the dividends where these are paid by a company which is a resident of the Ivory Coast and which is exempt from tax on its profits or does not pay tax on its profits at the normal rates;

(b) 15 per cent of the gross amount of the dividends in all other cases.

The provisions of this paragraph shall not affect the taxation of the company in respect of the profits out of which the dividends are paid.

(3) The term "dividends" as used in this Article means income from shares, jouissance shares or jouissance rights, mining shares, founders' shares or other rights, not being debt-claims, participating in profits, as well as income from

other corporate rights which is subjected to the same taxation treatment as income from shares by the laws of the State of which the company making the distribution is a resident.

(4) The provisions of paragraphs (1) and (2) of this Article shall not apply if the beneficial owner of the dividends, being a resident of a Contracting State, carries on business in the other Contracting State of which the company paying the dividends is a resident, through a permanent establishment situated therein, or performs in that other State independent personal services from a fixed base situated therein, and the holding in respect of which the dividends are paid is effectively connected with such permanent establishment or fixed base. In such case, the provisions of Article 7 or of Article 15, as the case may be, shall apply.

(5) Where a company which is a resident of a Contracting State derives profits or income from the other Contracting State, that other State may not impose any tax on the dividends paid by the company, except insofar as such dividends are paid to a resident of that other State or insofar as the holding in respect of which the dividends are paid is effectively connected with a permanent establishment or a fixed base situated in that other State, nor subject the company's undistributed profits to a tax on undistributed profits, even if the dividends paid or the undistributed profits consist wholly or partly of profits or income arising in such other State.

ARTICLE 11

Interest

(1) Interest arising in a Contracting State and paid to a resident of the other Contracting State may be taxed in that other State.

(2) However, such interest may also be taxed in the Contracting State in which it arises, and according to the law of that State, but if the recipient is the beneficial owner of the interest the tax so charged shall not exceed 15 per cent of the gross amount of the interest.

(3) Notwithstanding the provisions of paragraph (2) of this Article, interest arising in a Contracting State shall be exempt from tax in that State if it is derived and beneficially owned by the Government of the other Contracting State or a local authority thereof or any agency or instrumentality wholly owned by that Government or local authority.

(4) The term "interest" as used in this Article means income from debt-claims of every kind, whether or not secured by mortgage, and whether or not carrying a right to participate in the debtor's profits, and in particular, income from government securities and income from bonds or debentures, as well as all other income assimilated to income from money lent by the taxation law of the State in which the income arises.

(5) The provisions of paragraphs (1) and (2) of this Article shall not apply if the beneficial owner of the interest, being a resident of a Contracting State, carries on business in the other Contracting State in which the interest arises, through a permanent establishment situated therein, or performs in that other State independent personal services from a fixed base situated therein, and the debt-claim in respect of which the interest is paid is effectively connected with

such permanent establishment or fixed base. In such case, the provisions of Article 7 or Article 15, as the case may be, shall apply.

(6) Interest shall be deemed to arise in a Contracting State when the payer is that state itself, a political subdivision, a local authority or a resident of that State. Where, however, the person paying the interest, whether he is a resident of a Contracting State or not, has in a Contracting State a permanent establishment or a fixed base in connection with which the indebtedness on which the interest is paid was incurred, and such interest is borne by that permanent establishment or fixed base, then such interest shall be deemed to arise in the State in which the permanent establishment or fixed base is situated.

(7) Where, by reason of a special relationship between the payer and the beneficial owner or between both of them and some other person, the amount of the interest paid exceeds, for whatever reason, the amount which would have been agreed upon by the payer and the beneficial owner in the absence of such relationship, the provisions of this Article shall apply only to the last-mentioned amount. In such case, the excess part of the payments shall remain taxable according to the law of each Contracting State, due regard being had to the other provisions of this Convention.

ARTICLE 12

Royalties

(1) Royalties arising in a Contracting State and paid to a resident of the other Contracting State may be taxed in that other State.

(2) However, such royalties may also be taxed in the Contracting State in which they arise and according to the law of that State, but if the recipient is the beneficial owner of the royalties the tax so charged shall not exceed 10 per cent of the gross amount of the royalties.

(3) The term "royalties" as used in this Article means payments of any kind received as a consideration for the use of, or the right to use, any copyright of literary, artistic or scientific work (including cinematograph films, and films or tapes for radio or television broadcasting), any patent, trade mark, design or model, plan, secret formula or process or for the use of, or the right to use agricultural, industrial, commercial or scientific equipment.

(4) The provisions of paragraphs (1) and (2) of this Article shall not apply if the beneficial owner of the royalties, being a resident of a Contracting State, carries on business in the other Contracting State in which the royalties arise, through a permanent establishment situated therein, or performs in that other State independent personal services from a fixed base situated therein, and the right or property in respect of which the royalties are paid is effectively connected with such permanent establishment or fixed base. In such case, the provisions of Article 7 or Article 15, as the case may be, shall apply.

(5) Royalties shall be deemed to arise in a Contracting State when the payer is that State itself, a political subdivision, a local authority or a resident of that State. Where, however, the person paying the royalties, whether he is a resident of a Contracting State or not, has in a Contracting State a permanent establishment or a fixed base in connection with which the contract giving rise

to the payment of the royalties was concluded and the royalties are borne by that permanent establishment or fixed base, then the royalties shall be deemed to arise in the State in which the permanent establishment or fixed base is situated.

(6) Where, by reason of a special relationship between the payer and the beneficial owner or between both of them and some other person, the amount of the royalties, having regard to the use, right or information for which they are paid, exceeds the amount which would have been agreed upon by the payer and the beneficial owner in the absence of such relationship, the provisions of this Article shall apply only to the last-mentioned amount. In such case, the excess part of the payments shall remain taxable according to the laws of each Contracting State, due regard being had to the other provisions of this Convention.

ARTICLE 13

Management fees

(1) Management fees arising in a Contracting State and paid to a resident of the other Contracting State may be taxed in that other State.

(2) However, such management fees may also be taxed in the Contracting State in which they arise, and according to the law of that State, but if the recipient is the beneficial owner of the management fees the tax so charged shall not exceed 10 per cent of the gross amount of the management fees.

(3) The term "management fees" as used in this Article means payments of any kind to any person, other than to an employee of the person making the payments, in consideration for any services of a managerial, technical or consultancy nature.

(4) The provisions of paragraphs (1) and (2) of this Article shall not apply if the beneficial owner of the management fees, being a resident of a Contracting State, carries on business in the other Contracting State in which the management fees arise through a permanent establishment situated therein, or performs in that other State independent personal services from a fixed base situated therein, and the obligation in respect of which the management fees are paid is effectively connected with such permanent establishment or fixed base. In such case the provisions of Article 7 or Article 15, as the case may be, shall apply.

(5) A resident of one of the Contracting States who derives and beneficially owns management fees which arise in the other Contracting State may elect, for any year of assessment or financial year, that the tax chargeable in respect of those management fees in the Contracting State in which they arise shall be calculated as if he had a permanent establishment or fixed base in the last-mentioned Contracting State and as if those management fees were taxable in accordance with Article 7 or Article 15, as the case may be, as profits attributable to that permanent establishment or fixed base.

(6) Management fees shall be deemed to arise in a Contracting State when the payer is that State itself, a political subdivision, a local authority or a resident of that State. Where, however, the person paying the management fees, whether he is a resident of a Contracting State or not, has in a Contracting

State a permanent establishment or a fixed base in connection with which the obligation to pay the management fees was incurred, and where such management fees are borne by such permanent establishment or fixed base, then such management fees shall be deemed to arise in the Contracting State in which the permanent establishment or fixed base is situated.

(7) Where, by reason of a special relationship between the payer and the beneficial owner or between both of them and some other person, the amount of the management fees paid exceeds, for whatever reason, the amount which would have been agreed upon by the payer and the beneficial owner in the absence of such relationship, the provisions of this Article shall apply only to the last-mentioned amount. In such case, the excess part of the payments shall remain taxable according to the law of each Contracting State, due regard being had to the other provisions of this Convention.

ARTICLE 14

Capital gains

(1) Gains derived by a resident of a Contracting State from the alienation of immovable property referred to in Article 6 and situated in the other Contracting State may be taxed in that other State.

(2) Gains from the alienation of movable property forming part of the business property of a permanent establishment which an enterprise of a Contracting State has in the other Contracting State or of movable property pertaining to a fixed base available to a resident of a Contracting State in the other Contracting State for the purpose of performing independent personal services, including such gains from the alienation of such a permanent establishment (alone or with the whole enterprise) or of such fixed base, may be taxed in that other State.

(3) Gains from the alienation of ships or aircraft operated in international traffic, or movable property pertaining to the operation of such ships or aircraft shall be taxable only in the Contracting State in which the place of effective management of the enterprise is situated.

(4) Gains from the alienation of any property other than that mentioned in paragraphs (1), (2) and (3) of this Article shall be taxable only in the Contracting State of which the alienator is a resident.

ARTICLE 15

Independent personal services

(1) Subject to the provisions of Article 13, income derived by a resident of a Contracting State in respect of professional services or other activities of an independent character shall be taxable only in that State unless he:

(a) has a fixed base regularly available to him in the other Contracting State for the purpose of performing his activities; or

(b) carries on such professional services or such other activities of independent character in the other Contracting State for a period or periods exceeding in the aggregate 183 days in any period of 12 months.

In these cases the income shall be taxable in that other State but only so much of it as is attributable to the activities carried on through the fixed base or for the said period or periods.

(2) The term "professional services" includes especially independent scientific, literary, artistic, educational or teaching activities as well as the independent activities of physicians, lawyers, engineers, architects, dentists and accountants.

ARTICLE 16

Dependent personal services

(1) Subject to the provisions of Articles 17, 19, 20 and 21, salaries, wages and other similar remuneration derived by a resident of a Contracting State in respect of an employment shall be taxable only in that State unless the employment is exercised in the other Contracting State. If the employment is so exercised, such remuneration as is derived therefrom may be taxed in that other State.

(2) Notwithstanding the provisions of paragraph (1) of this Article, remuneration derived by a resident of a Contracting State in respect of an employment exercised in the other Contracting State shall be taxable only in the first-mentioned State if:

(a) the recipient is present in the other State for a period or periods not exceeding in the aggregate 183 days, including normal interruptions in work, in any period of 12 months; and

(b) the remuneration is paid by, or on behalf of, an employer who is not a resident of the other State; and

(c) the remuneration is not borne by a permanent establishment or a fixed base which the employer has in the other State.

(3) For the purpose of paragraph (2)(a) of this Article, "normal interruptions in work" means any period or periods during the twelve months in question for which the recipient is temporarily absent from that other State for purposes relating to his duties in that State, including any period or periods of leave, provided the recipient was exercising an employment in that State both before and after any such absence.

(4) Notwithstanding the preceding provisions of this Article, remuneration in respect of an employment exercised aboard a ship or aircraft operated in international traffic may be taxed in the Contracting State in which the place of effective management of the enterprise is situated.

ARTICLE 17

Directors' fees

Directors' fees and other similar payments derived by a resident of a Contracting State in his capacity as a member of the board of directors of a company which is a resident of the other Contracting State may be taxed in that other State.

ARTICLE 18

Artistes and athletes

(1) Notwithstanding the provisions of Articles 15 and 16, income derived by a resident of a Contracting State as an entertainer, such as a theatre, motion picture, radio or television artiste, or a musician, or as an athlete, from his personal activities as such exercised in the other Contracting State, may be taxed in that other State.

(2) Where income in respect of personal activities exercised by an entertainer or an athlete in his capacity as such accrues not to the entertainer or athlete himself but to another person, that income may, notwithstanding the provisions of Articles 7, 15 and 16, be taxed in the Contracting State in which the activities of the entertainer or athlete are exercised.

(3) The provisions of paragraphs (1) and (2) of this Article shall not apply to profits, remunerations, wages, salaries and similar income derived from activities performed in a Contracting State by entertainers or athletes if the visit of such entertainers or athletes to that State is wholly or substantially supported by public funds of the other Contracting State.

ARTICLE 19

Pensions

(1) Subject to the provisions of paragraphs (1) and (2) of Article 20, pensions and other similar remuneration paid in consideration of past employment to a resident of a Contracting State and any annuity paid to such a resident shall be taxable only in that State.

(2) The term "annuity" means a stated sum payable periodically at stated times during life or during a specified or ascertainable period of time under an obligation to make the payments in return for adequate and full consideration in money or money's worth.

ARTICLE 20

Government remuneration and pensions

(1) (a) Remuneration, other than a pension, paid by a Contracting State or a political subdivision or a local authority thereof to an individual in respect of services rendered to that State or subdivision or authority shall be taxable only in that State.

(b) However, such remuneration shall be taxable only in the other Contracting State if the services are rendered in that State and the individual is a resident of that State who:

(i) is not a national of the first-mentioned State; or

   (ii) did not become a resident of that other State solely for the purpose of rendering the services.

(2) (a) Any pension paid by, or out of funds created by, a Contracting State or a political subdivision or a local authority thereof to an individual in respect of services rendered to that State or subdivision or authority shall be taxable only in that State.

   (b) However, such pension shall be taxable only in the other Contracting State if the individual is a resident of that State and is not a national of the first-mentioned State.

(3) The provisions of Articles 16, 17 and 19 shall apply to remuneration and pensions in respect of services rendered in connection with a business carried on by a Contracting State or a political subdivision or a local authority thereof.

ARTICLE 21

Students and business apprentices

Payments which a student or business apprentice who is, or was immediately before visiting a Contracting State, a resident of the other Contracting State and who is present in the first-mentioned State solely for the purpose of his education or training or to carry out research receives for the purpose of his maintenance, education, training or research shall not be taxed in that State, provided that such payments arise from sources outside that State.

ARTICLE 22

Income not expressly mentioned

Items of income of a resident of a Contracting State, wherever arising, not dealt with in the foregoing Articles of this Convention shall be taxable only in that State.

ARTICLE 23

Elimination of double taxation

(1) Subject to the provisions of the law of the United Kingdom regarding the allowance as a credit against United Kingdom tax of tax payable in a territory outside the United Kingdom (which shall not affect the general principle hereof):

   (a) Ivory Coast tax payable under the laws of the Ivory Coast and in accordance with this Convention, whether directly or by deduction, on profits, income or chargeable gains from sources within the Ivory Coast (excluding in the case of a dividend, tax payable in respect of the profits out of which the dividend is paid) shall be allowed as a credit against any United Kingdom tax computed by reference to the same profits, income or chargeable gains by reference to which the Ivory Coast tax is computed; and

   (b) in the case of a dividend paid by a company which is a resident of the Ivory Coast to a company which is a resident of the United Kingdom and which controls directly or indirectly at least 10 per cent of the voting power in the company paying the dividend, the credit shall take into account (in addition to any Ivory Coast tax for which credit may be allowed under the provisions of sub-paragraph (a) of this paragraph) the Ivory Coast tax payable by the company in respect of the profits out of which such dividend is paid.

Provided that this paragraph shall not apply to a company which is a resident of the United Kingdom and is a Petroleum Company as defined for the purposes of Schedule 9 to the Oil Taxation Act 1975.

(2) For the purposes of paragraph (1) of this Article, the term "Ivory Coast tax payable" shall be deemed to include any amount which would have been payable as Ivory Coast tax for any year but for an exemption or reduction of tax granted for that year or any part thereof under:

(a) paragraphs IIA2(a), (b) and (c) and IIA4(1), (2) and (3) of the Annex to Law No 59–134 of 3 September 1959 so far as they were in force on, and have not been modified since, the date of signature of this Convention or have been modified only in minor respects so as not to affect their general character, or

(b) any other provision which may subsequently be made granting an exemption or reduction which is agreed by the competent authorities of the Contracting States to be of a substantially similar character, if it has not been modified thereafter or has been modified only in minor respects so as not to affect its general character.

Provided that:

(c) relief from United Kingdom tax shall not be given by virtue of this paragraph in respect of income from any source, if the income arises in a period starting more than ten years after the exemption from, or reduction of, Ivory Coast tax was first granted in respect of that source;

(d) where an exemption or reduction of tax is granted to any enterprise under paragraph IIA2(c)(i) or paragraph IIA4(1) of the Annex to Law No 59–134 of 3 September 1959 the tax which would have been payable but for that exemption or reduction shall be taken into account for the purposes of this paragraph only where the exemption or reduction is certified by the competent authority of the Ivory Coast as having been given with a view to promoting industrial, commercial, scientific or educational development in the Ivory Coast.

(3) Subject to the provisions of the law of the Ivory Coast regarding the allowance as a credit against Ivory Coast tax of tax payable in a territory outside the Ivory Coast (which shall not affect the general principle hereof):

(a) United Kingdom tax payable under the laws of the United Kingdom and in accordance with this Convention, whether directly or by deduction, on profits, income or chargeable gains from sources within the United Kingdom (excluding in the case of a dividend, tax payable in respect of the profits out of which the dividend is paid) shall be allowed as a credit against any Ivory Coast tax computed by reference to the same profits, income or chargeable gains by reference to which the United Kingdom tax is computed; and

(b) in the case of a dividend paid by a company which is a resident of the United Kingdom to a company which is a resident of the Ivory Coast and which controls directly or indirectly at least 10 per cent of the voting power in the company paying the dividend, the credit shall take into account (in addition to any United Kingdom tax for which credit may be allowed under the provisions of sub-paragraph (a) of this paragraph) the United Kingdom tax payable by the company in respect of the profits out of which such dividend is paid.

(4) For the purposes of paragraphs (1) and (3) of this Article profits, income and capital gains owned by a resident of a Contracting State which may be taxed in the other Contracting State in accordance with this Convention shall be deemed to arise from sources in that other Contracting State.

ARTICLE 24

Non-discrimination

(1) The nationals of a Contracting State shall not be subjected in the other Contracting State to any taxation or any requirement connected therewith which is other or more burdensome than the taxation and connected requirements to which nationals of that other State in the same circumstances are or may be subjected.

(2) The taxation on a permanent establishment which an enterprise of a Contracting State has in the other Contracting State shall not be less favourably levied in that other State than the taxation levied on enterprises of that other State carrying on the same activities.

(3) Enterprises of a Contracting State, the capital of which is wholly or partly owned or controlled, directly or indirectly, by one or more residents of the other Contracting State, shall not be subjected in the first-mentioned State to any taxation or any requirement connected therewith which is other or more burdensome than the taxation and connected requirements to which other similar enterprises of that first-mentioned State are or may be subjected.

(4) Nothing contained in this Article shall be construed as obliging either Contracting State to grant to individuals not resident in that State any of the personal allowances, reliefs and reductions for tax purposes which are granted to individuals so resident.

(5) Notwithstanding the provisions of this Article the period of exemption from tax on profits, under any relief referred to in paragraph (2)*(a)* of Article 23 or any relief of a substantially similar character under paragraph (2)*(b)* of that Article, from which a United Kingdom enterprise established in the Ivory Coast could benefit in the Ivory Coast, shall not under any circumstances exceed 10 years.

(6) In this Article the term "taxation" means taxes referred to in Article 2 of this Convention.

ARTICLE 25

Mutual agreement procedure

(1) Where a resident of a Contracting State considers that the actions of one or both of the Contracting States result or will result for him in taxation not in

accordance with this Convention, he may, notwithstanding the remedies provided by the domestic law of those States, present his case to the competent authority of the Contracting State of which he is a resident.

(2) The competent authority shall endeavour, if the objection appears to it to be justified and if it is not itself able to arrive at an appropriate solution, to resolve the case by mutual agreement with the competent authority of the other Contracting State, with a view to the avoidance of taxation not in accordance with the Convention.

(3) The competent authorities of the Contracting States shall endeavour to resolve by mutual agreement any difficulties or doubts arising as to the interpretation or application of the Convention.

(4) The competent authorities of the Contracting States may communicate with each other directly for the purpose of reaching an agreement in the sense of the preceding paragraphs.

ARTICLE 26

Exchange of information

(1) The competent authorities of the Contracting States shall exchange such information as is necessary for carrying out the provisions of this Convention or of the domestic laws of the Contracting States concerning taxes covered by the Convention insofar as the taxation thereunder is not contrary to the Convention. The exchange of information is not restricted by Article 1. Any information received by a Contracting State shall be treated as secret in the same manner as information obtained under the domestic laws of that State and shall be disclosed only to persons or authorities (including courts and administrative bodies) involved in the assessment or collection of, the enforcement or prosecution in respect of, or the determination of appeals in relation to, the taxes covered by the Convention. Such persons or authorities shall use the information only for such purposes. They may disclose the information in public court proceedings or in judicial decisions.

(2) In no case shall the provisions of paragraph (1) of this Article be construed so as to impose on a Contracting State the obligation:

(a) to carry out administrative measures at variance with the laws and administrative practice of that or of the other Contracting State;

(b) to supply information which is not obtainable under the laws or in the normal course of the administration of that or of the other Contracting State;

(c) to supply information which would disclose any trade, business, industrial, commercial or professional secret or trade process, or information, the disclosure of which would be contrary to public policy (ordre public).

ARTICLE 27

Diplomatic agents and consular officials

(1) Nothing in this Convention shall affect the fiscal privileges of members of diplomatic or consular missions under the general rules of international law or under the provisions of special agreements.

(2) Insofar as, by reason of the fiscal privileges from which members of diplomatic or consular missions benefit under the general rules of international law or under the provisions of special international agreements, income is not taxable in the accredited State, the right of assessment shall be retained by the accrediting State.

(3) For the purposes of this Convention the members of a diplomatic or consular mission of a Contracting State accredited in the other Contracting State or in a third State who are nationals of the accrediting State, shall be considered as residents of the accrediting State if they are subject to the same obligations there, regarding income taxes, as residents of the said State.

(4) This Convention shall not apply to international organisations, their organs and officials nor to persons who, as members of a diplomatic or consular mission of a third State, are present in a Contracting State and are not deemed to be residents of either Contracting State in respect of taxes on income.

ARTICLE 28

Entry into force

(1) This Convention shall be ratified and the instruments of ratification exchanged at Abidjan as soon as possible.

(2) This Convention shall enter into force immediately after the expiration of thirty days following the date on which the instruments of ratification are exchanged(a) and shall thereupon have effect:

(a) in the United Kingdom:

  (i) in respect of income tax and capital gains tax, for any year of assessment beginning on or after 6 April in the calendar year next following that in which the instruments of ratification are exchanged;

  (ii) in respect of corporation tax, for any financial year beginning on or after 1 April in the calendar year next following that in which the instruments of ratification are exchanged;

(b) in the Ivory Coast:

  (i) in respect of taxes on industrial, commercial and agricultural profits levied for any taxable period commencing on or after 1 October in the calendar year next following that in which the instruments of ratification are exchanged;

  (ii) in respect of other taxes on income levied for any taxable period beginning on or after 1 January in the calendar year next following that in which the instruments of ratification are exchanged;

(a) Instruments of ratification were exchanged on 24th December 1986.

(iii) in respect of taxes deducted at source on income credited or paid, on or after 1 January in the calendar year next following that in which the instruments of ratification are exchanged.

ARTICLE 29

Termination

This Convention shall remain in force until terminated by one of the Contracting States. Either Contracting State may terminate the Convention, through diplomatic channels, by giving notice of termination at least six months before the end of any calendar year beginning after the expiration of five years from the date of entry into force of the Convention. In such event, the Convention shall cease to have effect:

(a) in the United Kingdom:

    (i) in respect of income tax and capital gains tax, for any year of assessment beginning on or after 6 April in the calendar year next following that in which the notice is given;

    (ii) in respect of corporation tax, for any financial year beginning on or after 1 April in the calendar year next following that in which the notice is given;

(b) in the Ivory Coast:

    (i) in respect of taxes on industrial, commercial and agricultural profits assessed on income of taxable periods beginning on or after 1 October in the calendar year next following that in which the notice is given;

    (ii) in respect of other taxes on income assessed on income of taxable periods commencing on or after 1 January in the calendar year next following that in which the notice is given;

    (iii) in respect of taxes payable at source on income credited or paid, on or after 1 January in the calendar year next following that in which the notice is given.

In witness whereof the undersigned, duly authorised thereto, have signed this Convention.

Done in duplicate at Abidjan this 26th day of June 1985, in the English and French languages, both texts being equally authoritative.

For the Government of
the United Kingdom
of Great Britain and
Northern Ireland:

For the Government
of the Republic
of the Ivory Coast:

J. M. Willson

Simeon Aké

EXPLANATORY NOTE

(This note is not part of the Order)

The Convention with the Republic of the Ivory Coast is set out in the Schedule to this Order.

The Convention provides for business profits not arising through a permanent establishment to be taxed only in the country of the taxpayer's residence. Profits attributable to a permanent establishment may be taxed in the country in which the permanent establishment is situated (Articles 5 and 7). Profits arising from the operation of ships and aircraft are to be taxed only in the country in which the place of effective management of the enterprise is situated (Article 8).

Provision is made for income arising from immovable property and gains from the alienation of that property to be taxed in the country in which the property is situated (Articles 6 and 14).

The rate of tax imposed in the country of source on dividends derived by a resident of the other country is not to exceed 15% of the gross amount of the dividends. Where the company paying the dividend is a resident of the Ivory Coast and is exempt from tax on its profits or does not pay tax on its profits at the normal rate, then the rate of tax is not to exceed 18% of the gross amount of the dividends (Article 10).

The rate of tax imposed in the source country on interest is not to exceed 15%. However, the country of source will exempt from tax interest payable to the Government or a local authority of the other country or any agency or instrumentality wholly owned by that Government or local authority (Article 11).

The rate of tax in the source country on royalties flowing to the other country is not to exceed 10% (Article 12).

The rate of tax in the source country on management fees flowing to the other country is not to exceed 10% of the gross amount, but the payee may elect that the tax chargeable on those fees be calculated as if he had a permanent establishment in the source state i.e. net of expenses (Article 13).

The earnings of temporary business visitors are, subject to certain conditions, to be taxed only in the country of the taxpayer's residence (Articles 15 and 16).

Government service salaries and pensions are normally to be taxed by the paying Government only (Article 20) while other pensions are to be taxed only in the country of the taxpayer's residence (Article 19). Income derived by artistes and athletes may be taxed in the country where the activities are exercised. Where the activities exercised in one country are supported by public funds of the other country the income is taxable only in that other country (Article 18). Some payments made to visiting students and business apprentices are to be exempt from tax in the country visited (Article 21).

Where income continues to be taxable in both countries credit will be given by the country of the taxpayer's residence in respect of tax imposed by the other country. The credit to be given in the United Kingdom for tax payable in the Ivory Coast includes credit for tax spared under certain provisions of Ivorian law (Article 23).

There are provisions safeguarding nationals and enterprises of one country against discriminatory taxation in the other country (Article 24) and for consultation and exchange of information between the taxation authorities of the two countries (Articles 25 and 26).

The Convention will enter into force thirty days after the date on which instruments of ratification are exchanged and shall have effect in the calendar year next following that in which the instruments of ratification are exchanged (Article 28).

STATUTORY INSTRUMENTS

1987 No. 170

TRADE MARKS

The Trade Marks and Service Marks (Relevant Countries) (Amendment) Order 1987

Made - - - -	*10th February 1987*
Laid before Parliament	*18th February 1987*
Coming into force	*11th March 1987*

At the Court at Buckingham Palace, the 10th day of February 1987

Present

The Queen's Most Excellent Majesty in Council.

Whereas Her Majesty is satisfied that provision has been or will be made under the laws of Belgium, Brazil, the Federal Republic of Germany (and Berlin (West)), Luxembourg and the Netherlands (including Aruba and the Netherlands Antilles) whereby priority for the protection of service marks in respect of which application for registration under the Trade Marks Act 1938(**a**) has been made will be given on a basis comparable to that for which provision is made by section 39A of that Act(**b**) in relation to applications for registration made in a relevant country (as defined in that section):

Now, therefore, Her Majesty, in exercise of the powers conferred on Her by section 39A(7) of the said Act, is pleased, by and with the advice of Her Privy Council, to order, and it is hereby ordered, as follows:

1. This Order may be cited as the Trade Marks and Service Marks (Relevant Countries) (Amendment) Order 1987 and shall come into force on 11th March 1987.

2. Schedule 2 to the Trade Marks and Service Marks (Relevant Countries) Order 1986(**c**) shall be amended by the inclusion of references to Belgium, Brazil, the Federal Republic of Germany (and Berlin (West)), Luxembourg and the Netherlands (including Aruba and the Netherlands Antilles).

G.I. de Deney
Clerk of the Privy Council

(**a**) 1938 c. 22; the Act was applied, with modifications, to service marks by the Trade Marks (Amendment) Act 1984 (c. 19), section 1, as amended by the Patents, Designs and Marks Act 1986 (c. 39), section 2(1) and Schedule 3.
(**b**) Section 39A was added by the Patents, Designs and Marks Act 1986 (c. 39), Schedule 2, paragraph 5, and is applied to service marks by the Trade Marks (Amendment) Act 1984 (c. 19), section 1(2) and Schedule 1, paragraph 18C, as respectively substituted and inserted by the Patents, Designs and Marks Act 1986, section 2(1)(a) and Schedule 2, paragraph 11.
(**c**) S.I. 1986/1303, amended by S.I. 1986/1890, 2236.

EXPLANATORY NOTE

(This note is not part of the Order)

This Order adds Belgium, Brazil, the Federal Republic of Germany (and Berlin (West)), Luxembourg and the Netherlands (including Aruba and the Netherlands Antilles) to the list of countries specified as those in which an application for the registration of a service mark will give priority in respect of an application made in the United Kingdom within the following six months.

STATUTORY INSTRUMENTS

1987 No. 172

BUILDING SOCIETIES

The Building Societies (Provision of Services) Order 1987

Made - - -	*5th February 1987*
Laid before Parliament	*12th February 1987*
Coming into force	*5th March 1987*

The Building Societies Commission, in exercise of the powers conferred on it by section 34(2) of the Building Societies Act 1986(**a**), hereby makes the following Order:–

Citation and commencement

1. This Order may be cited as the Building Societies (Provision of Services) Order 1987 and shall come into operation on 5th March 1987.

Interpretation

2. In this Order, "the Act" means the Building Societies Act 1986.

Variation of restrictions in relation to certain services

3.—(1) This Article varies Part III of Schedule 8 to the Act as follows.

(2) In paragraph 5 (arranging for investment services), before "Arranging" there shall be inserted "(1)" and after "individuals" there shall be inserted the following sub-paragraph –

"(2) The power to arrange for the provision of investment services does not include power –

(a) to buy or sell any investment, either as principal or agent, or

(b) to give advice concerning any investment.".

(3) In place of paragraph 7 (arranging for the provision of credit), there shall be substituted the following paragraph –

"7. Arranging for the provision of credit and connected services is restricted to their provision by –

(a) any recognised bank or licensed institution;

(b) any body corporate connected with the person arranging for the services to be provided; or

(c) any other body for the time being approved for the purposes of this Schedule by the Commission, whether in relation to all building societies, to specified classes of building society, or to a particular building society.".

(**a**) 1986 c.53.

(4) In paragraph 12 (conditions applying to estate agency subsidiaries), after sub-paragraph (c) there shall be added the following sub-paragraph –

> "(d) its business must not include any activity which the society could not undertake by reason of the fact that –
>
> > (i) the society has not adopted a particular adoptable power, whether because the power is not available to it or for any other reason, or
> >
> > (ii) the activity would be in contravention of a restriction upon the extent of a power the society has adopted, being either a restriction specified in this Part of this Schedule and relating to a power to provide a financial service or a restriction assumed by the society.".

(5) In place of paragraph 13 (prohibition on acting as agent for estate agency subsidiary), there shall be substituted the following paragraph –

> "13. No employee of a building society whose duties include –
>
> > (a) making a report on the value of land which is to secure an advance,
> >
> > (b) making an assessment of the adequacy of the security for an advance to be secured on land, or
> >
> > (c) authorising the making of an advance to be secured on land,
>
> shall perform any service for any subsidiary of the society which provides estate agency services.".

Variation of supplementary provisions

4.—(1) This Article varies Part IV of Schedule 8 to the Act as follows.

(2) After paragraph 4, there shall be inserted the following paragraphs –

"Provision of credit by connected bodies

4A.—(1) For the purposes of paragraph 7(b) of Part III of this Schedule, a body corporate is connected with a person arranging for credit and connected services to be provided if and only if –

> (a) one is a building society and the other is a subsidiary or relevant associated body of that society; or
>
> (b) both are subsidiaries of the same building society.

(2) For the purposes of sub-paragraph (1) above an associated body of a building society which is not a corresponding European body as referred to in section 18(2)(b) of this Act is a relevant associated body of that society.

Subsidiaries providing estate agency services

4B. For the purpose of determining whether the condition in paragraph 12(d) of Part III of this Schedule is fulfilled as regards a subsidiary of a building society, the continuation, during the first fifteen months following the date on which an undertaking became or the business of an undertaking was transferred to a subsidiary of the society, of any activity carried on as part of the business of the undertaking immediately before that date shall be disregarded.".

(3) In paragraph 5 (sanctions for breach of restrictions), in place of "acts as agent" there shall be substituted "performs any service".

In witness whereof the common seal of the Building Societies Commission is hereto fixed, and is authenticated by me, a person authorised under paragraph 14 of Schedule 1 to the Building Societies Act 1986 on 5th February 1987.

G. M. Binns
Secretary to the Commission

EXPLANATORY NOTE

(This note is not part of the Order)

This Order varies Schedule 8 to the Building Societies Act 1986, which specifies financial services and services relating to land which building societies may provide (in some cases only through subsidiaries) and restrictions which apply in relation to the provision of particular services.

The power of societies to arrange for the provision of services relating to the acquisition or disposal of investments is made subject to an additional restriction, set out in article 3(2) of the Order. A society is not to be able, in the course of providing this service, either to buy or sell an investment itself or to give advice concerning a particular investment.

A restriction which appears in Schedule 8 concerning the powers of societies to arrange for the provision of credit by third parties is varied by article 3(3). Societies are enabled to make arrangements not only with recognised banks, licensed deposit-takers and bodies approved by the Building Societies Commission in relation to all societies or classes of society, as hitherto, but also with certain connected bodies and bodies approved by the Commission in relation to the society concerned.

Article 3(4) imposes an additional restriction regarding the power of societies to provide estate agency services. While such services may be provided through a subsidiary which undertakes other business besides estate agency work (as defined in the Estate Agents Act 1979 (c.38)), the business of an estate agency subsidiary must not include any activity which is outside the powers of its parent society, either because of the society's failure to adopt a power or because of a restriction of certain kinds upon the extent of a power it has adopted. Article 4 of the Order makes an exception in the case of newly-acquired estate agencies, which will give a society an opportunity to adopt additional powers or to vary or remove restrictions upon its powers that the society has assumed.

Article 3(4) also varies the restriction in Schedule 8 which prohibits employees of a society from acting as agent for an estate agency subsidiary. In consequence, the prohibition will apply to any service which an employee undertakes for the subsidiary, but will not apply in relation to employees who do not have responsibilities relating to the society's mortgage lending business.

STATUTORY INSTRUMENTS

1987 No. 177

IMMIGRATION

The Immigration (Ports of Entry) Order 1987

Made - - - - *10th February 1987*

Coming into force *1st March 1987*

In exercise of the powers conferred upon me by section 33(3) of the Immigration Act 1971**(a)**, I hereby make the following Order—

1.—(1) This Order may be cited as the Immigration (Ports of Entry) Order 1987 and shall come into force on 1st March 1987.

(2) The Immigration (Ports of Entry) Order 1972**(b)**, the Immigration (Ports of Entry) (Amendment) Order 1975**(c)** and the Immigration (Ports of Entry) (Amendment) Order 1979**(d)** are hereby revoked.

2. The ports specified in the Schedule to this Order shall be ports of entry for the purposes of the Immigration Act 1971.

Home Office
10th February 1987

Douglas Hurd
One of Her Majesty's Principal Secretaries of State

(a) 1971 c.77.   (b) S.I. 1972/1668.   (c) S.I. 1975/2221.   (d) S.I.1979/1635.

SCHEDULE

PORTS OF ENTRY

Seaports and Hoverports

Dover	Plymouth
Felixstowe	Portsmouth
Folkestone	Ramsgate
Harwich	Sheerness
Hull	Southampton
London	Tyne
Newhaven	

Airports

Aberdeen	Leeds/Bradford
Belfast	Liverpool
Birmingham	Luton
Bournemouth (Hurn)	Manchester
Bristol	Newcastle
Cardiff (Wales)	Norwich
East Midlands	Prestwick
Edinburgh	Southampton
Gatwick–London	Southend
Glasgow	Stansted–London
Heathrow–London	Tees-side

EXPLANATORY NOTE

(This note is not part of the Order)

Under paragraph 26 of Schedule 2 to the Immigration Act 1971 the owners or agents of a ship or aircraft employed to carry passengers for reward are prohibited from arranging, without the approval of the Secretary of State, for the ship or aircraft to call at a port in the United Kingdom other than a designated port of entry for the purpose of disembarking passengers, if any of them require leave to enter the United Kingdom and have not been given leave, or for the purpose of embarking passengers unless the owners or agents have reasonable cause to believe all of them to be British citizens. An owner or agent who contravenes the provisions of paragraph 26 commits an offence under section 27 of the Act.

Under section 13(3) a person who is entitled to appeal against a refusal of leave to enter the United Kingdom may do so only if (in addition to holding an entry clearance or a work permit) he was refused leave at a designated port of entry.

This Order consolidates with amendments previous orders designating ports of entry for the purposes of the Act. The only changes of substance are the addition of Ramsgate to the list of Seaports and Hoverports and the deletion of Ramsgate Hoverport from that list and the addition of Leeds/Bradford to the list of Airports and the deletion of Lydd (Ferryfield) from that list.

STATUTORY INSTRUMENTS

1987 No. 178 (C.3)

TOWN AND COUNTRY PLANNING, ENGLAND AND WALES

The Housing and Planning Act 1986 (Commencement No. 2) Order 1987

Made -   -   -   -   10th February 1987

The Secretary of State for the Environment, as respects England, and the Secretary of State for Wales, as respects Wales, in exercise of the powers conferred on them by section 57(2) of the Housing and Planning Act 1986**(a)** and of all other powers enabling them in that behalf hereby make the following Order:

1. This Order may be cited as the Housing and Planning Act 1986 (Commencement No. 2) Order 1987.

2. Paragraph 8 of Schedule 11 to the Housing and Planning Act 1986 shall come into force on 2nd March 1987.

Transitional provision

3. Subsections (2) to (5) of section 250 of the Local Government Act 1972**(b)** shall continue to apply to any inquiry held under paragraph 5 of Schedule 9 to the Town and Country Planning Act 1971**(c)** which began before 2nd March 1987 as those provisions applied immediately before that date.

9th February 1987

Nicholas Ridley
Secretary of State for the Environment

10th February 1987

Nicholas Edwards
Secretary of State for Wales

(a) 1986 c.63.
(b) 1972 c.70.
(c) 1971 c.78.

EXPLANATORY NOTE

(This note is not part of the Order)

This Order brings into operation on 2nd March 1987 paragraph 8 of Schedule 11 to the Housing and Planning Act 1986.

Paragraph 8(1) substitutes a new subsection (2) in section 282 of the Town and Country Planning Act 1971. This is a minor drafting improvement which makes no change of substance.

Paragraph 8(2) substitutes a new paragraph 5(3) of Schedule 9 to the Town and Country Planning Act 1971 (determination of appeals by appointed person) applying section 250(2) to (5) of the Local Government Act 1972 (local inquiries: evidence and costs) to an inquiry held under paragraph 5 of Schedule 9. At present only the Secretary of State is entitled under paragraph 5(3) to make orders as to the costs of the parties to an inquiry and as to the parties by whom the costs are to be paid. The substituted paragraph entitles a person appointed by the Secretary of State to hold an inquiry to make such orders as well.

1987 No. 180

HEALTH AND SAFETY

The Control of Industrial Air Pollution (Transfer of Powers of Enforcement) Regulations 1987

Made - - - -	*9th February 1987*
Laid before Parliament	*20th February 1987*
Coming into force	*1st April 1987*

The Secretary of State, in exercise of the powers conferred on him by sections 15(1), (3)(a) and (3)(c) and 82(3)(a) of the Health and Safety at Work etc. Act 1974**(a)** and of all other powers enabling him in that behalf, and after consulting, in accordance with section 50(1) of the 1974 Act**(b)**, the Health and Safety Commission being the only body which it appeared to him to be appropriate to consult, hereby makes the following Regulations:

Citation and operation

1. These Regulations may be cited as the Control of Industrial Air Pollution (Transfer of Powers of Enforcement) Regulations 1987 and shall come into force on 1st April 1987.

Transfer of powers of enforcement

2. The Secretary of State shall be the authority responsible for the enforcement of the following relevant statutory provisions:

(a) section 5 of the Health and Safety at Work etc. Act 1974**(c)**, and

(b) the Alkali, &c. Works Regulation Act 1906**(d)** ("the 1906 Act").

Consequential provisions

3.—(1) In section 27(1) of the 1906 Act (interpretation of terms), the definition of the expression "inspector" shall be omitted and the following substituted therefor:

"The expression "inspector" means an inspector appointed by the Secretary of State under section 19 of the Health and Safety at Work etc. Act 1974:".

(2) Paragraph 1 of Schedule 2 to the Clean Air Enactments (Repeals and Modifications) Regulations 1974**(e)** ("the 1974 Regulations"), to the extent that it relates to the definition of the expression "inspector", is hereby revoked.

(a) 1974 c.37; section 15(1) was substituted by the Employment Protection Act 1975 (c.71), Schedule 15, paragraph 6.   **(b)** Section 50(1) of the 1974 Act was substituted by the Employment Protection Act 1975 (c.71), Schedule 15, paragraph 16(1).   **(c)** Section 5 imposes a duty on persons having control of premises of a class prescribed for the purposes of section 1(1)(d) of the 1974 Act; classes of premises are prescribed for those purposes by S.I. 1983/943.   **(d)** 1906 c.14; the Control of Pollution Act 1974 (c.40) repealed sections 3, 4, 5, 8, 12(1)(d), 14, 15, 17, 18(4) and 19, repealed in part sections 9(1), 18(1) and 22(1), and amended section 27(1); S.I. 1974/2170 repealed sections 11, 12, 13, 18, 20 and 21 and amended section 27(1); S.I. 1983/943 repealed sections 6 and 7 and Schedule 1 and amended sections 1, 2, 9(1) and (5), 16 and 27(1); the Local Government Act 1972(c.70) amended section 27(1).   **(e)** S.I. 1974/2170.

4.—(1) Section 9(5) and (7) of the 1906 Act shall have effect as if the references therein to the Local Government Board, or for Scotland the Secretary for Scotland, were references to the Secretary of State.

(2) Paragraph 2 of Schedule 2 to the 1974 Regulations (which requires the references mentioned in paragraph 1 of this Regulation to have effect as if they were references to the Health and Safety Executive) is hereby revoked.

5.—(1) In Articles 3, 5, 6, 7 and 8, of the Alkali, &c. Works Regulation Order (Scotland) 1933(**a**), references to the Department shall have effect as if they were references to the Secretary of State.

(2) Paragraph (f) of Regulation 5 of the 1974 Regulations (which requires the references mentioned in paragraph 1 of this Regulation to be construed as references to the Health and Safety Executive) is hereby revoked.

6.—(1) In Articles 3, 5, 6 and 7 of the Alkali, &c. Works (Registration) Order 1957(**b**), references to the Minister of Housing and Local Government shall have effect as if they were references to the Secretary of State.

(2) Regulation 8 of the 1974 Regulations (which requires the references mentioned in paragraph 1 of this Regulation to have effect as if they were references to the Health and Safety Executive) is hereby revoked.

7. In Regulation 11 of the 1974 Regulations (references to inspectors), for the words "Health and Safety Executive" there shall be substituted the words "Secretary of State".

Transitional provision

8. These Regulations shall not affect the validity of anything done before they come into force under any provision of an enactment or subordinate legislation which is amended or the effect of which is modified by these Regulations; and anything which at the coming into force of these Regulations is in process of being done for the purposes of that provision by or in relation to the Health and Safety Executive may be continued by or in relation to the Secretary of State.

Signed by order of the Secretary of State

K. Clarke
Paymaster General,
Department of Employment

9th February 1987

EXPLANATORY NOTE

(This note is not part of the Regulations)

These Regulations transfer from the Health and Safety Executive to the Secretary of State the responsibility for enforcing enactments restricting the emission from certain industrial premises of substances which pollute the atmosphere and, consequentially, modify certain legislation related to those enactments so that it refers or is treated as referring to the Secretary of State. The Regulations contain a transitional provision designed to ensure that anything in the process of being done by or in relation to the Health and Safety Executive before the transfer can be continued by or in relation to the Secretary of State after it.

(**a**) S.R. & O. 1933/878 Rev.II, p.57.   (**b**) S.I. 1957/2208.

1987 No. 181

LOCAL GOVERNMENT, ENGLAND AND WALES

The Local Government (Direct Labour Organisations) (Competition) (Amendment) Regulations 1987

Made	-	-	-	*10th February 1987*
Laid before Parliament				*19th February 1987*
Coming into force				*1st April 1987*

The Secretary of State for the Environment, in relation to England, and the Secretary of State for Wales, in relation to Wales, in exercise of the powers conferred on them by sections 7 and 9(3) of the Local Government, Planning and Land Act 1980(a) and of all other powers enabling them in that behalf, hereby make the following Regulations —

1. These Regulations may be cited as the Local Government (Direct Labour Organisations) (Competition) (Amendment) Regulations 1987 and shall come into force on 1st April 1987.

2. The Local Government (Direct Labour Organisations) (Competition) Regulations 1983(b) are hereby amended as follows —

(a) in regulation 2(1), in the definitions of "contractual highway work" and "relevant highway work", there shall in each case be substituted for head (i) —

"(i) general highway works, does not exceed £25,000, or"

(b) in regulation 3(a) for "£50,000" there shall be substituted "£25,000";

(c) for regulation 6 there shall be substituted the following regulation —

"**6.**—(1) Regulation 5 applies —

(a) to any works contract of a value which does not exceed £25,000 providing or providing principally for the carrying out of general highway works (other than a contract described in Regulation 7(1)) if the value of the contract together with the value of all relevant highway work previously undertaken by the authority otherwise than in accordance with section 7 or the conditions mentioned in section 9(3)(a) of the Act in the same financial year exceeds the relevant limit;

(b) to any works contract of a value which does not exceed £50,000 providing or providing principally for the carrying out of works of new construction (other than a contract described in Regulation 7(1)) if the value of the contract together with the value of all relevant construction work previously undertaken as mentioned in sub-paragraph (a) exceeds the relevant limit;

(c) to any works contract of a value which does not exceed £10,000 providing or providing principally for the carrying out of works of maintenance

---

(a) 1980 c.65.   (b) S.I. 1983/685.

(other than a contract described in regulation 7(1)) if the value of the contract together with the value of all relevant maintenance work previously undertaken as mentioned in sub-paragraph (a) exceeds the relevant limit.

(2)   In this regulation the relevant limit, in relation to a works contract which provides, or provides principally, for —

(a) the carrying out of general highway works, is 70% of the aggregate value of all relevant highway work undertaken and all contractual highway work carried out by the authority in the immediately preceding financial year; or

(b) the carrying out of works of new construction, is 40% of the aggregate of all relevant construction work undertaken and all contractual construction work carried out by the authority in the immediately preceding financial year; or

(c) the carrying out of works of maintenance, is 40% of the aggregate value of all relevant maintenance work undertaken and all contractual maintenance work carried out by the authority in the immediately preceding financial year or £300,000, whichever is greater.";

(d) for regulation 8 there shall be substituted the following regulation —

"**8.**—(1)   Subject to regulation 9, a local authority or development body may not undertake functional work of the following descriptions unless they have first complied with the conditions mentioned in section 9(3)(a) of the Act as well as with those in section 9(2) —

(a) a job consisting or consisting principally of general highway works where the estimated cost of the job exceeds £25,000;

(b) a job consisting or consisting principally of the construction or maintenance of a sewer where the estimated cost of the job exceeds £50,000;

(c) a job consisting or consisting principally of works of new construction where the estimated cost of the job exceeds £50,000;

(d) a job consisting or consisting principally of works of maintenance where the estimated cost of the job exceeds £10,000;

(e) a job consisting or consisting principally of general highway works where the estimated cost of the job does not exceed £25,000 if the estimated cost of the job together with the aggregate value of all relevant highway work previously undertaken by the authority or body otherwise than in accordance with section 7 or the conditions mentioned in section 9(3)(a) of the Act in the same financial year exceeds the relevant limit;

(f) a job consisting or consisting principally of works of new construction where the estimated cost of the job does not exceed £50,000 if the estimated cost of the job together with the aggregate value of all relevant construction work previously undertaken as mentioned in subparagraph (e) exceeds the relevant limit;

(g) a job consisting or consisting principally of works of maintenance where the estimated cost of the job does not exceed £10,000 if the estimated cost of the job together with the aggregate value of all relevant maintenance work previously undertaken as mentioned in sub-paragraph (e) exceeds the relevant limit.

(2)   In this regulation the relevant limit in relation to a job which consists, or consists principally, of —

(a) general highway works, is 70% of the aggregate value of all relevant highway work undertaken and all contractual highway work carried out by that authority or body in the immediately preceding financial year;

(b) works of new construction, is 40% of the aggregate value of all relevant construction work undertaken and all contractual construction work carried out by that authority or body in the immediately preceding financial year;

    (c) works of maintenance, is 40% of the aggregate value of all relevant maintenance work undertaken and all contractual maintenance work carried out by the authority or body in the immediately preceding financial year or £300,000, whichever is greater.";

  (e) regulation 10 shall be deleted.

Nicholas Ridley
Secretary of State for the Environment

9th February 1987

Nicholas Edwards
Secretary of State for Wales

10th February 1987

EXPLANATORY NOTE

(This note is not part of the Regulations)

These Regulations amend the Local Government (Direct Labour Organisations) (Competition) Regulations 1983 in their application to highway work.

The 1983 Regulations prescribe £50,000 as the maximum value of a contract for highway works which a local authority may enter into without prior competitive tendering. They also apply tendering requirements to highway functional work worth more than £50,000 and to certain highway works contracts and highway functional work worth £50,000 or less if the value of the contract or work and the value of all similar work worth £50,000 or less previously contracted for or done by the authority in the current financial year exceeds a prescribed percentage of the total value of similar work contracted for or done in the previous year.

These Regulations substitute £25,000 for £50,000.

Regulations 6 and 8 of the 1983 Regulations are rewritten. Provisions which are now spent are omitted.

STATUTORY INSTRUMENTS

1987 No. 182

PUBLIC HEALTH, ENGLAND AND WALES
PUBLIC HEALTH, SCOTLAND
PUBLIC HEALTH, NORTHERN IRELAND
CONTAMINATION OF FOOD

The Food Protection (Emergency Prohibitions) (Wales) (No. 2) Amendment Order 1987

Made - - - -	*12th February 1987*
Laid before Parliament	*12th February 1987*
Coming into force -	*16th February 1987*

Whereas the Secretary of State is of the opinion, as mentioned in section 1(1)(a) of the Food and Environment Protection Act 1985(a), that there has been or may have been an escape of substances of such descriptions and in such quantities and such circumstances as are likely to create a hazard to human health through human consumption of food;

And whereas the Secretary of State is of the opinion, as mentioned in section 1(1)(b) of the said Act, that in consequence of the said escape of substances food which is or may be in the future in the area described in Schedule 1 to the Food Protection (Emergency Prohibitions) (Wales) (No.2) Order 1986(b), or which is derived or may be in the future derived from anything in that area, is, or may be, or may become, unsuitable for human consumption;

Now, therefore, the Secretary of State, in exercise of the powers conferred on him by the said section 1(1) and (2) and section 24(1) and (3) of the said Act, and of all other powers enabling him in that behalf, hereby makes the following Order:–

Title and commencement

1. This Order may be cited as the Food Protection (Emergency Prohibitions) (Wales) (No. 2) Amendment Order 1987 and shall come into force on 16th February 1987.

Partial revocation and amendment

2. The Food Protection (Emergency Prohibitions) (Wales) (No. 2) Order 1986 is revoked to the extent that it imposes prohibitions on–

    (a) the slaughter of a sheep which–

        (i) was moved from a place in accordance with a consent given under section

---

(a) 1985 c.48.
(b) S.I. 1986/1681, amended by S.I. 1986/1707, 1756, 1775, 1849 and 2242.

2(1) of the Food and Environment Protection Act 1985 which consent was subject to the condition that the sheep to which it applies should be marked with a red mark; and

    (ii) has been examined and marked by an ear-tag by a person authorised in that behalf by one of the Ministers**(a)**; and

  (b) the supply or having in possession for supply of meat, or food containing meat, derived from such a sheep,

and accordingly that Order is further amended in accordance with the following provisions of this Order.

3. Article 4 shall be re-numbered article 4(1) and after that paragraph there shall be inserted the following paragraph–

    "(2) Paragraph (1) above shall not apply in the case of any sheep which–

      (a) was moved from any place in accordance with a consent given under the said section 2(1) which consent was subject to the condition that the sheep to which it applies should be marked with a red mark; and

      (b) has been examined and marked by an ear-tag by a person authorised in that behalf by one of the Ministers.".

4. In article 6(2)(b)(i), after the words "blue mark" there shall be inserted the words "or with a red mark".

Nicholas Edwards
12th February 1987   Secretary of State for Wales

EXPLANATORY NOTE

(This note is not part of the Order)

The Food Protection (Emergency Prohibitions) (Wales) (No. 2) Order 1986 as amended by S.I. 1986/1707, 1756, 1775, 1849 and 2242 contains emergency prohibitions restricting various activities in order to prevent human consumption of food which has been or which may have been rendered unsuitable for that purpose in consequence of the escape of radioactive substances from a nuclear reactor situated at Chernobyl in the USSR.

This order excepts from the prohibition on slaughter in the area of land in Wales designated by the Order and from the prohibition on slaughter and supply throughout the United Kingdom any sheep (and in the latter case any meat derived from such sheep) identified by a red paint mark which have been examined and subsequently marked by an ear-tag by an official of the Ministry of Agriculture, Fisheries and Food, Scottish Office or Welsh Office (articles 3 and 4).

Maps showing the designated area are available for inspection during normal office hours at the offices of the Welsh Office Agriculture Department at Penrallt, Caernarfon, Gwynedd LL55 1EP; Government Buildings, Spa Road East, Llandrindod Wells, Powys LD1 5HA; Station Road, Ruthin, Clwyd LL15 1BP and Cathays Park, Cardiff, South Glamorgan CF1 3NQ.

(a) The definition of "the Ministers" is in section 24(1) of the Food and Environment Protection Act 1985.

STATUTORY INSTRUMENTS

1987 No. 188

SEEDS

The Seeds (National Lists of Varieties) (Fees) Regulations 1987

Made - - - -	9th February 1987
Laid before Parliament	20th February 1987
Coming into force	1st April 1987

The Minister of Agriculture, Fisheries and Food, the Secretary of State for Scotland, the Secretary of State for Wales and the Secretary of State for Northern Ireland, acting jointly, in exercise of the powers conferred by section 16(1), (1A) (e) and (8) of the Plant Varieties and Seeds Act 1964(a) as extended to Northern Ireland(b) and now vested in them(c), and of all other powers enabling them in that behalf, after consultation with representatives of such interests as appear to them to be concerned in accordance with section 16(1) of the said Act, hereby make the following Regulations:—

Title and commencement

1. These Regulations may be cited as the Seeds (National Lists of Varieties) (Fees) Regulations 1987 and shall come into force on 1st April 1987.

Interpretation

2.—(1) In these Regulations, unless the context otherwise requires—

"the Act" means the Plant Varieties and Seeds Act 1964;

"maintainer" means a person indicated in a National List as responsible for the maintenance of a plant variety;

"the Minister" means the Minister of Agriculture, Fisheries and Food, and "the Ministers" means the Minister of Agriculture, Fisheries and Food, the Secretary of State for Scotland, the Secretary of State for Wales and the Secretary of State for Northern Ireland acting jointly;

"National List" means a list of plant varieties prepared and published in accordance with the principal Regulations;

"plant breeders' rights" means rights which may be granted in accordance with Part I of the Act, and "plant breeders' rights scheme" means a scheme made under that Part of the Act to enable a grant of such rights;

"the principal Regulations" means the Seeds (National Lists of Varieties) Regulations 1982(d);

"renewal fee" means a fee payable in respect of the retention of a plant variety in a National List.

(a) 1964 c.14; section 16 was amended by the European Communities Act 1972 (c.68), section 4(1) and Schedule 4, paragraph 5(1), (2) and (3).
(b) By the Plant Varieties and Seeds (Northern Ireland) Order 1973 (S.I. 1973/609).
(c) In the case of the Secretary of State for Wales, by virtue of S.I. 1978/272.
(d) S.I. 1982/844, amended by S.I. 1985/1529.

(2) Any reference in these Regulations to a numbered Schedule shall be construed as a reference to the Schedule bearing that number in these Regulations.

Payment of fees

3.—(1) Subject to paragraph (2) below, there shall be paid to the Minister in respect of matters arising under the principal Regulations—

(a) a fee on making an application for the entry of a plant variety in a National List, being the fee set out in the second column of Part I of Schedule 1 opposite the reference in the first column of the said Part I to the plant variety of the kind to which the application relates, such fee being payable on making the application;

(b) a fee payable in respect of tests for one year for distinctness, uniformity and stability of a plant variety which is the subject of an application for entry in a National List, being the new fee set out in the second column of Part II of Schedule 1 opposite the reference in the first column of the said Part II to the plant variety of the kind to which the tests relate, such fee being payable within 14 days of a demand made by the Minister;

(c) a fee payable in respect of trials for value for cultivation and use of a plant variety which is the subject of an application for entry in a National List and is referred to in the first column of Part III of Schedule 1, being the new fee set out in the second column of the said Part III opposite that reference, such fee being payable in respect of each year of a trials cycle and so payable within 14 days of a demand made by the Minister;

(d) a renewal fee, being the new fee set out in the second and third columns of Part IV of Schedule 1 in relation to the particular year of retention of a plant variety in a National List opposite the reference in the first column of the said Part IV to the plant variety of the kind retained in the National List, such fee being payable, subject to regulation 4(3) below, before the beginning of the particular year of retention in the National List;

(e) the fees payable in respect of the matters referred to in the first column of Part V of Schedule 1, being the new fees set out in the third column of the said Part V opposite the respective references to those matters, such fees being payable at the times specified in respect of each such matter in the second column of the said Part V.

(2) The fees prescribed in Part II of Schedule 1 shall not be payable—

(a) by an applicant who has paid the fees prescribed by regulations made under the Act in respect of tests carried out on his behalf for the purposes of a grant of plant breeders' rights in respect of the same variety, or

(b) except as provided in paragraph (3) below, in respect of tests undertaken at a time when there is no plant breeders' rights scheme in operation in respect of the plant variety tested.

(3) If, while a plant variety in respect of which no plant breeders' rights scheme has operated is undergoing tests in connection with an application for its entry in a National List, a plant breeders' rights scheme comes into operation with respect to such variety, the person on whose behalf those tests are being carried out shall forthwith—

(a) apply for plant breeders' rights in respect of the plant variety (and become liable to pay any fees which may become payable under regulations made under the Act in connection with such application), or

(b) become liable to pay to the Minister the fees prescribed in Part II of Schedule 1 within 14 days of a demand made by the Minister.

(4) If the fee payable by a person in connection with tests of a plant variety shall not have been paid within 14 days of a demand made by the Minister or, as appropriate, in accordance with paragraph (3) above, the Minister shall not be obliged to take any further steps in relation to the tests until the fee shall have been paid.

Renewal fees

4.—(1) The renewal fee shall be paid by the maintainer who is indicated in the National List in compliance with regulation 18(1) of the principal Regulations.

(2) Where two or more maintainers are indicated in a National List as responsible for the maintenance of a plant variety there shall when the occasion arises be paid by each of them, in place of the renewal fee prescribed in Part IV of Schedule 1, a fee equal to one-half of such fee and if a fee so payable by a maintainer is not paid the Ministers shall remove from the National List the reference to such person as a maintainer of the plant variety.

(3) The Ministers may extend the time for the payment of a renewal fee if they consider that it is reasonable in all the circumstances to do so.

Revocation

5. The Regulations specified in Schedule 2 are revoked.

In Witness whereof the Official Seal of the Minister of Agriculture, Fisheries and Food is hereunto affixed on 5th February 1987.

Michael Jopling
Minister of Agriculture, Fisheries and Food

5th February 1987

John J. Mackay
Parliamentary Under-Secretary of State, Scottish Office

9th February 1987

Nicholas Edwards
Secretary of State for Wales

9th February 1987

Tom King
Secretary of State for Northern Ireland

SCHEDULE 1   Regulation 3

FEES

PART I

FEES PAYABLE ON AN APPLICATION FOR ENTRY OF A PLANT VARIETY IN A NATIONAL LIST

	Plant variety	*Fee*
		£
1.	A wheat (excluding durum wheat and spelt wheat) or barley variety	385
2.	A durum wheat, spelt wheat, rye, oat, oilseed rape, ryegrass, timothy, white clover, fescue or potato variety	310
3.	A maize, sugar beet or fodder beet variety	340
4.	A field pea or field bean variety	205
5.	Any other herbage, fodder, oil and fibre or cereal variety	150
6.	A vegetable variety subject to a plant breeders' rights scheme	150
7.	Any other vegetable variety	110

PART II

FEES PAYABLE IN RESPECT OF TESTS FOR DISTINCTNESS, UNIFORMITY AND STABILITY OF A PLANT VARIETY WHICH IS THE SUBJECT OF AN APPLICATION FOR ENTRY IN A NATIONAL LIST

		Amount	
	Plant variety	*New fee*	*Old fee*
		£	£(a)
1.	A wheat (excluding durum wheat and spelt wheat), barley or maize variety	680	*(535)*
2.	A durum wheat, spelt wheat, rye, oat, oilseed rape, ryegrass, timothy, white clover, fescue, potato, field pea or field bean variety	460	*(360–535)*
3.	Any other herbage, fodder, oil and fibre, cereal or vegetable variety	260	*(205–535)*

Note
(a) The figures in italics are the fees which were charged under the Seeds (National Lists of Varieties) (Fees) (Amendment) Regulations 1986 (S.I. 1986/338) before the coming into force of these Regulations.

PART III

FEES PAYABLE IN RESPECT OF TRIALS FOR VALUE FOR CULTIVATION AND USE OF A PLANT VARIETY WHICH IS THE SUBJECT OF AN APPLICATION FOR ENTRY IN A NATIONAL LIST

		Amount	
	Plant variety	*New fee*	*Old fee*
		£	£(a)
1.	A wheat (excluding durum wheat and spelt wheat) or barley variety	2,090	*(1,115)*
2.	A durum wheat, spelt wheat, rye, oat, oilseed rape, ryegrass, timothy, white clover, fescue, potato, maize, sugar beet, field bean, field pea, swede or fodder kale variety	720	*(1,115)***(b)**

Notes
(a) The figures in italics are the fees which were charged for the first year of a trials cycle under the Seeds (National Lists of Varieties) (Fees) (Amendment) Regulations 1986 before the coming into force of these Regulations.
(b) Applied only to oat varieties.

PART IV

RENEWAL FEES

		Renewal fees during the years of retention in a National List			
	Plant variety	*Second to fifth year — each year*		*Sixth and each subsequent year*	
		New fee	*Old fee*	*New fee*	*Old fee*
		£	£(a)	£	£(a)
1.	A wheat (excluding durum wheat and spelt wheat) or barley variety	240	*(130)*	405	*(220)*
2.	A durum wheat, spelt wheat, rye, oat, oilseed rape, ryegrass, timothy, white clover, fescue, potato, maize, sugar beet, fodder beet, field bean or field pea variety	225	*(120–130)*	345	*(185–220)*
3.	Any other herbage, fodder, oil and fibre or cereal variety	140	*(85–130)*	225	*(130–220)*
4.	A vegetable variety subject to a plant breeders' rights scheme	140	*(85)*	225	*(130)*
5.	Any other vegetable variety	120	*(85)*	180	*(130)*

Note
(a) The figures in italics are the fees which were charged under the Seeds (National Lists of Varieties) (Fees) (Amendment) Regulations 1986 before the coming into force of these Regulations.

PART V

FEES PAYABLE IN RESPECT OF OTHER MATTERS

Matter	When payable	Amount New fee	Old fee
		£	£(a)
1. Application for the substitution of a name in a National List	On making the application	21	(20)
2. Making written representations to the Ministers	On delivering the representations	3	(3)
3. Attending to be heard by a person appointed by the Ministers	Before the hearing	21	(20)
4. Inspection of the National List record	Before the inspection	1	(1)
5. Inspection of the file maintained for a plant variety in a National List	Before the inspection	1	(1)
6. Purchase of a report from a testing authority in another country	Within 14 days of demand by the Minister	112	(106)
7. Observation plot—trials for value for cultivation and use	Within 14 days of demand by the Minister	100	(—)
8. Entry in a National List—	Before entry in a National List		
(a) of a variety referred to in items 1 to 4 in Part I of this Schedule		110	(—)
(b) of a variety referred to in items 5 to 7 in Part I of this Schedule		60	(—)

Note
(a) The figures in italics are the fees which were charged under the Seeds (National Lists of Varieties) (Fees) (Amendment) Regulations 1986 before the coming into force of these Regulations. No fees were charged under those Regulations in respect of items 7 and 8 above.

Regulation 5

SCHEDULE 2

REVOCATIONS

Regulations revoked	References
The Seeds (National Lists of Varieties) (Fees) Regulations 1980	S.I. 1980/330
The Seeds (National Lists of Varieties) (Fees) (Amendment) Regulations 1981	S.I. 1981/342
The Seeds (National Lists of Varieties) (Fees) (Amendment) Regulations 1983	S.I. 1983/293
The Seeds (National Lists of Varieties) (Fees) (Amendment No. 2) Regulations 1983	S.I. 1983/1500
The Seeds (National Lists of Varieties) (Fees) (Amendment) Regulations 1984	S.I. 1984/243
The Seeds (National Lists of Varieties) (Fees) (Amendment) Regulations 1985	S.I. 1985/356
The Seeds (National Lists of Varieties) (Fees) (Amendment) Regulations 1986	S.I. 1986/338

EXPLANATORY NOTE

(This note is not part of the Regulations)

These Regulations consolidate with amendments the Seeds (National Lists of Varieties) (Fees) Regulations 1980, as amended. They prescribe fees in respect of various matters arising under the Seeds (National Lists of Varieties) Regulations 1982, as amended (regulation 3 and Schedule 1). The fees are payable to the Minister of Agriculture, Fisheries and Food.

The changes of substance are—

(a) the introduction of fees on making an application for the entry of a plant variety in a National List (regulation 3(1)(a) and Part I of Schedule 1);

(b) the introduction of fees in respect of trials for value for cultivation and use on an observation plot and in respect of entry of a plant variety in a National List (regulation 3(1)(e) and items 7 and 8 in Part V of Schedule 1);

(c) the introduction of a fee in respect of trials for value for cultivation and use of additional plant varieties (regulation 3(1)(c) and item 2 in Part III of Schedule 1);

(d) a general increase in fees payable in respect of tests and other trials of plant varieties, the retention of a plant variety in a National List and various miscellaneous matters (regulation 3(1)(b) to (e), Part II, item 1 in Part III and Parts IV and V of Schedule 1). Some fees remain the same and a few are reduced. Old fees are shown in Schedule 1 in italics.

The regulations continue to make provision for non-payment of fees for tests of a plant variety in certain circumstances (regulation 3(2) and (3)).

STATUTORY INSTRUMENTS

1987 No. 189

PLANT BREEDERS' RIGHTS

The Plant Breeders' Rights (Fees) Regulations 1987

Made - - - -	*11th February 1987*
Laid before Parliament	*20th February 1987*
Coming into force	*1st April 1987*

The Minister of Agriculture, Fisheries and Food, the Secretary of State for Scotland, the Secretary of State for Wales and the Secretary of State for Northern Ireland, acting jointly, in exercise of the powers conferred by sections 9(1) and 36 of the Plant Varieties and Seeds Act 1964(a) as extended to Northern Ireland(b) and now vested in them(c), and the said Minister and the Secretary of State, acting jointly, in exercise of the said powers as extended to the Isle of Man(d), and in exercise of all other powers enabling them in that behalf, with the approval of the Treasury in accordance with section 9(1) of the said Act of 1964 and after consultation with the Council on Tribunals in accordance with section 10(1) of the Tribunals and Inquiries Act 1971(e), hereby make the following Regulations:—

Title and commencement

1. These Regulations may be cited as the Plant Breeders' Rights (Fees) Regulations 1987 and shall come into force on 1st April 1987.

Interpretation

2.—(1) In these Regulations—

"the Act" means the Plant Varieties and Seeds Act 1964;

"the Controller" means the Controller of Plant Variety Rights;

"National List" means a list of plant varieties prepared and published in accordance with the Seeds (National Lists of Varieties) Regulations 1982(f);

"plant breeders' rights" means rights which may be granted in accordance with Part I of the Act;

"the principal Regulations" means the Plant Breeders' Rights Regulations 1978(g);

"renewal fee" means a fee payable in respect of the continued exercise of plant breeders' rights in a plant variety.

(2) Any reference in these Regulations to "the Schedule" shall be construed as a reference to the Schedule to these Regulations.

Payment of fees

3.—(1) There shall be paid to the Controller in respect of matters relating to plant breeders' rights arising under the Act or the principal Regulations—

(a) 1964 c.14.
(b) By the Plant Varieties and Seeds (Northern Ireland) Order 1964 (S.I. 1964/1574).
(c) In the case of the Secretary of State for Wales, by virtue of S.I. 1978/272.
(d) By the Plant Varieties and Seeds (Isle of Man) Order 1969 (S.I. 1969/1829).
(e) 1971 c.62.
(f) S.I. 1982/844, amended by S.I. 1985/1529.
(g) S.I. 1978/294, to which there are amendments not relevant to these Regulations.

(a) a fee on making an application for a grant of plant breeders' rights, being the new fee set out in the second column of Part I of the Schedule opposite the reference in the first column of the said Part I to the plant variety of the kind to which the application relates, such fee being payable on making the application;

(b) a fee payable in respect of tests or examination of a plant variety which is the subject of an application for a grant of plant breeders' rights, being the new fee set out in the third column of Part II of the Schedule opposite the reference in the first column of the said Part II to the plant variety of the kind to which the tests or examination relate, such fee being payable for the tests or examination referred to in the second column of the said Part II and so payable within fourteen days of a written demand made by the Controller;

(c) a renewal fee, being the new fee set out in relation to the particular year of the exercise of such rights in the second and third columns of Part III of the Schedule opposite the reference in the first column of the said Part III to the plant variety of the kind for which the rights were granted, such fee being due on, but not payable more than three months before, the anniversary of the date of the grant of the rights with which the particular year begins or within such later period as may have been allowed by the Controller;

(d) subject to paragraph (4) below, the fees payable in respect of the matters referred to in the first column of Part IV of the Schedule, being the new fees set out in the third column of the said Part IV opposite the respective references to those matters, such fees being payable at the times specified in respect of each such matter in the second column of the said Part IV.

(2) If at the time of the application for a grant of plant breeders' rights the plant variety in respect of which the application is made is or has been the subject of an application for its entry in a National List but no fee is or has been payable under the Seeds (National Lists of Varieties) (Fees) Regulations 1987(a) in respect of tests which have been or are being undertaken in connection with such application, then there shall be paid to the Controller in addition to the fee payable under paragraph (1)(b) above a fee in respect of such tests calculated in accordance with Part II of the Schedule as if references to tests in relation to an application for a grant of plant breeders' rights were references to tests in relation to an application for the entry of a plant variety in a National List.

(3) The fee payable in accordance with paragraph (2) above shall be payable within fourteen days of a written demand made by the Controller.

(4) No fee shall be payable in accordance with paragraph (1)(d) above in respect of any application to amend a document in any application or proceeding or in respect of any application for the amendment of the register of plant varieties where that application relates solely to the change of the end of the name of a body corporate to "public limited company" or its Welsh equivalent pursuant to the Companies Act 1985(b).

Renewal fees

4.—(1) The renewal fee shall be paid only by the holder of the plant breeders' rights or by a person acting on his behalf, being either an agent duly authorised in accordance with regulation 16 of the principal Regulations or a person who shall deliver to the Controller with the fee an authority in writing to pay the same, signed by the holder of the rights and if any such fee is tendered or paid otherwise than in accordance with this paragraph, the liability to pay the same shall not be regarded as having been thereby discharged.

(2) In a case where the period for which any plant breeders' rights are exercisable has been terminated in accordance with the principal Regulations on the ground that a renewal fee has not been paid, there shall only be recoverable by the Controller such a proportion of that fee as the period during which those rights have continued to be enjoyed since the date when the fee became payable bears to the period of 12 months.

(3) Notwithstanding regulation 3 above and paragraph (2) of this regulation, in a case where the period for which any plant breeders' rights are exercisable has been

---

(a) S.I. 1987/188.
(b) 1985 c.6.

terminated in accordance with the principal Regulations on the ground that a renewal fee has not been paid and—

    (a) the person entitled to exercise those rights has, not later than fourteen days before the date when that fee became payable, informed the Controller that he did not propose to exercise any of those rights at any time after that date, and

    (b) that person has not exercised any of those rights during the period beginning with the date when the fee became payable and ending with the date when the period for which the rights are exercisable was terminated,

the Controller shall not be entitled to recover from such person, by any legal proceedings or otherwise, the fee or any part of it.

Revocation

5. The Plant Breeders' Rights (Fees) Regulations 1985**(a)** and the Plant Breeders' Rights (Fees) (Amendment) Regulations 1986**(b)** are revoked.

In Witness whereof the Official Seal of the Minister of Agriculture, Fisheries and Food is hereunto affixed on 5th February 1987.

Michael Jopling
Minister of Agriculture, Fisheries and Food

John J. Mackay
Parliamentary Under-Secretary of State,
5th February 1987   Scottish Office

Nicholas Edwards
9th February 1987   Secretary of State for Wales

Tom King
9th February 1987   Secretary of State for Northern Ireland

Douglas Hurd
Secretary of State for the Home Department
(being the Secretary of State concerned
8th February 1987   with matters relating to the Isle of Man)

We approve,

T. Sainsbury
Michael Neubert
11th February 1987   Two of the Lords Commissioners of Her Majesty's Treasury

---

(a) S.I. 1985/357.
(b) S.I. 1986/339.

Regulation 3(1)

SCHEDULE

FEES

PART I

FEES PAYABLE ON AN APPLICATION FOR A GRANT OF PLANT BREEDERS' RIGHTS

	Plant variety	*Amount*	
		New fee	*Old fee*
		£	£(a)
1.	A wheat (excluding durum wheat and spelt wheat) or barley variety	520	(*280*)
2.	A durum wheat, spelt wheat, rye, oat, oilseed rape, ryegrass, timothy, white clover, fescue or potato variety	400	(*215–280*)
3.	A maize variety	480	(*280*)
4.	A field pea or field bean variety	310	(*215*)
5.	Any other herbage, fodder (including fenugreek), oil and fibre, cereal or vegetable variety	185	(*110–280*)
6.	Any other variety not mentioned above (including a decorative or fruit variety)	115	(*110*)

Note

(a) The figures in italics are the fees which were charged under the Plant Breeders' Rights (Fees) (Amendment) Regulations 1986 (S.I. 1986/339) before the coming into force of these Regulations.

PART II

FEES PAYABLE IN RESPECT OF TESTS OR EXAMINATION OF A PLANT VARIETY WHICH IS THE SUBJECT OF AN APPLICATION FOR A GRANT OF PLANT BREEDERS' RIGHTS

	Plant variety	*Tests or examination for which payable*	*Amount*	
			New fee	*Old fee*
			£	£(a)
1.	A wheat (excluding durum wheat and spelt wheat), barley or maize variety	Tests in any one year	680	(*535*)
2.	A durum wheat, spelt wheat, rye, oat, oilseed rape, ryegrass, timothy, white clover, fescue, potato, field pea or field bean variety	Tests in any one year	460	(*360–535*)
3.	Any other herbage, fodder (including fenugreek), oil and fibre, cereal or vegetable variety	Tests in any one year	260	(*205–535*)
4.	A year-round perennial chrysanthemum variety	Tests in each flowering season	215	(*205*)
5.	A cymbidium variety	Each examination	215	(*205*)
6.	Any other variety not mentioned above (including a decorative or fruit variety)	Tests in any one year	215	(*205*)

Note

(a) The figures in italics are the fees which were charged under the Plant Breeders' Rights (Fees) (Amendment) Regulations 1986 before the coming into force of these Regulations.

PART III

RENEWAL FEES

Plant variety	Renewal fees during the years of the exercise of plant breeders' rights indicated below			
	Second to fifth year — each year		Sixth and each subsequent year	
	New fee	Old fee	New fee	Old fee
	£	£(a)	£	£(a)
1. A wheat (excluding durum wheat and spelt wheat) or barley variety	455	(245)	605	(325)
2. A durum wheat, spelt wheat, rye, oat, oilseed rape, ryegrass, timothy, white clover, fescue, potato, maize, field bean or field pea variety	320	(175–245)	545	(295–325)
3. Any other herbage, fodder (including fenugreek), oil and fibre, cereal or vegetable variety	185	(110–245)	245	(145–325)
4. Any other variety not mentioned above (including a decorative or fruit variety)	120	(110)	155	(145)

Note

(a) The figures in italics are the fees which were charged under the Plant Breeders' Rights (Fees) (Amendment) Regulations 1986 before the coming into force of these Regulations.

PART IV

FEES PAYABLE IN RESPECT OF OTHER MATTERS

Matter	When payable	Amount	
		New fee	Old fee
		£	£(a)
1. Application for a compulsory licence	On making the application	21	(20)
2. Application to extend, limit, vary or revoke a compulsory licence	On making the application	21	(20)
3. Application to amend a document in any application or proceeding	On making the application	3	(3)
4. Application to rectify an error or omission in the register of plant varieties	On making the application	3	(3)
5. Application for extension of time for the service or delivery of a document or thing or for the doing of an act	On making the application	3	(3)
6. Making representations in writing to the Controller, by any person other than the applicant, in connection with any application	On delivering the representations	3	(3)
7. Making representations in writing to the Controller, by any person other than the holder of plant breeders' rights, in connection with a proposal to terminate those rights or to revoke or terminate any extension of such rights	On delivering the representations	3	(3)

PART IV – *continued*

Matter	*When payable*	Amount	
		New fee	*Old fee*
		£	£(a)
8. Attending to be heard by the Controller, or by a person appointed by him for the purpose	Before the hearing	21	(20)
9. Grant of plant breeders' rights in—			
(a) a variety referred to in items 1 to 4 in Part I of this Schedule	Before the issue of the document constituting evidence of the grant	145	(80)
(b) a variety referred to in item 5 in Part I of this Schedule		135	(80)
(c) a variety referred to in item 6 in Part I of this Schedule		85	(80)
10. Giving a protective direction	Before the issue of the document constituting evidence of the giving of the protective direction	21	(20)
11. Application for an extension of the period for payment of a renewal fee	On making the application	21	(20)
12. Payment of a renewal fee after the expiration of 7 days from the date when it fell due, except in a case where an application has been made for the period for payment to be extended	On payment of the renewal fee	21	(20)
13. Application for the approval of a substituted name for a plant variety	On making the application	21	(20)
14. Application for the amendment of the register of plant varieties, except in a case where the plant breeders' rights are transferred to another person	On making the application	3	(3)
15. Registration of title and amendment of the register of plant varieties on a transfer of plant breeders' rights or a share in such rights	On making the application for registration	21	(20)
16. Inspection of the register of plant varieties or of a document in the possession of the Controller	Before the inspection	1	(1)
17. Supplying copies of documents, per page	Before the delivery of the copies	0.30	(0.30)
18. Supplying a duplicate of a document constituting evidence of a grant of plant breeders' rights or protective direction	On ordering the duplicate	6	(6)
19. Purchase of a report from a testing authority in another country	Within 14 days of demand by the Controller	112	(106)

Note

(a) The figures in italics are the fees which were charged under the Plant Breeders' Rights (Fees) (Amendment) Regulations 1986 before the coming into force of these Regulations.

EXPLANATORY NOTE

(This note is not part of the Regulations)

These regulations consolidate with amendments the Plant Breeders' Rights (Fees) Regulations 1985, as amended. They prescribe fees in respect of various matters relating to plant breeders' rights arising under the Plant Varieties and Seeds Act 1964 or the Plant Breeders' Rights Regulations 1978, as amended (regulation 3 and Schedule). The fees are payable to the Controller of Plant Variety Rights.

There is a general increase in fees payable on making an application for a grant of plant breeders' rights (regulation 3(1)(a) and Part I of Schedule) or payable in respect of tests or examination of a plant variety (regulation 3(1)(b) and Part II of Schedule), the continued exercise of plant breeders' rights in a plant variety (regulation 3(1)(c) and Part III of Schedule) and various miscellaneous matters (regulation 3(1)(d) and Part IV of Schedule). Some fees remain the same and a few are reduced. Old fees are shown in the Schedule in italics.

1987 No. 191

PENSIONS

The Personal Injuries (Civilians) Amendment Scheme 1987

Made - - - -	*11th February 1987*
Laid before Parliament	*18th February 1987*
Coming into force	*6th April 1987*

The Secretary of State for Social Services, with the consent of the Treasury, in exercise of the powers conferred by sections 1 and 2 of the Personal Injuries (Emergency Provisions) Act 1939(**a**) and now vested in him(**b**), and of all other powers enabling him in that behalf, hereby makes the following Scheme:-

Citation, commencement and interpretation

1.—(1) This Scheme may be cited as the Personal Injuries (Civilians) Amendment Scheme 1987 and shall come into force on 6th April 1987.

(2) In this Scheme the expression "the principal Scheme" means the Personal Injuries (Civilians) Scheme 1983(**c**).

Amendment of Article 18 of the principal Scheme

2. In Article 18 of the principal Scheme (unemployability allowances) in paragraph (2) for the amount "£1,326" there shall be substituted the amount "£1,352".

Abolition of funeral grants

3.—(1) The principal Scheme shall be amended in accordance with the following provisions of this Article.

(2) Article 40 (funeral grants), and paragraph 12 of Schedule 4 are hereby revoked.

(3) In Article 53 the words "(other than a funeral grant)" and the words "and the expression 'funeral grant' means a funeral grant under Article 40" shall be omitted.

(4) In Article 54(3) the words "or of a funeral grant" shall be omitted.

(5) In Article 58(1) the words "(other than a funeral grant)" shall be omitted.

(6) In Article 63(1) and (2) the words "or funeral grant" shall be omitted wherever they appear.

(7) In Article 66(1) the words "or funeral grant" shall be omitted wherever they appear.

(**a**) 1939 c.82.　(**b**) *See* Transfer of Functions (Ministry of Pensions) Order 1953 (S.I. 1953/1198), Article 2; Ministry of Social Security Act 1966 (c.20), section 2; Secretary of State for Social Services Order 1968 (S.I. 1968/1699), Article 2.　(**c**) S.I. 1983/686, as amended by S.I. 1983/1164, 1540, 1984/1289, 1675, 1985/1313, 1986/628.

(8)   In Article 67(1) and (2) the words "or funeral grant" shall be omitted wherever they appear.

(9)   In Article 79 the words "or funeral grant" shall be omitted wherever they appear.

Substitution of Schedules 3 and 4 to the principal Scheme

4.   For Schedules 3 and 4 to the principal Scheme (rates of pensions and allowances payable in respect of disablement and death) there shall respectively be substituted the Schedules set out in the Schedule hereto and numbered 3 and 4.

Signed by authority of the Secretary of State for Social Services.

Trumpington
Parliamentary Under-Secretary of State,
6th February 1987   Department of Health and Social Security

We consent,

Tim Sainsbury
Michael Neubert
11th February 1987   Two of the Lords Commissioners of Her Majesty's Treasury

---

SCHEDULE   Article 4

Schedules to be substituted in the principal Scheme

"SCHEDULE 3   Article 11

Rates of Pensions and Allowances Payable in Respect of Disablement

Description of Pension or Allowance	Rate
1. Pension for 100 per cent. disablement under Article 11	£ 64.50 per week
2. Education allowance under Article 13	£120.00 per annum*
3. Constant attendance allowance—	
(a) under the proviso to Article 14	£ 51.60 per week*
(b) in any other case under that Article	£ 25.80 per week*
4. Exceptionally severe disablement allowance under Article 15	£ 25.80 per week
5. Severe disablement occupational allowance under Article 16	£ 12.90 per week
6. Allowance for wear and tear of clothing—	
(a) under Article 17(1)(a)	£ 56.00 per annum
(b) under Article 17(1)(b) and 17(2)	£ 88.00 per annum
7. Unemployability allowances—	
(a) personal allowance under Article 18(1)(i)	£ 41.95 per week
(b) additional allowances for dependants by way of—	
(i) increase of allowance in respect of a wife or a dependent husband under Article 18(5)(b)	£ 23.75 per week*
(ii) allowance in respect of an adult dependant under Article 18(5)(c)	£ 23.75 per week*
(iii) increase of allowance in respect of each child under Article 18(5)(d)	£ 8.05 per week

SCHEDULE 3:*continued*

Description of Pension or Allowance	Rate
8. Invalidity allowance payable under Article 19	
(a) if—	
(i) the relevant date fell before 5th July 1948; or	
(ii) on the relevant date the disabled person was under the age of 35; or	
(iii) on the relevant date the disabled person was under the age of 40 and had not attained the age of 65, in the case of the disabled person being a man, or 60, in the case of that person being a woman, before 6th April 1979 and the period in respect of which payment of the allowance is to relate begins on or after 6th April 1979	£ 8.30 per week
(b) if—	
(i) on the relevant date the disabled person was under the age of 45; or	
(ii) on the relevant date the disabled person was under the age of 50 and had not attained the age of 65, in the case of the disabled person being a man, or 60, in the case of that person being a woman, before 6th April 1979 and the period in respect of which payment of the allowance is to relate begins on or after 6th April 1979	£ 5.30 per week
(c) if heads (a) and (b) do not apply and on the relevant date the disabled person was a man under the age of 60 or a woman under the age of 55	£ 2.65 per week
9. Comforts allowance—	
(a) under Article 20(1)(a)	£ 11.10 per week
(b) under Article 20(1)(b) or 45(1)	£ 5.55 per week
10. Allowance for lowered standard of occupation under Article 21	£ 25.80 per week*
11. Age allowance under Article 22 where the degree of pensioned disablement is—	
(a) 40 or 50 per cent.	£ 4.50 per week
(b) 60 or 70 per cent.	£ 7.00 per week
(c) 80 or 90 per cent.	£ 10.05 per week
(d) 100 per cent.	£ 14.00 per week
12. Treatment allowances— increase of personal allowance under Article 23(2)	£ 14.00 per week*
13. Part-time treatment allowance under Article 25	£ 25.40 per day*
14. Mobility supplement under Article 25A	£ 24.55 per week

*Maximum

SCHEDULE 4

Article 27

Rates of Pensions and Allowances Payable in Respect of Death

Description of Pension or Allowance	Rate
1. Pension to widow—	
(a) under Article 27(1)	£ 51.35 per week
(b) under Article 27(2)	£ 11.85 per week

SCHEDULE 4:*continued*

Description of Pension or Allowance	Rate
2. Rent allowance under Article 28	£ 19.55 per week*
3. Allowance under Article 29 or 50 to an elderly surviving spouse—	
(a) if age 65 but under age 70	£ 5.50 per week
(b) if age 70 but under age 80	£ 11.00 per week
(c) if age 80 or over	£ 13.85 per week
4. Pension under Article 30 to unmarried dependant who lived as spouse	£ 1.00 per week*
5. Pension to dependent widower under Article 32	£ 51.35 per week*
6. Allowances under Article 33 in respect of each child under the age of 15	£ 11.60 per week
7. Pensions under Article 34(1) to motherless or fatherless children under the age of 15	£ 12.70 per week
8. Pension or allowance under Article 35(3) to or in respect of a child over the age of 15—	
(a) where the child has attained the age of 18 and is incapable of self-support by reason of an infirmity which arose before he attained the age of 15	£ 39.50 per week*
(b) any other case	£ 12.70 per week*
9. Education allowance under Article 36	£120.00 per annum*
10. Pensions to parents—	
(a) minimum rate under Article 38(4)	£ 0.25 per week
(b) maximum rate under Article 38(4)—	
(i) where there is only one eligible parent	£ 1.00 per week
(ii) where there is more than one eligible parent	£ 1.38 per week
(c) increase under the proviso to Article 38(4)—	
(i) where there is only one eligible parent	£ 0.38 per week*
(ii) where there is more than one eligible parent	£ 0.62 per week*
11. Pensions to other dependants—	
(a) for each juvenile dependant under Article 39(4)	£ 0.30 per week*
(b) aggregate rate under Article 39(4)	£ 1.00 per week*
(c) under Article 39(5)	£ 1.00 per week*

*Maximum".

EXPLANATORY NOTE

(This note is not part of the Scheme)

This Scheme, which takes effect from 6th April 1987, further amends the Personal Injuries (Civilians) Scheme 1983 ("the principal Scheme") which makes provision for the payment of pensions and allowances to or in respect of civilians who were killed or injured in the 1939–45 War.

Article 40 of the principal Scheme (funeral grants) is revoked to accord with the abolition of death grant payable under section 32 of the Social Security Act 1975 (c.14) by the Social Security Act 1986 (c.50), section 41 (Article 3).

This Scheme also raises the maximum amount of annual earnings which may be received by a disabled person while he is deemed to be unemployable for the purposes of unemployability allowances under Article 18 of the principal Scheme, and varies the rates of pensions and allowances in respect of disablement and death in the 1939–45 War (Articles 2 and 4, and the Schedule).

STATUTORY INSTRUMENTS

1987 No. 192

NATIONAL HEALTH SERVICE, ENGLAND AND WALES

The Special Hospital Boards (Amendment of Constitution) Order 1987

Made - - - -	*11th February 1987*
Laid before Parliament	*20th February 1987*
Coming into force	*13th March 1987*

The Secretary of State for Social Services, in exercise of powers conferred on him by section 11 of the National Health Service Act 1977**(a)**, and of all other powers enabling him in that behalf, hereby makes the following Order:—

Citation and commencement

1. This Order may be cited as the Special Hospital Boards (Amendment of Constitution) Order 1987 and shall come into force on 13th March 1987.

Amendment of Orders

2.—(1) Article 4 (constitution) of the Rampton Hospital Board (Establishment and Constitution) Order 1986**(b)** shall be amended by substituting "9" for "7".

(2) Article 4 (constitution) of the Broadmoor Hospital Board (Establishment and Constitution) Order 1986**(c)** shall be amended by substituting "9" for "7".

(3) Article 4 (constitution) of the Moss Side and Park Lane Hospitals Board (Establishment and Constitution) Order 1986**(d)** shall be amended by substituting "9" for "7".

Signed by authority of the Secretary of State for Social Services.

Trumpington
Parliamentary Under-Secretary of State,
Department of Health and Social Security

11th February 1987

(a) 1977 c. 49.
(b) S.I. 1986/963.
(c) S.I. 1986/2004.
(d) S.I. 1986/2006.

EXPLANATORY NOTE

(This note is not part of the Order)

This Order amends the Rampton Hospital Board (Establishment and Constitution) Order 1986, the Broadmoor Hospital Board (Establishment and Constitution) Order 1986, and the Moss Side and Park Lane Hospitals Board (Establishment and Constitution) Order 1986 so as to increase maximum membership of the three special health authorities established by those Orders from, in each case, seven members to nine members.

STATUTORY INSTRUMENTS

1987 No. 198 (C.4)

PUBLIC ORDER

The Public Order Act 1986 (Commencement No. 2) Order 1987

Made - - - - *13th February 1987*

In exercise of the powers conferred upon me by section 41 of the Public Order Act 1986**(a)**, I hereby make the following Order:

1.—(1) This Order may be cited as the Public Order Act 1986 (Commencement No. 2) Order 1987.

(2) In this Order "the 1986 Act" means the Public Order Act 1986.

2. The provisions of the 1986 Act specified in the Schedule to this Order shall come into force on 1st April 1987.

Douglas Hurd
Home Office   One of Her Majesty's Principal Secretaries of State
13th February 1987

(a) 1986 c.64.

Article 2   **SCHEDULE**

PROVISIONS OF THE PUBLIC ORDER ACT 1986 COMING INTO FORCE ON 1st APRIL 1987.

Provisions of the Act	*Subject matter of provisions*
In Part I–	
Section 1	Offence of riot.
Section 2	Offence of violent disorder.
Section 3	Offence of affray.
Section 4	Offence involving fear or provocation of violence.
Section 5	Offence involving harassment, alarm or distress.
Section 6	Mental element for offences under sections 1 to 5.
Section 7	Procedure in connection with offences under sections 1 to 5.
Section 8	Interpretation of terms in Part I.
Section 9	Abolition of offences.
Section 10	Construction of "riot" and cognate expressions in other instruments.
In Part II–	
Section 12	Imposing conditions on public processions.
Section 13	Prohibiting public processions.
Section 14	Imposing conditions on public assemblies.
Section 15	Delegation of powers of Chief Officer of Police under sections 12 to 14.
In Part III–	
Section 17	Meaning of "racial hatred" in Part III.
Section 18	Offence of using racially inflammatory words or behaviour or displaying racially inflammatory written material.
Section 19	Offence of publishing or distributing racially inflammatory written material.
Section 20	Offence of giving a public performance of a racially inflammatory play.
Section 21	Offence of distributing, showing or playing a racially inflammatory recording.
Section 22	Offence of broadcasting a racially inflammatory programme or including such a programme in a cable programme service.
Section 23	Offence of possession of racially inflammatory material.
Section 24	Powers of entry and search.
Section 25	Power to order forfeiture.
Section 26	Savings for reports of parliamentary or judicial proceedings.
Section 27	Procedure in connection with and punishment for offences under sections 18 to 23.
Section 28	Liability of director and others where body corporate guilty of offence under Part III.
Section 29	Interpretation of terms in Part III.
In Part V–	
Section 39	Power to direct trespassers to leave land.
Section 40, to the extent not already in force	Amendments, repeals and savings.
Schedule 2, to the extent not already in force	Miscellaneous and consequential amendments.
Schedule 3, to the extent not already in force	Repeals.

EXPLANATORY NOTE

(This note is not part of the Order)

This Order brings into force on 1st April 1987 the provisions of the Public Order Act 1986 specified in the Schedule to the Order.

NOTE AS TO EARLIER COMMENCEMENT ORDERS

(This note is not part of the Order)

Provisions	*Date of Commencement*	*S.I. No.*
Sections 11, 16 and 38 and section 40 partially, sections 41 to 43 and Schedule 1 and Schedules 2 and 3 partially	1.1.87	1986/2041

STATUTORY INSTRUMENTS

1987 No. 199

OFFSHORE INSTALLATIONS

The Offshore Installations (Safety Zones) (Revocation) (No. 2) Order 1987

Made - - -	*12th February 1987*
Coming into force -	*14th February 1987*

The Secretary of State, in exercise of the power conferred on him by section 21(1) of the Oil and Gas (Enterprise) Act 1982(**a**), and of all other powers enabling him in that behalf, hereby makes the following Order:—

1. This Order may be cited as the Offshore Installations (Safety Zones) (Revocation) (No. 2) Order 1987 and shall come into force on 14th February 1987.

2. The Offshore Installations (Safety Zones) Orders specified in the Schedule hereto are hereby revoked.

Alick Buchanan-Smith
Minister of State,
Department of Energy

12th February 1987

(**a**) 1982 c. 23.

SCHEDULE

Article 2

OFFSHORE INSTALLATIONS (SAFETY ZONES) ORDERS REVOKED

Order	Reference	Name of installation to which Order relates
The Offshore Installations (Safety Zones) (No. 94) Order 1986	S.I. 1986/1741	Dyvi Omega
The Offshore Installations (Safety Zones) (No. 100) Order 1986	S.I. 1986/1839	Dyvi Sigma
The Offshore Installations (Safety Zones) (No. 108) Order 1986	S.I. 1986/2052	Penrod 80
The Offshore Installations (Safety Zones) (No. 80) Order 1986	S.I. 1986/1464	Penrod 85
The Offshore Installations (Safety Zones) (No. 10) Order 1987	S.I. 1987/67	Rowan Gorilla II
The Offshore Installations (Safety Zones) (No. 14) Order 1987	S.I. 1987/71	Sedco 714

EXPLANATORY NOTE

(This note is not part of the Order)

This Order revokes the Offshore Installations (Safety Zones) Orders specified in the Schedule. The installations specified in the Schedule which were protected by the safety zones established by those Orders have been removed and accordingly those Orders are no longer required.

STATUTORY INSTRUMENTS

1987 No. 200

OFFSHORE INSTALLATIONS

The Offshore Installations (Safety Zones) (No. 16) Order 1987

Made - - - -	*12th February 1987*
Coming into force	*14th February 1987*

The Secretary of State, in exercise of the powers conferred on him by section 21(1), (2) and (3) of the Oil and Gas (Enterprise) Act 1982**(a)** (hereinafter referred to as "the Act"), and of all other powers enabling him in that behalf, hereby makes the following Order:—

1. This Order may be cited as the Offshore Installations (Safety Zones) (No. 16) Order 1987 and shall come into force on 14th February 1987.

2.—(1) A safety zone is hereby established around the installation specified in Column 1 of the Schedule hereto (being an installation maintained in waters to which section 21 of the Act**(b)** applies) having a radius of five hundred metres from the point as respects that installation which has the co-ordinates of latitude and longitude according to European Datum (1950) specified in Columns 2 and 3 of the Schedule.

(2) The prohibition under section 21(3) of the Act on a vessel entering or remaining in a safety zone without the consent of the Secretary of State shall not apply to a vessel entering or remaining in the safety zone established under paragraph (1) above—

(*a*) in connection with the laying, inspection, testing, repair, alteration, renewal or removal of any submarine cable or pipe-line in or near that safety zone;

(*b*) to provide services for, to transport persons or goods to or from, or under the authority of a government department to inspect, any installation in that safety zone;

(*c*) if it is a vessel belonging to a general lighthouse authority performing duties relating to the safety of navigation;

(*d*) in connection with the saving or attempted saving of life or property;

(*e*) owing to stress of weather; or

(*f*) when in distress.

12th February 1987

Alick Buchanan-Smith
Minister of State, Department of Energy

SCHEDULE

Article 2(1)

SAFETY ZONE

1	2	3
Name or other designation of the offshore installation	Latitude North	Longitude East
Audrey Template	53° 32′ 25·86″	02° 00′ 57·01″

EXPLANATORY NOTE

(This note is not part of the Order)

This Order establishes, under section 21 of the Oil and Gas (Enterprise) Act 1982, a safety zone, having a radius of 500 metres from a specified point, around the installation specified in the Schedule to this Order and maintained in waters to which the section applies (these include territorial waters and waters in areas designated under section 1(7) of the Continental Shelf Act 1964 (c.29)).

Vessels (which for this purpose include hovercraft, submersible apparatus and installations in transit) are prohibited from entering or remaining in the safety zone except with the consent of the Secretary of State or in the circumstances mentioned in Article 2(2) of the Order.

1987 No. 201

OFFSHORE INSTALLATIONS

The Offshore Installations (Safety Zones) (No. 17) Order 1987

Made - - - -	*12th February 1987*
Coming into force	*14th February 1987*

The Secretary of State, in exercise of the powers conferred on him by section 21(1), (2) and (3) of the Oil and Gas (Enterprise) Act 1982**(a)** (hereinafter referred to as "the Act"), and of all other powers enabling him in that behalf, hereby makes the following Order:—

1. This Order may be cited as the Offshore Installations (Safety Zones) (No. 17) Order 1987 and shall come into force on 14th February 1987.

2.—(1) A safety zone is hereby established around the installation specified in Column 1 of the Schedule hereto (being an installation maintained in waters to which section 21 of the Act**(b)** applies) having a radius of five hundred metres from the point as respects that installation which has the co-ordinates of latitude and longitude according to European Datum (1950) specified in Columns 2 and 3 of the Schedule.

(2) The prohibition under section 21(3) of the Act on a vessel entering or remaining in a safety zone without the consent of the Secretary of State shall not apply to a vessel entering or remaining in the safety zone established under paragraph (1) above—

(*a*) in connection with the laying, inspection, testing, repair, alteration, renewal or removal of any submarine cable or pipe-line in or near that safety zone;

(*b*) to provide services for, to transport persons or goods to or from, or under the authority of a government department to inspect, any installation in that safety zone;

(*c*) if it is a vessel belonging to a general lighthouse authority performing duties relating to the safety of navigation;

(*d*) in connection with the saving or attempted saving of life or property;

(*e*) owing to stress of weather; or

(*f*) when in distress.

12th February 1987

Alick Buchanan-Smith
Minister of State, Department of Energy

(a) 1982 c.23.　　　　　　**(b)** *See* section 21(9).

SCHEDULE

Article 2(1)

SAFETY ZONE

1	2	3
Name or other designation of the offshore installation	Latitude North	Longitude West
Benvrackie	58° 27′ 51·30″	00° 03′ 41·18″

EXPLANATORY NOTE

(This note is not part of the Order)

This Order establishes, under section 21 of the Oil and Gas (Enterprise) Act 1982, a safety zone, having a radius of 500 metres from a specified point, around the installation specified in the Schedule to this Order and maintained in waters to which the section applies (these include territorial waters and waters in areas designated under section 1(7) of the Continental Shelf Act 1964 (c.29)).

Vessels (which for this purpose include hovercraft, submersible apparatus and installations in transit) are prohibited from entering or remaining in the safety zone except with the consent of the Secretary of State or in the circumstances mentioned in Article 2(2) of the Order.

STATUTORY INSTRUMENTS

1987 No. 202

OFFSHORE INSTALLATIONS

The Offshore Installations (Safety Zones) (No. 18) Order 1987

Made - - - -	*12th February 1987*
Coming into force	*14th February 1987*

The Secretary of State, in exercise of the powers conferred on him by section 21(1), (2) and (3) of the Oil and Gas (Enterprise) Act 1982(a) (hereinafter referred to as "the Act"), and of all other powers enabling him in that behalf, hereby makes the following Order:—

1. This Order may be cited as the Offshore Installations (Safety Zones) (No. 18) Order 1987 and shall come into force on 14th February 1987.

2.—(1) A safety zone is hereby established around the installation specified in Column 1 of the Schedule hereto (being an installation maintained in waters to which section 21 of the Act(b) applies) having a radius of five hundred metres from the point as respects that installation which has the co-ordinates of latitude and longitude according to European Datum (1950) specified in Columns 2 and 3 of the Schedule.

(2) The prohibition under section 21(3) of the Act on a vessel entering or remaining in a safety zone without the consent of the Secretary of State shall not apply to a vessel entering or remaining in the safety zone established under paragraph (1) above—

(*a*) in connection with the laying, inspection, testing, repair, alteration, renewal or removal of any submarine cable or pipe-line in or near that safety zone;

(*b*) to provide services for, to transport persons or goods to or from, or under the authority of a government department to inspect, any installation in that safety zone;

(*c*) if it is a vessel belonging to a general lighthouse authority performing duties relating to the safety of navigation;

(*d*) in connection with the saving or attempted saving of life or property;

(*e*) owing to stress of weather; or

(*f*) when in distress.

Alick Buchanan-Smith
Minister of State, Department of Energy

12th February 1987

(a) 1982 c.23.   (b) *See* section 21(9).

SCHEDULE

Article 2(1)

SAFETY ZONE

1	2	3
Name or other designation of the offshore installation	Latitude North	Longitude East
Dan Earl	53° 22′ 06·22″	01° 37′ 14·56″

EXPLANATORY NOTE

(This note is not part of the Order)

This Order establishes, under section 21 of the Oil and Gas (Enterprise) Act 1982, a safety zone, having a radius of 500 metres from a specified point, around the installation specified in the Schedule to this Order and maintained in waters to which the section applies (these include territorial waters and waters in areas designated under section 1(7) of the Continental Shelf Act 1964 (c.29)).

Vessels (which for this purpose include hovercraft, submersible apparatus and installations in transit) are prohibited from entering or remaining in the safety zone except with the consent of the Secretary of State or in the circumstances mentioned in Article 2(2) of the Order.

1987 No. 203

OFFSHORE INSTALLATIONS

The Offshore Installations (Safety Zones) (No. 19) Order 1987

Made	-	-	-	-	*12th February 1987*
Coming into force					*14th February 1987*

The Secretary of State, in exercise of the powers conferred on him by section 21(1), (2) and (3) of the Oil and Gas (Enterprise) Act 1982**(a)** (hereinafter referred to as "the Act"), and of all other powers enabling him in that behalf, hereby makes the following Order:—

1. This Order may be cited as the Offshore Installations (Safety Zones) (No. 19) Order 1987 and shall come into force on 14th February 1987.

2.—(1) A safety zone is hereby established around the installation specified in Column 1 of the Schedule hereto (being an installation maintained in waters to which section 21 of the Act**(b)** applies) having a radius of five hundred metres from the point as respects that installation which has the co-ordinates of latitude and longitude according to European Datum (1950) specified in Columns 2 and 3 of the Schedule.

(2) The prohibition under section 21(3) of the Act on a vessel entering or remaining in a safety zone without the consent of the Secretary of State shall not apply to a vessel entering or remaining in the safety zone established under paragraph (1) above—

(*a*) in connection with the laying, inspection, testing, repair, alteration, renewal or removal of any submarine cable or pipe-line in or near that safety zone;

(*b*) to provide services for, to transport persons or goods to or from, or under the authority of a government department to inspect, any installation in that safety zone;

(*c*) if it is a vessel belonging to a general lighthouse authority performing duties relating to the safety of navigation;

(*d*) in connection with the saving or attempted saving of life or property;

(*e*) owing to stress of weather; or

(*f*) when in distress.

3. The Offshore Installations (Safety Zones) (No. 111) Order 1986**(c)** is hereby revoked.

12th February 1987

Alick Buchanan-Smith
Minister of State, Department of Energy

(a) 1982 c.23.   **(b)** *See* section 21(9).   **(c)** S.I. 1986/2055.

SCHEDULE   Article 2(1)

SAFETY ZONE

1	2	3
Name or other designation of the offshore installation	Latitude North	Longitude East
High Seas Driller	59° 33′ 36·51″	01° 25′ 53·32″

EXPLANATORY NOTE

(This note is not part of the Order)

This Order establishes, under section 21 of the Oil and Gas (Enterprise) Act 1982, a safety zone, having a radius of 500 metres from a specified point, around the installation specified in the Schedule to this Order and maintained in waters to which the section applies (these include territorial waters and waters in areas designated under section 1(7) of the Continental Shelf Act 1964 (c.29)).

Vessels (which for this purpose include hovercraft, submersible apparatus and installations in transit) are prohibited from entering or remaining in the safety zone except with the consent of the Secretary of State or in the circumstances mentioned in Article 2(2) of the Order.

The Order also revokes the Offshore Installations (Safety Zones) Order which created a safety zone around the installation specified in the Schedule to this order on its previous location.

STATUTORY INSTRUMENTS

1987 No. 204

OFFSHORE INSTALLATIONS

The Offshore Installations (Safety Zones) (No. 20) Order 1987

Made	- - - -	*12th February 1987*
Coming into force		*14th February 1987*

The Secretary of State, in exercise of the powers conferred on him by section 21(1), (2) and (3) of the Oil and Gas (Enterprise) Act 1982**(a)** (hereinafter referred to as "the Act"), and of all other powers enabling him in that behalf, hereby makes the following Order:—

1. This Order may be cited as the Offshore Installations (Safety Zones) (No. 20) Order 1987 and shall come into force on 14th February 1987.

2.—(1) A safety zone is hereby established around the installation specified in Column 1 of the Schedule hereto (being an installation maintained in waters to which section 21 of the Act**(b)** applies) having a radius of five hundred metres from the point as respects that installation which has the co-ordinates of latitude and longitude according to European Datum (1950) specified in Columns 2 and 3 of the Schedule.

(2) The prohibition under section 21(3) of the Act on a vessel entering or remaining in a safety zone without the consent of the Secretary of State shall not apply to a vessel entering or remaining in the safety zone established under paragraph (1) above—

(a) in connection with the laying, inspection, testing, repair, alteration, renewal or removal of any submarine cable or pipe-line in or near that safety zone;

(b) to provide services for, to transport persons or goods to or from, or under the authority of a government department to inspect, any installation in that safety zone;

(c) if it is a vessel belonging to a general lighthouse authority performing duties relating to the safety of navigation;

(d) in connection with the saving or attempted saving of life or property;

(e) owing to stress of weather; or

(f) when in distress.

12th February 1987

Alick Buchanan-Smith
Minister of State, Department of Energy

(a) 1982 c.23.   **(b)** *See* section 21(9).

SCHEDULE

Article 2(1)

SAFETY ZONE

1	2	3
Name or other designation of the offshore installation	Latitude North	Longitude West
Ocean Benarmin	50° 37′ 35·70″	01° 49′ 55·90″

EXPLANATORY NOTE

(This note is not part of the Order)

This Order establishes, under section 21 of the Oil and Gas (Enterprise) Act 1982, a safety zone, having a radius of 500 metres from a specified point, around the installation specified in the Schedule to this Order and maintained in waters to which the section applies (these include territorial waters and waters in areas designated under section 1(7) of the Continental Shelf Act 1964 (c.29)).

Vessels (which for this purpose include hovercraft, submersible apparatus and installations in transit) are prohibited from entering or remaining in the safety zone except with the consent of the Secretary of State or in the circumstances mentioned in Article 2(2) of the Order.

STATUTORY INSTRUMENTS

1987 No. 205

OFFSHORE INSTALLATIONS

The Offshore Installations (Safety Zones) (No. 21) Order 1987

Made - - - -	*12th February 1987*
Coming into force	*14th February 1987*

The Secretary of State, in exercise of the powers conferred on him by section 21(1), (2) and (3) of the Oil and Gas (Enterprise) Act 1982(a) (hereinafter referred to as "the Act"), and of all other powers enabling him in that behalf, hereby makes the following Order:—

1. This Order may be cited as the Offshore Installations (Safety Zones) (No. 21) Order 1987 and shall come into force on 14th February 1987.

2.—(1) A safety zone is hereby established around the installation specified in Column 1 of the Schedule hereto (being an installation maintained in waters to which section 21 of the Act(b) applies) having a radius of five hundred metres from the point as respects that installation which has the co-ordinates of latitude and longitude according to European Datum (1950) specified in Columns 2 and 3 of the Schedule.

(2) The prohibition under section 21(3) of the Act on a vessel entering or remaining in a safety zone without the consent of the Secretary of State shall not apply to a vessel entering or remaining in the safety zone established under paragraph (1) above—

(*a*) in connection with the laying, inspection, testing, repair, alteration, renewal or removal of any submarine cable or pipe-line in or near that safety zone;

(*b*) to provide services for, to transport persons or goods to or from, or under the authority of a government department to inspect, any installation in that safety zone;

(*c*) if it is a vessel belonging to a general lighthouse authority performing duties relating to the safety of navigation;

(*d*) in connection with the saving or attempted saving of life or property;

(*e*) owing to stress of weather; or

(*f*) when in distress.

3. The Offshore Installations (Safety Zones) (No. 63) Order 1986(c) is hereby revoked.

Alick Buchanan-Smith
Minister of State, Department of Energy

12th February 1987

(a) 1982 c.23.   (b) *See* section 21(9).   (c) S.I. 1986/1193.

SCHEDULE

Article 2(1)

SAFETY ZONE

1	2	3
Name or other designation of the offshore installation	Latitude North	Longitude East
Sedneth 701	56° 48′ 24·90″	01° 27′ 06·30″

EXPLANATORY NOTE

(This note is not part of the Order)

This Order establishes, under section 21 of the Oil and Gas (Enterprise) Act 1982, a safety zone, having a radius of 500 metres from a specified point, around the installation specified in the Schedule to this Order and maintained in waters to which the section applies (these include territorial waters and waters in areas designated under section 1(7) of the Continental Shelf Act 1964 (c.29)).

Vessels (which for this purpose include hovercraft, submersible apparatus and installations in transit) are prohibited from entering or remaining in the safety zone except with the consent of the Secretary of State or in the circumstances mentioned in Article 2(2) of the Order.

The Order also revokes the Offshore Installations (Safety Zones) Order which created a safety zone around the installation specified in the Schedule to this order on its previous location.

1987 No. 206

OFFSHORE INSTALLATIONS

The Offshore Installations (Safety Zones) (No. 22) Order 1987

Made	-	-	-	-	*12th February 1987*
Coming into force					*14th February 1987*

The Secretary of State, in exercise of the powers conferred on him by section 21(1), (2) and (3) of the Oil and Gas (Enterprise) Act 1982**(a)** (hereinafter referred to as "the Act"), and of all other powers enabling him in that behalf, hereby makes the following Order:—

1. This Order may be cited as the Offshore Installations (Safety Zones) (No. 22) Order 1987 and shall come into force on 14th February 1987.

2.—(1) A safety zone is hereby established around the installation specified in Column 1 of the Schedule hereto (being an installation maintained in waters to which section 21 of the Act**(b)** applies) having a radius of five hundred metres from the point as respects that installation which has the co-ordinates of latitude and longitude according to European Datum (1950) specified in Columns 2 and 3 of the Schedule.

(2) The prohibition under section 21(3) of the Act on a vessel entering or remaining in a safety zone without the consent of the Secretary of State shall not apply to a vessel entering or remaining in the safety zone established under paragraph (1) above—

(*a*) in connection with the laying, inspection, testing, repair, alteration, renewal or removal of any submarine cable or pipe-line in or near that safety zone;

(*b*) to provide services for, to transport persons or goods to or from, or under the authority of a government department to inspect, any installation in that safety zone;

(*c*) if it is a vessel belonging to a general lighthouse authority performing duties relating to the safety of navigation;

(*d*) in connection with the saving or attempted saving of life or property;

(*e*) owing to stress of weather; or

(*f*) when in distress.

3. The Offshore Installations (Safety Zones) (No. 116) Order 1986**(c)** is hereby revoked.

Alick Buchanan-Smith
Minister of State, Department of Energy

12th February 1987

(a) 1982 c.23.   **(b)** *See* section 21(9).   **(c)** S.I. 1986/2272.

SCHEDULE

Article 2(1)

SAFETY ZONE

1	2	3
Name or other designation of the offshore installation	Latitude North	Longitude East
Treasure Seeker	57° 04′ 52·27″	02° 05′ 07·18″

EXPLANATORY NOTE

(This note is not part of the Order)

This Order establishes, under section 21 of the Oil and Gas (Enterprise) Act 1982, a safety zone, having a radius of 500 metres from a specified point, around the installation specified in the Schedule to this Order and maintained in waters to which the section applies (these include territorial waters and waters in areas designated under section 1(7) of the Continental Shelf Act 1964 (c.29)).

Vessels (which for this purpose include hovercraft, submersible apparatus and installations in transit) are prohibited from entering or remaining in the safety zone except with the consent of the Secretary of State or in the circumstances mentioned in Article 2(2) of the Order.

The Order also revokes the Offshore Installations (Safety Zones) Order which created a safety zone around the installation specified in the Schedule to this order on its previous location.

STATUTORY INSTRUMENTS

1987 No. 207 (C.5)

REPRESENTATION OF THE PEOPLE

The Representation of the People Act 1985 (Commencement No. 4) Order 1987

Made - - - - *13th February 1987*

In exercise of the powers conferred upon me by section 29(2) of the Representation of the People Act 1985(a), I hereby make the following Order:—

1. This Order may be cited as the Representation of the People Act 1985 (Commencement No. 4) Order 1987.

2. Paragraph 34 of Schedule 4 to the Representation of the People Act 1985 shall come into force on 30th March 1987 except for the purposes of an election in respect of which the notice of election is published before that date.

Home Office
13th February 1987

Douglas Hurd
One of Her Majesty's Principal Secretaries of State

EXPLANATORY NOTE

(This note is not part of the Order)

This Order brings into force the last remaining provision of the Representation of the People Act 1985 which may be brought into force by order under section 29(2) of that Act. Separate provision is made by section 10 of that Act about the bringing into force of Schedule 1 to that Act.

(a) 1985 c.50.

STATUTORY INSTRUMENTS

1987 No. 208 (S. 12)

EDUCATION, SCOTLAND

The Education (Grants for Training of Teachers and Community Education Workers) (Scotland) Amendment Regulations 1987

Made - - - -	*10th February 1987*
Laid before Parliament	*23rd February 1987*
Coming into force	*22nd March 1987*

The Secretary of State, in exercise of the powers conferred on him by sections 73(a), (f) and (g) and 74(1) of the Education (Scotland) Act 1980(**a**), and of all other powers enabling him in that behalf, hereby makes the following Regulations:

Citation and commencement

1. These Regulations may be cited as the Education (Grants for Training of Teachers and Community Education Workers) (Scotland) Amendment Regulations 1987 and shall come into force on 22nd March 1987.

Amendment of principal regulations

2. For the Schedule to the Education (Grants for Training of Teachers and Community Education Workers) (Scotland) Regulations 1986(**b**) there shall be substituted the Schedule to these Regulations.

John J. MacKay
New St. Andrew's House, Edinburgh
10th February 1987
Parliamentary Under Secretary of State,
Scottish Office

(**a**) 1980 c.44.
(**b**) S.I. 1986/510.

Regulation 2   **SCHEDULE**

SUBJECT AREAS IN RESPECT OF WHICH GRANTS MAY BE PAID

Nursery and primary education

Environmental studies in the context of primary education development programme packages.
The management of change in the primary school.
Information technology: the impact on learning and teaching in the primary school.

Secondary education

Technological education in the secondary school.
Information technology: the impact on learning and teaching in the secondary school curriculum.
Monitoring and evaluating the effectiveness of secondary education for purposes of accountability and professional development.
Current issues for management in the secondary school.
Courses in support of Standard Grade.

Secondary and further education

The impact of the Technical and Vocational Education Initiative on the secondary curriculum and the professional development of teachers.
Extension of the Technical and Vocational Education Initiative.
Managing change at 16+.

Special educational needs

Education and personal development in the physically disabled young person.

General

The problem of drugs misuse.
The use of microcomputers.
Management for promoted staff in schools.
Multicultural education and anti-racist perspectives in relation to school education in Scotland.

EXPLANATORY NOTE

(This note is not part of the Regulations)

These Regulations amend the Education (Grants for Training of Teachers and Community Education Workers) (Scotland) Regulations 1986.

The Schedule to the 1986 Regulations lists subject areas in respect of which grants may be paid under the 1986 Regulations to enable teachers or community education workers to attend courses. These Regulations substitute a new list of subject areas reflecting the courses now available.

STATUTORY INSTRUMENTS

1987 No. 209

PENSIONS

The Superannuation (Children's Pensions) (Earnings Limit) Order 1987

Made	- - -	*10th February 1987*
Laid before Parliament		*24th February 1987*
Coming into force	-	*6th April 1987*

The Treasury, in exercise of the powers conferred by section 21(5) of the Judicial Pensions Act 1981(**a**) and now vested in them(**b**), and of all other powers enabling them in that behalf, hereby make the following Order:—

Citation and commencement

1. This Order may be cited as the Superannuation (Children's Pensions) (Earnings Limit) Order 1987 and shall into operation on 6th April 1987.

Increase in children's earnings limit

2. The sum mentioned in section 21(1)(c)(ii) of the Judicial Pensions Act 1981 (which excludes from the definition of "period of childhood and full-time education" a person over 16 who is undergoing training if the emoluments payable by his employer are more than the said sum) is hereby increased from £1154 to £1178.

Revocation of previous order

3. The Superannuation (Children's Pensions) (Earnings Limit) Order 1986(**c**) is hereby revoked.

Tim Sainsbury
Michael Neubert
Two of the Lords Commissioners
of Her Majesty's Treasury

10th February 1987

(**a**) 1981 c.20.
(**b**) *See* the Transfer of Functions (Minister for the Civil Service and Treasury) Order 1981 (S.I. 1981/1670), article 2(1)(c).
(**c**) S.I. 1986/814.

EXPLANATORY NOTE

(This note is not part of the Order)

Subject to certain conditions section 21 of the Judicial Pensions Act 1981 permits the payment of a children's pension under that Act to continue after the child reaches the age of 16 if the child is undergoing training for a trade, profession or vocation. One of the conditions is that the emoluments received during training, excluding any emoluments receivable or payable by way of return of any premium paid in respect of the training, do not exceed £1154 a year. This Order revokes the Superannuation (Children's Pensions) (Earnings Limit) Order 1986 and increases the limit on such emoluments from £1154 to £1178 a year.

1987 No. 211

ANIMALS

ANIMAL HEALTH

The Export of Sheep (Prohibition) Order 1987

Made - - - -	*15th February 1987*
Coming into force -	*17th February 1987*

The Minister of Agriculture, Fisheries and Food, in exercise of the power conferred by section 11 of the Animal Health Act 1981**(a)** and of all other powers enabling him in that behalf, hereby makes the following Order:–

Title and commencement

1. This Order may be cited as the Export of Sheep (Prohibition) Order 1987 and shall come into force on 17th February 1987.

Prohibition of export of sheep

2.—(1) No person shall export from Great Britain to a member State any sheep to which this Order applies.

(2) Subject to paragraphs (3) and (4) below, this Order applies to any sheep which—

(a) was moved from a place situated in an area which is a designated area for the purposes of Part I of the Food and Environment Protection Act 1985**(b)** by virtue of—

 (i) article 3 of the Food Protection (Emergency Prohibitions) (England) (No. 2) Order 1986**(c)**;

 (ii) article 3 of the Food Protection (Emergency Prohibitions) (Wales) (No. 2) Order 1986**(d)**; or

 (iii) article 3 of the Food Protection (Emergency Prohibitions) (No. 10) Order 1986**(e)**,

 in accordance with the terms of a consent under section 2(1) of that Act (consent to the doing of things prohibited by an emergency order under section 1 of that Act) which required that the sheep to which it applies should be marked in a manner specified therein; or

(b) was moved from such an area in contravention of a prohibition on its movement imposed by an order made under section 1(1) of that Act (which empowers the making of emergency Orders) which applied to that sheep at the time it was moved.

(a) 1981 c.22.
(b) 1985 c.48.
(c) S.I. 1986/1689, amended by S.I. 1986/2208 and 1987/153.
(d) S.I. 1986/1681, amended by S.I. 1986/1707, 1756, 1775, 1849 and 2242.
(e) S.I. 1986/2248.

(3) This Order applies to a sheep only for so long as the area from which it has been moved remains a designated area for the purposes of any of the Orders referred to in paragraph ´`)(a) above.

(4) Paragraph (2)(a) above shall not apply in the case of any sheep which has been examined and marked by an ear-tag by a person authorised in that behalf by the appropriate Minister.

Enforcement

3. This Order shall be executed and enforced by local authorities.

Revocation

4. The Export of Sheep (Prohibition) (No. 2) Order 1986**(a)** is hereby revoked.

In witness whereof the Official Seal of the Minister of Agriculture, Fisheries and Food was hereunto affixed on 15th February 1987.

Michael Jopling
Minister of Agriculture, Fisheries and Food

EXPLANATORY NOTE

(This note is not part of the Order)

The Orders mentioned in article 2(2) ("emergency Orders") among other things designate areas which have been affected by an accident at a nuclear reactor at Chernobyl in the USSR ("designated areas").

This Order (which revokes and re-enacts the Export of Sheep (Prohibition) (No. 2) Order 1986) prohibits the export from Great Britain to a member State of the European Communities of sheep moved from a place in such a designated area in the circumstances described in article 2. The principal change is that the present Order does not apply in the case of sheep which have been examined and subsequently marked by an ear-tag by an officer authorised by the Minister of Agriculture, Fisheries and Food or the Secretary of State for Scotland or Wales (article 2(4)).

Export of a sheep is prohibited only for so long as the area from which it was moved continues to be a designated area. The prohibition extends to sheep which have been moved in accordance with a Ministerial consent which required that the sheep to which it applies should be marked in a specified manner and to sheep which have been moved in contravention of a restriction, but it does not apply to those sheep which have been examined and subsequently marked by an ear-tag by an official referred to in the preceeding paragraph.

(a) S.I. 1986/1734.

1987 No. 212

FOOD

MILK AND DAIRIES

The Milk and Dairies and Milk (Special Designation) (Charges) Regulations 1987

Made - - - -	*15th February 1987*
Laid before Parliament	*17th February 1987*
Coming into force -	*30th March 1987*

The Minister of Agriculture, Fisheries and Food, the Secretary of State for Social Services and the Secretary of State for Wales, acting jointly, in exercise of the powers conferred on them by sections 33, 38 and 118 of the Food Act 1984**(a)** and of all other powers enabling them in that behalf, hereby make the following Regulations after consultation in accordance with section 118(6) of that Act with such organisations as appear to them to be representative of interests substantially affected by the Regulations:–

Title and commencement

1. These Regulations may be cited as the Milk and Dairies and Milk (Special Designation) (Charges) Regulations 1987, and shall come into force on 30th March 1987.

Interpretation

2.—(1) In these Regulations–

"the Act" means the Food Act 1984;

"the Board" means the Milk Marketing Board for England and Wales established under the Agricultural Marketing Act 1958**(b)**;

"cow" means a cow kept for milking purposes whether dry or in milk but does not include a heifer which has never calved;

"dairy farm visit" includes any visit to a registered dairy farm by an inspector or authorised officer of the Minister for the purpose of ascertaining whether the principal Regulations are being complied with;

"the Minister" means the Minister of Agriculture, Fisheries and Food and the Secretary of State, acting jointly;

"the principal Regulations" means the Milk and Dairies (General) Regulations 1959**(c)** and the Milk (Special Designation) Regulations 1986**(d)**;

(a) 1984 c.30.
(b) 1958 c.47.
(c) S.I. 1959/277; relevant amending instruments are S.I. 1973/1064, 1977/171, 1979/1567.
(d) S.I. 1986/723.

"registered dairy farm" means a farm registered under regulation 6 of the Milk and Dairies (General) Regulations 1959;

"registered dairy farmer" means a person registered under regulation 6 of the Milk and Dairies (General) Regulations 1959;

"served" means served in accordance with section 125 of the Act.

(2) Any reference in these Regulations to a numbered regulation or to a schedule shall, unless the reference is to a regulation of, or schedule to, specified Regulations, be construed as a reference to the regulation so numbered in or to the schedule to these Regulations.

Liability to charges

3.—(1) For the purposes of the principal Regulations and for services performed under them, and subject to paragraphs (2) and (3) hereof, there shall be due from the registered dairy farmer to the Minister, in respect of any matter specified in the first column of the Schedule, the charge specified in relation thereto in the second column thereof.

(2) The charge due under the first item of the Schedule shall be the higher rate of charge unless the number of cows on the registered dairy farm at the time of the dairy farm visit is less than twenty and the registered dairy farmer makes a written declaration to that effect, in which case the charge due shall be the lower rate of charge.

(3) Notwithstanding paragraphs (1) and (2) hereof, no charge shall be due in respect of any dairy farm visit–

(a) for the purpose of ascertaining whether there is a particular threat to public health, or for the purpose of taking measures to reduce such a threat,

(b) arising out of the findings of a previous dairy farm visit for which a charge has been made under these Regulations,

(c) in connection with an untreated milk producer's licence granted in accordance with the Milk (Special Designation) Regulations 1986 solely for the sale of milk under the conditions described in Schedule 2 Part I Condition A4(1)(c) of those regulations (farmhouse catering), or

(d) in connection with a consent granted under section 42 of the Act to sell milk without the use of a special designation.

Recovery of charges

4.—(1) Where–

(a) a charge is due under regulation 3,

(b) there is due from the Board to the registered dairy farmer a sum of money not less than that charge, and

(c) no determination has been made by the Minister that the charge should be collected directly by him,

such charge shall be recovered by the Board on behalf of the Minister by deduction of a sum equal to that charge from such sum of money.

(2) The Minister shall notify the registered dairy farmer before any deduction is made by the Board under paragraph (1) hereof.

(3) The Minister shall meet such reasonable costs as the Board may incur in recovering charges under paragraph (1) hereof.

(4) Any charge due under regulation 3 which is not recoverable under paragraph (1) hereof shall become payable on a demand being served on the registered dairy farmer by the Minister.

(5) Any sum remaining unpaid may be recovered by the Minister from the registered dairy farmer summarily as a civil debt.

In Witness whereof the Official Seal of the Minister of Agriculture, Fisheries and Food is hereunto affixed on 15th February 1987.

Michael Jopling
Minister of Agriculture, Fisheries and Food

10th February 1987

Trumpington
for the Secretary of State for Social Services

12th February 1987

Nicholas Edwards
Secretary of State for Wales

SCHEDULE

Regulation 3

Matter	Charge
	£
1. Dairy farm visit other than a dairy farm visit for the sole purpose of taking samples of milk or of water or both.	
(a) higher rate of charge	90.00
(b) lower rate of charge	80.00
2. Dairy farm visit for the sole purpose of taking samples of milk or of water or both.	22.00

EXPLANATORY NOTE

(This note is not part of the Regulations)

These Regulations introduce charges for the purposes of the Milk and Dairies (General) Regulations 1959 (S.I. 1959/277) and the Milk (Special Designation) Regulations 1986 (S.I. 1986/723), and for services performed under those Regulations.

A charge is to be made at the rate of £90 for each visit made by an authorised officer of the Minister of Agriculture, Fisheries and Food and the Secretary of State for Wales to a registered dairy farm for the purpose of ascertaining whether the principal Regulations are being complied with. Where there are less than 20 cows, the charge is £80. A visit solely for the purpose of sampling milk or water or both is to incur a charge of £22 (regulation 3 and the Schedule).

Regulation 3(3) provides exemption for–

    (a) visits relating to particular threats to public health,

    (b) follow up visits,

    (c) visits relating solely to farmhouse catering licences,

    (d) visits relating to consents under section 42 of the Food Act 1984.

Unless the Minister and the Secretary of State determine otherwise, the Milk Marketing Board for England and Wales will be the collecting agency where they hold a sum sufficient to meet the charges (regulation 4).

1987 No. 213

SEA FISHERIES

CONSERVATION OF SEA FISH

The Sole (North Sea) (Enforcement of Community Conservation Measures) Order 1987

Made - - - -	*15th February 1987*
Laid before Parliament	*17th February 1987*
Coming into force	*18th February 1987*

The Minister of Agriculture, Fisheries and Food and the Secretaries of State respectively concerned with sea fishing in Scotland, Wales and Northern Ireland, in exercise of the powers conferred on them by section 30(2) of the Fisheries Act 1981(a) and of all other powers enabling them in that behalf, hereby make the following Order:–

Title, commencement, duration and interpretation

1.—(1) This Order may be cited as the Sole (North Sea) (Enforcement of Community Conservation Measures) Order 1987, shall come into force on 18th February 1987 and shall cease to have effect on 16th April 1987.

(2) In this Order, "the Commission Regulation" means the Regulation adopted by the Commission of The European Communities on 6th February 1987 establishing temporary limits on landings of sole from the North Sea(b).

Offences

2.—(1) Where there is, in respect of–

(a) any British fishing boat registered in the United Kingdom wherever it may be, or

(b) any other fishing boat which is within British fishery limits,

a contravention of, or failure to comply with, article 1 of the Commission Regulation as respects the retention on board of sole (*Solea solea*), the master, the owner and the charterer (if any) shall each be guilty of an offence.

(2) Any person who, in the United Kingdom, lands any sole in contravention of article 1 of the Commission Regulation shall be guilty of an offence.

Penalties

3.—(1) A person guilty of an offence under article 2(1) or (2) of this Order shall be liable on summary conviction–

(a) to a fine not exceeding £5,000; and

(b) either–

(i) to a fine not exceeding the value of any fish in respect of which the offence was committed, or

---

(a) 1981 c.29.
(b) Commission Regulation (EEC) No. 384/87, O.J. No. L.36, 7.2.87, p.14.

    (ii) to the forfeiture of any fish in respect of which the offence was committed; and

  (c) to the forfeiture of any net or other fishing gear which was used for catching any fish in respect of which the offence was committed.

(2) A person guilty of an offence under article 2(1) or (2) of this Order shall be liable on conviction on indictment–

  (a) to a fine; and

  (b) to the forfeiture of any fish in respect of which the offence was committed; and

  (c) to the forfeiture of any net or other fishing gear which was used for catching any fish in respect of which the offence was committed.

Recovery of fines

4.—(1) Where a fine is imposed by a magistrates' court in England and Wales or Northern Ireland on the master, owner or charterer, or a member of the crew, of a fishing boat who is convicted by the court of an offence under article 2 of this Order, the court may–

  (a) issue a warrant of distress against the boat and its gear and catch and any property of the person convicted for the purpose of levying the amount of the fine; and

  (b) order the boat to be detained for a period not exceeding three months from the date of the conviction or until the fine is paid or the amount of the fine is levied in pursuance of any such warrant, whichever occurs first.

(2) Where a fine is imposed by a sheriff in Scotland on the master, owner or charterer, or a member of the crew, of a fishing boat who is convicted by the sheriff of an offence under article 2 of this Order, the sheriff may–

  (a) issue a warrant for the poinding and sale of the boat and its gear and catch and any property of the person convicted; and

  (b) order the boat to be detained for a period not exceeding three months from the date of the conviction or until the fine is paid, whichever occurs first.

(3) Sections 77(1) and 78 of the Magistrates' Courts Act 1980**(a)** (postponement of issue of, and defects in, warrants of distress) shall apply to a warrant of distress issued under this article in England and Wales as they apply to a warrant of distress issued under Part III of that Act.

(4) Article 114(2) of the Magistrates' Courts (Northern Ireland) Order 1981**(b)** (postponement of issue of certain warrants) shall apply to a warrant of distress issued under this article in Northern Ireland as it applies to a warrant referred to in that article.

Powers of British sea-fishery officers

5.—(1) For the purpose of enforcing article 2(1) of this Order, a British sea-fishery officer–

  (a) may go on board any British fishing boat wherever it may be or any other fishing boat which is within British fishery limits;

  (b) may require any such boat to stop and do anything else to enable him to board it;

  (c) may require the attendance of the master of the boat or any other person on board;

  (d) may require any person on board to assist him in the performance of his functions;

  (e) may take with him, to assist him in performing his functions, any other person and any equipment or materials; and

  (f) may make any examination or inquiry which appears to him to be necessary and, without prejudice to the generality of the foregoing, he may in particular–

    (i) examine any fish on the boat and the equipment of the boat, including the fishing gear;

(a) 1980 c.43.
(b) S.I. 1981/1675 (NI 26).

(ii) require the production of any document relating to the boat or to its fishing operations or other operations ancillary to its fishing operations;

(iii) search the boat for any such document, and require any person on board the boat to do anything which appears to the officer to be necessary for facilitating the search; and

(iv) take copies of any such document.

(2) If a British sea-fishery officer has reasonable grounds to suspect that an offence under article 2(1) of this Order has been committed in respect of a boat that he has power to go on board under paragraph (1)(a) of this article, he may seize and detain any document produced to him or found on board the boat, and, if he has reasonable grounds to suspect that such an offence has been committed within British fishery limits, the officer–

(a) may require the master to take, or may himself take, the boat and its crew to the port which appears to the officer to be the nearest convenient port; and

(b) may detain the boat in the port.

(3) Nothing in paragraph (2) of this article shall permit any document required by law to be carried on board any boat to be seized or detained except while the boat is detained in a port.

(4) If a British sea-fishery officer detains a boat, he shall serve on the master a notice stating that it is to be detained until the notice is withdrawn by the service on him of a further notice in writing signed by a British sea-fishery officer.

(5) For the purpose of enforcing article 2 of this Order, a British sea-fishery officer–

(a) may enter at any reasonable time any premises (other than a dwelling) used for carrying on any business in connection with the operation of fishing boats or activities connected therewith or ancillary thereto or with the treatment, storage or sale of sea fish;

(b) may search the premises for and examine any fish thereon;

(c) may require any person on the premises to produce any documents which are in his custody or possession relating to the catching, landing, trans-shipment, sale or disposal of sea fish;

(d) may take copies of any such document;

and, if he has reason to suspect that an offence under article 2 of this Order has been committed, the officer–

(e) may search the premises for any such document and require any person on the premises to do anything which appears to the officer to be necessary for facilitating the search; and

(f) may seize and detain any such document produced to him or found on the premises.

(6) A British sea-fishery officer may seize–

(a) any fish in respect of which he has reasonable grounds to suspect that an offence under article 2 of this Order has been committed; and

(b) any net or other fishing gear which he has reasonable grounds to suspect was used for catching any fish in respect of which any such offence has been committed.

Obstruction of officers

6. Any person who–

(a) fails without reasonable excuse to comply with any requirement imposed by a British sea-fishery officer under the powers conferred on British sea-fishery officers by article 5 of this Order;

(b) without reasonable excuse prevents, or attempts to prevent, any other person from complying with any such requirement; or

(c) assaults any such officer who is exercising any of the powers conferred on him by article 5 of this Order or intentionally obstructs any such officer in the exercise of any of those powers shall be guilty of an offence and liable–

      (i) on summary conviction to a fine not exceeding £5,000; or

      (ii) on conviction on indictment to a fine.

Protection of officers

7. An officer shall not be liable in any civil or criminal proceedings for anything done in the purported exercise of the powers conferred on him by article 5 of this Order if the court is satisfied that the act was done in good faith, that there were reasonable grounds for doing it and that it was done with reasonable skill and care.

Offences by bodies corporate

8. Where an offence under article 2 of this Order committed by a body corporate is proved to have been committed with the consent or approval of any director, manager, secretary or other officer of the body corporate, he, as well as the body corporate, shall be deemed to be guilty of the offence and shall be liable to be proceeded against and punished accordingly.

Proceedings

9. Proceedings for an offence under this Order may be taken, and the offence may for all incidental purposes be treated as having been committed, in any place in the United Kingdom.

In Witness whereof the Official Seal of the Minister of Agriculture, Fisheries and Food is hereunto affixed on 15th February 1987.

Michael Jopling
Minister of Agriculture, Fisheries and Food

12th February 1987

John J. Mackay
Parliamentary Under-Secretary of State,
Scottish Office

10th February 1987

Nicholas Edwards
Secretary of State for Wales

13th February 1987

Tom King
Secretary of State for Northern Ireland

EXPLANATORY NOTE

(This note is not part of the Order)

This Order makes provision for the enforcement of the prohibition on retaining on board or landing more than 30 per cent of sole (*Solea solea*) taken in the North Sea, measured as a percentage by weight of the total catch of fish, crustaceans and molluscs, contained in article 1 of the Regulation adopted by the Commission of the European Communities on 6th February 1987 establishing temporary limits on landings of sole from the North Sea ("the Commission Regulation").

Article 2 of the Order creates offences in respect of breaches of the provisions of article 1 of the Commission Regulation. Penalties, which may include the forfeiture of fish, nets and other fishing gear are specified for such offences (article 3). A provision corresponding to section 12 of the Sea Fisheries Act 1968 (c.77) is made for the enforcement of fines by way of the issue of a warrant of distress (in Scotland a warrant of poinding and sale) and a detaining Order (article 4).

The Order confers powers of enforcement on British sea-fishery officers (article 5), and provision is made for the punishment of anyone found guilty of obstructing or assaulting such an officer (article 6).

The Order ceases to have effect on 16th April 1987 (article 1).

STATUTORY INSTRUMENTS

1987 No. 214

SOCIAL SECURITY

The Social Security Commissioners Procedure Regulations 1987

Made	- - -	*13th February 1987*
Laid before Parliament		*18th February 1987*
Coming into force	-	*6th April 1987*

ARRANGEMENT OF REGULATIONS

PART 1

Introduction

PART II

Making Applications, Appeals and References

PART III

General Procedure

PART IV

Decisions

PART V

Miscellaneous and Supplementary

The Lord Chancellor, in exercise of the powers conferred by the provisions set out in the Schedule to these Regulations and now vested in him**(a)** and of all other powers enabling him in that behalf, after consultation with the Lord Advocate and, in accordance with section 10 of the Tribunals and Inquiries Act 1971**(b)**, with the Council on Tribunals, hereby makes the following Regulations.

PART I

INTRODUCTION

Citation and commencement

1. These Regulations may be cited as the Social Security Commissioners Procedure Regulations 1987 and shall come into force on 6th April 1987.

(a) By virtue of the Transfer of Functions (Social Security Commissioners) Order 1984 (S.I. 1984/1818) and paragraph 20 of Schedule 5 to the Social Security Act 1986 (c.50).
(b) 1971 c.62.

Interpretation

2. In these Regulations, unless the context otherwise requires:—

"the Act" means the Social Security Act 1975(a);

"adjudicating authority" means, as the case may be, the Chief or any other adjudication officer, an appeal tribunal, the Attendance Allowance Board, or a medical appeal tribunal and, in cases where a forfeiture rule question arises, includes the Secretary of State;

"adjudication officer" means an officer appointed in accordance with section 97(1) of the Act;

"appeal tribunal" means a social security appeal tribunal constituted in accordance with section 97(2) to (2E) of the Act;

"the Attendance Allowance Board" means the Board constituted in accordance with section 105 of the Act and for the purpose of section 106(2) of the Act, unless the context otherwise requires, includes a delegate appointed in pursuance of paragraph 5 of Schedule 11 to the Act;

"the chairman" for the purposes of Regulations 3 and 4 means:

(i)   the person who was the chairman of the appeal tribunal or medical appeal tribunal, as the case may be, when the decision was given against which leave to appeal is being sought; or

(ii) any other chairman of an appeal tribunal or medical appeal tribunal, as the case may be, duly authorised for the purposes of applications for leave to appeal to a Commissioner under the Social Security (Adjudication) Regulations 1986(b);

"Chief Adjudication Officer" means the Chief Adjudication Officer appointed under section 97(1B) of the Act;

"Chief Commissioner" means the Chief Social Security Commissioner appointed under section 97(3) of the Act;

"Commissioner" means the Chief or any other Social Security Commissioner appointed in accordance with section 97(3) of the Act or section 13(5) of the Social Security Act 1980(c) and includes a Tribunal of 3 such Commissioners constituted in accordance with section 116 of the Act;

"forfeiture rule question" means any question referred to in section 4(1) or 4(1A) to 4(1H) of the Forfeiture Act 1982(d);

"medical appeal tribunal" means a medical appeal tribunal constituted in accordance with Schedule 12 to the Act;

"nominated officer" means an officer authorised by the Lord Chancellor (or in Scotland, by the Secretary of State) in accordance with section 114(2C)(e) of the Act;

"proceedings" means any proceedings before a Commissioner, whether by way of an application for leave to appeal to, or from, a Commissioner, by way of an appeal or reference, or otherwise;

"respondent" means any person or organisation other than the applicant, appellant or person making the reference who would be entitled under Regulation 17(5) to be present and to be heard at any oral hearing;

"the specified time" for the purposes of Regulations 3(2) and 4(3) means the time specified under the Social Security (Adjudication) Regulations 1986 for applying to a chairman of an appeal tribunal or, as the case may be, a medical appeal tribunal for leave to appeal to a Commissioner;

"summons", in relation to Scotland, means "citation" and Regulation 18 shall be construed accordingly.

(a) 1975 c.14.
(b) S.I. 1986/2218.
(c) 1980 c.30.
(d) 1982 c.34. Subsections 4(1A) to 4(1H) of the Forfeiture Act 1982 were inserted by section 76 of the Social Security Act 1986 (c.50).
(e) Section 114(2C) of the Social Security Act 1975 was inserted by paragraph 16 of Schedule 5 to the Social Security Act 1986.

PART II

MAKING APPLICATIONS, APPEALS AND REFERENCES

Application to a Commissioner for leave to appeal

3.—(1) Subject to paragraph (2) of this Regulation, an application may be made to a Commissioner for leave to appeal against a decision of an appeal tribunal or a medical appeal tribunal only where the applicant has been refused leave to appeal by the chairman of an appeal tribunal or, as the case may be, of a medical appeal tribunal.

(2) Where there has been a failure to apply to the chairman for such leave within the specified time, an application for leave to appeal may be made to a Commissioner who may, if for special reasons he thinks fit, accept and proceed to consider and determine the application.

(3) An application for leave to appeal under paragraph (1) above must be made within 42 days from the date on which notice in writing of the refusal of leave to appeal was given to the applicant.

(4) An application to a Commissioner for leave to appeal against a determination by the Attendance Allowance Board of any question of law arising

(i) on a review by the Board in pursuance of section 106(1) of the Act; or

(ii) in connection with a refusal by the Board to review a determination made in pursuance of section 105(3) of the Act,

must be made within 3 months from the date on which notice in writing of the determination was given to the applicant.

(5) A Commissioner may accept and proceed to consider and determine an application for leave to appeal under paragraphs (1) and (4) above notwithstanding that the period specified for making the application has expired, if for special reasons he thinks fit.

Notice of application to a Commissioner for leave to appeal

4.—(1) Subject to the following provisions of this Regulation, an application to a Commissioner for leave to appeal shall be brought by a notice to a Commissioner containing:

(a) the name and address of the applicant;

(b) the grounds on which the applicant intends to rely;

(c) an address for service of notices and other documents on the applicant;

and the notice shall have annexed to it a copy of the decision against which leave to appeal is being sought.

(2) Where the applicant has been refused leave to appeal by the chairman of an appeal tribunal or of a medical appeal tribunal, otherwise·than by a decision recorded in the record of the proceedings of the tribunal, the notice shall also have annexed to it a copy of the decision refusing leave and shall state the date on which the applicant was given notice in writing of the refusal of leave.

(3) Where the applicant has failed:

(i) to apply within the specified time to the chairman of an appeal tribunal or of a medical appeal tribunal for leave to appeal; or

(ii) to comply with Regulation 3(3) above; or

(iii) to apply within the period specified in Regulation 3(4) to a Commissioner for leave to appeal against a determination by the Attendance Allowance Board

the notice of application for leave to appeal shall, in addition to complying with paragraphs (1) and (2) above, state the grounds relied upon for seeking acceptance of the application notwithstanding that the relevant period has expired.

(4) Where an application for leave to appeal is made by an adjudication officer or by the Secretary of State the applicant shall, as soon as may be practicable, send each respondent a copy of the notice of application for leave to appeal.

Determination of application

5.—(1) The office of the Social Security Commissioners shall notify the applicant and each respondent in writing of the determination by a Commissioner of the application.

(2) Subject to a direction by a Commissioner to the contrary, where a Commissioner grants leave to appeal on an application made in accordance with Regulation 4 above, notice of appeal shall be deemed to have been duly given on the date when notice of the determination is given to the applicant and the notice of application shall be deemed to be a notice of appeal duly served under Regulation 7 below.

(3) If on consideration of an application for leave to appeal to him from the decision of an adjudicating authority the Commissioner grants leave he may, with the consent of the applicant and each respondent, treat the application as an appeal and determine any question arising on the application as though it were a question arising on an appeal.

Notice of appeal

6. Subject to Regulation 5(2) above, an appeal shall be brought by a notice to a Commissioner containing:

(a) the name and address of the appellant;

(b) the date on which leave to appeal was granted;

(c) the grounds on which the appellant intends to rely;

(d) an address for service of notices and other documents on the appellant;

and the notice shall have annexed to it a copy of the determination granting leave to appeal and a copy of the decision against which leave to appeal has been granted.

Time limit for appealing

7.—(1) Subject to paragraph (2) below, a notice of appeal shall not be valid unless it is served on a Commissioner within 42 days of the date on which the applicant was given notice in writing that leave to appeal had been granted.

(2) A Commissioner may accept a notice of appeal served after the expiry of the period prescribed by paragraph (1) above if for special reasons he thinks fit.

References

8.—(1) Where a forfeiture rule question arises in a case before an adjudicating authority and that authority is not satisfied that the case can be disposed of without that question being determined, the adjudicating authority shall—

(a) if not the Secretary of State, require the Secretary of State to arrange for the case to be referred to a Commissioner to determine the forfeiture rule question; and

(b) if the Secretary of State, refer the case to a Commissioner to determine that question,

and shall inform the person in relation to whom the forfeiture rule question arises that his case is being referred to a Commissioner to determine that question.

(2) Any reference to a Commissioner under the Forfeiture Act 1982**(a)** or from a medical appeal tribunal shall be made in writing and shall include:

(a) a statement of the question for determination by the Commissioner and the facts upon which it arises;

(b) the grounds upon which the reference is made;

(c) the address for service of notices and other documents on the person making the reference and on any respondent.

Acknowledgement of a notice of appeal or a reference and notification to each respondent

9. There shall be sent by the office of the Social Security Commissioners:

(a) to the appellant or person making the reference an acknowledgement of the receipt of the notice of appeal or the reference; and

(b) to each respondent a copy of the notice of appeal or of the reference.

(a) 1982 c.34.

PART III

GENERAL PROCEDURE

Respondent's written observations

10.—(1) A respondent who wishes to submit to a Commissioner written observations on the appeal or on the reference shall do so within 30 days of being given notice in writing of it.

(2) Any such written observations shall include:
  (a) the respondent's name and address and address for service; and
  (b) in the case of observations on an appeal, a statement as to whether or not he opposes the appeal; and
  (c) in any case, the grounds upon which the respondent proposes to rely.

(3) A copy of any written observations from a respondent shall be sent by the office of the Social Security Commissioners to the other parties.

Written observations in reply

11.—(1) Any party may, within 30 days of being sent written observations submitted in accordance with Regulation 10 above, submit to a Commissioner written observations in reply.

(2) Regulation 10(3) above shall apply in relation to written observations in reply as it does in relation to written observations under Regulation 10 above.

Directions

12.—(1) Where it appears to a Commissioner that an application, appeal or reference which is made to him gives insufficient particulars to enable the question at issue to be determined, he may direct the party making the application, appeal or reference, or any respondent, to furnish such further particulars as may reasonably be required.

(2) In the case of an application for leave to appeal, or an appeal, from the Attendance Allowance Board, or of an application for leave to appeal or an appeal from, or of a reference by, a medical appeal tribunal, a Commissioner may, before determining the application, appeal or reference, direct the Board or tribunal, as the case may be, to submit a statement of such facts as he considers necessary for the proper determination of that application, appeal or reference.

(3) At any stage of the proceedings, a Commissioner may, either of his own motion or on application, give such directions as he may consider necessary or desirable for the efficient and effective despatch of the proceedings.

(4) Without prejudice to the provisions of Regulations 10 and 11, or to paragraph (3) above, a Commissioner may direct any party to any proceedings before him to make such written observations as may seem to him necessary to enable the question at issue to be determined.

(5) An application under paragraph (3) above shall be made in writing to a Commissioner and shall set out the direction which the applicant is seeking to have made and the grounds for the application.

(6) Unless a Commissioner shall otherwise determine, an application made pursuant to paragraph (3) above shall be copied by the office of the Social Security Commissioners to the other parties.

Medical references

13. A Commissioner may refer to a medical practitioner for examination and report any question arising in proceedings before him except in proceedings on an application for leave to appeal, or an appeal, from a medical appeal tribunal or the Attendance Allowance Board or on a reference by a medical appeal tribunal.

Non-disclosure of medical evidence

14.—(1) Where, in connection with any application, appeal or reference there is before a Commissioner medical advice or medical evidence relating to a person which has not been disclosed to that person and in the opinion of the Commissioner the disclosure to that person of that advice or evidence would be harmful to his health, such advice or evidence shall not be required to be disclosed to that person.

(2) Advice or evidence such as is mentioned in paragraph (1) above:

(a) shall not be disclosed to any person acting for or representing the person to whom it relates

(b) in a case where a claim for benefit is made by reference to the disability of a person other than the claimant and the advice or evidence relates to that other person, shall not be disclosed to the claimant or any person acting for or representing the claimant

unless the Commissioner is satisfied that it is in the interests of the person to whom the advice or evidence relates to do so.

(3) The Commissioner shall not by reason of non-disclosure under paragraphs (1) or (2) above be precluded from taking the advice or evidence concerned into account for the purpose of the proceedings.

Requests for oral hearings

15.—(1) Subject to paragraphs (2) and (3) below, a Commissioner may determine an application for leave to appeal or an appeal or a reference without an oral hearing.

(2) Where, in any proceedings before a Commissioner, a request is made by any party thereto for an oral hearing the Commissioner shall grant the request unless, after considering all the circumstances of the case and the reasons put forward in the request for the hearing, he is satisfied that the application or appeal or reference can properly be determined without a hearing, in which event he may proceed to determine the case without a hearing and he shall in writing either before giving his determination or decision, or in it, inform the person making the request that it has been refused.

(3) A Commissioner may of his own motion at any stage, if he is satisfied that an oral hearing is desirable, direct such a hearing.

Representation at an oral hearing

16. At any oral hearing a party may conduct his case himself (with assistance from any person if he wishes) or be represented by any person whom he may appoint for the purpose.

Oral hearings

17.—(1) This Regulation applies to any oral hearing of an application, appeal or reference to which these Regulations apply.

(2) Reasonable notice (being not less than 10 days beginning with the day on which notice is given and ending on the day before the hearing of the case is to take place) of the time and place of any oral hearing before a Commissioner shall be given to the parties by the office of the Social Security Commissioners.

(3) If any party to whom notice of an oral hearing has been given in accordance with these Regulations should fail to appear at the hearing, the Commissioner may, having regard to all the circumstances including any explanation offered for the absence, proceed with the case notwithstanding that party's absence, or may give such directions with a view to the determination of the case as he thinks fit.

(4) Any oral hearing before a Commissioner shall be in public except where the Commissioner is satisfied that intimate personal or financial circumstances may have to be disclosed or that considerations of public security are involved, in which case the hearing or any part thereof shall be in private.

(5) Where a Commissioner holds an oral hearing the following persons or organisations shall be entitled to be present and be heard:—

(a) the person or organisation making the application, appeal or reference;

(b) the claimant;

(c) the Secretary of State;

(d) an adjudication officer;

(e) a trade union, employers association or other association which would have had a right of appeal under sections 101(2) and 101(4) of the Act (including those sections as substituted by section 52(7)(d) of the Social Security Act 1986**(a)**);

(f) in cases concerning statutory sick pay and statutory maternity pay, the alleged employer and the alleged employee concerned;

(g) a person from whom it is determined that any amount is recoverable under or by virtue of section 27 or 53 of the Social Security Act 1986;

(h) any other person with the leave of a Commissioner.

(6) Any person entitled to be heard at an oral hearing may:

(i) address the Commissioner;

(ii) with the leave of the Commissioner but not otherwise, give evidence, call witnesses and put questions directly to any other person called as a witness.

(7) Nothing in these Regulations shall prevent a member of the Council on Tribunals or of the Scottish Committee of the Council in his capacity as such from being present at an oral hearing before a Commissioner, notwithstanding that the hearing is not in public.

Summoning of witnesses

18.—(1) A Commissioner may summon any person to attend as a witness, at such time and place as may be specified in the summons, at an oral hearing of an application to a Commissioner for leave to appeal, or of an appeal or of a reference, to answer any questions or produce any documents in his custody or under his control which relate to any matter in question in the proceedings.

Provided that no person shall be required to attend in obedience to such a summons unless he has been given at least 7 days notice of the hearing or, if less than 7 days, has informed the Commissioner that he accepts such notice as he has been given.

(2) A Commissioner may upon the application of a person summoned under this Regulation set the summons aside.

Postponement and adjournment

19.—(1) A Commissioner may, either of his own motion or on an application by any party to the proceedings, postpone an oral hearing.

(2) An oral hearing, once commenced, may be adjourned by the Commissioner at any time either on the application of any party to the proceedings or of his own motion.

Withdrawal of applications for leave to appeal, appeals and references

20.—(1) At any time before it is determined, an application to a Commissioner for leave to appeal against a decision of an appeal tribunal, a medical appeal tribunal or the Attendance Allowance Board may be withdrawn by the applicant by giving written notice to a Commissioner of his intention to do so.

(2) At any time before the decision is made, an appeal or reference made to a Commissioner under these Regulations may be withdrawn by the appellant or person making the reference, with the leave of a Commissioner.

(3) A Commissioner may, on application by the party concerned, give leave to reinstate any application, appeal or reference which has been withdrawn in accordance with paragraphs (1) and (2) above and, on giving leave, he may make such directions as to the future conduct of the proceedings as he thinks fit.

(a) 1986 c.50.

Irregularities

21. Any irregularity resulting from failure to comply with the requirements of these Regulations before a Commissioner has determined the application, appeal or reference shall not by itself invalidate any proceedings, and the Commissioner, before reaching his decision, may waive the irregularity or take such steps as he thinks fit to remedy the irregularity whether by amendment of any document, or the giving of any notice or directions or otherwise.

PART IV

DECISIONS

Determinations and decisions of a Commissioner

22.—(1) The determination of a Commissioner on an application for leave to appeal shall be in writing and signed by him.

(2) The decision of a Commissioner on an appeal or on a reference shall be in writing and signed by him and, except in respect of a decision made with the consent of the parties, he shall record the reasons.

(3) A copy of the determination or decision and any reasons shall be sent to the parties by the office of the Social Security Commissioners.

(4) Without prejudice to paragraphs (2) and (3) above, a Commissioner may announce his determination or decision at the conclusion of an oral hearing.

Procedure after determination of a forfeiture rule question

23.—(1) Subject to paragraph (2) below, the Commissioner who has determined a forfeiture rule question shall remit the case to the adjudicating authority which caused it to be referred to him together with a copy of his decision on that question and that authority shall then dispose of the case in the light of the Commissioner's decision on the forfeiture rule question.

(2) Where, disregarding the forfeiture rule question, the case referred to a Commissioner is one where an appeal tribunal has, or in the event of an appeal from a decision of an adjudication officer would have, jurisdiction to dispose of the case, the Commissioner may, with the consent of the parties, dispose of the case.

Correction of accidental errors in decisions

24.—(1) Subject to Regulation 26, accidental errors in any decision or record of a decision may at any time be corrected by the Commissioner who gave the decision.

(2) A correction made to, or to the record of, a decision shall become part of the decision or record thereof and written notice thereof shall be given by the office of the Social Security Commissioners to any party to whom notice of the decision had previously been given.

Setting aside of decisions on certain grounds

25.—(1) Subject to this Regulation and Regulation 26, on an application made by any party a decision may be set aside by the Commissioner who gave the decision in a case where it appears just to do so on the ground that—

  (a) a document relating to the proceedings was not sent to, or was not received at an appropriate time by, a party or his representative or was not received at an appropriate time by the Commissioner; or

  (b) a party or his representative had not been present at an oral hearing which had been held in the course of the proceedings; or

  (c) the interests of justice so require.

(2) An application under this Regulation shall be made in writing to a Commissioner,

within 30 days from the date on which notice in writing of the decision was given by the office of the Social Security Commissioners to the party making the application.

(3) Where an application to set aside a decision is made under paragraph (1), each party shall be sent by the office of the Social Security Commissioners a copy of the application and shall be afforded a reasonable opportunity of making representations on it before the application is determined.

(4) Notice in writing of a determination of an application to set aside a decision shall be given by the office of the Social Security Commissioners to each party and shall contain a statement giving the reasons for the determination.

Provisions common to Regulations 24 and 25

26.—(1) In Regulations 24 and 25 the word "decision" shall include determinations of applications for leave to appeal as well as decisions on appeals and on references.

(2) Subject to a direction by a Commissioner to the contrary, in calculating any time for applying for leave to appeal against a Commissioner's decision there shall be disregarded any day falling before the day on which notice was given of a correction of a decision or the record thereof pursuant to Regulation 24 or on which notice was given of a determination that a decision shall not be set aside under Regulation 25, as the case may be.

(3) There shall be no appeal against a correction or a refusal to correct under Regulation 24, or a determination given under Regulation 25.

(4) If it is impracticable or likely to cause undue delay for a decision or record of a decision to be dealt with pursuant to Regulation 24 or 25 by the Commissioner who gave the decision, the Chief Commissioner or another Commissioner may deal with the matter.

PART V

MISCELLANEOUS AND SUPPLEMENTARY

General powers of a Commissioner

27.—(1) Subject to the provisions of these Regulations, and without prejudice to Regulation 12, a Commissioner may adopt such procedure in relation to any proceedings before him as he sees fit.

(2) A Commissioner may, if he thinks fit:—
 (a) subject to Regulations 3(5) and 7(2) above, extend the time specified by or under these Regulations for doing any act, notwithstanding that the time specified may have expired;
 (b) abridge the time so specified;
 (c) expedite the proceedings in such manner as he thinks fit.

(3) A Commissioner may, if he thinks fit, either on the application of a party or of his own motion, strike out for want of prosecution any application for leave to appeal, appeal or reference.

Provided that before making any such order, the Commissioner shall send notice to the party against whom it is proposed that it shall be made giving him an opportunity to show cause why it should not be made.

(4) A Commissioner may, on application by the party concerned, give leave to reinstate any application, appeal or reference which has been struck out in accordance with paragraph (3) above and, on giving leave, he may make such directions as to the future conduct of the proceedings as he thinks fit.

(5) Nothing in these Regulations shall be construed as derogating from any inherent or other power which is exercisable apart from these Regulations.

Miscellaneous provisions relating to references of forfeiture rule questions

28.—(1) Section 116 of the Act (tribunal of Commissioners to deal with cases involving questions of law of special difficulty) shall apply in relation to forfeiture rule questions as it applies in relation to the Act.

(2) Section 104(1) of the Act (review of decisions) shall apply to a decision on a forfeiture rule question by a Commissioner with the modification that the power of review shall be exercisable only by a Commissioner, to whom any application for review shall be made.

(3) Subject to paragraph (2) above and section 14 of the Social Security Act 1980**(a)**, the decision of a Commissioner on any reference of a forfeiture rule question shall be final, but any finding of fact or other determination embodied in or necessary to the decision or on which it is based shall not be conclusive for the purpose of any further decision.

Delegation of functions to nominated officers

29.—(1) All or any of the following functions of a Commissioner may be exercised by a nominated officer, that is to say:
  (a) making any direction under Regulations 12(1), (3) and (4);
  (b) making orders for oral hearings under Regulations 15(2) and (3);
  (c) summoning witnesses under Regulation 18(1) and setting aside a summons made by a nominated officer under Regulation 18(2);
  (d) ordering the postponement of oral hearings under Regulation 19(1);
  (e) giving leave for the withdrawal of any appeal or reference under Regulation 20(2);
  (f) making any order for the extension or abridgement of time, or for expediting the proceedings, under Regulations 27(2)(a), (b) and (c);
  (g) making an order under paragraph (2) of this Regulation.

(2) Any party may, within 10 days of being given the decision of a nominated officer, in writing request a Commissioner to consider, and confirm or replace with his own, that decision, but such a request shall not stop the proceedings unless so ordered by the Commissioner.

Manner of and time for service of notices, etc

30.—(1) Any notice or other document required or authorised to be given or sent to any party under the provisions of these Regulations shall be deemed to have been given or sent if it was sent by post properly addressed and pre-paid to that party at his ordinary or last notified address.

(2) Any notice or other document given, sent or served by post shall be deemed to have been given on the day on which it was posted.

(3) Any notice or document required to be given, sent or submitted to or served on a Commissioner:—
  (a) shall be given, sent or submitted to an office of the Social Security Commissioners;
  (b) shall be deemed to have been given, sent or submitted if it was sent by post properly addressed and pre-paid to an office of the Social Security Commissioners.

Application to a Commissioner for leave to appeal to the Courts

31.—(1) An application to a Commissioner under section 14(3) of the Social Security Act 1980 for leave to appeal against a decision of a Commissioner shall be made in writing and shall be made within 3 months from the date on which the applicant was given written notice of the decision.

(a) 1980 c.30.

(2) In a case where the Chief Commissioner considers that it is impracticable, or would be likely to cause undue delay, for such an application to be determined by the Commissioner who decided the case, that application shall be determined—

(a) where the decision was a decision of an individual Commissioner, by the Chief Commissioner or a Commissioner selected by the Chief Commissioner, and

(b) where the decision was a decision of a Tribunal of Commissioners, by a differently constituted Tribunal of Commissioners selected by the Chief Commissioner.

(3) If the office of Chief Commissioner is vacant, or if the Chief Commissioner is unable to act, paragraph (2) above shall have effect as if the expression "the Chief Commissioner" referred to such other of the Commissioners as may have been nominated to act for the purpose either by the Chief Commissioner or, if he has not made such a nomination, by the Lord Chancellor.

(4) Regulation 28 of the Social Security (Claims and Payments) Regulations 1979**(a)** (persons unable to act) shall apply to the right of appeal conferred by section 14 of the Social Security Act 1980**(b)** (appeal from Commissioners etc. on point of law) as it applies to rights arising under the Act.

(5) In relation to a decision of a Commissioner which was given in consequence of a reference under section 112(4) of the Act (references of questions of law by medical appeal tribunals), section 14(3) of the Social Security Act 1980 shall have effect with the modification that an application for leave to appeal against the Commissioner's decision may be made only by—

(a) the claimant in relation to whose claim the question of law arose before the medical appeal tribunal; or

(b) a person appointed to apply on behalf of the claimant under paragraph (4) above; or

(c) a trade union of which the claimant is a member at the material time; or

(d) any other association which exists to promote the interests and welfare of its members and of which the claimant is a member at the material time; or

(e) an adjudication officer; or

(f) the Secretary of State.

(6) In paragraph (5)(c) and (d), "the material time" means, where the question of law arose in relation to—

(a) an accident, the time of that accident; or

(b) a prescribed disease, the date of onset (within the meaning of the Social Security (Industrial Injuries) (Prescribed Diseases) Regulations 1985**(c)**) of that disease; or

(c) a claim for mobility allowance, the date on which the reference was made.

(7) In relation to such a decision of a Commissioner as is referred to in paragraph (5), section 14(5) of the Social Security Act 1980 shall have effect with the modification that "the relevant place" means the premises where the medical appeal tribunal which has referred the question of law to the Commissioner usually exercises its functions.

(8) A person in respect of whom a forfeiture rule question arises and, as appropriate, an adjudication officer or the Secretary of State shall be authorised to apply for leave to appeal from a Commissioner's decision of a forfeiture rule question.

(9) Regulations 20(1) and 20(3) shall apply to applications to a Commissioner for leave to appeal from a Commissioner as they do to the proceedings therein set out.

(a) S.I. 1979/628.
(b) 1980 c.30.
(c) S.I. 1985/967.

Revocation

32. The following Regulations are hereby revoked to the extent that they relate to proceedings before the Commissioners:

    (i) the Statutory Sick Pay (Adjudication) Regulations 1982**(a)**;

    (ii) the Social Security (Adjudication) Regulations 1984**(b)**;

    (iii) the Social Security (Adjudication) Amendment Regulations 1984**(c)**;

    (iv) the Social Security (Adjudication) Amendment (No. 2) Regulations 1984**(d)**.

Transitional provisions

33.—(1) Subject to paragraphs (2) and (3) below, these Regulations shall apply to proceedings before the Commissioners commenced before the date on which they come into operation as well as to proceedings commenced on or after that date.

(2) Where he considers that the application of these Regulations to proceedings before a Commissioner would be inappropriate, a Commissioner may give such directions for the future conduct of the proceedings as he thinks fit and, in particular, he may order the proceedings to continue as if the Social Security (Adjudication) Regulations 1984**(e)** were still applicable to the proceedings to such extent as he may specify.

(3) Notwithstanding paragraphs (1) and (2) above, where before these Regulations came into operation the time limit for making an application, appeal or reference to a Commissioner had begun to run, then nothing in these Regulations shall operate so as to reduce that time limit.

Hailsham of St Marylebone, C.

Dated 13th February 1987

(a) S.I. 1982/1400.
(b) S.I. 1984/451.
(c) S.I. 1984/613.
(d) S.I. 1984/1991.
(e) S.I. 1984/451, as amended by the Social Security (Adjudication) Amendment Regulations 1984 (S.I. 1984/613) and the Social Security (Adjudication) Amendment (No. 2) Regulations 1984 (S.I. 1984/1991).

SCHEDULE

PROVISIONS CONFERRING POWERS EXERCISED IN MAKING THESE REGULATIONS

Section 6 of the National Insurance Act 1974**(a)**.
Sections 101(5A), 101(5B), 106(2), 112(3), 114(2C) and (5) and 115(1), (5) and (6) of, and the definitions of "prescribed" and "regulations" in Schedule 20 to, the Social Security Act 1975**(b)**.
Sections 14 and 15 of the Social Security Act 1980**(c)**.
Section 4 of the Forfeiture Act 1982**(d)**.

(a) 1974 c.14; section 6 was amended by the Social Security (Consequential Provisions) Act 1975 (c.18) Schedule 2, paragraph 70, the Social Security Pensions Act 1975 (c.60) Schedule 4, paragraph 35, the Child Benefit Act 1975 (c.61) Schedule 4, paragraph 8, the Supplementary Benefits Act 1976 (c.71) Schedule 7, paragraph 36, the Social Security and Housing Benefits Act 1982 (c.24) Schedule 4, paragraph 7 and the Social Security Act 1986 (c.50) Schedule 11.
(b) 1975 c.14; sections 101, 106, 112 and 114 and the definition of "regulations" in Schedule 20 were amended by section 52 of and Schedule 5 to the Social Security Act 1986.
(c) 1980 c.30; section 15(1) was amended by the Health and Social Services and Social Security Adjudications Act 1983 (c.41) Schedule 8, paragraph 18.
(d) 1982 c.34.

EXPLANATORY NOTE

(This note is not part of the Regulations)

1. These Regulations regulate the procedure of the Social Security Commissioners in determining claims and questions, generally arising from decisions of social security appeal tribunals, medical appeal tribunals or the Attendance Allowance Board, under social security legislation including the Family Income Supplements Act 1970 (c. 55), the Social Security Act 1975, the Child Benefit Act 1975, the Supplementary Benefits Act 1976 and the Social Security Act 1986. The Regulations take account of changes made in the system of social security adjudication by section 52 of, and Schedules 5 and 7 to, the Social Security Act 1986.

2. Hitherto, the procedure before the Social Security Commissioners has been governed by Regulations—principally the Social Security (Adjudication) Regulations 1984 (as amended)—which have applied also to procedures before the other adjudicating authorities. The present Regulations apply only to the Social Security Commissioners, and proceedings before the other adjudicating authorities are the subject of separate Regulations made by the Secretary of State.

3. Part II contains provisions for making applications, appeals and references, Part III provides for the procedure to be followed on appeals and references, Part IV contains provisions relating to the decisions of Commissioners and Part V contains miscellaneous and supplementary provisions (including the procedure for seeking leave from a Commissioner to appeal to the Courts), transitional provisions and revocations.

4. The Regulations reflect, with modifications, the procedure before the Commissioners under the 1984 Regulations. Principal changes include the following:—

   (i)   initiating documents will be lodged directly with the Office of the Social Security Commissioners, rather than at local offices of the Department of Health and Social Security;

   (ii) time limits for certain interlocutory matters have been reduced;

   (iii) Regulation 29 provides for certain interlocutory matters to be dealt with on behalf of the Commissioners by officers authorised by the Lord Chancellor in England and Wales or, in Scotland, by the Secretary of State.

5. These Regulations revoke the 1984 Regulations (as amended) in their application to proceedings before the Social Security Commissioners, and will apply, subject to the provisions of Regulation 33 (transitional provisions), to all proceedings before the Commissioners whether they were started before, on or after 6th April 1987.

STATUTORY INSTRUMENTS

1987 No. 215

CUSTOMS AND EXCISE

The Export of Goods (Control) (Amendment No. 8) Order 1987

Made	-	-	-	-	*23rd January 1987*
Coming into force					*24th January 1987*

The Secretary of State, in exercise of powers conferred by section 1 of the Import, Export and Customs Powers (Defence) Act 1939**(a)** and now vested in him**(b)**, and of all other powers enabling him in that behalf, hereby makes the following Order:

1. This Order may be cited as the Export of Goods (Control) (Amendment No. 8) Order 1987 and shall come into force on 24th January 1987.

2. For paragraph (*e*) of article 4 of the Export of Goods (Control) Order 1985**(c)** there shall be substituted the following:

"**Cocoa**

(*e*) cocoa beans, whole or broken, raw or roasted, and the following cocoa products namely cocoa paste (in bulk or block) whether or not defatted, cocoa butter (fat or oil) and unsweetened cocoa powder to any destination if there is produced to the proper officer of Customs and Excise at the place of export the appropriate certificate prescribed for this purpose by the economic and control rules of the International Cocoa Agreement 1986**(d)** which were adopted by the International Cocoa Council on 23rd January 1987".

E. W. Beston
An Assistant Secretary,
Department of Trade and Industry

23rd January 1987

(a) 1939 c.69.
(b) *See* S.I. 1970/1537.
(c) S.I. 1985/849, amended by S.I. 1985/1085, 1293, 1294, 1986/82, 540, 1446 and 1934.
(d) Cmnd. 9905.

EXPLANATORY NOTE

(This note is not part of the Order)

This Order further amends the Export of Goods (Control) Order 1985 to take into account the International Cocoa Agreement 1986. Copies of the economic and control rules can be obtained from the International Cocoa Organisation, 22 Berners Street, London W1.

STATUTORY INSTRUMENTS

1987 No. 216

WEIGHTS AND MEASURES

The Weights and Measures (Carriage of Solid Fuel by Rail) Order 1987

Laid before Parliament in draft

Made - - -	*16th February 1987*
Coming into force	*1st March 1987*

Whereas the Secretary of State pursuant to section 86(2) of the Weights and Measures Act 1985(**a**) has consulted with organisations appearing to him to be representative of interests substantially affected by this Order and considered the representations made to him by such organisations with respect to the subject matter of this Order:

And whereas a draft of this Order has been laid before Parliament and approved by resolution of each House of Parliament pursuant to section 86(5) of that Act:

Now, therefore, the Secretary of State, in exercise of his powers under sections 22(1) and (2), 24 and 86(1) of that Act and of all other powers enabling him in that behalf, hereby makes the following Order:—

1.—(1) This Order may be cited as the Weights and Measures (Carriage of Solid Fuel by Rail) Order 1987 and shall come into operation on 1st March 1987.

(2) In this Order, "the Act" means the Weights and Measures Act 1985.

2. Paragraph 23 of Schedule 5 to the Act is hereby amended as follows:—

  (a) for the words "Subject to paragraph 24 below" there shall be substituted the words "(1) Subject to subparagraph (2) and paragraph 24 below"; and

  (b) there shall be added as subparagraph (2) the following subparagraph:—

  "(2) Subparagraph (1) above shall not apply if, at the time of departure of the vehicle from the place of loading, the seller causes to be transmitted to the buyer, for receipt not later than the time of arrival of the vehicle at the buyer's premises, the information required by subparagraphs *(a)* to *(f)* of subparagraph (1) above:

  Provided that where such information is transmitted otherwise than in a legible form—

    (a) the seller and the buyer have agreed in writing that the information may be so transmitted;

    (b) the places of loading and destination of the vehicle are suitably equipped for the transmission and receipt of information in such form; and

---

(**a**) 1985 c. 72.

(c) the information is capable of being reproduced in a permanent legible form by the system effecting the transmission, and is so reproduced if required by an inspector, subject to the production, if so requested, of his credentials."

3. Paragraph 24 of the said Schedule 5 is hereby amended in subparagraph (1) as follows:

(a) after the words "the seller shall" there shall be inserted the words "either *(a)*"; and

(b) after the words "subparagraph (3) below" there shall be added the words "or *(b)* at the time of departure of the train which includes that vehicle transmit to the buyer, for receipt not later than the time of arrival of the train at the buyer's premises, the information required by subparagraph (2) or, as the case may be, subparagraph (3) below:

Provided that where such information is transmitted otherwise than in a legible form—

(a) the seller and buyer have agreed in writing that the information may be so transmitted;

(b) the places of loading and destination of the train are suitably equipped for the transmission and receipt of information in such form; and

(c) the information is capable of being reproduced in a permanent legible form by the system effecting the transmission, and is so reproduced if required by an inspector, subject to the production, if so requested, of his credentials."

Lucas of Chilworth
Parliamentary Under-Secretary of State,
Department of Trade and Industry

16th February 1987

EXPLANATORY NOTE

(This note is not part of the Order)

This Order amends the provisions of Part IV of Schedule 5 to the Weights and Measures Act 1985 relating to the carriage of solid fuel by rail. It enables a system of electronic data transfer to be used as an alternative to the present requirements for coal trains to be accompanied by either individual wagon documents or a train bill (paragraphs 23 and 24 of the said Schedule). As a condition of using such a system, the information so transmitted must be capable of being reproduced in a permanent legible form.

1987 No. 217

SEA FISHERIES

SHELLFISH

The Several and Regulated Fisheries (Form of Application) Regulations 1987

Made - - - -	*9th February 1987*
Coming into force	*1st March 1987*

The Minister of Agriculture, Fisheries and Food in relation to England, the Secretary of State for Scotland in relation to Scotland and the Secretary of State for Wales in relation to Wales, in exercise of the powers conferred on them by section 1(2) of the Sea Fisheries (Shellfish) Act 1967(**a**) and now vested in them(**b**), and of all other powers enabling them in that behalf, hereby make the following Regulations:

Title and commencement

1. These Regulations may be cited as the Several and Regulated Fisheries (Form of Application) Regulations 1987 and shall come into force on 1st March 1987.

Interpretation

2. In these Regulations–
"the Act" means the Sea Fisheries (Shellfish) Act 1967;
"application" means an application for an order under section 1 of the Act and "applicant" shall be construed accordingly.

Form of application

3. An application shall be in the form set out in the Schedule hereto.

Manner of application

4.—(1) An application shall be submitted to the appropriate Minister and shall be accompanied by–
    (a) evidence in writing that all consents required under sub-sections (4) and (5) of section 1 of the Act have been obtained;
    (b) two copies of the current Admiralty chart for the area to which the application relates with that area accurately indicated on one copy;
    (c) if the applicant is a company incorporated under the Companies Acts, a copy of the memorandum and Articles of Association and any registered Special Resolution of the company relating to its objects;
    (d) if the applicant is a corporate body incorporated in any other manner, a copy of every instrument of incorporation, charter or private or local Act of Parliament relating to that body.

(**a**) 1967 c.83.
(**b**) In the case of the Secretary of State for Wales, by virtue of S.I. 1969/388 and 1978/272.

(2) An application shall be signed by the applicant and, in the case of a corporate body, may be signed by an authorised officer of that body.

(3) The applicant shall furnish such further information as the appropriate Minister requires.

Revocation

5.   The Several and Regulated Fisheries (Form of Application) Regulations 1962(**a**) are hereby revoked.

In Witness whereof the Official Seal of the Minister of Agriculture, Fisheries and Food is hereunto affixed on 5th February 1987.

Michael Jopling
Minister of Agriculture, Fisheries and Food

Nicholas Edwards
Secretary of State for Wales

9th February 1987

John J. MacKay
Parliamentary Under Secretary of State, Scottish Office

26th January 1987

(**a**) S.I. 1962/2158.

Article 3   SCHEDULE

Application For An Order Under Section 1 of the Sea Fisheries (Shellfish) Act 1967, as amended by the Sea Fisheries Act 1968 and the Fishery Limits Act 1976, and as extended by the Fisheries Act 1981

To the *Minister of Agriculture, Fisheries and Food
        *Secretary of State for Wales
        *Secretary of State for Scotland

1.   Application is hereby made by ....
....
                            (Name of person(s) or corporate body)

of...
....
under Section 1 of the Sea Fisheries (Shellfish) Act 1967 (as amended by the Sea Fisheries Act 1968 and the Fishery Limits Act 1976, and as extended by the Fisheries Act 1981) ("the Act") for the making of an order granting to the applicant a *several/regulated fishery for *(type of shellfish)* situated at
....

2.   The land to which this application relates is known as
....
is owned by ....
and has an area of .... hectares, and its boundaries are as follows:–
....
....
....

3.   The past and present use of the land for shellfish cultivation and the type and extent of infestation by marine pests and diseases are as follows:–
....
....
....

4.   (a) If a Several Order is made it is intended to:
*stock/cleanse/restock/cultivate
*erect the following structures:–...
....
It is proposed to employ the following labour force
....
and adopt the following methods...
....

OR (b) If a Regulating Order is made it is intended:

(i) to make the following regulations, restrictions on fishing, tolls and charges and provisions for improving and cultivating the fishery *(indicate general intentions)*:–
....
....

(ii) to exercise, for the purpose of regulating the fishery, authority under *(here indicate statutory powers which the applicant is in a position to exercise)*
....

5.   The applicant considers the following additional information to be relevant to this application:–

Signature ....

Date ....

                              *Delete as appropriate

EXPLANATORY NOTE

(This note is not part of the Regulations)

These Regulations prescribe the form of application to be submitted and the manner of submission of such application to the Minister of Agriculture, Fisheries and Food in relation to England, and the Secretary of State in relation to Scotland and in relation to Wales, by applicants for the grant of several or regulating orders in respect of oyster, mussel, cockle, clam, scallop or queen fisheries under section 1 of the Sea Fisheries (Shellfish) Act 1967.

The Regulations replace the Several and Regulated Fisheries (Form of Application) Regulations 1962, which made similar provision in respect of England and Wales only.

STATUTORY INSTRUMENTS

1987 No. 218

SEA FISHERIES

SHELLFISH

The Shellfish (Specification of Molluscs) Regulations 1987

Made - - - -	*9th February 1987*
Coming into force	*1st March 1987*

The Minister of Agriculture, Fisheries and Food in relation to England, the Secretary of State for Scotland in relation to Scotland and the Secretary of State for Wales in relation to Wales, in exercise of the powers conferred on them by section 1(1) of the Sea Fisheries (Shellfish) Act 1967(**a**) and now vested in them(**b**), and of all other powers enabling them in that behalf, hereby make the following Regulations:

Title and commencement

1.   These Regulations may be cited as the Shellfish (Specification of Molluscs) Regulations 1987 and shall come into force on 1st March 1987.

Specification of Molluscs

2.   Scallops and queens are hereby specified for the purposes of section 1(1) of the Sea Fisheries (Shellfish) Act 1967.

In witness whereof the Official Seal of the Minister of Agriculture, Fisheries and Food is hereunto affixed on 5th February 1987.

Michael Jopling
Minister of Agriculture, Fisheries and Food

Nicholas Edwards
9th February 1987   Secretary of State for Wales

John J. MacKay
26th January 1987   Parliamentary Under Secretary of State, Scottish Office

---

(**a**) 1967 c.83; section 1(1) was amended by the Sea Fisheries Act 1968 (c.77) section 15(2) and by the Fishery Limits Act 1976 (c.86) Schedule 2, paragraph 15 and was extended by the Fisheries Act 1981 (c.29) section 34.
(**b**) In the case of the Secretary of State for Wales, by virtue of S.I. 1969/388 and 1978/272.

EXPLANATORY NOTE

(This note is not part of the Regulations)

These Regulations add scallops and queens to the list of shellfish in section 1(1) of the Sea Fisheries (Shellfish) Act 1967. This addition enables several or regulated fisheries for these species to be established by order on the sea shore and in the seas adjacent to Great Britain.

STATUTORY INSTRUMENTS

1987 No. 220

MARINE POLLUTION

The Merchant Shipping (Indemnification of Shipowners) Order 1987

Made - - - -	*17th February 1987*
Laid before Parliament	*27th February 1987*
Coming into force -	*1st May 1987*

The Secretary of State for Transport, in exercise of powers conferred on him by section 5(4)(a) and (6) of the Merchant Shipping Act 1974**(a)** (hereinafter called "the Act") and of all other powers enabling him in that behalf, hereby makes the following Order:

1.—(1) This Order may be cited as the Merchant Shipping (Indemnification of Shipowners) Order 1987 and shall come into force on 1st May 1987.

(2) The Merchant Shipping (Indemnification of Shipowners) Order 1985**(b)** and the Merchant Shipping (Indemnification of Shipowners) (Amendment) Order 1986**(c)** are hereby revoked.

2. The requirements prescribed for the purpose of section 5(4) of the Act, being those which appear to the Secretary of State appropriate to implement the provisions of Article 5(3) of the Fund Convention, are those contained in:

(a) Chapters II and III of Annex I to the International Convention for the Prevention of Pollution from Ships 1973**(d)** as amended by the Protocol of 1978 relating thereto**(e)**;

(b) Chapters II-1, II-2, IV and V of the Annex to the International Convention for the Safety of Life at Sea 1974**(f)** ("SOLAS") as amended by the Protocol of 1978 relating thereto**(g)** and as amended by the amendments adopted on 20th November 1981 and 17th June 1983 respectively by the Maritime Safety Committee of the International Maritime Organization at its 45th and 48th Sessions**(h)**;

(c) Annex I to the International Convention on Load Lines 1966**(i)**;

(a) 1974 c.43.
(b) S.I. 1985/1665, amended by S.I. 1986/296.
(c) S.I. 1986/296.
(d) Cmnd. 5748.
(e) Cmnd. 7347.
(f) Cmnd. 7874.
(g) Cmnd. 7346.
(h) Set out in the IMO Publications "Amendments to the International Convention for the Safety of Life at Sea" (Sales No. 092 82.01.E) and "The 1983 Amendments to the International Convention for the Safety of Life at Sea: Volume 1" (Sales No. 096 83.10.E).
(i) Cmnd. 3070.

(d) the International Regulations for Preventing Collisions at Sea 1972**(a)** ("the Collision Regulations").

3. The requirements of the amendments to the Collision Regulations adopted on 19th November 1981 by the Assembly of the International Maritime Organization at its Twelfth Session by resolution A464**(b)** are prescribed as alternatives to the requirements of the Collision Regulations prescribed in article 2.

Signed by the authority
of the Secretary of State
17th February 1987

Michael Spicer
Parliamentary Under-Secretary of State,
Department of Transport

EXPLANATORY NOTE

(This note is not part of the Order)

This Order revokes, and replaces with an amendment, the Merchant Shipping (Indemnification of Shipowners) Order 1985, as amended.

The amendment (which appears in article 2(b) of the Order) is to include the amendments made in 1983 to the Safety of Life at Sea Convention 1974, among the Conventions with which a shipowner must comply if he is to get indemnification in the circumstances set out in article 5 of the Convention on the Establishment of an International Fund for Compensation for Oil Pollution Damage 1971.

(a) Cmnd. 5471.
(b) Cmnd. 8500.

1987 No. 232

ANIMALS

ANIMAL HEALTH

The Diseases of Animals (Waste Food) (Amendment) Order 1987

Made - - - -	*17th February 1987*
Coming into force	*10th March 1987*

The Minister of Agriculture, Fisheries and Food and the Secretary of State for Scotland and the Secretary of State for Wales, acting jointly, in exercise of the powers conferred on them by sections 1 and 8(1) of the Animal Health Act 1981(a), and of all other powers enabling them in that behalf, order as follows:–

Title and commencement

1. This Order may be cited as the Diseases of Animals (Waste Food) (Amendment) Order 1987 and shall come into force on 10th March 1987.

Amendment

2. The Diseases of Animals (Waste Food) Order 1973(b) shall be amended as follows:–

(a) after paragraph (3) of article 2 there shall be inserted the following paragraph —

"(4) Any reference in this Order to granting a licence includes a reference to renewing a licence before it ceases to be valid.";

(b) in article 3 (prohibitions relating to unprocessed waste food etc)

(i) in paragraph (1) the words "Subject to paragraph (4) of this article," shall be omitted;

(ii) in paragraph (2) for the words "Subject to paragraph (4) of this article (but without prejudice to the provisions of article 4 of this order)" there shall be substituted the words, "without prejudice to the provisions of article 4 of this Order"; and

(iii) paragraph (4) shall be omitted; and

(c) after article 11 (applications for licences) there shall be inserted the following article —

"**11A.** The issuing authority may —

(a) before granting a licence under article 7 authorising the operation of plant and equipment for processing waste food on any premises; or

(b) before granting a licence under article 8 authorising the reception of waste food on any premises,

---

(a) 1981 c.22.   (b) S.I. 1973/1936.

carry out such inspections, examinations and tests as it considers necessary for the purpose of ascertaining —

    (i) whether the premises conform to the specifications set out in Part I of Schedule 1 or Part I of Schedule 2 to this Order (as appropriate) or are of a standard substantially equivalent to those specifications; and

    (ii) whether the operation of plant and equipment on the premises for processing waste food or (as the case may be) the use of the premises for the reception of waste food would give rise to a risk of the spread of disease."

In Witness whereof the Official Seal of the Minister of Agriculture, Fisheries and Food is hereunto affixed on 12th February 1987.

Michael Jopling
Minister of Agriculture, Fisheries and Food

John J. Mackay
17th February 1987   Parliamentary Under-Secretary of State, Scottish Office

Nicholas Edwards
17th February 1987   Secretary of State for Wales

EXPLANATORY NOTE

(This note is not part of the Order)

This Order amends the Diseases of Animals (Waste Food) Order 1973 ("the 1973 Order") which prohibits a person from possessing any unprocessed waste food for the purpose of feeding to livestock or poultry, unless he is the holder of a licence granted under that order authorising him to operate plant and equipment for processing waste food, and from feeding any waste food to livestock or poultry, unless it has first been processed by means of plant and equipment operated under such a licence. The 1973 Order further provides that these prohibitions do not apply to the possession by any person of any waste food originating from his own household or to the feeding of such waste food to livestock or poultry provided it has first been processed. This Order removes such exemptions from the 1973 Order so that the prohibitions referred to apply to all unprocessed waste food (article 2(a)).

This Order also enables an issuing authority (as defined in the 1973 Order) before granting, or renewing, a licence authorising the operation of plant and equipment on any premises for processing waste food or the reception of waste food intended for feeding to livestock or poultry on any premises to carry out such inspections, examinations and tests as it considers necessary in order to ascertain whether the premises comply with the constructional specifications set out in the 1973 Order and whether their use for waste food processing or the reception of waste food would give rise to the risk of the spread of disease (article 2(b)).

1987 No. 233

ANIMALS

ANIMAL HEALTH

The Movement and Sale of Pigs (Amendment) Order 1987

Made -	-	-	-	*17th February 1987*
Coming into force				*10th March 1987*

The Minister of Agriculture, Fisheries and Food and the Secretary of State for Scotland and the Secretary of State for Wales, acting jointly, in exercise of the powers conferred on them by sections 1, 7(1), 8(1) and 25 of the Animal Health Act 1981(a) and of all other powers enabling them in that behalf, order as follows:–

Title and commencement

1. This Order may be cited as the Movement and Sale of Pigs (Amendment) Order 1987 and shall come into force on 10th March 1987.

Amendment

2. The Movement and Sale of Pigs Order 1975(b) shall be amended as follows:–

(a) at the end of article 2(3) (movements of pigs exempt from movement restrictions) there shall be added the following sub-paragraph:–

"(f) movement of pigs for breeding purposes under the authority of a licence issued under article 5 of this Order, being a licence in the form set out in Schedule 4, and the return home of those pigs under the authority of such a licence.";

(b) in article 5(3) (licences for movements of pigs)–

(i) after the words "to which the licence is to relate" there shall be inserted the words "or his agent authorised in writing for this purpose"; and

(ii) after the words "at which the mating is to take place" there shall be inserted the words "or his agent authorised in writing for this purpose"; and

(c) for Schedule 5 (form of declarations to be made before a licence for the movement of pigs will be issued) there shall be substituted the Schedule to this Order.

(a) 1981 c.22.
(b) S.I. 1975/203, as amended by S.I. 1975 346.

In Witness whereof the Official Seal of the Ministry of Agriculture, Fisheries and Food is hereunto affixed on 12th February 1987.

Michael Jopling
Minister of Agriculture, Fisheries and Food

17th February 1987

John J. Mackay
Parliamentary Under-Secretary of State, Scottish Office

17th February 1987

Nicholas Edwards
Secretary of State for Wales

SCHEDULE

SCHEDULE 5   Article 5(3)

THE MOVEMENT AND SALE OF PIGS ORDER 1975

PART I

DECLARATION TO BE MADE BY OWNER OF PIGS (OR HIS AGENT) FOR USE IN CASE OF A LICENSED MOVEMENT OF PIGS (OTHER THAN A LICENSED MOVEMENT FROM A MARKET, FAIRGROUND, SALEYARD OR LICENSED COLLECTING CENTRE, ARTIFICIAL INSEMINATION CENTRE, PERFORMANCE TESTING STATION, EXHIBITION OR SHOW)

I,   of
                 hereby declare as follows:–

(a) that I am the owner of (or the agent authorised in writing for this purpose by the owner of) the pigs to be moved which are described below;

(b) that no pigs have been moved on to the premises described below from which the said pigs are to be moved ("my premises") since .... (day/month/year) (being 21 days before the date of the proposed movement) except for pigs which have:

(i) returned from an exhibition or show; or

(ii) been moved on for breeding purposes under a licence issued under article 5 of the Movement and Sale of Pigs Order 1975 and in the form set out in Schedule 4 to that Order or returned home under the authority of such a licence; or

(iii) been moved on from a performance testing station or artificial insemination centre; or

(iv) been moved on from premises known as ....
(being a source of breeding pigs approved by the Minister in respect of my premises for the purposes of article 2(3)(d) of the Movement and Sale of Pigs Order 1975);

(c) that no pigs will be moved on to my premises before the movement takes place other than pigs in the categories mentioned in (b)(i), (ii), (iii) and (iv) above;

(d) that to the best of my knowledge and belief the said pigs are not affected or suspected of being affected with a notifiable disease,[1] and have not been in any way exposed to infection from any such disease;

(e) that no pigs on my premises have been fed or brought into contact with any waste food[2] (including any waste food originating from my own household) during the past three months;

(f) that no waste food[2] intended for feeding to livestock or poultry has been brought on to my premises for any purpose;

(g)   that no waste food[2] has been kept on my premises for disposal as refuse otherwise than in covered refuse containers.

Dated ....

Signed ....

Name in block letters ....

Number and description of pigs to be moved	Address of premises from which pigs are to be moved, stating District of Local Authority in which situate	Address of place of destination to which pigs are to be moved, stating District of Local Authority in which situate

[1] Notifiable diseases of pigs are Foot-and-Mouth Disease, Swine Vesicular Disease, Swine Fever, Anthrax, Teschen Disease, African swine fever and Aujeszky's disease.

[2] Waste food means—

(a) any meat, bones, blood, offal or other part of the carcase of any livestock or of any poultry, or products derived therefrom or hatchery waste or eggs or egg shell, or

(b) any broken or waste foodstuffs (including table or kitchen refuse, scraps or waste) which contain or have been in contact with any meat, bones, blood, offal or with any other part of the carcase of any livestock or of any poultry,

but does not include meal manufactured from protein originating from livestock or poultry.

Note:– This declaration is to be retained by the person granting the licence to which it relates.

PART II

ADDITIONAL DECLARATION TO BE MADE BY OCCUPIER OF PREMISES AT WHICH MATING IS TO TAKE PLACE (OR HIS AGENT) FOR USE IN CASE OF A LICENSED MOVEMENT OF PIGS FOR BREEDING PURPOSES

I,   of
               hereby declare as follows:–

(a)   that I am the occupier of (or the agent authorised in writing for this purpose by the occupier of) the premises known as ....
("my premises") on which there is the boar/sow* to be mated with the sow/boar* described in the declaration made under Part I by
;

(b)   that the boar/sow* has been on my premises continuously for the past twenty-one days, and no pigs have been moved on to my premiises since .... (day/month/year) (being 21 days before the date of the proposed movement) except for pigs which have:

(i) returned from an exhibition or show; or

(ii) been moved on for breeding purposes under a licence issued under Article 5 of the Movement and Sale of Pigs Order 1975 and in the form set out in Schedule 4 to that Order or returned home under the authority of such a licence; or

(iii) been moved on from a performance testing station or artificial insemination centre or

(iv) been moved on from premises known as ....
(being a source of breeding pigs approved by the Minister in respect of my premises for the purposes of article 2(3)(d) of the Movement and Sale of Pigs Order 1975);

(c)   that no pigs other than pigs in the categories mentioned in (b)(i), (ii), (iii) and (iv) above will be moved on to my premises before the movement takes place or while the boar/sow* described in the said declaration is on my premises;

(d)   that to the best of my knowledge and belief the pigs on my premises are not affected or suspected of being affected with a notifiable disease,[1] and have not been in any way exposed to infection from any such disease;

(e)   that no pigs on my premises have been fed or brought into contact with any waste food[2] (including any waste food originating from my own household) during the past three months;

(f)   that no waste food[2] intended for feeding to livestock or poultry has been brought on to my premises for any purpose;

(g)   that no waste food[2] has been kept on my premises for disposal as refuse otherwise than in covered refuse containers;

(h)   that the boar/sow* on my premises which is involved in this breeding movement will be kept on my premises for a period of 21 days after the last date of contact with the boar/sow* described in the said declaration.

Dated..

Signed ....

Name in block letters ....

*Delete as appropriate.

---

[1] Notifiable diseases of pigs are Foot-and-Mouth Disease, Swine Vesicular Disease, Swine Fever, Anthrax, Teschen Disease, African swine fever and Aujeszky's disease.

[2] Waste food means–
   (a) any meat, bones, blood, offal or other part of the carcase of any livestock or of any poultry, or products derived therefrom or hatchery waste or eggs or egg shell, or
   (b) any broken or waste foodstuffs (including table or kitchen refuse, scraps or waste) which contain or have been in contact with any meat, bones, blood, offal or with any other part of the carcase of any livestock or of any poultry,
but does not include meal manufactured from protein originating from livestock or poultry.

Note:– This declaration is to be retained by the person granting the licence to which it relates.

EXPLANATORY NOTE

(This note is not part of the Order)

This Order amends the Movement and Sale of Pigs Order 1975 ("the 1975 Order") which, amongst other provisions, contains a prohibition on the movement of pigs from any premises within 21 days of the movement of any pigs on to those premises, subject to certain specified exemptions. The Order adds a further exemption to such prohibition where pigs are moved for breeding purposes under the authority of a licence in the form set out in Schedule 4 to the 1975 Order issued under article 5 of that Order (article 2(a)).

The Order also amends the form of the declarations required to be made before a licence is issued under article 5 of the 1975 Order authorising the movement of pigs from any premises (article 2(c)), the movement of pigs from all premises being subject to licensing control under the 1975 Order, with the exception of certain specified movements. A person making such a declaration is now required to declare that no pigs on his premises have been fed or brought into contact with any waste food (including waste food originating from his own household) during the previous three months.

1987 No. 235

TERMS AND CONDITIONS OF EMPLOYMENT

The Statutory Maternity Pay (Medical Evidence) Regulations 1987

Made - - - -	*19th February 1987*
Laid before Parliament	*20th February 1987*
Coming into force	*15th March 1987*

The Secretary of State for Social Services, in exercise of the powers conferred by sections 49 and 84(1) of and paragraph 6 of Schedule 4 to the Social Security Act 1986**(a)**, and of all other powers enabling him in that behalf, by this instrument, which is made before the end of the period of 12 months from the commencement of the enactments contained in the 1986 Act under which it is made, makes the following regulations:–

Citation, commencement and interpretation

1.—(1) These regulations may be cited as the Statutory Maternity Pay (Medical Evidence) Regulations 1987 and shall come into force on 15th March 1987.

(2) In these regulations, unless the context otherwise requires–

"the Act" means the Social Security Act 1986;

"registered midwife" means a midwife who is registered as a midwife with the United Kingdom Central Council for Nursing, Midwifery and Health Visiting under the Nurses, Midwives and Health Visitors' Act 1979**(b)**;

"doctor" means a registered medical practitioner;

"signature" means, in relation to any statement or certificate given in accordance with these regulations, the name by which the person giving that statement or certificate, as the case may be, is usually known (any name other than the surname being either in full or otherwise indicated) written by that person in his own handwriting; and "signed" shall be construed accordingly.

Evidence of pregnancy and confinement

2. The evidence as to pregnancy and the expected date of confinement which a woman is required to provide to a person who is liable to pay her statutory maternity pay shall be furnished in the form of a maternity certificate given by a doctor or by a registered midwife, not earlier than the beginning of the 14th week before the expected week of confinement, in accordance with the rules set out in Part I of the Schedule to these regulations–

(a) in the appropriate form as set out in Part II of that Schedule, or

---

(a) 1986 c.50; section 84(1) is cited because of the meaning ascribed to the words "prescribed" and "regulations".
(b) 1979 c.36.

(b) in a form substantially to the like effect with such variations as the circumstances may require.

Signed by authority of the Secretary of State for Social Services.

Nicholas Lyell
Parliamentary Under-Secretary of State,
19th February 1987   Department of Health and Social Security

---

SCHEDULE   Regulation 2

PART I

RULES

1. In these rules any reference to a woman is a reference to the woman in respect of whom a maternity certificate is given in accordance with these rules.

2. A maternity certificate shall be given by a doctor or registered midwife attending the woman and shall not be given by the woman herself.

3. The maternity certificate shall be on a form provided by the Secretary of State for the purpose and the wording shall be that set out in the appropriate part of the form specified in Part II of this Schedule.

4. Every maternity certificate shall be completed in ink or other indelible substance and shall contain the following particulars–
   (a)   the woman's name;
   (b)   the week in which the woman is expected to be confined or, if the maternity certificate is given after confinement, the date of that confinement and the date the confinement was expected to take place where this is later than the actual confinement;
   (c)   the date of the examination on which the maternity certificate is based;
   (d)   the date on which the maternity certificate is signed; and
   (e)   the address of the doctor or where the maternity certificate is signed by a midwife either her registered number or address,
and shall bear opposite the word "Signature", the signature of the person giving the maternity certificate written after there has been entered on the maternity certificate the woman's name and the expected date or, as the case may be, the date of the confinement.

5. After a maternity certificate has been given, no further maternity certificate based on the same examination shall be furnished other than a maternity certificate by way of replacement of an original which has been lost or mislaid, in which case it shall be clearly marked "duplicate".

PART II

FORM OF CERTIFICATE

MATERNITY CERTIFICATE

Please fill in this form in ink

Name of patient ....

Part A	Part B
Fill in this part if you are giving the certificate before the confinement	*Fill in this part if you are giving the certificate after the confinement*
Do not fill this in more than 14 weeks before the expected week of confinement	I certify that I attended you in connection with your confinement which took place on
I certify that I examined you on the date given below and in my opinion you can be expected to be confined in the week that includes / /	/ / when you were delivered of a child (...... children)
	Fill in the rest of Part B if the birth was before the expected week of confinement
	In my opinion your confinement was expected in the week that includes / /

Date of examination   / /

Date of signing   / /

Registered midwives

please give your registered number or address here

Signature

Definitions. Confinement: The Social Security Act 1986 defines confinement as 'labour resulting in the issue of a living child, or labour after 28 weeks of pregnancy resulting in the issue of a child whether alive or dead'. Part B of the Maternity Certificate must not be used in any other circumstances. Week: This means the 7 days beginning on a Sunday.

EXPLANATORY NOTE

(This note is not part of the Regulations)

These regulations prescribe the form in which evidence of her pregnancy or her expected date of confinement is to be provided by a woman to a person who is liable to pay her statutory maternity pay.

The provisions of the Social Security Act 1986 under which these regulations were made have not yet been in force for 12 months. The regulations are therefore exempt by section 61(5) of the Act of 1986 from reference to the Social Security Advisory Committee and have not been so referred.

STATUTORY INSTRUMENTS

1987 No. 236

EDUCATION, ENGLAND AND WALES

The Remuneration of Teachers (Primary and Secondary Education) (Amendment) (No. 2) Order 1987

Made - - - -	*18th February 1987*
Coming into force	*25th February 1987*

WHEREAS:

(1) in pursuance of section 2(2) of the Remuneration of Teachers Act 1965(a) ("the Act"), the Committee constituted under section 1 of the Act for the purpose of considering the remuneration payable to teachers in primary and secondary schools maintained by local education authorities and to other persons employed by such authorities as teachers in the provision of primary and secondary education (except teachers in an establishment maintained by a local authority in the exercise of a social services function) ("the Committee") have transmitted to the Secretary of State for Education and Science ("the Secretary of State") recommendations agreed on by them with respect to the remuneration of such teachers ("primary and secondary education teachers");

(2) there are in force Orders made under sections 2(4) and (6) of the Act with respect to the remuneration of the teachers in question, such Orders being those specified in the Schedule to this Order;

(3) it appears to the Secretary of State that effect can most conveniently be given to the recommendations of the Committee by amending the scales and other provisions set out in the document referred to in the said Orders, namely the document published by Her Majesty's Stationery Office on 7th October 1983 under the title "Scales of Salaries for Teachers: Primary and Secondary Education, England and Wales 1983"(b) ("the 1983 Document"), as amended by the said Orders;

(4) in pursuance of section 2(5) of the Act, the Secretary of State has prepared a draft Order setting out the amendments to the 1983 Document which, in his opinion, are requisite for giving effect to the recommendations of the Committee, and

(5) the Secretary of State, as required by section 2(6) of the Act, has consulted the Committee with respect to the draft Order and the Committee have made no representations with respect thereto:

Now, therefore, the Secretary of State, in pursuance of sections 2(6) and 7(3) of the Act, hereby makes the following Order, which is in the form of the draft:

1.—(1) This Order may be cited as the Remuneration of Teachers (Primary and Secondary Education) (Amendment) (No.2) Order 1987.

(2) This Order shall come into force on 25th February 1987.

2. The provisions contained in the 1983 Document, as amended, are hereby further amended, with effect from 25th February 1987 in the manner specified in sub-paragraphs (2), (3), (5), (6) and (11) and with effect from 16 July 1986 in the manner specified in sub-paragraphs (1), (4), (7), (8), (9) and (10) as follows–

(a) 1965 c.3.
(b) ISBN 0 11 270550 2.

(1) In section 1 (Remuneration) the word "and" where it appears after the words "(Section 18)" shall be deleted and there shall be inserted after the words "(Section 19)" the words "and unqualified teachers with comparable qualifications who are to be paid as qualified teachers (Section 20A)".

(2) In section 16 (Safeguarding)–
   (a) there shall be added after sub-paragraph (ii) the following sub-paragraph–
      "(iiA) where in the circumstances described in sub-paragraph (i) or (ii) a full-time teacher or a teacher in regular part-time service loses his post or would (but for this sub-section) suffer a diminution of salary or be placed on a salary scale with a lower maximum, and is thereupon employed as stated in sub-paragraph (i) but as a teacher in regular part-time service, he shall (subject, in the circumstances described in sub-paragraph (ii), to the same consent) be entitled to that proportion of the salary and allowances to which he was entitled immediately before the relevant change in circumstances which his part-time employment bears to full-time employment;";
   (b) in sub-paragraph (iii) for the words "(i) or (ii)" there shall be substituted the words "(i), (ii) or (iiA)".

(3) In section 17 (Part-time Teachers and Teachers employed on a Short Notice Basis)–
   (a) sub-section (c) shall be deleted; and
   (b) in sub-section (d) for the words "sub-sections (b) or (c) apply" there shall be substituted the words "sub-section (b) applies".

(4) After section 20 there shall be added the following paragraphs–

"20A. Circumstances in which an unqualified teacher is to be paid as a qualified teacher

Where an unqualified teacher–
   (i) has successfully completed a course which the authority by whom the teacher's remuneration is paid is satisfied is comparable to a course such as is mentioned in paragraph 2(*a*)(i) of Schedule 5 to the Education (Teachers) Regulations 1982**(a)** and
   (ii) unless he so completed the course before 1st September 1984, has attained in mathematics and in English the standard required to attain in the subject in question either a grade C in the examinations for the General Certificate of Education at ordinary level or a grade 1 for the examinations for the Certificate of Secondary Education

he shall, for a period not exceeding one year from the date of his first appointment as a teacher in England and Wales after successfully completing the said comparable course or until the Secretary of State declines to approve that course as comparable for the purposes of paragraph 2(*b*) of that Schedule, whichever is the sooner, be paid as a qualified teacher.

20B. Lump sum on becoming a qualified teacher

On being notified after 16th July 1986 that he is a qualified teacher a teacher shall be paid a lump sum by any authority by whom his remuneration has been paid in the year preceding his date of qualification or (if a shorter period) in the period between his relevant date (as defined for the purpose of Appendix III and its annexes) and his date of qualification, such lump sum to be equivalent to the difference (if any) between the remuneration he received from that authority during that period and the remuneration he would have received from them as a qualified teacher."

(5) In Appendix II, Part A, paragraph 6(3)**(b)**–
   (a) there shall be substituted for sub-paragraph (*d*) the following sub-paragraph–
      "*(d) the year beginning 1 April 1983*
      from the period 1 April 1987 to 31 March 1988 on (a) the average of unit totals for 1985, 1986 and 1987 or (b) the unit total for 1987 or (c) the estimated unit total for 1987 whichever is the greatest. Where a new head or deputy head teacher is appointed during the period 1 April 1987 to 31 March 1988, the head or deputy head teacher scale applicable shall be based on whichever of (a) or (b) is the greater;";

(a) S.I. 1982/106.
(b) Sub-paragraph (*d*) was substituted by S.I. 1986/559 and sub-paragraph (*g*) added by S.I. 1987/137.

(b) there shall be added after sub-paragraph (g) the following sub-paragraph–
"*(h) the year beginning 1 April 1987*
from the date of opening or reorganisation until 31 March 1991 on the estimated unit total for 1991.".

(6) In Appendix II, Part B, in paragraphs 3 and 4**(a)** there shall be substituted for the date 1986 wherever it appears the date 1987.

(7) In Appendix III–

(a) in sub-paragraphs (1) and (2) of paragraph 5 the word "post-qualified" wherever it appears shall be deleted; and there shall be inserted after the words "remunerated experience" wherever they appear the words "following his relevant date";

(b) after paragraph 5 there shall be added the following paragraph–
"5A. In this Appendix and its annexes "relevant date" shall mean–

(a) in the case of a teacher qualified before 16 July 1986 his date of qualification;

(b) in the case of a teacher qualified after 16 July 1986 the date on which–

(i) he obtained the qualification or successfully completed the course, or (if later)

(ii) he completed any requisite period of service or experience

which led to his being notified by the Secretary of State, pursuant to Schedule 5 to the Education (Teachers) Regulations 1982 that he was a qualified teacher; and

(c) in the case of an unqualified teacher to whom section 20A applies the date on which he successfully completed the comparable course there mentioned;".

(8) In paragraph 3(b) of annex A to Appendix III there shall be substituted for the words "after service as a qualified teacher" the words "following service after the relevant date".

(9) In annex B to Appendix III–

(a) in the heading, for the words "date of qualification" there shall be substituted the words "relevant date";

(b) in paragraph 1, for the words "Pre-qualified gainful employment" there shall be substituted the words "Gainful employment undertaken prior to the relevant date";

(c) in paragraph 1(ii), for the words "date of qualification" there shall be substituted the words "relevant date";

(d) in paragraph 2 the words from "either" to "and who" shall be deleted and for the words "date of qualification", wherever they appear, there shall be substituted the words "relevant date";

(e) in paragraph 3, for the words "date of qualification" there shall be substituted the words "relevant date".

(10) In annex C to Appendix III–

(a) in the heading, for the words in brackets there shall be substituted the following words "other than gainful employment undertaken, in the case of a qualified teacher, before the relevant date";

(b) for sub-paragraph 2(b) there shall be substituted the following sub-paragraph–
"(b) in the case of qualified teachers, before the relevant date.".

(11) In annex D to Appendix III for the note to paragraph 2 there shall be substituted–
"(NOTE—The courses referred to in sub-paragraphs (i) and (ii) above are prefixed by the letters C or D in the Department of Education and Science and Welsh Office Education Department publication entitled "Long Courses for Teachers 1986–1987". In the 1983–1984 publication they are described in sections A and S and in earlier equivalent publications in the corresponding sections.)".

(a) These paragraphs were substituted by S.I. 1984/1650 and most recently amended by S.I. 1987/137.

SCHEDULE

Orders in force relating to the remuneration of primary and secondary education teachers.

Order	Reference
The Remuneration of Teachers (Primary and Secondary Education) Order 1983	S.I. 1983/1463
The Remuneration of Teachers (Primary and Secondary Education) (Amendment) Order 1984	S.I. 1984/1650
The Remuneration of Teachers (Primary and Secondary Education) (Amendment) Order 1986	S.I. 1986/559
The Remuneration of Teachers (Primary and Secondary Education) (Amendment) Order 1987	S.I. 1987/137

Kenneth Baker

18th February 1987   Secretary of State for Education and Science

EXPLANATORY NOTE

(This note is not part of the Order)

This Order amends, with effect from 25th February 1987 (paragraph 2(2), (3), (5), (6) and (11)) or with effect from 16 July 1986 (paragraph 2(1), (4), (7), (8), (9) and (10)) the provisions contained in the document setting out the scales and other provisions for determining the remuneration of teachers in primary and secondary schools maintained by local education authorities and certain other teachers employed by such authorities. This document, entitled "Scales of Salaries for Teachers: Primary and Secondary Education, England and Wales 1983", which has been amended by the Orders listed in the Schedule, is published by Her Majesty's Stationery Office and may be obtained from Government bookshops or through booksellers. The Order gives effect to recommendations of the appropriate Burnham Committee under section 2 of the Remuneration of Teachers Act 1965 ("the Act").

The main amendments are, first, that the provisions in section 16 of the document designed to safeguard the remuneration payable to a teacher who loses his post or would suffer a diminution in salary or be placed on a salary scale with a lower maximum are extended to teachers in regular part-time service (paragraph 2(2)). Secondly, section 17(c), which provides that a teacher employed throughout a term on a day to day basis shall be paid the same as if he had been employed in regular service, is deleted (paragraph 2(3)). The pay of such teachers will in future be governed by section 17(b). Thirdly, provision is made for unqualified teachers to be paid as qualified teachers where they have comparable qualifications (paragraph 2(4)). Fourthly, provision is made for payment of a lump sum to a teacher who becomes a qualified teacher while employed by an authority (paragraph 2(4)). Finally, provision is made so that, for a teacher who qualifies after 16 July 1986, the point of reference for certain incremental credit is the date on which he obtained the qualification, successfully completed the course or completed any requisite period of service or experience which led to his becoming a qualified teacher (paragraph 2(7)(b)).

The retrospective effect of paragraph 2(1), (4), (7), (8), (9) and (10) is authorised by section 7(3) of the Act.

STATUTORY INSTRUMENTS

1987 No. 242

BETTING, GAMING AND LOTTERIES

The Gaming Act (Variation of Fees) Order 1987

Made - - - -	*19th February 1987*
Laid before Parliament	*2nd March 1987*
Coming into force	*1st April 1987*

In pursuance of sections 48(5) and 51(4) of the Gaming Act 1968**(a)**, I hereby make the following Order:–

1.—(1)   This Order may be cited as the Gaming Act (Variation of Fees) Order 1987 and shall come into force on 1st April 1987.

(2)   This Order shall not extend to Scotland.

2.   The provisions of section 48 of the Gaming Act 1968 specified in column 1 of the Schedule to this Order (which relate to fees charged in respect of the matters mentioned in column 2 of that Schedule) shall have effect as if, for the references to the sums specified in those provisions (for which the sums mentioned in column 3 of that Schedule were substituted by the Gaming Act (Variation of Fees) Order 1984**(b)**), there were substituted references to the sums specified in column 4 of that Schedule.

3.   The Gaming Act (Variation of Fees) Order 1984**(b)** is hereby revoked.

Home Office	*Douglas Hurd*
19th February 1987	One of Her Majesty's Principal Secretaries of State

---

(a) 1968 c.65.   **(b)** S.I. 1984/166.

Article 2

SCHEDULE

1 Provisions of section 48 referring to fees	2 Matter to which fee relates	3 Previous sum	4 New sum
Subsection (3)	Fees chargeable:		
paragraph (a)	Grant of gaming licence	£20,300	£22,350
paragraph (b)	Renewal of licence	£ 4,070	£ 4,500
paragraph (c)	Transfer of licence	£ 3,240	£ 3,800
paragraph (d)	Registration of club or institute (Part II) Renewal of registration	£ 108 £ 54	£ 125 £ 60
paragraph (e)	Registration of club or institute (Part III) Renewal of registration	£ 54 £ 27	£ 60 £ 30
paragraph (f)	Issue of certificate of approval	£ 20	£ 22
paragraph (g)	Issue of machine certificate Renewal of certificate	£ 1,635 £ 645	£ 1,800 £ 710
Subsection (4)	Fees chargeable where gaming limited to bingo:		
paragraph (a)	Grant of gaming licence	£ 1,635 £20,300	£ 1,800 £22,350
paragraph (b)	Renewal of licence	£ 645 £ 4,070	£ 710 £ 4,500
	Transfer of licence	£ 360 £ 3,240	£ 420 £ 3,800

EXPLANATORY NOTE

(This note is not part of the Order)

   This Order increases the fees to be charged in England and Wales under the Gaming Act 1968 for the matters mentioned in the Schedule to the Order.

STATUTORY INSTRUMENTS

1987 No. 243

BETTING, GAMING AND LOTTERIES

The Lotteries (Gaming Board Fees) Order 1987

Made - - - -	*19th February 1987*
Laid before Parliament	*2nd March 1987*
Coming into force	*1st April 1987*

In pursuance of section 18(1)(e) and (2) and section 24(2) of the Lotteries and Amusements Act 1976**(a)**, I hereby make the following Order:–

1. This Order may be cited as the Lotteries (Gaming Board Fees) Order 1987 and shall come into force on 1st April 1987.

2. The fee payable to the Board on an application for the registration of a scheme shall be of such amount as the Board may determine:

Provided that,–

   (a) where the total value of the tickets or chances which may lawfully be sold in each lottery under the scheme does not exceed £10,000, the fee shall not exceed £70; and

   (b) in any other case, the fee shall not exceed £265.

3. The further fee payable to the Board, where more than one lottery is to be promoted under a scheme registered by the Board, for each lottery promoted under that scheme shall be of such amount as the Board may determine:

Provided that,–

   (a) where the total value of the tickets or chances sold in the lottery does not exceed £10,000, the fee shall not exceed £20; and

   (b) where the total value of the tickets or chances sold in the lottery exceeds £10,000 but does not exceed £20,000, the fee shall not exceed £40; and

   (c) in any other case, the fee shall not exceed £55.

4. The Lotteries (Gaming Board Fees) Order 1983**(b)** is hereby revoked.

Douglas Hurd

Home Office   One of Her Majesty's Principal Secretaries of State
19th February 1987

(a) 1976 c.32.
(b) S.I. 1983/126.

EXPLANATORY NOTE

(This note is not part of the Order)

This Order increases the maximum fees which the Gaming Board may, under the provisions of this Order, determine to be payable under paragraph 7(1) of Schedule 2 to the Lotteries and Amusements Act 1976 in connection with the registration of lottery schemes and with the lotteries promoted under schemes registered by the Board. The maximum fees (which were previously prescribed by the Lotteries (Gaming Board Fees) Order 1983) are increased as follows. The maximum fees prescribed by provisos (a) and (b) of Article 2 are increased from £60 and £240 to £70 and £265, respectively. Those prescribed by provisos (a), (b) and (c) of Article 3 are increased from £18, £36 and £48 to £20, £40 and £55, respectively.

STATUTORY INSTRUMENTS

1987 No. 244

MERCHANT SHIPPING

The Merchant Shipping (Light Dues) (Amendment) Regulations 1987

Made - - - -	*23rd February 1987*
Laid before Parliament	*27th February 1987*
Coming into force -	*1st April 1987*

The Secretary of State for Transport, in exercise of powers conferred on him by section 5(2) of the Merchant Shipping (Mercantile Marine Fund) Act 1898**(a)** and of all other powers enabling him in that behalf, hereby makes the following Regulations:–

1. These Regulations may be cited as the Merchant Shipping (Light Dues) (Amendment) Regulations 1987 and shall come into force on 1st April 1987.

2. The Merchant Shipping (Light Dues) (Amendment) Regulations 1986**(b)** are hereby revoked.

3. The Schedule to the Merchant Shipping (Light Dues) Regulations 1981**(c)** shall be amended as follows:–

(a) For the scale of payments relating to the levying of light dues set out in Part I thereof there shall be substituted the following scale:–

SCALE OF PAYMENTS

1. Home-trade sailing ships: 86.5p per 10 tons per voyage.
2. Foreign-going sailing ships: £1.73 per 10 tons per voyage.
3. Home-trade steamers:
   Full rate: £1.73 per 10 tons per voyage.
   Reduced rate (visiting cruise ships): 86.5p per 10 tons per voyage.
4. Foreign-going steamers:
   Full rate: £3.46 per 10 tons per voyage.
   Reduced rate (visiting cruise ships): £1.73 per 10 tons per voyage.
5. In the place of payments per voyage, the following payments:–

   (a) for pleasure yachts which the general lighthouse authority is satisfied are ordinarily kept or used outside any of the following countries and territories (including the territorial waters thereof), namely the United Kingdom, Isle of Man, Republic of Ireland, a payment in respect of any visit of 86.5p per 10 tons for every period of 30 days or less comprised in such visit;

(a) 1898 c.44; section 5(2) was substituted by the Merchant Shipping Act 1979 (c.39), section 36(2).
(b) S.I. 1986/334.
(c) S.I. 1981/354, amended by S.I. 1986/334.

    (b) for tugs and pleasure yachts not included in sub-paragraph (a) of this paragraph an annual payment of £10.38 per 10 tons.

(b) In Part II thereof:–

    (i) in the proviso to Rule (1), for "£21.28" and "£10.64" there shall be substituted respectively "£24.22" and "£12.11";

    (ii) in Rule (7), for "76p" there shall be substituted "86.5p".

Signed by authority of the Secretary of State

23rd February 1987

Michael Spicer
Parliamentary Under-Secretary of State,
Department of Transport

EXPLANATORY NOTE

(This note is not part of the Regulations)

These Regulations provide for an increase of about 14% in the scale of light dues payable under the Merchant Shipping (Mercantile Marine Fund) Act 1898 as set out in the Merchant Shipping (Light Dues) Regulations 1981 (as amended) and revokes previous amending Regulations. The last change took effect on 1st April 1986.

STATUTORY INSTRUMENTS

1987 No. 245

NATIONAL HEALTH SERVICE, ENGLAND AND WALES

The National Health Service Functions (Amendment of Directions to Authorities) Regulations 1987

Made - - - -	*20th February 1987*
Laid before Parliament	*27th February 1987*
Coming into force -	*1st April 1987*

The Secretary of State for Social Services, in exercise of the powers conferred upon him by sections 13 and 18 of the National Health Service Act 1977(a), and of all other powers enabling him in that behalf, hereby makes the following regulations:–

Citation and commencement

1. These regulations may be cited as the National Health Service Functions (Amendment of Directions to Authorities) Regulations 1987 and shall come into force on 1st April 1987.

Amendment of Regulations

2.—(1) In the National Health Service Functions (Directions to Authorities and Administration Arrangements) Regulations 1982(b) regulation 3(e) (functions in the National Health Service Act 1977 to be exercisable by Regional Health Authorities) shall be amended as follows:–

(a) for head (xxviii) there shall be substituted the following–

"(xxviii) section 63, with respect to authorising hospital accommodation described in the section to be made available, determining the extent to which it is to be made available, determining the charges for part of its cost, recovering those charges, and allowing deductions from the amount due during periods when it is temporarily vacated;"

(b) in head (xxix) for the reference to "section 65(2)" there shall be substituted a reference to "section 65(2) and (5)" and after the words "resident patients" there shall be added the words "and allowing in respect of that treatment deductions from the amount due during periods when the accommodation is temporarily vacated;"

(c) for head (xxx) there shall be substituted the following–

(a) 1977 c.49; section 13 was amended by paragraph 33 of Schedule 1 to the Health Services Act 1980 (c.53) and section 18 was amended by paragraphs 38 and 92 of that Schedule. *See* section 128(1) of the National Health Service Act 1977 for the definition of "regulations".
(b) S.I. 1982/287; the relevant amending instrument is S.I. 1984/1577.

"(xxx) section 65(1), (3) and (4) and section 66(a), with respect to determining under those provisions the charges to be paid for accommodation and services authorised by the Secretary of State to be made available under sections 65(1) and 66(1) and with respect to recovering those charges;"

(2) In the Authorities for London Post-Graduate Teaching Hospitals Regulations 1982(b), regulation 6(2)(c) (functions under the National Health Service Act 1977 to be exercisable by the Authorities) shall be amended as follows:-

(a) for head (xxvii) there shall be substituted the following–

"(xxvii) section 63, with respect to authorising the hospital accommodation described in the section to be made available, determining the extent to which it is to be made available, determining the charges for part of its cost, recovering those charges, and allowing deductions from the amount due during periods when it is temporarily vacated;"

(b) in head (xxix) for the reference to "section 65(2)" there shall be substituted a reference to "section 65(2) and (5)" and after the words "resident patients" there shall be added the words "and allowing in respect of that treatment deductions from the amount due during periods when the accommodation is temporarily vacated;"

(c) for head (xxx) there shall be substituted the following–

"(xxx) section 65(1), (3) and (4) and section 66(a), with respect to determining under those provisions the charges to be paid for accommodation and services authorised by the Secretary of State to be made available under sections 65(1) and 66(1), and with respect to recovering those charges;"

Signed by authority of the Secretary of State for Social Services.

Tony Newton
Minister of State,
20th February 1987   Department of Health and Social Security

---

EXPLANATORY NOTE

(This note is not part of the Regulations)

These Regulations amend the directions given in regulations to regional health authorities in England, to District Health Authorities in Wales, and to the special health authorities established for certain London post-graduate teaching hospitals ("the authorities") relating to the exercise on behalf of the Secretary of State of his functions concerning health service accommodation and services available for private patients. The effect of the amendments is to extend to the authorities the function of determining the charges to be paid in respect of such accommodation and services.

In accordance with directions given in the National Health Service Functions (Directions to Authorities and Administration Arrangements) Regulation 1982 district health authorities in England exercise these functions on behalf of regional health authorities.

(a) Sections 65(1) and 66(1) were amended by section 11(1) of the Health Services Act 1980 (c.53).
(b) S.I. 1982/315.

STATUTORY INSTRUMENTS

1987 No. 248

ANIMALS

ANIMAL HEALTH

The Export of Sheep (Prohibition) (Amendment) Order 1987

Made - - - -	*22nd February 1987*
Coming into force	*27th February 1987*

The Minister of Agriculture, Fisheries and Food, in exercise of the power conferred by section 11 of the Animal Health Act 1981**(a)** and of all other powers enabling him in that behalf, hereby makes the following order:–

Title and commencement

1. This Order may be cited as the Export of Sheep (Prohibition) (Amendment) Order 1987 and shall come into force on 27th February 1987.

Amendment of the Export of Sheep (Prohibition) Order 1987

2. The Export of Sheep (Prohibition) Order 1987**(b)** is hereby amended by substituting for article 2(4) the following paragraph:–

   "(4) Paragraph (2)(a) above shall not apply in the case of–

   (a) any sheep which has been examined and marked with an ear-tag by a person authorised in that behalf by the appropriate Minister; or

   (b) any sheep which was marked with a blue mark.".

In witness whereof the Official Seal of the Minister of Agriculture, Fisheries and Food was hereunto affixed on 22nd February 1987.

Michael Jopling
Minister of Agriculture, Fisheries and Food

(a) 1981 c.22.
(b) S.I. 1987/211.

EXPLANATORY NOTE

(This note is not part of the Order)

This Order amends the Export of Sheep (Prohibition) Order 1987 ("the principal Order") which prohibits, subject to an exception, the export from Great Britain to a member State of the European Communities of–

(a) sheep moved from a place in an area designated for the purposes of Part I of the Food and Environment Protection Act 1985 in accordance with the terms of a consent under section 2(1) of that Act which required that the sheep to which it applies should be marked in a specified manner; and

(b) sheep which have been moved in contravention of a restriction imposed by an order made under section 1 of that Act.

The principal Order does not apply to those sheep which have been examined and subsequently marked with an ear-tag by an officer authorised by the Minister of Agriculture, Fisheries and Food or the Secretary of State for Scotland or Wales. This Order extends that exception to any sheep moved from a place in a designated area in accordance with the terms of a consent which required it to be marked with a blue paint mark.

STATUTORY INSTRUMENTS

1987 No. 249

PUBLIC HEALTH, ENGLAND AND WALES
PUBLIC HEALTH, SCOTLAND
PUBLIC HEALTH, NORTHERN IRELAND

CONTAMINATION OF FOOD

The Food Protection (Emergency Prohibitions) (England) (No. 2) Amendment No. 2 Order 1987

Made - - - -	*22nd February 1987*
Laid before Parliament	*25th February 1987*
Coming into force	*27th February 1987*

Whereas the Minister of Agriculture, Fisheries and Food is of the opinion, in accordance with section 1(1)(a) of the Food and Environment Protection Act 1985(a), that there has been or may have been an escape of substances of such descriptions and in such quantities and such circumstances as are likely to create a hazard to human health through human consumption of food;

And whereas the said Minister is of the opinion, in accordance with section 1(1)(b) of the said Act, that in consequence of the said escape of substances food which is or may be in the future in the area described in the Schedule to the Food Protection (Emergency Prohibitions) (England) (No. 2) Order 1986(b), or which is derived or may be in the future derived from anything in that area, is, or may be, or may become, unsuitable for human consumption;

Now, therefore, the said Minister, in exercise of the powers conferred on him by the said section 1(1) and section 24(3) of the said Act, and of all other powers enabling him in that behalf, hereby makes the following Order:–

Title and commencement

1. This Order may be cited as the Food Protection (Emergency Prohibitions) (England) (No. 2) Amendment No. 2 Order 1987 and shall come into force on 27th February 1987.

Partial revocation and amendment

2. The Food Protection (Emergency Prohibitions) (England) (No. 2) Order 1986 is revoked to the extent that it imposes prohibitions on–

    (a) the slaughter of a sheep which was moved from a place in accordance with a consent given under section 2(1) of the Food and Environment Protection Act 1985 which consent was subject to the condition that the sheep to which it applies should be marked with a blue mark; and

    (b) the supply or having in possession for supply of meat, or food containing meat, derived from such a sheep,

---

(a) 1985 c.48.
(b) S.I. 1986/1689, amended by S.I. 1986/2208 and 1987/153.

and accordingly that Order is further amended in accordance with the following provisions of this Order.

3. In article 6, for paragraph (2) there shall be substituted the following paragraph–

"(2) Paragraph (1) above shall not apply in the case of–

(a) any sheep which was moved to a market in accordance with a consent given under section 2(1) of the Act which consent did not require that the sheep to which it applies should be marked in a manner specified therein;

(b) any sheep which was moved from any place in accordance with a consent given under the said section 2(1) which consent was subject to the condition that the sheep to which it applies should be marked with a blue mark; or

(c) any sheep which–

    (i) was moved from any place in accordance with a consent given under the said section 2(1) which consent was subject to the condition that the sheep to which it applies should be marked with a red mark; and

    (ii) has been examined and marked with an ear-tag by a person authorised in that behalf by one of the Ministers.".

In witness whereof the Official Seal of the Minister of Agriculture, Fisheries and Food is hereunto affixed on 22nd February 1987.

Michael Jopling
Minister of Agriculture, Fisheries and Food

EXPLANATORY NOTE

(This note is not part of the Order)

The Food Protection (Emergency Prohibitions) (England) (No. 2) Order 1986 contains emergency prohibitions restricting various activities in order to prevent human consumption of food which has been or which may have been rendered unsuitable for that purpose in consequence of the escape of radioactive substances from a nuclear reactor situated at Chernobyl in the USSR.

This Order excepts from the prohibition on slaughter throughout the United Kingdom any sheep identified by a blue paint mark, and from the prohibition on supply throughout the United Kingdom any meat derived from such a sheep, which are no longer required to be examined and marked with an ear-tag by a person authorised by the Minister of Agriculture, Fisheries and Food or the Secretary of State for Scotland or Wales.

STATUTORY INSTRUMENTS

1987 No. 250

SOCIAL SECURITY

The Social Security (Notification of Deaths) Regulations 1987

Made - - - -	*23rd February 1987*
Laid before Parliament	*2nd March 1987*
Coming into force	*6th April 1987*

The Secretary of State for Social Services, in exercise of the powers conferred upon him by sections 60, 83(1) and 84(1)**(a)** of the Social Security Act 1986**(b)**, and of all other powers enabling him in that behalf, by this instrument, which is made before the expiry of the period of 12 months beginning with the commencement of those sections, makes the following regulations:–

Citation, commencement and interpretation

1.—(1) These regulations may be cited as the Social Security (Notification of Deaths) Regulations 1987 and shall come into force on 6th April 1987.

(2) In these regulations "data material" has the same meaning as in section 41 of the Data Protection Act 1984**(c)**.

Notification of particulars of deaths

2. The particulars of death which are required to be furnished to the Secretary of State under these regulations are required to be so furnished for the purposes of his functions under the benefit Acts and the functions of the Department of Health and Social Services for Northern Ireland under any corresponding Northern Ireland legislation.

Deaths in England or Wales

3. In respect of deaths occurring in England or Wales, it shall be the duty of each registrar of births and deaths, in relation to deaths registered by him, to furnish the Secretary of State with such particulars of the death of a person as are specified in Schedule 1 to these regulations, or as many of such particulars as are available to him, as soon as it is reasonably practicable to do so.

Deaths in Scotland

4. In respect of deaths occurring in Scotland, it shall be the duty of the Registrar General of Births, Deaths and Marriages for Scotland in relation to deaths notified to him, to furnish the Secretary of State with such particulars of the death of a person as are specified in Schedule 2 to these regulations, or as many of such particulars as are available to him, as soon as it is reasonably practicable to do so.

(a) *See* the definitions of "prescribed" and "regulations".   **(b)** 1986 c.50.   **(c)** 1984 c.35.

Manner in which particulars are to be furnished

5. The prescribed manner in which particulars are required to be furnished to the Secretary of State under these regulations, is either in writing or on data material.

Signed by authority of the   *John Major*
Secretary of State for Social Services.   Minister of State,
23rd February 1987   Department of Health and Social Security

---

Regulation 3   SCHEDULE 1

PARTICULARS OF A DEATH OCCURRING IN ENGLAND OR WALES REQUIRED TO BE NOTIFIED TO THE SECRETARY OF STATE

1. The surname and forenames of the deceased.

2. The date and place of death.

3. The sex of the deceased.

4. The maiden surname of a deceased married, widowed or divorced woman.

5. The date and place of birth of the deceased.

6. The occupation of the deceased.

7. The usual address of the deceased at the date of death.

Regulation 4   SCHEDULE 2

PARTICULARS OF A DEATH OCCURRING IN SCOTLAND REQUIRED TO BE NOTIFIED TO THE SECRETARY OF STATE

1. The surname and forenames of the deceased.

2. The date of death.

3. The sex of the deceased.

4. The maiden surname of a deceased married, widowed or divorced woman.

5. The date of birth of the deceased.

6. The place of usual residence of the deceased.

7. The district where the death was registered.

EXPLANATORY NOTE

(This note is not part of these Regulations)

These Regulations require registrars of births and deaths, in England and Wales, and the Registrar General of Births, Deaths and Marriages for Scotland to provide specified particulars of death to the Secretary of State for Social Services.

These Regulations are made under sections 60, 83(1) and 84(1) of the Social Security Act 1986 and are also made before the expiry of a period 12 months of the commencement of those sections, that is on 6th April 1987 and 25th July 1986. Accordingly they are exempt by section 61(5) of that Act, from the requirement of section 10(1) of the Social Security Act 1980 (c.30) to refer proposals to the Social Security Advisory Committee and are made without reference to that Committee.

STATUTORY INSTRUMENTS

1987 No. 255 (S. 13)

BETTING, GAMING AND LOTTERIES

The Gaming Act (Variation of Fees) (Scotland) Order 1987

Made - - -	*17th February 1987*
Laid before Parliament	*4th March 1987*
Coming into force	*1st April 1987*

The Secretary of State, in exercise of the powers conferred on him by sections 48(5) and 51(4) of the Gaming Act 1968(**a**), and of all other powers enabling him in that behalf, hereby makes the following Order:

1. This Order may be cited as the Gaming Act (Variation of Fees) (Scotland) Order 1987, shall extend to Scotland only and shall come into force on 1st April 1987.

2. The provisions of section 48 of the Gaming Act 1968 specified in column 1 of the Schedule to this Order (which relate to fees charged in respect of the matters mentioned in column 2 of that Schedule) shall have effect as if, for the references to the sums specified in those provisions (for which the sums mentioned in column 3 of that Schedule were substituted by the Gaming Act (Variation of Fees) (Scotland) Order 1984(**b**)), there were substituted references to the sums specified in column 4 of that Schedule.

3. The Gaming Act (Variation of Fees) (Scotland) Order 1984 is revoked.

Ian Lang
New St Andrew's House, Edinburgh   Parliamentary Under Secretary of State,
17th February 1987   Scottish Office

(**a**) 1968 c.65.
(**b**) S.I. 1984/338.

SCHEDULE

(1) *Provisions of section 48 referring to fees*	(2) *Matter to which fee relates*	(3) *Previous sum*	(4) *New Sum*
Subsection (3)	Fees chargeable:		
paragraph (a)	Grant of gaming licence	£20,300	£22,350
paragraph (b)	Renewal of licence	£ 4,070	£ 4,500
paragraph (c)	Transfer of licence	£ 3,240	£ 3,800
paragraph (d)	Registration of club or institute (part II)	£ 108	£ 125
	Renewal of registration	£ 54	£ 60
paragraph (e)	Registration of club or institute (Part III)	£ 54	£ 60
	Renewal of registration	£ 27	£ 30
paragraph (f)	Issue of certificate of approval	£ 20	£ 22
paragraph (g)	Issue of machine certificate	£ 1,635	£ 1,800
	Renewal of certificate	£ 645	£ 710
Subsection (4)	Fees chargeable where gaming limited to bingo:		
paragraph (a)	Grant of gaming licence	£ 1,635 £20,300	£ 1,800 £22,350
paragraph (b)	Renewal of licence	£ 645 £ 4,070	£ 710 £ 4,500
	Transfer of licence	£ 360 £ 3,240	£ 420 £ 3,800

EXPLANATORY NOTE

(This note is not part of the Order)

This Order increases the fees to be charged in Scotland under the Gaming Act 1968 for the matters mentioned in the Schedule to the Order.

1987 No. 256

POLICE

The Police Pensions (Supplementary Provisions) Regulations 1987

Made - - -		*20th February 1987*
Laid before Parliament		*9th March 1987*
Coming into force -		*1st April 1987*

In exercise of the powers conferred on me by sections 1 to 8 of the Police Pensions Act 1976(**a**), and after consultation with the Police Negotiating Board for the United Kingdom, I hereby, with the consent of the Treasury(**b**), make the following Regulations:—

Citation and commencement

1. These Regulations may be cited as the Police Pensions (Supplementary Provisions) Regulations 1987 and shall come into force on 1st April 1987.

Revocation and amendment of the Police Pensions Regulations 1973

2. The Police Pensions Regulations 1973(**c**) and the other Regulations specified in Part I of Schedule 1 hereto are hereby revoked to the extent there mentioned but, in respect of any period beginning on or after 1st April 1972 and ending before the coming into force of these Regulations, the said Regulations of 1973 as from time to time in force shall have effect subject to the amendment set out in Part II of that Schedule.

Commencement of the Police Pensions Regulations 1987 and transitional provisions

3. The Police Pensions Regulations 1987(**d**) shall come into force on 1st April 1987 and shall have effect subject to the transitional provisions set out in Part III of Schedule 1 hereto.

Old cases Regulations

4. The old cases Regulations, that is to say the Regulations set out in Part I of Schedule 2 hereto, shall, subject to the amendment contained in Part II of that Schedule, continue to apply in the case of an award or payment to or in respect of, or relating to—
   (*a*) a person who retired or otherwise ceased to be a member of a police force before 1st April 1972, or
   (*b*) a person, being a serviceman who did not resume service as a regular policeman, whose period of relevant service in the armed forces ended before 1st April 1972,
including an award on the death of such a person on or after the said date.

(**a**) 1976 c. 35, as amended by section 2(3) of the Police Negotiating Board Act 1980 (c. 10).
(**b**) Formerly the Minister for the Civil Service; *see* S.I. 1981/1670.
(**c**) S.I. 1973/428.
(**d**) S.I. 1987/257.

War Service Regulations

5. The Police Pensions (War Service) Regulations 1979(**a**) shall have effect subject to the amendments set out in Schedule 3 hereto.

War Service (Transferees) Regulations

6. The Police Pensions (War Service) (Transferees) Regulations 1985(**b**) shall have effect subject to the amendments set out in Schedule 4 hereto.

Injury Benefit Regulations

7. The Police (Injury Benefit) Regulations 1987(**c**) shall have effect subject to the amendments set out in Schedule 5 hereto.

Provisions supplemental to Regulations 5, 6 and 7

8.— (1) In accordance with Regulations 5, 6 and 7 of these Regulations, the Police Pensions Regulations 1987 shall have effect subject to the provisions of the Regulations amended thereby.

(2) Anything done before the coming into force of these Regulations under or for the purposes of the Regulations amended by Regulation 5, 6 or 7 thereof shall have effect as if done under or for the purposes of the Regulations in question as so amended.

Douglas Hurd
One of Her Majesty's Principal Secretaries of State

Home Office
6th February 1987

We consent

Peter Lloyd
Michael Neubert
Two of the Lords Commissioners of Her Majesty's Treasury

20th February 1987

(**a**) S.I. 1979/1259.
(**b**) S.I. 1985/2029.
(**c**) S.I. 1987/156.

SCHEDULE 1

Regulation 2   PART I

REGULATIONS REVOKED

Instrument	Reference	Extent of revocation
The Police Pensions Regulations 1973	S.I. 1973/428	The whole instrument
The Police Pensions (Transitory Provisions) Regulations 1973	S.I. 1973/429	The whole instrument
The Police Pensions (Amendment) Regulations 1974	S.I. 1974/1533	Regulation 8 and, to the extent that it relates to the Police Pensions Regulations 1973 ("the Regulations of 1973"), Regulation 9
The Police Pensions (Amendment) (No. 2) Regulations 1974	S.I. 1974/1673	The whole instrument
The Police Pensions (Amendment) (No. 3) Regulations 1974	S.I. 1974/1796	Regulation 7 and, to the extent that they amend the Regulations of 1973, Regulations 4, 5 and 8
The Police Pensions (Amendment) Regulations 1975	S.I. 1975/1718	Regulations 4 and 8 and, to the extent that they amend the Regulations of 1973, Regulations 5, 6 and 9
The Police Pensions (Amendment) Regulations 1976	S.I. 1976/306	The whole instrument
The Police Pensions (Amendment) (No. 2) Regulations 1976	S.I. 1976/1707	Regulation 7 and, to the extent that they amend the Regulations of 1973, Regulations 4, 5 and 8
The Police Pensions (Amendment) Regulations 1977	S.I. 1977/1705	Regulation 7 and, to the extent that they amend the Regulations of 1973, Regulations 4, 5 and 8
The Police Pensions (Amendment) (No. 2) Regulations 1977	S.I. 1977/2173	The whole instrument
The Police Pensions (Amendment) Regulations 1978	S.I. 1978/375	The whole instrument
The Police Pensions (Amendment) (No. 2) Regulations 1978	S.I. 1978/1348	The whole instrument
The Police Pensions (Amendment) (No. 3) Regulations 1978	S.I. 1978/1578	Regulation 7 and, to the extent that they amend the Regulations of 1973, Regulations 4, 5 and 8

SCHEDULE 1 (*continued*)

Instrument	Reference	Extent of revocation
The Police Pensions (Amendment) Regulations 1979	S.I. 1979/406	The whole instrument
The Police Pensions (Amendment) (No. 2) Regulations 1979	S.I. 1979/1287	Regulations 5, 6 and 9 and, to the extent that they amend the Regulations of 1973, 4, 7 and 10
The Police Pensions (Amendment) Regulations 1980	S.I. 1980/82	The whole instrument
The Police Pensions (Amendment) (No. 2) Regulations 1980	S.I. 1980/272	The whole instrument
The Police Pensions (Amendment) (No. 3) Regulations 1980	S.I. 1980/1616	Regulations 6, 9, 10 and 13 and, to the extent that they amend the Regulations of 1973, Regulations 3, 4 and 7
The Police Pensions (Amendment) Regulations 1982	S.I. 1982/1151	The whole instrument
The Police Pensions (Amendment) Regulations 1983	S.I. 1983/996	The whole instrument
The Police Pensions (Amendment) Regulations 1985	S.I. 1985/156	The whole instrument
The Police Pensions (Amendment) Regulations 1986	S.I. 1986/1379	The whole instrument

PART II   Regulation 2

AMENDMENT OF THE POLICE PENSIONS REGULATIONS 1973

In paragraph 1 of Part II of Schedule 3 to the Police Pensions Regulations 1973 (transitional modifications of provisions relating to a widow's pension) the following provision shall be inserted after sub-paragraph (2)(a), namely:—

"(aa) section 10 of the Police Pensions Act 1921(**a**), or".

(**a**) 1921 c. 31.

Regulation 3   PART III

TRANSITIONAL PROVISIONS

1. The Police Pensions Regulations 1987 shall have effect as if anything done, or treated as done, under or for the purposes of the Police Pensions Regulations 1973 had been done under or for the purposes of the corresponding provision of the said Regulations of 1987.

2. Without prejudice to the generality of paragraph 1 references therein to anything done shall include—
   (a) the determination of a question;
   (b) the exercise of a discretion;
   (c) the decision that a provision should apply;
   (d) the making of a payment;
   (e) the giving of a notice; and
   (f) the commutation or allocation of a portion of a pension.

SCHEDULE 2

Regulation 4   PART I

OLD CASES REGULATIONS

Instrument	Reference
The Police Pensions Regulations 1971	S.I. 1971/232
The Police Pensions (Amendment) Regulations 1971	S.I. 1971/583
The Police Pensions (Amendment) (No. 2) Regulations 1971	S.I. 1971/1327
The Police Pensions (Amendment) (No. 3) Regulations 1971	S.I. 1971/1466
The Police Pensions (Amendment) Regulations 1972	S.I. 1972/1642
The Police Pensions (Lump Sum Payments to Widows) Regulations 1986	S.I. 1986/1380
So far as they are not revoked by Regulation 2:—	
The Police Pensions (Amendment) Regulations 1974	S.I. 1974/1533
The Police Pensions (Amendment) (No. 3) Regulations 1974	S.I. 1974/1796
The Police Pensions (Amendment) Regulations 1975	S.I. 1975/1718
The Police Pensions (Amendment) (No. 2) Regulations 1976	S.I. 1976/1707
The Police Pensions (Amendment) Regulations 1977	S.I. 1977/1705
The Police Pensions (Amendment) (No. 3) Regulations 1978	S.I. 1978/1578
The Police Pensions (Amendment) (No. 2) Regulations 1979	S.I. 1979/1287
The Police Pensions (Amendment) (No. 3) Regulations 1980	S.I. 1980/1616

SCHEDULE 2 (*continued*)

PART II   Regulation 4

AMENDMENT OF OLD CASES REGULATIONS

At the end of Part IX of the Police Pensions Regulations 1971 there shall be added the following Regulation:—

"Transfer value payable under inter-change arrangements—application of Regulation F9 of the Police Pensions Regulations 1987

82A. — (1) If the police authority so determine in the case of a particular regular policeman—

(a) who retired on or after 5th July 1948,

(b) in whose case a transfer value, calculated in accordance with these or the former Regulations has not been paid,

Regulation F9 of the Police Pensions Regulations 1987 ("the Regulations of 1987") and Sections 1 and 3 of Part II of Schedule F thereto shall have effect as if set out herein but subject to the exceptions and modifications mentioned in paragraphs (2) and (3) and any other necessary modifications.

(2) Regulation F9 of the Regulations of 1987 shall have effect for the purposes hereof as hereinafter provided, namely, as if—

(a) in paragraph (1)(a) after the word "who" there were inserted the word "retired" and the words "retires or retired on or after 1st April 1972" were omitted, and

(b) the requisite payment mentioned in paragraph (5)(b) were one of an amount equal to that of the policeman's award mentioned in paragraph (1)(a)(ii) when increased by an amount equal to compound interest thereon at the rate of 6% per annum, calculated with yearly rests, in respect of the period before 1st January 1974 beginning with the date he received the award.

(3) Section 1 of Part II of Schedule F to the Regulations of 1987 shall have effect for the purposes hereof as hereinafter provided, namely—

(a) subject as hereinafter provided, the notional pensions referred to in paragraph 1(1)(b) and (c) shall be calculated in accordance with the Regulations of 1987 but by reference to—

(i) the policeman's average pensionable pay within the meaning of these Regulations, or

(ii) in the case of a policeman who retired before 1st July 1949, his pensionable pay within the meaning of the Police Pensions Regulations 1948 or the Police Pensions (Scotland) Regulations 1948;

(b) where immediately before his retirement the policeman was paying pension contributions at a rate related to 5% of his pensionable pay, the widow's notional accrued pension referred to in paragraph 1(1)(c) shall not be less than would have been the widow's ordinary pension which would have been payable to his widow under these or the former Regulations (as in force at the time of his retirement) had he died when he retired in circumstances entitling her to such an award, calculated however at the flat rate specified in Scheme I of the appropriate provision of the Regulations in question (as then in force);

(c) where immediately before his retirement the policeman was paying pension contributions at a rate related to 6.25% of his pensionable pay, the widow's notional accrued pension shall be calculated as if, at the time of his retirement—

(i) Regulation 57 of the Police Pensions Regulations 1973 had been in force in place of such of the relevant provisions, as defined in paragraph (2) of the said Regulation 57, as were then in force, and

(ii) paragraph 2 of Part VIII of Schedule B to the Police Pensions Regulations 1987 had been in force in place of the corresponding provisions of these or the former Regulations, as were then in force, and, accordingly, for the purposes of that calculation any additional contributions that he may have paid or any reduction that may have fallen to be made under the said relevant or corresponding provisions shall be deemed to have been paid or have fallen to be made under the said Regulation 57 or paragraph 2, as the case may be, and

    (d) the reference in paragraph 6 to Part I of Schedule F shall be construed as a reference to the corresponding provision of these or the former Regulations (as in force immediately before he ceased to be a member of his former force).

(4) This Regulation shall have effect as if anything done under or for the purposes of Regulation 85 of the Police Pensions Regulations 1973 as it had effect by virtue of paragraph (4) thereof had been done under or for the purposes of this Regulation.".

Regulation 5   SCHEDULE 3

AMENDMENT OF THE POLICE PENSIONS (WAR SERVICE) REGULATIONS 1979

In the provisions of the Police Pensions (War Service) Regulations 1979 specified in the first column of the following Table, for the words set out opposite thereto in the second column of that Table there shall be substituted the words so set out in the third column thereof.

TABLE

Provision amended	Existing words	Substituted words
Regulation 3(1)	"the Police Pensions Regulations 1973"	"the Police Pensions Regulations 1987"
Regulation 7(2)	"Regulation 85"	"Regulation F9"
Regulation 9(5)	"Regulation 85", in both places where the words occur	"Regulation F9"
Regulation 11	"Part VIII of Schedule 2"	"Part VIII of Schedule B"
Regulation 12(1)	"Part IV of Schedule 3"	"paragraph 8 of Part II of Schedule J"
Regulation 12(2)	"Part IV of Schedule 3 and Part III of Schedule 4"	"paragraph 8 of Part II and paragraph 3 of Part III of Schedule J"
Regulation 12(2)(a)	"sub-paragraphs (a) and (b) of paragraph 1(1) of the said Part IV"	"entries (a) and (c) in Table A in paragraph 7(3) of the said Part II"
Regulation 13(1)	"has allocated a portion of his pension under Regulation 25"	"has, or is treated as having, allocated a portion of his pension under Regulation B9"
Regulation 13(2)(a)	"allocated as provided in Regulation 25"	"allocated, or is treated as having allocated, as provided in Regulation B9"
Regulation 13(3)	"given thereunder"	"given or treated as given thereunder"
Regulation 14(1)(a)	"sub-paragraphs (a), (b), (d) or (e) of Regulation 21(1) of the principal Regulations"	"Regulation B2(1) of the principal Regulations or in circumstances treated as such by paragraph 5(3) or 6(2) of Part VII of Schedule J to those Regulations"

TABLE (*continued*)

Provision amended	Existing words	Substituted words
Regulation 14(2)	"Regulation 24", where the words first occur	"Regulation B7"
Regulation 14(3)(b)	"the principal Regulations"	"the Police Pensions Regulations 1973"
Regulation 15(2)	"commuted for a lump sum, as provided in Regulation 24"	"commuted for a lump sum, or is treated as having so commuted, as provided in Regulation B7"
	"the said Regulation 24"	"the said Regulation B7"
	"given thereunder"	"in question"
	"paragraph (6)"	"paragraph (7)"
Regulation 15(3)	"Regulation 24 of the principal Regulations as applied by Regulation 14"	"for the purposes of Regulation B7 of the principal Regulations, Regulation 24 of the Police Pensions Regulations 1973, as applied by Regulation 14 as originally made,"
Paragraph 2(a) of Part II of the Schedule	"it shall be calculated without regard to"	"or the Police Pensions Regulations 1973, it shall be calculated without regard to Regulation E8 of the principal Regulations or, in the case of the said Regulations of 1973, without regard to"
Paragraph 2(b) of the said Part II	"Part XIII of the principal Regulations"	"Regulation E9 of the principal Regulations or in accordance with Part XIII of the Police Pensions Regulations 1973"

Regulation 6 **SCHEDULE 4**

AMENDMENTS TO THE POLICE PENSIONS
(WAR SERVICE) (TRANSFEREES) REGULATIONS 1985

In the provisions of the Police Pensions (War Service) (Transferees) Regulations 1985 specified in the first column of the following Table, for the words set out opposite thereto in the second column of that Table there shall be substituted the words so set out in the third column thereof.

TABLE

Provisions amended	Existing words	Substituted words
Regulation 2(1)	"which"	"as amended by Regulation 4 of the Police Pensions (Supplementary Provisions) Regulations 1987; and the said Regulations of 1979 which"
Regulation 2(3)	"the Police Pensions Regulations 1973" and "the said Regulations of 1973"	"the Police Pensions Regulations 1987" and "the said Regulations of 1987", respectively.
Regulation 4(1)(b)	"the principal Regulations or, as the case may be, the old cases Regulations"	"the former Regulations"
Regulation 6(1)(d)	"the principal Regulations or, as the case may be, the old cases Regulations"	"the former Regulations"
Regulation 8(1)(b)	"paragraph 1(1) of Part IV of Schedule 3"	"paragraph 7(2) of Part II of Schedule J"
Regulation 8(2)(a)	"Regulation 27(3) and paragraph 4 of Part I of Schedule 4"	"paragraphs 3, 4 and 5 of Part II and paragraph 2 of Part III of Schedule J"
Regulation 8(2)(b)	"Part IV of Schedule 3"	"paragraph 8 of Part II of Schedule J"
Regulation 9(2)(b)	"Regulation 85" and "previous Regulations"	"Regulation F9" and "former Regulations", respectively
Regulation 11(c)	"paragraph 8(2) of Part I of Schedule 9"	"paragraph 9(2) of Section 1 of Part II of Schedule F"

SCHEDULE 5   Regulation 7

AMENDMENTS TO THE POLICE (INJURY BENEFIT) REGULATIONS 1987

In the provisions of the Police (Injury Benefit) Regulations 1987 specified in the first column of the following Table, for the words set out opposite thereto in the second column of that Table there shall be substituted the words so set out in the third column thereof.

TABLE

Provisions amended	Existing words	Substituted words
Regulation 3(1)	"Police Pensions Regulations 1973"	"Police Pensions Regulations 1987"
Regulation 3(2)	"Regulation 13(3)"	"Regulation A12(3)"
	"Regulation 13(1)"	"Regulation A12(1)"
Regulation 5(2)	"Regulation 71"	"Regulation H1"
Regulation 5(3)	"Regulation 33(2) or 34"	"Regulation C5(2) or C8"
	"Regulation 28"	"Regulation C2"
	"Regulation 42"	"Regulation D5(1), (3), (4) or (5)"
	"Regulation 38"	"Regulation D2"
	"Regulation 36"	"Regulation E1"
Regulation 7(1)	"paid to him under Regulation 20(4), 21(4) or 22"	"paid, or treated as paid, to him under Regulation B2(4), B3(4) or B4"
Regulation 7(2)	"paid to the member or his estate under Regulation 20(4), 21(4), 22 or 43"	"paid, or treated as paid, to the member or his estate under Regulation B2(4), B3(4), B4 or E3"
	"Regulation 28(2)", in both places where the words occur	"Regulation C2(2)"
	"Regulation 29(3)"	"Regulation C3(2)"
	"Regulation 29"	"Regulation C3"
	"Regulation 20"	"Regulation B3"
	"Regulation 39"	"Regulation D3"
	"Regulation 43"	"Regulation E2"
Regulation 10(2)	"Regulation 22"	"Regulation B4"
	"Regulation 28"	"Regulation C2"
	"Regulation 39"	"Regulation D3"
	"Regulation 43"	"Regulation E2"
Regulation 10(3)	"Part VIII (determination of questions)"	"Part H (appeals and medical questions)"
	"Regulation 71(2)"	"Regulation H1(2)"

EXPLANATORY NOTE

(This note is not part of the Regulations)

These Regulations come into force on 1st April 1987 and are supplementary to the Police Pensions Regulations 1987, "the principal Regulations", (which consolidate, with amendments, the Police Pensions Regulations 1973, as amended).

Regulation 2 revokes the 1973 Regulations and the other Regulations specified in Part I of Schedule 1 but provides for the application of those Regulations, as amended by Part II of Schedule 1, in respect of any period between 1st April 1972 and the date of commencement of these Regulations (retrospection is authorised by section 1(5) of the Police Pensions Act 1976). Regulation 3 brings the principal Regulations into force, subject to the transitional provisions in Part III of Schedule 1, on the same date as these Regulations, in compliance with section 8 of the Police Pensions Act 1976.

Regulation 4 and Schedule 2 continue in force the Police Pensions Regulations 1971 and the other Regulations there specified (subject to the amendment in Part II of that Schedule) in respect of persons whose service ended before 1st April 1972.

Regulations 5 to 7 and Schedules 3 to 5 amend the Police Pensions (War Service) Regulations 1979, the Police Pensions (War Service) (Transferees) Regulations 1985 and the Police (Injury Benefit) Regulations 1987 to take account of the principal Regulations; Regulation 8 provides for the principal Regulations to have effect subject to those Regulations and for the continuance in effect of things done under those Regulations before the commencement of these Regulations.

STATUTORY INSTRUMENTS

1987 No. 257

POLICE

The Police Pensions Regulations 1987

Made - - - -	*20th February 1987*
Laid before Parliament	*9th March 1987*
Coming into force	*1st April 1987*

ARRANGEMENT OF REGULATIONS

PART A

GENERAL PROVISIONS AND RETIREMENT

Part B

Personal Awards

B1.   Policeman's ordinary pension.

B2.   Policeman's short service award.

B3.   Policeman's ill-health award.

B4.   Policeman's injury award.

B5.   Policeman's deferred pension.

B6.   Award by way of repayment of aggregate pension contributions.

B7.   Commutation—general provision.

B8.   Commutation—small pensions.

B9.   Allocation.

B10.   Limitation of surrendered portion of a pension for the purposes of Regulation B7 or B9.

B11.   Deduction of tax from certain awards.

Part C

Widows' Awards

C1.   Widow's ordinary pension.

C2.   Widow's special award.

C3.   Widow's augmented award.

C4.   Widow's accrued pension.

C5.   Limitation on award to widow with reference to date of marriage and pension in case of post-retirement marriage.

C6.   Widow's requisite benefit and temporary pension.

C7.   Widow's award where no other award payable.

C8.   Limitation on award to widow living apart from her husband and widow's requisite benefit pension.

C9.   Termination of widow's award on remarriage.

Part D

Children's Awards

D1.   Child's ordinary allowance.

D2.   Child's special allowance.

D3.   Child's special gratuity.

Part G

Pensionable Pay and Contributions

Part H

Appeals and Medical Questions

Part I

Servicemen

Part J

Special Cases

In exercise of the powers conferred on me by sections 1 to 8 of the Police Pensions Act 1976(**a**), and after consultation with the Police Negotiating Board for the United Kingdom and, so far as Regulation H6 is concerned, with the Council on Tribunals in pursuance of section 10 of the Tribunals and Inquiries Act 1971(**b**), I hereby, with the consent of the Treasury(**c**), make the following Regulations:—

PART A

GENERAL PROVISIONS AND RETIREMENT

Citation and commencement

A1. These Regulations may be cited as the Police Pensions Regulations 1987 and come into force on the date specified in that behalf in the Police Pensions (Supplementary Provisions) Regulations 1987(**d**).

Supplementary provisions

A2. These Regulations have effect subject to—

(a) the transitional provisions set out in Part III of Schedule 1 to the Police Pensions (Supplementary Provisions) Regulations 1987 ("the Supplementary Regulations"), and

(b) the Police Pensions (War Service) Regulations 1979(**e**), the Police Pensions (War Service) (Transferees) Regulations 1985(**f**) and the Police (Injury Benefit) Regulations 1987(**g**) as amended by Regulations 5, 6 and 7 of the Supplementary Regulations.

Exclusion of old cases

A3.— (1) Nothing in these Regulations shall apply in a case in which the old cases Regulations apply, that is to say, in the case of an award or payment to or in respect of, or relating to—

(a) a person who retired or otherwise ceased to be a member of a police force before 1st April 1972, or

(b) a person, being a serviceman who did not resume service as a regular policeman, whose period of relevant service in the armed forces ended before 1st April 1972.

(2) The reference in paragraph (1) to the old cases Regulations is a reference to the Police Pensions Regulations 1971(**h**) and other Regulations set out in Part I of Schedule 2 to the Police Pensions (Supplementary Provisions) Regulations 1987, as amended by Part II of that Schedule.

(**a**) 1976 c. 35, as amended by section 2(3) of the Police Negotiating Board Act 1980 (c. 10).
(**b**) 1971 c. 62.
(**c**) Formerly the Minister for the Civil Service; *see* S.I. 1981/1670.
(**d**) S.I. 1987/256; Regulation 3 provides that the present Regulations shall come into force on 1st April 1987.
(**e**) S.I. 1979/1259.   (**f**) S.I. 1985/2029.   (**g**) S.I. 1987/156.
(**h**) S.I. 1971/232, revoked with savings by S.I. 1973/428.

Meaning of certain expressions and references—general provisions

A4.— (1) In these Regulations, unless the context otherwise requires—

    (a) the expressions contained in the glossary set out in Schedule A shall be construed as therein provided;

    (b) any reference to a member of a police force, however expressed, includes a reference to a person who has been such a member;

    (c) any reference to an award, however expressed, is a reference to an award under these Regulations.

(2) In these Regulations, unless the context otherwise requires, a reference to a Regulation or a Part shall be construed as a reference to a Regulation contained in these Regulations or a Part thereof, a reference to a Schedule shall be construed as a reference to a Schedule to these Regulations, a reference to a paragraph shall be construed as a reference to a paragraph in the same Regulation or, as the case may be, the same Part of the same Schedule or the same Section thereof and a reference to a sub-paragraph shall be construed as a reference to a sub-paragraph contained in the same paragraph.

Meaning of certain expressions related to the National Insurance and Social Security Acts

A5.— (1) In these Regulations the following expressions shall have the meanings respectively which they had for the purposes of the National Insurance Act 1965(**a**) immediately before its repeal by the Social Security (Consequential Provisions) Act 1975(**b**)—

    "employed contributor's employment";

    "graduated contribution";

    "graduated retirement benefit";

    "non-participating employment";

    "payment in lieu of contributions".

(2) In these Regulations any reference to state pensionable age is a reference to the age of 65 years in the case of a man, or 60 years in the case of a woman.

(3) In these Regulations any reference to a participating period of relevant employment is a reference to a period of employed contributor's employment after 5th April 1961 and before state pensionable age other than—

    (a) service in the armed forces, and

    (b) non-participating employment at the end of which no payment in lieu of contributions fell to be made;

and for the purposes of this paragraph a period of employed contributor's employment or of non-participating employment shall be treated as continuing during periods of holiday, temporary incapacity for work and similar temporary interruptions.

(**a**) 1965 c. 51.   (**b**) 1975 c. 18.

(4) In these Regulations any reference to the secured portion of a pension is a reference to the portion of the pension which equals the graduated retirement benefit which would be payable to the pensioner, on the assumption that he retired from regular employment on attaining state pensionable age, in return for a payment in lieu of contributions in respect of the whole of any period of non-participating employment by reason of which he is entitled to reckon pensionable service for the purposes of the pension, being a period of non-participating employment at the end of which no payment in lieu of contributions in fact fell to be made; and any reference to the unsecured portion of a pension shall be construed accordingly.

For the purposes of this paragraph a period of non-participating employment shall be treated as continuing during periods of holiday, temporary incapacity for work and similar temporary interruptions.

(5) For the purposes of these Regulations the annual rate of graduated retirement benefit shall be calculated as if there were 52 $\frac{1}{6}$ weeks in each year.

(6) In these Regulations the following expressions shall have the meanings respectively which they have for the purposes of the Social Security Pensions Act 1975(a)—

"contracted-out employment";

"contracted-out scheme";

"guaranteed minimum" and "guaranteed minimum pension";

"contributions equivalent premium".

(7) In these Regulations any reference to a case in which a contributions equivalent premium has been paid includes a reference to a case in which such a premium is payable but has not been paid by virtue of regulations under Schedule 2 to the Social Security Pensions Act 1975 dispensing with the payment of such a premium where its amount would be inconsiderable.

(8) In these Regulations any reference to the guaranteed minimum in relation to a pension under a pension scheme at a particular time is a reference to the amount certified by the Department of Health and Social Security as that minimum at that time.

Meaning of certain expressions in relation to persons who are not members of a home police force

A6.— (1) A reference in these Regulations to a rank, being a rank in a home police force, shall, in relation to a member of an overseas corps, be construed as a reference to such rank in that corps as the Secretary of State may from time to time direct.

(2) For the purposes of these Regulations—

(a) a central police officer, or

(b) an overseas policeman who is not a member of an overseas corps,

shall be deemed to hold the rank in which he is entitled to revert to his home

---

(a) 1975 c. 60.

police force at the end of his tour of overseas service or, as the case may be, of central service.

(3) For the purposes of these Regulations—

    (a) an inspector of constabulary shall be deemed to hold the rank and office of chief constable;

    (b) an assistant inspector of constabulary shall be deemed to hold the rank of chief superintendent.

(4) Except where the context otherwise requires, for the purposes of these Regulations—

    (a) an inspector or assistant inspector of constabulary or a central police officer shall be deemed to be a member of a home police force;

    (b) an overseas policeman who is not a member of an overseas corps shall be deemed to be a member of such a corps;

and any reference to such a person joining or leaving a police force or transferring from one force to another, however expressed, shall be construed accordingly.

(5) In relation to an inspector or assistant inspector of constabulary, a central police officer or an overseas policeman, any reference in these Regulations to the police authority shall be construed as a reference to the Secretary of State.

(6) This Regulation has effect subject to paragraph 3 of Part VII of Schedule J.

Weekly rate of pensions and allowances

A7. Where the rate at which a pension or allowance is payable or the amount thereof is expressed as an annual rate or amount then, for the purposes of these Regulations, the weekly rate or amount of that pension or allowance shall be determined as if there were 52 $\frac{1}{6}$ weeks in each year.

Persons treated as being in receipt of a pension

A8. For the purposes of these Regulations, except where otherwise expressly provided, a person shall be treated as being in receipt of an ordinary, short service, ill-health or, as the case may be, injury pension if he would be in receipt of such a pension—

    (a) in the case of an ordinary pension—

        (i) had he attained the age of 50 years, or

        (ii) had it not been wholly withdrawn under Regulation K4 (*withdrawal of pension during service as a regular policeman*);

    (b) in the case of a short service or ill-health pension, had it not been withdrawn as mentioned in sub-paragraph *(a)*(ii);

    (c) in the case of an injury pension, had the aggregate reductions therein under paragraphs 3 and 4 of Part V of Schedule B not exceeded the amount of the pension calculated in accordance with paragraph 2 thereof.

Reckoning of service for purposes of awards

A9.— (1) Subject to paragraph (3), for the purpose of calculating an award payable to or in respect of a member of a police force by reference to any period in years (including a period of pensionable or other service)—

(a) that period shall be reckoned in completed years and a fraction of a year;

(b) a part of a year shall be taken to be that fraction of a year whereof the denominator is 365 and the numerator is the number of completed days in that part and, accordingly, a part of a year which includes 29th February in a leap-year and comprises 365 days shall be treated as a whole year.

(2) Where, for the purpose of calculating an award to or in respect of a regular policeman—

(a) it is necessary to determine his pensionable service reckonable by reason of service or employment before or after a particular date, and

(b) by virtue of the receipt by a police authority of a transfer value, he is entitled to reckon a period of pensionable service by reason of service or employment for a period which includes the date in question,

then that part of the said period of pensionable service shall be deemed to be reckonable by reason of service or employment before or after the date in question which bears the same proportion to the whole of that period as the part of the previous service or employment before, or as the case may be after, that date bears to the whole thereof.

(3) Paragraph (1) has effect subject to paragraphs 1, 2 and 3 of Part IV of Schedule J.

Aggregate pension contributions for purposes of awards

A10.— (1) For the purpose of calculating the amount of an award by reference to the aggregate pension contributions of a regular policeman in respect of the relevant period of service, the relevant period of service shall be taken to be the period ending in the retirement, dismissal or death on which the award is payable and beginning with the date on which he became a regular policeman in the force from which he retired or was dismissed or in which he died or, if he has more than once been a regular policeman in that force, the date on which he last joined that force otherwise than as a serviceman resuming service in his former force within a month of the end of his period of relevant service in the armed forces.

(2) For the purpose aforesaid the aggregate pension contributions in respect of the relevant period of service shall be taken to be the sum of the following amounts—

(a) the aggregate of the pension contributions (including additional, further or special contributions) made in respect of that period by the person concerned to the police authority by whom the award is payable and any rateable deductions made in respect of that period by that authority from his pay under the former Acts;

(b) any additional, further or special payment by way of a lump sum made during the relevant period by that person to that police authority;

(c) the amount of any sums paid by the person concerned to the said police authority (including sums paid in pursuance of an undertaking) as a condition of being entitled to reckon pensionable service or, as the case may be, approved service, by reason of service before the said period;

(d) where the person concerned has transferred to the force of the police authority by whom the award is payable, any sum which had he retired instead of transferring would have been calculable under this paragraph as aggregate pension contributions at the time of transfer;

(e) where the person concerned, while a member of the force of the said police authority, became entitled, in the circumstances mentioned in Regulation F3(1)(d), (e) or (f), Regulation F6 or Regulation F7, to reckon pensionable service by reason of a period of previous service or employment otherwise than as a member of a police force, the amount of any award by way of return of contributions or of any analogous payment which would have been made to him at the end of that period of previous service or employment had he voluntarily retired therefrom in circumstances entitling him to such an award or payment under the superannuation arrangements applicable thereto, and

(f) where the person concerned previously retired with an ill-health pension from the force of the police authority by whom the current award is payable, that pension was terminated in whole or in part under Regulation K1 or any corresponding provision of the former Regulations and he rejoined the force, any sum which would have been calculable under this paragraph as aggregate pension contributions at the time of the previous retirement.

(3) The references in paragraph (2)(a) and (b) to additional, further or special contributions or payments are references to such contributions or payments made in pursuance of an election under any of the provisions mentioned in Regulation 57(2), under Regulation 58 or under Regulation 61A of the Regulations of 1973 subject, however, to Regulations F4(3) and F5(2)(c) (*previous service reckonable on payment or at discretion of police authority*).

Injury received in the execution of duty

A11.— (1) A reference in these Regulations to an injury received in the execution of duty by a member of a police force means an injury received in the execution of that person's duty as a constable and, where the person concerned is an auxiliary policeman, during a period of active service as such.

(2) For the purposes of these Regulations an injury shall be treated as received by a person in the execution of his duty as a constable if—

(a) the member concerned received the injury while on duty or while on a journey necessary to enable him to report for duty or return home after duty, or

(b) he would not have received the injury had he not been known to be a constable, or

(c) the police authority are of the opinion that the preceding condition may be satisfied and that the injury should be treated as one received as aforesaid.

(3) In the case of a person who is not a constable but is within the definition of "member of a police force" in the glossary set out in Schedule A by reason of his being an officer there mentioned, paragraphs (1) and (2) shall have effect as if the references therein to a constable were references to such an officer.

(4) For the purposes of these Regulations an injury shall be treated as received without the default of the member concerned unless the injury is wholly or mainly due to his own serious and culpable negligence or misconduct.

(5) Notwithstanding anything in these Regulations relating to a period of service in the armed forces, an injury received in the execution of duty as a member of the armed forces shall not be deemed to be an injury received in the execution of duty as a member of a police force.

(6) In the case of a regular policeman who has served as a police cadet in relation to whom the Police Cadets (Pensions) Regulations had taken effect, a qualifying injury within the meaning of those Regulations shall be treated for the purposes of these Regulations as if it had been received by him as mentioned in paragraph (1); and, where such a qualifying injury is so treated, any reference to duties in Regulation C3(1) (*widow's augmented award*) shall be construed as including a reference to duties as a police cadet.

In this paragraph the reference to the Police Cadets (Pensions) Regulations is a reference to the Regulations from time to time in force under section 35 of the Police Act 1964(**a**), as extended by section 13 of the Superannuation (Miscellaneous Provisions) Act 1967(**b**), or under section 27 of the Police (Scotland) Act 1967(**c**), read with the said section 13.

Disablement

A12.— (1) A reference in these Regulations to a person being permanently disabled is to be taken as a reference to that person being disabled at the time when the question arises for decision and to that disablement being at that time likely to be permanent.

(2) Subject to paragraph (3), disablement means inability, occasioned by infirmity of mind or body, to perform the ordinary duties of a male or female member of the force, as the case may be, except that, in relation to a child or the widower of a member of a police force, it means inability, occasioned as aforesaid, to earn a living.

(3) Where it is necessary to determine the degree of a person's disablement it shall be determined by reference to the degree to which his earning capacity has been affected as a result of an injury received without his own default in the execution of his duty as a member of a police force:

Provided that a person shall be deemed to be totally disabled if, as a result of such an injury, he is receiving treatment as an in-patient at a hospital.

(4) Where a person has retired before becoming disabled and the date on which he becomes disabled cannot be ascertained, it shall be taken to be the

---

(**a**) 1964 c. 48.   (**b**) 1967 c. 28.   (**c**) 1967 c. 77.

date on which the claim that he is disabled is first made known to the police authority.

Disablement, death or treatment in hospital the result of an injury

A13. For the purposes of these Regulations disablement or death or treatment at a hospital shall be deemed to be the result of an injury if the injury has caused or substantially contributed to the disablement or death or the condition for which treatment is being received.

Relevant service in the armed forces

A14. A reference in these Regulations to relevant service in the armed forces shall be construed as a reference to—

    (a) service specified in Schedule 1 to the Reserve and Auxiliary Forces (Protection of Civil Interests) Act 1951(**a**), other than service specified in paragraph 5*(b)* thereof;

    (b) part-time service under the National Service Act 1948(**b**), otherwise than pursuant to a training notice under that Act;

    (c) service for the purposes of training only performed by a person mentioned in paragraph 7 of Schedule 1 to the Reserve and Auxiliary Forces (Protection of Civil Interests) Act 1951, for a period shorter than 7 days;

    (d) in relation to a serviceman other than a serviceman (1939–1945), whole-time service in the armed forces under the National Service Acts 1939 to 1946(**c**), the National Service Act 1947(**d**) or, without prejudice to sub-paragraph *(a)*, the National Service Act 1948;

    (e) in relation to a serviceman (1939–1945), service in the armed forces up to such date as the Secretary of State on the application of the police authority of his former force may in his case have fixed.

Alterations in police areas

A15.— (1) Where a police area is or has been combined with another police area, the police force, police authority and police fund for the combined police area of which the first-named area for the time being forms part shall, for the purposes of these Regulations, be deemed to be the same force, authority and fund as the force, authority and fund for the first-named area.

(2) Where a police area is or has been divided, in relation to any person—

    (a) who is transferred by the instrument effecting the division from the force for the divided area to another force, the other force and the police authority and police fund for the area thereof shall, for the purposes of these Regulations, be deemed to be the same force,

---

(**a**) 1951 c. 65.   (**b**) 1948 c. 64.
(**c**) 1939 c. 81, 1940 c. 22, 1941 c. 15, 1942 c. 3, 1946 c. 38.
(**d**) 1947 c. 31.

authority and fund as the force, authority and fund for the divided area;

(b) who ceased to be a member of the force for the divided area before the division thereof, if the instrument effecting the division makes provision in that behalf, the force, authority and fund designated for the purpose thereby shall, for the purposes of these Regulations, be deemed to be the same force, authority and fund as the force, authority and fund for the divided area.

(3) In this Regulation—

(a) a reference to the combination or division of a police area includes a reference to an agreement under section 14 of the County Police Act 1840(**a**) or, as the case may be, the termination of such an agreement, and a reference to the force, authority or fund for a combined area shall be construed accordingly;

(b) a reference to the division of a police area includes a reference to the transfer of part of a police area, on or after 1st April 1966, on the date on which an order affecting the area, made under section 140 of the Local Government Act 1933(**b**) or under Part II of the Local Government Act 1958(**c**), comes into force, and

(c) a reference to the combination of a police area with another police area includes a reference to the inclusion of a police area in a county or county borough police area, on or after 1st April 1968, on a date on which an order affecting the area, made under Part II of the Local Government Act 1958, comes into force and, in such case, a reference to the combined police area shall be construed as a reference to the county or, as the case may be, the county borough police area.

(4) In its application to Scotland, this Regulation shall have effect as if—

(a) any reference to a police fund were omitted;

(b) any reference to the police authority for a combined area or to a combined authority were a reference to the joint police committee for a combined area; and

(c) the reference to section 14 of the County Police Act 1840 were a reference to section 61 of the Police (Scotland) Act 1857(**d**).

Transfers

A16. A reference in these Regulations to a regular policeman transferring from one force to another shall be construed as a reference to a regular policeman—

(a) leaving a home police force for the purpose of joining another home police force as a regular policeman and joining that other force in that capacity, where—

(i) not being the chief officer of police of, or a constable on probation

---

(**a**) 1840 c. 88.   (**b**) 1933 c. 51.   (**c**) 1958 c. 55.   (**d**) 1857 c. 72.

in, the force first mentioned in this sub-paragraph, he leaves or left that force on or after 1st January 1963 for the purpose aforesaid, after giving a month's notice in writing of his intention to do so to the police authority of that force or such shorter period of notice as may have been accepted by that authority on or after 15th February 1971, or

(ii) he left the said force before 1st January 1963 or, being the chief officer of police of, or a constable on probation in, the said force, he leaves or left that force on or after that date, in either case for the purpose aforesaid and with the written consent of the chief officer of police or, in the case of the chief officer of police, of the police authority of that force;

(b) leaving a home police force with the consent of the Secretary of State and with the written consent of the chief officer of police of that force acting with the consent of the police authority or, if he is the chief officer of police of that force, of the police authority, for the purpose of engaging for a tour of overseas service as a reversionary member of a home police force and engaging in such a tour of service;

(c) transferring or being transferred from one overseas corps to another;

(d) exercising his right of reversion to a home police force, under section 2(1) of the Police (Overseas Service) Act 1945(a), at the end of a tour of overseas service; or

(e) at the end of a tour of overseas service joining another home police force as a regular policeman subject, in the cases hereinafter mentioned, to his doing so with the consent so mentioned, namely—

(i) in the case of a person who was, at the time he left the home police force to which he had the right of reversion referred to in sub-paragraph (d), the chief officer of that force, the written consent of the police authority of that force;

(ii) in the case of any other person whose tour of overseas service ended before 15th February 1971, the written consent of the chief officer of police of the home police force to which he had such right of reversion, acting with the consent of the police authority of that force.

Retirement

A17.— (1) A reference in these Regulations to retirement includes a reference to the services of a member of a police force being dispensed with under regulations for the time being in force under section 33 of the Police Act 1964 or section 26 of the Police (Scotland) Act 1967 (other than regulations relating to the maintenance of discipline), to an auxiliary policeman ceasing to be called up for active service and to the termination of a tour of overseas service otherwise than by dismissal or transfer, but does not include a reference to leaving a force on transferring from one force to another, or on joining the Royal Ulster Constabulary with such consent as is mentioned in paragraph (2) and a reference to a continuous period of service is a reference to a period of service uninterrupted by any such retirement.

(a) 1945 c. 17 (9 & 10 Geo. 6).

(2) The consent referred to in paragraph (1) is—

(a) in the case of a member of a police force who left his force before 17th December 1969 or was a chief officer of police, an assistant chief constable or a deputy chief constable and left his force on or after that date, the consent of the police authority;

(b) in any other case, the consent of the chief officer of police acting with the consent of the police authority.

(3) If a regular policeman is dismissed but is entitled to an ordinary pension by virtue of Regulation B1(6), these Regulations shall apply in his case as if he had retired as mentioned in Regulation B1(6)(b).

Compulsory retirement on account of age

A18.— (1) Subject to paragraph (2), every regular policeman—

(a) who is not a member of the metropolitan police or an overseas policeman shall be required to retire—

(i) if he is the commissioner or assistant commissioner of police for the City of London or is a chief constable, deputy chief constable or assistant chief constable, on attaining the age of 65 years,

(ii) if he is a superintendent or inspector, on attaining the age of 60 years,

(iii) if he is a sergeant or constable, on attaining the age of 55 years;

(b) who is a member of the metropolitan police shall be required to retire—

(i) if he is an assistant commissioner, on attaining the age of 60 years,

(ii) if he is a deputy assistant commissioner or commander, on attaining the age of 57 years,

(iii) if he holds any lower rank, on attaining the age of 55 years.

(2) The time at which, under paragraph (1), a person shall be required to retire may be postponed, if the person concerned holds a rank above that of superintendent, by the police authority, and, if he holds the rank of superintendent or any lower rank, by the chief officer of police:

Provided that no such postponement or postponements shall extend beyond 5 years from the time at which, under paragraph (1), he would have been required to retire.

(3) Paragraph (1) has effect subject to paragraphs 5(2) and 6(3) of Part VII of Schedule J.

Compulsory retirement on grounds of efficiency of the force

A19.— (1) This Regulation shall apply to a regular policeman, other than a chief officer of police, deputy chief constable or assistant chief constable, who if required to retire would be entitled to receive a pension of an amount not less than 2 thirds of his average pensionable pay or would be entitled to receive a pension of such an amount if it did not fall to be reduced in accordance with

Part VIII of Schedule B (*reduction of pension related to up-rating of widow's pension*).

(2) If a police authority determine that the retention in the force of a regular policeman to whom this Regulation applies would not be in the general interests of efficiency, he may be required to retire on such date as the police authority determine.

Compulsory retirement on grounds of disablement

A20. Every regular policeman may be required to retire on the date on which the police authority determine that he ought to retire on the ground that he is permanently disabled for the performance of his duty:

Provided that a retirement under this Regulation shall be void if, after the said date, on an appeal against the medical opinion on which the police authority acted in determining that he ought to retire, the medical referee decides that the appellant is not permanently disabled.

Effective date of retirement

A21.— (1) For the purposes of these Regulations—

(a) a member of a police force shall be taken to retire or cease to serve immediately following his last day of service;

(b) a member of a police force required to retire under Regulation A18, A19 or A20 shall be deemed to retire on the date on which he is so required to retire and his last day of service shall be the immediately preceding day;

(c) a continuous period of active service as an auxiliary policeman or a tour of overseas service shall be taken to end immediately following the last day of service of the person concerned.

(2) The references in paragraph (1) to a person's last day of service are references to his last such day during the relevant period of service or, as the case may be, tour of overseas service.

PART B

PERSONAL AWARDS

Policeman's ordinary pension

B1.— (1) Subject to paragraphs (2), (4) and (6), this Regulation shall apply to a regular policeman who retires or has retired when entitled to reckon at least 25 years' pensionable service unless Regulation B3 (*policeman's ill-health award*) applies in his case.

(2) Except in the circumstances mentioned in paragraph (3), this Regulation shall not apply to a regular policeman where—

(a) he retires or retired without having given to the police authority a month's written notice of his intention to retire or such shorter notice as may have been accepted by the police authority, or

(b) being a chief officer of police, assistant commissioner of police of the metropolis, assistant commissioner of police for the City of London, deputy chief constable, assistant chief constable, commander, or deputy assistant commissioner in the metropolitan police force, he retires or retired before attaining the age of 60 years.

(3) The circumstances referred to in paragraph (2) are that—

(a) the police authority have decided that this Regulation should apply in his case, or

(b) being such a regular policeman as is mentioned in paragraph (2)(b), he retires or retired on or after attaining the age of 55 years having given to the police authority 3 months' written notice of his intention to retire, or

(c) he is or was required to retire on account of age, or on the ground that his retention in the force would not be in the general interests of efficiency, or as an alternative to dismissal, or

(d) he is or was required to retire under section 5(4) of the Police Act 1964(a) or section 4(4)(d) of the Police (Scotland) Act 1967(b).

(4) This Regulation shall not apply to an overseas policeman or central police officer who retires or retired before the completion of the tour of overseas service or, as the case may be, of central service (if any) applicable in his case.

(5) Subject to the provisions of these Regulations, a regular policeman to whom this Regulation applies shall be entitled to an ordinary pension of an amount calculated in accordance with Part I of Schedule B, subject however to Parts VII and VIII of that Schedule; but, in the case of a person entitled to reckon less than 30 years' pensionable service, no payments shall be made on account of the pension in respect of the period (if any) after his retirement and before he has attained the age of 50 years or, if he sooner becomes permanently disabled, before he becomes so disabled.

(6) If a regular policeman entitled to reckon at least 25 years' pensionable service—

(a) is dismissed otherwise than for a cause for which, if a pension were granted to him, it could be forfeited under Regulation K5, and

(b) would have been entitled to an ordinary pension if he had retired on the date his dismissal took effect, having given such notice to the police authority of his intention to retire as is mentioned in paragraph (2)(a) or (3)(b),

this regulation shall apply to him and, accordingly, he shall be entitled to an ordinary pension under paragraph (5).

(7) Paragraphs (2), (3) and (5) have effect subject to paragraphs 1, 2 and 3 of Part I, and paragraphs 5(2) and (4) and 6(2) of Part VII, of Schedule J.

(a) 1964 c. 48.   (b) 1967 c. 77.

Policeman's short service award

B2.— (1) This Regulation shall apply to a regular policeman who retires or has retired when entitled to reckon less than 25 years' pensionable service and who—

(a) is or was required to retire on account of age;

(b) being a reversionary member of a home police force, in pursuance of a notice in that behalf given to the Secretary of State and having attained the age of 60 years, retires or retired on the termination of the tour of overseas service (if any) applicable in his case, or

(c) is or was required to retire under section 5(4) of the Police Act 1964 or section 4(4)*(d)* of the Police (Scotland) Act 1967.

(2) A regular policeman to whom this Regulation applies shall be entitled to a short service award as hereinafter provided.

(3) In the case of a policeman entitled at the time of his retirement to reckon at least 5 years' pensionable service, the award under paragraph (2) shall be a short service pension calculated in accordance with Part II of Schedule B, subject however to Parts VII and VIII of that Schedule.

(4) In the case of any other policeman, the award under paragraph (2) shall be a short service gratuity calculated in accordance with Part IV of Schedule B.

(5) Paragraph (1) has effect subject to paragraphs 5(3) and 6(2) of Part VII of Schedule J.

Policeman's ill-health award

B3.— (1) This Regulation shall apply to a regular policeman who retires or has retired on the ground that he is or was permanently disabled.

(2) A regular policeman to whom this Regulation applies shall be entitled to an ill-health award as hereinafter provided.

(3) In the case of a policeman who is or was at the time of his retirement—

(a) entitled to reckon at least 5 years' pensionable service, or

(b) disabled as the result of an injury received in the execution of duty,

the award under paragraph (2) shall be an ill-health pension calculated in accordance with Part III of Schedule B, subject however to Parts VII and VIII of that Schedule.

(4) In the case of any other policeman the award under paragraph (2) shall be an ill-health gratuity calculated in accordance with Part IV of Schedule B.

Policeman's injury award

B4.— (1) This Regulation shall apply to a person who ceases or has ceased to be a member of a police force and is permanently disabled as a result of an injury received without his own default in the execution of his duty (in Part V of Schedule B referred to as the "relevant injury").

(2) A person to whom this Regulation applies shall be entitled to a gratuity and, in addition, to an injury pension, in both cases calculated in accordance with Part V of Schedule B; but payment of an injury pension shall be subject to the provisions of paragraph 5 of the said Part V and, where the person concerned ceased to serve before becoming disabled, no payment shall be made on account of the pension in respect of any period before he became disabled.

Policeman's deferred pension

B5.— (1) This Regulation shall apply to a regular policeman who—

(a) is entitled to reckon at least 5 years' pensionable service, or

(b) though not so entitled, has service as a regular policeman which, disregarding breaks in service of not more than a month, is continuous and which, when aggregated with any period of other service or employment by reason of which he is entitled to reckon pensionable service, is at least 5 years.

(2) A regular policeman to whom this Regulation applies who ceases or has ceased to be such in circumstances—

(a) in which no transfer value is payable in respect of him, and

(b) which do not entitle him to any award under any of the preceding provisions of this Part,

shall, on so ceasing to be a regular policeman, be entitled to a deferred pension as hereinafter provided.

(3) Where the unsecured portion of the ill-health pension of a regular policeman to whom this Regulation applies—

(a) is terminated under Regulation K1(4), or

(b) has been terminated on or after 1st April 1973 under Regulation 65(4) of the Regulations of 1973,

otherwise than on his rejoining his force he shall, as from the date of termination, be entitled to a deferred pension as hereinafter provided.

(4) A deferred pension under paragraph (2) or (3) shall be calculated in accordance with Part VI of Schedule B, subject however to Parts VII and VIII of that Schedule; but no payment shall be made on account of the pension—

(a) in respect of the period before the regular policeman attains the age of 60 years or, if he sooner becomes permanently disabled, before he becomes so disabled, or

(b) where he has relinquished his entitlement as mentioned in Regulation F4(3) or F5(3) (*previous service reckonable on payment or at discretion of police authority*), by written notice to the police authority, in respect of any period after the giving of that notice.

(5) This Regulation has effect subject to paragraph 8 of Part I of Schedule J.

Award by way of repayment of aggregate pension contributions

B6.— (1) This Regulation shall apply to a regular policeman who ceases to serve as such in circumstances—

(a) in which no transfer value is payable in respect of him, and

(b) which do not entitle him to an award under any of the preceding provisions of this Part or to an award under Regulation J1 or paragraph 9 of Part I of Schedule J.

(2) A regular policeman to whom this Regulation applies shall be entitled to an award by way of repayment of his aggregate pension contributions in respect of his relevant period of service.

Commutation—general provision

B7.— (1) This Regulation shall apply to an ordinary, short service, ill-health or deferred pension under this Part, but in relation to—

(a) a deferred pension, or

(b) an ordinary pension which is not payable as from the date of the policeman's retirement,

paragraphs (5), (6) and (7) shall have effect as if any reference therein to retirement or the date thereof were a reference to the coming into payment of the pension or the date thereof.

(2) A regular policeman may, subject to and in accordance with this Regulation, commute for a lump sum a portion of any pension to which this Regulation applies to which he is or may become entitled.

(3) For the purpose of commuting a portion of his pension in accordance with this Regulation a person shall give notice in writing to the police authority ("notice of commutation") of his wish to surrender and commute for a lump sum so much of his pension as, subject to the limitations contained in paragraph (4) and in Regulation B10, he may specify ("the surrendered portion").

(4) The surrendered portion shall be such that—

(a) the basic rate of the pension does not fall to be reduced in accordance with this Regulation by more than a quarter and, for the purposes hereof, that rate shall be taken to be the rate at which the pension would be payable not only if it did not fall to be so reduced but also disregarding any reduction—

(i) in accordance with Regulation B9 (*allocation*),

(ii) in accordance with Part VII of Schedule B (*reduction of pension at state pensionable age*),

(iii) as provided in paragraph 6(1) of Part VIII of Schedule B (*reduction of pension equivalent to outstanding additional or further contributions*), in accordance therewith, and

(b) in the case of a regular policeman who retires or retired with an ordinary pension when entitled to reckon less than 30 years' pensionable service otherwise than in the circumstances mentioned in sub-paragraph *(a)* or *(c)* of Regulation B2(1), the lump sum calculated

in accordance with paragraph (7) (disregarding any reduction in accordance with the proviso thereto) does not exceed an amount equal to $2\frac{1}{4}$ times the annual amount of his pension calculated in accordance with Part I of Schedule B (disregarding any reduction therein under paragraph (7) of this Regulation or any other provision of these Regulations):

Provided that, where a person wishes to surrender and commute for a lump sum a portion of a pension which falls to be reduced under paragraph (8)*(b)*, the portion which, in accordance with the preceding provisions of this paragraph, may be surrendered shall be reduced by the reduction under paragraph (8)*(b)* expressed in like manner.

(5) The notice of commutation shall be given by a person not earlier than 4 months before his intended retirement nor later than 6 months after his retirement.

(6) The notice of commutation given by a person shall become effective—

(a) as from the date of his retirement, or

(b) as from the date on which the notice is received by the police authority,

whichever is the later:

Provided that the notice of commutation shall not become effective if—

(i) it was given more than 4 months before his retirement, or

(ii) it relates to an ill-health pension and the unsecured portion of that pension has sooner been terminated under Regulation K1.

(7) Where the person retires or has retired and a notice of commutation given by him becomes or has become effective, the police authority shall reduce the pension to which the notice relates in accordance with the notice as from the time from which the notice is effective and shall pay him a lump sum of such amount as is the actuarial equivalent of the surrendered portion of the pension at the date of his retirement, calculated from tables prepared by the Government Actuary:

Provided that where the notice is effective as from the date mentioned in paragraph (6)*(b)*, the lump sum shall be reduced by an amount equal to the difference between the aggregate payments made in respect of the pension and the aggregate payments which would have been so made had it been reduced from the date of the retirement.

(8) Where the unsecured portion of an ill-health pension is terminated under Regulation K1 after a notice of commutation in relation to the pension has become effective—

(a) no reduction shall be made under paragraph (7) in the secured portion of the pension, insofar as it is payable under Regulation K1;

(b) if thereafter the person concerned becomes entitled to a pension, other than an injury pension, and is entitled to reckon for the purposes thereof the period of pensionable service reckonable for the purposes of the ill-health pension first mentioned in this paragraph, the unsecured portion of the other pension shall be reduced, in respect of any period, by the amount by which the ill-health pension would have

been reduced under paragraph (7) if it had not been terminated as aforesaid but had been payable in respect of that period.

(9) This Regulation has effect subject to paragraphs 4 and 8(11) of Part I, and paragraphs 5(3) and 6(2) of Part VII, of Schedule J.

Commutation—small pensions

B8.— (1) Where the annual amount of any pension payable under this Part to a regular policeman who has attained state pensionable age, together with any increase under the Pensions (Increase) Acts, does not exceed £104, the police authority may, at their discretion, commute the pension for a gratuity.

(2) A gratuity under this Regulation shall be of such amount as is the actuarial equivalent of the pension, calculated from tables prepared by the Government Actuary.

(3) Where the regular policeman is entitled to more than one pension, those pensions shall be treated as one for the purposes of this Regulation.

(4) This Regulation has effect subject to Regulation J1(6)*(a)* and paragraphs 8(11) and 9(4) of Part I of Schedule J.

Allocation

B9.— (1) This Regulation shall apply to an ordinary, short service, ill-health or deferred pension under this Part.

(2) A regular policeman who is entitled to reckon not less than 25 years' pensionable service may, subject to and in accordance with this Regulation, allocate a portion of any ordinary or ill-health pension to which he is or may become entitled and, notwithstanding that he has already allocated a portion of such a pension, he may—

> *(a)* allocate a further portion of that pension in favour of the beneficiary of a previous allocation;
>
> *(b)* where that beneficiary has died, allocate a further portion of that pension in favour of some other beneficiary, or
>
> *(c)* where (not having attained the age of 70 years) he proposes to marry or remarry, allocate a further portion of that pension in favour of his spouse by that marriage.

(3) A regular policeman may, subject to and in accordance with this Regulation, allocate a portion of any short service pension to which he is or may become entitled or of a deferred pension and, notwithstanding that he has already allocated a portion of such a pension, he may, where (not having attained the age of 70 years) he proposes to marry or remarry, allocate a further portion of that pension in favour of his spouse by that marriage.

(4) For the purpose of allocating a portion of his pension a policeman shall—

> *(a)* within the time limits mentioned in paragraph (5), give notice in writing to the police authority of the force in which he is serving or by whom his pension is payable ("notice of allocation") stating—

    (i) his wish to surrender so much of his pension as, subject to the limitations contained in Regulation B10, he may specify,

    (ii) the person in whose favour the surrender is to take effect ("the beneficiary") being his wife or some other person who the police authority are satisfied is substantially dependent upon him,

    (iii) in the case of a policeman entitled to reckon not less than 25 years' pensionable service who has not retired, whether or not he wishes the notice to become effective while he is serving, and

(b) satisfy the police authority of his good health and for that purpose submit himself to such medical examination as they may require.

(5) Notice of allocation shall be given—

(a) where in such case as is mentioned in paragraph (4)*(a)*(iii) the policeman wishes the notice to become effective while he is serving, before his intended retirement;

(b) where a person in receipt of a pension who has not attained the age of 70 years proposes to marry or remarry and the beneficiary is his spouse by that marriage, before but not earlier than 4 months before his intended marriage;

(c) where the pension is a deferred pension but the preceding sub-paragraph does not apply, before but not earlier than 4 months before the pension comes into payment;

(d) in any other case, before but not earlier than 4 months before the person's intended retirement.

(6) Where a person has complied with the provisions of sub-paragraphs *(a)* and *(b)* of paragraph (4), the police authority shall forthwith send to him a written notification that they have accepted the notice of allocation, which shall become effective—

(a) in any such case as is mentioned in paragraph (5)*(a)* where he wishes the notice of allocation to become effective while he is serving, as from the time when the notification is received by him or, if sent by post, as from the time when it would be received by him in the ordinary course of post, except that it shall have effect as from the date of his retirement if that is earlier;

(b) in any such case as is mentioned in paragraph (5)*(b)*, if, and only if, the proposed marriage takes place within 4 months of giving the notice of allocation and in that event as from the date of the marriage;

(c) in any such case as is mentioned in paragraph (5)*(c)*, if, and only if, the deferred pension comes into payment within 4 months of giving the notice of allocation and in that event as from the date it comes into payment;

(d) in any other case, if, and only if, the person retires within 4 months of giving the notice of allocation and in that event as from the date of retirement.

(7) Where a person retires or has retired in circumstances entitling him to a pension to which a notice of allocation given by him relates and that notice becomes effective—

(a) that pension shall be reduced in accordance with the notice (notwith-

standing the previous death of the beneficiary) as from the date from which the pension is payable or on which the notice becomes effective, whichever is the later, and

(b) the police authority shall, as from the person's death, pay to the beneficiary specified in the notice, if that person survives him, a pension of such amount as is the actuarial equivalent of the surrendered portion of the pension.

(8) For the purposes of paragraph (7)(b) the actuarial equivalent of the surrendered portion of the pension shall be calculated from tables prepared by the Government Actuary and in force at the time when the notice of allocation became effective, which tables shall—

(a) take account of the age of the regular policeman and of the age of the beneficiary at that time, and

(b) make different provision according to whether or not the notice of allocation became effective in accordance with paragraph (6)(a),

and separate calculations shall be made in respect of separate allocations.

(9) Where a person was entitled to reckon at least 25 years' pensionable service when he gave the notice of allocation and stated therein his wish that it should become effective while he was serving, then, if he dies before retiring, the police authority shall pay to the beneficiary the like pension that they would have paid by virtue of that notice if he had retired with a pension immediately before he died.

(10) Any reference in these Regulations to a widow's pension, however expressed, shall be construed as excluding a reference to a pension payable to a widow under this Regulation.

(11) This Regulation has effect subject to paragraph 8(11) of Part I of Schedule J.

Limitation of surrendered portion of a pension for the purposes of Regulation B7 or B9

B10. The portion of a pension which a regular policeman may surrender under either Regulation B7 or Regulation B9 shall be limited as hereinafter provided, namely, it shall not be—

(a) in the case of any pension, such that the pension becomes payable at a rate less than two-thirds of the rate at which it would have been payable but for the provisions of the said Regulations and of Parts VII and VIII of Schedule B;

(b) in the case of a deferred pension, where the policeman has a guaranteed minimum in relation to the pension on the date on which it becomes payable, such that the weekly amount of the pension at that date, including any increase under the Pensions (Increase) Act 1971(**a**), is less than that guaranteed minimum;

and the limitation contained in sub-paragraph *(b)* is without prejudice to that contained in sub-paragraph *(a)*.

(**a**) 1971 c. 56.

Deduction of tax from certain awards

B11.— (1) This Regulation shall apply to any payment on account of an award made to a member of a police force during his lifetime which constitutes a repayment of contributions within the meaning of paragraph 2 of Part II of Schedule 5 to the Finance Act 1970(**a**).

(2) The police authority may deduct from any payment to which this Regulation applies the tax for the time being chargeable thereon under paragraph 2 of the said Part II.

Part C

Widows' Awards

Widow's ordinary pension

C1.— (1) This Regulation shall apply to a widow of a regular policeman entitled to reckon at least 3 years' pensionable service—

(a) who, having retired with an ordinary, short service or ill-health pension, dies or has died while in receipt of that pension;

(b) who, having retired with both an ill-health and an injury pension, dies or has died otherwise than while in receipt of the ill-health pension but while in receipt of the injury pension;

(c) who, having retired with an ill-health gratuity, dies or has died as a result of the same injury as resulted in his disablement, or

(d) who dies or has died while serving as a regular policeman,

except that this Regulation shall not apply by virtue of sub-paragraph *(c)* to the widow of a regular policeman in respect of whom a transfer value was, or was required to be, paid, following his retirement, in pursuance of Regulation F9 (*interchange arrangements*).

(2) A widow to whom this Regulation applies shall be entitled to an ordinary pension calculated in accordance with Part I of Schedule C subject, however, to Regulation E8 (*increase during first 13 weeks*).

(3) Paragraph (1) has effect subject to paragraph 1 of Part II of Schedule J.

Widow's special award

C2.— (1) This Regulation shall apply to a widow of a member of a police force who dies or has died as the result of an injury received without his own default in the execution of his duty.

(2) A widow to whom this Regulation applies shall be entitled to an award which shall comprise—

(a) a widow's special pension calculated in accordance with Part II of

---

(**a**) 1970 c. 24.

Schedule C subject, however, to Regulation E8 (*increase during first 13 weeks*), and

(b) subject to paragraphs (3) and (4), a gratuity of an amount equal to 25% of her husband's average pensionable pay together with, where he died while serving as a member of a police force, an amount equal to whichever is the greater of the following amounts—

(i) her husband's average pensionable pay,

(ii) $2\frac{1}{4}$ times the annual amount of the ill-health pension which would have been payable under Regulation B3 to her husband had he retired on the ground that he was permanently disabled on the day on which he died.

(3) Where the husband was entitled to an injury gratuity under Regulation B4 then—

(a) if it equalled, or exceeded, the gratuity under paragraph (2)(b), the gratuity under paragraph (2)(b) shall not be payable, and

(b) in any other case, the gratuity under paragraph (2)(b) shall be reduced by the amount of the husband's gratuity.

(4) The amount of a widow's gratuity determined in accordance with the preceding provisions of this Regulation shall be increased in accordance with Regulation E9 (*increase by reference to the Pensions (Increase) Acts*).

(5) Paragraph (2)(b) has effect subject to paragraph 6 of Part II of Schedule J.

Widow's augmented award

C3.— (1) This Regulation shall apply to a widow of a member of a police force whose death is the result of an injury received without his own default in the execution of his duty where one of the following conditions is satisfied, namely that—

(a) he was attacked by a person or persons in a manner which was intrinsically likely to cause death and death ensued as a result of the attack, or

(b) the injury was received in the course of duties performed for the immediate purpose of effecting an arrest or of preventing an escape or rescue from legal custody, or

(c) the injury was received in the course of duties performed—

(i) for the immediate purpose of saving the life of another person or of preventing loss of human life, and

(ii) in circumstances in which there was an intrinsic likelihood of his receiving a fatal injury, or

(d) the police authority are of the opinion that one of the preceding conditions may be satisfied and that this Regulation should apply, or

(e) the police authority are of the opinion that the injury was received otherwise than as aforesaid but in the course of duties performed in such circumstances that it would be inequitable if there were not payable in respect of him such an award as would have been payable had one of the conditions specified in sub-paragraphs *(a)*, *(b)* and *(c)* been satisfied.

(2) An award under Regulation C2(2) to a widow to whom this Regulation applies shall comprise—

(a) a widow's special pension calculated as provided in Regulation C2(2)*(a)* but as if for the reference in paragraph 1 of Part II of Schedule C to 45% of the husband's average pensionable pay for a week there were substituted a reference to 50% thereof, and

(b) a gratuity of an amount equal to twice the annual pensionable pay, at the date of her husband's death, of a man—

(i) holding the rank of constable in the metropolitan police force, and

(ii) entitled to reckon 30 years' service for the purposes of pay,

and the provisions of Regulation C2(2)*(b)*, (3) and (4) shall not apply except that where those provisions are more favourable in her case the gratuity shall be of an amount determined in accordance therewith.

Widow's accrued pension

C4.— (1) This Regulation shall apply to a widow of a regular policeman who dies or has died while entitled to a deferred pension, whether or not that pension has or had come into payment.

(2) For the purposes of paragraph (1) a policeman shall be treated as entitled to a deferred pension if he would have been so entitled but for its commutation for a lump sum under Regulation B8.

(3) A widow to whom this Regulation applies shall be entitled to an accrued pension calculated in accordance with Part III of Schedule C subject, however, to Regulation E8 (*increase during first 13 weeks*).

Limitation on award to widow with reference to date of marriage and pension in case of post-retirement marriage

C5.— (1) A widow shall not be entitled to a widow's ordinary or accrued pension under Regulation C1 or C4 unless she was married to her husband during a period before he last ceased to be a regular policeman.

(2) A widow shall not be entitled to a widow's special award under Regulation C2 unless she was married to her husband during a period—

(a) before he last ceased to be a regular policeman, if he received the injury while serving as a regular policeman;

(b) before the end of the continuous period of service during which he received the injury, in any other case.

(3) A widow of a regular policeman who, but for paragraph (1) or (2)*(a)*, would be entitled to an award under Regulation C1, C2 or C4 shall, instead, be entitled to a pension calculated in accordance with Part IV of Schedule C subject, however, to Regulation E8 (*increase during first 13 weeks*).

Widow's requisite benefit and temporary pension

C6.— (1) This Regulation shall apply to a widow of a regular policeman not mentioned in Regulation C1(1), C2(1) or C4(1) where, after the beginning of the tax year in which he attained or would have attained state pensionable age, the husband either—

(a) has died while serving as a regular policeman, or

(b) has ceased to serve as such.

(2) A widow to whom this Regulation applies shall be entitled to an award which, subject to paragraph (3), shall comprise—

(a) if the husband died while serving as a regular policeman or in receipt of a pension, a temporary pension in respect of the first 13 weeks following his death of such amount in respect of each such week as, when aggregated with that of any children's allowances payable in respect of the husband's death, is of the like weekly amount as was his pensionable pay or, as the case may be, as was his pension, together with any increase therein, immediately before he died, under the Pensions (Increase) Acts;

(b) where such a temporary pension is not payable, or after the 13 weeks for which it is payable, a widow's requisite benefit pension calculated in accordance with Part V of Schedule C;

and, for the purposes of sub-paragraph (a), where the husband died while in receipt of both an ordinary, short service or ill-health pension and an injury pension, the reference therein to the weekly amount of his pension shall be construed as a reference to the aggregate weekly amount of those pensions.

(3) If the capitalised value of the pension payable under paragraph (2)(b) to a widow whose husband died while serving as a regular policeman, as calculated by the Government Actuary, is less than the husband's average pensionable pay, the widow shall also be entitled to a gratuity equal to the amount by which that capitalised value falls short of the husband's average pensionable pay.

(4) For the purposes of paragraph (2)(a)—

(a) the provisions of Regulation A8 shall be disregarded, and, accordingly, a person shall not by virtue thereof be treated as in receipt of an injury pension, but

(b) he shall be treated as in receipt of an injury pension if he would have been in receipt of such a pension but for his entitlement to additional benefit within the meaning of paragraph 4 of Part V of Schedule B and, where he is, or is so treated as being, in receipt of such a pension, the provisions of the said paragraph 4 shall be disregarded in determining the weekly amount of that pension.

Widow's award where no other award payable

C7.— (1) This Regulation shall apply to a widow of a member of a police force to whom neither Regulation C1, C2 nor C6 applies where the husband has died while serving as a member of a police force or, in the case of an auxiliary policeman, while called up for service as such.

(2) A widow to whom this Regulation applies shall be entitled to an award which shall comprise—

(a) in respect of the first 13 weeks following the husband's death, a temporary pension of such amount as secures that, in respect of each such week, the aggregate amount of the payment under this sub-paragraph and of any children's allowances payable in respect of the husband's death is of the like amount as his pensionable pay for a week immediately before he died, and

(b) an ordinary gratuity of an amount equal to the husband's average pensionable pay.

Limitation on award to widow living apart from her husband and widow's requisite benefit pension

C8.— (1) A widow shall not be entitled to an award under any of the preceding provisions of this Part if, at the time of her husband's death—

(a) she was separated from him by an order or decree of a competent court, and

(b) he was not required by an order or decree of a competent court to contribute to her support and was not in fact regularly contributing to her support;

and, for the purposes hereof, contributions to a woman for the support of her child shall be treated as contributions for her support.

(2) A widow of a member of a police force who, but for paragraph (1), would be entitled to an award under any of the preceding provisions of this Part shall, instead, be entitled to a widow's requisite benefit pension calculated in accordance with Part V of Schedule C.

Termination of widow's award on remarriage

C9.— (1) Where a widow entitled to a pension under this Part remarries or has remarried, she shall not be entitled to receive any payment on account of the pension in respect of any period after her remarriage:

Provided that if at any time after her remarriage she has again become a widow or that marriage has been dissolved, the police authority may, in their discretion, bring the pension into payment.

(2) Where a widow entitled to a gratuity under this Part remarries or has remarried, so much of the gratuity as has not been paid before her remarriage shall not be payable thereafter:

Provided that if at any time after her remarriage she has again become a widow or that marriage has been dissolved, the police authority may, in their discretion, pay to her the sums which they were actually or contingently liable to pay to her in respect of the gratuity immediately before her remarriage.

(3) Where, after her husband's death, a woman and a man to whom she is not married are living together as husband and wife, this Regulation shall apply as if for the period for which they so live together she were married to him and

any reference therein to her remarriage, her again becoming a widow or the marriage being dissolved shall be construed accordingly.

Part D

Children's Awards

Child's ordinary allowance

D1.— (1) This Regulation shall apply to a child of a regular policeman—

(a) who, having retired with an ordinary, short service or ill-health pension, dies or has died while in receipt of that pension;

(b) who, having retired with both an ill-health and an injury pension, dies or has died otherwise than while in receipt of the ill-health pension but while in receipt of the injury pension;

(c) who dies or has died having retired with a gratuity when entitled to reckon at least 3 years' pensionable service, or

(d) who dies or has died while serving as a regular policeman,

except that this Regulation shall not apply by virtue of sub-paragraph *(c)* to the child of a regular policeman in respect of whom a transfer value was, or was required to be, paid following his retirement, in pursuance of Regulation F9.

(2) Subject to Regulations D5 (*limitations*) and E8 (*increase during first 13 weeks*), a child to whom this Regulation applies shall be entitled to an ordinary allowance calculated in accordance with Part I of Schedule D.

(3) Paragraph (1) has effect subject to paragraph 1(2) of Part III of Schedule J.

Child's special allowance

D2.— (1) This Regulation shall apply to a child of a member of a police force who dies or has died as the result of an injury received without his own default in the execution of his duty.

(2) Subject to Regulations D5 (*limitations*) and E8 (*increase during first 13 weeks*), a child to whom this Regulation applies shall be entitled to a special allowance calculated in accordance with Part II of Schedule D.

Child's special gratuity

D3.— (1) This Regulation shall apply to a child of a member of a police force who dies or has died as the result of an injury received without his own default in the execution of his duty where one of the conditions set out in Regulation C3(1) is satisfied and—

(a) in the case of a man, does not leave a widow entitled to a gratuity in pursuance of Regulations C2 and C3, or

(b) in the case of a woman, was the child's only surviving parent.

(2) Subject to Regulation D5 (*limitations*) but without prejudice to the

provisions of Regulation D2 (*child's special allowance*), a child to whom this Regulation applies shall be entitled to a gratuity as hereinafter provided.

(3) The gratuity under paragraph (2) shall be of the amount mentioned in paragraph (4) except that, where two or more such gratuities are payable in respect of the same person, each gratuity shall be of the said amount divided by the number of such gratuities.

(4) The said amount shall be of an amount equal to twice the annual pensionable pay, at the date of that parent's death, of a man—

(a) holding the rank of constable in the metropolitan police force, and

(b) entitled to reckon 30 years' service for the purposes of pay.

Child's accrued allowance

D4.— (1) This Regulation shall apply to a child of a regular policeman who dies while entitled to a deferred pension, whether or not that pension has come into payment.

(2) Subject to Regulations D5 (*limitations*) and E8 (*increase during first 13 weeks*), a child to whom this Regulation applies shall be entitled to an accrued allowance calculated in accordance with Part III of Schedule D.

Child's allowance or special gratuity—limitations

D5.— (1) A child's allowance or gratuity under any of the preceding provisions of this Part ("an allowance" and "a special gratuity") shall not be granted—

(a) to a child born on or after the relevant date specified in paragraph (2) otherwise than of a marriage which took place before the relevant date;

(b) by reason of his being a step-child, to the child of a spouse whose marriage to the relevant parent took place on or after the relevant date;

(c) by reason of his being substantially dependent on the relevant parent, to a child who was not so dependent before the relevant date;

(d) by reason of his being an adopted child, to a child adopted on or after the relevant date;

(e) except in the case of a legitimate or adopted child of the relevant parent, to a child who was not substantially dependent on that parent at the time of his death.

(2) For the purposes of paragraph (1) the relevant date—

(a) in the case of an ordinary or accrued allowance, is the date on which the relevant parent last ceased to be a regular policeman;

(b) in the case of a special allowance or a special gratuity—

(i) if the relevant parent received the injury while serving as a regular policeman, is the date on which he last ceased to be a regular policeman,

(ii) if he received the injury while called up for service as an auxiliary policeman, is the date of the end of the continuous period of active service during which he received the injury,

(iii) if he received the injury while serving as a member of an overseas corps otherwise than as a regular policeman, is the date of the end of the tour of overseas service during which he received the injury.

(3) In the case of a child who has attained the age of 16 years but not that of 17 years, an allowance shall not be payable in respect of any period for which he is in full-time employment unless that employment constitutes full-time training, of at least a year's duration, for a trade, profession or calling.

(4) In the case of a child who has attained the age of 17 years but not that of 19 years, an allowance shall only be payable in respect of a period throughout which he satisfies one of the conditions set out in paragraph (8).

(5) Without prejudice to paragraph (1), in the case of a child who has attained the age of 19 years, an allowance shall not be payable (and, where he attained that age before the date of the relevant parent's death, shall not be granted) unless—

(a) he satisfies one of the conditions set out in paragraph (8), and

(b) in the case of condition (a), also satisfied that condition immediately before he attained the age of 19 years and throughout the entire period thereafter,

except that the payment (or granting) of an allowance shall not be precluded by reason only of sub-paragraph (b) if the police authority, having regard to all the circumstances of the case, in their discretion so decide.

(6) Without prejudice to paragraphs (3), (4) and (5), in the case of a child entitled to an allowance who is—

(a) in full-time training for a trade, profession or calling, and

(b) in receipt of remuneration in respect thereof,

and in the case of any other child entitled to an allowance in respect of the death of the same person, Part IV of Schedule D shall have effect in relation to their allowances.

(7) A special gratuity shall not be granted to a child who attained the age of 17 years before the date of the relevant parent's death unless at that date he satisfied one of the conditions set out in paragraph (8) (disregarding conditions (b)(ii) and (iii)).

(8) The conditions referred to in paragraphs (4), (5) and (7) are that the child—

(a) is or was undergoing full-time education or in full-time training of at least a year's duration for a trade, profession or calling, or

(b) is or was permanently disabled and either—

(i) was both so disabled and substantially dependent on the relevant parent at the time of his death,

(ii) became so disabled while in receipt of an allowance, or

(iii) the police authority, having regard to all the circumstances of the case, in their discretion decide to pay (or grant) an allowance to him.

(9) Any reference in this Regulation to the relevant parent is a reference to the parent in respect of whose death the allowance or special gratuity is or, but for the provisions thereof, would be payable.

(10) This Regulation has effect subject to paragraph 5 of Part III of Schedule J.

PART E

AWARDS ON DEATH—ADDITIONAL PROVISIONS

Dependent relatives and estate

Adult dependent relative's special pension

E1.— (1) This Regulation shall apply in the case of a member of a police force who dies as the result of an injury received without his own default in the execution of his duty and, in such case, shall apply—

(a) to a parent or (without prejudice to the following sub-paragraph) to a brother or sister of the member who had attained the age of 19 years before the member's death;

(b) subject to his having attained the age of 19 years, to any child of the member whether or not he had attained that age before the member's death, or

(c) where the member was a married woman whose husband was permanently disabled at the time she died, to her widower,

subject, in each case, to the person in question being substantially dependent on the member immediately before the member's death.

(2) If the police authority, having regard to all the circumstances of the case, so determine, they may grant a special pension to any such dependent relative.

(3) A dependent relative's special pension shall be calculated in accordance with Part I of Schedule E and, subject to paragraph 4 thereof, shall be payable for such period or periods as the police authority may, in their discretion, from time to time determine.

Gratuities—dependent relatives

E2.— (1) This Regulation shall apply in the case of a regular policeman—

(a) who dies while in receipt of a pension or while entitled to a deferred pension, whether or not that pension has come into payment, if death—

(i) results from an injury received in the execution of his duty, or

(ii) takes place within 2 years of his becoming entitled to his pension, or

(b) who dies while serving as such and in respect of whom no award is

payable otherwise than by virtue of this or the next following Regulation or by virtue of Regulation B9(9) (*allocation*).

(2) In the case of such a regular policeman the police authority may, in their discretion, grant a gratuity to any relative of the policeman who was dependent on him to any degree at the time of his death but the aggregate amount of any gratuities granted under this Regulation shall not exceed the aggregate pension contributions in respect of the policeman's relevant period of service.

Gratuity—estate

E3.— (1) This Regulation shall apply in the case of a regular policeman—

(a) who dies while entitled to an ordinary, short service, ill-health or deferred pension, whether or not that pension has come into payment, or

(b) who dies while serving as such.

(2) If, in the case of such a regular policeman, the aggregate of—

(a) any payments made or due to him on account of his ordinary, short service, ill-health or deferred pension or by way of a lump sum under Regulation B7 where a portion of such a pension has been commuted, or on account of an injury pension, together with any increase therein under the Pensions (Increase) Acts;

(b) where he has, or is deemed to have, exercised the right of election conferred by paragraph 8 of Part I of Schedule J (*award in certain cases in lieu of deferred pension under Regulation B5*), any payment made or due to him (or his estate) on account of the award mentioned in sub-paragraph (6)(a) of that paragraph;

(c) the capitalised value (calculated in accordance with tables prepared from time to time by the Government Actuary) of any pension or allowance granted in respect of his death (including, where he has allocated a portion of his pension under Regulation B9, any pension payable thereunder to the beneficiary of that allocation); and

(d) any gratuity granted in respect of his death otherwise than under this Regulation,

is less than his aggregate pension contributions in respect of his relevant period of service, the police authority shall pay a gratuity equal to the difference to his legal personal representative.

Supplementary provisions relating to awards on death

Gratuity in lieu of widow's pension

E4.— (1) Save as provided in paragraph (2), this Regulation shall apply to any pension under Part C ("a widow's pension").

(2) Where on the death of her husband before he attained state pensionable age a woman became entitled to a widow's ordinary or special pension under Regulation C1 or C2, the police authority may, subject to Regulation E6, commute for a gratuity that part of the pension (expressed as a weekly amount)

which is in excess of her guaranteed minimum pension or so much of that part as may be commuted without contravening Regulation E6:

Provided that a police authority shall not exercise their discretion under this paragraph unless—

(a) the widow consents, and

(b) they are satisfied that there are sufficient reasons for so doing.

(3) Where the annual amount of any widow's pension does not exceed £104 (other than a pension which does not exceed that amount by reason of the commutation of part thereof under paragraph (2)), the police authority may, at their discretion, commute it for a gratuity.

(4) The provisions of Regulation C9 relating to the termination of a widow's award on remarriage and certain other matters shall apply in relation to a gratuity under this Regulation as they apply in relation to a gratuity under Part C.

(5) A gratuity under this Regulation shall be calculated in accordance with Part II of Schedule E.

(6) Where a widow is entitled to more than one widow's pension in respect of the death of the same person but, in pursuance of Regulation E7, is not entitled to receive, in respect of any particular period, payment on account of more than one of those pensions, those widow's pensions shall be treated for the purposes of this Regulation and of Part II of Schedule E as a single widow's pension and, where one of those pensions is a widow's ordinary or special pension, that single pension shall be treated for the purposes of paragraph (2) as if it were a widow's ordinary or special pension.

(7) This Regulation has effect subject to Regulation J1(6)*(b)* and paragraph 9 of Part II of Schedule J.

Gratuity in lieu of child's allowance

E5.— (1) This Regulation shall apply to any allowance under Part D ("a child's allowance").

(2) Where a child is entitled to a child's allowance, the police authority may, subject to Regulation E6, commute it for a gratuity:

Provided that a police authority shall not exercise their discretion under this paragraph unless—

(a) the child's surviving parent or guardian consents or, where he has no such parent or guardian, the child himself consents, and

(b) they are satisfied that there are sufficient reasons for so doing.

(3) Where the police authority are precluded by reason of the provisions of Regulation E6 from exercising their discretion under the preceding paragraph but otherwise would exercise it, they may, subject to those provisions, exercise that discretion in relation to part only of the allowance.

(4) A gratuity under this Regulation shall be calculated in accordance with Part III of Schedule E.

(5) Where a child is entitled to more than one child's allowance in respect of the death of the same person but, in pursuance of Regulation E7, is not entitled to receive, in respect of any particular period, payment on account of more than one of the allowances, those child's allowances shall be treated for the purposes of this Regulation and of Part III of Schedule E as a single child's allowance.

(6) Paragraph (5) has effect subject to paragraph 6 of Part III of Schedule J.

Limitation on discretion to grant a gratuity in lieu of a pension or allowance

E6.— (1) This Regulation shall apply in the case of a regular policeman who has died while in receipt of an ordinary, short service, ill-health or deferred pension ("the principal pension").

(2) The police authority shall not under Regulation E4(2) or E5 substitute for the whole or any part of a widow's pension or child's allowance payable in respect of such a policeman a gratuity the actuarial equivalent of which (within the meaning of paragraph (3)) when added to that of—

(a) any other gratuity so substituted under Regulation E4(2) or E5, and

(b) any lump sum paid or payable under Regulation B7, where a portion of the principal pension has been commuted,

exceeds a quarter of the capitalised value of the principal pension, any reduction therein under Regulation B7 being ignored.

(3) For the puposes of this Regulation the actuarial equivalent of a gratuity or lump sum and the capitalised value of the principal pension shall, in each case, be that at the time of the husband's or parent's retirement, as calculated by the Government Actuary.

Prevention of duplication

E7.— (1) Subject to paragraph (2), where, but for this Regulation, a person would be entitled to receive, in respect of any particular period, payments on account of more than one award in respect of the death of the same person—

(a) each of the awards being a widow's pension under Part C, or

(b) each of the awards being either a child's allowance under Part D or an adult dependent relative's pension under Regulation E1,

he shall be entitled to receive, in respect of that period, payment on account of one only of those awards; and the award payable shall be that from time to time selected by the person concerned or, in default of such selection where one award is for the time being greater than any other such award, the award which is for the time being the greater.

(2) Nothing in paragraph (1) shall prevent a person from being entitled to receive more than one such pension or allowance as is mentioned in sub-paragraph *(a)* or *(b)* thereof if—

(a) the awards in question are calculated, directly or indirectly, by reference to different periods of pensionable service, and

(b) no award in question falls to be increased in accordance with Regulation E8 or to be determined in accordance with Regulation E10 *(flat-rate award)*.

Increase of widow's pension or child's allowance during first 13 weeks

E8.— (1) This Regulation shall apply to a widow's ordinary, special or accrued pension or a pension under Regulation C5(3) *(pension in case of post-retirement marriage)* and to a child's ordinary, special or accrued allowance where the person in respect of whose death the award is payable was, immediately before his death—

(a) serving as a member of a police force and, in the case of an auxiliary policeman, called up for service as such, or

(b) in receipt of a pension,

and, for the purposes of sub-paragraph *(b)*, the provisions of Regulation A8 relating to persons treated as being in receipt of an ordinary pension shall be disregarded.

(2) A widow's pension to which this Regulation applies shall, so far as necessary, be increased in respect of the first 13 weeks for which it is payable so as to secure that, in respect of each such week, the aggregate amount of the pension and of any children's allowances payable in respect of the same person's death is not less than—

(a) in the case mentioned in paragraph (1)*(a)*, the policeman's pensionable pay for a week immediately before he died, or

(b) in the case mentioned in paragraph (1)*(b)*, the weekly amount of his pension together with any increase therein, immediately before he died, under the Pensions (Increase) Acts;

and, for the purposes of sub-paragraph *(b)*—

(i) there shall be disregarded any reduction in the policeman's pension in consequence of Part VIII of Schedule B *(reduction of pension related to uprating of widow's pension)* or his entitlement to any additional benefit within the meaning of paragraph 4 of Part V of that Schedule *(policeman's injury award)*, and

(ii) where the policeman died while in receipt of both an ordinary, short service or ill-health pension and of an injury pension, the reference therein to the weekly amount of his pension shall be construed as a reference to the aggregate weekly amount of those pensions.

(3) Where a child's allowance to which this Regulation applies is payable in respect of the death of a person who—

(a) in the case of a man, did not leave a widow entitled to a pension which was payable for a continuous period of 13 weeks, or

(b) in the case of a woman, was the child's only surviving parent,

the allowance shall, so far as necessary, be increased in respect of the first 13 weeks for which it is payable so as to secure that, in respect of each such week, it is not less than the amount specified in paragraph (2)*(a)* or *(b)* except that,where 2 or more such allowances are payable in respect of the death of the same person, each allowance shall be so increased that it is of that amount divided by the number of such allowances:

Provided that where a widow's pension is payable in respect of any such week, a child's allowance in respect of the death of the same person shall not be so increased in respect of that week.

(4) Paragraph (1) has effect subject to paragraph 10 of Part II of Schedule J.

Increase of awards (other than flat-rate awards) by reference to the Pensions (Increase) Acts

E9.— (1) Where it is provided that, for the purpose of calculating an award by way of periodical payments or a gratuity ("the relevant award"), an amount shall be increased in accordance with this Regulation, it shall be increased by the amount, if any, by which a corresponding pension, within the meaning of the Pensions (Increase) Act 1971**(a)**, of the amount first mentioned would from time to time be increased under the Pensions (Increase) Acts if—

(a) it were payable to the person entitled to the relevant award and, in relation thereto, he had the like guaranteed minimum pension (if any) as he has in relation to the relevant award;

(b) it were one of the pensions specified in paragraph 43 of Part II of Schedule 2 to the said Act of 1971;

(c) it were not a pension to which section 1(2)*(a)* of the Pensions (Increase) Act 1974**(b)** applies, and

(d) it began, within the meaning of the said Act of 1971, and became payable when the relevant award so began and became payable.

(2) Where the relevant award is a child's allowance, the Pensions (Increase) Acts as applied by paragraph (1) shall have effect as if section 3 were omitted from the Pensions (Increase) Act 1971 and, accordingly, the amount first mentioned in paragraph (1) shall be increased so long as the allowance is payable.

Determination of amount of widow's or child's flat-rate award and increase thereof by reference to the Pensions (Increase) Act 1971

E10.— (1) Where, in respect of any week, the amount of a widow's ordinary or accrued pension or a child's ordinary or accrued allowance falls to be determined by reference to the husband's or relevant parent's rank by reason of an election under paragraph 3 of Part I or paragraph 3 of Part III of Schedule C or under paragraph 5 of Part I, or that paragraph as applied by Part III, of Schedule D, the amount of the award ("the relevant award") shall be the appropriate sum for the purposes of this Regulation increased in accordance with paragraph (6).

(2) In the case of a widow's pension the appropriate sum for the purposes of this Regulation shall be, subject to paragraphs (3) and (5)—

(**a**) 1971 c. 56.   (**b**) 1974 c. 9.

(a) where the husband at the time when he ceased to be a regular policeman held a rank higher than that of inspector, £11.39;

(b) where he so held the rank of inspector, £9.48, or

(c) where he so held a rank lower than inspector, £7.28.

(3) Each of the sums mentioned in paragraph (2) shall be increased by 56p where the relevant award is—

(a) a widow's ordinary pension and the husband was entitled to reckon at least 10 years' pensionable service, or

(b) a widow's accrued pension and the husband ceased to serve as a regular policeman on or after 6th April 1975 and would, had he continued so to serve until he could have been required to retire on account of age, have become entitled to reckon at least 10 years' pensionable service.

(4) In the case of a child's allowance the appropriate sum for the purposes of this Regulation shall be, subject to paragraph (5)—

(a) where the relevant parent at the time when he ceased to be a regular policeman held a rank higher than that of inspector, £3.01 if the allowance would otherwise be determined in accordance with paragraph 1 of Part I of Schedule D or £4.47 if it would otherwise be determined in accordance with paragraph 2 of that Part;

(b) where he so held the rank of inspector, £2.44 if the allowance would otherwise be determined in accordance with the said paragraph 1 or £3.62 if it would otherwise be determined in accordance with the said paragraph 2, or

(c) where he so held a rank lower than that of inspector, £2.07 if the allowance would otherwise be determined in accordance with the said paragraph 1 or £3.05 if it would otherwise be determined in accordance with the said paragraph 2,

and in this paragraph any reference to Part I of Schedule D includes a reference to that Part as applied by Part III of that Schedule.

(5) For the purposes of paragraphs (2) and (4) a chief inspector in the City of London police force shall be treated as if he held a rank higher than that of inspector.

(6) The appropriate sum shall be increased by the amount by which a corresponding pension, within the meaning of the Pensions (Increase) Act 1971, of a weekly amount equal to the said sum would from time to time be increased under the said Act of 1971 in respect of a week if—

(a) it were payable to the person entitled to the relevant award, in relation thereto he had the like guaranteed minimum pension (if any) as he has in relation to the relevant award and he satisfied the qualifying conditions within the meaning of the said Act of 1971;

(b) it were an official pension within the meaning aforesaid;

(c) it began, within the meaning aforesaid, on 30th June 1978, and

(d) no account were taken of the provisions of the Pensions Increase (Annual Review) Order 1978(**a**),

but, in performing the necessary calculations, sums shall be expressed to the nearest penny (a half penny counting as a whole penny).

PART F

PENSIONABLE SERVICE AND TRANSFER VALUES

Reckoning of pensionable service

F1.— (1) The pensionable service reckonable by a member of a police force at any date (in these Regulations referred to as the "relevant date") shall be determined in accordance with the succeeding provisions of these Regulations:

Provided that there shall not be reckonable by a regular policeman any period of unpaid maternity leave granted in the case of a woman.

(2) Any reference in this Part to approved service reckonable under the former Acts shall include—

(a) a reference to approved service which would have been so reckonable if there had been omitted from section 7(1) of the Police Pensions Act 1921(**b**) the words "but shall not include" to the end, and

(b) a reference to approved service which would have been so reckonable if there had been omitted from section 8(1) of the said Act the words "in which he has completed not less than one year's approved service, and".

(3) Paragraph (1) has effect subject to paragraphs 5 and 6 of Part IV of Schedule J.

Current service

F2.— (1) Subject to the provisions of these Regulations, there shall be reckonable by a regular policeman in respect of his service as such in the force in which he is or was serving on the relevant date, being service since he last joined or rejoined that force before that date—

(a) all such service on or after 5th July 1948, and

(b) where he last joined or rejoined the force before 5th July 1948, any period of approved service which he was entitled to reckon immediately before that date under the former Acts.

(2) There shall be reckonable by an auxiliary policeman as pensionable service, in respect of his service in the force in which he is or was serving on the relevant date, all his active service as such since he was last called up for active service before that date.

(3) There shall be reckonable as pensionable service by a member of an overseas corps who is not, or was not, on the relevant date a reversionary

---

(**a**) S.I. 1978/1211.　　(**b**) 1921 c. 31.

member of a home police force all his service as a member of an overseas corps, while not being such a reversionary member, since he last became a member of an overseas corps before the relevant date.

(4) Paragraph (1) has effect subject to paragraph 6(2) of Part VII of Schedule J.

Previous service reckonable without payment

F3.— (1) There shall be reckonable by a regular policeman as pensionable service—

(a) where from being a regular policeman in another force he transferred on or after 5th July 1948 to the force in which he is or was serving on the relevant date, any period of pensionable service reckonable by him immediately before the transfer;

(b) where he previously retired with an ill-health pension or a pension under the former Acts from the force in which he is or was serving on the relevant date, that pension was terminated in whole or in part under Regulation K1 or any corresponding provision of the former Regulations or former Acts, and he rejoined the force on or after 5th July 1948, any period of pensionable service or of approved service under the former Acts, as the case may be, reckonable by him at the time he retired;

(c) where he previously retired with a pension under the former Acts in respect of a non-accidental injury from the force in which he is or was serving on the relevant date, and the approved service under the former Acts reckonable by him at the time he retired is reckonable as pensionable service under sub-paragraph *(b)*, the period during which he was in receipt of the pension;

(d) where the relevant date is 15th May 1950 or any later date and he left the Royal Ulster Constabulary with the consent of the chief officer of that force and the approval of the Police Authority for Northern Ireland for the purpose of becoming a regular policeman in a home police force, any period of approved or pensionable service which was reckonable by him, immediately before he so left, for the purposes of the Royal Ulster Constabulary pensions legislation;

(e) where he previously engaged for a period of service in the Royal Ulster Constabulary as mentioned in section 2(1) of the Police Act 1969**(a)** and he exercises the right of reversion to a home police force conferred by the said section 2(1) or, on that right arising, does not exercise it but joins another home police force, any period of pensionable service which was reckonable by him for the purposes mentioned in sub-paragraph *(d)*, immediately before he left the Royal Ulster Constabulary;

(f) where from being a member of the British Airports Authority constabulary he was transferred to the force in which he is or was serving on the relevant date by an order under section 6 of the Policing of Airports Act 1974**(b)**, any period of pensionable service reckonable by him immediately before the transfer for the purposes of the superannuation scheme then applicable to him:

(a) 1969 c. 63.   (b) 1974 c. 41.

Provided that—

(i) where he was then, for the purposes of that scheme, purchasing added years by annual payments, those added years shall only be taken into account to the extent that they would have been taken into account for the purposes of a deferred pension under the said scheme if he had become entitled to such a pension immediately before he in fact transferred;

(ii) where he had been granted a back service credit within the meaning of the said scheme which exceeded the previous service by reason of which it was granted, otherwise than by reason of the previous service being wholly or partly service in a particular territory overseas, only that part of the credit which does not exceed the previous service shall be taken into account.

(2) Where a regular policeman—

(a) transferred as mentioned in paragraph (1)(a) during a leap-year beginning on or after 1st January 1984, or

(b) became a regular policeman in a home police force in the circumstances mentioned in paragraph (1)(d) or (e), during a leap-year beginning on or after 1st January 1988,

and throughout the leap-year in question had continuous service as a regular policeman or, as the case may be, as either a regular policeman or a member of the Royal Ulster Constabulary then, notwithstanding anything in paragraph (1)(a), (d) or (e), the pensionable service reckonable by him by reason of his continuous service in that year shall be a year's, and not 366 days', pensionable service.

Previous service reckonable on payment

F4.— (1) Subject to Regulation F9(4) (*interchange arrangements*), there shall be reckonable by a regular policeman as pensionable service, in the circumstances specified in this Regulation, the periods so specified before he last joined or rejoined the force before the relevant date, subject to his having made to the police authority the appropriate payment.

(2) Where before the relevant date he retired without a pension (including a pension under the former Acts) from the same force as that in which he is or was serving on the relevant date—

(a) the period shall be any period of pensionable service or approved service under the former Acts reckonable by him at the time he retired, not being a period of approved service reckonable by virtue of Regulation F2(1)(b), and

(b) the appropriate payment shall be an amount equal to any gratuity, return of pension contributions or rateable deductions, as the case may be, which he may have received on his retirement together with the balance outstanding immediately before his retirement of any sum he had undertaken to pay as mentioned in Part I of Schedule F, so however that where, before his retirement and in pursuance of an election under Regulation 58 or 59 of the Regulations of 1973 or under any of the provisions mentioned in Regulation 57(2) of those Regulations, he had paid additional or further contributions or had made an additional or further payment by way of a lump sum, the appropriate payment shall be reduced by the amount he had paid by way of such contributions or lump sum and he shall be treated for the purposes of these Regulations as having neither paid nor elected to pay such contributions or lump sum.

(3) Where before the relevant date he retired with a deferred pension but has relinquished his entitlement thereto by written notice given to the police authority for the purposes of this Regulation or Regulation F5 (or of the corresponding provisions of the Regulations of 1973), paragraph (2) shall have effect as though he had retired without a pension and, where immediately before his retirement he was paying such additional or further contributions as are mentioned in paragraph (2)(b), the amount he had paid by way of such contributions shall be repaid to him and he shall be treated for the purposes of these Regulations as having neither paid nor elected to pay such contributions.

(4) Where he previously served as a member of the first class of the police reserve, of the Police War Reserve or of Class A of the Women's Auxiliary Police Corps or, subject to paragraph (6), as a special constable—

(a) the period shall be half the period of active service as a member of the first class of the police reserve during which he was not in receipt of a pension (including a pension under the former Acts), half the period of active service as a member of the Police War Reserve, half the period of active service as a member of the Women's Auxiliary Police Corps, whether in Class A of that Corps or otherwise, or half the period of service as a special constable while serving as such in a whole-time capacity and in receipt of pay in respect of such service, as the case may be, and

(b) the appropriate payment shall be 5% of, in the case of a man, £4.50, or in the case of a woman, £3.95, in respect of each week which he is entitled under this paragraph to reckon as pensionable service.

(5) Where he was a person to whom section 1 of the Police and Firemen (War Service) Act 1939(a), as extended by Regulation 60DA of the Defence (General) Regulations 1939(b), applied—

(a) the period shall be the period during which he was engaged in war work within the meaning of the said Defence Regulation during the year 1947, and

(b) the appropriate payment shall be the aggregate of the payments that he would have been required to make under the said Act as so extended in respect of the said period if the emergency that was the occasion of the passing of that Act had not come to an end.

(6) Except where the appropriate payment has been made before 1st January 1963, the references in paragraph (4) to a special constable shall be construed as references only to a special constable appointed—

(a) in England and Wales, under the Special Constables Act 1831(c) or section 196 of the Municipal Corporations Act 1882(d);

(a) 1939 c. 103.
(b) S.R.&O. 1939/927; Regulation 60DA was added by S.R.&O. 1941/1038.
(c) 1831 c. 41.   (d) 1882 c. 50.

(b) in Scotland, under section 96 of the Burgh Police (Scotland) Act 1892(**a**) or the corresponding provisions of any local enactment.

(7) Paragraph (3) has effect subject to paragraph 4 of Part IV of Schedule J.

Previous service reckonable at discretion of police authority

F5.— (1) Subject to Regulation F9(4) (*interchange arrangements*), if the appropriate police authority in their discretion have so decided, there shall be reckonable by a regular policeman as pensionable service, in the circumstances specified in this Regulation, the periods so specified before he last joined or rejoined the force before the relevant date, subject, in the case of such a period as is mentioned in paragraph (2), to his having made to that police authority the appropriate payment.

(2) Where before the relevant date he ceased to serve as a regular policeman without a pension (including a pension under the former Acts)—

(a) the period shall be the whole of any period of pensionable service, or approved service under the former Acts, reckonable by him at the time he ceased to serve, not being a period reckonable by virtue of Regulation F2(1)*(b)* or F4(2), or so much of that period as the appropriate police authority in their discretion think fit;

(b) the appropriate police authority shall be the authority of the force in which he is or was serving on the relevant date, and

(c) the appropriate payment shall be the whole or the proportionate part of an amount equal to any gratuity or return of pension contributions or rateable deductions, as the case may be, which he may have received on ceasing to serve together with the balance outstanding immediately before so ceasing of any sum he had undertaken to pay as mentioned in Part I of Schedule F so however that where, before so ceasing and in pursuance of an election under Regulation 58 or 59 of the Regulations of 1973 or under any of the provisions mentioned in Regulation 57(2) of those Regulations, he had paid additional or further contributions or had made an additional or further payment by way of a lump sum, the appropriate payment shall be reduced by the whole or the proportionate part of the amount he had paid by way of such contributions or lump sum and he shall be treated for the purposes of these Regulations as having neither paid nor elected to pay such contributions or lump sum.

For the purposes of sub-paragraph *(c)* where the police authority exercise their discretion under sub-paragraph *(a)* so as to allow the policeman to reckon as pensionable service part only of the period first mentioned therein, "the proportionate part" means the part which bears the same proportion to the whole as that part of the period so mentioned bears to the whole thereof.

(3) Where before the relevant date he ceased to serve with a deferred pension but has relinquished his entitlement thereto by written notice given to the police authority for the purposes of this Regulation or of Regulation F4 (or of the corresponding provisions of the Regulations of 1973), paragraph (2) shall have effect as though he had ceased to serve without a pension and, where

---

(**a**) 1892 c. 55.

immediately before ceasing to serve he was paying such additional or further contributions as are mentioned in paragraph (2)*(c)*, the amount he had paid by way of such contributions shall be repaid to him by the police authority of the force in which he ceased to serve and he shall be treated for the purposes of these Regulations as having neither paid nor elected to pay such contributions:

Provided that the police authority shall not so exercise their discretion under paragraph (2)*(a)* that the period of pensionable service reckonable thereunder is less than that taken into account for the purposes of calculating the deferred pension.

(4) Where a serviceman (1939–1945), after receiving a pension under the Police and Firemen (War Service) Acts 1939 and 1944(**a**), rejoined the force in which he is or was serving on the relevant date, being the force of the police authority by whom the pension was payable—

(a) the period shall be the whole of the period for which he was in receipt of the said pension or such part thereof as the said police authority have, in their discretion, decided shall be reckonable;

(b) the appropriate police authority shall be the police authority of the force in which he is or was serving on the relevant date.

(5) Paragraphs (2) and (3) have effect subject to paragaph 4 of Part IV of Schedule J.

Previous service reckonable under current interchange arrangements

F6.— (1) Save as provided in paragraphs (2) and (5), this Regulation shall apply to a regular policeman—

(a) who before he last became a regular policeman before the relevant date was in service or employment (otherwise than as a member of a police force) by reason of which he was subject to superannuation arrangements in pursuance of which a transfer value may be paid to the police authority (in this Regulation and in Section 2 of Part II of Schedule F such service or employment and such superannuation arrangements are referred to as "former service" and "former superannuation arrangements");

(b) subject to paragraph (3), who, before the relevant date, last became a regular policeman on or after 1st April 1972, and

(c) in respect of whom a transfer value relating to his former service has, in pursuance of his former superannuation arrangements, been paid to the police authority of the force in which he is serving on the relevant date.

(2) This Regulation shall not apply in the case of a regular policeman who, before the relevant date, last became such before 6th April 1978 if either—

(a) he or his widow elected under paragraph (1A) of Regulation 51 of the Regulations of 1973 that that Regulation should apply in his case, or

(b) such a transfer value as is mentioned in paragraph (1)*(c)* was received in his case before 1st January 1974.

(**a**) 1939 c. 103, 1944 c. 22.

(3) If the police authority have so determined in the case of a particular regular policeman who, before the relevant date, last became such on or after 5th July 1948 but before 1st April 1972, this Regulation shall have effect as if paragraph (1)*(b)* were omitted.

(4) There shall be reckonable by a regular policeman to whom this Regulation applies, in respect of his former service, a period of pensionable service calculated in accordance with Sections 2 and 3 of Part II of Schedule F.

(5) Notwithstanding anything in this Regulation, the provisions thereof shall not apply—

(a) where the regular policeman concerned is entitled to reckon pensionable service under Regulation F3(1)*(d)*, *(e)* or *(f)* by reason of former service in the Royal Ulster Constabulary or in the British Airports Authority constabulary; or

(b) where the regular policeman concerned had a guaranteed minimum in relation to the pension provided by the former superannuation arrangements unless—

(i) those arrangements are of a kind mentioned in paragraph 1(2) of Section 2 of Part II of Schedule F, or

(ii) that guaranteed minimum is no greater than a notional deferred pension calculated by reference to the pensionable service which, under the said Section 2, would be reckonable if the transfer value were paid.

Previous service reckonable under preserved interchange arrangements

F7.— (1) Save as provided in paragraph (2) and subject to paragraph 5 of Section 1 of Part III of Schedule F, this Regulation shall apply to a regular policeman—

(a) who before he last became a regular policeman before the relevant date was in such service or employment as is mentioned in Section 1, 2 or 3 of Part III of Schedule F by reason of which he was subject to superannuation arrangements (in this Regulation such service or employment and the Section in which it is mentioned are referred to as "former service" and "the Section in question" and such superannuation arrangements are referred to as "former superannuation arrangements");

(b) who has served as a regular policeman on or after the date specified in the Section in question in relation to his former service;

(c) who last became a regular policeman before the relevant date within 12 months of the termination of his former service or within such longer period as may be agreed, in the circumstances of his case, between the police authority and the authority specified in the Section in question in relation to his former service;

(d) in respect of whom such a transfer value relating to his former service as is mentioned in the Section in question has been paid to the police authority of the force in which he is or was serving on the relevant date, and

(e) who, within 6 months of the date specified in the Section in question in relation to the former service or 3 months of last becoming a regular

policeman before the relevant date, whichever is the later, or within such longer period as the police authority may allow in his case—

(i) has paid, or has undertaken to pay as mentioned in Part I of Schedule F, a sum equal to the balance of any liability outstanding, immediately before he ceased to be engaged in his former service, in respect of payments or contributions he was then making as a condition of reckoning past service as contributing service or otherwise for the purposes of the former superannuation arrangements, being service taken into account for the purpose of calculating the transfer value referred to in sub-paragraph *(d)*, and

(ii) has paid to the police authority a sum equal to the amount, if any, by which the transfer value referred to in sub-paragraph *(d)* falls to be reduced on account of any sum paid to him under the former superannuation arrangements by way of return of contributions.

(2) Nothing in this Regulation shall apply—

(a) in the case of a regular policeman who, before the relevant date, last became a regular policeman on or after 1st April 1972 unless he last so became such before 6th April 1978 and either—

(i) paragraph (1)*(d)* was satisfied in his case before 1st January 1974, or

(ii) he or his widow elected under paragraph (1A) of Regulation 51 of the Regulations of 1973 that that Regulation should apply in his case;

(b) in relation to the transfer of a member of the British Airports Authority constabulary to a police force by an order under section 6 of the Policing of Airports Act 1974(**a**), or

(c) in relation to a regular policeman in whose case Regulation F6 applies in consequence of the exercise by the police authority of the discretion mentioned in paragraph (3) of that Regulation.

(3) Subject to paragraph (4), there shall be reckonable by a regular policeman to whom this Regulation applies, as pensionable service in respect of his former service, 3 quarters of the period specified in paragraph (5).

(4) Where under the former superannuation arrangements—

(a) the maximum pension payable (otherwise than on retirement occasioned by injury or ill-health) is payable where the person concerned has been engaged for a period of 30 years in service which counts in full for the purposes of those arrangements, or

(b) after 20 years of such service, each year of service counts as 2 years service for the said purposes,

paragraph (3) shall not apply but there shall be reckonable as therein mentioned the whole of the period specified in paragraph (5) so, however, that, where under the former superannuation arrangements such provision as is mentioned in sub-paragraph *(a)* or *(b)* is made in relation only to service or employment of a description designated therein (in this paragraph referred to as "designated

---

(**a**) 1974 c. 41.

service") and the regular policeman's former service included designated service, there shall be reckonable as aforesaid—

> (i) the whole of that part of the period specified in paragraph (5) as is referable to designated service, and
>
> (ii) 3 quarters of that part of that period as is not so referable.

(5) The period referred to in paragraphs (3) and (4) shall be—

> *(a)* the period of service which is reckonable for the purpose of calculating the transfer value referred to in paragraph (1)*(d)*, or
>
> *(b)* where separate calculations are made in respect of contributing and non-contributing service reckonable for the purpose of calculating the said transfer value, the aggregate of the period of contributing service and half the period of non-contributing service which is so reckonable.

Transfer values payable between police authorities

F8.— (1) This Regulation shall apply where a regular policeman—

> *(a)* by reason of previous service in a police force becomes entitled to reckon pensionable service either—
>
>> (i) by virtue of Regulation F3(1)*(a)*, or
>>
>> (ii) by virtue of Regulation F5 in the circumstances mentioned in paragraph (2) of that Regulation (including that paragraph as it has effect by virtue of paragraph (3) thereof), or
>
> *(b)* has left a police force and joined the Royal Ulster Constabulary with such consent as is mentioned in Regulation A17(2) and the police authority for Northern Ireland are contingently liable to make payments to or in respect of him under the Royal Ulster Constabulary pensions legislation;

and in this Regulation any reference to the former force or police authority is a reference to the police force mentioned in sub-paragraph *(a)* or, as the case may be, sub-paragraph *(b)* or the police authority of that force and any reference to the current police authority is a reference to the police authority of the force of which the regular policeman is a member, or, as the case may be, to the police authority for Northern Ireland.

(2) Where this Regulation applies the former police authority shall pay to the current police authority a transfer value calculated in accordance with Sections 1 and 3 of Part II of Schedule F:

Provided that where the current police authority exercise their discretion under Regulation F5(2)*(a)* to permit the reckoning as pensionable service of part only of the period mentioned therein, only the corresponding proportion of the transfer value calculated as aforesaid shall be payable.

(3) Where this Regulation applies and the person concerned was entitled to an award on retiring from his former force but has received no payment in respect thereof, he shall cease to be so entitled.

(4) Paragraph (2) has effect subject to paragraph 1(2) of Part V of Schedule J.

Transfer values payable under interchange arrangements

F9.— (1) Save as provided in paragraph (2) and subject to paragraph (5), this Regulation shall apply to a regular policeman—

(a) who, not having attained state pensionable age, retires or retired on or after 1st April 1972 and—

(i) was not entitled to a pension on so retiring or, if so entitled, has neither received any payment in respect thereof nor given any notice of commutation relating thereto which has become effective, and

(ii) has not received any award on so retiring by way of repayment of his aggregate pension contributions or a gratuity;

(b) who subsequently enters or entered service or employment (otherwise than as a member of a police force) by reason of which he is subject to superannuation arrangements (hereafter in this Regulation referred to as "new service") and in his new service is, or subject to the payment of a transfer value would be, entitled to reckon service for superannuation purposes by reason of his service as a member of a police force, and

(c) who, within 6 months of entering the new service, or within such longer period as the police authority may allow in the circumstances of the particular case, has given written notice to the police authority maintaining his former force of his desire that this Regulation should apply in his case.

(2) Nothing in this Regulation shall apply to a regular policeman—

(a) in whose case a transfer value—

(i) is payable or has been paid to the police authority for Northern Ireland under Regulation F8 or Regulation 84 of the Regulations of 1973, or

(ii) where he retired before 6th April 1978, has been paid before that date under the Regulations of 1973 as originally made, or

(b) who has a guaranteed minimum in relation to the pension provided by these Regulations unless either—

(i) the superannuation arrangements applicable to the new service constitute a contracted-out scheme in relation to him when the transfer value is paid, or

(ii) a contributions equivalent premium relating to the period ending with his retirement has been paid in respect of him by the police authority and not repaid.

(3) Where this Regulation applies the police authority of the force from which the regular policeman retired ("the former police authority") may pay a transfer value calculated in accordance with Sections 1 and 3 of Part II of Schedule F to the authority or person empowered to receive such payments for the purposes of the superannuation arrangements applicable to the new service and shall so pay such a transfer value where those superannuation arrangements—

(a) are contained in a public general Act of Parliament or were made under such an Act by a Minister of the Crown, or

    (b) are contained in Northern Ireland legislation being public general legislation or were made under such legislation by a Minister of the Crown (including a Northern Ireland Minister) or by a Northern Ireland ministry, department or head of department, or

    (c) are contained in a retirement benefits scheme approved under Chapter II of Part II of the Finance Act 1970(**a**) or section 222 of the Income and Corporation Taxes Act 1970(**b**), or

    (d) provide for the purposes thereof for a superannuation fund which is wholly approved under section 208 of the Income and Corporation Taxes Act 1970, or

    (e) provide, in the event of the regular policeman again becoming such in his former police force, for the payment of a transfer value which the police authority are satisfied would be calculated in like manner as under any superannuation arrangements contained in, or made by a Minister of the Crown under, a public general Act of Parliament.

(4) Where the former police authority decided, or were required, to pay a transfer value as mentioned in paragraph (3)—

    (a) if the regular policeman concerned was, on retiring, entitled to a pension or such an award as is mentioned in paragraph (1)*(a)*(ii), he shall cease to be so entitled, and

    (b) if he again becomes a regular policeman, neither Regulation F4 nor F5 (*reckoning of previous service*) shall apply in relation to the pensionable service which he was entitled to reckon at the time he retired unless before 1st April 1987 the former police authority had decided, or were required, to pay a transfer value in pursuance of Regulation 85 of the Regulations of 1973.

(5) In the case of a regular policeman who has received such an award as is mentioned in paragraph (1)*(a)*(ii) but has—

    (a) entered the new service within 12 months of retiring or such longer period as the former police authority may allow in the circumstances of his case, and

    (b) within 6 months of entering the new service, or within such longer period as the former police authority may allow in the circumstances of his case, has paid to that authority an amount equal to that of the said award,

paragraph (1) shall have effect as if sub-paragraph *(a)*(ii) were omitted.

Part G

Pensionable Pay and Contributions

Pensionable and average pensionable pay

G1.— (1) The pensionable pay of a member of a police force at any time means his pay at the rate to which he is or was then entitled, account being taken of any retrospective increase in that rate.

    (**a**) 1970 c. 24.   (**b**) 1970 c. 10.

(2) The average pensionable pay of a member of a police force shall, subject to paragraphs (3) and (4), be the aggregate of his pensionable pay in respect of the period of a year ending with the relevant date:

Provided that where he was entitled to pensionable pay for part only of that period, the said aggregate shall be multiplied by the reciprocal of the fraction of the year for which he was entitled to pensionable pay.

(3) Where the amount of a member of a police force's average pensionable pay, determined in accordance with paragraph (2), is less than the amount it would have been had he not suffered a temporary reduction in rate of pay by way of punishment, it shall be increased by the difference between the two said amounts.

(4) Where the amount of a member of a police force's average pensionable pay, determined in accordance with paragraphs (2) and (3), is less than the amount it would have been had the relevant date been the corresponding date in one of the two preceding years (whichever year yields the higher amount), it shall be increased by the difference between the two said amounts.

(5) Where an award is made to or in respect of a member of a police force the relevant date for the purpose of determining his average pensionable pay shall be—

  (a) in the case of a regular policeman, the date of his last day of service as such in the force of the police authority by whom the award is payable;

  (b) in the case of an auxiliary policeman, the date of the last day of the continuous period of active service as such during which he received the injury which resulted in disablement or death;

  (c) in the case of an overseas policeman who is not a reversionary member of a home police force, the date of the last day of the tour of overseas service during which he received the injury which resulted in disablement or death.

(6) Where a regular policeman has served as a member of the Royal Ulster Constabulary on or after 1st May 1970 and during part of the period of 3 years ending with the date mentioned in paragraph (5)*(a)*, then paragraphs (2), (3) and (4) shall have effect in his case as if any reference in paragraph (2) to pensionable pay included a reference to such pay within the meaning of the Royal Ulster Constabulary pensions legislation.

(7) For the purposes of these Regulations, a serviceman shall be deemed to be entitled, in respect of his period of relevant service in the armed forces, to the pay to which he would have been entitled if he had continued to serve in his former force.

(8) Where for the purpose of calculating an award to a widow, child or dependent relative it is necessary to determine average pensionable pay for a week, it shall be taken to be average pensionable pay divided by 52 $\frac{1}{6}$.

(9) Paragraph (2) has effect subject to paragraph 5(4)*(c)* of Part VII of Schedule J.

Pension contributions payable by regular policeman

G2.— (1) A regular policeman shall pay to the police authority pension contributions at the rate of 1p a week less than—

(a) in the case of a man, 11% of his pensionable pay, or

(b) in the case of a woman, 8% of her pensionable pay.

(2) The pension contributions payable under paragraph (1) upon each instalment of pay shall fall due at the same time as that instalment and may, without prejudice to any other method of payment, be discharged by way of a reduction of the appropriate amount made by the police authority from the said instalment.

Additional and further contributions

G3.— (1) This Regulation shall apply to a regular policeman who elected, in accordance with Regulation 58(2) or (3) of the Regulations of 1973, to pay additional or further pension contributions, and whose liability thereunder to pay those contributions did not cease before 1st April 1987.

(2) A man to whom this Regulation applies shall continue to pay additional or, as the case may be, further pension contributions until, subject to paragraph (4), the relevant date mentioned in paragraph (3), and Schedule G shall have effect for the purpose of calculating the amount of such additional or further pension contributions.

(3) For the purposes of paragraph (2), the relevant date is the date on which the man becomes entitled to reckon 25 years' pensionable service so, however, that in determining the said date there shall be disregarded pensionable service reckonable by reason of service or employment before 1st April 1973 which he was not entitled to reckon on 1st April 1973.

(4) Additional or further pension contributions payable under this Regulation shall cease to be payable on retirement; but where a regular policeman was paying such contributions immediately before retiring with an ordinary pension that pension shall be reduced in accordance with paragraph 6 of Part VIII of Schedule B.

(5) Regulation G2(2) shall apply in relation to the payment of additional or further contributions under this Regulation as it applies in relation to the payment of pension contributions under Regulation G2(1).

PART H

APPEALS AND MEDICAL QUESTIONS

Reference of medical questions

H1.— (1) Subject as hereinafter provided, the question whether a person is entitled to any and, if so, what awards under these Regulations shall be determined in the first instance by the police authority.

(2) Where the police authority are considering whether a person is

permanently disabled, they shall refer for decision to a duly qualified medical practitioner selected by them the following questions—

(a) whether the person concerned is disabled;

(b) whether the disablement is likely to be permanent;

and, if they are further considering whether to grant an injury pension, shall so refer the following questions:—

(c) whether the disablement is the result of an injury received in the execution of duty, and

(d) the degree of the person's disablement;

and, if they are considering whether to revise an injury pension, shall so refer question (d) above.

(3) A police authority, if they are considering the exercise of their powers under Regulation K3 (reduction of pension in case of default), shall refer for decision to a duly qualified medical practitioner selected by them the question whether the person concerned has brought about or substantially contributed to the disablement by his own default.

(4) The decision of the selected medical practitioner on the questions referred to him under this Regulation shall be expressed in the form of a certificate and shall, subject to Regulations H2 and H3, be final.

Appeal to medical referee

H2.— (1) Where a person has been informed of the determination of the police authority on any question which involves the reference of questions under Regulation H1 to a selected medical practitioner, he shall, if, within 14 days after being so informed or such further period as the police authority may allow, he applies to the police authority for a copy of the certificate of the selected medical practitioner, be supplied with such a copy.

(2) If the person concerned is dissatisfied with the decision of the selected medical practitioner as set out in his certificate, he may, within 14 days after being supplied with the certificate or such longer period as the police authority may allow, and subject to and in accordance with the provisions of Schedule H, give notice to the police authority that he appeals against the said decision, and the police authority shall notify the Secretary of State accordingly, and the Secretary of State shall appoint an independent person or persons (hereafter in these Regulations referred to as the "medical referee") to decide the appeal.

(3) The decision of the medical referee shall, if he disagrees with any part of the certificate of the selected medical practitioner, be expressed in the form of a certificate of his decision on any of the questions referred to the selected medical practitioner on which he disagrees with the latter's decision, and the decision of the medical referee shall, subject to the provisions of Regulation H3, be final.

Further reference to medical authority

H3.— (1) A court hearing an appeal under Regulation H5 or a tribunal hearing an appeal under Regulation H6 may, if they consider that the evidence before the medical authority who has given the final decision was inaccurate or inadequate, refer the decision of that authority to him for reconsideration in the light of such facts as the court or the tribunal may direct, and the medical authority shall accordingly reconsider his decision and, if necessary, issue a fresh certificate which, subject to any further reconsideration under this paragraph, shall be final.

(2) The police authority and the claimant may, by agreement, refer any final decision of a medical authority who has given such a decision to him for reconsideration on fresh evidence, and he shall accordingly reconsider his decision and, if necessary, issue a fresh certificate, which, subject to any further reconsideration under this paragraph or paragraph (1), shall be final.

(3) If a court or tribunal decide, or a claimant and the police authority agree, to refer a decision to the medical authority for reconsideration under this Regulation and that medical authority is unable or unwilling to act, the decision may be referred to a duly qualified medical practitioner selected by the court or tribunal or, as the case may be, agreed upon by the claimant and the police authority, and his decision shall have effect as if it were that of the medical authority who gave the decision which is to be reconsidered.

(4) In this Regulation a medical authority who has given a final decision means the selected medical practitioner, if the time for appeal from his decision has expired without an appeal to a medical referee being made, and the medical referee, if there has been such an appeal.

Refusal to be medically examined

H4. If a question is referred to a medical authority under Regulation H1, H2 or H3 and the person concerned wilfully or negligently fails to submit himself to such medical examination or to attend such interviews as the medical authority may consider necessary in order to enable him to make his decision, then—

  (a) if the question arises otherwise than on an appeal to a medical referee, the police authority may make their determination on such evidence and medical advice as they in their discretion think necessary;

  (b) if the question arises on an appeal to a medical referee, the appeal shall be deemed to be withdrawn.

Appeal by a member of a home police force

H5.— (1) Where a member of a home police force, or a person claiming an award in respect of such a member, is aggrieved by the refusal of the police authority to admit a claim to receive as of right an award or a larger award than that granted, or by the forfeiture under Regulation K5 by the police authority of any award granted to or in respect of such a member, he may, subject to Regulation H7, appeal to the Crown Court and that court, after enquiring into the case, may make such order in the matter as appears to it to be just.

(2) In the case of a member of a Scottish police force, paragraph (1) shall have effect as if any reference to the Crown Court were a reference to the sheriff having jurisdiction in the place where the person concerned last served as such a member.

(3) The provisions of section 5(1) and (5) of the Police Pensions Act 1948(**a**) (*appeals*), as they have effect under section 12(2) of the Police Pensions Act 1976(**b**), shall not apply in relation to an award under these Regulations.

Appeal by overseas policeman, inspector of constabulary or central police officer

H6.— (1) This Regulation shall apply in relation to—

(a) an overseas policeman;

(b) an inspector or assistant inspector of constabulary, or

(c) a central police officer,

and any such person is hereafter in this Regulation referred to as an officer to whom this Regulation applies.

(2) Where an officer to whom this Regulation applies, or a person claiming an award in respect of such an officer, is aggrieved by the refusal of the Secretary of State as police authority to admit a claim to receive as of right an award or a larger award than that granted, or by the forfeiture under Regulation K5, by the Secretary of State as police authority, of any award granted to or in respect of such an officer, he may, subject to Regulation H7, give notice of appeal to the Secretary of State; and any such notice shall be in writing and shall specify the grounds of the appeal.

(3) The Secretary of State, on receiving such notice of appeal, shall appoint an appeal tribunal (hereafter in this Regulation referred to as the tribunal), consisting of 3 persons, including a barrister or solicitor of not less than 7 years' standing and a retired member of a police force who, before he retired, held a rank not lower than that of superintendent.

(4) The time and place for the hearing, or any postponed or adjourned hearing, of the appeal shall be determined by the tribunal, which shall give reasonable notice thereof to the appellant and to the Secretary of State as police authority (hereafter in this Regulation described as the parties).

(5) Either party may be represented before the tribunal by counsel, by a solicitor or by such other person as appears to him appropriate, adduce evidence and cross-examine witnesses.

(6) In the case of an appeal under this Regulation the tribunal shall have regard to the practice of the Crown Court in the case of an appeal under Regulation H5 and the rules of evidence applicable in the case of such an appeal shall apply in the case of an appeal under this Regulation.

(7) Subject to the preceding provisions of this Regulation, the tribunal shall determine its own procedure.

(8) The tribunal, after enquiring into the case and arriving at a decision thereon, may make such order in the matter as appears to it just, which order shall state the reasons for the decision; and each of the parties shall be entitled to a copy of any such order.

(**a**) 1948 c. 24.   (**b**) 1976 c. 35.

(9) An appeal shall lie on a point of law from any decision of a tribunal under this Regulation to the High Court in accordance with rules of court.

(10) In the case of an officer to whom this Regulation applies and who—

    (a) in the case of an overseas policeman or a central police officer, immediately before becoming such, was a member of a Scottish police force, or

    (b) in the case of an inspector or assistant inspector of constabulary, was appointed (or treated as appointed) under section 33 or 34 of the Police (Scotland) Act 1967(**a**);

this Regulation shall have effect as if—

    (i) any reference to a barrister were a reference to an advocate, and

    (ii) any reference to the Crown Court or the High Court were a reference to the sheriff or, as the case may be, the Court of Session.

Limitations on appeals

H7.— (1) An appeal shall not lie under Regulation H5 or H6 against anything done by a police authority in the exercise of a power conferred by these Regulations which is expressly declared thereby to be a power which they are to exercise in their discretion.

(2) Subject to Regulation H3(1), in any proceedings under Regulation H5 or H6 the court or tribunal shall be bound by any final decision of a medical authority within the meaning of Regulation H3.

PART I

SERVICEMEN

Servicemen to whom Part I applies

I1. This Part shall, subject to Regulation A3 (*exclusion of old cases*) and Regulation I8(1) (*pension contributions*), have effect in the case of a serviceman whose period of relevant service in the armed forces ends or has ended on or after 5th July 1948 or who, having resumed service as a regular policeman, has served as such on or after 1st April 1972:

Provided that only Regulation I4 shall have effect in the case of a serviceman other than a serviceman (1939–1945), whose period of relevant service in the armed forces ended on or after 5th July 1948 but before 15th July 1950 and that Regulation shall have effect only where he was called up for service in the armed forces under the National Service Acts 1939 to 1946(**b**), the National Service Act 1947(**c**) or the National Service Act 1948(**d**), or required for training or called into actual service or called out for training or for permanent service in the armed forces in pursuance of his obligations as a member of the territorial army or any reserve of the armed forces.

(**a**) 1967 c. 77.
(**b**) 1939 c. 81, 1940 c. 22, 1941 c. 15, 1942 c. 3, 1946 c. 38.
(**c**) 1947 c. 31.   (**d**) 1948 c. 64.

Awards to servicemen

I2.— (1) This Regulation shall apply to a serviceman who at the end of his period of relevant service in the armed forces is or was permanently disabled for the performance of duty as a regular policeman.

(2) A serviceman to whom this Regulation applies shall be entitled to an ill-health award under Regulation B3 on the same conditions in all respects as if he were such a regular policeman as is mentioned in paragraph (1) of that Regulation, subject, however, to the following paragraphs.

(3) Where the disablement is the result of an injury received during the serviceman's period of relevant service in the armed forces, in lieu of an ill-health gratuity in pursuance of paragraph (2) (or, where the period of relevant service in the armed forces ended before 1st April 1987, in pursuance of the corresponding provision of the former Regulations), the police authority may, in their discretion, pay him a pension at the rate of a twelfth of his average pensionable pay, subject, however, to paragraph (4).

(4) Where the disablement is the result of such an injury as aforesaid, any pension payable to the serviceman in pursuance of paragraph (2) or (3) may, subject to the limitation in paragraph 1 of Schedule I, from time to time be increased at the discretion of the police authority but, where an ill-health pension payable in pursuance of paragraph (2) is so increased, no account of the increase shall be taken for the purposes of Regulation B7 or B9 (*commutation and allocation*) or of Part VIII of Schedule B (*reduction of pension related to up-rating of widow's pension*).

Awards on death of servicemen

I3.— (1) If a serviceman entitled to reckon 3 years' pensionable service—

(a) dies or has died during his period of relevant service in the armed forces, or

(b) having been permanently disabled for duty as a regular policeman at the end of the said period (without any intervening period of service as such) dies or has died either as a result of the same injury as resulted in his disablement or while in receipt of a pension,

his widow shall be entitled to a widow's ordinary pension under Regulation C1 on the same conditions in all respects as if he were such a regular policeman as is mentioned in paragraph (1) of that Regulation, subject, however, to paragraphs (5) and (6) of this Regulation.

(2) If a serviceman dies during his relevant period of service in the armed forces and his widow is not entitled to a pension under paragraph (1), she shall, subject to paragraph (3), be entitled to a gratuity of an amount equal to her husband's average pensionable pay.

(3) Where the death of a serviceman is the result of an injury received during his period of relevant service in the armed forces, in lieu of a gratuity under paragraph (2) (or, where he died before 1st April 1987, in lieu of a gratuity under the corresponding provision of the former Regulations) the police authority may, in their discretion, pay his widow a pension the amount whereof shall be the appropriate sum for the purposes of this paragraph, that is to say

£7.28, increased in accordance with Regulation E10(6) (*increase of flat-rate award*), subject, however, to paragraphs (5) and (6) of this Regulation.

(4) If a serviceman—

(a) dies or has died during his period of relevant service in the armed forces, or

(b) having been permanently disabled for duty as a regular policeman at the end of the said period (without any intervening period of service as such) dies or has died while in receipt of a pension, or, being a person entitled to reckon not less than 3 years' pensionable service, dies or has died having received a gratuity,

then each of his children shall be entitled to a child's ordinary allowance under Regulation D1 on the same conditions in all respects as if he were such a regular policeman as is mentioned in paragraph (1) of that Regulation, subject, however, to paragraphs (5) and (6) of this Regulation.

(5) Where the death of a serviceman is the result of an injury received during his period of relevant service in the armed forces, any pension or allowance payable in respect of him in pursuance of paragraph (1), (3) or (4) may, subject to the limitation in paragraph 2 or 3 of Schedule I, from time to time be increased at the discretion of the police authority.

(6) Without prejudice to anything in paragraph (1) or (4)—

(a) in relation to a widow's pension or gratuity in pursuance of paragraph (1), (2) or (3), Regulation C8 (*limitation on award to widow living apart from her husband and widow's requisite benefit pension*) and Regulation E7 (*prevention of duplication*) shall apply, and

(b) in relation to a child's allowance in pursuance of paragraph (4), Regulation E7 shall apply,

as those Regulations apply in relation to the awards therein mentioned.

Application of Regulations E2 and E3

I4. In the case of a serviceman—

(a) who dies while in receipt of a pension or while entitled to a deferred pension, whether or not that pension has come into payment, and whose death results from an injury received during his relevant period of service in the armed forces, Regulation E2 (*gratuities—dependent relatives*) shall apply as it applies in the case of a regular policeman who so dies and whose death results from an injury received in the execution of his duty;

(b) who dies during his relevant period of service in the armed forces, Regulation E2 and Regulation E3 (*gratuity—estate*) shall apply as they apply in the case of a regular policeman who dies while serving as such.

Servicemen who resume service as regular policemen

I5. If a serviceman, after resuming service, or returning to duty, as a regular policeman—

(a) is permanently disabled as a result of an injury received during his period of relevant service in the armed forces, the police authority may, in relation to any pension payable to him, other than a deferred pension, exercise the like discretion as that conferred by Regulation I2(4) but, where a pension is increased in pursuance of this sub-paragraph, no account of the increase shall be taken for the purposes of Regulation B7 or B9 (*commutation and allocation*) or of Part VIII of Schedule B (*reduction of pension related to up-rating of widow's pension*);

(b) dies or has died as a result of such an injury, the police authority may, in relation to any widow's pension or gratuity and any child's allowance payable in respect of him, exercise the like discretions as those conferred by Regulation I3(3) and (5).

Servicemen who do not resume service in their former force

I6. Where a serviceman who ceased to serve as a regular policeman in order to undertake a period of relevant service in the armed forces does not or did not resume service in his former force within a month of the end of that period, he shall be treated for the purposes of Regulations A10, A16, B5(2), B6, F3, F4 and F5 as having left his former force at the end of his period of relevant service in the armed forces.

Pensionable service

I7.— (1) A serviceman who ceased to serve as a regular policeman in order to undertake a period of relevant service in the armed forces shall be entitled to reckon that period as pensionable service in his former force except that so much, if any, of that period as fell before 5th July 1948 shall not be so reckonable under this paragraph.

(2) A serviceman (1939–1945) shall also be entitled so to reckon as pensionable service—

(a) such further period as the Secretary of State may fix or has fixed, not exceeding 3 months after the end of his period of relevant service in the armed forces and before becoming a member of a police force, and

(b) any period of approved service under the former Acts reckonable by him immediately before 5th July 1948.

(3) The reference in paragraph (2)(b) to approved service reckonable under the former Acts shall be construed as provided in Regulation F1(2) in the case of such a reference in Part F.

Pension contributions etc.

I8.— (1) This Part shall have effect in the case of a serviceman who ceased to serve as a regular policeman in order to undertake a period of relevant service in the armed forces only if he pays or has paid pension contributions (other than additional or further pension contributions) to the police authority of his former force, as though he had remained a regular policeman in that force, in respect of his period of relevant service in the armed forces and, in the case of a serviceman (1939–1945), such further period as the Secretary of State may have fixed which is reckonable as pensionable service:

Provided that this Part shall have effect notwithstanding that pension contributions are not or have not been paid as aforesaid—

    (a) by a serviceman other than a serviceman (1939–1945) in respect of—

        (i) any period during which his service pay when aggregated with any payments under Part V of the Reserve and Auxiliary Forces (Protection of Civil Interests) Act 1951(**a**) is less than his pensionable pay, or

        (ii) any period before 1st January 1952 for which he has been required to serve in the armed forces as mentioned in the proviso to Regulation I1 and in respect of which no payments under Part V of the Reserve and Auxiliary Forces (Protection of Civil Interests) Act 1951 have been made;

    (b) by a serviceman (1939–1945) in respect of any period in respect of which he would not have been compelled to pay sums equal to rateable deductions if the Police Pensions Act 1948 had not been passed.

(2) Where this Part has effect in the case of a serviceman by virtue of proviso *(a)* to paragraph (1), he shall be deemed, except for the purposes of Regulation A10 (*aggregate pension contributions for purposes of awards*), to have paid pension contributions in respect of any period beginning on or after 1st April 1956 and ending before 1st April 1972 at the rate at which he last paid such contributions or, where he was on 1st April 1956 performing relevant service in the armed forces and did not give the notice referred to in the relevant provisions of the former Regulations, at a rate related to 6.25% of his pensionable pay.

In this paragraph the reference to the relevant provisions of the former Regulations is a reference to the provisions of the proviso to Regulation 35(2) of the Police Pensions Regulations 1955(**b**) as set out in Regulation 13 of the Police Pensions Regulations 1956(**c**), or of the proviso to Regulation 37(2) of the Police Pensions (Scotland) Regulations 1955(**d**), as set out in Regulation 13 of the Police Pensions (Scotland) Regulations 1956(**e**).

(3) Where this Part has effect in the case of a serviceman, any reference in these Regulations to service as a member of a police force or of the Royal Ulster Constabulary on or after 1st April 1972 or in respect of which he has paid pension contributions at a rate related to 6.25% of his pensionable pay shall be construed as including a reference to his period of relevant service in the armed forces on or after that date or, as the case may be, in respect of which he has paid, or is deemed to have paid, pension contributions at that rate.

PART J

SPECIAL CASES

Policeman with a guaranteed minimum for the purposes of the Social Security Pensions Act 1975

(**a**) 1951 c. 65.   (**b**) S.I. 1955/480.   (**c**) S.I. 1956/385.
(**d**) S.I. 1955/485.   (**e**) S.I. 1956/434.

J1.— (1) This Regulation shall apply in the case of a regular policeman who, for the purposes of the Social Security Pensions Act 1975(**a**), has a guaranteed minimum in relation to the pension provided by these Regulations by reason of service which is contracted-out employment by reference thereto:

Provided that it shall not apply in the case of a regular policeman in respect of whom a transfer value has been, or is required to be, paid under Regulation F9.

(2) In a case in which this Regulation applies the regular policeman shall be entitled to a pension of a weekly amount equal to his guaranteed minimum but no payment shall be made on account of the pension—

(a) in respect of any period before he attains state pensionable age;

(b) if he is also entitled to a pension under Part B, in respect of any period for which that pension, together with any increase therein under the Pensions (Increase) Act 1971(**b**), exceeds the pension which, disregarding this sub-paragraph, would be payable hereunder subject, however, to paragraph (3)(a), or

(c) in respect of any period within the 5 years following his attaining state pensionable age during which he is serving as a regular policeman if either—

(i) he has so served for a continuous period beginning before he attained that age, or

(ii) he is entitled to a pension under Part B but for the period in question that pension has been withdrawn, in whole or in part, in pursuance of a decision taken by the police authority for the purposes of Regulation K4 before he attained state pensionable age.

(3) Where a regular policeman is entitled both to a pension under Part B and a pension under paragraph (2) then—

(a) for the purposes of paragraph (2)(b), in the case of a pension under Part B other than an injury pension, any secured portion thereof shall be disregarded but, subject as aforesaid, where he is entitled to both an injury pension and some other pension under Part B, those pensions shall be treated as a single pension;

(b) in respect of any period in respect of which a payment is made on account of the pension under paragraph (2), no payment shall be made on account of the pension under Part B otherwise than, in the case of a pension other than an injury pension, on account of any secured portion thereof.

(4) In a case in which this Regulation applies, where the regular policeman dies or has died at any time leaving a widow then, unless any pension to which he has been entitled has been forfeited under Regulation K5(2), she shall be entitled to a pension of a weekly amount equal to a half of his guaranteed minimum increased in accordance with Regulation E9 (*increase by reference to*

(**a**) 1975 c. 60.   (**b**) 1971 c. 56.

the Pensions (Increase) Acts) but that entitlement shall cease if she remarries or has remarried before attaining the age of 60 years and no payment shall be made on account of the pension—

> *(a)* if she is also entitled to a pension under Part C, in respect of any period for which the amount of that pension exceeds the pension which, disregarding this sub-paragraph, would be payable hereunder, or
>
> *(b)* in respect of any period before she attains the age of 60 years during which she and a man to whom she is not married are living together as husband and wife.

(5) Where a widow is entitled both to a pension under Part C and a pension under paragraph (4) then, in respect of any period in respect of which a payment is made on account of the pension under paragraph (4), no payment shall be made on account of the pension under Part C.

(6) The following provisions shall apply in relation to a pension under this Regulation as hereinafter provided, that is to say—

> *(a)* Regulation B8 (*commutation—small pensions*) shall apply in relation to a pension under paragraph (2) as it applies in relation to a pension under Part B;
>
> *(b)* Regulation E4(3) (*gratuity in lieu of widow's pension*) shall apply in relation to a pension under paragraph (4) as it applies in relation to a pension under Part C, and
>
> *(c)* Regulation K5 (*forfeiture of pension*) shall apply in relation to a pension under paragraph (2) or (4) as it applies in relation to a pension under Part B or C but as if paragraph (4) thereof were omitted,

but, save as aforesaid or as provided in paragraph (2) or (4), nothing in any other Regulation shall affect a person's entitlement to a pension under this Regulation, the amount of such a pension or the circumstances in which it may be withdrawn or forfeited.

Former member of the Royal Ulster Constabulary

J2.— (1) This Regulation shall apply in the case of a regular policeman who has been a member of the Royal Ulster Constabulary.

(2) Where such a regular policeman is entitled to reckon pensionable service by reason of previous service in the Royal Ulster Constabulary then, except where the context otherwise requires, these Regulations shall have effect as if anything done by him or in his case under, or for the purposes of, a provision of the Royal Ulster Constabulary pensions legislation which corresponds to a provision of these Regulations or of the former Regulations had been done under, or for the purposes of, that corresponding provision.

(3) Without prejudice to the generality of paragraph (2), if such a regular policeman elected to pay additional or further contributions under any provision of the Royal Ulster Constabulary pensions legislation corresponding to Regulation 58(2) or (3) of the Regulations of 1973 and his liability to pay such contributions, either under that legislation or by reason of Regulation 63

of the Regulations of 1973, did not cease before 1st April 1987 or, if later, the date on which he became a regular policeman then, notwithstanding that he is not such a regular policeman as is mentioned in paragraph (1) of Regulation G3 (*additional and further contributions*), that Regulation shall apply to him and Schedule G shall have effect subject to any necessary modifications.

Former reversionary member of home police force

J3. Notwithstanding anything in these Regulations, where a person who has been a reversionary member of a home police force becomes or has become a regular policeman in a home police force and an award is payable to or in respect of him by reason of his having received an injury in the execution of his duty as an overseas policeman without his own default, the award shall not be less than it would have been if he had not after being a reversionary member of a home police force become such a regular policeman.

Other special provisions

J4. The provisions of Schedule J shall have effect in the cases, and as respects the matters, mentioned therein.

Part K

Revision and Withdrawal or Forfeiture of Awards

Cancellation of ill-health and injury pensions

K1.— (1) As long as a person—

(a) is in receipt of an ill-health pension;

(b) would not, if he had continued to serve as a regular policeman instead of retiring with an ill-health pension, have been entitled to reckon 25 years' pensionable service, and

(c) if he had continued so to serve, could not have been required to retire on account of age,

the police authority may, if they wish to exercise the powers conferred by this Regulation, consider, at such intervals as they in their discretion think proper, whether his disability has ceased.

(2) If on any such consideration it is found that his disability has ceased, the police authority may give the person concerned notice that if he wishes to rejoin the force as a regular policeman within a period of not less than 3 months from the date on which he has been given such notice he will be permitted to do so.

(3) If the person concerned within the period referred to in paragraph (2) offers to rejoin the force as a regular policeman, he shall be permitted to do so in a rank not lower than that he held immediately before he retired with the ill-health pension.

(4) On the person concerned rejoining the force as mentioned in paragraph (3) or, where he does not offer to rejoin within the period referred to in paragraph (2), at the end of that period, there shall be terminated—

(a) the unsecured portion of his ill-health pension, and

(b) any injury pension to which he is entitled;

and where the unsecured portion of an ill-health pension is terminated under this paragraph, the secured portion of that pension shall not be payable in respect of any period before state pensionable age.

(5) Where the unsecured portion of an ill-health pension is terminated under paragraph (4) otherwise than on the policeman rejoining his force, but he is not a regular policeman to whom Regulation B5 applies, then, if the aggregate of—

(a) the sums paid in respect of the pension;

(b) the actuarial value of the secured portion of the pension (in so far as it is payable under paragraph (4)) determined in accordance with tables prepared by the Government Actuary, and

(c) the actuarial value of any pension to which he is entitled under Regulation J1 determined as aforesaid,

is less than his aggregate pension contributions in respect of the relevant period of service, the police authority shall pay the difference to the policeman.

(6) Paragraph (5) has effect subject to paragraph 5 of Part I of Schedule J.

Reassessment of injury pension

K2.— (1) Subject as hereinafter provided, where an injury pension is payable under these Regulations, the police authority shall, at such intervals as may be suitable, consider whether the degree of the pensioner's disablement has altered; and if after such consideration the police authority find that the degree of the pensioner's disablement has substantially altered, the pension shall be revised accordingly.

(2) Where the person concerned is not also in receipt of an ordinary, ill-health or short service pension, if on any such reconsideration it is found that his disability has ceased, his injury pension shall be terminated.

Reduction of pension in case of default

K3. Where a member of a police force or a person who has been a member of a police force becomes permanently disabled and has brought about or substantially contributed to the disablement by his own default, the police authority may reduce the amount of any ill-health or injury award payable to him by them by an amount not exceeding a half of that to which he would otherwise be entitled:

Provided that—

(a) this Regulation shall not apply where the person concerned has been a regular policeman and is in receipt of an ill-health pension and would, if he had continued to serve instead of retiring with that pension, have been entitled to reckon 25 years' pensionable service; and

(b) where the pension of a regular policeman has been reduced under this Regulation, then if when he attains the age of 60 years the reduced pension is less than the amount of the deferred pension which would have been payable had he been granted such a pension on the date of his ceasing to serve it shall be increased to that amount.

Withdrawal of pension during service as a regular policeman

K4.— (1) Subject to paragraph (2), a police authority by whom a pension is payable under Part B of these Regulations or under Regulation E1 (*adult dependent relative's special pension*) may, in their discretion, withdraw the whole or any part of the pension for any period during which the pensioner is serving as a regular policeman in any police force and, where they have done so, they shall be discharged from all actual or contingent liability in respect of the pension or the part thereof withdrawn for the period in question.

(2) This Regulation does not apply to a pension under Regulation B9(7)*(b)* (*allocation*).

Forfeiture of pension

K5.— (1) This Regulation shall apply to a pension payable to or in respect of a member of a police force under Part B or C or under Regulation E(1) (*adult dependent relative's special pension*).

(2) Subject to paragraph (5), a police authority responsible for payment of a pension to which this Regulation applies may determine that the pension be forfeited, in whole or in part and permanently or temporarily as they may specify, if the pensioner has been convicted of an offence mentioned in paragraph (3) and, in the case of a widow's pension, that offence was committed after the death of the pensioner's husband.

(3) The offences referred to in paragraph (2) are—

(a) an offence of treason;

(b) one or more offences under the Official Secrets Acts 1911 to 1939**(a)** for which the grantee has been sentenced on the same occasion to a term of imprisonment of, or to two or more consecutive terms amounting in the aggregate to, at least 10 years.

(4) Subject to paragraph (5), a police authority responsible for payment to a member of a police force of a pension to which this Regulation applies may determine that the pension be forfeited, in whole or in part and permanently or temporarily as they may specify, if the grantee has been convicted of an offence committed in connection with his service as a member of a police force which is certified by the Secretary of State either to have been gravely injurious to the interests of the State or to be liable to lead to serious loss of confidence in the public service.

(5) In the case of a pension to which this Regulation applies, other than an injury pension, the police authority in determining whether a forfeiture should be permanent or temporary and affect a pension in whole or in part, may make different determinations in respect of the secured and unsecured portions of the pension; but the secured portion of such a pension shall not be forfeited permanently and may be only forfeited temporarily for a period expiring before the grantee attains state pensionable age or for which he is imprisoned or otherwise detained in legal custody.

(6) To the extent to which a pension is forfeited under this Regulation, the

---

(a) 1911 c. 28, 1920 c. 75, 1939 c. 121.

police authority shall be discharged from all actual or contingent liability in respect thereof.

(7) The provisions of section 4(1) and (2) of the Police Pensions Act 1948(a), as they have effect by virtue of section 12(2) of the Police Pensions Act 1976(b) (*forfeiture of pensions*), shall not apply in relation to an award under these Regulations.

(8) This Regulation has effect subject to Regulation J1(6)*(c)*.

Part L

Payments by and to Police Authorities

Authorities responsible for payment of awards

L1.— (1) An award which is payable to or in respect of a person by reason of his having served as a regular policeman shall be payable by the police authority of the force in which he last served as such.

(2) An award which is payable to or in respect of a person by reason of his having been injured while serving as a member of a police force other than a regular policeman shall be payable by the police authority of the force in which he was serving when he received the injury.

Funds out of which and into which payments are to be made

L2.— (1) All payments for the purposes of these Regulations made by or to a police authority (including the Secretary of State as police authority for the metropolitan police district) shall be paid out of or into the police fund except in so far as is otherwise provided by the following paragraphs.

(2) There shall be paid out of moneys provided by Parliament—

(a) any award to or in respect of a person who last served as commissioner of police of the metropolis, and

(b) any transfer value payable in respect of such a person.

(3) There shall be paid into the Consolidated Fund—

(a) any transfer value received in respect of a person who has become commissioner of police of the metropolis, and

(b) the pension contributions (including additional and further contributions) paid by the said commissioner,

and, on a member of the metropolitan police force becoming commissioner of police of the metropolis, a payment shall be made out of the metropolitan police fund into the Consolidated Fund of an amount equal to the transfer value which would have been payable had the member in question instead transferred to another police force.

(a) 1948 c. 24.   **(b)** 1976 c. 35.

(4) There shall be paid out of moneys provided by Parliament or, as the case may be, into the Consolidated Fund all payments for the purposes of these Regulations made by or to the Secretary of State by reason that he is treated as the police authority in relation to—

(a) an overseas policeman;

(b) an inspector or assistant inspector of constabulary;

(c) a central police officer.

(5) Paragraph (1) shall not extend to Scotland.

Payment and duration of awards

L3.— (1) Subject to the provisions of these Regulations, in particular, of—

(a) Regulation B1(5) (*limitation on payment of an ordinary pension to a person entitled to reckon less than 30 years' pensionable service*);

(b) Regulation B4(2) (*limitation on payment of an injury pension to a person who ceased to serve before becoming disabled*);

(c) Regulation B5(4) (*limitation on payment of a deferred pension*);

(d) Regulation J1 (*policeman with a guaranteed minimum for the purposes of the Social Security Pensions Act 1975*);

(e) Part K (*revision and withdrawal or forfeiture of awards*), and

(f) paragraph 9(3)(a) of Part I of Schedule J (*pension by way of equivalent pension benefit*),

the pension of a member of a police force shall be payable in respect of each year as from the date of his retirement.

(2) Subject to the provisions of these Regulations, in particular, of—

(a) Regulation D5(3) to (6) (*limitations on child's allowance*), and

(b) Regulation J1 (*policeman with a guaranteed minimum for the purposes of the Social Security Pensions Act 1975*)

a widow's pension or child's allowance shall be payable in respect of each week as from the death of the husband or, as the case may be, the parent or, in the case of an allowance payable to a posthumous child, as from the birth of the child, except—

(i) where the husband or parent was in receipt of a pension and dies during a period in respect of which he has already received his pension, in which case the pension or allowance shall not be payable before the end of that period;

(ii) where the husband or parent has received a gratuity other than an injury gratuity under Regulation B4, in which case the pension or allowance shall be payable as from such time as the police authority may, in their discretion, determine to be reasonable, not being more than a year after his death, having regard to all the circumstances, including the amount of the gratuity.

(3) Subject to the provisions of these Regulations, in particular, of—

(a) Regulation C7(2)(a) (*widow's temporary pension*);

   (b) Regulation C9 *(termination of widow's award on remarriage etc.)*;

   (c) Regulation D5(3) to (6) *(limitations on child's allowance)*;

   (d) Regulation E1(3) *(adult dependent relative's special pension)*;

   (e) Regulation J1(2), (3)*(b)* and (4) *(policeman with a guaranteed minimum for the purposes of the Social Security Pensions Act 1975)*, and

   (f) Part K *(revision and withdrawal or forfeiture of awards)*,

a pension or allowance shall be payable for life and shall be discharged by payments in advance at such reasonable intervals as the police authority may, in their discretion, determine except that payment on account of a pension or allowance may be delayed, in whole or in part, pending the determination of any question as to the liability of the police authority in respect thereof, including any question as to the continuance of that liability.

(4) Where a person dies after receiving a sum paid in advance on account of a pension or allowance, neither the said sum nor any part thereof shall be recoverable although referable to a period after his death.

(5) Where a widow remarries after receiving a sum paid in advance on account of a pension, neither the said sum nor any part thereof shall be recoverable although referable to a period after her remarriage.

(6) Subject to the provisions of these Regulations, a gratuity, lump sum or award by way of repayment of aggregate pension contributions shall become payable as soon as the entitlement thereto arises and shall be paid forthwith in one sum except that—

   (a) payment on account thereof may be delayed, in whole or in part, pending the determination of any question as to the liability of the police authority in respect thereof, and

   (b) where the police authority are satisfied that it would be for the advantage of the beneficiary to pay a gratuity in instalments, they may pay it in instalments of such reasonable amounts and over such reasonable period as they think fit.

Payment of awards otherwise than to beneficiary and application of payments

   L4.— (1) This Regulation shall apply to the payment of any award to or in respect of a member of a police force, whether a pension, allowance, gratuity or other award, and any reference therein to the beneficiary is a reference to the person to whom, this Regulation apart, the award is payable.

(2) Where the beneficiary is a minor, the police authority may, if they think fit, in lieu of paying any sum on account of an award to the minor, pay it to such other person as they may determine.

A person who receives any sum in pursuance of this paragraph shall, subject to and in accordance with any directions of the police authority, apply the said sum for the benefit of the minor.

(3) On the death of the beneficiary to whom a sum is due on account of an award which does not exceed £5,000 or such higher amount as may from time to time be prescribed for the purposes of section 6 of the Administration of Estates (Small Payments) Act 1965(**a**), the police authority may, without

---

(**a**) 1965 c. 32.

probate, confirmation or any other formality or proof of title, pay the said sum to the persons appearing to the authority to be beneficially entitled to the personal estate of the deceased or, as the authority think fit, pay the said sum to one or more of those persons or distribute it among all or any of those persons in such proportions as the authority may determine.

(4) Where it appears to the police authority that a beneficiary is by reason of mental disorder or otherwise incapable of managing his affairs, in lieu of paying any sum on account of an award to that beneficiary—

(a) they may, in their discretion, pay it in whole or in part to a person having the care of the beneficiary or such other person as they may determine, and

(b) in so far as they do not so discharge their liability in respect thereof, the authority shall apply it in such manner as they think fit for the benefit of the beneficiary or his dependants.

A person who receives any sum in pursuance of sub-paragraph (a) shall, subject to and in accordance with any directions of the police authority, apply the said sum for the benefit of the beneficiary or his dependants.

(5) Where, as a result of any fraud, theft or negligence on the part of a regular policeman in connection with his service as such, a loss has occurred to the fund out of which an award is payable to him, in lieu of paying the whole or any part of any sum on account of the award to that beneficiary, the police authority may, if they think fit but subject to paragraph (6), apply it in making good the loss by retaining it in that fund:

Provided that the aggregate amount retained in pursuance of this paragraph shall not exceed whichever is the less of the following amounts, namely—

(a) the amount which is the actuarial value, at the time of the first retention, of the sums then or prospectively due to the regular policeman on account of the award, and

(b) the amount of the said loss,

and, in the event of any dispute as to the amount of that loss, the power conferred by this paragraph shall not be exercisable save to the extent of any sum adjudged due to the police authority in respect of the loss by an order of a competent court.

(6) Where the police authority exercise the power conferred by paragraph (5) they shall furnish the regular policeman concerned with a certificate showing the amount retained and the effect on the award and—

(a) where the award is an ordinary, short service or ill-health pension and the sum due on account thereof is in respect of a period beyond state pensionable age, only so much of that sum as is due on account of the unsecured portion of the pension may be retained and applied as mentioned in paragraph (5), and

(b) where the regular policeman is entitled to reckon pensionable service otherwise than by reason of service as a member of a police force, only the following proportion of any sum due on account of the award may be so retained and applied, that is to say, the proportion which his pensionable service reckonable by reason of service as a member of a police force bears to his total pensionable service.

(7) A police authority shall obtain a good discharge by paying or applying any sum in the manner provided by this Regulation.

(8) In the application of this Regulation to Scotland—

    (a) the references in paragraph (2) to a minor shall be construed as including references to a pupil, and

    (b) the reference in paragraph (3) to the personal estate of the deceased shall be construed as a reference to his movable estate.

Douglas Hurd
One of Her Majesty's Principal Secretaries of State

Home Office
9th February 1987

We consent,

Peter Lloyd
Michael Neubert
Two of the Lords Commissioners of Her Majesty's Treasury
20th February 1987

Regulation A4(1)   SCHEDULE A

GLOSSARY OF EXPRESSIONS

In these Regulations, unless the context otherwise requires, the following expressions shall be construed as hereinafter provided, that is to say:—

"the Act" means the Police Pensions Act 1976(**a**);

"aggregate pension contributions", for the purpose of calculating an award, has the meaning assigned to it by Regulation A10;

"approved service" has the same meaning as in the former Acts;

"armed forces" means the naval, military or air forces of the Crown, including any women's service administered by the Defence Council or formerly administered by the Admiralty, Army Council or Air Council;

"auxiliary policeman" means a member of the first class of the police reserve, a member of the Police War Reserve or a member of Class A of the Women's Auxiliary Police Corps;

"average pensionable pay" has the meaning assigned to it by Regulation G1;

"central police officer" means a member of a home police force engaged on central service who enjoys a right of reversion under section 43(1) of the Police Act 1964(**b**) or section 38(1) of the Police (Scotland) Act 1967(**c**) as the case may be;

  (**a**) 1976 c. 35.   (**b**) 1964 c. 48.   (**c**) 1967 c. 77.

SCHEDULE A *(continued)*

"central service" means temporary service under the Crown performed on or after 1st August 1964, being such service as is mentioned in section 43(5) of the Police Act 1964 or section 38(5) of the Police (Scotland) Act 1967;

"chief officer of police" in relation to an overseas corps means the senior member of that corps;

"child" means (without regard to age) legitimate or illegitimate child, step-child or adopted child and any other child who is substantially dependent on the member of a police force concerned and either is related to him or is the child of his spouse; and the expressions "father", "mother" and "parent" shall be construed accordingly;

"contracted-out employment" and "contracted-out scheme" have the meanings assigned to them by Regulation A5(6);

"contributions equivalent premium" has the meaning assigned to it by Regulation A5(6) (subject however, to Regulation A5(7));

"disablement" and cognate expressions have the meanings assigned to them by Regulation A12;

"employed contributor's employment" has the meaning assigned to it by Regulation A5(1);

"former Acts" means the Police Pensions Acts 1921 and 1926(**a**), including those Acts as applied and extended by or under any enactment, and any Act repealed by those Acts;

"former force", in relation to a serviceman, means the police force in which he was serving immediately before undertaking a period of relevant service in the armed forces;

"former Regulations" means the Regulations made under the Act or the Police Pensions Act 1948(**b**) before the making of these Regulations;

"graduated contribution" and "graduated retirement benefit" have the meanings assigned to them by Regulation A5(1);

"guaranteed minimum" and "guaranteed minimum pension" have the meanings assigned to them by Regulation A5(6) (subject, however, to Regulation A5(8));

"home police force" means any police force within the meaning of the Police Act 1964 or the Police (Scotland) Act 1967;

"injury" includes any injury or disease, whether of body or of mind, "injury received in the execution of duty" has the meaning assigned to it by Regulation A11 and "the result of an injury" shall be construed in accordance with Regulation A13;

"inspector" includes chief inspector;

"medical referee" has the meaning assigned to it by Regulation H2(2);

"member of a police force" includes—

(a) the commissioner and assistant commissioners of police of the metropolis;

(b) the commissioner of police for the City of London;

(**a**) 1921 c. 31, 1926 c. 34.   (**b**) 1948 c. 24.

SCHEDULE A *(continued)*

(c) an overseas policeman;

(d) an inspector or assistant inspector of constabulary appointed on or after 1st August 1964; and

(e) a central police officer;

"member of the first class of the police reserve" includes any member of a home police force appointed temporarily;

"non-participating employment" has the meaning assigned to it by Regulation A5(1);

"overseas corps" means any body in which persons such as are mentioned in section 1(1) of the Police (Overseas Service) Act 1945(**a**) are serving and in relation to which regulations made under section 1(2) of that Act have been made;

"overseas policeman" means—

(a) a member of an overseas corps, or

(b) an officer to whom section 10 of the Overseas Development and Co-operation Act 1980(**b**) or the Overseas Service Act 1958(**c**) applies or applied and whose service as such an officer is or was for the time being service in respect of which section 11 of the said Act of 1980 or section 5 of the said Act of 1958 has or had effect;

"overseas service" means service as an overseas policeman;

"participating period of relevant employment" has the meaning assigned to it by Regulation A5(3);

"payment in lieu of contributions" has the meaning assigned to it by Regulation A5(1);

"pensionable pay" has the meaning assigned to it by Regulation G1;

"the Pensions (Increase) Acts" means the Pensions (Increase) Act 1971(**d**) and the Pensions (Increase) Act 1974(**e**);

"police authority" has the same meaning as in the Act, and accordingly in relation to a Scottish police force has the same meaning as in the Police (Scotland) Act 1967;

"police force" means a home police force or an overseas corps;

"regular policeman" means—

(a) a member of a home police force who is not an auxiliary policeman;

(b) an overseas policeman who is a reversionary member of a home police force;

(c) an inspector or assistant inspector of constabulary appointed on or after 1st August 1964; and

(d) a central police officer;

(**a**) 1945 c. 17 (9 & 10 Geo. 6).   (**b**) 1980 c. 63.
(**c**) 1958 c. 14.   (**d**) 1971 c. 56.
(**e**) 1974 c. 9.

SCHEDULE A *(continued)*

"the Regulations of 1973" means the Police Pensions Regulations 1973(**a**) as from time to time in force;

"relevant service in the armed forces" has the meaning assigned to it by Regulation A14;

"retirement" and cognate expressions shall be construed in accordance with Regulations A17 to A21;

"reversionary member of a home police force" means an overseas policeman who has been a member of a home police force and has not lost his right of reversion under section 2(1) of the Police (Overseas Service) Act 1945, and includes a person who has transferred to an overseas corps from being either a civil servant within the meaning of the Superannuation Act 1887(**b**) or a member of the metropolitan civil staffs within the meaning of section 15 of the Superannuation (Miscellaneous Provisions) Act 1967(**c**);

"Royal Ulster Constabulary pensions legislation" means the Northern Ireland legislation for the time being in force relating to the superannuation of members of the Royal Ulster Constabulary;

"secured portion" and "unsecured portion", in relation to a pension, have the meanings assigned to them by Regulation A5(4);

"sergeant" includes station sergeant and first class sergeant (C.I.D.);

"serviceman" means a person who immediately before undertaking a period of relevant service in the armed forces was a regular policeman and includes a serviceman (1939–1945);

"serviceman (1939–1945)" means a person who ceased to serve as a regular policeman in such circumstances that he became a person to whom section 1 of the Police and Firemen (War Service) Act 1939(**d**) applied;

"state pensionable age" has the meaning assigned to it by Regulation A5(2);

"superintendent" includes chief superintendent;

"tax year" means the 12 months beginning with 6th April in any year;

"tour of central service" means the period of central service for which a central police officer has engaged with the consent of the appropriate authority for the purposes of section 43 of the Police Act 1964 or section 38 of the Police (Scotland) Act 1967, as the case may be, and, if such a period has been varied, means the period as so varied, so however that where the officer engaged for an indefinite period of central service the said expression means his actual period of such service;

"tour of overseas service" means the period of overseas service for which an overseas policeman has engaged with the consent, in the case of a reversionary member of a home police force, of the appropriate authority for the purposes of the Police (Overseas Service) Act 1945 and of the Secretary of State, and, if such a period has been varied under regulations made under section 1 of that Act, means the period as so varied, so however that where the overseas policeman has engaged for an indefinite period of overseas service the said expression means his actual period of such service;

"transfer" shall be construed in accordance with Regulation A16.

(**a**) S.I. 1973/428.   (**b**) 1887 c.67.
(**c**) 1967 c. 28.   (**d**) 1939 c. 103.

SCHEDULE B

PERSONAL AWARDS

Regulation B1   PART I

POLICEMAN'S ORDINARY PENSION

1. Subject to paragraph 2 and Parts VII and VIII of this Schedule (*reductions at state pensionable age and related to up-rating of widow's pension*), the pension shall be of an amount equal to 30 sixtieths of the policeman's average pensionable pay with the addition, subject to a maximum of 40 sixtieths, of an amount equal to 2 sixtieths of that pay multiplied by the period in years by which his pensionable service exceeds 25 years.

2. If the amount of the pension calculated in accordance with the preceding paragraph would be less than the amount it would have been had the person in question become entitled to receive an ordinary pension by retiring after due notice from the same police force at an earlier date, then, subject to Parts VII and VIII of this Schedule, the pension shall be of the last-mentioned amount.

Regulation B2   PART II

POLICEMAN'S SHORT SERVICE PENSION

Subject to Parts VII and VIII of this Schedule (*reductions at state pensionable age and related to up-rating of widow's pension*), the pension shall be of an amount which is the aggregate of—

  (a) an amount equal to a sixtieth of the policeman's average pensionable pay multiplied by the period in years of his pensionable service up to 20 years, and

  (b) an amount equal to 2 sixtieths of that pay multiplied by the period in years by which his pensionable service exceeds 20 years.

Regulation B3   PART III

POLICEMAN'S ILL-HEALTH PENSION

1. Subject to Regulation K1(5) (*termination of unsecured portion of ill-health pension*) and to Parts VII and VIII of this Schedule (*reductions at state pensionable age and related to up-rating of widow's pension*), the amount of the pension shall be determined in accordance with paragraph 2, 3 or 4 as the case may require.

2. Where the policeman has less than 5 years' pensionable service, the amount of the pension shall not be less than a sixtieth of his average pensionable pay and, subject as aforesaid, shall be of an amount equal to a sixtieth of that pay multiplied by the period in years of his pensionable service.

SCHEDULE B *(continued)*

3. Where the policeman has 5 or more years', but not more than 10 years' pensionable service, subject to paragraph 5, the pension shall be of an amount equal to 2 sixtieths of his average pensionable pay multiplied by the period in years of his pensionable service.

4. Where the policeman has more than 10 years' pensionable service, the pension shall be not less than 20 sixtieths, nor more than 40 sixtieths, of his average pensionable pay and, subject as aforesaid and to paragraph 5, shall be equal to 7 sixtieths of that pay with the addition—

(a) of an amount equal to a sixtieth of that pay multiplied by the period in years of his pensionable service up to 20 years, and

(b) of an amount equal to 2 sixtieths of that pay multiplied by the period in years by which his pensionable service exceeds 20 years.

5. In the case of a policeman who, had he continued to serve until he could be required to retire on account of age, would have become entitled to an ordinary or short service pension, a pension calculated in accordance with paragraph 3 or 4 shall not exceed the pension to which he would so have become entitled calculated, however, by reference to the average pensionable pay by reference to which the ill-health pension is calculated.

PART IV   Regulations B2 and B3

POLICEMAN'S SHORT SERVICE OR ILL-HEALTH GRATUITY

1. Where the policeman has not completed a year's pensionable service, the gratuity shall be of an amount equal to the policeman's aggregate pension contributions in respect of the relevant period of service subject, however, to paragraph 3.

2. Where the policeman has completed at least a year's pensionable service, the gratuity shall be of an amount equal to whichever is the greater of the two following amounts—

(a) a twelfth of the policeman's average pensionable pay multiplied by the period in years of his pensionable service;

(b) the policeman's aggregate pension contributions in respect of the relevant period of service,

subject, however, to paragraph 3.

3. Where the policeman retired after the beginning of the tax year in which he attains state pensionable age, the gratuity calculated in accordance with the preceding provisions of this Part shall be reduced by an amount equal to the capitalised value, as calculated by the Government Actuary, of the annual rate of any pension paid to him under Regulation J1(2) *(policeman with a guaranteed minimum for the purposes of the Social Security Pensions Act 1975)*.

SCHEDULE B *(continued)*

Regulation B4   PART V

POLICEMAN'S INJURY AWARD

1. A gratuity under Regulation B4 shall be calculated by reference to the person's degree of disablement and his average pensionable pay and shall be the amount specified as appropriate to his degree of disablement in column (2) of the following Table.

2. An injury pension shall be calculated by reference to the person's degree of disablement, his average pensionable pay and the period in years of his pensionable service, and, subject to the following paragraphs, shall be of the amount of his minimum income guarantee specified as appropriate to his degree of disablement in column (3), (4), (5) or (6) of the following Table, whichever is applicable to his period of pensionable service.

TABLE

Degree of disablement	Gratuity expressed as % of average pensionable pay	Minimum income guarantee expressed as % of average pensionable pay			
		Less than 5 years' service	5 or more but less than 15 years' service	15 or more but less than 25 years' service	25 or more years' service
(1)	(2)	(3)	(4)	(5)	(6)
25% or less (slight disablement)	12.5%	15%	30%	45%	60%
More than 25% but not more than 50% (minor disablement)	25%	40%	50%	60%	70%
More than 50% but not more than 75% (major disablement)	37.5%	65%	70%	75%	80%
More than 75% (very severe disablement)	50%	85%	85%	85%	85%

3.— (1) The amount of an injury pension, calculated as aforesaid, shall be reduced, where the person concerned received the relevant injury (within the

SCHEDULE B *(continued)*

meaning of Regulation B4) during a period of service as a regular policeman, by three-quarters of any other pension calculated by reference to pensionable service reckonable by reason of that period of service.

(2) For the purposes of sub-paragraph (1), such other pension as is there mentioned which is reduced in accordance with the provisions of Regulation B7 or B9 *(commutation and allocation)* or of Part VIII of this Schedule *(reduction related to up-rating of widow's pension)* shall be deemed not to have been so reduced.

4.— (1) The amount of the injury pension in respect of any week, calculated as aforesaid, shall be reduced on account of any such additional benefit as is mentioned in sub-paragraph (3) to which the person concerned is entitled in respect of the same week and, subject to sub-paragraph (2), the said reduction shall be of an amount equal to that of the additional benefit or, in the case of benefit mentioned in sub-paragraph (3)*(a)* or *(b)*, of so much thereof as is there mentioned.

(2) Where the provisions governing scales of additional benefits have changed after the person concerned ceased to be a member of a police force, the amount of the reduction in respect of any week on account of a particular benefit shall not exceed the amount which would have been the amount thereof in respect of that week had those provisions not changed, it being assumed, in the case of such benefit as is mentioned in sub-paragraph (3)*(a)*(ii), that it would have borne the same relationship to the former maximum amount thereof.

(3) The following benefits are the additional benefits referred to in this paragraph—

(a) any disablement pension under section 57 of the Social Security Act 1975**(a)** in respect of the relevant injury or so much of any such pension as relates to that injury (hereinafter referred to as the relevant part of the pension), together with—

   (i) any increase in such pension by way of unemployability supplement under section 58 of that Act or so much of any such increase as is proportionate to the relevant part of the said pension so, however, that where the person concerned is entitled to an unemployability supplement which is increased under section 59 of that Act, the unemployability supplement shall be deemed not to have been so increased,

   (ii) any increase in such pension under section 60 of that Act *(special hardship)* or so much of any such increase as is proportionate to the relevant part of the said pension,

   (iii) any increase in such pension under section 64 or 66 of that Act *(dependants)* or so much of any such increase as is proportionate to the relevant part of the said pension, and

   (iv) so long as the person concerned is receiving treatment as an in-

---

(a) 1975 c. 14, amended (as respects the provisions mentioned in this paragraph) by 1975 c. 60, s. 18(1) and Sch. 4, Pt. I; 1975 c. 61, Schs. 4 and 5; 1977 c.5, ss. 5 and 22 and Sch. 2; 1979 c. 18, Schs. 1 and 3; 1980 c. 30, Schs. 1 and 5; 1980 c. 39, s. 3; 1982 c. 24, s. 39, Sch. 2, Sch. 4, Pt. I and Sch. 5; 1986 c. 50, Sch. 3.

SCHEDULE B *(continued)*

patient at a hospital as a result of the relevant injury, any increase in such pension under section 62 of that Act (*hospital treatment*);

(b) any reduced earnings allowance under section 59A of the said Act of 1975**(a)** in respect of the relevant injury or so much of any such allowance as relates to that injury;

(c) until the first day after his retirement which is not, or is deemed not to be, a day of incapacity for work within the meaning of section 14 or 15, or, as the case may be, a day on which he is incapable of work within the meaning of section 36, of the said Act of 1975—

(i) any sickness benefit under the said section 14, including such benefit to which the person concerned is only entitled by virtue of section 50A**(b)** of that Act,

(ii) any invalidity pension under the said section 15, including any additional component comprised therein in pursuance of section 14 of the Social Security Pensions Act 1975**(c)**, or

(iii) any severe disablement allowance under the said section 36,

including, in each case, any increase under any provision of Chapter III of the Social Security Act 1975 (*dependants*).

(4) Where a person has become entitled to a disablement gratuity under section 57 of the Social Security Act 1975 in respect of the relevant injury, this paragraph shall have effect as if he were entitled during the relevant period to a disablement pension of such amount as would be produced by converting the gratuity into an annuity for the said period.

In this sub-paragraph the expression "the relevant period" means the period taken into account, in accordance with section 57 of the said Act of 1975, for the purpose of making the assessment by reference to which the gratuity became payable.

5. No payment shall be made in respect of an injury pension for any week in which the aggregate reductions under paragraphs 3 and 4 exceed the amount of the pension calculated in accordance with paragraph 2.

6. This Part has effect subject to paragraphs 6 and 7 of Part I, and paragraph 4 of Part VII, of Schedule J.

Regulation B5   PART VI

POLICEMAN'S DEFERRED PENSION

1. The amount of a policeman's deferred pension shall be calculated by reference to—

(a) the pensionable service he is entitled to reckon (here referred to as "actual service");

(b) the pensionable service he would have become entitled to reckon had he continued to serve until he could retire with a maximum ordinary

---

(a) S. 59A inserted by 1986 c. 50, Sch. 3, para. 5.
(b) S. 50A inserted by 1982 c. 24, s. 39.
(c) 1975 c. 60.

SCHEDULE B *(continued)*

pension (disregarding Regulation B1(2)) or until he could be required to retire on account of age, whichever is the earlier, (here referred to as "hypothetical service"), and

(c) his average pensionable pay.

2. Subject to Parts VII and VIII of this Schedule *(reductions at state pensionable age and related to up-rating of widow's pension)*, the policeman's pension shall be such that it is the same proportion of the hypothetical pension mentioned in paragraph 3 as his actual service is of his hypothetical service except that it shall not exceed 40 sixtieths of his average pensionable pay.

3. The hypothetical pension referred to in paragraph 2 is a pension of an amount which is the aggregate of—

(a) an amount equal to a sixtieth of his average pensionable pay multiplied by the period in years of his hypothetical service up to 20 years, and

(b) an amount equal to 2 sixtieths of that pay multiplied by the period in years by which his hypothetical service exceeds 20 years.

PART VII   Regulations B1, B2, B3 and B5

REDUCTION OF PENSION AT STATE PENSIONABLE AGE

Pension modifications connected with state flat-rate retirement benefit

1.— (1) Where, in respect of service as a regular policeman or as a member of the Royal Ulster Constabulary before 1st April 1980, a person has paid pension contributions at a rate of 6p a week (or 1s. 2d. a week) less than the appropriate percentage of his pensionable pay then, in respect of any period beyond state pensionable age, the unsecured portion of any ordinary, short service, ill-health or deferred pension payable to him shall be reduced in accordance with sub-paragraph (2) or, as the case may be, sub-paragraph (3).

(2) In the case of a person who paid contributions as aforesaid by reason of the giving of a notice—

(a) under Regulation 41(3) of the Police Pensions Regulations 1948(**a**);

(b) under Regulation 43(3) of the Police Pensions (Scotland) Regulations 1948(**b**), or

(c) without prejudice to the generality of Regulation J2(2), under any corresponding provision of the Royal Ulster Constabulary pensions legislation,

the reduction under sub-paragraph (1) shall be calculated at an annual rate obtained by multiplying the sum in the second column of the following Table set opposite to the age in the first column of the said Table which he had attained at the appropriate date by the number of years specified in sub-paragraph (4):—

(**a**) S.I. 1948/1531.   (**b**) S.I. 1948/1530.

SCHEDULE B *(continued)*

TABLE

Age in years at appropriate date	Sums to be multiplied
	£
Under 23	1.70
23	1.65
24	1.60
25	1.55
26	1.525
27	1.50
28	1.475
29	1.45
30	1.425
31	1.40
32	1.375
33	1.35
34	1.325
35	1.30
36	1.30
37	1.275
38	1.25
39	1.25
40	1.225
41	1.225
42	1.20
43	1.20
44 or over	1.175

In this sub-paragraph the expression "appropriate date" means, subject to sub-paragraph (5), 5th July 1948, or, in the case of a person who was then an auxiliary policeman, the date on which he first thereafter became a regular policeman.

(3) In the case of a person who paid contributions as aforesaid, otherwise than as mentioned in sub-paragraph (2), the reduction under sub-paragraph (1) shall be calculated at an annual rate obtained by multiplying £1.70 by the number of years specified in sub-paragraph (4).

(4) The number of years referred to in sub-paragraph (2) or (3) is, subject to the following sub-paragraphs, the period in years of service before 1st April 1980 either as a regular policeman or as a member of the Royal Ulster Constabulary in respect of which the person concerned paid pension contributions at such a rate as is mentioned in sub-paragraph (1):

Provided that there shall be excluded from the said period any period or periods—

(a) by reason of which the person concerned is not entitled to reckon pensionable service for the purposes of the pension in question, or

(b) which fell after the date on which the person concerned would have been entitled, if he had retired, to a pension equal to two thirds of his average pensionable pay.

SCHEDULE B *(continued)*

(5) In the case of a person who—

(a) first became a regular policeman on or after 1st January 1963;

(b) before 1st April 1980 became entitled to reckon pensionable service by reason of service or employment (otherwise than as a member of a police force or of the Royal Ulster Constabulary) in respect of which he was subject to superannuation arrangements ("the former service");

(c) was subject to the operation of any regulations made under section 69(4) of the National Insurance Act 1946(**a**) or section 110(1) of the National Insurance Act 1965(**b**) or of other provisions modifying those superannuation arrangements in connection with the passing of the said Act of 1946 ("the modifications"), and

(d) is entitled to reckon that pensionable service for the purposes of the pension in question,

the period in years specified in sub-paragraph (4) shall be increased by that period of pensionable service and, if he was subject to the modifications by virtue of an election made or notice given, the expression "appropriate date" in sub-paragraph (2) shall mean the date on which that election or notice became effective:

Provided that where only a proportion of the former service would have been taken into account for the purposes of the modifications, only that proportion of the pensionable service reckonable by virtue thereof shall be taken into account in determining the increase hereunder in the period specified in sub-paragraph (4).

Pension modifications connected with state graduated retirement benefit

2.— (1) Where a person in receipt of an ordinary, short service, ill-health or deferred pension has been in service or employment otherwise than as a regular policeman—

(a) in respect of which he was subject to superannuation arrangements;

(b) by reason of which he is entitled to reckon pensionable service for the purposes of the pension; and

(c) the period of which includes a participating period of relevant employment,

then, for the purpose of abating the pension in relation to that participating period of relevant employment, any provision of the said arrangements in operation when he left the said service or employment the effect of which is that pensions payable thereunder are to be reduced in connection with the operation of the National Insurance Act 1959(**c**) or of any provision of the National Insurance Act 1965 relating to graduated contributions or graduated retirement benefit shall apply, subject to the necessary adaptations and modifications, as though the provision were contained in this paragraph and as if—

(i) the pension were payable under the said arrangements, and

(ii) any other period of service or employment by reason of which he is entitled to reckon pensionable service for the purposes of the pension

---

(**a**) 1946 c. 67.   (**b**) 1965 c. 51.   (**c**) 1959 c. 47.

SCHEDULE B *(continued)*

were a period of non-participating employment at the end of which no payment in lieu of contributions falls to be made.

(2) A police authority, in determining any question arising under subparagraph (1) and relating to a particular service or employment, shall be entitled to treat as conclusive any relevant certificate issued, with the agreement of the person concerned, by his employer in that service or employment.

(3) Where for the purposes of the superannuation arrangements applicable to such service or employment as is mentioned in sub-paragraph (1) the person concerned was entitled to reckon service by reason of some previous service or employment, that previous service or employment shall be treated for the purposes of this paragraph as if it were part of the service or employment first mentioned in this sub-paragraph.

3.— (1) Where a person in receipt of an ordinary, short service, ill-health or deferred pension is entitled to reckon pensionable service for the purposes thereof by reason of a period of service as a regular policeman which is a participating period of relevant employment then, in respect of any period beyond state pensionable age, the unsecured portion of that pension shall be reduced in accordance with sub-paragraph (2).

(2) The reduction shall be calculated at the annual rate which is that of the graduated retirement benefit which would be payable to the pensioner, on the assumption that he retired from regular employment on attaining state pensionable age, in return for a payment in lieu of contributions in respect of the whole of the period referred to in sub-paragraph (1), whether or not such a payment was made.

4.— (1) Where a person in receipt of the secured portion of an ill-health pension, the unsecured portion of which has been terminated in the circumstances mentioned in Regulation K1(4), is also in receipt of some other pension, being an ordinary, short service, ill-health or deferred pension, and is entitled to reckon for the purposes of that other pension the period of pensionable service reckonable for the purposes of the ill-health pension then, in respect of any period beyond state pensionable age, the unsecured portion of that other pension shall be reduced in accordance with sub-paragraph (2).

(2) The reduction shall be calculated at the annual rate which is that of the secured portion of the ill-health pension.

Regulations B1, B2, B3 and B5   PART VIII

REDUCTION OF PENSION RELATED TO UP-RATING OF WIDOW'S PENSION

1.— (1) An ordinary, short service, ill-health or deferred pension payable to a man shall, in the cases hereinafter mentioned, be reduced in accordance with this Part except that a deferred pension payable in pursuance of paragraph 8(6)*(b)* of Part I of Schedule J shall not be so reduced.

(2) Any reference in this Part to a pension is a reference to a pension which falls to be reduced as aforesaid and any reference to police service is a reference to service as a member of a police force or of the Royal Ulster Constabulary.

SCHEDULE B *(continued)*

2.— (1) Subject to sub-paragraph (2), this paragraph shall apply in the case of a man entitled to reckon pensionable service otherwise than—

(a) by reason of police service on or after 1st April 1972;

(b) by reason of police service before that date in respect of which he paid pension contributions at a rate related to 6.25% of his pensionable pay;

(c) by virtue of Regulation F3(1)*(f)* (*British Airports Authority constabulary service*), or

(d) by virtue of Regulation F6 (*current interchange arrangements*).

(2) Where the man was a regular policeman to whom Regulation 59 or 60 of the Regulations of 1973 applied (that is to say, where on 1st April 1973 either he was serving as such or, having retired on or after 1st April 1972, he was entitled to a pension) and he last paid pension contributions before 1st April 1972 at a rate related to 5% of his pensionable pay, this paragraph shall not apply unless either—

(a) he elected or agreed, under paragraph (2)*(b)* or (4)*(a)* of the said Regulation 59 or under paragraph (2)*(b)* of the said Regulation 60, that his pension be reduced, or

(b) pensionable service became reckonable by him on or after 1st April 1987 by virtue of Regulation F4, F5 or F7 (*previous service and preserved interchange arrangements*).

(3) The pension of a man in whose case this paragraph applies shall, subject to the provisions of this Part, be reduced by the percentage specified in the second column of the Table in paragraph 7 opposite the number of completed years of pensionable service he is entitled to reckon other than pensionable service falling within either or both of the following sub-paragraphs, namely—

(a) pensionable service reckonable as mentioned in sub-paragraph (1), and

(b) where (subject to Regulations F4(3) and F5(2)*(c)*) he elected under Regulation 58(3) or 59(3) of the Regulations of 1973 to pay further pension contributions or to make a further payment by way of a lump sum, pensionable service reckonable by him immediately before 1st April 1973 otherwise than by reason of police service on or after 1st April 1972.

3.— (1) Subject to sub-paragraph (2), this paragraph shall apply in the case of a man entitled to reckon pensionable service otherwise than—

(a) by reason of police service on or after 1st April 1972;

(b) by virtue of Regulation F3(1)*(f)*, or

(c) by virtue of Regulation F6.

(2) Where the man was a regular policeman to whom Regulation 59 or 60 of the Regulations of 1973 applied, this paragraph shall not apply unless either—

(a) he elected or agreed, under paragraph (3)*(b)* or (4)*(b)* of the said Regulation 59 or paragraph (3)*(b)* of the said Regulation 60, that his pension be reduced, or

SCHEDULE B *(continued)*

(b) pensionable service became reckonable by him, on or after 1st April 1987, by virtue of Regulation F4, F5 or F7.

(3) The pension of a man in whose case this paragraph applies shall be reduced by the percentage specified in the third column of the Table in paragraph 7 opposite the number of completed years of pensionable service he is entitled to reckon other than pensionable service falling within either or both of the following sub-paragraphs, namely—

(a) pensionable service reckonable as mentioned in sub-paragraph (1), and

(b) where (subject to Regulations F4(3) and F5(2)(c)) he elected under Regulation 58(2) or 59(3) of the Regulations of 1973 to pay additional contributions or to make an additional payment by way of a lump sum, pensionable service reckonable by him immediately before 1st April 1973 otherwise than by reason of police service on or after 1st April 1972.

4. In calculating the amount of a reduction in a man's pension under paragraph 2 or 3 no account shall be taken—

(a) of any service he is entitled to reckon as pensionable service by virtue of section 10 of the Police Pensions Act 1921(**a**), or

(b) of any service on or after 1st April 1956 which he is entitled to reckon as pensionable service by virtue of Regulation I7 and the proviso to Regulation I8(1) *(relevant service in the armed forces)*.

5. In calculating the amount of a reduction in a man's pension under paragraph 2 or 3 no account shall be taken of any reduction in the amount of the pension in accordance with the provisions of Regulation B7 or B9 *(commutation and allocation)* or of Part VII of this Schedule *(reduction at state pensionable age)*; and, where the pension falls to be reduced under both those paragraphs, for the purpose of calculating each reduction, no account shall be taken of the other reduction.

6.— (1) Where a man entitled to an ordinary pension was, immediately before he retired, paying additional or further contributions in pursuance of an election under Regulation 58(2) or (3) of the Regulations of 1973, the annual amount of his ordinary pension shall be reduced for the period mentioned in sub-paragraph (2) by the annual amount of those contributions immediately before his retirement, calculated by reference to his pensionable pay at that time so, however, that no account of the said reduction shall be taken for the purpose of calculating any other reduction in the pension under these Regulations.

(2) The period referred to in sub-paragraph (1) shall be one corresponding to that for which the additional or further contributions would have remained payable had the man not retired but starting, where the pension is not payable as from the date of his retirement, with the date from which it is payable.

7. The following Table is that referred to in paragraphs 2 and 3:—

(**a**) 1921 c. 31.

TABLE

Completed years of pensionable service taken into account	Percentage reduction in pension	
	Under paragraph 2	Under paragraph 3
1	0.2	0.2
2	0.4	0.4
3	0.5	0.5
4	0.6	0.7
5	0.8	0.8
6	0.9	0.9
7	1.0	1.0
8	1.2	1.1
9	1.3	1.2
10	1.5	1.3
11	1.6	1.4
12	1.7	1.5
13	1.8	1.6
14	1.9	1.6
15	2.0	1.7
16	2.1	1.8
17	2.2	1.9
18	2.3	2.0
19	2.4	2.0
20	2.5	2.1
21	2.6	2.1
22	2.7	2.2
23	2.8	2.2
24	2.9	2.3
25	2.9	2.3
26	3.0	2.4
27	3.1	2.4
28	3.1	2.5
29	3.2	2.5
30 or more	3.3	2.5

8. Paragraph 6 has effect subject to paragraph 3 of Part VI of Schedule J.

SCHEDULE C

WIDOWS' AWARDS

PART I   Regulation C1

WIDOW'S ORDINARY PENSION

1.— (1) Subject to paragraphs 2 and 3, the annual amount of a widow's ordinary pension shall be whichever is the greater of the two following amounts, namely—

 (a) an amount equal to a half of the pension or notional pension mentioned in sub-paragraph (2), and

 (b) an amount equal to her husband's average pensionable pay divided by 160 and multiplied by the period in years of so much of his

SCHEDULE C *(continued)*

pensionable service as is reckonable by reason of service or employment after 5th April 1978.

(2) The pension or notional pension referred to in sub-paragraph (1)*(a)* is—

(a) where the husband died while entitled to an ordinary, short service or ill-health pension, that pension;

(b) where, having retired with both an ill-health and an injury pension, he died while no longer entitled to the ill-health pension but while entitled to the injury pension, the ill-health pension to which he would have been entitled had he not ceased to be entitled thereto;

(c) where, having retired with an ill-health gratuity, he died as a result of the same injury as resulted in his disablement, the ill-health pension to which he would have been entitled had he retired in circumstances entitling him to such a pension, or

(d) where he died while serving as a regular policeman, the ill-health pension to which he would have been entitled had he retired immediately before he died in circumstances entitling him to such a pension,

calculated, in each case, in accordance with sub-paragraph (3).

(3) For the purposes of sub-paragraph (1)*(a)*, the pension or notional pension referred to in sub-paragraph (2)*(a)*, *(b)*, *(c)* or *(d)* shall be calculated without regard to—

(a) the restrictions on payments on account of an ordinary pension contained in Regulation B1(5);

(b) the provisions for the reduction of a pension contained in Regulation B7(7) and (8)*(b)* *(commutation)*, in Regulation B9(7) *(allocation)* and in Parts VII and VIII of Schedule B *(reductions at state pensionable age and related to up-rating of widow's pension)*.

Where the husband died before 1st April 1987, any reference in this sub-paragraph to a provision of these Regulations shall be construed as including a reference to the corresponding provision of the former Regulations.

2. The amount of a widow's ordinary pension calculated in accordance with paragraph 1 shall be increased in accordance with Regulation E9 *(increase by reference to the Pensions (Increase) Acts)*.

3. Where in respect of any period a widow so elects, the weekly amount of her ordinary pension in respect of that period shall not be calculated as aforesaid but shall be determined by reference to the rank held by her husband in accordance with Regulation E10 *(flat-rate award)*.

4. This Part has effect subject to paragraphs 2 to 5 of Part II of Schedule J.

Regulations C2 and C3   PART II

WIDOW'S SPECIAL PENSION

1. Subject to paragraphs 2 and 3, the weekly amount of a widow's special pension calculated in accordance with this Part of this Schedule shall be equal to 45% of her husband's average pensionable pay for a week.

SCHEDULE C *(continued)*

2.— (1) Where, in respect of any week, a pension is payable to the widow in pursuance of section 67 of the Social Security Act 1975(**a**) in consequence of her husband's death and the amount of that pension exceeds that of a widow's pension under section 26 of that Act as specified in Part I of Schedule 4 thereto at the time of the husband's death, then the amount of her special pension in respect of that week shall be reduced by that excess.

(2) Where the provisions governing the amount of pensions under section 67 of the Social Security Act 1975 have changed after the death of the husband, the reduction under sub-paragraph (1) in respect of any week shall not exceed the amount which would have been the amount thereof in respect of that week had those provisions not changed.

3. The weekly amount of a widow's special pension calculated in accordance with paragraphs 1 and 2, shall be increased in accordance with Regulation E9 (*increase by reference to the Pensions (Increase) Acts*).

4. Paragraph 2 has effect subject to paragraph 4 of Part VII of Schedule J.

PART III   Regulation C4

WIDOW'S ACCRUED PENSION

1.— (1) Subject to paragraphs 2 and 3, the annual amount of a widow's accrued pension shall equal a half of her husband's deferred pension.

(2) For the purposes of sub-paragraph (1), the husband's deferred pension shall be calculated without regard to—

(a) the restrictions on payments contained in Regulation B5(4), and

(b) the provisions for the reduction of a pension contained in Regulation B7(7) and (8)*(b)* (*commutation*), in Regulation B9(7) (*allocation*) and in Parts VII and VIII of Schedule B (*reductions at state pensionable age and related to up-rating of widow's pension*),

and, where the pension has been commuted for a lump sum under Regulation B8 (*commutation of small pensions*), as if it had not been so commuted.

Where the husband died before 1st April 1987, any reference in this subparagraph to a provision of these Regulations shall be construed as including a reference to the corresponding provision of the former Regulations.

2. The amount of a widow's accrued pension calculated in accordance with paragraph 1 shall be increased in accordance with Regulation E9 (*increase by reference to the Pensions (Increase) Acts*).

3.— (1) Subject to sub-paragraph (2), where in respect of any period a widow so elects, the weekly amount of her accrued pension in respect of that period

---

(**a**) 1975 c. 14, amended (as respects the provisions mentioned in this paragraph) by 1975 c. 18, Sch. 3, Pt. III; 1975 c. 60, Sch. 4, Pt. I; by virtue of 1986 c. 50, Sch. 3, para. 8, s.67 ceases to have effect on a day to be appointed, subject to the transitional provisions in para. 9.

SCHEDULE C *(continued)*

shall not be calculated as aforesaid but shall be determined by reference to the rank held by her husband in accordance with Regulation E10 (*flat-rate award*).

(2) This paragraph shall only apply in the case of a widow whose husband was such a regular policeman entitled to reckon less than 5 years' pensionable service as is mentioned in Regulation B5(1)*(b)* (*policeman's deferred pension*) if, by reason of the period of service or employment otherwise than as a regular policeman there mentioned, he was entitled to reckon a period of pensionable service which was not shorter than that period of service or employment.

4. Paragraph 1(1) has effect subject to paragraphs 7 and 8 of Part II of Schedule J.

Regulation C5(3)   PART IV

WIDOW'S PENSION IN CASE OF POST-RETIREMENT MARRIAGE

1. Where under Regulation C5(3) the widow of a regular policeman is entitled to such a pension as is there mentioned instead of a widow's ordinary pension or special award under Regulation C1 or C2, the annual amount of that pension shall be calculated in accordance with Part I of this Schedule in like manner as the annual amount of a widow's ordinary pension except that, for the purposes hereof, the said Part I shall have effect—

(a) as if the reference in paragraph 1(1)*(a)* thereof to a half of a pension or notional pension were a reference to a half of the appropriate proportion thereof within the meaning of paragraph 3 of this Part;

(b) as if paragraph 3 thereof (*election for flat-rate award*) were omitted, and

(c) where the pension is instead of a widow's special award under Regulation C2, as if the pension or notional pension referred to in paragraph 1(1)*(a)* were the ill-health pension to which the husband would have been entitled had he, when he ceased to serve, retired because he was disabled in circumstances entitling him to such a pension.

2. Where under Regulation C5(3) the widow of a regular policeman is entitled to such a pension as is there mentioned instead of a widow's accrued pension under Regulation C4, the annual amount of that pension shall be calculated in accordance with Part III of this Schedule in like manner as the annual amount of a widow's accrued pension except that, for the purposes hereof, the said Part III shall have effect as if—

(a) the reference in paragraph 1(1) thereof to a half of the husband's deferred pension were a reference to whichever is the greater of the two following amounts, namely—

(i) an amount equal to a half of the appropriate proportion of that pension within the meaning of paragraph 3 of this Part, and

(ii) an amount equal to the husband's average pensionable pay divided by 160 and multiplied by the period in years of so much of his pensionable service as is reckonable by reason of service or employment after 5th April 1978, and *(b)* paragraph 3 thereof (*election for flat-rate award*) were omitted.

3. In this Part the appropriate proportion means the proportion which the husband's pensionable service reckonable by reason of service or employment after 5th April 1978 bears to his total pensionable service.

PART V   Regulations C6 and C8

WIDOW'S REQUISITE BENEFIT PENSION

1. Subject to paragraph 2, the annual amount of a widow's requisite benefit pension shall be an amount equal to her husband's average pensionable pay divided by 160 and multiplied by the period in years of his pensionable service reckonable by reason of service or employment after 5th April 1978.

2. The amount of a pension calculated in accordance with paragraph 1 shall be increased in accordance with Regulation E9 (*increase by reference to the Pensions (Increase) Acts*).

SCHEDULE D

CHILDREN'S AWARDS

PART I   Regulation D1

CHILD'S ORDINARY ALLOWANCE

1.— (1) Where one of the child's parents is alive, the child's ordinary allowance in respect of the death of a regular policeman ("the relevant parent") shall, subject to paragraphs 4 and 5, be determined in accordance with this paragraph.

(2) Subject to sub-paragraphs (3) and (4), an allowance determined in accordance herewith shall be of an annual amount equal to 18.75% of the amount of the relevant parent's pension or notional pension mentioned in paragraph 3.

(3) Subject to sub-paragraph (4), where 3 or more children's allowances are for the time being payable in respect of the death of the same person, an allowance determined in accordance herewith shall be of an annual amount equal to 37.5% of the relevant parent's pension or notional pension mentioned in paragraph 3 divided by the total number of allowances so payable.

(4) Where in respect of any week the aggregate rate at which—

    (a) any widow's ordinary pension, and

    (b) any children's allowances determined in accordance herewith,

would be payable in respect of a person who died while entitled to an ordinary, short service, ill-health or injury pension ("the principal pension") exceeds the rate at which the principal pension was payable immediately before that person's death, the children's allowances shall be reduced by such factor as will ensure that the said aggregate rate does not exceed the rate at which the principal pension was so payable.

SCHEDULE D *(continued)*

(5) For the purposes of sub-paragraph (4) there shall be ignored—

   (a) in the case of a widow's pension or child's allowance, any increase therein in accordance with Regulation E9 (*increase by reference to the Pensions (Increase) Acts*), and

   (b) in the case of the principal pension—

   (i) the restrictions on payments on account of an ordinary pension contained in Regulation B1(5), and

   (ii) the provisions for the reduction of a pension contained in Parts VII and VIII of Schedule B (*reductions at state pensionable age and related to up-rating of widow's pension*),

and where the relevant parent was entitled both to an ordinary, short service or ill-health pension and to an injury pension, the reference in sub-paragraph (4) to the rate at which the principal pension was payable shall be construed (subject to sub-paragraph *(b)*) as a reference to the aggregate rate at which those pensions were payable.

2.— (1) Where the relevant parent was the child's only surviving parent or in respect of any period after the death of the child's other parent, the child's ordinary allowance shall, subject to paragraphs 4 and 5, be determined in accordance with this paragraph.

(2) Subject to sub-paragraph (3), an allowance determined in accordance herewith shall be of an annual amount equal to 25% of the relevant parent's pension or notional pension mentioned in paragraph 3.

(3) Where 3 or more children's ordinary allowances are for the time being payable in respect of the death of the same person, an allowance determined in accordance herewith shall be of an annual amount equal to 50% of the relevant parent's pension or notional pension mentioned in paragraph 3 divided by the total number of allowances so payable.

3.— (1) The pension or notional pension referred to in paragraphs 1 and 2 is—

   (a) where the relevant parent died while entitled to an ordinary, short service or ill-health pension, that pension;

   (b) where, having retired with both an ill-health and an injury pension, he died while no longer entitled to the ill-health pension but while entitled to the injury pension, the ill-health pension to which he would have been entitled had he not ceased to be entitled thereto;

   (c) where he retired with a gratuity when entitled to reckon at least 3 years' pensionable service, the ill-health pension to which he would have been entitled had he retired in circumstances entitling him to such a pension, or

   (d) where he died while serving as a regular policeman, the ill-health pension to which he would have been entitled had he retired immediately before he died in circumstances entitling him to such a pension,

calculated, in each case, in accordance with sub-paragraph (2).

(2) The pension or notional pension referred to in sub-paragraph (1)*(a)*, *(b)*, *(c)* or *(d)* shall be calculated without regard to—

SCHEDULE D *(continued)*

(a) the restrictions on payments on account of an ordinary pension contained in Regulation B1(5), and

(b) the provisions for the reduction of a pension contained in Regulation B7(7) and (8)*(b)* *(commutation)*, in Regulation B9(7) *(allocation)* and in Parts VII and VIII of Schedule B *(reductions at state pensionable age and related to up-rating of widow's pension)*.

4. The amount of a child's ordinary allowance determined in accordance with sub-paragraph (2) or (3) of paragraph 1 or, as the case may be, of paragraph 2 shall be increased in accordance with Regulation E9 *(increase by reference to the Pensions (Increase) Acts)*.

5. Where in respect of any period a person to whom a child's ordinary allowance is paid so elects, the amount of that allowance in respect of that period shall not be calculated as aforesaid but shall be determined by reference to the rank held by the relevant parent in accordance with Regulation E10 *(flat-rate award)*.

6. Where the relevant parent died before 1st April 1987, any reference in paragraph 1(5)*(b)* or 3(2) to a provision of these Regulations shall be construed as including a reference to the corresponding provision of the former Regulations.

7. This Part has effect subject to paragraphs 1(3), 2 and 3 of Part III of Schedule J.

PART II   Regulation D2

CHILD'S SPECIAL ALLOWANCE

1.— (1) Where one of the child's parents is alive, the child's special allowance in respect of the death of a member of a police force ("the relevant parent") shall, subject to paragraph 3, be determined in accordance with this paragraph.

(2) Subject to sub-paragraph (3), an allowance determined in accordance herewith shall be of an amount equal to 10% of the average pensionable pay for a week of the relevant parent.

(3) Where 5 or more children's special allowances are payable in respect of the death of the same person, an allowance determined in accordance herewith shall be of an amount equal to 40% of the average pensionable pay for a week of the relevant parent divided by the total number of allowances so payable.

2.— (1) Where the relevant parent was the child's only surviving parent, or in respect of the period after the death of the child's other parent, the child's special allowance shall, subject to paragraph 3, be determined in accordance with this paragraph.

(2) Subject to sub-paragraph (3), an allowance determined in accordance herewith shall be of an amount equal to 20% of the average pensionable pay for a week of the relevant parent.

(3) Where 5 or more children's special allowances are payable in respect of

SCHEDULE D *(continued)*

the death of the same person, an allowance determined in accordance herewith shall be of an amount equal to 80% of the average pensionable pay for a week of the relevant parent divided by the total number of allowances so payable.

3. The amount of a child's special allowance determined in accordance with paragraph 1 or 2 shall be increased in accordance with Regulation E9 *(increase by reference to the Pensions (Increase) Acts)*.

Regulation D4   PART III

CHILD'S ACCRUED ALLOWANCE

1. Subject to paragraphs 2 and 3, a child's accrued allowance shall be determined in like manner as an ordinary allowance would be determined under Part I of this Schedule ("Part I") if the child were entitled to such an allowance.

2.— (1) Paragraphs 1(2) and (3) and 2(2) and (3) of Part I as applied hereby shall have effect without regard to paragraph 2 of Part III of Schedule J but as if for any reference in the said paragraphs of Part I to the relevant parent's pension or notional pension there were substituted a reference to his deferred pension calculated in accordance with the following sub-paragraph.

(2) For the purposes of paragraph 1(2) and (3) or 2(2) and (3) of Part I as so applied, the relevant parent's deferred pension shall be calculated without regard to—

   (a) the restrictions on payments contained in Regulation B5(4);

   (b) the provisions for the reduction of a pension contained in Regulation B7(7) and (8)*(b) (commutation)*, in Regulation B9(7) *(allocation)* and in Parts VII and VIII of Schedule B *(reductions at state pensionable age and related to up-rating of widow's pension)*.

3.— (1) Paragraph 1(4) and (5) of Part I as applied hereby shall have effect as if—

   (a) the reference to a widow's ordinary pension were a reference to a widow's accrued pension, and

   (b) any reference to an ordinary pension or to the principal pension were a reference to the relevant parent's deferred pension calculated in accordance with the following sub-paragaph.

(2) For the purposes of paragraph 1(4) of Part I as so applied, the relevant parent's deferred pension shall be calculated without regard to the restrictions on payments contained in Regulation B5(4).

4. Where the relevant parent died before 1st April 1987, any reference in paragraph 2(2) or 3(2) to a provision of these Regulations shall be construed as including a reference to the corresponding provision of the former Regulations.

5. Paragraph 2 has effect subject to paragraph 4 of Part III of Schedule J.

SCHEDULE D *(continued)*

Part IV   Regulation D5

REDUCTION IN CHILD'S ALLOWANCE DURING FULL-TIME REMUNERATED TRAINING ETC.

1.— (1) In this Part—

"relevant child" means, subject to sub-paragraph (2), a child entitled to an allowance who is—

(a) in full-time training for a trade, profession or calling, and

(b) in receipt of remuneration in respect of that training at an annual rate in excess of the specified rate;

"specified rate" means the annual rate (rounded up to the nearest £1) at which an official pension within the meaning of the Pensions (Increase) Act 1971(a) would be payable when increased under that Act if, within the meaning thereof, the basic rate of the pension were £250, it began on 1st June 1972 and the pensioner satisfied the qualifying conditions and if the pension fell to be paid in respect of periods for which the relevant child's remuneration falls to be paid;

"excess remuneration" means the annual amount by which the annual rate of the relevant child's remuneration exceeds the specified rate;

"relevant provision" means paragraph 1(3) or 2(3) of Part I of this Schedule (including those provisions as applied by Part III thereof) or paragraph 1(3) or 2(3) of Part II thereof.

(2) A child shall not be a relevant child for the purposes of this Part—

(a) if he is entitled to an allowance in respect of the death of a member of a police force who ceased to be such before 15th August 1983, unless and until he has attained the age of 19 years;

(b) if and so long as his allowance falls to be increased in accordance with Regulation E8 *(increase during first 13 weeks)*.

2. In the case of any relevant child—

(a) if the annual amount of the allowance is greater than the amount of his excess remuneration, it shall be reduced by the amount of that excess remuneration, or

(b) if the amount of that excess remuneration is equal to or greater than the annual amount of the allowance which, but for this sub-paragraph, would be payable to him, the allowance shall not be payable.

3.— (1) Where as well as any relevant child there are other children to whom allowances are payable in respect of the death of the same person and any of the relevant provisions apply, the allowances payable to those other children ("the other allowances") shall be increased as hereinafter provided.

(2) If paragraph 2(a) applies in the case of any relevant child, then, without prejudice to sub-paragraph (3), the annual amount of each of the other allowances shall be increased by an amount equal to his excess remuneration divided by the number of other allowances.

(3) If paragraph 2(b) applies in the case of any relevant child, then, without

(a) 1971 c. 56.

prejudice to sub-paragraph (2), each of the other allowances shall be recalculated as if the relevant child were not entitled to an allowance.

(4) Notwithstanding the provisions of sub-paragraphs (2) and (3), no child shall by virtue of those provisions receive an allowance greater than that to which he would be entitled if no relevant provision applied in his case.

SCHEDULE E

Awards on Death—Additional Provisions

Regulation E1   PART I

Dependent Relative's Special Pension

1. Subject to paragraphs 2, 3 and 4, a dependent relative's special pension shall be of a weekly amount equal to 45% of the average pensionable pay for a week of the member of a police force in respect of whose death it was granted ("the deceased").

2. In respect of any week for which there are payable in respect of the deceased's death both—

(a) a widow's special pension or, where the deceased was a married woman, a dependent relative's special pension granted to her widower, and

(b) a dependent relative's special pension other than, where the deceased was a married woman, one granted as aforesaid,

the dependent relative's special pension mentioned in sub-paragraph *(b)* shall not be of the amount mentioned in paragraph 1 but, subject to paragraphs 3 and 4, of an amount equal to 20% of the deceased's average pensionable pay for a week.

3. The amount of a dependent relative's special pension determined in accordance with paragraph 1 or 2 shall be increased in accordance with Regulation E9 *(increase by reference to the Pensions (Increase) Acts)*.

4.— (1) Where in respect of any week the aggregate amount of—

(a) any widow's special pension, and

(b) any child's special allowance,

payable in respect of the deceased's death equals or exceeds the amount of the deceased's average pensionable pay for a week, no dependent relative's special pension shall be payable in respect of that week.

(2) Where in respect of any week the aggregate amount of—

(a) any widow's special pension,

(b) any child's special allowance, and

(c) any dependent relative's special pension,

payable in respect of the deceased's death would exceed the amount of the deceased's average pensionable pay for a week, the dependent relative's pension shall be reduced by such factor as will ensure that the said aggregate does not exceed the said amount.

(3) For the purposes of this paragraph any increase in a pension or allowance in accordance with Regulation E9 (*increase by reference to the Pensions (Increase) Acts*) shall be ignored.

PART II   Regulation E4

GRATUITY IN LIEU OF WIDOW'S PENSION

The gratuity referred to in Regulation E4 shall be of an amount equal to 11 times the annual value of the pension or, as the case may be, of that part thereof which is commuted or of such greater amount as may be agreed between the police authority and the widow, not exceeding the capitalised value of the pension or, as the case may be, that part thereof which is commuted, calculated in accordance with tables prepared from time to time for the purpose by the Government Actuary.

PART III   Regulation E5

GRATUITY IN LIEU OF CHILD'S ALLOWANCE

The gratuity referred to in Regulation E5 shall be of such amount as may be agreed between the police authority and the child's surviving parent or guardian, or between the police authority and the child where he has no such parent or guardian, not exceeding the capitalised value of the allowance or, as the case may be, of that part thereof which is commuted, calculated in accordance with tables prepared from time to time for the purpose by the Government Actuary.

SCHEDULE F

PENSIONABLE SERVICE AND TRANSFER VALUES

PART I   Regulations F4, F5 and F7

PAYMENT BY POLICEMAN IN RESPECT OF PREVIOUS SERVICE OTHER THAN POLICE SERVICE

1.— (1) Where a regular policeman undertakes to pay a sum in accordance with this Part he shall, subject as hereafter in this Part provided, pay by regular instalments of such amount that the payment of the sum will be completed within a period of 5 years and before he becomes liable to be required to retire on account of age:

Provided that he may at any time discharge his liability under the undertaking, in whole or in part, by paying the whole or part of the balance of the sum then outstanding.

(2) Any payment in accordance with this paragraph shall be made by the policeman to the police authority of the force in which he is serving when the payment falls to be made and, without prejudice to any other method of

SCHEDULE F *(continued)*

payment, the liability to make any such payment may be discharged by way of a deduction by the said authority from his pay.

2. If, before he has discharged his liability under the undertaking, a regular policeman—

  (a) retires without an award other than one of the amount of his aggregate pension contributions in respect of the relevant period of service;

  (b) leaves his police force on joining the Royal Ulster Constabulary with the consent of the police authority;

  (c) dies, or

  (d) is dismissed,

all further liability under that undertaking shall cease.

3. If, before he has discharged his liability under the undertaking, a regular policeman retires with an award other than one of the amount of his aggregate pension contributions in respect of the relevant period of service, the police authority by whom the award is payable shall be empowered to deduct the balance of the sum then outstanding from payments on account of the award:

Provided that where a payment is made on account of an ordinary or ill-health pension and in respect of a period beyond state pensionable age no deduction shall be made from so much of the payment as is on account of the secured portion of the pension.

Regulations F6, F8 and F9   PART II

TRANSFERS AND CURRENT INTERCHANGE ARRANGEMENTS

Section 1—Transfer value payable by police authority under Regulation F8 or F9

1.— (1) A transfer value payable by a police authority under Regulation F8 or F9 in respect of a regular policeman shall be calculated in accordance with this Section and the Table set out in Section 3 of this Part of this Schedule by reference to—

  (a) his age in years on ceasing to be a member of his former force;

  (b) his notional deferred pension, that is to say the deferred pension to which he would have been entitled had he, on so ceasing, been entitled to such a pension, and any reduction therein in accordance with Part VII of Schedule B (*reduction at state pensionable age*);

  (c) in the case of a man, his widow's notional accrued pension, that is to say the widow's accrued pension to which, on the assumption aforesaid, his widow would become entitled were he to die while entitled to a deferred pension leaving a widow entitled to an accrued pension;

  (d) in the case of a regular policeman who had undertaken to make payments by way of regular instalments as mentioned in Part I of this Schedule, the payments not completed before he ceased to be a member of his former force;

  (e) in the case of a regular policeman who, at the time of his ceasing to be a member of his former force, has a guaranteed minimum in relation to

SCHEDULE F (continued)

the pension provided by these Regulations, the amount of that guaranteed minimum, and

(f) the amount of any contributions equivalent premium relating to the period ending with his retirement which has been paid by the police authority and not repaid;

and any reference in this Section to the policeman's notional deferred pension or widow's notional accrued pension shall be construed accordingly.

(2) In this Section any reference to the Table is a reference to the Table set out in Section 3 of this Part of this Schedule and any reference to the appropriate factor specified in a column of that Table is a reference to the factor specified in the column in question in relation to the policeman's age within the meaning of sub-paragraph (1)(a).

(3) In this Section any reference to a policeman's former force is a reference to the force maintained by the police authority by whom the transfer value is payable.

2.— (1) The annual amount of the policeman's notional deferred pension, disregarding any reduction therein at state pensionable age, shall be multiplied by the appropriate factor specified in the second column of the Table or, in the case of a woman, in the fifth column thereof.

(2) Where the policeman's notional deferred pension would fall to be reduced under paragraph 1 of Part VII of Schedule B (reduction connected with state flat-rate benefit), the product under sub-paragraph (1) shall be reduced by an amount equal to the annual amount of that reduction multiplied by the appropriate factor specified in the third column of the Table or, in the case of a woman, in the sixth column thereof.

(3) In the case of a policeman entitled to reckon pensionable service, immediately before he ceased to be a member of his former force, by reason of a participating period of relevant employment, the product under sub-paragraph (1) shall be reduced by an amount equal to the annual amount by which the policeman's notional deferred pension would fall to be reduced under paragraphs 2 and 3 of Part VII of Schedule B (reduction connected with state graduated retirement benefit) multiplied by the appropriate factor specified in the third column of the Table or, in the case of a woman, in the sixth column thereof.

(4) For the purposes of sub-paragraph (3) a period shall be treated as a participating period of relevant employment notwithstanding that a payment in lieu of contributions only fell to be made after the policeman ceased to be a member of his former force.

(5) The product under sub-paragraph (1), subject to any reduction under sub-paragraphs (2) and (3), is in paragraph 5 referred to as the basic element of the transfer value.

3.— (1) In the case of a man, the annual amount of the policeman's widow's notional accrued pension, disregarding paragraphs 2 and 3 of Part III of Schedule C (increase by reference to the Pensions (Increase) Acts and flat-rate award), shall be multiplied by the factor 4.

SCHEDULE F *(continued)*

(2) The said product is in paragraph 5 referred to as the widow's element of the transfer value.

4. For the purpose of calculating a transfer value payable as mentioned in paragraph 1, Part VI of Schedule B *(policeman's deferred pension)* shall apply as if references to the policeman's average pensionable pay were references to his average pensionable pay immediately before he ceased to serve except that in the case of a transfer value which falls to be paid in pursuance of Regulation F8 or of Regulation F9(3)*(a)* or *(b)* no account shall be taken of any retrospective increase in pay granted after the transfer value has been paid.

5. Subject to the following paragraphs, the transfer value shall be of an amount—

> *(a)* in the case of a man, equal to the sum of the basic element calculated in accordance with paragraph 2 and the widow's element calculated in accordance with paragraph 3;
>
> *(b)* in the case of a woman, equal to the basic element calculated in accordance with paragraph 2.

6.— (1) This paragraph shall apply in the case of a policeman who had undertaken to make payments by regular instalments in accordance with Part I of this Schedule but had not completed those payments before he ceased to be a member of his former force; and the payments not completed before he so ceased are, in this paragraph, referred to as the outstanding instalments.

(2) The transfer value shall be reduced by the actuarial equivalent of the outstanding instalments calculated, in accordance with tables prepared by the Government Actuary, by reference to the amount of each instalment, the interval at which instalments were payable and the number of outstanding instalments.

7. Where a regular policeman at the time of ceasing to be a member of his former force has a guaranteed minimum in relation to the pension provided by these Regulations, the transfer value shall be reduced by the amount of that guaranteed minimum, expressed as an annual pension, multiplied by the appropriate factor specified in the fourth column of the Table or, in the case of a woman, in the seventh column thereof.

8. Where a contributions equivalent premium relating to the period ending with the policeman's retirement has been paid by the police authority and has not been repaid, the transfer value shall be reduced by the amount of that premium.

9.— (1) This paragraph shall apply where a transfer value payable between police authorities under Regulation F8 is so payable in respect of previous service reckonable under Regulation F5.

(2) Where this paragraph applies the transfer value shall be reduced by an amount equal to the appropriate payment, within the meaning of Regulation F5(2)*(c)*, which falls to be made by the policeman under Regulation F5(1) except that, where the appropriate payment would have been of a greater amount but for Regulation B11 or Regulation 82 of the Regulations of 1973 *(deduction of tax from certain awards)*, the transfer value shall be reduced by that greater amount.

SCHEDULE F *(continued)*

10.— (1) This paragraph shall apply where a transfer value is payable under Regulation F9 in respect of a regular policeman who has given a notice of allocation under Regulation B9(4)*(a)* and that notice has become effective under Regulation B9(6).

(2) Where this paragraph applies the transfer value shall be adjusted by such amount, calculated by the Government Actuary, as takes account of the effect which the notice of allocation had on the benefits prospectively payable to or in respect of the policeman as at the time when the transfer value became payable.

11.— (1) This paragraph shall apply where a transfer value is not paid within 6 months of the policeman ceasing to be a member of his former force.

(2) The transfer value calculated in accordance with the preceding provisions of this Section shall be increased by an amount equal to compound interest thereon at the rate of $2\frac{1}{4}$ per cent for each completed 3 months of the period beginning with the date he ceased to be a member of his former force and ending with the date of payment of the transfer value (disregarding any residual period of less than 3 months).

12. This Section has effect subject to paragraphs 2 and 3 of Part V of Schedule J.

Section 2—Pensionable service reckonable on receipt of transfer value

1.— (1) The period of pensionable service reckonable by a regular policeman under Regulation F6 by virtue of the receipt of a transfer value by the police authority shall be calculated in accordance with this Section and the Table set out in Section 3 of this Part of this Schedule by reference to—

(a) the amount of the transfer value and of any increase therein by way of interest subject, however, to sub-paragraph (4);

(b) his age in years at the date mentioned in sub-paragraph (2), (3) or (4), whichever applies in his case;

(c) his pensionable emoluments within the meaning of the sub-paragraph in question;

(d) the provisions of Part VII of Schedule B relating to reduction of pension at state pensionable age, and

(e) where he, on ceasing to be in his former service, had a guaranteed minimum in relation to the pension provided by his former superannuation arrangements, the amount of that guaranteed minimum;

and any reference in this Section to the policeman's age or pensionable emoluments shall be construed accordingly.

(2) Subject to sub-paragraph (4), this sub-paragraph shall apply where—

(a) by reason of his former service the policeman was subject to superannuation arrangements which—

(i) were contained in a public general Act of Parliament or were made under such an Act by a Minister of the Crown, or

SCHEDULE F *(continued)*

(ii) were contained in Northern Ireland legislation being public general legislation or were made under such legislation by a Minister of the Crown (including a Northern Ireland Minister) or by a Northern Ireland ministry, department or head of department, or

(b) the police authority are satisfied that the transfer value was calculated in like manner as under some such superannuation arrangements as aforesaid;

and, in such case, the policeman's age for the purposes of sub-paragraph (1)*(b)* shall be his age on ceasing to be in his former service and his pensionable emoluments for the purposes of sub-paragraph (1)*(c)* shall be the annual value of the emoluments (including averaged emoluments) in relation to which the transfer value was calculated or would have been calculated if part thereof had not been disregarded on account of provisions of the superannuation arrangements connected with state retirement pensions under section 28 of the Social Security Act 1975**(a)**.

(3) Subject to sub-paragraph (4), in a case in which sub-paragraph (2) does not apply, the policeman's age for the purposes of sub-paragraph (1)*(b)* and his pensionable emoluments for the purposes of sub-paragraph (1)*(c)* shall be, respectively, his age and his annual pensionable pay as a regular policeman—

(a) on his becoming such, where the transfer value is received within 12 months of his ceasing to be in his former service, or

(b) on the date the transfer value is received, where it is received later.

(4) Where pensionable service reckonable under Regulation F6 is so reckonable by virtue of paragraph (3) of that Regulation in the case of a regular policeman who became such before 1st April 1972, then, notwithstanding the preceding provisions of this paragraph—

(a) if, before or within 3 months of receiving the transfer value the police authority are notified that, inclusive of any increase by way of interest, it would have been of a different amount, specified by the payor thereof, had it been calculated and paid on 1st January 1974, then, for the purposes of this Section the transfer value shall be treated as though it were of the amount so specified;

(b) the policeman's age for the purposes of sub-paragraph (1)*(b)* shall be his age on 1st January 1974, and

(c) his pensionable emoluments for the purposes of sub-paragraph (1)*(c)* shall be his annual pensionable pay as a regular policeman on 1st January 1974 or, if he was not serving as such on that date, on the date on which he first thereafter became a regular policeman.

(5) In this Section any reference to the Table is a reference to the Table set out in Section 3 of this Part of this Schedule and any reference to the appropriate factor specified in a column of that Table is a reference to the factor specified in the column in question in relation to the policeman's age within the meaning of sub-paragraph (1)*(b)*.

(6) In this Section any reference to a policeman's former service is a reference to the service in respect of which the transfer value is paid.

(**a**) 1975 c. 14.

SCHEDULE F *(continued)*

2.— (1) Where in a case to which paragraph 1(2) applies the transfer value was increased by the inclusion therein of interest calculated from the date when the policeman ceased to be in his former service, it shall be adjusted by the deduction of that interest.

(2) Where in any case any such pension as is mentioned in paragraph 2 of Part VII of Schedule B *(reduction connected with state graduated retirement benefit)* as might become payable to the policeman would fall to be abated in accordance with that paragraph, the annual amount of that abatement shall be calculated and multiplied by the appropriate factor specified in the third column of the Table or, in the case of a woman, in the sixth column thereof; and the transfer value shall be adjusted by the addition of that product.

(3) Where on the date that the policeman ceased to be in his former service he had a guaranteed minimum in relation to the pension provided by his former superannuation arrangements, the amount of that guaranteed minimum, expressed as an annual pension, shall be multiplied by the appropriate factor specified in the fourth column of the Table or, in the case of a woman, in the seventh column thereof, and the transfer value shall be adjusted by the addition of that product.

(4) The transfer value, subject to any such adjustment as aforesaid, is in paragraph 4 referred to as the adjusted transfer value.

3.— (1) The policeman's pensionable emoluments shall be multiplied by a factor 2.00 greater than the appropriate factor specified in the second column of the Table or, in the case of a woman, by the appropriate factor specified in the fifth column thereof.

(2) The said product shall be divided by 45.

(3) Where any such pension as is mentioned in paragraph 1 of Part VII of Schedule B *(reduction connected with state flat-rate retirement benefit)* as might become payable to the policeman would fall to be reduced in accordance with that paragraph and sub-paragraph (5) thereof applies, the amount of the reduction for each year of service relevant for the purposes of that paragraph shall be multiplied by the appropriate factor specified in the third column of the Table or, in the case of a woman, in the sixth column thereof; and the quotient under sub-paragraph (2) shall be adjusted by the deduction of the said product.

(4) The quotient under sub-paragraph (2), subject to any such adjustment as aforesaid, is in paragraph 4 referred to as the divisor.

4. The adjusted transfer value calculated in accordance with paragraph 2 shall be divided by the divisor calculated in accordance with paragraph 3 and the quotient (including any fraction) shall be the number of years reckonable as pensionable service.

5. Paragraph 1(2) has effect subject to paragraph 7 of Part IV of Schedule J.

SCHEDULE F *(continued)*

*Section 3—Table referred
to in Sections 1 and 2*

Age last birthday before date of cessation	Men			Women		
	Basic factor	N.I. factor	GMP factor	Basic factor	N.I. factor	GMP factor
(1)	(2)	(3)	(4)	(5)	(6)	(7)
Less than 20	5.00	.25	1.47	7.00	.50	2.20
20	5.05	.25	1.50	7.05	.50	2.24
21	5.10	.25	1.53	7.10	.55	2.28
22	5.15	.30	1.56	7.15	.60	2.32
23	5.20	.30	1.59	7.20	.65	2.36
24	5.25	.30	1.62	7.25	.70	2.40
25	5.30	.35	1.65	7.35	.75	2.45
26	5.35	.40	1.68	7.40	.80	2.50
27	5.40	.40	1.71	7.45	.85	2.55
28	5.45	.45	1.74	7.50	.90	2.60
29	5.50	.50	1.78	7.55	.95	2.66
30	5.55	.50	1.81	7.65	1.05	2.71
31	5.60	.55	1.85	7.70	1.15	2.77
32	5.65	.60	1.88	7.80	1.25	2.82
33	5.70	.65	1.92	7.90	1.35	2.88
34	5.75	.70	1.95	7.95	1.45	2.93
35	5.80	.80	1.99	8.05	1.55	2.99
36	5.85	.90	2.02	8.15	1.65	3.05
37	5.90	1.00	2.06	8.25	1.75	3.11
38	5.95	1.10	2.10	8.35	1.85	3.17
39	6.00	1.20	2.14	8.45	1.95	3.24
40	6.05	1.30	2.18	8.55	2.10	3.31
41	6.10	1.40	2.22	8.65	2.25	3.38
42	6.15	1.50	2.26	8.75	2.45	3.45
43	6.20	1.60	2.30	8.85	2.65	3.52
44	6.25	1.70	2.34	8.95	2.90	3.59
45	6.30	1.80	2.39	9.05	3.15	3.66
46	6.40	1.90	2.44	9.15	3.40	3.74
47	6.50	2.00	2.48	9.25	3.70	3.82
48	6.60	2.20	2.53	9.35	4.00	3.90
49	6.70	2.40	2.58	9.45	4.35	3.98
50	6.80	2.60	2.62	9.55	4.75	4.06
51	6.90	2.90	2.67	9.65	5.15	4.15
52	7.10	3.20	2.72	9.80	5.60	4.24
53	7.30	3.50	2.78	9.95	6.10	4.33
54	7.50	3.80	2.84	10.10	6.65	4.43
55	7.70	4.20	2.90	10.30	7.25	4.53
56	8.00	4.60	2.97	10.50	7.95	4.63
57	8.30	5.00	3.04	10.75	8.75	4.74
58	8.60	5.40	3.12	11.05	9.65	4.85
59	9.00	5.80	3.20	11.40	10.65	4.97
60	9.50	6.30	3.28	11.75	11.75	—
61	9.50	6.80	3.36	11.75	11.75	—
62	9.50	7.40	3.44	11.75	11.75	—
63	9.50	8.10	3.53	11.75	11.75	—
64	9.50	9.00	3.64	11.75	11.75	—
65	9.50	9.50	—	11.75	11.75	—

SCHEDULE F *(continued)*

PART III   Regulation F7

PRESERVED INTERCHANGE ARRANGEMENTS

Section 1—Civil service and Metropolitan Police Civil Staff service

1. This Section shall apply in relation to service or employment—

   (a) as a civil servant, or

   (b) in the metropolitan civil staffs within the meaning of section 15 of the Superannuation (Miscellaneous Provisions) Act 1967(**a**).

2. In relation to the said service or employment the specified date for the purposes of Regulation F7 shall be 1st January 1967.

3. In relation to the said service or employment the transfer value for the purposes of Regulation F7 shall be one payable under the provisions of a scheme made under section 1 of the Superannuation Act 1972(**b**) or of Rules made under sections 2 and 15 of the Superannuation (Miscellaneous Provisions) Act 1948(**c**), including such provisions as they have effect by virtue of section 15(2) of the Superannuation (Miscellaneous Provisions) Act 1967.

4. The specified authority for the purposes of Regulation F7 shall be—

   (a) in relation to service or employment as a civil servant, the Treasury or the Minister for the Civil Service;

   (b) in relation to service or employment in the metropolitan civil staffs, the Secretary of State.

5. In relation to such service or employment as is mentioned in paragraph 1, Regulation F7(1) shall have effect—

   (a) where the relevant date was before 1st April 1972, as if sub-paragraph *(c)* were omitted, and

   (b) where the relevant date was before 15th February 1971, as if sub-paragraph *(e)*(ii) were also omitted.

Section 2—Local Government, Fire, Education and Health service

1. This Section shall apply in relation to service or employment—

   (a) such as is mentioned in section 2(2)*(c)*, *(cc)*, *(d)*, *(e)* or *(ee)* of the Superannuation (Miscellaneous Provisions) Act 1948;

   (b) in respect of which awards may be made under the Firemen's Pensions Scheme, that is to say, under the Scheme for the time being in force under section 26 of the Fire Services Act 1947(**d**), or

   (c) in respect of which awards may be made under Regulations for the time being in force under section 10 of the Superannuation Act 1972,

---

(**a**) 1967 c. 28.   ⁻   (**b**) 1972 c. 11.
(**c**) 1948 c. 33, amended by 1972 c. 11, Sch. 6, para. 25.
(**d**) 1947 c. 41.

SCHEDULE F *(continued)*

section 67 of the National Health Service Act 1946(**a**), or section 66 of the National Health Service (Scotland) Act 1947(**b**).

2.— (1) Subject to sub-paragraph (2), in relation to the said service or employment the specified date for the purposes of Regulation F7 shall be 15th February 1971.

(2) Where in relation to a particular service or employment no provisions were in operation on 15th February 1971 for the payment of a transfer value to the police authority, as mentioned in Regulation F7(1)*(d)*, then in relation thereto the specified date for the purposes of Regulation F7 shall be the date on which such provisions first thereafter came into operation.

3. In relation to such service or employment as is mentioned in paragraph 1, the transfer value for the purposes of Regulation F7 shall be one payable under Rules made under sections 2 and 15 of the Superannuation (Miscellaneous Provisions) Act 1948 or under Regulations made under section 67 of the National Health Service Act 1946, section 66 of the National Health Service (Scotland) Act 1947 or section 7, 8, 9 or 10 of the Superannuation Act 1972.

4. The specified authority for the purposes of Regulation F7 shall be—

(a) in relation to such employment as is mentioned in section 2(2)*(c)*, *(cc)* or *(d)* of the Superannuation (Miscellaneous Provisions) Act 1948, the local authority maintaining the superannuation fund in the benefits of which the person concerned was entitled to participate;

(b) in relation to service in a fire brigade maintained by a local authority and in respect of which awards may be made under the Firemen's Pension Scheme, the fire authority concerned;

(c) in relation to any other service or employment, the Secretary of State.

Section 3—Other service or employment

1. This Section shall apply in relation to service or employment in which a person is subject to any superannuation arrangements specified in the second column of the following Table.

2. Subject to paragraph 5 in relation to any such service or employment the specified date for the purposes of Regulation F7 shall be 15th February 1971.

3.— (1) In relation to any such service or employment the transfer value for the purposes of Regulation F7 shall, subject to sub-paragraphs (2) and (3), be one of the like amount, and calculated in the like manner, as the transfer value which would have been receivable under Part III of the Superannuation (Local Government and Approved Employment) Interchange Rules 1969(**c**) had the person concerned entered local government employment, within the meaning of those Rules, on the date on which he became a regular policeman and in circumstances in which the said Part III applied.

(**a**) 1946 c. 81.   (**b**) 1947 c. 27.   (**c**) S.I. 1969/997.

SCHEDULE F *(continued)*

(2) For the purposes of sub-paragraph (1)—

(a) to the extent that the Table in Schedule 1 to the said Rules of 1969 does not contain entries in columns (1) and (2) thereof corresponding to the entries in the following Table, it shall be deemed to do so, and

(b) subject to paragraph 5, paragraph 6 of Schedule 1 to the said Rules of 1969 shall have effect as if any references therein to 18th August 1968 and to 18th August 1969 were, respectively, references to 15th February 1970 and to 15th February 1971 and sub-paragraphs (1)*(a)* and *(b)* and (3) were omitted.

(3) In relation to service in which a person is subject to the Isle of Man Police Pensions Regulations, that is to say, the Regulations for the time being in operation under section 16 of the Police (Isle of Man) Act 1962 (an Act of Tynwald), the transfer value shall be one payable under those Regulations.

4. In relation to any such service or employment the specified authority for the purposes of Regulation F7 shall be the persons having the general control and management of the relevant superannuation arrangements specified in the second column of the following Table.

5. In relation to service or employment in which a person is subject to—

(a) an Area Gas Board Protected Persons Superannuation Scheme,

(b) an Area Gas Board Staff Pension Scheme,

(c) the Gas Council Staff Pension Scheme, or

(d) the Independent Broadcasting Authority Staff Superannuation Fund and Staff Life Assurance Scheme,

the specified date for the purposes of Regulation F7 shall be 1st April 1973 and paragraph 3(2)*(b)* shall have effect as if for the dates "15th February 1970" and "15th February 1971" there were substituted, respectively, the dates "1st April 1971" and "1st April 1972".

TABLE

Employing body	Superannuation arrangements
Agricultural Research Council	Industrial Superannuation Scheme Agricultural Research Council Superannuation Scheme 1951
Area Electricity Board	British Electricity Authority Superannuation (Protected Persons) Scheme Electricity Board Superannuation (Protected Persons) Scheme Electricity Supply (Manual Workers) Superannuation Scheme Electricity Supply (Staff) Superannuation Scheme
British Airports Authority	The British Airports Authority Superannuation Scheme
British Broadcasting Corporation	The B.B.C. New Pension Scheme
British Council	British Council Superannuation Scheme

SCHEDULE F (continued)

Employing body	Superannuation arrangements
British European Airways Corporation	The Airways Corporations Joint Pension Scheme for General Staff members
British Gas Corporation or Area Gas Board	Area Gas Board Protected Persons Superannuation Scheme Area Gas Board Staff Pension Scheme
British Gas Corporation or Gas Council	Gas Council Staff Pension Scheme
British Overseas Airways Corporation	The Airways Corporations Joint Pension Scheme for General Staff members
British Waterways Board	Cheshire County Council Superannuation Fund—Divided Grand Union Canal Company Superannuation Fund Nottingham Corporation Superannuation Fund—Divided Scheme embodied in section 23 of and Schedule 4 to the Regent Canal and Dock Company (Grand Junction Canal Purchase) Act 1928(**a**) Scheme embodied in the Superannuation Act 1965(**b**) (as applied to former staff of the Lee Conservancy Board)
Central Electricity Generating Board	British Electricity Authority Superannuation (Protected Persons) Scheme Electricity Board Superannuation (Protected Persons) Scheme Electricity Supply (Manual Workers) Superannuation Scheme Electricity Supply (Staff) Superannuation Scheme
Commonwealth War Graves Commission	The Commonwealth War Graves Commission Superannuation Scheme (1952)
Corporation of Trinity House	Trinity House Service Superannuation Scheme
Crown Agents for Oversea Governments and Administrations	Crown Agents' Pension Scheme
Crown Estate Commissioners	Crown Estate Commissioners Superannuation Scheme
Development Commission	The Development Commission Superannuation Scheme 1940
Electricity Council	British Electricity Authority Superannuation (Protected Persons) Scheme Electricity Board Superannuation (Protected Persons) Scheme Electricity Supply (Manual Workers) Superannuation Scheme Electricity Supply (Staff) Superannuation Scheme

(**a**) 1928 c. xcviii.   (**b**) 1965 c. 74.

SCHEDULE F (continued)

Employing body	Superannuation arrangements
Forestry Commission	The Forestry Commission Superannuation Scheme
General Lighthouse Authority	General Lighthouse Fund Superannuation Scheme
Horserace Betting Levy Board	Horserace Betting Levy Board Pension Schemes A and B
Independent Broadcasting Authority	Independent Broadcasting Authority Staff Superannuation Fund and Staff Life Assurance Scheme
Industrial Training Boards	Industrial Training Boards Pension Fund
—	The Isle of Man Police Pensions Regulations
Metropolitan Water Board	Metropolitan Water Board Superannuation and Provident Fund Scheme
National Coal Board	National Coal Board Staff Superannuation Scheme
National Industrial Fuel Efficiency Service	National Industrial Fuel Efficiency Service Superannuation Scheme
National Institute of Agricultural Botany	Industrial Superannuation Scheme
Natural Environment Research Council	Natural Environment Research Council Superannuation Arrangements
North of Scotland Hydro-Electric Board	Hydroboard Superannuation Fund
Port of London Authority	Port of London Authority Pension Fund
Post Office	Post Office Staff Superannuation Scheme
Scottish Agricultural Colleges and Research Institutes	Industrial Superannuation Scheme
Science Research Council	Science Research Council Superannuation Scheme The Principal Non-Industrial Superannuation Scheme of the United Kingdom Atomic Energy Authority The United Kingdom Atomic Energy Authority's Industrial Superannuation Scheme
South of Scotland Electricity Board	The South of Scotland Electricity Board's Superannuation Scheme
United Kingdom Atomic Energy Authority	The Principal Non-Industrial Superannuation Scheme of the United Kingdom Atomic Energy Authority Protected Persons Superannuation Scheme of the United Kingdom Atomic Energy Authority The United Kingdom Atomic Energy Authority's Industrial Superannuation Scheme

Regulation G3   SCHEDULE G

ADDITIONAL AND FURTHER CONTRIBUTIONS

1. Where, in pursuance of paragraph (2) of Regulation G3 and such an election as is mentioned in paragraph (1) of that Regulation, additional or further pension contributions continue to be payable by a regular policeman, those contributions shall be payable at the rate specified in the second or, as the case may be, in the third column of the following Table opposite to the number of completed years of pensionable service in the first column thereof reckonable by the regular policeman immediately before 1st April 1973 otherwise than by reason of service on or after 1st April 1972 as a member of a police force or of the Royal Ulster Constabulary subject, however, to paragraph 2.

2. For the purposes of paragraph 1, no account shall be taken of any service reckonable as pensionable service by virtue of section 10 of the Police Pensions Act 1921(a).

TABLE

Completed years of pensionable service taken into account	Rate expressed as a percentage of pensionable pay	
	Additional contributions	Further contributions
1	0.1	0.1
2	0.1	0.1
3	0.2	0.2
4	0.3	0.2
5	0.3	0.3
6	0.4	0.3
7	0.5	0.4
8	0.6	0.5
9	0.7	0.6
10	0.9	0.7
11	1.1	0.8

(a) 1921 c. 31.

SCHEDULE H

Regulation H2

MEDICAL APPEALS

1. Every notice of appeal under Regulation H2(2) shall be in writing.

2. On receipt of the notice of appeal the police authority shall forward to the Secretary of State 2 copies thereof and of the certificate appealed against, with the name and address of the appellant.

3. A medical referee shall appoint a time and place for interviewing the appellant and for any such further interviews or examinations as he may consider necessary and shall give reasonable notice thereof to the appellant and the police authority.

4. At any time before any interview with the medical referee the appellant or the police authority may submit to the medical referee a statement relating to the subject matter of the appeal, and if they so submit a statement they shall send a copy thereof to the other party.

5. Any interview or examination may be attended by—

    (a) the selected medical practitioner; and

    (b) any duly qualified medical practitioner appointed for the purpose by either party.

6. The medical referee shall give written notice to the police authority and appellant of his decision and, if that decision is that he disagrees with any part of the certificate of the selected medical practitioner, shall send a copy of his certificate to the police authority and the appellant.

7.— (1) The medical referee shall be entitled to such fees and allowances as the Secretary of State may from time to time determine.

(2) The said fees and allowances shall be paid by the police authority and shall be treated as part of the police authority's expenses for the purposes of this Schedule.

8.— (1) Save as hereinafter provided, the expenses of each party to the appeal shall be borne by that party.

(2) Where the medical referee decides in favour of the police authority, the authority may require the appellant to pay towards the cost of the appeal such sum not exceeding the referee's total fees and allowances as the authority think fit.

(3) Where the medical referee decides in favour of the appellant, the police authority shall refund to the appellant any expenses actually and reasonably incurred by the appellant in respect of any such interview or examination as is mentioned in paragraph 3.

Regulations I2 and I3   SCHEDULE I

SERVICEMEN—INCREASE OF AWARDS

1.— (1) This paragraph shall apply where a pension payable to a serviceman in pursuance of paragraph (2) or (3) of Regulation I2 is increased in pursuance of paragraph (4) of that Regulation.

(2) The increased amount of the pension payable to the serviceman for any period shall not, when aggregated with the amount of any armed forces award which is also payable to or in respect of him for that period, exceed the amount of the award which would have been payable for that period if the injury as a result of which he is permanently disabled had been treated as if it were an injury received without his own default in the execution of his duty as a regular policeman.

(3) The reference in the preceding sub-paragraph to an armed forces award shall not include an allowance for constant attendance, wear and tear of clothing or comforts.

2.— (1) This paragraph shall apply where a pension payable to the widow of a serviceman in pursuance of paragraph (1) or (3) of Regulation I3 is increased in pursuance of paragraph (5) of that Regulation.

(2) The increased amount of the pension payable to the widow for any period shall not, when aggregated with the amount of any armed forces award which is also so payable for that period in respect of her husband, exceed the amount of the pension which would have been payable for that period if the injury as a result of which her husband had died had been treated as if it were an injury received without his own default in the execution of his duty as a regular policeman.

3.— (1) This paragraph shall apply when an allowance payable to the child of a serviceman in pursuance of paragraph (4) of Regulation I3 is increased in pursuance of paragraph (5) of that Regulation.

(2) The increased amount of the allowance payable to the child for any period shall not, when aggregated with the amount of any armed forces award payable to or for the child for that period in respect of the serviceman, exceed the amount of the allowance which would have been payable for that period if the injury as a result of which he had died had been treated as if it were an injury received without his own default in the execution of his duty as a regular policeman.

4.— (1) In this Schedule a reference to an armed forces award is a reference to an armed forces pension or other award payable in pursuance of a Royal Warrant or other instrument.

(2) Where such an armed forces award as mentioned in paragraph 1(2), 2(2) or 3(2) is a gratuity, the amount thereof payable for any period shall, for the purposes of the provision in question, be deemed to be the amount which would have been payable for that period in respect of such an annuity as is hereinafter mentioned if, at the date on which the gratuity became payable, it had been applied in the purchase of such an annuity.

The annuity referred to in this sub-paragraph is an immediate life annuity, dependent on the life of the serviceman, the widow or, as the case may be, the child concerned, granted under Part I of the Government Annuities Act 1929(**a**).

SCHEDULE J   Regulation J4

SPECIAL CASES—EXCEPTIONS AND MODIFICATIONS

PART I

PERSONAL AWARDS

Policeman's ordinary pension

Policeman serving on 15th February 1971 and retiring in the rank of commander (otherwise than in metropolitan police force)

1. In the case of a member of a home police force who was serving as a regular policeman on 15th February 1971 and first retired on or after that date when a commander in a police force other than the metropolitan police force, in relation to that first retirement Regulation B1(2) shall have effect as if sub-paragraph *(b)* were omitted therefrom.

Policeman with service before 8th August 1961

2. In the case of a regular policeman who served as such before 8th August 1961, Regulation B1(5) shall have effect as if the words "but, in the case of" to the end were omitted.

Policeman who retired before 25th October 1984

3. In the case of a regular policeman who retired before 25th October 1984, Regulation B1(3) shall have effect as if sub-paragraph *(b)* thereof were omitted.

Commutation by policeman who retires or retired before 1st October 1987

4.— (1) This paragraph shall apply in the case of a regular policeman who—

   (a) retired with an ordinary pension under the Regulations of 1973, or

   (b) retires with an ordinary pension under these Regulations before 1st October 1987.

(2) Regulation B7(1) shall have effect as if sub-paragraph *(b)* thereof were omitted in the case of such a regular policeman—

   (a) who retired as mentioned in sub-paragraph (1)*(a)* of this paragraph and commuted a portion of his pension under the Regulations of 1973, or

   (b) other than a policeman such as is referred to in paragraph *(a)* of this

---

(**a**) 1929 c. 29.

SCHEDULE J *(continued)*

sub-paragraph who not later than 6 months after his retirement elects that this sub-paragraph should apply in his case;

and any election under paragraph *(b)* of this sub-paragraph shall be made by notice in writing given to the police authority.

Policeman's ill-health pension

Policeman who is serving on 1st April 1987 or retired before that date

5. In the case of a regular policeman who either is serving as such on 1st April 1987 or retired before that date, Regulation K1(5) shall have effect as if the words "but he is not a regular policeman to whom Regulation B5 applies" and sub-paragraph *(c)* were omitted therefrom.

Policeman's injury award

Policeman serving on 1st April 1972 or ceasing to serve before 1st April 1973 who has less than 5 years' pensionable service

6.— (1) This paragraph shall apply in the case of a member of a police force who—

> *(a)* received a relevant injury (within the meaning of Regulation B4) during a period of service which included 1st April 1972 or ended before 1st April 1973, and

> *(b)* is entitled to reckon less than 5 years' pensionable service.

(2) In the case of such a member an injury pension shall be calculated and payable either in accordance with Part V of Schedule B (where the next following paragraph also applies, as modified thereby) or in accordance with Regulation 22 of the Police Pensions Regulations 1971(**a**) as from time to time amended (*supplemental pension*), whichever would have been the more favourable in his case if applied thereto when he first became entitled to the pension.

Policeman ceasing to serve before 1st April 1987

7.— (1) This paragraph shall apply in the case of a member of a police force who received a relevant injury (within the meaning of Regulation B4) during a period of service which ended before 1st April 1987.

(2) In the case of such a member paragraph 4 of Part V of Schedule B shall have effect as if—

> *(a)* the sickness benefit referred to in sub-paragraph (3)*(c)*(i) thereof did not include such benefit to which the member is only entitled by virtue of section 50A of the Social Security Act 1975(**b**), and

---

(**a**) S.I. 1971/232. (**b**) 1975 c. 14; s. 50A inserted by 1982 c. 24, s. 39.

SCHEDULE J *(continued)*

(b) sub-paragraph (3)*(c)*(iii) thereof were omitted.

Policeman's deferred pension

Policeman with service or employment both before, and on or after, 6th April 1978

8.— (1) This paragraph shall apply in the case of a regular policeman who (subject to the provisions hereof) is entitled to a deferred pension under Regulation B5 where—

(a) the period of pensionable service referred to in paragraph (1)*(a)* of that Regulation is reckonable by reason of service or employment partly before, and partly on or after, 6th April 1978, or

(b) the aggregate period of service or employment referred to in paragraph (1)*(b)* of that Regulation includes service or employment partly before, and partly on or after, that date.

(2) Such a regular policeman may elect that Regulation B5 shall not apply in his case by notice in writing given to the police authority, subject to sub-paragraph (4), within 3 months of his ceasing to be a member of a police force.

(3) Where immediately before his death such a regular policeman enjoyed, but had not exercised, the right of election conferred by sub-paragraph (2), his widow may request that these Regulations should have effect as if he had exercised that right by notice in writing given to the police authority, subject to sub-paragraph (4), within 3 months of his death; and, in such case, the policeman shall be deemed to have exercised that right.

(4) Where the police authority so allow, a notice for the purposes of sub-paragraph (2) or (3) may be given after the expiry of the 3 month period there mentioned if it is given within such longer period as they may allow in the circumstances of the case; and, without prejudice to Regulation 3 of the Police Pensions (Supplementary Provisions) Regulations 1987**(a)**, a notice duly given for the purposes of paragraph (2) or (3) of Regulation 23D of the Regulations of 1973 shall be effective for the purposes of sub-paragraph (2) or (3) of this paragraph.

(5) Where such a regular policeman has, or is deemed to have, exercised the right of election conferred by sub-paragraph (2)—

(a) Regulation B5 shall not apply in his case and, accordingly, he shall not thereunder be entitled to a deferred pension, but

(b) in lieu thereof he (or his estate) shall be entitled to an award under this paragraph.

(6) Subject to sub-paragraph (7), an award under this paragraph shall comprise—

(a) an award by way of repayment of the policeman's aggregate pension contributions in respect of the relevant period of service calculated, however, in accordance with sub-paragraph (8), and

---

(a) S.I. 1987/256.

SCHEDULE J *(continued)*

(b) a deferred pension calculated and payable as provided in sub-paragraph (9).

(7) Where a policeman whose contracted-out employment is less than 5 years ceases to serve before he has attained the age of 26 years—

(a) sub-paragraph (8) shall not apply for the purposes of calculating the award by way of repayment of his aggregate contributions, but

(b) he shall not be entitled to a deferred pension in pursuance of sub-paragraph (6)*(b)*.

(8) Save where sub-paragraph (7) applies, for the purposes of calculating the award mentioned in sub-paragraph (6)*(a)*—

(a) account shall be taken of such contributions or payments as are mentioned in sub-paragraph *(a)*, *(b)* or *(c)* of Regulation A10(2) only to the extent that either—

(i) they were made by the policeman before the end of the service appropriate in his case mentioned in sub-paragraph (10), or

(ii) they were made otherwise than as aforesaid but account was taken in their calculation of that service,

and sub-paragraph *(d)* thereof shall have effect accordingly, and

(b) in the circumstances mentioned in sub-paragraph *(e)* of Regulation A10(2), the award there mentioned shall be that which would have been made if it took into account only contributions or analogous payments—

(i) made by the person concerned before the end of the service appropriate in his case, or

(ii) made otherwise than as aforesaid but specified by the person responsible for the superannuation arrangements applicable to the previous service or employment mentioned in the said sub-paragraph *(e)* as having been made for the purpose of increasing any benefit which might become payable in respect of so much of that previous service or employment as forms part of the service appropriate in the policeman's case.

(9) A deferred pension in pursuance of sub-paragraph (6)*(b)* shall be calculated and be payable as mentioned in Regulation B5(4) except that in calculating the pension no account shall be taken of so much of the policeman's pensionable service as is reckonable by reason of the service appropriate in his case mentioned in sub-paragraph (10).

(10) The appropriate service referred to in sub-paragraphs (8) and (9) is—

(a) service or employment before 6th April 1978, in the case of a policeman who either—

(i) ceases to serve before he has attained the age of 26 years, or

(ii) would not be such a regular policeman as is mentioned in Regulation B5(1)*(a)* or *(b)* if, for the purposes thereof, there were

SCHEDULE J *(continued)*

disregarded any period of pensionable service reckonable by reason of, or any period of, service or employment before the said date;

(b) service or employment before 6th April 1975, in any other case.

(11) Regulations B7 to B11 *(commutation, allocation and deduction of tax)* shall apply in relation to an award in pursuance of sub-paragraph (6)*(a)* or *(b)* as though this paragraph were included in Part B of these Regulations.

Pension by way of equivalent pension benefit

Policeman serving on 5th April 1975

9.— (1) This paragraph shall apply in the case of a regular policeman who was serving as such on 5th April 1975 and ceases or has ceased so to serve in circumstances—

(a) in which no transfer value is payable or has been paid in respect of him;

(b) which do not entitle him to a pension otherwise than in pursuance of paragraph 8(6)*(b)* or of this paragraph, and

(c) in which no payment in lieu of contributions has been made.

(2) This paragraph shall also apply in the case of a regular policeman who was serving as such on 5th April 1975 and ceases or has ceased so to serve in circumstances in which either a transfer value is payable under Regulation F8 by reason of paragraph 1*(b)* thereof or under Regulation F9 or a transfer value was payable under Regulation 84 or 85 of the Regulations of 1973 if, but only if, he satisfies the police authority that he is not entitled under any superannuation arrangements (including these Regulations) to a pension—

(a) in the calculation of which account would be taken of the service which would be taken into account in calculating a pension under this paragraph, and

(b) which would be at least as favourable in his case as a pension under this paragraph.

(3) Such a regular policeman as is mentioned in sub-paragraph (1) or (2)—

(a) on attaining state pensionable age, and

(b) in the case mentioned in sub-paragraph (2), satisfying the police authority as there mentioned,

shall be entitled to a pension which equals the graduated retirement benefit mentioned in Regulation A5(4).

(4) Regulation B8 *(commutation—small pensions)* shall apply in relation to a pension in pursuance of sub-paragraph (3) as though this paragraph were included in Part B of these Regulations.

SCHEDULE J (continued)

PART II

WIDOWS' AWARDS

Widow's ordinary pension

Widow whose husband retired before 1st April 1987

1.— (1) This paragraph shall apply in the case of the widow of a regular policeman who retired before 1st April 1987.

(2) In the case of such a widow, Regulation C1(1) shall have effect as if the words "except that" to the end were omitted.

Application of paragraphs 3, 4 and 5

2. Paragraphs 3, 4 and 5 shall only apply in the case of a widow whose husband either was serving as a regular policeman or was entitled to a pension other than a deferred pension—

   (a) on 1st April 1973, or

   (b) at the date of his death where that date was before 1st July 1973.

Pre-1972 pensionable service not up-rated

3.— (1) This paragraph shall apply in the case of such a widow as is mentioned in paragraph 2 where—

   (a) her husband last before 1st April 1972 paid pension contributions at a rate related to 5% of his pensionable pay, and

   (b) neither he nor the widow exercised any right of election accorded by Regulation 58(2), 59(2), 60(2) or 61(2) of the Regulations of 1973,

and, in such a case Part I of Schedule C ("Part I") shall have effect as if for sub-paragraphs (1), (2) and (3) of paragraph 1 thereof there were substituted the like provision as is made by the following sub-paragraph.

(2) Where this paragraph applies the annual amount of the widow's ordinary pension shall, subject to paragraphs 2 and 3 of Part I, equal a half of the amount specified in paragraph 5(1) of this Part:

Provided that the amount payable in respect of any week on account of the pension shall not be less than it would have been either—

   (a) had the weekly amount thereof fallen to be calculated as provided in Scheme II of Part II of Schedule 3 to the Police Pensions Regulations 1971(**a**), or

   (b) had the annual amount thereof fallen to be calculated in accordance with Part V of Schedule C in like manner as a widow's requisite benefit pension.

(**a**) S.I. 1971/232.

SCHEDULE J *(continued)*

Pre-1972 pensionable service up-rated to third but not to half rate

4.— (1) This paragraph shall apply in the case of such a widow as is mentioned in paragraph 2 where—

(a) paragraph 3 does not apply, and

(b) neither her husband nor the widow exercised any right of election accorded by Regulation 58(3), 59(3), 60(3), or 61(3) of the Regulations of 1973,

and, in such a case, Part I of Schedule C ("Part I") shall have effect as if for sub-paragraph (1) of paragraph 1 thereof there were substituted the like provision as is made by the following sub-paragraph.

(2) Where this paragraph applies, the annual amount of the widow's ordinary pension shall, subject to paragraphs 2 and 3 of Part I, be the aggregate of—

(a) an amount equal to a third of the annual amount of the pension or notional pension mentioned in sub-paragraph (2) of paragraph 1 of Part I, and

(b) a sixth of the amount specified in paragraph 5(1) of this Part,

except that, where the husband died otherwise than while in receipt of an ordinary or short service pension and the said aggregate is less than a half of the amount specified in paragraph 5(2) of this Part, the annual amount of the widow's ordinary pension shall equal a half of the amount so specified:

Provided that the annual amount of the widow's ordinary pension shall not be less than it would have been had it fallen to be calculated in accordance with Part V of Schedule C in like manner as a widow's requisite benefit pension.

Specified amounts for purposes of paragraphs 3 and 4

5.— (1) The references in paragraphs 3(2) and 4(2) to the amount specified in this sub-paragraph are references to the amount which is, subject to sub-paragraph (3) of this paragraph, the difference between the two following amounts, namely—

(a) an amount which is the aggregate of—

(i) an amount equal to a sixtieth of the husband's average pensionable pay multipled by the period in years of his pensionable service up to 20 years, and

(ii) an amount equal to 2 sixtieths of that pay multiplied by the period in years by which his pensionable service exceeds 20 years;

(b) an amount calculated as aforesaid but by reference only to the husband's pre-1972 pensionable service.

(2) The reference in paragraph 4(2) to the amount specified in this sub-paragraph is a reference to the annual amount of the pension or notional pension mentioned in sub-paragraph (2) of paragraph 1 of Part I of Schedule C calculated in accordance with sub-paragraph (3) thereof but, subject to sub-paragraph (3) of this paragraph—

(a) where the husband's weighted relevant pensionable service does not exceed 20 years, by reference thereto;

SCHEDULE J *(continued)*

(b) where that service exceeds 20 years, by reference to his relevant pensionable service with the addition of a half of his pre-1972 pensionable service,

instead of by reference to his pensionable service.

(3) Where the husband's pensionable service exceeds 30 years there shall be reduced by that excess—

(a) his pensionable service taken into account for the purposes of sub-paragraph (1)*(a)*;

(b) his pre-1972 pensionable service taken into account for the purposes of sub-paragraph (1)*(b)*;

(c) his pre-1972 pensionable service taken into account for the purposes of sub-paragraph (2)*(b)* (otherwise than for the purpose of determining his relevant pensionable service).

(4) Subject to sub-paragraph (5), in this paragraph—

"pre-1972 pensionable service" means the period of pensionable service in years reckonable by the husband—

(a) otherwise than by reason of service as a member of a police force or of the Royal Ulster Constabulary on or after 1st April 1972;

(b) otherwise than by virtue of—

(i) Regulation F3(1)*(f)* (*British Airports Authority constabulary service*),

(ii) Regulation F4, F5 or F7 (*previous service and preserved interchange arrangements*) where the conditions specified in the Regulation in question were satisfied on or after 1st April 1973,

(iii) Regulation F6 (*current interchange arrangements*), or

(iv) section 10 of the Police Pensions Act 1921**(a)**, and

(c) other than pensionable service reckonable by him immediately before 1st April 1973, which was reckonable otherwise than as mentioned in sub-paragraph (a) above and did not exceed a year;

"relevant pensionable service" means the period in years of the husband's pensionable service reduced by his pre-1972 pensionable service;

"weighted relevant pensionable service" means the husband's relevant pensionable service, so much of such service as exceeds his relevant number of years (if any) being counted twice and, for the purposes hereof, "relevant number of years" means the period in years by which his pre-1972 pensionable service falls short of 20 years.

(5) Where the husband ceased to serve as a regular policeman before 24th January 1975 (without prejudice to the provisions of paragraphs 1, 2 and 3 of Part IV of this Schedule), sub-paragraph (4) shall have effect as if for the

---

(a) 1921 c. 31.

SCHEDULE J *(continued)*

definitions therein of "relevant pensionable service" and "weighted relevant pensionable service" there were substituted the following definitions:—

"relevant pensionable service" means the period in years of the husband's pensionable service reduced by his completed years of pre-1972 pensionable service;

"weighted relevant pensionable service" means the husband's completed years of relevant pensionable service up to the relevant number of years with the addition of a year for each completed half-year by which his relevant pensionable service exceeds the relevant number of years and, for the purposes hereof, "relevant number of years" means the period in years by which his completed years of pre-1972 pensionable service fall short of 20 years.

Widow's special gratuity

Widow whose husband died before 25th November 1982

6.— (1) This paragraph shall apply in the case of a widow of a member of a police force who died while serving as such before 25th November 1982.

(2) In the case of such a widow, Regulation C2(2)*(b)* shall have effect as if the words "together with" to the end were omitted.

Widow's accrued pension

Application of paragraph 8 and service for the purposes thereof

7.— (1) Paragraph 8 shall apply in the case of the widow of a regular policeman—

(a) who was not entitled to his deferred pension in pursuance of paragraph 8(6)*(b)* of Part I of this Schedule, and

(b) in relation to whom any of the conditions specified in the first column of either Table B or C are satisfied.

(2) The husband's half-rate and mixed-rate service for the purposes of paragraph 8 shall depend upon the conditions specified in the first column of Table A, B or C which are satisfied in relation to him and shall be the aggregate of the periods of pensionable service specified opposite the conditions which are so satisfied—

(a) in the case of half-rate service, in the second column of the Table in question, and

(b) in the case of mixed-rate service, in the third column thereof,

so, however, that where a period of pensionable service falls within more than one of the entries in Table A it shall not be taken into account more than once.

(3) The following Tables are those referred to in sub-paragraphs (1) and (2):—

SCHEDULE J *(continued)*

Table A: Service Counting Fully as both Half-Rate and Mixed-Rate Service

Condition	Half-rate service	Mixed-rate service
(a) If the husband has pensionable service reckonable by reason of police service on or after 1st April 1972.	That pensionable service	That pensionable service
(b) If he has pensionable service reckonable by virtue of Regulation F6 *(current interchange arrangements)*.	,,	,,
(c) If he has pensionable service reckonable by virtue of section 10 of the Police Pensions Act 1921.	,,	,,
(d) If he has pensionable service reckonable by virtue of Regulation I7(1) and the proviso to Regulation I8(1) by reason of a period of relevant service in the armed forces on or after 1st April 1956.	,,	,,
(e) If he has pensionable service which, immediately before 1st April 1973, was reckonable by him otherwise than by reason of police service on or after 1st April 1972 and was for a period of less than a complete year.	,,	,,
(f) If he has pensionable service reckonable by virtue of Regulation F3(1)*(f)* *(British Airports Authority constabulary service)* otherwise, where he has been granted a back service credit, than by reason of that credit (subject, however, to sub-paragraph (5) below).	,,	,,
(g) If he has pensionable service reckonable by virtue of Regulation F3(1)*(f)* by reason that he had been granted a back service credit and he had elected as mentioned in Regulation 61A(2)*(a)* of the Regulations of 1973 to make a special payment by way of a lump sum (subject, however, to sub-paragraphs (5) and (6) below).	,,	,,

SCHEDULE J *(continued)*

TABLE B: SERVICE COUNTING IN PART AS BOTH HALF-RATE AND MIXED-RATE SERVICE

Condition	Half-rate service	Mixed-rate service
(a) If the husband has pensionable service reckonable by virtue of Regulation F3(1)*(f)* by reason that he had been granted a back service credit and he had elected as mentioned in Regulation 61A(2)*(b)* of the Regulations of 1973 to pay special contributions (subject, however, to sub-paragraphs (5) and (6) below).	The proportion specified in sub-paragraph (7) below of that pensionable service.	The proportion specified in sub-paragraph (7) below of that pensionable service.
(b) If he has pensionable service reckonable by virtue of Regulation F3(1)*(f)* by reason that he had been granted a back service credit and his deferred pension fell to be reduced as mentioned in paragraph 3 of Part VI of this Schedule (subject, however, to sub-paragraph (5) below).	The proportion specified in sub-paragraph (8) below of that pensionable service.	The proportion specified in sub-paragraph (8) below of that pensionable service.

TABLE C: SERVICE COUNTING FULLY OR IN PART EITHER AS HALF-RATE OR AS MIXED-RATE SERVICE

Condition	Half-rate service	Mixed-rate service
(a) If the husband has pensionable service reckonable by reason of police service in respect of which he paid pension contributions at a rate related to 6.25% of his pensionable pay.	—	That pensionable service.
(b) If he has pensionable service not mentioned in the first column of Table A which, immediately before 1st April 1973, was reckonable by him and he had elected as mentioned in Regulation 59(3)*(a)* of the Regulations of 1973 to make a further payment by way of a lump sum.	That pensionable service.	—
(c) If he has such pensionable service as aforesaid and he had elected as mentioned in Regulation 59(2)*(a)* of the Regulations of 1973 to make an additional payment by way of a lump sum.	—	That pensionable service.
(d) If he has such pensionable service as aforesaid, he had elected as mentioned in Regulation 58(3) of the Regulations of 1973 and, immediately before he retired, was paying further contributions in pursuance of that election.	The proportion specified in sub-paragraph (9) below of that pensionable service.	—

SCHEDULE J *(continued)*

TABLE C *(continued)*

Condition	Half-rate service	Mixed-rate service
(e) If he has such pensionable service as aforesaid, he had elected as mentioned in Regulation 57 and 58(2) of the Regulations of 1973 and, immediately before he retired, was paying additional contributions in pursuance of that election.	—	The proportion specified in sub-paragraph (9) below of the period of pensionable service by reference to which the rate of payment of additional contributions was determined (including any fraction of a year disregarded for that purpose).
(f) If he has such pensionable service as aforesaid and his deferred pension fell to be reduced as mentioned in paragraph 3 of Part VIII of Schedule B.	The proportion mentioned in sub-paragraph (8) below of the period of pensionable service by reference to which that reduction was determined (including any fraction of a year disregarded for that purpose).	—
(g) If he has such service as aforesaid and his deferred pension fell to be reduced as mentioned in paragraph 2 of Part VIII of Schedule B.	—	The proportion specified in sub-paragraph (8) below of the period of pensionable service by reference to which that reduction was determined (including any fraction of a year disregarded for that purpose).

SCHEDULE J *(continued)*

(4) In this paragraph (including the Tables)—

(a) any reference to police service is a reference to service as a member of a police force or of the Royal Ulster Constabulary;

(b) the expressions "Airports Scheme" and "Scheme deduction" have the same meanings as in Regulation 61A of the Regulations of 1973 and the proviso to paragraph (3) of that Regulation shall have effect for the purposes of sub-paragraph (5) as it has effect for the purposes of the said paragraph (3), and

(c) any reference to a person having been granted a back service credit is a reference to his having been granted such a credit, within the meaning of the Airports Scheme, before his transfer from the British Airports Authority constabulary.

(5) Where, for the purposes of the Airports Scheme, any payments were made by, or on behalf of, the husband for securing family benefits thereunder in respect of a back service credit, entries *(f)* and *(g)* in Table A and the entries in Table B shall have effect as though, by virtue of Regulation F3(1)*(f)*, there were reckonable by him, by reason of the back service credit, only that part of the pensionable service so reckonable which bears the same proportion to the whole as the Scheme deduction in his case bears to what BAA plc certifies it would have been if the payments first mentioned in this sub-paragraph had not been made so, however, that, where the Scheme deduction is zero, entry *(f)* in Table A shall have effect as though the husband had no back service credit.

(6) Without prejudice to sub-paragraph (5), where the husband satisfies the conditions specified in both entry *(g)* in Table A and entry *(a)* in Table B, the references in those entries to his pensionable service reckonable by virtue of Regulation F3(1)*(f)* by reason of a back service credit shall be construed—

(a) in the case of entry *(g)* in Table A, as a reference to that part of that service which bears the same proportion to the whole as the lump sum payment under Regulation 61A of the Regulations of 1973 bears to the Scheme deduction;

(b) in the case of entry *(a)* in Table B, as a reference to the other part of that service.

(7) The proportion referred to in entry *(a)* in Table B shall be the proportion which the period for which the husband paid special contributions under Regulation 61A of the Regulations of 1973 bore to the period from the date of his transfer from the British Airports Authority constabulary until the date mentioned in paragraph (4)*(a)* or *(b)* of that Regulation.

(8) The proportion referred to in entry *(b)* in Table B and in entries *(f)* and *(g)* in Table C shall be the proportion which the husband's actual police service—

(a) on or after his transfer from the British Airports constabulary, in the case of entry *(b)* in Table B,

(b) on or after 1st April 1972, in the case entry *(f)* in Table C, or

(c) on or after 1st April 1956, in the case of entry *(g)* in Table C,

bears to the period of such service as he would have had if (irrespective of the date of his death) he had continued to serve until entitled to an immediately payable ordinary pension or until he could be required to retire on account of

SCHEDULE J *(continued)*

age, whichever is the earlier, each period being reckoned in completed years and completed months:

Provided that where on ceasing to serve as a regular policeman he had already served as aforesaid, the said proportion shall be the whole.

(9) The proportion referred to in entries *(d)* and *(e)* in Table C shall be the proportion which the period for which the husband paid further contributions or, as the case may be, additional contributions, bore to the period by which the pensionable service he was entitled to reckon on the relevant date fell short of 25 years or, where that period is less than 5 years, to a period of 5 years, each period being reckoned in completed years and completed months.

In this sub-paragraph "the relevant date" means—

    (a) where the husband last served as a regular policeman before 6th April 1978, the date on which he made the election referred to in the entry in question;

    (b) in any other case, the date from which the further contributions or, as the case may be, additional contributions were payable in pursuance of the election referred to in the entry in question.

Husband's pensionable service not fully up-rated

8.— (1) In the case of such a widow as is mentioned in paragraph 7(1), Part III of Schedule C shall have effect as if paragraph 1(1) thereof provided that the annual amount of her accrued pension should equal the aggregate of the following amounts namely—

    (a) in respect of her husband's half-rate service, a sixth of the corresponding proportion of his deferred pension;

    (b) in respect of his mixed-rate service, a third of the corresponding proportion of his deferred pension.

(2) For the purposes of sub-paragraph (1) "the corresponding proportion", in relation to the husband's deferred pension, means the proportion which his half-rate or, as the case may be, his mixed-rate service bears to the pensionable service reckonable by him.

(3) Unless the husband ceased to serve as a regular policeman before 1st April 1987 where—

    (a) the husband's half-rate service;

    (b) his mixed-rate service, or

    (c) the pensionable service reckonable by him,

exceeds 30 years, then, for the purposes of this paragraph, the period by which, in each case, it exceeds 30 years shall be disregarded.

Gratuity in lieu of widow's pension

Widow whose husband ceased to serve before 1st April 1987

9.— (1) This paragraph shall apply in the case of a widow of a member of a police force who ceased to serve before 1st April 1987.

SCHEDULE J *(continued)*

(2) In the case of such a widow, Regulation E4 shall have effect as if paragraph (6) thereof were omitted.

Widow's pension in case of post-retirement marriage

Widow whose husband ceased to serve before 1st April 1987

10.— (1) This paragraph shall apply in the case of a widow of a regular policeman who ceased to serve before 1st April 1987.

(2) Where such a widow is entitled to a pension under Regulation C5(3), Regulation E8 shall apply in relation to that pension as if, in paragraph (1) thereof, the words "and, for the purposes" to the end were omitted.

PART III

CHILDREN'S AWARDS

Child's ordinary allowance

Child whose parent retired before 1st April 1987

1.— (1) This paragraph shall apply in the case of the child of a regular policeman who retired before 1st April 1987.

(2) In the case of such a child, Regulation D1(1) *(child's ordinary allowance)* shall have effect as if the words "except that" to the end were omitted.

(3) In the case of such a child, paragraph 1 of Part I of Schedule D *(child's ordinary allowance)* shall have effect as if the provisions for the reduction of a pension to be ignored for the purposes of sub-paragraph (4) in pursuance of sub-paragraph (5)*(b)*(ii) thereof included those of Regulation B7(8)*(b)* *(commutation)*.

Transitional modification of Part I of Schedule D

2.— (1) This paragraph shall apply in the case of a child whose father was serving as a regular policeman or entitled to a pension other than a deferred pension either—

(a) on 1st April 1973, or

(b) at the date of his death where that date is before 1st July 1973,

where neither he nor his widow exercised any right of election accorded by Regulation 58, 59, 60 or 61 of the Regulations of 1973.

(2) Where this paragraph applies, Part I of Schedule D shall have effect as if for any reference in paragraph 1 or 2 thereof to the relevant parent's pension or notional pension there were substituted a reference to the amount specified in the following sub-paragraph and as if paragraph 3 were omitted.

(3) The reference in sub-paragraph (2) to the amount specified in this sub-paragraph is, subject to sub-paragraph (4), the difference between the two following amounts, namely—

SCHEDULE J *(continued)*

(a) an amount which is the aggregate of—

(i) an amount equal to a sixtieth of the father's average pensionable pay multiplied by the period in years of his pensionable service up to 20 years,

(ii) an amount equal to 2 sixtieths of that pay multiplied by the period in years by which his pensionable service exceeds 20 years;

(b) an amount calculated as aforesaid but by reference only to the father's pre-1972 pensionable service.

(4) Where the father's pensionable service exceeds 30 years, then there shall be reduced by that excess—

(a) his pensionable service taken into account for the purposes of sub-paragraph (3)*(a)*;

(b) his pre-1972 pensionable service taken into account for the purposes of sub-paragraph (3)*(b)*.

(5) In this paragraph "pre-1972 pensionable service" has the meaning assigned thereto by paragraph 5(4) of Part II of this Schedule.

Child whose relevant parent died before 1st April 1973

3.— (1) This paragraph shall apply in the case of the child of a regular policeman who died before 1st April 1973.

(2) Where the relevant parent was the child's only surviving parent or in respect of any period after the death of the child's other parent, the child's ordinary allowance determined—

(a) in accordance with paragraphs 2 and 4 of Part I of Schedule D, or

(b) in accordance with paragraph 5 of the said Part I,

may be increased in accordance with Part III of Schedule 4 to the Police Pensions Regulations 1971(**a**).

Child's accrued allowance

Transitional modification of Part III of Schedule D

4.— (1) This paragraph shall apply in the case of a child where the relevant parent is the father and he both—

(a) was not entitled to his deferred pension in pursuance of paragraph 8(6)*(b)* of Part I of this Schedule, and

(b) was entitled to reckon pensionable service otherwise than—

(i) by reason of service as a member of a police force or of the Royal Ulster Constabulary on or after 1st April 1972,

(ii) by virtue of Regulation F7 *(preserved interchange arrangements)* where the conditions specified in paragraph (1) thereof are satisfied on or after 1st April 1973,

(iii) by virtue of Regulation I7(1) and the proviso to Regulation I8(1)

(**a**) S.I. 1971/232.

SCHEDULE J *(continued)*

by reason of a period of relevant service in the armed forces on or after 1st April 1956, or

(iv) by virtue of section 10 of the Police Pensions Act 1921(**a**).

(2) Where this paragraph applies, Part III of Schedule D shall have effect as if for any reference in paragraph 2(1) thereof to the relevant parent's deferred pension were a reference to the proportion thereof specified in sub-paragraph (4).

(3) In accordance with sub-paragraph (2), where this paragraph applies, paragraphs 1(2) and (3) and 2(2) and (3) of Part I of Schedule D as applied by Part III thereof shall have effect without regard to paragraph 2 of this Part but as if for any reference therein to the relevant parent's pension or notional pension there were substituted a reference to the proportion specified in the following sub-paragraph of a deferred pension calculated in accordance with paragraph 2(2) of the said Part III.

(4) The reference in sub-paragraphs (2) and (3) to the proportion specified in this sub-paragraph are references to the proportion which the relevant parent's half-rate service (within the meaning of paragraph 7(2) of Part II of this Schedule) bears to the pensionable service reckonable by him.

Limitations on child's award

Child's allowance or special gratuity

5.— (1) This paragraph shall apply in the case of a child who is permanently disabled where the relevant parent (within the meaning of Regulation D5) ceased to be a member of a police force before 15th August 1983.

(2) Where this paragraph applies nothing in Regulation D5 shall preclude the grant of a child's allowance or special gratuity if the child was permanently disabled at the date of the relevant parent's death.

(3) Where this paragraph applies nothing in Regulation D5 shall preclude the payment of a child's allowance if—

(a) he has not attained the age of 19 years, or

(b) he has attained the age of 19 years and has been permanently disabled throughout the period after his attaining that age or, where later, after the death of the relevant parent.

Gratuity in lieu of child's allowance

Child whose relevant parent ceased to serve before 1st April 1987

6.— (1) This paragraph shall apply in the case of the child of a member of a police force who ceased to serve before 1st April 1987.

(2) In the case of such a child, Regulation E5 shall have effect as if paragraph (5) were omitted.

(**a**) 1921 c. 31.

SCHEDULE J *(continued)*

Part IV

Pensionable Service

Policeman who ceased to serve before 24th January 1975

Application of paragraphs 2 and 3 and reckoning of service etc. for purposes of awards

1.— (1) This paragraph and paragraphs 2 and 3 shall apply in the case of a member of a police force who ceased to serve as such before 24th January 1975.

(2) For the purposes of calculating an award payable to or in respect of such a member, Regulation A9 shall have effect subject to paragraphs 2 and 3 (without prejudice, however, in the case of an ordinary pension payable to such a widow as is mentioned in paragraph 2 of Part II of this Schedule, to the provisions of paragraph 5(5) of that Part).

Periods to be computed in completed years

2.— (1) This paragraph shall apply for the purposes mentioned in paragraph 1(2)—

(a) in the case of—

paragraphs 2 and 3 of Part III of Schedule B,
Part IV of Schedule B,
paragraph 1(4) of Part VII of Schedule B,
paragraph 5(3) of Part II of this Schedule, and
paragraph 2(4) of Part III of this Schedule;

(b) without prejudice to paragraph 3(3), in the case of—

Part II of Schedule B,
paragraph 4 of Part III of Schedule B,
paragraph 3 of Part VI of Schedule B,
paragraph 5(1) of Part II of this Schedule, and
paragraph 2(3) of Part III of this Schedule;

(c) without prejudice to paragraph 3(5), in the case of—

paragraph 8 of Part II of this Schedule,
paragraph 3 of Part III of this Schedule.

(2) Save as otherwise provided in paragraph 3(3) or (5), in the case of the provisions listed in sub-paragraph (1), a period shall be computed in completed years and, accordingly, a part of a year shall be ignored.

Periods to be computed in completed half-years

3.— (1) This paragraph shall, in the case of the provisions hereinafter mentioned, apply for the purposes mentioned in paragraph 1(2).

(2) In the case of paragraph 1 of Part I of Schedule B, the period in years by which a period exceeds 25 years shall be computed in half-years.

(3) In the case of the provisions listed in paragraph 2(1)*(b)* of this Part, the period in years by which a period exceeds 20 years shall be computed in half-years.

SCHEDULE J *(continued)*

(4) In the case of paragraph 5(2)*(b)* of Part II of this Schedule, a half of a person's pre-1972 pensionable service shall be computed in half-years.

(5) In the case of the provisions listed in paragraph 2(1)*(c)* of this Part, in so far as a period exceeds 20 years it shall be computed in half-years.

(6) Where in accordance with any of the preceding sub-paragraphs a period falls to be computed in half-years, it shall be computed in completed half-years and accordingly—

> *(a)* a part of a year less than half shall be ignored, and

> *(b)* a period of a year exceeding a half shall be treated as a half.

Policeman with service or employment both before, and on or after, 6th April 1978

Application of Regulation F4 or F5 to policeman who has relinquished deferred pension under paragraph 8 of Part I of this Schedule

4.— (1) This paragraph shall apply in the case of such a regular policeman as is mentioned in sub-paragraph (1) of paragraph 8 of Part I of this Schedule ("the principal paragraph") who—

> *(a)* has exercised the right of election conferred by sub-paragraph (2) of that paragraph and has become entitled to such a deferred pension as is mentioned in sub-paragraph (6)*(b)* thereof, but

> *(b)* has relinquished his entitlement to that pension by written notice given to the police authority for the purposes of Regulation F4 or F5 (*previous service reckonable on payment or at discretion of police authority*).

(2) In the case of such a policeman, no account shall be taken for the purposes of Regulation F4(3) or F5(3) of any additional or further contributions or of any additional or further payment by way of a lump sum of which account was taken for the purposes of an award under the principal paragraph by way of repayment of his aggregate contributions.

(3) Notwithstanding anything in Regulation F5(2), for the purposes of sub-paragraph *(c)* thereof where the police authority have exercised their discretion under sub-paragraph *(a)* thereof so as to allow such a policeman to reckon as pensionable service part only of the period first mentioned therein, "the proportionate part" shall mean that part which bears the same proportion to the whole as the first of the following periods bears to the second such period, namely—

> *(a)* the period of pensionable service the policeman is so allowed to reckon reduced by that taken into account under the principal paragraph for the purposes of calculating his deferred pension, and

> *(b)* the period of pensionable service first mentioned in sub-paragraph *(a)* of Regulation F5(2) so reduced.

SCHEDULE J *(continued)*

Policeman suspended before 15th February 1971

Pensionable service—period of suspension not reckonable

5.— (1) This paragraph shall apply in the case of a regular policeman who—

(a) before 15th February 1971 was suspended under regulations from time to time in operation under section 4 of the Police Act 1919(**a**), section 11 of the Police (Scotland) Act 1956(**b**); section 33 of the Police Act 1964(**c**) or section 26 of the Police (Scotland) Act 1967(**d**), and

(b) did not return to duty at the end of the period of suspension without having been found guilty of an offence under such regulations.

(2) Notwithstanding anything in Reglation F1, if the police authority so direct there shall not be reckonable by such a regular policeman the whole or such part of the period of suspension as may be specified in the direction.

Displaced chief constable

Pensionable service—added years in case of chief constable displaced under Police Act 1946 or corresponding Scottish enactments

6.— (1) This paragraph shall apply in the case of the chief constable of a force for a police area which was amalgamated with another police area by a scheme under the Police Act 1946(**e**) who was deemed to have retired under section 11(3) of that Act.

(2) The reference in paragraph (1) to the chief constable of a force for a police area which was amalgamated includes a reference to a person who engaged for a tour of overseas service and, immediately before he so engaged, was the chief constable of the force for an area which, while he was so engaged, was amalgamated as mentioned in sub-paragraph (1) and any reference in this paragraph to section 11(3) of the Police Act 1946 includes a reference to that provision as applied by section 14(3)*(a)* of that Act.

(3) Notwithstanding anything in Regulation F1—

(a) if during the period of 3 months referred to in section 11(3) of the said Act of 1946 such a chief constable joined the combined police force he shall be entitled to treat the period during which he was in receipt of a salary thereunder as service in the combined force for the purposes of reckoning pensionable service;

(b) if during the said period of 3 months he did not join the combined force, the pensionable service reckonable by him at the expiration of that period shall be the pensionable service which he was entitled to reckon at the date when he was deemed to have retired with the addition of the said period of 3 months and also of the shortest of the following periods, namely—

(i) a period of 10 years,

(**a**) 1919 c. 16.   (**b**) 1956 c. 26.   (**c**) 1964 c. 48.
(**d**) 1967 c. 77.   (**e**) 1946 c. 46.

SCHEDULE J *(continued)*

(ii) the period between the date on which he was deemed to have retired from his force and the date on which he would, if he had continued to serve therein, have become entitled to reckon 30 years' pensionable service, and

(iii) the period between the date on which he was deemed to have so retired and the date on which he would (if alive) attain the age of 65 years.

(4) In the application of these Regulations to Scotland, references in this paragraph to the Police Act 1946 and to sections 11(3) and 14(3)*(a)* thereof shall be construed as references to—

(a) the Police (Scotland) Act 1946(**a**) and to sections 7(2) and 9(3)*(a)* thereof, respectively;

(b) the Police (Scotland) Act 1956 and to sections 22(2) and 23(2) thereof, respectively, or,

(c) the Police (Scotland) Act 1967 and to sections 23(2) and 24(2) thereof, respectively.

Policeman who became such before 1st April 1987

Calculation of pensionable service reckonable under Regulation F6

7.— (1) This paragraph shall apply in the case of a regular policeman entitled to reckon pensionable service under Regulation F6 by virtue of the receipt by the police authority of a transfer value which was paid or became payable before 1st April 1987.

(2) In relation to such a policeman the reference in paragraph 1(2) of Section 2 of Part II of Schedule F to state retirement pensions shall be construed as a reference to state retirement pensions under section 28 of the Social Security Act 1975(**b**) section 24 of the Social Security Act 1973(**c**) or section 30 of the National Insurance Act 1965(**d**).

PART V

TRANSFER VALUES

Policeman who last became such before 6th April 1978

Transfer value payable between police authorities

1.— (1) This paragraph shall apply in the case of a regular policeman who becomes entitled to reckon pensionable service in the circumstances mentioned in paragraph (2) of Regulation F5 by virtue thereof where, before becoming so entitled, he last became a regular policeman before 6th April 1978.

(2) In the case of such a regular policeman Regulation F8(2) shall have effect

---

(**a**) 1946 c. 71.   (**b**) 1975 c. 14.   (**c**) 1973 c. 38.   (**d**) 1965 c. 51.

SCHEDULE J *(continued)*

as if it authorised but did not require the payment of a transfer value by the former police authority to the current police authority.

(3) Where such a regular policeman's former police authority, in pursuance of sub-paragraph (2), do not pay a transfer value but he has relinquished (as mentioned in Regulation F5(3)) a deferred pension with which he ceased to serve in his former force, the former police authority shall pay to the current police authority a sum equal to the award by way of repayment of his aggregate pension contributions in respect of the relevant period of service which would have been payable to him had he ceased to serve in circumstances entitling him to such an award:

Provided that where any sum is repaid to the policeman under Regulation F5(3) the payment to the current police authority shall be reduced by that sum.

Person who ceased to be a member of a police force before 1st April 1977

Transfer value in respect of person who ceased to be a member of a police force before 1st April 1977

2.— (1) This paragraph shall apply in the case of a regular policeman who ceased to serve as a member of a police force before 1st April 1977 and in respect of whom a transfer value is payable.

(2) In the case of such a regular policeman, in calculating a transfer value in accordance with Sections 1 and 3 of Part II of Schedule F, he shall be treated for the purposes of determining the increase in the transfer value under paragraph 11(2) of the said Section 1 as if he had ceased to be a member of his former force on 1st April 1977 but the transfer value shall be further increased by an amount equal to compound interest thereon (disregarding the increase under the said paragraph 11(2)) at the rate of 6% for each complete year in the period beginning with the date he ceased to be a member of his former force and ending with 31st March 1977 (disregarding any fraction of a year).

Transfer value in respect of policeman who ceased to serve before 24th January 1975

3.— (1) This paragraph shall apply in the case of a regular policeman who—

(a) ceased to serve as a member of his former force before 24th January 1975;

(b) was entitled to reckon less than a year's pensionable service immediately before he ceased so to serve, and

(c) in respect of whom a transfer value is payable under Regulation F8 or F9.

(2) In respect of such a regular policeman a transfer value calculated in accordance with Sections 1 and 3 of Part II of Schedule F shall be the appropriate proportion of the transfer value which would have been payable under Regulation F8 or F9 if he had been so entitled to reckon a year's pensionable service, that is to say, the proportion which the pensionable service he was so entitled to reckon bears to a year.

SCHEDULE J (continued)

PART VI

PENSIONABLE PAY AND CONTRIBUTIONS ETC.

Notional pensionable pay

Certain senior officers with service on or after 1st August 1975

1.— (1) This paragraph shall apply in the case of a regular policeman of a rank above that of superintendent who has served as such during a period beginning on or after 1st August 1975 ("the relevant period").

(2) Notwithstanding anything in these Regulations, an award to or in respect of such a regular policeman shall not be less than it would have been had the pay to which he was entitled as a member of a police force, in respect of the relevant period, fallen to be calculated in accordance with the scale of pay in force immediately before 1st August 1975 for a member of that force holding the rank, or the rank and office, held by him during the relevant period:

Provided that where the award is an ordinary pension which falls to be reduced in accordance with paragraph 6 of Part VIII of Schedule B, the reduction shall be calculated without regard to this paragraph.

Policeman with service between 31st August 1978 and 1st May 1979

2.— (1) This paragraph shall apply in the case of a member of a police force who has served as such for any period beginning on or after 1st September 1978 and ending before 1st May 1979 ("the relevant period").

(2) Notwithstanding anything in these Regulations, an award to or in respect of such a regular policeman shall be calculated as if the pay to which he was entitled in respect of the relevant period had been that to which a regular policeman would have been entitled in respect of a corresponding period beginning with 1st May 1979, disregarding any increase in pay which took effect after that date, if his circumstances had been identical to those during the relevant period of the regular policeman concerned.

Transferred member of the British Airports Authority constabulary

Payments by way of special contributions or reduction in pension

3.— (1) This paragraph shall apply in the case of a regular policeman entitled to reckon pensionable service by virtue of Regulation F3(1)*(f)* (*British Airports Authority constabulary service*) and, in this paragraph, "the Airports Scheme" means the superannuation scheme applicable to him before his transfer from the said constabulary.

(2) Where such a regular policeman elected, in accordance with paragraph (2)*(b)* of Regulation 61A of the Regulations of 1973, to pay special contributions and his liability thereunder to pay those contributions did not cease before 1st April 1987, he shall continue to pay special contributions until he attains the age of 50 years or sooner retires, and those contributions shall be so payable at the rate, expressed as a percentage of pensionable pay, at which they were payable under the said Regulation 61A before 1st April 1987.

SCHEDULE J *(continued)*

(3) Where immediately before retiring when entitled to an ordinary pension such a regular policeman was paying special contributions under this paragraph or under the said Regulation 61A, paragraph 6 of Part VIII of Schedule B shall have effect in relation to his ordinary pension as if any reference therein to additional or further contributions in pursuance of an election under Regulation 58(2) or (3) of the Regulations of 1973 included a reference to such special contributions.

(4) Where such a regular policeman—

(a) before his transfer was granted a back service credit within the meaning of the Airports Scheme,

(b) has been married at any time during his membership of that Scheme or while entitled to reckon pensionable service by virtue of Regulation F3(1)*(f)* or of Regulation 48*(f)* of the Regulations of 1973, and

(c) did not elect, in accordance with Regulation 61A(2)*(a)* or *(b)* of the Regulations of 1973, to make a special payment or to pay special contributions,

any ordinary, short service, ill-health or deferred pension (other than a deferred pension in pursuance of paragraph 8(6)*(b)* of Part I of this Schedule) payable to him shall be reduced by such percentage, determined by the Government Actuary or in accordance with tables prepared by him, that the reduction is the actuarial equivalent of the amount certified by BAA plc to be the actuarial equivalent at the date of his transfer of the contributions requisite under the Airports Scheme for securing family benefits in respect of the back service credit (after taking account of any payments made by him, or on his behalf, for that purpose before that date) subject, however, to sub-paragraph (5).

(5) Where the back service credit exceeded the previous service by reason of which it was given (otherwise than by reason of that service being wholly or partly service in a particular territory overseas), for the purposes of the certificate mentioned in sub-paragraph (4)—

(a) account shall be taken of that part only of the back service credit which does not exceed the previous service, but

(b) any payments made before the date of transfer for the purpose of securing family benefits in respect of the back service credit shall be treated as having been made in respect of that part.

(6) Except where the context otherwise requires, in the case of such a regular policeman any reference in these Regulations—

(a) to additional or further contributions shall be construed as including a reference to special contributions under this paragraph or Regulation 61A of the Regulations of 1973;

(b) to an additional or further payment by way of a lump sum shall be construed as including a reference to a special payment by way of a lump sum under the said Regulation 61A;

(c) to the reduction of a pension in accordance with Part VIII of Schedule B shall be construed as including a reference to such a reduction in accordance with the said Part VIII as it has effect in pursuance of sub-paragraph (3).

SCHEDULE J *(continued)*

PART VII

GENERAL AND ADDITIONAL PROVISIONS

Construction of references

Certain civilian employees treated as members of the City of London police force

1. These Regulations shall apply in the case of a person who on 5th July 1948 was a clerk or other person employed in, or in connection with, the City of London police force as if he were a member of that force.

Police authority for Northern Ireland before 15th February 1971

2. In these Regulations any reference to the Police Authority for Northern Ireland includes, in relation to a period before 15th February 1971, a reference to the Ministry of Home Affairs for Northern Ireland.

References to the police authority and to the Secretary of State in relation to overseas policemen in relation to period 1st April 1968 to 12th November 1970

3. As respects anything done on or after 1st April 1968 but before 12th November 1970 in relation to an overseas policeman—

(a) any reference in these Regulations to the police authority, and

(b) any reference in Regulation A6 or B2(1)*(b)* to the Secretary of State,

shall be construed as including a reference to the Minister of Overseas Development.

References to Social Security Act 1975 in relation to time before its coming into force

4.— (1) This paragraph shall apply in the case of—

(a) a member of a police force who ceased to serve as such before the coming into force of the provisions of the Social Security Act 1975 referred to in paragraph 4 of Part V of Schedule B *(policeman's injury award)*, or

(b) a widow whose husband died before the coming into force of the provisions of that Act referred to in paragraph 2 of Part II of Schedule C *(widow's special pension)*.

(2) In the case of any such member of a police force or any such widow, any reference in paragraph 4 of Part V of Schedule B or, as the case may be, paragraph 2 of Part II of Schedule C to a provision of the said Act of 1975 shall, in relation to a time before the coming into force thereof, be construed as including a reference to the corresponding enactment then in force and, accordingly, any such reference to a provision of the said Act of 1975 specified in the first column of the following Table shall be so construed as including a reference to the enactment specified opposite thereto in the second column of that Table.

SCHEDULE J *(continued)*

TABLE

Provision of Social Security Act 1975	Corresponding earlier enactment
Section 14	Section 19 of the National Insurance Act 1965(**a**) or section 10 of the Social Security Act 1973(**b**)
Section 15	Section 3 of the National Insurance Act 1971(**c**) or section 11 of the Social Security Act 1973
Section 26	Section 28 of the National Insurance Act 1965 or section 21 of the Social Security Act 1973
Section 57	Section 12 of the National Insurance (Industrial Injuries) Act 1965(**d**)
Section 58	Section 13 of the said Act of 1965
Section 59	Section 13A of the said Act of 1965
Section 60	Section 14 of the said Act of 1965
Section 62	Section 16 of the said Act of 1965
Section 64	Section 17 of the said Act of 1965
Section 66	Section 18 of the said Act of 1965
Section 67	Section 19 of the said Act of 1965
Part I of Schedule 4	Part I of Schedule 3 to the National Insurance Act 1965 or Part I of Schedule 4 to the Social Security Act 1973

Displaced chief constable

Chief constable affected by an amalgamation scheme under the Police Act 1946 or corresponding Scottish enactments

5.— (1) This paragraph shall apply in the case of a chief constable of an area that has been amalgamated with another area by a scheme made under the Police Act 1946(**e**).

(2) Where such a chief constable—

(a) was transferred to the combined police force in pursuance of an agreement made by him before the date of the transfer, or

(b) joined that force within the period of 3 months beginning with the date of transfer,

in any capacity other than that of chief constable or assistant chief constable, then, subject to any agreement to the contrary made between him and the police authority for the combined area, he shall be treated for the purposes of Regulations A18 and B1 as if, while serving in that force, he were a chief constable.

(**a**) 1965 c. 51.   (**b**) 1973 c. 38.   (**c**) 1971 c. 50.
(**d**) 1965 c. 52; s. 13A inserted by 1971 c. 50, s. 9.
(**e**) 1946 c. 46.

SCHEDULE J *(continued)*

(3) Where such a chief constable—

(a) was not transferred to the combined police force by the scheme, and

(b) did not join that force during the period of 3 months referred to in section 11(3) of the said Act of 1946 or, as the case may be, that provision as applied by section 14(3)*(a)* of that Act,

these Regulations shall apply as though he had retired at the end of that period from the force of which he was a chief constable and, for the purposes of Regulations B2(1) and B7(4)*(b)*, as though the circumstances of the retirement were mentioned in Regulation B2(1)*(a)*.

(4) In the application of these Regulations to Scotland—

(a) references in this paragraph to the Police Act 1946 and to sections 11(3) and 14(3)*(a)* thereof shall be construed as references to—

(i) the Police (Scotland) Act 1946**(a)** and to sections 7(2) and 9(3)*(a)* thereof, respectively,

(ii) the Police (Scotland) Act 1956**(b)** and to sections 22(2) and 23(2) thereof, respectively, or

(iii) the Police (Scotland) Act 1967**(c)** and to sections 23(2) and 24(2) thereof, respectively,

the reference in sub-paragraph (2) to the police authority for the combined area shall be construed as a reference to the joint police committee for that area and references in this paragraph to things done in the past shall include references to things done in the future;

(b) in relation to such a chief constable as is mentioned in sub-paragraph (3) and without prejudice thereto, Regulation B1 shall have effect as if—

(i) paragraph (2) thereof were omitted, and

(ii) the limitation imposed by paragraph (5) thereof on the making of payments in respect of a pension before a person has attained the age of 50 years did not apply, and

(c) for the purposes of calculating a pension payable by virtue hereof in the circumstances mentioned in sub-paragraph (3) to the chief constable of an area which has been amalgamated with another area by a scheme made under the Police (Scotland) Act 1967, his average pensionable pay shall include—

(i) where he was immediately before the date on which the area was amalgamated in receipt of a rent allowance the annual rate of that rent allowance,

(ii) where he was immediately before the said date provided with a house or quarters free of rent and rates, the annual worth of the house or quarters as determined in their discretion by the police authority of the force of which he was chief constable,

but, in respect of any period beyond state pensionable age the unsecured portion of such a pension shall be reduced to such amount

---

(a) 1946 c. 71.   **(b)** 1956 c. 26.   **(c)** 1967 c. 77.

SCHEDULE J *(continued)*

that the pension is payable at the rate at which it would have been payable had the chief constable's average pensionable pay not been so increased.

Chief constable affected by local government re-organisation or an amalgamation scheme under the Police Act 1964

6.— (1) This paragraph shall apply in the case of a chief constable of a police force who becomes or has become a member of another force ("the successor force") by virtue of an order mentioned in sub-paragraph (4) and section 58(1) of the Police Act 1964(**a**).

(2) In relation to such a member of a police force who suffers loss of office as such which is attributable to the provisions of an order mentioned in sub-paragraph (4)—

> *(a)* these Regulations shall apply as though he had retired from the successor force, having given to the police authority 3 months' written notice of his intention to retire;
>
> *(b)* where he becomes a member of another police force on or before the end of his resettlement period, Regulation F2 shall apply as though he had become a member of that other force immediately after ceasing to be a member of the successor force, and
>
> *(c)* where he was serving as a chief constable on 1st July 1964, Regulation B1 shall apply as though paragraph (2)*(b)* thereof were omitted and, for the purposes of Regulation B2(1) and B7(4)*(b)*, he shall be treated as though he had retired in the circumstances mentioned in Regulation B2(1)*(a)*.

(3) In relation to such a member of a police force as is mentioned in sub-paragraph (1) who suffers reduction in rank attributable to the provisions of an order mentioned in sub-paragraph (4), Regulation A18 shall apply as though he had not suffered such reduction in rank, unless he elects otherwise in writing to the police authority.

(4) Any reference in this paragraph to an order mentioned in this sub-paragraph is a reference to an order under Part I of the Police Act 1964 or Part II of the Local Government Act 1958(**b**); and the reference in sub-paragraph (2)*(b)* to a person's resettlement period is a reference to the period of 13 weeks next succeeding the week in which he ceased to be a member of the successor force or, in the case of a person who has attained the age of 45 years, the said 13 weeks extended by an additional week for every year of his age after attaining the age of 45 years and before he ceased to be a member of that force, subject to a maximum extension of 13 such weeks.

Miscellaneous

Member of an overseas corps with previous service outside Great Britain

7. Notwithstanding anything in these Regulations, where the Secretary of

---

(**a**) 1964 c. 48.   (**b**) 1958 c. 55.

SCHEDULE J *(continued)*

State is satisfied that a member of an overseas corps before becoming such had been engaged in the performance of police duties in any country or territory outside Great Britain, and that under legislation in force in that country or territory grants were, at the time he became such a member, payable to or in respect of persons similarly engaged on their retirement or, as the case may be, death, the Secretary of State may in accordance with any agreement made with that person in consideration of his becoming a member of an overseas corps, pay awards, in addition to any award payable under these Regulations, to or in respect of that person, on such conditions and of such a nature and amount as will ensure that the awards and any grants under the said legislation taken together are on the whole not less favourable to the person concerned than they would have been if the said police duties had been performed as a regular member of a home police force and the member of the overseas corps had been a reversionary member of a home police force.

Former lieutenant in Scottish police force

8. Where a member of a Scottish police force immediately before 5th July 1948 held the rank of lieutenant and on ceasing to be a member of a police force held the rank of chief inspector, his widow and any child of his shall be entitled to receive the like awards as if, on ceasing to be a member of a police force, he had held the rank of superintendent.

Lincolnshire

9. Notwithstanding anything in these Regulations, the police forces maintained before 1st April 1967 for the three divisions of Lincolnshire shall be treated for the purposes of these Regulations as having been one force and Regulation A15 shall have effect accordingly.

River Tyne police force

10. In relation to a person who served as a member of the River Tyne police force (which was dissolved on 1st July 1968 by the Port of Tyne Reorganisation Scheme 1967(**a**)), the police force for the Durham police area shall for the purposes of these Regulations, be deemed to be the same force as the River Tyne police force.

(**a**) S.I. 1968/942.

EXPLANATORY NOTE

(This note is not part of the Regulations)

These Regulations consolidate, with amendments, the Police Pensions Regulations 1973 and the regulations amending those Regulations. Those Regulations are revoked by the Police Pensions (Supplementary Provisions) Regulations 1987 (S.I. 1987/256), which also provide for the present Regulations to come into force on 1st April 1987 and contain transitional provisions.

Some apparent changes constitute no more than the omission of spent provisions. For example, Part G is considerably shorter than Part VI of the 1973 Regulations, because all the provisions which related to the making of elections and the payment of lump sums (which had to be completed in 1973) have been omitted.

There are apparent changes which constitute no more than the spelling out of something which was to be implied in the Regulations of 1973. Regulation A9(2) is an example of such an express provision.

A number of changes, however, affect the substance of the Regulations.

Under Regulation B7, the time at which a policeman may commute a portion of a pension which does not come into payment immediately on his retirement is related to the date on which it comes into payment and not his retirement date (transitory provisions are contained in paragraph 4 of Part I of Schedule J). Paragraph (4)*(a)*(ii) of that Regulation provides that, in determining the portion of a pension which may be commuted, any reduction at state pensionable age is to be disregarded (see, also, as respects both commutation and allocation, Regulation B10). The provisions of Regulation B8 relating to the commutation of small pensions apply to pensions of an annual amount not exceeding £104, instead of £52.

Where a policeman retired with an entitlement to an ill-health gratuity which he relinquished on transferring his pension rights to some other scheme, under Regulation C1 his widow is no longer entitled to an ordinary pension should he die from the disablement which occasioned his retirement (the widows of policemen who have already retired are protected by paragraph 1 of Part II of Schedule J). Regulation D1 (and paragraph 1 of Part III of Schedule J) provides similarly in the case of a child's ordinary allowance.

Under Regulation C4, a widow is entitled to an accrued pension even though her husband's deferred pension may have been commuted under Regulation B8.

Regulation E2 permits of the grant of a gratuity to a dependent relative notwithstanding that an award is payable under Regulation B9(9).

Changes are made in Regulations E4, E5 and E6 as respects the commutation of a widow's pension or child's allowance for a gratuity (paragraph 9 of Part II, and paragraph 6 of Part III, of Schedule J contain safeguards where the husband or parent has already ceased to serve).

Regulation E7 relaxes the provisions as respects the non-duplication of awards to widows and children where the awards are in respect of different policemen or different periods of service.

Changes are made in Regulation E8 affecting the increase of a widow's pension during the first 13 weeks of widowhood (see, also, Regulation C6 and paragraph 10 of Part II of Schedule J).

The provisions of Regulation F3(2) relating to the counting of service by policemen who transfer in a leap-year are extended to policemen who transfer from the Royal Ulster Constabulary.

Pension contributions are no longer payable under Regulation G2 by anyone other than regular policemen, who are the only members entitled to full pension benefits under the Regulations.

A policeman who is entitled to a deferred pension is excluded from the benefit of Regulation K1(5) and a payment thereunder takes account of any pension entitlement under Regulation J1 (see, however, paragraph 5 of Part I of Schedule J).

Regulation L2 provides for the payment of a transfer value out of the metropolitan police funds into the Consolidated Fund on a member of the metropolitan police force becoming commissioner.

Regulation L4 increases the amount which may be paid without probate where a person entitled to an award dies.

Part V of Schedule B provides (subject to paragraph 7 of Part I of Schedule J in the case of a policeman who has already ceased to serve) that in calculating an injury award account shall be taken of a social security severe disablement allowance or of sickness benefit payable by virtue of section 50A of the Social Security Act 1975 (1975 c. 14, as amended by 1982 c. 24, s. 39).

The provisions of Part IV of Schedule C relating to a widow's award in case of a post-retirement marriage deal with an exceptional case not dealt with by the Regulations of 1973.

Paragraph 1(5)*(b)* of Part I of Schedule D incorporates changes which, in particular circumstances, are favourable to a child entitled to an ordinary allowance. (Where changes might prove unfavourable, paragraph 1(3) of Part III of Schedule J contains safeguards where the parent has already ceased to serve.)

Part III of Schedule E enables a child with no parent or guardian himself to agree the amount of a gratuity under Regulation E5.

A change of limited application is made in paragraph 9 of Part I of Schedule J as respects policemen who might become entitled to a pension by way of equivalent pension benefit.

Changes of limited application are made in Part II of Schedule J as respects widows' ordinary pensions.

The structure of the present Regulations and the changes made thereby are discussed in detail in the *Memorandum on the Police Pensions Regulations 1987: changes made on consolidation*, copies of which are being sent to all police authorities under cover of H.O. Circular 1987/20 and Scottish Office Superannuation (Police Services) Circular 1987/2. Any person with an interest in the present Regulations will, on request and without charge, be supplied with a copy of that memorandum; requests should be addressed to Finance Division 2, Home Office, Queen Anne's Gate, London SW1H 9AT, or Scottish Office Superannuation Division, St. Margaret's House, 151 London Road, Edinburgh EH8 7TG, as the case may be.

STATUTORY INSTRUMENTS

1987 No. 258

TRADE UNIONS

The Certification Officer (Amendment of Fees) Regulations 1987

Made - - - -	*23rd February 1987*
Laid before Parliament	*6th March 1987*
Coming into force	*1st April 1987*

The Secretary of State, in exercise of the powers conferred on him by section 7 of the Trade Union (Amalgamations, etc.) Act 1964 (**a**) and section 8(4) of the Trade Union and Labour Relations Act 1974 (**b**) and section 8(2) of the Employment Protection Act 1975 (**c**) and of all other powers enabling him in that behalf, and as respects Regulation 2 with the approval of the Treasury, hereby makes the following Regulations:

Citation, commencement and revocation

1.—(1) These Regulations may be cited as the Certification Officer (Amendment of Fees) Regulations 1987 and shall come into force on 1st April 1987.

(2) The Certification Officer (Amendment of Fees) Regulations 1986 (**d**) are hereby revoked.

Increases in fees payable to the Certification Officer

2.   In Regulation 11 of the Trade Unions and Employers' Associations (Amalgamations, etc.) Regulations 1975 (**e**) for the words "£123" (fee for registration of an instrument of amalgamation or transfer) there shall be substituted the words "£130", for the words "£7.75" (fee for approval of a change of name) there shall be substituted the words "£8.00" and for the words "£1.60" (fee for every inspection on the same day of documents kept by the Certification Officer under the 1964 Act relating to one and the same organisation) there shall be substituted the words "£2.00".

3.   In section 8(4) of the Trade Union and Labour Relations Act 1974 for the words "£25" (fee on application by an organisation of workers or of employers to have its name entered in the list of trade unions or employers' associations, as the case may be) there shall be substituted the words "£26".

4.   In section 8(2) of the Employment Protection Act 1975 for the words "£150" (fee on application by a trade union for a certificate of independence) there shall be substituted the words "£156".

(**a**) 1964 c.24.   (**b**) 1974 c.52.   (**c**) 1975 c.71.   (**d**) S.I. 1986/302.
(**e**) S.I. 1975/536, amended by S.I. 1978/1344, 1981/1631, 1986/302.

Signed by order of the Secretary of State.

K. Clarke
Paymaster General

19th February 1987

We approve Regulation 2.

Peter Lloyd
T. Sainsbury

23rd February 1987   Two of the Lords Commissioners of Her Majesty's Treasury

---

EXPLANATORY NOTE

(This note is not part of the Regulations)

These Regulations, which come into force on 1st April 1987, increase the fees specified herein payable to the Certification Officer.

The Regulations revoke the Certification Officer (Amendment of Fees) Regulations 1986, which previously prescribed these fees.

Regulation 3 of the Certification Officer (Amendment of Fees) Regulations 1981 remains in force and prescribes the fee payable to the Certification Officer for the entry of an amalgamated organisation on the list of trade unions or employers' associations maintained by the Certification Officer under section 8 of the Trade Union and Labour Relations Act 1974 where each of the amalgamating organisations is already entered on the list (£12.50), which has not been increased.

1987 No. 259

TAXES

The Capital Gains Tax (Gilt-edged Securities) Order 1987

Made - - - - *25th February 1987*

The Treasury, in exercise of the powers conferred on them by paragraph 1 of Schedule 2 to the Capital Gains Tax Act 1979**(a)**, hereby make the following Order:

1. This Order may be cited as the Capital Gains Tax (Gilt-edged Securities) Order 1987.

2. The following securities are hereby specified for the purposes of Schedule 2 to the Capital Gains Tax Act 1979–

$2\frac{1}{2}$%	Exchequer Stock 1990
11 %	Exchequer Loan 1990
3 %	Treasury Stock 1991
10 %	Treasury Convertible Stock 1991
10 %	Treasury Loan 1993
10 %	Conversion Stock 1996
$9\frac{1}{2}$%	Conversion Loan 2001
10 %	Treasury Stock 2003
$9\frac{1}{2}$%	Conversion Stock 2005
$9\frac{3}{4}$%	Conversion Stock 2006
$8\frac{1}{2}$%	Treasury Loan 2007
8 %	Treasury Stock 2009
9 %	Conversion Loan 2011
$2\frac{1}{2}$%	Index-linked Treasury Stock 2016 "A"

Mark Lennox-Boyd
Tony Durant
25th February 1987   Two of the Lords Commissioners of Her Majesty's Treasury

---

(a) 1979 c.14.

EXPLANATORY NOTE

(This note is not part of the Order)

This Order specifies gilt-edged securities which are exempt from tax on capital gains if held for more than twelve months or if disposed of on or after 2nd July 1986 (section 67 of the Capital Gains Tax Act 1979 as amended by section 67(1) of the Finance Act 1985 (c.54)).

The following other specified gilt-edged securities enjoy like exemption and are listed in Part II of Schedule 2 to the Capital Gains Tax Act 1979 and in S.I. 1979/1231, 1676, 1980/507, 922, 1910, 1981/615, 1879, 1982/413, 1774, 1983/1774, 1984/1966, 1986/12.

Stocks and bonds charged on the National Loans Fund

$11\frac{1}{2}$%	Treasury Stock 1979
3 %	Treasury Stock 1979
$10\frac{1}{2}$%	Treasury Stock 1979
9 %	Treasury Convertible Stock 1980
4 %	British Overseas Airways Stock 1974–80
$9\frac{1}{2}$%	Treasury Stock 1980
$3\frac{1}{2}$%	Treasury Stock 1977–80
$5\frac{1}{4}$%	Funding Stock 1978–80
13 %	Exchequer Stock 1980
$11\frac{1}{2}$%	Treasury Stock 1981
$3\frac{1}{2}$%	Treasury Stock 1979–81
$9\frac{3}{4}$%	Treasury Stock 1981
$8\frac{1}{4}$%	Exchequer Stock 1981
$9\frac{1}{2}$%	Exchequer Stock 1981
3 %	Exchequer Stock 1981

Variable Rate Treasury Stock 1981

$12\frac{3}{4}$%	Exchequer Stock 1981
$8\frac{1}{2}$%	Treasury Loan 1980–82
3 %	Treasury Stock 1982
14 %	Treasury Stock 1982
$2\frac{1}{2}$%	British Overseas Airways Stock 1977–82

Variable Rate Treasury Stock 1982

$8\frac{1}{4}$%	Treasury Stock 1982
$9\frac{1}{4}$%	Exchequer Stock 1982
$8\frac{3}{4}$%	Exchequer Stock 1983
3 %	British Overseas Airways Stock 1980–83
3 %	Exchequer Stock 1983
12 %	Treasury Loan 1983
12 %	Treasury Loan 1983 "A"
$9\frac{1}{4}$%	Treasury Stock 1983
10 %	Exchequer Stock 1983

Variable Rate Treasury Stock 1983

$13\frac{1}{2}$%	Exchequer Stock 1983
3 %	Exchequer Stock 1983 "A"
$5\frac{1}{2}$%	Funding Stock 1982–84
12 %	Treasury Stock 1984
3 %	Exchequer Stock 1984
$11\frac{1}{4}$%	Exchequer Stock 1984
14 %	Exchequer Stock 1984
$12\frac{1}{4}$%	Exchequer Stock 1985
15 %	Treasury Stock 1985
3 %	Treasury Stock 1985
3 %	Treasury Stock 1985 "A"
$12\frac{1}{2}$%	Exchequer Stock 1985 "A"
12 %	Exchequer Convertible Stock 1985
$11\frac{1}{2}$%	Treasury Stock 1985

$8\frac{3}{4}$% Treasury Convertible Stock 1985
$8\frac{1}{2}$% Treasury Stock 1984–86
$2\frac{1}{2}$% Exchequer Stock 1986
$11\frac{3}{4}$% Exchequer Stock 1986
14 % Exchequer Stock 1986
$10\frac{1}{2}$% Exchequer Convertible Stock 1986
3 % Treasury Stock 1986
12 % Treasury Stock 1986
$12\frac{1}{4}$% Treasury Convertible Stock 1986
10 % Treasury Convertible Stock 1986
$6\frac{1}{2}$% Funding Loan 1985–87
$13\frac{1}{4}$% Exchequer Stock 1987
$13\frac{1}{4}$% Exchequer Stock 1987 "A"
$2\frac{1}{2}$% Exchequer Stock 1987
$10\frac{1}{2}$% Exchequer Stock 1987
$10\frac{1}{2}$% Exchequer Stock 1987 "A"
12 % Treasury Stock 1987
3 % Treasury Stock 1987
12 % Treasury Stock 1987 "A"
$10\frac{1}{4}$% Treasury Convertible Stock 1987
10 % Treasury Stock 1987
$7\frac{3}{4}$% Treasury Loan 1985–88
3 % British Transport Stock 1978–88
(issued under section 89 of the Transport Act 1947 (c.49))
3 % British Transport Stock 1978–88
(issued under section 12 of the National Loans Act 1968 (c.13))
2 % Index-linked Treasury Stock 1988
$10\frac{1}{2}$% Exchequer Stock 1988
$9\frac{1}{2}$% Treasury Stock 1988
$9\frac{1}{2}$% Treasury Stock 1988 "A"
$9\frac{3}{4}$% Treasury Convertible Stock 1988
5 % Treasury Stock 1986–89
$11\frac{1}{2}$% Treasury Stock 1989
$11\frac{1}{2}$% Treasury Stock 1989 "A"
3 % Treasury Stock 1989
$10\frac{1}{2}$% Treasury Stock 1989
$9\frac{1}{2}$% Treasury Convertible Stock 1989
10 % Exchequer Stock 1989
10 % Exchequer Stock 1989 "A"
11 % Exchequer Stock 1989
$10\frac{1}{4}$% Exchequer Convertible Stock 1989
$8\frac{1}{4}$% Treasury Loan 1987–90
2 % Index-linked Treasury Stock 1990
13 % Treasury Stock 1990
3 % Treasury Stock 1990
10 % Treasury Convertible Stock 1990
11 % Exchequer Stock 1990
$12\frac{1}{2}$% Exchequer Stock 1990
$11\frac{3}{4}$% Treasury Stock 1991
$11\frac{3}{4}$% Treasury Stock 1991 "A"
11 % Exchequer Stock 1991
$5\frac{3}{4}$% Funding Loan 1987–91
$12\frac{3}{4}$% Treasury Loan 1992
10 % Treasury Stock 1992
$10\frac{1}{2}$% Treasury Convertible Stock 1992
$12\frac{1}{4}$% Exchequer Stock 1992
$13\frac{1}{2}$% Exchequer Stock 1992
$12\frac{1}{2}$% Treasury Loan 1993
6 % Funding Loan 1993
$13\frac{3}{4}$% Treasury Loan 1993
$14\frac{1}{2}$% Treasury Loan 1994
$12\frac{1}{2}$% Exchequer Stock 1994

9 % Treasury Loan 1994
$13\frac{1}{2}$% Exchequer Stock 1994
3 % Exchequer Gas Stock 1990–1995 (formerly 3% British Gas Stock 1990–95)
12 % Treasury Stock 1995
$10\frac{1}{4}$% Exchequer Stock 1995
$12\frac{3}{4}$% Treasury Loan 1995
9 % Treasury Loan 1992–96
$15\frac{1}{4}$% Treasury Loan 1996
$13\frac{1}{4}$% Exchequer Loan 1996
14 % Treasury Stock 1996
2 % Index-linked Treasury Stock 1996
$13\frac{1}{4}$% Treasury Loan 1997
$10\frac{1}{2}$% Exchequer Stock 1997
$8\frac{3}{4}$% Treasury Loan 1997
15 % Exchequer Stock 1997
$6\frac{3}{4}$% Treasury Loan 1995–98
$15\frac{1}{2}$% Treasury Loan 1998
12 % Exchequer Stock 1998
12 % Exchequer Stock 1998 "A"
$9\frac{3}{4}$% Exchequer Stock 1998
$9\frac{1}{2}$% Treasury Loan 1999
$10\frac{1}{2}$% Treasury Stock 1999
$2\frac{1}{2}$% Index-linked Treasury Convertible Stock 1999
$10\frac{1}{4}$% Conversion Stock 1999
$12\frac{1}{4}$% Exchequer Stock 1999
$12\frac{1}{4}$% Exchequer Stock 1999 "A"
$12\frac{1}{4}$% Exchequer Stock 1999 "B"
9 % Conversion Stock 2000
13 % Treasury Stock 2000
14 % Treasury Stock 1998–2001
$2\frac{1}{2}$% Index-linked Treasury Stock 2001
10 % Treasury Stock 2001
$9\frac{3}{4}$% Conversion Stock 2001
12 % Exchequer Stock 1999–2002
12 % Exchequer Stock 1999–2002 "A"
$9\frac{3}{4}$% Treasury Stock 2002
$9\frac{1}{2}$% Conversion Stock 2002
10 % Conversion Stock 2002
$13\frac{3}{4}$% Treasury Stock 2000–2003
$13\frac{3}{4}$% Treasury Stock 2000–2003 "A"
$2\frac{1}{2}$% Index-linked Treasury Stock 2003
$3\frac{1}{2}$% Funding Stock 1999–2004
$11\frac{1}{2}$% Treasury Stock 2001–2004
10 % Treasury Stock 2004
$9\frac{1}{2}$% Conversion Stock 2004
$12\frac{1}{2}$% Treasury Stock 2003–2005
$12\frac{1}{2}$% Treasury Stock 2003–2005 "A"
$10\frac{1}{2}$% Exchequer Stock 2005
8 % Treasury Loan 2002–2006
2 % Index-linked Treasury Stock 2006
$11\frac{3}{4}$% Treasury Stock 2003–2007
$11\frac{3}{4}$% Treasury Stock 2003–2007 "A"
$13\frac{1}{2}$% Treasury Stock 2004–2008
$2\frac{1}{2}$% Index-linked Treasury Stock 2009
$2\frac{1}{2}$% Index-linked Treasury Stock 2011
$5\frac{1}{2}$% Treasury Stock 2008–2012
$2\frac{1}{2}$% Index-linked Treasury Stock 2013
$7\frac{3}{4}$% Treasury Loan 2012–2015
$2\frac{1}{2}$% Treasury Stock 1986–2016
$2\frac{1}{2}$% Index-linked Treasury Stock 2016
12 % Exchequer Stock 2013–2017
$2\frac{1}{2}$% Index-linked Treasury Stock 2020

$2\frac{1}{2}$%   Annuities 1905 or after
$2\frac{3}{4}$%   Annuities 1905 or after
$2\frac{1}{2}$%   Consolidated Stock 1923 or after
4 %   Consolidated Loan 1957 or after
$3\frac{1}{2}$%   Conversion Loan 1961 or after
$2\frac{1}{2}$%   Treasury Stock 1975 or after
3 %   Treasury Stock 1966 or after
$3\frac{1}{2}$%   War Loan 1952 or after

Securities issued by the Treasury under Part II of the Tithe Act 1936 (c.43)
3 %   Redemption Stock 1986–96

Securities issued by certain public corporations and guaranteed by the Treasury
$4\frac{1}{4}$%   North of Scotland Electricity Stock 1974–79
$4\frac{1}{4}$%   British Electricity Stock 1974–79
$3\frac{1}{2}$%   British Electricity Stock 1976–79
$3\frac{1}{2}$%   North of Scotland Electricity Stock 1977–80
3 %   British European Airways Stock 1980–83
3 %   North of Scotland Electricity Stock 1989–92

1987 No. 260

REPRESENTATION OF THE PEOPLE

The Local Elections (Parishes and Communities) (Amendment) Rules 1987

Made - - - -		*25th February 1987*
Laid before Parliament		*4th March 1987*
Coming into force		*11th March 1987*

In exercise of the powers conferred upon me by section 36(2) of the Representation of the People Act 1983(**a**), I hereby make the following Rules:

1.—(1) These Rules may be cited as the Local Elections (Parishes and Communities) (Amendment) Rules 1987.

(2) These Rules do not extend to Scotland or Northern Ireland.

(3) These Rules shall come into force on the fourteenth day after the day on which they were made, except for the purposes of an election at which the last day for the delivery of nomination papers was on or before that fourteenth day.

2.—(1) The rules in Schedule 2 to the Local Elections (Parishes and Communities) Rules 1986(**b**) shall be amended in accordance with the following paragraphs.

(2) In rule 23(5) (notices in polling stations) for the words "Vote for . . . . . candidate(s) only." there shall be substituted the words "[Vote for no more than . . . . . candidates.] [Vote for one candidate only.]".

(3) In the Appendix of forms, in the form of a candidate's consent to nomination, in paragraph (d), before the words "those twelve months" there shall be inserted the words "the whole of".

(4) In the Appendix of forms, in the form of the front of the ballot paper, for the words "VOTE FOR . . . . . CANDIDATE(S) ONLY" there shall be substituted the words "VOTE FOR NO MORE THAN . . . . . CANDIDATES".

(5) In the Appendix of forms, in the directions as to printing the ballot paper, for paragraph 2(a) there shall be substituted:

"(a) no word shall be printed on the face except the direction "VOTE FOR NO MORE THAN . . . . . CANDIDATES" or, where only one candidate is to be elected, "VOTE FOR ONE CANDIDATE ONLY" and the particulars of the candidates;".

(6) In the Appendix of forms, in the form of the declaration of identity, for the words "Vote for . . . . . candidate(s) only." in paragraph 2 of the instructions to the voter on the back of the form, there shall be substituted the words "[Vote for no more than . . . . . candidates.] [Vote for one candidate only.]".

(**a**) 1983 c. 2.
(**b**) S.I. 1986/2215.

(7) In the Appendix of forms, in the form of the elector's official poll card, for the words "Vote for . . . . . candidate(s) only." on the back of the card, there shall be substituted the words "[Vote for no more than . . . . . candidates.] [Vote for one candidate only.]".

(8) In the Appendix of forms, in the form of directions for the guidance of the voters in voting, for the words "Vote for . . . . . candidate(s) only." in paragraph 4, there shall be substituted "[Vote for no more than . . . . . candidates.] [Vote for one candidate only.]".

Home Office
25th February 1987

Douglas Hurd
One of Her Majesty's Principal Secretaries of State

EXPLANATORY NOTE

(This note is not part of the Rules)

These Rules amend the Local Elections (Parishes and Communities) Rules 1986 to remove a possible ambiguity from the directions to voters as to the number of candidates for whom they may vote. The original direction was "Vote for . . . . . candidate(s) only"; (the blank space being filled according to the number of vacancies to be filled). The direction was intended to indicate the maximum number of candidates for whom a voter could vote. However, a voter could also construe the direction as indicating the minimum number of candidates for whom he could vote. The substituted direction for use where more than one vacancy is to be filled ("Vote for no more than . . . . . candidates") removes this ambiguity.

Rule 2(3) amends the form of a candidate's consent to nomination to make it clear that a candidate whose qualification rests on residence in, or within three miles of, the parish or community during the twelve months before the date of his nomination and the day of election must have been so resident during the whole of that period.

STATUTORY INSTRUMENTS

1987 No. 261

REPRESENTATION OF THE PEOPLE

The Local Elections (Principal Areas) (Amendment) Rules 1987

Made - - - -	*25th February 1987*
Laid before Parliament	*4th March 1987*
Coming into force	*11th March 1987*

In exercise of the powers conferred upon me by section 36(2) of the Representation of the People Act 1983**(a)**, I hereby make the following Rules:-

1.—(1) These Rules may be cited as the Local Elections (Principal Areas) (Amendment) Rules 1987.

(2) These Rules do not extend to Scotland or Northern Ireland.

(3) These Rules shall come into force on the fourteenth day after the day on which they were made, except for the purposes of an election at which the last day for the delivery of nomination papers was on or before that fourteenth day.

2.—(1) The rules in Schedule 2 to the Local Elections (Principal Areas) Rules 1986**(b)** shall be amended in accordance with the following paragraphs.

(2) In rule 23(5) (notices in polling stations) for the words "Vote for .... candidate(s) only." there shall be substituted the words "[Vote for no more than .... candidates.] [Vote for one candidate only.]".

(3) In the Appendix of forms, in the form of a candidate's consent to nomination, in paragraph (d), before the words "those twelve months" there shall be inserted the words "the whole of".

(4) In the Appendix of forms, in the form of the front of the ballot paper, for the words "VOTE FOR .... CANDIDATE(S) ONLY" there shall be substituted the words "VOTE FOR NO MORE THAN .... CANDIDATES".

(5) In the Appendix of forms, in the directions as to printing the ballot paper, for paragraph 2(a) there shall be substituted:
"(a) no word shall be printed on the face except the direction "VOTE FOR NO MORE THAN .... CANDIDATES" or, where only one candidate is to be elected, "VOTE FOR ONE CANDIDATE ONLY" and the particulars of the candidates;".

(6) In the Appendix of forms, in the form of the declaration of identity, for the words "Vote for .... candidate(s) only." in paragraph 2 of the instructions to the voter on the back of the form, there shall be substituted the words "[Vote for no more than .... candidates.] [Vote for one candidate only.]".

(a) 1983 c.2.   **(b)** S.I. 1986/2214.

(7) In the Appendix of forms, in the form of the elector's official poll card, for the words "Vote for .... candidate(s) only." on the back of the card, there shall be substituted the words "[Vote for no more than .... candidates.] [Vote for one candidate only.]".

(8) In the Appendix of forms, in the form of directions for the guidance of the voters in voting, for the words "Vote for .... candidate(s) only." in paragraph 4, there shall be substituted "[Vote for no more than .... candidates.] [Vote for one candidate only.]".

Home Office   *Douglas Hurd*
25th February 1987   One of Her Majesty's Principal Secretaries of State

---

EXPLANATORY NOTE

(This note is not part of the Rules)

These Rules amend the Local Elections (Principal Areas) Rules 1986 to remove a possible ambiguity from the directions to voters as to the number of candidates for whom they may vote. The original direction was "Vote for .... candidate(s) only"; (the blank space being filled according to the number of vacancies to be filled). The direction was intended to indicate the maximum number of candidates for whom a voter could vote. However, a voter could also construe the direction as indicating the minimum number of candidates for whom he could vote. The substituted direction for use where more than one vacancy is to be filled ("Vote for no more than .... candidates") removes this ambiguity.

Rule 2(3) amends the form of a candidate's consent to nomination to make it clear that a candidate whose qualification rests on residence in the area of the local authority during the twelve months before the date of his nomination and the day of election must have been so resident during the whole of that period.

1987 No. 262

REPRESENTATION OF THE PEOPLE

The Parish and Community Meetings (Polls) (Amendment) Rules 1987

Made - - - -	*25th February 1987*
Laid before Parliament	*4th March 1987*
Coming into force	*11th March 1987*

In exercise of the powers conferred upon me by paragraph 18(5) of Part III of, and paragraph 34(5) of Part V of, Schedule 12 to the Local Government Act 1972(**a**), I hereby make the following Rules:

1.—(1) These Rules may be cited as the Parish and Community Meetings (Polls) (Amendment) Rules 1987.

(2) These Rules do not extend to Scotland or Northern Ireland.

(3) These Rules shall come into force on the fourteenth day after the day on which they were made, except for the purposes of a poll consequent on a parish or community meeting which has been demanded before that fourteenth day.

2.—(1) The rules in the Schedule to the Parish and Community Meetings (Polls) Rules 1987(**b**) shall be amended in accordance with the following paragraphs.

(2) In rule 11(5) (notices in polling stations) for the words "Vote for . . . . . candidate(s) only" there shall be substituted the words "[Vote for no more than . . . . . candidates] [Vote for one candidate only]".

(3) In the Appendix of forms, in the form of the front of the ballot paper on a question of appointment to an office for the words "VOTE FOR . . . CANDIDATE(S) ONLY" there shall be substituted the words "VOTE FOR NO MORE THAN . . . CANDIDATES".

(4) In the Appendix of forms, in the directions as to printing the ballot paper on a question of appointment to an office, for paragraph 2(a) there shall be substituted:

"(a) no word shall be printed on the face except the direction "VOTE FOR NO MORE THAN . . . . . CANDIDATES" or, where only one candidate is to be elected, "VOTE FOR ONE CANDIDATE ONLY" and the particulars of the candidates;".

(5) In the Appendix of forms, in the form of directions for the guidance of the voters in voting where the poll is on a question of appointment to an office, for the word "Vote for . . . . . candidate(s) only." in paragraph 4, there shall be substituted "[Vote for no more than . . . . . candidates.] [Vote for one candidate only.]".

(**a**) 1972 c. 70; those paragraphs were amended by paragraph 14 of Schedule 8 to the Representation of the People Act 1983 (c. 2).
(**b**) S.I. 1987/1.

Home Office
25th February 1987

Douglas Hurd
One of Her Majesty's Principal Secretaries of State

EXPLANATORY NOTE

(This note is not part of the Rules)

These Rules amend the Parish and Community Meetings (Polls) Rules 1987 to remove a possible ambiguity from the directions to voters as to the number of candidates for whom they may vote where the poll is on a question of appointment to an office. The original direction was "Vote for . . . . . candidate(s) only"; (the blank space being filled according to the number of vacancies to be filled). The direction was intended to indicate the maximum number of candidates for whom a voter could vote. However, a voter could also construe the direction as indicating the minimum number of candidates for whom he could vote. The substituted direction for use where more than one vacancy is to be filled ("Vote for no more than . . . . . candidates") removes this ambiguity.

STATUTORY INSTRUMENTS

1987 No. 263

PUBLIC HEALTH, ENGLAND AND WALES
PUBLIC HEALTH, SCOTLAND
PUBLIC HEALTH, NORTHERN IRELAND

CONTAMINATION OF FOOD

The Food Protection (Emergency Prohibitions) (Wales) (No. 2) Amendment No. 2 Order 1987

Made - - - -	*26th February 1987*
Laid before Parliament	*26th February 1987*
Coming into force	*27th February 1987*

Whereas the Secretary of State is of the opinion, as mentioned in section 1(1)(a) of the Food and Environment Protection Act 1985(**a**), that there has been or may have been an escape of substances of such descriptions and in such quantitites and such circumstances as are likely to create a hazard to human health through human consumption of food;

And whereas the Secretary of State is of the opinion, as mentioned in section 1(1)(b) of the said Act, that in consequence of the said escape of substances food which is or may be in the future in the area described in Schedule 1 to the Food Protection (Emergency Prohibitions) (Wales) (No. 2) Order 1986(**b**), or which is derived or may be in the future derived from anything in that area, is, or may be, or may become, unsuitable for human consumption;

Now, therefore, the Secretary of State, in exercise of the powers conferred on him by the said section 1(1) and (2) and section 24(1) and (3) of the said Act, and of all other powers enabling him in that behalf, hereby makes the following Order:–

Title and commencement

1. This Order may be cited as the Food Protection (Emergency Prohibitions) (Wales) (No. 2) Amendment No. 2 Order 1987 and shall come into force on 27th February 1987.

Partial revocation and amendment

2. The Food Protection (Emergency Prohibitions) (Wales) (No. 2) Order 1986 is revoked to the extent that it imposes prohibitions on –

(a) the slaughter of a sheep which was moved from a place in accordance with a consent given under section 2(1) of the Food and Environment Protection Act 1985 which consent was subject to the condition that the sheep to which it applies should be marked with a blue mark; and

---

(**a**) 1985 c.48. (**b**) S.I. 1986/1681, amended by S.I. 1986/1707, 1756, 1775, 1849, 2242 and 1987/182.

(b) the supply or having in possession for supply of meat, or food containing meat, derived from such a sheep,

and accordingly that Order is further amended in accordance with the following provisions of this Order.

3.   In article 6, for paragraph (2) there shall be substituted the following paragraph –

"(2) Paragraph (1) above shall not apply in the case of –

(a) any sheep which was moved to a market in accordance with a consent given under section 2(1) of the Act which consent did not require that the sheep to which it applies should be marked in a manner specified therein;

(b) any sheep which was moved from any place in accordance with a consent given under the said section 2(1) which consent was subject to the condition that the sheep to which it applies should be marked with a blue mark; or

(c) any sheep which –

(i) was moved from any place in accordance with a consent given under the said section 2(1) which consent was subject to the condition that the sheep to which it applies should be marked with a red mark; and

(ii) has been examined and marked with an ear-tag by a person authorised in that behalf by one of the Ministers.".

26th February 1987

Nicholas Edwards
Secretary of State for Wales

EXPLANATORY NOTE

(This note is not part of the Order)

The Food Protection (Emergency Prohibitions) (Wales) (No. 2) Order 1986 as amended by S.I. 1986/1707, 1756, 1775, 1849, 2242 and 1987/182 contains emergency prohibitions restricting various activities in order to prevent human consumption of food which has been or which may have been rendered unsuitable for that purpose in consequence of the escape of radioactive substances from a nuclear reactor situated at Chernobyl in the USSR.

This order excepts from the prohibition on slaughter throughout the United Kingdom any sheep identified by a blue paint mark, and from the prohibition on supply throughout the United Kingdom any meat derived from such a sheep, which are no longer required to be examined and marked with an ear-tag by a person authorised by the Minister of Agriculture, Fisheries and Food or the Secretary of State for Scotland or the Secretary of State for Wales (article 3).

1987 No. 264

LANDLORD AND TENANT

The Rent (Relief from Phasing) Order 1987

Made - - - -	*23rd February 1987*
Coming into force	*4th May 1987*

The Secretary of State for the Environment, as respects England, and the Secretary of State for Wales, as respects Wales, in exercise of the powers conferred on them by sections 60(5) and (7) and 151(3) of the Housing Act 1980(**a**), and of all other powers enabling them in that behalf, hereby make the following Order, a draft of which has been laid before, and has been approved by resolution of, each House of Parliament:

1. This Order may be cited as the Rent (Relief from Phasing) Order 1987 and shall come into force on the expiry of the period of ten weeks beginning with the day on which this Order is made.

2.—(1) The following provisions of the Rent Act 1977(**b**) are repealed–
  (a) section 55;
  (b) Schedule 8, in so far as it relates to section 55.

(2) The following provisions of the Rent (Agriculture) Act 1976(**c**) are repealed–
  (a) section 15;
  (b) Schedule 6.

(3) The consequential amendments to the Rent Act 1977 specified in Schedule 1 to this Order are made.

3. The repeals and amendments made by this Order do not have effect in the circumstances and to the extent specified in Schedule 2 to this Order.

(**a**) 1980 c.51.   (**b**) 1977 c.42.   (**c**) 1976 c.80.

SCHEDULE 1

Article 2(3)

CONSEQUENTIAL AMENDMENTS

RENT ACT 1977

1. In section 44(1) for "sections 55 and 71(3)" substitute "section 71(3)".

2. In section 45(2)–
(a) for "sections 55 and 71(3)" substitute "section 71(3)";
(b) omit "paragraph 10 of Schedule 8,".

3. In section 51(4)(b) omit sub-paragraph (ia).

4. In section 71(3)(a) omit "or, in relation to any such contractual period as is mentioned in paragraph (b) of section 55(1) of this Act, to the limit imposed by that paragraph".

5. In paragraph 3(2) of Schedule 20–
(a) at the end of paragraph (a) insert "and";
(b) at the end of paragraph (b) omit "and";
(c) omit paragraph (c).

SCHEDULE 2

Article 3

CIRCUMSTANCES WHERE PHASING IS TO CONTINUE

1.—(1) Subject to sub-paragraph (2), where a relevant application has been made, in relation to any increase in rent pursuant to that application following a determination by the rent officer or a determination, whether before or after this Order comes into force, by a rent assessment committee.

(2) Sub-paragraph (1) does not apply to a case to which section 72(3) of the Rent Act 1977 or section 13(6) of the Rent (Agriculture) Act 1976 applies if the resulting registration takes effect after this Order comes into force.

(3) In this paragraph "a relevant application" means an application under section 67 or section 68 of the Rent Act 1977 pursuant to which, before this Order comes into force, a rent has been registered or confirmation noted on the register following a determination by a rent officer.

2. Where a controlled tenancy has been converted into a regulated tenancy and no rent for it has been registered under Part IV of the Rent Act 1977 before this Order comes into force, in relation to any increase in rent pursuant to the first application under section 67 or section 68 of that Act.

23rd February 1987

Nicholas Ridley
Secretary of State for the Environment

19th February 1987

Nicholas Edwards
Secretary of State for Wales

EXPLANATORY NOTE

(This note is not part of the Order)

This Order removes the requirements for the phasing of rent increases in respect of registered rents for regulated tenancies in the Rent Act 1977 and for statutory tenancies in the Rent (Agriculture) Act 1976. It does not alter the phasing requirements in relation to registered rents for housing association tenancies in Part VI of the 1977 Act.

The Order does not affect the phasing of a rent increase (whether the increase is as a result of a determination by the rent officer or a rent assessment committee) in relation to an application for which a rent has been registered or confirmed following a determination by the rent officer before this Order comes into force. This is subject to the exception in paragraph 1(2) of Schedule 2 to the Order. The Order also does not affect the phasing of a rent increase in connection with the first application for registration of a rent for a former controlled tenancy.

The Order makes consequential amendments to the 1977 Act.

STATUTORY INSTRUMENTS

1987 No. 265

LANDLORD AND TENANT

The Protected Shorthold Tenancies (Rent Registration) Order 1987

Made - - - -	*23rd February 1987*
Coming into force	*4th May 1987*

The Secretary of State for the Environment, as respects England, and the Secretary of State for Wales, as respects Wales, in exercise of the powers conferred upon them by section 52(4) of the Housing Act 1980 (**a**) and of all other powers enabling them in that behalf, hereby make the following Order, a draft of which has been laid before, and has been approved by resolution of, each House of Parliament:

1. This Order may be cited as the Protected Shorthold Tenancies (Rent Registration) Order 1987 and shall come into force on the expiry of the period of ten weeks beginning with the day on which this Order is made.

2. Section 52(1) of the Housing Act 1980 shall have effect as if paragraph (c) of that subsection were omitted.

3. The Protected Shorthold Tenancies (Rent Registration) Order 1981(**b**) is hereby revoked.

23rd February 1987

Nicholas Ridley
Secretary of State for the Environment

19th February 1987

Nicholas Edwards
Secretary of State for Wales

(**a**) 1980 c.51.   (**b**) S.I. 1981/1578.

I/1x*

EXPLANATORY NOTE

(This note is not part of the Order)

Under section 52(1)(c) of the Housing Act 1980, for a tenancy to be a protected shorthold tenancy, either a fair rent for the dwelling-house must be registered under the Rent Act 1977 (c.42) at the time the tenancy is granted, or a certificate of fair rent must have been obtained at that time and an application for registration must be made within 28 days and not withdrawn. The Protected Shorthold Tenancies (Rent Registration) Order 1981 removed this requirement for all registration areas outside Greater London. This Order revokes the 1981 Order and removes this requirement generally, i.e. for all registration areas within, as well as outside, Greater London.

STATUTORY INSTRUMENTS

1987 No. 266

LANDLORD AND TENANT

The Rent Act 1977 (Forms etc.) (Amendment) Regulations 1987

Made	-	-	-	-	*23rd February 1987*
Laid before Parliament					*6th March 1987*
Coming into force	-		-		*4th May 1987*

The Secretary of State for the Environment, as respects England, and the Secretary of State for Wales, as respects Wales, in exercise of the powers conferred upon them by sections 49, 60 and 61 of the Rent Act 1977 **(a)**, and of all other powers enabling them in that behalf, hereby make the following Regulations:—

1. These Regulations may be cited as the Rent Act 1977 (Forms etc.) (Amendment) Regulations 1987 and shall come into force on 4th May 1987.

2. The Rent Act 1977 (Forms etc.) Regulations 1980 **(b)** are amended as follows—

(i) For sub-paragraphs (a) and (b) of regulation 3(1) substitute—

" (a) in the case of a notice under section 45(2) of the 1977 Act where the rent is not subject to the phasing provisions of Schedule 8 to the Act, form No. 1;

(b) in the case of a notice under section 45(2) of the 1977 Act where a rent is subject to the phasing provisions of Schedule 8 to the Act, form No. 2; and ".

(ii) In the list of contents in Schedule 1 for the entries relating to forms Nos. 1 to 3 substitute—

" 1. Notice of increase of rent under regulated tenancy where the increase is not subject to the phasing provisions of Schedule 8 to the Act.

2. Notice of increase of rent under regulated tenancy where the increase is subject to the phasing provisions of Schedule 8 to the Act.".

(iii) In Schedule 1, for forms Nos. 1 and 2 substitute the forms bearing those numbers in the Schedule to these Regulations and omit form No. 3.

(a) 1977 c.42; in section 61, *see* the definition of "prescribed".
(b) S.I. 1980/1697, to which there are amendments not relevant to these Regulations.

Regulation 2(iii)   **SCHEDULE**

                                                   FORM 1

RENT ACT 1977, SECTION 45(2), AS AMENDED BY HOUSING ACT 1980 AND
RENT (RELIEF FROM PHASING) ORDER 1987

See Notes 1 to 3   NOTICE OF INCREASE OF RENT UNDER REGULATED TENANCY
                          WHERE A FAIR RENT HAS BEEN REGISTERED AND THE
                          INCREASE IS *NOT* SUBJECT TO THE PHASING PROVISIONS OF
                          SCHEDULE 8 TO THE RENT ACT 1977

See Note 4   PLEASE READ THE NOTES CAREFULLY AND KEEP THIS FORM

                          To ...., tenant of ....

Cross out   1.   A rent of £ .... per .... (exclusive of rates) has been
words which   [registered by the Rent Officer] [determined by a Rent Assessment Committee]
do not apply   for the above premises and takes effect from ....
                          ....

                          2.   Unless—

See Note 5   (a) a different rent is registered by the Rent Officer or determined by a
                              Rent Assessment Committee, or

See Note 6   (b) the Rent Officer agrees to cancel the registration, or

See Note 7   (c) the rent is registered as variable—

                          the maximum rent (exclusive of rates) you can be charged from the date in
                          paragraph 1 is the full registered rent as shown in that paragraph.

                          3.   I hereby give you notice that your rent (exclusive of rates) will be
                          increased as follows—

                                              Present rent | £   per |

                          New rent from ....* | £   per |

                          The date at * must not be earlier than the date in paragraph 1 above nor 4 weeks
                          before the date of service of this Notice.

Cross out this   [It is noted in the rent register that rates in respect of the above premises are
paragraph if tenant   borne by me or a superior landlord. I am entitled to add the amount for rates
pays rates   to the rent and to pass on to you future increases in rates without serving a
                          Notice of Increase.]

                          Signed ....

Cross out   [On behalf of ....]
words in square   Address of Landlord ....
brackets if they   ....
do not apply
                          [Name and Address of Agent ....
                          ....]

                          Date ....

Notes

Use of Notice

1.   This notice is for use for rent increases which are **not** subject to phasing. Except in the circumstances described in paragraph 2 below, phasing does not apply to increases which result from a determination by the rent officer or rent assessment committee if the registration (or confirmation of the existing registration) resulting from the rent officer's determination of the fair rent takes effect *on or after 4th May 1987*.

2.   Phasing does apply in the circumstances described above if the registration of rent is the first such registration for a tenancy which has been converted from a controlled tenancy to a regulated tenancy. Form No. 2 should be used for these cases.

3.   This Notice can only be used for increases which are to take effect when the tenancy is a statutory tenancy. A statutory tenancy comes into being when a tenancy agreed between the landlord and tenant (known as a contractual tenancy) has come to an end and the tenant has security of tenure under the Rent Act 1977. The Notice can be served while there is still a contractual tenancy. If the contractual tenancy can be terminated before the date in paragraph 3, this notice can be used instead of a notice to quit to turn the contractual tenancy into a statutory tenancy from that date.

Explanatory booklet

4.   The Department of the Environment and Welsh Office booklet " Regulated Tenancies " explains in more detail than these Notes how the fair rent system works and the rights and duties of landlords and tenants under the Rent Act. It is available free from Rent Officers, and Citizens' Advice Bureaux, and you are advised to obtain a copy.

Re-registration

5.   No application for a new registration may be made during the two years from the date in paragraph 1 of the Notice unless either—

(a) it is made by the landlord and the tenant acting together, or

(b) there has been such a change in the circumstances taken into account when the rent was registered (e.g. the making of an improvement to the premises) as to make the registered rent no longer a fair rent.

But the landlord may apply three months in advance for a new registration to take effect after the end of the two year period.

Cancellation

6.   As long as there is a regulated tenancy an application to the Rent Officer to cancel the registration can only be made jointly by landlord and tenant.

Limitation of rent increases

7.   The rent shown in paragraph 1 of the Notice may not be exceeded unless the rent is registered as variable. It will only be registered as variable if the terms of the tenancy provide for the rent to be varied according to the cost of services or works of maintenance and repair carried out by the landlord or superior landlord and the Rent Officer considers the terms reasonable.

Help with rent and rates

8.   If the tenant has difficulty in paying his rent or rates he should apply to the local council offices for details of the rent allowance and rate rebate schemes. The council will also advise if he may be better off receiving supplementary benefit from the Department of Health and Social Security.

FORM 2

RENT ACT 1977, SECTION 45(2), AS AMENDED BY HOUSING ACT 1980

See Notes 1
and 2

NOTICE OF INCREASE OF RENT UNDER REGULATED TENANCY WHERE A FAIR RENT HAS BEEN REGISTERED AND THE INCREASE IS SUBJECT TO THE PHASING PROVISIONS OF SCHEDULE 8 TO THE RENT ACT 1977

See Note 3

PLEASE READ THE NOTES CAREFULLY AND KEEP THIS FORM

To ...., tenant of ....

See Note 4
Cross out words
which do not
apply

1.   A rent of £..................... per .... (exclusive of rates) has been [registered by the Rent Officer] [determined by a Rent Assessment Committee] for the above premises and takes effect from ....

2.   Unless—

See Note 5

(a) a different rent is registered by the Rent Officer or determined by a Rent Assessment Committee, or

See Note 6

(b) the Rent Officer agrees to cancel the registration, or

(c) the rent is registered as variable—

the maximum rent (exclusive of rates) you can be charged during the first year from the date in paragraph 1 is

See Note 7

£	per

This is calculated as follows:—

New registered rent

£	per

+

See Note 8

Previous rent limit

£	per

+

See Note 9

Service element (if any)

£	per

=

£	per

÷ 2

£	per

=

£	per

3.   After the end of the first year from the date in paragraph 1 the maximum rent (unless 2(a), (b) or (c) applies) is the full registered rent as shown in 1 above of

£	per

4.   I hereby give notice that your rent (exclusive of rates) will be increased as follows:—

Present rent	£ per
New rent from ....*	£ per
New rent from	£ per

If two increases are shown above I am not obliged to remind you when the second increase becomes payable. The date at * must not be earlier than the date in paragraph 1 above nor 4 weeks before the date of service of this Notice.

Cross out this paragraph if tenant pays rates

[It is noted in the rent register that rates in respect of the above premises are borne by me or a superior landlord. I am entitled to add the amount for rates to the rent and to pass on to you future increases in rates without serving a Notice of Increase.]

Cross out words in square brackets if they do not apply

Signed ....

[On behalf of ....]

Address of Landlord ....

....

[Name and Address of Agent ....

....]

Date ....

Notes

Use of Notice

1.   This Notice is only for use for rent increases which are subject to phasing. Phasing applies in the following circumstances—

(a) if the registration of rent is the first such registration for a tenancy which has been converted from a controlled tenancy to a regulated tenancy, or

(b) if the rent was determined by a rent officer or rent assessment committee and the registration (or confirmation of the existing registration) resulting from the rent officer's determination of the fair rent took effect *before 4th May 1987.*

2.   The Notice can only be used for increases which are to take effect when the tenancy is a statutory tenancy. A statutory tenancy comes into being when a tenancy agreed between the landlord and tenant (known as a contractual tenancy) has come to an end and the tenant has security of tenure under the Rent Act 1977. The Notice can be served while there is still a contractual tenancy. If the contractual tenancy can be terminated before the (earliest) date in paragraph 4, this Notice can be used instead of a notice to quit to turn the contractual tenancy into a statutory tenancy from that date.

Explanatory booklet

3.   The Department of the Environment and Welsh Office booklet " Regulated Tenancies " explains in more detail than these Notes how the fair rent system works and the rights and duties of landlords and tenants under the Rent Act. It is available free from Rent Officers, and Citizens' Advice Bureaux, and you are advised to obtain a copy.

Limitation of rent increase

4.   The rent shown in paragraph 1 of the Notice may not be exceeded unless the rent is registered as variable. It will only be registered as variable if the terms of the tenancy provide for the rent to be varied according to the cost of services or works of maintenance and repair carried out by the landlord or superior

landlord and the Rent Officer considers the terms reasonable. Secondly, the landlord may only increase the rent during the first year from the date in paragraph 1 of the notice to the extent allowed under the provisions for the phasing of increases.

Re-registration

5.   No application for a new registration may be made during the two years from the date in paragraph 1 of the Notice unless either—

(a) it is made by the landlord and the tenant acting together, or

(b) there has been such a change in the circumstances taken into account when the rent was registered (e.g. the making of an improvement to the premises) as to make the registered rent no longer a fair rent.

But the landlord may apply three months in advance for a new registration to take effect after the end of the two year period.

Cancellation

6.   As long as there is a regulated tenancy an application to the Rent Officer to cancel the registration can only be made jointly by landlord and tenant.

How phasing works

7.   During the first year from the date in paragraph 1 of the Notice the landlord is permitted to charge half of the increase, except that where there is a service element he may charge this in full at once. After the end of the first year he can charge the full registered rent shown in paragraph 1.

Previous rent limit

8.   The amount of increase permitted has to be worked out by taking as a starting point the previous rent limit. The previous rent limit is the amount the landlord was permitted by the Rent Act to charge immediately before the Rent Officer registered the rent (whether or not there has been an appeal to a Rent Assessment Committee). (Rates are disregarded for this purpose.) The landlord may not actually have been charging this amount.

Service element

9.   The service element is the increase in the rent permitted on account of services provided by the landlord or a superior landlord. If there is a service element it has to be recorded in the Rent Officer's register.

Help with rent and rates

10.   If the tenant has difficulty in paying his rent or rates he should apply to the local council offices for details of the rent allowance and rate rebate schemes. The council will also advise if he may be better off receiving supplementary benefit from the Department of Health and Social Security.

23rd February 1987

Nicholas Ridley
Secretary of State for the Environment

19th February 1987

Nicholas Edwards
Secretary of State for Wales

EXPLANATORY NOTE

(This note is not part of the Regulations)

These Regulations amend the Rent Act (Forms etc.) Regulations 1980 and are consequential on the provisions of the Rent (Relief from Phasing) Order 1987 (S.I. 1987/264). They replace the forms to be used for giving notice of increase of rent under a regulated tenancy where the rent is registered.

1987 No. 267

LANDLORD AND TENANT

The Protected Shorthold Tenancies (Notice to Tenant) Regulations 1987

Made - - - -	*23rd February 1987*
Coming into force	*4th May 1987*

The Secretary of State for the Environment, as respects England, and the Secretary of State for Wales, as respects Wales, in exercise of the powers conferred upon them by section 52(3) of the Housing Act 1980 (a) and of all other powers enabling them in that behalf, hereby make the following Regulations:

1. These Regulations may be cited as the Protected Shorthold Tenancies (Notice to Tenant) Regulations 1987 and shall come into force on 4th May 1987.

2. The requirement with which a notice has to comply in order to be valid for the purposes of section 52(1)(b) of the Housing Act 1980 is that it shall be in the form set out in the Schedule to these Regulations or in a form substantially to the like effect.

3. The Protected Shorthold Tenancies (Notice to Tenant) Regulations 1981 (b) are hereby revoked.

(a) 1980 c.51. (b) S.I. 1981/1579.

SCHEDULE

NOTICE OF A PROTECTED SHORTHOLD TENANCY — SECOND REVISION

(The landlord must give this to the tenant *before* a protected shorthold tenancy is granted. It does not commit the tenant to take the tenancy.)

To ....

(Name of proposed tenant)

IMPORTANT — PLEASE READ THIS NOTICE CAREFULLY. IF THERE IS ANYTHING YOU DO NOT UNDERSTAND YOU SHOULD GET ADVICE (FOR EXAMPLE, FROM A SOLICITOR OR A CITIZENS' ADVICE BUREAU) BEFORE YOU AGREE TO TAKE A SHORTHOLD TENANCY.

NB: This document is important; keep it in a safe place.

---

1. You are proposing to take a tenancy of the dwelling known as ....

....

from .... 19.... to .... 19....

    (day)   (month)   (year)   (day)   (month)   (year)

2. This notice is to tell you that your tenancy is to be a *protected shorthold tenancy*. Under shorthold, provided you keep the terms of the tenancy, you are entitled to remain in the dwelling for the fixed period agreed at the start of the tenancy. At the end of this period the landlord has the right to repossession if he wants. Full details about shorthold are given in the Department of the Environment and Welsh Office booklet "Shorthold Tenancies. Second Revision" obtainable free from Rent Officers, council offices and housing aid centres. You are advised to read this booklet before you agree to take a shorthold tenancy.

---

*The landlord must cross out the version of paragraph 3 below which does not apply.

---

*3. A fair rent of   per   is already registered for the dwelling under the Rent Act 1977.

This is the most you can be required to pay as rent until such time as a higher rent is registered. If I apply for a higher rent to be registered you will be told about my application and you will have the opportunity of a consultation with the Rent Officer.

*3. The rent for this tenancy is the rent that we have agreed, and has not been registered by the Rent Officer. But this does not affect your right as tenant or my right as landlord to apply at any time to the Rent Officer for the registration of a fair rent. This is fully explained in the booklet "Shorthold Tenancies. Second Revision.".

4. This notice is given to you on .... 19....

Signed ....

(on behalf of) ....

....

....

(Name and address of landlord)

SPECIAL NOTE FOR EXISTING TENANTS

IF YOU ARE ALREADY A PROTECTED OR STATUTORY TENANT UNDER THE RENT ACT 1977 YOUR PRESENT TENANCY CANNOT LAWFULLY BE CONVERTED INTO A SHORTHOLD. BUT SHOULD YOU GIVE IT UP AND TAKE A SHORTHOLD TENANCY IN SOME OTHER ACCOMMODATION, INCLUDING ANOTHER FLAT IN THE SAME BUILDING, YOU WILL ALMOST CERTAINLY HAVE *LESS* SECURITY UNDER SHORTHOLD THAN UNDER YOUR EXISTING TENANCY.

Nicholas Ridley
23rd February 1987   Secretary of State for the Environment

Nicholas Edwards
19th February 1987   Secretary of State for Wales

EXPLANATORY NOTE

(This note is not part of the Regulations)

One of the conditions which has to be satisfied for a tenancy to be a protected shorthold tenancy is that, before the grant of the tenancy, the landlord has given the tenant a valid notice stating that the tenancy is to be a protected shorthold tenancy.

Section 52(3) of the Housing Act 1980 provides that a notice is not valid unless it complies with the requirements of Regulations made by the Secretary of State. These Regulations require the notice to be in the form set out in the Schedule. These Regulations revoke the Protected Shorthold Tenancies (Notice to Tenant) Regulations 1981 and are consequential on the provisions of the Protected Shorthold Tenancies (Rent Registration) Order 1987 (S.I. 1987/265).

STATUTORY INSTRUMENTS

1987 No. 268

HOUSING, ENGLAND AND WALES
HOUSING, SCOTLAND

The Home Purchase Assistance (Price-limits) Order 1987

Made - - - -	*24th February 1987*
Laid before the House of Commons	*6th March 1987*
Coming into force	*27th March 1987*

The Secretary of State for the Environment, as respects England, and the Secretary of State for Wales, as respects Wales, in exercise of their powers under sections 445(2) and (3) of the Housing Act 1985(**a**), and the Secretary of State for Scotland, as respects Scotland, in exercise of his powers under sections 1(2) and 2(7) of the Home Purchase Assistance and Housing Corporation Guarantee Act 1978(**b**), and of all other powers enabling them in that behalf, hereby make the following Order:

Citation and commencement

1. This Order may be cited as the Home Purchase Assistance (Price-limits) Order 1987 and shall come into force on 27th March 1987.

Prescribed price-limits

2. The amounts mentioned in the Schedule to this Order are hereby prescribed as the price-limits for the purposes of section 445 of the Housing Act 1985 or section 1 of the Home Purchase Assistance and Housing Corporation Guarantee Act 1978 (as the case may be) in respect of house property situated in the areas mentioned in relation thereto in that Schedule.

Revocation

3. The Home Purchase Assistance (Price-limits) Order 1986 (**c**) is hereby revoked.

(**a**) 1985 c.68.   (**b**) 1978 c.27.   (**c**) S.I. 1986/1511.

SCHEDULE

The counties of Cleveland, Durham, Northumberland and Tyne and Wear	£25,500
The counties of Humberside, North Yorkshire, South Yorkshire and West Yorkshire	£24,800
The counties of Derbyshire, Leicestershire, Lincolnshire, Northamptonshire and Nottinghamshire	£27,400
The counties of Cambridgeshire, Norfolk and Suffolk	£34,600
Greater London	£55,400
The counties of Bedfordshire, Berkshire, Buckinghamshire, East Sussex, Essex, Hampshire, Hertfordshire, Isle of Wight, Kent, Oxfordshire, Surrey and West Sussex	£44,600
The counties of Avon, Cornwall, Devon, Dorset, Gloucestershire, Somerset and Wiltshire and the Isles of Scilly	£35,600
The counties of Hereford and Worcester, Shropshire, Staffordshire, Warwickshire and West Midlands	£26,900
The counties of Cheshire, Cumbria, Greater Manchester, Lancashire and Merseyside	£26,100
Wales	£26,700
Scotland	£29,800

18th February 1987

Nicholas Ridley
Secretary of State for the Environment

23rd February 1987

Nicholas Edwards
Secretary of State for Wales

24th February 1987

Malcolm Rifkind
Secretary of State for Scotland

EXPLANATORY NOTE

(This note is not part of the Order)

Assistance for first-time purchasers of house property, under section 446 of the Housing Act 1985 as respects England and Wales and under section 1 of the Home Purchase Assistance and Housing Corporation Guarantee Act 1978 as respects Scotland, can take the form of a bonus of up to £110 on savings and a loan of £600 additional to that which the lending institution would otherwise have made and free of any obligation to repay principal or interest for up to five years. Assistance is only available where the purchase price of the property is within the limit prescribed by the Secretary of State by order. This Order prescribes limits for different areas which are higher than those prescribed by the Home Purchase Assistance (Price-limits) Order 1986, which is revoked.

STATUTORY INSTRUMENTS

1987 No. 269

CIVIL AVIATION

The Civil Aviation (Navigation Services Charges) (Second Amendment) Regulations 1987

Made - - - -	*23rd February 1987*
Laid before Parliament	*5th March 1987*
Coming into force -	*1st April 1987*

The Secretary of State for Transport, in exercise of his powers under sections 73 and 74 of the Civil Aviation Act 1982**(a)** and of all other powers enabling him in that behalf, and with the consent of the Treasury, hereby makes the following Regulations–

1. These Regulations may be cited as the Civil Aviation (Navigation Services Charges) (Second Amendment) Regulations 1987 and shall come into force on 1st April 1987.

2. The Civil Aviation (Navigation Services Charges) Regulations 1986**(b)** shall be further amended as follows–

(1) In regulation 2(1), for the Table there shall be substituted the following new Table–

Table

Column 1	Column 2	Column 3
Heathrow-London		
For each metric tonne and each fraction of a metric tonne up to 100 metric tonnes	£1.40	£1.18
For each additional metric tonne, and for each fraction of a metric tonne, over 100 tonnes	£0.60	£0.49
Gatwick-London		
For each metric tonne and for each fraction of a metric tonne up to 100 metric tonnes	£1.40	£1.18
For each additional metric tonne, and for each fraction of a metric tonne, over 100 metric tonnes	£0.60	£0.49

(a) 1982 c.16; section 73(4) was amended by section 3(2) of the Civil Aviation (Eurocontrol) Act 1983 (c.11).
(b) S.I. 1986/403, as amended by S.I. 1986/2170.

Table—*continued*

Column 1	Column 2	Column 3
Stansted-London		
For each metric tonne and for each fraction of a metric tonne up to 100 metric tonnes	£1.40	£1.18
For each additional metric tonne, and for each fraction of a metric tonne, over 100 metric tonnes	£0.60	£0.49
Aberdeen (Dyce)	£3.85	£3.25
Edinburgh	£3.85	£3.25
Glasgow	£2.85	£2.40
Prestwick	£3.85	£3.25

(2) In regulation 5 for "a charge of sixty-eight pounds" there shall be substituted "a charge of seventy pounds".

(3) In regulation 6(1) for "a charge of eighty-five pounds" there shall be subsituted "a charge of one hundred and ten pounds".

Signed by authority of the Secretary of State

Michael Spicer
Parliamentary Under Secretary of State,
Department of Transport

19th February 1987

We consent to the making of these Regulations,

Tim Sainsbury
Michael Neubert
23rd February 1987   Two of the Lords Commissioners of Her Majesty's Treasury

EXPLANATORY NOTE

(This note is not part of the Regulations)

These Regulations further amend the Civil Aviation (Navigation Services Charges) Regulations 1986. The following changes are made–

(1) The charges payable to the Civil Aviation Authority for navigation services provided in connection with the use of aerodromes specified in the Table have been changed as follows–

    (a) In respect of the three London Airports, the standard charge for the first 100 metric tonnes maximum total weight authorised of an aircraft is reduced from £1.44 per metric tonne to £1.40 for aircraft engaged on international flights and from £1.21 per metric tonne to £1.18 for aircraft engaged on domestic flights. For each additional metric tonne, or part thereof, in excess of 100 metric tonnes, the charge is reduced from £0.62 per metric tonne to £0.60 for aircraft engaged on international flights and from £0.51 per metric tonne to £0.49 for aicraft engaged on domestic flights.

    (b) Charges at Aberdeen (Dyce) are reduced by 1.5% for domestic flights (and are unchanged for international flights), charges at Edinburgh are reduced by 8.5% for domestic flights and 9.4% for international flights, charges at Glasgow are reduced by 14.3% for domestic flights and 14.9% for international flights and charges at Prestwick are reduced by 8.5% for domestic flights and 11.5% for international flights (regulation 2(1)).

(2) The charge payable to the Civil Aviation Authority by the operator of an aircraft which flies within the Shanwick Oceanic Control Area and in respect of which a flight plan is communicated to the appropriate air traffic control unit is increased from sixty-eight pounds to seventy pounds (regulation 2(2)).

(3) The charge payable to the Civil Aviation Authority for a flight made by a helicopter from a point in the United Kingdom to an off-shore installation within the area of the northern North Sea specified in regulation 6(1) of the Regulations is increased from eighty-five pounds to one hundred and ten pounds (regulation 2(3)).

STATUTORY INSTRUMENTS

1987 No. 270

PUBLIC HEALTH, ENGLAND AND WALES
PUBLIC HEALTH, SCOTLAND
PUBLIC HEALTH, NORTHERN IRELAND

CONTAMINATION OF FOOD

The Food Protection (Emergency Prohibitions) (No.10) Revocation Order 1987

Made - - - -	*25th February 1987*
Laid before Parliament	*26th February 1987*
Coming into force	*27th February 1987*

The Secretary of State, in exercise of the powers conferred on him by section 1(1) of the Food and Environment Protection Act 1985(**a**), and of all other powers enabling him in that behalf, hereby makes the following Order:

Citation and commencement

1. This Order may be cited as the Food Protection (Emergency Prohibitions) (No. 10) Revocation Order 1987 and shall come into force on 27th February 1987.

Revocation

2. The Food Protection (Emergency Prohibitions) (No. 10) Order 1986(**b**) is hereby revoked.

New St. Andrew's House, Edinburgh
25th February 1987

D. J. Essery
Under Secretary,
Scottish Office

(**a**) 1985 c.48.
(**b**) S.I. 1986/2248.

EXPLANATORY NOTE

(This note is not part of the Order)

This Order revokes the Food Protection (Emergency Prohibitions) (No. 10) Order 1986 (which contained a prohibition on the slaughter of certain sheep following the escape of radioactive substances from a nuclear reactor situated at Chernobyl, in the Ukraine, USSR). In consequence the prohibition which applied throughout the United Kingdom on the slaughter, for human consumption or for use in the preparation of feeding stuffs, of sheep which had been moved from the designated areas described in column 1 of Schedule 2 to that Order, between the dates specified in column 2 of that Schedule no longer applies.

STATUTORY INSTRUMENTS

1987 No. 271

CUSTOMS AND EXCISE

The Export of Goods (Control) (Amendment No. 9) Order 1987

Made - - - -	*16th February 1987*
Coming into force	*10th March 1987*

The Secretary of State, in exercise of powers conferred by section 1 of the Import, Export and Customs Powers (Defence) Act 1939(**a**) and now vested in him,**b**), and of all other powers enabling him in that behalf, hereby makes the following Order:

1. This Order may be cited as the Export of Goods (Control) (Amendment No. 9) Order 1987 and shall come into force on 10th March 1987.

2. The Export of Goods (Control) Order 1985(**c**) shall be further amended as follows:

  (a) in Group 3E of Part II of Schedule 1 –

    (i) in entry IL1416 (Ships, surface-effect vehicles, water-screw propellers, and specially designed components), for head (5B) there shall be substituted the following:

      "(5B) Ships having special structural features for landing personnel and/or vehicles on a beach .... I";

    (ii) in the same entry, after head (5C), there shall be inserted the following additional heads:

      "(5D) Ships capable of supporting helicopter operations and maintenance I

      (5E) Ships capable of submerging I

      (5F) Ships not elsewhere specified in this Part of this Schedule of below 100 tons GRT, including inflatable craft in an inflated or uninflated state, except lightvessels, fire floats and dredgers .... I";

    (iii) in head (6) of the same entry, for "(1) to (5C)", there shall be substituted "(1) to (5F)";

  (b) in Group 3I of Part II of Schedule 1, in the entry Chemicals –

    (i) after head (7), there shall be inserted the following additional head:

      "(7A) Phosphorus trichloride .... A";

    (ii) after head (9), there shall be inserted the following additional head:

      "(10) Trimethylphosphite .... A".

E. W. Beston

16th February 1987   An Assistant Secretary, Department of Trade and Industry

---

(**a**) 1939 c. 69.   (**b**) *See* S.I. 1970/1537.   (**c**) S.I. 1985/849, amended by S.I. 1985/1085, 1293, 1294, 1986/82, 540, 1446, 1934 and 1987/215.

EXPLANATORY NOTE

(This note is not part of the Order)

This Order further amends the Export of Goods (Control) Order 1985.

Export control is:

(a) *extended* on certain small boats to any destination in Iran or Iraq, *and relaxed* for certain larger ones;

(b) *introduced* on phosphorus trichloride and trimethylphosphite.

STATUTORY INSTRUMENTS

1987 No. 272

DATA PROTECTION

The Data Protection (Fees) Regulations 1987

Made - - - -	*25th February 1987*
Laid before Parliament	*3rd March 1987*
Coming into force	*16th March 1987*

In exercise of the powers conferred upon me by sections 8(5), 40(7) and 41 of the Data Protection Act 1984(**a**) and after consultation with the Data Protection Registrar and with the approval of the Treasury in accordance with the said section 40(7), I hereby make the following Regulations:–

1. These Regulations may be cited as the Data Protection (Fees) Regulations 1987 and shall come into force on 16th March 1987.

2. The fee payable under section 8(5) of the Data Protection Act 1984 on the renewal of an application for registration shall be £22.

Home Office.   *Douglas Hurd*
24th February 1987   One of Her Majesty's Principal Secretaries of State

We approve these Regulations.

Tony Durant
Tim Sainsbury
25th February 1987   Two of the Commissioners of Her Majesty's Treasury

EXPLANATORY NOTE

(This note is not part of the Regulations)

These Regulations prescribe a fee of £22 which is to accompany the renewal of an application to the Data Protection Registrar for registration under the Data Protection Act 1984. (The fee payable on an initial application for registration is prescribed by the Data Protection Regulations 1985 (S.I. 1985/1465).)

(**a**) 1984 c.35; *see* the definition of "prescribed" in section 41.

STATUTORY INSTRUMENTS

1987 No. 273

PREVENTION AND SUPPRESSION OF TERRORISM

The Prevention of Terrorism (Temporary Provisions) Act 1984 (Continuance) Order 1987

Made - - - -	*25th February 1987*
Coming into force	*22nd March 1987*

Whereas a draft of this Order has been approved by resolution of each House of Parliament:

Now, therefore, in exercise of the powers conferred upon me by section 17(2)*(a)* of the Prevention of Terrorism (Temporary Provisions) Act 1984(**a**), I hereby make the following Order:

1. This Order may be cited as the Prevention of Terrorism (Temporary Provisions) Act 1984 (Continuance) Order 1987 and shall come into force on 22nd March 1987.

2. In this Order, "the temporary provisions of the Act of 1984" means sections 1 to 13, 14 (except in so far as it relates to orders under subsection (2)*(a)* or *(b)* of section 17) and 17(2)*(c)* of the Prevention of Terrorism (Temporary Provisions) Act 1984 and Schedules 1 to 3 thereto.

3. The temporary provisions of the Act of 1984 shall continue in force for a period of twelve months beginning with 22nd March 1987.

Home Office	*Douglas Hurd*
25th February 1987	One of Her Majesty's Principal Secretaries of State

EXPLANATORY NOTE

(This note is not part of the Order)

This Order continues in force the temporary provisions of the Prevention of Terrorism (Temporary Provisions) Act 1984 for a period of 12 months from 22nd March 1987. These provisions are currently in force by virtue of the Prevention of Terrorism (Temporary Provisions) Act 1984 (Continuance) Order 1986 (S.I. 1986/417).

(**a**) 1984 c.8.

STATUTORY INSTRUMENTS

1987 No. 275 (S. 14)

LOCAL GOVERNMENT, SCOTLAND

The Rate Support Grant (Scotland) Order 1987

Approved by the House of Commons

Made - - - -	*2nd February 1987*
Laid before the House of Commons	*4th February 1987*
Coming into force	*19th February 1987*

In exercise of the powers conferred upon me by the enactments set out in Schedule 1 to this Order and of all other powers enabling me in that behalf, and after consultation with such associations of local authorities as appear to me to be concerned and with the consent of the Treasury, I hereby make the following Order:

Title, commencement and interpretation

1.—(1) This Order may be cited as the Rate Support Grant (Scotland) Order 1987 and shall come into force on the day after the day on which it is approved by a resolution of the House of Commons.

(2) In this Order–

"the 1963 Act" means the Local Government (Financial Provisions) (Scotland) Act 1963(**a**);

"the 1966 Act" means the Local Government (Scotland) Act 1966(**b**);

"the 1973 Act" means the Local Government (Scotland) Act 1973(**c**);

"the 1975 Act" means the Local Government (Scotland) Act 1975(**d**);

"the 1982 Act" means the Local Government and Planning (Scotland) Act 1982(**e**);

"the 1984 Act" means the Rating and Valuation (Amendment) (Scotland) Act 1984(**f**);

"the 1985 No. 4 Order" means the Rate Support Grant (Scotland) (No. 4) Order 1985(**g**); and

"the 1986 Order" means the Rate Support Grant (Scotland) Order 1986(**h**).

Aggregate grants for 1987-88

2.—(1) The estimated aggregate amount of the rate support grants for the year 1987-88, as determined in accordance with the provisions of section 2(2) of the 1966 Act, is hereby fixed and prescribed as £1,896,760,000.

(**a**) 1963 c.12.
(**b**) 1966 c.51.
(**c**) 1973 c.65.
(**d**) 1975 c.30.
(**e**) 1982 c.43.
(**f**) 1984 c.31.
(**g**) S.I. 1986/140.
(**h**) S.I. 1986/1965.

(2) The amounts of the needs element and the domestic element and the estimated amount of the resources element of the rate support grants for the year 1987-88 shall be the amounts set out in the following table:–

	£
Amount of the needs element	1,608,560,000
Amount of the domestic element	91,100,000
Estimated amount of the resources element	197,100,000

Apportionment of the needs element for 1987-88

3. There shall be apportioned to each local authority set out in column 1 of the table in Schedule 2 to this Order the amount of the needs element for the year 1987-88 set out in column 2 of that table opposite to the name of that authority.

Domestic rate reduction for 1987-88

4. The amount prescribed for the year 1987-88 for the purposes of section 7(1) of the 1966 Act (reduction of rates on dwellings by reference to the domestic element) shall be 7 pence in the pound, being the amount which in my opinion corresponds to the amount of the domestic element for that year, as prescribed by article 2(2) of this Order.

Weighted population and national standard amount per head for 1987-88

5. For the purposes of section 9(3) of the 1963 Act (definition of standard penny rate product) the weighted population of an area for the year 1987-88 shall be the total population of the area as first estimated by the Registrar General of Births, Deaths and Marriages in Scotland in relation to 30th June 1985(**a**) and the national standard amount per head for the year 1987-88 shall be such as will result as nearly as may be in the distribution of the whole of the resources element for that year.

Redetermined estimated aggregate grants for 1986-87

6. The estimated aggregate amount of the rate support grants for the year 1986-87 (which was fixed as £1,636,083,991 by article 2 of the 1986 Order), as redetermined in accordance with the provisions of section 2(2) of the 1966 Act, is hereby fixed and prescribed as £1,636,183,991.

Variation of needs element for 1986-87 and its apportionment

7. The amount of the needs element for the year 1986-87, which was varied to £1,359,583,991 by article 3 of the 1986 Order, is hereby further varied to £1,360,583,991.

8. There shall be apportioned to each local authority set out in column 1 of the table in Schedule 3 to this Order the amount of the needs element for the year 1986-87 set out in column 2 of that table opposite to the name of that authority.

Variation of resources element for 1986-87

9. The estimated amount of the resources element for the year 1986-87, which was prescribed as £185,200,000 by article 2(2) of the 1985 No. 4 Order, is hereby varied to £184,300,000.

Redetermined estimated aggregate grants for 1985-86

10. The estimated aggregate amount of the rate support grants for the year 1985-86 (which was fixed as £1,692,749,142 by article 5 of the 1986 Order), as redetermined in accordance with the provisions of section 2(2) of the 1966 Act, is hereby fixed and prescribed as £1,700,108,228.

Variation of needs element for 1985-86 and its apportionment

11. The amount of the needs element for the year 1985-86, which was varied to £1,383,949,142 by article 6 of the 1986 Order, is hereby further varied to £1,391,308,228.

(**a**) *See* the Registrar General Scotland Annual Report 1985 (HMSO No. 131).

12. There shall be apportioned to each local authority set out in column 1 of the table in Schedule 4 to this Order the amount of the needs element for the year 1985-86 set out in column 2 of that table opposite to the name of that authority.

Redetermined estimated aggregate grants for 1984-85

13. The estimated aggregate amount of the rate support grants for the year 1984-85 (which was fixed as £1,671,517,328 by article 11 of the 1985 No. 4 Order), as redetermined in accordance with the provisions of section 2(2) of the 1966 Act, is hereby fixed and prescribed as £1,671,736,538.

Variation of needs element for 1984-85 and its apportionment

14. The amount of the needs element for the year 1984-85 which was varied to £1,442,117,328 by article 12 of the 1985 No. 4 Order, is hereby further varied to £1,442,336,538.

15. There shall be apportioned to each local authority set out in column 1 of the table in Schedule 5 to this Order the amount of needs element for the year 1984-85 set out in column 2 of that table opposite to the name of that authority which amounts are, in total, £1,440,036,538.

Revocation

16. Article 4 of, and Schedule 2 to, the 1986 Order (which made provision for the apportionment of the needs element for 1986-87), article 7 of, and Schedule 3 to, that Order (which made provision for the apportionment of the needs element for 1985-86) and article 13 of, and Schedule 4 to, the 1985 No. 4 Order (which made provision for the apportionment of the needs element for 1984-85) are hereby revoked.

Malcolm Rifkind
One of Her Majesty's Principal
Secretaries of State

New St. Andrew's House, Edinburgh
28th January 1987

We consent,

Peter Lloyd
Mark Lennox-Boyd

2nd February 1987   Two of the Lords Commissioners of Her Majesty's Treasury

SCHEDULE 1

(1) Relevant enactment conferring power	(2) Relevant amending enactment	(3) Relevant provision of this Order
Section 9(5) of the 1963 Act.	Section 13 of the 1966 Act. Paragraph 24 of Part II of Schedule 6 to the 1975 Act.	Article 5.
Section 2(4) of the 1966 Act.	Paragraph 1 of Schedule 2 to the 1975 Act.	Article 2(2).
Section 3 of the 1966 Act.	Section 120(1)(a) of the 1973 Act. Paragraph 2 of Schedule 2 to the 1975 Act. Paragraph 6 of Schedule 3 to the 1982 Act.	Articles 2(1), 6, 10 and 13.
Sections 4 and 45(2) of the 1966 Act.	Section 3 of and paragraph 7 of Schedule 3 to the 1982 Act.	Articles 7, 9, 11, 14 and 16.
Paragraph 3, as read with paragraph 3A, of Part I of Schedule 1 to the 1966 Act.	Paragraph 5(b) of Schedule 2 to the 1975 Act. Section 1(1) of the 1984 Act.	Articles 3, 8, 12, 15 and Schedules 2, 3, 4 and 5.
Paragraph 1 of Part III of Schedule 1 to the 1966 Act.	Paragraph 7 of Schedule 2 to the 1975 Act.	Article 4.

SCHEDULE 2

Article 3

APPORTIONMENT OF NEEDS ELEMENT 1987-88

(1) Authority	(2) Amount £
Regional Councils	
Borders	32,105,330
Central	69,323,590
Dumfries and Galloway	44,173,290
Fife	91,312,733
Grampian	137,202,042
Highland	80,804,146
Lothian	172,936,521
Strathclyde	715,092,141
Tayside	104,991,270
District Councils	
Berwickshire	213,835
Ettrick and Lauderdale	383,018
Roxburgh	887,561
Tweeddale	166,888
Clackmannan	549,295
Falkirk	1,650,467
Stirling	933,493
Annandale and Eskdale	413,507
Nithsdale	657,168
Stewartry	265,232
Wigtown	349,710

(1) Authority	(2) Amount £
Dunfermline	1,485,223
Kirkcaldy	1,953,516
North East Fife	759,010
Aberdeen City	4,180,520
Banff and Buchan	958,713
Gordon	806,970
Kincardine and Deeside	537,904
Moray	977,378
Badenoch and Strathspey	120,125
Caithness	478,375
Inverness	676,472
Lochaber	284,064
Nairn	117,071
Ross and Cromarty	1,028,758
Skye and Lochalsh	237,359
Sutherland	405,867
East Lothian	944,896
Edinburgh City	12,513,104
Midlothian	936,546
West Lothian	1,631,730
Argyll and Bute	2,630,941
Bearsden and Milngavie	559,180
Clydebank	3,075,044
Clydesdale	669,933
Cumbernauld and Kilsyth	724,204
Cumnock and Doon Valley	912,041
Cunninghame	1,932,617
Dumbarton	1,006,527
East Kilbride	942,090
Eastwood	638,522
Glasgow City	42,525,369
Hamilton	1,237,428
Inverclyde	2,453,304
Kilmarnock and Loudoun	1,012,858
Kyle and Carrick	1,379,049
Monklands	2,470,557
Motherwell	2,354,567
Renfrew	4,396,435
Strathkelvin	1,111,105
Angus	1,084,667
Dundee City	5,741,682
Perth and Kinross	1,407,344
Islands Councils	
Orkney	9,247,635
Shetland	10,925,602
Western Isles	22,676,461

SCHEDULE 3

APPORTIONMENT OF NEEDS ELEMENT 1986-87

(1) Authority	(2) Amount £
Regional Councils	
Borders	29,323,241
Central	62,885,461
Dumfries and Galloway	40,268,343
Fife	79,847,952
Grampian	126,200,331
Highland	75,957,220
Lothian	140,814,750
Strathclyde	580,784,554
Tayside	97,678,811
District Councils	
Berwickshire	195,923
Ettrick and Lauderdale	355,587
Roxburgh	870,401
Tweeddale	155,344
Clackmannan	522,248
Falkirk	1,541,190
Stirling	313,713
Annandale and Eskdale	386,290
Nithsdale	613,258
Stewartry	244,756
Wigtown	324,781
Dunfermline	1,396,520
Kirkcaldy	1,918,512
North East Fife	707,474
Aberdeen City	2,638,132
Banff and Buchan	895,500
Gordon	739,899
Kincardine and Deeside	412,947
Moray	799,862
Badenoch and Strathspey	109,959
Caithness	456,268
Inverness	629,465
Lochaber	278,416
Nairn	108,750
Ross and Cromarty	1,000,356
Skye and Lochalsh	230,218
Sutherland	397,898
East Lothian	869,452
Edinburgh City	289,829
Midlothian	564,651
West Lothian	1,271,240
Argyll and Bute	2,583,256
Bearsden and Milngavie	546,625
Clydebank	2,712,070
Clydesdale	573,021

(1) Authority	(2) Amount £
Cumbernauld and Kilsyth	662,971
Cumnock and Doon Valley	666,144
Cunninghame	1,636,194
Dumbarton	648,397
East Kilbride	865,567
Eastwood	597,377
Glasgow City	34,491,402
Hamilton	1,160,494
Inverclyde	1,935,430
Kilmarnock and Loudoun	507,623
Kyle and Carrick	1,217,424
Monklands	2,255,479
Motherwell	2,307,889
Renfrew	3,723,983
Strathkelvin	1,049,427
Angus	1,014,292
Dundee City	4,670,768
Perth and Kinross	1,295,184
Islands Councils	
Orkney	7,592,938
Shetland	10,045,627
Western Isles	20,824,907

Article 12

SCHEDULE 4

APPORTIONMENT OF NEEDS ELEMENT 1985-86

(1) Authority	(2) Amount £
Regional Councils	
Borders	26,816,364
Central	59,613,657
Dumfries and Galloway	35,235,557
Fife	75,875,090
Grampian	121,203,862
Highland	70,514,161
Lothian	158,939,636
Strathclyde	623,800,433
Tayside	91,378,650
District Councils	
Berwickshire	180,478
Ettrick and Lauderdale	326,658
Roxburgh	965,631

(1) Authority	(2) Amount £
Tweeddale	141,209
Clackmannan	233,688
Falkirk	1,636,010
Stirling	847,880
Annandale and Eskdale	351,308
Nithsdale	514,800
Stewartry	115,790
Wigtown	297,607
Dunfermline	1,335,903
Kirkcaldy	2,064,639
North East Fife	688,098
Aberdeen City	3,523,437
Banff and Buchan	730,967
Gordon	610,569
Kincardine and Deeside	427,525
Moray	720,042
Badenoch and Strathspey	100,556
Caithness	486,685
Inverness	488,571
Lochaber	309,050
Nairn	98,630
Ross and Cromarty	1,263,378
Skye and Lochalsh	223,790
Sutherland	357,094
East Lothian	870,004
Edinburgh City	9,566,739
Midlothian	512,259
West Lothian	1,116,975
Argyll and Bute	2,575,310
Bearsden and Milngavie	607,354
Clydebank	2,095,956
Clydesdale	611,848
Cumbernauld and Kilsyth	546,663
Cumnock and Doon Valley	682,700
Cunninghame	1,185,275
Dumbarton	853,477
East Kilbride	889,691
Eastwood	575,477
Glasgow City	31,804,085
Hamilton	214,962
Inverclyde	1,976,362
Kilmarnock and Loudoun	1,011,967
Kyle and Carrick	1,183,733
Monklands	2,124,931
Motherwell	2,007,042
Renfrew	2,393,715
Strathkelvin	1,151,538
Angus	982,510
Dundee City	4,552,965

(1) Authority	(2) Amount £
Perth and Kinross	1,252,076
Islands Councils	
Orkney	7,459,314
Shetland	9,961,998
Western Isles	18,123,899

Article 15

SCHEDULE 5

APPORTIONMENT OF NEEDS ELEMENT 1984-85

(1) Authority	(2) Amount £
Regional Councils	
Borders	25,558,996
Central	64,944,416
Dumfries and Galloway	33,419,058
Fife	74,084,917
Grampian	119,540,756
Highland	66,913,532
Lothian	168,817,955
Strathclyde	643,345,094
Tayside	88,129,308
District Councils	
Berwickshire	318,953
Ettrick and Lauderdale	669,381
Roxburgh	695,896
Tweeddale	248,509
Clackmannan	995,233
Falkirk	3,048,781
Stirling	1,202,476
Annandale and Eskdale	600,790
Nithsdale	990,469
Stewartry	397,994
Wigtown	524,799
Dunfermline	2,667,531
Kirkcaldy	3,626,230
North East Fife	1,375,941
Aberdeen City	5,504,703
Banff and Buchan	1,749,273
Gordon	1,423,608
Kincardine and Deeside	832,392
Moray	1,614,640
Badenoch and Strathspey	205,041
Caithness	464,671
Inverness	794,371

(1) Authority	(2) Amount £
Lochaber	446,830
Nairn	141,535
Ross and Cromarty	978,514
Skye and Lochalsh	221,573
Sutherland	310,156
East Lothian	1,315,158
Edinburgh City	6,601,217
Midlothian	1,108,356
West Lothian	2,586,591
Argyll and Bute	2,034,939
Bearsden and Milngavie	1,022,037
Clydebank	1,748,972
Clydesdale	1,213,497
Cumbernauld and Kilsyth	1,316,956
Cumnock and Doon Valley	1,110,728
Cunninghame	2,724,130
Dumbarton	1,505,228
East Kilbride	1,751,701
Eastwood	930,284
Glasgow City	31,552,557
Hamilton	1,535,568
Inverclyde	2,542,744
Kilmarnock and Loudoun	1,952,872
Kyle and Carrick	2,382,325
Monklands	2,631,792
Motherwell	3,573,036
Renfrew	4,358,739
Strathkelvin	1,930,764
Angus	1,955,642
Dundee City	3,886,080
Perth and Kinross	2,515,804
Islands Councils	
Orkney	7,690,279
Shetland	10,243,710
Western Isles	17,510,510

EXPLANATORY NOTE

(This note is not part of the Order)

This Order–
(a) In relation to the year 1987-88–
   (i) fixes the estimated aggregate amount of the rate support grants payable under Part I of the Local Government (Scotland) Act 1966 to regional, islands and district councils in Scotland, and prescribes the division of this amount among the needs element, the domestic element and the estimated resources element (article 2);
   (ii) prescribes the amount in the pound by which rating authorities are to reduce the rate in the pound which they would otherwise levy on dwellinghouses in their areas so as to take account of the amount of domestic element for the year (article 4); and
   (iii) prescribes matters relating to the distribution of the needs and resources elements of rate support grants among local authorities (articles 3 and 5);
(b) In relation to the year 1986-87–
   (i) redetermines the estimated aggregate amount of the rate support grants and varies the amount of the needs element and the estimated amount of the resources element payable for that year (articles 6, 7 and 9);
   (ii) varies the needs element distribution (article 8); and
   (iii) revokes article 4 of, and Schedule 2 to, the Rate Support Grant (Scotland) Order 1986 (article 16);
(c) In relation to the year 1985-86–
   (i) redetermines the estimated aggregate amount of the rate support grants and varies the amount of the needs element payable for that year (articles 10 and 11);
   (ii) varies the needs element distribution (article 12); and
   (iii) revokes article 7 of, and Schedule 3 to, the Rate Support Grant (Scotland) Order 1986 (article 16);
(d) In relation to the year 1984-85–
   (i) redetermines the estimated aggregate amount of the rate support grants and varies the amount of the needs element payable for that year (articles 13 and 14);
   (ii) varies the needs element distribution (article 15); and
   (iii) revokes article 13 of, and Schedule 4 to, the Rate Support Grant (Scotland) (No. 4) Order 1985 (article 16).

STATUTORY INSTRUMENTS

1987 No. 281

SOCIAL SECURITY

The Family Income Supplements (General) Amendment Regulations 1987

Made - - - -	*27th February 1987*
Laid before Parliament	*27th February 1987*
Coming into force -	*24th March 1987*

The Secretary of State for Social Services, in exercise of the powers conferred on him by section 6(3) of the Family Income Supplements Act 1970**(a)** and of all other powers enabling him in that behalf, after agreement by the Social Security Advisory Committee that the proposals to make these regulations should not be referred to it**(b)**, hereby makes the following regulations:–

Citation and commencement

1. These regulations may be cited as the Family Income Supplements (General) Amendment Regulations 1987 and shall come into force on 24th March 1987.

Insertion of new regulation 3A in the Family Income Supplements (General) Regulations 1980

2. After regulation 3 of the Family Income Supplements (General) Regulations 1980**(c)** there shall be inserted the following regulation:—

"Termination of awards

3A. Notwithstanding any provision in the Act or these regulations, where a claim is made on or after 24th March 1987 the period for which benefit is payable on the claim shall expire on a date not later than 11th April 1988.".

Signed by authority of the Secretary of State for Social Services.

John Major
Minister of State,
Department of Health and Social Security

27th February 1987

(a) 1970 c.55; section 6(3) was amended by section 25 of, and paragraph 1(1) and (3) of Schedule 8 to, the Health and Social Services and Social Security Adjudications Act 1983 (c.41).
(b) *See* section 10(2) of the Social Security Act 1980 (c.30).
(c) S.I. 1980/1437; there are no relevant amending instruments.

EXPLANATORY NOTE

(This note is not part of the Regulations)

These regulations insert a new regulation 3A in the Family Income Supplements (General) Regulations 1980 which makes provision for awards of family income supplements to terminate not later than 11th April 1988, the day of the coming into operation of the new Family Credit legislation.

STATUTORY INSTRUMENTS

1987 No. 282

AGRICULTURE

The Potato Marketing Scheme (Amendment) Order 1987

Made - - - -	*23rd February 1987*
Coming into force	*1st March 1987*

Whereas the Potato Marketing Board duly submitted to the Minister of Agriculture, Fisheries and Food, the Secretary of State concerned with agriculture in Scotland and the Secretary of State for Wales (hereinafter called "the Ministers") certain amendments of the Potato Marketing Scheme 1955(**a**), which amendments as subsequently modified by the Ministers are set out in the Schedule hereto;

And whereas the Ministers laid before each House of Parliament the amendments set out in the said Schedule and the House of Commons resolved on 5th February 1987 and the House of Lords resolved on 5th February 1987 that they should be approved;

Now, therefore, the Ministers, acting jointly, in exercise of the powers conferred by section 2 of, and Schedule 1 to, the Agricultural Marketing Act 1958(**b**), and now vested in them(**c**), hereby make the following Order:

1. This Order may be cited as the Potato Marketing Scheme (Amendment) Order 1987.

2. The amendments of the Potato Marketing Scheme 1955 which are set out in the Schedule hereto are hereby approved and shall come into force on 1st March 1987.

In Witness whereof the Official Seal of the Minister of Agriculture, Fisheries and Food is hereunto affixed on 22nd February 1987.

Michael Jopling
Minister of Agriculture, Fisheries and Food

23rd February 1987

John J. Mackay
Parliamentary Under Secretary of State, Scottish Office

23rd February 1987

Nicholas Edwards
Secretary of State for Wales

(**a**) Approved by S.I. 1955/690, amended by S.I. 1962/883, 1971/711, 1976/133, 1985/312.
(**b**) 1958 c.47.
(**c**) In the case of the Secretary of State for Wales, by virtue of S.I. 1969/388 and 1978/272.

Article 2   SCHEDULE

The Potato Marketing Scheme 1955 shall be further amended as follows:

1. In paragraph 83(1)(a), for the words "two hundred pounds" there shall be substituted the words "two thousand pounds".

2. In paragraph 84(2)(b), for the words "five times the formula rate as defined in paragraph 84(3)(a)", there shall be substituted the words "seven times the formula rate with effect from 1st March 1987 and ten times the formula rate with effect from 1st January 1989".

EXPLANATORY NOTE

(This note is not part of the Order)

This Order approves further amendments of the Potato Marketing Scheme 1955, ("the Scheme").

The amendments–
- (a) increase the maximum monetary penalty which the Disciplinary Committee may impose on any registered producer under the provisions of paragraph 83(1)(a) of the Scheme from two hundred to two thousand pounds;
- (b) increase the maximum excess area contribution provided for in paragraph 84(2)(b) of the Scheme, which is currently fixed at five times the formula rate (as defined in paragraph 84(3)(a) of the Scheme) as follows–
  - (i) with effect from 1st March 1987 to seven times the formula rate;
  - (ii) with effect from 1st January 1989 to ten times the formula rate.

STATUTORY INSTRUMENTS

1987 No. 286

CONSUMER PROTECTION

The Nightwear (Safety) (Amendment) Regulations 1987

Made - - - -	*27th February 1987*
Coming into force	*1st March 1987*

Whereas the Secretary of State has, in accordance with section 1(4) of the Consumer Safety Act 1978(**a**), consulted such organisations as appear to him to be representative of interests substantially affected by these Regulations and such other persons as he considers appropriate:

And whereas a draft of these Regulations has been approved by a resolution of each House of Parliament pursuant to section 7(7) of the said Act of 1978:

Now, therefore, the Secretary of State, in exercise of the powers conferred on him by section 1 of, and paragraph 13 of Schedule 2 to, the said Act of 1978(**a**), hereby makes the following Regulations:

1. These Regulations may be cited as the Nightwear (Safety) (Amendment) Regulations 1987 and shall come into force on 1st March 1987.

2. Regulation 1 of the Nightwear (Safety) Regulations 1985(**b**) shall be amended by adding at the end the words—

", except that, for the purposes of the requirements imposed by them in relation to babies' garments, they shall come into operation on 1st September 1987".

Michael Howard
Parliamentary Under Secretary of State,
Department of Trade and Industry

27th February 1987

(**a**) 1978 c.38; a new Schedule 2 was substituted by section 14 of the Consumer Safety (Amendment) Act 1986 (c.29).
(**b**) S.I. 1985/2043.

EXPLANATORY NOTE

(This Note is not part of the Regulations)

These Regulations amend the Nightwear (Safety) Regulations 1985. As a result, those Regulations come into force on 1st September 1987 as regards requirements relating to babies' garments. 1st March 1987 remains the date on which all other requirements of the 1985 Regulations come into force.

The 1985 Regulations impose requirements relating to the flammability performance of nightwear (which includes any babies' garments, as defined in Regulation 3(1)), its testing and labelling. Babies' garments are not required to comply with the flammability performance requirements but must be labelled so as to indicate whether or not they are capable of complying with those requirements.

1987 No. 287

DESIGNS

The Designs (Amendment) Rules 1987

Made - - - -	*23rd February 1987*
Laid before Parliament	*2nd March 1987*
Coming into force	*24th March 1987*

The Secretary of State, in exercise of the powers conferred upon him by sections 36 and 39(1) the Registered Designs Act 1949**(a)** and now vested in him**(b)** and after consultation with the Council on Tribunals pursuant to section 10(1) of the Tribunals and Inquiries Act 1971**(c)**, hereby makes the following Rules:–

1. These Rules may be cited as the Designs (Amendment) Rules 1987 and shall come into force on 24th March 1987.

2. For rule 69 of the Designs Rules 1984**(d)** there shall be substituted the following:
"**69.**—(1) The following shall be excluded days for all purposes under the Act:
 (a) all Sundays,
 (b) Good Friday and Christmas Day;
 (c) any day specified as or proclaimed to be a bank holiday in England in or under section 1 of the Banking and Financial Dealings Act 1971**(e)**;
 (d) any Saturday immediately preceded by one of the above.

(2) Saturdays not falling within paragraph (1) above shall be excluded days for all purposes except the filing of new applications for the registration of designs which are not Convention applications."

Geoffrey Pattie
Minister of State,
Department of Trade and Industry

23rd February 1987

(a) 1949 c.88.
(b) S.I. 1970/1537.
(c) 1971 c.62.
(d) S.I. 1984/1989, to which there are amendments not relevant to these Rules.
(e) 1971 c.80.

EXPLANATORY NOTE

(This note is not part of the Rules)

These Rules revise rule 69 of the Designs Rules 1984, which specifies days as excluded days.

STATUTORY INSTRUMENTS

1987 No. 288

PATENTS

The Patents (Amendment) Rules 1987

Made - - - -	*27th February 1987*
Laid before Parliament	*2nd March 1987*
Coming into force	
Rules 1, 8, 9, 10, 11 and 12,	
and rules 2 and 3 as provided in	
rule 1(2)	*24th March 1987*
Remainder	*1st September 1987*

The Secretary of State, in exercise of the powers conferred upon him by sections 77(9), 78(8), 120(1) and 123(1), (2) and (3) of the Patents Act 1977(**a**), after consultation with the Council on Tribunals pursuant to section 10(1) of the Tribunals and Inquiries Act 1971(**b**), and as to rule 3 with the consent of the Treasury pursuant to subsection (4) of the said section 123, hereby makes the following Rules:

Preliminary

1.—(1) These Rules may be cited as the Patents (Amendment) Rules 1987.

(2) The following rules and Schedules shall come into force on 24th March 1987–
  (a) this rule;
  (b) rule 2 and Schedule 1 so far as they relate to Patents Forms Nos. 50/77, 52/77 and 53/77;
  (c) rule 3 and Schedule 2 so far as they relate to the fees payable in respect of those forms; and
  (d) rules 8, 9, 10, 11 and 12.

(3) The following rules and Schedules shall come into force on 1st September 1987–
  (a) rule 2 and Schedule 1 so far as they relate to Patents Forms Nos. 54/77, 55/77, 56/77 and 57/77;
  (b) rule 3 and Schedule 2 so far as they relate to the fees payable in respect of those forms; and
  (c) rules 4, 5, 6 and 7.

(4) Rules 20(9), 25(4), 28 and 80 of the Patents Rules 1982(**c**) are hereby revoked, and the reference to rule 80 in Patents Form No. 40/77 set out in Schedule 2 to the said Rules shall be omitted.

2.—(1) There shall be substituted for Patents Form No. 50/77 as set out in Schedule 2 to the Patents Rules 1982 the form set out in Part I of Schedule 1 hereto.

(2) The forms set out in Part II of Schedule 1 hereto shall be inserted at the end of the said Schedule 2.

(**a**) 1977 c.37.
(**b**) 1971 c.62.
(**c**) S.I. 1982/717; the relevant amending instrument is S.I. 1985/785.

3. Part A of the Schedule to the Patents (Fees) Rules 1986(**a**) shall be amended in accordance with Schedule 2 hereto.

Translations

4.—(1) 1st September 1987 is the day appointed under section 77(9) of the Patents Act 1977 for the purpose of the coming into force of subsection (6) of that section.

(2) This rule shall not apply in the case of a European patent (UK) mention of whose grant is published in the European Patent Bulletin before that day.

5.—(1) 1st September 1987 is the day appointed under section 78(8) of the Patents Act 1977 for the purpose of the coming into force of subsection (7) of that section.

(2) This rule shall not apply in the case of an application for a European patent (UK) which is published by the European Patent Office before that day.

6. The following rules shall be inserted after rule 79 of the Patents Rules 1982–

"Translations of European patents (UK) filed under section 77(6)

79A.—(1) A translation filed under section 77(6) shall be filed in duplicate and shall be accompanied by Patents Form No. 54/77 in duplicate, in the case of a translation filed under section 77(6)(a), or by Patents Form No. 55/77 in duplicate, in the case of a translation filed under section 77(6)(b).

(2) A translation filed under section 77(6)(a) shall comprise a translation of the entirety of the published specification of the patent, irrespective of whether a translation of all or any part of the claims contained in the specification has previously been filed under section 78(7) but subject to paragraph (5) below, and shall include any drawings in the specification, irrespective of whether the drawings contain textual matter.

(3) A translation filed under section 77(6) shall comply with the following requirements as to presentation, subject to paragraph (4) below in the case of any drawings–

  (a) it shall permit of direct reproduction by photography, electrostatic processes, photo offset and micro-filming, in an unlimited number of copies;

  (b) it shall be on A4 paper (29.7cm x 21cm.) which shall be pliable, strong, white, smooth, matt and durable;

  (c) each sheet of paper shall be free from cracks, creases and folds and used on one side only;

  (d) each sheet shall be used with its short sides at the top and bottom (upright position);

  (e) the minimum margins shall be–
    top   2 cm.
    left side   2.5 cm.
    right side   2 cm.
    bottom   2 cm.;

  (f) the margins of the sheets shall be completely blank;

  (g) the translation shall be typed or printed in single-line spacing (unless the comptroller otherwise permits), in a dark, indelible colour and in characters of which the capital letters are not less than 0.21cm. high, save that graphic symbols and characters and chemical and mathematical formulae may, instead of being typed or printed, be written or drawn;

  (h) the translation shall be reasonably free from deletions and other alterations, overwritings and interlineations and shall, in any event, be legible;

  (i) each sheet (other than a sheet of drawings) shall be numbered consecutively in arabic numerals.

(a) S.I. 1986/583.

(4) Where a translation including any drawings is filed, the sheets of drawings shall correspond exactly in content and presentation to the sheets of drawings which were published by the European Patent Office, except that–

(a) each sheet shall be numbered consecutively in arabic numerals, as a separate series from that used for the other sheets of the translation, if not so numbered when published by the European Patent Office; and

(b) any textual matter contained in the published drawings shall be replaced with a translation into English.

(5) For the purposes of paragraph (2) above, the published specification of the patent shall be taken not to include–

(a) anything which does not consist of, or form part of, the description of the invention, the claims or the drawings referred to in the description or the claims, or

(b) any claim not having effect in the United Kingdom, or

(c) anything published in a language other than the language of the proceedings (within the meaning of Article 14 of the European Patent Convention).

Periods prescribed under section 77(6)

79B.—(1) The period prescribed under section 77(6)(a) for filing a translation of the specification of a European patent (UK) and paying the prescribed fee shall be three months from the date of publication of the mention of the grant of the patent in the European Patent Bulletin.

(2) The period prescribed under section 77(6)(b) for filing a translation of an amendment to a European patent (UK) and paying the prescribed fee shall be three months from the date of publication by the European Patent Office of the specification of the patent as amended.

Translations of claims of applications for European patents (UK) filed under section 78(7)

79C.—(1) A translation filed under section 78(7) shall be filed in duplicate and shall be accompanied by Patents Form No. 56/77 in duplicate.

(2) The translation shall comply with the requirements contained in rule 79A(3).

Corrected translations filed under section 80(3)

79D.—(1) A corrected translation filed under section 80(3) shall be filed in duplicate.

(2) The corrected translation shall comply with the requirements contained in rule 79A(3) and (4).

(3) Publication of the corrected translation shall be requested on Patents Form No. 57/77, which shall be filed in duplicate.

(4) The period prescribed under section 80(3) for payment of the prescribed fee shall be fourteen days from the day on which the corrected translation is filed.

Verification of translation

79E. A translation shall be verified to the satisfaction of the comptroller as corresponding to the original text of–

(a) the specification, in the case of a translation filed under section 77(6)(a), or

(b) the amendment, in the case of a translation filed under section 77(6)(b), or

(c) the claims of the specification of the application, in the case of a translation filed under section 78(7), or

(d) the specification of the patent or the claims of the application, as the case may be, in the case of a translation filed under section 80(3);

and if such verification does not accompany the translation when filed it shall be filed within one month of the sending by the comptroller of a written request for such verification.

Inspection of translations

79F. A request for inspection of a translation published under section 77(8), 78(7) or 80(3) shall be made on Patents Form No. 23/77."

7. There shall be inserted at the end of rule 113(4) of the Patents Rules 1982 the words, "unless such a translation has already been filed under section 77(6)"; and in Patents Form No. 23/77 set out in Schedule 2 to the said Rules there shall be substituted for the reference to rules 48, 49 and 93 a reference to rules 48, 49, 79F and 93.

Miscellaneous

8. In paragraph (16) of rule 20 of the Patents Rules 1982 the words "free from" in the second place where they occur shall be deleted.

9. In rule 26(3) of the Patents Rules 1982 there shall be inserted after the words "rule 110(3)" the words "or (3C)".

10. For rule 99 of the Patents Rules 1982 there shall be substituted the following–

"**99.**—(1) The following shall be excluded days for all purposes under the Act–
   (a) all Sundays;
   (b) Good Friday and Christmas Day;
   (c) any day specified as or proclaimed to be a bank holiday in England in or under section 1 of the Banking and Financial Dealings Act 1971(**a**);
   (d) any Saturday immediately preceded by one of the above.

(2) Saturdays not falling within paragraph (1) above shall be excluded days for all purposes except the filing of applications in respect of which no declaration for the purposes of section 5(2) is made."

11. For rule 100 of the Patents Rules 1982 there shall be substituted the following–

"**100.**—(1) Subject to paragraph (2) below, any document filed in any proceedings before the comptroller may, if he thinks fit, be amended, and any irregularity in procedure in or before the Patent Office may be rectified, on such terms as he may direct.

(2) Where the irregularity in procedure consists of a failure to comply with any limitation as to times or periods specified in the Act or the 1949 Act or prescribed in these Rules or the Patents Rules 1968(**b**), as they continue to apply, the comptroller may direct that the time or period in question shall be altered if the irregularity is attributable wholly or in part to an error, default or omission on the part of the Patent Office, but not otherwise.

(3) Paragraph (2) above is without prejudice to the comptroller's power to extend any times or periods under rule 110 below."

12.—(1) In paragraph (1) of rule 110 of the Patents Rules 1982 there shall be substituted for the words "paragraph (3)" the words "paragraphs (3) and (3A)".

(2) For paragraphs (2) and (3) of the said rule 110 there shall be substituted the following–

"(2) The rules referred to in paragraph (1) above are rules 6(1), 17(3), 26 (so far as it relates to rule 6(1)), 39(1) and (2), 40(2), 43(2), 60(2), 65(1), 66(1), 71(1), 78(1), 81(1), 82(1) and 91(4).

(3) A time or period prescribed in rules 6(2) and (6), 15(1), 17(2), 23, 25(2), 25(3) (except so far as it relates to the filing of claims for the purposes of the application and the filing of the abstract), 26 (except so far as it relates to rule 6(1)), 33(2), (3) and (4), 34, 79B, 81(2) and (3), 82(2) and (3), 83(3) and 85(1) and (3) above shall, if not previously extended, be extended for one month upon filing Patents Form No.

(**a**) 1971 c.80.
(**b**) S.I. 1968/1389, amended by S.I. 1970/955, 1971/1917, 1973/66, 1975/891, 1021 and 1262 and revoked with savings by S.I. 1978/216.

50/77; and where in any proceedings more than one such time or period expires on the same day (but not otherwise), those times or periods may be extended upon the filing of a single such form.

(3A) Without prejudice to paragraph (3) above, a time or period prescribed in the rules referred to in that paragraph may, upon request made on Patents Form No. 52/77, be extended or further extended by the comptroller if he thinks fit, upon such terms as the comptroller may direct, and whether or not the time or period, including any extension obtained under paragraph (3), has expired:

> Provided that no extension may be granted under this paragraph in relation to any time or period expiring before 24th March 1987.

(3B) A single request may be made under paragraph (3A) above for the extension of more than one time or period in the same proceedings if the extensions are to be to a common date (but not otherwise).

(3C) If on consideration of a request under paragraph (3A) above the comptroller decides that the extension requested (or, in a case falling within paragraph (3B) above, any or all of the extensions requested) may be granted he shall notify the applicant accordingly and invite him to file Patents Form No. 53/77, upon receipt of which the comptroller shall effect the extension or extensions in accordance with the decision."

23rd February 1987

Geoffrey Pattie
Department of Trade and Industry

We consent to the making of rule 3 of these Rules.

Mark Lennox-Boyd
Michael Neubert
27th February 1987   Two of the Lords Commissioners of Her Majesty's Treasury

Rule 2

SCHEDULE 1

PART I

REVISED PATENTS FORM NO 50/77

For official use only

THE PATENT OFFICE

PATENTS ACT 1977   PATENTS FORM NO. 50/77

REQUEST FOR EXTENSION OF TIME OR
PERIOD UNDER RULE 110(3)

Please write or type in BLOCK
LETTERS using dark ink. For
details of current fees please
contact the Patent Office

Enter the full name(s) of the
person(s) making the request

Mark the appropriate box(es) with
an 'x'. This form may not be used
to extend more than one time or
period unless the times or periods
expire on the same day

Please sign here ▶

Attention is drawn to rules 90 and
106 of the Patents Rules 1982

1. Application Number

2. Name

3. Rule(s) prescribing the time(s) or period(s) to be
   extended

   ☐ 6(2)   ☐ 25(2)   ☐ 33(4)   ☐ 82(2)
   ☐ 6(6)   ☐ 25(3)   ☐ 34   ☐ 82(3)
   ☐ 15(1)   ☐ 26   ☐ 79B   ☐ 83(3)
   ☐ 17(2)   ☐ 33(2)   ☐ 81(2)   ☐ 85(1)
   ☐ 23   ☐ 33(3)   ☐ 81(3)   ☐ 85(3)

4. Signature:

   Date: _____
         Day   Month   Year

PART II
ADDITIONAL FORMS

THE PATENT OFFICE

PATENTS ACT 1977   PATENTS FORM NO. 52/77

REQUEST FOR EXTENSION OF TIME OR
PERIOD UNDER RULE 110(3A)

For official use only

Please write or type in BLOCK
LETTERS using dark ink. For
details of current fees please
contact the Patent Office

Enter the full name(s) of the
person(s) making the request

Mark the appropriate box(es) with
an 'x'. This form may not be used
to extend more than one time or
period unless the times or periods
are to be extended to a common
date

Enter the date on which the
extension would expire if allowed

Please sign here   ▶

Attention is drawn to rules 90 and
106 of the Patents Rules 1982

**This form must be accompanied by
a statement setting out fully the
reasons for requesting the
extension**

1. Application Number

2. Name

3. Rule(s) prescribing the time(s) or period(s) to be
   extended

   ☐ 6(2)   ☐ 25(2)   ☐ 33(4)   ☐ 82(2)
   ☐ 6(6)   ☐ 25(3)   ☐ 34   ☐ 82(3)
   ☐ 15(1)   ☐ 26   ☐ 79B   ☐ 83(3)
   ☐ 17(2)   ☐ 33(2)   ☐ 81(2)   ☐ 85(1)
   ☐ 23   ☐ 33(3)   ☐ 81(3)   ☐ 85(3)

4. Extension required

   _____
   Day   Month   Year

5. Signature:

   Date: _____
          Day   Month   Year

Reminder

Have you attached

Statement of reasons for requesting
an extension of time or period   ☐

For official use only

THE PATENT OFFICE

PATENTS ACT 1977   PATENTS FORM NO. 53/77

ADDITIONAL FEE FOR EXTENSION OF TIME
OR PERIOD UNDER RULE 110(3C)

Please write or type in BLOCK
LETTERS using dark ink. For
details of current fees please
contact the Patent Office

Enter the full name(s) of the
applicant(s)

Please sign here ▶

Attention is drawn to rules 90 and
106 of the Patents Rules 1982

1. Application Number

2. Name

3. Signature:

Date: _____
      Day   Month   Year

For official use only

THE PATENT OFFICE

PATENTS ACT 1977   PATENTS FORM NO. 54/77

FILING OF TRANSLATION OF EUROPEAN
PATENT (UK) UNDER SECTION 77(6)(a)

Please write or type in BLOCK
LETTERS using dark ink. For
details of current fees please
contact the Patent Office

Enter the name and address of the
proprietor(s) of the European
Patent (UK). If you do not have
enough space please continue on a
separate sheet

Enter the date on which the
mention of the grant of the
European Patent (UK) was
published in the European Patent
Bulletin, or, if it has not yet been
published, the date on which it will
be published

A UK Address for Service MUST
be provided to which all
communications from the Patent
Office will be sent

Please sign here ▶

Attention is drawn to rules 90 and
106 of the Patents Rules 1982

**This form must be filed in duplicate
and must be accompanied by a
translation into English in
duplicate of:**
1) **the whole description**
2) **those claims appropriate to the
   UK (in the language of the
   proceedings)**
3) **all drawings, whether or not
   these contain any textual matter**
but **excluding the front page which
contains bibliographic
information. The translation must
be verified to the satisfaction of the
comptroller as corresponding to
the original text**

1. European Patent
   Number

2. Name

   Address

3. European Patent Bulletin Date:

   _____
   Day   Month   Year

4. Name of Agent (if any)

   Agent's Patent Office
   ADP number (if known)

5. Address for Service

   Postcode

6. Signature:

   Date: _____
   Day   Month   Year

Reminder

Have you attached

One duplicate copy of this form ☐

Two copies of the Translation ☐

Any continuation sheets (if appropriate) ☐

For official use only

THE PATENT OFFICE

PATENTS ACT 1977   PATENTS FORM NO. 55/77

FILING OF TRANSLATION OF AMENDMENT OF
EUROPEAN PATENT (UK) UNDER SECTION 77(6)(b)

Please write or type in BLOCK LETTERS using dark ink. For details of current fees please contact the Patent Office	1. European Patent Number
Enter the name and address of the proprietor(s) of the European Patent (UK). If you do not have enough space please continue on a separate sheet	2. Name Address
Enter the date on which the amended European Patent (UK) was published by the European Patent Office, or, if it has not yet been published, the date on which it will be published	3. Amended European Patent Publication Date: ——————————— Day Month Year
	4. Name of Agent (if any) Agent's Patent Office ADP number (if known)
A UK Address for Service MUST be provided to which all communications from the Patent Office will be sent	5. Address for Service Postcode
Please sign here ▶	6. Signature: Date: ——————————— Day Month Year
Attention is drawn to rules 90 and 106 of the Patents Rules 1982	
This form must be filed in duplicate and must be accompanied by a translation into English in duplicate of either the amendment or preferably the whole of the amended European Patent (UK). The translation must be verified to the satisfaction of the comptroller as corresponding to the original text	Reminder Have you attached One duplicate copy of this form ☐ Two copies of the Translation ☐ Any continuation sheets (if appropriate) ☐

For official use only

THE PATENT OFFICE

PATENTS ACT 1977   PATENTS FORM NO. 56/77

REQUEST FOR PUBLICATION OF TRANSLATION
OF CLAIMS OF APPLICATION FOR EUROPEAN
PATENT (UK) FILED UNDER SECTION 78(7)

Please write or type in BLOCK
LETTERS using dark ink. For
details of current fees please
contact the Patent Office

Enter the name and address of the
applicant(s) for the European
Patent (UK). If you do not have
enough space please continue on a
separate sheet

1. European Publication
Number

2. Name

    Address

3. Name of Agent (if any)

    Agent's Patent Office
    ADP number (if known)

A UK Address for Service MUST
be provided to which all
communications from the Patent
Office will be sent

4. Address for Service

               Postcode

Please sign here ▶

Attention is drawn to rules 90 and
106 of the Patents Rules 1982

5. Signature:

        Date: _____
              Day Month Year

**This form must be filed in duplicate
and must be accompanied by a
translation into English in
duplicate of the claims of the
Application for a European Patent
(UK). The translation must be
verified to the satisfaction of the
comptroller as corresponding to
the original text**

Reminder

Have you attached

One duplicate copy of this form ☐

Two copies of the Translation ☐

Any continuation sheets (if appropriate) ☐

For official use only

THE PATENT OFFICE

PATENTS ACT 1977   PATENTS FORM NO. 57/77

REQUEST FOR PUBLICATION OF CORRECTED
TRANSLATION OF EUROPEAN PATENT (UK) OR
APPLICATION FOR EUROPEAN PATENT (UK)
FILED UNDER SECTION 80(3)

Please write or type in BLOCK
LETTERS using dark ink. For
details of current fees please
contact the Patent Office

Enter the name and address of the
proprietor(s) of, or the
applicant(s) for, the European
Patent (UK). If you do not have
enough space please continue on a
separate sheet

A UK Address for Service MUST
be provided to which all
communications from the Patent
Office will be sent

Please sign here ▶

Attention is drawn to rules 90 and
106 of the Patents Rules 1982

**This form must be filed in duplicate
and must be accompanied by a
corrected version, in duplicate, of
the whole of the incorrect
translation. The translation must
be verified to the satisfaction of the
comptroller as corresponding to
the original text**

1. European Patent or
   Publication Number

2. Name

   Address

3. Name of Agent (if any)

   Agent's Patent Office
   ADP number (if known)

4. Address for Service

                    Postcode

5. Signature:

            Date: _____
                  Day   Month   Year

Reminder

Have you attached

One duplicate copy of this form

Two copies of the Translation

Any continuation sheets (if appropriate)

SCHEDULE 2   Rule 3

AMENDMENTS TO THE PATENTS (FEES) RULES 1986

In Part A of the Schedule to the Patents (Fees) Rules 1986–

  (a) in the entry relating to Patents Form No. 50/77, after the words "On request for extension of time" there shall be inserted the words "or period under Rule 110(3)".

  (b) after the entry relating to Patents Form No. 51/77 the following entries shall be inserted:

"52/77	On request for extension of time or period under Rule 110(3A)	100
53/77	Additional fee for extension of time or period under Rule 110(3C)	100
54/77	On filing of translation of European Patent (UK) under section 77(6)(a)	25
55/77	On filing of translation of amendment of European Patent (UK) under section 77(6)(b)	25
56/77	On request for publication of translation of claims of application for European Patent (UK) filed under section 78(7)	25
57/77	On request for publication of a corrected translation filed under section 80(3)	25".

EXPLANATORY NOTE

(This note is not part of the Rules)

These Rules bring into force section 77(6) and section 78(7) of the Patents Act 1977 which provide for the filing of translations into English of specifications and amendments of European patents (UK) and claims of applications for European patents (UK) which have been published in French and German under the European Patent Convention by the European Patent Office. They also amend the Patents Rules 1982 so as to prescribe forms and to introduce other requirements for these translations and they amend the Patents (Fees) Rules 1986 to prescribe fees in connection with these translations. Similar provision is made for corrected translations filed under section 80(3) of the 1977 Act where the translation originally filed confers narrower protection than that conferred by the French or German text published by the European Patent Office. A consequential amendment is made to rule 113 of the 1982 Rules.

Other amendments to the 1982 and 1986 Rules are also made, namely–

  (a) rule 20 of the 1982 Rules, which prescribes the size and presentation of documents contained in a patent application, is amended;

  (b) rules 25(4) and 80 of the 1982 Rules, which are no longer of practical effect, are revoked;

  (c) rule 28 of the 1982 Rules, which provides for the determination of the time when the preparations for publication of a patent application under section 16 of the 1977 Act are completed, is revoked;

  (d) rule 99 of the 1982 Rules, which specifies days as excluded days, is revised;

  (e) rule 100 of the 1982 Rules, which provides for the amendment of documents and the correction of irregularities in procedure, is revised;

  (f) rule 110 of the 1982 Rules, which provides for the alteration of time limits, is amended and new forms and fees are prescribed.

STATUTORY INSTRUMENTS

1987 No. 289 (C. 6) (S. 15)

LEGAL AID AND ADVICE, SCOTLAND

The Legal Aid (Scotland) Act 1986 (Commencement No. 2) Order 1987

Made - - - - *25th February 1987*

The Secretary of State, in exercise of the powers conferred on him by section 46 of the Legal Aid (Scotland) Act 1986(**a**), and of all other powers enabling him in that behalf, hereby makes the following Order:

1. This Order may be cited as the Legal Aid (Scotland) Act 1986 (Commencement No. 2) Order 1987.

2. The provisions of the Legal Aid (Scotland) Act 1986 (other than Part V and section 30), insofar as they are not already in force, shall come into force on 1st April 1987.

New St. Andrew's House, Edinburgh
25th February 1987

Ian Lang
Parliamentary Under Secretary of State,
Scottish Office

EXPLANATORY NOTE

(This note is not part of the Order)

This Order brings into force on 1st April 1987 all the provisions of the Legal Aid (Scotland) Act 1986 which are not already in force, except for Part V (which relates to the employment of solicitors by the Scottish Legal Aid Board) and section 30 (which makes special provision for legal aid in contempt proceedings).

(**a**) 1986 c.47.

NOTE AS TO EARLIER COMMENCEMENT ORDERS

(This note is not part of the Order)

The following provisions of the Act have been brought into force by commencement order made before the date of this Order:–

Provision	Date of commencement	S.I. No.
section 1 (partially), section 2 (partially), section 3 (partially), section 40 (partially), section 41, section 45 (partially), Schedule 1, and Schedule 3 (partially)	1.10.1986	1986/1617

STATUTORY INSTRUMENTS

1987 No. 290 (S. 16)

EDUCATION, SCOTLAND

The Schools General (Scotland) Amendment Regulations 1987

Made - - - -	*23rd February 1987*
Laid before Parliament	*9th March 1987*
Coming into force	*1st April 1987*

The Secretary of State, in exercise of the powers conferred on him by section 2 of the Education (Scotland) Act 1980(**a**) and of all other powers enabling him in that behalf, hereby makes the following Regulations:

Citation and commencement

1. These Regulations may be cited as the Schools General (Scotland) Amendment Regulations 1987 and shall come into force on 1st April 1987.

Amendment of the principal regulations

2. For regulation 5 of the Schools General (Scotland) Regulations 1975(**b**) there shall be substituted the following regulation:–

"**Minimum number of school days**

5. An education authority shall, except where prevented by circumstances outwith their control, secure that every school under their management shall be open for at least–

(a) 198 school days (excluding Saturdays and Sundays) in the school year which ends on 31st July 1987; and

(b) 190 school days (excluding Saturdays and Sundays) in each subsequent school year."

John J. MacKay
Parliamentary Under Secretary of State,
Scottish Office

New St. Andrew's House, Edinburgh
23rd February 1987

(**a**) 1980 c.44.
(**b**) S.I. 1975/1135, to which there are amendments not relevant to these Regulations.

EXPLANATORY NOTE

(This note is not part of the Regulations)

These Regulations reduce from 200 to 198 days the minimum number of school days that an education authority school in Scotland must be open during the school year 1986/1987. They further reduce to 190 the minimum number of school days that such a school must be open during 1987/1988 and subsequent school years. A school year runs from 1st August in one year to 31st July in the next.

STATUTORY INSTRUMENTS

1987 No. 291 (S. 17)

EDUCATION, SCOTLAND

The Education (Grants for Further Training of Teachers and Educational Psychologists) (Scotland) Regulations 1987

Made - - - -	*25th February 1987*
Laid before Parliament	*9th March 1987*
Coming into force - -	*30th March 1987*

The Secretary of State, in exercise of the powers conferred on him by sections 73(a),(c), and (d), 74(1) and 75 of the Education (Scotland) Act 1980(**a**), and of all other powers enabling him in that behalf, hereby makes the following Regulations:

Citation, commencement and interpretation

1.—(1) These Regulations may be cited as the Education (Grants for Further Training of Teachers and Educational Psychologists) (Scotland) Regulations 1987 and shall come into force on 30th March 1987.

(2) In these Regulations–

"assessors" means persons whose duties are–

  (i) the provision of advice to the Secretary of State as to the suitability of projects prepared or engaged in by educational psychologists undergoing further training; and

  (ii) assistance in the conduct of further training of educational psychologists;

"grant-aided special school" means a school in respect of which annual maintenance grants are paid in terms of regulation 2 of the Residential Special Schools and Orphanages (Scotland) Grant Regulations 1948(**b**).

Grants by the Secretary of State

2. The Secretary of State may, subject to the provisions of these Regulations, pay to–

  (a) education authorities and managers of grant-aided special schools grants of such amounts as he thinks necessary or expedient in respect of teachers and educational psychologists in their employment undergoing further training; and

  (b) assessors grants of such amounts as he thinks necessary or expedient in respect of remuneration for, and expenses incurred in connection with, their duties.

Training in respect of which grants may be paid

3. A grant may be paid in respect of–

  (a) teachers in respect only of training consisting of attendance at a one year full-time course leading to the Diploma in Special Educational Needs (Recorded Pupils); and

---

(**a**) 1980 c.44.
(**b**) S. R. & O. 1948/2768; the relevant amending instrument is S.I. 1976/1431.

(b) educational psychologists in respect only of training consisting of the preparation of, or engagement in, a project approved as suitable by the Secretary of State, on the advice of an assessor.

Application for, payment of, and conditions of, grants

4.—(1) Applications for grants described in regulation 2(a) above shall be made in writing to the Secretary of State by education authorities or managers of grant-aided special schools, and the Secretary of State shall in any year advise education authorities and managers of grant-aided special schools by circular of the procedure for making application and the last day by which applications must be received by him.

(2) Payment of grants described in regulation 2(a) above shall be made to education authorities or managers of grant-aided special schools by two instalments paid half-yearly in arrears.

(3) If any teacher or educational psychologist in respect of whom a grant described in regulation 2(a) above has been approved fails to complete the course the Secretary of State may revoke and recover from the education authority or managers of a grant-aided special school the whole or such part as he considers appropriate of such grant.

(4) Applications for grants described in regulation 2(b) above shall be made in writing to the Secretary of State by assessors within 6 months of the completion of the duties to which the applications relate and shall consist of a statement of the duties performed, the remuneration claimed in respect of those duties and the expenses of travel and subsistence incurred in connection with those duties, and shall be accompanied by such evidence as to the duties performed and expenses incurred as the Secretary of State may require.

(5) Payment of grants described in regulation 2(b) above may be made to assessors at such time and in such manner as the Secretary of State may determine.

(6) If an assessor has not performed any duty, or has not incurred or has incorrectly stated the amount of any expense, in respect of which a grant described in regulation 2(b) above has been approved the Secretary of State may revoke and recover from the assessor the whole or such part as he considers appropriate of such grant.

(7) Assessors shall not be required to keep accounts of income and expenditure and the condition specified in section 75 (examination of accounts) of the Education (Scotland) Act 1980 shall not apply to them.

Revocation

5. The Education (Grants for Further Training of Teachers) (Scotland) Regulations 1984**(a)** are hereby revoked.

New St. Andrew's House, Edinburgh
25th February 1987

John J. MacKay
Parliamentary Under Secretary of State,
Scottish Office

(a) S.I. 1984/432.

EXPLANATORY NOTE

(This note is not part of the Regulations)

Under section 73 of the Education (Scotland) Act 1980 the Secretary of State may in accordance with Regulations made by him make payment of such sums as he thinks necessary and expedient for various purposes. Section 74(1) of the Act enables the Secretary of State to prescribe in Regulations conditions with which the recipients of grant are required to comply.

These Regulations provide for payment to education authorities and managers of grant-aided special schools of grants in respect of teachers and educational psychologists employed by them undergoing further training, and regulate the procedure for applying for such grants. Provision is made for revocation of grant and recovery of any payment already made should a teacher or educational psychologist fail to complete a course.

The Regulations also provide for payment of grants in respect of remuneration and expenses to persons who act as assessors in the further training of educational psychologists and regulate the procedure for applying for such grants. Provision is made for revocation of grant and recovery of any payment already made where grant was improperly claimed. Assessors are not required to keep accounts of income and expenditure.

Previous Regulations, which provided for grants only in respect of further training of teachers and are superseded by these Regulations, are revoked.

1987 No. 292

SEA FISHERIES

COMMUNITY RESTRICTIONS

The Third Country Fishing (Enforcement) Order 1987

Made - - - -	*27th February 1987*
Laid before Parliament	*9th March 1987*
Coming into force	*30th March 1987*

The Minister of Agriculture, Fisheries and Food and the Secretaries of State respectively concerned with sea fishing in Scotland, Wales and Northern Ireland, in exercise of the powers conferred on them by section 30(2) of the Fisheries Act 1981 (**a**) and of all other powers enabling them in that behalf, hereby make the following Order:

Title, commencement and interpretation

1.—(1) This Order may be cited as the Third Country Fishing (Enforcement) Order 1987 and shall come into force on 30th March 1987.

(2) In this Order, "relevant Community provision" means any provision of a Regulation of the European Communities referred to in column 1 of Schedule 1 to this Order which is specified in column 2 of that Schedule opposite the reference to that Regulation, as read with any qualifying words relating to that provision in that column of that Schedule.

Offences and penalties

2.   If there is, in respect of any fishing boat to which a relevant Community provision applies, a contravention of, or failure to comply with, that provision within British fishery limits, the master of that boat shall be guilty of an offence and liable–

(a) on summary conviction to a fine not exceeding the amount specified in column 4 of Schedule 1 to this Order opposite the reference to that provision in column 2; or

(b) on conviction on indictment to a fine.

Recovery of fines

3.—(1) Where a fine is imposed by a magistrates' court in England and Wales or Northern Ireland on the master or a member of the crew of a fishing boat who is convicted by the court of an offence under article 2 or 5 of this Order, the court may–

(a) issue a warrant of distress against the boat and its gear and catch and any property of the person convicted for the purpose of levying the amount of the fine; and

(b) order the boat to be detained for a period not exceeding three months from the date of the conviction or until the fine is paid or the amount of the fine is levied in pursuance of any such warrant, whichever occurs first.

(**a**) 1981 c.29.

(2) Where a fine is imposed by a sheriff in Scotland on the master or a member of the crew of a fishing boat who is convicted by the sheriff of an offence under article 2 or 5 of this Order, the sheriff may–

(a) issue a warrant for the poinding and sale of the boat and its gear and catch and any property of the person convicted; and

(b) order the boat to be detained for a period not exceeding three months from the date of the conviction or until the fine is paid, whichever occurs first.

(3) Sections 77(1) and 78 of the Magistrates' Courts Act 1980(a) (postponement of issue of, and defects in, warrants of distress) shall apply to a warrant of distress issued under this article in England and Wales as they apply to a warrant of distress issued under Part III of that Act.

(4) Article 114(2) of the Magistrates' Courts (Northern Ireland) Order 1981(b) (postponement of issue of certain warrants) shall apply to a warrant of distress issued under this article in Northern Ireland as it applies to a warrant referred to in that article.

Powers of British sea-fishery officers in relation to fishing boats

4.—(1) For the purpose of enforcing article 2 of this Order, a British sea-fishery officer–

(a) may go on board any fishing boat to which a relevant Community provision applies and which is within British fishery limits;

(b) may take with him, to assist him in performing his functions, any other person and any equipment or materials;

(c) may require any such boat to stop and do anything else to enable him to board it;

(d) may require the attendance of the master of the boat or any other person on board;

(e) may require any person on board to assist him in the performance of his functions; and

(f) may make any examination or inquiry which appears to him to be necessary and, without prejudice to the generality of the foregoing, he may in particular–

  (i) examine any fish on the boat and the equipment of the boat, including the fishing gear;

  (ii) require the production of any document relating to the boat or to its fishing operations or other operations ancillary to its fishing operations;

  (iii) search the boat for any such document; and require any person on board the boat to do anything which appears to the officer to be necessary for facilitating the search; and

  (iv) take copies of any such document.

(2) If a British sea-fishery officer has reasonable grounds to suspect that an offence under article 2 of this Order has been committed within British fishery limits in respect of a boat that he has power to go on board under paragraph (1)(a) of this article, he may seize and detain any document produced to him or found on board the boat, and the officer–

(a) may require the master to take, or may himself take, the boat and its crew to the port which appears to the officer to be the nearest convenient port; and

(b) may detain the boat in the port.

(3) Nothing in paragraph (2) of this article shall permit any document required by law to be carried on board any boat to be seized or detained except while the boat is detained in a port.

(4) If a British sea-fishery officer detains a boat, he shall serve on the master a notice stating that it is to be detained until the notice is withdrawn by the service on him of a further notice in writing signed by a British sea-fishery officer.

(a) 1980 c.43.
(b) S.I. 1981/1675 (NI 26).

Obstruction of officers

5.   Any person who, on any fishing boat which is within British fishery limits and to which a relevant Community provision applies–

(a) fails without reasonable excuse to comply with any requirement imposed by a British sea-fishery officer under the powers conferred on British sea-fishery officers by article 4 of this Order;

(b) without reasonable excuse prevents any other person from complying with any such requirement; or

(c) assaults an officer who is exercising any of the powers conferred on him by article 4 of this Order or intentionally obstructs any such officer in the exercise of any of those powers

shall be guilty of an offence and liable–

(i)   on summary conviction to a fine not exceeding £5,000; or

(ii) on conviction on indictment to a fine.

Protection of officers

6.   An officer shall not be liable in any civil or criminal proceedings for anything done in the purported exercise of the powers conferred on him by article 4 of this Order if the court is satisfied that the act was done in good faith, that there were reasonable grounds for doing it and that it was done with reasonable skill and care.

Proceedings

7.   Proceedings for an offence under this Order may be taken, and the offence may for all incidental purposes be treated as having been committed, in any place in the United Kingdom.

Revocation

8.   The Orders specified in Schedule 2 to this Order are hereby revoked.

In witness whereof the Official Seal of the Minister of Agriculture, Fisheries and Food is hereunto affixed on 25th February 1987.

Michael Jopling
Minister of Agriculture, Fisheries and Food

25th February 1987

John J. Mackay
Parliamentary Under-Secretary of State, Scottish Office

24th February 1987

Nicholas Edwards
Secretary of State for Wales

27th February 1987

Tom King
Secretary of State for Northern Ireland

Articles 1(2) and 2   # SCHEDULE 1

PENALTIES

(1) *Regulation of the European Communities*	(2) *Provision*	(3) *Subject Matter*	(4) *Maximum fine on summary conviction*
1. Council Regulation (EEC) No. 4029/86 laying down for 1987 certain measures for the conservation and management of fishery resources applicable to vessels flying the flag of Norway (O.J. . No. L376, 31.12.86, p.25).	Article 2(2)	Keeping of log book	£2,000
	Article 2(3)	Transmission of information	£2,000
	Article 2(4)	Marking on vessels of registration letters and numbers	£2,000
	Article 3(1)	Holding on board of licence and observance of conditions thereof	£5,000
	Article 5	Restriction on methods of fishing for blue ling, ling and tusk	£5,000
2. Council Regulation (EEC) No. 4037/86 laying down for 1987 certain measures for the conservation and management of fishery resources applicable to vessels flying the flag of Sweden (O.J. No. L376, 31.12.86, p.85).	Article 2(2)	Keeping of logbook	£2,000
	Article 2(3)	Transmission of information	£2,000
	Article 2(4)	Marking on vessels of registration letters and numbers	£2,000
	Article 3(1)	Holding on board of licence and observance of conditions thereof	£5,000
3. Council Regulation (EEC) No. 4039/86 laying down for 1987 certain measures for the conservation and management of fishery resources applicable to vessels registered in the Faroe Islands (O.J. No. L376, 31.12.86, p.94).	Article 2(2)	Keeping of logbook	£2,000
	Article 2(3)	Transmission of information	£2,000
	Article 2(4)	Marking on vessels of registration letters and numbers	£2,000
	Article 3(1)	Holding on board of licence and observance of conditions thereof	£5,000

Article 8   # SCHEDULE 2

REVOCATIONS

Order revoked	*References*
The Third Country Fishing (Enforcement) Order 1982	S.I. 1982/1161
The Third Country Fishing (Enforcement) Order 1983	S.I. 1983/258
The Third Country Fishing (Enforcement) (No. 2) Order 1983	S.I. 1983/720
The Third Country Fishing (Enforcement) Order 1984	S.I. 1984/516
The Third Country Fishing (Enforcement) Order 1985	S.I. 1985/313
The Third Country Fishing (Enforcement) Order 1986	S.I. 1986/779

EXPLANATORY NOTE

(This note is not part of the Order)

This Order, which replaces the Third Country Fishing (Enforcement) Order 1986, ("the 1986 Order"), makes breaches of specified articles of the Community Regulations set out in column 1 of Schedule 1 to the Order offences for the purposes of United Kingdom law where they occur within British fishery limits.

The Community Regulations authorise fishing in certain specified areas within Member States' fishery limits for specified descriptions of fish by vessels of third countries, namely, Sweden, the Faroe Islands and Norway. The offences arise out of breaches of the provisions of the Community Regulations concerning methods of fishing, the holding on board of licences and observance of the conditions thereof, the keeping of log books, the making of radio reports and similar matters; all are triable summarily or on indictment. On summary conviction, the master of an offending vessel will be liable to a fine not exceeding the sum specified in relation to the offence in column 4 of Schedule 1 to the Order and, on conviction on indictment, to a fine (article 2).

The Order confers powers of enforcement on British sea-fishery officers (article 4). Provision is made for the punishment of anyone found guilty of obstructing or assaulting an officer (article 5).

The Order revokes the 1986 order and the earlier orders listed in Schedule 2, which have ceased to have effect (article 8).

1987 No. 293

PENSIONS

The Local Government Superannuation (Miscellaneous Provisions) Regulations 1987

Made - - - -	*26th February 1987*
Laid before Parliament	*11th March 1987*
Coming into force	*1st April 1987*

The Secretary of State for the Environment, in exercise of the powers conferred upon him by sections 7 and 12 of the Superannuation Act 1972(a), and of all other powers enabling him in that behalf, after consultation with such associations of local authorities as appeared to him to be concerned, the local authorities with whom consultation appeared to him to be desirable and such representatives of other persons likely to be affected by the Regulations as appeared to him to be appropriate, hereby makes the following Regulations:—

Citation, commencement and interpretation

1.—(1) These Regulations may be cited as the Local Government Superannuation (Miscellaneous Provisions) Regulations 1987, and shall come into force on 1st April 1987, but regulations 10, 14 and 21 shall have effect as from 1st March 1986.

(2) In these Regulations "the principal Regulations" means the Local Government Superannuation Regulations 1986(b), and unless the context otherwise requires expressions which are also used in the principal Regulations have the same meaning as they have in those Regulations.

Employees of public airport companies

2.—(1) Where a passenger transport authority or a principal council have formed a company in pursuance of section 13 of the Airports Act 1986(c)—

(a) that authority, or

(b) any principal council of which the company is for the purposes of Part II of that Act an associated company,

may, subject to paragraph (3), with the agreement of the company, by a statutory resolution resolve that every qualified employee of the company shall for the purposes of the principal Regulations be deemed to be in employment with the body passing the resolution.

(2) A qualified employee is one who—

(a) during a period ending no earlier than 12 months before the start of his employment with the company was in an employment with the body passing the resolution in which he was a pensionable employee, or

(b) immediately before the start of his employment with the company was in an employment with that body in which, if he had continued in it, he might have become a pensionable employee.

(a) 1972 c.11.
(b) S.I. 1986/24; relevant amendments were made by S.I. 1986/380.
(c) 1986 c.31.

(3) No resolution may be passed under this regulation after a scheme has come into force under section 15 of the Airports Act 1986.

(4) in this regulation "principal council" means the council of a non-metropolitan county, of a district, or of a London borough.

Resolutions ceasing to have effect

3. Where—

(a) a resolution has been passed under regulation 4 of the Local Government Superannuation (Miscellaneous Provisions) Regulations 1986**(a)** (employees of public transport companies) or regulation 2 of these Regulations, and

(b) the company to which it relates makes an admission agreement,

the resolution ceases to have effect in relation to any employee who becomes an admitted employee by virtue of the agreement.

Pensionable employees

4. Regulation B1 of the principal Regulations is amended—

(a) in paragraph (1), by substituting for the words "paragraphs (16) and (17)" the words "paragraphs (15A) to (17)";

(b) in paragraph (3)(a), by deleting the words "whole-time" and by inserting after the words "that body" the words "in which the contractual hours were 15 or more";

(c) in paragraph (4), by inserting after the words "whole-time", in both places in which they occur, the words "or part-time";

(d) by inserting after paragraph (13) the following:

"(13A) A justices' clerk (outside the inner London area) is a pensionable employee.

(13B) A registration officer is a pensionable employee.";

(e) by inserting after paragraph (15) the following:

"(15A) Part IV of Schedule 2 has effect for determining whether—

(a) in a part-time employment in which he is not already a pensionable employee by virtue of paragraphs (2) to (15), or

(b) in any whole-time employment in which the contractual weeks are fewer than 45,

an employee of a scheduled body is for the time being a pensionable employee.

(15B) A person who is in a part-time employment in which he is, by virtue of paragraphs (2) to (15), a pensionable employee may at any time, by notice in writing given to the employing authority, elect to cease to be a pensionable employee in that employment from the day after the date to which the next payment of wages or salary will be calculated.";

(f) in paragraph (16), by substituting for the words "paragraph (2), (3) or (4)" the words "paragraph (2), (3), (4) or (15A)(a)";

(g) in paragraph (17)—

(i) by substituting for the words "paragraphs (2) to (15)" the words "paragraphs (2) to (15A)", and

(ii) in sub-paragraph (b), by substituting for the words "a person" the words "subject to paragraph (18), a person"; and

(h) by inserting after paragraph (17) the following:

"(18) A person—

(a) who falls within paragraph (17)(b), or

(b) who gave a notification under regulation G10(2) of the 1974 Regulations (certain transferred water employees electing not to be pensionable employees),

but who would otherwise be a pensionable employee by virtue of paragraph (3) may at any time, by notice in writing given to the body by whom he is

---

(a) S.I. 1986/380.

employed, elect to become a pensionable employee from the day after the date to which the next payment of wages or salary will be calculated.".

Persons treated as employees of a scheduled body

5. Regulation B2 of the principal Regulations is amended—
   (a) in paragraph (1), by inserting at the end of the entry in column (1) of the Table relating to members of, and directors of subsidiaries of, passenger transport executives the words "or who are pensionable employees by virtue of, or of an election under, Part IV of Schedule 2";
   (b) in paragraph (2)—
      (i) by inserting after sub-paragraph (b) the following:
         "or
         (c) Part IV of Schedule 2, or an election under that Part,", and
      (ii) by substituting for the words "who passed the resolution" the words "who passed the relevant resolution";
   (c) in paragraph (4B)—
      (i) by substituting for the words "had effect" the words "had continued to have effect", and
      (ii) by inserting after the words "he shall" the words ", unless he then becomes an admitted employee,";
   (d) in paragraph (4C), by substituting for the words "had effect shall" the words "had continued to have effect shall, unless he then becomes an admitted employee,";
   (e) in paragraph (4F), by deleting the words " "public transport company" "; and
   (f) by inserting after paragraph (4F) the following:
      "(4G) Every employee of a public airport company ("the first airport company") in relation to whom a resolution under regulation 2 of the Local Government Superannuation (Miscellaneous Provisions) Regulations 1987 has effect shall for the purposes of these Regulations be deemed to be in employment with the body who passed the resolution.
      (4H) If a person in relation to whom such a resolution had continued to have effect becomes an employee of another public airport company ("the second airport company") whose controlling authority—
         (a) is not the body who passed the resolution or a composite authority of which that body was a constituent council, but
         (b) is an authority which has, or a composite authority one at least of whose constituent councils has, also passed such a resolution,
      for the purposes of these Regulations he shall, unless he then becomes an admitted employee, be deemed to be in employment with the controlling authority of the second airport company or, where that authority is a composite authority, with such one of its constituent councils as the authority may decide.
      (4I) If a person to whom paragraph (4G) or (4H) applies becomes an employee of a subsidiary of, as the case may be, the first airport company or the second airport company, the relevant paragraph continues to apply to him as if he had remained an employee of the company in question.
      (4J) Paragraph (4G) and paragraph (4H) cease to apply to a person if the first airport company or, as the case may be, the second airport company ceases to be a public airport company.
      (4K) In paragraph (4G) to (4J) "controlling authority", "composite authority" and "constituent council" have the meanings given in section 16 of the Airports Act 1986 and "subsidiary" has the meaning given in section 82(1) of that Act.".

Power to admit employees of other bodies

6. Regulation B3 of the principal Regulations is amended—
   (a) by inserting after paragraph (1) the following:

"(1A) Where an administering authority have under regulation P1(2) established a further fund, in relation to a body identified in the notification required by regulation P1(3)—

(a) the superannuation fund referred to in paragraph (1) is the further fund, and

(b) any admission agreement made before its establishment is to be construed as providing for participation in the benefits of the further fund."; and

(b) in paragraph (4), by inserting after the words "an admitted employee" the words ", or for any part-time employee to become an admitted employee otherwise than as provided in Part IV of Schedule 2, which shall, in relation to a part-time employee to whom the agreement applies, be taken to apply as if the employing body were a scheduled body described in column (1) of Part I of Schedule 2".

Appropriate superannuation fund

7. Regulation C1 of the principal Regulations is amended by inserting after paragraph (10) the following:

"(11) Where an administering authority have under regulation P1(2) established a further fund—

(a) references in the preceding paragraphs of this regulation to "the fund" are to be construed as references to the fund maintained by that authority under regulation P1(1), and

(b) in relation to a person to whom these Regulations apply by virtue of an admission agreement with a body identified in the notification required by regulation P1(3), the appropriate superannuation fund is the further fund."

Payment and amount of employee's contributions

8. Regulation C2 of the principal Regulations is amended by inserting after paragraph (5) the following:

"(6) For the purposes of this regulation the remuneration of a part-time employee for any period, except a period during which he was on leave of absence from duty by reason of illness or injury with reduced remuneration or without remuneration, is to be taken to be the remuneration he would have received if during that period he had worked no more and no less than the contractual hours.".

Additional payments by certain pensionable employees in respect of previous service

9. The principal Regulations are amended by substituting for regulation C7 the following:

"Additional payments by certain pensionable employees in respect of previous service

C7.—(1) A whole-time manual worker who becomes a pensionable employee by virtue of regulation B1(3)(c) may make a payment into the appropriate superannuation fund in order to become entitled under regulation D9 to reckon as reckonable service in relation to the employment in which he is a pensionable employee the period during which he was in that employment before becoming a pensionable employee.

(2) If he was not immediately before 1st April 1987 a pensionable employee, a justices' clerk (outside the inner London area) or a registration officer may by notice in writing given to his employing authority within 12 months after that date elect to make a payment into the appropriate superannuation fund in order to become entitled under regulation D9 to reckon a period as reckonable service in relation to his local government employment.

(3) The period mentioned in paragraph (2) is to be specified in the notice, and may be any period beginning after 31st March 1974 and ending with

31st March 1987 during which the person was a justices' clerk (outside the inner London area) or, as the case may be, a registration officer.

(4) The amount of a payment under paragraph (1) or (2) is an amount equal to the contributions which the person would have been required to make under regulation C2 if he had throughout the period been a pensionable employee.

(5) A payment under paragraph (1) is to be made, unless the employing authority allow a longer period, within 6 months after the date on which the person became a pensionable employee.

(6) A payment under paragraph (2) is to be made, unless the employing authority allow a longer period, within 12 months after the date on which the person is notified by the employing authority of its amount.

(7) A payment under paragraph (1) or (2) is to be treated for the purposes of these Regulations as if it consisted of contributions made under regulation C2 in respect of employment in which the person was a pensionable employee.".

Return of employee's contributions in certain cases

10. Regulation C12(1) of the principal Regulations is amended by substituting for the words "pensionable employee", where first occurring, the word "person".

Qualifying service

11. Regulation D2(2)(a) of the principal Regulations is amended by substituting for the words "regulation D10, D11 or J9(1)(b)" the words "regulation D10, D11, D12 or J9(1)(b)".

Previous service of certain pensionable employees

12 The principal Regulations are amended by substituting for regulation D9 the following:

"Previous service of certain pensionable employees

D9.—(1) A pensionable employee who has made a payment under regulation C7(1) is entitled to reckon as reckonable service in relation to the employment in which he became a pensionable employee the period during which he was in that employment before becoming a pensionable employee.

(2) A pensionable employee who has made a payment under regulation C7(2) is entitled to reckon as reckonable service in relation to his local government employment the period in respect of which the payment was made.".

Previous service of part-time employees

13. The principal Regulations are amended by inserting after regulation D11 the following:

"Previous service of part-time employees

D12.—(1) A person who—

(a) has become a pensionable employee by virtue of an election under paragraph 1(1) of Part IV of Schedule 2 made before 1st April 1988 or by virtue of paragraph 4 of that Part, or

(b) has become a pensionable employee in a whole-time employment at any time after 31st March 1974 and before 1st April 1988 and had previously been in a part-time employment under a scheduled body,

is entitled to reckon as qualifying service in relation to the employment in which he is a pensionable employee any previous period of employment under a scheduled body after the material date, except a period which was followed by one of 12 months or more during which he was not employed by a scheduled body.

(2) The material date is the earliest date from which, if Part IV of Schedule 2 had come into force on 1st April 1974, an election or, as the case may be, a deemed election by him could have had effect.".

Death grant

14. Regulation E11 of the principal Regulations is amended—

(a) in paragraph (2)(a), by substituting for the words "the deceased's reckonable service" the words "the reckonable service taken into account in calculating the pension"; and

(b) in paragraph (2)(b), by substituting for the words "his reckonable service" the words "the reckonable service taken into account in calculating the pension".

Calculation of service in certain employments

15. Regulation E25 of the principal Regulations is amended by inserting after paragraph (2) the following:

"(3) Paragraph (4) applies to any period which became reckonable as reckonable service by virtue of a payment made by a registration officer under regulation C7(2) (previous service reckonable on additional payment).

(4) For the purposes of calculating any benefit service in each income tax year during any period to which this paragraph applies is to be multiplied by $\frac{A}{B}$, where—

A is the remuneration the employee would have received during the income tax year on the assumption that there had been no discontinuance or reduction of remuneration during any absence from duty owing to illness or injury, and

B is the remuneration that would, on that assumption, have been paid during the income tax year in respect of a single comparable employment under a scheduled body in which the contractual weeks were 52.

(5) In paragraph (4) "income tax year" means a period of 12 months ending with 5th April.

(6) For the purposes of calculating the amount of any benefit, service during any period which became reckonable as reckonable service by virtue of paragraph 5(2)(a) or an election under paragraph 5(2)(b) of Part IV of Schedule 2 (whole-time employment in which contractual weeks are fewer than 45) shall be multiplied by $\frac{52}{C}$, where C is the number of contractual weeks.".

Gratuities

16. The principal Regulations are amended by substituting for Part K the following:

"PART K
GRATUITIES

Interpretation

K1.—(1) In this Part, unless the context otherwise requires—

"annual rate of remuneration" means the annual rate of the employee's remuneration in respect of the relevant employment (ascertained as if paragraphs 4 and 5 of Part V of Schedule 16 had applied) at whichever of the following times yields the highest figure:

(a) the date on which he ceased to be employed,

(b) 12 months before that date, or

(c) 24 months before that date;

"lower earnings limit" and "upper earnings limit" mean the annual equivalents of, respectively, the lower earnings limit and the upper earnings limit in force under section 4(1) of the Social Security Act 1975(a) at the time at which the annual rate of remuneration falls to be ascertained; and

"service" is to be construed in accordance with paragraphs (2) to (4).

(2) Subject to paragraphs (3) and (4), a person's service is the time spent by him in employment with any scheduled body or former local authority.

(a) 1975 c.14; section 4(1) was amended by the Social Security Pensions Act 1975 (c.60), Schedule 4, Part I, paragraph 36(a).

(3) A person's service does not in any case include any period—

(a) before attaining the age of 18 or after attaining the age of 70, or

(b) in excess of a total of 40 years, or

(c) in respect of which a gratuity has been granted under a local Act, section 18 of the Act of 1953, the former Regulations, or these Regulations.

(4) Where regulation K2(a) or (b) applies, a person's service does not include any period—

(a) in respect of which he has retained rights in a scheme which was a relevant scheme for the purposes of regulation G14 of the 1974 Regulations, or

(b) which has been or may be taken into account for the purpose of calculating any benefit under any public service scheme,

but where regulation K2(c) (death while in employment) applies it includes periods of those kinds before 1st April 1987.

Persons to whom Part K applies

K2. This Part applies to a person employed, otherwise than as a teacher, by a scheduled body if he—

(a) has been employed by the body for not less than 5 years and ceases to be employed by them, or

(b) has been employed by them for not less than one year and—

  (i) has attained the age of 60, or

  (ii) is incapable of discharging efficiently the duties of his employment by reason of permanent ill-health or infirmity of mind or body,

  and ceases to be employed by them, or

(c) has been employed by them for not less than one year and dies while in their employment.

Power to grant gratuities

K3.—(1) The body who employed a person to whom this Part applies may grant to him or, where regulation K2(c) (death while in employment) applies, to his widow or any other dependant of his, a gratuity which may consist of a lump sum or an annuity or both.

(2) Where—

(a) the gratuity granted under paragraph (1) is or includes an annuity granted to the person himself, and

(b) he dies before receiving payments of the annuity of an aggregate amount equal to its capital value,

the body may grant a further gratuity by way of an annuity to his widow or any other dependant of his.

Amount of gratuity

K4.—(1) The amount of a gratuity, which is to be taken as including the capital value of an annuity, granted under regulation K3(1) is not to exceed

$$\left(\frac{5 \times A}{100} \times B\right) + \left(\frac{5 \times C}{100} \times D\right) + \left(\frac{5 \times E}{100} \times D\right), \text{ where—}$$

A is the annual rate of remuneration,

B is the total of the length in years and days of the person's service before 1st April 1987 and 50% of any war service in respect of which a period might have become reckonable as reckonable service under regulation F6 if the conditions in regulation F3(2) to (10) had been satisfied,

C is the lesser of the annual rate of remuneration and the lower earnings limit,

D is the length in years and days of the person's service after 31st March 1987 except, in the case of a person who had not before 1st April 1987 attained the age of 55, any service which would have become reckonable as reckonable service if he had on 1st April 1987 made any election which he was entitled to make under regulation B1(18) or paragraph

1(1) or 5(2) of Part IV of Schedule 2 and, if he has made an election under regulation B1(15B), any service which would have become so reckonable if he had not made the election, and

E is any amount by which the annual rate of remuneration exceeds the upper earnings limit.

(2) The capital value of an annuity granted under regulation K3(2) is not to exceed the difference between the capital value of the annuity granted under regulation K3(1) and the aggregate amount received by the person to whom that annuity was granted.

Finance

K5. The cost of a gratuity granted under this Part is not to be met out of any superannuation fund.

Application to certain bodies and employees

K6.—(1) This Part applies in relation to the committee of magistrates for the inner London area as if that committee were a scheduled body, and paragraphs (2) to (5) have effect for modifying its application in relation to that committee and to probation committees and magistrates' courts committees.

(2) The probation committee for an area other than the inner London area are to report any decision made by them under regulation K3 to the body responsible for defraying the expenses of the committee, or, where two or more bodies contribute to the defraying of those expenses, to each of those bodies.

(3) A magistrates' courts committee are to report any decision made by them under regulation K3 to the body who paid the employee's remuneration.

(4) Where a report is made under paragraph (2) or (3) above, regulation N8 has effect as if any body receiving the report were a person mentioned in paragraph (3) of regulation N8 (service of notice of appeal) and paragraph (2) of regulation N8 were omitted.

(5) Any decision made under regulation K3 by—

(a) the probation committee for the inner London area, or

(b) the committee of magistrates for that area,

is to be reported by the committee to the Secretary of State, and has no effect until approved by him; and any gratuity granted by virtue of such an approved decision is to be paid by the Receiver for the Metropolitan Police District.

(6) Where—

(a) a person is employed, otherwise than as a teacher, by the governors of a voluntary school maintained but not provided by a local education authority for such education as may be provided by a local education authority under Part II of the Education Act 1944**(a)**, and

(b) the local education authority have by a statutory resolution specified him as an employee, or specified a class of employees to which he belongs as a class of employees, to whom this Part is to apply,

this Part applies to him as if he were employed by the local education authority."

Superannuation funds

17. Regulation P1 of the principal Regulations is amended—

(a) by inserting before the words "The superannuation funds" the figure "(1)"; and

(b) by adding at the end the following:

"(2) An administering authority (other than the Severn-Trent Water Authority) who are a party to any admission agreement may establish a further superannuation fund (a "further fund"), to be maintained by them in addition to the fund they maintain under paragraph (1) ("the main fund").

(a) 1944 c.31.

(3) An authority who establish a further fund shall notify the Secretary of State forthwith, in writing, that they have done so, identifying the bodies (which must be bodies specified in regulation B3(8)) whose employees are to participate in the benefits of the further fund.

(4) On the establishment of a further fund the authority shall cease to hold as part of the main fund assets of a value to be specified by an actuary, which shall then become part of the further fund.

(5) When the authority first obtain under regulation P5 valuations of both the main fund and the further fund, they shall also obtain from the actuary a statement specifying the value to which further assets should in his opinion cease to be held by them as part of the main fund and become part of the further fund.

(6) On a day to be selected by them, which shall be as soon as is reasonably practicable after they obtain the statement mentioned in paragraph (5), the authority shall cease to hold as part of the main fund assets to the value specified, which shall then become part of the further fund.

(7) As soon as is reasonably practicable after the establishment of the further fund the authority shall obtain from the actuary consulted by them for the purposes of paragraph (5) a certificate specifying in respect of the further fund, for each remaining year of the period of 5 years to which the most recent certificate obtained by them under regulation P6 relates, the matters referred to in regulation P6(1) (common rate of employer's contribution and any individual adjustments).

(8) For each of the remaining years mentioned in paragraph (7), regulation P7 (employer's contributions) shall in relation to any body identified in the notification required by paragraph (3) have effect as if for references to a certificate under regulation P6 there were substituted references to the certificate required by paragraph (7).

(9) On the establishment of the further fund all rights to payment out of the main fund in respect of service in employment under a body identified in the notification required by paragraph (3) shall become rights to payment out of the second fund.".

Pensions increase

18. The principal Regulations are amended by inserting after regulation P13 the following:

"**Pensions increase**

P14.—(1) Where—

(a) an administering authority have—

  (i) at any time made an admission agreement with a public transport company or a public airport company, or

  (ii) after 31st March 1987 made such an agreement with any other body, and

(b) a pension (within the meaning of the Pensions (Increase) Act 1971(**a**)) has become payable under these Regulations to or in respect of a person who has at any time been an admitted employee by virtue of the agreement,

the prescribed part of any increase of the pension under that Act shall be paid out of the appropriate fund.

(2) The prescribed part of an increase is $A \times \dfrac{B}{C}$, where—

A is the amount of the increase,

B is the length of the reckonable service attributable to the period during which the person was an admitted employee by virtue of the agreement, and

C is the length of the reckonable service taken into account in calculating the pension.

(**a**) 1971 c.56.

(3) The reckonable service attributable to the period during which a person was an admitted employee does not include—

(a) service resulting from—

(i) any transfer value received, or

(ii) any election under these Regulations made,

before the period began, or

(b) service resulting from any election made during the period which falls to be treated for any purposes of these Regulations as service before the period began.

(4) The appropriate fund is the fund which was the appropriate superannuation fund immediately before the person ceased to be an admitted employee by virtue of the agreement.

(5) As soon as is reasonably practicable after making an admission agreement to which this regulation applies an administering authority shall obtain from an actuary a certificate specifying, for each remaining year of the period to which the most recent certificate obtained by them under relation P6 relates, any individual adjustment (within the meaning of that regulation) to be made in respect of the body with whom the agreement was made.

(6) For the purposes of regulation P7 (employer's contributions) an individual adjustment specified under paragraph (5) has effect as if it had been specified under regulation P6.".

Definitions in principal Regulations

19. Schedule 1 to the principal Regulations is amended—

(a) by inserting after the entry relating to the expression "Admission agreement" the following:

" "Admitted employee"	The meaning given in regulation B3(2).";

(b) by inserting after the entry relating to the expression "Contracted-out employment" the following:

" "The contractual hours"	The number of hours the employing authority are entitled to require the employee to work in each of the contractual weeks; but where there is any cyclical variation in those hours the contractual hours are the average of those hours over the cycle.
"The contractual weeks"	The number of weeks in every period of 12 months for which (assuming that there will be no unpaid leave of absence) wages or salary is payable to the employee.";

(c) by inserting after the entry relating to the expression "Probation Officer" the following:

" "Public airport company"	The meaning given in section 16 of the Airports Act 1986(a)."; and

(d) by inserting after the entry relating to the expression "Public service scheme" the following:

(a) 1986 c.31.

| " "Public transport company" | The meaning given in section 72 of the Transport Act 1985(a).". |

Pensionable employees

20. Schedule 2 to the principal Regulations is amended by inserting after Part III the following:

"PART IV

1.—(1) Subject to sub-paragraphs (2) to (6), a person who is in a qualifying part-time employment may elect to become a pensionable employee in that employment.

(2) Subject to sub-paragraphs (3) and (4), a qualifying part-time employment is—

(a) an employment under a scheduled body,

(b) an employment under a body mentioned in regulation B1(6)(a) or (b) (governors of certain educational institutions), or

(c) an employment as a member of a passenger transport executive or a director of a subsidiary of a passenger transport executive,

in which the contractual weeks are 35 or more and the contractual hours are 15 or more but fewer than 30.

(3) If a person is in two or more employments under a single such body, and—

(a) in each of the employments the contractual weeks are 35 or more and the contractual hours are fewer than 30, and

(b) the total of the contractual hours in all the employments is 15 or more,

then each of the employments is a qualifying part-time employment, but any election under sub-paragraph (1) must be made in respect of all of them.

(4) An employment is not a qualifying part-time employment if—

(a) it is an employment in which the person is a manual worker, unless, subject to sub-paragraph (5), he has completed 12 months' continuous employment with the same body in which the contractual hours were 15 or more, or

(b) it is an employment under a scheduled body not described in column (1) of Part I, unless they have by a statutory resolution—

(i) specified him as a person, or

(ii) specified a class of persons to which he belongs as a class of persons,

to whom sub-paragraph (1) is to apply, or

(c) it is an employment falling within sub-paragraph (2)(b), unless the local education authority have, with the general or specific consent of the employer, by a statutory resolution specified as mentioned in (b)(i) or (ii) above, or

(d) it is an employment falling within sub-paragraph (2)(c), unless the passenger transport executive have by a statutory resolution specified as so mentioned.

(5) An employment which would but for sub-paragraph (4)(a) be a qualifying part-time employment becomes one if the employee—

(a) became employed by the body in question as a manual worker after ceasing to be employed in non-local government employment, and

(b) provides that body with a declaration in writing that his pension rights under his non-local government scheme will be preserved or that he has applied, or will apply, for their transfer to the appropriate administering authority.

(6) An election under sub-paragraph (1) may be made at any time by giving notice in writing to the body which will become the person's employing authority and—

(a) 1985 c.67.

(a) has effect from the day after the date to which the next payment of wages or salary will be calculated, and

(b) so long as there is no break in service, and subject to sub-paragraph (7), has effect in relation to any subsequent qualifying part-time employment under that body even though not made in respect of it.

(7) If the contractual hours in the employment, or as the case may be the total of the contractual hours in all the employments, in relation to which the election has effect fall below 15, the person may elect to cease to be a pensionable employee in the employment or employments.

2. If a person who is in a part-time employment under a body mentioned in paragraph 1(2) was, immediately before the commencement of that employment, a pensionable employee in a whole-time employment under that body, he remains a pensionable employee in the part-time employment unless he elects to cease to be one.

3. An election under paragraph 1(7) or 2—

(a) must be made, by giving notice in writing to the employing authority, within 6 months after the date on which the provision in question becomes applicable or such longer period as the authority may allow, and

(b) has effect from the day after the date to which the next payment of wages or salary will be calculated,

and the person making it is to be treated for the purposes of these Regulations, except regulation C12 (return of contributions), as if he had on that day ceased to hold the employment or employments.

4. Where—

(a) at any time after 31st March 1974 a body mentioned in paragraph 1(2) decided that a person in a part-time employment under them was in that employment a pensionable employee, and

(b) he was not at that time a pensionable employee by virtue of regulation B1(2) to (15), and

(c) if this Part had then been in force he could have made an election under paragraph 1(1),

he is to be treated as if this Part had then been in force and he had made such an election.

5.—(1) Subject to sub-paragraph (2), a person who is in a whole-time employment under a body mentioned in paragraph 1(2) in which the contractual weeks are fewer than 45 is not in that employment a pensionable employee.

(2) Where a person is in such an employment—

(a) if he was in the employment immediately before 1st April 1987 and the employing authority had decided that he was in the employment a pensionable employee, he remains so unless he otherwise elects, and

(b) in any other case, he may elect to become a pensionable employee in the employment.

(3) An election under sub-paragraph (2) may be made at any time by giving notice in writing to the employing body or, as the case may be, the body which will become the employing authority, and has effect from the day after the date to which the next payment of wages or salary will be calculated.".

Amount to be paid for additional period

21. Schedule 4 to the principal Regulations is amended—

(a) in paragraph 2, by inserting in the second column in Table 1, opposite the figure "64" in the first column, the figure "21.10";

(b) by inserting after paragraph 3 the following:

"4. For the purposes of paragraphs 1 to 3, where the employee is a pensionable employee by virtue of—

(a) an election or deemed election under paragraph 1(1) of Part IV of Schedule 2 (elections by part-time employees), or

(b) paragraph 2 of that Part (part-time employee remaining pensionable if previously whole-time),

and the election under regulation C5 or C6 was made after 31st March 1987, references to his remuneration and to the remuneration that he would have received are to be construed as references to the remuneration that would have been paid for a single comparable whole-time employment.".

Modification of earlier provisions as to return of contributions

22. Regulation C8 of the Local Government Superannuation Regulations 1974(a) shall be deemed to have had effect during the period beginning on 1st April 1974 and ending with 28th February 1986 as if in paragraph (1)—

(a) for the words "a pensionable employee of an employing authority" there had been substituted the words "an employee of a scheduled body"; and

(b) for the words "by that authority" there had been substituted the words "by that body".".

Modification of earlier provisions as to gratuities

23.—(1) Section 18 of the Act of 1953 shall be deemed to have had effect during the period beginning on 1st July 1973 and ending with 28th February 1986, and the regulation which on 1st March 1986 took effect as regulation K1 of the principal Regulations shall be deemed to have had effect, notwithstanding the provisos numbered (ii), as if they had—

(a) in the circumstances described in paragraph (2) below, authorised, and

(b) in the circumstances described in paragraph (3) below, required

a gratuity to be granted in accordance with paragraphs (4) to (6).

(2) The circumstances mentioned in paragraph (1)(a) are that the employee was entitled to a payment out of the superannuation fund, other than a return of contributions, in the calculation of which less than the whole of his service was, at whatever length, taken into account.

(3) The circumstances mentioned in paragraph (1)(b) are that the employee—

(a) became a contributory employee on 1st July 1973 by virtue of regulations 5(1) and 10 to 13 of the Miscellaneous Provisions Regulations, and

(b) was one of a class or description of employees in relation to whom, immediately before that date, it was the prevailing practice of the employing body to exercise beneficially their power under section 18 of the Act of 1953.

(4) A gratuity granted where paragraph (1)(a) applies is not to exceed $\frac{5 \times A}{100} \times B$, where—

A is the annual rate of the employee's remuneration at the date on which he ceased to be employed, ascertained as if paragraph 4 of Part V of Schedule 16 to the principal Regulations had applied, and

B is the length in years and days of the service which was not taken into account in calculating the payment mentioned in paragraph (2).

(5) The gratuity to be granted where paragraph (1)(b) applies is $\frac{C}{D} \times E$, where—

C is the length in years and days of any of the employee's service before 1st July 1973 that was reckonable neither as contributing service nor as non-contributing service,

D is the length in years and days of all his service, and

E is the amount of the gratuity that would have been granted in accordance with the prevailing practice mentioned in paragraph (3)(b) if he had continued in that employment with the body until the date of the relevant cessation of employment and his age and the length of his service had then been such that that practice would have applied.

(a) S.I. 1974/520; a relevant amendment was made by S.I. 1978/266.

(6) Where the employee has died in employment with the body concerned, any gratuity granted by virtue of this regulation is payable to his widow or any other dependant of his.

(7) In this regulation "service"—

(a) in relation to any time before 1st April 1974, has the meaning given in section 40(1) of the Act of 1937,

(b) in relation to any time after 31st March 1974 and before 1st March 1986, has the meaning given in regulation A3(1) of the 1974 Regulations, and

(c) in relation to any time after 28th February 1986, means time spent in employment with a scheduled body.

Transitional and supplemental

24.—(1) A person is not to be taken to have become a pensionable employee by virtue of regulation 4(b) of these Regulations at any time before 1st April 1986.

(2) Any admission agreement made before 1st April 1987 which made provision for any part-time employees to become admitted employees is to be treated as having been varied on 1st April 1987 so as to comply with regulation B3(4) of the principal Regulations as amended by regulation 6(b) of these Regulations.

(3) Paragraph (2) does not affect the position of any person who became an admitted employee before 1st April 1987.

Retrospective effect

25.—(1) Any resolution passed after 31st December 1986 and before 1st April 1987 which, if regulation 2 above had been in force, could have been passed under that regulation shall be treated for the purposes of the principal Regulations as having been so passed.

(2) A superannuation fund established after 31st December 1986 and before 1st April 1987 by the London Residuary Body for the purposes of the principal Regulations shall be treated for those purposes as having been established under regulation P1(2) of those Regulations (inserted by regulation 17 above).

(3) Where—

(a) if these Regulations had come into operation on 1st April 1986, a person would at any time before 1st April 1987 have been entitled to make an election under regulation B1(15B) or (18) of the principal Regulations or under paragraph 1(1) or (7), 2 or 5(2) of Part IV of Schedule 2 to those Regulations, and

(b) he gives notice of such an election within 6 months after 1st April 1987,

the election may be expressed to have effect as if these Regulations had come into operation on 1st April 1986 and the notice had been given on the first day on which he would in that case have been entitled to give notice of the election or, where that day is 1st April 1986, to have effect from that date.

26th February 1987

Nicholas Ridley
Secretary of State for the Environment

EXPLANATORY NOTE

(This note is not part of the Regulations)

These Regulations are concerned principally with employees of public transport and airport companies formed under the Transport Act 1985 and the Airports Act 1986, with gratuities, and with employees who work less than a full week or year.

Regulation 2 is a transitory provision enabling a passenger transport authority or principal council to resolve that former employees who have become employees of a public airport company are to be deemed still to be employed by them for the purposes of the Local Government Superannuation Regulations 1986 ("the principal Regulations"). Regulation 5(c) to (f) makes related amendments to the principal Regulations which secure that the employees remain pensionable employees while employed by, or by a subsidiary of, that or another public airport company, unless they become admitted employees by virtue of an admission agreement under regulation B3 of the principal Regulations. Regulation 3 of these Regulations provides that a resolution under regulation 2, or under an earlier similar provision relating to public transport company employees, ceases to have effect in relation to employees who become admitted employees.

Regulation 18 provides that where an admission agreement has been made with a public transport or airport company, or after 31st March 1987 with any other body, so much of any pensions increase (under the Pensions (Increase) Act 1971) as is attributable to a person's service with the body as an admitted employee is to be paid out of the superannuation fund, and provides for a related increase in the employer's contributions payable by the body. These provisions are made by virtue of section 7(3) of the Superannuation Act 1972, and accordingly provisions of the Pensions (Increase) Act 1971, and of regulations made under section 5 of that Act, relating to liability for the cost of increases have effect subject to them.

Regulation 17 empowers an authority administering a superannuation fund to establish further funds. Where they do so, the further fund becomes the appropriate fund for employees of specified admitted bodies (regulations 6(a) and 7).

Regulation 16 substitutes a new Part for Part K of the principal Regulations (gratuities). New regulations K2 and K3 set out the cases in which a gratuity may be granted and the forms it may take. Entitlement to superannuation benefits will no longer be a bar in all cases. New regulation K4, with the definitions in new regulation K1, fixes the maximum amounts. New regulation K5 provides that the cost of gratuities is not to be met out of superannuation funds, and new regulation K6 provides for the modified application of Part K in relation to certain bodies and for its application to non-teaching staff in maintained schools.

Regulation 23 retrospectively modifies earlier gratuity provisions so as to authorise, and in some circumstances to require, payment of a gratuity notwithstanding that the former employee was entitled to superannuation benefits in respect of part of his service.

Regulation 20 inserts into Schedule 2 to the principal Regulations a new Part IV. Paragraphs 1 to 4 of this, with related provisions in regulations 4(a), (b), (c), (e) and (f), 5(a) and (b), 6(b), 8, 11, 13, 19(b), 21(b), 24 and 25(3) make provision for part-time employees to elect to be pensionable employees. The basic qualification for making an election is that the employee has a contractual obligation to work at least 15 hours a week for at least 35 weeks a year. In some circumstances part-time employees remain or become pensionable without an election, and elections to cease to be pensionable may be made in certain cases.

The new Part IV of Schedule 2 also provides (in paragraph 5) that a whole-time employee with an obligation to work fewer than 45 weeks a year is pensionable only if his employing authority has so decided in the past or if he elects to be pensionable.

Regulation 4(d) makes certain office-holders (justices' clerks outside inner London and registration officers) pensionable employees. Regulation 9 amends regulation C7 of the principal Regulations so as to allow them to pay for a past period in office to become reckonable service under regulation D9 of the principal Regulations, which is consequentially amended by regulation 12 of these Regulations.

For employees working less than 45 weeks a year and for registration officers, service is adjusted for benefit purposes by regulation E25(3) to (6) of the principal Regulations, inserted by regulation 15 of these Regulations.

The remaining provisions of these Regulations deal with miscellaneous matters. Regulation 4(g) and (h) allows manual workers who had elected not to be pensionable to elect to be so. Regulations 10 and 22 remedy, with retrospective effect, an anomaly which has prevented the return of contributions, on cessation of employment, to persons whose continuing employment had ceased to be pensionable. Regulation 14 clarifies provisions relating to death grants, and regulation 21(a) supplies a missing figure. Regulation 25(1) and (2) validates actions taken in anticipation of regulations 2 and 17.

Section 12 of the Superannuation Act 1972 confers express power to make regulations retrospective in effect. These Regulations are to a certain extent retrospective, but rights in relation to former employees are not adversely affected.

STATUTORY INSTRUMENTS

1987 No. 295

MERCHANT SHIPPING

PILOTAGE

The Pilotage Commission Provision of Funds Scheme 1987 (Confirmation) Order 1987

Made - - - -	*27th February 1987*
Laid before Parliament	*11th March 1987*
Coming into force	*1st April 1987*

The Secretary of State for Transport, there having been no objections made to him in pursuance of section 3(2)(b)(iii) of the Pilotage Act 1983**(a)** in respect of the Scheme set out in the Schedule hereto, in exercise of the powers conferred on him by section 3(3) of the said Act and of all other powers enabling him in that behalf, hereby makes the following Order:

1. This Order may be cited as the Pilotage Commission Provision of Funds Scheme 1987 (Confirmation) Order 1987 and shall come into force on 1st April 1987.

2. The Scheme made by the Pilotage Commission under section 3(1) of the said Act and set out in the Schedule hereto is hereby confirmed.

3. The Pilotage Commission Provision of Funds Scheme 1986 (Confirmation) Order 1986**(b)** is hereby revoked.

Michael Spicer
Parliamentary Under Secretary of State,
Department of Transport

Signed by authority of the Secretary of State
27th February 1987

(a) 1983 c.21.
(b) S.I. 1986/402.

SCHEDULE

THE PILOTAGE COMMISSION
SCHEME UNDER SECTION 3 OF THE PILOTAGE ACT 1983

The Pilotage Commission, in exercise of its powers under Section 3 of the Pilotage Act, 1983, hereby makes the following Scheme:–

1.   This Scheme may be cited as the Pilotage Commission Provision of Funds Scheme, 1987.

2.   In this Scheme:–
"the Act" means the Pilotage Act, 1983;
"the Commission" means the Pilotage Commission;
"month" means calendar month;
"operative period" means twelve months from the date of coming into force of this Scheme;
"relevant receipts" means, in relation to each pilotage authority, all pilotage dues received for the pilotage district or districts for which it is the pilotage authority, excluding charges for the boarding and landing of pilots.

3.   Each pilotage authority shall pay to the Commission three-quarters of one per cent of the relevant receipts received from the date of coming into force of this Scheme until 31st March 1988, inclusive. Payments shall be made monthly and payment in respect of any one month's receipts shall be made within the month following.

4.—(1)   Each pilotage authority shall furnish the Commission with information reasonably required by the Commission for the purpose of ascertaining or confirming the amount of relevant receipts in any month within the operative period.

(2)   If it appears to the Commission that a pilotage authority has failed to furnish it with reliable information as to the relevant receipts in any month within the operative period, it may estimate as best it can the amount of relevant receipts in that month and payment shall be made by the authority on that basis.

5.—(1)   Pursuant to Section 3(1)(b) of the Act, a statement prepared by the Commission indicating how the sums payable under this Scheme are related to the Commission's estimates of its expenditure during the operative period shall accompany this Scheme when it is submitted to the Secretary of State and when it is copied to pilotage authorities and any licensed pilot, harbour authority and shipowner in accordance with section 3(2) of the Act.

EXPLANATORY NOTE

(This note is not part of the Order)

By this Order the Secretary of State confirms a Scheme made by the Pilotage Commission under section 3 of the Pilotage Act 1983 for imposing on pilotage authorities charges to provide funds for the Commission for the purposes mentioned in section 3(1). The Scheme is set out in the Schedule.

The Order revokes the Pilotage Commission Provision of Funds Scheme 1986 (Confirmation) Order 1986 to which was scheduled the text of the previous Scheme.

The Scheme is in a form similar to the previous Scheme and the general levy on pilotage receipts remains at $\frac{3}{4}$%. The operative period of the Scheme is twelve months.

STATUTORY INSTRUMENTS

1987 No. 298

DANGEROUS DRUGS

The Misuse of Drugs (Licence Fees) (Amendment) Regulations 1987

Made - - - -	*26th February 1987*
Laid before Parliament	*9th March 1987*
Coming into force	*1st April 1987*

In pursuance of sections 30, 31 and 37(1) of the Misuse of Drugs Act 1971(**a**), and after consultation with the Advisory Council on the Misuse of Drugs, I hereby make the following Regulations:–

1. These Regulations may be cited as the Misuse of Drugs (Licence Fees) (Amendment) Regulations 1987 and shall come into force on 1st April 1987.

2. Regulation 3(1) of the Misuse of Drugs (Licence Fees) Regulations 1986(**b**) shall be amended as follows–

(a) in sub-paragraph (a), for "£318" there shall be substituted "£324";

(b) in sub-paragraph (b), for "£212" there shall be substituted "£216";

(c) in sub-paragraph (c), for "£106" there shall be substituted "£108";

(d) in sub-paragraph (d), for "£106" there shall be substituted "£108"; and

(e) in sub-paragraph (e), for "£53" there shall be substituted "£54".

Home Office
26th February 1987

Douglas Hurd
One of Her Majesty's Principal Secretaries of State

EXPLANATORY NOTE

(This note is not part of the Regulations)

Section 30 of the Misuse of Drugs Act 1971 provides that a licence issued by the Secretary of State for the purposes of that Act or of Regulations made under it may be issued subject to the condition of payment of a fee. The Misuse of Drugs (Licence Fees) Regulations 1986 prescribe the fee payable in relation to a licence to produce, supply, offer to supply or possess controlled drugs; the present Regulations amend those Regulations so as to increase the fees there prescribed by approximately 2 per cent.

(**a**) 1971 c. 38: *see* the definition of "prescribed" in section 37(1).
(**b**) S.I. 1986/416.

STATUTORY INSTRUMENTS

1987 No. 299

CRIMINAL LAW, ENGLAND AND WALES

The Prosecution of Offences (Custody Time Limits) Regulations 1987

Made - - - -	*26th February 1987*
Laid before Parliament	*6th March 1987*
Coming into force	*1st April 1987*

ARRANGEMENT OF REGULATIONS

In exercise of the powers conferred on me by sections 22(1) and (2) and 29(2) of the Prosecution of Offences Act 1985(**a**), I hereby make the following Regulations:–

Citation and commencement

1. These Regulations may be cited as the Prosecution of Offences (Custody Time Limits) Regulations 1987 and shall come into force on 1st April 1987.

Interpretation

2.—(1) In these Regulations –

"the 1980 Act" means the Magistrates' Courts Act 1980(**b**);
"the 1985 Act" means the Prosecution of Offences Act 1985.

(**a**) 1985 c.23.   (**b**) 1980 c.43.

(2) In these Regulations a reference to a person's first appearance in relation to proceedings in a magistrates' court for an offence is a reference to the time when first he appears or is brought before the court on an information charging him with that offence.

(3) In these Regulations a reference to the commencement of a summary trial is a reference to the time when the court begins to hear evidence for the prosecution at the trial or, if the court accepts a plea of guilty without hearing such evidence, the time when the plea is accepted.

(4) Any maximum period set by these Regulations during which a person may be in the custody of a court does not include the day on which the custody commenced.

(5) A custody time limit which would, apart from this paragraph, expire on any of the days to which this paragraph applies shall be treated as expiring on the next preceding day which is not one of those days.

The days to which this paragraph applies are Saturday, Sunday, Christmas Day, Good Friday and any day which under the Banking and Financial Dealings Act 1971(a) is a bank holiday in England and Wales.

Application

3.—(1) Subject to paragraph (3) below these Regulations shall apply in relation to proceedings instituted in any of the areas mentioned in paragraph (2) below, but shall not apply in relation to proceedings instituted elsewhere.

(2) The areas referred to in paragraph (1) above are the following counties, namely –

> Avon
> Kent
> Somerset
> West Midlands.

(3) These Regulations shall not apply in relation to proceedings for an offence instituted before the date of commencement of these Regulations, except where the accused is committed on or after that date for trial in the Crown Court.

Custody time limits in magistrates' courts

4.—(1) In proceedings in relation to which these Regulations apply, the maximum period during which a person accused of an indictable offence other than treason may be in the custody of a magistrates' court in relation to that offence while awaiting completion of any preliminary stage of the proceedings specified in the following provisions of this Regulation shall be as stated in those provisions.

(2) Except as provided in paragraph (3) below, in the case of an offence triable either way the maximum period of custody between the accused's first appearance and the commencement of summary trial or, as the case may be, the time when the court decides whether or not to commit the accused to the Crown Court for trial shall be –

(a) in the case of proceedings instituted in the county of West Midlands, 98 days; and

(b) in the case of proceedings instituted elsewhere, 70 days.

(3) In the case of an offence triable either way if, before the expiry of 56 days following the day of the accused's first appearance, the court decides to proceed to summary trial in pursuance of sections 19 to 24 of the 1980 Act the maximum period of custody between the accused's first appearance and the commencement of the summary trial shall be 56 days.

(4) In the case of an offence triable on indictment exclusively the maximum period of custody between the accused's first appearance and the time when the court decides whether or not to commit the accused to the Crown Court for trial, shall be –

(a) in the case of proceedings instituted in the county of West Midlands, 98 days; and

---

(a) 1971 c.80.

(b) in the case of proceedings instituted elsewhere, 70 days.

(5) Where a court proceeds to inquire into an information as examining justices in pursuance of section 6(1) of the 1980 Act, the foregoing provisions of this Regulation shall have effect as if any reference therein to the time when the court decides whether or not to commit the accused to the Crown Court for trial was a reference to the time when it begins to hear evidence for the prosecution at the inquiry.

Custody time limits in the Crown Court

5.—(1) In this Regulation "specified Crown Court centre" means the Crown Court sitting at any of the following places, namely –

> Birmingham
> Bristol
> Maidstone.

(2) In proceedings in relation to which these Regulations apply, where –

(a) a person accused of an indictable offence other than treason is committed for trial at a specified Crown Court centre; or

(b) a bill of indictment is preferred against such a person under section 2(2)(b) of the Administration of Justice (Miscellaneous Provisions) Act 1933(a) at a specified Crown Court centre,

the maximum period during which he may be in the custody of the Crown Court in relation to that offence, or any other offence included in the indictment preferred against him, while awaiting the preliminary stage of the proceedings specified in the following provisions of this Regulation shall be as stated in those provisions.

(3) The maximum period of custody –

(a) between the time when the accused is committed for trial and his arraignment; or

(b) where a bill of indictment is preferred against him under the said section 2(2)(b), between the preferment of the bill and his arraignment,

shall, subject to the following provisions of this Regulation, be 112 days.

(4) Where, following a committal for trial, the bill of indictment preferred against the accused (not being a bill preferred under the said section 2(2)(b)) contains a count charging an offence for which he was committed for trial at that committal together with a count charging an offence for which he was committed for trial on a different occasion, paragraph (3) above applies in relation to each offence separately.

(5) Where, following a committal for trial, a bill of indictment is preferred under the said section 2(2)(b) and the bill does not contain a count charging an offence for which he was not committed for trial, the maximum period of custody between the preferment of the bill and the accused's arraignment shall be 112 days less any period, or the aggregate of any periods, during which the accused has, since the committal, been in the custody of the Crown Court in relation to an offence for which he was committed for trial.

(6) Where, following a committal for trial, the bill of indictment preferred against the accused (not being a bill preferred under the said section 2(2)(b)) contains a count charging an offence for which he was not committed for trial, the maximum period of custody –

(a) between the preferment of the bill and his arraignment, or

(b) if the count was added to the bill after its preferment, between that addition and his arraignment,

shall be 112 days less any period, or the aggregate of any periods, during which he has, since the committal, been in the custody of the Crown Court in relation to an offence for which he was committed for trial.

(a) 1933 c.36; section 2(2)(b) was amended by the Supreme Court Act 1981 (c.54), Schedule 5, and by the Prosecution of Offences Act 1985 (c.23), Schedule 2.

(7) For the purposes of this Regulation, the arraignment of the accused shall be regarded as occurring at the time when he is asked to plead, notwithstanding that he has not done so.

Bail on expiry of Crown Court custody time limit

6.—(1) Subject to the following provisions of this Regulation where an accused who is in custody pending trial in the Crown Court has the benefit of a custody time limit under Regulation 5 above the prosecution shall –

   (a) not less than 5 days before the expiry of the time limit give notice in writing to the appropriate officer of the Crown Court and to the accused or his representative stating whether or not it intends to ask the Crown Court to impose conditions on the grant of bail in respect of the accused and, if it intends to do so, the nature of the conditions to be sought; and

   (b) make arrangements for the accused to be brought before the Crown Court within the period of 2 days preceding the expiry of the time limit.

(2) If the Crown Court is satisfied that it is not practicable in all the circumstances for the prosecution to comply with sub-paragraph (a) in paragraph (1) above, the Crown Court may direct that the prosecution need not comply with that sub-paragraph or that the minimum period of notice required by that sub-paragraph shall be such lesser minimum period as the Crown Court may specify.

(3) The prosecution need not comply with paragraph (1)(a) above if it has given notice under Regulation 7(2) below of its intention to make an application under section 22(3) of the 1985 Act.

(4) On receiving notice under paragraph (1)(a) above stating that the prosecution intends to ask the Crown Court to impose conditions on the grant of bail, the accused or his representative shall –

   (a) give notice in writing to the appropriate officer of the Crown Court and to the prosecution that the accused wishes to be represented at the hearing of the application; or

   (b) give notice in writing to the appropriate officer and to the prosecution stating that the accused does not oppose the application; or

   (c) give to the appropriate officer, for the consideration of the Crown Court, a written statement of the accused's reasons for opposing the application, at the same time sending a copy of the statement to the prosecution.

(5) The Crown Court may direct that the prosecution need not comply with paragraph (1)(b) above.

(6) The Crown Court, on being notified that an accused who is in custody pending trial there has the benefit of a custody time limit under Regulation 5 above and that the time limit is about to expire, shall grant him bail in accordance with the Bail Act 1976**(a)**, as from the expiry of the time limit, subject to a duty to appear before the Crown Court for trial.

Application for extension of custody time limit

7.—(1) An application to a court for the extension or further extension of a custody time limit under section 22(3) of the 1985 Act may be made orally or in writing.

(2) Subject to paragraphs (3) and (4) below the prosecution shall –

   (a) not less than 5 days before making such an application in the Crown Court; and

   (b) not less than 2 days before making such an application in a magistrates' court,

give notice in writing to the accused or his representative and to the appropriate officer of the Crown Court stating that it intends to make such an application.

(a) 1976 c.63.

(3) It shall not be necessary for the prosecution to comply with paragraph (2) above if the accused or his representative has informed the prosecution that he does not require such notice.

(4) If the court is satisfied that it is not practicable in all the circumstances for the prosecution to comply with paragraph (2) above, the court may direct that the prosecution need not comply with that paragraph or that the minimum period of notice required by that paragraph to be given shall be such lesser minimum period as the court may specify.

Application of Bail Act 1976

8.—(1) The Bail Act 1976 shall apply in relation to cases to which a custody time limit applies subject to the modifications specified in paragraph (2) below, being modifications necessary in consequence of the foregoing provisions of these Regulations.

(2) That Act shall apply as if –

   (a) in section 3 (general provisions) at the end there were inserted the following subsection:–

   "(10) Where a custody time limit has expired this section shall have effect as if –

      (a) subsections (4) and (5) (sureties and security for his surrender to custody) were omitted;

      (b) in subsection (6) (conditions of bail) for the words "before release on bail or later" there were substituted the words "after release on bail"";

   (b) in section 4 (general right to bail of accused persons and others) at the end there were inserted the following subsection:–

   "(8) Where a custody time limit has expired this section shall have effect as if, in subsection (1), the words "except as provided in Schedule 1 to this Act" were omitted.";

   (c) in section 7 (liability to arrest for absconding or breaking conditions of bail) at the end there were inserted the following subsection:–

   "(7) Where a custody time limit has expired this section shall have effect as if, in subsection (3), paragraphs (a) and (c) were omitted.".

Home Office
26th February 1987

Douglas Hurd
One of Her Majesty's Principal Secretaries of State

EXPLANATORY NOTE

(This note is not part of the Regulations)

These Regulations make provision, with effect from 1st April 1987, as to the maximum period during which a person accused of any indictable offence except treason (including an offence triable either way) in the counties of Avon, Kent, Somerset and West Midlands may be kept in custody while awaiting trial or committal for trial.

Regulation 4 is concerned with custody time limits in relation to proceedings in magistrates' courts. The limit between the first appearance of the accused in court and the commencement of summary trial or, as the case may be, committal for trial is 70 days, except where the proceedings are commenced in the West Midlands in which case the limit is 98 days. If a decision to proceed to summary trial is taken within 56 days following the accused's first appearance, the limit up to the commencement of the trial is reduced to 56 days in all cases.

Regulations 5 and 6 are concerned with custody time limits in relation to proceedings in the Crown Court sitting at Birmingham, Bristol or Maidstone. The limit between committal (or the preferment of a voluntary bill of indictment) and arraignment is 112 days.

Regulation 7 deals with the procedure for applying to the Crown Court or a magistrates' court for an extension of a custody time limit. In particular, the prosecution is normally required to give the accused 5 days notice before applying to the Crown Court and 2 days before applying to a magistrates' court.

Regulation 8 makes consequential modifications in the application of the Bail Act 1976 in cases where a custody time limit applies.

STATUTORY INSTRUMENTS

1987 No. 304 (C.7)

TOWN AND COUNTRY PLANNING, ENGLAND AND WALES

The Housing and Planning Act 1986 (Commencement No. 3) Order 1987

<table>
<tr><td>Made -</td><td>-</td><td>-</td><td>-</td><td>26th February 1987</td></tr>
</table>

The Secretary of State for the Environment, as respects England, and the Secretary of State for Wales, as respects Wales, in exercise of the powers conferred on them by section 57(2) of the Housing and Planning Act 1986(**a**) and of all other powers enabling them in that behalf hereby make the following Order:

1. This Order may be cited as the Housing and Planning Act 1986 (Commencement No. 3) Order 1987.

2. Section 49 of the Housing and Planning Act 1986 insofar as it relates to paragraph 8 of Schedule 11 to that Act shall come into force on 2nd March 1987.

Transitional provision

3. Subsections (2) to (5) of section 250 of the Local Government Act 1972(**b**) shall continue to apply to any inquiry held under paragraph 5 of Schedule 9 to the Town and Country Planning Act 1971(**c**) which began before 2nd March 1987 as those provisions applied immediately before that date.

Revocation

4. The Housing and Planning Act 1986 (Commencement No. 2) Order 1987(**d**) is hereby revoked.

26th February 1987

Nicholas Ridley
Secretary of State for the Environment

25th February 1987

Nicholas Edwards
Secretary of State for Wales

(**a**) 1986 c.63.   (**b**) 1972 c.70.   (**c**) 1971 c.78.   (**d**) S.I. 1987/178.

EXPLANATORY NOTE

(This note is not part of the Order)

This Order revokes and replaces S.I. 1987/178 which was made on 10th February 1987.

This Order brings into operation on 2nd March 1987 paragraph 8 of Schedule 11 to the Housing and Planning Act 1986.

Paragraph 8(1) substitutes a new subsection (2) in section 282 of the Town and Country Planning Act 1971. This is a minor drafting improvement which makes no change of substance.

Paragraph 8(2) substitutes a new paragraph 5(3) of Schedule 9 to the Town and Country Planning Act 1971 (determination of appeals by appointed person) applying section 250(2) to (5) of the Local Government Act 1972 (local inquiries: evidence and costs) to an inquiry held under paragraph 5 of Schedule 9. At present only the Secretary of State is entitled under paragraph 5(3) to make orders as to the costs of the parties at an inquiry and as to the parties by whom the costs are to be paid. The substituted paragraph entitles a person appointed by the Secretary of State to hold an inquiry to make such orders as well.

NOTE AS TO EARLIER COMMENCEMENT ORDERS

(This note is not part of the Order)

An earlier commencement order (S.I. 1986/2262) brought into force on 7th January 1987 sections 1 to 4, 10 to 14, 16, 17, 19, 20, 22, 23, 24 (partially), 27 to 29, 44 to 48, 49 (partially), 53 (partially), 54 and 55, and paragraphs 1 to 7, 14, 15, 17, 21 to 26, 28, 30, 32, 33, 39, 41 and 42 of Schedule 5, paragraphs 1 to 7, 10 to 14, 16 to 18, 20 to 22, 24 and 25, 28 to 38, 41 to 56 and 59 to 62 of Schedule 11 and certain repeals effected by Schedule 12.

STATUTORY INSTRUMENTS

1987 No. 306

MERCHANT SHIPPING

SAFETY

The Merchant Shipping (Submersible Craft) (Amendment) Regulations 1987

Made - - - -	*26th February 1987*
Laid before Parliament	*11th March 1987*
Coming into force -	*1st April 1987*

The Secretary of State for Transport, in exercise of his powers under sections 16 and 17 of, and Schedule 5 to the Merchant Shipping Act 1974(**a**) and of all other powers enabling him in that behalf, hereby makes the following Regulations:—

Citation, commencement and interpretation

1. These Regulations may be cited as the Merchant Shipping (Submersible Craft) (Amendment) Regulations 1987 and shall come into force on 1st April 1987.

2. The Merchant Shipping (Registration of Submersible Craft) Regulations 1976(**b**) shall be amended as follows:—

    (a)   (i) in regulation 1(2), for the definition of "submersible craft" there shall be substituted the following:—

        " "submersible craft" means any description of manned mobile submersible apparatus which is designed to maintain some or all of its occupants at or near atmospheric pressure including free, self-propelled, tethered, towed or bottom contact propelled apparatus and atmospheric diving suits. A diving bell is not a submersible craft for the purposes of these Regulations; and "diving bell" means any compression chamber which is capable of being manned and is used or designed for use under the surface of water in supporting human life being a chamber in which any occupant is or may be subjected to a pressure of more than 300 millibars above atmospheric pressure during normal operation;";

        (ii) there shall be added at the end the following definition:—

        " "United Kingdom ship" means such a ship as is defined in section 21(2) of the Merchant Shipping Act 1979(**c**);

    (b) in regulation 2(1) for paragraph (b) the following shall be substituted:—

        "(b) launched, recovered, operated or supported from or comprises a United Kingdom ship";

    (c) there shall be inserted after regulation 2(1) the following:—

        "(1A) These Regulations do not apply to submersible craft which are not

---

(**a**) 1974 c.43.   (**b**) S.I. 1976/940, to which there is an amendment not relevant to these Regulations.
(**c**) 1979 c.39. As to the meaning of "Citizen of the United Kingdom and Colonies" referred to in section 21(2), *see now* the British Nationality Act 1981 (c.61), section 51(3).

used in the course of or in connection with any trade or business or by any person for hire or reward.".

3. The Merchant Shipping (Submersible Craft Construction and Survey) Regulations 1981(**a**) shall be amended as follows:—
  (a) in regulation 1(2):—
      (i) there shall be inserted (after the definition of "autonomous submersible craft") the following definition:
          " "Certifying Authority" means the Secretary of State or any person authorised by the Secretary of State and includes (if so authorised) Lloyds Register of Shipping, the British Committee of Bureau Veritas, the British Committee of Det Norske Veritas, the British Committee of Germanischer Lloyd and the British Technical Committee of the American Bureau of Shipping;";
      (ii) for the definition of "crew", there shall be substituted the following:—
          " "crew" means the person or persons within the submersible craft required to operate the craft and its equipment";
      (iii) for the definition of "submersible craft" there shall be substituted the following:—
          " "submersible craft" means any description of manned mobile submersible apparatus which is designed to maintain some or all of its occupants at or near atmospheric pressure including free, self-propelled, tethered, towed or bottom contact propelled apparatus and atmospheric diving suits. A diving bell is not a submersible craft for the purposes of these Regulations; and "diving bell" means any compression chamber which is capable of being manned and is used or designed for use under the surface of water in supporting human life being a chamber in which any occupant is or may be subjected to a pressure of more than 300 millibars above atmospheric pressure during normal operation;";
      (iv) for the definition of "surveyor" there shall be substituted the following:—
          " "surveyor" means a surveyor appointed by a Certifying Authority;";
      (v) there shall be added at the end the following definition:—
          " "United Kingdom ship" means such a ship as is defined in section 21(2) of the Merchant Shipping Act 1979;
  (b) for regulation 2(1)(b) there shall be substituted:—
          "(b) launched recovered or operated or supported from or comprises a United Kingdom ship.";
  (c) for regulation 2(2) there shall be substituted:—
          "(2) These Regulations do not apply to submersible craft which are not used in the course of or in connection with any trade or business or by any person for hire or reward.";
  (d) in regulation 3(2), for "Secretary of State" (in both places) there shall be substituted "Certifying Authority";
  (e) in regulation 3(3), for the second sentence there shall be substituted:—
          "The owner or his agent shall afford all necessary facilities for such survey and shall at the request of the Certifying Authority furnish such further documents or information as may be required";
  (f) in regulation 3(4), for "Secretary of State" there shall be substituted "Certifying Authority";
  (g) in regulation 4, for "Secretary of State" there shall be substituted "Certifying Authority";
  (h) in regulation 5(1) for "Secretary of State" where it first appears there shall be substituted "Certifying Authority";

(**a**) S.I. 1981/1098.

(i) in regulation 8, there shall be added as paragraph (3) the following:—

"(3) In any proceedings for an offence under these Regulations an averment in any process of the fact that anything was done or situated within waters to which these Regulations apply shall, until the contrary is proved, be sufficient evidence of that fact as stated in the averment.";

(j) there shall be inserted in Schedule 1 as a new sub-paragraph 5.2.9. and in Schedule 2 as a new sub-paragraph 5.2.6. the following sub-paragraph:—

"be equipped with such medical stores as the Secretary of State may direct.".

Michael Spicer

Signed by authority of the Secretary of State   Parliamentary Under Secretary of State,
26th February 1987   Department of Transport

EXPLANATORY NOTE

(This note is not part of the Regulations)

These Regulations amend the Merchant Shipping (Registration of Submersible Craft) Regulations 1976 and the Merchant Shipping (Submersible Craft Construction and Survey) Regulations 1981, to bring certain definitions and other provisions into line with the Merchant Shipping (Submersible Craft Operations) Regulations 1987 (S.I. No. 311). In particular the definition of "submersible craft" now excludes diving bells (as defined); the application of the Regulations in connection with submersible craft used outside the United Kingdom or its territorial waters is revised; and there is an exclusion for submersible craft not used commercially.

The Regulations also introduce into the 1981 Regulations a requirement that submersible craft be equipped with medical stores, and can enable survey and certification to be performed by Classification Societies.

I/1aa*

1987 No. 307 (S. 18)

LEGAL AID AND ADVICE, SCOTLAND

The Criminal Legal Aid (Scotland) Regulations 1987

Made - - - -	*26th February 1987*
Laid before Parliament	*5th March 1987*
Coming into force	*1st April 1987*

ARRANGEMENT OF REGULATIONS

The Secretary of State, in exercise of the powers conferred on him by sections 31 and 36 of the Legal Aid (Scotland) Act 1986(**a**), and of all other powers enabling him in that behalf, hereby makes the following Regulations:

Citation and commencement

1. These Regulations may be cited as the Criminal Legal Aid (Scotland) Regulations 1987 and shall come into force on 1st April 1987.

(**a**) 1986 c.47.

Interpretation

2. In these Regulations, unless the context otherwise requires–
"the Act" means the Legal Aid (Scotland) Act 1986;
"the 1975 Act" means the Criminal Procedure (Scotland) Act 1975(**a**);
"assisted person" means a person to whom criminal legal aid has been made available in relation to the proceedings in question.

Revocation

3. Without prejudice to their continuation in effect for certain purposes by virtue of paragraph 3 of Schedule 4 to the Act, the Legal Aid (Scotland) (Criminal Proceedings) Regulations 1975(**b**) are hereby revoked.

Distinct proceedings for purposes of criminal legal aid

4.—(1) For purposes of criminal legal aid, the following shall be treated as distinct proceedings:–

(a) any such identification parade as is referred to in section 21(4)(b) of the Act;

(b) any such proceedings as are described in section 22(1)(b) of the Act;

(c) solemn proceedings other than the proceedings referred to in sub-paragraph (b) above;

(d) any such proceedings as are described in section 22(1)(c) of the Act;

(e) summary proceedings other than the proceedings referred to in sub-paragraph (d) above;

(f) appeals to the High Court of Justiciary against conviction, sentence or acquittal;

(g) petitions to the *nobile officium* of the High Court of Justiciary (whether arising in the course of any proceedings or otherwise);

(h) references by the Secretary of State under section 263 of the 1975 Act(**c**);

(i) such proceedings as are described in section 22(1)(e) of the Act.

(2) The distinct proceedings specified in paragraph (1) above shall be treated as including the following related proceedings (which are accordingly not to be treated as distinct proceedings for purposes of criminal legal aid):–

(a) applications for bail or review of bail, or appeals in respect of bail;

(b) in relation to paragraph (1)(c) above, proceedings following a remit for sentence to the High Court of Justiciary under section 104 of the 1975 Act(**d**);

(c) in relation to paragraph (1)(f) above, proceedings following a remit from the High Court of Justiciary to the inferior court in accordance with section 452A of the 1975 Act(**e**).

Duty solicitors

5.—(1) The Board shall make arrangements for there to be available, in each sheriff court district and district court district, at all times throughout the year, when required, solicitors, hereinafter referred to as "duty solicitors", for the following purposes:–

(a) attending (other than in the circumstances specified in sub-paragraph (b) below), whether in person or by means of a representative who is a solicitor, at any such identification parade as is referred to in section 21(4)(b) of the Act at which the services of the duty solicitor are required;

(b) attending on any person who has been taken into custody on a charge of murder, attempted murder or culpable homicide and who requires the services of the duty solicitor, and advising and acting for such a person until he is admitted to bail or is committed until liberated in due course of law;

(**a**) 1975 c.21.
(**b**) S.I. 1975/717, amended by S.I. 1982/1553, 1984/520.
(**c**) Section 263 was amended by the Criminal Justice (Scotland) Act 1980 (c.62), Schedule 6, paragraph 22(b) and Schedule 8.
(**d**) A new section 104 was inserted by the Criminal Justice (Scotland) Act 1980, Schedule 4, paragraph 15.
(**e**) Section 452A was inserted by the Criminal Justice (Scotland) Act 1980, Schedule 3, paragraph 11.

(c) advising and acting for any person in custody (other than a person referred to in sub-paragraph (b) above) whose case is being prosecuted under solemn procedure, on the day when that person is first brought before a sheriff for examination and thereafter until he is admitted to bail or is committed until liberated in due course of law;

(d) advising and acting for any person who is being prosecuted under summary procedure and who is either in custody or has been liberated under section 295(1)(a) of the 1975 Act(a) (liberation by police on undertaking to appear) on the day when that person is first brought before a court to answer to any complaint and thereafter–

(i) until the conclusion of the first diet at which he is called upon to plead and in connection with any application for liberation following upon that diet; and

(ii) where he has tendered a plea of guilty at that diet, until his case is finally disposed of.

(2) Where a duty solicitor is available by virtue of arrangements made by the Board in accordance with sub-paragraphs (a) or (d) of paragraph (1) above, section 31(1) of the Act shall not apply, and criminal legal aid for the purposes specified in the said sub-paragraphs (a) and (d) shall be provided only by such solicitor.

Applications for criminal legal aid in solemn proceedings

6. An application for criminal legal aid under section 23(1)(a) of the Act shall be made in writing and shall be in such form as the court may require.

Availability of other rights and facilities in proceedings to which section 23 of the Act applies

7.—(1) Where it appears to the court that an applicant for criminal legal aid under section 23 of the Act has available to him rights and facilities making it unnecessary for him to obtain legal aid, or has a reasonable expectation of receiving financial or other help from a body of which he is a member, the court shall not, unless it is satisfied that there is special reason for doing so, make legal aid available to him.

(2) The court, before making legal aid available under section 23 of the Act to a person who is a member of a body which might reasonably have been expected to give him financial help towards his defence, shall require him to undertake in writing that he will pay to the Board any sum received from that body on account of the expenses of his defence.

Applications for criminal legal aid in summary proceedings

8.—(1) An application for criminal legal aid under section 24 of the Act in relation to summary proceedings shall–

(a) be made in writing in such form as the Board may require and be signed by the applicant;

(b) subject to paragraph (2) below, be lodged with the Board within 14 days after the conclusion of the first diet at which the applicant has tendered a plea of not guilty; and

(c) include a statement signed by or on behalf of the solicitor nominated by the applicant as to his willingness to act for the applicant.

(2) Paragraph (1)(b) above shall not apply where either–

(a) in the circumstances specified in section 24(6) of the Act the court has adjourned the trial diet to enable an application for legal aid to be made to the Board and that application is lodged with the Board within 14 days of the adjournment;

(b) the Board considers that there is special reason for it to consider a late application; or

(c) the first diet at which the applicant tendered a plea of not guilty was concluded prior to 1st April 1987 and the application is lodged with the Board not later than 15th April 1987.

(a) A new section 295 was inserted by the Bail etc. (Scotland) Act 1980 (c.4), section 8.

Attendance for interview and supply of information

9. An applicant for criminal legal aid under section 24 of the Act shall, if required by the Board to do so, attend for interview by a representative of the Board or supply such further information or such documents as the Board may require to enable it to determine the application.

Availability of other rights and facilities in summary proceedings

10.—(1) Where it appears to the Board that an applicant for criminal legal aid under section 24 of the Act has available to him rights and facilities making it unnecessary for him to obtain legal aid, or has a reasonable expectation of receiving financial or other help from a body of which he is a member, the Board shall not, unless it is satisfied that there is special reason for doing so, make legal aid available to him.

(2) The Board, before making criminal legal aid available under section 24 of the Act to a person who is a member of a body which might reasonably have been expected to give him financial help towards his defence, shall require him to undertake in writing that he will pay to the Board any sum received from that body on account of the expenses of his defence.

Notification of decision

11.—(1) The Board shall inform an applicant for criminal legal aid under section 24 of the Act, and the solicitor nominated by him, of its decision in regard to the application.

(2) Where the Board refuses an application for criminal legal aid under section 24 of the Act, it shall inform the applicant and the solicitor that the application has been refused on one or more of the following grounds, that -

(a) the proceedings in question are not proceedings for which such legal aid is available;

(b) the Board is not satisfied that the expenses of the case cannot be met without undue hardship to the accused person or his dependants;

(c) the Board is not satisfied that in all the circumstances of the case it is in the interests of justice that legal aid should be made available to him; or

(d) it appears to the Board that the applicant has available to him rights and facilities making it unnecessary for him to receive legal aid or has a reasonable expectation of receiving financial or other help from a body of which he is a member, and the Board is not satisfied that there is special reason for making legal aid available to him.

Applications for review

12.—(1) An application for a review under section 24(5) of the Act shall–

(a) be in writing;

(b) be signed by the applicant; and

(c) subject to paragraph (2) below, be lodged with the Board within 7 days of the time when notice of the refusal of his application was given to the applicant.

(2) Paragraph (1)(c) above shall not apply where the Board considers that there is special reason for it to consider a late application for a review.

Legal aid for criminal appeals

13.—(1) An application under section 25 of the Act for legal aid in relation to an appeal against conviction, sentence or acquittal in criminal proceedings shall–

(a) be in writing in such form as the Board may require and be signed by the applicant;

(b) include a statement signed by or on behalf of the solicitor nominated by the applicant as to his willingness to act for the applicant; and

(c) except where the appeal is against acquittal, include, where the solicitor nominated by the applicant is of the opinion that in all the circumstances there are substantial grounds for taking an appeal, a statement as to the nature of those grounds.

(2) Regulations 9, 10 and 11(1) above shall apply in relation to legal aid under section 25 as they apply in relation to legal aid in summary proceedings under section 24.

Employment of counsel and expert witnesses

14.—(1) Subject to paragraph (2) below, the prior approval of the Board shall be required—

(a) where the proceedings are in the High Court and are not proceedings relating to a prosecution or conviction for murder, for the employment of senior counsel alone, of senior counsel with junior counsel, or of more than one junior counsel;

(b) where the proceedings are in the sheriff court or the district court, for the employment of counsel; and

(c) for the employment of an expert witness.

(2) Paragraph (1) above shall not apply where the Board, on an application made to it for retrospective approval for the employment of counsel or, as the case may be, of an expert witness, considers that the employment would have been approved by them and that there was special reason why prior approval was not applied for.

Matters of special urgency

15.—(1) Where an applicant seeks legal aid under section 24 or section 25 of the Act in a matter of special urgency, the Board may, if it thinks fit, make criminal legal aid available to him notwithstanding that it has not been satisfied—

(a) in the case of an application under section 24 of the Act, as to the matters specified in subsection (1) of that section; and

(b) in the case of an application under section 25 of the Act, as to the matters specified in subsection (2) of that section.

(2) Where criminal legal aid is made available under paragraph (1) above, the Board shall—

(a) specify that it is available only for such limited purposes as it thinks appropriate in the circumstances;

(b) require the assisted person as soon as practicable to satisfy it that the requirements of section 24 or, as the case may be, section 25 of the Act are met;

(c) in the case of the assisted person not so satisfying it, cease to make criminal legal aid available to him.

Duty to report completion of proceedings

16. It shall be the duty of the solicitor acting for an assisted person to inform the Board of the conclusion and outcome of the proceedings in respect of which criminal legal aid was made available to the assisted person.

Changes of solicitor

17.—(1) Where the solicitor nominated by an assisted person determines that he should cease to act for him, the solicitor shall notify the Board and, where possible, the assisted person accordingly, and shall supply to the Board a statement of his reasons for ceasing to act.

(2) Where an assisted person has required the solicitor nominated by him to cease to act for him, the solicitor shall notify the Board accordingly and shall supply the Board with a statement of the circumstances, so far as they are known to him, in which he was required to cease to act.

(3) Where an assisted person desires that a solicitor other than the solicitor presently nominated by him shall act for him, he shall apply to the Board for authority to nominate another specified solicitor to act for him, and shall inform the Board of the reason for his application; and the Board, if it is satisfied that there is good reason for the application and, in the case of legal aid made available under section 24 or section 25 of the Act, that it is in the interests of justice or, as the case may be, is reasonable, for him to receive or continue to receive criminal legal aid, may grant the application.

Duty of Board to cease to make criminal legal aid available and right to recover sums paid out of the Fund

18.—(1) The Board shall cease to make criminal legal aid available if it is satisfied that the assisted person has wilfully failed to comply with the provisions of these Regulations as to the information to be furnished by him or, in furnishing such information, has knowingly made a false statement or false representation.

(2) Where the Board, in accordance with paragraph (1) above, ceases to make legal aid available–

    (a) the Board shall have the right to recover from the assisted person the amount paid out of the Fund in respect of the fees and outlays of his solicitor and counsel; and

    (b) the solicitor who acted for the assisted person shall have the right to receive from him the difference between the amount payable out of the Fund and the full amount which would be payable to him on a solicitor and client basis in respect of fees and outlays.

New St. Andrew's House, Edinburgh
26th February 1987

Ian Lang
Parliamentary Under Secretary of State,
Scottish Office

EXPLANATORY NOTE

(This note is not part of the Regulations)

These Regulations make provision for the administration of criminal legal aid in Scotland following the coming into force on 1st April 1987 of the main provisions of the Legal Aid (Scotland) Act 1986. In particular, the Regulations take account of the transfer of responsibility for the administration of legal aid from the Law Society of Scotland to the Scottish Legal Aid Board, and of responsibility for granting legal aid in summary criminal proceedings from the courts to the Board. They supersede in relation to applications for criminal legal aid granted on or after 1st April 1987 the Legal Aid (Scotland) (Criminal Proceedings) Regulations 1975, which are revoked, and the Legal Aid (Scotland) (Criminal Proceedings) Scheme 1975.

The Regulations make provision as to–

    (i) what are to be treated as distinct proceedings for purposes of criminal legal aid (regulation 4);

    (ii) the availability of duty solicitors and the circumstances in which criminal legal aid is to be provided only by the duty solicitor (regulation 5);

    (iii) how to apply for criminal legal aid (regulations 6, 8 and 13);

    (iv) the availability of criminal legal aid where other rights and facilities may be available (regulations 7 and 10);

    (v) attendance for interview and supply of information by applicants (regulation 9);

    (vi) notification of decisions by the Scottish Legal Aid Board as to the availability of criminal legal aid for summary proceedings, and applications for review of such decisions (regulations 11 and 12);

    (vii) employment of counsel and expert witnesses (regulation 14);

    (viii) applications in matters of special urgency (regulation 15);

    (ix) the duty of the solicitor to notify the Board of the conclusion and outcome of the proceedings (regulation 16);

    (x) changes of nominated solicitor (regulation 17); and

    (xi) the duty of the Board in certain circumstances to cease to make criminal legal aid available, and its right to recover sums paid out of the Scottish Legal Aid Fund (regulation 18).

STATUTORY INSTRUMENTS

1987 No. 308 (S. 19)

LOCAL GOVERNMENT, SCOTLAND

The Colleges of Education (Allowances to Governors: Prescribed Bodies) (Scotland) Regulations 1987

Made - - - -	*2nd March 1987*
Laid before Parliament	*11th March 1987*
Coming into force -	*1st April 1987*

The Secretary of State, in exercise of the powers conferred on him by section 49(1)(e) of the Local Government (Scotland) Act 1973(**a**) (as read with the definition of "prescribed" in section 235(1) of that Act) and of all other powers enabling him in that behalf, hereby makes the following Regulations:

Citation and commencement

1. These Regulations may be cited as the Colleges of Education (Allowances to Governors: Prescribed Bodies) (Scotland) Regulations 1987 and shall come into force on 1st April 1987.

Prescription of governing bodies of colleges of education

2. The governing bodies of colleges of education, constituted by the Colleges of Education (Scotland) Regulations 1987(**b**), are hereby prescribed for the purposes of sections 45 to 47 of the Local Government (Scotland) Act 1973(**c**).

John J. MacKay
New St. Andrew's House, Edinburgh
2nd March 1987

Parliamentary Under Secretary of State,
Scottish Office

EXPLANATORY NOTE

(This note is not part of the Regulations)

These Regulations prescribe the governing bodies of colleges of education in Scotland as bodies to which the provisions of sections 45 to 47 of the Local Government (Scotland) Act 1973 apply, so that members of the governing bodies will be entitled to the relevant allowances under those sections.

(**a**) 1973 c.65.
(**b**) S.I. 1987/309.
(**c**) Section 45 was amended and section 45A inserted by section 60(1) of the Local Government and Planning (Scotland) Act 1982 (c.43); section 46 was amended by the Local Government, Planning and Land Act 1980 (c.65), section 25(1) and Schedule 34, Part XVI; section 47 was amended by section 25(5) of the said Act of 1980.

STATUTORY INSTRUMENTS

1987 No. 309 (S. 20)

EDUCATION, SCOTLAND

The Colleges of Education (Scotland) Regulations 1987

Made - - - -	*2nd March 1987*
Laid before Parliament	*11th March 1987*
Coming into force	*1st April 1987*

ARRANGEMENT OF REGULATIONS

PART IX

SUPPLEMENTARY, TRANSITIONAL AND REVOCATION

SCHEDULES

The Secretary of State, in exercise of the powers conferred on him by sections 73, 74 and 77 of the Education (Scotland) Act 1980(**a**) and of all other powers enabling him in that behalf, and after consultation, in accordance with section 5(1)(b) of the Teaching Council (Scotland) Act 1965(**b**), with the General Teaching Council for Scotland and with the governing bodies of the colleges of education appearing to him to be concerned regarding the functions in relation to colleges of education assigned to the said Council by these Regulations, hereby makes the following Regulations:

PART I

COMMENCEMENT AND INTERPRETATION

Citation and commencement

1.   These Regulations may be cited as the Colleges of Education (Scotland) Regulations 1987 and shall come into force on 1st April 1987.

Interpretation

2.—(1) In these Regulations, unless the context otherwise requires, the following expressions have the meanings respectively assigned to them:–

"academic board" means an academic board constituted under regulation 32;

"college" means a college of education;

"dissolved college" means a college dissolved by regulation 4;

"governing body" means the governing body of a college;

"governor" means a member of a governing body;

"higher academic staff", in relation to a central institution, means the principal or director, any vice-principal, deputy principal or deputy director, and any person holding a post equivalent to those posts, in the institution;

"principal" means the principal of a college;

"relevant receiving college" means the college to the governing body of which the staff, property, rights, liabilities and obligations of the governing body of a dissolved college are transferred under Part III;

"students' representative council" means the students' representative council in a college, constituted under regulation 33;

(**a**) 1980 c.44; section 77 was amended by the Education (Scotland) Act 1981 (c.58), Schedule 6, paragraph 2.
(**b**) 1965 c.19.

"vice-principal" means a vice-principal of a college.

(2) In these Regulations, unless the context otherwise requires, any reference to a regulation, Part or Schedule is a reference to a regulation or Part of these Regulations or a Schedule to these Regulations.

PART II

ESTABLISHMENT OF COLLEGES OF EDUCATION

Establishment of colleges of education

3.   There are hereby established institutions being colleges of education under the names of Moray House College of Education (Incorporating the Scottish Centre for Physical Education, Movement and Leisure Studies) and Northern College of Education.

PART III

DISSOLUTION OF CERTAIN COLLEGES OF EDUCATION AND TRANSFER OF STAFF AND PROPERTY, ETC.

Dissolution of certain colleges of education

4.   Aberdeen College of Education, Dundee College of Education, Dunfermline College of Physical Education, Edinburgh, and Moray House College of Education shall be dissolved on 1st April 1987.

Application of transfer provisions

5.   The provisions of these Regulations for the transfer of staff of a dissolved college apply to any member of staff who immediately before 1st April 1987 was in whole time or part time employment of the governing body of a dissolved college.

Transfer of staff of dissolved colleges

6.   On 1st April 1987–
   (a) the staff of Aberdeen College of Education and Dundee College of Education shall be transferred to Northern College of Education; and
   (b) the staff of Dunfermline College of Physical Education, Edinburgh, and Moray House College of Education shall be transferred to Moray House College of Education (Incorporating the Scottish Centre for Physical Education, Movement and Leisure Studies).

Savings for training arrangements

7.—(1) Where a member of staff transferred by virtue of regulation 6 is undergoing or is to undergo a course of training or has entered or is about to enter an apprenticeship in accordance with arrangements made by the governing body of a dissolved college, which have not been discharged before 1st April 1987, those arrangements shall continue in force on and after that date as if they had been made by the governing body of the relevant receiving college into whose employment he is so transferred.

(2) Where any such member of staff was immediately before 1st April 1987 undergoing a course of training or undertaking research work these Regulations shall apply–
   (a) if it was part of the arrangements by virtue of which he is undergoing such a course that at the completion of the course he should be transferred to employment different from that in which he was engaged prior to the commencement of the course, as if he was immediately before 1st April 1987 so employed; or

(b) in the absence of any such arrangement, as if he was immediately before 1st April 1987 in the employment in which he was engaged immediately prior to the commencement of such training.

Transfer of property, rights, liabilities and obligations

8.—(1) On 1st April 1987 the whole property, heritable and moveable, and the rights, liabilities and obligations to which the governing body of a dissolved college specified in Column (2) of the following Table (opposite a serial number specified in Column (1) of the Table) was entitled or subject immediately before that day shall, by virtue of this regulation and subject to the provisions of these Regulations, be transferred to, vest in and become the property, rights, liabilities and obligations of the governing body of the relevant receiving college specified in Column (3) of the Table opposite that serial number:-

Table

(1) Serial No.	(2) Dissolved college	(3) Relevant receiving college
1.	Aberdeen College of Education	Northern College of Education
2.	Dundee College of Education	Northern College of Education
3.	Dunfermline College of Physical Education, Edinburgh	Moray House College of Education (Incorporating the Scottish Centre for Physical Education, Movement and Leisure Studies)
4.	Moray House College of Education	Moray House College of Education (Incorporating the Scottish Centre for Physical Education, Movement and Leisure Studies).

(2) Any agreement made, transaction effected or other thing done in connection with a dissolved college by, to or in relation to the governing body of that college which is in force or effective immediately before 1st April 1987 shall have effect on and after that day as if made or done in connection with the relevant receiving college by, to or in relation to the governing body of that college in all respects as if the governing body of the relevant receiving college were the same person in law as the governing body of the dissolved college and accordingly references to the governing body of a dissolved college–

(a) in any agreement whether or not in writing and in any deed, bond, instrument or notice;

(b) in any action or proceeding pending or existing at 1st April 1987 by or against that governing body before any court or other tribunal; and

(c) in any other document whatsoever (other than an enactment) relating to or affecting any property, right, liability or obligation of or relating to that dissolved college which vests by virtue of this regulation in a relevant receiving college,

shall be taken on and after 1st April 1987 as referring to the governing body of the relevant receiving college.

(3) Without prejudice to the generality of paragraphs (1) and (2) above—

(a) the rights, liabilities and obligations transferred and vested by virtue of paragraph (1) of this regulation shall include the rights, liabilities and obligations of the governing body of a dissolved college under any contract of employment in force immediately before 1st April 1987 between them and any member of staff of the dissolved college transferred by virtue of regulation 6;

(b) by virtue of paragraph (2) of this regulation, any such contract of employment shall be modified by substituting for any reference therein to the governing body of the dissolved college a reference to the governing body of the relevant receiving college;

(c) without prejudice to sub-paragraph (b) of this paragraph, for the purposes of any such contract of employment (as it has effect by virtue of paragraphs (1) and (2) of this regulation in relation to the governing body of the relevant receiving college) any period of employment with the governing body of a dissolved college under that contract shall count as employment with the governing body of the relevant receiving college; and

(d) nothing in these Regulations shall have the effect of terminating any such contract of employment or of varying it in any other way.

(4) The governing body of the relevant receiving college may, and shall if so required by the Secretary of State, sell or otherwise dispose of the whole or any part of any heritable property transferred by virtue of paragraph (1) of this regulation on such terms and conditions as may be approved by the Secretary of State and shall pay to the Secretary of State the whole or such part of any proceeds of such sale or disposal as he may require.

(5) Where accommodation in any property of a dissolved college, transferred to and vested in the relevant receiving college by virtue of paragraph (1) of this regulation, is used (or in the case of accommodation not yet in occupation, proposed to be used), otherwise than temporarily, for the purpose of any functions which on and after 1st April 1987 are not dischargeable by the governing body of the relevant receiving college, the user shall subject to paragraph (4) above be entitled to the use of such accommodation for such purposes as were authorised by the governing body of the dissolved college.

Vehicle licences

9. Any excise licence, operators' licence, public service vehicle licence, road service licence, plating certificate or other document issued in respect of any vehicle transferred by regulation 8 shall have effect as if it had been issued to the governing body of the relevant receiving college and any reference to the governing body of the dissolved college from whom the vehicle is transferred in any such licence or certificate or in any registration book or other document issued in respect of such vehicle shall have effect as if it were a reference to the governing body of the relevant receiving college.

PART IV

GOVERNING BODIES OF COLLEGES OF EDUCATION

Constitution and incorporation of governing bodies

10. The governing bodies of Craigie College of Education, Jordanhill College of Education, Moray House College of Education (Incorporating the Scottish Centre for Physical Education, Movement and Leisure Studies), Northern College of Education and St. Andrew's College of Education are hereby constituted as bodies corporate with perpetual succession and a common seal under the following respective names:–

"The Governors of Craigie College of Education";

"The Governors of Jordanhill College of Education";

"The Governors of Moray House College of Education (Incorporating the Scottish Centre for Physical Education, Movement and Leisure Studies)";

"The Governors of Northern College of Education"; and

"The Governors of St. Andrew's College of Education".

General powers of governing bodies

11.—(1) Subject to the provisions of these Regulations, each governing body shall have power in its own name–

(a) to sue and be sued;

(b) to enter into contracts or agreements for the purposes of its functions under these Regulations;

(c) to purchase, acquire, hold and dispose of property, heritable or moveable, for those purposes;

(d) to accept any endowments, whether subject to special conditions or not, for the furtherance of those purposes; and

(e) to invest any monies and funds held by it which are not immediately required to be expended for the said purposes in any investments for the time being authorised by law for the investment of trust funds, and to change any investments held by it into investments of a nature so authorised;

and shall have all other rights, powers and privileges of a body corporate.

(2) Notwithstanding the provisions of the foregoing paragraph, a governing body shall not have power to borrow money except with the consent of the Secretary of State.

Composition of governing bodies

12.—(1) Each governing body shall be composed in the manner prescribed in Schedule 1.

(2) Each governing body shall be entitled at any time to co-opt additional persons to serve as governors for such period, not exceeding two years, as the governing body thinks fit:
Provided that it shall not be competent–

(a) for more than 3 persons to be such governors at any time, in the case of Jordanhill College of Education, Moray House College of Education (Incorporating the Scottish Centre for Physical Education, Movement and Leisure Studies) or Northern College of Education;

(b) for more than 2 persons to be such governors at any time, in the case of Craigie or St Andrew's College of Education.

Period of office of governors

13.—(1) The period of office of the governors first appointed or elected under these Regulations (not being governors to whom regulation 12(2) relates) shall, subject to the provisions of regulation 14, end on 31 March 1991, and the period of office of the governors appointed to succeed these governors shall, subject also to the said provisions, end on 31 March 1995, and so on at intervals of 4 years.

(2) Each governing body shall, on or about 5th January in each year in which the period of office of the governors expires in terms of paragraph (1) above, intimate to each of the bodies or persons referred to in Schedule 1, who are entitled to appoint governors, the number of places for which they are entitled to appoint governors, and each of those bodies or persons shall appoint governors for the period of office of the governors beginning on 1st April in that year before or as soon as possible after that date.

(3) Each governing body shall–

(a) after consultation with the academic staff of the college, make rules for the election of the governors to be elected by the academic staff from among such staff;

(b) after consultation with the non-academic staff of the college, make rules for the election of the governors to be elected by the non-academic staff from among such staff; and

(c) after consultation with the students' representative council, make rules for the election of the governors to be elected by the matriculated students from among such students.

(4) Any rules made by a governing body under paragraph (3) above may, after consultation with the academic staff of the college, with the non-academic staff of the college, or with the students' representative council, whichever is appropriate, be revoked and replaced, or varied, by further rules made by that governing body.

Vacancies among governors

14.—(1) A governor shall be deemed to have vacated his office as governor, and the governing body shall declare his place vacant, in the following circumstances:–

(a) where he intimates in writing his resignation as a governor;

(b) where he ceases to hold an office in respect of which he was qualified for appointment or election to the governing body, provided that he shall be deemed not to have ceased to hold that office if he is at the first opportunity re-appointed or re-elected to it;

(c) where his estate is sequestrated or a bankruptcy order is made against him or he has granted a trust deed for, or entered into an arrangement with, his creditors;

(d) where he becomes unable to carry out his duties as a governor by reason of physical or mental illness;

(e) where he fails without leave of the governing body to attend any meeting of the governing body or of a committee or sub-committee of the governing body for a period of 6 months; or

(f) in the case of a governor who has been elected to be a governor in accordance with rules made under regulation 13(3) or (4), where he ceases to be a member of the academic or non-academic staff or a matriculated student, as the case may be.

(2) Where the place of a governor who has been appointed to the office of governor has been declared vacant under paragraph (1) of this regulation, or where such a governor has died, the governing body shall intimate the vacancy to the body or person referred to in Schedule 1 which is entitled to appoint that governor and that body or person may appoint a governor to fill the vacancy.

(3) Where the place of a governor who has been elected to be a governor in accordance with rules made under regulation 13(3) or (4) has been declared vacant under paragraph (1) of this regulation, or where such a governor has died, or where, in one of the elections held under those rules no person is declared to have been duly elected or the number of the persons declared to have been duly elected is less than the number of places to be filled, the governing body shall hold a further election to fill the vacant place or places.

(4) A governor appointed or elected in terms of paragraph (2) or (3) of this regulation shall hold office until the expiry of the period of office of the governors in terms of regulation 13(1).

Age limit for governors

15. A person who has attained the age of 65 years shall not be eligible for appointment, election or co-option to the office of governor, but a person who attains the said age while he is a governor may continue to be a governor until the expiry of his period of office.

Chairman and vice-chairman

16.—(1) The chairman of each governing body shall be appointed by the Secretary of State from among the governors and shall hold office until the expiry of his period of office as governor:

Provided that if the chairman is deemed to have vacated office as governor under regulation 14 he shall also cease to be chairman.

(2) The principal shall be vice-chairman of the governing body *ex officio*.

(3) In the absence of both the chairman and the vice-chairman the governing body may appoint one of their own number to preside at any meeting.

Business arrangements

17.—(1) The governing body may appoint such committees of its own number as it thinks fit, and may appoint, as additional members of any committee, persons, not being governors, whom it considers specially fitted to assist the work of the committee, and may delegate such of its functions as it considers expedient to any such committee.

(2) The governing body shall hold at least four ordinary meetings in the year, at such times and places as it may determine.

(3) At all meetings of the governing body one-third of the current membership of the governing body shall be a quorum. All questions shall be determined by a majority of the governors present, and the chairman of any meeting shall have both a deliberative vote and a casting vote.

(4) Where any meeting of a governing body is to consider the salary or conditions of service of a particular category of staff, any governor who is within that category shall withdraw from the meeting while such matters are considered, unless invited to remain by virtue of a resolution of the members of the governing body present at the meeting who are not within that category:

Provided that nothing in this paragraph shall require the principal or a vice-principal to withdraw from a meeting.

(5) Where any meeting of a governing body or any committee of it is to consider the salary, conditions of service, appointment, promotion, suspension or dismissal of any member of the staff of the college of education, any governor who is a student of that college shall withdraw from the meeting while such matters are considered, unless invited to remain by

virtue of a resolution of the members of the governing body or committee present at the meeting who are not such students.

(6) All deeds and other writings, sealed by the common seal of the governing body and signed by one governor and an officer of the governing body appointed for the purpose, shall be held to be validly executed on behalf of the governing body.

Standing orders

18. Subject to the provisions of these Regulations, each governing body may make such standing orders as it thinks fit for regulating its proceedings and the proceedings (including the quorum) of its committees and for regulating the exercise of its functions under these Regulations.

Validity of proceedings of governing body

19. No failure or defect in the appointment or co-option of any governor and no vacancy in the office of governor shall prevent the governing body from acting in the execution of these Regulations, nor shall any act or proceeding of the governing body or of any committee appointed by it be invalidated or be illegal by reason of or in consequence of any such vacancy or of any such defect in the appointment or co-option of any one or more governors.

PART V

FUNCTIONS

General

20. Each governing body shall provide, administer and conduct the college of education specified in its name.

Provision of courses

21.—(1) At or in connection with the college of education under its administration and, where appropriate, in co-operation with other colleges of education and other educational institutions and agencies, each governing body shall provide such courses of the following kinds as the Secretary of State may approve or direct to be provided:–

(a) courses leading to the teaching qualifications specified in the Teachers (Education, Training and Registration) (Scotland) Regulations 1967(a);

(b) courses for the further training of teachers;

(c) courses leading to a qualification in youth and community work;

(d) courses for the further training of leaders or workers in youth and community work;

(e) courses leading to a qualification in social work;

(f) courses for the further training of social workers;

(g) special courses suitable for persons who have undertaken or propose to undertake duties outside the United Kingdom which may include teaching in, or the supervision of, schools or colleges;

(h) courses leading to a qualification in the training of the handicapped, a qualification in speech therapy or a qualification relevant to any other profession ancillary to medicine;

(i) courses in leisure and recreation training; and

(j) such other courses of education or training as the college is reasonably able to provide.

(2) The provision of courses may include the arrangement of conferences and the giving of assistance or advice to education authorities or other bodies providing such courses or arranging such conferences.

(a) S.I. 1967/1162, to which there are amendments not relevant to these Regulations.

(3) Each governing body may award diplomas and certificates to students who have successfully completed courses at or in connection with the college under its administration provided that no external body has awarded diplomas and certificates to the student for the successful completion of those courses.

(4) Each governing body shall comply with any direction given by the Secretary of State, after consultation with the governing body, as to the discontinuance of any course of instruction provided in the college under its administration or the number of students of different categories to be admitted to the college in any period.

Research

22.—(1) Each governing body may–
- (a) undertake, or assist any body or person to undertake, any research related to the subjects in which it is entitled to provide courses;
- (b) provide consultancy or similar services to any body or person provided that such services shall be related to the subjects in which it is entitled to provide courses;
- (c) arrange for affiliation of the college to or affiliation to the college of, or enter into arrangements or co-operation with, any educational institution, association or other body for purposes connected with the functions of the governing body;
- (d) raise income from research.

(2) Where a governing body, in exercise of its powers under paragraph (1)(a) or (b) of this regulation, provides a service to any body or person outwith the college, it shall make a charge for the service, and in determining the charge shall, unless satisfied that in the particular circumstances of the case it is inappropriate to do so, seek to recover the cost to the governing body of providing the service.

Land, buildings and facilities

23.—(1) Each governing body shall provide, maintain, furnish and equip such land and buildings as are required for the exercise of its functions.

(2) Each governing body shall provide such facilities as are required for the exercise of its functions and such provision may include facilities for sports, social and recreational purposes, libraries and reading rooms, and residential accommodation and meals for students and members of staff.

(3) Subject to the following paragraphs, governing bodies shall not provide a school.

(4) Until regulations provide otherwise, the governing body of Jordanhill College of Education may continue to provide the school previously provided at that college and any facilities, including meals for staff and pupils, required for the school.

(5) Until regulations provide otherwise, the governing body of Moray House College of Education (Incorporating the Scottish Centre for Physical Education, Movement and Leisure Studies) may continue to provide the nursery school previously provided at Moray House College of Education and any facilities, including meals for staff and pupils, required for the nursery school.

Co-operation

24.—(1) Governing bodies shall where appropriate co-operate with one another and other educational institutions and agencies for the purpose of facilitating the exercise of any of their functions or reducing their expenditure.

(2) Governing bodies may arrange for the discharge of any function of the governing body of one college by the governing body of another college or for the discharge of any function of a governing body by another educational institution or agency.

(3) Two or more governing bodies may arrange for the discharge of any of their functions jointly, and may where appropriate empower a joint committee or sub-committee appointed under this regulation to discharge those functions for them.

(4) Two or more governing bodies may appoint a joint committee or committees to facilitate co-operation or consultation between the governing bodies in relation to the exercise of their functions or any matter of common interest and may empower any such joint committee to appoint sub-committees and delegate functions to them.

(5) A joint committee or sub-committee appointed under this regulation shall consist of members of the governing bodies concerned and such other persons, if any, not exceeding one-third of the members of the committee or sub-committee, as may be arranged.

(6) Expenditure incurred in connection with the work of a joint committee or sub-committee appointed under this regulation shall be shared by agreement among the governing bodies concerned.

PART VI
STAFF

Employment of Staff

25.—(1) Subject to paragraphs (2) to (5) of this regulation, each governing body shall employ a principal and such other full-time and part-time staff as it may require.

(2) Subject to paragraphs (3) to (5) of this regulation–

(a) the governing body of a college shall not appoint any person to a teaching post in that college unless that person is a registered teacher; and

(b) if a person appointed to such a post after 1st September 1986 ceases to be a registered teacher, his appointment shall be terminated by the governing body.

(3) Where a person who is not a registered teacher was appointed to a teaching post before 1st September 1986, his appointment shall not be terminated on the ground that he is not a registered teacher, save as provided in paragraph (4) of this regulation.

(4) Where a person who is not a registered teacher was appointed to a teaching post before 1st September 1986 and since his appointment has become a registered teacher, his appointment shall be terminated by the governing body if he ceases to be a registered teacher.

(5) If the governing body of a college is unable to appoint a registered teacher to a teaching post it may, with the approval of the General Teaching Council for Scotland, appoint a person to such a post who is not a registered teacher, but who, in the opinion of the governing body, possesses sufficient qualifications and experience for the purposes of the instruction to be given in the post.

(6) The governing body of a college shall intimate to the General Teaching Council for Scotland the name of any person appointed to a teaching post in the college who is a registered teacher and the Council shall have the function of notifying to the governing body the removal from the register kept by them in accordance with section 6 of the Teaching Council (Scotland) Act 1965(**a**) of any name so intimated to them.

(7) In paragraphs (2) to (6) of this regulation–

"teaching post" means a post in a college being a post the duties of which include instruction of students; and for the purposes of this definition "student" means a person engaged in a course of training leading to a teaching qualification or a teacher engaged on a course of further training; and

"registered teacher" means–

(a) a person registered other than provisionally in the category of primary or secondary education by the General Teaching Council for Scotland under section 6 of the Teaching Council (Scotland) Act 1965; or

(b) a person employed to teach lecturers from further education colleges if he is registered other than provisionally in the category of primary, secondary or further education by the said Council.

(8) This regulation shall not apply to a person with specialist knowledge where he is to be employed only in imparting that specialist knowledge, such knowledge being other than the theory, methods or practice of teaching, and not in teaching a subject in which it is possible to obtain a Teaching Qualification (Secondary Education) as defined in the Teachers (Education, Training and Registration) (Scotland) Regulations 1967.

(**a**) 1965 c.19.

(9) In the case of St. Andrew's College of Education no person shall be appointed by the governing body to the teaching staff unless he is approved as regards religious belief and character by the Scottish Hierarchy of the Roman Catholic Church.

(10) Each governing body may require any person employed by it whose responsibility includes intromission with its funds to find such caution as it may determine for his duly accounting for his intromissions.

Pensions, Allowances and Gratuities

26.—(1) Subject to the following provisions of this regulation, each governing body may, with the approval of the Secretary of State, pay such sum or sums by way of pension, allowance or gratuity as it thinks fit to any person who has been employed by the governing body on his retirement, through age or permanent incapacity, from such employment in respect of any period of his service in the employment of the governing body.

(2) In paragraph (1) of this regulation "permanent incapacity" means disability of mind or body of such a nature or to such an extent as, in the opinion of the governing body, renders a person permanently incapable of continuing to serve efficiently in its employment.

(3) A pension, allowance or gratuity under this regulation shall not be payable in respect of any period of service which is reckoned for the purpose of any other pension, allowance, gratuity, or like benefit, payable–

    (a) out of any superannuation scheme or fund established by or under any enactment; or

    (b) directly or indirectly out of monies provided by Parliament.

(4) In paragraph (3) of this regulation the reference to "any other pension" does not include a retirement pension under Part II of the Social Security Act 1975(**a**) and the reference to "like benefit" does not include any benefit payable under the Social Security Acts 1975 to 1986.

PART VII

ADMINISTRATION

Powers and duties of the principal: general

27.—(1) The principal shall have under his direct control, and shall be responsible to the governing body for, the whole organisation and discipline of a college.

(2) In the absence of the principal, his powers and duties under these Regulations shall be exercised by the vice-principal, or where there is more than one vice-principal by the vice-principal nominated by the governing body to substitute for the principal in exercising those powers and duties.

Power of principal to suspend member of staff

28. The principal may suspend any member of the staff of the college who is in his opinion guilty of serious misconduct, provided that–

    (a) he shall report the suspension to the chairman of the governing body or, if the chairman is not available, to another governor, within 2 days; and

    (b) the suspension shall not affect the rights of the person suspended to the salary or other emoluments of his post.

Discipline of students

29.—(1) The principal may suspend from attendance at the college any student who is, in his opinion, guilty of serious misconduct.

(**a**) 1975 c.14.

(2) At the time of such suspension or as soon as practicable thereafter the principal shall inform the student in writing of the grounds on which he has been suspended and shall give him an opportunity to reply; and shall thereupon decide whether the student should be reinstated, should continue to be suspended or should be expelled.

(3) Where the principal decides that a student should continue to be suspended, or should be expelled, he shall inform the student in writing and the student may, within 14 days of the principal's decision being so intimated to him, appeal to the governing body.

(4) Where the student so desires, the governing body shall give him the opportunity to appear before them and be heard in relation to the appeal, in person or through a representative, and in the consideration of any such appeal no governor who has been concerned with the suspension of the student under paragraph (1) of this regulation shall act as a member of the governing body.

(5) The decision of the governing body upon an appeal shall be final.

Unsatisfactory progress of students

30. Where in the opinion of the academic board a student is failing to make satisfactory progress, the principal shall warn the student, or shall cause warning to be given to him, that if his progress continues to be unsatisfactory he may be required to leave the college, and if after a reasonable period the academic board is still of the opinion that the student's progress is unsatisfactory, the principal may require the student to leave the college, and the student shall leave forthwith.

Requirement to leave for medical reasons

31.—(1) Where the principal, after consultation with the college medical officer, is of the opinion that a student should discontinue his studies for medical reasons, he may require the student, by notice in writing, to leave the college.

(2) Within a period of 14 days after receiving notice under paragraph (1) of this regulation, the student may appeal in writing against the principal's decision to the governing body.

(3) Where a student has appealed under paragraph (2) of this regulation, the principal may, at his discretion, allow the student to continue attendance at the college pending the decision of the governing body.

(4) Where the student so desires, the governing body shall give him the opportunity to appear before it and be heard in relation to the appeal, in person or through a representative.

(5) The decision of the governing body on an appeal shall be final.

(6) Where a student has been required to withdraw from a college for medical reasons, he may not resume his course of studies at the college until he has satisfied proviso (b) to regulation 5(1) of the Teachers (Education, Training and Registration) (Scotland) Regulations 1967, and where he satisfies that condition the principal shall, after consulting the academic board, decide at what stage in his course he may resume his studies.

Academic Boards

32.—(1) An academic board shall be constituted in each college.

(2) The academic board shall be composed in the manner prescribed in Part I of Schedule 2 and its procedure shall be regulated in the manner prescribed in Part II of that Schedule.

(3) The functions of the academic board shall be to advise the principal in relation to the co-ordination of studies, the maintenance of academic standards and questions falling within the ambit of the responsibilities of the teaching staff of the college.

Students' representative councils

33. Each governing body shall, in consultation with representatives of students attending the college under its administration, and subject to the approval of the Secretary of State, make a scheme for the constitution and the functions of a students' representative council in the college; and the scheme shall also prescribe rules under which the said council shall be entitled to make representations to the governing body.

Reports and returns

34. Each governing body shall make such reports and returns and give such information to the Secretary of State as he may require.

PART VIII

GRANTS

Making of grants

35. Subject to the provisions of this part of these Regulations, the Secretary of State may pay to the governing body of a college–

(a) non-recurrent grants, being grants in aid of its expenditure on the acquisition of lands, or rights therein, and buildings, on the erection, enlargement and improvement of buildings, on the supply of equipment and furnishings, on the provision and laying out of premises, including playing fields and other facilities for social activities and physical recreation; and

(b) recurrent grants, being grants in aid of its expenditure on the administration and maintenance of the college, including the employment of members of staff, and on other purposes connected with such administration and maintenance.

Assessment of grants

36. A grant under this Part of these Regulations shall be of such amount or at such rate and in respect of such period as the Secretary of State may determine.

Conditions of grants

37.—(1) The following conditions shall apply to the payment and acceptance of all grants under this Part of these Regulations:–

(a) the governing body shall furnish such estimates of income and expenditure and shall give such other information to the Secretary of State as he may require;

(b) the accounts shall be audited to the satisfaction of the Secretary of State, and the governing body shall, if the Secretary of State intimates to it that he is not so satisfied, make such arrangements for the audit of its accounts as satisfy him; and

(c) the governing body shall comply with any requirement imposed on it by these Regulations.

(2) The following additional conditions shall apply to the payment and acceptance of non-recurrent grant:–

(a) the governing body shall obtain the sanction of the Secretary of State to the purchase of any land, or rights therein, and buildings proposed to be acquired, and his approval of any building and other works proposed to be undertaken, with the aid of grant; and

(b) where any property which is in the ownership of the governing body, whether or not it was provided with the aid of the grant, is no longer required by the governing body for the purpose for which it was provided, the governing body may with the consent of the Secretary of State, and shall if the Secretary of State so directs, sell or otherwise dispose of the said property, and shall repay to the Secretary of State such part as he may require of any proceeds of the sale or disposal.

(3) The following additional conditions shall apply to the payment and acceptance of recurrent grant:–

(a) the scales of tuition and other fees charged to students attending the college shall be approved by the Secretary of State; and

(b) the governing body in determining the scales of charges to students resident in hostels, the scales of charges for meals, and the scales of charges for other services provided to staff or students under its administration shall have regard to the principle that hostels, facilities for meals and other services should, save in exceptional circumstances, be self-supporting.

Payment of grants

38. A grant under this Part of these Regulations shall be paid by instalments of such amount and at such times as the Secretary of State may determine.

Power to withhold grants

39. The Secretary of State may reduce or withhold a grant if any condition imposed by this Part of these Regulations is not fulfilled.

PART IX

SUPPLEMENTARY, TRANSITIONAL AND REVOCATION

Colleges which continue: rights, obligations, etc.

40.—(1) This regulation shall apply to Craigie College of Education, Jordanhill College of Education and St. Andrew's College of Education.

(2) The governing body constituted by these Regulations of each college to which this regulation applies shall be treated for all purposes as the same legal person as the previously existing governing body of that college, and accordingly, without prejudice to the foregoing generality–

(a) the property, rights, liabilities and obligations of the previously existing governing body (including rights, liabilities and obligations under any contract of employment) shall be the property, rights, liabilities and obligations of the governing body constituted by these Regulations; and

(b) any reference in any deed, any writ relating to court proceedings or any other document to the governing body of the college shall be a reference to the governing body constituted by these Regulations.

(3) In this regulation, a reference to the previously existing governing body is a reference to the governing body which existed immediately before commencement of these Regulations(**a**).

Revocation

41. The Regulations specified in Schedule 3 are hereby revoked.

John J. MacKay
New St. Andrew's House, Edinburgh   Parliamentary Under Secretary of State,
2nd March 1987   Scottish Office

(**a**) The governing bodies were constituted for St. Andrew's College of Education by S.I. 1981/1017 and for all other colleges of education by S.I. 1967/29, the relevant amending instruments being S.I. 1975/640 and 1981/1017.

Regulation 12

SCHEDULE 1

COMPOSITION OF GOVERNING BODIES

CRAIGIE COLLEGE OF EDUCATION

The Governors of Craigie College of Education shall be composed as follows:–

   (1) One person appointed by Strathclyde Regional Council from the members of their education committee;

   (2) One person appointed by the Convention of Scottish Local Authorities from members of education committees of regional and islands councils;

   (3) One person appointed by the Association of Directors of Education in Scotland from their own number;

   (4) One person appointed by the Senate of the University of Strathclyde from their own number;

   (5) The principal and vice-principal of the college;

   (6) Two persons elected by the academic staff of the college from their own number;

   (7) One person elected by the non-academic staff of the college from their own number;

   (8) Two teachers appointed by the General Teaching Council for Scotland of whom–

      (a) one shall be the head teacher of a primary school; and

      (b) one shall be a registered teacher employed in a primary school;

   (9) One person elected by the matriculated students of the college from their own number who is an office bearer in the students' representative council in the college;

   (10) One person appointed by the Education Committee of the General Assembly of the Church of Scotland;

   (11) Three persons appointed by the Secretary of State.

JORDANHILL COLLEGE OF EDUCATION

The Governors of Jordanhill College of Education shall be composed as follows:–

   (1) One person appointed by Strathclyde Regional Council from the members of their education committee;

   (2) One person appointed by the Convention of Scottish Local Authorities from members of education committees of regional and islands councils;

   (3) One person appointed by the Association of Directors of Education in Scotland from their own number;

   (4) One person appointed by the Senate of the University of Glasgow from their own number;

   (5) One person appointed by the governing body of Paisley College of Technology from among the higher academic staff of that institution;

   (6) The principal and vice-principal of the college and the Director of the School of Further Education at the college;

   (7) Three persons elected by the academic staff of the college from their own number;

   (8) One member elected by the non-academic staff of the college from their own number;

   (9) Four teachers appointed by the General Teaching Council for Scotland of whom–

      (a) one shall be the headteacher of a primary school;

      (b) one shall be the headteacher of a secondary school;

      (c) one shall be the principal of a further education college; and

      (d) one shall be a registered teacher appointed without regard to the post in which he or she is employed;

   (10) One person elected by the matriculated students of the college from their own number who is an office bearer in the students' representative council in the college;

   (11) One person appointed by the Education Committee of the General Assembly of the Church of Scotland;

   (12) One person appointed by the Association of Directors of Social Work from their own number;

   (13) One person appointed by the Association of Directors of Education in Scotland being a person who in their opinion is a person of experience in youth and community work;

   (14) Four persons appointed by the Secretary of State.

MORAY HOUSE COLLEGE OF EDUCATION (INCORPORATING THE SCOTTISH CENTRE FOR PHYSICAL EDUCATION, MOVEMENT AND LEISURE STUDIES)

The Governors of Moray House College of Education (incorporating the Scottish Centre for Physical Education, Movement and Leisure Studies) shall be composed as follows:-

(1) One person appointed by Lothian Regional Council from the members of their education committee;

(2) One person appointed by the Convention of Scottish Local Authorities from members of education committees of regional and islands councils;

(3) One person appointed by the Association of Directors of Education in Scotland from their own number;

(4) One person appointed by the Senate of the University of Edinburgh from their own number;

(5) One person appointed by the governing body of Napier College of Commerce and Technology from among the higher academic staff of that institution;

(6) The principal and vice-principal of the college and the Director of the Scottish Centre for Physical Education, Movement and Leisure Studies;

(7) Three persons elected by the academic staff of the college from their own number;

(8) One member elected by the non-academic staff of the college from their own number;

(9) Three teachers appointed by the General Teaching Council for Scotland of whom–

    (a) one shall be the head teacher of a primary school;

    (b) one shall be the head teacher of a secondary school; and

    (c) one shall be a registered teacher appointed without regard to the post in which he or she is employed;

(10) One person elected by the matriculated students of the college from their own number who is an office bearer in the students' representative council in the college;

(11) One person appointed by the Education Committee of the General Assembly of the Church of Scotland;

(12) One person appointed by the Association of Directors of Social Work from their own number;

(13) One person appointed by the Association of Directors of Education in Scotland being a person who in their opinion is a person of experience in youth and community work;

(14) One person appointed by the Association of Directors of Recreation, Leisure and Tourism from their own number;

(15) One medical practitioner appointed by the British Medical Association (Scottish Council);

(16) Four persons appointed by the Secretary of State.

NORTHERN COLLEGE OF EDUCATION

The Governors of Northern College of Education shall be composed as follows:-

(1) One person appointed by Tayside Regional Council from the members of their education committee;

(2) One person appointed by Grampian Regional Council from the members of their education committee;

(3) One person appointed by the Convention of Scottish Local Authorities from members of education committees of regional and islands councils;

(4) One person appointed by the Association of Directors of Education in Scotland from their own number;

(5) One person appointed from their own number by the Senate of–

    (a) the University of St Andrews for the first period of office of governors;

    (b) the University of Aberdeen for the second such period;

    (c) the University of Dundee for the third such period;

    (d) the University of Aberdeen for the fourth such period,

and by one of those Senates in the same sequence for each period of office of governors thereafter;

(6) One person appointed from among the higher academic staff of the institution under its administration by the governing body of -

    (a) Robert Gordon's Institute of Technology for the first period of office of governors;

    (b) Duncan of Jordanstone College of Art for the second such period;

    (c) Robert Gordon's Institute of Technology for the third such period;

    (d) Dundee College of Technology for the fourth such period, and by one of those governing bodies in the same sequence for each period of office of governors thereafter;

(7) The principal and vice-principals of the college;

(8) Three persons elected by the academic staff of the college from their own number;

(9) One person elected by the non-academic staff of the college from their own number;

(10) Three teachers appointed by the General Training Council for Scotland of whom—

    (a) one shall be the head teacher of a primary school;

    (b) one shall be the head teacher of a secondary school; and

    (c) one shall be a registered teacher appointed without regard to the post in which he or she is employed;

(11) One person elected by the matriculated students of the college from their own number who is an office bearer in the students' representative council in the college;

(12) One person appointed by the Education Committee of the General Assembly of the Church of Scotland;

(13) One person appointed by the Association of Directors of Social Work from their own number;

(14) One person appointed by the Association of Directors of Education in Scotland being a person who in their opinion is a person of experience in youth and community work;

(15) Four persons appointed by the Secretary of State.

ST ANDREW'S COLLEGE OF EDUCATION

The Governors of St Andrew's College of Education shall be composed as follows:–

(1) One person appointed by Strathclyde Regional Council from the members of their education committee;

(2) One person appointed by the Convention of Scottish Local Authorities from members of education committees of regional and islands councils;

(3) One person appointed by the Association of Directors of Education in Scotland from their own number;

(4) One person appointed jointly by the Senates of the Universities of Scotland from their own number;

(5) One person appointed by the governing body of Glasgow College of Technology from among the higher academic staff of that institution;

(6) The principal and vice-principal of the college;

(7) Two persons elected by the academic staff of the college from their own number;

(8) One member elected by the non-academic staff at the college from their own number;

(9) Three teachers appointed by the General Teaching Council for Scotland from registered teachers approved as regards their religious belief and character by the Scottish Hierarchy of the Roman Catholic Church who are serving in schools in Scotland, of whom—

    (a) one shall be the head teacher of a primary school;

    (b) one shall be the head teacher of a secondary school; and

    (c) one shall be a registered teacher appointed without regard to the post in which he or she is employed;

(10) One person elected by the matriculated students of the college from their own number who is an office bearer in the students' representative council in the college;

(11) Two persons appointed by the Scottish Hierarchy of the Roman Catholic Church;

(12) Three persons appointed by the Secretary of State, of whom at least one shall be member of the Roman Catholic Church.

Regulation 32

SCHEDULE 2

ACADEMIC BOARDS

PART I

COMPOSITION

1. The academic board of a college of education shall comprise members of the academic staff as follows:–

(1) the principal and all holders of posts in the grades of vice-principal and assistant principal *ex officio*;

(2) such number of holders of promoted posts as the governing body, with agreement of the Secretary of State, considers necessary to reflect the range of activities undertaken by the academic staff;

(3) such number of holders of non-promoted posts as the governing body, with agreement of the Secretary of State, considers appropriate having regard to the size of the board and to the need to ensure an appropriate breadth of specialist expertise.

2. The governing body shall appoint the members of the academic board referred to in paragraph 1(2) and (3) of this Schedule.

3. The principal shall be chairman of the academic board.

PART II

PROCEDURE

4. The procedure of the academic board shall be regulated by a scheme drawn up by the board and approved by the governing body.

5. The said scheme shall include provision for–

(1) the appointment of a vice-chairman;

(2) co-option to the board for specific purposes of persons who are not members of the academic staff;

(3) a minimum number of meetings a year;

(4) the appointment of such committees comprising both members of the board and others as the board thinks necessary; and

(5) such other matters connected with the board's business as the board thinks fit.

SCHEDULE 3   Regulation 41

REGULATIONS REVOKED

The Teachers (Colleges of Education) (Scotland) Regulations 1967(**a**)

The Teachers (Colleges of Education) (Scotland) Amendment Regulations 1972(**b**)

The Teachers (Colleges of Education) (Scotland) Amendment Regulations 1975(**c**)

The Teachers (Colleges of Education) (Scotland) Amendment Regulations 1977(**d**)

The Teachers Colleges of Education (Scotland) Regulations 1981(**e**)

The Teachers (Colleges of Education) (Scotland) Amendment Regulations 1986(**f**)

EXPLANATORY NOTE

(This note is not part of the Regulations)

These Regulations provide for the dissolution of 4 colleges of education in Scotland and the establishment of 2 new colleges of education to take their place. The Regulations also

---

(**a**) S.I. 1967/29.
(**b**) S.I. 1972/1891.
(**c**) S.I. 1975/640.
(**d**) S.I. 1977/634.
(**e**) S.I. 1981/1017.
(**f**) S.I. 1986/1353.

set out the arrangements for colleges of education in Scotland, superseding the Teachers (Colleges of Education) (Scotland) Regulations 1967, the Teachers Colleges of Education (Scotland) Regulations 1981 and various amending instruments.

Part II of the Regulations establishes two new colleges of education, namely Moray House College of Education (Incorporating the Scottish Centre for Physical Education, Movement and Leisure Studies) and Northern College of Education.

Part III dissolves the existing Aberdeen College of Education and Dundee College of Education and provides for transfer of their staff and their property, rights and obligations to the new Northern College of Education. Part III also dissolves the existing Dunfermline College of Physical Education, Edinburgh, and Moray House College of Education and provides for transfer of their staff and their property, rights and obligations to the new Moray House College of Education (Incorporating the Scottish Centre for Physical Education, Movement and Leisure Studies).

Part IV provides for the constitution of governing bodies to administer the 5 colleges of education in Scotland, namely Craigie, Jordanhill, Northern and St. Andrew's Colleges of Education and Moray House College of Education (Incorporating the Scottish Centre for Physical Education, Movement and Leisure Studies). Part IV gives these governing bodies general powers for the purpose of carrying out their functions. It makes provision, together with Schedule 1, for the composition of governing bodies and regarding the appointment or election and tenure of office of governors. It provides also for the procedures of governing bodies.

Part V sets out the functions of governing bodies, namely to administer the college of education, to provide courses of education or training for teachers and others, to undertake or promote research, to provide land, buildings and facilities necessary for these purposes, and to co-operate with other colleges and other educational bodies where appropriate.

Part VI provides for employment of the staff required. It prescribes in particular that staff in teaching posts, who teach students who are training to be teachers or are receiving further training as teachers, must subject to certain exceptions be teachers registered under the Teaching Council (Scotland) Act 1965. This requirement does not apply to staff appointed before 1st September 1986, when this requirement was first introduced by previous regulations, unless they have become registered teachers. Part VI also gives governing bodies, with approval of the Secretary of State, a power to pay pensions, allowances or gratuities to employees who retire through age or ill-health, and who are not already covered by other pension schemes.

Part VII makes various provisions regarding administration of colleges. It provides for the general powers and duties of the principal, for his power to suspend staff, for the discipline of students, and for the cases where students can be required to leave on academic or medical grounds. It provides, together with Schedule 2, for the constitution and functions of an academic board in each college and provides for the setting up of a students' representative council in each college.

Part VIII provides for the payment by the Secretary of State to the governing bodies of colleges of non-recurrent grants in respect of capital expenditure and recurrent grants in respect of the administration and maintenance of colleges, and prescribes the conditions for payment of those grants.

Part IX contains transitional provisions to ensure the transfer of property, rights, liabilities and obligations from the old to the new governing body, in the case of those colleges which are not affected by the provisions for establishment and dissolution of colleges. It revokes the previous regulations superseded by these Regulations.

STATUTORY INSTRUMENTS

1987 No. 310

SUGAR

The Sugar Beet (Research and Education) Order 1987

Made - - - -	*2nd March 1987*
Laid before Parliament	*11th March 1987*
Coming into force	*1st April 1987*

The Minister of Agriculture, Fisheries and Food and the Secretary of State, acting jointly, in exercise of the powers conferred on them by section 68(1) and (2) of the Food Act 1984(a), and of all other powers enabling them in that behalf, after consultation in accordance with subsection (1) of the said section with British Sugar p.l.c. and with such bodies as in their opinion are substantially representative of growers of home-grown beet, and having prepared a programme for carrying out research and education in matters affecting the growing of home-grown beet as required by the said subsection, hereby make the following Order:–

Title, commencement and interpretation

1.—(1) This Order, which extends to England and Wales only, may be cited as the Sugar Beet (Research and Education) Order 1987 and shall come into force on 1st April 1987.

(2) In this Order –

"adjusted beet tonne" has the same meaning as in the inter-professional agreement made on 3rd October 1983, as amended on 30th November 1984, between British Sugar p.l.c. of the one part and the National Farmers' Union of the other part;

"the Company" means British Sugar p.l.c.;

"the Ministers" means the Minister of Agriculture, Fisheries and Food and the Secretary of State acting jointly;

"the year 1987–8" means the year beginning on 1st April 1987.

Programme of research and education for 1987–8

2. The programme of research and education set out in the Schedule to this Order, together with the estimate therein contained of the amount of the expenditure to be incurred in carrying it out, shall be the programme for the year 1987–8.

Assessment of contributions

3. The contributions from the Company, and from every grower of home-grown beet who delivers beet to the Company during the year 1987–8, towards defraying the expenditure to be incurred in carrying out the programme for that year shall be assessed as follows:–

(a) 1984 c.30.

(a) in the case of any grower of home-grown beet the contribution shall be at the rate of 10.0p for every adjusted beet tonne of home-grown beet sold by him for delivery to the Company in that year;

(b) in the case of the Company, the contribution shall be at the rate of 10.0p for every adjusted beet tonne of home-grown beet purchased by the Company in that year.

Collection and recovery of contributions

4.—(1) All contracts made between the Company and any grower for the sale of home-grown beet for delivery to the Company during the year 1987–8 shall provide that the amount of the grower's contribution assessed in accordance with paragraph (a) of article 3 of this Order shall be payable by the grower to the Company out of any sums standing to the credit of that grower in account with the Company and be deducted by the Company from the amount payable to the grower.

(2) The Company shall pay the proceeds, together with the amount of the Company's contribution assessed in accordance with paragraph (b) of article 3 of this Order, to the Ministers on or before 30th April 1988.

(3) The amount of any contribution which has not been paid to the Ministers by the date on which it has become due for payment shall be recoverable by them summarily as a civil debt.

In Witness whereof the Official Seal of the Minister of Agriculture, Fisheries and Food is hereunto affixed on 25th February 1987.

Michael Jopling
Minister of Agriculture, Fisheries and Food

Nicholas Edwards
Secretary of State for Wales

2nd March 1987

SCHEDULE

PART I

PROJECTS OF RESEARCH AND EDUCATION IN MATTERS AFFECTING THE GROWING OF HOME-GROWN BEET TO BE CARRIED OUT BY THE PERSONS OR BODIES DESCRIBED IN RELATION THERETO, AND ESTIMATES OF EXPENDITURE TO BE INCURRED IN CARRYING THEM OUT

A. Research

	£	£	£
1. Variety trials : National Institute of Agricultural Botany, Cambridge		73,982	
2. Agronomy, physiology, nutrition, pest and disease control : Broom's Barn Experimental Station	1,165,562		
Less income from Broom's Barn Experimental Station	132,550		
		1,033,012	
3. Crop husbandry : Norfolk Agricultural Station		89,281	
4. Machinery experiments : Institute of Engineering Research		10,000	
5. Physiology : Rothamsted Experimental Station		42,238	
6. Rhizomania : MAFF Harpenden Laboratory		27,786	
7. Beet Yellows Virus : John Innes Institute		6 637	
8. Soil erosion : MAFF (ADAS), Cambridge		7,012	
			1,289,948

B. Education

British Sugar p.l.c.:

1. Publicity:			
(a) British Sugar Beet Review		30,000	
(b) Film unit		1,150	
(c) Warning schemes		9,200	
			40,350
2. Demonstrations:			
(d) Salaries, programme and equipment		359,533	
(e) Spring demonstration		27,600	
(f) Autumn demonstration		57,500	
(g) Silsoe College/British Sugar Soil Management project		40,250	
			484,883
3. Audit fee			1,092
		c/f	1,816,273

b/f £1,816,273

PART II

GENERAL EXPENSES RELATING TO THE PROGRAMME OF RESEARCH AND EDUCATION

	£	£	£
1. Travelling and subsistence expenses of members and officers of the Sugar Beet Research and Education Committee and its sub-committees			3,675
2. Administrative charges:			
(a) Ministry of Agriculture, Fisheries and Food		19,448	
(b) National Audit Office		1,470	
			20,918
3. Institut International de Recherches Betteravières:			
(a) Subscriptions	9,550		
Less recoverable subscriptions	1,350		
		8,200	
(b) Expenses and visits		12,090	
			20,290
4. Other items:			
(a) Visits		450	
(b) Contingencies		50,000	
			50,450
			1,911,606

EXPLANATORY NOTE

(This note is not part of the Order)

This Order provides for the carrying into effect for the year 1987–8 of the programme, as set out in the Schedule, of research and education in matters affecting the growing of home-grown beet.

It also provides for the assessment of contributions towards the expenditure on this programme and for their collection from British Sugar p.l.c. and growers of sugar beet in England and Wales. The rates of contribution are increased to 10.0p per adjusted beet tonne bought and sold, from the 1986–7 rates of 9.5p.

"Adjusted beet tonne" is defined by reference to the interprofessional agreement of 3rd October 1983, as amended on 30th November 1984, between British Sugar p.l.c. and the National Farmers' Union. A copy of the agreement incorporating the amendments made to it on 30th November 1984 may be inspected during usual office hours at the offices of British Sugar (p.l.c.), Oundle Road, Peterborough PE2 9QU, the National Farmers' Union, Agriculture House, Knightsbridge, London SW1X 7NJ, or the Ministry of Agriculture, Fisheries and Food, Whitehall Place, London SW1A 2HH.

STATUTORY INSTRUMENTS

1987 No. 311

MERCHANT SHIPPING

SAFETY

The Merchant Shipping (Submersible Craft Operations) Regulations 1987

Made - - - -	*26th February 1987*
Laid before Parliament	*11th March 1987*
Coming into force -	*1st October 1987*

The Secretary of State for Transport, in exercise of his powers under sections 16 and 17 of, and Schedule 5 to the Merchant Shipping Act 1974(**a**) and of all other powers enabling him in that behalf, hereby makes the following Regulations:—

Citation, commencement and interpretation

1.— (1) These Regulations may be cited as the Merchant Shipping (Submersible Craft Operations) Regulations 1987 and shall come into force on 1st October 1987.

(2) In these Regulations, unless the context otherwise requires—

"approved doctor" means a doctor approved by the Secretary of State as competent to examine pilots and crew;

"casualty" means—

(a) loss or presumed loss or abandonment of or damage to a submersible craft or supporting apparatus; or

(b) loss of life or serious injury to any person occurring in the course of a submersible operation; or

(c) any incident involving serious danger to the life or health of any person in a submersible craft;

"crew" means the person or persons within the submersible craft required to operate the craft or its equipment;

"diver lock out submersible craft" means a submersible craft a compartment of which allows underwater access for personnel and with a means of controlling the differential pressure between the inside and outside environment;

"Diving Operation Regulations" means the Merchant Shipping (Diving Operations) Regulations 1975(**b**), the Submarine Pipe-lines (Diving Operations) Regulations 1976(**c**), and the Diving Operations at Work Regulations 1981(**d**), and, except for the purposes of regulation 12(2), includes any laws or other regulations of other countries having similar effect in such countries or their territorial waters or other waters under their jurisdiction;

"master" means the person in charge of the parent craft;

(**a**) 1974 c. 43.
(**b**) S.I. 1975/116, amended by S.I. 1981/399.
(**c**) S.I. 1976/923.
(**d**) S.I. 1981/399.

"operations controller" means the person appointed by the owner pursuant to regulation 5(1)(d);

"operations manual" means the manual referred to in regulation 5(1)(h) and Schedule 1;

"parent craft" means any vessel, structure or place from which a submersible craft is launched or recovered or from which it is supported or operated;

"pilot" means the person appointed to command the submersible craft or, in the case of a submersible craft which is an atmospheric diving suit, to operate that diving suit;

"submersible craft" means any description of manned mobile submersible apparatus which is designed to maintain some or all of its occupants at or near atmospheric pressure including free, self-propelled, tethered, towed or bottom contact propelled apparatus and atmospheric diving suits. A diving bell is not a submersible craft for the purposes of these Regulations; a "diving bell" means any compression chamber which is capable of being manned and is used or designed for use under the surface of water in supporting human life being a chamber in which any occupant is or may be subjected to a pressure of more than 300 millibars above atmospheric pressure during normal operation;

"submersible operation" means any operation of a submersible craft and its supporting equipment to which these Regulations apply;

"supporting equipment" means the launching and recovery gear used in connection with a submersible craft;

"United Kingdom ship" means such a ship as defined in section 21(2) of the 1979 Merchant Shipping Act(a).

(3) References in the Regulations to the owner of a submersible craft or supporting equipment, are for the purpose of the application of any provisions of these Regulations in relation to any particular submersible craft or supporting equipment, references to the person who at the relevant time has the management of that submersible craft or supporting equipment.

(4) In these Regulations:—

(a) a reference to a numbered regulation is, unless otherwise stated, a reference to the regulation of that number in these Regulations;

(b) a reference to a numbered schedule is a reference to the schedule of that number of these Regulations.

Application and performance

2.— (1) These Regulations apply to every operation of a submersible craft and its supporting equipment—

(a) which takes place within the United Kingdom or in waters which are adjacent thereto and within the seaward limits of territorial waters, or

(b) wherever it takes place, in which the submersible craft is launched, recovered, operated or supported from, or comprises a United Kingdom ship.

(2) These Regulations do not apply to submersible operations which are not carried on in the course of or in connection with any trade, or business or by any person for hire or reward.

(3) These Regulations do not affect the operation of any Regulations relating to diving operations from diver lock-out submersible craft.

Master of parent craft

3. The master of a parent craft shall—

(a) ensure that no operation or activity which is likely to be a danger to any person engaged in the submersible operation is carried on from or on the parent craft;

(b) before commencing any activity which in his view might affect the safety of the submersible operation, advise the operations controller;

(a) 1979 c. 39. As to the meaning of "citizen of the United Kingdom and Colonies" referred to in section 21(2), *see now* the British Nationality Act 1981 (c. 61), section 51(3).

(c) ensure that the area of the parent craft on or from which any part of the submersible operation is carried out is maintained in a condition suitable and safe for that purpose;

(d) ensure that the operations controller is provided before the submersible operation begins and at adequately frequent intervals during the course of such operation with meteorological and oceanological forecasts for the relevant area;

(e) warn the operations controller of the approach of any vessel which is or might become a hazard to the parent craft or the submersible craft;

(f) take such steps as circumstances may require to warn vessels in the vicinity that a submersible operation is in progress from or near the parent craft;

(g) in the event of a casualty ensure notification by the operations controller to the owner as required under regulation 13.

Owners of submersible craft

4. The owner of a submersible craft shall take all practicable steps to ensure that these Regulations are in all respects complied with by those persons upon whom duties are imposed by these Regulations.

5.— (1) The owner of a submersible craft which is engaged or about to engage in a submersible operation shall make adequate arrangements for the safe conduct of the submersible operation and in particular and without prejudice to the generality of the foregoing shall—

(a) ensure that there is a safe and suitable platform or other area of the parent craft from which the submersible craft can be launched, recovered or supported;

(b) ensure that all plant and equipment necessary for the safe conduct of the submersible operation is available for use;

(c) ensure that there are adequate and effective means of communication and means of recording communications between the submersible craft and the place from which the submersible operation is controlled;

(d) appoint in writing a person to control the submersible operation (in these Regulations called "the operations controller"); such person shall be competent and have adequate knowledge of the techniques to be used in the submersible operation;

(e) appoint in writing to command the submersible craft one or more persons who are qualified under regulation 9 to pilot that submersible craft;

(f) appoint sufficient personnel other than those required by sub-paragraphs (d) and (e) of this paragraph to enable the submersible operation to be carried out in a safe manner;

(g) subject to the provisions of regulation 2(3) require all persons engaged in the submersible operation to obey the instructions of the operations controller;

(h) issue an operations manual relating to the matters specified in this regulation and Schedule 1 for regulating the safety and conduct of all persons engaged in the submersible operation (under his control);

(i) where the submersible operation includes diving operations from a diver lock out submersible craft, ensure that the operations controller is provided with a copy of the diving manual or Rules issued in accordance with the relevant Diving Operation Regulations applicable at that time;

(j) provide the operations controller with an operations log book;

(k) prepare a contingency plan taking into account all rescue services which are readily available and that can be called upon in an emergency, and make copies of that plan available to the operations controller, the master, the pilot and to all the authorities and rescue services necessary for its effective execution;

(l) where the submersible craft is a one-man submersible craft, provide—

(i) a second fully operational submersible craft capable of operating in the maximum depth of water in which the craft is to be located together with a pilot, present at the work site; or

(ii) a second fully operational submersible craft and pilot capable, together with all necessary equipment, of being transported to the work site and being ready to dive within a period of not more than one third of the life support time which would remain on completion of any planned operation of the submersible craft originally taking part in the operation or within 24 hours of the emergency arising whichever is the shorter; or

    (iii) an operational diving team fully mobilised at the work site capable of diving into the depth in which the submersible craft is to operate within a period of 10 hours; or

    (iv) an equivalent proven effective arrangement approved by the Secretary of State available for immediate deployment and capable of effecting a recovery within the time limits prescribed in sub-paragraph (ii) of this paragraph;

(m) inform any harbour or marine traffic control authority whose authority extends to the area where the submersible operation is to take place of the nature and proposed time and location of the submersible operation;

(n) ensure that there are in force in respect of the submersible craft and supporting equipment the safety certificates issued under regulation 5 of the Merchant Shipping (Submersible Construction and Survey) Regulations 1981(**a**);

(o) ensure a list is maintained of all personnel involved in the submersible operation which shall include the following information about each person:—

    (1) his name;

    (2) his address;

    (3) capacity in which he is employed;

    (4) the name, address and relationship of his next of kin.

(2) The owner of a submersible craft shall retain the operations log-book referred to in regulation 5(1)(j) for at least two years after the date of the last entry made therein.

Operations controller

6. Every operations controller shall ensure that the submersible operation for which he has been appointed is being carried out safely and in accordance with the operations manual issued by the owner of the submersible craft pursuant to regulation 5(1)(h).

7.— (1) The operations controller shall not permit the submersible operations to begin unless—

(a) the master has confirmed in the light of his duties under regulation 3 that it is safe to do so;

(b) there is produced to him a valid safety certificate issued by the Secretary of State under the Merchant Shipping (Submersible Craft Construction and Safety) Regulations 1981 in respect of the submersible craft and its supporting equipment;

(c) regulation 5(1)(m) has been complied with;

(d) records show that post-dive checks carried out on the submersible craft and all its associated systems after its last previous dive and that any defects indicated by such checks have been made good and signed for by the person responsible for maintenance of the submersible craft and countersigned by the operations controller;

(e) a pre-dive check on the submersible craft and its associated systems has been carried out within 6 hours of the commencement of the dive by the pilot and the pre-dive check list has been signed by the pilot and countersigned by the operations controller;

(f) he has ensured that the pilot is familiar with the matters referred to in Schedule 1 and has been briefed on and provided with a copy of the emergency procedures laid down in the operational manual;

(g) the pilot and the crew (if any) of the submersible craft have been fully briefed as to their duties and mission;

(h) the wind, sea state, visibility and predicted tidal currents are within the specified limits for safe operation as detailed in the operations manual;

(**a**) S.I. 1981/1098, amended by S.I. 1987/306.

(i) the submersible craft has adequate mid-water control, and the water depth is not greater than the maximum operating depth of the submersible craft;

(j) the pilot and crew have had adequate rest;

(k) the supporting equipment has been checked and is in working order;

(l) a sufficient number of competent persons are present to operate any plant, equipment, or other facilities necessary for the safe conduct of the submersible operation.

(2) The operations controller shall ensure that the communications systems referred to in regulation 5(1)(c) are tested at the earliest possible opportunity in the submersible operation and are in good order.

8. The operations controller shall ensure that an accurate record of the matters specified in Schedule 2 in respect of each dive made by the submersible craft shall be entered in the operations log book referred to in regulation 5(1)(j) and shall countersign the entries after each dive by the submersible craft has been completed.

Qualifications of pilots

9. No person shall be qualified to pilot a submersible craft unless he has—

(a) had previous experience in, and is competent in, the operation of the submersible craft which he is to pilot; or

(b) (i) received adequate theoretical and practical instruction in the operation of that submersible craft under the supervision of a person who is himself qualified under paragraph (a) above to operate that submersible craft; and

(ii) demonstrated his ability to control the submersible craft and shown himself to have the necessary practical and theoretical knowledge of the submersible craft; and

(c) holds a current medical certificate issued not more than 12 months previously by an approved doctor certifying that he is fit to perform the duties of a pilot in that type of submersible craft.

10. Notwithstanding regulation 9(b), a pilot in a one-man submersible craft or atmospheric diving suit while undergoing instruction for the purpose of obtaining the practical experience referred to in regulation 9(b) shall be exempt from the requirements of that paragraph provided that—

(i) the training dives are being carried out in suitable environmental conditions; and

(ii) during the training dives he is continuously under the direct supervision of a person qualified under regulation 9(a) to operate that submersible craft.

Duties of pilot

11. The pilot of a submersible craft shall—

(a) so operate the submersible craft as to ensure its safe operation and the safety of any crew and passengers;

(b) carry out the pre- and post-dive checks described in regulation 7;

(c) be fully conversant with the operational and emergency procedures to be adopted and shall brief any passengers and crew accordingly;

(d) ensure that the submersible craft has an adequate reserve of buoyancy and stability;

(e) keep a pilot's log book, which shall contain his signature and photograph, and enter therein the matters specified in Schedule 3 which entries shall be countersigned after each dive by the operations controller;

(f) retain that pilot's log book for a period not less than 2 years from the date of the last entry made therein.

Crew and passengers

12.— (1) Every member of the crew of, and every passenger in or on a submersible craft, subject to the provisions of regulation 2(3) shall—

(a) obey the orders of the pilot;

(b) observe all safety precautions; and

(c) be conversant with emergency procedures.

(2) Every member of the crew shall unless holding a current medical certificate issued pursuant to the relevant Diving Operations Regulations hold a current medical certificate issued not more than 12 months previously by an approved doctor certifying that he is fit to participate in a submersible operation.

Reports of casualties

13. Where a casualty has occurred the operations controller shall—

(a) in the most expeditious manner practicable immediately inform the owner of the submersible craft when and where it occurred giving him the name of any person killed, lost or injured;

(b) enter in the operations log book the particulars of the casualty as specified in Schedule 4 and sign that entry;

(c) within three days of the casualty deliver a copy of such particulars to the owner of the submersible craft.

14. The owner of a submersible craft shall—

(a) upon being informed of a casualty as soon as reasonably practicable give the Secretary of State such information about the casualty as he may have;

(b) within three days of receiving the copy particulars referred to in regulation 13(c) deliver a copy of those particulars together with his own name and address and the name and address of the pilot of the submersible craft to the Secretary of State;

(c) if it comes to his knowledge that any person has died as a result of the casualty, inform the Secretary of State of the death notwithstanding, if such be the case, that he is required to send a return of the death to the Registrar General of Shipping and Seamen.

Returns of injuries

15.— (1) The owner of a submersible craft shall make a return of every accident, injury or disease (other than an injury already notified under regulation 14) suffered by any person, in connection with or working from the submersible craft who is injured in the course of any submersible operation and by reason of which such person is disabled from work for a continuous period of three days or more.

(2) A return under this regulation—

(a) shall relate to a period of three months ending on the last day of March, June, September or December;

(b) shall be made to the Secretary of State within 10 days after the end of the period to which it relates; and

(c) shall contain particulars of the following—

(i) the registration number, name or other designation of the submersible craft;

(ii) the name and address of the owner of the submersible craft;

(iii) the name of each person who suffered an accident, injury or disease and the name and address of his employer; and

(iv) the date and time of any accident or injury and the date when the symptoms of any disease were first observed;

and a brief description of the accident, injury or disease.

Inquiries and investigations

16. Section 728 of the Merchant Shipping Act 1894(**a**), sections 55 to 58 of the Merchant Shipping Act 1970(**b**), section 27 of the Merchant Shipping Act 1979 and the Merchant Shipping (Formal Investigations) Rules 1985(**c**) shall apply (subject to the modifications set out in Schedule 5 to the Regulations) to casualties to which these Regulations apply when they involve any submersible craft or supporting apparatus which is not a ship, as those sections and Rules apply to casualties involving ships, and as if references in those sections and Rules, in whatever terms, to ships or activities connected therewith included references to submersible craft or supporting apparatus, or activities connected therewith.

17. When a casualty involving submersible craft, or supporting apparatus has been investigated by an Inspector appointed under the provisions referred to in regulation 16, the Secretary of State may cause a report on the incident to be made public at such time and in such manner as he thinks fit.

Offences

18.— (1) A person who contravenes any provision of these Regulations shall be guilty of an offence.

(2) The punishment for an offence created by these Regulations shall be—
  (a) on summary conviction a fine not exceeding £2,000;
  (b) on conviction on indictment imprisonment for a term not exceeding two years, or a fine, or both.

(3) In proceedings for an offence under this regulation it shall be a defence for the accused to prove—

  (a) that he exercised all due diligence to prevent commission of the offence; and
  (b) that the offence was committed without his consent, connivance or default.

Proceedings

19.— (1) In any proceedings for an offence under these Regulations an averment in any process of the fact that anything was done or situated within waters to which the Act applies shall, unless the contrary be proved, be sufficient evidence of the fact as stated in the averment.

(2) Any proceedings for an offence under these Regulations may be taken, and the offence be treated for all incidental purposes as having been commmitted, in any place in the United Kingdom.

(3) These Regulations shall apply to persons, whether or not British subjects, and to companies, whether or not incorporated under the law of any part of the United Kingdom.

Michael Spicer
Signed by authority of   Parliamentary Under Secretary of State,
the Secretary of State   Department of Transport
26th February 1987

(**a**) 1894 c. 60.
(**b**) 1970 c. 36: sections 55 and 56 were amended by section 32 of the Merchant Shipping Act 1979 (c. 39).
(**c**) S.I. 1985/1001.

SCHEDULE 1

MATTERS IN RESPECT OF WHICH WRITTEN PROCEDURES ARE TO BE MADE IN THE OPERATIONS MANUAL

Personnel:

1. Chain of command.

2. Responsibilities, authority and duties.

Operational Planning:

1. Mission planning.

2. Safety planning.

3. Movement and position reporting.

4. Operational environmental limitations.

Operational Procedures:

1. Planned maintenance.

2. Pre and post dive check-lists.

3. Maintenance of pilots, submersible operations, surface and underwater communications logbooks.

4. Pre and post dive briefings.

5. Routine operational procedures.

6. Submersible craft communications procedures.

7. Support craft position.

8. Estimation of stability and reserve of buoyancy.

9. In the case of diver lock-out submersible craft particular aspects relating to diving from it.

Emergency Planning:

1. Problem identification.

2. Status of equipment and support services.

3. Self-help plan.

4. Outside help plan.

5. Diving or other medical services.

Emergency Procedures:

1. Position marking.

2. Initiation responsibilities.

3. Search procedures for lost submersible craft.

4. Recovery of disabled submersible craft.

5. Submersible craft emergency procedures.

Emergency Equipment:

1. Parent craft.

2. Submersible craft.

3. Launch and recovery.

4. Ancillary equipment.

5. Communications.

SCHEDULE 2

Regulation 8

MATTERS IN RESPECT OF WHICH ENTRIES ARE TO BE MADE IN THE SUBMERSIBLE CRAFT OPERATIONS LOGBOOK

(a) the name of the submersible craft owner;

(b) the name or designation of the submersible craft;

(c) the date(s) on which, and the period during which the submersible craft made its dive;

(d) the name or other designation of the parent craft, offshore installation or work site from which the submersible operation is carried on and the location of that craft, offshore installation or work site;

(e) the names of the submersible craft crew, and of any passengers, engaged in the dive and their respective duties;

(f) the times of the main events of the dive;

(g) the maximum depth reached in the course of the dive;

(h) the nature of the submersible operation with a description of the work carried out and problems encountered;

(i) the weather and bottom conditions;

(j) any other factors relevant to the safety or health of the persons engaged in the operation;

(k) particulars of any emergency which occurred during operation and of any action taken;

(l) particulars of any environmental factors affecting the operation;

(m) particulars of any casualty which occurred during the operation.

SCHEDULE 3

Regulation 11(e)

MATTERS IN RESPECT OF WHICH ENTRIES ARE TO BE MADE IN THE SUBMERSIBLE CRAFT PILOT'S LOGBOOK

The following matters shall be entered in the pilot's logbook in respect of each submersible operation in which he takes part:—

(a) the name and address of the submersible craft owner;

(b) the name or designation of the submersible craft;

(c) the date and dive number of the submersible craft;

(d) the name or other designation and the location of the parent craft;

(e) the area of operation and the maximum depth reached;

(f) the time from shutting the submersible craft hatch to opening the hatch on completion of the dive;

(g) the task(s) undertaken by the submersible craft;

(h) details of any diving operations carried out from the submersible craft;

(i) any other factors relevant to the safety or health of the crew or passengers of the submersible craft.

SCHEDULE 4

Regulation 13(b)

PARTICULARS OF A CASUALTY

1. The date and time of the casualty.

2. Where the casualty occurred on board the submersible craft, the place on board the craft where, and the position of the craft when, the casualty occurred.

3. Where the casualty occurred other than on board the submersible craft, the place where, and the position of the craft when, the casualty occurred.

4. A description of the casualty, and of any submersible operation being carried out, and any plant or equipment being used, at the time the casualty occurred.

5. A description of any damage sustained by the submersible craft or any plant or equipment at the time the casualty occurred and the name or other designation and port or place of registry (if any) of any other craft involved.

6. The name of any person killed, lost or injured in the casualty, the name and address of his employer and a description of any injury, including an injury resulting in death, sustained by any person in the casualty.

7. The name and address of any witness to the casualty and the name and address of his employer.

Regulation 16

SCHEDULE 5

MODIFICATION OF ENACTMENTS

The following are the modifications of enactments referred to in regulation 16:—

I. SECTION 728 OF THE MERCHANT SHIPPING ACT 1894

In section 728 the following shall be substituted for paragraph (b)—
  "(b) whether the provisions of the Merchant Shipping (Submersible Craft Operations) Regulations 1986 have been complied with".

II. SECTIONS 55 TO 58 OF THE MERCHANT SHIPPING ACT 1970

(1) Wherever the words "this Act" occurs there shall be substituted "this Act as modified by the Merchant Shipping (Submersible Craft Operations) Regulations 1986".

(2) For section 55 there shall be substituted—
  "(Where any casualty has occurred to which the Merchant Shipping (Submersible Craft Operations) Regulations 1986 apply, the Secretary of State—
  (i) may cause a preliminary inquiry into the casualty to be held by a person appointed for the purpose by the Secretary of State and any person so appointed shall have the powers conferred on an inspector by section 27 of the Merchant Shipping Act 1979;
  (ii) may (whether or not a preliminary inquiry into the casualty has been held) cause a formal investigation into the casualty to be held, if in England, Wales or Northern Ireland, by a Wreck Commissioner and, if in Scotland by the Sheriff.".

(3) In section 56(1) the words "and if any question as to the cancellation or suspension of an officer's certificate is likely to arise, the assistance of not less than two assessors" shall be omitted.

(4) In section 58(1) the words "for the conduct of inquiries under sections 52 and 54 of this Act and" shall be omitted.

III. THE MERCHANT SHIPPING (FORMAL INVESTIGATIONS) RULES 1985

(1) For the words "shipping casualty" and "shipping casualties" wherever they appear there shall be substituted the words "casualty" and "casualties" respectively.

(2) For rule 12 there shall be substituted—
  "12. At the end of the formal investigation the wreck commissioner shall make a report on the case to the Secretary of State including his and the assessor's, or assessors', findings as to the reasons for the casualty or incident or as to any particular matter relating thereto, or as to the conduct or any person implicated therein".

EXPLANATORY NOTE

(This note is not part of the Regulations)

These Regulations relate to the operation of manned submersible craft in United Kingdom waters, or elsewhere when the submersible craft is operated from, or comprises a United Kingdom ship.

The Regulations impose operational safety requirements and provide for the reporting of casualties and other accidents which may occur in the course of such operations.

The Regulations lay duties on the owner of the submersible craft relating to the provision of the necessary equipment and an Operations Manual detailing the procedures to be followed in submersible operations and on the master of the parent craft in ensuring that the operation is carried on from a safe place and in a safe manner.

They provide for the appointment of an Operations Controller to exercise immediate control of the submersible operations, for ensuring the maintenance of log books, and for ensuring that the submersible pilot is familiar with the operational and emergency procedures and is fully briefed as to the mission and on the anticipated environmental conditions during the mission. The Regulations require the submersible craft pilot to be competent to command that particular type of submersible craft and that all the crew hold a current medical certificate. Requirements are laid down as to matters which are to be included in the operations manual and log books.

They introduce requirements relating to casualties involving submersible craft and the powers conferred on the Secretary of State to direct an inspector to investigate such casualties.

STATUTORY INSTRUMENTS

1987 No. 312

CUSTOMS AND EXCISE

The General Betting Duty (Amendment) Regulations 1987

Made - - - -	*3rd March 1987*
Laid before the House of Commons	*6th March 1987*
Coming into force	*29th March 1987*

The Commissioners of Customs and Excise, in exercise of the powers conferred on them by section 12(2) of, and paragraph 2 of Schedule 1 to, the Betting and Gaming Duties Act 1981(**a**) and of all other powers enabling them in that behalf, hereby make the following Regulations:–

1. These Regulations may be cited as the General Betting Duty (Amendment) Regulations 1987 and shall come into force on 29th March 1987.

2.—(1) For regulation 13(2) of the General Betting Duty Regulations 1986(**b**) there shall be substituted the following–

"(2) A return under this regulation shall be made monthly in the form numbered 4 in the Schedule to these Regulations and such return shall be furnished not later than the 15th day following the end of the month to which it relates.".

(2) The form numbered 3 in the Schedule to the General Betting Duty Regulations 1986 shall be omitted.

(3) This regulation does not apply in respect of bets made before 29th March 1987.

King's Beam House, Mark Lane,
London EC3R 7HE
3rd March 1987

Peter Jefferson-Smith
Commissioner of Customs and Excise

(**a**) 1981 c. 63.
(**b**) S.I. 1986/400.

EXPLANATORY NOTE

(This note is not part of the Regulations)

The administration of general betting duty has been centralised by stages at a national Betting Duty Control Centre (BDCC) at Manchester. These regulations enable this programme to be completed by simplifying the accounting procedures for off-course bookmakers.

The Regulations come into force from 29th March 1987 when the current system of weekly returns and payments is replaced by a monthly payment system. From that date Regulation 13(2)(a) of the General Betting Duty Regulations 1986 is revoked.

STATUTORY INSTRUMENTS

1987 No. 313

NORTHERN IRELAND

The General Betting Duty (Northern Ireland) (Amendment) Regulations 1987

Made - - - -	*3rd March 1987*
Laid before the House of Commons	*6th March 1987*
Coming into force	*29th March 1987*

The Commissioners of Customs and Excise, in exercise of the powers conferred on them by sections 24(2) and 72(1) of the Miscellaneous Transferred Excise Duties Act (Northern Ireland) 1972(**a**) and paragraphs 1 and 7 of Schedule 2 to that Act and now vested in them by virtue of Article 4(2) of the Northern Ireland (Modification of Enactments—No. 1) Order 1973(**b**) and of all other powers enabling them in that behalf, hereby make the following Regulations:–

1. These Regulations may be cited as the General Betting Duty (Northern Ireland) (Amendment) Regulations 1987 and shall come into force on 29th March 1987.

2.—(1) For regulation 13(2) of the General Betting Duty Regulations (Northern Ireland) 1986(**c**) there shall be substituted the following–

   "(2) A return under this regulation shall be made monthly in the form numbered 4 in the Schedule to these Regulations and such return shall be furnished not later than the 15th day following the end of the month to which it relates.".

(2) The form numbered 3 in the Schedule to the General Betting Duty Regulations (Northern Ireland) 1986 shall be omitted.

(3) This regulation does not apply in respect of bets made before 29th March 1987.

King's Beam House, Mark Lane,
London EC3R 7HE
3rd March 1987

Peter Jefferson-Smith
Commissioner of Customs and Excise

(**a**) 1972 c. 11 (N.I.).
(**b**) S.I. 1973/2163.
(**c**) S.I. 1986/404.

EXPLANATORY NOTE

(This note is not part of the Regulations)

The administration of general betting duty has been centralised by stages at a national Betting Duty Control Centre (BDCC) at Manchester. These regulations enable this programme to be completed by simplifying the accounting procedures for off-course bookmakers.

The Regulations come into force from 29th March 1987 when the current system of weekly returns and payments is replaced by a monthly payment system. From that date Regulation 13(2)(a) of the General Betting Duty Regulations (Northern Ireland) 1986 is revoked.

1987 No. 314

CUSTOMS AND EXCISE

The Spoilt Beer (Remission and Repayment of Duty) Regulations 1987

Made - - - -	*3rd March 1987*
Laid before Parliament	*11th March 1987*
Coming into force	*1st April 1987*

The Commissioners of Customs and Excise, in exercise of the powers conferred on them by sections 2, 3 and 46 of the Alcoholic Liquor Duties Act 1979(**a**) and of all other powers enabling them in that behalf, hereby make the following Regulations:–

Citation and Commencement

1. These Regulations may be cited as the Spoilt Beer (Remission and Repayment of Duty) Regulations 1987 and shall come into force on 1st April 1987.

Interpretation

2. In these Regulations, unless the context otherwise requires–

"accounting period" means one month or such other period as the Commissioners may in any particular case determine;

"approved" means approved by the Commissioners;

"brewing record" means the record maintained pursuant to regulation 7(1) or, as the case may be, regulation 7(5) of the principal Regulations;

"calculated original gravity" means original gravity calculated in accordance with regulation 14(3) of the principal Regulations;

"diluted" means diluted by the addition of water;

"the principal Regulations" means the Beer Regulations 1985(**b**);

"return of duty" means the return prepared pursuant to regulation 15(1) of the principal Regulations.

Revocation

3. Part VII of and Schedules 3, 4, 5 and 6 to the principal Regulations (Spoilt Beer) are revoked.

Introduction

4. Remission or repayment of duty in respect of beer which has been removed from the entered premises of a brewer for sale and which has become spoilt or otherwise unfit for use, is subject to compliance with the conditions set out in these Regulations.

(**a**) 1979 c.4; section 2 was substituted by the Alcoholic Liquors (Amendment of Enactments Relating to Strength and to Units of Measurement) Order 1979 (S.I. 1979/241), article 6, and was amended by the Finance Act 1981 (c.35), section 11(1) and Schedule 8, paragraph 10; section 3 was amended by the Alcoholic Liquors (Amendment of Enactments Relating to Strength and to Units of Measurement) Order 1979, article 7; and section 46 was amended by the Finance Act 1986 (c.41).
(**b**) S.I. 1985/1627.

Vessels and premises

5.—(1) The brewer for sale shall–

(a) make entry of an area of his premises to be used for the storage of spoilt beer or of other premises approved for that purpose; and

(b) except as the Commissioners otherwise allow, provide and make entry of a container (hereinafter called a "spoilt beer vessel") of a size acceptable to the Commissioners.

(2) The area entered under paragraph (1)(a) above shall be kept free of beer which has been diluted or had any substance added other than as permitted by or under the Alcoholic Liquor Duties Act 1979 and, if this condition is not complied with, there will be no remission or repayment of duty on spoilt beer in the area at that time unless allowed by the proper officer.

(3) Except in the case of cellar tank beer, bottled beer and canned beer, spoilt beer shall be returned to the brewer in the container in which it left the entered premises and shall be kept in that container until it is emptied in accordance with these Regulations.

(4) Remission or repayment of duty shall not be allowed unless the volume of the beer exceeds 3 per cent. of the volume of the container in which it left the entered premises or of the cellar tank to which it was transferred.

Determination of original gravity

6. Except as the Commissioners otherwise allow, the original gravity of spoilt beer shall be determined in accordance with regulation 14 of the principal Regulations.

Destruction

7.—(1) Except as the Commissioners otherwise allow, spoilt beer shall be destroyed in the following manner–

(a) destruction shall take place in the spoilt beer vessel; and

(b) destruction shall be by the addition of 0.3 per cent. by volume of acetic, formic or propionic acid, or by the addition of an approved dye in an approved proportion.

(2) Following destruction spoilt beer shall remain in the spoilt beer vessel in which it was destroyed for at least 2 hours or until inspected by the proper officer, if earlier.

(3) Destruction shall not take place on a Saturday, Sunday or public holiday.

Procedure

8.—(1) Except as the proper officer otherwise allows, the brewer for sale shall, at least 24 hours before emptying spoilt beer from any container, enter in the brewing record the proposed date and time of the beginning of that operation.

(2) Where destruction is to take place in a spoilt beer vessel the brewer for sale shall, before emptying any spoilt beer into the vessel, ensure that it is empty and certify in the brewing record that the vessel is empty.

(3) Except as the proper officer otherwise allows, the brewer for sale shall, at least 24 hours before destroying spoilt beer–

(a) enter the date and time of the proposed destruction in the brewing record; and

(b) notify the proper officer in an approved manner of the date and time of the proposed destruction.

(4) Except as the proper officer otherwise allows, the brewer for sale shall, at least one hour before destroying the spoilt beer–

(a) enter in the brewing record the dry dip of the spoilt beer vessel and the quantity of the spoilt beer;

(b) enter in the brewing record the quantity and type of acid or dye to be used to destroy the spoilt beer;

(c) ensure that the spoilt beer is thoroughly roused;

(d) take a sample for the use of the proper officer, and add an approved substance for the purpose of preservation;

(e) keep the sample until the end of the second accounting period following that in which the beer was destroyed, or until authorised by the proper officer, if earlier; and

(f) determine the original gravity in accordance with regulation 6 above and enter the result in the brewing record when it is known to him.

(5) Within one hour of the completion of destruction the brewer for sale shall enter the date and time of completion in the brewing record.

Claims

9.—(1) The brewer for sale shall make a claim for remission or repayment of duty to the proper officer and, except as the Commissioners otherwise allow, that claim shall contain the particulars set out in the Schedule to these Regulations.

(2) Except as the proper officer otherwise allows, claims shall be made by the end of the accounting period following that in which the spoilt beer was destroyed.

(3) When there is a change in the rate of duty, separate claims shall be made for spoilt beer liable to the old and new rates of duty.

Remission and repayment

10.—(1) Remission or repayment of duty shall not be made unless the claim is authorised by the proper officer.

(2) Except as the proper officer otherwise allows, authorised claims shall be accounted for on the next return of duty.

Records

11.—(1) The brewer for sale shall keep records establishing that duty has been charged or paid on the spoilt beer and the amount of that charge or payment.

(2) The brewer for sale shall retain the records required under paragraph (1) above for at least 2 years from the date of the claim and shall allow the proper officer to inspect, copy and take extracts from them at any reasonable time.

(3) Where the records required under paragraph (1) above are preserved in a form which is not readily legible or which is legible only with the aid of equipment the brewer for sale shall, at the proper officer's request, produce a transcript or other permanently legible reproduction of the records and shall permit the proper officer to retain that reproduction.

King's Beam House,
Mark Lane,
London, EC3R 7HE
3rd March 1987

Peter Jefferson-Smith
Commissioner of Customs and Excise

SCHEDULE

PARTICULARS REQUIRED UNDER REGULATION 9(1)

Particulars in respect of each destruction

(a) the total volume destroyed;

(b) the date and time of the destruction;

(c) the volume destroyed in each spoilt beer vessel;

(d) the original gravity, less 1°, in each spoilt beer vessel or in each other container in which destruction took place;

(e) the rate of duty charged or paid;

(f) the amount of remission or repayment claimed;

(g) the description of the beer returned by each purchaser in respect of which a claim is made;

(h) the name and address of each purchaser;

(i) unless the beer is returned in bottles or cans, the distinguishing marks, numbers and size of each container in which the beer was returned and the quantity in litres returned in each container or tanker;

(j) if the beer is returned in bottles or cans, the total number of bottles or cans returned by each purchaser, the number of bottles or cans according to each size of bottle or can and the total number of litres returned by each purchaser;

(k) where any of the operations mentioned in this paragraph have taken place in the United Kingdom the address of the premises where the beer was brewed, last diluted or last blended, the date or dates on which the beer was brewed, last diluted or last blended and delivered from the entered or approved premises concerned, and the original gravity of the beer as brewed or, in the case of blended or diluted beer, the calculated original gravity of the beer as last blended or diluted.

Additional particulars where beer is imported into the United Kingdom or removed to the United Kingdom from the Isle of Man

(l) a statement that none of the beer was brewed in the United Kingdom, and the name of the country in which it was brewed; or

a statement that the beer has been imported into or removed to the United Kingdom after having been previously exported, removed to the Isle of Man or shipped as stores;

(m) the date and place of importation into or removal to the United Kingdom or (where the beer has been deposited there without payment of duty on importation) the date and place of clearance from warehouse and the name, address and code number of the warehouse;

(n) the particulars of the ship, aircraft or vehicle in which the beer was imported or removed to the United Kingdom;

(o) the volume in litres and original gravity in respect of each container;

(p) the rate and total amount of excise duty charged at importation or removal from warehouse, and the amount of such duty charged on total bulk litres at each original gravity;

(q) in the case of imported beer and where the claimant is the importer the following declaration:–

"I/We ....
(name in block letters)

declare that I have not made nor will I make any other claim in respect of the beer which is the subject of this claim for remission or repayment of excise duty.";

(r) in the case of imported beer and where the claimant is not the importer, the following undertaking:–

"I/We ....
(name in block letters)

hereby undertake to indemnify the Commissioners of Customs and Excise against payment by them of any other claim for repayment or remission of excise duty in respect of the beer which is the subject of this claim.".

Additional particulars where beer has not been delivered to another person

(s) the place in which the beer was stored between its removal from the entered premises of the brewer for sale and the date of the claim together with the description and distinguishing marks of the containers in which it was stored.

EXPLANATORY NOTE

(This note is not part of the Regulations)

The Finance Act 1986 amendment of section 46(2) of the Alcoholic Liquor Duties Act 1979 altered the basis for claiming relief from excise duty on returned beer which has become spoilt or otherwise unfit for use after delivery from brewery premises.

The Regulations specify the conditions to be complied with in claiming relief on the new basis. The regulations come into force on 1 April 1987 and revoke Part VII of, and Schedules 3, 4, 5 and 6 to, the Beer Regulations 1985.

STATUTORY INSTRUMENTS

1987 No. 315

ROAD TRAFFIC

The Motor Vehicles (Type Approval and Approval Marks) (Fees) (Amendment) Regulations 1987

Made - - - -	*2nd March 1987*
Laid before Parliament	*11th March 1987*
Coming into force -	*1st April 1987*

The Secretary of State for Transport, in exercise of the powers conferred by section 50(1) of the Road Traffic Act 1972**(a)**, now vested in him**(b)**, and of the powers conferred by section 56(1) of the Finance Act 1973**(c)** with the consent of the Treasury, and of all other enabling powers, and in relation to the exercise of the powers conferred by section 50(1) of the Road Traffic Act 1972, after consultation with representative organisations in accordance with section 199(2) of that Act, hereby makes the following Regulations:–

1. These Regulations may be cited as the Motor Vehicles (Type Approval and Approval Marks) (Fees) (Amendment) Regulations 1987 and shall come into force on 1st April 1987.

2. The Motor Vehicles (Type Approval and Approval Marks) (Fees) Regulations 1984**(d)** are hereby further amended in accordance with the following provisions of these Regulations.

3. In regulation 4 (Fees—basic scale for examinations of vehicles or parts of vehicles), in paragraph (2) for the words "column 2" there shall be substituted the words "column 1".

4. In regulation 8 (Fees—final examination of complete vehicle), in paragraph (2)(c) for sub-paragraph (ii) there shall be substituted–

" (ii) in column (3)(b) of Schedule 3 if the vehicle is in category N2, and

(iii) in column (3)(c) of Schedule 3 if the vehicle is in category N3.".

5. In regulation 13 (Fees on withdrawals and cancellations), for paragraph (1) there shall be substituted–

"(1) Subject to the provisions of regulation 14, if an applicant:–

(a) after he has been notified of the time and place for the examination withdraws his application, or

(b) does not submit the vehicle or vehicle part for the examination at the time and place fixed therefor,

---

(a) 1972 c.20, amended by section 10 of, and Schedule 2 to, the Road Traffic Act 1974 (c.50).
(b) S.I. 1979/571 and 1981/238.
(c) 1973 c.51.
(d) S.I. 1984/1404, as amended by S.I. 1985/1656.

he shall be liable to pay a cancellation fee to cover the abortive work involved in dealing with the application and making arrangements for the examination:–

  (i) in the case of an examination of a vehicle or vehicle part to which a fee specified in regulation 5 or Schedule 1 applies–

  (A) of £66, if the Secretary of State is notified of the withdrawal or of the intention not to submit the vehicle or vehicle part for the examination not less than 7 days before the date fixed for the examination, or

  (B) in any other case—

    (aa) where the fee is specified in column (a) of Schedule 1, of a quarter of that fee plus any wasted expenses reasonably incurred by the Secretary of State in the provision of any facility for the particular examination, or

    (bb) where the fee is specified in regulation 5 or column (b) of Schedule 1, of half that fee or £150 if that is less;

  (ii) in the case of a further or partial examination of a vehicle or vehicle part in the circumstances described in regulation 7, of such proportion of the fee as the Secretary of State considers to be appropriate;

  (iii) in the case of an examination of a vehicle to which a fee specified in Schedule 2 or Schedule 3 applies–

  (A) of £66, if the Secretary of State is notified of the withdrawal or of the intention not to submit the vehicle for examination not less than 14 days before the date fixed for the examination, or

  (B) of £200 in any other case.".

6. In the regulations listed in column 1 of the table below there shall be substituted for the present fees listed in column 2 in relation to those regulations the new fees listed in column 3 of the table.

1	2	3
Regulation	Present Fee	New Fee
5(a)	£520	£570
5(b)	£530	£580
6(a)	£520 or £530	£570 or £580
11(1)(b)	£27	£30
15(1)(a)(i)	£15	£17
15(1)(a)(ii)	£20	£23
15(2)(b)	£ 4	£ 5
15(3)(b)	£ 4	£ 5

7. For Schedules 1 to 5 there shall be substituted the schedules contained in the Schedule to these Regulations.

Signed by authority of the Secretary of State

Peter Bottomley
Parliamentary Under Secretary of State,
Department of Transport

26th February 1987

We consent to the making of these Regulations to the extent that they are made in exercise of the powers conferred by section 56(1) and (2) of the Finance Act 1973.

Mark Lennox-Boyd
Tony Durant

2nd March 1987　　Two of the Lord's Commissioners of Her Majesty's Treasury

Regulation 7

SCHEDULE

The Schedules substituted for Schedules 1–5 to the Regulations

Regulation 4

"SCHEDULE 1

TABLE OF FEES FOR THE EXAMINATION OF VEHICLES OR PARTS OF VEHICLES

Note. The Community Instruments specified in column 2(b) of this Schedule are listed in Schedule 2 to the Type Approval Regulations and particulars of the dates and Official Journal references of these instruments may be found in that Schedule.

1	2		3	4	
	Approval requirements		Particulars of type of examination, vehicle or vehicle part where not uniform in relation to each approval requirement	Amount of fee for examination	
Fee No	(a) Subject matter	(b) Document in which requirement is specified		(a) £	(b) £
0100G	Headlamps emitting an asymmetrical passing beam or a driving beam or both	Directive 76/761/EEC of 27th July 1976		460	—
		or			
		ECE Regulation 1 as revised on 26th October 1964 and corrected on 8th June 1965			
		or			
		Item 6 in Schedule 1 to the Great Britain Regulations			

1	2	3	4	
	Approval requirements	Particulars of type of examination, vehicle or vehicle part where not uniform in relation to each approval requirement	Amount of fee for examination	
Fee No	(b) Document in which requirement is specified		(a) £	(b) £
(a) Subject matter				
0200N	Incandescent electric filament lamps for head-lamps emitting an asymmetrical passing beam or a driving beam or both — Directive 76/761/EEC of 27th July 1976 / or / Item 6 in Schedule 1 to the Great Britain Regulations		610	—
0300V 0301R	Reflex reflecting devices — Directive 76/757/EEC of 27th July 1976 / or / ECE Regulation 3 of 1st November 1963 / or / Item 8 in Schedule 1 to the Great Britain Regulations	Universal mounting Left and right versions	440 510	— —
0310H 0311E	Reflex reflecting device — ECE Regulation 3 as revised on 20th March 1982 / or / Item 8A in Schedule 1 to the Great Britain Regulations	Universal mounting Left and right versions	450 530	— —
0320W 0321T	Reflex reflecting device — ECE Regulation 3 as revised on 20th March 1982 and amended on 1st July 1985 / or	Universal mounting Left and right versions	450 530	— —

	Item 8A in Schedule 1 to the Great Britain Regulations				
0400B	Devices for the illumination of rear registration plates	Directive 76/760/EEC of 27th July 1976	First examination	410	—
0401Y			Each additional examination at same time	220	—
		or			
		ECE Regulation 4 of 15th April 1964, as amended on 6th May 1974			
0500H	Sealed-beam headlamps emitting a European asymmetrical passing beam or a driving beam or both	ECE Regulation 5 as revised on 29th August 1982	Type SR	420	—
0501E		or	Type SCR	500	—
		Item 6 in Schedule 1 to the Great Britain Regulations			
0600P	Direction indicators	Directive 76/759/EEC of 27th July 1976		410	—
		or			
		ECE Regulation 6 of 22nd May 1967			
		or			
		Item 9 in Schedule 1 to the Great Britain Regulations			
0700W	Lamps-side, rear, stop	Directive 76/758/EEC of 27th July 1976		410	—
		or			
		ECE Regulation 7 of 22nd May 1967, as corrected on 9th February 1971			

1		2	3	4	
		Approval requirements	Particulars of type of examination, vehicle or vehicle part where not uniform in relation to each approval requirement	Amount of fee for examination	
Fee No	(a) Subject matter	(b) Document in which requirement is specified		(a) £	(b) £
		or			
		Item 7 in Schedule 1 to the Great Britain Regulations			
0800C	Headlamps emitting an asymmetrical passing beam or a driving beam or both and equipped with halogen filament lamps (H1, H2 and H3 lamps) and the filament lamps	ECE Regulation 8 as revised on 6th May 1974 and corrected on 2nd May 1977 and 21st June 1978	Type HR	390	—
0801Z			Type HCR	460	—
0802W			Filament lamp	550	—
		or			
		Item 6 in Schedule 1 to the Great Britain Regulations			
1010T	Radio-interference suppression	Directive 72/245/EEC of 20th June 1972	First examination	450	640
1011P			Each additional examination at same time	320	380
		or			
		ECE Regulation 10 as revised on 19th March 1978			
		or			
		Item 2A in Schedule 1 to the Great Britain Regulations			
		or			

		Item 5A in Schedule 1 to the Great Britain Regulations Goods Vehicles		
1111W	Door latches and hinges	Directive 70/387/EEC of 27th July 1970 — Vehicle test to Annex I on M vehicles only	330	240
		or		
		Item 1 in Schedule 1 to the Great Britain Regulations		
1120M	Door latches and hinges	Directive 70/387/EEC of 27th July 1970 — Laboratory and vehicle test on M1 and N1 vehicles, excluding work covered in fee number 1121J below	1,760	510
		or		
1121J		ECE Regulation 11 as revised on 15th March 1981 and corrected on 9th August 1982 — Witness of 30g dynamic test for each deceleration or 30g calculation per door system	200	180
		or		
		Item 1A in Schedule 1 to the Great Britain Regulations		
1200T	Protective steering	Directive 74/297/EEC of 4th June 1974 — Steering control test	2,230	530
1201P		Barrier test	6,550	750
		or		
		ECE Regulation 12 as revised on 20th October 1974		
		or		
		Item 3 in Schedule 1 to the Great Britain Regulations		

1		2	3	4	
		Approval requirements	Particulars of type of examination, vehicle or vehicle part where not uniform in relation to each approval requirement	Amount of fee for examination	
Fee No	(a) Subject matter	(b) Document in which requirement is specified		(a) £	(b) £
1220U	Protective steering	ECE Regulation 12 as revised on 14th November 1982	Steering control test of original equipment wheel by the method of Annex 4	2,230	530
1221Q		or	Steering control test of original equipment wheel by the method of Annex 5	2,230	590
1222M		Item 3A in Schedule 1 to the Great Britain Regulations	Steering control test of non-original equipment wheel by the method of Annex 4	2,230	530
1223J			Steering control test of non-original equipment wheel by the method of Annex 5	2,230	590
1224F			Barrier test	6,550	750
1310M	Brakes	Directive 71/320/EEC of 26th July 1971, as amended by Directive 74/132/EEC of 11th February 1974, Directive 75/524/EEC of 25th July 1975 and Directive 79/489/EEC of 18th April 1979, as corrected on 26th July 1979	Trailers of category 01 not fitted with brakes	290	410
		or	Trailers fitted only with overrun		

Fee number		Description		
1311J		brakes:- compatibility	960	—
1312F		control device	1,400	—
1313C		foundation brake	1,000	—
1320A		Other trailers	3,370	—
		ECE Regulation 13 as revised on 4th January 1979 and amended on 11th August 1981 but excluding the requirements of Annex 13		
		or		
		Items 13A and 13B in Schedule 1 to the Great Britain Regulations		
1330N		M1, M2 and N1 vehicles	2,790	1,800
1331K		M3, N2 and N3 vehicles, excluding those vehicles covered in fee number 1333D below	5,030	2,490
		or		
		Items, 6, 6B and 6C in Schedule 1 to the Great Britain Regulations for Goods Vehicles		
1332G		L5 vehicles	1,570	660
1333D		N3 vehicles heavier than 50 tonnes or having individual axle weights over 11 tonnes	7,060	—
1340B	Brakes	Trailers, except those of category 0L and those fitted with overrun brakes	3,980	—
		ECE Regulation 13 as revised on 4th January 1979 amended on 11th August 1981		
		or		
		Items 13C and 13D in Schedule 1 to the Great Britain Regulations		
1350P		M1, M2 and N1 vehicles	3,420	2,620
		or		
		Items 6A and 6D in Schedule 1 to the Great Britain Regulations for Goods Vehicles		
1351L		M3, N2 and N3 vehicles	5,910	4,560

1	2	3	4	
	Approval requirements	Particulars of type of examination, vehicle or vehicle part where not uniform in relation to each approval requirement	Amount of fee for examination	
Fee No	(b) Document in which requirement is specified		(a) £	(b) £
(a) Subject matter				
1360C Brakes	Annex 13 of ECE Regulation 13 as mentioned above	Anti-lock devices for:– trailers, except those of overrun brakes	1,130	—
1361Z 1362W	or Items 13C and 13D in Schedule 1 to the Great Britain Regulations or Items 6 and 6C in Schedule 1 to the Great Britain Regulations for Goods Vehicles	M1 and N1 vehicles M2, M3, N2 and N3 vehicles	1,110 1,690	990 1,650
1390R Brakes	Item 6E in Schedule 1 to the Great Britain Regulations for Goods Vehicles	Slow vehicles and public works vehicles	670	680
1420G Seat belt anchorages	Directive 76/115/EEC of 18th December 1975 as amended by Directive 81/575/EEC of 20th July 1981 and Directive 82/318/EEC of 2nd April 1982 or ECE Regulation 14 as revised on 28th April 1976, corrected on 4th August 1977, 19th July 1978, September 1979 and amended and corrected on 22nd November 1984 or		4,100	870

1500M	Exhaust emissions (spark ignition)	Item 12A(ii) in Schedule 1 to the Great Britain Regulations		310	280
1531Y	Exhaust emissions (spark ignition)	Item 2A in Schedule 1 to the Great Britain Regulations for Goods Vehicles			
		Directive 70/220/EEC of 20th March 1970, as amended by Directive 74/290/EEC of 28th May 1974, Directive 77/102/EEC of 30th November 1976 and Directive 78/665/EEC of 14th July 1978	Phase I	1,290	640
1532V			Piase II	520	140
1533R			Phase III	520	140
		or			
		ECE Regulation 15 as revised on 6th March 1978 and corrected on 31st October 1978			
		or			
		Item 4B in Schedule 1 to the Great Britain Regulations			
		or			
		Item 2 in Schedule 1 to the Great Britain Regulations for Goods Vehicles			
1541L	Exhaust emissions (spark ignition)	Directive 70/220/EEC of 20th March 1970, as amended by Directive 74/290/EEC of 28th May 1974, Directive 77/102/EEC of 30th November 1976, Directive 78/665/EEC of 14th July 1978 and Directive 83/351/EEC of 16th June 1983	Phase I	1,360	640
1542H			Phase II	610	140
1543E			Phase III	610	140
1544B			Subsequent phases	610	140
		or			

1	2	3	4	
	Approval requirements	Particulars of type of examination, vehicle or vehicle part where not uniform in relation to each approval requirement	Amount of fee for examination	
Fee No	(b) Document in which requirement is specified		(a) £	(b) £
(a) Subject matter				
	ECE Regulation 15 as revised on 20th October 1981, corrected on 9th June 1982 and amended on 1st June 1984			
	or			
	Item 4C in Schedule 1 to the Great Britain Regulations			
	or			
	Item 2 in Schedule 1 to the Great Britain Regulations for Goods Vehicles			
1601Q Seat belts	Directive 77/541/EEC of 28th June 1977, as amended by Directive 81/576/EEC and Directive 82/319/EEC of 2nd April 1982	Examination of installation	230	290
1602M Seat belts	Item 12A(iii) in Schedule 1 to the Great Britain Regulations	Examination of installation on front seats only	210	270
1610G Seat belts	ECE Regulation 16 as revised on 9th December 1979 and corrected on 25th June 1981	Two or three point static belt assembly	1,570	—
1620V	or	Two or three point belt with an emergency locking retractor	1,910	—
1630H	Item 12A(ia) in Schedule 1 to the Great Britain Regulations	Additional test of restraint system	1,270	—

1611D	Seat belts	Directive 77/541/EEC of 28th June 1977, as amended by Directive 81/576/EEC of 20th July 1981 and Directive 82/319/EEC of 2nd April 1982	Two or three point static belt assembly	1,600	—
1621R			Two or three point belt with an emergency locking retractor	1,940	—
1631E			Additional test of restraint system	1,270	—
		or			
		ECE Regulation 16 as revised on 9th December 1979, corrected on 25th June 1981 and amended on 22nd December 1985			
1720B	Seats and anchorages	Directive 74/408/EEC of 22nd July 1974, as amended by Directive 81/577/EEC of 20th July 1981	M1 vehicles – static test of two seats, including up to two seat back moment tests	4,770	480
		or			
1721Y		ECE Regulation 17 as revised on 11th September 1973 and amended on 9th March 1981	M1 vehicles – dynamic test, including up to two seat back moment tests	5,190	480
		or			
1722V		Item 16 in Schedule 1 to the Great Britain Regulations	Inspection of other vehicles in accordance with Annex III of Directive 74/408/EEC	240	240
1800G	Anti-theft devices	Directive 74/61/EEC of 17th December 1973, as corrected on 6th August 1974		640	510
		or			
		ECE Regulation 18 of 14th September 1970			
		or			
		Item 11 in Schedule 1 to the Great Britain Regulations			

1	2 Approval requirements		3 Particulars of type of examination, vehicle or vehicle part where not uniform in relation to each approval requirement	4 Amount of fee for examination	
Fee No	(a) Subject matter	(b) Document in which requirement is specified		(a) £	(b) £
1810D	Anti-theft devices	ECE Regulation 18 of 14th September 1970, as revised on 24th November 1980		970	590
		or			
		Item 11A in Schedule 1 to the Great Britain Regulations			
1900N	Front fog lamps	Directive 76/762/EEC of 27th July 1976		430	—
		or			
		ECE Regulation 19 as revised on 18th December 1974			
2010X	Headlamps emitting an asymmetrical passing beam or a driving beam or both and equipped with halogen filament lamps (H4 lamps) and the filament lamps	ECE Regulation 20 as revised on 15th August 1976	Type HR	420	—
2011U		or	Type HCR	500	—
2012Q		Item 6A in Schedule 1 to the Great Britain Regulations	Type HC	450	—
2013M			Filament lamp	680	—
2100Q	Interior fittings	ECE Regulation 21 of 21st June 1971, as corrected in 1972	Up to 6 impact tests	3,290	1,730
2101M		or	Each additional impact test	390	80

Code	Description	Community Instrument	Test		
	Interior fittings	Item 18 in Schedule 1 to the Great Britain Regulations			
2110D		Directive 74/60/EEC of 17th December 1973, as corrected on 6th August 1974 and 25th February 1977 and amended by Directive 78/632/EEC of 19th May 1978	Up to 6 impact tests Each additional impact test	3,290 390	1,730 80
		or			
		ECE Regulation 21 of 1st March 1971, as revised on 8th October 1980			
		or			
2111A		Item 18A in Schedule 1 to the Great Britain Regulations			
2300D	Reversing lamps	Directive 77/539/EEC of 28th June 1977, as corrected on 10th October 1978		410	—
		or			
		ECE Regulation 23 of 20th August 1971			
2310R	Reversing lamps	ECE Regulation 23 of 20th August 1971, as amended on 22nd March 1977		410	—
2400K	Exhaust emissions (compression ignition)	Item 3B in Schedule 1 to the Great Britain Regulations for Goods Vehicles		240	160
2410Y	Exhaust emissions (compression ignition)	Directive 72/306/EEC of 2nd August 1972, as corrected on 6th August 1974	Vehicle test	2,100	440
		or			

1	2 Approval requirements		3 Particulars of type of examination, vehicle or vehicle part where not uniform in relation to each approval requirement	4 Amount of fee for examination	
Fee No	(a) Subject matter	(b) Document in which requirement is specified		(a) £	(b) £
2411V		ECE Regulation 24 of 23rd August 1971, as corrected on 1st December 1972, amended on 11th September 1973 and corrected on 15th July 1975	Engine test	4,410	500
		or			
2412R		Item 5 in Schedule 1 to the Great Britain Regulations	Engine test concurrent with power measurement to 80/1269/EEC	—	620
		or			
		Item 3 in Schedule 1 to the Great Britain Regulations for Goods Vehicles			
2420L	Exhaust emissions (compression ignition)	ECE Regulation 24 as revised on 11th February 1980 and amended on 15th February 1984	Engine test, concurrent with power measurement on Annex 10 of Regulation 24.02	4,760	750
		or			
2421H		Item 5A in Schedule 1 to the Great Britain Regulations	Vehicle test where engine power has previously been measured to Annex 10 of Regulation 24.02	2,090	420
		or			
2422E		Item 3A in Schedule 1 to the Great Britain Regulations for Goods Vehicles	Measurement of engine power to Annex 10 of Regulation 24.02	4,260	540

2500R	Head restraints	Directive 78/932/EEC of 16th October 1978	Including static moment test	1,470	570
		or			
		ECE Regulation 25 of 30th December 1971			
2510E	Head restraints	ECE Regulation No 25 of 30th December 1971, as amended on 11th August 1981		1,470	570
2610L	External projections	Directive 74/483/EEC of 17th September 1974, as amended by Directive 79/488/EEC of 18th April 1979	Test on separate technical units:–	740	860
2611H			luggage or ski racks	380	200
2612E			radio aerials	200	130
		or			
		ECE Regulation 26 of 28th April 1972, as amended on 11th September 1973			
		or			
		Items 19 and 19A in Schedule 1 to the Great Britain Regulations			
2700E	Advance warning triangles	ECE Regulation 27 of 7th June 1972, as amended on 11th September 1973 and 1st July 1977	Including fluorescent material	900	—
2701B			Excluding fluorescent material	640	—
2710T	Advance warning triangles	ECE Regulation 27 of 7th June 1972, as amended on 11th September 1973, 1st July 1977 and 3rd March 1985		1,020	—
2800L	Audible warning device	Directive 70/388/EEC of 27th July 1970	Laboratory test	2,340	570
		or			

1		2		3	4	
		Approval requirements		Particulars of type of examination, vehicle or vehicle part where not uniform in relation to each approval requirement	Amount of fee for examination	
Fee No	(a) Subject matter	(b) Document in which requirement is specified			(a) £	(b) £
2810Z		ECE Regulation 28 of 31st October 1972, as amended on 7th February 1984		Vehicle test	430	350
3020P	Tyres	ECE Regulation 30 of 1st April 1975, as amended on 25th September 1977, corrected on 21st June 1978 and amended on 15th March 1981			—	380
		or				
		Items 17 and 17A in Schedule 1 to the Great Britain Regulations				
3100V 3101R 3102N	Halogen sealed-beam (H4SB) headlamps emittings an asymmetrical passing beam or driving beam or both	ECE Regulation 31 of 2nd June 1975		Type HSCR Type HSR Type HSC	620 490 550	— — —
		or				
		Item 6 in Schedule 1 to the Great Britain Regulations				
3110H 3111E 3112B	Halogen sealed-beam (HSB) headlamps emitting an asymmetrical passing beam or driving beam or both	ECE Regulation 31 of 2nd June 1975, as amended on 7th February 1983		Type HSCR Type HSR Type HSC	620 490 550	— — —
3200B	Rear end impact	ECE Regulation 32 of 14th July 1975, as corrected on 25th April 1977			5,440	910
3300H	Head on impact	ECE Regulation 33 of 25th July 1975, as corrected on 25th April 1977			5,320	910

3410C	Fire risks	ECE Regulation 34 of 25th July 1975, as amended on 18th January 1979	Excluding Annex 5 test	9,690	1,570
3411Z			Annex 5 test only	—	1,240
3500W	Foot controls	ECE Regulation 35 of 18th September 1975		570	440
3600C	Public service vehicles	ECE Regulation 36 of 12th November 1975	Rigid vehicles	1,960	2,360
3601Z			Articulated vehicles	2,380	2,920
3610Q	Public service vehicles	ECE Regulation 36 of 12th November 1975, as amended on 8th February 1982	Rigid vehicles	1,960	2,360
3611M			Articulated vehicles	2,380	2,920
3700J	Filament lamps	ECE Regulation 37 of 4th October 1977, as corrected on 28th June 1978	Type R2	610	—
3701F			Type H4	680	—
3702C		or	Types H1, H2 and H3	550	—
3703Z			Type P25–2	400	—
3704W		Item 6 and 6A in Schedule 1 to the Great Britain Regulations	Types P25–1, R19, C11, C15, T8/4, W10/5, W10/3, F1, F2 and F3	340	—
3710X	Filament lamps	ECE Regulation 37 of 4th October 1977, as corrected on 28th June 1978 and amended on 29th October 1981	Type R2	610	—
3711U			Types H4	680	—
3712Q			Types H1, H2 and H3	550	—
3713M			Type P25–2	400	—
3714J		or	Types P25–1, R19, C11, C15, T8/4, W10/5, W10/3, F1, F2 and F3	340	—
3715F		Item 6 and 6A in Schedule 1 to the Great Britain Regulations	Types S1 and S2	610	—
3720K	Filament lamps	ECE Regulation 37 as revised on 27th October 1983 and 1st June 1984	Type R2	610	—
3721G			Type H4	680	—
3722D			Types H1, H2 and H3	550	—
3723M			Type P21/5W	400	—
3724X		or	Types P21/W, R5W, R10W, C5W, C21W T4W, W5W, F1, F2 and F3	340	—
		Item 6 and 6A in Schedule 1 to the			

1	2		3	4	
	Approval requirements		Particulars of type of examination, vehicle or vehicle part where not uniform in relation to each approval requirement	Amount of fee for examination	
Fee No	(a) Subject matter	(b) Document in which requirement is specified		(a) £	(b) £
3725U		Great Britain Regulations	Types S1 and S2	610	—
3726Q			Type S3	540	—
3727M			Type P21/4W	410	—
3800Q	Rear fog lamps	Directive 77/538/EEC of 28th June 1977, as corrected on 10th October 1978 or ECE Regulation 38 of 1st August 1978 or Item 21 in Schedule 1 to the Great Britain Regulations		500	—
3900X	Speedometers and reverse gear	Directive 75/443/EEC of 26th June 1975 or ECE Regulation 39 of 20th November 1978 or Item 20 in Schedule 1 to the Great Britain Regulations		420	340

Code	Category	Description	Reference		
4300M	Safety glass	Windscreen toughened	ECE Regulation 43 of 15th February 1981, as amended on 14th October 1982 or	1,110	—
4301J		Windscreen laminated		1,430	—
4302F		Windscreen, treated and laminated		1,490	—
4303C		Windows other than windscreens, toughened		670	—
4304Z		Windows other than windscreens, laminated	Item 15B in Schedule 1 to the Great Britain Regulations	770	—
4305W		Additional test on plastic coated glass		220	—
4306T		Additional test on double-glazed units		280	—
4307P	Safety glass	Conversion of a BSAU 178 approval to ECE Regulation 43		160	—
4308H	Safety glass	Glass manufactured under a licence issued by the British Standards Institution	Item 15 or 15A in Schedule 1 to the Great Britain Regulations	90	—
4400U	Child restraints	Assembly without retractors	ECE Regulation 44 of 1st February 1981	1,300	—
4401Q		Assembly with an automatic locking retractor		1,510	—
4402M		Assembly with an emergency locking retractor		1,570	—
4403J		Children's seat, forward facing		1,400	—
4404F		Children's seat, rearward facing		1,880	—
4410G	Child restraints	Assembly without retractors	ECE Regulation 44 of 1st February 1981, as amended on 17th November 1982	1,300	—
4411D		Assembly with an automatic locking retractor		1,510	—
4412A		Assembly with an emergency locking retractor		1,570	—
4413X		Children's seat, forward facing		1,400	—
4414U		Children's seat, rearward facing		1,880	—
4420V	Child restraints	Assembly without retractors	ECE Regulation 44 of 1st February 1981, as amended on 17th November 1982 and 4th April 1986	1,300	—
4421R		Assembly with an automatic locking retractor		1,510	—

1	2		3	4	
Fee No	Approval requirements		Particulars of type of examination, vehicle or vehicle part where not uniform in relation to each approval requirement	Amount of fee for examination	
(a) Subject matter		(b) Document in which requirement is specified		(a) £	(b) £
4422N			Assembly with an emergency locking retractor	1,570	—
4423K			Children's seat, forward facing	1,400	—
4424G			Children's seat, rearward facing	1,880	—
4425D			Group O—infant restraints	1,460	—
5000X	Motor cycle and moped lighting	ECE Regulation 50 of 1st June 1982, as corrected 14th August 1985	Any single lamp	410	—
5001U			Any two lamps	500	—
5002Q			Any three lamps	610	—
5400Y	Tyres for commercial vehicles	ECE Regulation 54 of 1st March 1983	Examination of a test report and initial documentation from authorised laboratory for issue of initial certificate	140	—
5401V			Examination of documents submitted at the same time as initial documentation for issue of subsequent certificates	70	—
5402R			Test conducted at non-authorised laboratory	—	1,990
6400C	Temporary-use spare wheels/tyres	ECE Regulation 64 of 1st October 1985		730	300
7100M	Multi-function lamp assemblies	ECE Regulation 6, 7 and 23, as mentioned above	Any two of the lamps listed at fee numbers 0600P, 0700W, 2300D and 2310R	540	—
7101J			Any three of the lamps listed at fee numbers 0600P, 0700W, 2300D and 2310R	640	—
7102F		or	Any four of the lamps listed at fee numbers 0600P, 0700W, 2300D and 2310R	720	—
		Items 7 and 9 in Schedule 1 to the Great Britain Regulations			

Code	Item	Reference	Detail		
7200U	Recording equipment for road transport vehicles	Community Regulation 1463/70 of 20th July 1970, as amended by Community Regulation 1787/73 of 25th June 1973, Community Regulation 2828/77 of 12th December 1977 and Community Regulation 3821/85 of 20th December 1985	Instrument and chart	2,330	—
7201Q			Chart only, instrument supplied by applicant	850	—
7310N	Sound levels	Item 14B in Schedule 1 to the Great Britain Regulations	Drive by:— M1 or N1 vehicles	670	420
7311K		or	other vehicles	950	520
7312G		Items 4B, 4C and 4D in Schedule 1 to the Great Britain Regulations for Goods Vehicles	Exhaust system conditioning procedure:— on engine test bed	240	350
7313S			on track or road, vehicle driven by driver supplied by applicant	240	280
7320B	Sound levels	Directive 70/157/EEC of 6th February 1970, as amended by Directive 73/350/EEC of 7th November 1973, Directive 77/212/EEC of 8th March 1977 and Directive 81/334/EEC of 13th April 1981	Drive by:— M1 or N1 vehicles	950	460
7321Y			other vehicles	1,260	570
		Item 14C in Schedule 1 to the Great Britain Regulations	Exhaust system conditioning procedure:—		
		or			
7322V		Items 4B, 4C and 4D in Schedule 1 to the Great Britain Regulations for Goods Vehicles	on engine test bed	240	350
7323R			on track or road vehicle driven by driver supplied by appellant	240	280
7324N			pulsation method	790	270
7325K			Replacement silencers	1,000	530

1 Fee No	1 (a) Subject matter	2 Approval requirements (b) Document in which requirement is specified	3 Particulars of type of examination, vehicle or vehicle part where not uniform in relation to each approval requirement	4 Amount of fee for examination (a) £	4 (b) £
7330P	Sound levels	Directive 70/157 EEC of 6th February 1970, as amended by Directive 73/350/EEC of 7th November 1973, Directive 77/212/EEC of 8th March 1977, Directive 81/334/EEC of 13th April 1981 and Directive 84/372/EEC of 3rd July 1984	Drive by:— M1 or N1 vehicles	950	460
7331L			other vehicles	1,260	570
			Exhaust system conditioning procedure		
7332H			on engine test bed	240	350
7333E			on track or road vehicle driven by driver supplied by applicant	240	280
7334B		or	pulsation method	790	270
7335Y		Item 14C in Schedule 1 to the Great Britain Regulations	Replacement silencers	1,000	530
		or			
		Items 4B, 4C and 4D in Schedule 1 to the Great Britain Regulations for Goods Vehicles			
7340C	Sound levels	Directive 70/157/EEC of 6th February 1970, as amended by Directive 73/350/EEC of 7th November 1973, Directive 77/212/EEC of 8th March 1977, Directive 81/334/EEC of 13th April 1981, Directive 84/372/EEC of 3rd July 1984 and Directive 84/424/EEC of 3rd September 1984	Drive by:— M1 or N1 vehicles	950	460
7341Z			other vehicles	1,260	570
		or	Exhaust system conditioning procedure:—		

Code	Directive	Description		
7342W	Item 14D in Schedule 1 to the Great Britain Regulations	on engine test bed	240	350
7343T		on track or road vehicle driven by driver supplied by applicant pulsation method	240	280
7344T	or		790	270
7345L	Items 4B, 4C and 4D in Schedule 1 to the Great Britain Regulations for Goods Vehicles	Replacement silencers	1,000	530
7400G	Fuel tanks	Directive 70/221/EEC of 20th March 1970, as amended by Directive 79/490/EEC of 18th April 1979, corrected on 26th July 1979 and as amended by Directive 81/333/EEC of 13th April 1981	M1 or N1 vehicles	1,070	470
7401D			Other vehicles	1,540	430
7500N	Rear protective devices	Directive 70/221/EEC of 20th March 1970, as amended by Directive 79/490/EEC of 18th April 1979, corrected on 26th July 1979 and as amended by Directive 81/333/EEC of 13th April 1981	Inspection of M1, M2, M3, N1, O1 and O2 vehicles	240	260
7501K			Installation of separate technical unit	240	220
7502G			Force test on separate technical unit or on N2, N3, O3 and O4 vehicles	630	470
7503D			Separate technical unit on N2, N3, O3 and O4 vehicles, by calculation	460	430
7600V	Space for mounting and fitting of rear registration plates	Directive 70/222/EEC of 20th March 1970		320	300
7700B	Steering equipment	Directive 70/311/EEC of 8th June 1970	Without power steering	690	520
7701Y			With power steering	890	640
7820J	Rear-view mirrors	Directive 71/127/EEC of 1st March 1971, as amended by Directive 79/795/EEC of 20th July 1979	Component test	—	410
7821F		or	Component test on single mirror of moderate dimensions and simple mounting system involving two impact tests	440	—

1			2	3	4	
Fee No	(a) Subject matter	(b) Document in which requirement is specified	Approval requirements	Particulars of type of examination, vehicle or vehicle part where not uniform in relation to each approval requirement	Amount of fee for examination	
					(a) £	(b) £
7822C				Component test on single mirror of large dimensions or complex mounting system involving two impact tests	550	—
		Item 10 and 10A in Schedule 1 to the Great Britain Regulations		Installation test:—		
7830X				2 mirrors	1,150	440
7831U				3 mirrors	1,480	520
7840K	Rear-view mirrors	Directive 71/127/EEC of 1st March 1971, as amended by Directive 79/795/EEC of 20th July 1979 and Directive 85/205/EEC of 18th February 1985		Component test	—	410
7841E				Component test on single mirror moderate dimensions and simple mounting system, involving two impact tests	440	—
7842D		or Item 10B in Schedule 1 to the Great Britain Regulations		Component test on single mirror of large dimensions or complex mounting system, involving two impact tests	550	—
				Installation test:—		
7843A				—1 mirror	1,150	420
7844X				—2 mirrors	1,150	440
7845W				—3 mirrors	1,480	520
7846Q				—4 mirrors	2,000	670
7910C	Statutory plates	Directive 76/114/EEC of 18th December 1975, as corrected on 4th March 1976 and amended by Directive 78/507/EEC of 19th May 1978			290	300

Item	Description	Reference			
8030Z 8032T	Installation of lighting and light signalling devices	Directive 76/756/EEC of 27th July 1976, as amended by Directive 80/233/EEC of 21st November 1979, Directive 82/244/EEC of 17th March 1982, Directive 83/276/EEC of 26th May 1983 and Directive 84/8/EEC of 14th December 1983	M category vehicles N category vehicles	1,190 1,190	920 1,280
		or			
8034L 8036E		ECE Regulations 48 of 1st January 1982	Vehicles with retractable headlamps Trailers	1,360 640	1,070 340
8090C	Installation of lighting and signalling equipment	Item 24 in Schedule 1 to the Great Britain Regulations		1,070	590
8091Z	Installation of lighting and signalling equipment	Item 24A in Schedule 1 to the Great Britain Regulations		990	590
8100R	Towing hooks	Directive 77/389/EEC of 17th May 1977		1,090	380
8200Y 8201V	Parking lamps	Directive 77/540/EEC of 28th June 1977, as corrected in 10th October 1978	Single function Two functions	420 510	— —
8300E	Forward field of vision	Directive 77/649/EEC of 27th September 1977, as corrected on 6th June 1978 and amended by Directive 81/643/EEC of 29th July 1981		1,180	630
8400L	Identification of controls, tell-tales and indicators	Directive 78/316/EEC of 21st December 1977		310	300
8500T	Defrosting and demisting systems	Directive 78/317/EEC of 21st December 1977, as corrected on 19th July 1978		3,200	1,400
		or			

1 Fee No	1 (a) Subject matter	2 Approval requirements (b) Document in which requirement is specified	3 Particulars of type of examination, vehicle or vehicle part where not uniform in relation to each approval requirement	4 Amount of fee for examination (a) £	4 (b) £
		Item 23 in Schedule 1 to the Great Britain Regulations			
8600Z	Wiper and washer systems	Directive 78/318/EEC of 21st December 1977, as corrected on 19th July 1978	Vehicle test of wiper/washer system	5,100	1,480
8601W			Vehicle test of wiper system with approved washer system	820	750
8602T		or	Washer system as a separate technical unit	2,270	750
		Item 22 in Schedule 1 to the Great Britain Regulations			
8700F	Heating systems	Directive 78/548/EEC of 12th June 1978	Vehicles fitted with a system for heating the passenger compartment using heat from the engine cooling fluid	210	220
8701C			Vehicles fitted with a system for using heat from the exhaust gases or the engine cooling air	830	910
8800M	Wheel guards	Directive 78/549/EEC of 12th June 1978		280	320
9100W	Rear-view mirrors for motorcycles	Directive 80/780/EEC 22nd July 1980	Component test	—	410
9200C	Fuel consumption	Directive 80/1268/EEC 16th December 1980		1,260	660
		or			
		Annex 9 to ECE Regulation No. 15 as revised on 20th October 1981			

9300J	Engine power	Directive 80/1269/EEC of 16th December 1980		780	750
9390B	Power to weight ratio	Item I in Schedule 1 to the Great Britain Regulations for Goods Vehicles	Vehicles whose power to weight ratio is less than 6 kilowatts per tonne	190	130
9391Y			Vehicles whose power to weight ratio is 6 kilowatts per tonne or more	150	110
9392V	Power to weight ratio	Item 1A in Schedule 1 to the Great Britain Regulations for Goods Vehicles	Vehicles whose power to weight ratio is less than 6 kilowatts per tonne	220	140
9393R			Vehicles whose power to weight ratio is 6 kilowatts per tonne or more	190	130

SCHEDULE 2

Regulation 8(1)

FEES FOR THE FINAL EXAMINATION OF A COMPLETE VEHICLE TO WHICH THE GREAT BRITAIN REGULATIONS APPLY WITH A VIEW TO THE ISSUE OF CERTAIN DOCUMENTS

(1) Fee No.	(2) Description of examination	(3) Amount of fee for examination £
1	Complete examination of a type vehicle with a view to the issue of a type approval certificate	660
2	Complete examination of a vehicle with a view to the issue of a Minister's approval certificate under section 47(8)	615
3	Complete examination of a vehicle with a view to the issue of a Minister's approval certificate under section 47(11)	440

SCHEDULE 3

Regulation 8(2)

FEES FOR THE FINAL EXAMINATION OF A COMPLETE VEHICLE TO WHICH THE GREAT BRITAIN REGULATIONS FOR GOODS VEHICLES APPLY WITH A VIEW TO THE ISSUE OF CERTAIN DOCUMENTS

(1) Fee No.	(2) Description of examination	(3) Amount of fee for examination		
		(a) Vehicles of category L2, L5 or N1 £	(b) Vehicles of category N2 £	(c) Vehicles of category N3 £
1	Complete examination of a type vehicle consisting of 50 or less variants with a view to the issue of a type approval certificate	525	955	1,020
2	Complete examination of a type vehicle consisting of more than 50 variants with a view to the issue of a type approval certificate	540	1,000	1,070
3	Complete examination of a vehicle with a view to the issue of a Minister's approval certificate under section 47(8)	540	920	980
4	Complete examination of a vehicle with a view to the issue of a Minister's approval certificate under section 47(11)	490	785	910

SCHEDULE 4

Regulation 10(1)

FEES FOR THE ISSUE OF DOCUMENTS IN RESPECT OF VEHICLE PARTS

(1) Fee No.	(2) Description of document	(3) Amount of fee for document £
	A. Documents for the purposes of a Community Instrument or ECE Regulation	
1	EEC or ECE type approval certificate	40
2	EEC or ECE type approval certificate modifying an EEC or ECE type approval certificate	70
	B. Documents for the purposes of the national type approval scheme	
3	Type approval certificate	40
4	Type approval certficate modifying a type approval certificate	70
5	Minister's approval certificate under section 47(8)	40
6	Minister's approval certificate modifying a Minister's approval certificate	70
	C. Duplicate certificates	
7	Duplicate type approval, Minister's approval, EEC or ECE type approval certificate or duplicate certificate of conformity	20

NB Where both EEC and ECE certificates are issued concurrently in respect of the same vehicle part, the total fee for the two certificates shall be one and a half times Nos 1 or 2 above, as appropriate.

SCHEDULE 5   Regulation 10(2) and (3)

FEES FOR THE ISSUE OF DOCUMENTS IN RESPECT OF VEHICLES

PART I

VEHICLES TO WHICH THE GREAT BRITAIN REGULATIONS APPLY

(1) Fee No.	*(2)* Description of document	*(3)* Amount of fee for document £
	A. TYPE APPROVAL CERTIFICATES	
1	Type approval certificate in respect of a type vehicle	370
2	Type approval certificate in respect of a type vehicle issued in replacement of one or more Minister's approval certificates	60
3	Type approval certificate modifying a type approval certificate issued in respect of a type vehicle	80
4	Duplicate type approval certificate	20
5	Updated type approval certificate in respect of a type vehicle	175
	B. MINISTER'S APPROVAL CERTIFICATES	
6	Minister's approval certificate under section 47(8) when issued after a complete examination of a vehicle	290
7	Minister's approval certificate under section 47(8) when issued after a partial examination of a vehicle	80
8	Minister's approval certificate under section 47(11) in respect of a vehicle	0.60
9	Duplicate Minister's approval certificate	20
10	Updated Minister's approval certificate in respect of a vehicle	130
	C. CERTIFICATES OF CONFORMITY	
11	Duplicate certificate of conformity	20

PART II

VEHICLE TO WHICH THE GREAT BRITAIN REGULATIONS FOR GOODS VEHICLES APPLY

(1) Fee No.	(2) Description of document	(3) Amount of fee for examination	
		(a) Vehicles of category L2, L5 or N1 £	(b) Vehicles of category N2 or N3 £
	A. TYPE APPROVAL CERTIFICATES		
1	Type approval certificate in respect of a type vehicle	150	180
2	Type approval certificate in respect of a type vehicle issued in replacement of one or more Minister's approval certificate	70	70
3	Further type approval certificate in respect of a vehicle issued under section 47(9)	25	25
4	Type approval certificate modifying a type approval certificate issued in respect of a type vehicle	45	45
5	Duplicate type approval certificate	20	20
6	Updated type approval certificate in respect of a type vehicle	110	110
	B. MINISTER'S APPROVAL CERTIFICATES		
7	Minister's approval certificate under section 47(8) when issued after a complete examination of a vehicle	90	115
8	Minister's approval certificate under section 47(8) when issued after a partial examination of a vehicle	35	35
9	Minister's approval certificate under section 47(11) in respect of a vehicle	0.90	0.90
10	Duplicate Minister's approval certificate	20	20
11	Updated Minister's approval certificate in respect of a vehicle	90	115
	C. CERTIFICATE OF CONFORMITY		
12	Duplicate certificate of conformity	20	20

"

EXPLANATORY NOTE

(This note is not part of the Regulations)

1. These Regulations further amend the Motor Vehicles (Type Approval and Approval Marks) (Fees) Regulations 1984 in the following ways—
    (a) regulation 3 corrects an error in regulation 4(2) of the principal Regulations;
    (b) regulation 4 amends regulation 8(2)(c)(ii) so as to distinguish between fees applied to vehicles in category N2 and those in category N3;
    (c) regulation 5 amends regulation 13 and restructures the fees payable on withdrawals and cancellations. The new structure prescribes a cancellation fee of £66—
       (i) if the Secretary of State is notified not less than 7 days before the date fixed for the examination of the withdrawal or of the intention not to submit a vehicle or vehicle part for an examination in relation to which a fee in regulation 5 or Schedule 1 applies, or
       (ii) if the Secretary of State is so notified not less than 14 days before the date fixed for the final examination of a vehicle in relation to which a fee in Schedule 2 or Schedule 3 applies.
    The cancellation fees in other cases are—
       (A) where the examination fee is specified in column (a) of Schedule 1, a quarter of that fee plus any wasted expenses incurred by the Secretary of State;
       (B) where the examination fee is specified in regulation 5 or column (b) of Schedule 1, a half of that fee or £150 if less;
       (C) where the examination fee is specified in Schedule 2 or 3, £200; and
       (D) where a partial examination under regulation 7 is involved, such proportion of the fee as the Secretary of State considers to be appropriate;
    (d) regulation 6 amends regulations 5, 6, 11 and 15 and increases the fees payable for certain examinations, towards certain expenses, and when particulars and notifications are sent to the Secretary of State; and
    (e) regulation 7 substitutes new Schedules for Schedules 1 to 5 to the principal Regulations. Almost 75% of the fees are increased by varying amounts, almost equally in the ranges of 0–20% and 20–50% but with a small number increasing by amounts greater than 50%. A small number of fees remain unchanged or are new fees. The remaining fees are decreased by varying amounts, mostly in the range of 0–20%.

2. Copies of the ECE Regulations and EEC Directives referred to in these Regulations may be obtained from Her Majesty's Stationery Office.

1987 No. 316

SOCIAL SECURITY

The Social Security (Earnings Factor) Amendment Regulations 1987

Made - - - -	*3rd March 1987*
Laid before Parliament	*6th March 1987*
Coming into force	*29th March 1987*

The Secretary of State for Social Services, in exercise of the powers conferred upon him by section 13(5) and (5A) of and Schedule 20 to the Social Security Act 1975(a) and section 6(5A) of the Social Security Pensions Act 1975(b), and of all other powers enabling him in that behalf, after agreement by the Social Security Advisory Committee that proposals to make these regulations should not be referred to it(c), hereby makes the following regulations:

Citation and commencement

1. These regulations may be cited as the Social Security (Earnings Factor) Amendment Regulations 1987 and shall come into force on 29th March 1987.

Earnings Factors for the tax year 1986–87

2. For the tax year commencing 6th April 1986, paragraph 2 of Schedule 1 to the Social Security (Earnings Factor) Regulations 1979(d) shall have effect as if for sub-paragraphs (e) and (f) there were substituted the following sub-paragraphs–

"(e) F is–

(i) in relation to any Class 1 contributions paid at a rate specified in section 4(6)–(6B) of the Act–

(aa) 1.8 where P–Q is less than £156;

(bb) $\dfrac{142}{P-Q} + 0.89$ where P–Q is not less than £156 but not greater than £1,290.91;

(cc) 1, where P–Q is greater than £1,290.91;

(ii) in relation to any Class 1 contributions paid at a rate so specified as modified by regulations under section 128 of the Act–

(aa) 1.976, where P is less than £127.90;

(bb) $\dfrac{140.2}{P} + 0.88$, where P is not less than £127.90 but not greater than £1,161.82;

(cc) 1, where P is greater than £1,161.82;

(**a**) 1975 c.14; section 13(5A) was inserted by the Social Security Act 1985 (c.53), section 29(1), Schedule 5, paragraph 6.
(**b**) 1975 c.60; section 6(5A) was inserted by the Social Security Act 1985, section 29(1); Schedule 5, paragraph 16; Schedule 20 is cited because of the meaning ascribed to the words "prescribed" and "regulations".
(**c**) *See* section 10(2)(b) of the Social Security Act 1980 (c.30).
(**d**) S.I. 1979/676; the relevant amending instrument is S.I. 1985/1417.

(iii) in relation to any Class 1 contributions paid at a rate so specified as modified by regulations under section 129 of the Act–

(aa) 1.842, where P is less than £148.18;

(bb) $\dfrac{141.5}{P} + 0.887$, where P is not less than £148.18 but not greater than £1,255.05;

(cc) 1, where P is greater than £1,255.05;

(iv) in relation to such part of any Class 1 contributions as is paid at the normal percentage in accordance with section 27(1)(a) of the Pensions Act in a year in which no payment is made of contributions to which head (i) above applies–

(aa) 1.8, where P–Q is less than £98.80;

(bb) $\dfrac{177.84}{P-Q}$, where P–Q is not less than £98.80 but not greater than £177.84;

(cc) 1, where P–Q is greater than £177.84;

(v) in relation to such part of any Class 1 contributions as is paid at the normal percentage in accordance with section 27(1)(a) of the Pensions Act in a year in which there are also paid contributions to which head (i) applies–

(aa) 1.8, where P–Q is less than £156;

(bb) $\dfrac{142}{P-Q} + 0.89$ where P–Q is not less than £156 but not greater than £1,290.91;

(cc) 1, where P–Q is greater than £1,290.91;

(vi) in relation to such part of any Class 1 contributions as is paid at the normal percentage in accordance with section 27(1)(a) of the Pensions Act as modified by regulations under section 128 of the Act–

(aa) 1.976, where P–Q is less than £81.02;

(bb) $\dfrac{160.06}{P-Q}$, where P–Q is not less than £81.02 but not greater than £160.06;

(cc) 1, where P–Q is greater than £160.06;

(vii) in relation to such part of any Class 1 contributions as is paid at the normal percentage in accordance with section 27(1)(a) of the Pensions Act as modified by regulations under section 129 of the Act–

(aa) 1.842, where P–Q is less than £93.86;

(bb) $\dfrac{172.90}{P-Q}$, where P–Q is not less than £93.86 but not greater than £172.90;

(cc) 1, where P–Q is greater than £172.90;

(f) G is–

(i) in relation to any Class 1 contributions paid at the highest of the rates specified in section 4(6)–(6B) of the Act or to any contracted-out contributions ascertained by reference to section 27(2)(a) of the Pensions Act–

(aa) 2.4, where Q is less than £48.48;

(bb) $\dfrac{72}{Q} + 0.915$, where Q lies between £48.48 and £847.06;

(cc) 1, where Q is greater than £847.06;

(ii) in relation to any contracted-out contributions ascertained by reference to section 27(2)(a) of the Pensions Act, as modified by regulations under section 128 of the Act–

(aa) 3.05, where Q is less than £33.05;

(bb) $\dfrac{71}{Q} + 0.902$, where Q lies between £33.05 and £724.49;

(cc) 1, where Q is greater than £724.49;

(iii) in relation to any contracted-out contributions ascertained by reference to section 27(2)(a) of the Pensions Act, as modified by regulations under section 129 of the Act–

(aa) 2.54, where Q is less than £44.20;

(bb) $\dfrac{72}{Q}$ + 0.911, where Q lies between £44.20 and £808.99;

(cc) 1, where Q is greater than £808.99;

and the amount resulting shall be rounded to the nearest whole penny."

Signed by authority of the Secretary of State for Social Services.

John Major
3rd March 1987   Minister of State, Department of Health and Social Security

---

EXPLANATORY NOTE

(This note is not part of the Regulations)

The Social Security (Earnings Factor) Amendment Regulations 1985 made provision for employed earners who paid primary Class 1 contributions at a reduced rate as from 6th October 1985 to have the earnings factor derived from those contributions boosted in accordance with a formula.

Regulation 2 of these regulations applies new figures to that formula for the tax year 1986–87. These figures reflect the increases made as from 6th April 1986 in the amount of weekly earnings specified in the earnings brackets in section 4(6B) of the Social Security Act 1975, and so preserve the value of the formula for the tax year 1986–87.

STATUTORY INSTRUMENTS

1987 No. 317

SOCIAL SECURITY

The Social Security (Unemployment, Sickness and Invalidity Benefit) Amendment Regulations 1987

Made - - - -	*3rd March 1987*
Laid before Parliament	*3rd March 1987*
Coming into force	*4th March 1987*

The Secretary of State for Social Services in exercise of the powers conferred on him by sections 17(2)(a) and 166 of, and Schedule 20(**a**) to, the Social Security Act 1975(**b**) and of all other powers enabling him in that behalf, without having referred any proposals to make these regulations to the Social Security Advisory Committee because it appears to him that by reason of the urgency of the matter it is inexpedient to do so(**c**), hereby makes the following Regulations:–

Citation and commencement

1. These Regulations may be cited as the Social Security (Unemployment, Sickness and Invalidity Benefit) Amendment Regulations 1987 and shall come into force on 4th March 1987.

Amendment of the Social Security (Unemployment, Sickness and Invalidity Benefit) Regulations 1983

2. After sub-paragraph (m) of paragraph (1) of regulation 7 of the Social Security (Unemployment, Sickness and Invalidity Benefit) Regulations 1983(**d**) there shall be inserted the following sub-paragraph–

"(n) a day shall not be treated as a day of unemployment in relation to any person if it falls in a week during any part of which that person is employed in employment under arrangements made by the Secretary of State under section 5 of the Employment and Training Act 1973(**e**); but this sub-paragraph does not apply to any day before the first day of employment in the first week in which he is employed under such arrangements or after the last day of employment in the last week in which he is so employed.".

Signed by authority of the Secretary of State for Social Services.

John Major
3rd March 1987 Minister of State, Department of Health and Social Security

---

(**a**) *See* the definition of "Regulations".
(**b**) 1975 c. 14.
(**c**) *See* section 61(1)(a) of the Social Security Act 1986 (c. 50).
(**d**) S.I. 1983/1598; the relevant amending instrument is S.I. 1986/1011.
(**e**) 1973 c. 50. Section 5 was amended by the Employment Protection Act 1975 (c. 71), Schedule 14, paragraph 2 and the Employment Subsidies Act 1978 (c. 6), section 3(7).

EXPLANATORY NOTE

(This note is not part of the Regulations)

These Regulations amend regulation 7(1) of the Social Security (Unemployment, Sickness and Invalidity Benefit) Regulations 1983 so as to provide that a day shall not be treated as a day of unemployment if it falls in a week for any part of which the claimant is employed under arrangements made by the Secretary of State under section 5 of the Employment and Training Act 1973.

STATUTORY INSTRUMENTS

1987 No. 327

SOCIAL SECURITY

The Social Security Benefits Up-rating Regulations 1987

Made - - - -	*3rd March 1987*
Laid before Parliament	*10th March 1987*
Coming into force -	*6th April 1987*

The Secretary of State for Social Services, in exercise of the powers conferred upon him by sections 17(1)(a), 58(3) and 131 of, and Schedule 20 to, the Social Security Act 1975**(a)** and section 64(2) of the Social Security Act 1986**(b)**, and of all other powers enabling him in that behalf, by this instrument, which contains only provisions in consequence of an order under section 63 of the Act of 1986, makes the following regulations:–

Citation, commencement and interpretation

1.—(1) These regulations may be cited as the Social Security Benefits Up-rating Regulations 1987 and shall come into force on 6th April 1987.

(2) In these regulations, unless the context otherwise requires–

"the Act" means the Social Security Act 1975;

"the 1986 Act" means the Social Security Act 1986;

"the up-rating order" means the Social Security Benefits Up-rating Order 1987**(c)**;

and any reference in a regulation to a numbered paragraph is to the paragraph of that regulation bearing that number.

Conditions relating to payment of additional benefit under awards made before the appointed or prescribed day

2.—(1) This regulation applies to a case where–

(a) either–

    (i) an award of any benefit under Chapters I to III of Part II of the Act has been made before the day appointed or prescribed for the payment of the benefit in question at a higher rate provided in or by virtue of the up-rating order, or

    (ii) an award of any benefit under Part II of the Act has been made before the day appointed or prescribed for the payment of the benefit in question at a lower rate provided in or by virtue of the up-rating order;

(b) the period to which the award relates has not ended before that day; and

(c) the award does not, in accordance with the provisions of section 64(3) of the

---

(a) 1975 c.14; section 58(3) ceases to have effect except in relation to certain beneficiaries – *see* section 39 of and paragraph 4 of Schedule 3 to the Social Security Act 1986 (c.50).
(b) 1986 c.50.
(c) S.I. 1987/45.

1986 Act, provide for the payment of the benefit at a higher or lower rate (as the case may be) as from that day.

(2) In a case to which this regulation applies, section 64(1)–(3) of the 1986 Act shall have effect subject to the condition that if a question arises as to either–

(a) the weekly rate at which the benefit is payable by virtue of the up-rating order; or

(b) whether the conditions for the receipt of the benefit at the altered rate are satisfied,

the benefit shall, unless the question has been determined in accordance with the provisions of the Act, be or continue to be payable at the weekly rate specified in paragraph (3).

(3) The weekly rate referred to in paragraph (2) is the weekly rate specified in the award or the weekly rate at which the benefit would have been paid if the question had not arisen, whichever is the lower.

Persons not ordinarily resident in Great Britain

3. Regulation 5 of the Social Security Benefit (Persons Abroad) Regulations 1975**(a)** (application of disqualification in respect of up-rating of benefit) shall apply to any additional benefit payable by virtue of the up-rating order.

Amendment of the Social Security (Unemployment, Sickness and Invalidity Benefit) Regulations 1983

4. Regulation 3 of the Social Security (Unemployment, Sickness and Invalidity Benefit) Regulations 1983**(b)** (persons deemed to be incapable of work) shall be further amended by the substitution in paragraph (3) for "£25.50" of "£26.00".

Amendment of the Social Security (General Benefit) Regulations 1982

5. Regulation 16 of the Social Security (General Benefit) Regulations 1982**(c)** (earnings level for the purpose of unemployability supplement) shall be further amended by the substitution for "£1326.00" of "£1352.00".

Revocation

6. The Social Security Benefits Up-rating Regulations 1986**(d)** are hereby revoked.

Signed by authority of the Secretary of State for Social Services

3rd March 1987

John Major
Minister of State, Department of Health and Social Security

(a) S.I. 1975/563; the relevant amending instruments are S.I. 1977/342, 1979/1432.
(b) S.I. 1983/1598; the relevant amending instrument is S.I. 1986/1118.
(c) S.I. 1982/1408; the relevant amending instrument is S.I. 1986/1118. Unemployability Supplement is only payable to those beneficiaries in receipt of it immediately before 6th April 1987 – *see* Social Security Act 1986, section 39, Schedule 3, paragraph 4.
(d) S.I. 1986/1118.

EXPLANATORY NOTE

(This note is not part of the Regulations)

This instrument contains only provisions in consequence of an order under section 63 of the Social Security Act 1986 (up-rating of benefit). Accordingly, by virtue of paragraph 8 of Schedule 16 to the Social Security Act 1975 and paragraph 12(2) of Schedule 3 to the Social Security Act 1980 (c.30), the Secretary of State has not referred proposals to make the regulations contained in this instrument to the Industrial Injuries Advisory Council or to the Social Security Advisory Committee. Paragraph 8 and paragraph 12(2), mentioned above, were amended by the Social Security Act 1986, section 86 and Schedule 10, paragraphs 90 and 99 respectively.

Regulation 2 provides that in certain cases where a question has arisen about the effect of the up-rating order on a benefit already in payment the altered rates will not apply until the question is determined by an adjudicating authority.

Regulation 3 applies the provisions of regulation 5 of the Social Security Benefit (Persons Abroad) Regulations 1975 so as to restrict the application of the increases specified in the order in cases where the beneficiary lives abroad.

Regulation 4 raises from £25.50 to £26.00 the earnings limit which applies to those undertaking work in certain circumstances while receiving sickness or invalidity benefit.

Regulation 5 raises to £1352.00 a year the earnings limit which applies to unemployability supplement.

Regulation 6 contains a revocation consequential upon the coming into force of these regulations.

STATUTORY INSTRUMENTS

1987 No. 329

SAVINGS BANKS

The National Savings Bank (Investment Deposits) (Limits) (Amendment) Order 1987

Laid before Parliament in draft

Made - - - -	*2nd March 1987*
Coming into force	*3rd March 1987*

Whereas a draft of this Order has been laid before Parliament and a period of 40 days beginning with the day of laying has expired and neither House of Parliament has resolved that the Order be not made;

Now, therefore, the Treasury, in exercise of the powers conferred on them by section 4 of the National Savings Bank Act 1971(**a**), and of all other powers enabling them in that behalf, hereby make the following Order:-

1. This Order may be cited as the National Savings Bank (Investment Deposits) (Limits) (Amendment) Order 1987, and shall come into force on 3rd March 1987.

2. The National Savings Bank (Investment Deposits) (Limits) Order 1977(**b**) shall be amended in article 4(1) by the addition of the following sub-paragraph:

"(d) the receipt or crediting of any amount received or credited in contravention of that Article from being treated as having been lawfully received or credited for such period as the Director, in his discretion, thinks appropriate provided that at the time the amount was received or credited the Director was unaware of the contravention and provided also that the Director considers it just and reasonable that the amount should be so treated.".

Mark Lennox-Boyd
Tony Durant
Two of the Lords Commissioners
of Her Majesty's Treasury

2nd March 1987

EXPLANATORY NOTE

(This note is not part of the Order)

The Order, which further amends the National Savings Bank (Investment Deposits) (Limits) Order 1977, permits the Director of Savings to treat as a lawful deposit any amount received by way of investment deposit in excess of the prescribed limit where the Director was unaware, at the time the deposit was made, that it was in excess of the limit.

(**a**) 1971 c.29; section 4 was amended by the Finance Act 1982 (c.39), Schedule 20, paragraph 3.
(**b**) S.I. 1977/1210, amended by S.I. 1981/108, 1984/640 and 1986/1217.

STATUTORY INSTRUMENTS

1987 No. 330

SAVINGS BANKS

The Savings Banks (Ordinary Deposits) (Limits) (Amendment) Order 1987

Laid before Parliament in draft

Made - - - - *2nd March 1987*

Coming into force *3rd March 1987*

Whereas a draft of this Order has been laid before Parliament and a period of 40 days beginning with the day of laying has expired and neither House of Parliament has resolved that the Order be not made;

Now, therefore, the Treasury, in exercise of the powers conferred on them by section 4 of the National Savings Bank Act 1971**(a)**, and of all other powers enabling them in that behalf, hereby make the following Order:-

1. This Order may be cited as the Savings Banks (Ordinary Deposits)(Limits) (Amendment) Order 1987, and shall come into force on 3rd March 1987.

2. The Savings Banks (Ordinary Deposits)(Limits) Order 1969**(b)** shall be amended in Article 3(2) by the addition of the following sub-paragraph:

"(c) the receipt or crediting of any amount received or credited by the Director of Savings in contravention thereof from being treated as having been lawfully received or credited for such period as the Director of Savings, in his discretion, thinks appropriate provided that at the time the amount was received or credited the Director of Savings was unaware of the contravention and provided also that the Director considers it just and reasonable that the amount should be so treated.".

Mark Lennox-Boyd
Tony Durant
Two of the Lords Commissioners
of Her Majesty's Treasury

2nd March 1987

(a) 1971 c.29; section 4 was amended by the Finance Act 1982 (c.39), Schedule 20, paragraph 3.
(b) S.I. 1969/939, amended by S.I. 1969/1699; by virtue of section 28(2) of the National Savings Bank Act 1971 the Order is deemed to have been made under section 4 of that Act.

EXPLANATORY NOTE

(This note is not part of the Order)

The Order, which further amends the Savings Banks (Ordinary Deposits) (Limits) Order 1969, permits the Director of Savings to treat as a lawful deposit any amount received by way of ordinary deposit in excess of the prescribed limit where the Director was unaware, at the time the deposit was made, that it was in excess of the limit.

1987 No. 331 (S. 21)

HOUSING, SCOTLAND

The Housing Support Grant (Scotland) Variation Order 1987

Made - - - -	*25th February 1987*
Coming into force	*26th February 1987*

The Secretary of State, in exercise of the powers conferred on him by sections 1, 2 and 3 of the Housing (Financial Provisions) (Scotland) Act 1978(**a**), and of all other powers enabling him in that behalf, since it appears to him that after the time when the amount mentioned in section 1(2)(a) of the said Act was estimated for 1986-87 the eligible expenditure of local authorities for that year has been substantially decreased by reason of changes which have taken place in the level of the matters specified in section 1(3)(b) of the said Act, and that account was not taken of those changes when the amount mentioned as aforesaid was estimated, and after such consultation with such associations of local authorities as appear to him to be concerned as is required by the said sections 1, 2 and 3, and with the consent of the Treasury, hereby makes the following Order, a draft of which has been approved by the House of Commons:

Citation, commencement and interpretation

1.—(1) This Order may be cited as the Housing Support Grant (Scotland) Variation Order 1987 and shall come into force forthwith.

(2) In this Order "the Order of 1986" means the Housing Support Grant (Scotland) Order 1986(**b**).

(3) Unless the context otherwise requires, expressions used in this Order shall have the same meaning as in the Order of 1986.

Aggregate grant for 1986-87

2. For the aggregate amount of housing support grants and the general and hostel portions thereof fixed for the year 1986-87 by articles 2 and 3 of the Order of 1986 (as indicated in parenthesis in the second column of the following table) there shall be substituted the amount and portions set out in the third column thereof:–

	£	£
Aggregate amount	(50,728,464)	44,469,760
General portion	(49,775,753)	43,531,491
Hostel portion	(952,711)	938,269.

Apportionment of housing support grants for 1986-87

3.—(1) The general portion of housing support grants shall be apportioned among appropriate local authorities in proportion to their estimated net expenditures assessed in the manner provided in the Schedule to the Order of 1986.

(**a**) 1978 c.14; sections 1 and 2 were amended by the Local Government (Miscellaneous Provisions) (Scotland) Act 1981 (c.23), sections 21 and 22, both read with section 23.   (**b**) S.I. 1986/388.

(2) The hostel portion shall be apportioned among appropriate local authorities in proportion to their estimated net expenditures for the year 1986-87 on the provision of hostels and lodging houses.

New St. Andrew's House, Edinburgh
17th February 1987

Michael Ancram
Parliamentary Under Secretary of State,
Scottish Office

We consent,

25th February 1987

Mark Lennox-Boyd
Tony Durant
Two of the Lords Commissioners of Her Majesty's Treasury

EXPLANATORY NOTE

(This note is not part of the Order)

This Order in relation to the year 1986-87 decreases the aggregate amount of housing support grants and the portions thereof payable to certain local authorities in Scotland.

1987 No. 332 (S. 22)

HOUSING, SCOTLAND

The Housing Support Grant (Scotland) Order 1987

Made	-	-	-	*25th February 1987*
Coming into force				*1st April 1987*

The Secretary of State, in exercise of the powers conferred on him by sections 1 and 2 of the Housing (Financial Provisions) (Scotland) Act 1978(**a**) and of all other powers enabling him in that behalf, and after such consultation with such associations of local authorities as appear to him to be concerned as is required by the said sections 1 and 2, and with the consent of the Treasury, hereby makes the following Order, a draft of which has been approved by the House of Commons:

Citation, commencement and interpretation

1.—(1) This Order may be cited as the Housing Support Grant (Scotland) Order 1987 and shall come into force on 1st April 1987.

(2) In this Order–

"the 1978 Act" means the Housing (Financial Provisions) (Scotland) Act 1978;

"appropriate local authority" means a local authority other than an authority whose eligible expenditure and relevant income have been left out of account by virtue of section 1(4A)(a) of the 1978 Act;

"hostel" means a hostel as defined in section 138(4) of the Housing (Scotland) Act 1966(**b**);

"the number of houses of the authority" means the estimate of the number of houses to which the housing revenue account of the authority at 30th September 1987 relates.

(3) Except where the context otherwise requires–

(a) any reference to a numbered Article or Schedule is a reference to the Article or Schedule bearing that number in this Order; and

(b) any reference to an estimate is a reference to an estimate made by the Secretary of State.

Aggregate grant for 1987-88

2. The aggregate amount of the housing support grants for 1987-88 shall be £46,489,693.

Apportionment of housing support grants for 1987-88

3.—(1) The aggregate amount of the housing support grants for the year 1987-88 shall be divided into two portions hereinafter referred to as the "general portion" and the "hostel portion".

(**a**) 1978 c.14; sections 1 and 2 were amended by the Local Government (Miscellaneous Provisions) (Scotland) Act 1981 (c.23), sections 21 and 22, both read with section 23.   (**b**) 1966 c.49.

(2) The general portion shall amount to £45,849,924 and shall be apportioned among appropriate local authorities in proportion to their estimated net expenditures assessed in the manner provided in the Schedule to this Order.

(3) The hostel portion shall amount to £639,769 and shall be apportioned among appropriate local authorities in proportion to their estimated net expenditures for the year 1987-88 on the provision of hostels and lodging houses.

New St. Andrew's House, Edinburgh
17th February 1987

Michael Ancram
Parliamentary Under Secretary of State,
Scottish Office

We consent,

Mark Lennox-Boyd
Tony Durant

25th February 1987   Two of the Lords Commissioners of Her Majesty's Treasury

Article 3(2)   **SCHEDULE**

ASSESSMENT OF NET EXPENDITURE FOR APPORTIONMENT OF GENERAL PORTION OF HOUSING SUPPORT GRANTS AMONG APPROPRIATE LOCAL AUTHORITIES FOR 1987-88

The net expenditure of an appropriate local authority shall be the amount arrived at by addition of the amounts specified in items 1 to 7 below less the amounts specified in items 8 to 10 below.

1. Estimated loan charges due to be debited to the authority's housing revenue account for the year 1987-88 under paragraph 2 of Schedule 4 to the Housing (Financial Provisions) (Scotland) Act 1972(**a**) (other than loan charges in respect of hostels and lodging houses).

Basic amount for supervision and management (SM).

2. £69.592977 multiplied by the number of houses of the authority.

Additional SM factor for certain houses.

3. (a) £27.837190 in the case of an authority with not more than 3,000 houses, or
   (b) £13.918595 in the case of an authority with more than 3,000 but not more than 6,000 houses, or
   (c) £6.959297 in the case of an authority with more than 6,000 but not more than 9,000 houses,
multiplied in each case by the number of houses of the authority.

Basic amount for repairs and maintenance (RM).

4. £209.336120 multiplied by the number of houses of the authority.

Additional RM factors for certain urban expenditure.

5. £324.470989 multiplied by the number of high-rise houses of the authority contained in blocks of flats which are of fifteen or more storeys.

6. £146.535285 multiplied by the number of high-rise houses of the authority contained in blocks of flats which are of more than four but not more than fourteen storeys, with lifts.

7. Estimated other miscellaneous expenditure which may properly be included in the authority's housing revenue account.

Basic income amount.

8. £824.31 multiplied by the number of houses of the authority excluding certain houses leased by the authority for short term occupation without, or with nominal, rental income.

9. A figure, to represent rate fund contributions, calculated for each authority–
   i. by multiplying £30 million by the most up to date estimate then available for that authority's council house stock at 30 September 1987 and dividing by the estimated council house stock in Scotland, again at 30 September 1987;
   ii. by taking the lower of the figure thus derived and the 1986/87 rate fund contribution limit for the Council as specified in the Housing Revenue Account Rate Fund Contribution Limits (Scotland) Order 1986(**b**).

10. Estimated other miscellaneous income which may properly be included in the authority's housing revenue account.

(**a**) 1972 c.46; paragraph 2 of Schedule 4 was amended by the Housing Rents and Subsidies (Scotland) Act 1975 (c.28), Schedule 4, and by the Housing (Financial Provisions) (Scotland) Act 1978 (c.14), section 11 and Schedule 2, paragraph 38.   (**b**) S.I. 1986/7.

EXPLANATORY NOTE

(This note is not part of the Order)

This Order in relation to the year 1987-88–

(i) fixes the estimated aggregate amount of the housing support grants payable under section 1 of the Housing (Financial Provisions) (Scotland) Act 1978 to certain local authorities in Scotland; and

(ii) prescribes the method of apportionment of housing support grants among those authorities.

STATUTORY INSTRUMENTS

1987 No. 333 (S. 23)

LEGAL PROFESSION

The Scottish Solicitors' Discipline Tribunal (Increase of Maximum Fine) Order 1987

Made - - - -	*26th February 1987*
Laid before Parliament	*11th March 1987*
Coming into force	*1st April 1987*

Whereas it appears to the Secretary of State that there has been a change in the value of money since 1980;

And whereas the sum substituted by this Order for the sum specified in section 53(2)(c) of the Solicitors (Scotland) Act 1980(**a**) appears to him to be justified by that change:

Now therefore, in exercise of the powers conferred on him by section 53(8) of that Act, and of all other powers enabling him in that behalf, the Secretary of State hereby makes the following Order:

1. This Order may be cited as the Scottish Solicitors' Discipline Tribunal (Increase of Maximum Fine) Order 1987 and shall come into force on 1st April 1987.

2. In section 53(2)(c) of the Solicitors (Scotland) Act 1980, for the reference to "£2,500" there shall be substituted a reference to "£4,000".

Ian Lang
Parliamentary Under Secretary of State,
Scottish Office

New St. Andrew's House, Edinburgh
26th February 1987

EXPLANATORY NOTE

(This note is not part of the Order)

This Order increases from £2,500 to £4,000 the maximum fine which may be imposed by the Scottish Solicitors' Discipline Tribunal.

(**a**) 1980 c.46; section 53(2)(c) was amended by the Law Reform (Miscellaneous Provisions) (Scotland) Act 1980 (c.55), section 24(a)(i) and by the Law Reform (Miscellaneous Provisions) (Scotland) Act 1985 (c.73), Schedule 1, Part I, paragraph 28(b); section 53(8) was added by the Law Reform (Miscellaneous Provisions) (Scotland) Act 1980, section 24(a)(ii).

STATUTORY INSTRUMENTS

1987 No. 335

SOCIAL SECURITY

The Social Security (Industrial Injuries) (Prescribed Diseases) Amendment Regulations 1987

Made - - - -	*4th March 1987*
Laid before Parliament	*4th March 1987*
Coming into force	
for the purposes of regulations 1, 2, 3 and 4	*1st April 1987*
for the purposes of regulation 5	*6th April 1987*

The Secretary of State for Social Services, in exercise of the powers conferred upon him by sections 76, 77 and 113 of, and Schedule 20 to, the Social Security Act 1975 (**a**) and of all other powers enabling him in that behalf, after reference to the Industrial Injuries Advisory Council, hereby makes the following regulations:

Citation, commencement and interpretation

1.—(1) These regulations, which may be cited as the Social Security (Industrial Injuries) (Prescribed Diseases) Amendment Regulations 1987, shall come into force for the purposes of regulations 1, 2, 3 and 4 on 1st April 1987 and for the purposes of regulation 5 on 6th April 1987.

(2) In these regulations "the principal regulations" means the Social Security (Industrial Injuries) (Prescribed Diseases) Regulations 1985(**b**).

Amendment of the principal regulations relating to prescription of lung cancer

2.—(1) Part 1 of Schedule 1 to the principal regulations shall be amended by the addition after the disease numbered D9 (Bilateral diffuse pleural thickening), of the disease specified in the first column of the Schedule hereto and of the occupations set against this disease in the second column of that Schedule.

(2) For the definition of "lung cancer" in regulation 1(2) of the principal regulations shall be substituted " 'lung cancer' means the diseases numbered D8 and D10 in Part I of Schedule 1 to these regulations except in Part I of Schedule 1 and in Schedule 4 where it means the disease numbered D10.".

(3) In Schedule 4 to the principal regulations after the entry relating to the disease numbered D9 (Bilateral diffuse pleural thickening) there shall be inserted–

(a) in the first column the words "D10 lung cancer";

(b) in the second column the date "1st April 1987".

(**a**) 1975 c.14; Schedule 20 is cited because of the meaning ascribed to the words "prescribe" and "regulations".
(**b**) S.I. 1985/967; the only relevant amending instrument is S.I. 1986/1561.

Date before which there will not be entitlement to payment of benefit

3. There shall be no entitlement to payment of benefit in the case of a person suffering from prescribed disease D10 in respect of any day which is earlier than the relevant date or in respect of any death which occurs before the relevant date.

Amendment of the Social Security (Adjudication) Regulations 1984

4.—(1) The Social Security (Adjudication) Regulations 1984(**a**) shall be amended in accordance with the following provisions of this regulation.

(2) In regulation 32(2) (determination of medical questions) for the words "or D9" there shall be substituted the words ", D9 or D10".

(3) In regulation 36(2) (disqualification from acting as an adjudicating medical authority) for the words "or D9" there shall be substituted the words ", D9 or D10".

(4) In regulation 41(2)(b) (application of adjudication regulations to prescribed diseases) for the words "and D9" there shall be substituted the words ", D9 and D10".

(5) In regulation 43(2) (reference of diagnosis and recrudescence questions for medical report) for the words "and D9" there shall be substituted the words ", D9 and D10".

Amendment of the Social Security (Adjudication) Regulations 1986

5.—(1) The Social Security (Adjudication) Regulations 1986(**b**) shall be amended in accordance with the following provisions of this regulation.

(2) In regulation 29(2) (determination of medical questions) for the words "or D9" there shall be substituted the words ", D9 or D10".

(3) In regulation 33(2) (disqualification from acting as an adjudicating medical authority) for the words "or D9" there shall be substituted the words ", D9 or D10".

(4) In regulation 41(2)(b) (application of adjudication regulations to prescribed diseases) for the words "and D9" there shall be substituted the words ", D9 and D10".

(5) In regulation 42(1) (reference of diagnosis and recrudescence questions for medical report) for the words "and D9" there shall be substituted the words ", D9 and D10".

Signed by authority of the Secretary of State for Social Services.

John Major
4th March 1987   Minister of State, Department of Health and Social Security

---

Regulation 2(1)   **SCHEDULE**

Description of disease or injury	Nature of occupation
D10. Lung Cancer.	(a) Work underground in a tin mine; or
	(b) exposure to bis(chloromethyl)ether produced during the manufacture of chloromethyl methyl ether; or
	(c) exposure to zinc chromate calcium chromate or strontium chromate in their pure forms.

(**a**) S.I. 1984/451.   (**b**) S.I. 1986/2218.

EXPLANATORY NOTE

(This note is not part of the Regulations)

These regulations which come into effect on 1st April 1987 provide for a further industrial disease of lung cancer to be prescribed under Chapter V of Part II of the Social Security Act 1975.

Regulation 2(2) amends the definition of lung cancer in regulation 1(2) of the principal regulations. Benefit is not payable for any period before 1st April 1987 (regulations 2(3) and 3). The Social Security (Adjudication) Regulations 1984 and 1986 are amended by regulations 4 and 5 so as to provide for diagnosis of the newly prescribed disease to be for special medical boards and for medical reports to be obtained from specially qualified medical practitioners.

STATUTORY INSTRUMENTS

1987 No. 337

TRANSPORT

The Transport Act 1985 (Modifications in Schedule 4 to the Transport Act 1968) (Amendment) Order 1987

Made - - - -	*2nd March 1987*
Laid before Parliament	*13th March 1987*
Coming into force	*3rd April 1987*

The Secretary of State for Transport (as respects England) and the Secretary of State for Wales (as respects Wales) in exercise of the powers conferred by section 129(5) of the Transport Act 1985(**a**), and of all other enabling powers, hereby make this Order:

1.   This Order may be cited as the Transport Act 1985 (Modifications in Schedule 4 to the Transport Act 1968) (Amendment) Order 1987 and shall come into force on 3rd April 1987.

2.   In article 3 of the Transport Act 1985 (Modifications in Schedule 4 to the Transport Act 1968) Order 1985(**b**), after the word "section" there shall be inserted the word "50(4),".

Signed by authority of the Secretary of State.

David Mitchell
Minister of State,
24th February 1987   Department of Transport

Nicholas Edwards
2nd March 1987   Secretary of State for Wales

EXPLANATORY NOTE

(This note is not part of the Order)

This Order extends the Transport Act 1985 (Modifications in Schedule 4 to the Transport Act 1968) Order 1985, so that it applies to transfers under section 50(4) of the Transport Act 1985. These are transfers under schemes made by the National Bus Company.

(**a**) 1985 c.67.
(**b**) S.I. 1985/1903.

STATUTORY INSTRUMENTS

1987 No. 340

PLANT HEALTH

The Import and Export (Plant Health Fees) (England and Wales) Order 1987

Made - - - -	*2nd March 1987*
Laid before Parliament	*11th March 1987*
Coming into force	*1st April 1987*

The Minister of Agriculture, Fisheries and Food in relation to England and the Secretary of State in relation to Wales, in exercise of the powers conferred by sections 2, 3(1) and 4A of the Plant Health Act 1967(a) and now vested in them(b) and of all other powers enabling them in that behalf, with the consent of the Treasury, hereby make the following Order:–

Title, extent and commencement

1. This Order may be cited as the Import and Export (Plant Health Fees) (England and Wales) Order 1987, shall apply to England and Wales and shall come into force on 1st April 1987.

Interpretation

2.—(1) In this Order, unless the context otherwise requires–

"alternative fee" means a fee prescribed in column 4 of Schedule 1;

"the appropriate Minister" means, in relation to England, the Minister and, in relation to Wales, the Secretary of State for Wales;

"basic fee" means a fee prescribed in column 3 of Schedule 1;

"certificate" means a phytosanitary certificate or a re-forwarding phytosanitary certificate;

"district" means, in Wales, a community and, in England, a parish or where there is no parish a district ward;

"financial year" means the twelve months ending with 31st March;

"import licence" means a licence issued by the appropriate Minister under article 17 of the Import and Export (Plant Health) (Great Britain) Order 1980(c);

"micro-plant" means a micro-propagated plant in vitro or a plant which is–

   (i) produced by micro-propagation,

   (ii) weaned, and

   (iii) not more than 5 centimetres in height;

"the Minister" means the Minister of Agriculture, Fisheries and Food;

"national list" means a list of plant varieties prepared and published in a Member State which corresponds to that prepared and published under regulation 4 of the Seeds (National List of Varieties) Regulations 1982(d);

(a) 1967 c. 8; sections 2(1) and 3(1) were amended by the European Communities Act 1972 (c. 68), section 4(1) and Schedule 4, paragraph 8, and section 4A was inserted by the Agriculture Act 1986 (c. 49), section 3.
(b) In the case of Secretary of State by virtue of S.I. 1978/272.
(c) S.I. 1980/420; article 17 was amended by S.I. 1985/873, 1986/1135.
(d) S.I. 1982/844, amended by S.I. 1985/1529.

"phytosanitary certificate" means a phytosanitary certificate issued by an inspector or other officer of the appropriate Minister under article 9 of the Import and Export (Plant Health) (Great Britain) Order 1980 and "re-forwarding phytosanitary certificate" means a re-forwarding phytosanitary certificate issued by such an inspector or officer under that article;

"premises" includes any land, building, vessel, vehicle, aircraft, hovercraft or freight container;

"reduced fee" means a fee equal to one-half of a basic fee or an alternative fee;

"small consignment" means a consignment–

(i) of the following articles not more than 100 that is to say plants, fruits, bulbs, corms, rhizomes, tubers, bud sticks or cut flowers, or

(ii) of the following articles not more than 1,000 that is to say rooted seedlings, or rooted or unrooted cuttings, not more than 15 centimetres in height or micro-plants, or

(iii) whose gross value, to the satisfaction of the appropriate Minister, is less than £100;

"soil" includes any growing medium;

"stock" means the whole or part of a single crop of a single cultivar from a single field.

(2) Where a fee prescribed by this Order is prescribed in relation to an inspection, examination or test as well as the issue of a certificate, the refusal to issue a certificate by reason of the results of the inspection, examination or test being unsatisfactory shall not affect the amount of the fee otherwise payable.

(3) Any reference in this Order to a numbered article or Schedule shall be construed as a reference to the article or Schedule bearing that number in this Order.

Fees for export certification services

3.   Subject to the following provisions of this Order, there shall be paid to the Minister in respect of any service described in column 2 of Schedule 1 the basic fee prescribed opposite the reference to that service.

Alternative fees for export certification services

4.—(1) Subject to the following provisions of this Order where–

(a) opposite the reference to any service described in column 2 of Schedule 1 there is also prescribed an alternative fee, and

(b) the applicant applies for the performance of more than one such service, or more than one performance of any such service, under a single application, and

(c) two or more such services are performed consecutively

there shall be paid to the Minister, in place of the basic fee, the alternative fee so prescribed.

(2) Paragraph (1) above shall not apply to—

(a) the first, fifteenth and twenty-ninth service nor to any other service which follows this sequence (that is to say every 14th service), other than a service described in column 2 of Schedule 1 opposite item number 9, or

(b) the first service, being a service described opposite the said item 9.

(3) Where the applicant applies, under a single application—

(a) for the performance of more than one of the services described in column 2 of Schedule 1 opposite item numbers 1, 2 and 3, or more than one performance of any of those services, or

(b) for more than one performance of the service described in column 2 of Schedule 1 opposite item number 5

the services shall, for the purposes of paragraphs (1) and (2) above, be treated as performed consecutively whether or not they are so performed.

(4) No application shall be treated as an application made for the purposes of this article unless the services are to be performed on premises farmed, worked, occupied or administered as a single unit within the same district or any district adjoining it.

(5) For the purposes of this article services shall be treated as performed consecutively if–

(a) they are performed in immediate succession, or

(b) notwithstanding that they are not so performed, the articles in respect of which the services are performed were so presented by the applicant as to have enabled the services to be performed in immediate succession.

Further provisions for the payment of alternative fees

5.—(1) Where an inspector is on any premises for the purpose of performing any service for which a fee is payable to the Minister otherwise than under this order as well as any service for which a fee is prescribed in Schedule 1, there shall be paid to the Minister, in place of the basic fee, the alternative fee prescribed opposite the reference to the appropriate service.

(2) Without prejudice to article 7, where an inspector is on any premises for the purpose of performing any service for which a fee is prescribed in Schedule 2 as well as a service for which a fee is prescribed in Schedule 1, there shall be paid to the Minister, in place of the basic fee, the alternative fee prescribed opposite the reference to the appropriate service.

Reduced fees for export certification services

6.—(1) Subject to paragraph (2) below, there shall be paid to the Minister, in place of any basic fee or alternative fee, a reduced fee where the appropriate Minister is satisfied that—

(a) the applicant is not a taxable person for the purposes of the Value Added Tax Act 1983(**a**) or if he is a taxable person, he makes no taxable supplies of plants, plant products, soil or agricultural machinery for the purposes of that Act, or

(b) the gross value of the articles exported, or sold for export, by the applicant from Great Britain and accompanied by a certificate in the previous financial year was less than £5,000.

(2) Paragraph (1) above shall not apply in respect of services performed in any financial year the reduced fees for which would cause the total amount of the reduced fees, otherwise payable by the applicant under that paragraph, to exceed £250 in that financial year.

Fees for import licensing services

7. Subject to the following provisions of this Order, there shall be paid to the Minister in respect of any service described in column 2 of Schedule 2 the fee prescribed in column 3 of Schedule 2 opposite the reference to that service.

Time for payment of fees

8. The fees prescribed in Schedule 1 shall be paid on demand made by the Minister and the fees prescribed in Schedule 2 shall be paid at the time of application for the services to which they relate.

Refund of fees

9. If an application for a service described in column 2 of Schedule 2 is withdrawn by a written request made by the applicant and received by the appropriate Minister within 7 days of the date of the application, the fee paid under article 7 less an amount of £5 shall be refunded to the applicant.

In Witness whereof the Official Seal of the Minister of Agriculture, Fisheries and Food is hereunto affixed on 26th February 1987.

Michael Jopling
Minister of Agriculture, Fisheries and Food

Nicholas Edwards
Secretary of State for Wales

2nd March 1987

(**a**) 1983 c. 55.

Articles 2 to 5 and 8

SCHEDULE 1

FEES IN RESPECT OF EXPORT CERTIFICATION SERVICES

(1) Item	(2) Service	(3) Basic fee £	(4) Alternative fee £
1	The taking of one soil sample from a field, or part of a field, which is not more than 4 hectares	28	10
2	The taking of two soil samples on the same visit from fields on the same holding, the combined area of which is not more than 3 hectares	28	10
3	The taking of up to three samples of compost for container grown plants	28	10
4	Laboratory testing of one soil sample	13	
5	Growing Season Inspection Where the basic fee is payable, one Growing Season Inspection of– (a) up to 0.1 hectares of outdoor plants (including bulbs and plants in containers), or (b) up to 1,000 indoor plants, or (c) up to 1.0 hectares of seed crops; and where the alternative fee is payable, one Growing Season Inspection of– (a) up to 1.5 hectares of bulbs, or (b) up to 1.0 hectares of outdoor plants other than bulbs, or (c) up to 6.0 hectares of seed crops, or (d) up to 10,000 indoor plants	28	10
6	Pre-export inspection of and the issue of certificates, for– (a) up to 7 small consignments, to be exported under up to 7 certificates, or (b) up to 25 tonnes, to be exported under one certificate, of plants, plant products or soil other than bulbs, potatoes and seeds	28	10
7	Pre-export inspection of up to 25 tonnes of potatoes, to be exported under one certificate, and the issue of that certificate	28	15
8	Pre-export inspection of– (a) a stock of bulbs up to 25 tonnes and the issue of such certificates as may be required for the export of bulbs from that stock issued while the inspector is on the premises for the purposes of this inspection or any other official purpose, or (b) up to 25 tonnes of bulbs of one stock, to be exported under one certificate, and the issue of that certificate	28	15
9	The taking of samples of seed for examination or testing– (a) where the basic fee is payable the taking of 3 samples, and (b) where the alternative fee is payable the taking of one sample	28	2.50
10	The issue of one certificate for the export of a consignment of seeds where they, or the bulk from which they are taken, have already been sampled and examined or tested	10	

SCHEDULE 1 – continued

(1) Item	(2) Service	(3) Basic fee £	(4) Alternative fee £
11	The issue of one certificate for the export of a consignment of seeds where the appropriate Minister is satisfied that the export is for national listing purposes and where they, or the bulk from which they are taken, have already been sampled and examined or tested	5	
12	The inspection for any traces of soil or plant debris and the issue of one or more certificates for the export of used agricultural machines– (a) where the basic fee is payable the inspection of up to 5 agricultural machines, and (b) where the alternative fee is payable the inspection of up to 10 agricultural machines	28	10
13	The issue of one certificate, including any prior examination or test, without a visit by an inspector to the applicant's premises	10	
14	The issue of up to 20 certificates for the export of articles not requiring inspection on that occasion but requiring a visit to the applicant's premises	28	10
15	The issue of one certificate by an inspector where an inspector has not had to visit the applicant's premises in respect of the articles to be certified or to inspect those articles and where no examination or testing has been necessary	1	

SCHEDULE 2

Articles 7 and 8

FEES IN RESPECT OF IMPORT LICENSING SERVICES

(1) Item	(2) Service	(3) Fee £
1	Consideration of an application for the issue of an import licence and the performance of any connected service, including the issue of the licence where appropriate	150
2	The inspection of articles imported for the purposes of a trade or business, being an inspection required by the terms of the import licence under which the articles were imported	28
3	Where the application for an import licence is for the import of articles for a scientific purpose and the number of types of article to be imported under the same licence exceeds 5, the inclusion of one type of article in the licence in addition to the first five	5
4	Where an import licence is issued for the importation of articles for a scientific purpose, the variation of the licence so as to enable the importation of additional articles under that licence	20 plus 5 for each article
5	The issue of an import licence for the importation of articles not for the purposes of a trade or business nor for a scientific purpose	25

EXPLANATORY NOTE

(This note is not part of the Order)

This Order prescribes fees in respect of the services listed in Schedules 1 and 2 to the Order (articles 3 to 7). These services are performed in connection with applications received for the issue of phytosanitary certificates or licences in accordance with the provisions of the Import and Export (Plant Health) (Great Britain) Order 1980. The certificates are required to accompany exports of certain plants, plant products etc and licences are issued to enable the importation of those articles which would otherwise be prohibited.

As regards the export certification services the Order prescribes a basic fee in column 3 of Schedule 1 and in certain circumstances provides for the payment of a lower alternative fee instead of the basic fee. The alternative fees are shown in column 4 of Schedule 1 (articles 3, 4 and 5). The Order also makes provision for the payment of reduced fees (ie at half-rate up to a maximum total value at full fee of £500 in any financial year) by persons who are not taxable for the purposes of the Value Added Tax Act 1983 or who make no taxable supplies of plants, plant products, soil or agricultural machinery for the purposes of that Act or whose certificated exports or sales for exports in the previous financial year were of a value less than £5,000 gross (article 6). Where an application for an import licensing service is withdrawn within the specified time, a refund shall be made (article 9).

In the case of certificates, the fee is payable on demand and in the case of licences the fee is payable on application (article 8).

STATUTORY INSTRUMENTS

1987 No. 341

• POLICE

The Police (Injury Benefit) (Amendment) Regulations 1987

Made - - - -	*2nd March 1987*
Laid before Parliament	*9th March 1987*
Coming into force	*17th March 1987*

In exercise of the powers conferred on me by sections 1, 3, 4 and 6 of the Police Pensions Act 1976**(a)**, and after consultation with the Police Negotiating Board for the United Kingdom, I hereby, with the consent of the Treasury**(b)**, make the following Regulations:–

1. These Regulations may be cited as the Police (Injury Benefit) (Amendment) Regulations 1987.

2. These Regulations shall come into force on 17th March 1987 and shall have effect as from 25th November 1982.

3.—(1) The Police (Injury Benefit) Regulations 1987**(c)** shall be amended in accordance with the following provisions of this Regulation.

(2) In Regulation 4(1)(c), the words "on or after that date and" shall be omitted.

(3) In Regulation 5(2)–

(a) for the words "a duly qualified medical practitioner under Regulation 71" there shall be substituted the words "a medical authority under Regulation 71, 72 or 73"; and

(b) at the end there shall be added the words "and where this Regulation so applies it shall apply to the exclusion of Regulation 4".

(4) In Regulation 8, for paragraphs (3), (4) and (5) there shall be substituted the following paragraphs–

"(3) No payment in respect of a gratuity under these Regulations shall be made to a person unless he has given to the police authority a written undertaking that if he recovers any damages or compensation in respect of the death or disability to which the gratuity relates he will inform them thereof and, unless the damages or compensation have been taken into account in pursuance of paragraph (1), will pay to the police authority such sum as they may demand not exceeding–

(a) where the amount of the payment made by the police authority is less than the net amount of the damages or compensation, the amount of that payment;

(b) where the amount of that payment is not less than the net amount of the damages or compensation, an amount equal to the net amount of the damages or compensation;

(a) 1976 c.35, as amended by the Police Negotiating Board Act 1980 (c.10).
(b) Formerly the Minister for the Civil Service: *see* S.I. 1981/1670.
(c) S.I. 1987/156.

and, in this paragraph, "the net amount" in relation to damages or compensation recovered by any person means the amount of the damages or compensation after deducting tax payable in the United Kingdom or elsewhere to which the damages or compensation are subject.

(4) The police authority shall not demand any payment in pursuance of such an undertaking as is mentioned in paragraph (3)–

(a) after the death of the person to whom the payment in respect of a gratuity under these Regulations was made, or

(b) after the expiration of 2 years from the date on which the final determination of the amount of the damages or compensation first came to the knowledge of the police authority.".

(5) Regulation 9 shall be omitted.

4. The Police Pensions (Supplementary Provisions) Regulations 1987**(a)** shall be amended as follows–

(a) in Regulation 7, after the words "Police (Injury Benefit) Regulations 1987" there shall be inserted the words "(as amended by the Police (Injury Benefit) (Amendment) Regulations 1987";

and

(b) in Schedule 5, for the entry in the Table relating to Regulation 5(2), there shall be substituted the following entry:

"Regulation 5(2)/"Regulation 71, 72 or 73"/"Regulation H1, H2 or H3" ".

5. The Police Pensions Regulations 1987**(b)** shall be amended by the insertion, at the end of Regulation A2, of the words "and, in this Regulation, references to the Police (Injury Benefit) Regulations 1987 and to Regulation 7 of the Supplementary Regulations are to those Regulations as amended by the Police (Injury Benefit) (Amendment) Regulations 1987".

Douglas Hurd
One of Her Majesty's Principal Secretaries of State

Home Office
2nd March 1987

We consent

Tony Durant
Tim Sainsbury
2nd March 1987   Two of the Lords Commissioners of Her Majesty's Treasury

---

(a) S.I. 1987/256.   **(b)** S.I. 1987/257.

EXPLANATORY NOTE

(This note is not part of the Regulations)

These Regulations amend the Police (Injury Benefit) Regulations 1987 (the principal Regulations) in order to correct a number of errors of substance and drafting.

Regulation 4 of the principal Regulations (disablement gratuity) is amended to remove the condition of eligibility that the disablement must have occurred on or after 25th November 1982 even where the injury from which it resulted was received before that date.

Regulation 5 of the principal Regulations (death gratuity) is amended to include a reference to the decision of a medical authority on appeal or reconsideration that a person is permanently and totally disabled, and to exclude the exceptional applicability of both Regulation 4 and Regulation 5.

Regulation 8 of the principal Regulations (abatement in respect of damages or compensation) is amended to substitute, for the police authority's right to take proceedings for the recovery of the amount of any damages or compensation, a provision that the recipient of a gratuity under the Regulations must have given an undertaking to repay such an amount to the police authority. Regulation 9 of the principal Regulations (admissibility of certificates in evidence) is omitted.

These Regulations also make consequential amendments to the Police Pensions Regulations 1987 and the Police Pensions (Supplementary Provisions) Regulations 1987 in their reference to the principal Regulations.

As in the case of the principal Regulations, these Regulations come into force on 17th March 1987 and have effect as from 25th November 1982 (retrospection is authorised by section 1(5) of the Police Pensions Act 1976).

STATUTORY INSTRUMENTS

1987 No. 342

POLICE

The Police Cadets (Injury Benefit) (Amendment) Regulations 1987

Made - - - -	*3rd March 1987*
Laid before Parliament	*9th March 1987*
Coming into force	*17th March 1987*

In exercise of the powers conferred on me by section 35 of the Police Act 1964**(a)**, as extended by section 13 of the Superannuation (Miscellaneous Provisions) Act 1967**(b)** and sections 12 and 15 of the Superannuation Act 1972**(c)**, and after consulting the Police Negotiating Board for the United Kingdom in accordance with section 2(3) of the Police Negotiating Board Act 1980**(d)**, I hereby make the following Regulations:–

1.   These Regulations may be cited as the Police Cadets (Injury Benefit) (Amendment) Regulations 1987.

2.   These Regulations shall come into force on 17th March 1987 and shall have effect as from 25th November 1982.

3.   Regulation 4(1) of the Police Cadets (Injury Benefit) Regulations 1987**(e)** shall be amended as follows–

   (a) after the words "Police (Injury Benefit) Regulations 1987"**(f)** there shall be inserted the words "(as amended by the Police (Injury Benefit) (Amendment) Regulations 1987)"**(g)**; and

   (b) in paragraph (a)(iii), the words "on or after that date and" shall be omitted.

Douglas Hurd
Home Office   One of Her Majesty's Principal Secretaries of State
3rd March 1987

(**a**) 1964 c.48.   (**b**) 1967 c.28.   (**c**) 1972 c.11.
(**d**) 1980 c.10.   (**e**) S.I. 1987/158.   .(**f**) S.I. 1987/156.
(**g**) S.I. 1987/341.

EXPLANATORY NOTE

(This note is not part of the Regulations)

These Regulations amend the Police Cadets (Injury Benefit) Regulations 1987 in consequence of the Police (Injury Benefit) (Amendment) Regulations 1987 (which correct certain errors in the Police (Injury Benefit) Regulations 1987).

As in the case of each of the above mentioned instruments, these Regulations come into force on 17th March 1987 and have effect as from 25th November 1982 (retrospection is authorised by sections 12 and 15 of the Superannuation Act 1972).

STATUTORY INSTRUMENTS

1987 No. 343

POLICE

The Special Constables (Injury Benefit) (Amendment) Regulations 1987

Made - - - -	*3rd March 1987*
Laid before Parliament	*9th March 1987*
Coming into force	*17th March 1987*

In exercise of the powers conferred on me by section 34 of the Police Act 1964(**a**) (read with section 1(2) of the Police Pensions Act 1961(**b**)), as amended and extended by sections 12 and 15 of the Superannuation Act 1972(**c**), I hereby make the following Regulations:

1.   These Regulations may be cited as the Special Constables (Injury Benefit) (Amendment) Regulations 1987.

2.   These Regulations shall come into force on 17th March 1987 and shall have effect as from 25th November 1982.

3.   Regulation 4 of the Special Constables (Injury Benefit) Regulations 1987(**d**) shall be amended as follows–
   (a) after the words "Police (Injury Benefit) Regulations 1987"(**e**) there shall be inserted the words "(as amended by the Police (Injury Benefit) (Amendment) Regulations 1987)" (**f**) ; and
   (b) in paragraph (a)(iii), the words "on or after that date and" shall be omitted.

Home Office	*Douglas Hurd*
3rd March 1987	One of Her Majesty's Principal Secretaries of State

EXPLANATORY NOTE

(This note is not part of the Regulations)

These Regulations amend the Special Constables (Injury Benefit) Regulations 1987 in consequence of the Police (Injury Benefit) (Amendment) Regulations 1987 (which correct certain errors in the Police (Injury Benefit) Regulations 1987).

As in the case of each of the above-mentioned instruments, these Regulations come into force on 17th March 1987 and have effect as from 25th November 1982 (retrospection is authorised by sections 12 and 15 of the Superannuation Act 1972).

(**a**) 1964 c.48.   (**b**) 1961 c.35.   (**c**) 1972 c.11.   (**d**) S.I. 1987/159.
(**e**) S.I. 1987/156.   (**f**) S.I. 1987/341.

S T A T U T O R Y   I N S T R U M E N T S

1987 No. 344 (C.8)

EDUCATION, ENGLAND AND WALES
EDUCATION, SCOTLAND

The Education (No. 2) Act 1986 (Commencement No. 2) Order 1987

Made - - - - *2nd March 1987*

In exercise of the powers conferred on the Secretary of State by section 66 of the Education (No. 2) Act 1986 (**a**), I hereby make the following Order:–

Citation

1. This Order may be cited as the Education (No. 2) Act 1986 (Commencement No. 2) Order 1987.

Interpretation

2. In this Order –

"the Act" means the Education (No. 2) Act 1986;
"the 1944 Act" means the Education Act 1944 (**b**);
"the 1968 (No. 2) Act" means the Education (No. 2) Act 1968 (**c**); and
"the 1980 Act" means the Education Act 1980 (**d**).

Coming into force of certain provisions of the Act

3. The provisions of the Act specified in column 1 of Schedule 1 to this Order (which relate to the matters mentioned in column 2 thereof) shall come into force on 15th August 1987, and the provisions of the Act specified in column 1 of Schedule 2 to this Order (which relate to the matters mentioned in column 2 thereof) shall come into force on 1st September 1987.

Transitional Provisions

4. The transitional provisions contained in Schedule 3 to this Order shall have effect in connection with the provisions brought into force by this Order which are referred to in that Schedule.

(**a**) 1986 c.61.　　(**b**) 1944 c.31.　　(**c**) 1968 c.37.　　(**d**) 1980 c.20.

SCHEDULE 1

PROVISIONS COMING INTO FORCE ON 15TH AUGUST 1987

Provisions of the Act	Subject matter of provisions
Section 47, so far as it is not already in force, that is to say subsections (1) to (10).	Abolition of corporal punishment.
Section 48.	Abolition of corporal punishment: Scotland.

SCHEDULE 2

PROVISIONS COMING INTO FORCE ON 1ST SEPTEMBER 1987

Provisions of the Act	Subject matter of provisions
Section 1.	Instruments of government and articles of government.
Section 2.	Procedure in relation to making etc. of instruments and articles.
Section 3.	Governing bodies for county, controlled and maintained special schools.
Section 4.	Governing bodies for aided and special agreement schools.
Section 5.	Appointment of parent governors by governing body.
Section 6.	Connection with local business community.
Section 7.	Appointment of representative governors in place of co-opted governors.
Section 8.	Governors' proceedings and tenure of office.
Section 9.	Grouping of schools under single governing body.
Section 10.	Requirements as to consent to grouping.
Section 11.	Review of constitution of governing bodies of county, controlled and maintained special schools.
Section 12.	Temporary governing bodies for new schools.
Section 13.	Effect of change of circumstances on instrument of government.
Section 14.	Adjustment in number of governors.
Section 15.	Miscellaneous.
Section 16.	General responsibility for conduct of certain schools.
Section 18.	Curriculum: county, controlled and maintained special schools.

SCHEDULE 2 – *continued*

Provisions of the Act	Subject matter of provisions
Section 19.	Curriculum: aided and special agreement schools.
Section 20.	Information for parents.
Section 21.	Terms, sessions and holidays.
Section 22.	Discipline: general duties.
Section 23.	Exclusion of pupils: duty to inform parents etc.
Section 24.	Reinstatement of excluded pupils: county, controlled and maintained special schools.
Section 25.	Reinstatement of excluded pupils: aided and special agreement schools.
Section 26.	Exclusion: appeals.
Section 27.	Exclusion: additional provision for appeals.
Section 28.	Local education authority's reserve power.
Section 29.	Finance.
Section 32.	Reports by governing body and head teacher.
Section 34.	Determination of staff complement for schools.
Section 35.	Appointment and dismissal of staff: introductory.
Section 36.	The selection panel.
Section 37.	Appointment of head teacher.
Section 38.	Appointment of certain other staff.
Section 39.	Appointment of deputy head teacher.
Section 40.	Appointment and dismissal of clerk to governing body.
Section 41.	Dismissal etc. of staff.
Section 42.	School premises.
Section 43.	Freedom of speech in universities, polytechnics and colleges.
Section 57.	Information and training for governors.
Section 58.	Travelling and subsistence allowances for governors of schools and establishments of further education.
Section 61.	Minimum age for governors of establishments of further education.
Section 62.	Access to papers etc. of governing bodies.
Section 67(4), so far as it is not already in force, that is to say, so far as it relates to paragraphs 2, 3, 4 and 6 of Schedule 4.	Consequential amendments.
Section 67(5).	Transitional provisions.
Section 67(6), so far as it relates to the repeals set out in the Appendix to this Schedule.	Repeals.
Schedule 1.	Grouped schools.
Schedule 2.	New schools.
Schedule 3.	Exclusion on discipline grounds: appeals.

SCHEDULE 2 – *continued*

Provisions of the Act	Subject matter of provisions
Schedule 4, so far as it is not already in force, that is to say, paragraphs 2, 3, 4 and 6.	Consequential amendments.
Schedule 5.	Transitional provisions.
Schedule 6, so far as it relates to the repeals set out in the Appendix to this Schedule.	Repeals.

APPENDIX TO SCHEDULE 2

REPEALS TAKING EFFECT FROM 1ST SEPTEMBER 1987

Chapter	Short title	Extent of repeal
1944 c.31.	The Education Act 1944.	Section 17. Section 18. Section 19. Section 20. Section 21. Section 23. Section 24(1). In section 27(3), from "but before" to end.
1962 c.12.	The Education Act 1962.	In section 3, paragraph (*a*) and from "in the case of" to "this section". In Section 4(3), "(*a*) or".
1968 c.37.	The Education (No. 2) Act 1968.	Section 2. In section 3(2), the words "or subsection (4) of section 2".
1980 c.20.	The Education Act 1980.	Section 2. Section 3. Section 4. In section 35(1), the words from "(other" to "(*b*))".

SCHEDULE 3

TRANSITIONAL PROVISIONS

1.—(1) Subject to sub-paragraph (2) below, this paragraph applies in relation to every county, voluntary and maintained special school.

(2) This paragraph –
    (a) shall not apply in relation to a school unless, immediately before 1st September 1987, there were in force for the school –
        (i) an instrument of government made under section 17 of the 1944 Act or section 2 of the 1968 (No. 2) Act; or an arrangement made under section 3 of the 1980 Act; and
        (ii) articles of government made under section 17 of the 1944 Act or section 2 of the 1968 (No. 2) Act; and
    (b) shall cease to apply in relation to a school on whichever is the earliest of the following dates:–
        (i) the date of the coming into force of an instrument of government for the school made under the Act;

(ii) the date of the coming into force of articles of government for the school made under the Act;

(iii) the relevant date.

(3) In sub-paragraph (2)(b)(iii) above, "the relevant date" means, in relation to any county or maintained special school, 1st September 1988; or, in relation to any voluntary school, 1st September 1989.

(4) During such time as this paragraph applies in relation to a school –

(a) the instrument of government or (as the case may be) arrangement for the school, and the articles of government for the school, shall continue in force and be treated as having been made under the Act;

(b) Article 3 of this Order, so far as it brings into force –

(i) sections 3 to 7, 8(2) to (5), 11, 13 to 15, 16(1) and (3), 18 and 19, 21 to 27, 34 to 42 and 57 of the Act;

(ii) paragraphs 3 to 5 of Schedule 1 to the Act; and

(iii) Schedule 3 to the Act;

shall not apply in relation to the school;

(c) subsection (4) of section 22 of the 1944 Act shall, notwithstanding the bringing into force by this Order of paragraph 2 of Schedule 4 to the Act (which amends that subsection), continue to have effect in relation to the school as though paragraph 2 of that Schedule had not come into force;

(d) the repeals of the enactments referred to in the Appendix to this Schedule shall not affect the operation of those enactments in relation to the school; and

(e) the requirements contained in sections 29 and 32 of the Act shall have effect, in relation to the school, as though they were requirements imposed directly by those sections, instead of requirements to be imposed under the articles of government for the school.

2.—(1) This paragraph applies in relation to county, voluntary and maintained special schools and shall have effect until 1st September 1989.

(2) Subsections (9) and (10) of section 8 of the Act shall have effect as though the references in those subsections to an instrument of government included references to an arrangement made under section 3 of the 1980 Act.

3.—(1) Article 3 of this Order, so far as it brings into force section 12 of, and Schedule 2 to, the Act, shall not apply in relation to a new school if the date on which the relevant proposal falls to be implemented is earlier than 1st April 1988.

(2) Subject to sub-paragraph (1) above, where a local education authority have, by a resolution passed before 1st September 1987, resolved to establish a new special school, subsection (3)(b) of section 12 of the Act shall, in relation to that new special school, have effect with the substitution for the words "the day on which their resolution to establish the school is passed ", of the words "1st October 1987".

4.—(1) This paragraph applies in relation to county, controlled, special agreement and maintained special schools.

(2) The procedures laid down in the articles of government for such a school by virtue of sections 37 to 39 of the Act shall not apply in relation to the filling of any vacancy in a post at such a school occurring before the date on which the articles of government came into force, if arrangements have been made for any of the candidates for the post to be interviewed on a date earlier than one month after the date on which those articles came into force and the candidates concerned were, before those articles came into force, informed of those arrangements.

(3) Where, by reason of sub-paragraph (2) above, the procedures laid down by the articles of government for a school by virtue of sections 37 to 39 of the Act do not apply in relation to the filling of a particular vacancy in a post at a school, that vacancy shall be filled in accordance with the procedures which would have applied in relation to the filling of such a vacancy immediately before the coming into force of those articles.

APPENDIX TO SCHEDULE 3

Chapter	Short title	Extent of repeal
1944 c.31.	The Education Act 1944.	Section 21(1). Section 23. Section 24(1). In section 27(3), from "but before" to end.
1968 c.37.	The Education (No. 2) Act 1968.	Section 2(5).
1980 c.20.	The Education Act 1980.	Section 2. Section 3(4).

Kenneth Baker
One of Her Majesty's Principal Secretaries of State

2nd March 1987

EXPLANATORY NOTE

(This note is not part of the Order)

This Order brings into force all the provisions of the Education (No. 2) Act 1986 which are not already in force, with the exception of the repeals (by Schedule 6 to the Act) of section 31(8) of the London Government Act 1963 (c.33) (the application of which is, by virtue of a transitional provision in the first commencement Order (S.I.1986/2203), now confined to further education) and paragraph 6 of Schedule 5 to the Local Government Act 1966 (c.42) (both of which enactments relate to recoupment).

The provisions specified in Schedule 1 to the Order are brought into force on 15th August 1987. Those specified in Schedule 2 are brought into force on 1st September 1987, subject to certain transitional provisions set out in Schedule 3 to the Order.

The principal effect of paragraph 1 of Schedule 3 (which applies to county, voluntary and maintained special schools) is to enable such schools to continue to be governed in accordance with existing instruments (or arrangements made under section 3 of the Education Act 1980) and articles of government (sub-paragraph (4)(a)), provided that the requirements as to the making and content of instruments and articles of government brought into force by the Order are complied with by "the relevant date" as defined by sub-paragraph (3). While a school continues to be so governed, most of the provisions of the Act which are brought into force by the Order and are concerned with school government will not apply to the school (sub-paragraph (4)(b) to (d)). The requirements in sections 29 and 32 will, however, apply as though they were direct statutory requirements (sub-paragraph (4)(e)).

Paragraph 2 of Schedule 3, which makes transitional provision in connection with section 8(9) and (10) of the Act, recognises the possibility that (by virtue of the transitional provisions explained above) the governing bodies of some schools may, until 1st September 1989, continue to be constituted under arrangements made under section 3 of the Education Act 1980.

By virtue of paragraph 3 of Schedule 3 to the Order, section 12 of, and Schedule 2 to, the Act do not apply to a new school, if the date on which the proposal to establish or, as the case may be, maintain the school falls to be implemented, is earlier than 1st April 1988. Paragraph 3 also makes transitional provision in connection with section 12(3)(b) so that, where a local education authority have, before 1st September 1987, passed a resolution to establish a new special school, the temporary governing body will be required to be constituted at least one year before the date on which the first pupils are expected to be admitted or on 1st October 1987.

Although, once a school has articles of government made under the Act, the appointment of staff of a kind mentioned in sections 37 to 39 of the Act will normally be subject to the procedures set out in the articles by virtue of those sections, paragraph 4 of Schedule 3 to the Order provides for the procedures applicable immediately before those articles came into force, to continue to apply in relation to such an appointment if arrangements have been made for any of the candidates for the post to be interviewed on a date earlier than one month from the date on which those articles came into force and the candidates concerned were, before those articles came into force, informed of those arrangements.

NOTE AS TO EARLIER COMMENCEMENT ORDER

Section 66(1) of the Act provides for sections 60 and 63 to 65, section 66 and section 67(1) to (3) and (7) to come into force on the passing of the Act (7th November 1986); and section 66(2) provides for sections 49 and 59 to come into force two months from that date (7th January 1987).

The remainder of those provisions of the Act which are already in force were brought into force by the Education (No. 2) Act 1986 (Commencement No. 1) Order 1986 (S.I. 1986/2203) as indicated below –

Provision	Date of commencement
Sections 17, 30, 31, 33, 44, 45, 46, 47(11), 50 to 53, 56, 67(4) (partially), 67(6) (partially); and Schedules 4 and 6 (both partially).	7th January 1987.
Sections 54, 55, 67(4) (partially); and Schedule 4 (partially).	1st April 1987.

STATUTORY INSTRUMENTS

1987 No. 345 (S. 25)

RATING AND VALUATION

The Revaluation Rate Rebates (Scotland) Order 1986

Approved by the House of Commons

Made - - - -	*17th December 1986*
Laid before the House of Commons	*19th December 1986*
Coming into force	*19th February 1987*

In exercise of the powers conferred on me by section 1(1) and (6) of the Rating (Revaluation Rebates) (Scotland) Act 1985(**a**) and of all other powers enabling me in that behalf, and with the consent of the Treasury, I hereby make the following Order:

Citation and commencement

1. This Order may be cited as the Revaluation Rate Rebates (Scotland) Order 1986 and shall come into force on the day after the day on which it is approved by a resolution of the House of Commons.

Interpretation

2. In this Order–

"the 1985 Act" means the Rating (Revaluation Rebates) (Scotland) Act 1985;

"financial year" means the period of twelve months ending with 31st March 1988.

Grant of rebates

3. Subject to article 5 below, rebates under the 1985 Act of such amounts as are provided in article 4 of this Order shall be granted by rating authorities in respect of rates levied by them in respect of the financial year on lands and heritages in their area which qualify for rebate under section 1(2) of the 1985 Act.

Amount and calculation of rebates

4.—(1) Subject to paragraphs (2) and (3) below the amount of rebate shall be 50 per cent of the amount by which the amount payable in respect of rates levied on the lands and heritages for the financial year according to their revaluation rateable value exceeds the amount of rates which would have been payable in respect of the same lands and heritages for the financial year according to 3 times their pre-revaluation rateable value.

(2) In calculating the amount payable in respect of rates levied on the lands and heritages for the financial year no account shall be taken of the provisions of section 9 of the Local Government (Scotland) Act 1975(**b**) (restriction on rates payable when valuation appeal is pending).

(**a**) 1985 c.33.
(**b**) 1975 c.30.

(3) The maximum amount of rebate in respect of any particular lands and heritages is £5,000.

Procedure for granting rebates

5.—(1) The rating authority for each area shall ascertain those lands and heritages which qualify for a rebate under section 1(2) of the 1985 Act and by 1st June 1987 shall grant the rebate appropriate to those lands and heritages.

(2) A rebate may be granted either by making a payment of the amount of the rebate or by reducing the amount of rates payable by the amount of the rebate.

(3) By 8th June 1987 the rating authority shall publish in a newspaper circulating in their area a notice notifying ratepayers that any ratepayer who considers that he is entitled to a rebate but who either–

(a) has not been granted a rebate, or

(b) considers that the amount of the rebate granted is incorrect,

may within 28 days of the date of publication of the notice submit an application for a rebate under the 1985 Act in writing to the rating authority, in or as nearly as may be in the form contained in the Schedule to this Order.

(4) An application submitted under paragraph (3) above shall be determined by the rating authority and on determining the application the rating authority shall forthwith–

(a) where they have refused the application, advise the applicant in writing, and

(b) where they have granted the application either in whole or in part, grant the rebate.

(5) If the rating authority fail to make a determination in accordance with paragraph (4) above within 28 days of the submission of an application under paragraph (3) above they shall be deemed to have refused the application.

Subsequent alterations

6. Where any alteration is made in the rates levied by the rating authority, or in the pre-revaluation rateable value or in the revaluation rateable value of any lands and heritages–

(a) the question of the grant of a rebate, and

(b) the calculation of any such rebate

shall be determined anew; and the amount of any rebate already paid or allowed, or of any rebate or balance thereof found to be due shall be paid or allowed by or, as the case may require, repaid to, the rating authority accordingly.

Appeals

7.—(1) Subject to paragraph (2) below any ratepayer who is dissatisfied with a determination of the rating authority under articles 5(4) or 6 above or with a deemed refusal under article 5(5) above may, within 28 days of that determination or deemed refusal, appeal by way of summary application to the sheriff, whose decision shall not be subject to review; and if the sheriff allows the appeal he may direct that the rating authority grant the rebate.

(2) An appeal under paragraph (1) above shall be competent only if the ratepayer within 14 days of the determination or deemed refusal intimates to the rating authority by recorded delivery service that he intends to appeal.

(3) Nothing in this order affects any right of appeal in respect of any entry in the valuation roll.

New St. Andrew's House, Edinburgh
16th December 1986

Malcolm Rifkind
One of Her Majesty's Principal
Secretaries of State

We consent,

Tony Durant
Michael Neubert

17th December 1986   Two of the Lords Commissioners of Her Majesty's Treasury

Article 5

SCHEDULE

APPLICATION FOR REVALUATION RATE REBATE

In terms of article 5(3) of the Revaluation Rate Rebates (Scotland) Order 1986 I hereby apply for a rebate under the Rating (Revaluation Rebates) (Scotland) Act 1985 in respect of the property known as

Full address (in BLOCK CAPITALS) of the property for which rebate is claimed

Reference number if known (see your rates demand notice)

The rateable value of the property in the valuation roll for 1984-85 as at 31st March 1985 was   £

The rateable value of the property in the valuation roll as at 1st April 1985 was   £

Signature   Date

Name (in BLOCK CAPITALS)

Address (in BLOCK CAPITALS) to which reply should be sent (if different from above)

Daytime telephone number

Note

(1) Rebate can be claimed only where the rateable value as at 1st April 1985 is more than 3 times the rateable value as at 31st March 1985.

(2) The maximum amount of rebate is £5,000.

(3) It would be helpful, but not essential, to enclose copies of your 1984-85 and 1987-88 rates demand notices.

EXPLANATORY NOTE

(This note is not part of the Order)

This Order requires rating authorities to grant rebates of rates levied in 1987-88 in respect of those lands and heritages specified in section 1 of the Rating (Revaluation Rebates) (Scotland) Act 1985 (article 3); specifies the amount of and the method of calculation of the rebates (article 4); prescribes the procedure for the granting of rebates (article 5 and Schedule); provides for the adjustment of any rebates as a result of alterations in rateable values or in rates levied (article 6) and makes provision for appeals to the sheriff (article 7). The Order provides for 50 per cent rebate and the maximum rebate is to be £5,000. (For the financial year ending 31st March 1987 75 per cent rebate was paid and the maximum rebate was £7,500 in terms of the Revaluation Rate Rebates (Scotland) (No. 2) Order 1985 (S.I. 1986/150)).